The
Thinker's
Thesaurus

The Thinker's Thesaurus

SOPHISTICATED ALTERNATIVES *to* COMMON WORDS

Expanded Second Edition

W. W. NORTON & COMPANY

NEW YORK • LONDON

For information about permission to reproduce selections from this book,
write to Permissions, W. W. Norton & Company, Inc.,
500 Fifth Avenue, New York, NY 10110

For information about special discounts for bulk purchases, please contact
W. W. Norton Special Sales at specialsales@wwnorton.com or 800-233-4830

Manufacturing by Courier Westford
Book design by Judith Stagnitto Abbate / Abbate Design
Production manager: Devon Zahn

Library of Congress Cataloging-in-Publication Data

Meltzer, Peter E., 1958–
The thinker's thesaurus : sophisticated alternatives to
common words / Peter E. Meltzer. — Expanded 2nd ed.
p. cm.
ISBN 978-0-393-07824-4 — ISBN 978-0-393-33794-5 (pbk.)
1. English language—Synonyms and antonyms. I. Title.
PE1591.M464 2010
423'.12—dc22

                                        2010005416

W. W. Norton & Company, Inc.
500 Fifth Avenue, New York, N.Y. 10110
www.wwnorton.com

W. W. Norton & Company Ltd.
Castle House, 75/76 Wells Street, London W1T 3QT

    8 9 0

word (just the right . . . or phrase) *n.*: **mot juste** [French]. ❖ That words matter has few dissenters, especially among those who try to make sense with them. The right word is the writer's Holy Grail. Often elusive, the mot juste is the lullaby that sends one into rapturous sleep, while its evil twin—the ill-chosen word—can have the opposite effect. (Kathleen Parker, "Putting Words to Rest," *Oakland Tribune*, 7/8/2006.)

ABOUT THIS THESAURUS

Ⅰ The Limitations Inherent in Existing Thesauruses and How This Thesaurus Came into Being

We seek in vain the words we need, and strive ineffectually to devise forms of expression which shall faithfully portray our thoughts and sentiments. The appropriate terms, notwithstanding our utmost efforts, cannot be conjured up at will. Like "spirits from the vasty deep," they come not when we call; and we are driven to the employment of a set of words and phrases either too general or too limited, too strong or too feeble, which suit not the occasion, which hit not the mark we aim at.

DR. PETER MARK ROGET—introduction to his original 1852 thesaurus

This book had its genesis in a 1994 discussion with a group of friends and colleagues, all of whom were involved directly or indirectly in the writing profession. The issue of thesauruses arose. To a person, our reactions were virtually identical: While in theory a thesaurus is a marvelous reference aid, the reality tends to be quite different. That "eureka" moment we all hope for when consulting a thesaurus ("That's just the word I need!") occurs far too rarely. Conventional thesauruses present "le mot juste" far less frequently than they should (and never present the term "le mot juste" itself). Moreover, as a vocabulary enhancement tool, a regular thesaurus is almost useless, since the synonyms tend to be just as common as the base words.

Thus, in fulfilling Dr. Roget's original goals, other thesauruses today exist primarily only to remind us of words we already know but which we have temporarily forgotten, those "tip-of-the-tongue" words that "cannot be conjured up at will." I therefore had an ambitious (some might say foolhardy) goal: to create a new kind of thesaurus that is intended to be a genuine improvement over existing versions for the benefit of casual and serious writers alike who want to be able to use just the right word for a given occasion. One may ask: "Isn't that precisely what conventional thesauruses are for?" The answer is yes, but only in theory. The reality is that existing thesauruses suffer from two primary flaws.

The first problem is that one usually finds that no matter how many synonyms an ordinary thesaurus contains, it rarely seems to offer interesting choices. Typically the synonyms offered have already been considered and rejected before the user even consulted the thesaurus. This is because those synonyms, while numerous, are mostly uninteresting. The mere fact that people own thesauruses means not only that they care enough about words to want to be able to find precisely the right one for the right occasion, but also that their basic vocabulary is probably such that any synonyms that are of equal or lesser complexity than the base word given are generally not going to be of much use, because they will have thought of those synonyms anyway. To address this problem, a thesaurus was needed that would contain interesting, rather than mundane, synonyms.

The second problem is that all thesauruses (other than this one) start with one word—the base word—and then list a number of synonyms for that one word. In addition, they inevitably compare like word forms—adjective to adjective, noun to noun, and so forth. What if, however, the would-be synonym does not easily lend itself to a single base word? This can occur in numerous different ways. For example, some words involve two distinct concepts. "Nephew" requires reference both to "son" and to "sister" or "brother"; "claustrophobia" requires reference to both "fear" and "confined spaces." In other words, there is no one-word synonym for "nephew" or "claustrophobia." Similarly, the most common definition of "elopement" is flight with a lover with the intention of getting married. However, it is obviously not a synonym for "flight" or "marriage" standing alone. Nevertheless, *Roget's International Thesaurus* (6th ed., HarperCollins, 2001), lists "flight" and "wedding" as synonyms for "elopement." "Embezzlement" is stealing something that has been entrusted to one's care.

Another example of the "one base word" limitation is where the most logical base word–synonym comparison involves different word forms. Consider the adjective "maternal," in the sense of "maternal grandfather." If this were the synonym, what would be the most logical connecting base word? The answer is obviously "mother," but that word is a noun. Because traditional thesauruses will only list other nouns as synonyms for "mother," there is no way they can lead the user to the synonym "maternal," as simple as that word may be.

The most serious problem, however, with the single base word system is its inability to deal with nuance. Take, for example, the word "smile." Most thesauruses will include "grin," "smirk," "snicker," and "grimace" as potential synonyms for this word. Each of these words means something totally different from the others, yet they are invariably all listed as synonyms for "smile." "Embezzlement" is a type of theft. But one does not break into a stranger's house and "embezzle" her belongings. Nevertheless, *Roget's International* lists "embezzle" as a synonym for "steal" and "misuse."

How can the writers of these thesauruses get away with these types of comparisons? Easy, because (precisely in accordance with Dr. Roget's original vision) they start with the premise that the user already knows the synonyms. For example, the foreword to *Webster's New World Thesaurus* states that "the editors asked themselves which bodies of synonymic expressions are sufficiently common so that they belong in a general reference work." Similarly, in recommending one common thesaurus, Will Weng, a former *New York Times* crossword puzzle editor, stated: "Every so often one finds oneself trying to think of a certain exact word, buried frustratingly in the back of the mind."[1] In other words, the user is familiar with the synonym but has simply forgotten it temporarily, and thus uses the thesaurus to jog his or her memory.

After consulting numerous thesauruses, I realized that no thesaurus like this one exists. On one side are all the traditional thesauruses that tend to avoid inclusion of hard words and which are limited to a single base word. On the other side are the numerous word books and Web sites that delight in presenting unusual or complex words, but which do not give the user any logical system or means by which to find these gems, since they are inevitably alphabetized by the hard synonym rather than by base word.[2] Thus they are useless as reference tools since the reader doesn't know what the synonyms mean in the first place. Presumably one reads them for amusement only, not as thesauruses or reference guides, since that would not be possible.

It was therefore my intent to create a thesaurus that would bridge the large gap between these two kinds of books and give the user a logical and organized means by which to find (and then use) synonyms that are less mundane rather than more; that is, synonyms that users would be unlikely to consider on their own, but which nevertheless are legitimate words that are not archaic, obsolete, rare, dialectical, regional, outdated, or relegated to and findable in only the most obscure reference sources. In other words, this thesaurus is not designed primarily to help users recall words that they already know, but which are temporarily "buried frustratingly in the back of the mind." That is the purpose of traditional thesauruses. Rather, it is designed to present words that users may never have heard of in the first place, but which, one hopes, will meet their exact needs.

To fill the void between conventional thesauruses and rare-book words, this thesaurus offers three features, each of which makes it unique, and each of which is demonstrated in the example above.

1. Nearly all of the synonyms, while completely legitimate, are harder or more sophisticated words than one would find in a regular thesaurus.
2. Because the synonyms are more interesting and generally more unusual than those found in conventional thesauruses, the entries have examples from current books or periodicals. There are numerous reasons for providing these examples:
   a. They demonstrate how the words are properly used.
   b. They show that these are real words currently used by real writers in the real world, not obsolete words that are never used anymore. Besides showing proper usage, the

---

1. There is actually a word for not being able to remember the word you want, namely "lethologica."
2. Take, for example, *The Superior Person's Book of Words* (Godine, 2002), which is just one of dozens of such books available. Under the letter "n," the first five entries are "napiform," "natterjack," "naumachia," "naupathia," and "nefandous." If one ever wanted to use any of these words in lieu of some other word (which is unlikely in the first place, given their definitions), the book has no means of guiding the user to them. A few other examples of many unusual word dictionaries that are alphabetized according to the unusual words include *Weird and Wonderful Words* (Oxford University Press, 2003), *Foyle's Philaver*, (Chambers, 2007), *Wordsmanship* (Verbatim, 1991), *Mrs. Byrne's Dictionary of Unusual, Obscure and Preposterous Words* (Citadel Press, 1990), and *The Logodaedalian's Dictionary* (University of South Carolina Press, 1989). In addition, many of the words in these books are obsolete and thus it would be impossible to find an example of their use, at least when relying on sources more recent than the nineteenth century.

examples serve as an anticipatory rebuttal to those who tend to scoff at harder words and ask rhetorically: "Who ever uses these words anyway? Aren't they obsolete?" (These questions are addressed in more detail below—see "In Defense of the Hard Word.") Moreover, from reading the examples, one can tell that in each instance, the word in question is being used within the natural flow of the passage; that is, the author is not straining to use the word or artificially forcing it on the reader.

    c. They bring the particular synonym to life and allow the user to focus on and consider its use more strongly than if the word was one among dozens buried in a conventional thesaurus (even putting aside the fact that most of the synonyms herein won't be found in other thesauruses anyway).

In sum, it is hoped that giving actual examples of the synonyms makes for a more interesting presentation and will help the reader remember the words next time.

3. Finally, I use what I call a Clarifier in about 75 percent of the entries. This allows for the use of thousands of words as synonyms that either cannot be found at all in other thesauruses or are used imprecisely. The technique is designed to address a problem with ordinary thesauruses: They are limited to single-word base words. How the Clarifier works is described in section III below.

Because of selectivity in the use of synonyms, the average base word in this thesaurus is, by design, not followed by the ten or twenty (boring) synonyms that accompany base words in most thesauruses. Instead, there is typically only one synonym for each base word. Let's use a few examples to show how this thesaurus works. There are two kinds of entries, the single base word entry and the Clarifier entry.

II The Single Base Word Entry

The first type of entry is the use of a single base word to define the synonym. There is no accompanying Clarifier. These entries have the same format as conventional thesaurus entries, but the synonyms are more interesting than those found in other thesauruses. Take the word "lethargy." Conventional thesauruses suggest synonyms such as "apathy," "idleness," "inactivity," "passivity," and "listlessness." It is likely that if readers were looking for a synonym for "lethargy," they would have already considered those synonyms on their own. Thus, this thesaurus offers the more interesting alternative "hebetude," together with an example.

> **lethargy** *n*.: **hebetude**. ❖ [Bend, Oregon is] a city with a bike rack on every car, a canoe in every garage and a restless heart in every chest. While too many Americans slouch toward a terminal funk of **hebetude** and sloth, Bendians race ahead with toned muscles, wide eyes and brains perpetually wired on adrenaline. (*Washington Times*, "Wild Rides in the Heart of Central Oregon—Bent Out of Shape in Bend," 8/11/2001.)

Another word for "cheerful"? Traditional thesauruses offer "gay," "merry," "joyful," and "happy." But how about "eupeptic" as a more interesting alternative?

cheerful *adj.*: **eupeptic**. ❖ [Artist Keith] Haring has little to express beyond a vague pleasantness, a whiff of happiness. Any attempt at true feeling is immediately deflected and thwarted by a blithely **eupeptic** tone that was intrinsic to his art: his AIDS image seems as innocuous as his radiant babies and his barking dogs. (James Gardner, "Radiant Baby," *National Review*, 10/27/1997, p. 58.)

Other typical examples follow. Every one has an example—to show that these are not archaic words but rather words in current usage.

In a traditional thesaurus:
   basic *adj.*: **elementary, introductory**

In *The Thinker's Thesaurus*:
   basic *adj.*: **abecedarian**. ❖ [Muhammad Ali] expressed himself in energetic, if **abecedarian**, rhymes. Listen to this excerpt from "Song of Myself": "Yes, the crowd did not dream—When they laid down their money—That they would see—A total eclipse of the Sonny. I am the greatest!" (Keith Mano, "Still the Greatest," *National Review*, 11/9/1998, p. 59.)

In a traditional thesaurus:
   tattle (on) *v.i.*: **inform, squeal**

In *The Thinker's Thesaurus*:
   tattle (on) *v.i.*: **peach** ❖ A few days ago a rumor spread like fire through a straw rick that "Deep Throat," the world's most famous news source, was [Alexander Haig]. What made this story far-fetched was not that Haig had been a big shot in the Nixon White House in Watergate days, so wouldn't have **peached** on his boss. . . . [Rather, it was implausible] on literacy grounds [since] he is utterly incapable of making anything perfectly clear once he starts to talk. (Russell Baker, Tiresome News Dept., *New York Times*, 10/7/1989.)

In a traditional thesaurus:
   harmful *adj.*: **damaging, detrimental**

In *The Thinker's Thesaurus*:
   harmful *adj.*: **nocent**. ❖ [W]ith respect to the disastrous imbalance in trade between the U.S. and the rest of the world, I would urge the administration and Congress to consider alternatives to import limitations. Besides the **nocent** effects on world trade that such limitations would cause, there is the very real threat of imposing exports of capital back to Europe[,] thus completely upsetting the American capital markets. (John Murphy, "Fighting the Trade Imbalance," *Chicago Tribune*, 10/31/1985.)

In a traditional thesaurus:
   laughable *adj.*: **funny, amusing**

In *The Thinker's Thesaurus*:

> **laughable** *adj.*: **risible**. [As with the word "laughable" itself, this word is sometimes used in the straightforward sense, but it is more frequently used pejoratively, as in "his argument was so ridiculous, it was laughable."] ❖ By endorsing Howard Dean before a single vote has been cast [in the primaries], Al Gore has done Democrats hoping for a victory next November a true disservice. . . . [I]t's hard to say what was more **risible** about Gore's remarks: His claim that he respected the prerogative of caucus and primary voters or his suggestion to the other candidates that they should "keep their eyes on the prize" and eschew attacks on the front-runner. (Scott Lehigh, "Gore Hurts Democrats with Premature Nod," *Boston Globe*, 12/12/2003.)

In a traditional thesaurus:

> **redundancy** *n.*: **repetition, duplication**

In *The Thinker's Thesaurus*:

> **redundancy** *n.*: **pleonasm**. ❖ It was, after all, public officials who gave us "safe haven" during the Persian Gulf War. Someone apparently grafted the "safe" from "safe harbor" (not all harbors are safe) onto "haven" (by definition, a safe place). The creation of this obnoxious **pleonasm** . . . illustrates the bureaucrat's familiar combination of self-importance, pretension, and ignorance. (John E. McIntyre, "Words That Survive the Test of Time," *Christian Science Monitor*, 12/30/1999.)

In a traditional thesaurus:

> **chat** *v.i.*: **talk, converse, discuss**

In *The Thinker's Thesaurus*:

> **chat** *v.i.*: **confabulate**. ❖ The hotel, on a highway outside Richmond, the state capital of Virginia, braced itself for [boxing promoter Don King's] arrival, as for that of a hurricane. In the lobby his minions **confabulated** in blobs: roly-poly men like waddling molecules, their bangles jangling, their pinky rings glinting, walkie-talkies jutting from their polyester rumps. (Peter Conrad, "The Joy of Slavery," *Independent on Sunday*, 3/10/1996.)

In short, with regard to the single base word entries, this thesaurus is unique not because other thesauruses won't have the same base words but because they typically won't have the same synonyms.

Ⅲ The Clarifier Entry

The second type of entry, which is not found in any traditional thesaurus, involves the use of a base word accompanied by a Clarifier. In this case, the base word may not be, by itself, a synonym for the entry, but rather the most likely word the user might be expected to consult to find the synonym. The intent is that the base word, when combined with the Clarifier, will accurately yield the synonym. About 75 percent of the entries herein contain a Clarifier.

The use of the Clarifier is essential to this thesaurus, since there are so many wonderful words in the English language that simply do not easily lend themselves to a one-word synonym, and which are not accessible without the Clarifier. In fact, this is one of the primary limitations of even the most compendious standard thesauruses. There are essentially three different occasions on which a Clarifier is necessary, and each of them demonstrates the shortcoming of ordinary thesauruses. These are as follows:

❶ The Use of a Clarifier to Provide More Exact Definitions or to Show Nuance

As virtually all thesaurus introductions point out, in a technical sense, there is rarely such a thing as an "exact" synonym. Thus, when using a single word to compare both the base word and the synonym, the base word and the synonym will often not mean the exact same thing. With the Clarifier, however, it is far easier to arrive at a more precise definition for the synonym, since we are no longer limited to a single base word. Let's consider just a few of the entries in this thesaurus to see how this problem is resolved. The word "malversation" means wrongdoing, but not just any wrongdoing. It means wrongdoing in public office. Let's put aside the fact that "malversation" would rarely appear in a regular thesaurus in the first place, despite being a perfectly legitimate word. Even if it did, that thesaurus could only offer the following: **wrongdoing** *n.*: **malversation**. That comparison would be faulty, however, because unless one is in public office, one cannot commit malversation. The example in this thesaurus is as follows:

> **wrongdoing** (in public office) *n.*: **malversation**. ❖ A third charge is that [President Clinton's first-term national security adviser Anthony] Lake is guilty of **malversation**, the evidence being a token $5,000 fine he was assessed by the Justice Department for failing to sell several stock holdings promptly. (Jacob Heilbrunn, "Dr. Maybe Heads for the CIA," *New Republic*, 3/24/1997.)

The word "neologism" means a word, phrase, or expression, but not just any kind. Thus, a regular thesaurus, even if it contained the word in the first place, which it would not, could not properly list it as a synonym for "word," "phrase," or "expression."

> **word** (new . . . , phrase, or expression) *n.*: **neologism**. ❖ Back during Watergate, the President's men were always having to announce that he had "misspoke himself," an odd **neologism** that made it sound as though Nixon had just wet his pants. Just once it would be nice to hear a White House press secretary say, "The President made a faux pas." (Christopher Buckley, "Hoof in Mouth," *Forbes FYI*, 5/4/1998, p. 31.)

"Aestivate" (or "estivate") is a synonym for "laze," but one would not "aestivate" by lying in the snow:

> **laze** (around during the summer) *v.i.*: **aestivate** (or **estivate**). ❖ Above all, my children **aestivate**. From May to September their life is a languorous stroll from pool to ham-

mock to beach to barbecue. Their biggest challenges are ice creams that melt before the first lick, and fireflies that resist capture in jam jars. (Gerald Baker, "The Long Hot Summer," *Financial Times* [London], 7/12/2003.)

One of the definitions of "virago" is a strong and courageous woman. But clearly it is not a synonym for "woman" or "courageous" standing alone. With the Clarifier, this is not a problem:

> **woman** (who is strong and courageous) *n.*: **virago**. ❖ Feminists don't like strong women because too many **viragos** would put them out of business. To prosper they need a steady supply of women who exemplify the other V-word, "victim." (Florence King, "The Misanthrope's Corner," *National Review*, 3/10/1997, p. 64.)[3]

Next, consider the word "nocturne," which means (among other things) a painting of a night scene. A standard thesaurus would obviously not list the word as a synonym for "painting." However, with the help of the Clarifier, we have the following:

> **painting** (dealing with evening or night) *n.*: **nocturne**. ❖ Making art outdoors on misty autumn evenings and brisk winter nights has its ups and downs for painter Mike Lynch and photographer Chris Faust, whose serene show of poetic nightscapes opens today at the Minneapolis Institute of Arts. [Faust] had admired Lynch's nocturnes for nearly 30 years, having first seen them when he was still in high school. (Mary Abbe, "Night Moves/Photographer Chris Faust and Painter Mike Lynch Do Their Best Work on the Third Shift," *Minneapolis Star Tribune*, 12/15/2000.)

Finally, the Clarifier is also useful for arriving at a closer match for the synonyms, especially when the synonym involves a nuance. This can be a particular failing in conventional thesauruses, which may well contain the synonyms but which can lead the user astray because the nuance is not provided. Indeed, nuance is a foreign concept to conventional thesauruses because, in order to convey nuance, one must necessarily use more than one base word to explain the synonym accurately.[4] The issue here is not whether the synonyms in question can be found in a regular thesaurus, but whether incorrect usage will result due to the lack of a Clarifier. For example, most thesauruses use the word "fecund" as a synonym for "prolific." While this is not necessarily inaccurate, it does not reflect that the closest synonym for "fecund" is "fertile." Thus, while a person who has given birth to many offspring may be fecund, it would certainly raise an eyebrow to say that Babe Ruth was a "fecund" home run hitter.

---

3. At the risk of stating the obvious, all examples used in this thesaurus were chosen solely for their effectiveness in conveying the meaning of the given word and never for editorial content. Absolutely no opinion of my own is expressed on any of the editorial opinions contained in the examples in this thesaurus, of which there are many.

4. The creators of most thesauruses are well aware of this inherent flaw in their "one word to one word" structure, particularly where the words are not familiar. In their introductions, they always warn the readers to use the thesauruses with caution and to use them in conjunction with a dictionary. As stated in one: "The nature of language and the behavior of words defy precision." And so they do—particularly when one is trying to compare one base word with one synonym. The Clarifier helps to supply that precision.

prolific (esp. as in fertile) *adj.*: **fecund** (*v.t.*: **fecundate**). ❖ The manatee population continues to grow despite the few that are killed in boating accidents, just as our deer populations continue to thrive despite the deer that are struck on the highways. Manatees are not particularly **fecund** animals, but they have no natural predators. (Frank Sargeant, "Manatees Are Not [an] Endangered Species," *Tampa Tribune*, 9/13/2000.)

Consider next the relatively common verb "keen." Virtually every thesaurus will include it as a synonym for "cry," without elaboration. If one is not familiar with the word, one may reasonably conclude that a baby who is crying is "keening," but such use of the word would be inaccurate:

cry (in lament for the dead) *v.i.*: **keen**. ❖ When word spread through the convent, recalls one nun, "Everybody rushed to [the Mother Teresa's] room. They were all around her, wailing and hugging the Mother's body." The sisters' **keening** was heard by the communists, whose party headquarters are next door, and they tipped off journalists that Teresa had died. (Tim McGirk, Religion: "'Our Mother Is Gone!'" *Time* International, 9/22/1997, p. 54.)

To have a "sinecure," one must be employed or hold office, but attempting to make that word a synonym for "occupation" or "officeholder" will quickly lead to trouble in most cases. Thus, it is impossible to list "sinecure" as a correct synonym for any single word in a conventional thesaurus.

occupation (requiring little work but paying an income) *n.*: **sinecure**. ❖ [After] nearly ten years in government service, where everything is geared to the lowest common denominator, I find it refreshing to have work that rewards initiative and effort. Certainly I would be happy to have a **sinecure** again, but I am no longer brokenhearted that I left one. (Lars Eighner, *Travels with Lizbeth*, St. Martin's Press [1993], p. 124.)

The verb "peculate" is sometimes listed as a synonym for "steal," yet one would not accuse a child of "peculating" from the cookie jar.

steal (as in embezzle) *v.t.*, *v.i.*: **peculate**. ❖ [The Mazda] Miata gets passers-by smiling and talking. . . . Other conspicuous cars are costly and imposing and draw hate waves, as they are intended to. Decent householders glare, knowing you couldn't own the thing unless you were a drug dealer or a **peculating** [bureaucrat]. (John Skow, Living: "Miatific Bliss in Five Gears, This Is Definitely Not Your Father's Hupmobile," *Time*, 10/2/1989, p. 91.)

The adjective "fatuous" is often listed as a synonym for "foolish," yet forgetting one's wallet at home would not properly be termed a "fatuous" mistake.

foolish (in a smug or complacent manner) *adj.*: **fatuous**. ❖ "Jerry Garcia destroyed his life on drugs," Rush Limbaugh fearlessly proclaimed. You don't have to advocate heroin addiction or alcoholism to feel that all this moralistic fury is inanely misdirected. Nothing is more **fatuous** than to indict some performer for his failure to conform to the prescribed virtues of the "role model." Smug, self-satisfied, sanctimonious, this line of thinking fails first of all to acknowledge the true complexities of human existence. (John Taylor, "Live and Let Die: In Praise of Mickey [Mantle], Jerry, and the Reckless Life," *Esquire*, 12/1/1995, p. 120.)

Sometimes a conventional thesaurus will provide a synonym that, due to its lack of a Clarifier, is nearly the opposite of the base word. For example, a "philosophaster" is one who pretends to be a philosopher but is not truly (or is a bad one). It is a derogatory term that may be used when, for example, an actor or athlete gives his views on the world which, in the view of the writer profiling him, are frivolous. And yet, "philosophaster"—if included in a regular thesaurus at all—is generally given as a synonym for "philosopher," as if to suggest that Aristotle was a philosophaster.

> **philosopher** (bad . . . , or one who pretends to be a . . .) *n.*: **philosophaster**. ❖ Reagan won the 1980 and 1984 debates and elections because he spoke plain sense to the American people. Simple phrases. Common words. Plainstuff. Broken sentences. So what? That's how normal people speak. . . . In contrast, Carter and Mondale spoke more in the highfalutin' lingo our professors and other **philosophasters** love. (*Orange County Register*, "Silliness about Senility," 12/27/1987.)

With words such as "fecund," "keen," "sinecure," and "peculate," the issue is not whether they would be contained in an ordinary thesaurus, but whether the ordinary thesaurus could easily lead the reader astray with regard to correct usage.

Finally, just the treatment of the word "woman" demonstrates the contrast between this thesaurus and others. For synonyms, most thesauruses give us "lady," "dame," "matron," "gentlewoman," "maid," "spinster," "debutante," "nymph," "virgin," "girl," and "old woman." While it is unlikely that a user would misuse any of these synonyms, since they are all simple, the lack of a Clarifier again points out one of the flaws of the conventional thesaurus, namely that virtually all of these synonyms have very different meanings, and yet they are all equated to "woman." In contrast, this thesaurus gives thirty-two synonyms using "woman" as a base word. Ten of those are as follows:

five good women to be:
woman (who is beautiful and alluring) *n.*: **houri** [French]
woman (who is slender and graceful) *n.*: **sylph**
woman (who is strong and courageous) *n.*: **virago**
woman (of a . . . who is stately and regal, esp. tending toward voluptuous) *adj.*: **Junoesque**
woman (who is charming and seductive) *n.*: **Circe**

five bad women to be:
woman (who is coarse and abusive) *n.*: **fishwife**
woman (regarded as ugly, repulsive, or terrifying) *n.*: **gorgon**
woman (regarded as vicious and scolding) *n.*: **harridan**
woman (who is scheming and evil) *n.*: **jezebel**
woman (frenzied or raging . . .) *n.*: **maenad**

These examples—and there are thousands of others—show how the Clarifier is used to provide more precise synonyms for base words and to show nuance in a way that conventional thesauruses do not.

❷ When the Base Word and Synonym Are Different Word Forms

Ordinarily, thesauruses compare identical word forms: verb to verb, adjective to adjective, and so on. But what happens when the best base word for a given synonym is a different word form, as is often the case? Clarifiers are extremely useful in such instances. For example, suppose one wants to use an adjective meaning "like a lion." Because "lion" is a noun, the synonyms in regular thesauruses—though numerous—will also be nouns, since they have no means to allow the switching of word forms. However, in this thesaurus, one will find the following entry:

> **lions** (of, relating to, or characteristic of) *adj.:* **leonine**. ❖ [The TV show *Lions* is] nowhere near the scope of the Disney classic *The African Lion* but includes some intriguing familial disputes—like an episode of a **leonine** soap opera. (Susan Reed, Picks & Pans: Video, *People*, 5/29/1989, p. 20.)

Here the Clarifier allows an adjectival synonym to be listed next to a base word that is a noun, and it also gives the user an easy and logical reference to a word that would not be found in most thesauruses.

The same is true for virtually any occasion on which the user is looking for an adjective that is "of, relating to, characteristic of, or resembling" a particular noun. A conventional thesaurus cannot help users make these connections because it does not change word forms, even if the synonyms, such as "leonine," are not necessarily unusual. Thus, the following types of entries will not and cannot be found in other thesauruses, and for each of them there is an example given:

> **clay** (relating to, resembling, or containing) *n.:* **argillaceous**
> **death** (of, relating to, or resembling . . .) *adj.:* **thanatoid**
> **dreams** (of, relating to, or suggestive of) *adj.:* **oneiric**
> **evening** (of, relating to, or occurring in) *adj.:* **vespertine**
> **old age** (of or relating to . . .) *adj.:* **gerontic**
> **wealth** (of or relating to the gaining of . . .) *adj.:* **chrematistic**

The Clarifier works equally well in converting from adjective to noun form. Consider the word "milquetoast," not a particularly unusual word. Although it is a noun, because it refers to a kind of person, the essence of the word is adjectival, namely "timid" (or "meek," "shy," or "unassertive"). Once again, the conventional thesaurus is unable to lead the user to the noun "milquetoast," because in order to do so, it must pass through an adjective. The Clarifier solves the problem:

> **timid** (and unassertive person) *n.:* **milquetoast**. ❖ [Warren Buffet]: "Mergers will be motivated by very good considerations. There truly are synergies in a great many mergers.

But whether there are synergies or not, they are going to keep happening. You don't get to be the CEO of a big company by being a **milquetoast**. You are not devoid of animal spirits." (Brent Schlender, "The Bill & Warren Show—What Do You Get When You Put a Billionaire Buddy Act in Front of 350 Students? $84 Billion of Inspiration," *Fortune*, 7/20/1998, p. 48.)

Have you heard of a "bashi-bazouk"? I'm guessing not, legitimate though it is. It's a person (read: noun), but its essence is someone who is undisciplined and uncontrollable (adjective). Obviously, a regular thesaurus could not put it as a synonym for "undisciplined" (and in fact won't have it as a synonym for any other word, either). But you'll find it in this thesaurus:

> **undisciplined** (and uncontrollable person) *n.*: **bashi-bazouk** [Turkish; derives from the irregular, undisciplined, mounted mercenary soldiers of the Ottoman army]. ❖ I admit it: I cut through. To get . . . to my daughter's school, I drive through residential streets in Homeland. . . . This commuter traffic does not please residents of Homeland, to whom, apparently, we motorists on our way to school and work are a crowd of **bashi-bazouks** galloping over the hill to plunder their houses and slaughter their cattle. (John McIntyre, "Cruising through Homeland," *Baltimore Sun*, 1/18/1999.)

Finally, the Clarifier can also be useful if one wants to switch a verb to an adjective:

> **persuading** (as in urging someone to take a course of action) *adj.*: **hortatory**. ❖ [Writer Meg Greenfield] loved argument and continued a tradition under which [*Washington*] *Post* editorials avoided **hortatory** calls to action in favor of making points by marshaling facts. (J. Y. Smith, obituary of Meg Greenfield, *Washington Post*, 5/14/1999.)

In short, almost any time the most likely base word a user would look up to find the right synonym is a word form other than that of the synonym, the Clarifier makes it possible.

❸ The Use of Clarifiers When a Synonym Involves Two Distinct Concepts

Many words in the English language cannot be included in thesauruses that only compare single base words to single synonyms, because the synonyms involve two distinct concepts that cannot possibly be conveyed with a single base word. Say a person has an abnormal fear of dirt or contamination—a condition called mysophobia. The single base word thesauruses cannot list it under "fear" (because it relates to a specific kind of fear) or under "dirt" or "contamination" (because it obviously is not a synonym for those words). The Clarifier solves this problem:

> **dirt** (abnormal fear of) *n.*: **mysophobia**. See *fear*

> **fear** (of dirt or contamination) *n.*: **mysophobia**. ❖ Dear Ann: My wife has developed an obsession for clean hands and wears cotton gloves constantly, even at mealtimes. She is also afraid to shake hands with anyone or even hold my hand. . . . Dear Concerned: Your

wife has **mysophobia**, which is an obsessive-compulsive disorder. This condition is not all that rare. (Ann Landers, *Newsday*, 11/16/1993.)

Consider next the word "malinger," again a relatively common verb meaning to fake a sickness or illness in order to avoid work. But what one base word could be used to come up with this synonym? Certainly not "sick" or "ill." The use of the verbs "pretend" or "shirk" get closer, but, without the Clarifier, no one could really suggest that those verbs, by themselves, could be considered synonyms for "malinger." The fact is that there is no one word that will do the trick, since one needs both the concepts of pretending and being sick to arrive at "malinger." In this thesaurus, the user can be led to "malinger" through both roads:

> **sickness** (pretend to have a . . . or other incapacity to avoid work) *v.i.*: **malinger**. See *shirk*

> **shirk** (work by pretending to be sick or incapacitated) *v.i.*: **malinger**. ❖ Players are regarded [by team owners] as overpaid louts who greedily want more than they deserve. . . . When a player is injured, he is suspected of **malingering** if he doesn't return to action immediately- —unless the bone is sticking through the meat. (Ron Mix, "So Little Gain for the Pain: Striking NFL Players Deserve Much, Much More," *Sports Illustrated*, 10/19/1987, p. 54.)

How about hatred of women (misogyny) or men (misandry)? By now, the reader gets the point that although words such as "misogyny" are not unusual, there is no way they could be found in a typical thesaurus. For the less common word "misandry," the entries are as follows:

> **men** (hatred of . . .) *n.*: **misandry**. See *hatred*

> **hatred** (of men) *n.*: **misandry**. ❖ I was shocked and horrified by your cover story, not only because of the recent rash of wife and child murders, but also by the strong suggestion that it is in the biological nature of males to be violent and abusive. . . . I suppose we can now expect another wave of **misandry** in this country such as the one that followed the Montreal Massacre by Marc Lépine. (Unsigned letter to the editor, *Maclean's*, 8/28/2000, p. 4.)

④ Summary of Ten Types of Entries in This Thesaurus

The following is a summary of the ten different kinds of entries in this book, together with an example of each, taken from the second edition. Only the first one is comparable in form to traditional thesauruses, but even then, the options offered are unlikely to be found in most such thesauruses. The last nine are unique to this thesaurus.

1. Entries with No Clarifier

> **subservient** *adj.*: **sequacious**. ❖ In 1945 . . . , Janet Kalven . . . called for "an education that will give young women a vision of the family . . . that will inspire them with the great ambitions of being queens in the home." By which she did not mean a **sequacious** help-

meet to the Man of the House, picking up his dirty underwear and serving him Budweisers during commercials, but rather a partner in the management of a "small, diversified family firm." (Bill Kauffman, "The Way of Love: Dorothy Day and the American Right," *Whole Earth*, 6/22/2000.)

2. Entries with Clarifier to Provide Nuance

impose (oneself or one's ideas in an unwelcome way, such as with undue insistence or without request) *v.t.*: **obtrude**. [This word is subtly distinct from the more common verb "intrude." To intrude is to thrust oneself into a place without permission or welcome, and often suggests violation of privacy. To obtrude is to unjustifiably force oneself or one's remarks, opinions, etc., into consideration. The example given here illustrates the distinction well because "intrude" could not be used interchangeably with "obtrude."] In these dark times, when war threatens to engulf a considerable portion of the globe, I hesitate to **obtrude** upon the public a merely personal problem; but the fact is that we in France— I mean my wife and I—have a border problem. Our neighbors' goats stray onto our land continually and cause us a great deal of irritation. (Anthony Daniels, "The Menace in France: In Which Our Correspondent Talks Goats," *National Review*, 8/28/2006.)

3. Entries That Provide Explanation as to Usage or Derivation

unfeeling (person, as in one who is interested only in cold, hard facts, with little concern for emotion or human needs) *n.*: **Gradgrind**. [This word is based on Thomas Gradgrind, from *Hard Times*, by Charles Dickens, who had such a personality and who valued practicality and materialism over all else]. ❖ In [her book on Julius Caesar, Colleen] McCullough is very much a Gradgrind when it comes to facts: They are all that is needful, presented, it must be said, without color or animation to detract from their merit. Even descriptions of battles—which are cursory for a work devoted to the life of one of the world's greatest generals—have all the movement and drive of origami instructions. . . . McCullough's [writing is] leaden [in the] way it sits on the page. (Katherine A. Powers, review of *The October Horse*, by Colleen McCullough, *Washington Post*, 12/15/2002.)

4. Entries Based on Foreign Words

essence (the . . . of a matter, as in the bottom line, the main point, the substance, etc.) *n.*: **tachlis** (esp. as in "talk tachlis") [Yiddish]. ❖ My current cookbook bible is *How to Cook Everything* by Mark Bittman. The author writes for the *New York Times* . . . and he's written several other good-read cookbooks. Yes he's opinionated, very. But this guy talks **tachlis**, he gets right to the point and tells you what you need to know in a clear, down to earth manner. (Ann Kleinberg, "Books for Cooks," *Jerusalem Post*, 6/18/2004.)

5. Entries in Which the Figurative Usage Is Distinguished from the Literal Usage

pale (and often sickly) *adj.*: **etiolated**. [This term specifically refers to plants becoming whitened due to lack of exposure to sunlight, but is also used more generally to describe a pale and sickly appearance or condition.] ❖ [After the concentration camp in Berga, Germany, was discovered in May 1945,] the **etiolated** bodies were exhumed—eloquent of malnutrition, sickness, abuse and suffering—and later many more bodies of GIs were found scattered on the route of the death march southward as the investigators retraced it. (Roger Cohen, *Soldiers and Slaves*, Knopf [2005], p. 221.)

6. Entries with Clarifier That Changes Word Form from Base Word to Synonym (for Example, from Noun to Adjective)

glass (of, resembling, or relating to) *adj.*: **vitreous**. ❖ Women have made tremendous progress in the labor market except for the area of management, where the glass ceiling still exists. . . . American research has also found that some of the few women who do crack the **vitreous** barrier feel so unsatisfied and undervalued that they leave early—and in proportionately greater numbers than their male rivals. (*Economist*, "Breaking the Glass Ceiling," 8/10/1996.)

7. Entries That Present Different Definitions of a Word

bigwig *n.*: **satrap**. [This word has various definitions, including (1) a leader or ruler generally, (2) a prominent or notable person generally, (3) a henchman, (4) a bureaucrat, and (5) the head of a state acting either as a representative or under the dominion and control of a foreign power. This is an example of the second definition. Often—but not always—it has a negative connotation.] ❖ Long protected by the senators and journalistic **satraps** who paid him court, [after uttering a racial slur against the Rutgers women's basketball team, radio personality Don] Imus found himself consumed by perhaps the only forces more powerful than those that elevated him to his place of privilege: the politics of race and gender. (*Newsweek*, "The Power That Was," 3/23/2007.)

8. Entries That Present Different Connotations of a Word

lordly *adj.*: **seigneurial**. [In the feudal system of landholding in Canada, seigneurs were lords granted lands by the king in return for their oath of loyalty and promise to support him in time of war. Like "lordly" itself, the word can have connotations that are either positive (such as dignified, noble, or exalted) or negative (such as arrogant, overbearing, or imperious). Examples of both are presented here, first the positive and then the negative.] ❖ *Vanity Fair*'s front cover is one of the prime slots in American show business, making [editor Graydon] Carter a Very Powerful Person. Everyone wants to stay sweet with him. He accepts his grandeur with **seigneurial** benevolence and drops the name of Robert De Niro as casually as a boy playing a yo-yo. (Quenton Letts, "Tinseltown," *Evening Standard* [London], 11/13/2002.)

The guy was driving his cream-colored Rolls-Royce Corniche along West Broadway in SoHo. Actually, to call it driving is giving him too much credit. Bobbing and weaving is more like it. Several times, he nearly hit parked cars. Once, he almost veered into oncoming traffic. Naturally, he was gabbing on a cell phone the whole time, with a **seigneurial** indifference to anything in his path. (Clyde Haberman, NYC: "We Need More Tickets, Not Fewer," *New York Times*, 6/13/2003.)

9. Entries That Combine More Than One of the Above Features

right-thinking *adj.*: **bien pensant**. [This French term, sometimes hyphenated, and literally meaning well-thinking, has two very different usages. In the complimentary sense, it simply means right-minded or correct. In the derogatory sense (which is more common), it is used in an ironic, facetious, or sarcastic sense to mean conformist or doctrinaire or politically correct, often self-righteously. Thus, though closer in actual definition to conservatism, when used in this latter sense, it is typically used by conservatives to criticize liberals. An example of each usage is presented here.]

❖ [In the French elections for president, the ability of seventy-three-year-old Jean-Marie Le Pen] to edge into the two-man run-off against incumbent Jacques Chirac . . . rightly made headlines. . . . Le Pen's good fortune provoked continental outrage. **Bien-pensant** Europeans vowed to turn back this candidate of the far-right fringe who—as almost every story on him points out—once called the Holocaust a "detail of history." (*National Review*, "Le Pen: Not So Mighty," 2/20/2002.)

❖ [With regard to the false accusation of rape against three white Duke University lacrosse players by an African American woman, a *New York*] *Times* alumnus recently e-mailed me, "You couldn't invent a story so precisely tuned to the outrage frequency of the modern, metropolitan, **bien-pensant** journalist." . . . But real facts are stubborn things. And today, the preponderance of facts indicate that [the woman's accusation was false]. Yet at the epicenter of bien-pensant journalism, the *New York Times*, reporters and editors . . . are declining to expose it. (Kurt Anderson, "Rape, Justice, and the *Times*," *New York*, 10/16/2006.)

10. Whimsical Entries

unfaithful (spouse) n.: bedswerver.
❖ When a **bedswerver**'s hungry for spice,
　It's unlikely she'll heed the advice
　When her conscience yells, "Don't!"
　And I'm guessing she won't
　Give a thought to adultery's price.
(Mike Scholtes, *The Omnificent English Dictionary in Limerick Form* [*oedilf.com*], 4/6/2006.)

Ⅳ Criteria for Entry and Rules Regarding the Examples

The following is a list of the general rules I attempted to abide by for each entry. There may be certain instances in which not every rule was followed, particularly when I felt that a given word was, on balance, a worthy and legitimate inclusion, even if it may not have satisfied every criterion to the letter.

❶ All Words Used Are "Legitimate"

What is meant by legitimate? A legitimate word is any word that appears in one or more recognized major dictionaries and which is not generally described as archaic, rare, obsolete, informal, slang, or anything similar. In other words, while less common than what is in one's typical word-hoard, the words are all in current use in the English language. The word should appear in one or more standard dictionaries of the entire English language, including the *Oxford English Dictionary*, the 4th Edition of *The American Heritage Dictionary of the English Language*, the 2nd Edition of *The Random House Dictionary of the English Language*, and *Webster's Third International Dictionary*. Foreign words are acceptable if they are included in English dictionaries or are relatively easily found in English-language periodicals or books. When a foreign word is used, the language is given as well.

Language evolves over time, such that not only are new words constantly entering the vocabulary, but old words are constantly leaving. When use of the older words has become sufficiently infrequent (but not perhaps extinct altogether), those words are designated in dictionaries as "archaic" or "obsolete."[5] None of those words is used here. Application of this rule arises frequently with respect to words used by Shakespeare. If the only instance of usage is found in Shakespeare or other old sources, the word is not included, on the assumption that it has become archaic.

> **argument** (esp. about a trifling matter) *n.*: **brabble**. ❖ Aaron: Why, how now, lords! / So near the emperor's palace dare you draw, / And maintain such a quarrel openly? . . . / Now, by the gods that warlike Goths adore, / This petty **brabble** will undo us all. (William Shakespeare, *Titus Andronicus*, act 2, scene 1.)

The American Heritage Dictionary (4th Edition) and other dictionaries do not list "brabble" as archaic though *Webster's Third* does). Nevertheless, every usage of the word located is from Shakespeare. As for the examples used, almost every one is less than twenty years old, and most are less than ten years old.

In short, the synonyms in the word base will not ordinarily fall into any of the following categories:

a. Words that appear only in specialized dictionaries such as medical dictionaries or (with a very few exceptions) slang dictionaries (such as *The Random House Historical Dictionary of American Slang*, by Eric Partridge, *A Dictionary of Slang and Unconventional English*, by Jonathan Green, *The Dictionary of Contemporary Slang and Thesaurus of American Slang*, by Robert Chapman) or dictionaries of regional usage; dialectical words; or nonce words (words coined for a particular occasion).

b. Words that appear only in rare or unusual word books, such as *The Superior Person's Book of Words* or *Weird and Wonderful Words*, but are not found in standard dictionaries.

---

5. In general, the difference between an obsolete word and an archaic word is that, although both have fallen into disuse, an obsolete word has done so more recently.

c. Words that appear only in the *Official Scrabble Players Dictionary* or the British equivalent, *Official Scrabble Words*.

d. Words that are specific to the fields of biology, chemistry, physics, botany, zoology, specialized or complex anatomy, or most other medical or scientific specialties.

e. Words that merely constitute specific varieties of a larger category of items. These words would not be considered synonyms for the items themselves. For example, "boudin" is a type of sausage, but it is not a synonym for sausage itself.

f. Words that are new or recently coined (neologisms), especially computer-related terminology such as "blogger" (from "Web blogger"), "google," and "dot-com," and also terms such as "metrosexual," "spin doctor," "infomercial," and the like. The purpose of this thesaurus is to focus on established (albeit not common) words, as opposed to words that have only recently come into vogue.

How is it determined which words go into dictionaries in the first place? Conversely, how is it determined which words already in the dictionary have fallen into sufficient disuse to be considered archaic or obsolete? This is clearly a subjective process on both ends. What constitutes a legitimate word is ultimately nothing more than a matter of opinion, based on popular vote. When a writer or speaker uses a given word, he is in essence casting a vote for its legitimacy, and no one vote counts more or less than any other. As stated by Stefan Fatsis in his book *Word Freak* (Houghton Mifflin, 2001), "dictionaries are as subjective as any other piece of writing. Which words are included in them and which words are removed or ignored are decisions made by lexicographers based on shifting criteria, varying standards and divergent publishing goals."

How are the new words found? Joseph Pickett, executive editor of the 4th Edition of *The American Heritage Dictionary of the English Language* (Houghton Mifflin, 2000), states that "we have a systematic program for reading publications like *Time*, looking for examples of new words and new uses of old words." Based on this review, the people who compile the *American Heritage Dictionary* decided that words like "multitasking," "day trader," "erectile dysfunction," and "shock jocks" were worthy of inclusion in the 4th Edition of *The American Heritage Dictionary*, published in 2000, but they were not included in the 3rd Edition, published in 1992. These words have been "voted for" enough to be considered part of the language. Other words have received some votes through usage, but apparently not enough, such as "stalkerazzi," which did not make the 4th Edition.

Of course, the reverse process is true as well, which explains how thousands of words become archaic or obsolete: Not enough people voted for them by using them over the years, so they dropped out of the public vocabulary and hence out of the dictionaries. This, too, is a subjective process. What happens if a dictionary lists a word as archaic, but it suddenly appears in a current issue of a mainstream publication such as the *New York Times* or *Newsweek* or *USA Today*? Is it no longer archaic? Or was the one vote not enough? To take but one example: The word "venery" has two different definitions—sexual intercourse and the sport of hunting. Most dictionaries describe the word as being archaic for both definitions. Yet, the word has popped up in both senses in several different publications over the past ten years. For example:

intercourse (sexual . . .) *n*.: **venery**. ❖ Among the Major government's other recent disasters in the **venery** department have been headlines about (a) the environment minister who was forced to resign for impregnating a local government legislatress established to be not his wife . . . (Daniel Seligman, "Keeping Up: Depravity Among Conservatives," *Fortune*, 5/2/1994, p. 129.)

The rule of thumb used here is that if a word appears to be in current usage, it is considered a legitimate word if at least one dictionary does not categorize it as archaic.

② The Synonym Should Generally Not Be Found in Conventional Thesauruses

As discussed above, one of the reasons for the creation of this thesaurus was the premise that conventional thesauruses rarely assist the literate writer. The synonyms provided are so bland and simple that they were likely considered and rejected before the writer even opened the thesauruses. On a scale of 1 to 10, the complexity of the synonyms in a conventional thesaurus may range from about 1 to 6. In this thesaurus, the range is from about 6 to 10. Thus, while it would not be accurate to say that there is no overlap between the synonyms in this thesaurus and in a regular thesaurus, there is very little. Even if overlap does occur, the regular thesaurus, which lacks Clarifiers, can easily lead the user astray. The overlap word is thus included in this thesaurus to protect the writer from misusing the synonyms. In addition, a typical thesaurus may list twenty synonyms for a word, and the word in question may be buried down at number seventeen.

Consider the following two examples: The word "eudemonia" is listed as a synonym for "happiness" in both this thesaurus and *The Synonym Finder* [Rodale], which is considered comprehensive. The latter book has two paragraphs for the word "happiness" (although there is no explanation of how it and "eudemonia" differ). Under the second sense, the following sixteen synonyms for "happiness" are listed:

paradise, heaven, seventh heaven, Eden, utopia, Elysium, Arcadia, sunshine, halcyon days, beatitude, serenity, peace, eudemonia, gratification, fulfillment, contentment

Thus, while "eudemonia" is there, it's so buried among other choices that it is difficult for the user to focus on the word and consider its use. The fact that the user probably won't know what the word means anyway merely heightens this probability—not to mention the fact that the absence of a Clarifier will get the user into immediate trouble if he or she thinks that "eudemonia" can be used synonymously with, say, "gratification" or "sunshine." While *The Thinker's Thesaurus* also lists "eudemonia" as a synonym for "happiness," the presentation is hardly similar:

happiness *n.*: **eudemonia** (or **eudaemonia**) [based on the Aristotelean concept that the goal of life is happiness, to be achieved through reaching one's full potential as opposed to through the hedonistic pursuit of pleasure]. ❖ [The] objective is a good life, an Aristotelean **eudemonia**, which embraces a substantial dose of self-interest, but also incorporates concern for others, fulfilment at work, and the respect earned from others by participating in activities, including economic activities, which they value. (John Kay, "Staking a Moral Claim," *New Statesman*, 10/11/1996.)

Similarly, both this thesaurus and *The Synonym Finder* list "excrescence" as a synonym for "outgrowth." So does it need to be included in this thesaurus? The presentation in *The Synonym Finder* is as follows:

> **outgrowth** *n.*: 1. product, consequence, result, outcome, payoff, effect, aftereffect, aftermath, conclusion, upshot, final issue, eventuation, yield.
>
> 2. addition, supplement, postscript, sequel.
>
> 3. excrescence, offshoot, shoot, sprout, bud, burgeon, blossom, flower, fruit, projection, protuberance, bulge, knob, node, nodule, process, caruncle.[6]

Compare that presentation of "excrescence" with the one in this thesaurus:

> **outgrowth** *n.*: **excrescence**. [This word is often used literally, such as to describe an abnormal growth on the body or of a bodily part, such as a wart, but just as often is used in the sense of being an offshoot or consequence of a prior event or circumstance.] ❖ [In *Ceasefire!* author Cathy Young's intention] is to unmask the false claims of these "thought police," especially as they concern the supposed continued inequality of women in the United States. [C]ourt cases involving gender violence and sex crimes, child abuse and domestic violence, child custody and school curricula [are] **excrescences** of a cultural agenda that has been put in place to support spurious feminist claims and provide employment for enforcers. (Elizabeth Powers, "What Our Mothers Didn't Tell Us: Why Happiness Eludes the Modern Woman," *Commentary*, 3/1/1999.)

Even in those rare instances where the same synonym is included in this thesaurus and others and where the use of the word straight out of a conventional thesaurus is not likely to get the user in trouble (such as it could, in the above two examples), the use in this thesaurus of an example and just one synonym will likely cause the user to focus more seriously on that synonym, since it is not hidden among many others. Consider the following from *The Synonym Finder*:

> **enchant** *v.*: 1. cast a spell upon, spellbind, bewitch, charm, mesmerize, hypnotize, ensorcell, bind by incantations, hoodoo, hex
>
> 2. captivate, allure, delight, enrapture, fascinate, enamor, transport, entice, enthrall, infatuate, catch, win, lead captive, enchain

Thus we are given twenty-four possible synonyms for "enchant." However, most of these are uninteresting and will already be familiar to the user anyway, with the exception of "hoodoo," which is an unusual word but which is in fact presented incorrectly in *The Synonym Finder*. ("Hoodoo" is not a synonym for "enchant" but rather for "bad luck" which is how it is presented in this thesaurus.) "Ensorcell," on the other hand, is an interesting word and is correctly listed as a synonym for

---

6. No dictionary seems to support the notion that "excrescence" is synonymous with all the floral-based words in this section, such as sprout, bud, burgeon, blossom, flower, and fruit, but that's another issue.

"enchant." But would the reader really think about using it when it is buried among twenty-three other synonyms? Possibly not. This thesaurus presents the word as follows:

> **enchant** *v.t.*: **ensorcell** (or **ensorcel**). ❖ Trying to soften his military image and lure more female voters in New Hampshire, Gen. Wesley Clark switched from navy suits to argyle sweaters. It's an odd strategy. It's also a little alarming that he thinks the way to **ensorcell** women is to swaddle himself in woolly geometric shapes that conjure up images of Bing Crosby on the links or Fred MacMurray at the kitchen table. (Maureen Dowd, "The General Is Sweating His Image," *New York Times*, 1/13/2004.)

In short, for every synonym herein that may be found in a conventional thesaurus, there are dozens of others that are not. Moreover, for those relatively few that are found in conventional thesauruses, (1) the user runs the risk of misuse due to the lack of a Clarifier, and (2) the user may not notice the words at all because they are buried among all the mundane choices.

❸ The Meaning of the Word Generally Must be Understood from the Given Example Alone

Mere correct usage of the word is generally insufficient if the context does not make the definition clear. (There are some exceptions to this rule, which are discussed in the next section.) Consider the following example:

> L.L. Cool J. Here's a guy who has fallen in love with the sound of his own voice. All right, that's an occupational hazard for rappers, but rarely has this sort of verbal vanity exerted such a baleful stylistic influence as it does on this young urban **poetaster**. (David Hiltbrand, Picks & Pans: Song, *People*, 9/4/1989, p. 19.)

If the reader did not know the meaning of "poetaster," this particular example would not be very helpful. Consider instead the example used in this thesaurus, in which the meaning of the word is made clear from the entire passage:

> **poet** (bad . . .) *n.*: **poetaster** ❖ And now her first book of poems, *Yesterday I Saw the Sun*, has become a cause for further hiding. Just before the book's publication last month, a *New York Post* gossip item ridiculed her as a **poetaster**, contributing to her latest headache. "Ally Sheedy from bad to verse," chortled the headline on the item. (*Entertainment Weekly*, "Heartbreak—Ally Sheedy Says She Wrote Her Poems to Heal Her Wounds, but Their Publication Has Only Made Them Another Source of Pain," 3/29/1991, p. 28.)

This rule has particular applicability when an author, discussing a specific famous person, television show, movie, or book, assumes familiarity with the subject. If that assumption is wrong, the meaning of the word may not be apparent. This does not of course mean that there is anything wrong with the writing or the usage, but simply that the given passage is not appropriate for this thesaurus.

> **midget** *n*.: **homunculus**. ❖ Conceived as a spoof of TV's old amateur hours, [*The Gong Show*] had all its oddball ingredients in place by episode 1. There was creator and host Chuck Barris, a hyper **homunculus** in a bad tux. (A. J. Jacobs, "Encore: Cool and the 'Gong,'" *Entertainment Weekly*, 6/11/1999, p. 80.)

Unless one is familiar with Chuck Barris, this example will not help the reader understand the meaning of "homunculus"; hence the above example was not used. However, on other occasions, a word might be used with reference to a particular person, but familiarity with that person may not be necessary if the rest of the example supplies context.

> **voluptuous** (woman, often with stately or regal bearing) *adj*.: **Junoesque** [after ancient Roman goddess Juno, wife of Jupiter]. ❖ After rejections from countless modeling agencies, [Anna Nicole Smith was selected to be in *Playboy* magazine]. Her **Junoesque** appeal led straight to a three-year contract with Guess? "I always wanted to get back to be smaller than I was," she says. "But I just couldn't. Now I feel very good about it, and I wouldn't change my figure for anything." (*People*, "Anna Nicole Smith Is Livin' Large and Loving It," 9/20/1993, p. 76.)

④ The Word Cannot Be Defined within the Example Given

Anytime a writer uses a word but then feels compelled to define it for the reader, that usage is not included. The purpose of giving the examples in the first place is not only to show that a word is legitimate, nonarchaic, and in current use, but also to give the reader a sense of how a word may be used in a sentence or passage. If the writer must define the word, then in a sense both purposes are defeated. The fact that it is necessary to provide the definition indicates that the word is not being used naturally within the passage. Instead, undue attention is being drawn to the word, which defeats the second purpose of using the examples. Consider the following:

> **postcards** (collection and study of) *n*.: **deltiology**. ❖ With National Postcard Week on May 6–12, now's a good time to consider expanding your collection, say fans of **deltiology** (a fancy word for postcard collecting). (Penny Walker, "A Passion for Postcards," *Arizona Republic*, 5/5/2001.)

Indeed, in theory, any word can be given a "usage," simply if one states, for example, "Deltiology means postcard collecting," but this obviously does not further the goal of putting a given word in a context. Consider the contrast between the next two examples involving the use of the word "kakistocracy."

> **government** (by the least qualified or least principled people) *n*.: **kakistocracy**
>
> ❖ No, Matthew. Don Fletcher is right. "**Kakistocracy**. Are you familiar with that word?" Fletcher asked while nursing his coffee at the Bill O' Fare. "It means government by the

worst elements. . . . It doesn't matter whether you vote Republican or Democratic." (Steve Lopez, Nation/Campaign 2000: "Campaign Diary: Is It Over Yet? Gore. No, Wait. Bush," *Time*, 11/6/2000, p. 69.)

❖ Cannon: Well, we couldn't convict [Bill Clinton]. But I think the American people understand what [the Clinton] administration is all about. . . . And we have the greatest system on earth, a system strong enough to withstand the assaults over the last six years of this **kakistocracy**. (Sean Hannity and Alan Colmes, Ken Starr Investigation, Hannity & Colmes, Fox News Network, 6/24/1999.)

The first example merely defines the word, while the second uses it within the flow of the statement. For that reason, it is the second usage that is found in this thesaurus, and the same concept holds true for every usage found herein.

5 A Literal Usage of the Word Is Generally Preferred over a Figurative Usage

In many instances, a writer will use a word correctly, but in a figurative sense. With some exceptions, discussed below, those usages are avoided here. This is because presenting readers with figurative examples only may be misleading.

> **murder** (of parent or close relative) *n.*: **parricide**. ❖ Sharpton says [Jesse] Jackson, 60, has been his mentor, friend and "surrogate father" but now is an exhausted volcano, viewed by young blacks as "an establishment figure." . . . Sharpton compares Jackson to Muhammad Ali: Great once; can't fight anymore. . . . **Parricide** isn't pretty. (George F. Will, "Sharpton Eyes the Prize," *Washington Post*, 1/10/2002.)

When one is trying to understand appropriate usage, it is easier to expand from the literal to the figurative. Conversely, when one is familiar with the figurative use of a word only, it can be a recipe for trouble. In the above example, George Will's use of the word "parricide" is perfectly appropriate for his purposes. Nevertheless, given his figurative use of the word, it is not the best example for purposes of this thesaurus, because it does not convey the fact that parricide is the literal killing of a parent or relative. Indeed, it could leave a reader who is unfamiliar with the word with the impression that the mere act of showing disrespect to or criticizing one's parents could be an act of parricide.

One exception to this general rule is those words that are almost always used in their figurative sense and only occasionally in their literal sense. The word "thralldom," meaning "slavery" or "bondage," is used in a figurative sense far more than in a literal sense, and thus this thesaurus gives the figurative usage:

> **bondage** *n.*: **thralldom**. ❖ We Western women, it appears, still have not shucked off male ideas of female beauty; the voluntary mutilation of plastic surgery bears witness to our **thralldom**. (Elizabeth Ward, "The Trouble with Women," *Washington Post*, 5/23/1999.)

Similarly, the verb "flagellate" means to "whip" or "flog," but it is almost always used in the figurative sense of self-criticism, often as in "self-flagellate." Therefore, a figurative example was again used.

> **criticize** (oneself) *v.t.*: **flagellate** (*n.*: **flagellation**). [This word means to whip or flog another, and is properly used in that sense, but is generally used figuratively, esp. as in criticism of oneself, sometimes as in self-flagellation.] ❖ Journalists belong to the only profession whose members regularly get together to **flagellate** themselves in public. (Sheryl McCarthy, "Here's How We Cover the Blob," *Newsday*, 4/12/1995.)

A second exception is where it was felt that the literal meaning of the word was clear, even where the example did not present a literal usage. For example, the word "theanthropic" means having both human and divine or godlike qualities. The tongue-in-cheek example presented here is as follows:

> **godlike** (having both human and . . . attributes) *adj.*: **theanthropic**. ❖ [After September 11, 2001,] our government should order the CIA to air drop to the Mullahs and their angry young men millions of pages from the *Victoria's Secret* catalogues. Anyone familiar with the September 11 atrocities knows that these fellows are sexually repressed. . . . Pursuing the **theanthropic** [Victoria's Secret model Laetitia Casta] through Google-space, they will be lured toward the pages of *The American Spectator*, where they will enjoy the health benefits of cultural diversity. (R. Emmett Tyrell Jr., "The Continuing Crisis," *American Spectator*, 1/1/2002.)

While Laetitia Casta may indeed be a lovely woman, one presumes that the user will understand that she is not literally a goddess. Just as important, however, so long as the writer understands the literal meaning of the word, there is nothing wrong with using it in a figurative sense, as Tyrell did here and Will did above.

⑥ The Base Word Must Logically Lead to the Synonym

The mere fact that a word may be too unusual for inclusion in a regular thesaurus does not automatically render it appropriate for inclusion in this one. This is because certain words refer to concepts, theories, or principles rather than single words. Thus if there is no single word that one might logically connect with a given synonym, that synonym was excluded, no matter how useful the concepts, theories, or principles were. For example, the word "meliorism," although a fine word, does not readily lend itself to a one-word base. The same is true for words such as "diglossia," "duopsony," "eponym," "featherbedding," "festschrift," "fideism," and "obscurantism," It does no good to include an interesting word if the user is not likely to ever find that word due to an inability to connect it to an appropriate base word.

On the opposite end, some synonyms, although unusual, are very close to a common base word but don't add anything to that word. For example, most people have probably never heard the word "botheration." However, it is no surprise that it means the act of bothering or state of being bothered. It is essentially just the noun form of the verb "to bother." Similarly, "perfectibilism" is a rare (though legitimate) synonym for . . . guess what? Perfectionism. Words such as "botheration" and "perfectibilism" (of which there are a surprising number) are not included in this thesaurus.

7 A Note on the Use of "As In"

In many instances, the base word is followed by a Clarifier that includes the words "as in." This is done either because the base word may have several different definitions or because the synonym given may not have precisely the same meaning as the base word but the user may nevertheless be inclined to look up the base word in hopes of finding a similar or related synonym. When the connection between the base word and the synonym may be unclear or even appear questionable, what follows "as in" is intended to explain or fine-tune the connection and hit closer to the mark.

For example, one of the definitions of "fatuous" is "delusional." "Delusional" in turn is related to, but not a direct synonym for, "imaginary" or "illusory." One might call the tooth fairy imaginary, but not delusional. Nevertheless, there are times when one might look to the word "imaginary" or "illusory" when searching for a good word that is in fact closer to "delusional." This situation, which arises frequently, is addressed in this thesaurus as follows:

unreal (as in delusional) *adj.*: **fatuous**. See *delusional*

illusory (as in delusional) *adj.*: **fatuous**. See *delusional*

imaginary (as in delusional) *adj.*: **fatuous**. See *delusional*

delusional *adj.*: **fatuous**. ❖ After the 1992 election, I wrote [an article] on Bill Clinton. . . . I did express high, and in retrospect rather **fatuous**, hopes for the coming Clinton Administration. . . . I cherished, for a time, a kind of fresh-start, non-partisan, post-ideological, post–Cold War faith that a new-paradigm Clinton might lead the nation brilliantly toward . . . toward, well, the bridge to the twenty-first century! (Lance Morrow, "U.S. v. Clinton," *National Review*, 9/28/1998, p. 39.)

In this example, "as in" is used not only to show that "delusional" is the closest synonym to "fatuous" but also to demonstrate that using "illusory" or "imaginary" as synonyms for "fatuous," while sometimes workable, can also be problematic. The "as in" Clarifier helps the user avoid this pitfall. Consider also the following example: The essence of "perspicuous" is something that is understandable. In the right context, "clear" and "simple" might be perfectly adequate synonyms for "perspicuous," which is why these words are included among the base words for perspicuous. However, in the wrong context, these words may have no connection whatsoever. One might call the Caribbean Sea "clear," but not "perspicuous." Once again, "as in" solves this problem.

clear (as in understandable) *adj.*: **perspicuous**. See *understandable*

simple (as in understandable) *adj.*: **perspicuous**. See *understandable*

understandable *adj.*: **perspicuous.** ❖ One [of the "Principles of Mathematics"] was the "theory of descriptions" which purported to solve a problem that Plato had wrestled with, namely how one can think and speak of non-existent things. The theory showed how various tricky propositions could be translated into something more **perspicuous** and less puzzling; it soon came to be seen as a model of how to philosophise. (*Economist*, "The Philosophers That Sophie Skipped," 12/7/1996, p. 79.)

In short, any word or phrase that follows "as in" as part of a Clarifer is considered the word or phrase that comes closest in meaning to the synonym used. If a given base word does not appear at first to connect logically to the synonym, then what follows "as in" should provide the logical connection.

8 A Note on the Use of "See"

As we saw above with the word "perspicuous," many synonyms are arrived at through multiple base words. However, so as to avoid repetition of examples, there is only one example presented for each synonym. The synonym that contains the example will follow the word "See," and is generally considered the synonym that is closest to the base word in question. Thus "See *understandable*" means that the example given will be found at "understandable."

9 Notes on the Presentation of the Examples

a. When the author of an example was known, he or she is listed.

b. When there were multiple authors of one passage, only the first author's name is listed.

c. When the author of the piece quoted another person who used the word in question, this is noted.

d. The titles were occasionally shortened or modified, particularly where there was verbiage that was not relevant to the passage.

e. Reference to the volume numbers of periodicals is not made.

f. The page on which the passage appeared is provided if known.

g. The source provided may not have been the initial source in which the passage appeared, particularly when the author is a syndicated columnist.

h. Any words in brackets (but not parentheses) are my own words and may represent (1) an addition to the text without any deletion, often for purposes of clarification or (2) a substitution of fewer words for longer deleted material, which could be of any length. Ellipses (. . .) represent deletion of material from the text, which also could be of any length. In general, the intent was to present as much of the passage as was deemed necessary to give the user a good sense of the word without changing the author's meaning. Small portions of the text were sometimes included as part of the example when I felt that inclusion of the sentence gave a sense of completeness to the passage. The premise is that if a passage is thought-provoking or if it serves to amuse, intrigue, entertain, or inspire, then the synonym itself might be better remembered than if the example was a mere sentence fragment.

Ⅴ In Defense of the Hard Word

A. Our Shrinking National Vocabulary

Exposure to progressively more rare words expands the verbal reservoir. Exposure to media with entirely common words keeps the reservoir at existing levels. Years of consumption of low rare-word media have a dire intellectual effect. A low-reading, high-viewing childhood and adolescence prevent a person from handling . . . civic and cultural media such as the New York Review of Books and the National Review. The vocabulary is too exotic.

MARK BAUERLEIN, *The Dumbest Generation*

These days, in matters of vocabulary, to use a word that is not understood by the lowest common denominator of our society is almost to be seen as politically incorrect or offensive. We are so bombarded by the mantra of "write clearly and simply" that to use any word that is not readily known by all is to be labeled "elitist" or "pretentious" or "bombastic," no matter that the word in question may be legitimate and perfectly suited for the occasion; indeed, that it may be the best word for the occasion.[7]

It often seems that when a writer uses a word that is not instantly recognized by everyone, it must be an example of poor writing, because (so the argument goes) the only good writing is that which is "clear"—using a limited vocabulary understood by all. Virtually anytime a writer's lexicon goes over the reader's head, you can be sure that the old gripe about "having to reach for a dictionary" is coming. The following is a typical criticism of the use of harder words:

Studies show that even the most educated Americans prefer to read at or below the 10th-grade reading level. . . . The way to credibility is to speak and write plainly without language that bewilders or misleads. And the way to lose credibility is to veil the message in showy blather.[8]

Given that very few of the words in this thesaurus—though all perfectly legitimate, dictionary-recognized words—would be recognized by those at or below the tenth-grade reading level, it stands to reason that the authors of every passage herein lose credibility because of their "showy blather."

---

7. ❖ Of course, at times, the directive to "write clearly" simply means to not be unnecessarily verbose, which is always good advice. For example, saying "If there are any points on which you require explanation or further particulars, we shall be glad to furnish such additional details as may be required by telephone" could be written simply as: "If you have any questions, please call." (Tamra Orr, "Getting Rid of Goobledygook: Don't Let Your Writing Become More Complicated Than It Has to Be," *Writing!* 9/1/2003.)

8. Paula LaRoque, "Dumb—or Dumber?" *Quill*, 5/1/2003.

But what would our world be like if we were all discouraged from using any words too sophisticated for a tenth grader?

Susan Jacoby, a leading observer of the increase of ignorance in America, in addressing the issue of our collective comfort with our lack of knowledge has written:

> [Another] factor behind the new American dumbness [is] not lack of knowledge per se but arrogance about that lack of knowledge. The problem is not just the things we do not know . . . it's the alarming number of Americans who have smugly concluded that they do not need to know such things in the first place. ("The Dumbing of America," *Washington Post*, 2/17/2008.)

This same smugness applies to our vocabularies. When a fifty-cent word is thrown out in public, you can be sure that it is the user of that word who will be put on the defensive, rather than readers or listeners feeling any sense of discomfort that they don't know what the word means in the first place. In her book *The Age of American Unreason* (Pantheon, 2008), Jacoby notes "the precipitous decline [since the 1960s and prior] of reading and writing skills, now attested to by every objective measure, from tests of both children and adults to the shrinking of the number of Americans who read for pleasure."

In addressing the consequences of the fact that we don't read as much as we used to, Harvard University professor Peter Gibbon has written: "Students spend more time with media than with teachers"; they are "raised in a visual culture," which results in "shrinking vocabularies, shorter attention spans, and less efficient reading skills."[9]

The dumbing down of our collective vocabularies is no accident and did not come about just by circumstance. In the age of e-mails and text messaging (and now Twitter), letter writing is becoming a lost art. We are also constantly exhorted to avoid using hard words by those who would teach us how to write. "Keep it simple. Forget the idea that long, complicated words make you sound smarter. Use clear, plain language. It gets your point across more efficiently without confusing your readers."[10]

One writer urges the use of the simplest possible words in direct mail ad copy: "Does the reader comprehend what you're saying or must [he] reach for the dictionary?. . . I recently read an advertisement for a new book in which the writer tells of the excitement of reading 'the bildungsroman of the main character.' [The dictionary defines that as] '[a] novel about the moral and psychological growth of the main character.' Why didn't they write those words?" Of course: Why use one interesting (and economical) word, when eleven dull words will do just as nicely? "Bildungsroman" is obviously not an everyday word. But does that mean we should never use it? Or perhaps we should just assume that all those who receive direct mail are especially unintelligent or too lazy to look up the word.

Is our vocabulary shrinking? Some studies demonstrate that we know and use fewer words today than we used to; others refute the claim. Studies cited in *Harper's* Index show that the average number of words in the written vocabulary of a six- to fourteen-year-old American child has gone

---

9. Quoted in "Don't Know Much About History," *American Enterprise*, 1/1/2003.
10. "Write Right," *Career World*, 11/1/2003.

from 25,000 in 1945 to 10,000 in 2000, though some question whether the decline is that substantial. In *Doing Our Own Thing—The Degradation of Language and Music and Why We Should, Like, Care* (Gotham Books, 2003), John McWhorter contrasts the eloquence with which we used to write and speak with how we do so now. What is particularly striking about his disquisition is the evidence of how this deterioration cuts across every socioeconomic and educational level, from those at the pinnacle of academia, politics, entertainment, and society to the most uneducated among us. As but one example, McWhorter quotes from one of many letters from Richard Robinson to Helen Jewett, an upscale prostitute, whom Robinson was later accused of murdering in the 1830s. He was a nineteen-year-old clerk with an eighth-grade education. He wrote:

> At best we live but one little hour, strut at our own conceit and die. How unhappy must those persons be who cannot enjoy life as it is, seize pleasure as it comes floating on like a noble ship, bound for yonder distant port with all sails set. Come will ye embark?—then on we go, gayly, hand in hand, scorning all petty and trivial troubles, eagerly gazing on our rising sun, till the warmth of its beams [i.e., love] causes our sparkling blood to o'erflow and mingle in holy delight, as mind and soul perchance some storms arise . . .[11]

McWhorter's emphasis is not on the abnormality of Robinson's writing skills in comparison to his level of education (except in comparison to how today's eighth graders would write) but rather on its very typicality, as he demonstrates with one example after another.

B. "My Vocabulary Is Perfect; Yours Is Deficient or Pompous"

We tend to believe that a word is unfamiliar because it is unfamiliar to us.

WILLIAM F. BUCKLEY

What is a hard word? It is not necessarily a long word. Rather, it is simply a word whose usage is sufficiently infrequent that many English speakers and writers, even the more literate ones, may not be familiar with the word or its definition.[12]

There are many who decry the use of hard words in writing or in speech and who feel we would all be better off if they simply didn't exist. One such person is James Kilpatrick, who has been waging a one-way war against William F. Buckley—or more precisely William F. Buckley's vocabulary—for many years. In article after article, Kilpatrick has railed against what he considers to be Buckley's

---

11. John McWhorter, *Doing Our Own Thing* (Gotham Books, 2003), pp. 123–24.

12. People often wonder whether there are any one-word synonyms for a hard word or the word "synonym" itself. It is ironic that out of the more than 600,000 words in the English language, the answer appears to be, not really. About the closest we come to a hard word is "sesquepedalian," a noun meaning "long word" or, as an adjective, "given to the use of long words." Also, an "inkhorn" word or term means one that is pedantic or affectedly learned. In addition "recondite" means not easily understood, but this can apply to many concepts and not simply words. Finally, the rare word "polyonymy" (*adj.*: polyonymous) means the use of various names for one thing. It comes from a Greek word meaning "having many names." As for "thesaurus," a "synonymicon" is a lexicon of synonyms.

unnecessary use of "recondite words." These articles include "Each Writer Must Choose to Be Erudite or Be Clear," in a syndicated column that appeared on February 16, 1997, and a critical review of Buckley's book *The Right Word*, which appeared in the December 23, 1996, issue of *National Review*. In addition, while not directly mentioning Buckley, Kilpatrick touched on the same themes in another syndicated column that appeared on November 30, 1997: "Essence of Writing: Have Something to Say and Say It Clearly."

In each of these pieces and many others, Kilpatrick's theme is the same: write so as to be understood by the widest possible audience and refrain from using words that may not be generally familiar to your readers. To help make his point, Kilpatrick often uses the technique frequently resorted to by him and others who would stand with him on this issue: mockery. Indeed, if one is so inclined, it is easy to try to make fun of those with larger vocabularies by forcing difficult words on the reader in an unnatural fashion, especially by stacking them on top of each other. Kilpatrick opens his December 1996 review of *The Right Word* as follows:

> If I were to say of Mr. Buckley's latest compendium that it is not at all an anodyne work, I could fairly be indicted for gross meiosis. Even a necessarily truncated review, such as this brief epitome, cannot offer more than a meager adumbration of this kaleidoscopic omnium gatherum. What an epiphany it is, to share his eudaemonia! What a nimiety of logomachical riches have we here! I am quite undone.

The primary problem with Kilpatrick's reasoning is that it requires veering away from the dictionary as the standard reference source for what does and does not constitute a "legitimate" English word and instead requires us to draw a completely arbitrary line in the sand as to what words are or are not appropriate. But who sets the standard? Clearly it can't be Buckley, since his standard is evidently too high. Is it then Kilpatrick himself? Should he be the official word arbiter? But why him? Or, to borrow from the standard set forth by Supreme Court Justice Potter Stewart when deciding what constituted obscene material, should our standard for inappropriately hard words be: "We know them when we see them"?

In attempting to answer these questions, it becomes immediately apparent that any attempt to reach the goal of a universally agreeable standard is a fool's errand. No two people have the same lexicon and thus no one of us can set a standard. Just as certain words in Buckley's vocabulary are unacceptable to Kilpatrick, there are undoubtedly words in Kilpatrick's vocabulary that are unfamiliar to others who may be less literate than he is.

Consider a traffic analogy: On a highway with no speed limit where all traffic is moving in the same direction, the left-hand lane is for passing. Those who are in the left-hand lane should move over to the right-hand lane when someone is trying to pass. That is true regardless of the speed of either the front car or the car trying to pass. If the front car is going 80 mph and the car trying to pass is going 90, then the front car should get out of the way. It is not for the driver of the front car to say: "I'm going fast enough; I'll set the standard speed here."

If we were to carry Kilpatrick's argument to its logical conclusion, where would that leave us? It would seem to require that all words that are on the wrong side of an imaginary standard would need to be jettisoned from the language, since there would no longer be any need for them—a reductio ad absurdum that few would endorse. Thus, just based on his paragraph above, we would likely have to say good-bye to "anodyne," "meiosis," "adumbration," "omnium gatherum," "epiphany," "nimiety" and "logomachical" as words in the English language, even though other writers have chosen to use all of them at one time or another. Presumably there are thousands of others that would also become extinct.[13]

Even within Kilpatrick's own mocking of Buckley's word choices, the unsolvable problem of the folly of trying to choose the appropriate standard immediately becomes clear. One knows right away that "meiosis," "omnium gatherum," "eudaemonia," and "nimiety" (all of which are in this thesaurus, incidentally) are unfamiliar words. But what about the other words he includes in the same passage, such as "compendium," "truncated," "epitome," "meager," and even "epiphany"? Though none of these words is unusual, it is probably safe to say that they are not necessarily familiar to everyone. But surely Kilpatrick is not suggesting that these words should be included with his list of words that have no place in the English language? Or should the reader know what those words mean, and thus they should be separated from words that would be placed on death row?

What Kilpatrick has done (likely subconsciously) is to set himself up as the proverbial "reasonable man" when it comes to vocabulary. This is something we all do (again, likely subconsciously). In other words, if I'm the reasonable man, and you're using words I don't know, the problem must necessarily be with your unnecessarily fancy writing or speech, not my limited vocabulary. However, if you don't understand a word I use, I may consider you a pretty dim bulb, since "everyone" should know the words I do. Since I'm the reasonable man, I'm always in the right and you're always in the wrong. Heads I win, tails you lose.

What are the possible reasons one might have for opposing the use of unfamiliar words? Consider the book *Witness*, the biography of Whittaker Chambers by Sam Tanenhaus, which was a Pulitzer Prize finalist in 1998. That book contains the following passages:

A **refulgent** star of the [Communist] movement, as indeed "the purest Bolshevik writer ever to function in the United States," Chambers involved himself in various projects. [Chambers] was an adept linguist, with idiomatic German still Communism's **lingua franca**, and so could easily communicate with agents sent from overseas.

They became a "tightly knit unit," bound together by the effort to maintain the household on the **exiguous** sum Jay sent them, eight dollars a week by Vivian's recollection.

Passports were essential for traveling Communist agents and American passports were preferred above all others because anyone, even non-English speakers, could travel on

---

13. Kilpatrick is hardly alone in his views. Indeed, he likely speaks for a majority of people. Virtually any time a book contains more than a handful of less commonly used words, the author is sure to be taken to task by reviewers for the use of words the reviewers did not know. It would seem that Kilpatrick, and many similarly minded people, can be advocating only one possible conclusion, namely that the kinds of words that appear in this thesaurus should never be used and thus should be removed from the dictionary altogether. But isn't that a rather sad result, with the upshot simply the dumbing down of our collective vocabulary?

them without arousing suspicion, thanks to the country's vast **polyglot** population, with its many immigrants.

Let us concede, first, that the words in bold are not common words known by everyone, and, second, that the author could have used, but chose not to use, "bright" in place of "refulgent," "common language" in place of "lingua franca," "meager" in place of "exiguous," and "multilingual" in place of "polyglot." So why didn't he? (Indeed, Kilpatrick might pose this very question, because, in his review of *The Right Word*, he asks: "[W]hat is gained in communication by speaking of the politician who tergiversates? The fellow waffles, or flip-flops, or reneges. Why not say so?")[14] One who deplores the use of hard words may offer the following arguments, the first of which is critical of Tanenhaus and the rest of which appear to be qualified defenses of his writing *but,* as discussed below, qualified in an erroneous way:

1. Tanenhaus made poor word choices, Pulitzer Prize credentials or not, and it would have been better writing for him to use the simpler synonyms.
2. I personally happen to be familiar with all of his word choices, and, because the words are within my own lexicon, I have no problem with them, even if others might not know their meaning.
3. These words are appropriate because Tanenhaus is writing for a sophisticated and particularly literate audience.
4. This writing is acceptable because the hard words are sporadic and interspersed with easy words; in other words, they are not crammed together.
5. Hard words are acceptable if and only if their meanings can be deduced from the context of the passage.

The first response makes no sense unless one is prepared to argue that the authors of virtually every passage in this thesaurus are poor writers because they didn't use the very simplest words at all times. This is obviously a ludicrous argument. The second response again raises the issue of whether we must adopt a hypothetical "reasonable person" standard. But as we have seen, that is impossible. Whose vocabulary do we make the exact dividing line? This too is a silly result.

As to the third response, it is quite true that we often hear it said that authors should "write suitably for their audience." Indeed, Kilpatrick makes this very point himself.[15] If we are talking

---

14. The words chosen from Tanenhaus's book actually represent easier targets of criticism than the vast majority of entries in this thesaurus because they at least have simpler one-word equivalents, and thus can be presented without a Clarifier. As for every entry in the book that *does* have a Clarifier, however, the whole point is that they have no one-word simpler equivalent in the first place. Thus, they exist not to be duplicative of existing words, but to economically fill a void. In other words, if one can successfully defend these particular choices of Tanenhaus's, it is even easier to defend all of the entries in this thesaurus that have Clarifiers.

15. In his review of *The Right Word*, he states: "Every person who writes or speaks for a living must begin his task with certain assumptions. The preacher assumes a certain level of biblical literacy. The reporter who covers Congress assumes that his readers know what is meant by a partisan vote. . . . Fair enough. But in [Buckley's] quotidian columns, he assumes too much." (One wonders why he didn't follow his own practice and use a more mundane word than "quotidian.")

about differentiating between readers by age, there is certainly merit to this advice. For example, these words would obviously not be appropriate for children. However, once we confine the "audience" to adults, the advice makes far less sense. Indeed, it's only possible to carry out the advice if we differentiate between "smart adults" and "dumb adults" (or, more precisely, "literate adults" and "not-so-literate adults"). A further consequence is that a word that might be appropriate in, say, the *National Review* or the *Nation* would not be appropriate in *People* magazine. But isn't that patronizing, and doesn't it discourage readers (and, just as important, writers) from ever learning new words?[16] Indeed, based on the fact that so many of the examples herein do in fact come from widely read (shall we say non-snooty?) periodicals, such as *People, Entertainment Weekly, Time,* and *Newsweek,* it would appear that the authors of those articles are implicitly expressing their disagreement with the foes of hard words through their frequent use of excellent but uncommon words, which undoubtedly would fall outside of any mythical and mystical "approved word list."

The fourth response—that the kinds of words used in this thesaurus are perfectly acceptable so long as they are not jammed together, two or three to a sentence, in sentence after sentence—presumes that this is in fact a prevalent problem among writers today. But in fact, who writes like that anyway? Certainly not the authors of any of the examples in this thesaurus. Indeed, virtually the only time one sees the types of sentences written by Kilpatrick above is, ironically, when other writers do exactly what Kilpatrick does, which is to make the multiple hard words the very raison d'être of the sentence for one reason or another, and string them together for humorous effect (often to make fun of writers who use hard words or to salute those who write all of the weird word books). Examples abound.[17] Are these tongue-in-cheek examples truly the kind of writing Kilpatrick is fulminating against? Doubtful. The authors cited in this thesaurus use hard words as useful conduits through which to make their points and not as the points themselves. Thus, if the argument is simply against using too many hard words in a row, then those making the argument are merely setting up a straw man so they can blow him down.

As to the final response, if one would approve of the use of all hard words if and only if their meanings can be determined from the context (even if the reader would otherwise have no clue as

---

16. Kilpatrick appears to engage in this patronization himself. Returning again to his review of *The Right Word*, he states, as we saw, that in Buckley's "quotidian columns, he assumes too much" and states that "the problem is that Bill writes solely for the discriminating ear and the fastidious eye." He then contrasts this with his own reluctance to use hard words because "my column is aimed at the general readership of the 220 papers that carry it." But what is he really saying here when one reads between the lines? He seems to be saying that his "general readers" may be incurious—unwilling to deal with hard words that appear in the "quotidian columns" they read. In fact, however, virtually every example in this thesaurus comes from a "quotidian column" (or book) that is in fact "aimed at the general readership." The examples are not from specialized sources and certainly are not written "solely for the discriminating ear and the fastidious eye."

17. ❖ In his first formal interview since being dumped as Treasurer, the erudite Mr. Ralph Willis seemingly could find no more eloquent way of expressing his emotion than "I'm very pissed off." [He should have said]: "Well, actually my untimely labefaction has left me feeling somewhat lactiferous and, although I do not intend to indulge in any longanimity, I do admit to a vague sense of lypophrenia. . . . And furthermore, I'm not diversivolent, but I feel there was absolutely no nonfeasance or murcidity on my part and I think the whole thing is a real proctalgia." (Megan Turner, "Five-Star Words," *Courier-Mail* [Brisbane, Australia], 3/14/1992.) ❖ Finding the Christmas shopping moliminous? Do you think the whole event is badot, over-promoted by kakistocracy and the gilly-gaupus? Do you drumble down the local High Street feeling nocent about all you haven't done, or are you quite pococurantish in the face of pressure to spend your hard-earned money on finnimbruns? (*Financial Times* [London] "Present Perfect," 12/13/2003.)

to their meaning out of context), this only means that those who take this position and I are on the same page, at least in those instances. The use of those specific hard words would need no defense. Even here, however, there are problems with this position. First, if the only goal is truly to be clear, then why (one might ask facetiously) even take a chance on an unfamiliar word that forces the reader to guess its meaning, a guess that may or may not be accurate? Why not just resort to the simplest possible words? Consider the following example, which is a perfectly appropriate use of the excellent word "sockdolager." In reading it, consider the following two questions: (1) Can you say for certain what it means? (2) Even if the answer is yes, might a simpler word have sufficed?

> The American Council for the Arts [wanted to] show how much the American people love the arts. . . . [T]hey retained pollster Lou Harris [who knows that] 99% of a public opinion poll lies in framing the questions to be asked. . . . Lou asked them, "How important do you think it is to the quality of life in the community to have such things as museums, theater and concert halls in the community?" That was a sockdolager [because 84% said very important or somewhat important.]

A "sockdolager" is a decisive or telling factor, remark, or blow, kind of like a knockout punch. It was the perfect word to use in the above passage, in that Harris knew what question to ask that would yield the telling response it did. And yet, might not the author have used a simpler (but less interesting) word or phrase, such as "knockout punch" or "telling factor," just to make sure that everyone understood the message? The author could have, but thankfully didn't. And guess who the author was? None other than Kilpatrick himself.[18]

Second, we are often on a slippery slope in terms of whether or not the context does the trick. For example, in the passages cited above, wouldn't it have been safer for Tanenhaus to have used simpler terms than "lingua franca" and "polyglot"? Was "refulgent" really necessary? Similarly, at several points in Kilpatrick's article, he is guilty of the very same crime of which he accuses Buckley (as he was in the use of "sockdolager"). At one point, he states that Buckley's editor "undertook this labor con amore, and all language lovers are in his debt." For those who don't know Italian, why not just say that he did it lovingly? Wouldn't that be simpler? Later, Kilpatrick states that "my objection, I suppose, is mostly a complaint pro bono publico." For those who don't know Latin, why not just say that his complaint is for the public good?

There are clearly many instances where the meaning of a hard word is not easily ascertainable from the context and yet the word is perfect for the situation. For example, if I were to advise readers that part of this essay is a "prolepsis," I highly doubt that most would know what I meant. And yet, it is the right word. It is a rebuttal made by responding to an anticipated objection to an argument before that objection has been made (namely the objection that we should not use hard words because they may prevent readers from understanding our writing).

The word "Luddite" is just the right word in the following passage, but even in context, its meaning is not necessarily clear, not to mention its derivation:

---

18. James J. Kilpatrick, "An Artfully Assembled Poll," *St. Petersburg (FL) Times*, 4/29/1992.

[Al Gore's] role as an enemy of medical progress should come as no surprise. When bio-tech Luddite Jeremy Rifkin wrote *Algeny*—a diatribe against gene-based drug development in which he implied that the human life span should revert to that enjoyed before the Bronze Age so that mankind could be closer to nature—it was Al Gore who wrote the glowing blurb that Rifkin has given us "an insightful critique of the changing way in which mankind views nature." (Robert Goldberg, "The Luddite: [Al Gore] Invented the Inter-net?" *National Review*, 8/14/2000.)[19]

In the following example, the writer uses "aptronym," again a perfect word for the situation, and again one that most readers couldn't define in most contexts. Can you figure it out?

Viewers apparently haven't minded that they already knew the ending [to the World Series of Poker]. The well-publicized competition, held in May, was won by Tennessee amateur Chris Moneymaker (talk about **aptronyms**!), whose only previous poker tournaments were on the Internet. (Jack Broom, "A Sure Bet: Poker Is Hot; Televised Games Spur Local Players to Up the Ante," *Seattle Times*, 9/14/2003.)[20]

This same point is especially true with respect to many of the entries that involve phrases rather than single words. Even though the context does not make the phrase clear, it is still le mot juste.

An electioneering budget is an **argumentum ad crumenam**, and most elections in democracies have a strong element of this old argument. It may not be idealistic, but it is the way people vote. (Philip Howard, "Rhetoric and All That Rot," *Times* [London], 4/12/1991.)[21]

An article entitled "The Importance of Being Simple," though being one of many that support Kilpatrick's point of view, unwittingly demonstrates its very dilemma. The writer states:

We must befuddle our readers with at least one rare word in each paragraph, with style and form and with quality of expression—so we tell ourselves. . . . Befuddle? Isn't this a rare mouthful? Goodness gracious me, I'm not practicing what I'm trying to preach! You're right. There must be simpler words than befuddle. How about baffle or confound then? You think that they're still not simple enough? Well, let's settle for confuse. Okay?[22]

It seems as if the writer is being facetious, but he is not. His viewpoint is apparently that writ-ers should never use the words "befuddle," "baffle," or "confound," because they could just as eas-

---

19. **traditionalist** (spec. a person who is opposed to advancements in technology) *n.*: **Luddite.** [The word is based on a group of British workers who destroyed laborsaving textile machinery between 1811 and 1816 for fear that the machinery would reduce employment. It is generally, but not always, used disparagingly.]
20. **name** (of a person well-suited to its owner) *n.*: **aptronym.**
21. **appeal** (making an . . . to one's monetary self-interest) *n*: **argumentum ad crumenam.**
22. Ang Seng Chai, "The Importance of Being Simple," *New Straits Times* [Malaysia], 1/17/2004.

ily resort to the most common synonym, namely "confuse." But isn't this an absurd argument? Can one imagine even Kilpatrick going to this extreme? Where do we ever draw the line? Clearly, if this writer is going to object to "befuddle," "baffle," or "confound," then what would he say about Kilpatrick's choices of "con amore" and "pro bono publico"?

Even if we assume, for argument's sake, that certain words have an exact simpler synonym, does that mean that the harder word should never be used? For example, an "ecdysiast" is simply a strip tease artist. Even though it is safe to assume that not everyone knows that, the word "ecdysiast" is still used all the time, often with the context providing no assistance as to the word's meaning.[23] Does that mean that we should simply do away with the word because we can insert "stripper" in its place? Or is the use of "ecdysiast" always poor writing unless presented in context?

As Buckley puts it: "It is a curious thing, this universal assumption . . . that the American people are either unaware of the unusual word or undisposed to hear it and find out what it means, thus broadening not merely their vocabulary—that isn't the important thing—but their conceptual and descriptive powers." In short, even if there is an exact simpler synonym, this thesaurus is useful if a writer does not want to keep using the same words again and again and wants to use more interesting words.[24]

The problem is not only where to draw the line, but the fact that the hard-word critics are encouraging us to work toward a lowest common denominator; to shrink our vocabulary as much as possible. Is it not a worthy goal to expand our vocabularies as much as possible rather than to prod writers in the opposite direction? The only imaginable response to this is to advocate (once again) a "standard of reason," in deciding which words pass muster and which do not. But that brings us right back to the original flaw in the argument: There is no single standard of reason. To many people, portions of Kilpatrick's own writing ("con amore"? "pro bono publico"?) must come off as abstruse (or would that word be rejected as well?)—just as Buckley's do to him. So there can never be a reasonable, let's-all-agree-what-words-are-acceptable-and-what-words-aren't standard. Nor should we even try to set such a standard, for the mere attempt is necessarily an exercise in slicing and dicing perfectly good and legitimate words out of the dictionary, all in the name of no one's feeling inadequate.

What if, however, one were to disagree with my argument entirely and wholly support Kilpatrick's worldview as to the use of unfamiliar words? Wouldn't it be nice to have a good word to describe the kind of writing that the hard-word critics bemoan? This thesaurus has several. One of them, although technically relating to the use of archaic words rather than merely hard words, is still

---

23. ❖ Through the years, disco has lived in the rear Rio Room, which is reliably crammed on weekends with off-duty **ecdysiasts** and microfiber-clad lunkheads. (Mr. Dallas, *Dallas Morning News*, "Orpheus Descending at the Sellar," 4/19/2002.)
24. While clearly in the minority, Buckley was not completely alone in his opposition to the dumbing down of our collective vocabulary. Michael Spear, an associate professor of journalism at the University of Richmond, has written: "What reporter, after using a word a bit above the level of a high-school dropout, hasn't heard an editor exclaim with a scowl: 'What is this word?' Or, 'Who do you think you are writing for, anyway? We're trying to communicate here.' I'd wonder: 'With whom? . . .' Unfortunately, the use of multisyllable words still often invites attack, or, at least, eye-rolling. But if we are influenced by this, aren't we relegating ourselves to a rather barren landscape of expression?" See Spear's article, "Lingually Challenged," in *Editor & Publisher*, 7/10/2000.

close, especially if one argues that hard words ought to be treated as if they were archaic anyway, and that using too many of them is a sign of poor writing:

writing (poor . . . , esp. characterized by the affected choice of archaic words) *n.*: **tushery**. ❖ This novel, set in the last days of Rome in the Eastern Empire, . . . tells the story of [a woman] who discovers that she is a born doctor . . . , but soon realises that there is no room for her in a society where medicine is the province of men. As a piece of historical romance it is saved from **tushery** by down-to-earth writing and a quite remarkable amount of information about early medicine which proves fascinating in itself. (Robert Nye, review of *The Beacon at Alexandria*, by Gillian Bradshaw," *Guardian* [London], 2/6/1987.)

Another word that describes the use of hard words in a derogatory fashion is "lexiphanicism":

writing (or speech characterized by the affected choice of obscure words) *n.*: **lexiphanicism** (*adj.*: **lexiphanic**). ❖ Can a book be both funny and tiresome? It is not the logorrhoea [wordiness] of the narrator, Harry Driscoll, that bothers me, nor his **lexiphanic** prose . . . (I love reading with a dictionary to hand). (Debra Adelaide, "In Short," *Sydney Morning Herald*, 3/29/2003.)

Can the defense of using unfamiliar words be reconciled with the risk of being lexiphanic? Absolutely. Note that the operative adjective in the definition of both "tushery" and "lexiphanicism" is "affected." That is, pretentious and/or unnatural. Thus, when in the course of just a few sentences Kilpatrick uses "anodyne," "meiosis," "adumbration," "omnium gatherum," "eudaemonia," "nimiety," and "logomachical," he is writing in an "affected" (albeit intentionally affected) fashion. But that kind of writing, in which the hard words are crammed together one right after the other, is a far cry from the examples found in this thesaurus, in which, almost without exception, the hard words are not being used in an affected way, but rather within the natural flow of the text. Indeed, any other conclusion (for example, that the use of any hard words is automatically lexiphanic) would necessarily lead to the corollary conclusion that virtually every writer quoted in this thesaurus must be a bad writer, which is, of course, absurd.

Turning back to John McWhorter's *Doing Our Own Thing* as evidence of the current mindset in this country regarding higher vocabulary, he quotes an educator who visited a classroom of twelve-year-olds and observed them studying verbal analogies in anticipation of the SAT. "I learned that they spend hours each month . . . studying long lists of verbal analogies such as 'untruthful is to mendaciousness' as 'circumspect is to caution.' The time involved was not aimed at developing the students' reading and writing abilities but rather their test-taking skills."

McWhorter stated that "the passage got around in the media" and was "intended to make people shake their heads at such a sad sight":

[I]t is telling that it spontaneously struck [the educator] as being so sad, so beside the point of education, that twelve-year-olds were being taught the meaning of written words. . . . [He] assumes that this learning of words is unrelated to developing students' reading abilities. . . . [H]is discomfort at seeing twelve-year-olds drilled on words like this marks him as a man of our times, for whom learned levels of English are less a main course than a garnish in an education [and for whom] learning high vocabulary [is] an imposition."

One suspects that those who would object to the use of the words contained in this thesaurus also concur with the notion that the teaching of analogies such as "'untruthful is to mendaciousness' as 'circumspect is to caution'" is a waste of time. However, McWhorter notes that this is "hardly self-evident" and quotes an English professor from Rutgers who conducted a study that found "an extraordinarily high correlation" between SAT verbal scores and final grades and a much lower correlation between grades and socioeconomic status. In other words, mastering the types of verbal skills tested by the SAT is not an exercise in trivia or one that is not predictive of future performance in broader academic areas. The same may be said of the synonyms in this thesaurus: Learning their use is not an exercise in trivia or becoming lexiphanic.

In a Utopian lexicographical world, the synonyms that appear in this thesaurus would be as familiar and accessible to everyone as the mundane synonyms in ordinary thesauruses. Perhaps this book is a small step in that direction. However, even though none of us can be expected to know every word in the English language, or even half of the words, that does not mean that one should be insouciant about ignorance of any particular word or that the person who uses the word should be subjected to rebuke or mockery.[25] If a writer uses a word I don't know, it is my job to learn the word, to look it up, and I should not be frustrated or critical because someone has stepped past my own "reasonable person" standard.

The bottom line is this: If a word appears in the dictionaries and is not qualified as being archaic or obsolete, it is a legitimate word, entitled to the same respect and holding the same qualifications for use as any other word. We cannot engage in a "hierarchy of legitimacy" with respect to words, since they are equally legitimate—especially the words in this thesaurus, whose validity is proven by examples showing their current usage. The fact that one word may be more familiar to the average person than another does not disqualify the less common word from use, nor should its user be subject to scorn. If a word is not described in the dictionaries as being archaic or obsolete (and at the risk of stating the obvious, that means it is not archaic or obsolete), that means it is considered current and thus legitimate—as legitimate as every other word.

---

25. The word "insouciant" once again points out the flaw in Kilpatrick's argument. About that word, we may safely assume, first, that Kilpatrick knows what it means (and has likely used it from time to time); second, that he would never equate it with any of Buckley's word choices that Kilpatrick mocks; and, third, that he would find ludicrous the notion that it should be jettisoned from the language. And yet, despite these assumptions, two things are true: First that the simpler words "nonchalant" or "carefree" could be substituted for "insouciant" just about every time. Second, and more important, there are many people who do not know the meaning of "insouciant." But, given the assumptions above, what can Kilpatrick say to those people? The only thing he could say is that literate people should know the word. Of course, that brings us right back to the problem of setting him up as the standard we would have to consult on every word. One wonders where, for example, would he stand on a less common synonym for "insouciant," such as "dégagé," which is used in this thesaurus? In any event, the point is clear.

C. On the Goal of Preserving the Beauty of the English Language

The majesty and grandeur of the English language—it's the greatest possession we have. The noblest thoughts that ever flowed through the hearts of men are contained in its extraordinary, imaginative and musical mixtures of sounds.

PROFESSOR HENRY HIGGINS to Eliza Doolittle in *My Fair Lady*

Like muscles, our lexicon atrophies when not used. However, most of the words in this book are not unusual because of being in disfavor, but rather because most people don't know they exist in the first place. I believe people would use these words if they knew about them, because they are such wonderful words. The problem is that there is no other tool available to introduce these words in any kind of logical fashion. Those who own traditional thesauruses clearly care about their writing and specifically their choice of words. They are unlikely to be people who would scoff at words they don't know. By the same token, it is unlikely that this audience needs to be "taught" that "big," "large," and "huge" are synonymous, as a regular thesaurus will tell them.

This thesaurus is my attempt to reverse the trend of the dumbing down of our collective vocabularies by (one hopes) building a better mousetrap and in the process, preserving "the majesty and grandeur of the English language," as Professor Higgins eloquently put it to Eliza Doolittle. The second edition, which has taken four years to create (on top of the ten years it took to create the first edition), is a continuation of that effort. It is nearly 50 percent longer than the first edition.

When people first heard about this thesaurus, their typical reaction (aside from concluding that I must be a little daffy) was: Don't we have plenty of thesauruses out there already? Well, based on the fact that the first edition of this book, despite being published by a very small company, was the top-selling thesaurus in the United States over twenty times on Amazon.com, apparently there was room for one more.

Having defended the hard word, let's go to the synonyms and the examples . . .

Both editions of this book were lengthy and complex undertakings, and to say that I could not have written either one by myself, while clichéd, is also true. I had significant amounts of help from many people at all stages of the process on levels tangible—such as providing ideas for words and examples—and intangible—such as providing enthusiasm and moral support (particularly in the early days when people would ingenuously ask me, "Hasn't someone already written a thesaurus?"). While those who chipped in with potential new entries for this new edition of the book are too numerous to mention, their contributions are known by me and are gratefully remembered. I am also appreciative of everyone who purchased and so warmly received the first edition.

I would also like to thank the following:

• My wonderful agent, Regina Ryan, who has been a delight to work with from day one.

• The entire team at Norton who helped me with all aspects of this project, including my primary editor, Amy Cherry, as well as Don Rifkin, Erica Stern, and Laura Romain.

• My copyeditor, Janet Bryne, who is as thorough as they come and who is definitely *not* sciolistic (and who is probably sick of analyzing that word with me).

• Orin Hargraves, word-master extraordinaire, whose early belief in the need for this book and my ability to create it started the dominoes falling, so as to lead to the publication of the first edition.

• My father, Dr. Lawrence Meltzer, who showed me that it is possible to be an author (in his case many times over) despite having another career.

• My mother, Helga; my sisters, Lilly, Lauren, and Zoe; and my brother, Konstantin. Thank you all for everything. Seriously.

• My children, Thomas and Charlotte, who remind me daily of what life is all about. Even the wondrous words in this book are inadequate to describe what they mean to me.

• Lastly to Deirdre. For those who know her, it's no wonder that I'm so uxurious.

abandonment (of one's religion, principles, or causes) *n.*: **apostasy**. ❖ It was during the 1980s and 1990s that [Barry] Goldwater developed a reputation for **apostasy**. He defended legal abortion and homosexual rights and criticized the religious right, famously arguing that Jerry Falwell deserved "a swift kick in the ass." Some conservatives felt betrayed, while liberals applauded. (Michael Gerson, "Mr. Right," *U.S. News & World Report*, 6/8/1998.)

(2) abandonment (esp. regarding one's belief, cause, or policy) *n.*: **bouleversement** [French]. See *change of mind*

(3) abandonment (of one's belief, cause, or policy) *n.*: **tergiversation** (*v.i.*: **tergiversate**). See *change of mind*

abate (attempt to . . . seriousness of an offense) *v.t.*: **palliate**. ❖ Every civilization needs its self-justifying myths. . . . America's great national myth of the settlement and taming of the frontier grew out of the slaughter of indigenous peoples, which it was meant to explain and **palliate**. (James Bowman, "Alien Menace: Lt. Ripley Is Hollywood's Mythical Woman—Butch and Ready to Kill," *National Review*, 1/26/1998, p. 35.)

abbreviated (something . . .) *n.*: **bobtail**. See *abridged*

abduct (a person, often to perform compulsory service abroad) *v.t.*: **shanghai**. See *kidnap*

aberration (as in someone or something that deviates from the norm) *n.*: **lusus** [Latin; almost always used as part of the term "lusus naturae," or freak of nature]. See *freak*

abhor *v.t.*: **execrate**. See *hate*

(2) abhor *v.t.*: **misprize**. See *hate*

abhorrence (develop an . . . for, as in dislike) *n.*: **scunner** (esp. as in "take a scunner") [British]. See *dislike*

abhorrent (or treacherous) *adj.*: **reptilian**. See *despicable*

(2) abhorrent *adj.*: **ugsome**. See *loathsome*

ability (area of . . .) *n.*: **métier** [French]. See *forte*

ablaze (with intense heat and light) *n.*: **deflagration**. See *explosion*

able (as in skillful) *adj.*: **habile**. See *skillful*

(2) able (to handle all matters) *adj.*: **omnicompetent**. See *competent*

(3) able (or adept) *adj.*: **au fait** [French]. See *skillful*

abnormal (as in departing from the standard or norm) *adj.*: **heteroclite**. ❖ Their mother was severely authoritarian. It is often from such repressive origins that rebels arise. "You have to assassinate your parents" was Philippe's advice to the young. He did it by running away to join the Foreign Legion. He attended, off and on, a suspiciously **heteroclite** array of schools before graduating with a degree in foreign languages from the Sorbonne. (James Kirkup, obituary of Philippe Leotard, *Independent* [London], 8/28/2001.)

(2) abnormal (as in unusual) *adj.*: **selcouth**. See *unusual*

abnormality (as in someone or something that deviates from the norm) *n.*: **lusus** [Latin; almost always used as part of the term "lusus naturae," or freak of nature]. See *freak*

abolish *v.t.*: **extirpate**. ❖ The argument: that if you are sufficiently fanatical in attempting to **extirpate** all sex discrimination, you will end up abolishing institutions you'd probably prefer to keep, like Wellesley, Hollins and other single-sex women's colleges. (Daniel Seligman, "Keeping Up: A Splash for the Secretary of Energy," *Fortune*, 2/05/1996, p. 138.)

(2) abolish (as in put an end to) *n.*: **quietus** (*v.t.*: "put the quietus to"). See *termination*

abolition *n.*: **quietus**. See *termination*

abominable *adj.*: **execrable**. ❖ My generation has lots of excuses for our **execrable** parenting. [For example,] the economy has forced most women into the workplace. (Katherine Dowling, "Parents Can't Duck Blame for Morally Abandoned Kids," *Milwaukee Journal Sentinel*, 3/11/1996.)

abortion (antiabortion term for an . . . clinic) *n.*: **abortuary**. ❖ Referring to a business where someone is killed as a "health-care facility" or "clinic" assaults the dignity of the one who is killed there. When the primary goal of an establishment is to violently kill human beings (in an embryonic or fetal stage of life), they are abortion sites, child killing centers, abortion chambers, abortion mills and **aborturaries.** They, again, are not "health-care facilities." (Susan Pine, "City Should Not Help Killing Center," *Fort Lauderdale Sun-Sentinel*, 9/27/2005.)

(2) abortion *n*.: **feticide.** ❖ [T]he equal-protection clause of the 14th Amendment would seem to require states to extend legal protection to the unborn. [In *Roe v. Wade*, Justice Harry] Blackmun, however, relying on grossly inaccurate legal history . . . concluded that the due-process clause of [the] amendment forbids states from providing any meaningful protection against deliberate **feticide**. (*National Review*, "Harry Blackmun, R.I.P.," 4/5/1999.)

abound *v.i.*: **pullulate**. See *teem*

about (as in concerning or regarding) *prep*.: **anent**. See *regarding*

about-face (as in reversal of policy or position) *n*.: **volte-face** [French]. ❖ More than 350 years have passed since Galileo was condemned by the Roman Catholic Church for the correct, if impolitic, declaration that the earth revolved around the sun. Now the church has solemnized its belated **volte-face** on the celestial dispute by mailing an apology [that is, issuing new stamps commemorating Galileo]. (*Time* International, Chronicles: "More than 350 Years Have Passed Since Galileo Was Condemned," 6/13/1994, p. 13.)

(2) about-face (as in abandonment of one's religion, principles, or causes) *n*.: **apostasy**. See *abandonment*

(3) about-face (esp. regarding one's beliefs, causes, or policies) *n*.: **bouleversement** [French]. See *change of mind*

(4) about-face (regarding one's belief, cause, or policy) *n*.: **tergiversation** (*v.i.*: **tergiversate**). See *change of mind*

above (lying . . .) *adj*.: **superjacent**. See *overlying*

abreast (being . . . of or familiar with something) *adj*.: **au fait** [French]. See *familiar*

abridged (something . . .) *n*.: **bobtail**. ❖ Senator Trent Lott, the majority leader, said that it would be "a big mistake" for the Senate to vote to dismiss the [impeachment] charges Monday. The Mississippi Republican said it would be a "**bobtail** action of a constitutional process." (Brian Knowlton, "Trial of Clinton Turns Bitter: Democrats 'Appalled' at Sudden Summons of Lewinsky," *International Herald Tribune*, 1/25/1999.)

abrupt (as in sudden, or unexpected) *adj*.: **subitaneous**. See *sudden*

abscond (as in leave hurriedly or secretly) *v.t.*: **absquatulate**. See *leave*

absent (anything better) *adv*.: **faute de mieux** [French]. See *lacking*

absentminded (as in distracted, esp. because of worries or fears) *adj*.: **distrait**. See *distracted*

(2) absentminded (person, as in an impractical, contemplative person with no clear occupation or income) *n*.: **luftmensch** [lit. man of air; German, Yiddish]. See *dreamer*

absolute (as in complete or unlimited, esp. as in . . . power) *adj*.: **plenary**. See *complete*

(2) absolute (as in inviolable) *adj*.: **infrangible**. See *inviolable*

(3) absolute (usually used with "nonsense") *adj*.: **arrant**. See *total*

absolution (as in place or occasion of humiliation and seeking . . .) *n*.: **Canossa**. See *penance*

absorb (as in incorporate, the ideas or attitudes of others, esp. parents, into one's own personality) *v.t.*: **introject**. See *incorporate*

abstract (as in intangible; lacking material form or substance) *adj*.: **incorporeal**. See *intangible*

absurd (as in acting foolishly, esp. in a smug or complacent manner) *adj*.: **fatuous**. See *foolish*

(2) absurd (as in laughable) *adj*.: **gelastic**. See *laughable*

(3) absurd (as in laughable) *adj*.: **risible**. See *laughable*

absurdity (as in foolishness or stupidity) *n*.: **bêtise** [French]. See *stupidity*

(2) absurdity (as in nonsense) *n*.: **codswallop** [British]. See *nonsense*

(3) absurdity (as in nonsense) *n.*: **piffle**. See *nonsense*

(4) absurdity (statement that contains a logical . . . , usually not recognized by the speaker) *n.*: **Irish bull**. See *incongruity*

(5) absurdity *n.*: **folderol** (or **falderal**). See *nonsense*

(6) absurdity *n.*: **trumpery**. See *nonsense*

abundance (illusion of . . . when in fact there is little) *adj.*: **Barmecidal** (esp. as in "Barmecidal feast"). See *illusion*

abuse (being subject to . . . , esp. public) *n.*: **obloquy**. ❖ Despite being the target of so much public **obloquy**, [John D.] Rockefeller seemed fearless. (Ron Chernow, *Titan*, Random House [1998], p. 262.)

abuse of power (often sexual) *n.*: **droit de seigneur** [French]. See *entitlement*

abusive (language) *n.*: **billingsgate**. See *language*

(2) abusive (language) *n.*: **vituperation** (*adj.*: **vituperative**). See *invective*

(3) abusive (woman who is also vulgar) *n.*: **fishwife**. See *woman*

abutting (as in surrounding) *adj.*: **circumjacent**. See *surrounding*

academic (as in pedantic) *adj.*: **donnish**. See *pedantic*

(2) academic (as in scholarly or bookish) *adj.*: **donnish**. See *bookish*

accept (as in approve, esp. to confirm officially) *v.t.*: **homologate**. See *approve*

acceptable (an . . . , as in proper or appropriate, thing to do) *n.*: **bon ton** [French]. See *appropriate*

(2) acceptable (in accord with . . . standards) *adj.*: **comme il faut** [French]. See *proper*

(3) acceptable *adj.*: **cromulent**. See *legitimate*

acceptance (joyful . . . of one's fate in life) *n.*: **amor fati**. [This Latin phrase, meaning "love of fate," comes from Friedrich Nietzsche, who stated, in *Ecce Homo*, "My formula for greatness in a human being is *amor fati*: that one wants nothing to be different, not forward, not backward, not in all eternity. Not merely bear what is necessary, still less conceal it—all idealism is mendaciousness in the face of what is necessary—but *love* it." The term is sometimes considered synonymous with stoicism or fatalism, but this matching is not technically accurate since those philosophies do not require a joyful acceptance of one's fate in life, merely an acceptance.] ❖ One of his greatest fears was the possibility of eternal recurrence, that everything he'd been through would keep repeating itself, that nothing would change. He knew that, as Nietzsche had said, he needed to embrace *amor fati*, his love of fate. He needed to trust that all the suffering and loss he'd endured was ultimately good, that everything that'd happened had a predestined purpose. (Don Lee, *Wrack and Ruin*, Norton [2008], p. 132.)

(2) acceptance (as in giving one's stamp of approval) *n.*: **nihil obstat** [Latin]. See *approval*

accepting (for the sake of argument) *adv.*: **concesso non dato** [Italian; sometimes **dato non concesso**]. See *stipulating*

(2) accepting (of other views and opinions) *adj.*: **latitudinarian**. See *open-minded*

access key (something such as an . . . or master key that permits one to gain access or pass at will) *n.*: **passe-partout**. See *passkey*

accessible (to the general public in terms of comprehension or suitability) *adj.*: **exoteric**. ❖ [Robert Penn Warren] saw nothing contradictory in his esoteric and **exoteric** activities, and wrote with equal facility for magazines such as *Life* and for those of small circulation. (Daniel Aaron, "A Minor Master," *New Republic*, 10/20/1997.)

accessories (as in finery) *n.*: **caparison**. See *finery*

(2) accessories (showy . . . , as in finery) *n.*: **frippery**. See *finery*

accidental (as in by chance) *adj.*: **adventitious**. See *chance*

acclaim *n.*: **éclat**. ❖ The City of Atlanta held a contest for a slogan that would best illustrate why the City was chosen for the international

éclat that goes with hosting the 1996 Olympic Games. The winner: "Atlanta—Come celebrate our dream." (Nat Hentoff, "Amnesty Focuses Light on Atlanta," *Denver Rocky Mountain News*, 7/22/1996.)

(2) acclaim (or to bestow . . . upon) *n., v.t.*: **garland**. See *accolade*

accolade (or to confer an . . . upon) *n., v.t.*: **garland**. ❖ The first American movie to be shot in Vietnam since the war, *Three Seasons* arrives **garlanded** with prizes from the Sundance Film Festival. (David Ansen, "Return to Vietnam; *Three Seasons* May Not Journey Far Enough," *Newsweek*, 5/3/1999.)

accompaniment *n.*: **appanage**. See *adjunct*

accompanying (as in incident to) *adj.*: **appurtenant**. See *pertaining*

accomplishment (celebrating . . . , as in victory) *adj.*: **epinician**. See *victory*

accomplishments *n.pl.*: **res gestae**. See *deeds*

accord (in . . .) *adj.*: **consonant**. See *harmony*

(2) accord (in . . . , as in harmonious or compatible) *adj.*: **simpatico**. See *compatible*

(3) accord (of the human race throughout history on an issue) *n.*: **consensus genitum** [Latin]. See *consensus*

accouterments (as in trappings) *n.*: **habiliment(s)**. See *trappings*

accumulation (confused or jumbled . . .) *n.*: **agglomeration**. See *jumble*

(2) accumulation (of objects, people, or ideas) *n.*: **congeries**. See *collection*

accurate (appearing to be . . .) *adj.*: **verisimilar**. See *realistic*

(2) accurate (as in reflecting reality or truth) *adj.*: **veridical**. See *realistic* and *truthful*

accusation (spec. accusing an accuser of having committed a similar offense) *n.*: **tu quoque** [Latin]. ❖ The Democrats, who still resent Mr. Barbour for raising the money that snatched Congress away from them in 1994, are trying to imply that Mr. Barbour's Republicans are just as sleazy as the Clinton people. . . . This **tu quoque** attack on Mr. Barbour begins to look like simple partisanship. (*Economist*, "Inside the Belly of the Beast," 7/26/1997.)

(2) accusation (which is false, defamatory, and published for political gain right before an election) *n.*: **roorback**. See *falsehood*

accuse *v.t.*: **inculpate**. See *blame*

accuser (esp. by being an informer) *n.*: **delator**. ❖ The right to file charges against a fellow citizen was not in itself new, but took on a new character when the state began awarding the **delator** a share of the property of the accused; a successful accusation of treason, for example, carried as a prize a quarter of the victim's estate. (Walter Olson, "Tripp Wire: How Informers Ended Up Behind Every Office Potted Plant," *Reason*, 4/1/1998, p. 60.)

accustomed *adj.*: **wonted**. See *customary*

acerbic (as in . . . remarks) *adj.*: **astringent**. See *harsh*

achievement (celebrating . . . , as in victory) *adj.*: **epinician**. See *victory*

achievements *n.pl.*: **res gestae**. See *deeds*

aching (as in longing, esp. for something one once had but has no more) *n.*: **desiderium**. See *longing*

acknowledgment (of sin) *n.*: **confiteor** (sometimes cap.). See *confession*

acme (as in highest point that can be attained or the ultimate degree, as of a condition or quality) *n.*: **ne plus ultra**. See *ultimate*

acne (tending to produce or aggravate . . .) *adj.*: **comedogenic**. ❖ The best skin care in the world isn't going to cure your acne so don't spend a fortune. Always look on labels for **noncomedogenic** products as these won't block follicles. (*Mirror*, "Health Zone: Tips from the Top Spot of Bother," 3/21/2002.)

acquainted (being . . . or familiar with something) *adj.*: **au fait** [French]. See *familiar*

acquire (by mooching or sponging off of) *v.t.*: **cadge**. See *mooch*

(2) acquire (for oneself without permission) *v.t.*: **expropriate**. See *seize*

(3) acquire (money unfairly and in excessive amounts) *v.t.*: **mulct**. See *extract*

(4) acquire (or claim for oneself without right) *v.t.*: **arrogate**. See *claim*

acquittal (finding . . . through testimony of others) *n.*: **compurgation**. ❖ [In medieval times], the ordeal, a form of proof which relied on [torture] to determine the guilt or innocence of the accused [, was used] in cases where normal juridical procedures, most notably **compurgation**, the sworn endorsement of friends and neighbors of the accused, were not deemed applicable. (Kathleen Biddick, "Aesthetics, Ethnicity, and the History of Art," *Art Bulletin*, 12/1/1996, p. 594.)

acrimony *n.*: **asperity**. ❖ Mr. Karsh's will assuredly not be the last word. In an exchange last year in *Middle East Quarterly*, Mr. Shlaim mounted a spirited (and, given the **asperity** of Mr. Karsh's attack, good-natured) defense of his collusion thesis. (*Economist*, "The Unchosen People," 7/19/1997.)

across *prep., adv.*: **athwart**. ❖ Dagestan is far more strategically vital than Chechnya: the Russians can build a bypass around Chechnya for Caspian Sea oil; Dagestan, however, lies **athwart** the only Russian route from Baku. (Owen Matthews, "Digging In for Worse to Come," *Newsweek* International, 9/20/1999, p. 26.)

act (which is official, as in with the authority of one's office) *adv., adj.*: **ex cathedra**. See *official*

action (as in course of . . .) *n.*: **démarche** [French]. See *course of action*

(2) action (gracious . . .) *n.*: **beau geste**. See *gesture*

actions (as in deeds) *n.pl.*: **res gestae**. See *deeds*

(3) actions (study of human . . .) *n.*: **praxeology**. See *behavior*

actors (in a play or story) *n.*: **dramatis personae**. See *characters*

actress (comic . . . , sometimes in musicals or opera, who plays a nonleading character who is saucy, flirtatious, and/or frivolous) *n.*: **soubrette**. ❖ If [Violet Carlson] is not an enduring household name, it is only because, unlike . . . other luminaries of the era, Miss Carlson was not a leading lady, or even a demure ingenue. She was a **soubrette**, that deliciously wicked and flirtatious featured player who never gets the leading man but who can steal a scene with a song and snare an audience's heart with a saucy shake of her curly head. (Robert Thomas, obituary of Violet Carlson, *New York Times*, 12/8/1997.)

acts (as in deeds) *n.pl.*: **res gestae**. See *deeds*

actual (as in genuine) *adj.*: **echt** [German]. See *genuine*

(2) actual (as in legitimate; acceptable) *adj.*: **cromulent**. See *legitimate*

(3) actual (as in reflecting reality) *adj.*: **veridical**. See *realistic*

actuality (state of . . . as opposed to potentiality) *n.*: **entelechy**. ❖ Animals are not only being assimilated to humans; they are being made into the destiny of humans, the **entelechy** of humanity in which it realizes its highest possibility. [Fully social] animals are assumed to have achieved a degree of success as social animals that we ourselves, who invented the idea of society, have not attained, argue the sociobiologists. (Richard Klein, "The Power of Pets: America's Obsession with the Cute and Cuddly," *New Republic*, 7/10/1995, p. 18.)

(2) actuality (historical . . .) *n.*: **historicity**. See *authenticity*

(3) actuality (relating to a story in which . . . and fiction are mixed together) *adj.*: **Pirandellian**. See *reality*

(4) actuality (as in the reality of something as it really is, as opposed to how it is perceived by the senses) *n.*: **noumenon**. See *thing-in-itself*

actualize (as in making an abstract concept seem real) *v.t.*: **reify**. See *materialize*

actually (as in, in fact) *adj., adv.*: **de facto** (as contrasted with de jure: legally or by law) [Latin]. See *in fact*

adage (pithy . . .) *n.*: **gnome** (*adj.*: **gnomic**). See *catchphrase*

(2) adage (witty or clever . . . or line) *n.*: **bon mot**. See *line*

(3) adage *n.*: **apothegm**. See *saying*

adages (given to stating . . . , esp. in a moralizing way) *adj.*: **sententious**. See *aphoristic*

Adam and Eve (belief that the human race is descended from two persons, such as . . .) *n*.: **monogenism**. ❖ The story of Adam and Eve, though mythical, is not understood [by Christians] merely as such. It is taken as a foundation of Christian anthropology and of subsequent theology. . . . [But] how can God's justice condemn the whole of humanity for the sin of the first parents? Is not the underlying hypothesis of **monogenism** itself questioned in the face of scientific evidence? (Tissa Balasuriya, "Companion to the Encyclical of Pope Benedict XVI on 'God Is Love,'" *Cross Currents*, 6/22/2006.)

adamant (as in stubborn) *adj*.: **pervicacious**. See *stubborn*

addictive (or nearly so; said esp. of food or drink that is so good that one wants more) *adj*.: **moreish** [chiefly British]. ❖ Freedom [lager] doesn't let the tastebuds down. It is said to marry with food very well, particularly pizza to compliment the rich yeastiness and, rather dangerously, it is very **moreish**. It's the lager for those who eagerly did their groundwork in the '80s and have a greater appreciation of bottled beers in the '90s. (Carol Ann Rice, "When Small Beer Is So Satisfying," *Birmingham Post*, 8/19/1998.)

addition (as in insertion of something between existing things) *n*.: **intercalation**. See *insertion*
(2) addition (as in something that is an accessory to something else) *n*.: **appurtenance**. See *appendage*

additionally *adv*.: **withal**. See *moreover*

address (to . . . an absent person or thing) *v.t*.: **apostrophize**. [This is the verb form of apostrophe—the words themselves. In dramatic works and poetry, this rhetorical form is often introduced by the word "O." For example: "O Romeo, Romeo! wherefore art thou Romeo?" (Shakespeare, *Romeo and Juliet*, act 2, scene 2). Or: "O eloquent, just, and mighty Death!" (Sir Walter Raleigh, *A Historie of the World*). A more recent example is when Ronald Reagan said: "Mr. Gorbachev, tear down this wall!"]. ❖ Benjamin Trotter [is a] writer-cum-rock-composer. . . . Cicely Boyd is "the willowy goddess who ran the junior wing of the Girls' School Dramatic Society"—at least in the awestruck estimation of Benjamin, her ardent worshiper-from-afar, who through most of the novel can **apostrophize** his love for her only in score upon score of labored progressive rock compositions. (Chris Lehman, "Dazed and Confused," *Washington Post*, 3/3/2002.)
(2) address (a subject at length in speech or writing) *v.i*.: **expatiate**. See *expound*
(3) address (a topic, esp. in a long-winded or pompous manner) *v.i*.: **bloviate**. See *speak*
(4) address (formal . . .) *n*.: **allocution**. See *speech*
(5) address (lengthy . . . , as in speech) *n*.: **peroration**. See *monologue*

adept (as in skillful) *adj*.: **habile**. See *skillful*
(2) adept (at handling all matters) *adj*.: **omnicompetent**. See *competent*
(3) adept (as in skillful) *adj*.: **au fait**. [French]. See *skillful*

adhere (together, as with glue) *v.t*.: **agglutinate**. ❖ The [rhinoceros] horn is nothing more than **agglutinated** hair with no medicinal value, but is highly coveted—said to contain legendary aphrodisiac properties—in Chinese pharmacopoeia. (Claire Scobie, "Nature Watch," *Sunday Telegraph* [London], 9/27/1998.)
(2) adhere (closely to a line, rule, or principle) *v.i*.: **hew**. See *conform*
(3) adhere (tightly and tenaciously, in the case of a person or thing) *n*.: **limpet**. See *clinger*
(4) adhere (tightly and tenaciously, in the case of a person or thing) *n*.: **remora**. See *clinger*

adherent (strong . . . of a cause, religion, or activity) *n*.: **votary**. See *supporter*
(2) adherent *adj*.: **acolyte**. See *follower*

adjunct *n*.: **appanage**. ❖ Some still believe the dream, insisting that [the town of Primorye in eastern Russia]—no longer a pliant **appanage** of Moscow—will unite with the Pacific Rim and arise from its Soviet hangover in a hearty economic rebound. (Andrew Meier, "Europe: Letter from Vladivostok: Surviving on the Edge," *Time* International, 2/7/2000, p. 25.)

ad-libbed *adj.*: **autoschediastic**. See *unrehearsed*

administrator (as in bureaucrat) *n.*: **satrap**. See *bureaucrat*

admiration (as in praise) *n.*: **approbation**. See *praise*

admirer (male ...) *n.*: **swain**. See *suitor*

admirers (group of fawning . . .) *n.*: **claque**. ❖ On a visit to Time Inc.'s new-media facility, [Bill Gates] answered questions from a collection of magazine editors as if by rote, but on his way out he asked to see the Internet servers and spent 45 minutes grilling the **claque** of awed techies there. (Walter Isaacson, "Business: In Search of the Real Bill Gates," *Time*, 1/13/1997, p. 44.)

admission (of sin) *n.*: **confiteor** (sometimes cap.). See *confession*

(2) admission (of sin) *n.*: **peccavi**. See *confession*

admit (as in confide one's thoughts or feelings) *v.t., v.i.*: **unbosom**. See *confide*

(2) admit (to one's sins, esp. in church) *v.t., v.i.*: **shrive**. See *confess*

admitting (for the sake of argument) *adv.*: **concesso non dato** [Italian; sometimes **dato non concesso**]. See *stipulating*

admonish (sharply) *v.t.*: **keelhaul**. See *rebuke*

(2) admonish *v.t.*: **objurgate**. See *criticize*

admonishing (as in criticism) *n.*: **animadversion** (*v.t.*: **animadvert**). See *criticism*

admonition (relating to the giving of an . . .) *adj.*: **paraenetic** (*n.*: **paraenesis**). See *advice*

ado (as in commotion) *n.*: **bobbery**. See *commotion*

(2) ado (as in commotion) *n.*: **kerfuffle**. See *commotion*

(3) ado (over a trifling matter) *n.*: **foofaraw**. See *fuss*

adopt (as in incorporate, the ideas or attitudes of others, esp. parents, into one's own personality) *v.t.*: **introject**. See *incorporate*

adoration (as in worship of dead people) *n.*: **necrolatry**. See *worship*

(2) adoration (mad or crazy . . .) *n.*: **amour fou** [French]. See *love*

(3) adoration (of women) *n.*: **philogyny**. See *women*

(4) adoration (spec. the emotional thrill and excitement one feels when initially in love) *n.*: **limerence** (*adj.*: **limerent**). See *love*

adorn (in a showy or excessive manner) *v.t.*: **bedeck**. ❖ The best albums preserve not just a show's score but the meaning and joy of the theatrical moment. Sitting at home, you can't see the deliriously gaudy haberdashery that **bedecks** the Guys and Dolls touts. (Richard Corliss, "Broadway's Record Year," *Time*, 9/14/1992, p. 71.)

(2) adorn (or dress in a showy or excessive manner) *v.t.*: **bedizen**. ❖ Occasionally, I've shown houses out this way, though their owners, fat and **bedizened** as pharaohs, and who should be giddy with the world's gifts, always seem the least pleasant people in the world. (Richard Ford, *Independence Day*, Knopf [1995], p. 128.)

adornment (which is showy or superfluous or frilly) *n.*: **furbelow**. See *ornamentation*

adornments (showy . . .) *n.*: **frippery**. See *finery*

(2) adornments *n.*: **caparison**. See *finery*

adroit *adj.*: **habile**. See *skillful*

(2) adroit (or adept) *adj.*: **au fait** [French]. See *skillful*

adroitness (or subtlety, esp. in political or business dealings) *n.*: **Italian hands** [often used in the phrase "fine Italian hands"]. See *subtlety*

adulation (one who seeks favor through . . . , esp. of one in power) *n.*: **courtier**. See *flattery*

adult education *n.*: **andragogy**. ❖ As more and more schools have discovered, the trick is not getting adults into the classroom, but keeping them there. Whether they're in search of professional credentials or expanding a hobby, adults thrive in classes that value their life experience. . . . **Andragogy** also assumes that adults are highly motivated, self-directed, and have become used to learning by solving problems. (*Chicago Sun-Times*, "Adults Thrive in Classes That Value Their Life Experience," 8/4/1998.)

adulterous (man married to . . . wife) *n*.: **cuckold** (*v.t.*: to make a . . . of). ❖ Married with two children, Don acquired a reputation as an incurable skirt chaser. . . . His conquests soon became the stuff of legend. One that is often told but has never been confirmed: A **cuckolded** husband got his revenge by dumping a load of wet cement into Don's convertible. (Kim Clark, "Tough Times for the Chicken King Don Tyson," *Fortune*, 10/28/1996, p. 88*.)*

advance (esp. a military . . .) *n*.: **anabasis**. ❖ Federer, carried forward by the momentum from his serve, picked [Andre Agassi's] return out of the air, effortlessly flicking a backhand volley from behind the service line, and continued his **anabasis** toward the net. (L. Jon Wertheim, "That Was as Good as It Gets: So Said a Certain Bald Superstar from Las Vegas About the Play of the Lavishly Talented Roger Federer, Who Elevated the Men's Game in 2003," *Sports Illustrated*, 12/29/2003.)

advantage (as in, "to whose . . . ?") *n*.: **cui bono**. [Latin. This phrase is generally posed as a question and usually one to which the writer knows the answer.] ❖ [W]hat if George Bush is a plant . . . put here by shadowy somebodies in order to undermine the United States? . . . You can ask, **cui bono**? Ah, there's a list: radical Islamicists, international oil cartels, China, the Russian mob, North Korea, Iran, the South American drug cartels, just about anyone who needs a diplomatically inept, chronically weak U.S. administration to consolidate its power. (Jon Carroll, Daily Datebook, *San Francisco Chronicle*, 6/24/2004.)

Advent (as in Second Coming) *n*.: **Parousia** [Greek]. See *Second Coming*

adverse (as in harmful) *adj*.: **nocent**. See *harmful*

   (2) adverse *adj*.: **oppugnant**. See *antagonistic*

advice (relating to the giving of . . .) *adj*.: **paraenetic** (*n*.: **paraenesis**) ❖ "Remember those who are in prison," admonishes the Christian

moralist. . . . Remembering the incarcerated is only one of what Harold W. Attridge calls a "series of discrete and staccato admonitions" in the final chapter of Hebrews. . . . The writer of Hebrews 13 groups this and other **paraenetic** points under a broader one: "Let mutual love continue," which echoes Jesus' "new command" to his disciples . . . (Bruce Wollenberg, "Guest List," *Christian Century*, 8/24/2004.)

   (2) advice (as in word to the wise) *phr*.: **verbum sap** [Latin]. See *word to the wise*

advisors (group of . . . , often scheming or plotting) *n*.: **camarilla**. ❖ An old-fashioned nationalist, Giesevius had been authorized by Admiral Wilhelm Canaris, the head of German intelligence, to make contact with the Allies on behalf of the German Resistance. He supplied Dulles with tantalizing information on the incessant infighting among Hitler's **camarilla**. (Jacob Heilbrunn, "Gentleman Spy: The Life of Allen Dulles," *New Republic*, 3/27/1995, p. 32.)

advocate (of a cause) *n*.: **paladin**. See *proponent*

   (2) advocate (or leader, esp. for a political cause) *n*.: **fugleman**. See *leader*

   (3) advocate (strong . . . of a cause, religion, or activity) *n*.: **votary**. See *supporter*

advocating (a particular point of view) *adj*.: **tendentious**. See *biased*

affability *n*.: **bonhomie**. ❖ But Peace with Dignity won't come easily [in the Clinton impeachment proceedings]. For all the bipartisan **bonhomie** that has marked the Senate proceedings, Democrats aren't inclined to do much to help Republicans save face with their party's Clinton-loathing right wing. (James Carney, "Nation: Waiting for the Bell," *Time*, 2/15/1999, p. 30.)

affable (and pleasant) *adj*.: **sympathique** [French]. See *genial*

affair (as in sex outside of marriage) *n*.: **hetaerism**. ❖ Of course, [historically] men still enjoyed conjugal infidelity referred to as **hetaerism**. . . . Monogamy was thus only meant for women. (Unsigned letter to the editor, *Edmonton Sun*, 5/7/2000.)

(2) affair (love . . .) *n.*: **amourette** [French]. See *love affair*

affected (and high-flown use of language) *adj.*: **euphuistic**. ❖ *Ryder*, [Djuna Barnes's] first novel, shows off her talent for baroque excess nearly as well, with spirited flights of invective, arias of verbal extravagance and mock-Elizabethan prose dotted with **euphuistic** exuberance. (*Washington Post*, New in Paperback, 6/10/1990.)

(2) affected (as in contrived) *adj.*: **voulu** [French]. See *contrived*

(3) affected (as in insincere) *adj.*: **crocodilian**. See *insincere*

(4) affected (as in pedantic) *adj.*: **donnish**. See *pedantic*

(5) affected (of an . . . , as in pedantic, word or term) *adj.*: **inkhorn**. See *pedantic*

(6) affected (speech or writing) *adj.*: **fustian**. See *pompous*

affectionate (as in amorous) *adj.*: **amative**. See *amorous*

affiliated (with, as in incident to) *adj.*: **appurtenant**. See *pertaining*

affinity (as in family ties) *n.*: **propinquity**. See *kinship*

affluence (study of or focus on . . . , esp. in artistic works) *n.*: **plutography**. See *wealth*

affluent (and/or prominent person) *n.*: **nabob**. See *bigwig*

(2) affluent (government by the . . .) *n.*: **plutocracy**. See *government*

affront (an . . . to another's dignity) *n.*: **lese majesty**. See *insult*

(2) affront (as in insult, delivered while leaving the scene) *n.*: **Parthian shot**. See *parting shot*

affronted (easily . . .) *adj.*: **umbrageous**. See *offended*

afraid (and cautious and indecisive) *adj.*: **Prufrockian**. See *timid*

(2) afraid (as in cowardly) *adj.*: **pusillanimous**. See *cowardly*

(3) afraid (as in spineless or indecisive, or such a person) *adj., n.*: **namby-pamby**. See *spineless*

(4) afraid (something that is dreaded, disliked, or to be . . . of) *n.*: **bête noire** [French]. See *dreaded*

(5) afraid (as in cowardly) *adj.*: **retromingent**. See *cowardly*

aftereffect (or secondary result) *n.*: **sequela** (pl. **sequelae**). [This term is frequently used to refer to the aftereffect of a disease or condition, although it is sometimes used more broadly, as in the example here.] ❖ With my clothes, I enjoy breaking stereotypes of women scientists, but it's not a calculated image. . . . I feel comfortable in trousers and short skirts. I feel uncomfortable in tweed suits. If the clothes I happen to like give off a certain image, then that's a **sequela**, it's not the trigger for choosing those clothes. It's a happy consequence that people find my look interesting as a role model for women. (Susan Greenfield, "How Do I Look? Lab Fab," *Independent* [London], 8/12/2000.)

aftermath (as in aftereffect) *n.*: **sequela** (pl. **sequelae**). See *aftereffect*

after-the-fact (an . . . analysis; i.e., to project into the past) *v.t.*: **retroject**. See *analyze*

(2) after the fact (as in a statement, thought, knowledge, or action that comes to mind or occurs when it is too late to act on it, such as locking the barn door after the cows have left) *n.*: **afterwit**. See *belated*

again (as in anew) *adv.*: **afresh**. See *anew*

against *adj.*: **oppugnant**. See *antagonistic*

against the world *adv., adj.*: **contra mundum** [Latin]. ❖ [Jack Straw said] that negotiations on a new European Constitution could end in failure, with Britain vetoing a deal. . . . Prime Minister [Tony Blair] feared the Government would be compared to [John Major and the Tories, who] habitually threatened to block EU business unless Britain got its way. [One source said:] "Jack's comments came out as too Major-esque, as if we were saying veto, veto, veto like the Tories. Blair does not want it to be Britain **contra mundum**." (Toby Helm, "Straw in Trouble with Blair for Sounding 'Too Major-esque,'" European Constitution, *Daily Telegraph* [London], 11/26/2003.)

age (as in generation or era) *n*.: **saeculum**. See *generation*

aged (and sick person) *n*.: **Struldbrug**. See *decrepit*

(2) aged (as in broken down and/or worn-out) *adj*.: **raddled**. See *worn-out*

(3) aged (of or like an . . . woman) *adj*.: **anile**. See *old woman*

agent (as in middleman) *n*.: **comprador**. See *intermediary*

(2) agent (such as an ambassador or diplomat who is fully authorized to represent a government) *n*.: **plenipotentiary**. See *diplomat*

aggravation (as in trouble) *n*.: **tsuris** [Yiddish]. See *trouble*

aggregation (of objects, people, or ideas) *n*.: **congeries**. See *collection*

aggressive (as in pugnacious or ready to fight) *adj*.: **bellicose**. See *belligerent*

aggrieved (easily . . . , as in offended) *adj*.: **umbrageous**. See *offended*

agile *adj*.: **lightsome**. See *nimble*

aging *adj*.: **senescent**. ❖ [The literature I received from the] American Association of Retired Persons . . . warranted that this organization fought unstintingly for the rights of **senescent** folks everywhere and hinted heavily that even though it already had 27 million members, it could make room for one more if only [I] would put up the highly affordable $5 dues. (Daniel Seligman, "Keeping Up, Staving Off the Old Folks," *Fortune*, 12/21/1987, p. 169.)

agitate *v.t*.: **commove**. ❖ Twelve years ago, Fuller founded [Habitat for Humanity to] provide the poor with "simple, decent, affordable housing." . . . Fuller, 53, is an Ichabod Crane look-alike who is incessantly joking, cajoling, **commoving**, pressing, pleading for Habitat. (Don Winbush, American Ideas: "Habitat for Humanity a Bootstrap Approach to Low-Cost Housing," *Time*, 1/16/1989, p. 12.)

agitated *adj*.: **in a dither**. See *flustered*

agitation (as in a state of tense and nervous . . .) *n*. **fantod**. See *tension*

(2) agitation (as in propaganda) *n*.: **agit-prop**. See *propaganda*

(3) agitation (state of . . .) *n*.: **swivet** (as in "in a swivet") *informal*. See *distress*

agitator (a political . . . , who often believes in violence to attain an end) *n*.: **sans-culotte**. See *extremist*

(2) agitator *n*.: **stormy petrel**. See *inciter*

agonize (or complain) *v.i*.: **repine**. See *complain*

agonizing (journey or experience) *n*.: **via dolorosa**. See *ordeal*

agony (as in occasion or place of great suffering) *n*.: **Gethsemane**. See *hell*

(2) agony (as in occasion or place of great suffering) *n*.: **Golgotha**. See *hell*

(3) agony (as in place or occasion of great suffering, or hell) *n*.: **Gehenna**. See *hell*

agreeable (as in genial, and pleasant) *adj*.: **sympathique** [French]. See *genial*

(2) agreeable (as in pleasing) *adj*.: **prepossessing**. See *pleasing*

agreeing (for the sake of argument) *adv*.: **concesso non dato** [Italian; sometimes **dato non concesso**]. See *stipulating*

agreement (as in pact) *n*.: **amicabilis concordia**. See *pact*

(2) agreement (in . . . on the arrangement of parts as part of a whole) *n*.: **concinnity**. See *harmony*

(3) agreement (in . . .) *adj*.: **consonant**. See *harmony*

(4) agreement (in . . . , as in harmonious or compatible) *adj*.: **simpatico**. See *compatible*

(5) agreement (of the human race throughout history on an issue) *n*.: **consensus genitum** [Latin]. See *consensus*

(6) agreement (temporary . . . between opposing parties pending final deal) *n*.: **modus vivendi** [Latin]. See *truce*

ahead (of, as in antecedent) *adj*.: **prevenient** (often as in "prevenient grace"). See *antecedent*

aid (as in, "to whose . . . ?") *n*.: **cui bono** [Latin]. See *advantage*

aide (esp. to a scholar or magician) *n*.: **famulus**. See *assistant*

(2) aide (esp. to organized crime leader) *n.*: **consigliere** [Italian]. See *assistant*

(3) aide (who is loyal and unquestioning) *n.*: **myrmidon**. See *assistant*

(4) aide *n.*: **adjutant**. See *assistant*

(5) aide *n.*: **factotum**. See *assistant*

aides (group of . . . or advisors, often scheming or plotting) *n.*: **camarilla**. See *advisors*

ailing (person, esp. one morbidly concerned with his own health) *n., adj.*: **valetudinarian**. See *sickly*

aim (as in the thing that is being looked for; also the answer to a problem) *n.*: **quaesitum**. See *objective*

(2) aim (directed toward an . . .) *adj.*: **telic**. See *purposeful*

(3) aim (esp. of life) *n.*: **telos** [Greek]. See *goal*

(4) aim (hidden or ulterior . . .) *n.*: **arrierepensee** (or **arrière-pensée**) [French]. See *motive*

(5) aim (the . . . to achieve a particular goal or desire) *n.*: **nisus**. See *goal*

(6) aim (which is elusive or not realistically obtainable) *n.*: **will-o'-the-wisp**. See *pipe dream*

aimless (talk or act in an . . . or incoherent fashion) *v.i.*: **maunder**. See *ramble*

air (as in aura or impalpable emanation) *n.*: **effluvium**. See *aura*

(2) air (as in demeanor) *n.*: **mien**. See *demeanor*

airborne (dancer's seeming ability to stay . . .) *n.*: **ballon** [French]. See *float*

airheaded (person) *n.*: **featherhead**. See *flighty*

(2) airheaded (person) *n.*: **flibbertigibbet**. See *flighty*

airtight *adj.*: **hermetic**. See *sealed*

airy *adj.*: **diaphanous**. See *transparent*

(2) airy *adj.*: **gossamer**. See *transparent*

akin (to, as in related) *adj.*: **cognate**. See *related*

alarm (bell) *n.*: **tocsin**. ❖ We are now facing a second spate of [Carol] Gilligan-inspired books and articles, this time sounding the **tocsin** about the plight of our nation's isolated, repressed and silenced young males. (Christina Sommers, *The War Against Boys*, Simon & Schuster [2000], p. 137.)

(2) alarm (as in panic) *n.*: **Torschlusspanik** [German]. See *panic*

(3) alarm (audio . . .) *n.*: **klaxon**. See *signal*

(4) alarm (serving as a warning or . . .) *adj.*: **aposemetic**. See *warning*

alcohol (given to or marked by consumption of . . .) *adj.*: **bibulous**. See *imbibing*

(2) alcohol (of superior quality) *n.*: **supernaculum**. See *wine*

alcoholic *n.*: **dipsomaniac** (*adj.*: **dipsomaniacal**). ❖ A matched pair of **dipsomaniacs**, Caitlin and Dylan [Thomas] led a depraved existence, roaring from pub to pub and brawling over countless infidelities. (David Grogan, Pages: "From Dylan Thomas' Widow, Caitlin, Comes a Portrait of the Poet as a [Mad] Young Dog," *People*, 7/6/1987, p. 79.)

alert (as in alarm bell) *n.*: **tocsin**. See *alarm*

(2) alert (as in on the . . .) *n.*: **on the qui vive** [idiom]. See *lookout*

(3) alert (audio . . .) *n.*: **klaxon**. See *signal*

(4) alert (person) *n.*: **Argus**. See *watchful*

(5) alert (serving as a warning or alarm) *adj.*: **aposematic**. See *warning*

(6) alert (esp. for changes in trends) *n.*: **weather eye** (esp. as in "keep a weather eye"). See *lookout*

alertness (lacking . . .) *adj.*: **bovine**. See *sluggish*

(2) alertness (lacking . . .) *adj.*: **logy**. See *sluggish*

(3) alertness *n.*: **acuity**. See *keenness*

alias (spec. woman's use of a man's name) *n.*: **pseudandry**. See *pseudonym*

(2) alias *n.*: **allonym**. See *pseudonym*

alien (as in foreigner) *n.*: **auslander**. See *foreigner*

(2) alien (as in foreigner, from another country or place) *n.*: **outlander**. See *foreigner*

(3) alien (as in originating elsewhere; nonnative) *adj.*: **allochthonous**. See *foreign*

alienation (spec. a negative attitude toward society or authority arising from repressed hostility or feelings of inadequacy, combined with a sense of powerlessness to express or act on those feelings) *n.*: **ressentiment**. See *resentment*

all at once *adv.*: **holus-bolus**. See *simultaneously*

all-around (often used of a performer or artist) *adj.*: **protean**. See *versatile*

(2) all-around *adj.*: **multifarious**. See *versatile*

all-comprehensive (state of being . . .) *n.*: **omneity**. See *all-inclusive*

allegation (made without proof or support) *n.*: **ipse dixit** [Latin]. ❖ I have long been convinced that authors of pro-choice literature have no concept of the ideology and philosophy which drive pro-life activities. The January 16 editorial admits that abortion is a deeply divisive, controversial issue, then by **ipse dixit**, declares the pro-choice side to be the right one. (Mary Duhon, Viewpoints, *Houston Chronicle*, 1/23/1998.)

alleged (as in invented or substituted with fraudulent intent) *adj.*: **supposititious**. See *supposed*

(2) alleged (as in supposed) *adj.*: **putative**. See *supposed*

allegiance *n.*: **vassalage** [This word derives from the allegiance that a vassal owed to a feudal lord.] ❖ I started a part-time teaching gig last week at the University of California at Berkeley, and part of the paperwork (which included a form on which you had to pledge allegiance to the state of California, an entity I had not thought needed my **vassalage**) was a form that asked what my ethnicity was. (Gary Kamiya, "Black vs. 'Black,'" *Salon.com*, 1/23/2007).

(2) allegiance *n.*: **fealty**. See *loyalty*

alleviating (as in reducing stress or anxiety, often used with respect to medications) *adj.*: **anxiolytic** (*n.*: a product that has this effect). See *relaxing*

alliance (secret . . . , as in conspiracy) *n.*: **cabal**. See *plot*

all-inclusive (state of being . . .) *n.*: **omneity**. ❖ Little wonder that many tribes and cults have worshiped the god of thunder. The inexplicable power, the enormity and the drama is enough to strike terror and awe into unsophisticated hearts. They could not have compre-

hended the totality of God any more than we can, but they were given a small glimpse of his **omneity**. (David Barlow, Theme for the Day, *Birmingham Post*, 6/4/1999.)

all-inclusiveness *n.*: **catholicity** (*adj.*: **catholic**). See *universality*

allocate (proportionately) *v.t.*: **admeasure**. See *apportion*

allot (proportionately) *v.t.*: **admeasure**. See *apportion*

allow (as in approve, esp. to confirm officially) *v.t.*: **homologate**. See *approve*

(2) allow (as in bestow, by one with higher power) *v.t.*: **vouchsafe**. See *bestow*

allowance (as in giving one's stamp of approval) *n.*: **nihil obstat** [Latin]. See *approval*

alluring *adj.*: **sirenic**. [In Greek mythology, the sirens were three bird-women who, through their beautiful singing, lured mariners to destruction on the rocks and cliffs surrounding their island. Today, the word often suggests something that is alluring, but dangerous if heeded; just as frequently, it refers to something simply alluring. See also the nouns *siren call* and *Lorelei call* under *lure*.] ❖ The A12 to La Spezia, swirling into tunnels, soaring over bridges, resembles a white-knuckle funfair ride. A tour de force by some Leonardo of motorway design, it burrows along the Ligurian coast with tantalising glimpses of impossibly-perched villages and azure water inlets whose **sirenic** string of exit signs reads like a travel brochure: Camogli, Portofino, Rapallo, Sestri Levante. (Ray Kershaw, "You and Italy: The Road Movie," *Independent* [London], 5/31/2003.)

(2) alluring *adj.*: **illecebrous**. [This word is usually considered rare or obsolete, but it is legitimate and has been used in the *New York Times* and thus is included here.] ❖ The first hour [of *Alien Empire*] has to do with insects' bodies, which confirm the rumor that God is a great engineer, and with the reproductive propensities of the randy little rascals, which humans can only envy. [The narrator is] an old-fashioned romantic waxing lyrical over the smells and sounds that lure males to females of many species. The background music [celebrates] the **illecebrous** [aspects of] of bugdom. (Walter Goodman, "Sex, Beauty, Home and Travel Tips on Bugs," *New York Times*, 2/9/1996.)

(3) alluring (and charming woman) *n.*: **Circe**. See *enchantress*

(4) alluring (but in a way that is solely based on deception or pretense or gaudiness) *adj.*: **meretricious**. See *attractive*

(5) alluring (person through magnetism or charm) *n.*: **duende**. See *charisma*

(6) alluring (young woman) *n.*: **houri** [French]. See *woman*

(7) alluring *adj.*: **piquant**. See *appealing*

alone (as in against the world) *adv., adj.*: **contra mundum** [Latin]. See *against the world*

aloof (as in haughty or condescending) *adj.*: **top-lofty**. See *haughty*

(2) aloof (as in haughty) *adj.*: **fastuous**. See *haughty*

(3) aloof (as in socially withdrawn or inexperienced and/or shy and/or sullen) *adj.*: **farouche** [French]. See *shy*

aloofness (as in chilliness in relations between people) *n.*: **froideur** [French]. See *chilliness*

aloud (fear of speaking . . .) *n.*: **phonophobia**. See *fear*

alphabet (one who is learning the . . .) *n.*: **abecedarian**. ❖ Why not be **abecedarians** with your family as you discover the sensory delights of spring? You can document spring firsts from A to Z when you make a "Spring ABC Book" together. On each of 26 large index cards, write a letter of the alphabet. (Donna Erickson, "Prime Time with Kids," *St. Louis Post-Dispatch*, 3/15/1995.)

(2) alphabet (sentence with every letter of) *n.*: **pangram**. ❖ [Will Shortz:] "It was inspired by a current novel, *Ella Minnow Pea* by Mark Dunn, which has a number of **pangrams** sprinkled through it . . . like 'Pack my box with five dozen liquor jugs.'" (Liane Hansen, "Analysis: Sunday Puzzle," Weekend Edition [Sunday], NPR, 9/29/2002.)

also (as in moreover) *adv.*: **withal**. See *moreover*

alter (esp. in a strange, grotesque, or humorous way) *v.t.*: **transmogrify**. See *transform*

alteration (complete . . .) *n.*: **permutation**. See *transformation*

(2) alteration (spec. a fundamental transformation of mind or character, esp. a spiritual conversion) *n.*: **metanoia**. See *conversion*

altercation (esp. public) *n.*: **affray**. See *brawl*

altogether (as in, in the entirety) *adv.*: **holus-bolus**. See *entirety*

altruistic *adj.*: **eleemosynary**. See *charitable*

always (as in forever) *adv.*: **in aeternum** [Latin]. See *forever*

amateur (or dabbler) *n.*: **dilettante** (pl. **dilettanti**). ❖ But [in the world of scavengers or homeless people] eating from dumpsters is what separates the **dilettanti** from the professionals. (Lars Eighner, *Travels with Lizbeth*, St. Martin's Press [1993], p. 112.)

amazing (as in wonderful) *adj.*: **mirific**. See *wonderful*

ambassador (or diplomatic agent who is fully authorized to represent a government) *n.*: **plenipotentiary**. See *diplomat*

ambiguity (as in subject to two different interpretations) *n.*: **amphibiology**. ❖ Robbe-Grillet wrote some incredibly dull books, if you'll allow me the discourtesy, but also some texts whose undeniable interest resides in what we might call his technical dexterity. For example, *Jealousy*. The title isn't very objective—quite a paradox!—since in French it means both "window blind" and "jealousy," an **amphibiology** that disappears in Spanish (and English). (Mario Vargas Llosa, "Levels of Reality," *Literary Review*, 3/22/2002.)

ambiguous (as in having multiple interpretations or signifying different things) *adj.*: **multivocal**. ❖ It is my contention that all revelation is **multivocal** and full of multiple levels of meaning. Indeed, all human words can be described in the same way—**multivocal** with a variety of levels of meaning. Shallow words and concepts exhaust their meanings quickly. . . . Classics (and divine revelations) have such richness of content that people in a wide variety of settings—and even in different civilizations—find the meaning and messages that speak to them. (Irving Greenberg, "On the Divine Plan and the Human Role in Development of Religion," *Journal of Ecumenical Studies*, 6/22/2007.)

(2) ambiguous (as in subject to two different interpretations) *adj.*: **amphibolous**. ❖ For example, in an old radio sketch, Bing Crosby says to Phil Silvers: "Should I take my children to the zoo?" and Phil replies, "No, if the zoo wants them, let it come and fetch them." [Crosby's sentence] admits only a unique parsing, nevertheless gets two quite different interpretations. . . . How can the meaning of a sentence be composed of the meanings of its constituents when a single sentence, not **amphibolous** and with no ambiguous components, has multiple meanings? (Laurence Goldstein, Introduction, *Monist*, 1/1/2005.)

(3) ambiguous (or obscure) *adj.*: **Delphic** [derives from the oracle of Apollo at Delphi in Greek mythology]. ❖ The star attraction was Colin Powell, and the big issue was whether he would run for president in 1996. And when a member of the audience put the question to him directly, Powell answered with **Delphic** aplomb. "There is no real passion in me to run for office," Powell said. "But I don't want to rule it out." (Robert Shogan, "A Novice, but Maybe a Frontrunner, Powell Leaves Himself on the List as a '96 Presidential Possibility," *Minneapolis Star Tribune*, 2/2/1995.)

(4) ambiguous (use of . . . words) *n.*: **parisology**. [Some dictionaries suggest that this word refers specifically to the deliberate use of ambiguous words, but this is a minority view.] ❖ [Throughout the film *Casablanca*, Claude Rains] delivers his lines with such inherent **parisology** that the viewer is never really sure as to where he actually stands. (Martin N. Kriegl, "Casablanca: A Comparison between the Classic Motion Picture and Its Stage Play Source," p-mi.com/ wordpress/wp-contentuploads/2006/08/ Essay_Casablanca.pdf.)

(5) ambiguous (or cryptic or equivocal) *adj.*: **sibylline** (or **sibilline**; often cap.). See *cryptic*

(6) ambiguous (or obscure speech or writing, esp. deliberately) *adj.*: **elliptical**. See *cryptic*

(7) ambiguous (word, phrase or expression) *n.*: **equivoque**. See *equivocal*

ambition (as in energy coupled with a will to succeed) *n.*: **spizzerinctum**. See *energy*

(2) ambition (highest . . . to be attained, lit. the greatest or highest good) *n.*: **summum bonum** [Latin]. See *ideal*

(3) ambition (to achieve a particular goal or desire) *n.*: **nisus**. See *goal*

ambitious (esp. as in . . . to equal or surpass another) *adj.*: **emulous**. [This word is used in a number of different ways including, variously, (1) competitive, (2) ambitious (as in ambitious to equal or surpass another), and (3) jealous/envious. The following, an example of the second definition, is a discussion of the Florida vote-counting issue in the aftermath of the 2000 presidential election.] ❖ Power and ambition continue to collide darkly in the Sunshine State. . . . But ambition is gender-neutral; it is not limited to those who seek the highest office in the land. . . . [I]t is on the face of Katherine Harris, Florida's ghoulishly made-up secretary of state. How fascinating and ironic that women like Harris . . . are playing pivotal roles in a national drama dominated by **emulous** men. (Joan Venochi, "Oh, What a Plot the Politicians Are Weaving in Florida," *Boston Globe*, 11/17/2000.)

ambivalence (as in the dilemma of being given a choice between two equally appealing alternatives and thus being able to choose neither one) *n.*: **Buridan's ass**. See *paralysis*

ambivalent (or undecided person, esp. regarding political issues) *n.*: **mugwump**. See *undecided*

ambushing (as in lying in wait for prey, often used of insects) *adj.*: **lochetic**. ❖ A spider ran beneath my couch. And I became **lochetic**. I perched and leaned into a crouch. That surely looked comedic. It showed; I jumped and missed; cried "ouch!" And now need ortho-pedic. (Dave Dickerson, "Vocabulary Poem," bourboncowboy.blogspot.com/2006/06, 6/7/2006.)

amend (text or language by removing errors or flaws) *v.t.*: **blue-pencil**. See *edit*

(2) amend (text or language by removing errors or flaws) *v.t.*: **emend**. See *edit*

amendment (as in correction, esp. in printed material) *n.*: **corrigendum**. See *correction*

(2) amendment (esp. a scholarly critical . . . , as in revision) *n.*: **recension**. See *revision*

amends (make . . . for) *v.t., v.i.*: **expiate**. See *atone*

(2) amends (making . . . for) *adj.*: **piacular**. See *atoning*

amiability *n.*: **bonhomie**. See *affability*

amiable (and pleasant) *adj.*: **sympathique** [French]. See *genial*

amnesia (spec. inability to recall meaning of words) *n.*: **paramnesia**. ❖ If you suffer from **paramnesia**, just do what I did: subscribe to the A.Word.A.Day service on the Internet . . . and enrich your vocabulary with a plethora of words that will express exactly what you want in the most efficient manner. (Dorothea Helms, "Reining in Rampant Verbosity," *Toronto Sun*, 9/13/2000.)

amoral (person) *n.*: **reprobate**. See *unprincipled*

amorous *adj.*: **amative**. ❖ Of course, there's the argument that the baby-boom generation of which the Clintons are a part don't express their **amative** feelings openly, that Hillary Rodham Clinton is a new breed of professional woman with her own political ambitions, or that, quite frankly, the Clintons' personal relationship is their own private business—and not the pub-lic's. (Thomas DiBacco, "Will the Real Clinton Stand Up? A Year Later, We're Still Waiting," *Orlando Sentinel*, 12/5/1993.)

(2) amorous (esp. in the sexual sense) *adj.*: **amatory**. See *lovemaking*

amuse (oneself in a light, frolicsome manner) *v.t., v.i.*: **disport**. See *frolic*

amused (having an ability or tendency to be . . .) *n.*: **risibility**. See *laugh*

amusing (as in witty) *adj.*: **waggish**. See *witty*

(2) amusing (in a sarcastic or biting way) *adj.*: **mordant**. See *sarcastic*

(3) amusing (line) *n.*: **bon mot** [French]. See *quip*

(4) amusing (line) *n.*: **epigram**. See *quip*

(5) amusing (person who tries to be . . . but is not) *n.*: **witling**. See *humorless*

(6) amusing *adj.*: **gelastic**. See *laughable*

(7) amusing *adj.*: **risible**. See *laughable*

analogous (as in related) *adj.*: **cognate**. See *related*

analysis (detailed . . . of a literary work) *n.*: **explication de texte** [French]. ❖ In [movie director Bertrand] Blier's male-dominated uni-verse, men routinely turn women into objects and toss them aside, then discuss it all as if doing some academic **explication de texte**. (John Morrone, "Too Beautiful for You," *New Leader*, 1/8/1990.)

(2) analysis (as in relating to . . . that sounds plausible but is false or insincere) *adj.*: **mere-tricious**. See *specious*

(3) analysis (as in formal . . . or discussion of a subject) *n.*: **disquisition**. See *discourse*

(4) analysis (esp. of a text) *n.*: **exegesis**. See *interpretation*

(5) analysis (of a subject, as in survey) *n.*: **conspectus**. See *survey*

(6) analysis (of a text by adding one's own ideas) *n.*: **eisegesis**. See *interpretation*

(7) analysis (one who is undergoing . . .) *n.*: **analysand**. See *psychoanalysis*

(8) analysis (specious . . . intended to mislead or rationalize) *n.*: **casuistry**. See *fallacious*

(9) analysis (which is complicated and often illogical) *n.*: **choplogic**. See *fallacy*

(10) analysis (which is fallacious or specious) *n.*: **syllogism**. See *specious*

(11) analysis (observation and . . . of matters outside oneself; that is, the outside world) *n.*: **extrospection** (*adj.*: **extrospective**). See *observation*

analyst (as in investigator or examiner) *n.*: **scru-tator**. See *examiner*

analytical (as in logical) *adj.*: **ratiocinative**. See *logical*

analyze (in minute detail) *v.t.*: **anatomize**.
❖ Few movies attempt to **anatomize** a whole sick society, to dissect the mortal betrayals of country, friend, lover and family; fewer films achieve this goal with such energy and wit. (Richard Corliss, Cinema: "From Failure to Cult Classic," *Time*, 3/21/1988, p. 84.)

(2) analyze (logically) *v.i.*: **ratiocinate**.
❖ [Author Stephen] Fry talks of his father's "misanthropy and arrogance," his "infuriatingly, cold, precise **ratiocinating** engine of a brain fuelled by a wholly egocentric passion" and says that whenever Fry Senior was in the house, "instantly, fun, freedom and relaxation turned into terrified silence." (Lynn Barber, Books: "But Who Cares About Tishes and Pollies?" *Daily Telegraph* [London], 10/18/1997.)

(3) analyze (that which has already occurred; i.e., to project into the past) *v.t.*: **retroject**.
❖ Nor is there any indication that [Joan of Arc] was repelled by the idea of sex. That would be a **retrojected** suspicion, based on the widespread later presumption that every sane woman marries, has romantic affairs, or is ready to tangle in easy sexual liaisons. But not all women act according to such (mostly) male expectations and preconceptions. (Donald Spoto, *Joan*, HarperCollins [2007], p. 31.)

(4) analyze (as in think about) *v.t.*: **cerebrate**. See *think*

(5) analyze (as in think about) *v.t.*: **cogitate**. See *think*

(6) analyze *v.t.*: **assay**. See *evaluate*

(7) analyze (closely, esp. for purposes of surveillance) *v.t.*: **perlustrate**. See *examine*

anarchist (spec. one who hates or mistrusts authority) *n.*: **misarchist**. See *rebel*

anarchy (as in government by the mob or the masses) *n.*: **mobocracy**. See *government*

(2) anarchy (as in government by the mob or the masses) *n.*: **ochlocracy**. See *government*

(3) anarchy (movement toward or degree of . . . in a system or society) *n.*: **entropy**. See *disorder*

ancestor (as in predecessor) *n.*: **progenitor**. See *predecessor*

(2) ancestor (of or derived from name of female . . .) *adj.*: **matronymic**. See *maternal*

(3) ancestor (of or derived from name of male . . .) *adj.*: **patronymic**. See *paternal*

ancestors (excessive reverence for . . . or tradition) *adj.*: **filiopietistic**. See *old-fashioned*

ancient (esp. as in outdated) *adj.*: **antediluvian**. See *outdated*

(2) ancient *adj.*: **hoary**. See *old*

anecdote (as in example, used to make a point) *n.*: **exemplum**. See *example*

anemic (as in pale, and often sickly) *adj.*: **etiolated**. See *pale*

(2) anemic (from loss or lack of body strength) *adj.*: **asthenic** (*n.*: **asthenia**). See *weak*

anesthetizing (as in sleep-inducing) *adj.*: **soporific**. See *sleep-inducing*

anew *adv.*: **afresh**. ❖ But now that the [Internet] mania is over, it's probably time to think **afresh** about the technological revolution, to toss out those wishful fantasies left over from the Romantic era, or the 1960s, and see how these gizmos are really going to change our lives. (David Brooks, "Finding the 'Next' Netheads," *Newsweek* International, 8/20/2001, p. 53.)

angelic *adj.*: **beatific** (to make . . .) *v.t.*: **beatify**. See *joyful*

(2) angelic *adj.*: **seraphic**. ❖ Songwriters Lynn Hollyfield and Nina Spruill . . . [favor a] soft-spun weave of musings and music, relying mostly on Hollyfield's **seraphic** soprano voice and Spruill's alto flute to cast an introspective spell, but not to the exclusion of more earthy and engaging material. (Mike Joyce, "Hollyfield & Spruill: Graceful Musing," *Washington Post*, 3/19/1993.)

anger *n.*: **choler** (*adj.*: **choleric**). ❖ [As Richard Marcinko] rages over and over again in [his] book, "Why the hell didn't they let us do what we were trained to do? Even in Vietnam, the system kept me from hunting and killing as many of the enemy as I would have liked." Marcinko's **choler** stems partly from the fact that in 1990 he was convicted of conspiracy to defraud the government. (Elizabeth Gleick,

Pages: "Master of Mayhem Richard Marcinko Was Too Loose a Cannon for the U.S. Navy," *People*, 5/04/1992, p. 155.)

(2) anger *v.t.*: **envenom**. See *embitter*

(3) anger (marked by a sudden or violent . . .) *adj.*: **vesuvian** (esp. as in . . . temper). See *temper*

(4) anger *n.*: **bile**. See *bitterness*

angered (easily . . . , as in offended) *adj.*: **umbrageous**. See *offended*

angry (extremely . . .) *adj.*: **apoplectic**. ❖ He's not a young man anymore, but John Mellencamp sure is angry. Guys with "suspenders and cigars" piss him off. No-smoking laws make him furious. And record-company execs, well, they make him absolutely **apoplectic**. (Rob Brunner, Music: "Ripe Mellencamp," *Entertainment Weekly*, 10/9/1998, p. 83.)

(2) angry *adj.*: **wroth**. ❖ [C]ondescending white liberals have been handing down to the supposedly grateful black man what they're patronizingly confident is good for him. And if an ungrateful black refuses this generous offering, white liberals, seemingly unaware of the racial vanity involved in their assumptions, are **wroth** indeed. But this is nothing compared to how **wroth** are this country's dominant black leaders presently attacking Justice [Clarence] Thomas with rare venom, now that he's assumed a position of real leadership on the Supreme Court. (Richard Grenier, "The Most Courageous Man in America," *Washington Times*, 7/10/1995, p. 29.)

(3) angry (as in grouchy person) *n.*: **crosspatch**. See *grouch*

(4) angry (as in indignant) *n.*: **dudgeon** (often expressed as "in high dudgeon"). See *indignant*

(5) angry (as in irritable) *adj.*: **liverish**. See *irritable*

(6) angry (as in irritable) *adj.*: **shirty**. See *irritable*

(7) angry (as in irritable) *adj.*: **splenetic**. See *irritable*

(8) angry (as in surly) *adj.*: **atrabilious**. See *surly*

(9) angry (extremely . . .) *adj.*: **furibund**. See *furious*

(10) angry *adj.*: **bilious**. See *surly*

anguish (as in sadness) *n.*: **dolor** (*adj.*: **dolorous**). See *sadness*

(2) anguish (expressing . . . often regarding something gone) *adj.*: **elegiac**. See *sorrowful*

(3) anguish (over) *v.t.*: **bewail**. See *lament*

(4) anguish (out of the depths of . . . or despair) *n., adv.*: **de profundis**. See *despair*

animal (lover) *n.*: **zoophilist**. ❖ Typical of the **zoophilist** who favors life's lower orders over humankind, Robinson Jeffers claimed he'd sooner kill a man than a hawk. (David Yezzi, review of *My Dog Tulip*, by J. R. Ackerley, *New Criterion*, 11/1/1999.)

(2) animal (which feeds mainly on plants) *n.*: **herbivore** (*adj.*: **herbivorous**). See *plants*

animals (sexual attraction to . . .) *n.*: **zoophilia**. (person attracted: **zoophile**) See *bestiality*

animosity (intense . . . , such as toward an enemy) *n.*: **enmity**. See *hatred*

announce *v.t.*: **annunciate**. ❖ Prior to the summit, U.N. Secretary General Kofi Annan sought to deflect criticism by acknowledging that the agenda was "absurdly ambitious." Mr. Annan saw this as a virtue—that **annunciating** impossibly high-minded aims was nobler and better than pursuing more realistic goals. (Bret Schaefer, "United Nations Nonevent," *Washington Times*, 9/23/2000.)

(2) announce (as in assert) *v.t.*: **asseverate**. See *declare*

(3) announce (as in declare, publicly, solemnly, or formally) *v.t.*: **nuncupate**. See *declare*

announcement (as in decree) *n.*: **diktat**. See *decree*

(2) announcement (made without proof or support) *n.*: **ipse dixit** [Latin]. See *allegation*

(3) announcement (of forthcoming marriage, esp. in a church) *n.*: **banns**. See *marriage*

(4) announcement (which is official, as in with the authority of one's office) *adv., adj.*: **ex cathedra**. See *official*

annoy (as in bother or inconvenience) *v.t.*: **discommode**. See *inconvenience*

(2) annoy (as in bother or inconvenience) *v.t.*: **incommode**. See *inconvenience*

(3) annoy *v.t.*: **chivvy**. See *pester*

annoyance (as in trouble) *n.*: **tsuris** [Yiddish]. See *trouble*

annoyed (as in irritable) *adj.*: **splenetic**. See *irritable*

(2) annoyed (easily . . . , as in offended) *adj.*: **umbrageous**. See *offended*

annoying (as in repellent) *adj.*: **rebarbative**. See *repellent*

(2) annoying *adj.*: **pestiferous**. See *bothersome*

annulment (as in termination) *n.*: **quietus**. See *termination*

anomalous (as in departing from the standard or norm) *adj.*: **heteroclite**. See *abnormal*

anomaly (as in someone or something that deviates from the norm) *n.*: **lusus** [Latin; almost always used as part of the term "lusus naturae," or freak of nature]. See *freak*

anonymous *adj.*: **innominate**. ❖ Situated in an otherwise **innominate** strip mall on Olive Boulevard in the heart of University City, Kelly's Golf Repair and Club Makers Center is a working man's laboratory of golf club fitting and construction. (Dan O'Neill, "Clubs That Don't Fit May Cause Bad Habits," *St. Louis Post-Dispatch*, 5/9/1998.)

answer (as in responding to an anticipated objection to an argument before that objection has been made) *n.*: **prolepsis**. See *rebuttal*

(2) answer (charging accuser with similar offense) *n.*: **tu quoque** [Latin]. See *accuse*

(3) answer (clever . . . that one thinks of after the moment has passed) *n.*: **esprit d'escalier** [French]. See *retort*

(4) answer (to a problem, or objective, as in the thing that is being looked for) *n.*: **quaesitum**. See *objective*

antagonism (as in event that causes or provokes war, literally or figuratively) *n.*: **casus belli** [Latin: occasion of war]. See *provocation*

antagonistic *adj.*: **oppugnant**. ❖ [I]f city officials [who are] **oppugnant** to the [monorail initiative that was enacted into law by the voters] had expended half of the energy of their opposition . . . in respectfully fulfilling the mandate and spirit of the law, we'd be well on our way to riding above the increasing gridlock. (Laurence Ballard, "Monorail—Effort to Repeal Vote—Disrespects Citizens' Decision and Needs," *Seattle Times*, 6/23/2000.)

antecedent *adj.*: **prevenient** (often as in "prevenient grace"). ❖ The symbolism behind Catholic doctrines of Mary is lost on most Protestants. The doctrine of the immaculate conception, for example, symbolizes **prevenient** grace—the grace that "comes before" faith in Christ, the grace that moves us to place our faith in Christ. It has nothing to do with Mary's virginity or with the virgin birth of Jesus. (James Gaughan, "Protestants Embrace New Vision of Mary," *Minneapolis Star Tribune*, 11/13/1999.)

anthology (as in collection of writings by an author) *n.*: **chrestomathy**. ❖ Book World readers need no introduction to the author of this collection. . . . *Readings* is an assortment of perambulations and reflections on literary, cultural and autobiographical themes reprinted from the author's monthly columns bearing the same name. It is, in other words, a **chrestomathy** of all things Dirda. (*Washington Post*, In Brief, review of *Readings: Essays and Literary Entertainments*, by Michael Dirda, 11/05/2000.)

antic *n.*: **dido**. See *prank*

anti-change (as in hatred or fear of anything new or different) *n.*: **misoneism** (person holding this view: **misoneist**). See *conservatism*

anticipation (spec. acting as if or threatening that a future event [usually unwanted] has already occurred by reference to an event that precedes it, for example "if you look at my diary, you're dead") *n.*: **prolepsis**. See *prediction*

(2) anticipation (nervously excited with . . .) *adj.*: **atwitter**. See *excited*

(3) anticipation (that something is going to occur) *n.*: **presentiment**. See *premonition*

anticipatory *adj.*: **prevenient**. ❖ Organizations set up to tell us about how to educate or otherwise raise our children usually have some ax to grind. Often they are driven by some ideological demon. . . . [Thus], what aroused my hackles when I saw the news reports on the Academy [of Pediatrics] findings [that young people should not specialize in one sport] was the **prevenient** sense that here again was another propaganda statement. But no, it is common sense based on research. (R. Emmett Tyrrell Jr., "Sporting Chance for the Young," *Washington Times*, 7/7/2000.)

anticlimax *n.*: **bathos**. ❖ [Watching a film about outer space on a giant IMAX screen] is a dizzy mixture of true grandeur and sudden **bathos**. . . . When an image is this large in scope as well as in area on the screen, it squeezes a silent gasp out of you. . . . On the other hand, when the IMAX is displaying things that aren't intrinsically giant, the size of the image registers as a grotesque inflation, and anticlimax swiftly follows. (Francis Spufford, Essay: "The Outerspace Documentary as Big as the Ritz," *Independent on Sunday*, 5/30/1999.)

antiquated *adj.*: **antediluvian**. See *outdated*

antisocial (as in socially withdrawn or inexperienced and/or shy and/or sullen) *adj.*: **farouche** [French]. See *shy*

ants (of or relating to) *adj.*: **formic**. ❖ Woody Allen voices worker ant Z-4195 ("the middle child in 5 million"), who becomes an accidental war hero in the **formic** army's battle against the termites. (Stuart Price, Preview: Film—Christmas Films, review of *Antz*, *Independent* [London], December 1998.)

(2) ants (study of) *n.*: **myrmecology**. ❖ Most kids are **myrmecologists** at one time or another. That's the great thing about **myrmecology**: no matter where you are or who you are, and no matter what resources you arrive with, ants are there too, awaiting study. (Bill Roorbach, "King of the Anthill," *Newsday*, 11/13/1994, p. 38.)

anxiety *n.*: **inquietude**. ❖ [In a survey], people felt the world has become unsafe and expressed a belief that real change is not in sight. It is true

that similar statements of dissatisfaction and **inquietude** might have been elicited during any decade in U.S. history. Now, however, one obtains responses of exasperation and desperation from all parts of the population about all types of events, communicating an urgency. (Ralph Hyatt, "American Hearts Have Hardened," *USA Today Magazine*, 3/01/1994.)

(2) anxiety (as part of depressed state) *n.*: **dysphoria**. See *depression*

(3) anxiety (in a state of . . .) *idiom*: [on] **tenterhooks**. See *suspense*

(4) anxiety (in a state of . . .) *n.*: **swivet** (as in "in a swivet") *informal*. See *distress*

(5) anxiety (positive form of . . . brought on, for example, by a job promotion or a new baby) *n.*: **eustress**. See *stress*

(6) anxiety *n.pl.* but sing. or pl. in construction: **collywobbles**. See *bellyache*

anyway (as in nevertheless) *adv.*: **withal**. See *nevertheless*

apart (from, as in separable) *adj.*: **dissociable**. See *separable*

apathetic *adj.*: **pococurante**. ❖ The only child of an interminably famous literary theorist, and now **pococurante** chair of the English Department, Hank published one critically acclaimed novel—*Off the Road*—20 years ago. . . . [His] fate [is that of] a middle-aged, middle-class guy trapped by his successes. . . . [T]he faculty meetings and search committees that footnote his daily existence [are not gratifying]. . . . Is this middle age, he thinks, the cruel punch line of prostate trouble visited on an irreverent man? (Gail Caldwell, "College Bound; Richard Russo's Comic/Sad Novel of Learning and Campus Politics," *Boston Globe*, 7/13/1997.)

(2) apathetic (as in sluggish or lethargic) *adj.*: **torpid**. See *lethargic*

apathy (sometimes in matters spiritual, and sometimes leading to depression) *n.*: **acedia**. ❖ What makes our situation today different from previous periods in American history—and fundamentally more serious—is the "de-moralization" of much of middle- and upper-middle-class life. The causes are varied and complicated—my list would include . . . modernity itself, affluence, spiritual **acedia**, intellectual trends, movies and television, advertising, and flawed government programs. (William Bennett, "Moral Corruption in America," *Commentary*, 11/1/1995, p. 29.)

(2) apathy (a matter of . . . , esp. in matters of religion and theology; that is, neither right nor wrong, beneficial nor harmful) *n.*: **adiaphoron** (*adj.*: **adiaphorous**). See *indifference*

(3) apathy (as in lethargy) *n.*: **hebetude**. See *lethargy*

(4) apathy (as in lethargy) *n.*: **torpor**. See *lethargy*

(5) apathy (esp. in matters of politics or religion) *n.*: **Laodiceanism**. See *indifference*

ape (of, relating to, or resembling) *adj.*: **anthropoid**. ❖ One limb [of the evolutionary tree] led to the prosimians, or lower primates, such as lemurs and bush babies, and the other to the **anthropoids**, or higher primates, such as monkeys, apes and humans. (Alice Park, "Linking Man to a Monkey: New Fossils Point to a Tiny, Tree-Dwelling Ancestor," *Time*, 3/27/2000.)

(2) ape (of, relating to, or resembling) *adj.*: **simian**. ❖ To the Flikshteins . . . Cookie Flikshtein is a beloved—albeit **simian**—member of the family. She may be a monkey, they say, but she has adjusted enough to the human condition to spend most evenings eating rocky road ice cream and watching the nightly news. (Alan Feuer, "Family Not Ready to Give Up Pet Monkey: State Wants to Put Rare Creature in Zoo," *Dallas Morning News*, 7/23/2000.)

apex (as in highest point that can be attained or the ultimate degree, as of a condition or quality) *n.*: **ne plus ultra**. See *ultimate*

(2) apex *n.*: **apogee**. See *height*

aphorism (pithy . . .) *n.*: **gnome** (*adj.*: **gnomic**). See *catchphrase*

(2) aphorism (witty or clever . . . or line) *n.*: **bon mot**. See *line*

(3) aphorism *n.*: **apothegm**. See *saying*

aphoristic (as in given to stating aphorisms, esp. in a moralizing way) *adj.*: **sententious**.

❖ [Rockefeller] delivered brief sermons along with the coins, exhorting children to work hard and be frugal if they wanted a fortune; the coins were for saving, not indulgence. . . . He informed children that the nickel represented a year's interest on a dollar. For someone of Rockefeller's **sententious** nature, this was a very comfortable persona to adopt. (Ron Chernow, *Titan*, Random House [1998], p. 614.)

aphrodisiac *n.*: **philter**. See *potion*

aplomb (esp. under pressure or trying circumstances) *n.*: **sang-froid** [French]. See *composure*

apology (which is formal, full, and genuine) *n.*: **amende honorable** [French]. ❖ [A]ppeasement fuels the appetite of the moral blackmailer. . . . Visiting the Yad Vashem memorial, [Pope John Paul II] expressed regret for historical antipathies "that led to the deaths of Jews by Christians at any time and in any place." That comprehensive **amende honorable** was immediately denounced as inadequate, because it did not condemn the Pope's predecessor, Pius XII, for alleged complicity in the Nazi murder of the Jews. (Gerald Warner, "Sorry Is the Most Dangerous Word for the Church in Crisis," *Scotland on Sunday*, 3/26/2000, p. 18.)

(2) apology (as in place or occasion to offer . . . and to seek forgiveness) *n.*: **Canossa**. See *penance*

apparel *n.*: **raiment**. See *clothing*

apparition *n.*: **phantasm**. ❖ In 1993 he brought out *The Ghosts of Virginia*, a much larger compilation of his stories. "I thought I was finished," he says, "but people from all over started writing me and calling me." That resulted in three more volumes on Old Dominion **phantasms**, each about 400 pages long. (Rick Britton, "Ghosts; Colonial Past Haunts Williamsburg," *Washington Times*, 10/28/1999.)

(2) apparition *n.*: **wraith**. ❖ We sat for hours in our crude tumbleweed blind. I can't remember if we heard the golden eagle or saw it first, but suddenly it was there, slipping through the fog like a **wraith**. (Larry Rice, "Nature's Wild Gifts: Abrupt and Fleeting Encounters with

Animals Leave Impressions That Last Forever," *Backpacker*, 5/1/1998, p. 118.)

appeal (as in plea) *n.*: **cri de coeur** [French; lit. cry of the heart]. See *plea*

(2) appeal (making an . . . to one's monetary self-interest) *n.*: **argumentum ad crumenam** [Latin]. See *argument*

(3) appeal (of an . . . to one's sense of pity or compassion) *adv., adj.*: **ad misericordiam**. See *argument*

(4) appeal (to earnestly) *v.t.*: **adjure**. See *plead*

appealing *adj.*: **piquant**. ❖ Philip Malbone, his antihero, is a puzzling mix of bad and good, of mal and bon. "There was for him something **piquant** in being . . . neither innocent nor guilty," Higginson writes, "but always on some delicious middle ground." (Caleb Crain, "The Monarch of Dreams," *New Republic*, 5/28/2001.)

(2) appealing (as in alluring) *adj.*: **illecebrous**. See *alluring*

(3) appealing (as in alluring) *adj.*: **sirenic**. [See also the nouns *siren call* and *Lorelei call* under *lure*.] See *alluring*

(4) appealing (but in a way that is solely based on deception or pretense or gaudiness) *adj.*: **meretricious**. See *attractive*

(5) appealing (in appearance in an unconventional way) *adj.*: **jolie laide** (or **belle laide**) [French]. See *pretty* or *handsome* or *beautiful*

(6) appealing (person through magnetism or charm) *n.*: **duende**. See *charisma*

(7) appealing (physically . . .) *n.*: **pulchritude**. See *beauty*

(8) appealing (said esp. of food or drink that is so good that one wants more) *adj.*: **moreish** [chiefly British]. See *addictive*

(9) appealing *adj.*: **prepossessing**. See *pleasing*

appear (as in emerge or materialize) *v.i.*: **debouch**. See *emerge*

appearance (outward . . . as opposed to the substance that lies beneath) *n., n.pl.*: **superficies**. ❖ But a candidate cannot live by policy alone.

Charisma counts at the presidential level. The president isn't just a bureaucrat with executive power. . . . Image counts. **Superficies** add up to substance. Someone running for president could benefit from a little celebrity power, some magic. (Joel Achenbach, "Old Hats in the Ring," *Washington Post*, 4/5/1995.)

(2) appearance (as in physique) *n.*: **somatotype**. See *physique*

(3) appearance (facial . . .) *n.*: **physiognomy**. See *facial features*

(4) appearance (of knowledge that is actually superficial) *n.*: **sciolism**. See *superficial*

(5) appearance (of plenty when in fact there is little) *adj.*: **Barmecidal** (esp. as in "Barmecidal feast"). See *illusion*

(6) appearance (as in demeanor) *n.*: **mien**. See *demeanor*

appease *v.t.*: **dulcify**. ❖ One of Pakistan's most notorious homegrown terrorists was elected to parliament—from prison. . . . His pro-Taliban, pro-al Qaeda outlawed party, Sipah-e-Sahaba (Guardians of the Friends of the Prophet), was one of five extremist groups banned by President Pervez Musharraf last January as he tried to **dulcify** U.S. concerns. (Arnaud de Borchgrave, "A Triumph for Taliban's Tutors," *Washington Times*, 11/12/2002.)

(2) appease *v.t.*: **propitiate**. See *placate*

appeasing (as in peacemaking) *adj.*: **irenic**. See *peacemaking*

appendage *n.*: **appurtenance**. ❖ To Baron, a firearm is an unpleasant, even repulsive **appurtenance** of life in L.A.—he would gladly throw his away, he says, if he ever moved back to New York. (Justin Davidson, "Guns in America," *Newsday*, 12/18/2000.)

appetite (abnormally increased . . . for food) *n.*: **hyperphagia**. ❖ It also is the time of year when all bears are going into "**hyperphagia**," a phase in which they are almost crazed by hunger and must try to put on two or three times their body weight in fat before winter. They feel like they are starving—they are ravenous—and it just doesn't seem like there is enough food. (Michael Babcock, "Tough Time of Year for Black Bears," Gannett News Service, 9/6/2001.)

(2) appetite (excessive . . .) *n.*: **polyphagia**. ❖ Beginning in the 1950s, obesity shifted to being considered a condition best dealt with through medical intervention. . . . Even the language changed to reflect the new perspective. . . . Instead of engaging in gluttonous or gorging behavior, [fat people] were considered victims of . . . "**polyphagia**." (Mike Powers, "In the Eye of the Beholder," *Human Ecology Forum*, 9/1/1996, p. 16.)

(3) appetite (condition involving . . . for eating nonfood items) *n.*: **pica**. See *craving*

(4) appetite (excessive . . .) *n.*: **gulosity**. See *gluttony*

(5) appetite (having a strong . . . , esp. sexual) *adj.*: **concupiscent** (*n.*: **concupiscence**). See *lustful*

(6) appetite (loss resulting from chronic disease) *n.*: **cachexia**. See *wasting*

appetizing (said esp. of food or drink that is so good that one wants more) *adj.*: **moreish** [chiefly British]. See *addictive*

(2) appetizing *adj.*: **esculent**. See *edible*

(3) appetizing *adj.*: **sapid**. See *tasty*

(4) appetizing *adj.*: **toothsome**. See *tasty*

applaud (persons hired to . . . at a performance) *n.*: **claque**. ❖ [New York Mayor Rudy Giuliani] brought a **claque** of 40 to 50 supporters and City Hall employees to envelop him as he walked in the Lesbian and Gay Pride March. Their job: to cheer and applaud the mayor whenever any of the spectators along the route booed him. (Sydney H. Schanberg, "Giuliani on Parade—with a Human Heat Shield, *Newsday*, 6/27/1995.)

applause (as in praise) *n.*: **approbation**. See *praise*

apples (of, relating to, or derived) *adj.*: **pomaceous**. ❖ Many apples are biennial, which in practise means they alternate between good and bad crops. Some fruit will be scabby and others have bitterpit, and the earwigs and wasps and moths will have their day. But that is an important part of their **pomaceous** charm. (Monty

Don, Life & Soul: Gardens: "Apple of His Eye," *Observer*, 10/29/2000, p. 82.)

appoint (as in delegate, authority or duties to another) *v.t.*: **depute**. See *delegate*

appointment (esp. for illicit sexual relations) *n.*: **assignation**. ❖ The next scene takes place two years earlier, in a flat that Jerry and Emma have been renting for years to accommodate their afternoon trysts. Only there's no trysting on this bleak winter's day. Neither has time for midday **assignations** any longer, nor are they willing to upend their lives by dumping their respective spouses. (Steve Parks, "The Genesis of a 'Betrayal,'" *Newsday*, 3/20/1998.)

apportion *v.t.*: **admeasure**. ❖ The Admiral, David Robinson, the admirable Tim Duncan and the **admeasuring** [i.e., ball distributing] point guard Avery Johnson will make the Spurs the favorites [in the NBA finals], on and off the court, whether they host the Knicks or the Pacers. (John Walters, SI View: The Week in TV Sports, *Sports Illustrated*, 6/14/1999, p. 19.)

appraise (as in analyze, that which has already occurred, i.e., to project into the past) *v.t.*: **retroject**. See *analyze*

appreciate (as in understand, thoroughly and/or intuitively) *v.t.*: **grok**. See *understand*

appreciation (as in perception or awareness) *n.*: **ken**. See *perception*

apprehend (based on past experience) *v.t.*: **apperceive**. See *comprehend*

(2) apprehend (through the senses) *adj.*: **sensate**. See *feel*

apprehension (positive form of . . . brought on, for example, by a job promotion or a new baby) *n.*: **eustress**. See *stress*

(2) apprehension (that something is going to occur) *n.*: **presentiment**. See *premonition*

apprehensive (and cautious and indecisive) *adj.*: **Prufrockian**. See *timid*

apprentice (as in beginner) *n.*: **abecedarian**. See *beginner*

approach *v.t.*: **appropinquate**. ❖ Got spurned, so I don't have a date, / **Appropinquated** Kate far too late. / Before my approach, / She fell for her coach, / Note to self: it does not pay to wait! (Oxford Victor, *The Omnificent English Dictionary in Limerick Form* [oedilf.com], 10/14/2006.)

approaching (spec. getting closer and closer to a goal but never quite reaching it) *adv.*: **asymptotically**. See *closer*

appropriate *adj.*: **felicitous**. ❖ [B]aseball never had it so good as it did in the era immediately after World War II. . . . But pivotal is the more **felicitous** expression for this period. . . . These, after all, were the years of Jackie Robinson, of the gestation of a players' union that would eventually topple the despised reserve clause, [and] of middle-class flight to the suburbs (which drastically altered the game's demographics). (Ron Fimrite, Books: "Those Were the Days," *Sports Illustrated*, 4/19/1999, p. R26.)

(2) appropriate (an . . . thing to do) *n.*: **bon ton** [French]. ❖ But what remains very similar after all these years is the sense of elitism and the sentiment of "we are better than them" which still unabashedly pervades Labor ranks. . . . [Labor leader Tiki Dayan] thought it **bon ton** to haughtily intimate that Likud supporters are unthinking low-class trash—definitely not as good as us. (Sarah Honig, "Barak's Delayed Reaction: Will It Help Netanyahu?" *Jerusalem Post*, 5/3/1999.)

(3) appropriate (as in relevant) *adj.*: **apposite**. See *relevant*

(4) appropriate (as in usurp) *v.t.*: **accroach**. See *usurp*

(5) appropriate (esp. in reference to a punishment) *adj.*: **condign**. See *deserved*

(6) appropriate (for oneself without right) *v.t.*: **arrogate**. See *claim*

(7) appropriate *adj.*: **comme il faut** [French]. See *proper*

approval *n.*: **nihil obstat**. [Latin for "nothing hinders." This term refers to a certification given by an official censor in the Roman Catholic Church approving a book as not being doctrinally or morally objectionable, and which may therefore be published. It is often used generally or metaphorically to refer to any kind of seal of approval, sanction, or blessing, as in the following example.] ❖ The [Royal Canadian Mounted Police] has engaged the Walt Disney organization of Hollywood, U.S.A., to take control of marketing the [Mounties'] image. From now on every item, from Mountie swizzle sticks to those awful Mountie dolls that make a rude noise when you squeeze them, must have the **nihil obstat** of one of Walt's minions. (Christopher Dafoe, "Walt Disney Deserves to Get His Man," *Ottawa Citizen*, 9/17/1995.)

(2) approval (as in praise) *n.*: **approbation**. See *praise*

approve (esp. to confirm officially) *v.t.*: **homologate**. ❖ The new model, called the TX1, is **homologated** for all of Europe, said Hugh Lang, chairman of London Taxi's parent, Manganese Bronze Holdings PLC. The first left-hand-drive versions will be built next spring for export into Europe. (William Diem, "Two U.K. Firms Eye American Market," *Automotive News*, 10/20/1997).

(2) approve (officially) *v.t.*: **approbate**. See *authorize*

approved (as in official, act, declaration, or statement, as in with the authority of one's office) *adv., adj.*: **ex cathedra**. See *official*

apt (as in relevant) *adj.*: **apposite**. See *relevant*

arbiter (on matters of taste, fashion, style, protocol, etc.) *n.*: **arbiter elegantiae** [Latin]. ❖ Suddenly, it seems, one's mother has become the latest, choicest fashion accessory. Forget Gucci—a mother on the arm is a better class of bag. Gwyneth Paltrow, Hollywood's new **arbiter elegantiae**, confirmed this at the Oscars. Her acceptance speech was a panegyric to her mother Blythe Danner: "I love her more than anyone in the world," she sobbed. . . . (Penelope Wyatt, "Mommy Dearest: Stars Stepping Out with Mothers at Their Sides," *Chicago Sun-Times*, 4/4/1999.)

arbitrary (as in haphazard) *adj., adv.*: **higgledy-piggledy**. See *haphazard*

(2) arbitrary (as in random) *adj.*: **stochastic**. See *random*

arch (slightly) *v.t.*, *v.i.*: **camber**. See *curve*

archaic (as in obsolete) *adj.*: **superannuated**. See *obsolete*

archconservative (in beliefs and often stuffy, pompous, and/or elderly) *adj.*, *n.*: **Colonel Blimp**. See *conservative*

arched (like a bow) *adj.*: **arcuate**. See *curved*

archer *n.*: **toxophilite**. ❖ Sir—Your reporter rather disparagingly refers to Robin Hood as having used "a makeshift wooden bow." . . . As a former keen **toxophilite**, I would point out that the longbow demands a higher degree of skill in use than the modern bow with all its hi-tech gadgetry. (Marcus Wells, letter to the editor, *Western Mail* [Cardiff, Wales], 9/10/2001.)

Arctic (of or relating to the . . . region) *adj.*: **hyperborean**. [Note: This word also means very cold, and, in the following example, both meanings would be appropriate.] ❖ [If there were drilling in the Arctic National Wildlife Refuge,] how many drilling rigs, it's fair to ask, would cause postpartum psychosis among caribou? . . . Would oil pipes and pumps in just 2,000 acres of the 9 million-acre refuge seriously harm animals and migrating birds? And if it does, is that the overriding consideration? Certainly no tourist jobs are at stake in that desolate, **hyperborean** plain. (Edwin A. Roberts Jr., "Ruminations on Oil and Its Origins," *Tampa Tribune*, 11/18/2001.)

ardent *adj.*: **perfervid**. See *impassioned*

ardor (excessive or unbridled . . . , as in enthusiasm) *n.*: **schwarmerei** (or **schwärmerei**) [German]. See *enthusiasm*

arduous (as in difficult or painful, journey or experience) *n.*: **via dolorosa**. See *ordeal*

    (2) arduous (task, esp. of cleaning up or remedying bad situations) *n.*: **Augean task**. See *Herculean*

    (3) arduous *adj.*: **operose**. See *laborious*

area (as in sphere or realm) *n.*: **ambit**. See *realm*

    (2) area (densely populated . . .) *n.*: **megalopolis**. See *crowded*

    (3) area (esp. small, between things or events) *n.*: **interstice**. See *gap*

    (4) area (physical . . .) *n.*: **vicinage**. See *vicinity*

    (5) area (populated by persons from many countries or backgrounds) *n.*: **cosmopolis**. See *diversity*

    (6) area (surrounding . . . served by an institution, such as a school or hospital) *n.*: **catchment area**. See *district*

    (7) area *n.*: **purlieu**. See *vicinity*

areas (as in vicinity or environs) *n.pl.*: **purlieus**. See *outskirts*

arguable (as in controversial opinion or person who holds one) *n.*: **polemic**. See *controversy*

argue (about petty matters) *v.i.*: **pettifog**. See *quibble*

    (2) argue (against a statement, opinion, or action) *v.t.*: **oppugn**. See *oppose*

    (3) argue (against) *v.t.*: **expostulate**. See *object*

argument (appealing to one's purse) *n.*: **argumentum ad crumenam** [Latin for "to the purse"]. ❖ An electioneering budget is an **argumentum ad crumenam**, and most elections in democracies have a strong element of this old argument. It may not be idealistic, but it is the way people vote. (Philip Howard, "Rhetoric and All That Rot," *Times* [London], 4/12/1991.)

    (2) argument (in which one of the propositions, usually the premise—which may or may not be accurate—is omitted, leading listeners to fill in the premise themselves) *n.*: **enthymeme** (*adj.*: **enthymematic**). ❖ On May 1, [2003,] President Bush said, "The battle of Iraq is one victory in a war on terror that began on September the 11th, 2001, and still goes on." . . . This is classic **enthymematic** argumentation: We were attacked on Sept. 11, so we went to war against Iraq. The missing piece of the argument—"Saddam was involved in 9/11"—didn't have to be said aloud for those listening to assimilate its message. (Paul Waldman, "Why the Media Don't Call It as They See It," *Washington Post*, 9/28/2003.)

    (3) argument (fallacious . . . , usually, but not necessarily, related to philosophy) *n.*: **phi-**

losophism. [To understand what this writer is saying would likely require, at a minimum, a degree in ontology, which is a branch of metaphysics relating to the nature of being. However, even without understanding the writer's point, the meaning of philosophism is nevertheless clear from the example given.] ❖ Like Nancy, however, de Beistegui falls into the trap of **philosophism** when he assumes that a differential ontology should be an ontology of differential being *as such* and, hence, should be untainted by any particular "beings" or ontic regions. (Oliver Marchart, *Post-Foundational Political Thought*, books .google.com/books?isbn=0748624988, 2007.)

(4) argument (of an . . . appealing to one's emotions or designed for crowd-pleasing) *adj.*, *adv.*: **ad captandum** (or **ad captandum vulgus**) [Latin]. ❖ [Prime Minister Blair] spent much of Monday trying to corner the market in opinions on the row [after a soccer coach made controversial comments about disabled people]. First, **ad captandum vulgus**, he took the role of prosecutor . . . , announcing that it would be "very difficult" for Mr. Hoddle to stay. Then, having failed to secure plaudits from the tabloids, he telephoned the England coach to make his peace. (*Daily Telegraph* [London], "The Correct Way Forward," 2/3/1999.)

(5) argument (of an . . . appealing to one's prejudices or sentiments rather than facts or logical reasoning) *adj.*, *adv.*: **ad populum** (*n.*: **argumentum ad populum**) [Latin]. ❖ "When contemplating college liberals, you really regret once again that John Walker is not getting the death penalty. We need to execute people like John Walker in order to physically intimidate liberals, by making them realize that they can be killed, too. . . ." Rife with its **ad populum** and slippery slope fallacies, the above statement came from former *National Review* columnist Ann Coulter during a speech to the Conservative Political Action Conference. (Blaine Sullivan, "Fanatical Officials Endanger Liberties," University Wire, 3/19/2002.)

(6) argument (of an . . . appealing to pity or compassion) *adv.*, *adj.*: **argumentum ad misericordiam** [Latin]. ❖ I empathize absolutely with Kit Marx, who has "qualms about 'taking' private lands." . . . Every one of us [has seen] heart-wringing stories about elderly couples, standing on their land and dolefully declaring, "This swamp was our retirement." There surely are injustices, and Kit Marx is not the only "radical preservationist" who is swayed by the endless resorts to **argumentum ad misericordiam**. (Harvey Manning, letter to the editor, *Seattle Times*, 8/13/1992.)

(7) argument (of an . . . based on the authority or say-so of another, but in an area that is outside his or her field of expertise; that is, improperly trading on the reverence and respect of another) *adj.*, *adv.*: **ad verecundiam** (*n.*: **argumentum ad verecundiam**) [Latin]. ❖ [In maintaining that Martin Luther King is now on a par with George Washington,] an op-ed writer in my local paper argues: "[A question about] Dr. King has already replaced [one about] George Washington on the most widely used individual intelligence test for adults, the Wechsler Revised. [This is] an example of **ad verecundiam**, . . . an appeal to an unsuitable authority, in this case the authors of the IQ test. (Florence King, QED, *National Review*, 10/7/1991.)

(8) argument (that if something cannot be proven false, then it must be true) *n.*: **argumentum ad ignorantiam**. [Latin. This is generally, though not always, considered to be a fallacious argument.] ❖ Conservatives occasionally [suggest] that even if we do not know that fetuses are fully human from conception, they never-the-less may be; and they should be given the benefit of the doubt. . . . What is wrong with the "benefit of the doubt" argument? . . . [T]he argument is a classic case of **argumentum ad ignorantiam**. From the "we do not know" admission, no positive conclusions logically follow, especially not that we should treat [fetuses] as if they were fully human. (Rem Edwards, "Why Conservatives Are Wrong," *National Forum*, 9/22/1989.)

(9) argument (that silence from an opposing side or absence of evidence is itself indicative of the fact that the person making the argument must be correct) *n.*: **argumentum ex silentio.** [Latin. This is generally, though not always, considered to be a fallacious argument.] ❖ Sir—Your report . . . quoted Prof Sean Freyne as claiming that "Ireland has one of Europe's oldest Jewish communities." This is plainly fallacious. . . . The earliest indication of a resident Jewish community in Ireland does not occur before the 1230s . . . although [I recognize that] this is an **argument[um] ex silentio.** (Anthony Gandon, "Jewish History in Ireland," *Irish Times*, 11/19/1997.)

(10) argument (about a philosophical or theological issue) *n.*: **quodlibet.** See *debate*

(11) argument (about words) *n.*: **logomachy.** See *words*

(12) argument (as in difference of opinion) *n.*: **divarication.** See *disagreement*

(13) argument (as in heated disagreement or friction between groups) *n.*: **ruction.** See *dissension*

(14) argument (characterized by internal . . .) *adj.*: **factious.** See *dispute*

(15) argument (fallacious . . . in logic in which a false conclusion is drawn from two premises, neither of which conveys information about all members of the designated class) *n.*: **undistributed middle.** See *fallacy*

(16) argument (fallacious . . . , spec. where one argues that because event B followed event A, then event A must have caused event B) *n.*: **post hoc ergo propter hoc** [Latin for "after this, therefore, because of this"]. See *fallacy*

(17) argument (given to . . . which may be specious or one who is so given) *adj., n.*: **eristic.** See *specious* and *debate*

(18) argument (minor . . .) *n.*: **velitation.** See *skirmish*

(19) argument (person who hates rational . . . or enlightenment) *n.*: **misologist.** See *closed-minded*

(20) argument (specious . . . intended to mislead or rationalize) *n.*: **casuistry.** See *fallacious*

(21) argument (suggesting the use of force to settle an issue) *n.*: **argumentum ad baculum** [Latin]. See *threat*

(22) argument (which is complicated and often illogical) *n.*: **choplogic.** See *fallacy*

(23) argument (which is fallacious) *n.*: **syllogism.** See *specious*

argumentative (as in combative) *adj.*: **agonistic.** See *combative*

(2) argumentative *adj., n.*: **eristic.** See *debate*

(3) argumentative *adj.*: **querulous.** See *peevish*

arid (of or adapted to an . . . habitat) *adj.*: **xeric.** See *dry*

arise (as in result) *v.i.*: **eventuate.** See *result*

aristocracy (as in fashionable society) *n.*: **beau monde** [French]. See *high society*

(2) aristocracy (as in fashionable society) *n.*: **bon ton** [French]. See *high society*

aristocratic (esp. those aspiring or pretending to be . . .) *adj.*: **lace-curtain.** See *well-bred*

arithmetic (difficulty with or inability to do . . .) *n.*: **acalculia**; **dyscalculia.** See *math*

(2) arithmetic (having ability with . . . and math generally) *adj.*: **numerate.** See *mathematical*

armistice (temporary . . . between opposing parties pending final deal) *n.*: **modus vivendi** [Latin]. See *truce*

armor *n.*: **cuirass.** ❖ [T]he difference [between dancing just topless and totally nude] is huge psychologically. . . . When you're completely naked, you're out there, sans **cuirass.** (Lily Burana, *Strip City*, Talk Miramax Books [2001], p. 170.)

armpit *n.*: **oxter** [Scottish]. ❖ 5pm: Stuck on the M8 in traffic. . . . Despite the early hour, I am buffed, puffed and dressed to kill. There is a minibus full of Polish football fans beside us. They notice I seem to be naked—well, from the **oxter** upwards—which causes much amusement. Grabbing Dave's dinner jacket from the back seat, I cover my arm nudity and off we crawl. (Alison Craig, "Finally at the Great Scots," *Sunday Mail* [Glasgow], 9/23/2007.)

(2) armpit *n.*: **axilla**. ❖ [In the] Old Spice Red Zone poll of the 50 sweatiest cities in the United States, St. Louis finished 15th—15th! We didn't even make the Top 10. Any St. Louis resident who has been up to the **axillas** in permanent 'pit rings and a sweaty back stuck to vinyl car seats may be surprised by the results. According to the poll, San Antonio is the sweatiest city. (Joe Holleman, "We're No. 15? Local Sweathogs Are Up in [Under]arms at City's Ranking," *St. Louis Post-Dispatch*, 7/11/2002.)

arms (move by swinging with . . . , like a monkey) *v.i.*: **brachiate**. See *swing*

army (of, relating to, or suggesting) *adj.*: **martial**. See *warlike*

arouse (as in encourage) *v.t.*: **inspirit**. See *encourage*

arousing (or inciting or inspiring to action) *adj.*: **proceleusmatic**. See *exhorting*

arrange (close together, side by side, or in proper order) *v.t.*: **collocate**. See *place*

arrangement (as in pact) *n.*: **amicabilis concordia**. See *pact*

(2) arrangement (temporary . . . between opposing parties pending final deal) *n.*: **modus vivendi** [Latin]. See *truce*

array (as in assortment) *n.*: **farrago**. See *assortment*

(2) array (as in assortment) *n.*: **gallimaufry**. See *assortment*

(3) array (as in assortment) *n.*: **olla podrida** [Spanish]. See *assortment*

(4) array (as in assortment) *n.*: **omnium gatherum** [Latin]. See *assortment*

(5) array (as in assortment) *n.*: **salmagundi**. See *assortment*

arrogance *adj.*: **hubris**. ❖ Like any Greek tragic hero, Clinton is also guilty of **hubris**: He indulged himself most of all when things were going well and he thought that his office, good polls and the election results made him invulnerable to his enemies and free to defy Congress. (Morton Kondracke, Roll Call,

"Impeachment Fight a Tragedy for All," *Arizona Republic*, 12/20/1998.)

(2) arrogance (as in boastful behavior) *n.*: **rodomontade**. See *bluster*

(3) arrogance (in behavior or speech) *n.*: **contumely**. See *contempt*

arrogant (and shameless person) *n.*: **jackanapes**. See *conceited*

(2) arrogant (as in being presumptuous; venturing beyond one's province) *adj.*: **ultracrepidarian**. See *presumptuous*

(3) arrogant (as in condescending) *adj., adv.*: **de haut en bas** [French]. See *condescending*

(4) arrogant (as in haughty or condescending) *adj.*: **toplofty**. See *haughty*

(5) arrogant (as in lordly) *adj.*: **seigneurial**. See *lordly*

(6) arrogant (as in pompous or haughty) *adj.*: **hoity-toity**. See *pompous*

(7) arrogant (as in pompous) *adj.*: **flatulent**. See *pompous*

(8) arrogant (as in pushy and assertive) *adj.*: **bumptious**. See *pushy*

(9) arrogant *adj.*: **fastuous**. See *haughty*

arrows (one who makes . . .) *n.*: **fletcher**. ❖ Kingmaker is a similar set-up at the castle, where children can watch the **fletcher** construct traditional bows and arrows. (Katie Bowman, "Ye Complete Guide to Ye Olde England," *Independent* [London], 12/15/2001.)

art (objects of . . . , esp. curios or crafts) *n.*: **virtu**. [French. This word is generally used as part of the expression "objets virtu," or occasionally the English form, "objects of virtue."] ❖ In sharp contrast, the technically innovative [crafts] in the second group are functional in form but are rarely used; they never would have been called crafts 100 years ago. These are the **objets virtu** of our time, labor-intensive works that are exuberant expressions of clay, glass, metal, wood or feathers. (Rita Reif, "Keeping Up with the Expanding Meaning of Craft," *New York Times*, 2/13/2000.)

(2) art (or writings created in the artist's or author's youth) *n.*: **juvenilia**. See *compositions*

(3) art (sale of . . . by a museum to purchase more) *v.t.*: **deaccession**. See *sell*

(4) art (work of . . . dealing with evening or night) *n.*: **nocturne**. See *painting*

arthritis (or joint pain) *n.*: **arthralgia**. ❖ Cave divers face the near certainty of [high-pressure nervous syndrome] on deep descents. The syndrome often hits in combination with a condition called compression **arthralgia**, known to Navy divers as "no joint juice" because it feels as if their knees, elbows and wrists have suddenly rusted solid. (Michael Ray Taylor, "Scuba Diving," *Sports Illustrated*, 10/3/1994, p. 5.)

artificial *adj.*: **factitious**. ❖ Moguls in a mythic land [that is, Hollywood, Louis B. Mayer and Samuel Goldwyn] lived extravagantly, inventing a **factitious** world peopled by gorgeous chorus girls and chaste heroines and handsome leading men. (Walter Guzzardi, "Laurels: The National Business Hall of Fame," *Fortune*, 3/12/1990, p. 118.)

(2) artificial (as in contrived) *adj.*: **voulu** [French]. See *contrived*

(3) artificial (something . . . , as in sham) *n.*: **postiche**. See *sham*

artistic (as in creative, and/or original) *adj.*: **Promethean**. See *creative*

(2) artistic (piece imitating previous pieces) *n.*: **pastiche**. See *imitation*

artwork (which looks like a photograph or something real) *n.*: **trompe l'oeil** [French]. See *illusion*

ascending (esp. too high for safety) *adj.*: **Icarian**. See *soaring*

(2) ascending *adj.*: **assurgent**. See *rising*

ascent (as in upward slope) *n.*: **acclivity** (*adj.*: **acclivitous**). See *incline*

ascertain (as in figure out) *v.t.*: **suss** (usually with "out"; slang). See *figure out*

ashen (and often sickly) *adj.*: **etiolated**. See *pale*

(2) ashen (as in pale or corpselike) *adj.*: **cadaverous**. See *corpselike*

ashes (resembling or having the color of . . .) *adj.*: **cinerous**. ❖ "The tribulations / Rise smokily [of our lives] . . . / . . . until we find

/ It becomes strangely easy to forgive / Even ourselves with this clouding of the mind / This **cinerous** blur and smudge in which we live." (David Yezzi, quoting an Anthony Hecht poem, "Sarabande on Attaining the Age of Seventy-seven," "Appreciation: Anthony Hecht," *New York Times*, 11/21/2004.)

aside (as in digression) *n.*: **excursus**. See *digression*

(2) aside (as in, as an . . .) *n.*: **obiter dictum** [Latin]. See *passing comment*

asinine (in a smug or complacent manner) *adj.*: **fatuous**. See *foolish*

ask (as in plead to earnestly) *v.t.*: **adjure**. See *plead*

(2) ask (for by mooching or sponging off of) *v.t.*: **cadge**. See *mooch*

(3) ask *v.t.*: **catechize**. See *question*

aspect (as in demeanor) *n.*: **mien**. See *demeanor*

aspersion (as in insult, which is clever or polite) *n.*: **asteism**. See *insult*

(2) aspersion (ethnic . . .) *n.*: **ethnophaulism**. See *slur*

aspiring (esp. as in ambitious to equal or surpass another) *adj.*: **emulous**. See *ambitious*

ass (a fat . . .) *n.*: **steatopygia** (having a fat . . .) *adj.*: **steatopygic**. See *rear end*

(2) ass (as in buttocks) *n.pl.*: **nates**. See *buttocks*

(3) ass (as in buttocks) *n.*: **fundament**. See *buttocks*

(4) ass (having a hairy . . .) *adj.*: **dasypygal**. See *rear end*

(5) ass (having a nicely proportioned . . .) *adj.*: **callipygian**. See *rear end*

assail (as in criticize, sharply) *v.t.*: **scarify**. See *criticize*

(2) assail *v.t.*: **flay**. See *criticize*

(3) assail *v.t.*: **oppugn**. See *oppose*

assault (as in attack in writing) *n.*: **coup de plume** [French; attack by pen]. See *attack*

(2) assault (surprise . . .) *n.*: **coup de main** [French; attack by hand]. See *attack*

assemble (cheaply and flimsily) *v.t.*: **jerrybuild**. See *build*

assembly (as in group) *n.*: **gaggle**. See *group*

assert *v.t.*: **asseverate**. See *declare*

assertion (made without proof or support) *n.*: **ipse dixit** [Latin]. See *allegation*

assertive (in an obnoxious or loud way) *adj.*: **bumptious**. See *pushy*

assess (as in analyze, that which has already occurred; i.e., to project into the past) *v.t.*: **retroject**. See *analyze*

(2) assess (under a new standard, esp. one that differs from conventional norms) *v.t.*: **transvaluate**. See *evaluate*

(2) assess *v.t.*: **assay**. See *evaluate*

assets (personal . . . , as in belongings) *n.pl.*: **personalia**. See *belongings*

assiduous (in effort or application) *adj.*: **sedulous**. See *diligent*

assign (authority or duties to another) *v.t.*: **depute**. See *delegate*

assimilate (as in incorporate, the ideas or attitudes of others, esp. parents, into one's own personality) *v.t.*: **introject**. See *incorporate*

assistant (esp. to a scholar or magician) *n.*: **famulus**. ❖ [T]elevision is trying to coolify magic by ridding it of its associations with slimeballs in sequined suits, assisted by a mute **famulus** bedecked in feathers, mascara, and an inane grin, together partaking in a mindless ritual of sawing, stabbing, and vanishing. (Victor Lewis-Smith, "Don't Shoot, This Is Live . . . ," *Evening Standard* [London], 10/6/2003.)

(2) assistant (esp. to organized crime leader) *n.*: **consigliere** [Italian]. ❖ Forbes.com rustled through [Mafia boss John] Gotti's wit and wisdom, as captured by FBI wiretaps, and put together these useful tips: . . . On caring for subordinates: "Chrissake, I love you (speaking to Gambino family **consigliere** Frank Locascio) more than I love myself. . . . I'm worried about you going to jail. I don't give two (bleeps) about my going to jail." (Michael Precker, "Working World," *Dallas Morning News*, 6/18/2002.)

(3) assistant (who is loyal and unquestioning) *n.*: **myrmidon**. ❖ Judge Wright concluded, "the record demonstrates by clear and

convincing evidence that [President Clinton] responded to plaintiff [Paula Jones's] questions by giving false, misleading, and evasive answers that were designed to obstruct the judicial process." (How many times did the president's **myrmidons** tell us he equivocated to spare his family embarrassment?) (Bruce Fein, "A Protracted List of Discredits," *Washington Times*, 4/20/1999.)

(4) assistant *n.*: **adjutant**. ❖ For 17 seasons as an assistant coach, Craig Esherick sat quietly and nondescriptly next to John Thompson on Georgetown's bench. [Thus, when Thompson resigned, it] was natural for the rest of the world to wonder whether this faceless, voiceless **adjutant** was up to the job he had unexpectedly inherited. (Seth Davis, Inside College Basketball, *Sports Illustrated*, 1/22/2001, p. 80.)

(5) assistant *n.*: **factotum**. ❖ At the time of Annie [Sullivan's] death in 1936, Polly Thompson, who was five years younger than Helen, had been with the household for twenty-two years as a secretary and general **factotum**. (Dorothy Herrmann, *Helen Keller*, Knopf [1998], p. 266.)

assistants (group of . . . or advisors, often scheming or plotting) *n.*: **camarilla**. See *advisors*

associate (tendency of people to . . . with, or be attracted to, those they perceive are similar to them) *n.*: **homophily**. ❖ In fact, research . . . shows that if you know whether a person's friends are Republicans, Democrats or independents, you can predict with near certainty that person's political views. **Homophily** may help explain some of the bitter partisanship of our times—when your friends are drawn exclusively from one half of the electorate, it is not surprising that you will find the views of the other half inexplicable. (Shankar Vedantam, "Why Everyone You Know Thinks the Same as You," *Washington Post*, 10/16/2006.)

(2) associate (as in comrade) *n.*: **tovarich** [Russian]. See *comrade*

(3) associate (close . . . or partner, often but

not always, one in marriage) *n.*: **yokefellow**. See *partner*

(4) associate *n.*: **confrere**. See *colleague*

associated (with, as in incident to) *adj.*: **appurtenant**. See *pertaining*

association (whose members act primarily in their own self-interest) *n.*: **gesellschaft** (sometimes cap.). [German. This is a sociological category introduced by the German sociologist Ferdinand Tönnies in 1887. It refers to an association whose members act primarily in their own self-interest. It is associated with modern industrial life, mobility, heterogeneity, and impersonality. Its contrasting association is "gemeinschaft," a community united by common ideals, beliefs about the appropriate behavior and responsibility of members of the association, and strong personal ties. Self-interest is deemphasized in favor of the greater good. See *community*.] ❖ Fifty years after the Normandy invasion, what is it that binds North America and Europe together in an "Atlantic community"? A North Atlantic **gesellschaft** clearly exists, in the form of the NATO treaty and all the buildings and bureaucrats that embody it. . . . In the post-Cold War era, only . . . strategic self-interest will endure as a glue to hold the community together while ideological and cultural bonds will decay. This will not be a healthy situation. (Francis Fukuyama, "For the Atlantic Allies Today, a Fraying of the Sense of Moral Community," *International Herald Tribune,* 6/6/1994.) [The following example uses both terms to illustrate the distinction.] ❖ [The] gemeinschaft society [of the antebellum South], with its emphasis on tradition, rural life, close kinship ties . . . persisted in the South long after the North began moving toward a **gesellschaft** society with its impersonal, bureaucratic, meritocratic, urbanizing, commercial, industrializing, mobile, and rootless characteristics. Above all, the South's folk culture valued tradition and stability. (James M. McPherson, "Antebellum Southern Exceptionalism: A New Look at an Old Question," *Civil War History*, 12/1/2004.)

(2) association (united by close personal bonds) *n.*: **gemeinschaft** [German]. See *community*

assortment *n.*: **farrago**. ❖ Though tickets cost only $25 and the dress code was casual, a fair number of attendees wore tuxedos and party gowns anyway. The band offered some '70s guitar-rock, and once it started playing, the wood-tile floor in front of the stage became a strange tangle of disparate body rhythms and dance styles, a **farrago** of denim, taffeta and tulle. (Romesh Ratnesar, "Lefties Left Out," *New Republic*, 2/10/1997.)

(2) assortment *n.*: **gallimaufry**. ❖ Old South Africa [journalists] have lived for decades with a **gallimaufry** of some 100 press restrictions. It has long been an offense to quote locally or transmit abroad the words of "listed" or "banned" activists. (Ezra Bowen, "Press: Whiteout on the Bad News," *Time*, 6/30/1986.)

(3) assortment *n.*: **olla podrida** [Spanish]. ❖ The trouble is, Petronius is so infernally readable, and his **olla podrida** of conmanship, bitchy lit. crit., absurd gastronomy, bed-bouncing, murder and anecdotes (werewolves, susceptible widows) is so enticing that we tend to forget the horrendous social implications of what we're reading. (Review of *The Satyricon*, translated by Peter Green, *New Republic*, 10/28/1996, p. 42A.)

(4) assortment *n.*: **omnium-gatherum** [Latin]. ❖ A kind of cyclonic **omnium-gatherum**, [the book] *The Tornado* packs in science and superstition [about tornados], lore and personal narratives, safety tips, forecasting breakthroughs, snapshots of famous storm chasers and their quarry, common myths . . . , tons of statistics . . . and all sorts of odd facts and findings. (David Laskin, "Ill Wind," *Washington Post*, 4/22/2001.)

(5) assortment *n.*: **salmagundi**. ❖ [Paraguay] is a place where dreamers, dictators, fugitives and fantasists have gone to find peace. Among these are conquistadors, Jesuits, Nazis, Mennonites, Australian socialists, Japanese utopians, German vegetarians, White Russians.

There are no misfits in Paraguay because in this particular **salmagundi** of a place, everyone fits, more or less. (Ben Macintyre, "You Don't Want to Live There," *New York Times Book Review*, 2/29/2004.)

(6) assortment (as in diversity) *n.*: **heterogeneity** (*adj.*: **heterogeneous**). See *diversity*

assuage (as in appease) *v.t.*: **dulcify**. See *appease*

(2) assuage *v.t.*: **propitiate**. See *placate*

assumption (or set of assumptions) *n.*: **donnée**. [French. This word is generally used to describe the premise on which an artistic work is based or a fact, notion, or condition that governs or shapes an act, viewpoint, or way of life, as in this example.] ❖ Liberalism . . . prescribes not only the terms of debate, but also the rhetorical atmosphere in which any debate must take place. . . . As [a historian noted, for many years now,] "to use liberal language has been taken to be intelligent: to reject it evidence of stupidity." That conviction has long since been elevated into a fundamental **donnée** of intellectual life: an unspoken assumption that colors every aspect of political and moral deliberation. (Roger Kimball, "One Very Simple Principle," *New Criterion*, 11/1/1998.)

assurance (as in self-assurance, and poise) *n.*: **aplomb**. See *self-confidence*

astute *adj.*: **perspicacious**. ❖ The companies below occupy market niches, have strong brand-name franchises or provide special services in a way that inspires long-term loyalty from a small number of **perspicacious** stock pickers. (Marguerite T. Smith, Wall Street: "Smart-Money Stocks: Homely Companies That Leading Pros Are Swooning Over," *Money*, 5/1/1990, p. 57.)

(2) astute (as in having a penetrating quality) *adj.*: **gimlet** (esp. as in "gimlet eye"). See *penetrating*

(3) astute *adj.*: **trenchant**. See *incisive*

atheist (as in one with no faith or religion) *n.*, *adj.*: **nullifidian**. See *nonbeliever*

atmosphere (as in setting or physical environment) *n.*: **mise-en-scène** [French; lit. putting on stage]. See *setting*

(2) atmosphere (distinctive . . . or spirit of a place) *n.*: **genius loci** [Latin]. See *spirit*

(3) atmosphere (which is thick and vaporous or noxious) *n.*: **miasma**. See *noxious*

at once *adv.*: **holus-bolus**. See *simultaneously*

atone (for) *v.t.*, *v.i.*: **expiate**. ❖ In recent years the American press has written countless stories about South Africa's efforts to **expiate** its racist past—about the Truth and Reconciliation Commission; about the renaming of streets, airports, and government buildings; about the conversion of Nelson Mandela's prison into a museum. (*New Republic*, "TRB from Washington," 9/17/2001.)

atonement (road to . . . , as in rehabilitation, or conversion) *n.*: **sawdust trail**. See *conversion*

(2) atonement (spec. the opportunity to withdraw from, or decide not to commit, an intended crime) *n.*: **locus poenitentiae** [Latin]. See *repentance*

(3) atonement (spec. a change of mind or heart, a recognition of one's errors, and a return to a sane, sound, or correct position) *n.*: **resipiscence**. See *reformation*

atoning *adj.*: **piacular**. ❖ [T]his high-ranking Greek guy actually came around to 1009 after Saturday's supper to assure me that raggednecked Lebanese heads were even at that moment rolling down various corridors in **piacular** recompense for my having had to carry my own bag. (Wallace, "Shipping Out: On the Nearly Lethal Comforts of a Luxury Cruise," *Harper's*, 1/1/1996, p. 33.)

atrocious *adj.*: **execrable**. See *abominable*

attack (in writing) *n.*: **coup de plume** [French; lit. attack by pen]. ❖ [I] understand Premier Parizeau's bigoted remarks about "les ethniques" on Quebec referendum night. . . . What offends me is that Mr. Rheaume chose to attack Mr. Richler rather than Mr. Parizeau's antagonistic speech itself. . . . Mr. Rheaume's awkward **coup de plume** serves to embarrass him while focusing an even brighter spotlight on the masterful "sleight of pen" of the literate

Mr. Richler. (Elizabeth Irving, letter to the editor, *Gazette* [Montreal], 7/21/1996.)

(2) attack (surprise . . .) *n.:* **coup de main** [French; lit. attack by hand]. ❖ When Coca-Cola cajoled Venezuela's only bottler to defect from Pepsi and join its own ranks, it exploited the strategic lessons of one of history's most successful covert ops, the Israeli attack on Entebbe. That **coup de main** was marked by minutely detailed planning, lightning fast execution, a shroud of secrecy, superb intelligence and the use of elite shock troops. (Dennis Laurie, "In War and in Business, Strategy Brings Success," *Washington Times*, 8/20/2001.)

(3) attack (a statement, opinion or action) *v.t.:* **oppugn**. See *oppose*

(4) attack (as in complaint) *n.:* **jeremiad**. See *complaint*

(5) attack (as in criticize) *v.t.:* **flay**. See *criticize*

(6) attack (as in criticize, sharply) *v.t.:* **scarify**. See *criticize*

(7) attack (as in insult another's dignity) *n.:* **lese majesty**. See *insult*

(8) attack (being subject to verbal . . . , esp. public) *n.:* **obloquy**. See *abuse*

(9) attack (esp. as in military advance) *n.:* **anabasis**. See *advance*

(10) attack (ethnic . . .) *n.:* **ethnophaulism**. See *slur*

(11) attack (harshly, as in criticize) *v.t.:* **fustigate**. See *criticize*

(12) attack (initiate an . . . , fighting, or violence) *v.i.:* **aggress**. See *fight*

(13) attack (of or relating to being under . . . or siege) *adj.:* **obsidional**. See *besieged*

attacking (as in lying in wait for prey, often used of insects) *adj.:* **lochetic**. See *ambushing*

attempt (the . . . to achieve a particular goal or desire) *n.:* **nisus**. See *goal*

attendant (esp. to a scholar or magician) *n.:* **famulus**. See *assistant*

(2) attendant (who is loyal and unquestioning) *n.:* **myrmidon**. See *assistant*

attendants (line or train of . . . as for an important person) *n.:* **cortege**. See *procession*

attention *n.:* **advertence**. ❖ As a church [that is, Catholics with differing views on birth control], we call to mind an estranged couple who carry on their individual business and fulfill their separate responsibilities without **advertence** to the differences which divide them. The silence is disturbed only by occasional outbursts of mutual recrimination. (Paul Murray, "The Power of 'Humanae Vitae': Take Another Look," *Commonweal*, 7/15/1994.)

(2) attention (treat another with excessive . . .) *n., v.t.:* **wet-nurse**. See *coddle*

(3) attention (as in publicity or a taste or flair for being in the limelight) *n.:* **réclame** [French]. See *publicity*

attentive (as in watchful person) *n.:* **Argus**. See *watchful*

at the same time *adv.:* **holus-bolus**. See *simultaneously*

attic (or loft or room on top floor) *n.:* **garret**. See *loft*

attire (as in clothes) *n.:* **habiliment(s)**. See *clothing*

(2) attire (as in clothes) *n.:* **raiment**. See *clothing*

(3) attire (showy article of . . .) *n.:* **froufrou**. See *clothing*

attired (being partially, carelessly, or casually . . .) *n.:* **dishabille** [French]. ❖ The average college football player is about as fashionably attired as a hotel guest fleeing an early-morning fire. Surely no one with any pride in his appearance would wish to be caught in such a state of **dishabille**. (Ron Fimrite, Point After: "Because My Own Taste in Men's Apparel Has Not Changed Appreciably," *Sports Illustrated*, 5/17/1993, p. 85.)

attitude (as in demeanor) *n.:* **mien**. See *demeanor*

(2) attitude (of an era) *n.:* **zeitgeist**. See *spirit*

(3) attitude (preconceived or biased . . . on an issue) *n.:* **parti pris** [French]. See *preconception*

attorney (who may be petty, dishonest, or disreputable) *n.:* **pettifogger**. See *lawyer*

attract (power to . . . through magnetism or charm) *n.*: **duende**. See *charisma*

attraction (as in lure or temptation) *n.*: **Lorelei call**. See *lure*

(2) attraction (sexual . . . to animals) *n.*: **zoophilia** (person attracted: **zoophile**). See *bestiality*

(3) attraction (sexual . . . to the elderly) *n.*: **gerontophilia**. See *lust*

attractive (but in a way that is solely based on deception or pretense or gaudiness) *adj.*: **meretricious**. ❖ Like Reagan, [Louis Farrakhan] knows how to wow an audience by telling cheap, shifty, suggestive anecdotes about "outgroups." He also knows how to include a special segment on the brotherhood of man. . . . [T]here is no mystery about the **meretricious** attraction exerted by a man who proudly says that ordinary standards mean nothing to him. (Christopher Hitchens, Minority Report: "Ronald Reagan's Tax Policies," *Nation*, 10/26/1985.)

(2) attractive (as in alluring) *adj.*: **illecebrous**. See *alluring*

(3) attractive (as in alluring) *adj.*: **sirenic**. [See also the nouns *siren call* and *Lorelei call* under *lure*.] See *alluring*

(4) attractive (as in pleasing) *adj.*: **prepossessing**. See *pleasing*

(5) attractive (esp. sexually) *adj.*: **toothsome**. See *sexy*

(6) attractive (in a superficial, romanticized, or sentimental way) *adj.*: **chocolate-box**. See *pretty*

(7) attractive (in an unconventional way) *adj.*: **jolie laide** (or **belle laide**) [French]. See *pretty* or *handsome* or *beautiful*

attractiveness (facetious way of measuring . . . by units) *n.*: **millihelen**. See *beauty*

(2) attractiveness (physical . . .) *n.*: **pulchritude**. See *beauty*

at will *adv., adj.*: **ad libitum**. [Latin for "at one's pleasure." This term is often used to refer to the extent to which food, drink, or drugs may be taken by people or animals as part of experimental testing.] ❖ Williams: So what about the claims that the Eclipse is a safer cigarette? . . . Dr. Debothesey: Well, first of all, there is no safe cigarette, and we're not making any claim that this is a safe cigarette. [But] we found that when smokers smoked the cigarette **ad libitum**, just walking around in their normal activities, we found a 70 percent reduction in exposure to mutagens, which are DNA-damaging chemicals. (Jan Debothesey, "R. J. Reynolds Claims That Their New Cigarette, Eclipse, Presents the Smoker with Less Risk for Cancer and Other Diseases than Other Cigarettes," Talk of the Nation, National Public Radio, 4/24/2000.)

atypical (as in unusual or rare) *adj.*: **recherché** [French]. See *rare*

(2) atypical (holding . . . opinions or having an . . . perspective) *adj.*: **heterodox** (*n.*: **heterodoxy**). See *unconventional*

(3) atypical (as in departing from the standard or norm) *adj.*: **heteroclite**. See *abnormal*

auction (act of bidding or selling at) *n.*: **licitation**. ❖ Brazil: Small players can be benefitted in auction. . . . The **licitation** to explore oil and natural gas areas . . . can benefit small players of the sector. Specialists believe the major companies already acquired their areas in 1999 and 2000. (*South American Business Information*, "Brazil: Small Players Can Be Benefitted in Auction," 6/12/2001.)

(2) auction (public . . .) *n.*: **vendue**. ❖ At last year's **vendue**, a Maryland-bred colt topped the sale at $280,000. (Cindy Deubler, "Daily Horse Racing Form: Maryland Breeding: Timonium Sale Offers 590 Juveniles," Sports Network, 5/16/2003.)

(3) auction (or sale by a museum of items in order to purchase more) *v.t.*: **deaccession**. See *sell*

audacious (as in being presumptuous; venturing beyond one's province) *adj.*: **ultracrepidarian**. See *presumptuous*

audacity *n.*: **hardihood**. See *gall*

augur *v.t.*: **adumbrate**. See *foreshadow*

aunt (of, like, or relating to an . . .) *adj.*: **materteral**. [One would think that the feminine equivalent of "avuncular" would be equally common, but not so. However, there is a legitimate word that fills the bill.] ❖ [Janet Trinkaus, the founder of Rise n' Shine, an organization devoted to helping children who have AIDS or whose lives have been touched by AIDS, stated]: "I had a lot of aunts and uncles, a wide net of support growing up, and I really wanted to create that for the Rise n' Shine kids." At Rise n' Shine, these avuncular and **materteral** roles are filled by the group's small army of volunteers, each of whom spends four hours a week with his or her Rise n' Shine charge. (David Schmader, "Rise n' Shine," *Stranger*, 1/25/2007.)

aura *n.*: **effluvium**. ❖ To record his return to [surfing] greatness, Harmon recruits down-and-out surf-mag photographer Jack Fletcher, who also needs another chance. Along with a couple of younger guys dripping with Southern California **effluvium**, they head for a place that may or may not exist, Heart Attacks, where the waves are said to be 30 feet or higher. (Ken Wisneski, "Adventure/Northern California Setting Rounds Out an Eerie Thriller," *Minneapolis Star Tribune*, 4/27/1997.)

(2) aura (having an . . . through magnetism or charm) *n.*: **duende**. See *charisma*

austere (as in strictly disciplined or regimented) *adj.*: **monastic**. See *strict*

austerity (as in person who practices extreme . . . , esp. for spiritual improvement) *n.*, *adj.*: **ascetic.** [The concept of living in this manner is called **ascesis**.] ❖ Always an **ascetic**, [Austrian philosopher Ludwig Wittgenstein] gave away his inheritance, relying on the generosity of his Cambridge champions, Russell and John Maynard Keynes, to secure academic employment for him, living frugally and in later life being cared for by his disciples. (Daniel Dennett, Time 100 "Philosopher Ludwig Wittgenstein," *Time*, 3/29/1999, p. 88.)

(2) austerity (as in marked by simplicity, frugality, self-discipline, and/or self-restraint) *adj.*: **Lacedaemonian**. See *spartan*

authentic (appearing to be . . . or accurate) *adj.*: **verisimilar**. See *realistic*

(2) authentic *adj.*: **echt** [German]. See *genuine*

(3) authentic *adj.*: **pukka**. See *genuine*

authenticity (historical . . .) *n.*: **historicity**. ❖ A naive early attempt to save the **historicity** of the [Gospels] was to assume that Joseph and Mary had told the evangelists' sources what happened. According to this theory, Joseph must have been the source for Matthew's Gospel . . . and Mary must have been Luke's ultimate source. The trouble with this view is that the two stories are contradictory [and it] "presupposes that Mary and Joseph never spoke to each other." (Garry Wills, *What the Gospels Meant*, Viking [2008], p. 61.)

author (of, by, or pertaining to) *adj.*: **auctorial**. ❖ [In the bookstore, I found] a dozen or so issues of a typewritten fanzine from the 1980s called, shamelessly, *Books Are Everything!* . . . I bought all the issues—as who would not?—and doled them out to myself over the next few weeks. . . . Of course, having duly secured such . . . **auctorial** largesse, I could hardly stop myself from poking around the bookstore a while longer. (Michael Dirda, "Pulp Fiction, Critical Journals and Other Ephemeral Pleasures," *Washington Post*, 2/25/2001.)

(2) author (professional . . .) *n.*: **wordmonger**. ❖ Jonathan Franzen . . . won the National Book Award for fiction here tonight for his novel *The Corrections*, about the breakdown of an American family. . . . The 52nd awards drew 800 or so dolled-up denizens of the publishing world—down 20 percent from last year—to the Marriott Marquis Hotel. In the grand ballroom, **wordmongers** supped on red meat, mushroom bisque and New York State apple pie. (Linton Weeks, "Oprah-Pick Franzen Wins National Book Award," *Washington Post*, 11/15/2001.)

(3) author (as in compose or write) *v.t.*: **indite**. See *compose*

(4) author (of fiction, esp. who writes in quantity) *n.*: **fictioneer**. See *novelist*

authoritative (as in influential person, esp. in

intellectual or literary circles) *n*.: **mandarin**. See *influential*

(2) authoritative (as in official, act, declaration, or statement, issued with the authority of one's office) *adv.*, *adj.*: **ex cathedra**. See *official*

authority (as in a person's area of expertise) *n*.: **bailiwick**. See *expertise*

(2) authority (of an argument based on the . . . or say-so of another, but in an area that is outside his or her field of expertise; that is, improperly trading on the reverence and respect of another) *adj.*, *adv.*: **ad verecundiam** (*n*.: **argumentum ad verecundiam**) [Latin]. See *argument*

(3) authority (of one political state over others) *n*.: **hegemony**. See *dominance*

(4) authority *n*.: **cognoscente**. See *connoisseur*

(5) authority (on matters of taste, fashion, style, protocol, etc.) *n*.: **arbiter elegantiae** [Latin]. See *arbiter*

authorize (officially) *v.t.*: **approbate**. ❖ [National Security Advisor] Sandy Berger said there is a widespread consensus, and he mentioned a number of states more or less **approbating** the use of force against Iraq in support of U.S. action. (Washington Transcript Service, "Iraqi Deputy Foreign Minister Holds News Conference," 2/13/1998.)

(2) authorize (as in approve, esp. to confirm officially) *v.t.*: **homologate**. See *approve*

(3) authorize (authority or duties to another) *v.t.*: **depute**. See *delegate*

autograph-collecting *n*.: **philography**. ❖ The fourth annual Houston Celebrity/Autograph Collector's Show, sponsored by Focus on **Philography,** will be 10 a.m.–5 p.m. Saturday. (*Houston Chronicle*, Around Houston, 1/30/2000.)

automatic (as in trained to show a conditioned response) *adj.*: **Pavlovian**. See *conditioned*

(2) automatic (reaction, as in reflex) *n*.: **tropism**. See *reflex*

avail (as in, "to whose . . . ?") *n*.: **cui bono** [Latin]. See *advantage*

avarice (as in worship of or devotion to money) *n*.: **plutolatry**. See *wealth*

(2) avarice *n*.: **cupidity**. See *greed*

(3) avarice *n*.: **pleonexia**. See *greed*

avenging (one who is intent on . . . something) *n*.: **tricoteuse**. See *knitter*. [See the note at "knitter" for why this word can be synonymous with avenging.]

aver *v.t.*: **asseverate**. See *declare*

aversion (develop a strong . . . to) *n*.: **scunner** (esp. as in "take a scunner") [British]. See *dislike*

avert *v.t.*: **forfend**. ❖ [The *New York Times*] had repeatedly demanded that Governor Cuomo forgo a scheduled state tax-rate reduction while also allowing the city to raise income-tax rates. . . . It suggested that for Mario to resist this course "smacked of national ambition." **Forfending** further charges of smackery, the governor has now set aside the state income-tax reduction for the second year in a row. (Daniel Seligman, "Incredible Shrinking Humans, a King's Troubles, Mario Cuomo's Ambition, and Other Matters," *Fortune*, 9/23/1991, p. 215.)

avocation (as in favorite topic or activity) *n*.: **cheval de bataille** [French for "battle-horse"]. See *hobby*

avoid (as in avert or ward off) *v.t.*: **forfend**. See *avert*

avoid (a straight answer) *v.t.*: **tergiversate**. See *evade*

avoidance (engaging in . . . tactics, esp. as a means to wear out an opponent or avoid confrontation) *adj.*: **Fabian**. See *dilatory*, *guerrilla*, and *caution*

avoided (something that is dreaded, disliked, or to be . . .) *n*.: **bête noire** [French]. See *dreaded*

avow *v.t.*: **asseverate**. See *declare*

avowedly *adv.*: **ex professo** [Latin]. See *expressly*

awakened (as in revived) *adj.*: **redivivus**. See *revived*

awakening (spec. a fundamental transformation of one's character or way of thinking, often spiritual) *n*.: **metanoia**. See *conversion*

award (a prize to) *v.t.*: **premiate**. ❖ This issue celebrates the fifth annual cycle of the ar+d awards . . . to hail the work of relatively young architects. All [jurors] agreed that we should not try to **premiate** by category, but to choose the best of what was before us. (Peter Davey, "Emerging Architecture," *Architectural Review*, 12/1/2003.)

(2) award (or to bestow an . . . upon, as in an accolade) *n.*, *v.t.*: **garland**. See *accolade*

aware (as in consciously perceiving) *adj.*: **sentient**. See *conscious*

(2) aware (as in watchful person) *n.*: **Argus**. See *watchful*

(3) aware (self-proclaimed . . . , as in enlightened, people) *n.pl.*: **illuminati**. See *enlightened*

awareness (spec. a recognition of one's errors, and a return to a sane, sound, or correct position and the . . . gained from the experience) *n.*: **resipiscence**. See *reformation*

(2) awareness (as in attention) *n.*: **advertence**. See *attention*

(3) awareness (moment of . . . , often the point in the plot at which the protagonist recognizes his or her or some other character's true identity or discovers the true nature of his or her own situation) *n.*: **anagnorisis**. See *recognition*

(4) awareness (sudden . . .) *n.*: **epiphany**. See *realization*

(5) awareness *n.*: **ken**. See *perception*

awash *adj.*, *adv.*: **aslosh**. ❖ Half the fun of the New Year clearance sales is the fossicking about, but the temptation to buy simply because the price has been slashed can leave unwanted omelette on your face and your limited cellar space **aslosh** with wine you rather wished you hadn't bought. (Anthony Rose, "Bargain Bottles," *Independent* [London], 1/20/1996.)

awesome (as in wonderful) *adj.*: **mirific**. See *wonderful*

awful (person) *n.*: **caitiff**. See *despicable*

(2) awful *adj.*: **execrable**. See *abominable*

(3) awful *adj.*: **ugsome**. See *loathsome*

awkward (and clumsy boy) *n.*: **hobbledehoy**. See *clumsy*

(2) awkward (as in clumsy) *adj.*: **lumpish**. See *clumsy*

(3) awkward (habitually . . . , as in bumbling person) *n.*: **schlemiel** [Yiddish]. See *bumbler*

(4) awkward (to make one feel . . . , as in disconcert) *v.t.*: **discomfit**. See *disconcert*

(5) awkward (as in clumsy) *adj.*: **bunglesome**. See *clumsy*

(6) awkward (as in clumsy) *adj.*: **ambisinister**. See *clumsy*

awkwardness (resulting from an inopportune occurrence) *n.*: **contretemps**. See *mishap*

ax *v.t.*: **hew**. ❖ [There are a] host of private Christmas tree farms to sate your appetite for axing. And there is an appetite: As many as 10,000 Forest Service trees in Colorado will be **hewn** and trimmed for the holidays. (James B. Meadow, "**Hew** It Yourself Forest Service Sites, Tree Farms Ensure a Merry Ax-mas for All," *Denver Rocky Mountain News*, 11/29/1997.)

babble (as in meaningless talk or nonsense) *n.*: **galimatias**. See *gibberish*

(2) babble (as in unintelligible baby talk) *n.*: **lallation**. See *baby talk*

(3) babble *v.i.*: **maunder**. See *ramble*

babbler (as in one who often talks foolishness) *adj.*: **blatherskite**. ❖ When [Governor Christine Todd Whitman's] campaign consultant, a Washington **blatherskite**, regaled reporters after the election with tales of money used to suppress the black turnout, Whitman's reaction—fury leavened by disdain—stamped her as an exception to the rule that in politics as in professional wrestling, there is no role for authentic passion. (George Will, "A Governor Who Makes Waves," *St. Louis Post-Dispatch*, 4/6/1994.)

baby (as in wimp or sissy) *n.*: **pantywaist**. See *sissy*

(2) baby (collection of clothing and equipment for a newborn . . .) *n.*: **layette**. See *newborn*

(3) baby (newborn . . . , esp. less than four weeks old) *n.*: **neonate**. See *newborn*

(4) baby (who is deserted or abandoned) *n.*: **foundling**. See *orphan*

baby talk (unintelligible . . .) *n.*: **lallation**. ❖ Actually Echo is given a very primordial and unaware use of her voice. . . . [I]n the human world it could be compared to the so-called **lallation** of infants, capable of uttering any sound (also having nothing to do with their mother tongue) with no phonetic value, or without any linguistic awareness. (D. Frigoli, "The Myth of Narcissus," www.aneb.it/pages/eng/myth_of_narcissus.php.)

back (in or toward the . . .) *adv.*: **astern**. ❖ Yet an estate car was, originally, exactly that: a car to cart the gentry around their country estates, hunting, shooting and fishing gear stowed **astern**. (John Simister, "Loaded with Style," *Independent* [London], 1/25/1997.)

(2) back (of, toward, or near the . . . of a person or an organ or body part of a person or animal) *adj.*: **dorsal**. ❖ *Tattoo*, reportedly the world's largest-selling tattoo magazine, is probably the best-written of the bunch. (And that's still not saying a lot.) . . . But, in the end, who wants to actually read any of these campy, trashy magazines when there are such distracting photos as the one of a **dorsal** homage to the rockers KISS or of a smiling, rotund Buddha image on an equally rotund tummy? (*Toronto Star*, "Tattoo Mags Get to the Needle-Sharp Point," 8/26/2000.)

back away *v.i.*: **resile**. See *recoil*

backbreaking (task, esp. of cleaning up or remedying bad situations) *n.*: **Augean task**. See *Herculean*

backer (esp. who supports or protects a political leader) *n.*: **Janissary**. See *supporter*

backward (as in intellectually or morally unenlightened) *adj.*: **benighted**. See *unenlightened*

(2) backward (or stagnant place or situation) *n.*: **backwater**. See *stagnant*

bacon *n.*: **flitch**. ❖ Uncle Charles, my mother's favourite brother, had a gift for curing bacon, using a secret recipe that he never even told her about. It produced **flitches** as stiff as boards, which, when the brine had done its work, hung from huge hooks set in the dairy ceiling. The bacon smelled sweet and dry. (Anna Pavord, "Border Crossings: How to Save Your Own Bacon," *Independent* [London], 10/27/2001.)

bad (as in evil or wicked) *adj.*: **iniquitous**. See *wicked*

(2) bad (as in evil or wicked) *adj.*: **malefic**. See *evil*

(3) bad (as in evil or wicked) *adj.*: **malevolent**. See *evil*

(4) bad (as in mischievous) *adj.*: **elfin**. See *mischievous*

(5) bad (very . . . , as in abominable) *adj.*: **execrable**. See *abominable*

bad dream (or episode having the quality of a . . .) *n.*: **Walpurgis Night**. See *nightmare*

bad faith (with or in . . .) *adv., adj.*: **mala fide** [Latin]. ❖ The inescapable conclusion, from the Indian point of view, is that either U.S. intentions in India are **mala fide**, or, even worse, India is so low on Clinton's list of priorities that it does not merit a serious policy.

(K. V. Bapa Rao, "Clinton's India Policy," *India Currents*, 4/30/1994.)

badger *v.t.*: **chivvy**. See *pester*

(2) badger *v.t.*: **hector**. See *bully*

bad luck *n., adj.*: **hoodoo** [sometimes as in "a hoodoo" when used in the sense of a curse or jinx; also used as an adjective, as in "hoodoo team"]. ❖ Mo Vaughn had no idea what he was stepping into April 6 when he plunged feet-first into the visitors' dugout during the first inning of his first game as an Anaheim Angel. Eighty million bucks [Vaughn's salary] might keep you toasty at night, but no truckload of cash covers . . . four decades of **hoodoo**. Vaughn dismissed the opening-day misstep as a freak accident. (Chris Dufresne, "The Hex Files; Angels Have Been Foiled by Something for Almost Four Decades," *Los Angeles Times*, 5/27/1999.)

bad temper *n.*: **bile**. See *bitterness*

(2) bad temper *n.*: **choler** (*adj.*: **choleric**). See *anger*

bad-tempered (as in grouchy person) *n.*: **crosspatch**. See *grouch*

(2) bad-tempered (as in irritable) *adj.*: **liverish**. See *irritable*

(3) bad-tempered (as in irritable) *adj.*: **shirty**. See *irritable*

(4) bad-tempered (as in irritable) *adj.*: **waspish**. See *irritable*

(5) bad-tempered (as in surly) *adj.*: **atrabilious**. See *surly*

(6) bad-tempered (as in surly) *adj.*: **bilious**. See *surly*

(7) bad-tempered *adj.*: **choleric**. See *angry*

baffling *adj.*: **quisquous**. See *perplexing*

bag (women's drawstring . . .) *n.*: **reticule**. See *handbag*

baggage (or equipment or supplies or any object that hinders progress or movement) *n.pl.*: **impedimenta**. [This word is generally, though not always, used in its literal sense. It can also be used figuratively. For example: "Candidates have since come to lug their character around as the ultimate impedimenta, and Mr. Clinton has written the campaigner's guidebook on how best to do it." (*New York Times*, "Reaction Off the Trail," 11/5/1992.)] ❖ If you have travelled recently and waited in security lines you know that people take entirely too much stuff with them on a trip. The people in front of you in line inevitably have a roller bag with a shoulder bag resting on it. Watch them as they take out their laptop, heave their bags onto the conveyor belt and then fill bin after bin with other **impedimenta**. And this is their carry-on luggage. Who knows what they checked. (Julia McCue, Working the Web, *Portland [ME] Press Herald*, 6/5/2006.)

bagpipes (high, shrill sound of . . .) *n.*: **skirl**. ❖ With eyes dried and hearts lifted—thanks to the **skirl** of bagpipes played by kilt-wearing pipers coming up the hill—Grant, Gill and the wedding guests arrived at Grant's rented home. (Karen S. Schneider, Weddings: "Perfect Harmony," *People*, 3/27/2000, p. 57.)

balance (as in equilibrium) *n.*: **equipoise**. See *equilibrium*

(2) balance (spec. to be or to make equal in weight) *v.t., v.i.*: **equiponderate**. See *equal*

balancer (as in one who balances things or balancing on things) *n.*: **equilibrist**. [This word is broader than *funambulist* (see *tightrope walker*) in that it includes one who performs feats of balance, whether balancing on something, as in the example given, or doing the balancing. It is also sometimes used figuratively.] ❖ Among the more bizarre stunts is the "Roller Boller Balancer" number by Pavel and Natasha Lavrik. Pavel is an **equilibrist** who balances himself atop a stack of rolling cylinders. While pivoting from this precarious perch, he and his wife Natasha play catch with a dozen juggling pins. (Steve Parks, "Russia's National Treasure: Moscow Circus," *Newsday*, 12/20/1994.)

bald (-headed man) *n.*: **pilgarlic**. ❖ Moving from pogonotrophy to **pilgarlics**, many politicians perceive that the voters won't go for a bald-headed candidate, according to John T. Capps III of (where else?) Moorehead City, North Carolina, President and Founder of

Bald-Headed Men of America. (*Newsday*, Eye on Long Island, 3/12/1995.)

(2) bald (or hairless) *adj.*: **glabrous**. ❖ In the Brazilian rainforests Dutch scientists have located the world's tiniest species of monkey. . . . Too small to eat or even to perform with an organ grinder, the diminutive monkey might be used as a hairpiece, and if these Dutch scientists are as bald as most middle-aged Dutchmen, they may return to Holland as saviors of their **glabrous** race. (*American Spectator*, "The Continuing Crisis: Scrabbled Brains," 10/1/1997.)

(3) bald (become . . . by shaving one's head) *v.t., n.*: **tonsure**. See *shave*

baldness *n.*: **alopecia**. ❖ Coming on the eve of the muckraking era, Rockefeller's **alopecia** had a devastating effect on his image: It made him look like a hairless ogre, stripped of all youth, warmth, and attractiveness, and this played powerfully on people's imaginations. (Ron Chernow, *Titan*, Random House [1998], p. 408.)

ball (formal . . . esp. for debutantes) *n.*: **cotillion**. ❖ [He is] one of six blacks in a Catholic school of 1,200 males wearing blazers to class each day. . . . He's at a **cotillion**. He's very quiet. Perfectly mannerly. But he's making one debutante's mother nervous. She asks what his family name is. "Wilkens," he replies. She asks what his father's profession is. "My father's dead." (Gary Smith, Bonus Piece, *Sports Illustrated*, 12/5/1994, p. 68.)

ballet (admirer or fan of . . .) *n.*: **balletomane**. ❖ Although he would go on to dance with more than 40 companies, [Rudolf] Nureyev's most successful relationship was with England's Royal Ballet, partnering Margot Fonteyn. In the body-conscious 1960s, his athletic, pantherlike approach enraptured audiences and created a whole new generation of **balletomanes**. (Eileen Clarke, "The Final Curtain—Eight Years Ago, Groundbreaking Dancer Rudolf Nureyev Succumbed to AIDS," *Entertainment Weekly*, 1/11/2002, p. 76.)

ballooned (as in swollen) *adj.*: **dropsical**. See *swollen*

balls (as in testicles; surgical removal of one or both . . .) *n.*: **orchiectomy**. See *testicles*

balm (or lotion that is soothing) *n.*: **demulcent**. See *soothing*

bamboozle *v.t.*: **hornswoggle**. See *deceive*

banal (as in insipid intellectual nourishment, like baby food) *n.*: **pabulum** (also **pablum**). See *insipid*

(2) banal (one who utters . . . remarks, as in platitudes) *n.*: **platitudinarian**. See *platitudes*

(3) banal (remark or statement) *n.*: **platitude**. See *cliché*

banality (in speech or writing) *n.*: **pablum**. See *triteness*

banditry *n.*: **brigandage** (**bandit** *n.*: **brigand**). See *robbery*

banished (or ostracized) *v.t.*: **sent to Coventry** [British]. See *ostracized*

bank (of or relating to a . . . of water) *adj.*: **riparian**. See *water bank*

banner (an inspiring . . .) *n.*: **oriflamme**. ❖ Nobody has raised an **oriflamme**—the scarlet banner to which scattered troops may repair—to rally all people to a great cause, saying, "This is an epic in which we all have a role. This is something we will be proud to bequeath to our children." (Jon Cypher, "Lights! Camera! Action! It's Time to Script a New Show for NASA," *Omni*, 7/1/1994, p. 4.)

(2) banner (suspended from a crossbar, as opposed to on a flagstaff) *n.*: **gonfalon**. ❖ [The New York] Rangers, who went 54 years between [Stanley] Cups, have . . . ascended to the championship throne . . . as the **gonfalon** was hoisted in New York. (Austin Murphy, Hockey: "It Was the Kind of Gaudy Excess That New York Does Best," *Sports Illustrated*, 1/30/1995, p. 24.)

bannister (and supports for) *n.*: **balustrade**. See *handrail*

banter *n.*: **badinage**. ❖ Front runners can stumble, but the mayor exudes confidence. In the middle of a formal Transport for London Board meeting, a white-haired woman got up to denounce him. Instead of having her ejected, Mr Livingstone engaged in a lively debate, calling her "darling." After five minutes of **badinage**, the woman sat down, apparently content. Few ministers could have handled her so deftly. (*Economist*, Britain: "A Shoo-in: London's Mayor," 2/23/2002, p. 33.)

(2) banter (as in good-natured teasing) *n.*: **raillery**. See *teasing*

(3) banter (one skilled at dinner . . .) *n.*: **deipnosophist**. See *conversation*

(4) banter *n.*: **persiflage**. See *chitchat*

(5) banter *v.t., v.i., n.*: **chaff**. See *teasing*

barb (as in insult, delivered while leaving the scene) *n.*: **Parthian shot**. See *parting shot*

barbarian (as in boor) *n.*: **grobian**. See *boor*

(2) barbarian (as in crude or uncouth person) *n.*: **yahoo**. See *boor*

(3) barbarian (as in indifferent or antagonistic to artistic or cultural values) *adj.*: **philistine**. See *uncultured*

(4) barbarian *n.*: **troglodyte**. See *Neanderthal*

barbaric *adj.*: **gothic**. ❖ "I am opposed to Asiatics being brought here," said the [congressman in 1870]. But "while they are here it is our duty to protect them [from] barbarous and cruel laws that place upon them unjust and cruel burdens." Over the past 100 years, California has passed a **gothic** variety of laws discriminating against aliens; but the Court has balked only when some aliens were discriminated against more than others. (Jeffrey Rosen, "The War on Immigrants: Why the Courts Can't Save Us," *New Republic*, 1/30/1995, p. 22.)

barbarous *adj.*: **Hunnish.** [This word is based on the reputation of the Huns, a confederation of equestrian nomads who established an empire in Central Asia in the fourth and fifth centuries.] ❖ [A 1981 piece entitled "Barbarians at the Gate"] said that the Reagan Administration and its allies were "abusing the environment in so many ways that it is as if the barbarians were swarming through the gates of Rome, burning and looting." And what precisely was it that agitated the author of this piece . . . to predict the fall of American civilization at the hands of

Hunnish Reaganites? (Peter Samuel, "Barbarians Within?" *National Review*, 8/31/1992.)

bargain (as in pact) *n.*: **amicabilis concordia**. See *pact*

bark (or yelp, squawk, or screech) *v.t., n.*: **yawp**. See *shriek*

barren *adj.*: **acarpous**. See *sterile*

barricade *n.*: **bulwark**. See *protection*

barrier (esp. a low, temporary, quickly built fortification) *n.*: **breastwork**. See *fortification*

(2) barrier (usually in the form of buffer states, against nations considered potentially aggressive or ideologically dangerous) *n.*: **cordon sanitaire** [French]. See *buffer*

base (as in nerve center) *n.*: **ganglion** (pl. **ganglia**). See *nerve center*

(2) base (on which something is built) *n.*: **warp and woof**. See *foundation*

(3) base *adj.*: **ignoble**. See *mean*

baseless (and/or illogical argument) *n.*: **choplogic**. See *fallacy*

(2) baseless (as in relating to reasoning that sounds plausible but is false or insincere) *adj.*: **meretricious**. See *specious*

(3) baseless (reasoning) *n.*: **syllogism**. See *specious*

bashful (and unassertive person) *n.*: **milquetoast**. See *unassertive*

(2) bashful (esp. from lack of self-confidence) *adj.*: **diffident**. See *timid*

basic (as in essential) *adj.*: **constitutive**. See *essential*

(2) basic *adj.*: **abecedarian**. ❖ [Muhammad Ali] expressed himself in energetic, if **abecedarian**, rhymes. Listen to this excerpt from "Song of Myself": "Yes, the crowd did not dream—When they laid down their money—That they would see—A total eclipse of the Sonny. I am the greatest!" (Keith Mano, "Still the Greatest," *National Review*, 11/9/1998, p. 59.)

basically *adv.*: **au fond** [French: at bottom]. ❖ Unlike most radicals, however, [British politician Tony] Benn has not mellowed with age and modified his views. [He believes that] the monarchy should be abolished. . . . **Au fond,**

Mr Benn is a Robespierre. That is to say, he has no grasp of the need for continuity and authority as well as that for radical change. He is strong on the dangers of authoritarianism. He does not seem to grasp the equal dangers of anarchy. (*Economist*, "Common Sense," 9/18/1993.)

basis (as in root) *n.*: **taproot**. See *root*

(**2**) **basis** (as in source and origin) *n.*: **fons et origo** [Latin]. See *source and origin*

(**3**) **basis** (as in that which set the standard or established the model from which others followed or on which others are based) *n.*: **locus classicus** [Latin]. See *model*

(**4**) **basis** (initial . . . as in prime mover) *n.*: **primum mobile** [Latin]. See *prime mover*

(**5**) **basis** (on which something is built) *n.*: **warp and woof**. See *foundation*

(**6**) **basis** (principal . . . or source) *n.*: **wellhead**. See *source*

(**7**) **basis** (as in assumption or set of assumptions) *n.*: **donnée** [French]. See *assumption*

basket (often one of a pair, on either side of a bike or animal) *n.*: **pannier**. ❖ In Vietnam the unemployed not only get on their bikes, they load them up with saleable goods. The contents of whole supermarkets are available from the **panniers** of trusty Flying Pigeon bicycles. (Stanley Stewart, Travel: "Oh What a Lovely Peace; The Vietnam War Helped Save Old Hanoi," *Daily Telegraph* [London], 11/15/1997.)

bat (one's eyes) *v.i.*: **nictitate**. See *blink*

batch (confused or jumbled . . .) *n.*: **agglomeration**. See *jumble*

baths (of or relating to . . . or bathing) *adj.*: **balneal**. ❖ When . . . boats are bobbing and becking on the blue water, Jayne Ikard likes nothing better than to draw a bath in her forest green bathroom and soak herself as she surveys the scene spread before her. . . . "You might call Jayne a sort of assistant harbormaster," said one friend of Ikard's **balneal** supervision of the boats. (William MacKaye, "Edgartown Harbor from the Second-Floor Bath," *Washington Post*, 5/4/1996.)

battered (as in decrepit) *adj.*: **spavined**. See *decrepit*

battle (act or event that causes or provokes . . . , literally or figuratively) *n.*: **casus belli** [Latin: occasion of war]. See *provocation*

battle (as in brawl, esp. public) *n.*: **affray**. See *brawl*

(**2**) **battle** (engaged in . . . , as in a struggle) *adj.*: **agonistes**. See *struggle*

(**3**) **battle** (minor . . . as in skirmish) *n.*: **velitation**. See *skirmish*

(**4**) **battle** (of or about words) *n.*: **logomachy**. See *words*

(**5**) **battle** (or conflict among the gods) *n.*: **theomachy**. See *gods*

(**6**) **battle** (over an idea or principle) *n.*: **jihad**. See *crusade*

(**7**) **battle** (people who . . . as if to the death) *n.*: **Kilkenny cats** (esp. as in "fight like Kilkenny cats"). See *fight*

bauble (as in gadget) *n.*: **whigmaleerie**. See *gadget*

(**2**) **bauble** (as in trinket) *n.*: **bibelot**. See *trinket*

(**3**) **bauble** (as in trinket) *n.*: **bijou**. See *trinket*

(**4**) **bauble** (as in trinket) *n.*: **gewgaw**. See *trinket*

bay window *n.*: **oriel**. ❖ The newer Renaissance section [of the Rothenburg town hall], built in 1572, replaced the portion destroyed in the fire. It's decorated with intricate friezes, an **oriel** extending the building's full height, and a large stone portico opening onto the square. (*Frommer's Europe*, "Germany: The Romantic Road," 1/1/1998.)

beaming (as in shining brightly) *adj.*: **effulgent**. See *bright*

(**2**) **beaming** (as in shining brightly) *adj.*: **fulgurant**. See *bright*

(**3**) **beaming** (as in shining brightly) *adj.*: **refulgent**. See *bright*

bear (of, resembling, or relating to) *adj.*: **ursine**. ❖ The worm of doubt that really eats at market watchers taurine and **ursine** [bull and bear] is the high price/earnings multiple, recently about 24.4 for the S&P 500. (Terence P. Pare, "Finding Buys When Stocks Are High," *Fortune*, 10/26/1992, p. 16.)

beard (having a . . .) *adj.*: **barbate**. ❖ It took the Western pioneers to make woolly faces fashionable again, and it took Abraham Lincoln in 1861 to bring a **barbate** visage to the White House. (David Wharton, "Face to Face with Hairy Situations," *Los Angeles Times*, 8/6/1991.)

bearing *n.*: **mien**. See *demeanor*

beat (as in defeat by upset) *v.t.*: **unhorse**. See *defeat*

(2) **beat** (as in whip, generally used figuratively) *v.t.*: **larrup**. See *whip*

(3) **beat** (repeatedly, often used figuratively) *v.t.*: **buffet**. See *hit*

(4) **beat** (with a club) *v.t.*: **cudgel**. See *club*

beaten (capable of being . . .) *n.*: **vincible**. ❖ Probably the worst thing the Yankees did in playing barely .500 ball for the last month is give heart to the players they'll meet later this month and in October. The invincible team has been distinctly **vincible**. (Steve Jacobson, "The Playoffs—Just Win, Baby," *Newsday*, 9/29/1998.)

beating (the soles of the feet with a stick as a form of punishment or torture) *n., v.t.*: **bastinado**. [This word is used both literally and figuratively, to refer to any kind of punishment or torture, as in the following example.] ❖ [O]ur story began last October, when candidate [George H. W.] Bush was winning the White House by cheerfully bashing Michael Dukakis about the head and shoulders with the ever-popular "Harvard-boutique-liberal, soft-on-crime, weak-on-defense" **bastinado**. (Jeff Greenfield, "A Haunted Honeymoon," *Chicago Sun-Times*, 2/28/1989.)

beat-up (as in broken-down and/or worn-out) *adj.*: **raddled**. See *worn-out*

(2) **beat-up (as in decrepit)** *adj.*: **spavined**. See *decrepit*

(3) **beat up** (sometimes in jest) *v.t.*: **spiflicate** [British slang]. ❖ My wife and daughter-in-law will **spiflicate** me for saying so, but

I find the invitation to Annika Sorenstam to play in a men's pro golf tournament laughable. There would be a huge hue and cry if Tiger Woods played in a girls' rich tournament and won by 20 strokes, playing left-handed. (Terry Tuckey, letter to the editor, *Sydney Morning Herald*, 5/22/2003.)

beau (as in boyfriend) *n.*: **inamorato**. See *boyfriend*

beau *n.*: **swain**. See *suitor*

beautiful (in an unconventional way) *adj.*: **belle laide** (or **belle-laide**). [French, for "beautiful-ugly." This term refers to being attractive in an unconventional or unusual way or, more literally, beautiful and ugly at the same time. It can also be applied to inanimate objects, and can be used as a noun to refer to the person or thing being described, which is in fact the way it is used here. A similar term is "jolie laide," which is "pretty-ugly." See *pretty*. Finally, a related (but rare) word meaning unattractive but sexy at the same time is "cacocallia."] ❖ [Fred Astaire is] the masculine equivalent of what the French call a **belle laide**: a feature-by-feature homely woman who is somehow nevertheless stunning. [In Joseph Epstein's book about Astaire, he] lovingly describes each peculiarity: Head and ears too large, face too long, hair too thin (he invariably wore a hairpiece in movies)—in sum, he had a sweet goofy look. (John Taylor, "Canadian Explorer, Dancer Sublime," *Washington Times*, 10/19/2008.)

(2) **beautiful** (esp. sexually) *adj.*: **toothsome**. See *sexy*

(3) **beautiful** (of a . . . and stately woman, esp. tending toward voluptuous) *adj.*: **Junoesque**. See *voluptuous*

(4) **beautiful** (young woman) *n.*: **houri** [French]. See *woman*

beautiful people (as in fashionable society) *n.*: **beau monde** [French]. See *high society*

(2) **beautiful people** (as in fashionable society) *n.*: **bon ton** [French]. See *high society*

beauty (facetious way of measuring . . . by units) *n.*: **millihelen**. [This word is not yet officially dictionary-recognized, but it is increasing in use and is a fun word to boot. The example explains the derivation and usage.] ❖ I saw [Princess] Diana once, up close. Lasering the room, batting her big eyes—so knowingly, so knowingly—she went off the scale. Measured in **millihelens** (Helen of Troy's beauty launched a thousand ships; a millihelen is enough to launch only one), Diana's was much greater than [Monica Lewinsky's]. But the president [Clinton] made up for it. Tall and light and handsome, he commands any room. (Paul Richard, Essay: "Big News," *Washington Post*, 4/26/2000.)

(2) beauty (highest . . . , esp. moral . . . , as conceived by Aristotle) *n.*: **kalon** [Greek]. ❖ The "great-souled man" had a character of such undiluted integrity, inspiration and achievement in the real world that his life expressed, for Aristotle, the **kalon**, moral beauty. Ronald Reagan was a morally beautiful human being. (Jack Wheeler, "The 'Great-Souled Man'; Reagan Was a Classic," *Washington Times*, 6/8/2004.)

(3) beauty (physical . . .) *n.*: **pulchritude**. ❖ [Baseball player Mike] Piazza has hit the mother lode of visual **pulchritude**. His girlfriend is Darlene Bernaola. He has her initials tattooed on his ankle. Bernaola and her twin sister are *Playboy*'s Playmates of the Millennium. (Richard Deitsch, "The Fans: Knowwhatimsayin'? Fuggedabowdit!" *Sports Illustrated*, 11/1/2000, p. 82.)

(4) beauty (perfect . . . or a beautiful example of something) *n.*: **beau ideal**. See *ideal*

bed (mattress filled with straw) *n.*: **palliasse**. See *mattress*

bedlam (and confusion, esp. from simultaneous voices) *n.*: **babel**. See *noise*

(2) bedlam (as in chaos) *n.*: **tohubuhu**. See *chaos*

(3) bedlam (as in commotion) *n.*: **maelstrom**. See *commotion*

bed-wetting *n.*: **nocturnal enuresis**. ❖ Severe "**nocturnal enuresis**," characterized by three or more bed-wetting episodes per week in children older than age seven, affects some 7 percent of the population. (Josie Glausiusz, "Strange Genes," *Discover*, 1/1/1996, p. 33.)

beehive *n.*: **skep**. ❖ Back on the ground, I turned the **skep** upside-down, with the bottom open, and propped up so that stragglers could rejoin the main tribe. Inward migration confirmed that the queen [bee] was inside, but it took nearly an hour for all to be gathered in. (Duff Hart-Davis, "Country: 'I'm Not Going Near Them,' Said Mr. X," *Independent* [London], 6/15/1996.)

beer-bellied *adj.*: **abdominous**. ❖ We chaps also know what it's like to be grossly **abdominous**, and if my byline photo were full length and in profile, you'd realise that I've been 14 months pregnant for the past five years. (Victor Lewis-Smith, "Womb for Improvement," *Evening Standard* [London], 8/9/2001.)

(2) beer-bellied *adj.*: **stomachy**. See *paunchy*

bees (of or relating to) *adj.*: **apian**. ❖ The buzz about the alarming disappearance of bees has been all about people food. Honeybees pollinate one-third of the fruits, nuts and vegetables that end up in our homey kitchen baskets. If the tireless **apian** workers didn't fly from one flower to the next, depositing pollen grains so that fruit trees can bloom, America could well be asking where its next meal would come from. (Kevin Berger, "Where Have All the Bees Gone?" *Seattle Post-Intelligencer*, 7/8/2007.)

befog (over one's vision) *v.t.*: **obnubilate**. See *obscure*

before (a meal, esp. dinner) *adj.*: **preprandial**. See *meal*

(2) before (coming . . .) *adj.*: **prevenient** (often as in "prevenient grace"). See *antecedent*

befuddled (esp. used of a person, as in . . . and stupid) *adj.*: **addlepated**. See *confused*

beg (as in plead) *v.t.*: **adjure**. See *plead*

(2) beg (from or sponge off of) *v.t.*: **cadge**. See *mooch*

beggar *n.*: **mendicant**. ❖ In [Graham Greene's] 1940 novel, *The Power and the Glory*, he created a character who was a street **mendicant**, and observed, "He had the grudging independence you find in countries where it is the right of a poor man to beg." (Philip Marchand, "He Goes Here," *Toronto Star*, 7/18/1998.)

(2) beggar (as in one who mooches) *n.*: **schnorrer** [Yiddish; slang]. See *moocher*

begging the question (as in assuming the truth of the premise that is to be proved) *n.*: **petitio principii.** [Latin. A common misusage of the phrase "begging the question" is in the sense of "raising or inviting a further question." However, its correct usage requires a conclusion that restates the premise. For example: "Affirmative action can never be just, because you cannot remedy one injustice by committing another." Here the premise is that affirmative action is unjust, and that premise is used as the basis for the exact same conclusion.] ❖ It has been objected, from Gassendi downward, that to say [as Descartes did], "I think, therefore I am," is a begging of the question; since existence has to be proved identical with thought. Certainly, if Descartes had intended to prove his own existence by reasoning, he would have been guilty of the **petitio principii** Gassendi attributes to him. (George Henry Lewes, "Birth of Modern Scientific Methods, Bacon and Descartes," *History of the World*, 1/1/1992.)

beginner *n.*: **abecedarian.** ❖ Apprentice alphabetarians are **abecedarians** (as are apprentice anythings). [But] Richard A. Firmage's entertaining and eclectic book . . . is chiefly aimed at more advanced readers who are fascinated by language and how letters are formed and used. (Andrew McKie, "Books: Nothing Simple About A, B, C," *Daily Telegraph* [London], 4/8/2000.) See *basic*

(2) beginner *n.*: **catechumen.** ❖ Sonny appears to be the only child of Jake and Lily Cantrell. Jake raises gamecocks as proprietor of the Snake Nation Cock Farm. . . . Sonny is an eager **catechumen** in his father's cockfighting religion. (Jonathan Taylor, "The Small Press/Journey to Manhood," *Newsday*, 3/15/1998.)

(3) beginner (as in amateur) *n.*: **dilettante**. See *amateur*

beginning (from the . . .) *adv.*: **ab initio** [Latin]. ❖ In contrast with "regular" wars where most nations agree to operate within certain rules, terrorism is characterized by the fact that its perpetrators permit themselves **ab initio** any means and any target. (Yigal Carmon, "A Very Costly Naivete," *Jerusalem Post*, 7/30/1996.)

(2) beginning (from the . . .) *adv.*: **ab ovo** [Latin]. ❖ To describe this project's gestation, **ab ovo**, I need to take you back to 1990, when Penguin published my comic-book version of *The Waste Land*. (Martin Rowson, Books, *Independent on Sunday*, 9/1/1996.)

(3) beginning (as in coming into being) *adj.*: **nascent**. See *emerging*

(4) beginning (again, as in renewal or restoration of something after decay, lapse of time, or dilapidation) *n.*: **instauration**. See *restoration*

(5) beginning (existing from the . . . , as in innate) *adj.*: **connate**. See *innate*

(6) beginning (often of a speech or writing) *n.*: **exordium**. See *introduction*

(7) beginning (stage of growth or development) *adj.*: **germinal**. See *earliest*

beginning and end *n.*: **alpha and omega**. ❖ From my room at the Holiday Inn [in Sarajevo], the **alpha and omega** of the war lay before me. [To the left, in 1979, a woman] took a sniper's bullet and so became the first of 10,615 of the city's residents to die. . . . The last fatality occurred not 75 yards to the right. (Alexander Wolff, *Big Game, Small World*, Warner Books [2002], p. 109.)

beguile *v.t.*: **ensorcell** (or **ensorcel**). See *enchant*

beguiling (as in alluring) *adj.*: **illecebrous**. See *alluring*

(2) beguiling (as in alluring) *adj.*: **siren**. [See also the nouns *siren call* and *Lorelei call* under *lure*.] See *alluring*

behavior (study of human . . .) *n.*: **praxeology**. ❖ [In the black church,] they talk about what Jesus did. Yes they will say what he did, but they won't do it themselves. The difference between what is being said in church (doctrine) and what action is being taken (**praxeology**) confuses people in and outside the church. (H. Dwight Sterling, "Black Church Must Act with Words and Deeds," *Oakland Post*, 6/12/1994.)

(2) behavior (appropriate . . .) *n.*: **correctitude**. See *propriety*

behind (a fat . . .) *n.*: **steatopygia** (having a fat . . .) *adj.*: **steatopygic**. See *rear end*

(2) behind (as in buttocks) *n.pl.*: **nates**. See *buttocks*

(3) behind (as in buttocks) *n.*: **fundament**. See *buttocks*

(4) behind (as in toward the back) *adv.*: **astern**. See *back*

(5) behind (having a hairy . . .) *adj.*: **dasypygal**. See *rear end*

(6) behind (having a nicely proportioned . . .) *adj.*: **callipygian**. See *rear end*

behold (wonderful to . . .) *adv.*: **mirabile visu** [Latin]. ❖ With their love of tradition and their formal dress code (no shorts even for children, and covered heads for women), the members of Mater Ecclesiae Church in Berlin Township can seem a tight-laced congregation of Roman Catholics. But on Sunday they were ringing bells, popping corks and slicing cake, and—**mirabile visu**!—some were even smoking cigars. (David O'Reilly, "Reviving a Latin Past," *Philadelphia Inquirer*, 7/10/2008.)

being (while coming into . . .) *adv.*: **aborning**. See *born*

belaboring (as in repeating a particular act over and over, often after initial stimulus has ceased) *n.*: **perseveration** (*v.i.*: **perseverate**). See *repeating*

belated (as in a statement, thought, or action, generally amusing, that comes to mind or occurs after the fact when it is too late to act on it) *n.*: **afterwit**. [This is an admittedly obscure word, but a good one nevertheless and one that deserves to be revived. A limerick about the word, referring to its "retort" sense, goes as follows: "I'm the wittiest guy in the hood / Snappy comebacks? I'm tops, understood? / Still, my best repartee / Keeps occurring to me / The next day, when it does me no good." For a related word, see *esprit d'escalier* under *retort*.] ❖ Conductor [Leopold] Stokowski bade Philadelphia goodbye "for a long time." "And I hope," he added, with pensive Polish **afterwit**, "your colds will all be better!" (*Time*, "Adieu," 5/9/1927.)

belch *v.t.*, *v.i.*: **eruct**. ❖ Scientists have been telling us for decades that the greatest contributors to smog, the greenhouse effect and global warming are automobiles. In response, we've choked our cities with spaghetti strands of interstates on which stalled, snorting tank cars **eruct** their fetid air. (Gary Corseri, letter to the editor, *Atlanta Journal-Constitution*, 6/26/2000.)

belief (as in reliance on . . . alone—as in faith—rather than reason, esp. in philosophical or religious matters) *n.*: **fideism**. See *faith*

(2) belief (which is false) *n.*: **pseudodoxy**. See *fallacy*

(3) belief (which is odd, stubborn, or whimsical) *n.*: **crotchet**. See *notion*

(4) belief *n.*: **shibboleth**. See *principle*

beliefs (spec. doctrines to be believed; articles of faith) *n.pl.*: **credenda** (sing.: **credendum**). ❖ Everyone (who cares) is focusing on the upcoming Republican leadership's convention, at which . . . the **credenda** for the 1999–2000 GOP will be given. A survey of individual Republicans' views reminds us how marked the divisions are. But lo!—the diaspora comes together on one point, which is that the GOP must be the sponsor of reduced taxes. (*National Review*, "Gephardt-Proof Tax Reform?" 12/21/1998.)

believable (as in appearing to be true or accurate) *adj.*: **verisimilar**. See *plausible*

believing (as in credulous) *adj.*: **ultrafidian** [Latin]. See *credulous*

belittle (oneself) *v.t.*: **self-flagellate** (*n.*: **self-flagellation**). See *criticize*

(2) belittle *v.t.*: **vilipend**. See *disparage*

belittlement (as in disdain) *n.*: **misprision** (*v.t.*: **misprize**). See *disdain*

belittling (another, often through insult or humiliation) *adj.*: **contumelious**. See *contemptuous*

belligerent *adj.*: **bellicose**. ❖ Ever since they split in a civil war 50 years ago, China has been a very real danger to Taiwan. The People's Republic has menaced the island with missile tests and **bellicose** threats of invasion. (Mahlon Meyer, "Risky Business," *Newsweek International*, 8/14/2000, p. 36.)
(2) belligerent (as in combative) *adj.*: **agonistic**. See *combative*

bell ringing (art of . . .) *n.*: **campanology**. ❖ Writer Christopher Russell set his story in the enclosed and slightly mysterious world of **campanology**. Bellringers are a little like many wicket keepers, goalies or steeplejacks—lonely, obsessive figures devoted to ancient rules and customs. (Peter Paterson, "It Always Rings a Bell . . . ," *Daily Mail* [London], 9/16/2002.)

bells (ringing or sounding of) *n.*: **tintinnabulation**. ❖ [*Beauty and The Beast's*] dancing clocks and singing teacups will blend marvelously with the **tintinnabulation** of bells this holiday season. (Mark Goodman, Picks & Pans, *People*, 11/18/1991, p. 21.)

bellyache *n.pl.* but *sing.* or *pl.* in construction: **collywobbles**. [This colloquial British term, sometimes preceded by "the," is often used as a synonym for nervousness, anxiety, tension, and the like.] ❖ Gone are the days when going away to a conference meant languishing in luxury for a few nights in deluxe accommodation with spa, fine dining and top service. Worldwide economic **collywobbles** and stock-market jitters are squeezing travel budgets, and executives now find themselves being downgraded to mid-market hotels or budget lodges. (Gaby Huddart, "Stop the Drain on Your Pocket," *Evening Standard* [London], 7/9/2001.)

belonging (as in associated with or incident to) *adj.*: **appurtenant**. See *pertaining*

belongings (personal . . .) *n.pl.*: **personalia**. ❖ [A] dress worn in late pregnancy by Princess Charlotte of Wales (1796–1817), the only child of George IV, revealed that her breasts were slightly unequal in size, by no means an unusual trait. This potential heir to the throne died in childbirth, aged only twenty-one, and her **personalia** have consequently become almost as revered as relics of Charles I. The discovery prompted a re-examination of other dresses associated with the princess . . . (Kay Staniland, "The Fabric of History," *History Today*, 11/1/2000.)

beloved (as in darling) *n.*: **acushla** [Irish]. See *darling*
(2) beloved (my . . .) *n.*: **mavourneen** [Irish]. See *darling*

below (lying . . .) *adj.*: **subjacent**. [I]t's high time we call on the American Lung Association et al. and the Apartment Owners Association to get together and constructively engage themselves on behalf of those tenants who are still being plagued by carcinogen carrying secondhand smoke; typically drifting upward from a **subjacent**, seemingly 24/7-smoking neighbor, who [shirks] any good neighbor, secondhand smoke mitigation, obligations whatsoever. (Harvey Pearson, letter to the editor, *Los Angeles Daily News*, 3/24/2002.)

bend (in and out) *v.i.*: **sinuate**. See *wind*
(2) bend (slightly) *v.t., v.i.*: **camber**. See *curve*

bendable *adj.*: **ductile**. See *pliable*

bending (as in winding or waving) *adj.*: **flexuous**. See *waving*

beneath (lying . . .) *adj.*: **subjacent**. See *below*

benediction *n.*: **benison**. See *blessing*

benefactor (generous . . . , esp. of the arts) *n.*: **Maecenas** [after Gaius Maecenas, a Roman statesman, who was a patron of Horace and Virgil.] ❖ Christie's star [auction] was the sale of 14 works from the collection of Paul Mellon, the octogenarian **Maecenas**, who must be considered America's premier collector; his father founded Washington's National Gallery and he has given literally hundreds of works to institutions. (Geraldine Norman, "Blue Period for High Prices," *Independent* [London], 11/25/1989.)

beneficial (as in having the power to cure or heal) *adj.*: **sanative**. See *healthful*

benefit (as in, "to whose . . . ?") *n.*: **cui bono** [Latin]. See *advantage*

(2) benefit (extra or unexpected . . . , sometimes given as thanks for a purchase) *n.*: **lagniappe**. See *gift*

benevolent *adj.*: **eleemosynary**. See *charitable*

bent (as in twisted) *adj.*: **tortile**. See *twisted*

(2) bent (like a bow) *adj.*: **arcuate**. See *curved*

berate (as in criticize, sharply) *v.t.*: **scarify**. See *criticize*

(3) berate *v.t.*: **flay**. See *criticize*

(4) berate *v.t.*: **objurgate**. See *criticize*

berating (as in criticism) *n.*: **animadversion** (*v.t.*: **animadvert**). See *criticism*

(2) berating (being subject to . . . , esp. public) *n.*: **obloquy**. See *abuse*

bereft *adj.*: **lorn**. See *forlorn*

beseech (as in begging for or sponging off of) *v.t.*: **cadge**. See *beg*

(2) beseech (as in plead) *v.t.*: **adjure**. See *plead*

besides *adv.*: **withal**. See *moreover*

besieged *adj.*: **obsidional**. ❖ The observation of the historian Michel Winock that in late-nineteenth-century France one sector of public opinion embraced—as if the country were under siege—a nationalism "whose mission was to defend the cohesive social organism against modernity"—could equally have been made about France in the 1920s. That "**obsidional**" nationalism, he continues, oriented itself toward the interior and the past. (Frederick Brown, "Perfumed Rot," *New Republic*, 6/26/2000.)

best (as in first-class) *adj.*: **pukka**. See *first-class*

(2) best (the . . . , lit. the greatest or highest good) *n.* **summum bonum**. [Latin]. See *ideal*

bestiality (as in sexual attraction to animals) *n.*: **zoophilia** (person attracted: **zoophile**). ❖ Zoophiles say they favour companionship with animals that can include unforced sexual contact. Woods said her patient told her that **zoophilia** today was where homosexuality was 20 years ago and before long could be considered normal, accepted behaviour. (Michael Conlon, "Web Skews Sex Education, U.S. Psychiatrist Warns," Reuters, 5/16/2000.)

bestow (by one with higher power) *v.t.*: **vouch-**

safe. ❖ [Foreign Secretary] Robin Cook . . . has become dismayed. There is too much regulation, he observes. The [European Union in Brussels is] too remote from the electors of Europe, he complains, with the air of a man who believes he has been **vouchsafed** a unique insight. (*Daily Telegraph* [London] "Look, but Don't Touch," 8/14/1998.)

(2) bestow (a prize on) *v.t.*: **premiate**. See *award*

betray (as in tattle) *v.i.*: **peach**. See *tattle*

(2) betray (oneself by selling one's soul to the devil) *adj.*: **Mephistophelean**. See *sellout*

betrayer (esp. under guise of friendship) *n.*: **Judas**. ❖ [Russian President Boris] Yeltsin has more than enough enemies. To fanatical nationalists he is the **Judas** who sold his country to the West for 30 silver dollars. (John Kohan, "Moscow, Russia: Looking for Mr. Good Czar," *Time*, 4/5/1993, p. 24.)

(2) betrayer (esp. who aids an invading enemy) *n.*: **quisling**. See *traitor*

betrayers (as in traitors or group of . . . working within a country to support an enemy and who may engage in espionage, sabotage, or other subversive activities) *n.*: **fifth column**. See *traitors*

betrothed (to be . . .) *v.t.*: **affianced**. See *marriage*

better (state of being . . .) *n.*: **meliority**. See *superiority*

between (as in intermediate or transitional state, phase, or condition) *adj.*: **liminal**. See *transitional*

bewitch *v.t.*: **ensorcell** (or **ensorcel**). See *enchant*

bewitching (as in alluring) *adj.*: **illecebrous**. See *alluring*

(2) bewitching (as in alluring) *adj.*: **siren**. [See also the nouns *siren call* and *Lorelei call* under *lure*.] See *alluring*

bias (develop a strong . . . against) *n.*: **scunner** (esp. as in "take a scunner") [British]. See *dislike*

(2) bias (preconceived . . . on an issue) *n.*: **parti pris** [French]. See *preconception*

biased (toward a particular point of view) *adj.*:

tendentious. ❖ This **tendentious** and unpleasant [and unflattering biography of New York mayor Rudy Giuliani] also reads like the revenge of a jilted lover, which is no coincidence. . . . [To the author, Giuliani] evidently personifies Evil. (Michael Grunwald, "Rudolph Giuliani's Means and Ends," *New Republic*, 1/15/2001.)

Bible (excessive adherence to literal interpretation of . . .) *n*.: **bibliolatary**. ❖ Christians who have a high view of Scripture—of its divine inspiration, infallibility and authority—are sometimes accused of **bibliolatry**. (*Dallas Morning News*, "Religion; Spirited Media.")

(2) Bible (seller) *n*.: **colporteur**. ❖ Named after the **colporteurs** who on horseback sold Bibles and other "edifying" books door-to-door, Moody's Colportage Library was a series of 10-cent reprints of sermons and tracts that sold well enough to establish his publisher, the Fleming H. Revell Co., as the largest publisher of religion books by the turn of the century. (John D. Spalding, "Stirring the Waters of Reflection: How the Anguish of the 1960s Transformed the Role of Religious Publishing," *Publishers Weekly*, 7/1/1997.)

(3) Bible (worshipper) *n*.: **bibliolater**. ❖ There is a form of heart disease defined, not by clogged arteries, but by blockage of the spirit. . . . There is no magical elixir here and no "quick fix," despite what many spiritual gurus proclaim. But, let me recommend one tried-and-true source of bracing tonic for a despairing, confused or starving spirit. Regular readers know that I am no **bibliolater**. But the remedy I'm talking about is from the Bible. It's the collection of poetry known as the Psalms. (Tom Harpur, "The Psalms Are Healing Tonic for an Ailing Spirit," *Toronto Star*, 7/14/1996.)

bid (the . . . to achieve a particular goal or desire) *n*.: **nisus**. See *goal*

bidding (act of . . . at an auction) *n*.: **licitation**. See *auction*

big (very . . .) *adj*.: **cyclopean** [derives from cyclops, the one-eyed giant in Greek mythology]. ❖ Size evidently mattered to the great builders of [Queen Victoria's] reign—not for them the diminutive . . . , but the high, the wide, the vast, their buildings **cyclopean**, . . . "the bigger the better" the motto of the day. (Brian Sewell, "Scale, Greed and Vanity—the Victorian Inheritance," *Evening Standard* [London], 1/19/2001.)

(2) big (very . . .) *adj*.: **mastodonic** [derives from the extinct species of mammals resembling elephants.]. ❖ Q: I'm looking for a hunting hand-gun that's more powerful than the .44 magnum and recently shot a .454 Casull, which packs a lot more punch but just about broke my hand. Is there anything in between? A: . . . If you can tolerate its **mastodonic** size and $1,000-plus price, the Smith & Wesson Model 500 is not bad to shoot, despite its awesome power. (David Petzal, Hunting Q & A, *Field and Stream*, 2/1/2005.)

(3) big (like an elephant) *adj*.: **pachydermatous**. See *elephant*

(4) big (very . . . object) *n*.: **leviathan**. See *huge*

(5) big (very . . .) *adj*.: **brobdingnagian** (often cap.). See *huge*

(6) big (very . . .) *adj*.: **Bunyanesque**. See *enormous*

(7) big (very . . .) *adj*.: **Pantagruelian**. See *gigantic*

(8) big (very . . .) *adj*.: **pythonic**. See *huge*

(9) big (like an elephant) *adj*.: **elephantine**. See *enormous*

bigot (as in one who clings to an opinion or belief even after being shown that it is wrong) *n*. **mumpsimus**. See *stubborn*

big picture (in the . . .) *adv*.: **sub specie aeternitatis** [Latin for "under the aspect of eternity." It means what is universally true, without reference to or dependence on temporal reality, and is used synonymously with taking a broad perspective.] ❖ Stress, the psychologists always tell us, is relative. [Manchester United manager] Sir Alex Ferguson now finds himself employed by a club 300 million pounds in debt. . . . [Southampton manager Harry Redknapp knows] that nothing short of a win

. . . will guarantee survival. To point out that both men are millionaires, . . . that **sub spe-cie aeternitatis** the result matters rather less than Monday's weather forecast is to ignore the gladiatorial substitute that these things have become. ("Better Red Than Relegated?" *Independent* [London], 5/15/2005.)

big toe *n.*: **hallux**. ❖ Left undiagnosed and untreated, turf toe can develop into a career-ending arthritic condition known as **hallux** rigidus. When this happens, the injured big toe stiffens and the player can no longer push off on the affected foot, thereby losing most of his mobility, a critical commodity in today's speed-dominated pro game. (Jill Lieber, Medicine: "Turf Toe: The NFL's Most Pesky Agony of Da Feet," *Sports Illustrated*, 12/12/1988, p. 8.)

bigwig (often arrogant or self-important) *n.*: **high muck-a-muck** (also **high-muck-a-muck**). ❖ Landing at Teterboro [Airport] also allows corporate fliers to avoid having to mingle with the perspiring masses—people who happen not to be **high muck-a-mucks**; people like you and the guy who lives across the street—they would encounter at Newark, Kennedy, and LaGuardia. (Jeffrey Page, "Fat Cats Are Left Cooling Their Jets," *Bergen County [NJ] Record*, 2/6/2004.)

(2) bigwig *n.*: **nabob**. ❖ "People look at Washington," said George W. [Bush] last week, "and they don't like what they see." Oh? Mr. Outsider went to a Washington, D.C., ballroom jammed with 2,000 entrenched political **nabobs**, mostly lobbyists and lawyers who wrote checks for more than $2 million. George W. liked what he saw. (*Columbian*, "Fireworks Lid Inflicts Undue Pain on Vendors," 7/6/1999.)

(3) bigwig *n.*: **panjandrum**. ❖ Still, for reasons known only to the preposterous **panjandrums** who run college athletics, we can watch 13 hours of New Year's Day bowl games and come away with only a suggestion as to the identity of the national college football champion. (Dave Kindred, "Here's a Super Bowl Solution," *Sporting News*, 1/10/1994.)

(4) bigwig *n.*: **satrap**. [This word has various definitions, including (1) a leader or ruler generally (see *leader*), (2) a prominent or notable person generally, (3) a henchman (see *henchman*), (4) a bureaucrat (see *bureaucrat*), and (5) the head of a state acting either as a representative or under the dominion and control of a foreign power (see *ruler*). This is an example of the second definition. Often—but not always—it has a negative connotation.] ❖ Long protected by the senators and journalistic **satraps** who paid him court, [after uttering a racial slur against the Rutgers women's basketball team, radio personality Don] Imus found himself consumed by perhaps the only forces more powerful than those that elevated him to his place of privilege: the politics of race and gender. (*Newsweek,* "The Power That Was," 3/23/2007.)

(5) bigwig *n.*: **padishah**. See *emperor*

(6) bigwig *n.*: **wallah**. See *notable*

bilingual *adj.*: **diglot**. ❖ A pocket size edition of the Constitution of India in **diglot** form is in the final stage of publication. It will be in the twin languages of English and Hindi. (M2 PressWire, "Indian Government: Pocket Size Edition of Constitution of India," 9/29/1999.)

bilk *v.t.*: **mulct**. See *defraud*

billboard *n.*: **hoarding** [British]. ❖ The most authentic element [of the 1967 movie *Star!* starring Julie Andrews as Gertrude Lawrence] was the use of several Broadway theatres, such as . . . the Music Box. . . . A temporary **hoarding**, "Gertrude Lawrence in *Skylark*," masked the Music Box's current attraction: Harold Pinter's *The Homecoming*. (Richard Stirling, *Julie Andrews*, St. Martin's Press [2007], p. 204.)

bind (a person by holding down their arms) *v.t.*: **pinion**. See *immobilize*

(2) bind (as in dilemma, except where there are three options, all of which are or seem to be unsatisfactory) *n.*: **trilemma**. See *dilemma*

(3) bind (together) *v.t.*: **colligate**. See *unite*

binding (act of . . . or tying up or together) *n.*: **ligature**. See *tying*

biographer (as in one who, out of admiration

or friendship, records the deeds and words of another) *n.*: **Boswell** [after James Boswell (1740–1795), the biographer of Samuel Johnson]. ❖ From the beginning, [Katharine] Hepburn knew that in Berg she had found not only a companion but her **Boswell**. Over the years, he kept notes on their many meetings. He knew that eventually he would do her bidding and write her story. . . . Throughout the 370-page reminiscence, Berg sets aside his biographer's independence and takes his cues from one of America's greatest movie stars. (Linton Weeks, "Hepburn and Her **Boswell**; A. Scott Berg's Memoir Caps a 20-Year Friendship with the Legend," *Washington Post*, 7/12/2003.)

biography (esp. in relation to other people or within a specific historical, social, or literary context) *n.*: **prosopography**. ❖ [U]ntil now, we have known surprisingly little about most of the men who ran [London between 1890 and 1914]. Youssef Cassis, in this pioneering study full of telling detail and perceptive analysis, does much to change that. The engine of his book is a sample of 460 leading bankers active in these years, in effect a collective biography of the City. . . . [T]his is **prosopography** on the grand scale. (David Kynaston, "Heyday of the Banking Purple [*sic*]," *Financial Times* [London], 3/30/1995.)

(2) biography (which is worshipful or idealizing) *n.*: **hagiography** (*adj.*: **hagiographic**). ❖ Nella hoped to write [Helen Keller's] biography. It would be similar to the one she had written of Annie Sullivan wherein she had painted a **hagiographic** portrait of Teacher as a true heroine and master teacher. (Dorothy Herrmann, *Helen Keller*, Knopf [1998], p. 269.)

bird dung (esp. that of sea birds) *n.*: **guano**. ❖ [Hucks Gibbs's] family had made much of their money from working the vast deposits of **guano** in Peru. (Doggerel of the day referred, not unkindly, to "The House of Gibbs That made Their Dibs by Selling Turds of Foreign Birds"). (Simon Winchester, *The Meaning of*

Everything, Oxford University Press [2003], p. 129.)

birdhouse *n.*: **aviary**. ❖ The bald eagle has a good buddy in Dolly Parton. At her Dollywood theme park in Tennessee, the country star will break ground next month for an **aviary** to house the U.S.'s largest collection of bald eagles unable to survive in the wild. (Emily Mitchell, People: "Best Little Birdhouse," *Time*, 7/30/1990, p. 71.)

birds (of, relating to or characteristic of) *adj.*: **avian**. ❖ Frank X. Ogasawara, one of the world's leading poultry scientists whose pioneer studies in **avian** reproduction helped create the plumper, meatier turkeys that grace U.S. tables on Thanksgiving, died June 8. He was 88. (Dennis McLellan, obituary of Frank X. Ogasawara, *Newsday*, 6/21/2002.)

(2) birds (of, relating to, or characteristic of) *adj.*: **ornithic**. ❖ But Johnson has other problems . . . of an **ornithic** nature. Pedro Borbon, the 48-year-old (he says) replacement pitcher cut by the Reds last week, sold Johnson two parrots for $500 each. At midnight Friday, Johnson had to take one of the parrots to a hospital in Lakeland, Fla., with some sort of infection. (Rick Hummel, "Reds Boss Bonds Better with Birds Than Replacements," *St. Louis Post-Dispatch*, 3/26/1995.)

birth (before . . .) *adj.*: **antenatal**. ❖ When I say I've no way of knowing [the sex of the unborn child] because I'm not having any **antenatal** tests—no, not even ultrasound scans—people are generally flabbergasted. Isn't ultrasound a routine part of **antenatal** care in this day and age? Doesn't everyone have to have a scan? The answer is no, and no again. (Joanna Moorhead, "Health: Ultrasound? I Don't Want to Know," *Independent* [London], 10/3/2001.)

(2) birth *n.*: **parturition**. ❖ He cannot forget that he was born a mere six months after his parents were married at a time when people counted the months between wedding and **parturition**. (Arnold Beichman, "A Rascal Looks Back on Life," *Washington Times*, 2/15/1998.)

(3) birth (giving . . . to, esp. a dog) *v.t., v.i.*: **whelp**. ❖ It was a block from her veterinarian's office, where she was going since she was **whelped**. (Lars Eighner, *Travels with Lizbeth*, St. Martin's Press [1993], p. 95.)

(4) birth (having given . . . one or more times) *n.*: **parous**. ❖ Women who have already had a child tend to be more likely than those who have not to recognize their pregnancy early; however, when there are significant differences in prenatal behavior, **parous** women are less likely to follow their provider's recommendations. (Kathryn Kost, "Predicting Maternal Behaviors During Pregnancy—Does Intention Status Matter?" *Family Planning Perspectives*, 3/1/1998, p. 85.)

(5) birth (of or relating to giving . . .) *adj.*: **parturient**. See *childbirth*

(6) birth (attitude or policy that encourages giving . . .) *n.*: **pronatalism**. See *childbearing*

(7) birth (period before giving . . .) *n.*: **antepartum** [Latin]. See *pregnancy*

(8) birth (relating to a woman during or right after . . .) *adj.*: **puerperal**. See *postpartum*

(9) birth (woman right after . . .) *n.*: **puerperium**. See *postpartum*

(10) birth (woman who has given . . . only once or is pregnant for the first time) *n.*: **primipara**. See *pregnant*

(11) birth *n.*: **accouchement**. See *childbirth*

(12) birth (existing from . . . , as in innate) *adj.*: **connate**. See *innate*

bisexual (as in one having characteristics or reproductive organs of both sexes) *n.*: **hermaphrodite**. ❖ For example, [James] Callendar . . . once described [John] Adams as a "hideous **hermaphroditical** character which has neither the force and firmness of a man, nor the gentleness and sensibility of a woman." (Stephen Ambrose, *Undaunted Courage*, Simon & Schuster [1996], p. 65.)

bistro (or café) *n.*: **estaminet** [French]. ❖ A survey of the many **estaminets** on the cobbled Rue de Gand [in Lille, France,] convinced us that there was good food to be had. We selected Bistrot Lillois which, that evening,

was hearteningly full of locals, many alone and nursing a single course and a beer. (Nick Curtis, "France Moves a Lille Closer," *Evening Standard* [London], 4/30/2008.)

bit (as in trace or small amount of) *n.*: **tincture**. See *trace*

bitchy (woman) *n.*: **harridan**. See *shrew*

(2) bitchy (woman) *n.*: **termagant**. See *shrew*

(3) bitchy (woman) *n.*: **virago**. See *shrew*

(4) bitchy (woman) *n.*: **vixen**. See *shrew*

(5) bitchy (woman) *n.*: **Xanthippe**. See *shrew*

biting (as in . . . remarks) *adj.*: **astringent**. See *harsh*

(2) biting (as in sarcastic) *adj.*: **mordant** (or **mordacious**). See *sarcastic*

(3) biting *adj.*: **acidulous**. See *tart*

bits and pieces (usually, but not necessarily, in reference to literary . . . , or to disjointed quotations) *n.pl.*: **disjecta membra** [Latin]. ❖ [*The Stone Diaries* by Carol Shields] ends with the death of Daisy as images are torn from a long life and pinned to the spinning wheel of her mind. Fragments of overheard conversation cross the page—disembodied, eerily displaced; lost recipes, bits of official paper, shopping lists, book titles: the **disjecta membra** of a life float by. (Jay Parini, "Men and Women, Forever Misaligned," *New York Times*, 3/27/1994.)

(2) bits and pieces *n.*: **flinders**. ❖ However . . . the one woman [Prince Charles] desperately wanted to wed—was Anna Wallace, a sexy Scottish lass with a rip-roaring sense of humor. Alas, Anna also had a fiery temper . . . and one night at a palace ball it blew their affair to **flinders**. The prince carelessly ignored his ladylove for several hours, and when at last he went looking for her she was gone—forever. (Brad Darrach, "Prince Charles—A Dangerous Age," *People*, 10/31/1988, p. 96.)

bitter (to make . . .) *v.t.*: **envenom**. See *embitter*

(2) bitter (to the taste or smell) *adj.*: **acrid**. See *pungent*

bitterness *n.*: **bile**. ❖ But in the wake of the

feminist movement, some men are beginning to pipe up. In the intimacy of locker rooms and the glare of large men's groups, they are spilling their **bile** at the incessant criticism, much of it justified, from women about their inadequacies as husbands, lovers, fathers. (Sam Allis, "The Changing Family: Essay—What Do Men Really Want?" *Time*, 11/8/1990, p. 80.)

(2) bitterness (and ill-will that occurs when disputes about religion arise) *n.*: **odium theologicum**. See *intolerance*

(3) bitterness (as in acrimony) *n.*: **asperity**. See *acrimony*

(4) bitterness (spec. a resentment toward society or authority arising from repressed hostility, feelings of inadequacy, combined with a sense of powerlessness to express or act on those feelings) *n.*: **ressentiment** [French]. See *resentment*

(5) bitterness *n.*: **choler** (*adj.*: **choleric**). See *anger*

bizarre (as in unconventional) *adj.*: **outré** [French]. See *unconventional*

(2) bizarre (as in unusual) *adj.*: **selcouth**. See *unusual*

black (admirer of . . . persons) *n.*: **negrophile**. ❖ [*Negrophilia*, by Petrine Archer-Shaw,] reveals that the Parisian obsession with black culture in the 1920s went far beyond the exuberant Josephine Baker. . . . Archer-Straw concludes that the **negrophile's** embrace of blacks was "a very difficult relationship." (Emma Hagestadt, Books: Paperbacks, *Independent* [London], 9/30/2000.)

(2) black (one who fears or dislikes . . . persons) *n.*: **negrophobe**. ❖ [Lincoln's] death [was] at the hands of John Wilkes Booth, a **negrophobe** and white supremacist who was enraged at Lincoln's endorsement of black civil equality. (Allen Guelzo, "Proclamation Takes Some Hits: 'How Abe Lincoln Lost the Black Vote,'" *Washington Times*, 5/11/2002.)

(3) black (person who is one-fourth . . .) *n.*: **quadroon**. ❖ The racial calculus employed by both print and television media to describe [golfer Tiger] Woods is a throwback to the

racial classifications used in the Old South. People were classified as mulatto if they were half white and half black, **quadroon** if they were a quarter black, octoroon if an eighth and so on. (Henry Yu, "The Profit in Counting Tiger's Stripes," *Newsday*, 12/5/1996.)

black and white (as in colorless) *adj.*: **achromatic**. See *colorless*

(2) black and white (spotted) *adj.*: **piebald**. See *spotted*

black magic *n.*: **necromancy** [See also *magic*]. ❖ Scattered around Meszaros's den are the paraphernalia of **necromancy**: a desiccated frog, a glass-encased tarantula, a lead crystal ball and two skulls, one with nails through the cranium. . . . The bookshelves sag under the weight of tomes detailing spells, voodooism, the formation of covens, the enactment of jinxes and other black lore. (Julius Strauss, "International: Taxman Casts Spell on Witches," *Sunday Telegraph* [London], 1/11/1998.)

blackmail *n.*: **chantage**. See *extortion*

blackness (or tending toward . . .) *n.*: **nigrescense**. [This word can refer to the black race, as in this example, or to the color, as in the following example.] ❖ The second major perspective of Black racial identity development consists of the **nigrescence** [model which is] the developmental process through which one "becomes Black" (Helms, 1990). Here, Black does not refer to complexion, but the manner in which African Americans evaluate themselves and their reference group (Helms, 1990). (Reginald Alston, "Racial Identity and African Americans with Disabilities," *Journal of Rehabilitation*, 4/15/1996, p. 11.)

(2) blackness (or tending toward . . .) *adj.*: **nigrescent**. [This word can refer to the color, as in this example, or to the black race, as in the above example.] ❖ I doubt there is any Manhattan neighborhood where you can find more trash on the street of a Monday morning, or where you must endure louder blastings of reggaeton "music" in those **nigrescent** hours before the cock crows, than in Inwood. (Jason Lee Steorts, "Dominican Republican: Our Man

Up North in Manhattan," *National Review*, 12/31/2006.)

blackout *n.* **syncope**. See *fainting*

blame *v.t.*: **inculpate**. ❖ There is a [proposed bill that] would make it illegal for any state law enforcement agency to maintain gun ownership records. This means the next time police recover a gun used in a felony, the trail of clues would begin and end with the gun. . . . [T]his outrageous bill would eliminate access to crucial forensic information—information that is often as likely to exonerate the innocent as **inculpate** the guilty. (Christopher D. Brown, "Taking Gun-Ownership Records from Police Is 'Pandering Legislation,'" *Miami Herald*, 12/23/2003.)

(2) blame (oneself) *v.t.*: **self-flagellate** (*n.*: **self-flagellation**). See *criticize*

bland (though wanting to appear grandiose or having pretensions of grandeur) *adj.*: **blandiose** ❖ The trouble with the American entertainment industry is there just aren't enough out-of-the-closet and in-your-face Jews. We know they're there, their names (Coen, Spielberg, Spelling, et al.) are in the credits as producers and directors and writers. Some actors have hidden behind **blandiose** names so as to be ethnically indistinguishable (and sexually unclear in the case of Jamie Lee Curtis, [daughter of] Tony Curtis, [born] Schwartz). (Penny Starr, "Who's a Jew on American TV Imports," *Jerusalem Post*, 12/6/1996.)

(2) bland *adj.*: **anodyne**. ❖ [John] McEnroe seemed to save his snittiest behaviour for No. 1: perhaps he found the acoustics more effective there than on Centre Court. It says something about the **anodyne** nature of contemporary tennis that the sight of McEnroe in full flood tugs so at the heart-strings. (Andrew Baker, "Emotional Farewell to Home of the Tantrum," *Independent on Sunday*, 6/16/1996.)

blank slate *n.*: **tabula rasa**. ❖ The dominant picture of mind since the Renaissance— it is common to classical empiricism, which embraced consciousness, and modern behaviorism, which eschewed it—is the **tabula rasa**: the blank ledger upon which the environment leaves its trace as the mind is given whatever structure and content it finally possesses. (Colin McGinn, "The Know-It-All," *New Republic*, 2/23/1998.)

blaring *adj., adv., n.*: **fortissimo** [Italian]. See *loud*

blasé *adj.*: **pococurante**. See *apathetic*

blaze (with intense heat and light) *v.t., v.i.*: **deflagrate** (*n.*: **deflagration**). See *explosion*

bleak (and dismal and gloomy) *adj.*: **acherontic**. See *gloomy*

(2) bleak *adj.*: **Cimmerian**. See *gloomy*

bleed (as in escape from proper channels, esp. a liquid or something that flows) *v.i.*: **extravasate**. See *exude*

blemished (or impure) *adj., v.t.*: **maculate**. See *impure*

blend *v.t., v.i.*: **inosculate**. ❖ After recombination [of districts], New Foshan will be the third largest city in Guangdong. . . . According to CCTV, experts stated that New Foshan must solve the problems of disordered city planning, overlapping layout and economic structure duplication. Some experts even suggest to build a super-administrative organization . . . , just like Tokyo Area, and to further **inosculate** with Hong Kong, Macau and Taiwan. (AsiaInfo Services, "New Foshan Government Starts to Function," 1/13/2003.)

(2) blend (as in bring together) *v.t.*: **conflate**. See *combine*

(3) blend (esp. involving dissimilar elements) *n.*: **admixture**. See *mixture*

(4) blend *v.t.*: **amalgamate**. See *combine*

blended (as in composed of a mixture of items) *adj.*: **farraginous**. See *mixed*

(2) blended (as in interwoven) *v.t.*: **interleaved**. See *interwoven*

(3) blended (of things that cannot be . . .) *adj.*: **immiscible**. See *incompatible*

blending (or reconciling of opposing viewpoints or beliefs) *adj.*: **syncretic** (or **syncretistic**). See *reconciling*

blessing *n.*: **benison**. ❖ [Bill Gates] looked upon cable this week and saw that it was good and sprinkled $1 billion of his spare $9 billion or so over the industry, in an investment in Comcast, America's fourth-largest cable-television operator. Barely had the **benison** arrived from [Gates] when the nearest thing in the cable companies' lives to Lucifer—Rupert Murdoch—turned out to be an angel after all. (*Economist*, "Cable Television: Enter God, with $1 Billion," 6/14/1997.)

(2) blessing (as in giving one's stamp of approval) *n.*: **nihil obstat** [Latin]. See *approval*

(3) blessing (as in praise) *n.*: **approbation**. See *praise*

blind (almost, but not quite . . .) *adj.*: **purblind**. ❖ At birth he was sightless in one eye and **purblind** in the other, so his father, a craftsman who made tatamis (straw mats), sent him at age six to the city of Kumamoto, where he could attend a subsidized school for the blind. (James Walsh, "Shoko Asahara: The Making of a Messiah," *Time*, 4/3/1995, p. 30.)

(2) blind (window . . . with adjustable horizontal slats) *n.*: **jalousie**. See *window blind*

blindly (in a disorderly and hasty manner) *adv.*: **pell-mell**. See *disorderly*

blindness (at night) *n.*: **nyctalopia**. ❖ Medical science now recognizes a pathological condition called Carsonogeneous Monocular **Nyctalopia**: temporary blindness in one eye caused by watching the [*Late Show with Johnny Carson*] with one visual organ buried in the pillow and the other on the box. (People, "Top 25 Stars: Johnny Carson H-e-e-e-r-r-e's TV's Top," 5/4/1989, p. 20.)

(2) blindness *n.*: **amaurosis**. ❖ Still, Pernice's professional heartaches [as a golfer] were no match for what he felt in 1995, when his daughter, Brooke, was born with a retinal disorder, Leber's **amaurosis**, so severe that she was legally blind. (L. Jon Wertheim, "Golf Plus," *Sports Illustrated*, 8/31/1998, p. G10.*)*

blind spot *n.*: **scotoma**. ❖ [A] short-sighted driver could be much more dangerous than an elderly chap who can compensate for a small **scotoma** in his field of vision by keeping his head and eyes moving (as a good driver should). (Honest John, "Motoring: Not Seeing Eye to Eye with Authority," *Daily Telegraph* [London], 8/9/1997.)

blink (one's eyes) *v.i.*: **nictitate**. ❖ Thanks to thick fur and loose skin, a badger can turn around with amazing ease in a tight burrow. And a **nictitating** membrane protects its beady eyes from flying dirt. Oh does the dirt fly! (Les Line, "The Benefits of Badgers," *National Wildlife*, 12/10/1995, p. 18.)

blinking (spasmodic . . . of the eyes) *n.*: **blepharospasm**. ❖ It is an unsightly affliction. Victims of **blepharospasm** suffer from continual eyelid muscle spasms that clamp the lids closed for seconds to minutes. In effect, sufferers are left blind. (*Time*, Medicine: "Eye Misery Insurance Loss Halts Drug Test," 10/27/1986, p. 71.)

bliss *n.*: **beatitude**. ❖ When he gets to talking about his stewardship of the 49ers' offense, [quarterback] Steve Young often lapses into a dreamlike state usually associated with religious rapture. His eyes glaze over with a kind of gauzy joy. . . . [But the 49ers' poor showing on offense recently is] enough to shatter Young's **beatitude** like a concrete pie to the face. (John Crumpacker, "Sharing the Load," *Denver Rocky Mountain News*, 11/23/1997.)

(2) bliss *n.*: **felicity**. See *happiness*

blissful *adj.*: **Elysian**. ❖ [In one TV makeover show, a man] and his partner supposedly turned their rundown garden into an **Elysian** vision in the space of a weekend, using only a spade and elbow grease. He never did work out how the director managed to keep two-dozen navvies, a gang of landscape gardeners and the heavy-duty diggers permanently out of shot. (Greg Wood, "Sweet Science," *Independent on Sunday*, 1/7/2001.)

(2) blissful *adj.*: **beatific** (to make . . .) *v.t.*: **beatify**. See *joyful*

blissfulness (causing or tending to produce . . .) *adj.*: **felicific**. See *happiness*

blisters (producing or tending to produce . . . or an agent that does so) *adj., n.*: **vesicant**. ❖ **Vesicants** such as Lewisite and sulfur mustard can cause irritation to the mouth and skin with terrible blistering, and death is possible within 12 to 24 hours after exposure. (Thomas Inglesby, "The Germs of War; How Biological Weapons Could Threaten Civilian Populations," *Washington Post*, 12/9/1998.)

bloated (as in pompous or bombastic) *adj.*: **flatulent**. See *pompous*

(2) bloated (as in pompous or bombastic) *adj.*: **tumid**. See *bombastic* and *swollen*

(3) bloated (or disheveled in appearance) *adj.*: **blowsy** (or **blowzy**). See *disheveled*

(4) bloated *adj.*: **dropsical**. See *swollen*

block (up) *v.t.*: **occlude**. ❖ It has clearly been shown that there is a higher incidence of Sudden Infant Death Syndrome when infants are put to sleep on their stomachs. Also, pillows should not be used in an infant bed because of the possibility of **occluding** the airway. (Unsigned letter to the editor, *St. Louis Post-Dispatch*, 1/24/1996.)

blockage (total . . . , as in constipation) *n.*: **obstipation**. See *constipation*

blockhead *n.*: **jobbernowl** [British]. See *idiot*

(2) blockhead *n.*: **mooncalf**. See *fool*

blood (of, relating to, or tinged with) *adj.*: **sanguinolent**. ❖ [A German magazine] tried to bring the violence done to women in war right into 520,000 readers' homes. American artist Jenny Holzer used blood donated by eight German and Yugoslav women volunteers in her design for the cover, a black page with a white card glued to it carrying the **sanguinolent** message: "Anywhere women are dying, I am wide awake." (*Time*, Chronicles: Talk of the Streets, 11/29/1993, p. 12.)

(2) blood (to cover or stain with . . .) *v.t.*: **ensanguine**. See *stain*

bloodletting *n.*: **phlebotomy**. ❖ About 1.3 million Americans have a disorder called hemochromatosis, an ailment in which the body improperly metabolizes iron. There is an effective treatment, though: old-fashioned bloodletting. Each year, more than 100,000 Americans get regular "therapeutic **phlebotomies**." (Dana Hawkins, "Throwing Out

Good Blood," *U.S. News & World Report*, 9/1/1997.)

blood-red *adj.*: **incarnadine**. See *crimson*

bloodthirsty (one who is . . .) *n.*: **tricoteuse**. See *knitter*. [See the note at "knitter" for why this word can be synonymous with bloodthirsty.]

bloody *adj.*: **sanguinary**. ❖ [In] *The Patriot*, a sadistic British colonel and his soldiers provoke the peace-minded Mel Gibson into a bloody bout of reprisals. . . . The film performs a service by reminding us that this war was a good deal more **sanguinary** than most think— per capita, it took more American lives than any but the Civil War. (*Washington Post*, "The Fourth of July," 7/4/2000.)

(2) bloody *adj.*: **sanguineous**. ❖ [The movie] *Quills* . . . is obviously not for the squeamish or the high-minded. The film opens with a victim's-eye view of an oversize (by 10 feet) guillotine and a basketful of severed heads, as spectators cheer on the **sanguineous** spectacle. (Glenn Lovell, "Idolizing Iconoclasts," *San Jose Mercury News*, 12/16/2000.)

(3) bloody (to make . . .) *v.t.*: **ensanguine**. See *stain*

bloom (as in burgeon or expand; lit: bear fruit) *v.i.*: **fructify**. See *burgeon*

blooming (more than once per season) *adj.*: **remontant**. [This adjective is usually applied to roses, but not always, as shown in the following example.] ❖ Out at The Morton Arboretum in Lisle, magnolias are blooming [in August]. What's going on? The heavy rains seem to have startled these shrubs into sudden activity after the long dry spell in May and June sent them into a winterlike slowdown. They've been fooled into thinking it's spring. This **remontant** late-summer blooming is not uncommon in magnolias. (Beth Botts, "Some Trees Put On a Surprise Display," *Chicago Gardener*, 8/26/2007.)

(2) blooming *n.*: **efflorescence** (*v.i.*: **effloresce**). ❖ Almost two decades later, black writers and artists, musicians, dancers and actors find themselves in an era of creativity unrivaled in American history. The current

efflorescence may have begun with the literature and criticism by black women published in the early '80s, especially the works of Ntozake Shange, Michele Wallace, Alice Walker and Toni Morrison. (Henry Louis Gates Jr., "Black Creativity: On the Cutting Edge," *Time*, 10/10/1994, p. 74.)

(3) blooming *n.*: **florescence**. ❖ Today's [fireworks] displays unfold in time [like flowers]. It is not surprising that the similes are floral. Not only is their blossom short-lived; as in nature, these chemical **florescences** are designed, but not down to the last detail. Their beauty lies, as so often, in the conjunction of perfection and imperfection. (Hugh Aldersey-Williams, "A Flaming Liberty," *New Statesman*, 10/30/1998.)

blooper (as in a transposition of letters or sounds, which creates a comic effect, usually unintentionally) *n.*: **spoonerism** [after William Spooner, a British cleric, whose first recorded Spoonerism was when he said to a groom at the end of a ceremony: "It is now kisstomary to cuss the bride"]. ❖ My vote for the prince of **spoonerisms** goes to a young announcer I helped break in to broadcasting. . . . [The copy read:] Good evening, ladies and gentlemen. This is your invitation to join the gay groups at the beautiful Park Lane cocktail lounge." [Instead he said:] "Good ladies, evening and gentlemen. This is your invitation to join the gray goops at the Park Tail cocklane lounge." (Gene Amole, "Spoonerisms Can Bangle Words Beyond Melief," *Denver Rocky Mountain News*, 12/21/2000.)

(2) blooper (such as a slip of the tongue or malapropism) *n.*: **parapraxis**. See *blunder*

blossoming *n.*: **efflorescence** (*v.i.*: effloresce). See *blooming*

(2) blossoming *n.*: **florescence**. See *blooming*

blotched (or impure) *adj.*, *v.t.*: **maculate**. See *impure*

blue (sky-. . .) *adj.*: **cerulean**. ❖ In contrast, Bryant, blessed with a much larger canvas, produces vibrant watercolors of summer green,

golden wheat, and **cerulean** blue that recall the visual sweetness of a technicolor movie. (Terri Heard, "Reflections of a Black Cowboy," *Philadelphia Tribune*, 1/27/1995.)

blue-blooded (esp. those aspiring or pretending to be . . .) *adj.*: **lace-curtain**. See *well-bred*

blue-collar (class of people) *adj.*: **plebian**. See *common*

blues (having the . . . , as in being depressed) *n.*: **cafard** [French]. See *depression*

(2) blues (having the . . . , as in being depressed) *n.*: **megrims** (pl. of **megrim**) [also means migraine headache]. See *headache*

bluff *v.t.*: **four-flush** (*n.*: **four-flusher**). ❖ [I]f the [job applicant] obviously doesn't fit the slot you're looking for, give him a "half-pitch" on the shop and ask for a resume. Don't waste a lot of time, but don't **four-flush** him, either. You may need someone with his lack of qualifications in the future. (*Dealernews*, "Uncle Paul: My Reality Check Bounced," 9/1/1999, p. 66.)

blunder (verbal . . . such as a slip of the tongue or malapropism) *n.*: **parapraxis**. ❖ In this construction, TV news in the Soviet Union becomes a tableau in which the journalist is cowering beneath the fist of the state. . . . More than one **parapraxis** while reading the glad tidings about the leader's health, and the newsreaders (news bimbskis employed for their looks) could lose their jobs. (Andrew Billen, "And Here Is Today's News of the World . . . ," *New Statesman*, 6/27/1997, p. 42.)

blunt (as in to dull or deaden) *v.t.*: **narcotize**. See *deaden*

(2) blunt *v.t.*: **obtund**. See *deaden*

blur (one's vision as if by clouds, fog, or vapor) *v.t.*: **obnubilate**. See *obscure*

blurred (as in a failure to perceive something clearly or accurately or not being based on clear observation or analysis as a result of being cross-eyed, literally or figuratively) *adj.*: **strabismic**. See *cross-eyed*

blushing (as in reddening) *adj.*: **erubescent** (or **rubescent**). See *reddening*

blushing (spec. having a red glow) *adj.*: **rutilant**. See *red*

bluster (as in boastful behavior) *n*.: **rodomontade**. ❖ The best those commentators could do [to support President Clinton's claim that radio was being used to spread hatred] was to quote an imprudent remark by Gordon Liddy, but what he said—that if any official came to his house to requisition his pistol, he'd better shoot straight—was more **rodomontade** than a call to arms or hatred. (William F. Buckley, "What Does Clinton Have in Mind?" *National Review*, 5/29/1995, p. 70.)

(2) bluster (full of . . . and vanity) *adj*.: **vainglorious**. See *boastful*

blusterer (who often talks foolishness) *adj*.: **blatherskite**. See *babbler*

blustering (behavior) *n*.: **fanfaronade**. See *bravado*

boast (esp. about the accomplishments of a relative) *v.t., n*.: **kvell** [Yiddish]. ❖ Our visit to Yale was highlighted by the admissions officer informing [my son] Michael that he had been accepted for the fall term, and then genially turning to congratulate me and shake my hand. Now, as a Jewish mother, I can **kvell** with the best of them, but this was truly my son's moment in the sun, not mine. (Esther Berger, "One Family's Perspective," *Town & Country*, 7/1/2000.)

(2) boast (false . . . , esp. one that is designed to harm or prejudice another) *n*.: **jactitation**. ❖ So as to raise their status and expand their influence in foreign countries and regions, some Chinese companies use names with words like "China," "National," "Group," and "Holding Company." The Chinese Ministry of Commerce has published a circular to rule out such **jactitation**, requiring all Chinese-funded enterprises overseas to use names suited to their capacity and size. (Xinhua News Agency, "Government Regulates Naming of Overseas Chinese-Funded Companies," 2/24/2006.)

boaster (who often talks foolishness) *adj*.: **blatherskite**. See *babbler*

boastful (and vain) *adj*.: **vainglorious**. ❖ The 1935 trial of Bruno Hauptmann, arrested for the kidnapping and murder of Charles Lind-

bergh's infant son, featured [columnist] Walter Winchell at his most **vainglorious**. . . . When the jury found Hauptmann guilty, Winchell reportedly leaped to his feet and shouted to the press pack: "I predicted he'd be guilty! Oh, that's another big one for me!" (Walter Shapiro, Arts & Media, *Time*, 10/10/1994, p. 86.)

(2) boastful (talk or person) *n*.: **cockalorum**. [This word can refer either to the talk itself or to the person doing the talking, although in the latter sense, it is typically used in reference to one who is small in stature.] ❖ The Blackstone Group announced last Monday that it plans on stepping up its buying of debt securities. . . . The same day, Goldman Sachs announced it was infusing $3 billion into one of its funds in order to take advantage of current debt prices. . . . And Blackstone and Goldman's pronouncements were not a lot of **cockalorum**. Buyout firms are still flush with cash. (Matthew Sheahan, "LBOs: One Way or Another, LBO Firms May Help Clear Pipeline," *High Yield Report*, 8/20/2007.)

(3) boastful *adj*.: **thrasonical**. ❖ In his earlier days, Roald Dahl [author of *Charlie and the Chocolate Factory* and *James and the Giant Peach*] was a **thrasonical** bully. (Gerald Windsor, "Portrait of Another Malodorous Old Fart," *Sydney Morning Herald*, 5/7/1994.)

(4) boastful (and vain person) *n*.: **coxcomb**. See *conceited*

(5) boastful (as in vain, person) *n*.: **popinjay**. See *vain*

(6) boastful (behavior) *n*.: **rodomontade**. See *bluster*

(7) boastful (behavior, as in bravado) *n*.: **fanfaronade**. See *bravado*

(8) boastful (being in a state of . . . exultation or elation) *adj*.: **cock-a-hoop**. See *elated*

(9) boastful (person) *n*.: **Gascon** (act of being . . . *n*.: **Gasconade**). See *braggart*

bodies (fascination with or erotic attraction to dead . . .) *n*.: **necrophilia**. See *corpses*

(2) bodies (repository for dead . . .) *n*.: **charnel**. See *repository*

body (human . . . , or a representation of same,

with the skin removed so as to show the bones and musculature underneath) *n.*: **écorché** [French]. ❖ There is evidence too [in the exhibit] of homo-eroticism, even of quiescent homosexuality, in the long-limbed, muscular and classically handsome superheroes of mythology and history, their forms those of the **écorché** figures from which the skin has been stripped to reveal the long strong muscles and tendons that lie immediately beneath . . . (Brian Sewell, "The Dreamy Stuff of Nightmares," *Evening Standard* [London], 2/17/2006.)

(2) body (of or relating to the . . .) *adj.*: **corporeal**. ❖ What the two [dance] works share is an almost forensic interest in the **corporeal**; in what happens when you push limbs beyond beauty and pain. In the age of virtual reality, the [dance] company focuses on what Obarzanek calls "the vulnerable human body that's vicious and beautiful and ugly and sweating." (Michael Fitzgerald, The Arts/Dance, *Time International*, 9/13/1999, p. 69.)

body build (esp. as relating to tendency to develop disease) *n.*: **habitus**. See *physique*

bodyguards (esp. who protect an evil leader or dictator) *n.*: **Praetorian guard**. See *guard*

body odor (from foul-smelling sweat) *n.*: **bromidrosis**. See *sweat*

body rub (with lotion) *n.*: **embrocation**. (*v.t.*: **embrocate**) ❖ [Golfer Colin Montgomerie] twice needed treatment for a back injury during yesterday's third round and he is worried it could be the difference between him winning and losing the Deutsche Bank-SAP Open. . . . The combination of **embrocation**, manipulation and painkillers got Montgomerie through yesterday and remarkably he shot a seven under-par 65 to stay out in front. (Mark Garrod, "Golf: Monty Playing the Pain Game," *Birmingham Evening Mail*, 5/20/2002.)

body type *n.*: **somatotype**. See *physique*

bog *n.*: **fen**. See *swamp*

bogus (something . . . , as in sham) *n.*: **postiche**. See *sham*

boil down (the flavor or essence of something) *v.t.*: **decoct**. ❖ "Shopping is a form of entertainment," as Riggio phrases it. . . . [Consumers shop] to mingle with others in a prosperous-feeling crowd, to see what's new, to enjoy the theatrical dazzle of the display, to treat themselves to something interesting or unexpected. So Riggio learned to craft stores that **decoct** the pure elixir of the shopping experience. In 1989, he began to perfect the formula: a high-visibility, upscale, usually suburban location to draw the crowds where they live. (Myron Magnet, "Let's Go for Growth," *Fortune*, 3/7/1994.)

boisterous (girl) *n.*, *adj.*: **hoyden**. See *tomboy*

(2) boisterous (to engage in . . . revelry or merrymaking) *v.i.*: **roister**. See *revel*

(3) boisterous *adj.*: **strepitous**. See *loud*

bold (as in creative and/or original) *adj.*: **Promethean**. See *creative*

(2) bold (offensively . . . and conceited person) *n.*: **jackanapes**. See *conceited*

(3) bold (or courageous while under the influence of alcohol) *adj.*: **potvaliant**. See *courageous*

boldness (and daring) *n.*: **hardihood**. See *courage*

bombastic *adj.*: **tumid**. ❖ Nothing is easier than for educated persons to mock "I move the reference back," "I must consult my executive" and the rest of it [as used by the Shadow Cabinet of the British Labour Party]. But the **tumid** phrases and tedious procedures have a long and honourable history, going back to the artisans' societies of the early 19th century. (Alan Watkins, "Shadow Cabinet Hokey-Cokey: Right Leg In, Left Leg Out," *Independent on Sunday*, 7/14/1996.)

(2) bombastic (as in affected and high-flown use of language) *adj.*: **euphuistic**. See *affected*

(3) bombastic (behavior) *n.*: **rodomontade**. See *bluster*

(4) bombastic (esp. regarding speaking or writing style) *adj.*: **orotund**. See *pompous*

(5) bombastic (of speech or writing that is . . .) *adj.*: **fustian**. See *pompous*

(6) bombastic (speech or writing) *n.*: **grandiloquence**. See *pomposity*

(7) bombastic (style) *n.*: **ampollosity**. See *pompousness*

(8) bombastic *adj.*: **flatulent**. See *pompous*

(9) bombastic *adj.*: **magniloquent**. See *pompous*

(10) bombastic *adj.*: **turgid**. See *pompous*

bond (or tie) *n.*: **vinculum**. ❖ In the current Iran-US imbroglio, Afghanistan figures as the key to economically isolated Iran, prominent member of "Axis of Evil" that Mr. Bush is worried of. These reasons do not[,] however, override the importance of Indo-US strategic **vinculum** against perceived Chinese threat in the South and South East Asia. (M. Sakhawat Hussain, "Behind the US Diplomatic Initiative in South Asia," *Independent* [Bangladesh], 6/19/2002.)

(2) bond (as in chain or link) *n.*: **catenation** (*v.t.*: **catenate**). See *chain*

(3) bond (tendency of people to . . . with, or be attracted to, others who they perceive are similar to them) *n.*: **homophily**. See *associate*

(4) bond (together, as with glue) *v.t.*: **agglutinate**. See *adhere*

bondage (free from . . .) *v.t.*: **manumit**. See *emancipate*

(2) bondage *n.*: **thralldom**. ❖ We Western women, it appears, still have not shucked off male ideas of female beauty; the voluntary mutilation of plastic surgery bears witness to our **thralldom**. (Elizabeth Ward, "The Trouble with Women," *Washington Post*, 5/23/1999.)

bone (composed of, relating to, or resembling) *adj.*: **osseous**. ❖ If you want to get ahead—or get down to the bare bones of the matter—you could do very much worse than meet the interactive skeleton. It's a fascinating new multimedia construct developed by University College of London's department of medical physics and bioengineering. . . . For student and interested amateurs, a fascinating insight into all things **osseous**. (Joe Donnelly, "Shake, Rattle and Scroll," *Herald* [Glasgow], 8/31/1996.)

(2) bone (or tooth decay) *n.*: **caries**. See *decay*

bones (repository for . . . of the dead) *n.*: **charnel**. See *repository*

bonkers *adj.*: **doolally**. See *crazy*

bonus (as in extra or unexpected gift or benefit, sometimes as thanks for a purchase) *n.*: **lagniappe**. See *gift*

bon vivant (as in man about town) *n.*: **boulevardier**. See *man about town*

bony (composed of, relating to, or resembling) *adj.*: **osseous**. See *bone*

book (published in installments) *n.*: **fascicle** (pronounced FAS-i-kuhl). ❖ To prime the financial pump, the university press had taken the vulgar step of issuing the [Oxford English] dictionary in serial form, like a Dickens novel. . . . Like a car manufactured on Friday, this first **fascicle** contained subtle flaws [editor James] Murray himself polished out in subsequent issues that inched the alphabet forward. (Henry Kisor, "Making the Mighty Oxford English Dictionary," *Chicago Sun-Times*, 9/28/2003.)

(2) book (worshipper) *n.*: **bibliolater**. ❖ The disorderly bins outside a secondhand bookshop are like a potter's field. . . . Their uniform token price—ANY BOOK THIS BOX $1—signifies their all-but-worthlessness. It was in just such a **bibliolater's** boneyard that I happened upon Scarne on Teeko. (Blake Eskin, "Cards and Gambling Authority John Scarne Claimed to Have Invented One of the Greatest Board Games of All Time," *Washington Post*, 7/15/2001.)

(3) book (for ready reference like a guidebook) *n.*: **vade mecum** [Latin]. See *guidebook*

bookish *adj.*: **donnish**. [This word, which means characteristic of a university don (the equivalent of a university professor), can have a positive or a neutral connotation, as when used to mean scholarly or bookish, or a negative connotation, as when used to mean pedantic. An example of the former follows. An example of the latter is found under *pedantic*.] With his owlish spectacles and academic background, Glaxo's boss, Sir Richard Sykes, could easily be mistaken for a **donnish** research scientist. (*Economist*, "Waging Sykological Warfare," 1/28/1995.)

books (aversion to or fear of . . .) *n.*: **bibliophobia**. ❖ Elizabeth Dipple [in *Reading Contemporary Fiction*] is anxious to dispel readers' fears about contemporary texts. Perfect for sufferers from Nabokov-angst, Beckett-fear, Borges-terror, and general undirected **bibliophobia**. (*Times* [London], New Books, 4/7/1988.)

(2) books (extreme desire to own or collect . . .) *n.*: **bibliomania**. ❖ There are detailed lists of his reading, which ranged voraciously from the most arcane corners of medieval German literature and philosophy to every new Simenon mystery . . . and not least importantly, unflagging reports on his **bibliomania** and latest acquisitions. (David Stern, "Profane Illumination," *New Republic*, 4/10/1995, p. 31.)

(3) books (lover or collector of . . .) *n.*: **bibliophile**. ❖ "I've always been a bit of a **bibliophile**," says Arthur Ashe, the former Wimbledon and U.S. Open champion who, in the 1960s, started collecting books written by and about African-Americans. (Daphne Hurford, Books, *Sports Illustrated*, 11/4/1991, p. 88.)

(4) books (one who steals . . .) *n.*: **biblioklept**. ❖ The author was—and, he implies, may still be—a compulsive **biblioklept**. The first book he stole as a schoolboy was *Dracula*; but it was at Cambridge, in the vast, irresistible canyons of Heffer's bookshop, that Mr. Rayner's literary thievery began in earnest. (Ben Macintyre, "A Gentleman, a Scholar, a Thief," *New York Times*, 10/22/1995.)

(5) books (or artistic works created in the author's or artist's youth) *n.*: **juvenilia**. See *compositions*

(6) books (people who read too many . . .) *n.*: **bibliobibuli**. See *read*

bookworm *n.*: **bibliophage**. [This word, like bookworm itself, can have both a literal meaning, as in a worm that eats through the paste in book bindings, or a figurative meaning, namely one who is an ardent reader.] ❖ Bookstores in urban cores across America have been exiled to the suburbs or extinction by onslaughts from the Internet, the big chains, and huge spikes in downtown commercial rents. . . . Even New York has been savaged. **Bibliophages** consider Manhattan a lunar landscape today compared to what it offered five years ago. (Sam Allis, "Bookstores' Demise a Sad Chapter," *Boston Globe*, 5/23/1999.)

boor *n.*: **grobian**. ❖ Me, I like melted cheese on my hot dogs. And more often than not I slap plenty of hot sauce on my morning ration of scrambled eggs. Factor in the notion that I'm basically a loud-mouth **grobian** who'd rather guffaw than grimace, and there's little reason why I shouldn't be on the right side of [the band] Sex Mob and their second opus de squawk. (Jim Macnie, review of *Solid Sender*, *Down Beat*, 5/1/2000.)

(2) boor *n.*: **yahoo**. ❖ The Dallas Cowboys showed up at their hotel in Santa Monica and there were more guys with yellow Event Staff jackets on than there were **yahoos**. An NFL event staff guy who ordinarily likes to flex some crowd-control muscle was thoroughly disappointed. "This is America's Team?" he said, disgusted, looking for a **yahoo** to wrestle to the ground. (Richard Hoffer, Super Bowl XXVII: "Dear Phoenix," *Sports Illustrated*, 2/8/1993, p. 14.)

boorish (or dull or ignorant or obtuse or stupid) *adj.*: **Boeotian**. See *dull*

(2) boorish (person with respect to artistic or cultural values) *adj.*: **philistine**. See *uncultured*

boost (as in stimulus) *n.*: **fillip**. See *stimulus*

bootlicker (esp. someone who seeks to associate with or flatter persons of rank or high social status) *n.*: **tuft-hunter**. See *hanger-on*

(2) bootlicker *n.*: **lickspittle**. See *sycophant*

border *n.*: **selvage**. See *edge*

bordering (as in surrounding) *adj.*: **circumjacent**. See *surrounding*

bored *adj.*: **pococurante**. See *apathetic*

boredom (sometimes in matters spiritual, and sometimes leading to depression) *n.*: **acedia**. See *apathy*

(2) boredom (of life) *n.*: **tedium vitae** [Latin]. See *tedium*

boring *adj.*: **anodyne**. See *bland*

(2) boring (writer or speaker) *n.*: **dryasdust**. ❖ [The Congressional Budget Office's] recent study *Long-Term Budgetary Pressures and Policy Options* describes the economic future our children and grandchildren are likely to face. The report is written in the CBO's **dryasdust** style, but for anyone with a tolerance for numbers and an interest in policy, it is as scary as a Stephen King novel. (N. Gregory Mankiw, "Government Debt: A Horror Story," *Fortune*, 8/3/1998, p. 52.)

(3) boring (as in bland, though wanting to appear grandiose or having pretensions of grandeur) *adj.*: **blandiose**. See *bland*

(4) boring (as in insipid, intellectual nourishment, like baby food) *n.*: **pabulum** (also **pablum**). See *insipid*

(5) boring (passage or section in a book or work of performing art) *n.*: **longueur**. See *tedious*

(6) boring (lit. sleep-inducing) *adj.*: **soporific**. See *sleep-inducing*

(7) boring (as in uninteresting) *adj.*: **jejune**. See *uninteresting*

born (while being . . .) *adv.*: **aborning**. ❖ One idea, briefly debated, was to merge Olds, GM's oldest and weakest franchise, with Saturn, its youngest and strongest, so that Oldsmobiles would become step-up vehicles from Saturns. The idea died **aborning**, but it had merit; today Saturn outsells Olds. (Alex Taylor III, "Giants of the Fortune 500," *Fortune*, 4/28/1997, p. 94.)

(2) born (being . . . , as in coming into being) *adj.*: **nascent**. See *emerging*

(3) born (being . . . , esp. a dog) *v.t., v.i.*: **whelp**. See *birth*

born again *adj.*: **renascent**. See *reborn*

borrow (without real intent to repay, as in sponging off of) *v.t.*: **cadge**. See *mooch*

bosom (condition of having overly small . . .) *n.*: **micromastia**. See *breasts*

(2) bosom (condition of having overly large . . .) *n.*: **macromastia**. See *breasts*

bosomy *adj.*: **bathycolpian**. See *busty*

(2) bosomy *adj.*: **hypermammiferous**. See *busty*

boss *n.*: **padrone** [Italian]. ❖ [E]rmando Rosa [is an] Italian small-business man who lives for his company and his family and often melds the two. [He and his family] help run his eponymous machine-tool company, an arrangement that typifies the triangular relationship linking the **padrone**, the business and the family that is an enormous source of strength in the Italian economy. (John Wyles, Italy: "Being Small Is Best," *Time* International, 7/11/1994, p. 43.)

(2) boss (as in manager or overseer) *n.*: **gerent**. See *manager*

(3) boss (brutal . . . , as in taskmaster) *n.*: **Simon Legree**. See *taskmaster*

botch (esp. a golf shot) *v.t., n.*: **foozle**. ❖ I am not any good at golf. At all. I have played for years, but that has only increased the variety of skulls, yips and **foozles** I can produce. When I started, for example, I hit everything on a low banana slice to the right. Today, I have improved to the point where I have no idea where the ball will go. (C. W. Nevius, "It's Time for the Truth About Golf—It's a Game, Not a Sport," *San Francisco Chronicle*, 4/28/2002.)

bother (as in bully or browbeat) *v.t.*: **hector**. See *bully*

(2) bother (as in fuss, over a trifling matter) *n.*: **foofaraw**. See *fuss*

(3) bother (as in trouble) *n.*: **tsuris** [Yiddish]. See *trouble*

(4) bother *v.t.*: **chivvy**. See *pester*

(5) bother *v.t.*: **discommode**. See *inconvenience*

(6) bother *v.t.*: **incommode**. See *inconvenience*

bothered (as if by a witch or by unfounded fears) *adj.*: **hagridden**. See *tormented*

(2) bothered *adj.*: **in a dither**. See *flustered*

bothersome *adj.*: **pestiferous**. ❖ No sooner did a federal judge bar a hugely popular ban on telemarketing than the House approved legal repairs to keep the do-not-call list alive. . . . Washington is right to offer the country a way to bar one of the unrelenting annoyances of the modern age: dinner-time sales pitches by **pestiferous** telemarketers. Since June 27, more than 50 million phone lines were entered on a national do-not-call list. (*San Francisco Chronicle*, "Don't Call Us," 9/26/2003.)

(2) bothersome (as in repellent) *adj.*: **rebarbative**. See *repellent*

bottom (a fat . . .) *n.*: **steatopygia** (having a fat . . .) *adj.*: **steatopygic**). See *rear end*

(2) bottom (as in buttocks) *n.pl.*: **nates**. See *buttocks*

(3) bottom (as in buttocks) *n.pl.*: **fundament**. See *buttocks*

(4) bottom (having a hairy . . .) *adj.*: **dasypygal**. See *rear end*

(5) bottom (having a nicely proportioned . . .) *adj.*: **callipygian**. See *rear end*

bottom line (as in basically) *adv.*: **au fond** [French]. See *basically*

(2) bottom line (the . . . of a matter, as in the substance, the main point, the essence, etc.) *n.*: **tachlis** (esp. as in "talk tachlis") [Yiddish]. See *essence*

bounce (a child on one's knees) *v.t.*: **dandle**. ❖ The Village Green in New Milford, Conn., is a snapshot of New England charm: a carefully manicured lawn flanked by scrupulously maintained colonial homes. Babysitters **dandle** Gap kids in the wooden gazebo, waiting for commuter parents to return from New York. (Debra Rosenberg, "Generation Depressed," *Newsweek*, 7/10/1995.)

bound (as in set the boundaries of) *v.t.*: **delimit**. See *demarcate*

(2) bound (together by a close relationship) *adj.*: **affined**. See *connected*

boundary (as in sphere or realm) *n.*: **ambit**. See *realm*

bouquet *n.*: **nosegay**. ❖ Corsages are history—something from the '50s that should stay there. If you want the mother of the bride or the grandmother to have flowers, give her a two-inch **nosegay**. (Heidi K. Schiller, "T&C's Guide to the Perfect Wedding," *Town & Country*, 2/1/1998, p. 141.)

bourgeois (esp. one indifferent or antagonistic to artistic or cultural values) *adj.*: **philistine**. See *uncultured*

bow (down, often in a servile manner) *v.i.*: **genuflect**. See *kneel*

bowl (shallow . . . or cup with a handle) *n.*: **porringer**. ❖ We had a pewter **porringer** with a lid in the shape of a mountain that was a trophy my brother had won before the war. The German soldier was holding the bowl and trying to open the lid, but he couldn't. (Sarah Ballard, Skiing, *Sports Illustrated*, 12/2/1991, p. 14.)

boxing *n.*: **fistiana**. ❖ Tex Rickard got off the New York-to-Boston train at North Station in late November 1927 with a plan but no money, which is typical of a boxing promoter. . . . He would open a string of Madison Square Gardens around the country, creating the McDonald's of **fistiana**. (Ron Borges, "Garden's Roots: Seeds Planted in '28, When Boxing Was Only Attraction, *Boston Globe*, 12/11/1994.)

(2) boxing (against a shadow or imaginary foe) *n.*: **sciamachy**. See *shadowboxing*

boy (just entering manhood, esp. in the late teens) *n.*: **ephebe** (*adj.*: **ephebic**). ❖ All that's been accomplished by [the scandal involving Rep. Mark Foley] is to call into question one of the central erotic archetypes of gay male tradition—the **ephebic** beauty of boys at their muscular peak between the ages of 16 and 18. . . . In ancient Greek culture, an adult man could publicly profess his love for a young man without necessarily having sexual contact with him. (Interview with Camille Paglia, *Salon.com*, 10/27/2006.)

(2) boy (man who has sexual relations with a . . .) *n.*: **pederast**. See *sodomizer*

(3) boy (who has sexual relations with a man) *n.*: **catamite**. See *sex*

(4) boy (who is awkward and clumsy) *n.*: **hobbledehoy**. See *clumsy*

boyfriend (of a married woman) *n.*: **cicisbeo**. ❖ Walpole, meanwhile, attached himself to the young and beautiful (and married) Elisabetta Grifoni. These were bloodless infidelities condoned in Florence. Walpole became Elisabetta's **cicisbeo**. (Richard Edmonds, review of *A Golden Ring*, by Charles Hobday, *Birmingham Post*, 5/2/1998.)

(2) boyfriend (or man with whom one is in love or with whom one has an intimate relationship) *n.*: **inamorato**. ❖ Instead of his usual manic intensity, Jack Nicholson acts his reined-in, middle-aged mafioso with little more than a stiff upper lip to give his patient, expressionless face character. Kathleen Turner plays his lover, a classy California professional woman, thunderstruck with vibrant passion for her Brooklyn-born **inamorato**. (*Magill's Survey of Cinema*, review of *Prizzi's Honor*, 6/15/1995.)

(3) boyfriend *n.*: **swain**. See *suitor*

bra (narrow . . .) *n.*: **bandeau**. ❖ The best new bras feel good—and look sexy—thanks to extra-soft microfiber, smooth styling, and sophisticated colors. Our favorites: Three in One Convertible straps let you wear this **bandeau** as shown, crisscrossed, or even strapless. (Tina McIntyre, "Beauty & Style: Is Your Bra the Right Size?" *Parenting*, 9/1/2000, p. 63.)

brag (esp. about the accomplishments of a relative) *v.t., n.*: **kvell** [Yiddish]. See *boast*

braggart *n.*: **Gascon** (act of bragging *n.*: **Gasconade**) [based on stereotype of people from Gascon, France, as being braggarts]. ❖ Italian journalist Luigi Barzin . . . cites Edmond Rostand's fictional Cyrano as the quintessence of French character, at least as outsiders exaggerate it: the boastful, cocksure **Gascon** whose fellow provincials are defined in Rostand's play as "free fighters, free lovers, free spenders, defenders of old homes, old names and old splendors . . . bragging of crests and pedigrees." (James Walsh, "If Geography Is Destiny . . . ," *Time* International, 7/15/1991, p. 8.)

(2) braggart (who often talks foolishness) *adj.*: **blatherskite**. See *babbler*

bragging (and vain) *adj.*: **vainglorious**. See *boastful*

(2) bragging (behavior) *n.*: **rodomontade**. See *bluster*

(3) bragging (false . . . , esp. that which is designed to harm or prejudice another) *n.*: **jactitation**. See *boast*

(4) bragging (talk or person) *n.*: **cockalorum**. See *boastful*

(5) bragging *adj.*: **thrasonical**. See *boastful*

brain (congenital absence of) *n.*: **anencephaly**. ❖ **Anencephaly** occurs in the very early stages of pregnancy, when the neural tube—an embryonic structure that normally develops into the brain and spinal cord—fails to close. (David Grogan, Scene: "The Baby Killer," *People*, 9/27/1993, p. 86.)

brainless *adj.*: **excerebrose**. ❖ The **excerebrose** followers of Pastor White, many of whom are convicted felons . . . are nothing more than easy prey for the Pastor to manipulate into a wild frenzy of disruptive distraction. (Dvija Michael Bertish, quoted in Brett Oppegaard, "City Cultural Center: A New Approach to Old Issue," *Columbia*, 5/18/2003.)

brainstorming (spec. a final effort made by architectural students to complete a solution to a problem within an allotted time, but sometimes is used to refer to any kind of . . . or workshop session) *n.*: **charette** (or **charrette**). See *workshop*

brainwashing *n.*: **menticide**. ❖ An African-centered curriculum is also essential to repair the **menticide** afflicting our [African-American] youth through racism, cultural aggression and the imposition of a Eurocentric education on our children in the schools. (Ron Daniels, "Vantage Point: Redefining the Role of Schools in the African-American Community," *New Pittsburgh Courier*, 4/23/1994.)

branch out *v.i.*: **ramify**. [This word is related to, but distinct from, the more well-known noun "ramification."] ❖ Decisions made in Washington **ramify** around the world in ways that are often discomfiting or worse to those affected by them but who have no say in them. This is never going to be a source of American popularity, including among democracies. Others want influence over the United States, and who can blame them? (Tod Lindberg, "The Treaty of the Democratic Peace; What the World Needs Now," *Weekly Standard* [London], 2/12/2007)

brash (as in reckless) *adj.*: **temerarious**. See *reckless*

(2) brash (as in reckless) *adj.*: **harum-scarum**. See *reckless*

brashness *n.*: **impudicity**. ❖ What needs to be emphasized is that [stealing a bust of Edgar Allan Poe from a bank] is not the sort of shenanigan that would occur to just anyone. The notion would come only to one of unique sensibility—playful and rash, with a dash of **impudicity**. (Jack Matthews, "The Raven Caper and the Writing Curse," *Antioch Review*, 1/1/1994, p. 157.)

brassiere (narrow . . .) *n.*: **bandeau**. See *bra*

bravado *n.*: **fanfaronade**. ❖ Here's some other [adult education] courses that could capture the public imagination: . . . [Stripping]. **Fanfaronade** will take you through the steps necessary to become a confident exotic dancer. Each participant is expected to have partially completed a semester each of Tassel Making, Cracking Walnuts with Your Own Buttocks on Stage and Booking the Light Entertainment Circuit. (*Sydney Morning Herald*, "One Bourbon, One Scotch and One Gin," 7/1/2000.)

(2) bravado (person with . . .) *n.*: **Gascon** (an act of a person with . . . *n.*: **Gasconade**). See *braggart*

(3) bravado *n.*: **rodomontade**. See *bluster*

brave *adj.*: **doughty**. ❖ Well, finally—the president we deserve, a morally square peg in the Oval Office. . . . He is also, as it turns out, physically brave and uncannily resourceful under life-threatening pressure. And he looks a lot like the reliably **doughty** Harrison Ford. (Richard Schickel, The Arts/Cinema, *Time*, 7/28/1997, p. 69.)

(2) brave (and strong woman) *n.*: **virago**. See *woman*

bravery *n.*: **hardihood**. See *courage*

brawl (esp. public) *n.*: **affray**. ❖ [John] Lewis added to his own reputation for bravery when, after being invited to join the Congress of Racial Equality (CORE)'s Freedom Ride bus demonstration, in May 1961, he led the group into its first **affray**, entering the "Whites Only" waiting room in the Rock Hill, South Carolina, bus terminal and getting knocked down and bloodied by a band of local toughs. (Sean Wilentz, "The Last Integrationist: John Lewis' American Odyssey," *New Republic*, 7/1/1996, p. 19.)

brawny (having a . . . body build) *adj.*: **mesomorphic**. See *muscular*

brazen (as in being presumptuous; venturing beyond one's province) *adj.*: **ultracrepidarian**. See *presumptuous*

brazenness *n.*: **impudicity**. See *brashness*

break (as in pause) *n.*: **caesura**. See *pause*

(2) break (in a sentence from one construction to a second, grammatically inconsistent construction) *n.*: **anacoluthon**. See *shift*

breakable *adj.*: **frangible**. ❖ The red-gray, meringuelike substance ices some of the cave's surfaces and ledges like cake frosting, from a millimeter to several inches thick, and is so **frangible** you could cut it with a butter knife. (Peter Nelson, "The Cave That Holds Clues to Life on Mars," *National Wildlife*, 8/18/1996, p. 36.) See *fragile*

break apart (tending to . . . or disintegrate) *adj.*: **fissiparous**. See *break up*

breakdown (of a group or social structure as a result of lack of standards or values) *n.*: **anomie**. ❖ "All of a sudden," said drummer Jerry Carrigan, "nobody cared [about how the Elvis Presley recording session was going]. We all felt, What can we do to get this over with? He'd settle for anything." In keeping with the spirit of general **anomie**, Carrigan failed to show up at all the second day. (Guralnick, *Careless Love: The Unmaking of Elvis Presley*, Little, Brown [1999], p. 437.)

(2) breakdown (violent or turbulent . . . of a society or regime) *n.*: **Götterdämmerung** [German]. See *collapse*

(3) breakdown (of or relating to a . . . , as in downfall, esp. after an innocent or carefree time) *adj.*: **postlapsarian**. See *downfall*

(4) breakdown (as in downfall, esp. from

a position of strength) *n*.: **dégringolade** [French]. See *downfall*

break in (suddenly or forcibly) *v.i.*: **irrupt**. See *burst in*

breaking (act of . . . up into parts) *n*.: **fission**. See *splitting*

breaking out (as in bursting forth or through) *adj*.: **erumpent**. See *bursting*

break up (tending to . . . or disintegrate) *adj*.: **fissiparous**. ❖ But however novel, when Elizabeth II was crowned, the idea [that a royal family should be an ideal family] was a powerful one. It didn't last: with her sister and three of her four children divorced, the queen's clan is even more **fissiparous** than most modern families. (*Economist*, Britain: "Twenty-five Out of Fifty; Queen Elizabeth II," 6/1/2002, p. 31.)

(2) break up (or apart, into component parts) *v.i.*: **disaggregate**. See *separate*

breasts (condition of having overly small . . .) *n*.: **micromastia**. ❖ [An FDA-approved] synthetic human growth hormone . . . would also contribute to the idea that being short can and should be fixed. A scientist from Eli Lilly & Company spoke of being short as a "growth failure problem." . . . This reminded me that doctors promoting breast implants once talked of correcting "**micromastia**," which turned being flat-chested into pathology. (John Schwartz, Ideas & Trends: "The View from 5-Foot-3," *New York Times*, 6/22/2003.)

(2) breasts (condition of having overly large . . .) *n*.: **macromastia**. ❖ Aside from physical complications, **macromastia** can carry a heavy emotional burden. Dr. Renata Calabria . . . says most girls he treats with this condition are unhappy with their breast size because of the psychological issues that come with teasing and stares. Unfortunately, the only way to correct **macromastia** is with breast reduction surgery. (*Girls' Life*, "Boobs! An Owner's Guide," 10/1/2002.)

breathe *v.t.*: **aspirate**. See *inhale*

breathing (temporary absence or cessation of) *n*.: **apnea** (*adj*.: **apneic**). ❖ They have a potentially life-threatening health condition even they have trouble describing, since it affects them only when they're deeply asleep. It's called sleep **apnea**, and it means that every night after they doze off, they go through regular periods in which they completely stop breathing. (Donovan Webster, "Dead Tired," *Men's Health*, 3/1/2002, p. 119.)

(2) breathing (characterized by loud snoring or . . . sounds) *adj*.: **stertorous**. See *snoring*

(3) breathing (heavily) *adj*.: **suspirious** (*v.t.*: **suspire**). See *panting*

breathing space (as in adequate space for living) *n*.: **lebensraum** [German; sometimes cap.]. ❖ Even the most gung-ho frontier boosters admit that Alaska is no longer the kind of wild and woolly place it was when the gold miners rushed in 100 years ago. . . . On the other hand, even if it is not the frontier it once was, it still has space, space, space, residents said, and that **lebensraum** is stamped on the state's psyche. (Carey Goldberg, "Has the Modern Age Overtaken 'The Last Frontier'?" *Minneapolis Star Tribune*, 8/15/1997.)

breeze (gentle . . .) *n*.: **zephyr**. ❖ From the south, there was a warm wind blowing, gentle **zephyrs** that barely rippled the surface of Long Island Sound. (Nick Karas, Outdoors: "Striped Bass Fishing on an Ideal Evening," *Newsday*, 10/13/1992.)

breezy (as in relaxed and easygoing) *adj*.: **dégagé** [French]. See *easygoing*

bribe (or protection money) *n*.: **Danegeld** (or **Danegelt**). See *protection money*

bribery (open to . . .) *adj*.: **venal**. See *corruptible*

bribes (one who accepts . . .) *n*.: **boodler**. See *corrupt*

bribe-taker *n*.: **boodler**. See *grafter*

bric-a-brac (esp. trivial or worthless) *n*.: **trumpery**. See *junk*

bride (personal possessions of) *n*.: **trousseau**. ❖ Crown Prince Naruhito of Japan & Masako Owada [were married on] June 9, 1993, [in] the Imperial Palace, Tokyo. The dress . . . reportedly cost $300,000. . . . [M]emorable detail: In the bride's **trousseau** was a small sword. Tradition dictates that it be used for self-defense or, in the case of dishonor such as adultery, suicide. (Hilary Sterne, "The Royals: The Princess Brides," *In Style*, 6/1/1999, p. 143.)

bridge (situated across a . . .) *adj.*: **transpontine**. ❖ The galleries of the Royal Academy of Arts have been transformed into a watery Lilliput by "Living Bridges," a celebration of the inhabited bridge. Visitors peer down at 20-odd immaculate models of bridges ancient and modern, extant and imagined, all of which have higher ambitions than the mere facilitation of **transpontine** traffic. (*Independent* [London], "The Weasel," 11/23/1996.)

brief (as in transient or fleeting) *adj.*: **evanescent**. See *transient*

(2) brief (saying) *n.*: **gnome** (*adj.*: **gnomic**). See *catchphrase*

(3) brief (speech or writing being very . . . , as in terse) *adj.*: **elliptical**. See *terse*

bright (as in shining . . .) *adj.*: **effulgent**. ❖ It's a glorious afternoon of **effulgent** sunshine and fresh western breezes. (John Brant, "Formula for Success," *Runner's World*, 11/1/1995, p. 78.)

(2) bright (as in shining . . .) *adj.*: **refulgent**. ❖ As a **refulgent** star of the [Communist] movement—as indeed the "purest Bolshevik writer ever to function in the United States"—Chambers involved himself in various projects. (Sam Tanenhaus, *Whittaker Chambers*, Random House [1997], p. 73.)

(3) bright (as in shining . . . , like lightning) *adj.*: **fulgurant**. ❖ The more we know about Hitler, the more enigmatic he—or rather, his **fulgurant** success—becomes. Here was a man without character, or with a most uninspiring personality. He had no vices; he did not drink or smoke, and he did not really care for women. . . . "Outside politics," Kershaw writes, "Hitler's life was largely a void." (Istvan Deak, "The Making of a Monster," *New Republic*, 4/12/1999.)

(4) bright (as in emitting flashes of light) *adj.*: **coruscant**. See *glittering*

(5) bright (as in happy and cheerful) *adj.*: **eupeptic**. See *cheerful*

(6) bright (as in radiant or glowing) *adj.*: **lucent**. See *glowing*

(7) bright (esp. as to talent, wit, or ability) *adj.*: **lambent**. See *brilliant*

(8) bright (softly . . .) *adj.*: **lambent**. See *shimmering*

brilliance (of performance or achievement) *n.*: **éclat**. See *success*

brilliant (esp. as to talent, wit, or ability) *adj.*: **lambent**. ❖ TV is about to become home to a pair of unusual British detectives. First, the medieval. On PBS, Sir Derek Jacobi (*I, Claudius*) portrays Brother Cadfael, the 12th-century Benedictine monk and hero of a popular series of mysteries by Ellis Peters (the nom de plume of Edith Pargeter). This [show] is a sort of *Murder, He Scribed*, illuminated by Jacobi's **lambent** talent. (David Hiltbrand, Picks & Pans, *People*, 1/16/1995, p. 13.)

(2) brilliant (as in shining brightly) *adj.*: **effulgent**. See *bright*

(3) brilliant (as in shining brightly) *adj.*: **fulgurant**. See *bright*

(4) brilliant (as in shining brightly) *adj.*: **refulgent**. See *bright*

(5) brilliant (like a diamond) *adj.*: **diamantine**. See *diamonds*

bring (together) *v.t.*: **colligate**. See *unite*

British (exaggerated fondness for . . . manners, customs, styles, etc.) *n.*: **Anglomania**. ❖ Within a relatively short time dandyism swept across the Channel to capture French fashion in a wave of **Anglomania**. While the British wore fitted jackets, the French made waists so tight they could barely breathe. English shirt collars reached up to the cheekbone; French collars almost obscured the vision. (G. Bruce Boyer, "The Return of Dandyism," *Forbes*, 3/9/1998, p. 248.)

(2) British (admiration of . . . manners, customs, styles, etc.) *n.*: **Anglophilia**. ❖ [Y]ou would expect George herself to be as British as high tea at Brown's Hotel. Not so. Born in Ohio, she grew up in northern California and now lives outside L.A., just a mile from the Pacific. Yet her rampant **Anglophilia**, which she says took root during a summer in England at age 16, has resulted in six Brit-based novels. (Marjorie Rosen, Pages: "No True Brit," *People*, 8/23/1993, p. 59.)

(3) British (fear, distrust, or disliking of . . . manners, customs, styles, etc.) *n.*: **Anglophobia**. ❖ The experience [of traveling around Europe] bred in the Colonel a lifelong love for the plainness of the American Midwest and an undying distaste for the Old World, particularly for England. His **Anglophobia** was world-class, though it never extended to his wardrobe, which was pure Savile Row, or his preference in athletics, which was polo. (Andrew Ferguson, Books in Review, *American Spectator*, 9/1/1997.)

brittle (as in breakable) *adj.*: **frangible**. See *breakable*

broad (and flat, like a spatula) *adj.*: **spatulate**. See *flat*

(2) broad (as in widespread) *adj.*: **pandemic**. See *widespread*

(3) broad (as in widespread) *adj.*: **regnant**. See *widespread*

(4) broad (in scope or applicability) *adj.*: **ecumenical**. See *universal*

broaden (in scope) *v.t.*: **aggrandize**. See *expand*

broad-minded *adj.*: **latitudinarian**. See *open-minded*

broadness (as in breadth of inclusiveness) *n.*: **catholicity** (*adj.*: **catholic**). See *universality*

broken-down (and/or worn-out) *adj.*: **raddled**. See *worn-out*

(2) broken-down (as in decrepit) *adj.*: **spavined**. See *decrepit*

brood (as in sulk) *v.t.*: **mump** [British]. See *sulk*

brooding (or grumpy mood) *n.pl.*: **mulligrubs**. See *grumpiness*

brook (small) *n.*: **rivulet**. See *stream*

broom (esp. made of twigs) *n.*: **besom**. ❖ The hit Harry Potter movie has sparked a magical spin-off for a Golden Bay man who has almost sold out of brooms. . . . Mr Greer said even though he had not promoted his **besom** business in conjunction with the movie, par-

ents have been buying the smaller ones for children. (Loney Kelly, "Wizardry Sparks Busy Spell," *Nelson Mail* [Nelson, New Zealand], 1/16/2002.)

brothel *n.*: **bagnio**. ❖ Minna [Everleigh] and her older sister, Ada, opened what would become the best little bordello in Chicago and, for a time, one of the best known in the world. . . . Raised in a prosperous Southern family, the sisters fled bad marriages to become touring actresses and ended up in Chicago after running a **bagnio** in Omaha during the Trans-Mississippi Exposition. (Louise Kiernan, "Events That Shaped Chicago," *Chicago Tribune*, 4/1/1997.)

brotherhood (as in fellowship or association) *n.*: **sodality**. See *fellowship*

browbeat *v.t.*: **hector**. See *bully*

brownish-red *adj.*: **ferruginous**. See *rust*

brown-nose *v.t.*: **bootlick**. See *kowtow*

brown-noser (esp. someone who seeks to associate with or flatter persons of rank or high social status) *n.*: **tuft-hunter**. See *hanger-on*

(2) brown-noser *n.*: **lickspittle**. See *sycophant*

browse (a quick cursory . . .) *n.*: **Cook's tour**. See *scan*

brush (as mass of bushes or shrubs) *n.*: **boscage**. See *bushes*

brutal (as in cruel) *adj.*: **fell** (*n.*: **fellness**). See *cruel*

(2) brutal (in the manner of an oppressive and despotic organization) *adj.*: **jackbooted**. See *oppressive*

(3) brutal (spectacle in which shame, degradation, or harm is inflicted on a person, often for the enjoyment of onlookers) *n.*: **Roman holiday**. See *spectacle*

bucolic (as in a place that is . . . , rustic, and simple) *adj.*: **Arcadian**. See *pastoral*

budding (as in coming into being) *adj.*: **nascent**. See *emerging*

buffalo (of, relating to, or resembling) *adj.*, *n.*: **bovine**. ❖ [In filming the movie *Dances with Wolves*,] the live, hoofed extras used in the hunt—some 2,300 buffalo from the herd of South Dakota rancher Roy Houck—were unpredictable. Wranglers worked for six hours to round up the fidgety, cantankerous, 1,600-lb. **bovines** and get them charging. (*People*, "Dances with Buffaloids," 3/27/1991, p. 100.)

buffer (usually in the form of buffer states, against nations considered potentially aggressive or ideologically dangerous) *n*.: **cordon sanitaire.** [French. The term is also often used figuratively to refer to any kind of buffer created to protect against something considered dangerous or unwanted.] ❖ [The argument for expanding NATO to the East is that] expansion of NATO could isolate Russia. Military alliances are always directed against some potential adversary; thus any strengthening of NATO is to be seen as affecting Russia's security interests. By embracing new members, NATO would create a **cordon sanitaire** separating Russia from the West. (Janusz Onyszkiewicz, "Why NATO Should Expand to the East; A Polish View," *Washington Post*, 1/6/1994.)

buffoon (who is sometimes boastful) *n*.: **Scaramouch.** ❖ Q—I can't seem to get a straight answer. Where will the Dow Jones averages be one year from now? A— . . . Because your question commands a "yes, but and if" answer, only a **Scaramouch** or a blind dog would venture an opinion in the market's direction. (Malcom Berko, "Bears Make Headlines, but . . . Likelihood That Dow Will Make New Highs Continues to Rise," *Chicago Tribune*, 8/20/1993.)

(2) buffoon *n*.: **balatron.** ❖ In the 2004 People vs. the Pros event at Pinehurst, [golf amateur] Phil Johnson of McKinney, Texas, defeated [golf pro Gary] McCord in a sudden death playoff. "The demeaning . . . has lived with me for too long," said McCord. "[In the 2006 event,] I plan to strike with lightning force and impale my competitor with verbal assaults that will render him a drooling **balatron**." (PR Newswire, "People vs. the Pros Returns to Pinehurst in 2006," 6/8/2006.)

(3) buffoon (one who resembles a short, fat . . . , as in clown) *n*.: **Punchinello.** See *clown*

bug *v.t.*: **chivvy**. See *pester*

bug-eyed *adj*.: **exophthalmic**. ❖ And then the conversation turns to condoms. McIlvenna hates condoms. They're antisex. They're stupid, and bad medicine. Suddenly, he is furious. Up go the lids. The eyes are practically **exophthalmic**: "The hell with condoms!" he spews. "I don't have faith in condoms!" (Rene Chun, "The Goo That Saved the World," *Esquire*, 1/1/1998.)

bugs (feeding on . . .) *adj*.: **entomophagous**. ❖ That's right, bugs are good food. At least that's the thrust behind the Eatbug.com Web site. Run by a 17-year old girl, it's a two-year-old online guide for insect eaters. From raising and slaughtering, to cooking and eating, this site has everything you never wanted to know about the gentle art of being **entomophagous**. (Edward Mazza, "Weird Wide Web," *New York Daily News*, 5/28/2000, p. 9.)

(2) bugs (of or relating to . . .) *adj*.: **entomic**. See *insects*

(3) bugs (sensation that . . . are crawling on you) *n*.: **formication**. See *insects*

(4) bugs (study of . . .) *n*.: **entomology**. See *insects*

build (cheaply and flimsily) *v.t.*: **jerry-build**. ❖ In truth, Britt is a sort of pioneer: His home, however, is a **jerry-built** wigwam on state-owned land near Boston's Chestnut Hill—a haute community of $500,000 mansions and country club sensibilities. (Cable Neuhaus, "Main Street: Facing Eviction from His Boston Hovel, Hermit Bill Britt Pleads There's No Place Like Home," *People*, 4/13/1987, p. 61.)

(2) build (as in physique) *n*.: **somatotype**. See *physique*

builder (of houses, spec. a carpenter) *n*.: **housewright**. See *carpenter*

building (art of . . . , esp. large buildings) *n*.: **tectonics**. See *construction*

built-in (as in innate) *adj*.: **connate**. See *innate*

(2) built-in *adj*.: **immanent**. See *inherent*

bulb-shaped (or rounded) *adj*.: **bulbous**. ❖ Like the coupe, its styling is reminiscent of the **bulbous** Porsche ragtops of the late 1950s and early '60s, with rounded contours and an industrial-strength high tech interior. (Frank

Aukofer, "Audi Gets TT Roadster Right," *Washington Times*, 5/19/2000.)

bulging (as in swollen or distended) *adj*.: **tumid**. See *swollen*

(2) bulging (as in swollen) *adj*.: **dropsical**. See *swollen*

(3) bulging (marked by . . . eyes) *adj*.: **exophthalmic**. See *bug-eyed*

(4) bulging (used often of body parts such as the penis) *adj*.: **tumescent**. See *swollen*

bull (of or resembling) *adj*.: **taurine**. ❖ The worm of doubt that really eats at market watchers **taurine** and ursine [bull and bear] is the high price/earnings multiple, recently about 24.4 for the S&P 500. (Terence P. Pare, "Finding Buys When Stocks Are High," *Fortune*, 10/26/1992, p. 16.)

bullfight *n*.: **corrida**. ❖ The bulls were in a corral, swishing their tails to ward off hordes of flies. They came in a variety of colors—black, brown, gray and even chestnut—and weighed about 900 pounds each. . . . They seemed calm, but that would change the instant the **corrida** started. (Bill Barich, Bullfighting, *Sports Illustrated*, 5/15/2000, p. R28.)

bullfighting (of or relating to) *adj*.: **tauromachy**. ❖ Animal rights activists are trying to close America's only bullfighting school—where, instead of facing a raging bull, students armed with wooden swords fight an instructor waving a pair of horns and snorting loudly. The Humane Society claims that although the California Academy of **Tauromachy**, in San Diego, does not use real bulls, it nevertheless desensitizes people to the "cruelty actually suffered by a bull in a ring." (Tunku Varadarajan, "Matador School a Red Rag to Activists," *Times* [London], 9/15/1997.)

bullish (as in one habitually expecting an upturn in one's fortunes, sometimes without justification) *adj*.: **Micawberish** (*n*.: **Micawber**). See *optimistic*

(2) bullish (esp. blindly or naively) *adj*.: **Panglossian**. See *optimistic*

bully *v.t*.: **hector**. ❖ I don't know about you but I'm getting mighty sick of Wilfred Brim-

ley **hectoring** me about Quaker Oats [in the TV commercial]. (Tony Kornheiser, *Pumping Irony*, Times Books [1995], p. 216.)

(2) bully (as in intimidate) *v.t*.: **bogart**. See *intimidate*

bum (off of) *v.t*.: **cadge**. See *mooch*

(2) bum *n*.: **clochard** [French]. See *vagrant*

bumbler (habitual . . .) *n*.: **schlemiel**. [Yiddish. The counterpart to this word is "schlimazel," a perpetually unlucky person. Thus, the schlemiel will spill his soup and it will land on the schlimazel.] ❖ Excited by the applause and growing confident, Avner seems to improvise ways to entertain the audience, finding and balancing a ladder on his chin, and walking across a rope. . . . [B]y the end of the show, Avner has transformed himself from an inept bumbler into a confident, occasionally competent performer. . . . "I want the audience to care about this poor **schlemiel** who is trying to do something beyond his capabilities because he wants to please the audience." (Patricia Lerner, "Li'l Avner," *Los Angeles Times*, 2/10/1991.)

bunch (of riders in a bike race) *n*.: **peloton** [French]. See *cluster*

bundle (as in group) *n*.: **gaggle**. See *group*

(2) bundle (of objects, people, or ideas) *n*.: **congeries**. See *collection*

bungle (esp. a golf shot) *v.t., n*.: **foozle**. See *botch*

bungler (habitual . . .) *n*.: **schlemiel** [Yiddish]. See *bumbler*

buoyancy (as in dancer's seeming ability to float) *n*.: **ballon** [French]. See *float*

buoyant (as in exuberant) *adj*.: **yeasty**. See *exuberant*

burden (which is oppressive) *n*.: **incubus**. ❖ The essays range over other topics, including attempts by some German historians in the 1980s to liberate Germans from the **incubus** of the Holocaust by placing it within the broader context of other mass murders of the twentieth century, especially those in Stalin's Soviet Union. (Daniel E. Rogers, "Murder in Our Midst," *National Forum*, 1/1/1997, p. 44.)

(2) burden *v.t., v.i., n*.: **cark**. See *worry*

bureaucracy (as in actions of government officials who are pompous but inefficient) *n.*: **bumbledom** [after a character in *Oliver Twist,* by Charles Dickens]. ❖ . . . Congress [has created a new job] to help a city [Washington, D.C.] with severe managerial and operational problems. [The appointee] will be responsible for . . . making sweeping changes in no less than 80 percent of the government. It's a tall order for someone new to Washington and to that unresponsive bureaucratic **bumbledom** known locally as the District government. (*Washington Post,* "The CMO's Challenge," 12/24/1997.)

bureaucrat (subordinate . . .) *n.*: **satrap**. [This word has various definitions, including (1) a leader or ruler (see *leader*), (2) a prominent or notable person (see *bigwig*), (3) a henchman (see *henchman*), (4) a bureaucrat, and (5) the head of a state acting either as a representative or under the dominion and control of a foreign power (see *ruler*). This is an example of the fourth definition. Often—but not always—it has a negative connotation. ❖ [T]enure is an idea whose time has gone. [It has deteriorated into] a cover for incompetence [and] an instrument of bureaucratization. Like the **satraps** of communism's dying empire, the members of the professoriate are insulated in their warrens of privilege and indifference, answerable to no one except themselves; but the bureaucrats of Eastern Europe are on the run, and so too in time will be tenure's apologists. (Jonathan Yardley, "Tenure, the Overdue Target," *Washington Post,* 1/8/1990.)

burgeon (lit. bear fruit) *v.i.*: **fructify**. ❖ What distinguishes her work is an ability, if not need, to write with her senses as well as her intellect. The sights and sounds of what she calls Hong Kong's "**fructifying** untidiness" are abundant and enthusiastically conveyed. (R. Z. Sheppard, review of *Wind and Water,* by Jan Morris, *Time,* 1/16/1989, p. 72.)

burglar (as in thief, caught red-handed) *n.*: **backberend**. See *thief*

burial (ground) *n.*: **necropolis**. See *graveyard*

burly (having a . . . body build) *adj.*: **mesomorphic**. See *muscular*

burn (with intense heat and light) *v.t., v.i.*: **deflagrate** (*n.*: **deflagration**). See *explosion*

burning (of, relating to, or resulting from) *adj.*: **pyric**. ❖ Still, most of us will sometimes long for a fire—for sociability, to grill a trout, to bake bread, or simply to avoid technology. So when the **pyric** urge does strike, first think habitat. (Ted Kerasote, "How to Build a Fire in 1996," *Sports Afield,* 3/1/1996, p. 18.)

(2) burning (as in of or relating to dog days of summer) *adj.*: **canicular**. See *dog days*

(3) burning (of heretics at the stake) *n.*: **auto-da-fé**. See *execution*

(4) burning (or prickling sensation on skin) *n.*: **paresthesia**. See *prickling*

burp (as in belch) *v.t., v.i.*: **eruct**. See *belch*

burrowing (adapted for . . .) *adj.*: **fossorial**. See *digging*

burst in (suddenly or forcibly) *v.i.*: **irrupt**. ❖ The Summer House (Samuel Goldwyn) proves again that even if you can't teach an old dog new tricks, the old tricks can still be amusing when neatly done. This film is one more go-round with the gimmick of the colorful stranger **irrupting** into some colorless lives and improving them. (Stanley Kauffmann, "The Summer House," *New Republic,* 1/10/1994, p. 31.)

bursting (forth or through) *adj.*: **erumpent**. ❖ The sustainability of [Voice over Internet Protocol] may be the deciding factor in the newly **erumpent** turf war between cable and the Bells, but it's too soon to tell. VoIP is still in its voice-cracking pubescent phase, and has a ways to go before it can reach its full potential, which is to become a workaday bundled offering. (Anthony Crupi, "Ask Not for Whom the Bell(s) Toll," *CableWorld,* 9/8/2003.)

burying (act of . . . someone alive) *n.*: **vivisepulture**. ❖ [The drama of the National Spelling Bee] can create the suffocating sense, certainly for the contestants' parents, of being subject to **vivisepulture** in a sarcophagus. (Linda Campbell, "Spellbound, Indeed," *Fort Worth Star-Telegram,* 6/1/2006.)

bushes (mass of . . .) *n.*: **boscage**. ❖ He also views the Allied nighttime drop of the 82nd and 101st Airborne in the **boscage** country . . . [as] a mistake and believes it would have been better to have landed them at first light. He faults Allied intelligence for not recognizing the difficulty of fighting in the hedgerows, thick bushes [that] enclosed every Normandy field and farm and provided natural defenses for the Germans. (Leah Rawls Atkins, review of *D-Day, June 6, 1944: The Climactic Battle of World War II*, by Stephen Ambrose, *National Forum*, 9/1/1994, p. 45.)

busty *adj.*: **bathycolpian**. ❖ [The Duchess of York] has ordered 12 new outfits from the London couturier Isabell Kristensen. [Kristensen] was unwilling to comment on the duchess's style, other than to say that her influences for this season's collections have been twofold: the **bathycolpian** cartoon character Jessica Rabbit and reed-slender Audrey Hepburn. "One of my great specialities is the corset," she says. "And they are padded for both bust and hips." (*Times* [London], "Haught Couture," 6/1/1995.)

(2) busty *adj.*: **hypermammiferous**. ❖ Salma Hayek officially earns the title of this year's Miss Golden Globe. There are only a few women in the world who can put huge, heaving yabbos on display and still come off as chic and refined, and the majestically **hypermammiferous** actress is one of them. She's a standout—literally and figuratively—in a va-va-voomy beige Bottega Veneta gown that accentuates her Jayne Mansfield-meets-Jessica Rabbit silhouette. (www.filesnews.com, "Golden Globes Hotties," 1/15/2009.)

busybody *n.*: **quidnunc**. ❖ To become enriched by the information that Beethoven might have had syphilis is of great moment to the **quidnunc**, but to do a forensic analysis of Beethoven's harmonics might give insight into what went on under his scalp and benefit us all. (Unsigned letter to the editor, *Time*, 7/1/1996, p. 5.)

(2) busybody (as in officious meddler who frustrates the success of a plan by stupidly getting in the way) *n.*: **marplot**. See *meddler*

butchery (as in slaughterhouse) *n.*: **abattoir**. See *slaughterhouse*

butler *n.*: **major-domo**. ❖ Mr. Roberts believes his previous jobs have prepared him for a life as a **major-domo** and considers his personality well suited to service. These days butlers are not so much man-servants à la Jeeves, as managers and administrators who may be responsible for 20 or 30 staff. (Barrie Clement, "Servants Back in Below-Stairs Britain," *Independent*, 7/1/1996.)

butt (a fat . . .) *n.*: **steatopygia** (having a fat . . . *adj.*: **steatopygic**). See *rear end*

(2) butt (as in buttocks) *n.pl.*: **nates**. See *buttocks*

(3) butt (as in buttocks) *n.pl.*: **fundament**. See *buttocks*

(4) butt (having a hairy . . .) *adj.*: **dasypygal**. See *rear end*

(5) butt (having a nicely proportioned . . .) *adj.*: **callipygian**. See *rear end*

butterfly (or, relating to, or resembling) *adj.*: **lepidopterous**. ❖ At the end of winter, as the weather warms up, the monarch [butterflies] mate in what can only be described as an orgy. "Everybody mates with everybody else. It is quite a fantastic sight, I assure you," says University of California, Davis, entomologist Arthur Shapiro, who has witnessed this spectacle of **lepidopterous** lechery. (*Sacramento Bee*, "Fluttering Peril—Are Bred Monarchs a Menace in the Wild?" 1/2/2002.)

buttocks *n.*: **fundament**. ❖ It's a vivid violet-blue that would be worthy of a Monet landscape if not for the fact that it's the **fundament** of a very large monkey named Nikko. Nikko's beautiful blue bottom is probably the most startling thing about the quartet of mandrills that have moved into the Virginia Zoo. "Ooh! He's mooning you!" one young visitor exclaimed Wednesday. (Meredith Kruse, "Monkeys, in Full Color," *Virginian-Pilot*, 5/1/2003)

(2) buttocks *n.pl.*: **nates**. ❖ This is followed by a fashion show, during which Andrea . . .

delicately shriek[s] as a bare-chested, chocolate-colored young chap saunters up and down the runway. "Is it hot in here," says Andrea, fanning her face with her Kwanza program and eyeing the lad's strutting, splendidly molded young **nates**, "or is it just me?" (E. Jean Carroll, "The Return of the White Negro," *Esquire*, 6/1/1994, p. 100.)

buxom *adj.*: **bathycolpian**. See *busty*

(2) buxom *adj.*: **hypermammiferous**. See *busty*

buying (mania for . . . things) *n.*: **oniomania**. See *shopping*

buzzing (a . . . and droning hum) *n.*: **bombilation**. ❖ The treatment of Darryl Strawberry at Shea Stadium this past season stands out in my mind, although Phil Simms and the entire Knick squad have also played to the **bombilations** of hometown booing. (*New York Times*, "Boos or Cheers?" 1/11/1987, p. 11.)

(2) buzzing (or ringing sound in one's ears) *n.*: **tinnitus**. See *ringing*

buzzword *n.*: **shibboleth**. See *catchphrase*

by choice *adj.*: **facultative**. See *optional*

by heart *adv.*: **memoriter**. See *memory*

by itself *adv.*: **eo ipso** [Latin; lit. by that act]. ❖ Pundits are coming out of the ground, responding to the challenge to interpret the move of King Hussein. They tend to follow the usual rule, which is usually safe. It is that anything that occurs in the Mideast is **eo ipso** inscrutable. (*National Review*, "The Enigma," 9/2/1988.)

by the book *idiom*: **according to Hoyle** [after Edmond Hoyle, c. 1672–1769, British writer on games and their rules]. ❖ [Saddam Hussein's use of] civilians as human shields "is not a military strategy." It is "a violation of the laws of armed conflict," [stated Defense Secretary Donald Rumsfeld]. Since the premise . . . is that Hussein is evil and ruthless, which is certainly true, it would be remarkable if he played the game of war **according to Hoyle**. Why should he? It's not going to improve his reputation and will do nothing for his life expectancy either. (Michael Kinsley, "Problems of International Law," *Washington Post*, 3/3/2003.)

cabaret (as in nightclub) *n.*: **boîte** [French]. See *nightclub*

cable (operated or moved by . . .) *adj., n.*: **funicular**. ❖ Last Saturday the weather was particularly fine, and the 9 a.m. **funicular** train to one of the country's most popular high-altitude ski resorts . . . was filled to capacity. As many as 180 people, including dozens of youngsters, were in the cable-driven car when it headed into a 3,200 m tunnel burrowed through the side of the mountain. Eight people would make it out alive. (Andrew Purvis, "Alpine Nightmare: A Fire in a Funicular Train Kills at Least 150 People at a Popular High-Altitude Ski Resort in Austria," *Time* International, 11/20/2000.)

cackle (as in guffaw) *v.i.*: **cachinnate** (*n.*: **cachinnation**). See *laugh*

cacophonous *adj.*: **scrannel**. ❖ There are burnings and beatings, there are feces and mud, there is animal torture and incestuous rape, and soaring above the cacophony in this pious Catholic village, where every nose is bulbous and every jaw undershot, are the screeches and **scrannel** note of the church organ which is, naturally, untuned. (Peter Walker, "Nasty, Brutish, Grimm," *Independent on Sunday*, 3/23/1997.)

(2) cacophonous (of a sound or noise that is . . . , as in grating, shrill, harsh, or otherwise unpleasant) *adj.*: **stridulous**. See *grating*

cadavers (abnormal fear of . . . or dead people) *n.*: **necrophobia**. See *fear*

(2) cadavers (fascination with or erotic attraction to . . .) *n.*: **necrophilia**. See *corpses*

café *n.*: **estaminet** [French]. See *bistro*

cagey *adj.*: **jesuitical** (sometimes cap.). See *crafty*

(2) cagey (as in deceitful conduct) *n.*: **skullduggery**. See *deceitfulness*

cajolery (to win over or obtain by . . .) *v.t.*: **inveigle**. See *lure*

cajoling (by flattery) *n.*: **blandishment** (*v.t.*: **blandish**). See *flattery*

calamity (as in episode having the quality of a nightmare) *n.*: **Walpurgis Night**. See *nightmare*

(2) calamity (one who is always predicting . . .) *n.*: **catastrophist**. See *pessimist*

calculated (as in contrived) *adj.*: **voulu** [French]. See *contrived*

calculating (act or process of . . . , as in measuring) *n.*: **mensuration**. See *measuring*

calendar (of months or of saints' days) *n.*: **menology**. ❖ Starting with the May issue [of *McCall's* magazine]—which, in accordance with typically bizarre magazine **menology**, will be out in the US on April 3—it is to undergo a radical makeover under the hands of unlikely new editorial director Rosie O'Donnell. (Sally Jackson, "*McCall's* Gets a Rosie Glow," *Australian*, 3/22/2001.)

callous (as in cruel) *adj.*: **fell** (*n.*: **fellness**). See *cruel*

(2) callous (as in thick-skinned) *adj.*: **pachydermatous**. See *thick-skinned*

(3) callous (as in unfeeling, person, as in one who is interested only in cold, hard facts, with little concern for emotion or human needs) *n.*: **Gradgrind**. See *unfeeling*

calm (and carefree time) *adj.*: **prelapsarian**. See *innocent*

(2) calm (as in unemotional or even-tempered) *adj.*: **phlegmatic**. See *even-tempered*

(3) calm (esp. with respect to the wind) *adj.*: **favonian**. See *mild*

(4) calm *adj.*: **equable**. See *serene*

(5) calm *v.t.*: **propitiate**. See *placate*

calming (as in reducing stress or anxiety, often used with respect to medications) *adj.*: **anxiolytic** (*n.*: a product that has this effect). See *relaxing*

calmness *n.*: **ataraxy** (or **ataraxia**). ❖ [I made an obscene gesture and he marched up to me nose-to-nose and shouted:] "You've got something to say to me?" . . . "No, I don't think so," I responded with a calm that would have earned me full marks from several schools of philosophy. Raw **ataraxy**. (Tabor Fischer, *The Thought Gang*, The New Press [1994], p. 219.)

(2) calmness (as in gentleness) *n.*: **mansuetude**. See *gentleness*

(3) calmness (as in peace of mind) *n.*: **heartsease**. See *peace of mind*

(4) calmness (as in tranquillity) *n.*: **quietude**. See *tranquillity*

(5) calmness (esp. under pressure or trying circumstances) *n.*: **sang-froid** [French]. See *composure*

(6) calmness (in the face of adversity or suffering) *n.*: **longaminity**. See *patience*

camaraderie (as in fellowship or association) *n.*: **sodality**. See *fellowship*

campus rules (or of relating to . . . , esp. regarding visiting privileges of the opposite sex in dormitories) *adj.*: **parietal**. See *college rules*

candidates *n.pl.*: **papabili**. [Italian. This word specifically refers to the list of men who might be elected pope (pope-able). However it is sometimes more generally used to refer to the slate of candidates for positions other than pope, as in the example given here, although the connection to the papal election is clear. See also *pope*.] ❖ While analysts of the Roman Catholic church have been parsing Vatican statements this month about the real state of the pope's health, halfway around the world a similar sort of sifting of the tea leaves has been under way in Hollywood. In sharp contrast to 2004, when *Lord of the Rings* won all 11 Oscars for which it was nominated, there are no obvious winners among this year's celluloid **papabili**. (*Economist*, "Winged Victors; The Oscars," 2/19/2005.)

cane (instrument such as a . . . for punishing children) *n.*: **ferule**. See *paddle*

cannibalistic *adj.*: **anthropophagous**. ❖ There seems to be an ingrained taboo, a knee-jerk response that simultaneously combines repulsion from, and fascination with, the **anthropophagous** act. From earliest times, cannibalism has been depicted as the ultimate horror. (Thomas Hodgkinson, The Essay: "Cannibalism: A Potted History," *Independent* [London], 3/17/2001.)

can't-miss (esp. with respect to a plan, deal, or investment that can be trusted completely because it is supposedly safe and sure to succeed) *adj.*: **copper-bottomed** [British]. See *sure-fire*

capable (as in skillful) *adj.*: **habile**. See *skillful*

(2) capable (as in skillful) *adj.*: **au fait** [French]. See *skillful*

caper (as in prank) *n.*: **dido**. See *prank*

capital letter *n.*: **majuscule**. See *uppercase*

caprice (as in whim) *n.*: **boutade** [French]. See *whim*

capricious (as in fickle, person whose opinion is always changing as the wind blows, like a weathervane) *n.*: **girouette** [French]. See *weathervane*

captivate *v.t.*: **ensorcell** (or **ensorcel**). See *enchant*

captivating (as in alluring) *adj.*: **sirenic**. [See also the nouns *siren call* and *Lorelei call* under *lure*.] See *alluring*

(2) captivating *adj.*: **illecebrous**. See *alluring*

(3) captivating *adj.*: **piquant**. See *appealing*

captivity (as in bondage) *n.*: **thralldom**. See *bondage*

captured (capable of being . . . , as in ensnared) *adj.*: **illaqueable**. See *ensnared*

care (as in attention) *n.*: **advertence**. See *attention*

(2) care (treat another with excessive . . .) *n.*, *v.t.*: **wet-nurse**. See *coddle*

carefree (behavior) *n.*: **rhathymia** (ruh-THY-mee-uh). [This is an uncommon but legitimate word.] ❖ This is the second in a series of irrelevant emails exploring the romance and **rhathymia** . . . of racing round and round some ragged rocks [in Colorado] during the recession. (Mike O'Donnell, "Economic Updates from Colorado Lending Source," www.coloradolendingsource.org/files/RR%202.pdf, 2/12/2009.)

(2) carefree (and innocent time) *adj.*: **prelapsarian**. See *innocent*

(3) carefree *adj.*: **dégagé** [French]. See *easygoing*

careless (and irresponsible) *adj.*: **feckless**. See *irresponsible*

(2) careless (as in irresponsible or reckless) *adj.*: **harum-scarum**. See *reckless*

(3) careless (as in reckless) *adj.*: **temerarious**. See *reckless*

carelessly (as in, in a disorderly and hasty manner) *adv.*: **pell-mell**. See *disorderly*

caress *v.i.*: **canoodle** (often as in "canoodle with"). ❖ Really, it would probably be worth aging into a saggy, babbling hack—as [John Phillips and Denny Doherty of the Mamas and the Papas] both now seem to be—if one could have spent a few nights **canoodling** with Michelle [Phillips] in her swivel-hipped prime. (Ken Tucker, Television: Hard Rock, *Entertainment Weekly*, 2/5/1999, p. 51.)

caressing (gentle . . . , as in stroking, used in massage) *n.*: **effleurage**. See *stroking*

(2) caressing *idiom*: **slap and tickle**. See *sex*

caring (as in compassionate) *adj.*: **ruthful**. See *compassionate*

carnal (relating to or exhibiting . . . behavior in many forms) *adj.*: **pansexual**. See *sexual*

carouse (noisily) *v.i.*: **roister**. See *revel*

carouser *n.*: **roisterer**. See *revel*

carpenter (who builds houses) *n.*: **housewright**. ❖ A 1754 white colonial with dark red shutters . . . built by a wealthy **housewright** for himself, still possessing original floorboards and a few original windowpanes. (Suzanne Berne, *A Perfect Arrangement*, Algonquin Books of Chapel Hill [2001], p. 19.)

carry (a person or group from one place to another against his or their will, whether literally or figuratively) *v.t.*: **frogmarch**. See *march*

carte blanche (as in entitlement, spec. one presumed arrogantly or asserted involuntarily against others) *n.*: **droit du seigneur** [French]. See *entitlement*

carved (into rock) *adj.*: **rupestrian**. ❖ One of her most poignant legacies lies in Cuba. . . . There she created her "**Rupestrian** Sculptures" (1981), a series of haunting, semiabstract figures carved into the soft rock of caves in Jaruco Park, on the outskirts of Havana. (Leslie Camhi, "Burning a Lasting Place in Art," *International Herald Tribune*, 6/26/2004.)

carving (esp. of gemstones) *n., adj.*: **glyptic**. ❖ [In his portrait of Madame de Pompadour,] Quentin de La Tour . . . conspicuously placed a large blue book, possibly P.-J. Mariette's treatise on the engraving of precious stones. . . . From under the book a print unfurls which shows a gem engraver at work. Pompadour was herself one of the few eighteenth-century practitioners of this **glyptic** art. (Melissa Hyde, "The 'Makeup' of the Marquise," *Art Bulletin*, 9/1/2000.)

case (as in example) *n.*: **exemplum**. See *example*

cast (of characters in a play or story) *n.*: **dramatis personae**. See *characters*

castle (master of a . . .) *n.*: **chatelain** (mistress: **chatelaine**). ❖ By virtue of their wealthy owners, many castles are graced by lovely gardens. In the days of the Tudor royal visits, a topiary garden or maze was a way to impress important guests, while Victorian **chatelains** sought to cultivate rare plants brought from exotic travels. (Allison Culliford, "The Complete Guide to British Castles," *Independent* [London], 5/4/2002.)

cast off (as in shed, a skin or covering) *v.t., v.i.*: **exuviate**. See *shed*

castrate *v.t.*: **geld**. ❖ Percy's problems, experts say, started when he was fed from a bottle soon after birth. Then the llama's handlers failed to castrate him. So it came as no surprise . . . that Percy pounced on an amusement park attendant on Friday. . . . While several llama authorities denounced the Weeki Wachee attraction for failing to **geld** Percy, the attraction said it had done nothing wrong. (Justin Blum, "Llama Attacks Park Attendant," *St. Petersburg Times*, 7/9/1995.)

castration *n.*: **orchidectomy**. ❖ [O]ne of the rare surviving examples of a castrato singing [is] a 1903 recording of Alessandro Moreschi, the last singer to be subjected to **orchidectomy** to preserve his unbroken voice. (Brian Morton, "Suffering for Your Art Is One Thing but Counter-Tenor Beats Castrato," *Scotland on Sunday*, 11/12/1995.)

casual (as in relaxed and easygoing) *adj.*: **dégagé** [French]. See *easygoing*

casualness (appearance of . . .) *n.*: **sprezzatura** [Italian]. See *effortlessness*

catalyst (as in creative inspiration) *n.*: **afflatus**. See *inspiration*

(2) catalyst *n.*: **fillip**. See *stimulus*

catastrophe (as in episode having the quality of a nightmare) *n.*: **Walpurgis Night**. See *nightmare*

catchphrase (or catchword) *n.*: **shibboleth**. ❖ The word self-esteem has become one of the obstructive **shibboleths** of education. Why do black children need Afrocentrist education? Because, its promoters say, it will create self-esteem. (Robert Hughes, Essay: "The Fraying of America," *Time*, 2/3/1992, p. 44.)

(2) catchphrase (pithy . . .) *n.*: **gnome** (*adj.*: **gnomic**). ❖ [Frank Yablans] had gotten a lot of the credit for *Love Story*, with its **gnomic**, but effective tag line: "Love means never having to say you're sorry." (Peter Biskind, *Easy Riders, Raging Bulls*, Simon & Schuster [1998], p. 145.)

cat hater *n.*: **ailurophobe**. ❖ Q: I received a modest inheritance from an aunt and wished to give some portion of it to charity. Did I have a moral obligation to donate to causes she specifically believed in? A: Once it passed into your hands, it became yours to do with as you wished. Even had your aunt been, say, a militant **ailurophobe**, you could have contributed honourably to a home for recalcitrant cats. (*Toronto Star*, "Tapping the Tourists for 20's," 2/17/2002.)

cat lover *n.*: **ailurophile**. ❖ An animal decked out in peasant garb is one thing, but—holy cat!—Herbert has tails peeking out from monks' robes and halos perched on furry heads. Judging from their pious expressions, though, these kitties mean no disrespect. And what **ailurophile** could resist a cat in a wimple? (Marlene McCampbell, Picks & Pans: Pages, *People*, 4/10/1995, p. 25.)

caught (capable of being . . . , as in ensnared) *adj.*: **illaqueable**. See *ensnared*

(2) caught (in the act, esp. of committing an offense or a sexual act) *adv.*: **in flagrante delicto**. See *in the act*

cause (as in prime mover) *n.*: **primum mobile** [Latin]. See *prime mover*

(2) cause (as in source and origin) *n.*: **fons et origo** [Latin]. See *source and origin*

cause (as in event that is . . . of war, literally or figuratively) *n.*: **casus belli** [Latin]. See *provocation*

causes (study of . . . , esp. relating to medical conditions) *n.*: **etiology**. ❖ An essential component of the initial assessment is a detailed and accurate history of the event in order to determine **etiology**. The causes of seizures vary with age, and knowledge of these age-related causes can also help establish the diagnosis. (Genell Hilton, "Seizure Disorders in Adults," *Nurse Practitioner*, 9/1/1997, p. 42.)

caustic (as in . . . remarks) *adj.*: **astringent**. See *harsh*

(2) caustic *adj.*: **acidulous**. See *tart*

(3) caustic *adj.*: **mordant**. See *sarcastic*

caution (as in word to the wise) *phr.*: **verbum sap** [Latin]. See *word to the wise*

cautionary (as in serving as a warning) *adj.*: **aposematic**. See *warning*

cautious (tactics, esp. as a means to wear out an opponent) *adj.*: **Fabian**. [This adjective derives from Roman general Quinton Fabius Maximus, who through caution, avoidance of direct confrontation, and harassment, defeated Hannibal in the Second Punic War. Today, it has become synonymous with, alternately, caution or conservativeness, delay or dilatoriness, or guerrilla tactics, and is often used in the phrase "Fabian tactics"]. ❖ [After becoming world chess champion in 1960, Mikhail] Tal immediately embarked upon a fresh challenge but at [a tournament in] 1962, instead of the anticipated race between the young lions, Mikhail Tal and Bobby Fischer, the tournament resulted in a narrow victory of attrition for the **Fabian** tactics of the ultra-cautious Armenian Tigran Petrosian. During this tournament Tal's health collapsed and he had to withdraw well before the end. (*Times* [London], "Mikhail Tal," 6/30/1992.)

(2) cautious (and timid and indecisive) *adj.*: **Prufrockian**. See *timid*

cave dweller *n.*: **troglodyte**. See *Neanderthal*

cavort *v.i.*: **gambol**. See *frolic*

(2) **cavort** *v.t., v.i.*: **disport**. See *frolic*

cease (as in put an end to) *v.t.*: **quietus** (as in "put the quietus to"). See *termination*

ceasefire (temporary . . . between opposing parties pending final deal) *n.*: **modus vivendi** [Latin]. See *truce*

cede (as in give back, often property or territory) *v.i.*: **retrocede**. See *return*

(2) **cede** (esp. responsibility or duty) *v.t.*: **abnegate**. See *renounce*

celebrate (with boisterous public demonstrations) *v.i.*: **maffick**. [British. This word derives from celebrating in England after a British military success during the Boer War on May 17, 1900, in Mafeking, South Africa.] ❖ Currently, on the southern shore of the Thames, from the archetypal working-class districts . . . , a large percentage of locals are preparing for **mafficking** on a scale not seen for decades; all subject to the dreamy prospect of Millwall beating Manchester United in this afternoon's FA Cup final. (Michael Collins, "Millwall: The Island That Time Forgot; Its Footballers Stand on the Brink of Sporting Glory," *Independent* [London], 5/22/2004.)

(2) **celebrate** (as in revel or carouse) *v.i.*: **roister**. See *revel*

(3) **celebrate** (or boast, esp. about the accomplishments of a relative) *v.t., n.*: **kvell** [Yiddish]. See *boast*

celebrating (victory) *adj.*: **epinician**. See *victory*

celebration (or to bestow . . . upon, as in an accolade) *n., v.t.*: **garland**. See *accolade*

(2) **celebration** (riotous . . .) *n., adj.*: **bacchanal**. See *revelry*

celebratory (and social) *adj.*: **Anacreontic**. See *convivial*

celebrity (as in publicity or a taste or flair for being in the spotlight) *n.*: **réclame** [French]. See *publicity*

celestial (as in of or related to the sky or heavens) *adj.*: **empyreal**. [This word, like heavenly itself, is often used figuratively (as in the example given) but of course can be used liter-

ally as well.] ❖ The sold-out production by the acclaimed Steppenwolf Theater Company is lifted to **empyreal** heights by the presence of Ladysmith Black Mambazo, the South African a cappella group. (Emily Mitchell, Sightings: Theater, *Time* International, 5/4/1992, p. 66.)

(2) **celestial** (as in of or relating to the skies or heavens) *adj.*: **supernal**. [Like empyreal, this word can be used figuratively or literally.] ❖ [At Per Se restaurant in New York,] dishes like sabayon of oysters and caviar, and cauliflower panna cotta, are nothing short of **supernal**, and dinner's many flourishes include a silver tray lined with rows of exquisite housemade chocolates. The catch: Only reservations to a state dinner at the White House may be tougher to snare. (Tom Sietsema, "My Recent Meals in New York City Included Something Old, Something New," *Washington Post*, 10/3/2004.)

(3) **celestial** *adj.*: **ethereal**. See *heavenly*

cell (as in dungeon) *n.*: **oubliette**. See *dungeon*

cemeteries (one who loves . . .) *n.*: **taphophile**. ❖ [Before] he died in 1994, [horror movie star Peter] Cushing, fearing that any tangible memorial would become a shrine for cinematic **taphophiles**, arranged for [his remains to be buried] at an undisclosed location. (Matthew Sweet, Film: "Why Do the Press Only Call Me a Horror Actor?" *Independent* [London], 2/25/2001.)

cemetery *n.*: **necropolis**. See *graveyard*

censor (a book or a piece of writing in a prudish manner) *v.t.*: **bowdlerize**. See *edit*

censorship (of arts, theater, or literature) *n.*: **Comstockery** [named for Anthony Comstock (1844–1915), secretary of the New York Society for the Suppression of Vice, who helped destroy 160 tons of literature and pictures that he deemed immoral]. ❖ The [Communication Decency Act says,] in effect, that if you display "indecent" or "patently offensive" material on the Internet, "in a manner available to a person under 18 years of age," you are a criminal. . . . The best argument for upholding this electronic **Comstockery** can be summed up in a single world: zoning. (Jeffrey Rosen, "Can the Government Stop Cyberporn?" *New Republic*, 3/31/1997.)

censure (as in criticism) *n.*: **animadversion** (*v.t.*: **animadvert**). See *criticism*

(2) censure (as in criticize) *v.t.*: **flay**. See *criticize*

(3) censure (as in denunciation) *n.*: **commination**. See *denunciation*

(4) censure (being subject to . . . , esp. public) *n.*: **obloquy**. See *abuse*

(5) censure (harshly) *v.t.*: **fustigate**. See *criticize*

(6) censure (sharply) *v.t.*: **scarify**. See *criticize*

censuring (or expressing disapproval) *adj.*: **dyslogistic**. See *uncomplimentary*

center (moving, directed, or pulled toward) *adj.*: **centripetal**. ❖ Sometimes wildly diverse interests may be a better bet. Keep in mind, one of the big threats to wedded bliss is **centripetal** force, the tendency for a marriage to . . . collapse in on itself. If both peas are from the same pod, it can get claustrophobic in there. (Hugh O'Neill, "Have You Met Your Match? Get a Wife!" *Men's Health*, 6/1/2001, p. 126.)

(2) center (as in central point) *n.*: **omphalos** [Greek; lit. navel]. ❖ [I]n 1400 BC, Delphi] was considered the center . . . of the world. Is Omaha today's **omphalos** of the world, and Warren Buffett its oracle? This weekend devotees will congregate, hoping to hear some prophecies. (Steve Jordon, "Warren Buffett's Past Pronouncements Show Mixed Results," *Omaha World-Herald*, 4/30/2004.)

(3) center (as in middle way) *n.*: **via media** [Latin]. See *middle way*

(4) center (as in nerve center) *n.*: **ganglion** (pl. **ganglia**). See *nerve center*

(5) center (into the . . .) *adv.*: **in medias res** [Latin.] See *into the middle*

center of attention *n.*: **cynosure**. ❖ **Cynosure** on the court though he was, [basketball star Bill] Russell never enjoyed being the celebrity alone. . . . Maybe that's one reason the team mattered so to him; it hugged him back. (Frank Deford, "The 20th Century: The Ring Leader," *Sports Illustrated*, 5/10/1999, p. 96.)

centerpiece (large table . . . , often used for holding fruit, flowers, etc.) *n.*: **epergne**. ❖ [In one house on the million-dollar house tour,] an open butler's pantry between kitchen and formal dining room is across the hall from a silver closet large enough to hold multiple tea services and still have room for a multilayer **epergne** guaranteed to prevent guests from seeing one another across the dinner table. (Brenda Warner Rotzell, "Million-Dollar Houses Offer Lap of Luxury," *Chicago Sun-Times*, 10/7/1988.)

ceremony (or ritual that is pretentious) *n.*: **mummery**. ❖ [In the London courtroom, Barrister] Richard Rampton, who wears a short gray-blond wig and the silk robes of a Queen's Counsel, and his black-robed junior Heather Rogers, whose wig partially covers her own gray hair, add yet a further note of **mummery** to the proceedings. (D. D. Guttenplan, *The Holocaust on Trial*, Norton [2001], p. 19.)

certain (as in sure-fire, esp. with respect to a plan, deal, or investment that can be trusted completely because it is supposedly safe and sure to succeed) *adj.*: **copper-bottomed** [British]. See *sure-fire*

certain (as in unavoidable) *adj.*: **ineluctable**. See *unavoidable*

certification (as in giving one's stamp of approval) *n.*: **nihil obstat** [Latin]. See *approval*

cessation (as in ending) *n.*: **desinence**. See *ending*

chafe *v.t.*: **abrade**. ❖ [If one uses chewing tobacco, the] gums may recede, the teeth loosen, biting surfaces are **abraded**, and tough, white patches called leukoplakia may appear on the gums and cheeks. After several years the mouth can be devastated. (Claudia Wallis, Medicine, *Time*, 7/15/1985, p. 68.)

chagrin (resulting from an inopportune occurrence) *n.*: **contretemps**. See *mishap*

chain *n.*: **catenation** (*v.t.*: **catenate**). ❖ The subject we're on is adultery. . . . Tonight [Sondra] will be Joan's fictitious sick aunt or her friend in dire need of a babysitter. Her alibi. This arrangement is ongoing, a round-robin [with two other women], a quid pro quo. Yet despite, or perhaps because of, this seamless **catenation** of adultery, these New York City women consider themselves very happily married. (Binnie Kirshenbaum, "The Cheaters' Club," *Harper's Bazaar*, 10/1/1995, p. 138.)

challenge (a statement, opinion, or action) *v.t.*: **oppugn**. See *oppose*

(2) challenge (as in hostile meeting) *n.*: **rencontre** [French]. See *duel*

champion (of a cause) *n.*: **paladin**. See *proponent*

chance (by . . .) *adj.*: **adventitious**. ❖ [F]or depth of experience, breadth of repertory, theatrical understanding and a touch of old-school maestro bossiness—not to mention the **adventitious** advantage of his British nationality—my vote for music director of the Royal Opera would go to Mark Elder any day. (Rupert Christiansen, The Arts, *Daily Telegraph* [London], 2/11/1999.)

(2) chance (as in random) *adj.*: **stochastic**. See *random*

(3) chance (pertaining to or dependent upon . . .) *adj.*: **aleatory**. See *unpredictable*

change (complete . . .) *n.*: **permutation**. See *transformation*

(2) change (esp. in a strange, grotesque, or humorous way) *v.t.*: **transmogrify**. See *transform*

(3) change (sudden . . . of events, often in a literary work) *n.*: **peripeteia**. See *turnaround*

changeable *adj.*: **labile**. ❖ The beautiful show of Guercino drawings . . . reminds you, moreover, how **labile** reputation can be. Guercino was one of those 17th century Italian artists who sank under the weight of an earlier age's revival [i.e., the Renaissance]. (Robert Hughes, review of Guercino, *Time* International, 7/13/1992, p. 49.)

(2) changeable (as in fickle, person whose opinion is always changing as the wind blows, like a weathervane) *n.*: **girouette** [French]. See *weathervane*

(3) changeable (one that is . . . or varies with trends) *n.*: **weathercock**. See *fickle*

change of heart (spec. a fundamental transformation of mind or character, esp. a spiritual conversion) *n.*: **metanoia**. See *conversion*

change of mind (esp. regarding one's beliefs, causes, or policies) *n.*: **bouleversement** [French]. ❖ The timing of this week's **bouleversement** [by British Prime Minister Tony Blair] in Brussels was rotten. It is less than a month since [Blair] decided to break cover, . . . launch his "national changeover plan," and make it plain to anyone who had ever doubted it that he really did intend to lead Britain into the promised land of the euro, the single European currency. (*Economist*, "Moses Blair and His Promised Euroland," 3/20/1999.) See *reversal*

(2) change of mind (esp. regarding one's beliefs, causes, or policies) *n.*: **tergiversation** (*v.i.*: **tergiversate**). ❖ [Rudolph Giuliani] had himself changed positions over the years, having been prolife and then pro-choice, and he knew the pain and punishment of **tergiversation**. But, after all, he was elected mayor, and like so many others, concluded that to oppose abortion is politically more dangerous than to tolerate it. (William F. Buckley, "Temporizing on the Abortion Issue," *Buffalo News*, 8/3/1994.)

(3) change of mind (as in abandonment, of one's religion, principles, or causes) *n.*: **apostasy**. See *abandonment*

(4) change of mind (as in reversal of policy or position) *n.*: **volte-face** [French]. See *about-face*

(5) change of mind (spec. a fundamental transformation of mind or character, esp. a spiritual conversion) *n.*: **metanoia**. See *conversion*

(6) change of mind (spec. the opportunity to withdraw from, or decide not to commit, an intended crime) *n.*: **locus poenitentiae** [Latin]. See *repentance*

(7) change of mind (spec. a recognition of one's errors, and a return to a sane, sound, or correct position) *n*.: **resipiscence**. See *reformation*

channel *v.t.*: **canalize**. ❖ [Gothic and Georgian buildings] were just the sort of buildings thought to be irrelevant by "fiery" modernists such as George Howe. . . . "The modern movement," Howe said, "is a conscious effort to direct and **canalize** the stupendous energy of modern civilization. . . . The Modern architect has created a new style based on the old common law of architecture reformulated to meet modern needs in the light of modern economic and engineering genius." (Benjamin Forgey, "Architecture in Time & Flux; The AIA's Retrospective," *Washington Post*, 3/12/1983.)

chant (as in hymn, expressing praise and glory to God) *n*.: **doxology**. See *hymn*

chanting (responsive . . . or singing) *n*.: **antiphony**. ❖ I left the church to the soft **antiphony** of monks chanting the liturgy. (Nancy Shute, *Into and Out of the Mystic, U.S. News & World Report*, 4/19/1999.)

chaos *n*.: **tohubuhu** [derives from the Hebrew "tohu wa-bhohu" in the second verse of Genesis, translated in the King James Version in 1611 as "And the earth was without form, and void"]. ❖ *Brother of Sleep* [by Robert Schneider includes] a meditation on the wiles, the vulnerabilities and the potential for mishap of the human body. . . . Time and again . . . Elias tunes in to the "mad **tohubohu**" of the body noises of his neighbours, "an incredible noise of swallowing, gurgling, snorting, and belching, a churning of gall-like stomach juices, a quiet splash of urine." (Valentine Cunningham, The Week in Reviews: Books: "Who Needs Enemas . . . ," *Observer*, 11/24/1996.)

(2) chaos (and confusion) *n., adj.*: **hugger-mugger**. See *confusion*

(3) chaos (as in commotion) *n*.: **maelstrom**. See *commotion*

(4) chaos (in a state of . . . or confusion) *idiom*: **at sixes and sevens**. See *disarray*

(5) chaos (movement toward or degree of . . . in a system or society) *n*.: **entropy**. See *disorder*

chaotic (situation that is . . . or confused or complicated) *n*.: **mare's nest**. ❖ Tyco is a dreadful company. [It's a] **mare's nest** of spare-part businesses. . . . Its financial statements are byzantine. . . . The company constantly buys and sells its own stock. . . . Owing $23 billion and possessing a conglomeration of slow-growing, badly matched businesses. Tyco should be a short seller's dream, a virtual laughingstock. It's even headquartered in Bermuda. (Ken Kurson, "Bermuda Shorts: Tyco's Long-Suffering Bears Are About to Get the Last Laugh," *Esquire*, 5/1/2002.)

(2) chaotic *adj., adv.*: **higgledy-piggledy**. See *haphazard*

character (of a person, people, or culture) *n*.: **ethos**. ❖ Copyright . . . involves the exclusive use of private property. And it often appears in conflict with the computer world, which values usable and immediate public access. "The **ethos** of the Internet," says Marci Hamilton . . . "is that anything online may be downloaded, cut, copied, and sent along to others." (Daniel Grant, "Copyright Law Faces Sea Change," *Christian Science Monitor*, 2/25/1999.)

(2) character (lit. humanity, often used in the sense of decency) *n*.: **menschlichkeit** [German, Yiddish]. See *decency*

(3) character (showing an idea without words, e.g., $, or Chinese or Japanese symbols) *n*.: **ideogram**. See *symbol*

characterize (as in describe, by painting or writing) *v.t.*: **limn**. See *describe*

characters (in a play or story) *n*.: **dramatis personae**. ❖ Jenkins just finished a second romance novel, due out this fall. (The setting: Michigan, 1876; the **dramatis personae**: a black woman doctor from California and a Civil War veteran.) (Betsy Israel, Pages: "Heat in Another Color," *People*, 2/13/1995, p. 153.)

charade (as in sham) *n*.: **postiche**. See *sham*

charge (an accuser with having committed a similar offense) *n*.: **tu quoque** [Latin]. See *accusation* and *answer*

(2) charge (as in order or direct) *v.t.*: **adjure**. See *order*

charisma *n.*: **duende**. ❖ [There is] a quality called **duende**. Fred Astaire had it, he said, Gene Kelly didn't, Joe DiMaggio did, Stan Musial didn't. Willie Mays had it, but not Henry Aaron. Ken Griffey Jr. has **duende** whether he gets sixty homers this season or not. He will always have it. . . . There is just something about him. A spark. A smile. A flair. (Mike Lupica, "Roger and Him," Esquire, 9/1/1994, p. 96.)

charitable *adj.*: **caritative**. ❖ This should appear, for instance, in the form of responsibility and consideration [by the nurse] and, above all, as reverence for the suffering patient. This also can be seen as an expression of an unconditional **caritative** ethic, involving responsibility and a desire to do good. (Dahly Matilainen, "Patterns of Ideas in the Professional Life and Writings of Karin Neuman-Rahn," *Advances in Nursing Science*, 9/1/1999, p. 78.)

(2) charitable *adj.*: **eleemosynary**. ❖ Nevertheless, paying the chief executive less than an underling often makes sense—and many good chief executives know it. . . . "I'm not **eleemosynary**, mind you," says [Bally's] Chairman[,] Robert E. Mullane, who pulled down $592,222 himself. "[Paying certain Bally's employees more than I make] is what's best for the company. I live very nicely. I like my job." (John Paul Newport Jr., Managing: "How to Outearn the Boss and Keep Your Job," *Fortune*, 5/27/1985, p. 73.)

charlatan (esp. who sells quack medicines) *n.*: **mountebank**. See *huckster*

charm (power to . . .) *n.*: **duende**. See *charisma*

(2) charm *v.t.*: **ensorcell** (or **ensorcel**). See *enchant*

charming (and seductive woman) *n.*: **Circe**. See *enchantress*

(2) charming *adj.*: **piquant**. See *appealing*

chaste *adj.*: **vestal**. ❖ [The bride] has the advantage that her dress is so distinct that nobody could mistake her for anyone else. She is not even to be confused with her bridesmaids, for although they too are "clothed in white samite, mystic, wonderful," they lack that supreme symbol of **vestal** virginity, the veil. Their time

will come. (Nigel Nicolson, "Marriage, Magic and Memories," *Sunday Telegraph*, 8/15/1999.)

chasten *v.t.*: **objurgate**. See *criticize*

chat (informal . . .) *n.*: **causerie**. ❖ [W]hile it is true that the people Mr. Terkel interviews are all old, and that sometimes he so far forgets himself as to ask some of them about death and the irreversible canter of time, this is not a gentle **causerie** with greying America. It is a defiant tribute to an "other America" that may indeed be dying. (*Economist*, "Coming of Age: The Story of Our Century by Those Who've Lived It," 10/7/1995, p. 100.)

(2) chat *n.*: **chinwag** [slang]. ❖ Recently Republican presidential hopeful George W. Bush decided he wanted CNN's schmoozy Larry King and NBC's somewhat tougher Tim Russert ("Meet the Press") to mediate two of his three potential TV appearances with Democratic rival Al Gore. . . . If George and Al opt for the King style of TV **chinwag**, they will place personality, vibes and image over issues and information. (Kinney Littlefield, "As Bush Pushes to Control Debates, Fragmentation of Viewership Continues," *Orange County Register*, 9/8/2000.)

(3) chat *v.i.*: **confabulate**. ❖ The hotel, on a highway outside Richmond, the state capital of Virginia, braced itself for [boxing promoter Don King's] arrival, as for that of a hurricane. In the lobby his minions **confabulated** in blobs: roly-poly men like waddling molecules, their bangles jangling, their pinky rings glinting, walkie-talkies jutting from their polyester rumps. (Peter Conrad, "The Joy of Slavery," *Independent on Sunday*, 3/10/1996.)

chat (esp. about art or literature) *n.*: **conversazione** [Italian]. See *conversation*

(4) chat (idle . . .) *n.*: **palaver**. See *small talk*

(5) chat (light or playful . . .) *n.*: **badinage**. See *banter*

(6) chat *n.*: **interlocution**. See *discussion*

chatter *n.*: **bavardage**. See *chitchat*

(2) chatter *n.*: **persiflage**. See *chitchat*

chatterbox *n.*: **magpie**. ❖ Whatever happened to "Hummmm, babe?" There was also that singsong staple of Little League: "Hey, batta; hey, batta; hey, batta; SWINNNNG, batta!" Chatter was held to be proof of invincible team spirit. In my rad-lib college days, I thought that the theme song for the robotic conformity of the sleepy '50s was the **magpie** monotony of little boys endlessly repeating the same baseball mantra. (Bill Livingston, "Infield Chatter Is Thing of Past," *Cleveland Plain Dealer*, 6/9/1996.)

chattering (mania for . . . too much) *n.*: **cacoëthes loquendi** [Latin]. See *talking*

chatting (one skilled at dinner . . .) *n.*: **deipnosophist**. See *conversation*

chatty (and flighty person) *n.*: **flibbertigibbet**. See *flighty*

cheap (and showy, or such an object) *adj., n.*: **brummagem**. See *showy*

(2) cheap (and tasteless or showy, or such an object) *adj., n.*: **gimcrack**. See *showy*

(3) cheap (as in made without regard to quality) *adj.*: **catchpenny**. See *inferior*

(4) cheap (as in stingy) *adj.*: **cheeseparing**. See *stingy*

(5) cheap (as in stingy) *adj.*: **costive**. See *stingy*

(6) cheap (as in stingy) *adj.*: **mingy**. See *stingy*

(7) cheap (as in stingy) *adj.*: **niggardly**. See *stingy*

(8) cheap (as in stingy) *adj.*: **penurious**. See *stingy*

cheapskate *n.*: **lickpenny**. See *miser*

cheat *v.t.*: **euchre**. ❖ Peepgass knew then, if not before, that whatever he could do to **euchre** PlannersBanc out of Croker's [assets] was justified. (Tom Wolfe, *A Man in Full*, Farrar, Straus and Giroux [1998], p. 606.)

(2) cheat (as in deceive or defraud) *v.t., v.i.*: **cozen**. See *defraud*

(3) cheat (as in deceive or defraud) *v.t.*: **hornswoggle**. See *deceive*

(4) cheat (as in defraud) *v.t.*: **mulct**. See *defraud*

(5) cheat (as in swindle) *n., v.t.*: **thimblerig**. See *swindle*

(6) cheat (as in swindle) *v.t.*: **bunco**. See *swindle*

(7) cheat (or deceive) *v.t.*: **gull**. See *deceive*

check (a quick cursory . . . , as in scan) *n.*: **Cook's tour**. See *scan*

checkered *adj.*: **tessellated**. ❖ Price: More than $400,000. Address: 1 Dunkley Ave. Type: Six-bedroom return-veranda sandstone villa, three bathrooms. All three bathrooms have black and white **tessellated** floors. (*Advertiser*, "Graceful Family Home with History," 7/7/2001.)

cheek (of or pertaining to) *adj.*: **buccal**. ❖ Eli Lilly is developing a **buccal** inhaler that delivers insulin by mouth, to be absorbed through the walls of the inner cheeks. (Laura Common, "Medicine 2010—Custom-Tailored Medicines Coming of Age," *Medical Post*, 5/22/2001.)

cheekbone (of or relating to) *adj.*: **malar**. ❖ Just because the **malar** fat pads, which started out over your cheekbones, have slipped an inch or two and are dragging down the corners of your mouth, should you have to go around looking like a perpetual sourpuss? (Patricia McLaughlin, "Face It: Forces of Gravity Are Beginning to Show in the Mirror," *St. Louis Post-Dispatch*, 8/4/1994.)

cheer (as in encourage) *v.t.*: **inspirit**. See *encourage*

(2) cheer (persons hired to . . . at a performance) *n.*: **claque**. See *applaud*

cheerful *adj.*: **eupeptic**. ❖ [Artist Keith] Haring has little to express beyond a vague pleasantness, a whiff of happiness. Any attempt at true feeling is immediately deflected and thwarted by a blithely **eupeptic** tone that was intrinsic to his art: his AIDS image seems as innocuous as his radiant babies and his barking dogs. (James Gardner, "Radiant Baby," *National Review*, 10/27/1997, p. 58.)

(2) cheerful *adj.*: **riant**. [This word comes from the French and is sometimes defined (in both French and English) as "cheerful" and sometimes as "laughing." Since those words are often not exactly synonymous, it is open to question whether it applies to a cheerful person who is not laughing, although based on the (few) examples found, it is submitted that the word does encompass the broader concept of cheerfulness, and not only the narrower concept of laughing.] ❖ My wife was enjoying the article by John van Tiggelen on Noel Pearson in the *Good Weekend* until she encountered the phrase "the **riant** Peter Costello." . . . I nodded understandingly. "Probably give him a good laugh when he reads it," I said. "He looks a cheerful bloke in the photo." (Paul Roberts, letter to the editor, *Sydney Morning Herald*, 2/18/1994.)

(3) cheerful (as in genial, and pleasant) *adj.*: **sympathique** [French]. See *genial*

(4) cheerful (as in rosy) *adj.*: **roseate**

(5) cheerful *adj.*: **Falstaffian**. See *jovial*

(6) cheerful *adj.*: **gladsome**. See *gladness*

cheerfulness (causing or tending to produce . . .) *adj.*: **felicific**. See *happiness*

cheerless (as in person who never laughs) *n.*: **agelast**. See *humorless*

cheese (of or resembling) *adj.*: **caseous**. ❖ A square of rare Tibetan [very old] cheese has [sold at Sotheby's]. . . . This cheese—don't snicker—has been named "Eye of the Tiger." Hence, the price that Simon Perry paid was stiff. However, **caseous** allure ripens with age. (Letter from a listener, *All Things Considered*, NPR, 2/11/1993.)

cherished (household items) *n.pl.*: **lares and penates**. See *treasures*

chew *v.t.*, *v.i.*: **masticate**. ❖ In its most pristine presentation, the best Kava is produced not with a grinder or a pestle, but **masticated** by young, chaste girls. The girls work the root chunk around in their mouths until the cuds become the consistency of pablum. Then they spit it out on to a leaf. (*Toronto Star*, "Chugga Cuppa Kava—The Drink That Bites Back," 12/22/1999.)

chewing (practice of very thorough . . .) *n.*: **Fletcherism**. ❖ Then there was Horace Fletcher, called the "Great Masticator" or the "chew-chew man," for his devotion to the act of chewing. . . . [I]n his book *The AB-Z of Our Nutrition*, written in 1903, . . . he took chewing to a new level. **Fletcherism** eventually fell out of favor, and diets, of course, are still subject to fashion. (Michael Stroh, "Some Diets Gain or Lose Weight over Time," *Baltimore Sun*, 7/15/2002.)

chic (and wealthy young people) *n.*: **jeunesse dorée** [French]. See *fashionable*

(2) chic *adj.*: **nobby** [British]. See *elegant*

chicken (as in coward) *n.*: **poltroon**. See *coward*

(2) chicken (of or relating to the domestic fowl, including . . .) *adj.*: **gallinaceous**. See *fowl*

chide *v.t.*: **objurgate**. See *criticize*

chiding (as in criticism) *n.*: **animadversion** (*v.t.*: **animadvert**). See *criticism*

chief (of a party, school of thought, or group of persons) *n.*: **coryphaeus**. See *leader*

(2) chief *n.*: **duce** (Italian). See *commander*

chiefly (as in basically) *adv.*: **au fond** [French]. See *basically*

child *n.*: **bairn** [Scottish]. ❖ The scan shows that there are four, possibly five babies. I can't believe it. I didn't think I could carry that amount of **bairns**. (Anna Smith, "I Can't Believe It . . . My Scan Shows Five Little Babies," *Daily Record* [Glasgow], 12/22/2000.)

(2) child *n.*: **moppet**. ❖ The Wiggles, Australia's most popular music group for **moppets**, are fast winning fans in the U.S. via live tours, clips on the Disney Channel and videos. . . . [They are] often billed [in Australia] as the "Fab Four for the Under 5s." (Don Groves, "Top Gaffney Property Wiggles Way into U.S. Moppet Market," *Variety*, 5/6/2002.)

(3) child (esp. infant, who is deserted or abandoned) *n.*: **foundling**. See *orphan*

(4) child (of or relating to) *adj.*: **filial**. See *offspring*

childbearing (attitude or policy that encourages) *n.*: **pronatalism**. ❖ Lafayette . . . calls [her ChildFree Network] "an alternative voice in this wilderness of **pronatalism**." She remembers, "When I started the ChildFree Network, no one was giving women a chance to think through their options. It seemed taboo to even bring it up." Lafayette has become the lone, brave Betty Friedan for the voluntarily childless. (Cynthia Kling, "Childless by Choice," *Harper's Bazaar*, 6/1/1996, p. 134.)

childbirth (of or relating to) *adj.*: **parturient**. ❖ But hormones aside, the stimulating role of motherhood itself would seem to play a role. When the investigators gave . . . rats [who had never given birth] another mother's pups to raise, the . . . foster moms did almost as well in tests as their truly **parturient** counterparts. (*Medical Post*, "Does Mothering Make Females Smarter?" 2/9/1999, p. 37.)

(2) childbirth (slow or difficult . . .) *n.*: **dystocia**. ❖ Significantly higher rates of virtually every complication of pregnancy [for women over 40], with the "most striking" differences in malpresentation and **dystocia**. (*Medical Post*, "First-Time Mothers over 40 Can Have Healthy Babies, but Largest Study to Date Shows Higher Complication Rates," 2/9/1999, p. 8.)

(3) childbirth *n.*: **accouchement**. ❖ Born on the island of Kiribat, [Millie] slid into the world on Jan. 1, 2000, at 12:00:01 a.m. . . . . Millie didn't just happen to be born on Kiribati. [Her] parents moved there a few months before the **accouchement** because the island sits along the international date line and, as such, it would be the first place on the planet to welcome the new year. (Elvira Cordileone, "The Frenzy of Baby Day," *Toronto Star*, 4/9/2000.)

(4) childbirth (before . . .) *adj.*: **antenatal**. See *birth*

(5) childbirth (period before . . .) *n.*: **antepartum** [Latin]. See *pregnancy*

(6) childbirth (relating to a woman right after . . .) *adj.*: **puerperal**. See *postpartum*

(7) childbirth (science of . . . , as in midwifery) *n.*: **tokology** (or tocology). See *midwifery*

(8) childbirth (woman right after . . .) *n.*: **puerperium**. See *postpartum*

(9) childbirth *n.*: **parturition**. See *birth*

childhood (period of . . .) *n.*: **nonage**. See *youth*

childish (retention of . . . characteristics into adulthood) *n.*: **paedomorphism** (person who retains these characteristics) *n.*: **paedomorph**. See *infantile*

(2) childish *adj.*: **jejune**. See *juvenile*

(3) childish *adj.*: **puerile**. See *juvenile*

childless (of or relating to a . . . female) *adj.*: **nulliparous**. ❖ But hormones aside, the stimulating role of motherhood itself would seem to play a role. When the investigators gave **nulliparous** rats another mother's pups to raise, the . . . foster moms did almost as well in tests as their . . . counterparts [who had given birth]. (*Medical Post*, "Does Mothering Make Females Smarter?" 2/9/1999, p. 37.)

childlike (and carefree time) *adj.*: **prelapsarian**. See *innocent*

(2) childlike (false or insincere showing of innocent, naive, or . . . behavior) *adj.*: **faux-naïf** [French]. See *naive*

children (attitude or policy that encourages having . . .) *n.*: **pronatalism**. See *childbearing*

(2) children (hatred of . . .) *n.*: **misopedia**. See *hatred*

(3) children (having had one or more . . .) *n.*: **parous**. See *birth*

(4) children (of or relating to a woman who has never had . . .) *adj.*: **nulliparous**. See *childless*

chilliness (often in relations between people) *n.*: **froideur** [French]. ❖ I used to run into [fellow teacher] Sue Hodges quite a lot. [But] there was something of a **froideur** between us, dating from an occasion a few years earlier when Sue had caught me sniggering over one of her class work sheets entitled "Dem Bones: The Cultural Roots of the Negro Spiritual." (Zoë Heller, *What Was She Thinking?* Henry Holt [2003], p. 35.)

chilling (as in causing coldness) *adj.*: **frigorific**. See *coldness*

chills (from having a cold or fever) *n.*: **ague**. ❖ When Moses finds me later, my head is throbbing, and my teeth chatter like the spoons Papa used to play. . . . I know what this is: fever and **ague**. And no Mama to cure me this time. (Liza Ketchum, "*Orphan Journey Home*; Chapter 15: 'Stop the Boat!'" *Washington Post*, 5/4/2000.)

chilly *adj.*: **algid**. See *cold*

chimpanzee (of, relating to, or resembling) *adj.*: **anthropoid**. See *ape*

Chinese (custom or trait peculiar to the . . .) *n.*: **Sinicism**. ❖ The Europeans were a different matter, and by 1900 it was clear that things must change radically—in a way that would break the old molds that had not been affected for several millennia. But what then? Could China acquire technology and awareness while keeping its inner **Sinicism**? (Joseph Losos, "Weaving the Long Strands of Chinese History," *St. Louis Post-Dispatch*, 4/15/1990.)

(2) Chinese (object reflecting . . . artistic influence) *n.*: **chinoiserie**. ❖ Four years ago, she lavished $22,000 on a bed built for a decorator show house using Chinese-style parasols as the canopy. . . . Mandarins and parasols are classic images of **chinoiserie**, the style that took Europe by storm in the 17th and 18th centuries. (Linda Hales, "The China Syndrome; Decorator Charlotte Moss Takes On a Tall Order," *Washington Post*, 4/17/1999.)

(3) Chinese (one who studies . . . history, culture, and language) *n.*: **Sinologist**. ❖ The great **Sinologist** Joseph Needham (1900–1995) is a legend for his *Science and Civilization in China*, an encyclopedic account of China's achievements in science and technology. (Judith Shapiro, "China's Greatest Student; The Making of Joseph Needham's Multi-Volume Masterpiece, *Newsweek*, 5/25/2008.)

chinks (full of . . .) *adj.*: **rimose**. See *cracks*

chirp (like a bird) *v.i.*: **chitter**. ❖ In Arlington [National Cemetery], the lens peered down the slope, over the row of clipped bushes and into the granite bowl that Jackie had helped design as President Kennedy's gravesite. The granite bowl is a haunted place, but it isn't quiet. Birds **chitter** loudly and full of life in the nearby magnolia trees. (Charlotte Grimes, "Once More, a Service in Arlington: Mrs. Onassis Laid to Rest Beside the Eternal Flame," *St. Louis Post-Dispatch*, 5/24/1994.)

chiseled (into rock) *adj.*: **rupestrian**. See *carved*

chitchat *n.*: **bavardage**. ❖ [The cookhouse is] small to the point of intimate. . . . It is a warm, bouncy, friendly, neighbourhood place. There is an appreciable volume of **bavardage** among people who know the place, if not each other, well, and that makes for an off-with-the-jacket-and-tie-roll-up-the-sleeves-and-pour-out-a-glass atmosphere. (Matthew Fort, Food & Drink: "Rhapsody in Blue," *Guardian* [London], 6/28/1997.)

(2) chitchat *n.*: **persiflage**. ❖ Well-coiffed American women say, "You look just like a little leprechaun, I could put you in my pocket and take you home." Of course, that's not the prime ambition of a male. . . . But I've always evoked indulgence, if not admiration, from women. It's good to have a capacity for **persiflage**. If you can't dazzle people with looks, at least fall back on some nifty bullshit. (Robert Marks, "Look on the Bright Side," *Independent* [London], 9/9/2000.)

(3) chitchat (idle . . .) *n.*: **palaver**. See *small talk*

(4) chitchat (light or playful . . .) *n.*: **badinage**. See *banter*

(5) chitchat (one skilled at dinner . . .) *n.*: **deipnosophist**. See *conversation*

choice (as in first-class) *adj.*: **pukka**. See *first-class*

(2) choice (as in personal preference) *n.*: **de gustibus** [Latin]. See *taste*

(3) choice (as in select or excellent) *adj.*: **eximious**. See *excellent*

(4) choice (bad . . . , as in the situation of having to make a move where any move made will weaken the position) *n.*: **zugzwang** [German]. See *predicament*

(5) choice (by . . .) *adj.*: **facultative**. See *optional*

(6) choice (of taking what is offered or nothing; i.e., no real choice at all) *n.*: **Hobson's choice**. See *predicament*

choke (as in strangle) *v.t.*: **garrote**. See *strangle*

(2) choke (as in strangle) *v.t.*: **jugulate**. See *strangle*

chop (with an ax) *v.t.*: **hew**. See *ax*

chorus (as in hymn, expressing praise and glory to God) *n.*: **doxology**. See *hymn*

chorus girl *n.*: **chorine**. ❖ [Pre-censorship code] musicals tell audiences how great it is to be young. *Roman Sandals* was just such a production, with all of the vital ingredients on hand: a comic star, comely **chorines**, a few melodies, and a happy ending to take the public mind away from the Depression for an hour and a half. (Stefan Kanfer, *Ball of Fire*, Knopf [2003], p. 40.)

Christ (depiction of . . . wearing crown of thorns) *n.*: **ecce homo**. See *Jesus*

Christian (who believes that faith alone, rather than obedience to moral or civil law, is necessary for salvation) *n.*: **antinomian**. ❖ [British Prime Minister Tony Blair's] own devotion to a supernatural cause is sincere and deep; and he has continually displayed a quite remarkable freedom from the principles and scruples of this world. [Blair] is **antinomian**. He believes that "to the pure all things are pure" and that if you are of the elect you can do anything at all still in the certainty of salvation. (Geoffrey Wheatcroft, "He Did Do God. And That, in the End, Is What Did for Him," *Independent on Sunday*, 5/13/2007.)

Christianity (one who is taught principles of . . . before baptism) *n.*: **catechumen**. ❖ "Orthodox Christians are not going to tell people they are lost and going to hell. There is never any pressure to join." And a convert's required year-long, weekly tutoring in the faith, in the **catechumen** tradition of first-century Christians, puts off some "church shoppers" seeking lively weekday activities, new music and entertaining worship styles, Schaeffer said. (Patricia Rice, "Converts Help Fuel Pan-Orthodox Efforts," *St. Louis Post-Dispatch*, 2/23/2002.)

(2) Christianity (teacher of) *n.*: **catechist**. ❖ The murders of six Jesuit priests, their housekeeper and her daughter in El Salvador in 1989 are among the higher profile killings. Haugen said a church he visited had written special music and had a plaque listing the names of the disappeared. A number were **catechists** who'd taught people to read and write as they taught them the gospel. (Susan Hogan, "Otherworldly Unplugged," *Minneapolis Star Tribune*, 12/12/1998.)

chronicler *n.*: **annalist**. ❖ The Queen was lucky with [photographer] Annie Leibovitz. Instead of [asking the queen merely to] "lose the crown," this pop chronicler of the American Seventies, glitzy **annalist** of the American Eighties and now international photographer extraordinary, extravagant and eminent, might well have asked Her Majesty to bathe in mud and be photographed with mustard and cress sprouting in her pubic hair. (Brian Sewell, "The Palace Denies Reports of a Row between the Queen and Photographer Annie Leibovitz," *Evening Standard* [London], 7/13/2007.)

chubby (as in paunchy) *adj.*: **stomachy**. See *paunchy*

(2) chubby (condition of having a . . . physique) *n.*: **embonpoint**. See *plump*

(3) chubby (having a short . . . physique) *adj.*: **pyknic**. See *stocky*

(4) chubby (person, esp. with a large abdomen) *n.*: **endomorph** (*adj.*: **endomorphic**). See *pot-bellied*

(5) chubby (woman) *adj.*: **zaftig** [Yiddish]. See *full-figured*

(6) chubby (as in beer-bellied) *adj.*: **abdominous**. See *beer-bellied*

(7) chubby *adj.*: **pursy**. See *fat*

chump (or fool or loser or idiot or anyone generally not worthy of respect) *n.*: **schmendrick** or **shmendrik** [Yiddish]. See *fool*

chunky (condition of having a . . . physique) *n.*: **embonpoint**. See *plump*

(2) chunky (having a short . . . physique) *adj.*: **pyknic**. See *stocky*

church (excessive devotion to the . . .) *n.*: **ecclesiolatry**. ❖ Perhaps older Catholics should take seriously the prophetic dimension of our suspicion of institutions. Many of us recognize that the church is a means to God, not an end in itself. The form of idolatry of which we are most suspicious is **ecclesiolatry**. (Tom Beaudoin,

"Irreverently Yours: A Message from Generation X," *U.S. Catholic*, 4/1/1999.)

(2) church (of or relating to) *adj.*: **ecclesiastical**. ❖ A Catholic annulment is an **ecclesiastical** finding that, due to some impediment under Church law, a true marriage never existed. (Susan Jacoby, "A Kennedy Wife Says No," *Newsday*, 5/11/1997.)

churches (concerned with establishing unity among . . .) *adj.*: **ecumenical**. ❖ [D]espite the signs of **ecumenical** progress, Christian splintering remains the dominant trend. Last year, according to the *World Christian Encyclopedia*, the number of denominations throughout the world surpassed 33,800, with an average of 10 new ones organized each week. (Jeffery L. Sheler, "In a Time of Division, an Urge to Merge," *U.S. News & World Report*, 1/15/2001.)

circle (around) *v.t.*: **girdle**. See *surround*

circling (as in surrounding) *adj.*: **circumjacent**. See *surrounding*

circular (argument, as in begging the question) *n.*: **petitio principii** [Latin]. See *begging the question*

(2) circular (or spiraling motion in an ocean current) *n.*: **gyre**. See *spiraling*

circularity (as in roundness) *n.*: **rondure**. See *roundness*

circulate (as in to spread news or a rumor about) *v.t.*: **bruit**. See *rumor*

circulating (as in surrounding) *adj.*: **ambient**. See *surrounding*

circumstance (occurring necessarily by force of . . .) *adv.*: **perforce**. See *necessarily*

(2) circumstance (which is difficult or complex) *n.*: **nodus**. See *complication*

citation (as in excerpt, esp. from the Bible) *n.*: **pericope**. See *excerpt*

citizen (of a town) *n.*: **burgher**. See *resident*

city (as in urban region) *n.*: **conurbation**. See *metropolis*

(2) city (densely populated . . . or region) *n.*: **megalopolis**. See *crowded*

(3) city (populated by persons from many countries or backgrounds) *n.*: **cosmopolis**. See *diversity*

civilities (relating to . . . , where the purpose is to establish a mood of sociability rather than to communicate information or ideas, such as "have a nice day") *adj.*: **phatic**. See *pleasantries*

Civil War (period prior to) *adj.*: **antebellum** [Latin]. ❖ Williamsburg itself is probably the most important historic town in the US, and was one of the last Confederate towns to fall during the Civil War. It has perfectly preserved **ante-bellum** buildings—dating from the 18th-Century. (Doc Holiday, "How to Roll Up in Olden Virginia," *Mirror* [London], 11/25/2000.)

claim (or take for oneself without right) *v.t.*: **arrogate**. ❖ Where the Olympic Charter goes astray is [where the International Olympic Committee] **arrogates** for itself Supreme Authority. When you're eight years old and have broken the antique crystal decanter, your mother is the supreme authority. So too are the deities in various, but not all, religions. Men in blazers, who have become powerful and imperious as a result of the Olympics, don't qualify. (Paul A. Witteman, Essay: "Less Wretched Excess, Please," *Time*, 8/17/1992, p. 72.)

(2) claim (as in assert) *v.t.*: **asseverate** See *declare*

(3) claim (false . . . , as in boast, esp. one that is designed to harm or prejudice another) *n.*: **jactitation**. See *boast*

(4) claim (or take for oneself without permission) *v.t.*: **expropriate**. See *seize*

clairvoyant *adj.*: **fey**. ❖ Crow is particularly **fey** when it comes to the economic future. He even knows precisely how much the Phoenix metropolitan area needs to invest to capture the next big thing for ourselves: $500 million to $600 million a year in fundamental science expenditures, at least half of it on biological endeavors. (Robert Robb, "Let's Keep Arizona's Economy 'Cool'—Not Chase It," *Arizona Republic*, 11/11/2001.)

clamor (and confusion, esp. from simultaneous voices) *n.*: **babel**. See *noise*

(2) clamor (as in hubbub) *n.*: **charivari**. See *hubbub*

(3) clamor *n.*: **bruit**. See *din*

clamorous *adj.*: **strepitous**. See *loud*

clandestine (activity) *n.*: **hugger-mugger**. See *secrecy*

(2) clandestine (as in of or relating to a court, legislative body, or other group that meets in private, and often makes decisions that are harsh or arbitrary) *adj.*: **star chamber**. See *closed-door*

clap (persons hired to . . . at a performance) *n.*: **claque**. See *applaud*

clarification *n.*: **éclaircissement** [French] ❖ It is the scope of the tale to recapture some, if not all, of the lost memories of an architect named Jorn. . . . Early on in the text the starting point for Jorn's gradual **éclaircissement** is described. . . . After the war and during Jorn's adolescence his insights and experiences increase, but there is never a linear progression of his development. (Franz P. Haberl, "Der Fehlende Rest," *World Literature Today*, 9/22/1997, p. 777.)

(2) clarification (additional . . . or explanation) *n.*: **epexegesis** (*adj.*: **epexegetic**). See *explanation*

clash (engaged in a . . . , as in struggle) *adj.*: **agonistes**. See *struggle*

(2) clash (minor . . . as in skirmish) *n.*: **velitation**. See *skirmish*

class (lowest . . . of society) *n.*: **lumpenproletariat**. See *underclass*

classify *v.t.*: **taxonomize**. ❖ I appreciate that there are those who feel that Michelle Obama has been "mom-ified" by the media. But given the centuries during which black women have been relentlessly **taxonomized** as mammy rather than mom, many black and brown women find this phenomenon paradoxically, even sweetly transgressive. (Patricia Williams, "Mrs. Obama Meets Mrs. Windsor," *Nation*, 4/8/2009.)

classy *adj.*: **nobby** [British]. See *elegant*

clay (relating to, resembling, or containing) *adj.*: **argillaceous**. ❖ Next day brother and I had to go further than the last row of peach trees in the orchard to fetch some potter's clay. My uncle came with us and, touching the **argillaceous** earth, pinching it with his agile fingers, he said, "This must be the best clay in the world," and I knew he would make a vase of this clay. (Ana Doina, "Village," *North American Review*, 1/1/2001.)

clean (and tidy) *adj.*: **in Bristol fashion** [British]. See *tidy*

cleaning (material or device) *n.*: **abstergent**. ❖ Regarding **abstergents**, I was glad to learn that medievals used hay balls and sticks to clean themselves [of human excrement, which got on the body while it was being applied to the soil as fertilizer], while Rabelais' Gargantua employed a live goose to do his dirty work. (Adam Bresnick, "Baedeker for the Bowels," *Los Angeles Times*, 11/14/1999.)

cleaning woman *n.*: **charwoman**. See *maid*

cleanse *v.t., v.i.*: **depurate**. ❖ It wasn't long ago when the bay's surface was covered with an oily sheen and Ed Dumont was as likely to haul up a bottle as a clam. Now, the clammers can see clear to the bay floor. Over the winter, they were allowed to clam a section of the Navesink River without having to **depurate** the clams. (Debra Lynn Vial, "Tide Turns for Clammers," *Record*, 5/27/1997.)

cleansing (like detergent) *v.t.*: **detersive**. ❖ Anionic surfactants are very effective detergents, and while they may be well suited for "clarifying" products, their **detersive** action may be too harsh in other systems, completely stripping the hair of its natural oils and lipids, and leaving the hair dull and brittle. (Marianne P. Berthiaume, "Formulation of Conditioning Shampoos," *Drug & Cosmetic Industry*, 5/1/1997, p. 54.)

(2) cleansing (of the body) *n.*: **ablution**. ❖ In my little down-Maine coastal growing-up town (the date would be 1918) . . . we had the town water piped in. However, there were times that the bathtub faucet delivered a rich, chocolate-brown fluid that was a bit too brisk for tidy **ablutions**. (John Gould, "How Baby Joe's Bath Made the Town Come Clean," *Christian Science Monitor*, 8/7/1998.)

clean slate *n.*: **tabula rasa**. See *blank slate*

clean up (a book or a writing in a prudish manner) *v.t.*: **bowdlerize**. See *edit*

clear (in thought or expression) *adj.*: **luculent**. ❖ This Act acknowledges and validates the right of the people to peacefully assemble and petition the government for grievances. . . . In **luculent** and unmistakable language, the police, the public officials concerned, the leaders and organizers of the rally or demonstrations are strictly enjoined to observe [the parameters of the act]. (Alfredo S. Lim, " 'No Permit, No Rally,' " speech delivered in the Senate, September 27, 2005, *Manila Bulletin*, 10/4/2005.)

(2) clear (in thought or expression) *adj.*: **pellucid**. ❖ Mr. Richardson, author of the magnificent *A Life of Picasso*, two volumes of which have appeared, is a shrewd judge of character. He's also the master of a **pellucid** prose that makes his portraits all the more powerful. (*Washington Times*, "Larger Than Life, 20th-Century Standouts, Both the Very Good and the Marvelously Bad," 12/16/2001.)

(3) clear (as in easily understood or seen through, likes motives) *adj.*: **transpicuous**. See *transparent*

(4) clear (as in unambiguous) *adj.*: **univocal**. See *unambiguous*

(5) clear (as in understandable) *adj.*: **limpid**. See *understandable*

(6) clear (as in understandable) *adj.*: **perspicuous**. See *understandable*

(7) clear (like glass) *adj.*: **hyaline**. See *glassy*

clearing up (as in clarification) *n.*: **éclaircissement** [French]. See *clarification*

clenching (or grinding of teeth during sleep) *n.*: **bruxism**. See *grinding*

clergy (government by . . .) *n.*: **hierocracy**. See *government*

clergyman (replacement . . .) *n.*: **locum tenens**. See *temporary*

clever (as in creative, and/or original) *adj.*: **Promethean**. See *creative*

(2) clever (as in resourceful, person) *n.*: **debrouillard** (or **débrouillard**) [French]. See *resourceful*

(3) clever (line) *n.*: **bon mot** [French]. See *quip*

cleverness (or subtlety, esp. in political or business dealings) *n.*: **Italian hands** [often used in the phrase "fine Italian hands"]. See *subtlety*

cliché *n.*: **bromide**. ❖ [In *Authentically Black: Essays for the Black Silent Majority*, John McWhorter] attacks "so-called black leaders" and scheming "white leftists" who peddle the **bromide** of black "victimization" over the balm of personal responsibility. "Since the late 1960s," McWhorter writes, "blacks have been taught that presenting ourselves and our people as victims when whites are watching is the essence of being 'authentically black.' " (Brian Palmer, "Black Like Who?" *Newsday*, 2/21/2003.)

(2) cliché *n.*: **platitude**. ❖ The night of that bowling date, we're sitting on a couch at Rebecca's house. The air is electric, fed by our percolating hormones. I seize the moment with a question: "What's going on here?" "Well, Brian. I love you." The L-word? Twice in one day? Since running from the room isn't an option, I stutter out a **platitude**. "Love is a big step, you know." (Joshua Mooney, "What I Learned from My Sex Coach," *Men's Health*, 4/1/1998, p. 130.)

clichés (one who utters . . . , as in platitudes) *n.*: **platitudinarian**. See *platitudes*

cliff (steep . . .) *n.*: **escarpment**. ❖ "We're gonna have to walk from here," Mr. Hayes tells me as he parks the truck at the bottom of an **escarpment** that—to my middle-aged legs and lungs—seems to shoot straight up. This is a harsh and desolate yet colorful environment: a rocky, sun-scorched palette of gray cliffs and brick-red buttes. (Tom Verde, "Indian Cliff-Dwelling Ruins Still Impressive, Mysterious," *Washington Times*, 2/19/2000.)

climax (of a drama) *n.*: **catastasis**. ❖ Just then a beautiful little white egg dropped through the scaffling hay, descended, and arrived on the barn floor. It didn't bounce. [My cat] Mephistopheles, plainly awaiting this **catastasis**, jumped to one side to escape spattering and then pounced and began to slurp and smack, soon reducing the hen-fresh egg to naught. (John Gould, "Getting the Drop on Feline and Fowl," *Christian Science Monitor*, 5/14/1982.)

climbing (esp. too high for safety) *adj.*: **Icarian**. See *soaring*

clinger (as in person or thing that clings to something tenaciously, whether literally or figuratively) *n.*: **limpet**. [A limpet is a conical-shelled mollusk that adheres tightly to rocks when disturbed. The word is also often used as part of the phrase "clings like a limpet," and, as an adjective, limpet-like, as in the following example.] ❖ George Bush's economic team—notably Paul O'Neill, the treasury secretary—still cling **limpet**-like to their view that the economic recovery is on track (Mr. O'Neill's only concession: that it is a "bumpy road"). Few others share that optimism. (*Economist*, "Economically, It's Looking Grim," 11/9/2002.)

(2) clinger (as in person or thing that clings to something tenaciously, whether literally or figuratively) *n.*: **remora**. [A remora is a marine fish with a sucking disk that it uses to attach itself to sharks and other large fish and to ships. It is in this sense used similarly to "limpet" above.] ❖ Swarms of comparisons to the Grateful Dead (a fascinating group until their temporary retirement in the '70s) clung to the band [Phish] like **remoras**, but always seemed like sucker fare. Phish had aspects in common with the Dead—dilute vocals, faint drumming, keyboards that drained vitality, rhythm problems throughout—but invariably sounded more like Jethro Tull. (Milo Miles, "Look Who Stopped Sucking!" *Village Voice*, 10/28/1997.)

clinging *adj.*: **osculant**. See *hugging*

clocks (science of making . . . or watches) *n.*: **horology**. See *time*

clomp (as in move heavily or clumsily) *v.i.*: **galumph**. See *tromp*

close (as in put an end to) *v.t.*: **quietus** (as in "put the quietus to"). See *termination*

(2) close (up) *v.t.*: **occlude**. See *block*

closed-door (of or relating to a court, legislative

body, or other group that meets in private, and often makes decisions that are harsh or arbitrary) *adj.*: **star chamber.** [This term derives from a courtroom in England that existed until 1641, which sat in closed session and which had stars on its ceiling.] ❖ [A] national problem [is that] colleges and universities are secretly "adjudicating" and hiding crimes as serious as sexual assault. Colleges hide crimes using **star chamber**–type proceedings to protect their enrollment and alumni donations from bad publicity. Unfortunately, they are accountable to nobody. They leave victims without justice and the student body at large at undue risk. (*Washington Post*, "Crimes on Campus," 3/11/2002.)

closed-minded (person who hates reasoning or enlightenment) *n.*: **misologist**. ❖ The typical rationalist's antipathy toward religion, like the **misologist's** resentment of intellectualism, is born of a misconception based on models and definitions that have given an incomplete picture at best or have been caricatures and travesties. (Larry A. Gray, "To Bind Again," *Humanist*, 3/1/2001.)

(2) closed-minded (as in one who clings to an opinion or belief even after being shown that it is wrong) *n.*: **mumpsimus**. See *stubborn*

(3) closed-minded *adj.*: **hidebound**. See *narrow-minded*

closeness (in place, time, or relation) *n.*: **propinquity**. ❖ He marched up for nose-to-nose contact, and in spite of our **propinquity**, shouted: "You've got something to say to me?" (Tabor Fischer, *The Thought Gang*, The New Press [1994], p. 219.)

closer (spec. getting closer and closer to a goal but never quite reaching it) *adv.*: **asymptotically**. [In geometry, an asymptote is a line whose distance to a given curve tends to zero, but never actually reaches it.] ❖ The objective has to be to reduce reasonably the number of people who are searched [at airports], and perhaps the scope of the search. . . . If the passenger has a clean police record, a family, a job, retirement savings—add these up, one at a time, as the needle on the dial inches **asymptotically** towards 0 likelihood, and you have accomplished something which translates into fewer strip searches for women—or, for that matter, men. (William F. Buckley, "Just Say No," *National Review*, 12/27/2004.)

closure *n.*: **quietus**. See *termination*

clothe (as in outfit or equip) *v.t.*: **accouter**. See *outfit*

(2) **clothe** (or adorn in a showy or excessive manner) *v.t.*: **bedizen**. See *adorn*

clothed (being partially, carelessly, or casually . . .) *n.*: **dishabille** [French]. See *attired*

(2) **clothed** (inappropriately . . .) *adj.*: **misclad**. See *dressed*

clothes *n.*: **habiliment(s)**. See *clothing*

clothier (for men) *n.*: **haberdasher**. ❖ The outlook for menswear retailers is, in fact, bright, insisted Len Kubas, president of Kubas Consultants, in Toronto. [One] reason for **haberdashers** to be optimistic [is that] the casual clothing sector is seeing yet another wave of U.S. retailers coming to Canada. (Steven Theobald, "Menswear Ripe for Consolidation," *Toronto Star*, 12/29/2000.)

clothing (showy article of . . .) *n.*: **froufrou**. ❖ The color-splashed cartoon couture of French fashion sensation Christian Lacroix may be fine for playful Parisiennes, but what's a working woman to do? Impress a client by turning up in a bustle? Show up for a board meeting wearing a **froufrou**? (Mary Vespa, Style, *People*, 11/23/1987, p. 149.)

(2) **clothing** *n.*: **habiliment(s)**. ❖ Anyone coming to London for the first time would be shocked at the extraordinary departure from the regulation black **habiliments** of an old-time Londoner's wardrobe to the wildest extravagances based on the time-honored elements of the rainbow and developed into half-holiday superlatives of a color mixer's dreams. (*International Herald Tribune*, In Our Pages: 100, 75 and 50 Years Ago—1897: Wild Fashion," 7/12/1997.)

(3) **clothing** *n.*: **raiment**. ❖ The All England Clubbies [at the Wimbledon Tennis Club] were quaking, remembering the 1972 contretemps over little Rosie Casals' nifty little dress adorned with violet squiggles. The frocked-up Casals was ordered to leave Court One and change to the prescribed "predominantly white" **raiment** forthwith. Presumably, the offending gown was sent to the Tower to be drawn-and-quartered. (Bud Collins, Wimbledon 2001: "Agassi at Peak of Arrogant Artistry," *Independent* [London], 6/25/2001.)

(4) **clothing** (and equipment for newborn baby) *n.*: **layette**. See *newborn*

(5) **clothing** (richly ornamented) *n.*: **caparison**. See *finery*

cloud (low, dark gray . . . that precedes rain) *n.*: **nimbostratus**. ❖ **Nimbostratus** clouds follow next, bringing with them a gray day. Rain tends to be widespread, coming steadily or in long showers alternating with drizzle. (Eliot Tozer, "An Eye to the Sky," *Horticulture*, 3/1/1998, p. 58.)

(2) **cloud** (type of . . . that is dense, white, and fluffy) *n.*: **cumulus**. ❖ Humidity in the air condenses to form puffy, **cumulus** clouds, which can grow to produce showers or even thunderstorms. (Bill Leonard, "Clouds Often Mark Seabreeze Front," *USA Today*, 7/7/1994.)

(3) **cloud** (over one's vision) *v.t.*: **obnubilate**. See *obscure*

clouds (used of . . . that are luminous at night) *adj.*: **noctilucent**. ❖ The clouds are called **noctilucent** because they are visible long after dusk. They float 50 miles up, Thomas said, reflecting sunlight during the long twilight hours of summer months in polar regions. (Robert Cooke, "A Lovely Glow in Sky Signals Ugly Warning," *Newsday*, 5/31/1994.)

cloudy (as in a failure to perceive something clearly or accurately, or not being based on clear observation or analysis as a result of being cross-eyed, literally or figuratively) *adj.*: **strabismic**. See *cross-eyed*

(2) **cloudy** (as in overcast) *adj.*: **lowering**. See *overcast*

clown (as in buffoon, who is sometimes boastful) *n.*: **Scaramouch**. See *buffoon*

(2) clown (one who resembles a short, fat . . .) *n.*: **Punchinello**. ❖ The ringmaster, a hunchbacked **Punchinello** with bright red coat and bright red hair, is only one performer among many. (John Gross, The Arts: "Incredible Feats Amid the Flames," *Sunday Telegraph*, 1/11/1998.)

(3) clown (unintentional . . .) *n.*: **balatron**. See *buffoon*

club (as in nightclub or cabaret) *n.*: **boîte** [French]. See *nightclub*

(2) club (as in to beat with a . . .) *v.t.*: **cudgel**. ❖ They were **cudgeling** people who could barely raise an arm in self-protection. (Daniel Goldhagen, *Hitler's Willing Executioners*, Knopf [1996], p. 357.)

clue (to solving a puzzle or deciphering a code that has not previously been solved or deciphered) *n.*: **Rosetta stone** [derives from a tablet found in 1799 in Rosetta, Egypt, that furnished the first clues to deciphering Egyptian hieroglyphics]. ❖ Cancer researchers say they've discovered a tumor control gene which, when abnormal, leads to several types of cancer. . . . "They've hit upon the **Rosetta stone** of cancer study," said Marston Linehan of the National Cancer Institute. . . . "We are already tremendously impressed and excited to hear about it." (*Newsday*, "Rosetta Stone of Cancer Study," 2/24/1996.)

clueless (as in ignorant) *adj.*: **nescient** (*n.*: **nescience**). See *ignorant*

(2) clueless (as in intellectually or morally unenlightened) *adj.*: **benighted**. See *unenlightened*

clumsy (and awkward boy) *n.*: **hobbledehoy**. ❖ To hear Republicans tell it, however, Clinton remains a **hobbledehoy**, stuck in the immature foreign policy of what might be called his first term, the period from 1992 to 1994. (Jacob Heilbrun, "Univisionary," *New Republic*, 11/11/1996, p. 6.)

(2) clumsy (like an elephant) *adj.*: **elephantine**. ❖ The bureaucracy in a company [Sears] that employs 526,000 people is **elephantine**, out of touch with the consumer, and too

unwieldy to coordinate change. (Patricia Sellers, "Selling: Why Bigger Is Badder at Sears," *Fortune*, 12/5/1988, p. 79.)

(3) clumsy *adj.*: **lumpish**. ❖ Farley may make people feel better, but his character, Tommy Callahan, just makes them nervous. Ever since he was a kid, the **lumpish** youth has been walking into glass doors and making a shambles of his life and furniture. (John Anderson, "Farley and Spade's *SNL* Skit Gone Long," *Newsday*, 3/31/1995.)

(4) clumsy *adj.*: **bunglesome**. ❖ If the up-and-coming Phillies have an Achilles' heel, it's at second base with Marlon Anderson, who's been **bunglesome** at best this spring. (Chris Jenkins, "Big Mac Takes Rip at Realignment Proposal," *San Diego Union-Tribune*, 3/12/2000.)

(5) clumsy *adj.*: **ambisinister** (lit. two left hands). ❖ An Anglican chum of my mum's / Is so clumsy, we say when he comes: / "It's the maladroit minister, / *Tres* **ambisinister**. / Left hand or right, he's all thumbs." (Tim Alborn, *The Omnificent English Dictionary in Limerick Form* [oedilf.com], 10/7/2004.)

(6) clumsy (habitually . . . person) *n.*: **schlemiel** [Yiddish]. See *bumbler*

cluster (of riders in a bike race) *n.*: **peloton** [French]. ❖ [Bicycle racer Greg LeMond] conquers the hills. He conquers the flat-out sprints. He conquers the piranhas of the **peloton**, the grand mass of 197 riders that surrounds him. (Leigh Montville, "Triumph," *Sports Illustrated*, 7/30/1990, p. 16.)

(2) cluster (as in group) *n.*: **gaggle**. See *group*

(3) cluster (of objects, people, or ideas) *n.*: **congeries**. See *collection*

clutch (person who maintains, or thing that maintains, a tenacious . . . on something, whether literally or figuratively) *n.*: **limpet**. See *clinger*

clutching (adapted for . . . , esp. a tail) *adj.*: **prehensile**. See *grasping*

clutter (as in confusion) *n., adj.*: **hugger-mugger**. See *confusion*

coach (as in teacher) *n.*: **pedagogue**. See *teacher*

(2) coach *v.t.*: **catechize**. See *teach*

coarse (language) *n.*: **billingsgate**. See *language*

(2) coarse (or poorly put together, esp. with respect to writing or speech) *adj.*: **incondite**. See *crude*

(3) coarse (woman who is also abusive) *n.*: **fishwife**. See *woman*

coast (as in glide, through the air like glider) *n., v.i.*: **volplane**. See *glide*

coastline *n.*: (of or on a . . .) *adj.*: **littoral**. See *shore*

coat of arms (bearing or entitled to bear) *adj.*: **armigerous**. ❖ Now we read of [Michael] Barrymore's fear that he has AIDS, while he has booked himself into the Meadows Clinic in Arizona. Yuck. Just as the **armigerous** have mottos on their coats of arms, so variety artistes have catchphrases. I never thought that Barrymore's "Aw-wight?" was really quite good enough. It must be the feeblest catchphrase ever. (A. N. Wilson, "It's Not Aw-wight, Michael," *Evening Standard* [London], 6/11/2001.)

coax (as in extract or pry or force out, whether from a place or position, or information) *v.t.*: **winkle** (usually used with *out*). See *extract*

coaxing (by flattery) *n.*: **blandishment** (*v.t.*: **blandish**). See *flattery*

(2) coaxing (to win over or obtain by . . .) *v.t.*: **inveigle**. See *lure*

cocky (and vain) *adj.*: **vainglorious**. See *boastful*

coddle *n., v.t.*: **wet-nurse**. ❖ [Tennis coach Nick Bollettieri on deciding to stop coaching Mary Pierce:] "It's been coming for quite a while now. Mary has to get her own coach. She needs somebody. I refuse to go on baby-sitting for Mary Pierce; I am not going to **wet-nurse** her. She has to commit herself all over again to her career." (*USA Today*, "Old Hand Woodforde Advances to Quarterfinals," 1/21/1996.)

(2) coddle (in an overprotective way or indulge) *v.t.*: **mollycoddle**. See *overprotect*

(3) coddle *v.t.*: **cosset**. See *pamper*

code (as in figure of speech, where a part is used to stand for the whole or vice versa) *n.*: **synecdoche**. See *figure of speech*

code name *n.*: **cryptonym**. ❖ [There was] a decade-long effort [by U.S. intelligence] to encourage a military coup in Iraq. For much of that time, the secret coup plot was known within the CIA by the **cryptonym** "DBACHILLES." Now, with Saddam Hussein's regime deposed, U.S. and Iraqi sources have provided a detailed account of a coup strategy that never delivered. (David Ignatius, "The CIA and the Coup That Wasn't," *Washington Post*, 5/16/2003.)

codes (secret . . . hidden in various forms of communication) *n.*: **steganography**. ❖ [Although some] who monitor terrorism decry **steganography** as a threat, it's also a liberating tool for people in countries like China, where Internet blocks, or "firewalls," prevent citizens from learning anything that is not advantageous to the regime. "For every Al Qaeda member who's using **steganography** to hide something, there's someone else using it to aid the democratic process," argues Diebert. (Olivia Ward, "Global Terror Battle Moves to Net," *Toronto Star*, 9/7/2003.)

code words (spec. words conveying an innocent meaning to an outsider but with a concealed meaning to an informed person, often to avoid censorship or punishment) *n.*: **Aesopian language** ❖ Previously [in the Soviet Union], students and teachers were forced to follow patently false and hypocritical programs of history and social thought. Any opposition was forced into covert speech in **Aesopian language**. Extraordinarily sharp political jokes and anecdotes abounded—the dark humor of suffering. (Irwin Weil, "The USSR's Creative Democrats Refused to Be Cowed," *Chicago Tribune*, 8/23/1991.)

codger (as in cranky or stubborn old man) *n.*: **alter kocker** [Yiddish]. See *old man*

codify (as in classify) *v.t.*: **taxonomize**. See *classify*

coerce (or trick someone into doing something, esp. by fraud) *v.t.*: **shanghai** (person who does so *n.*: **shanghaier**). ❖ They live apart and she can't remember the date they got married. But

Carmen Electra wants the world to know that she is very definitely Mrs. Dennis Rodman and that she's not a gold-digging, NBA-star **shanghaier**. "We are legally married," the actress and singer said yesterday. "We love each other very much and we're doing great." (Claire Bickley, "Together, Whatever; Marriage to Rodman's Real, Though Bizarre, Electra Says," *Edmonton Sun*, 1/8/1999.)

(2) coerce (to act, esp. by violent measures or threats) *v.t.*: **dragoon**. ❖ If the men and women using and **dragooning** slave laborers are included (over 7.6 million in the German Reich in August 1944), then the numbers of Germans who perpetrated grievous crimes might run into the millions. (Daniel Goldhagen, *Hitler's Willing Executioners*, Knopf [1996], p. 166.)

(3) coerce (a person or group to go from one place to another, whether literally or figuratively) *v.t.*: **frogmarch**. See *march*

coexisting (possibility of two things . . . together) *adj.*: **compossible**. See *compatible*

cognizance (as in attention) *n.*: **advertence**. See *attention*

cognizant (as in consciously perceiving) *adj.*: **sentient**. See *conscious*

cohabitation (as in marriage or sexual relations involving people of different races) *n.*: **miscegenation**. See *sex*

coincidence (as in discovering fortunate things by accident) *n.*: **serendipity** (*adj.*: **serendipitous**). See *fortuitous*

coincident (as in simultaneously) *adv.*: **holus-bolus**. See *simultaneously*

coincidental (as in random) *adj.*: **stochastic**. See *random*

coins (of or relating to . . . , including collecting) *adj.*: **numismatic**. ❖ [T]here are some very legitimate **numismatic** collectibles being promoted. For instance, the U.S. Mint regularly advertises highly polished mirror proof and uncirculated American coins—real coins that collectors eagerly snap up. (Peter Rexford, "How to Tell if Coin Is a Good Investment," *St. Louis Post-Dispatch*, 9/21/1995.)

cold (causing or producing) *adj.*: **frigorific**. ❖ Boston is ill-equipped for [a Mardi Gras–type celebration]. Picture it: people exposing sensitive body parts in the **frigorific** breezes. It just wouldn't happen, and if it did, these raucous individuals would be picked up for indecent exposure or end up at [the hospital]. Generally with painful and unusual cases of frostbite. (Christopher Muther, Go! Tuesday, *Boston Globe*, 2/12/2002.)

(2) cold (of or relating to very . . . temperatures) *adj.*: **cryogenic**. ❖ To deal with the outlaws [in the movie *Demolition Man*, set in 2032], Cocteau frees a killer named Simon Phoenix (Wesley Snipes) from **cryogenic** prison (they took to deep-freezing criminals as early as 1996, during the last convulsive phase of urban warfare). (Richard Schickel, The Arts, *Time* International, 11/1/1993, p. 47.)

(3) cold (very . . .) *adj.*: **gelid**. ❖ It's evening [in December]. I begin to walk across the parking lot toward my hotel. My exhalations are steamy in the **gelid** air. Suddenly, my feet slide out from under me on a sheer patch of ice. (Mark Leyner, "Xmas in Newark," *Esquire*, 12/1/1997, p. 52.)

(4) cold *adj.*: **algid**. ❖ Anyone who has read Paul Theroux's *Riding the Iron Rooster: By Train Through China* will know of the wonders of Harbin, the **algid** Chinese city where remarkable ice sculptures remain all winter long. (William Furney, "N'ice and Easy Does It at Ice Carving Contest," *Jakarta Post*, 7/9/2000.)

(5) cold (very . . .) *adj.*: **hyperborean**. See *freezing*

(6) cold (as in cruel) *adj.*: **fell** (*n.*: **fellness**). See *cruel*

(7) cold (as in of, like, or occurring in winter) *adj.*: **brumal**. See *winter*

(8) cold (as in unfeeling, person, as in one who is interested only in cold, hard facts, with little concern for emotion or human needs) *n.*: **Gradgrind**. See *unfeeling*

cold-blooded *adj.*: **ectothermic** ❖ The assumption that dinosaurs were **ectothermic** —cold-blooded—was originally based on a simple argument. Reptiles are **ectothermic**—they can't regulate their body heat. If they get too hot, they die. If they get too cold, they get sluggish. Dinosaurs were closely related to reptiles. End of argument. (Michael D. Lemonick, Science: "Rewriting the Book on Dinosaurs," *Time*, 4/26/1993, p. 42.)

coldhearted (as in cruel) *adj.*: **fell** (*n.*: **fellness**). See *cruel*

(2) coldhearted (as in unfeeling, person, as in one who is interested only in cold, hard facts, with little concern for emotion or human needs) *n.*: **Gradgrind**. See *unfeeling*

coldness (often in relations between people) *n.*: **froideur** [French]. See *chilliness*

collapse (violent or turbulent . . . of a society or regime) *n.*: **Götterdämmerung** [German]. ❖ What did happen to Hitler in the **Gotterdammerung** of the Third Reich? The widely accepted version . . . is that on April 30, 1945, Hitler committed suicide in his command bunker in Berlin and that his body was burned in the garden just outside, as he had expressly ordered. (Julie K. Dam, *Time* International, 5/8/1995, p. 45.)

(2) collapse (of a group or social structure as a result of lack of standards or values) *n.*: **anomie**. See *breakdown*

(3) collapse (of or relating to a . . . , esp. after an innocent or carefree time) *adj.*: **postlapsarian**. See *downfall*

(4) collapse (as in downfall, esp. from a position of strength) *n.*: **dégringolade** [French]. See *downfall*

colleague *n.*: **confrere**. ❖ [Lamar Alexander] defends the environmental legislation that his congressional **confreres** are trying to gut, arguing that Republicans "should be the champions of the great outdoors . . . of clean air, clean water, an open space to walk in. Our party is doing a poor job on conservation." (Ruth Shalit, "Sinking, Shining Tennessean: On the Road with Lamar Alexander," *New Republic*, 2/26/1996, p. 18.)

(2) colleague (as in comrade) *n.*: **tovarich** [Russian]. See *comrade*

(3) colleague (faithful . . . , as in companion) *n.*: **Achates**. See *companion*

(4) colleague (or close partner, often but not always, one in marriage) *n.*: **yokefellow**. See *partner*

collected (as in unemotional or even-tempered) *adj.*: **phlegmatic**. See *even-tempered*

collection (of objects, people, or ideas) *n.*: **congeries**. ❖ Unlike touch or taste, pain is not a simple sensation. It involves a complex **congeries** of senses, memories, attitudes, and emotions that affect how people perceive pain and how their bodies respond to it. (Gene Bylinsky, "Health: New Gains in the Fight Against Pain," *Fortune*, 3/22/1993, p. 107.)

(2) collection (confused or jumbled . . .) *n.*: **agglomeration**. See *jumble*

(3) collection (of writings by an author) *n.*: **chrestomathy**. See *anthology*

college rules (or of relating to . . . , esp. regarding visiting privileges of the opposite sex in dormitories) *adj.*: **parietal**. ❖ A group of students at Simon's Rock, part of Bard College, is fighting the **parietal** rules against nonresident students' staying overnight in single-sex freshmen dormitories. The administration is showing signs of retreat. (*New York Times*, Campus Life, 12/17/1989.)

collision (spec. the act of one object striking a stationary object, usually applied to ships) *n.*: **allision**. ❖ The analysis said more than 300 collisions and "**allisions**," which involve a moving vessel striking a stationary object, have occurred in the Port of New Orleans in the last 10 years. (George F. W. Tefler, "Casinos in New Orleans Port Increase Risks, Report Says," *Journal of Commerce*, 11/11/1994, p. 1B.)

colloquial (language of the people) *n.*: **vulgate**. See *vernacular*

color (having only one . . .) *adj.*: **monochromatic**. ❖ Turns out, quiz-show host Regis Philbin, a newly minted menswear purveyor, is the one legislating this summer's hot new look: a men's cotton dress shirt with a glossy necktie in the same color—solid black, tan, blue or green. . . . [Several designers] have sent the

monochromatic look down the runways. (Francine Parnes, "*Millionaire*'s Philbin Sets the Style," *Washington Times*, 7/26/2000.)

(2) color (relating to . . . or colors) *adj.*: **chromatic**. ❖ New York designers have wiped the slate clean of all that is dark, drab and dreary. Whether such colourful optimism is authentic or wishful thinking, this funky, **chromatic** vibration embraces spring's sleek, sexy clothing with lightness and brightness. (Sylvi Capelaci, "Colour Report," *Ottawa Sun*, 2/15/2000.)

colorblindness (total . . .) *n.*: **achromatopsia**. ❖ Olof Sundin, an assistant professor of ophthalmology at Johns Hopkins and a co-investigator of the **achromatopsia** study, said the condition results from the lack of a protein required for color detection and optimal daytime sight. (Delthia Ricks, "Origins of Our Diversity," *Newsday*, 6/27/2000.)

colorful (esp. in an iridescent way) *adj.*: **opalescent**. See *iridescent*

coloring (of or relating to . . . , as in dyeing) *adj.*: **tinctorial**. See *dyeing*

colorless *adj.*: **achromatic**. ❖ Men also typically dream in black and white. . . . **Achromatic** dreaming probably reflects the fact that men have more rigid boundaries—between thoughts and emotions, right and wrong, sanity and madness—than women do. (Michael Segell, "Dreams: His and Hers," *Esquire*, 2/1/1996, p. 42.)

(2) colorless (as in pale, and often sickly) *adj.*: **etiolated**. See *pale*

colors (use of many . . . , esp. in paintings, statues, and works of art) *n.*: **polychromy**. ❖ Riemenschneider was one of the first to abandon **polychromy**, relying on wood transfigured by his own virtuosic technique to boost religious devotion. . . . Avoiding color was a way to make his sculptures more safely abstract, distancing them from the accusations of idolatry that the Reformation continuously hurled at religious art. (Ariella Budick, "Sculpting an Enduring Name for a Gothic Great," *Newsday*, 2/10/2000.)

(2) colors (having different . . .) *n.*: **heterochromatic**. See *multicolored*

(3) colors (having many . . .) *n.*: **polychromatic**. See *multicolored*

combat (act or event that causes or provokes . . . , literally or figuratively) *n.*: **casus belli** [Latin; occasion of war]. See *provocation*

(2) combat (engaged in . . . , as in a struggle) *adj.*: **agonistes**. See *struggle*

combative *adj.*: **agonistic**. [Book reviews are] the only . . . endeavour where the object of study, and the review, are both made of the same stuff: prose. People don't review architecture with bricks, or ballet with free-form interpretive dance. So, at a fundamental level, reviewing is implicitly competitive: my prose beside (whether against or at the service of) yours. [Bad book reviews are] **agonistic.** The most spectacular are the attacks from below: David socking Goliath. (Sam Lieth, Commentary: "A Critic Can Go Too Far," *Daily Telegraph* [London], 5/21/2005.)

(2) combative *adj.*: **bellicose**. See *belligerent*

combine (as in bring together) *v.t.*: **conflate**. ❖ The women who passed through [Jerry Lewis's] life are cast by his words as mothers, not sex partners [Lewis often claimed that "they wanted to burp me"]. . . . It would be cheap Freudianism to suggest that he slept around because his mother hadn't shown him sufficient love, but he was the one who repeatedly **conflated** extramarital sex with the care and feeding of an infant. (Shawn Levy, *The King of Comedy*, St. Martin's Press [1996], p. 95.)

(2) combine *v.t.*: **amalgamate**. ❖ A key part of the program's ideology is to have special-needs children mix with other Jewish day-school pupils as much as possible [which] allows them "to see themselves more as normal children." Moreover, Leberman believes that **amalgamating** classes also helps the community as a whole. (*Jewish Exponent*, "A Light Unto the Schools," 3/18/1999, p. 1.)

(3) combine (in a series or chain) *v.t.*, *adj.*: **concatenate** (*n.*: **concatenation**). See *connect*

(4) combine *v.t.*, *v.i.*: **inosculate**. See *blend*

combined (closely . . .) *adj.*: **coadunate**. See *joined*

    (2) combined (of things that cannot be . . .) *adj.*: **immiscible**. See *incompatible*

combustible *adj.*: **tindery**. See *flammable*

comeback (clever . . . that one thinks of after the moment has passed) *n.*: **esprit d'escalier** [French]. See *retort*

    (2) comeback (of something after a period of dormancy or inactivity) *n.*: **recrudescence** (*v.i.*: **recrudesce**). See *reappearance*

comedown (as in anticlimax) *n.*: **bathos**. See *anticlimax*

comedy *n.*: **jocosity**. See *humor*

come in (suddenly or forcibly, as in burst in) *v.i.*: **irrupt**. See *burst in*

comeliness *n.*: **pulchritude**. See *beauty*

come near (as in approach) *v.t.*: **appropinquate**. See *approach*

comes back (one who . . . after lengthy absence or death) *n.*: **revenant**. See *returns*

come to pass (as in happen or occur) *v.t.*: **betide**. See *happen*

come up with (an idea, plan, theory, or explanation after careful thought) *v.t.*: **excogitate**. See *devise*

comfort (as in placate) *v.t.*: **propitiate**. See *placate*

comfortable (as in warm and cozy) *adj.*: **gemütlich** [German]. See *cozy*

comforter (false . . . , as in one who discourages another by offering remarks that supposedly have the opposite intent) *n.*: **Job's comforter**. [In the Bible, Job is a prosperous man whose patience and piety are tested by a series of undeserved misfortunes. The attempts of his friends to comfort him only add to his sense of despair, and he tells them: "miserable comforters are ye all" (Job 16:2). The effect of the remarks can be either tactless (i.e., unintentional) or malicious (i.e., intentional). In a newspaper contest asking for humorous examples, people offered the following: "You're much better in bed than your sister." "I can't believe your husband ran off with the nanny. Oh well, at least you know she'll be good with your kids if he marries her." (*Washington Post*,

"The Style Invitational," 2/13/2005.)] ❖ Newt Gingrich was forced to resign as Speaker of the House after] an enormously expensive campaign of nasty TV commercials [and] a series of Mickey Mouse ethics charges intended by the Democrats in the House to bedevil and distract him. . . . Nor had he through all this been lacking in **Job's comforters** in the conservative community to instruct him in the many different ways he had brought it all upon himself . . . (Midge Decter, "Comeback Kid?" *National Review*, 12/7/1998).

comforting (agent) *n.*: **anodyne**. See *pain reliever* and *soothing*

    (2) comforting (lotion or balm) *n.*: **demulcent**. See *soothing*

comical *adj.*: **gelastic**. See *laughable*

    (2) comical *adj.*: **risible**. See *laughable*

coming-of-age (spec. a novel that follows the development of its main character over time) *n.*: **bildungsroman** [German]. ❖ Taken as a whole, the trilogy is a **bildungsroman** about Patrick Melrose—a damaged 5-year-old in the first novel, a 22-year-old junkie in the second and, in the third, a drug-free 30-year-old trying to put the past behind him. (Leo Carey, "A Bag of Heroin and a Crisp White Shirt," *New York Times*, 1/4/2004.)

command (as in order or direct) *v.t.*: **adjure**. See *order*

commander *n.*: **duce** [Italian]. ❖ [In Bosnia and Kosovo, Serbian leader] Slobodan Milosevic unleashed a violent campaign of terror against an ethnicity that represents a challenge to the legitimacy of his rule and its fascist, racialist foundations. Once again it took a particular bloodbath to concentrate the minds of Washington, New York, and Brussels on the policies of the **duce** of Serbia. (*New Republic*, "The Villain," 10/26/1998.)

    (2) commander *n.*: **imperator**. [This word originally referred to the supreme commander in the Roman Empire, but now is also used to refer to commander and leaders generally.] ❖ [Baltimore Orioles owner] Peter Angelos, Lord Paramount of Baltimore, Most

Regal **Imperator** of Maryland and now Prime [Ruler] of the National Capital Area, long ago decreed that there shall be no baseball in the Washington region save His Very Own. (Marc Fisher, "To Angelos, the Power and the Money, *Washington Post*, 6/24/2002.)

(3) commander (or ruler, esp. hereditary) *n.*: **dynast**. See *ruler*

commendation (or to bestow a . . . upon, as in an accolade) *n.*, *v.t.*: **garland**. See *accolade*

(2) commendation *n.*: **approbation**. See *praise*

comment (additional . . . , as in explanation) *n.*: **epexegesis** (*adj.*: **epexegetic**). See *explanation*

(2) comment (as in insight or observation) *n.*: **aperçu** [French]. See *insight*

(3) comment (as in statement, which is left unfinished because the speaker is unwilling or unable to continue or because the rest of the message is implicit) *n.*: **aposiopesis**. See *statement*

(4) comment (in which one references an issue by saying that one will not discuss it; e.g., "I'm not even going to get into the character issue") *n.*: **apophasis**. See *figure of speech*

(5) comment (on a topic, esp. in a long-winded or pompous manner) *v.i.*: **bloviate**. See *speak*

(6) comment (on in a scholarly manner, often used in a derogatory fashion) *v.i.*: **lucubrate**. See *discourse*

(7) comment (or expression or phrase that is elegant, concise, witty, and/or well-put) *n.*: **atticism**. See *expression*

(8) comment (or line that is witty) *n.*: **epigram**. See *quip*

(9) comment (upon, esp. at length) *v.i.*, *n.*: **descant**. See *talk*

commentator (spec. one who provides comments, explanation, or interpretation of a text) *n.*: **glossator**. ❖ The texts of the Talmud . . . seem the very enemy of style, the very enemy of system. And yet, as the generations of **glossators** saw, they are never what they seem. They are, in fact, masterpieces of style, of a precise, chiseled, classical language rarely equaled for the intensity of its beauty. And they are the unsystematic records of some of the earliest monuments of systematic thought. (Leon Wieseltier, "Unlocking the Rabbis' Secrets," *New York Times*, 12/17/1989.)

commingled (of things that cannot be . . .) *adj.*: **immiscible**. See *incompatible*

commiserator (false . . . , as in one who discourages another by offering remarks that supposedly have the opposite intent) *n.*: **Job's comforter**. See *comforter*

commitment (as in allegiance) *n.*: **vassalage**. See *allegiance*

common (of or relating to the . . . people) *adj.*: **plebian**. ❖ [Queen] Victoria worked on two levels: She liked **plebian** pleasures, such as those offered by the showman P. T. Barnum and his midget Tom Thumb [but she also liked art,] ballet and the opera. (Stanley Weintraub, "In His Own Words: Victorian in Name Only, the Queen Was Amused in the Bedroom and Elsewhere," *People*, 6/22/1987, p. 58.)

(2) common (as in mundane; everyday) *adj.*: **sublunary**. See *earthly*

(3) common (in tastes and ideas and culture) *adj.*: **philistine**. See *uncultured*

(4) common (language of the people) *n.*: **vulgate**. See *vernacular*

(5) common (pertaining to the . . . people) *adj.*: **demotic**. See *masses*

(6) common (the . . . people, as in the masses) *n.*: **canaille**. See *masses*

commoners *n.*: **hoi polloi**. ❖ Fame has style, glamour, money, attention; ignites the sudden light of recognition in strangers' eyes, commands the comic deference of headwaiters as they sweep you past the serfs and **hoi polloi** to the best table. (Lance Morrow, "Fame Offers Delights and Burdens, Boredom and—Especially—Menace," *Time*, 9/15/1997, p. 76.)

(2) commoners (as in the masses) *n.*: **vulgus** [Latin]. See *masses*

commonplace *adj.*: **quotidian**. See *mundane*

common sense (person who hates . . . or enlightenment) *n.*: **misologist**. See *closed-minded*

commotion *n.*: **bobbery**. ❖ Big plans for a big

public safety building are creating bad vibes in Sausalito. The 7,300 people in this normally peaceful waterfront town are going apoplectic for and against plans to build a $7.8 million, 22,500-square-foot police and fire building at the foot of Caledonia Street. The whole **bobbery**, which has simmered for years, will finally come to a boil on Tuesday with a vote on advisory Measure B. (Peter Fimrite, "Feng Shui a Sausalito Voter Issue," *San Francisco Chronicle*, 2/27/2002.)

(2) commotion *n.*: **kerfuffle**. ❖ The Associated Press reports on an interesting political-correctness **kerfuffle**: "When a few . . . classmates razzed Rebekah Rice about her Mormon upbringing with questions such as, 'Do you have 10 moms?' she shot back: 'That's so gay.' After Rice got a warning . . . her parents sued, claiming [that the school] disciplined her for uttering a phrase 'which enjoys widespread currency in youth culture.'" (James Taranto, "Sensitivity vs. P.C.," *Chicago Sun-Times*, 3/4/2007.)

(3) commotion *n.*: **maelstrom**. ❖ Monica Lewinsky—the former White House intern—is at the center of the **maelstrom**, alleged to have had an extended sexual liaison with [President] Clinton. (Linda Feldmann, "The Stakes Suddenly Rise for Clinton," *Christian Science Monitor*, 1/23/1998.)

(4) commotion *n.*: **pother**. ❖ Australia's arts community is in a colossal **pother**. On March 7 it was revealed that the supposedly Aboriginal painter Mr. Eddie Burrup, whose daubings have recently been the wow of Australian museum curators and gallery owners, is no Aborigine at all. Mr. Burrup is actually an 82-year-old woman of Irish descent, Miss Elizabeth Durack. (*American Spectator*, "The Continuing Crisis: Al Gets Chinese, the Danes Get Wild," 5/1/1997.)

(5) commotion *n.*: **charivari**. See *hubbub*

(6) commotion (and confusion, esp. from simultaneous voices) *n.*: **babel**. See *noise*

(7) commotion (over a trifling matter) *n.*: **foofaraw**. See *fuss*

communicate (as in send a signal) *v.t.*, *v.i.*: **semaphore**. See *signal*

communication (spec. the study and analysis of symbols and signs as part of . . . , as in language, gesture, clothing, and behavior) *n.pl.*: **semiotics**. ❖ They boarded the plane ahead of the other passengers wearing to the very last minute their trademark trench coats—the sexy **semiotics**, as they interpreted it, of international mystery and intrigue. (Tova Reich, *My Holocaust*, HarperCollins [2007], p. 5.)

(2) communication (medium of . . . between people of different languages) *n.*: **lingua franca**. See *language*

(3) communication (with the dead or their spirits) *n.*: **necromancy**. See *divination*

(4) communication (having a good feel for what is linguistically appropriate in using spoken or written . . .) *n.*: **sprachgefühl** [German]. See *language*

community (united by close personal bonds) *n.*: **gemeinschaft** (sometimes cap.). [German. This is a sociological category introduced by the German sociologist Ferdinand Tönnies in 1887. It refers to a close-knit group or association united by common ideals, beliefs about the appropriate behavior and responsibility of members of the association, and strong personal ties. Self-interest is deemphasized in favor of the greater good. The contrasting type of association is "gesellschaft," where members act more in their own interest. Gesellschaft is associated with modern industrial life, mobility, heterogeneity, and impersonality. See *association*, which includes an example that uses both terms.] A chief source of the pleasure of the [*Washington Past*] Style section is its tone of intimacy with its readers, of Baby Boomer **Gemeinschaft**. The assumed "we" of its writers is a generation united by a rock-and-Hollywood, Vietnam-and-Watergate patrimony. It is taken for granted that "we" have all been to college and are liberals—probably liberals who work in government. (Joseph Sobran, "The Rise of Style," *National Review*, 6/21/1993.)

(2) community (Spanish-speaking) *n.*: **barrio**. See *Spanish*

compacted (something . . . , as in abridged) *n.*: **bobtail**. See *abridged*

companion (faithful . . .) *n.*: **Achates** (often as in "fidus Achates," "fidus" being Latin for "faithful") [derives from Achates, who was a close companion of Aeneas in Virgil's *Aeneid*]. ❖ In my teens, [Tony Mulligan] was the first in our little backwater who was "cool." . . . I cultivated him like a hothouse plant. And then I noticed the second advantage to being his fidus **Achates**—girls. He was exceptionally popular with girls—all of the good-looking, clean and clever ones that nobody else could get near. (Dennis O'Donnell, "Words of Wisdom: An Open-Sesame to the World of Romance," *Scotsman*, 11/13/1998.)

(2) companion (as in comrade) *n.*: **tovarich** [Russian]. See *comrade*

(3) companion (or close partner, often but not always, one in marriage) *n.*: **yokefellow**. See *partner*

companionship (as in fellowship or association) *n.*: **sodality**. See *fellowship*

company (as in fellowship or association) *n.*: **sodality**. See *fellowship*

compare (by way of setting in contrast) *adv.*: **per contra**. See *contrast*

(2) compare (by way of setting in contrast) *v.t.*: **counterpose**. See *contrast*

compassion (relating to an argument appealing to one's sense of . . .) *adv., adj.*: **ad misericordiam** [Latin]. See *argument*

compassionate *adj.*: **ruthful**. [While *ruthless* is of course a common word, most people are not aware that *ruth* is a noun, meaning pity or mercy or compassion, and that *ruthful* is an adjectival form of that word. The word can be used in the sense of genuine sympathy or compassion (as in the example given), or in the sense of pity. See *pitiful*.] ❖ [F]or many voters, the ideal legislative candidate remains the Republican Woman, a combination that suggests the blend of the tough-minded and tender-hearted. The late Robert Kennedy could safely empha-size compassion in his Democratic presidential campaign because so many critics had already branded him "ruthless." Voters, who are both **ruthful** and assertive, recognize that we live in a difficult and dangerous world, and therefore prefer national leaders who share that judgment. (Mark Shields, "The Feminine and Masculine Parties," *Washington Post*, 3/11/1986.)

compatibility (in the arrangement of parts as part of a whole) *n.*: **concinnity**. See *harmony*

compatible *adj.*: **consonant**. See *harmony*

(2) compatible (as in possibility of two things being . . . together) *adj.*: **compossible**. ❖ Issues of morality, social justice and genuine cosmopolitanism must be preceded . . . by a fundamental analysis of what makes . . . different virtues in our era of diversity and cultural pluralism **compossible** . . . (Geoffrey Hartman, review of *The Persistence of Romanticism: Essays in Philosophy and Literature*, by Richard Eldridge, *Wordsworth Circle*, 9/22/2001.)

(3) compatible *adj.*: **simpatico**. ❖ Hundt voices the "new Democrat" themes of economic expansion and job growth. "He's very **simpatico** with the Clinton economic principles," Allard says. (Del Jones, "FCC Chief Doesn't Take His Role Lightly," *USA Today*, 2/25/1994.)

compatriot *n.*: **paisano**. See *countryman*

compel (a person or group to go from one place to another, whether literally or figuratively) *v.t.*: **frogmarch**. See *march*

(2) compel (or trick someone into doing something, esp. by fraud or coercion) *v.t.*: **shanghai** (person who does so *n.*: **shanghaier**). See *coerce*

(3) compel (to act, esp. by violent measures or threats) *v.t.*: **dragoon**. See *coerce*

compelling (as in urgent) *adj.*: **necessitous**. See *urgent*

compensation (awarded for injured feelings, as opposed to financial loss or physical suffering) *n.*: **solatium**. ❖ Japan intends to review the way **solatium** payments are made to South Korean women who were forced into sexual slavery by Japanese soldiers before and during

World War II, Chief Cabinet Secretary Hiromu Nonaka indicated Monday. (Kyodo World News Service, Kyodo News Summary, 5/10/1999.)

(2) compensation (esp. as payment for damage or loss) *n.*: **quittance**. See *recompense*

(3) compensation (as in payment or wages) *n.*: **emolument**. See *wages*

competent (to handle all matters) *adj.*: **omnicompetent** [This word technically means having jurisdiction or legal capacity to act in all matters, but it is far more generally used to refer to one who can handle anything.] ❖ To label him a jack-of-all-trades is a colossal understatement. He's the kind of **omnicompetent** guy you wish were in charge of the New Orleans levee system. "The Swiss Army knife, they call me," admits Sam Ellis, describing his job as the wizard behind the curtain of *The New Mel Brooks Musical Young Frankenstein*, opening on Broadway Nov. 8. (Carol Strickland, "The Technical Wizard Behind Broadway's New Extravaganza, *Young Frankenstein*," *Christian Science Monitor*, 11/8/2007.)

competitive (as in marked by a spirit of rivalry) *adj.*: **emulous**. [This word is used in a number of different ways, including, variously, (1) competitive, (2) ambitious (as in ambitious to equal or surpass another), (3) jealous/envious. The following is an example of the first definition.] ❖ "We always like playing Boone County," Conner coach Chandra Dixon said. "It's always a good competitive game. You never get tired of playing against them because of the rivalry between the two teams." The previous three meetings between the Rebels and Cougars this season have been **emulous** to say the least. Each game has been decided by just one run with Conner owning two wins over the Rebels. (Matt Savoti, "On a Collision Course Boone, Conner May Meet for 4th Time," *Cincinnati Post*, 5/21/2001.)

(2) competitive *adj.*: **agonistic**. ❖ But the Greeks were a wildly **agonistic** people, which means they were keenly competitive at everything. It didn't take long before play and recreational fitness were formatted into local contests,

then inter-municipal meets. (Rosie DiManno, "But If, My Heart, You Wish to Sing of Contests, Look No Further for Any Star Warmer Than the Sun," *Toronto Star*, 9/14/2000.)

complain (or fret) *v.i.*: **repine**. ❖ [Jess and her husband took] up the burden of the three aged relatives living with them, [including her] mother-in-law . . . a spiteful Presbyterian. . . . Not that she noticed [but Jess] was an object of pious admiration among those who did, because of her strength and selflessness and refusal to **repine**. God had a stiffer test of her character in store, though: her husband disappeared without warning, and Jess feared he had gone into the river to escape his ghastly mother. (Thomas Sutcliffe, "The Weekend's Television: Hellishly Stiff Tests of Character," *Independent* [London], 9/13/2004.)

(2) complain (about petty matters) *v.i.*: **pettifog**. See *quibble*

(3) complain (against) *v.t.*: **expostulate**. See *object*

(4) complain (as in raise trivial objections) *v.t.*: **cavil**. See *quibble*

(5) complain (in a whiny or whimpering way) *v.i.*: **pule**. See *whimper*

(6) complain (in a whiny or whimpering way) *v.i.*: **girn** (Scottish). See *whine*

complaining *adj.*: **querulous**. See *peevish*

complaint (mournful or bitter lament or . . .) *n.*: **jeremiad**. ❖ So far Perot has trained most of his fire on the Republicans. And his **jeremiads** against "mean-spirited campaigning" could make it harder for Dole to chip away at Clinton on the "character issue." (John B. Judis, "The Third Rail—Ross Perot: America's Charles de Gaulle? *New Republic*, 5/20/1996, p. 22.)

(2) complaint (as in subservient) *adj.*: **sequacious**. See *subservient*

complementary (as in compatible) *adj.*: **simpatico**. See *compatible*

complete (esp. as in . . . power) *adj.*: **plenary**. ❖ In 1976 the [Supreme Court] held that Congress's **plenary** control over immigration gives it broad discretion to discriminate against aliens, and therefore it could restrict Medicare benefits to legal aliens who had lived in the United States for five years. "Citizens," the Court announced deferentially, "may reasonably be presumed to have a greater affinity with the United States." (Jeffrey Rosen, "The War on Immigrants: Why the Courts Can't Save Us," *New Republic*, 1/30/1995, p. 22.)

(2) complete (usually used with "nonsense") *adj.*: **arrant**. See *total*

completely (as in, in the entirety) *adv.*: **holus-bolus**. See *entirety*

(2) completely (as in, in the entirety) *adv.*: **in extenso** [Latin]. See *entirety*

complex (as in difficult to understand) *adj.*: **recondite**. See *complicated*

(2) complex (as in difficult to understand, sometimes due to being obscure) *adj.*: **abstruse**. See *difficult*

(3) complex (in design or function, as in intricate) *adj.*: **daedal**. See *intricate*

(4) complex (situation or problem) *n.*: **nodus**. See *complication*

(5) complex (situation that is . . . or chaotic or complicated) *n.*: **mare's nest**. See *chaotic*

(6) complex *adj.*: **involute**. See *intricate*

(7) complex (as in tortuous) *adj.*: **vermiculate**. See *tortuous*

(8) complex *adj.*: **byzantine**. See *complicated*

(9) complex (overly . . .) *adj.*: **Rube Goldberg**. See *complicated*

complexity *n.*: **cat's cradle**. See *intricacy*

compliance (as in marked by insistence on rigid conformity to a belief, system, or course of action without regard to individual differences) *adj.*: **Procrustean** (*n.*: **Procrustean bed**). See *conformity*

compliant *adj.*: **biddable**. See *obedient*

complicate (as in entangle) *v.t.*: **embrangle**. See *entangle*

complicated (as in difficult to understand) *adj.*: **recondite**. ❖ Paul Hoffman not only gives us a sympathetic and beautifully observed account of [mathematician Paul] Erdos's strange life, he also helps us to appreciate the appeal of this most **recondite** of human activities [pure

mathematics]. *The Man Who Loved Only Numbers* is one of the most accessible and engaging introductions to the world of pure mathematics you are ever likely to come across. (Graham Farmelo, Books: "The Prime Numbers of Mr. Paul Erdos," *Sunday Telegraph* [London], 7/19/1998.)

(2) complicated (overly . . .) *adj.*: **Rube Goldberg**. [Rube Goldberg (1883–1970) was an American cartoonist who drew incredibly complicated contraptions to perform simple tasks. For example, for the "self-operating napkin," the soup spoon is raised to the mouth, pulling a string, thereby jerking a ladle, which throws a cracker past a parrot, which then jumps at the cracker, causing the perch to tilt, thereby upsetting seeds into pail. The extra weight in the pail pulls a cord, which opens and lights an automatic cigar lighter, setting off a sky-rocket, which causes a sickle to cut a string, which causes a pendulum with the attached napkin to swing back and forth, thereby wiping the chin. Today, the word is more frequently used to describe something convoluted (such as a poorly designed political policy or a plotline), although not necessarily because a simple alternative exists. It can be used as an adjective ("a Rube Goldberg plan") and is also used in the sense of "designed by Rube Goldberg."] ❖ [T]he old-fashioned way of having shareholders elect corporate directors may be better than the **Rube Goldberg**–like plan that assures that the UAL board will be made up of factions that cannot be replaced no matter how badly things are going for the company. . . . Of the 12 members of the UAL board, 5 are chosen by public shareholders, 2 by unions and one by nonunion employees. Four are independent directors who choose their own successors. It hasn't worked. (Floyd Norris, "Pilot Woes: Why Employee Ownership Didn't Help UAL," *New York Times*, 8/11/2000.)

(3) complicated *adj.*: **byzantine**. ❖ Political life in Reed's day was dominated by powerful "bosses," and riddled with corruption. But Reed believed profoundly in representative government. Elected speaker in 1890, he launched a frontal assault on the **byzantine** system of House rules, an intricate maze "calculated better than anything else to obstruct legislation" and frustrate the will of the majority. (Katherine Kersten, "For Integrity in Politics, Take a Lesson from Tom Reed," *Minneapolis Star Tribune*, 3/12/1997.)

(4) complicated (as in tortuous) *adj.*: **vermiculate**. See *tortuous*

(5) complicated (as in difficult to understand, sometimes due to being obscure) *adj.*: **abstruse**. See *difficult*

(6) complicated (situation or problem) *n.*: **nodus**. See *complication*

(7) complicated (situation that is . . . or chaotic or confused) *n.*: **mare's nest**. See *chaotic*

(8) complicated *adj.*: **involute**. See *intricate*

complication (or difficult situation) *n.*: **nodus**. ❖ The status of Jerusalem has been the most difficult issue in the peace talks between the two sides, as Israel . . . and the Palestinians [have both claimed rights to the City]. . . . Meanwhile, the Knesset endorsed a bill on the return of Palestinian refugees, another **nodus** in the Israeli-Palestinian talks, in the first reading with a vote of 90 in favor and nine against. (Xinhua News Agency, "Israeli Parliament Adopts Bills on Jerusalem, Palestinian Refugees," 11/27/2000.)

compliment (empty, meaningless or insincere . . .) *n.*: **flummery**. ❖ "We've performed for hundreds of audiences over the years and I have to say, you were the best, the most perceptive, the most intelligent, the most attractive." Don't believe a word of Peter Lamont's **flummery**. He and his partner Richard Wiseman are natural born liars and the title of the show [*Lessons in Deception*] is about the only honest aspect of it (and even that's a half-truth). (Rory Ford, "A Trick Worth Checking Out," *Evening News* [Scotland], 4/12/2000.)

(2) compliment (as in giving praise or . . .) *n.*: **encomium** (one who delivers praise or . . . *n.*: **encomiast**). See *praise*

(3) compliment (as in tribute) *n.*: **panegyric** (one who does so, *n.*: **panegyrist**). See *tribute*

(4) compliment (or to bestow a . . . upon, as in an accolade) *n.*, *v.t.*: **garland**. See *accolade*

complimenting (insincerely . . .) *adj.*: **fulsome**. See *insincere*

comportment *n.*: **mien**. See *demeanor*

compose *v.t.*: **indite**. ❖ Second on my bill of rights would be a non-write clause. It would bar forever the **inditing** of letters to the editor by those of the frail facade. Women seem to dip their pens in their visceral fluids, eschewing the black ink of logic or the green ink of pure venom. (Christine Bertelson, "Old Curmudgeon at His Very Best," *St. Louis Post-Dispatch*, 7/9/1996.)

composed *adj.*: **equable**. See *serene*

(2) composed *adj.*: **phlegmatic**. See *even-tempered*

compositions (or artistic works created in the artist's or author's youth) *n.*: **juvenilia**. ❖ Like fox-hunting and badger-baiting, tracking down the "juvenile" works of writers and artists is a traditional British sport. Biography has never been so popular—the more revisionist the better. And **juvenilia** is one of biography's purest raw materials. (Adrian Turpin, "Drawing on Inexperience," *Independent on Sunday*, 11/19/2000.)

composure (esp. under pressure or trying circumstances) *n.*: **sang-froid** [French]. ❖ The message conveyed by [Kurt Waldheim's] demeanor [when Waldheim appeared with Ted Koppel on *Nightline*] was that he'd dealt with even ruder people than we, and that nothing could interfere with his **sang-froid**. (Ted Koppel, *Nightline*, Times Books [1996], p. 165.)

(2) composure (in the face of adversity or suffering) *n.*: **longanimity**. See *patience*

(3) composure *n.*: **ataraxy** (or **ataraxia**). See *calmness*

comprehend (based on past experience) *v.t.*: **apperceive**. ❖ Here, then, is [diet book author] Allen Carr's great strength: he understands. He's been there, done that, bought the stretchy cardigan and outsize trousers. Serial slimmers, like smokers, are not so much lacking in will as they are willful. No one, after all, likes to be told what to do. This Carr has clearly **apperceived**. (Rose Shepherd, "Slim Chance," *Independent* [London], 1/11/1997.)

(2) comprehend (as in understand, thoroughly and/or intuitively) *v.t.*: **grok**. See *understand*

(3) comprehend (as in figure out) *v.t.*: **suss** (usually with "out"; slang). See *figure out*

(4) comprehend (difficult to . . .) *adj.*: **recondite**. See *complicated*

(5) comprehend (inability to . . . spoken or written words due to brain injury) *n.*: **aphasia**. See *uncomprehending*

comprehensible (as in clear, in thought or expression) *adj.*: **luculent.** See *clear*

(2) comprehensible (in thought or expression) *adj.*: **pellucid**. See *clear*

(3) comprehensible (to the general public) *adj.*: **exoteric**. See *accessible*

(4) comprehensible *adj.*: **limpid**. See *understandable*

(5) comprehensible *adj.*: **perspicuous**. See *understandable*

comprehension (as in perception or awareness) *n.*: **ken**. See *perception*

(2) comprehension (sudden . . .) *n.*: **epiphany**. See *realization*

comprehensive (in scope or applicability) *adj.*: **ecumenical**. See *universal*

comprehensiveness (as in breadth of inclusiveness) *n.*: **catholicity** [*adj.*: **catholic**]. See *universality*

compromise (as in middle way) *n.*: **via media** [Latin]. See *middle way*

compulsion (irresistible . . .) *n.*: **cacoëthes**. ❖ [My girlfriend has asked me what I want for my birthday] so many times I've been this close to replying, "Well, I heard that [attractive actress] Sean Young is selling her [underwear] on her website." It's a **cacoëthes**, the words itch under my tongue—somewhere in the delusional, crumbling corridors of my mind, I picture her replying, "Yeah, okay, then.

I admire the quirkiness of that request." (Mil Millington, "Relationships: Things My Girlfriend and I Argue About," *Guardian* [London], 10/6/2001.)

(2) compulsion (to shop) *n.*: **oniomania**. See *shopping*

compulsive (person who is . . . about work) *n.*: **Stakhanovite**. See *workaholic*

computing (act or process of . . . , as in measuring) *n.*: **mensuration**. See *measuring*

comrade *n.*: **tovarich** [Russian]. ❖ Canadian company enters joint venture with Russian company. . . . Russian partner tells Canadian partner, "We want to buy you out, **tovarich**." Canadian company [says no. They send someone to check out the project and he is shot.] As soon as he hits the deck, a fax arrives at the Canadian company's headquarters, basically saying, "What are you gonna do now?" (Doug Beazley, "In Lawless, Corrupt Russia, Guns Do the Talking," *Edmonton Sun*, 7/11/2001.)

(2) comrade (or close partner, often but not always, one in marriage) *n.*: **yokefellow**. See *partner*

comradeship (as in fellowship or association) *n.*: **sodality**. See *fellowship*

con (as in deceive) *v.t.*: **hornswoggle**. See *deceive*

(2) con (as in deceive) *v.t.*: **humbug**. See *deceive*

(3) con (as in defraud) *v.t.*: **mulct**. See *defraud*

(4) con (as in swindle) *n.*, *v.t.*: **thimblerig**. See *swindle*

(5) con (as in deceive) *v.t.*: **gull**. See *deceive*

concealed (as in state of being absent from view, lost to notice or . . .) *n.*: **occultation**. See *disappearance*

(2) concealed *adj.*: **delitescent**. See *hidden*

concealment (in . . .) *adv.*: **doggo** (esp. as in "lying doggo"; slang). ❖ Even as his parents prepare to brag on their family values and family, First Son Neil Bush has been conspicuously absent, even though he now lives in Houston. In the wake of the Silverado Savings and Loan scandal, Mr. Bush has been lying **doggo**, and is expected to surface only when the Bush children appear on stage for Barbara Bush's speech on Wednesday night. (Maureen Dowd, "Republicans in Houston: The Houston Thing," *New York Times*, 8/17/1992.)

(2) concealment (deliberate . . . or misrepresentation of facts to gain an advantage) *n.*: **subreption**. See *misrepresentation*

(3) concealment *n.*: **hugger-mugger**. See *secrecy*

conceding (for the sake of argument) *adv.*: **concesso non dato** [Italian; sometimes **dato non concesso**]. See *stipulating*

conceit *adj.*: **hubris**. See *arrogance*

conceited (and shameless person) *n.*: **jackanapes**. ❖ [Actor Jim Carrey] is such a conceited, mugging lout that he makes us glum. If this **jackanapes** can attract large audiences, maybe we should worry a little less about the survival of the human race. (Stanley Kauffmann, Stanley Kauffmann on Films, *New Republic*, 4/28/1997.)

(2) conceited (and vain person) *n.*: **coxcomb**. ❖ [I]t sounds as if Vain Tours, a travel agency on Jerusalem's King George Street, specializes in making arrangements for these **coxcombs** to attend international conferences for the uncommonly conceited. (Alex Berlyne, "Circumstances Alter Faces," *Jerusalem Post*, 12/11/1998.)

(3) conceited (and vain) *adj.*: **vainglorious**. See *boastful*

(4) conceited (as in vain person) *n.*: **fop**. See *vain*

(5) conceited (as in vain person) *n.*: **popinjay**. See *vain*

(6) conceited (person) *n.*: **Gascon** (act of being . . . *n.*: **Gasconade**). See *braggart*

(7) conceited (talk or person) *n.*: **cockalorum**. See *boastful*

conceivable (as in appearing to be true or accurate) *adj.*: **verisimilar**. See *plausible*

conceivably *adv.*: **perchance**. See *possibly*

conceive (of, or form an image of) *v.t.*: **ideate**. See *visualize*

concentrate (emotional energy on) *v.t.*: **cathect**. See *focus*

(2) concentrate (the flavor or essence of something, as if by boiling down) *v.t.*: **decoct**. See *boil down*

concentration (of emotional energy on an object or idea) *n.*: **cathexis**. See *focus*

(2) concentration (area of . . . esp. in a military attack) *n.*: **schwerpunkt** [German]. See *focus*

concept (about which one is obsessed) *n.*: **idée fixe** [French]. See *obsession*

(2) concept (or idea that can be expressed in one word) *n.*: **holophrasis** (*adj.*: **holophrastic**). See *idea*

conception (to form a . . . of) *v.t.*: **ideate**. See *visualize*

concern (as in attention) *n.*: **advertence**. See *attention*

(2) concern (as in worry) *v.t.*, *v.i.*, *n.*: **cark**. See *worry*

(3) concern (in a state of . . .) *idiom*: [on] **tenterhooks**. See *suspense*

(4) concern (positive form of . . . , as in stress, brought on, for example, by a job promotion or a new baby) *n.*: **eustress**. See *stress*

(5) concern (treat another with excessive . . .) *n.*, *v.t.*: **wet-nurse**. See *coddle*

concerned (as if by a witch or without reason) *adj.*: **hagridden**. See *tormented*

(2) concerned (as in compassionate) *adj.*: **ruthful**. See *compassionate*

concerning *prep.*: **anent**. See *regarding*

concession (of sin) *n.*: **confiteor** (sometimes cap.). See *confession*

conciliate *v.t.*: **propitiate**. See *placate*

conciliating (or uniting of opposing viewpoints or beliefs) *adj.*: **syncretic** (or **syncretistic**). See *reconciling*

conciliatory (as in peacemaking) *adj.*: **irenic**. See *peacemaking*

concise (speech or writing being very . . .) *adj.*: **elliptical**. See *terse*

conclusion (as in inference) *n.*: **illation**. See *inference*

conclusive (as in indisputable or unquestionable) *adj.*: **irrefragable**. See *unquestionable*

(2) conclusive (as in unambiguous) *adj.*: **univocal**. See *unambiguous*

(3) conclusive (necessarily or demonstrably . . .) *adj.*: **apodictic**. See *incontrovertible*

(4) conclusive (remark, blow, or factor) *n.*: **sockdolager**. See *decisive*

concoct (an idea, plan, theory, or explanation after careful thought) *v.t.*: **excogitate**. See *devise*

concubine *n.*: **odalisque**. ❖ I was living his life, not mine. All the choices, plans, goals were his and would remain so. . . . Here I was, this liberated woman, and I was actually an **odalisque** out of la belle epoque. (Betty Fussell, "The Century's Almost Over . . . and You're Still Living through a Man?" *Cosmopolitan*, 6/1/1996, p. 200.)

concurrence (of the human race throughout history on an issue) *n.*: **consensus genitum** [Latin]. See *consensus*

concurrently *adv.*: **holus-bolus**. See *simultaneously*

condemn (as in criticize) *v.t.*: **flay**. See *criticize*

(2) condemn (as in criticize, sharply) *v.t.*: **scarify**. See *criticize*

(3) condemn (as in scold or rebuke) *v.t.*: **objurgate**. See *criticize*

(4) condemn *v.t.*: **execrate**. See *hate*

(5) condemn (or reject or disapprove) *v.t.*, *n.*: **discountenance**. See *reject*

condemnation (as in criticism) *n.*: **animadversion** (*v.t.*: **animadvert**). See *criticism*

(2) condemnation (as in damnation) *n.*: **perdition**. See *damnation*

(3) condemnation (as in denunciation) *n.*: **commination**. See *denunciation*

(4) condemnation (in speech) *n.*: **philippic**. See *tirade*

condemning (of convicted persons, spec. burning of heretics at the stake) *n.*: **auto-da-fé**. See *execution*

condense (as in thicken) *v.t.*, *v.i.*: **inspissate**. See *thicken*

(2) condense (the flavor or essence of something, as if by boiling down) *v.t.*: **decoct**. See *boil down*

condensed (something . . . , as in abridged) *n.*: **bobtail**. See *abridged*

condescend (as in bestow, by one with higher power) *v.t.*: **vouchsafe**. See *bestow*

condescending *adj.*, *adv.*: **de haut en bas** (sometimes hyphenated) [French; lit. from high to low]. ❖ Love it or hate it, everyone instantly acknowledges that the [*New York Review of Books*] is saturated with fashionable left-wing politics. . . . From its very first issue in 1963, the *Review* has epitomized the snotty **haut-en-bas** leftism of the academy. . . . [They believe that] their view of the world is not a political view but simply an accurate transcription of the way the world appears to any right-thinking (i.e., left-leaning) person. (*New Criterion*, Notes & Comments, 9/1/2003.)

(2) condescending (as in haughty) *adj.*: **fastuous**. See *haughty*

(3) condescending (as in lordly) *adj.*: **seigneurial**. See *lordly*

(4) condescending (or haughty) *adj.*: **top-lofty**. See *haughty*

condition *n.*: **fettle**. ❖ Given the importance of the bank's financial condition, it's possible for two borrowers in the same town, in similar financial **fettle**, to face drastically different loan prospects depending on where they bank. (Gary Hector, The Economy: "Victims of the Credit Crunch," *Fortune*, 1/27/1992, p. 100.)

conditioned (as in trained to show a . . . response) *adj.*: **Pavlovian** [based on Russian physiologist Ivan P. Pavlov (1849–1936), who trained dogs to respond instantly to various stimuli]. ❖ President Clinton's final, and longest, State of the Union address evoked a **Pavlovian** partisan response. Republicans denounced, in the words of their shaky heir apparent, George W. Bush, the "litany of spending." Democrats lined up to praise a speech that stroked every tender party cause from education to hate crimes. (*Nation*, "Two States of the Union," 2/21/2000.)

condolence (one offering false . . . , as in one who discourages or depresses another by offering remarks that supposedly have the opposite intent) *n.*: **Job's comforter**. See *comforter*

conduct (appropriate . . . , as in propriety) *n.*: **correctitude**. See *propriety*

(2) conduct (as in demeanor) *n.*: **mien**. See *demeanor*

(3) conduct (study of human . . .) *n.*: **praxeology**. See *behavior*

conference (as in dialogue in which neither side hears or understands or pays attention to the other) *n.*: **dialogue de sourds** [French]. See *dialogue*

(2) conference (esp. with an enemy or adversary) *n.*, *v.t.*: **parley**. See *discussion*

confess (one's sins, esp. in church) *v.t.*, *v.i.*: **shrive**. ❧ [Worldcom CEO Bernie Ebbers] made his first public comments about the fraud allegations to a Baptist church in Brookhaven, Miss. Churches are perfect places to **shrive** and be forgiven, but Ebbers was unapologetic, denying any knowledge of fraud. It's hard to imagine that a multibillion-dollar gaffe could slip by Ebbers undetected. (Ed Gubbins, "Scandalism," *Telephony*, 7/8/2002.)

(2) confess (one's thoughts or feelings) *v.t.*, *v.i.*: **unbosom**. See *confide*

confession (of sin) *n.*: **confiteor** (sometimes cap.). [The word technically refers to a prayer in which sin is confessed, but is occasionally used more broadly to describe any confession of sin, as in the example given.] ❧ [Baseball player Pete] Rose is telling the world that he bet on baseball. This is every bit as revelatory as learning that Hugh Hefner likes the ladies. . . . The circumstances surrounding Rose's **confiteor** are repulsive. In classic form for a guy who would set up a card table and charge for autographs in Nepal if he could make a buck, prodigal Pete has a profit motive. (Pat Forde, "Arrrrrgh! Let This Be the Last on Rose," *Louisville [KY] Courier-Journal*, 1/7/2004.)

(2) confession (of sin) *n.*: **peccavi**. ❧ Clinton performed miserably in his first public ceremonies of repentance [over the Monica Lewinsky affair], but then last Friday, at the White House prayer breakfast, delivered at last a persuasive **peccavi**, mea culpa. (Lance Morrow, Essay: "That Old Familiar Uncharted Territory: Clinton's Survival May Depend on

a Combination of Forgiveness and Boredom," *Time*, 9/21/1998, p. 120.)

confide (one's thoughts or feelings) *v.t.*, *v.i.*: **unbosom**. ❧ The President had received a copy of the page proofs and, in response, now confessed to Wattenberg that in his first two years in office he had "lost the language" of values, and thereby "let Democrats down." . . . Clinton's **unbosoming** certainly helped, however briefly, to call attention to this book, and to Wattenberg's cause. (Richard Brookhiser, review of *Values Matter Most*, by Ben J. Wattenberg, *Commentary*, 4/1/1996, p. 62.)

confidence (and poise) *n.*: **aplomb**. ❧ Obviously, style wasn't my native tongue. I got style more or less the way I got French, through a combination of study and osmosis. It was a long time before I had the nerve, the experience or the **aplomb** necessary to hold forth. (Judith Thurman, "The Search for Style," *InStyle*, 10/15/1998, p. 81.)

(2) confidence (excess . . .) *adj.*: **hubris**. See *arrogance*

confident (as in one habitually expecting an upturn in one's fortunes, sometimes without justification) *adj.*: **Micawberish** (*n.*: **Micawber**). See *optimistic*

(2) confident (behavior, as in bravado) *n.*: **fanfaronade**. See *bravado*

(3) confident (esp. blindly or naively . . . , as in optimistic) *adj.*: **Panglossian**. See *optimistic*

confidential (as in secret activity) *n.*: **huggermugger**. See *secrecy*

(2) confidential (as in, of, or relating to a court, legislative body, or other group that meets in private, and often makes decisions that are harsh or arbitrary) *adj.*: **star chamber**. See *closed-door*

confidentially (as in privately) *adv.*, *adj.*: **in camera**. See *privately*

confine *v.t.*: **immure**. ❧ In 1793, the 8-year-old son of the guillotined monarchs, King Louis XVI and Queen Marie Antoinette, was flung into Paris' Temple prison. Then, according to [one legend, he] was **immured** in a windowless dungeon, ignored, barely fed and left alone in his own filth. (*Minneapolis Star Tribune*, "The DNA Test That Solved a Royal Puzzle," 4/26/2000.)

(2) confine (a person's movement by holding down his arms) *v.t.*: **pinion**. See *immobilize*

(3) confine (as in overly restrict or . . . , as to amount or share) *v.t.*: **scant**. See *stint*

confined (by not affording enough space) *adj.*: **incommodious**. See *cramped*

confinement (as in imprisonment) *n.*: **durance vile**. See *jail*

(2) confinement (place of . . . as in dungeon) *n.*: **oubliette**. See *dungeon*

confiscate (property to compel payment of debts) *v.t.*: **distrain**. ❖ Mr. Yeltsin went on television to assure investors that Russia would weather the storm, but he made clear that it needs increased tax revenue to do so. . . . He also signed a decree giving tax police powers to **distrain** tax dodgers' property. (Genine Babakian, International: "Tax Chief Is Victim as Yeltsin Shields Rouble," *Daily Telegraph* [London], 5/30/1998.)

conflict (between laws, rules, or principles) *n.*: **antinomy**. ❖ [In Florida, people under the age of twenty-one cannot go to dance clubs or juice bars, because they are supposed to lack the necessary judgment. Despite that,] a 13-year-old boy arrested in a school shooting in Lake Worth was found to be vested with plenty enough judgment and maturity to stand trial as an adult on first-degree murder charges. This qualifies, perhaps, as an **antinomy** or a contradiction. (Fred Grimm, "Geezers' Revenge: Ban the Brats," *Miami Herald*, 6/4/2000.)

(2) conflict (act or event which causes or provokes . . . , literally or figuratively) *n.*: **casus belli** [Latin; occasion of war]. See *provocation*

(3) conflict (as in difference of opinion) *n.*: **divarication**. See *disagreement*

(4) conflict (as in heated disagreement or friction between groups) *n.*: **ruction**. See *dissension*

(5) conflict (characterized by internal . . .) *adj.*: **factious**. See *dispute*

(6) conflict (engaged in a . . . , as in struggle) *adj.*: **agonistes**. See *struggle*

(7) conflict (in literature) *n.*: **agon**. ❖ Bloom's view of literature as a ceaseless **agon** between challengers and titleholders is interesting and, in some instances, true. (Paul Gray, Ideas: "Hurrah for Dead White Males!" *Time*, 10/10/1994, p. 62.)

(8) conflict (in terms or ideas) *n.*: **antilogy**. See *contradiction*

(9) conflict (in the soul between good vs. evil) *n.*: **psychomachia**. See *good vs. evil*

(10) conflict (minor . . . as in skirmish) *n.*: **velitation**. See *skirmish*

(11) conflict (of or relating to . . . within a group or country) *adj.*: **internecine**. See *dissension*

(12) conflict (or battle among the gods) *n.*: **theomachy**. See *gods*

conflicting (as in things that do not mix together) *adj.*: **immiscible**. See *incompatible*

conform (closely to a line, rule, or principle) *v.i.*: **hew** ❖ But during his three decades in Congress, the upstate New Yorker [Samuel Stratton] **hewed** to the orthodox liberal line on many issues, supporting school busing and economic sanctions against South Africa. (*Time*, Milestones, 9/24/1990, p. 97.)

conforming (do things in a . . . manner, as in "by the book") *idiom*: **according to Hoyle**. See *by the book*

(2) conforming (or reconciling of opposing viewpoints or beliefs) *adj.*: **syncretic** (or **syncretistic**). See *reconciling*

conformist (esp. self-righteously . . .) *adj.*: **bienpensant**. See *right-thinking*

conformity (marked by insistence on rigid . . . to a belief, system, or course of action without regard to individual differences) *adj.*: **Procrustean** (*n.*: **Procrustean bed**) [after Procrustes, a mythical Greek giant who stretched or shortened captives to make them fit his beds]. ❖ Poor [former presidential candidate Al Gore] was abysmally self-satirizing on [*Saturday Night Live*], ripping the last shreds of dignity from his profile in attempted comedy.

. . . The chuckles and laughter in his conversation with Lesley Stahl on Sunday night were those of a private person struggling to be free of public life, a man trapped in a **Procrustean bed** built by a father who raised a son to be president. (Suzanne Fields, "It's Sunday Night Live: Gore Should Leave Comedy to the Comics," *Washington Times*, 12/19/2002.)

(2) conformity (precise . . . with formalities or etiquette) *n.*: **punctilio**. See *etiquette*

confounding (as in perplexing) *adj.*: **quisquous**. See *perplexing*

confrontation (engaged in a . . . , as in struggle) *adj.*: **agonistes**. See *struggle*

(2) confrontation (event that causes or provokes . . . , literally or figuratively) *n.*: **casus belli** [Latin; occasion of war]. See *provocation*

(3) confrontation (minor . . . as in skirmish) *n.*: **velitation**. See *skirmish*

confuse (as in entangle) *v.t.*: **embrangle**. See *entangle*

(2) confuse *v.t.*: **befog**. See *muddle*

confused (esp. used of a person, as in . . . and stupid) *adj.*: **addlepated**. ❖ *Bias: A CBS Insider Explains How the Media Distort the News* by Bernard Goldberg, is making a splash in the very media that are its target. . . . Some of the response to *Bias* has been more vitriolic than polemical. . . . [T]elevision critic Tom Shales dismisses Goldberg as an "**addlepated** windbag who is trying to make a second career out of trashing his former employer." (Cathy Young, "Skewed News: Fair and Balanced Coverage Requires Diversity of Opinion," *Boston Globe*, 2/4/2002.)

(2) confused (as in a failure to perceive something clearly or accurately or not being based on clear observation or analysis as a result of being cross-eyed, literally or figuratively) *adj.*: **strabismic**. See *cross-eyed*

(3) confused (as in haphazard) *adj., adv.*: **higgledy-piggledy**. See *haphazard*

(4) confused (situation that is . . . or chaotic or complicated) *n.*: **mare's nest**. See *chaotic*

confusion (disorderly . . .) *n., adj.*: **huggermugger**. ❖ If this all sounds complicated, it is: The first hour of *The Last of the Mohicans* plays like a convoluted history lesson. . . . When the English are defeated and skulk away, only to be massacred, it feels like a cheat: All that historical **hugger-mugger** just to get Hawkeye, the colonel's daughter, and her younger sister (Jodhi May) stranded in the wilderness. (Owen Gleiberman, "Native Son Michael Mann's *The Last of the Mohicans* Is a Powerfully Realistic Adventure Saga," *Entertainment Weekly*, 9/25/1992, p. 38.)

(2) confusion (as in chaos) *n.*: **tohubuhu**. See *chaos*

(3) confusion (as in disarrayed mass) *n.*: **welter**. See *jumble*

(4) confusion (in a state of . . . or disarray) *idiom*: **at sixes and sevens**. See *disarray*

(5) confusion (of one's memory with actual fact) *n.*: **paramnesia**. See *misremember*

congenial (and pleasant) *adj.*: **sympathique** [French]. See *genial*

congenital (as in innate) *adj.*: **connate**. See *innate*

conglomeration (as in assortment) *n.*: **farrago**. See *assortment*

(2) conglomeration (as in assortment) *n.*: **gallimaufry**. See *assortment*

(3) conglomeration (as in assortment) *n.*: **olla podrida** [Spanish]. See *assortment*

(4) conglomeration (as in assortment) *n.*: **omnium-gatherum** [Latin]. See *assortment*

(5) conglomeration (as in assortment) *n.*: **salmagundi**. See *assortment*

congratulate *v.t.*: **felicitate**. ❖ President Soeharto of Indonesia has also **felicitated** President Negasso Gidada and Prime Minister Meles Zenawi [in connection with the sixth anniversary of the day on which the Ethiopian people ousted the dictatorial Derg regime, May 28], who also received a congratulatory message sent from Mr. Ahmed Ouyahia, head of state of Algeria. (Africa News Service, "Clinton and Other Leaders Welcome Ethiopia's Achievements," 5/29/1997.)

congregation (at church) *n.*: **ecclesia**. ❖ These changes reflect changes in theology of worship and our understanding of the **ecclesia**—the Christian community meeting in worship. Today there is a preference for seats in a semi-circle round a nave altar; rather than worshipping a God out there, we feel it better to worship a God in the midst of us. (Alan D. Skyes, letter to the editor, *Independent* [London], 11/19/1997.)

(2) congregation (at church) *n.*: **laity**. See *parish*

congressperson *n.*: **solon**. See *legislator*

connect (in a series or chain) *v.t., adj.*: **concatenate** (*n.*: **concatenation**). ❖ [A]s anyone involved in the criminal trade will affirm (although I didn't know this at the time), the phrase "I don't know anything about it" is employed almost exclusively by those, paradoxically, who do know all about it; that this **concatenation** of words is a code, a slang, a camouflaged way of saying: prove it. (Tabor Fischer, *The Thought Gang*, The New Press [1994], p. 4.)

(2) connect (as in blend) *v.t., v.i.*: **inosculate**. See *blend*

(3) connect (as in bring together) *v.t.*: **conflate**. See *combine*

(4) connect (tendency of people to . . . with, or be attracted to, others who they perceive are similar to them) *n.*: **homophily**. See *associate*

connected (by a close relationship) *adj.*: **affined**. ❖ When Reinette says that next year she wants to go to art school in Paris, Mirabelle invites her to share her apartment since her present roommate is leaving. The matter is not immediately settled, because the two, the city sophisticate and the country enthusiast, are not completely **affined**. Next morning they experience the [beautiful hour before dawn] together. The moment is so lovely that it unites them. (Stanley Kauffman, review of *Four Adventures of Reinette and Mirabelle,* by Eric Rohmer, *New Republic,* 8/28/1989.)

(2) connected (closely . . .) *adj.*: **coadunate**. See *joined*

(3) connected (of things that cannot be . . .) *adj.*: **immiscible**. See *incompatible*

connection (as in bond or tie) *n.*: **vinculum**. See *bond*

(4) connection *n.*: **catenation** (*v.t.*: **catenate**). See *chain*

conniving (and evil or shameless woman) *n.*: **jezebel** (sometimes cap.). See *woman*

connoisseur *n.*: **cognoscente**. ❖ Become an art **cognoscente**. *ArtNet* Magazine, a new trade publication for the visual arts world, offers columns, auction reports and photos. (Sam Vincent Meddis, Net: New and Notable, *USA Today,* 5/30/1996.)

(2) connoisseur (of good food and drink) *n.*: **epicure**. See *gourmet*

(3) connoisseur (of good food and drink) *n.*: **gastronome**. See *gourmet*

conscientious (in effort or application) *adj.*: **sedulous**. See *diligent*

conscious *adj.*: **sentient**. ❖ Could a mechanical device ever duplicate human intelligence—the ultimate test being whether it could cause a real human to fall in love with it? And if such a machine could be built, would it actually be conscious? Would dismantling it be the snuffing out of a **sentient** being[?] (Steven Pinker, "Can a Computer Be Conscious?" *U.S. News & World Report,* 8/25/1997.)

consciousness (as in soul) *n.*: **anima**. See *soul*

consensus (of the human race throughout history on an issue) *n.*: **consensus gentium.** [Latin. Note that the consensus does not necessarily mean that the issue agreed upon is correct.] ❖ Despite prevailing attitudes at Yale, there is a **consensus gentium** against homosexuality, extending over millennia and transcending cultural differences. Yes, there was Sparta. But that was a drop in the bucket beside the overwhelming consensus. (Jeffrey Hart, "Show Opening in New Haven," *National Review,* 11/20/1987.)

(2) consensus (as in popular opinion) *n.*: **vox populi** [Latin]. See *popular opinion*

consent (as in giving one's stamp of approval) *n.*: **nihil obstat** [Latin]. See *approval*

consequence (as in outgrowth) *n.*: **excrescence**. See *outgrowth*

(2) consequence *n.*: **sequela** (pl. **sequelae**). See *aftereffect*

conservatism (as in hatred or fear of anything new or different) *n.*: **misoneism** (person holding this view: **misoneist**). [A rare equivalent for this word is "misocaneia."] ❖ With predictable corporate **misoneism** . . . the [music] industry anointed Jet [as the next hot rock band] not for their singularity, but their overfamiliarity. It's a neat execution of a tried and true formula: a faithful and loving synthesis of classic Stones, AC/DC, the Who and Kinks-era rock, put together by four young guys who love what they're playing, play well and look the part. (Kelsey Munro, "The Formula Works: Humming Along to an Overfamiliar Tune," *Sydney Morning Herald*, 7/22/2003.)

conservative (very . . . in beliefs and often stuffy or pompous) *adj.*, *n.*: **Colonel Blimp** [after a British cartoon character having these qualities]. ❖ [The campaign by those supporting a conversion of Britain's monetary system from the pound to the eurodollar (i.e., the Yes campaign) is based in part on the] assumption . . . that they will be able to portray the No campaign as a bunch of right-wing loonies: **Colonel Blimp** types desperately clinging to a vision of a long-forgotten Britain. (*Sunday Business* [London], "Murdoch Seals E1.5bn Italy Pay-TV Deal with Vivendi," 6/9/2002.)

(2) conservative (person, spec. a person who is opposed to advancements in technology) *n.*: **Luddite**. See *traditionalist*

(3) conservative (spec. a person who is opposed to individual or political reform or enlightenment) *n.*: **obscurant** (doctrine of such opposition: **obscurantism**). See *traditionalist*

(4) conservative (tactics, esp. as a means to wear out an opponent) *adj.*: **Fabian**. See *cautious*

consider (something; often used as a directive, as in "Consider this:") *v.t.*: **perpend**. ❖ Former Oxford teacher Bernard Richards says the first-year exams of the [language and literature students at Oxford] show an "alarming" decline in spelling skills over the past 10 years. **Perpend**: They misspelled gnats as "knats," unpalatable as "unpalletable," expressed as "escpressed," paddle as "padel," angry as "angery," vehicle as "vehicule," and so on. (Chris Floyd, Global Eye, *Moscow Times*, 1/24/1998.)

(2) consider (as in think about) *v.t.*: **cerebrate**. See *think*

(3) consider (as in think about) *v.t.*: **cogitate**. See *think*

(4) consider (logically) *v.i.*: **ratiocinate**. See *analyze*

consideration (of matters outside oneself, i.e., the outside world) *n.*: **extrospection** (*adj.*: **extrospective**). See *observation*

consistent (as in harmonious or compatible) *adj.*: **simpatico**. See *compatible*

consoler (false . . . , as in one who discourages another by offering remarks that supposedly have the opposite intent) *n.*: **Job's comforter**. See *comforter*

consolidate *v.t.*: **amalgamate**. See *combine*

conspiracy *n.*: **cabal**. See *plot*

constant (as in everlasting) *adj.*: **sempiternal**. See *everlasting*

(2) constant (as in unvarying) *adj.*: **equable**. See *unvarying*

(3) constant (in rhythm or tempo) *adj.*: **metronomic**. See *steady*

constantly (as in forever) *adv.*: **in aeternum** [Latin]. See *forever*

constellation *n.*: **asterism**. See *stars*

constellations (of or relating to) *adj.*: **sidereal**. See *stars*

constipated *adj.*: **costive**. ❖ "Buzzed" [is a] guide to the most used and abused drugs. . . . With typical cool, the good doctors quote an expert who decided that "if you didn't mind being impotent and constipated, opiate addiction really wasn't too bad." No wanly romantic early demise, but 20 or 30 years of flabby, **costive** desperation. Glamorous, or what? (Boyd Tonkin, Books, *Independent* [London], 4/25/1998.)

constipation (total . . .) *n.*: **obstipation**. ❖ If untreated, the condition [colonic obstruction] can proceed to **obstipation**, a more stubborn fecal impaction [than constipation] that can require prolonged hospitalization and more elaborate therapy—for example, manual removal of hardened fecal matter from an anesthetized dog's colon. (Tom Ewing, "Constipation: A Painful Disorder," *Dog Watch*, 5/1/2007.)

constrain (as in confine) *v.t.*: **immure**. See *confine*

constricted (by not affording enough space) *adj.*: **incommodious**. See *cramped*

construct (cheaply and flimsily) *v.t.*: **jerrybuild**. See *build*

constructed (finely or skillfully . . . , as in intricate) *adj.*: **daedal**. See *intricate*

construction (art of . . . , esp. of large buildings) *n.*: **tectonics**. ❖ The dangerous, shattering glass of I. M. Pei's controversial John Hancock Mutual Life Insurance Company Tower in Boston in the 1970s is a famous and graphic example of faulty **tectonics** as faulty publicity. There, problems with the skyscraper's glass curtain walls took months to repair at great expense. (Scott Berman, "Public Buildings as Public Relations," *Public Relations Quarterly*, 4/15/1999.)

consumable (as in edible) *adj.*: **esculent**. See *edible*

consume (as in ingest) *v.t.*: **incept**. See *ingest*

(2) consume (greedily) *v.t.*: **guttle**. See *devour*

consuming (act or process of . . . , as in swallowing) *n.*: **deglutition**. See *swallowing*

consummation (as opposed to potentiality) *n.*: **entelechy**. See *actuality*

contaminated (morally . . .) *v.t.*: **cankered**. See *corrupted*

contamination (abnormal fear of . . .) *n.*: **mysophobia**. See *fear*

contemplate (on something, often used as a directive, as in "Consider this:") *v.t.*: **perpend**. See *consider*

contemplation (of matters outside oneself, i.e., the outside world) *n.*: **extrospection** (*adj.*: **extrospective**). See *observation*

(2) contemplation (staring at one's belly button as an aid to . . .) *n.*: **omphaloskepsis**. See *meditation*

contemporaneous (as in over the same time period) *adj.*: **coetaneous**. ❖ This course was created to examine institutionalized prejudice in the field of psychology. Psychology, as a discipline, has been an arena for examining the structure and etiology of prejudice. . . . **Coetaneously**, psychology has been rife with institutionalized prejudice in terms of theories, especially Freud's theory. (Mary Ballard, "The Politics of Prejudice in Psychology: A Syllabus and Bibliography," Contemporary Women's Issues Database, 3/1/1995, p. 16.)

contemporary (as in of the same era) *adj.*, *n.*: **coeval**. ❖ Go ahead, baby. Wail. You're due. It sure is nice to hear [singer Gladys Knight] tear into some material with spirit in its soul. After more than 35 years, she still boasts one of the most assured and moving voices in the business. . . . Unlike her **coeval**, that big, bad wolf Patti LaBelle, Knight doesn't huff and puff and try to blow the roof off the sucker every time out of the box. (David Hiltbrand, Picks & Pans: Song, *People*, 2/22/1988, p. 13.)

contempt (in behavior or speech) *n.*: **contumely**. ❖ And now Madeleine Albright addresses Benjamin Netanyahu approximately as she addresses Slobodan Milosevic, as though he merited **contumely** rather than respect, as though he were the head of a hostile power rather than an ally. (*New Republic*, "A Crisis of Partnership," 6/1/1998.)

(2) contempt (develop a . . . for) *n.*: **scunner** (esp. as in "take a scunner") [British]. See *dislike*

(3) contempt (treat with . . .) *v.t.*: **contemn**. See *scorn*

(4) contempt *n.*: **misprision** (to hold in . . . *v.t.*: **misprize**). See *disdain*

contemptible (or treacherous) *adj.*: **reptilian**. See *despicable*

(2) contemptible (person) *n.*: **caitiff**. See *despicable*

(3) contemptible *adj.*: **ugsome**. See *loathsome*

contemptuous (of another, often by being insulting or humiliating) *adj.*: **contumelious**. ❖ I worked for part of a summer in a hellish Texarkanan carnival as the **contumelious** clown you get to drop into a tank of water after he calls you pencil-dick. (Michael Chabon, *Wonder Boys*, Villard [1995], p. 18.)

(2) contemptuous *adj.*: **opprobrious** (*n.*: **opprobrium**). ❖ While the label "fiscal conservative" might seem **opprobrious** to [Jesse] Jackson, it is a compliment in many places, including California, the cradle of the 1970s tax revolt. (Laurence I. Barrett, Nation: "The Grail of the Golden State," *Time*, 6/6/1988, p. 19.)

(3) contemptuous (as in lordly) *adj.*: **seigneurial**. See *lordly*

contemptuousness (as in disdain) *n.*: **misprision** (*v.t.*: **misprize**). See *disdain*

contend (as in assert) *v.t.*: **asseverate**. See *declare*

contention (as in heated disagreement or friction between groups) *n.*: **ruction**. See *dissension*

(2) contention (made without proof or support) *n.*: **ipse dixit** [Latin]. See *allegation*

contentious (as in combative) *adj.*: **agonistic**. See *combative*

(2) contentious (as in controversial opinion or person holding one) *n.*: **polemic**. See *controversy*

(3) contentious (as in pugnacious; ready to fight) *adj.*: **bellicose**. See *belligerent*

contentment (as in peace of mind) *n.*: **heartsease**. See *peace of mind*

(2) contentment (as in well-being) *n.*: **weal** (usu. as in *weal or woe* or *weal and woe*). See *well-being*

(3) contentment (delusive or illusory . . .) *n.*: **fool's paradise**. See *illusion*

(4) contentment *n.*: **eudemonia** (or **eudaemonia**). See *happiness*

contest (a statement, opinion, or action) *v.t.*: **oppugn**. See *oppose*

(2) contest (as in hostile meeting) *n.*: **rencontre** [French]. See *duel*

contort (one's face) *v.i.*: **girn** [Scottish]. See *grimace*

contorted (as in twisted) *adj.*: **tortile**. See *twisted*

contortion (gaping . . . of the face due to pain or disgust) *n.*: **rictus**. See *grimace*

contour (distinctive . . . or outline, often of a face) *adj.*: **lineament** (often **lineaments**). ❖ There's another low building behind the park: painted blue, almost lost in the weak light of evening. It's neglected-looking, the asphalt shingles of its roof patchy and stained. I pull into the parking lot before this building and its **lineaments** are unmistakable. At the center of America, an abandoned motel. (Mark Baechtel, "Dead Center America," *Washington Post*, 1/16/2000.)

contradict (as in oppose a statement, opinion, or action) *v.t.*: **oppugn**. See *oppose*

contradiction (in terms or ideas) *n.*: **antilogy**. ❖ "Travel consumer." The juxtaposition of terms rankles. To consume means, variously, "to eat up . . . waste or squander . . . destroy totally or ravage." If travel ideally is a productive and compassionate activity—nurturing both for individual and for cultures as they meet and mingle—how can we so blithely use such a blatant **antilogy**? (Jim Molnar, "To Consume, or Not to Consume? A Question for Every Traveler," *Seattle Times*, 8/20/1995.)

(2) contradiction (as in conflict between laws, rules, or principles) *n.*: **antinomy**. See *conflict*

(3) contradiction (statement that contains a logical . . . , usually unrealized by the speaker) *n.*: **Irish bull**. See *incongruity*

contradictory (as in things that do not mix together) *adj.*: **immiscible**. See *incompatible*

(2) contradictory (having . . . ideas or qualities) *adj.*: **bipolar**. See *opposite*

contrary (stubbornly . . . or disobedient) *adj.*: **froward**. ❖ "The pigeons hang out on the light fixtures and the droppings get on the sidewalk right in front of the front door," said Assistant City Manager George Brown. For the past year, city maintenance crews have frequently pressure-cleaned the sidewalks, but the birds have been relentless. Tired of cleaning, the city decided to go on the offensive against the **froward** fowl. (John Murawski, "Pigeons Foil Boca Efforts to Evict Them," *Palm Beach Post*, 11/25/2000.)

(2) contrary (as in peevish) *adj.*: **querulous**. See *peevish*

(3) contrary (on the . . .) *adv.*: **per contra**. See *contrast*

(4) contrary (as in discordant) *adj.*: **absonant**. See *discordant*

contrast (by way of . . .) *adv.*: **per contra**. ❖ The Israelis believe God gave them Israel in perpetuity. . . . The Palestinians, **per contra**, believe equally firmly that the land is theirs, and that it was simply seized in the late 1940s by an influx of Jewish refugees from Europe. (William Rusher, "Camp David Designs," *Washington Times*, 7/19/2000.)

(2) contrast (to set in . . .) *v.t.*: **counterpose**. ❖ A British appeals court ruled Friday that six-week-old conjoined twins will have to be separated, even though the operation will almost certainly mean the death of one of them. The desperate parents fought unsuccessfully against the surgery. [The question is, what should the government do] when medical science and the religion-based wishes of the parents are **counterposed**? (William Raspberry, "The Ultimate Sacrifice," *Washington Post*, 9/25/2000.)

contribution (which is all one can afford) *n.*: **widow's mite**. See *donation*

contrition (as in place or occasion to express . . . and to seek forgiveness) *n.*: **Canossa**. See *penance*

(2) contrition (spec. the opportunity to withdraw from, or decide not to commit, an intended crime) *n.*: **locus poenitentiae** [Latin]. See *repentance*

contrived *adj.*: **voulu.** [French. This word is the past participle of the verb "vouloir," meaning to want or wish.] ❖ The main problem with the film [*The New Age*] is that it feels contrived and programmatic—**voulu**. Mr. Tolkin is hell-bent on delivering a moral sermon on the emptiness of Los Angeles lives and does not concern himself with piddling problems such as motivation and believability. (John Simon, "The New Age," *National Review*, 10/24/1994.)

(2) contrived (as in artificial) *adj.*: **factitious**. See *artificial*

control (as in dominate) *v.t.*: **bestride**. See *dominate*

(2) control (as in domination, of a nation or group over another) *n.*: **suzerainty**. See *domination*

(3) control (as in marked by simplicity, frugality, self-discipline, and/or . . .) *adj.*: **Lacedaemonian**. See *spartan*

controlled (as in subjected to external controls and impositions; i.e., the opposite of autonomous) *adj.*: **heteronomous** (*n.*: **heteronomy**). See *subjugated*

controversy (point of view that is the subject of . . . , or person who holds one) *n.*: **polemic**. ❖ In *The Coming Collapse of China*, Gordon G. Chang launches directly into his controversial argument that the country's many woes add up to a terminal illness. [After describing a familiar litany of problems, Chang] takes his startling **polemic** one step further: He says that . . . the Communist Party will soon collapse—possibly within 5 years. (Dexter Roberts, "Pessimism on a Grand Scale," *Business Week*, 8/27/2001.)

(2) controversy (as in commotion) *n.*: **bobbery**. See *commotion*

(3) controversy (as in commotion) *n.*: **kerfuffle**. See *commotion*

(4) controversy (given to argument or . . . that may be specious) *adj., n.*: **eristic**. See *specious* and *debate*

(5) controversy (of or relating to . . . within a group or country) *adj.*: **internecine**. See *dissension*

convention (as in habit or custom) *n.*: **praxis**. See *custom*

conventional (of one who is . . . , as in conforming, often self-righteously) *adj.*: **bien-pensant**. See *right-thinking*

conventionality (intolerant insistence on . . .) *n.*: **Grundyism**. See *puritanical*

conversant (being . . . with or familiar with something) *adj.*: **au fait** [French]. See *familiar*

conversation (between three people) *n.*: **trialogue**. ❖ Greenberg was in Jakarta yesterday attending the International Scholars Annual **Trialogue**, a meeting of Christian, Muslim and Jewish scholars. (Jacqueline Trescott, "N.Y. Rabbi to Chair Holocaust Museum; Irving Greenberg Seen as Bridge Builder," *Washington Post*, 2/16/2000.)

(2) conversation (between two people) *n.*: **duologue**. ❖ The unlikely ice partners—tiny francophone Isabelle Brasseur and giant anglophone Lloyd Eisler—won Olympic bronze twice and the Worlds once. They share their lives on and off the ice in an interesting **duologue**. (Gina Mallet, "Various Positions," *Chatelaine*, 12/1/1996, p. 16.)

(3) conversation (esp. about art or literature) *n.*: **conversazione** [Italian] (pl. **conversazioni**). ❖ At times, in the corner of my eye, I think I can still see a skinny streak of mottled fur and hear a tiny, bossy [meow], demanding to be let in, [or] to be let out. . . . Perhaps she's summoning my husband and me, in her usual highhanded She-Who-Must-Be-Obeyed manner, for one of her elegant drawing-room **conversazioni** on great themes in art and literature. (Ann Leslie, "Farewell Posy, Most Magnificent of [Cats]," *Daily Mail* [London], 9/7/2001.)

(4) conversation (casual . . . , as in chitchat) *n.*: **bavardage**. See *chitchat*

(5) conversation (casual . . . , discussion of a subject, as in chitchat) *n.*: **persiflage**. See *chitchat*

(6) conversation (idle . . .) *n.*: **palaver**. See *small talk*

(7) conversation (in which neither side hears or understands or pays attention to the other): *n.*: **dialogue de sourds** [French]. See *dialogue*

(8) conversation (informal . . .) *n.*: **causerie**. See *chat*

(9) conversation (light or playful back and forth . . .) *n.*: **badinage**. See *banter*

(10) conversation *n.*: **interlocution**. See *discussion*

conversationalist (skilled dinner . . .) *n.*: **deipnosophist**. ❖ At the age of six his future as a **deipnosophist** seemed certain. Guzzling filched apples he loved to prattle. Hogging the pie he invariably piped up and rattled on. (MacDonald Daly, "Malice Aforethought: The Fictions of Ellis Sharp," *Critique: Studies in Contemporary Fiction*, 1/1/1998, p. 139.)

converse (casually) *n.*: **chinwag** [slang]. See *chat*

(2) converse (casually) *v.i.*: **confabulate**. See *chat*

(3) converse (esp. in a long-winded or pompous manner) *v.i.*: **bloviate**. See *speak*

conversion (road to . . . or rehabilitation) *n.*: **sawdust trail**. [This term derives from the old practice of going down sawdust-covered roads to a revival tent meeting for the purpose of conversion, rehabilitation.] ❖ There are no atheists in foxholes, as any dogface soldier could tell you, and neither are there any atheists in presidential politics. Looking death in the face . . . Democratic office-seekers are walking the **sawdust trail** to the mourner's bench, drenching their campaigns in religiosity if not necessarily authentic religion. Be prepared to hear a lot more about the "Religious Left." (Suzanne Fields, "Nobody Here but Believers," *Washington Times*, 3/12/2007.)

(2) conversion (spec. a fundamental transformation of mind or character or way of thinking, esp. a spiritual . . .) *n.*: **metanoia** [Greek.] ❖ Whether the theme [of the reality TV show] is interior decoration, home organization, fashion sense, or parenting . . . the outcome is predictable. The victim is tearful, breathless, and grateful: the victim's friends and acquaintances are amazed and thankful, and we are left assured that the external remodeling is matched by an internal **metanoia** that ensures the change will be permanent. (Dolores Puterbaugh, "Wanted: Secular Miracle Worker," *USA Today Magazine*, 9/1/2005.)

convert (recent . . . to a belief) *n.*: **neophyte**.

❖ For the story of the small but steadily expanding number of Westerners who are converting to the religion of Mohammed has something to say to us all. . . . The majority of **neophytes** are between 35 and 55, said Batool al-Toma, an Irishwoman who was once called Mary. (Paul Vallely, "The New Muslims," *Independent* [London], 11/3/1998.)

(2) convert (esp. in a strange, grotesque, or humorous way) *v.t.*: **transmogrify**. See *transform*

convey (as in send a signal) *v.t., v.i.*: **semaphore**. See *signal*

convict *n.*: **malefactor**. See *wrongdoer*

convivial *adj.*: **Anacreontic**. [The example gives the derivation of this word.] ❖ The less-than-glorious origin of our national anthem was indeed a drinking song, "To Anacreon in Heaven," the theme song of the **Anacreontic** Club of London. The melody, published in England around 1780, is attributed to [two] members of the club, a group of wealthy men who liked to celebrate music, food and drink. The club took its name from Anacreon, a sixth-century-B.C. Greek lyric poet who also celebrated, well, celebrating. (Mike Rudeen, "You Can Toss Batteries in Trash, but Shouldn't," *Denver Rocky Mountain News*, 3/1/2003.)

(2) convivial *adj.*: **Falstaffian**. See *jovial*

convoluted (as in twisted) *adj.*: **tortile**. See *twisted*

(2) convoluted (as in tortuous) *adj.*: **vermiculate**. See *tortuous*

(3) convoluted *adj.*: **Rube Goldberg**. See *complicated*

convulsions (during or after pregnancy) *n.*: **eclampsia**. ❖ Doctors try to keep pre-eclampsia from progressing to convulsions, a condition known as **eclampsia** that can be very harmful to mother and unborn child. (*Newsday*, "Gene Found That Links High Blood Pressure, Pregnancy," 5/11/1993.)

cool (as in unemotional or even-tempered) *adj.*: **phlegmatic**. See *even-tempered*

(2) cool *adj.*: **algid**. See *cold*

coolness (esp. under pressure or trying circum-stances) *n.*: **sang-froid** [French]. See *composure*

coop up (as in confine) *v.t.*: **immure**. See *confine*

coordination (loss of . . .) *n.*: **apraxia**. ❖ Most [Rett Syndrome] victims suffer from **apraxia**, in which the body can't do what the brain tells it to, such as moving and talking. (Judy Siegel-Itzkovich, "Autism or Cerebral Palsy? No, It's Rett," *Jerusalem Post*, 7/8/2001.)

copier (inferior . . . , often of an artist, writer, or entertainer) *n.*: **epigone**. See *imitator*

copulation *n.*: **houghmagandy** [Scottish]. See *intercourse*

(2) copulation *n.*: **venery**. See *intercourse*

copy (of a previous artistic, musical, or literary piece) *n.*: **pastiche**. See *imitation*

copying (of the real world in art or literature) *n.*: **mimesis** (*adj.*: **mimetic**). See *imitation*

(2) copying (pathological or uncontrollable . . . of another's actions) *n.*: **echopraxia**. See *repeating*

(3) copying (pathological or uncontrollable or a child's . . . of another's words) *n.*: **echolalia**. See *repeating*

coquettish (as in flirtatious glance) *n.*: **oeillade** [French]. See *glance*

(2) coquettish (glance at in a . . . way) *idiom*: **make sheep's eyes**. See *flirtatious*

cordial (and pleasant) *adj.*: **sympathique** [French]. See *genial*

cordiality *n.*: **empressement** [French]. ❖ In an atmosphere of international excitement, the mentors fretted about whether Albert was enough of a flirt. He had, Leopold's doctor friend Baron Stockmar ruefully acknowledged, "more success with men than with women," in whose company he showed, alas, "too little **empressement**." (Ben Pimlott, "A Bit Too Good to Be True?" *Independent on Sunday*, 5/4/1997.)

(2) cordiality *n.*: **bonhomie**. See *affability*

core (of a matter, as in the essence) *n.*: **quiddity**. See *essence*

(2) core (the . . . of a matter, as in the bottom line, the main point, the essence, etc.) *n.*:

tachlis (esp. as in "talk tachlis") [Yiddish]. See *essence*

corpselike (appearing . . . or pale) *adj.*: **cadaverous**. ❖ Jordan, for his part, felt [Ann] Rice's casting suggestions [to play the Vampire Lestat] all were too old and too predictable. He wanted to avoid the same cliched, **cadaverous**-looking actors familiar to audiences from Max Schreck and Bela Lugosi Dracula flicks. (Jennet Conant, "Lestat, C'est Moi," *Esquire*, 3/1/1994, p. 70.)

corpses (fascination with or erotic attraction to . . .) *n.*: **necrophilia**. ❖ Jeffrey Dahmer stood before a Milwaukee court last week, finally adding his voice to the tales of mutilation, cannibalism and **necrophilia** that had held the country in a macabre thrall since his crimes were discovered last July. . . . [He] had the presence of mind to wear a protective condom when having sex with corpses. (Karen S. Schneider, "Up Front: Day of Reckoning," *People*, 3/2/1992, p. 38.)

(2) corpses (abnormal fear of . . . or dead people) *n.*: **necrophobia**. See *fear*

correct (as in proper or suitable) *adj.*: **comme il faut** [French]. See *proper*

(2) correct (text or language by removing errors or flaws) *v.t.*: **blue-pencil**. See *edit*

(3) correct (text or language by removing errors or flaws) *v.t.*: **emend**. See *edit*

(4) correct (as in right-thinking) *adj.*: **bienpensant**. See *right-thinking*

correcting (as in atoning for) *adj.*: **piacular**. See *atoning*

correction (esp. of printed material) *n.*: **corrigendum**. ❖ [Delly Bonsange, editor of the daily newspaper *Alerte Plus*] was sentenced to six months on 6 September by a Kinshasa court for publishing a report that Democratic Republic of the Congo Security Minister Mwenze Kongolo had been poisoned. Next day, *Alerte Plus* had published a **corrigendum** stating that the information was false. (Africa News Service, "Media Watchdog Decries Poor Health of Jailed Journalist," 10/1/2002.)

correctly (as in "by the book") *idiom*: **according to Hoyle**. See *by the book*

correctness (precise observance of . . . , as in etiquette) *n.*: **punctilio**. See *etiquette*

correspondence (of or relating to . . . , as in letters) *adj.*: **epistolary**. See *letters*

corridor (spec. the . . . in a stadium that connects the outer concourse to the interior of the stadium itself) *n.*: **vomitory**. ❖ Yankees tradition will be personified at the new park, from a replica of the monuments at Yankee Stadium, which will be located outside the park, to the signs identifying rows and seats at the six **vomitories** entering Legends Field. (Bill Chastain, "To Honor Tradition, Yanks' Spring Park Called Legends Field," *Tampa Tribune*, 12/16/1995.)

corrugated (as in grooved) *adj.*: **striated**. See *grooved*

corrupt (group of . . . politicians) *n.*: **plunderbund**. ❖ In 1952, the *Chicago Daily News* reported that Big Joe [Dan Rostenkowski's father] had three no-show employees on his committee payroll. . . . The next year, in an anti-corruption editorial, the *Sun-Times* called . . . Big Joe and a couple of other aldermen "the council's worst specimens." In 1955, the same paper termed Big Joe "an undeviating member of the **plunderbund** that now controls the council." (Peter Carlson, "Dan Rostenkowski Goes Down in History," *Washington Post*, 10/17/1993.)

(2) corrupt (person, spec. one who accepts bribes) *n.*: **boodler**. ❖ [Bill Clinton] knew exactly what he was doing [when he pardoned Marc Rich], which returns us to the original point: Does anyone believe Denise Rich didn't pay for the pardon? Isn't this exactly what it seems to be: An unclad case of bribery? . . . Defending Clinton is hard for anyone with a conscience. He's a fraud, a **boodler**, a coward and a thief. (R. Cort Kirkwood, *Ottawa Sun*, 2/18/2001.)

(3) corrupt (politician) *n.*: **highbinder**. ❖ The theory that animated the term limits vogue (which is now clearly subsiding) is a populist one: These here **highbinders** get themselves into their cushy [jobs] and stay on forever, lining their pockets and their cronies' pockets with honest graft (or doing some other undesirable things), until in extreme old age they're carted off drooling. (Dan Polsby [interviewee], "Q&A on Gerrymandering with Dan Polsby," United Press International, 9/25/2002.)

(4) corrupt (as in unscrupulous) *adj.*: **jack-leg**. See *unscrupulous* and *grafter*

(5) corrupt (government by . . . persons) *n.*: **kleptocracy**. See *government*

corrupted (morally . . .) *v.t.*: **cankered**. ❖ [SS officer Blobel] testified to the difficulty his men faced [in perpetrating mass killings]—testimony **cankered** by his continued belittling of the victims: Blobel: "Our men . . . suffered more from nervous exhaustion than those who had to be shot." [Judge:] "In other words, your pity was more for the men who had to shoot than the victims?" Blobel: "Our men had to be cared for." (Richard Rhodes, *Masters of Death*, Knopf [2003], p. 162.)

(2) corrupted (morally . . .) *adj.*: **scrofulous**. See *depraved*

corruptible (esp. politically) *adj.*: **Praetorian**. [The Praetorian Guard was a special force of guards used by Roman emperors, created by the Emperor Augustus in 27 B.C. The Guard lasted until 312 A.D. The Guard propped up a number of ruthless regimes in its later years and became corrupt, which is the derivation of this adjective. The term "Praetorian guard" also today generally refers to any person who provides protection, or any group that does so—bodily or otherwise—to a political leader, especially dictators or those considered evil. See *guard*.] ❖ I'm madder than when we learned he had no valid reasons to have invaded Iraq. Madder, even, than when it became clear we actually had been lied to about the reasons [President George W. Bush] invaded Iraq, or that the **Praetorian** thugs around him were willing to destroy anyone who exposed the lies. (Bill Cope, "Crime and Commutation," *Boise Weekly*, 12/18/2007.)

(2) corruptible *adj.*: **venal**. ❖ In 1988 he took on Democrat Jim Wright, launching a yearlong ethics probe that ultimately brought Wright down. Gingrich's weapon of choice was always charges of corruption: by showing that the people who ran the system were **venal**, he could undermine the entire Democratic edifice. (Nancy Gibbs, Man of the Year: "Master of the House," *Time*, 12/25/1995, p. 54.)

corruption (place of . . . and filth) *n.*: **Augean stable** [after Augeas, a legendary Greek king who did not clean out his stable for thirty years, until it was cleaned by Hercules]. ❖ A federal judge ruled Thursday that the nearly-bankrupt International Brotherhood of Teamsters (IBT) must absorb at least $6 million of the estimated $7.4 million cost of its rerun election scheduled for this spring. Last week, U.S. District Judge David Edelstein ruled, "The time has come when the IBT must bear its own costs of cleansing its **Augean stable**. . . . In plainer words, [the Teamsters] made the mess. It is their job to clean it up at any price." (*Washington Times*, "The Teamsters' Augean Stables," 12/22/1997.)

(2) corruption *n.*: **knavery**. ❖ Woodrow Wilson warned of the **knavery** that results when the uninitiated gain public office. **Knavery** characterizes all of the Nigerian military government's actions, from its human rights record to foreign policy formulations. Journalists languish in prison; publishing houses are shut down at will; daring publishers appear on the hit lists of government agents. (Yereba Yemmy Kina, "The Tragic Misrule of Nigeria," *St. Louis Post-Dispatch*, 11/11/1996.)

cosmetics *n.*: **maquillage** [French]. See *makeup*

costar (spec. the character in a drama second in importance to the protagonist) *n.*: **deuteragonist**. ❖ The plot of [Umberto Eco's] latest concerns an antiquarian book dealer called Yambo who, on recovering from an accident, discovers that he can remember every word of every book he has ever read but nothing about his own life. [His] monologue . . . forms the bulk of the book [but] deprived of backstory or **deuteragonist**, Yambo has only the reader to talk to . . . (Tim Martin, Books: "Tell Me, Is That a Signpost Back to Myself?" *Independent* [London], 6/26/2005.)

cough (of, relating to, or caused by) *adj.*: **tussive**. ❖ And then there was the coughing. Believe me, I know all about coughing. When it comes to **tussive** endeavour, I've put in the hours. When they come to write the annals of the great expectorators, I'll get an embossed first paragraph. (John Walsh, "The Worst Bout of Flu Ever, the Worst Poetry Reading," *Independent* [London], 1/30/1997.)

cough syrup *n.*: **linctus**. ❖ A new weapon in the armoury of cough medication is being tested on sickly volunteers. [They] will be invited [to] a secret location in Birmingham city centre and given a supply of the medicine, under the supervision of a doctor. They will then [be] invited back a few days later to assess the effect of the new **linctus** on their coughs. (Louise Palfreyman, "Take Part in Secret Battle Against Cough," *Sunday Mercury* [Birmingham], 3/28/1999.)

counsel (relating to the giving of . . . , as in advice) *adj.*: **paraenetic** (*n.*: **paraenesis**). See *advice*

counterattack (esp. to recover lost territory or political standing) *n.*: **revanche** [French]. See *revenge*

counterbalance (spec. to be or to make equal in weight) *v.t., v.i.*: **equiponderate**. See *equal*

counterclockwise *adv.*: **widdershins**. ❖ More spiral stairs. Along with labyrinthine passages and skull-crushing door lintels, they seem to sprout from every turret in Fordell. Some wind clockwise, some go **widdershins**. This helps with navigation, but if you wind up in the wrong bedroom, at least you have a good excuse. (Tom Kidd, Property: "A Tower That Mary Queen of Scots Was Pleased to Sleep In," *Daily Telegraph* [London], 8/14/1999.)

counterfeit *adj.*: **pinchbeck** [after Christopher Pinchbeck (1670–1732), a London watchmaker, who invented an alloy of five parts copper and one part zinc, which looked a bit like gold, and was used in making cheap jewelry; now used more generally to refer to something counterfeit]. ❖ Lying comes easy in *Dreams of Dead Women's Handbags* [a collection of short stories by Shena Mackay]. In "The Blue Orchestra," a woman has reinvented herself as The Contessa, after "so many glass tiaras, aliases, false campaign ribbons, **pinchbeck** baubles, forged checks." Her scam is working until she's vacationing in the tropics and runs into a vagrant who turns out to be a girlfriend from school days. (Emily White, "Outside the Curve," *Newsday*, 11/27/1994.)

(2) counterfeit (as in sham) *n.*: **postiche**. See *sham*

counterpart (ghostly . . . or twin of a living person) *n.*: **doppelgänger**. See *twin*

country (as in rural) *adj.*: **villatic**. See *rural*

countryman *n.*: **paisano** [Spanish]. ❖ [Mexicans were abuzz because] Oklahoma star Eduardo Nájera became the first Mexican ever to be drafted to an NBA team. As one [Mexican] cab driver [said] "Presidents come and go, but placing a **paisano** in the NBA is not so common." (*Christian Science Monitor*, Today's Story Line, 6/30/2000.)

countryside (of or relating to) *adj.*: **bucolic**. See *rustic*

coup (sudden attempt at a . . .) *n.*: **putsch**. ❖ "But as the economic crisis worsens, active discontent is growing." . . . [Boris] Yeltsin sternly rejects any possibility of a **putsch**. But, in a new poll, 46 percent of his countrymen said they think a coup is possible; only 30 percent rule it out. (Robin Knight, "A Creeping Coup in Russia?" *U.S. News & World Report*, 7/20/1992.)

coup de grace *n.*: **quietus** (esp. as in "put the quietus to"). See *termination*

couple (arranged in or forming a . . .) *adj.*: **jugate**. See *pair*

(2) couple (as in pair of two people) *n.*: **duumvirate**. See *duo*

(3) couple (two individuals or units regarded as a . . .) *n.*: **dyad**. See *pair*

courage *n.*: **hardihood**. ❖ Gentle reader, this

is the truth, and you know it. Water is wet, the sky is blue, men fight wars, women don't—here are basic truths about the natural order. Sexual politics can't alter or amend such truths. . . . None of this is to depreciate the valor and **hardihood** of women: traits demonstrated so many times as to require no proof. (William Murchison, "Unisex Military Works Poorly," *Dallas Morning News*, 11/20/1996.)

courageous (or bold while under the influence of alcohol) *adj.*: **potvaliant**. ❖ While many music lovers will be at this weekend's non-alcoholic Irish festival, we'll be celebrating a different kind of Celtic culture—the 20-ounce variety, if you know what we mean. Call us old-fashioned lushes or **potvaliant** know-it-alls . . . , but we believe St. Paddy's Day is best celebrated with a 39- to 45-degree Guinness, properly poured in an imperial pint glass and lovingly delivered with a shamrock on top. (*Eugene [OR] Register-Guard*, "For a Stout Pour, Take It to New Max's," 3/12/2004.)

(2) courageous (and strong woman) *n.*: **virago**. See *woman*

(3) courageous *adj.*: **doughty**. See *brave*

course of action *n.*: **démarche** [French]. ❖ The decision by . . . the regulator of British Gas, to enforce a new round of price restrictions . . . produced vitriol from the company, which accused her of a "smash and grab raid." . . . Although British Gas's reaction to the week's **démarche** was exaggerated, it does have a point about the volatility and subjectivity of regulatory action over the years. (*New Statesman & Society*, "All Gas and Downsizing," 5/17/1996, p. 5.)

covenant (as in pact) *n.*: **amicabilis concordia**. See *pact*

cover (a surface in a scattered way) *v.t.*: **bestrew**. ❖ She was wearing a baby-blue cotton print summer dress which showed off her slender figure and exposed the constellation of freckles **bestrewing** her shoulders. (Erik Tarloff, *The Man Who Wrote the Book*, Crown [2000], p. 7.)

coverage (as in publicity or a taste or flair for

being in the limelight) *n.*: **réclame** [French]. See *publicity*

covering (protective . . . , like a turtle shell) *n.*: **carapace**. See *shell*

covert (activity) *n.*: **hugger-mugger**. See *secrecy*

covetous (as in lustful) *adj.*: **lickerish**. See *lustful*

(2) covetous (strongly . . .) *adj.*: **appetent** (*n.*: **appetence**). See *desirous*

(3) covetous *adj.*: **emulous**. See *envious*

covetousness (as in greed) *n.*: **pleonexia**. See *greed*

(2) covetousness (as in worship of or devotion to money) *n.*: **plutolatry**. See *wealth*

(3) covetousness (esp. for wealth) *n.*: **cupidity**. See *greed*

cow (of, relating to, or resembling) *adj., n.*: **bovine**. ❖ So far, cow theft hasn't been a problem, say police, but maybe that's because the fiberglass creatures weigh almost 600 pounds with their concrete bases. There have been a few incidents of vandalism, however. The worst case occurred at Oak Street Beach when thugs tried hauling away "Wow Cow" but dropped the abstract-design **bovine** and ran when they were spotted. (Lisa Newman, "Chicago's Udder Delight: Whimsical Herd of Sculptures Creates a Bull Market in Tourism," *Washington Post*, 8/11/1999.)

coward *n.*: **poltroon**. ❖ And the problem isn't even all these poor politiclones, either. It's us. We listen to them. We tolerate their existence. We vote for them. If we had a leader with moral character, we'd get rid of her in the blink of an eye. We demand **poltroons** and panderers. (Crispin Sartwell, "Nearly All U.S. Political Leaders Are Frauds," *Arizona Republic*, 10/21/1998.)

cowardly *adj.*: **pusillanimous**. ❖ Until now, the European countries have hesitated to back Washington fully [in the war against Iraq], even though they depend more on Middle East oil than the U.S. does. Last week's spurt of resolve came just in time to save continental governments from appearing totally **pusillanimous**

not only in the eyes of Washington but also in European public opinion. (Lisa Beyer, "The Gulf: The Center Holds—For Now," *Time*, 9/3/1990, p. 34.)

(2) cowardly *adj., n.*: **retromingent**. [The definition of this word is "urinating backwards" (when used as an adjective) or animals that do so (when used as a noun). See *urinating*. However, while the connection to the definition is vague, it has also taken on a slang meaning—"cowardly"—in addition to being used as a kind of general, all-purpose insulting way to describe a person, such as "idiotic" or "moronic." The most famous usage is when *Washington Post* executive editor Ben Bradlee called Reed Irvine, the founder of Accuracy in Media, a "miserable, carping, **retromingent** vigilante," a line that led off most obituaries of Irvine.] ❖ [After somebody spray-painted his house with [racist] messages, William Brewer saw a white guy climbing his tree.] But the guy climbing the tree was not a **retromingent** racist creep preparing to do further damage to Brewer's home: He was a neighbor using the lofty perch to see and help capture the punks if they came back the next night. (*Northwest Indiana Post-Tribune*, "Hate-Message Experience Brings Both Good Feelings and Bad Ones," 9/23/1992.)

(3) cowardly (and cautious and indecisive) *adj.*: **Prufrockian**. See *timid*

cower (as in recoil, due to fear or intimidation) *v.t.*: **quail**. See *recoil*

(2) cower *v.i.*: **blench**. See *flinch*

(3) cower *v.i.*: **resile**. See *recoil*

(4) cower *v.i.*: **truckle**. See *kowtow*

co-worker (as in colleague) *n.*: **confrere**. See *colleague*

coy (as in flirtatious, glance) *n.*: **oeillade** [French]. See *glance*

cozy (or warm or friendly) *adj.*: **gemütlich** [German] ❖ The public rooms give testimony to the Danish gift for interior design, for mixing the old with the modern, creating a cozy atmosphere without ever lapsing into cuteness. [W]hitewashed brick and ancient, wonderfully

irregular oak timber . . . are combined here to create a mood of warm, familiar, unostentatious well-being. The bedrooms are no less **gemütlich**. (Michel Arnaud, "A Great Little Dane," *Town & Country*, 10/1/1995, p. 118.)

crabby (mood) *n.pl.*: **mulligrubs**. See *grumpiness*

(2) crabby (old man) *n.*: **alter kocker** [Yiddish]. See *old man*

(3) crabby (person) *n.*: **crosspatch**. See *grouch*

(4) crabby *adj.*: **atrabilious**. See *surly*

(5) crabby *adj.*: **bilious**. See *surly*

(6) crabby *adj.*: **liverish**. See *irritable*

(7) crabby *adj.*: **shirty**. See *irritable*

(8) crabby *adj.*: **splenetic**. See *irritable*

(9) crabby *adj.*: **waspish**. See *irritable*

crack (open) *v.t., v.i., n.*: **fissure**. ❖ The steeple-shattering light was followed by quakes of thunder as violent as any shift in the San Andreas. The sky **fissured** and rain fell. (Dean Koontz, *Intensity*, Knopf [1995] p. 99.)

crackle *v.i.*: **crepitate**. ❖ The Sixties People are rapidly getting past it. Their knees are going, their hips **crepitate** as they walk, gravity is doing what gravity does, their juices are drying up, liberal relativism and pot-smoking have extinguished their inner spark, they're all going deaf, and soon all that will be left is the contemplation of past glories. (Michael Bywater, "Porn with a Silver Spoon in Its Mouth," *Independent on Sunday*, 3/15/1998.)

cracks (full of . . .) *adj.*: **rimose**. ❖ Sir—As one (of the many) who have been delivered from the grip of substance abuse, I can understand the reasoning of the pro-cannabis clique. However, I am bemused at the willingness of The Press to give it some credence by publishing (Soapbox, July 28) their shallow sophistry, and their **rimose** ruminations. (*Press* [Canterbury, New Zealand], "Marijuana Law," 8/10/2001.)

(2) cracks (network of hairline . . . on works of art, such as paintings, esp. old works of art) *n.*: **craquelure**. ❖ Restorers, who have scrutinized countless paintings and learned to recognize the signs of aging, are the great authorities on **craquelure**. To listen to them talk about age cracks in paintings is like listening to makeup artists talk about crow's feet and puffy eyes. (Edward Dolnick, *The Forger's Spell*, HarperCollins [2008], p. 174.)

crafts (as in handmade artwork) *n*.: **virtu** [French]. See *art*

crafty (or cunning) *adj*.: **jesuitical** (sometimes cap.). [While "crafty" or "cunning" can certainly be used in complimentary ways (e.g., as synonyms for "clever"), this word is invariably used disparagingly, especially in regard to the use of subtly fallacious arguments, as in this example.] ❖ [Senator Charles Robb] admitted to having received from [Miss Virginia] a "nude massage" but denied they'd had coital relations. [E]ven if everything he said is literally true, he has still been deeply dishonest— that his novel sexual code enabled him to issue declarations ("I've never slept with another woman") designed to mislead. [T]here is an obsessive, missing-the-point quality to all such **Jesuitical** sexual distinctions . . . (Michael Lewis, "The New Lust Loophole; On Chuck Robb and Too-Subtle Sexual Distinctions," *Washington Post*, 3/20/2004.)

(2) crafty (artfully . . . or shrewd) *adj*.: **pawky**. See *shrewd*

(3) crafty (behavior) *n*.: **knavery**. See *corruption*

(4) crafty (characterized by . . . and cunning conduct, esp. in regard to the pursuit and maintenance of political or other power) *adj*.: **Machiavellian**. See *deceitful*

(5) crafty (conduct) *n*.: **skullduggery**. See *deceitfulness*

cramped (by not affording enough space) *adj*.: **incommodious**. ❖ Trading a 67,200-sq.-ft. house (the White one) for a not-**incommodious** 5,232-sq.-ft. Dutch Colonial, Hillary Rodham Clinton, 52, spent the first night at her new home in Chappaqua, N.Y., on Jan. 5, as part of her bid to establish residency in the state and run for the senate. (David Cobb Craig, Passages, *People*, 1/24/2000, p. 95.)

cranky (and/or shy and/or socially withdrawn or inexperienced) *adj*.: **farouche** [French]. See *shy*

(2) cranky (mood) *n.pl*.: **mulligrubs**. See *grumpiness*

(3) cranky (old man) *n*.: **alter kocker** [Yiddish]. See *old man*

(4) cranky (person) *n*.: **crosspatch**. See *grouch*

(5) cranky *adj*.: **atrabilious**. See *surly*

(6) cranky *adj*.: **bilious**. See *surly*

(7) cranky *adj*.: **liverish**. See *irritable*

(8) cranky *adj*.: **querulous**. See *peevish*

(9) cranky *adj*.: **shirty**. See *irritable*

(10) cranky *adj*.: **splenetic**. See *irritable*

(11) cranky *adj*.: **tetchy**. See *grouchy*

(12) cranky *adj*.: **waspish**. See *irritable*

crash (spec. the act of one object striking a stationary object, usually applied to ships) *n*.: **allision**. See *collision*

craving (condition involving . . . to eat non-food items) *n*.: **pica**. ❖ Pica, which is normally observed in children and is thought to result from iron deficiencies or lead exposure, causes cravings for clay, sand, dirt, plaster and paint. (Jamie Talan, "New Research Zeros In on the Lead Question," *Newsday*, 11/25/1993.)

(2) craving (esp. something one once had but has no more) *n*.: **desiderium**. See *longing*

(3) craving (strong . . .) *n*.: **avidity**. ❖ [The movie *Crouching Tiger, Hidden Dragon*] concerns the theft of a sword, the Green Destiny. [Jen] arrives, and everything tips off-balance. The wiser, more cautious adults are both drawn to and upset by Jen's beauty and vagrant energy. They sense Jen's **avidity** for rare toys like the Green Destiny. (Richard Corliss, The Arts/Cinema: "Martial Masterpiece," *Time* International, 7/10/2000, p. 44.)

(4) craving *n*.: **appetence**. ❖ Male sexual **appetence**, monotonous and warlike, can be enough to make any unprepared young wife major in menstruation for life. Resort people know that. They set out to mitigate and feminize sexuality. (Keith D. Mano, "Honeymoon Hotels in the Pocono Mountains," *Playboy*, 2/1989, p. 118.)

(5) craving (having a strong . . .) *adj.*: **appetent** (*n*.: **appetence**). See *desirous*

(6) craving *adj.*: **athirst**. See *eager*

crawl (as in teem or swarm) *v.i.*: **pullulate**. See *teem*

crawling *adj.*: **reptant**. [This word is both an adjective and a noun that refers to crustaceans, such as lobsters and crabs.] ❖ **Reptants** occurred in 47.1% of the stomachs examined [of the thornback ray]. . . . Swimming crabs . . . were the most important **reptant** prey item in [their] diet. Other important **reptants** included the lesser locust lobster [and] the shamefaced crab. (Maria Gros, "Diets of Thornback Ray," *Fishery Bulletin*, 7/1/2003.)

craze (as in irresistible compulsion) *n.*: **cacoëthes**. See *compulsion*

(2) craze (the latest . . .) *n.*: **dernier cri** [French]. See *trend*

crazy (appearing . . . as if under a spell) *adj.*: **fey**. ❖ [O]ur host, now full of wine, failed to spot an approaching roundabout in the dark and drove straight up the central grassy mound and stopped on top. . . . [He] said genially: "Sorry about that, but I swear that roundabout came a good 200 yards earlier than usual." . . . That is an example of what Claud Cockburn once called the kind of **fey** logic peculiar to the Irish. (Miles Kington, "It's Enough to Drive You to Nuits-St-Georges," *Independent* [London], 6/5/1997.)

(2) crazy (informal, as in daffy or loony) *adj.*: **doolally** [British; often as in "going doolally." This word is an alteration of Deolali, a town near Bombay, India, where British soldiers awaited their return home and where sickness and boredom caused some to break down.] ❖ I see why big names feature in a [list of worst songs] of all time. It's hard not to remember the shock of a great artist going **doolally**. David Bowie (who does not feature in the list) must have had his reasons for recording "The Little Drummer Boy" with Bing Crosby, and one day he might tell them to a therapist. (David Lister, "Even the Biggest Stars Can Hit the Wrong Note," *Independent* [London], 4/24/2004.)

(3) crazy (slightly mentally . . . , often used humorously) *adj.*: **tetched**. ❖ A long, empty coffin sits on the rag rug, its lid propped open. . . . I shrug, as if I'm used to seeing empty coffins in parlors. "Who died?" I manage to ask. "No one." He laughs. "Mr. Cottland built it for himself. He's crazy; **tetched** in the head, as my mama would say. Keeps a jug of whiskey in there, 'case he gets thirsty on the way to heaven." (Liza Ketchum, "Orphan Journey Home," *Dallas Morning News*, 11/4/1998.)

(4) crazy (person) *n.*: **bedlamite**. See *lunatic*

(5) crazy (as in frenzied) *adj.*: **corybantic**. See *frenzied*

(6) crazy (as in not of sound mind) *adj.*: **non compos mentis** [Latin]. See *insane*

(7) crazy (as in foolish) *adj.*: **barmy** [British]. See *foolish*

(8) crazy (as in foolish) *adj.*: **balmy**. See *foolish*

crease (or wrinkle) *n.*, *v.t.*: **rimple**. See *wrinkle*

creased (very . . . , as in wrinkled) *adj.*: **rugose**. See *wrinkled*

create (an idea, plan, theory, or explanation after careful thought) *v.t.*: **excogitate**. See *devise*

creative (and/or original) *adj.*: **Promethean**. [Prometheus was the Titan god of forethought, who, based on some legends, was entrusted with the task of molding mankind out of clay.] ❖ Over the course of his decades-long career, Frank Zappa crafted a body of work as complex and **Promethean** as any artist in rock music's history. From his early efforts with the Mothers of Invention to his late-period attempts at crafting a kind of modern classical, Zappa's particular blend of exploration, iconoclasm and gutter humor remains as unique as it is musically intimidating. (*Denver Rocky Mountain News*, Weekend Round-Up, 11/16/2007.)

(2) creative (as in resourceful person) *n.*: **debrouillard** (or **débrouillard**) [French]. See *resourceful*

creativity (source of . . . , as in inspiration) *n.*: **Pierian spring**. See *inspiration*

creator *n.*: **demiurge** [In some philosophies, a

demiurge is the creator deity of the material world. It is also sometimes used more generally to refer to the creator of anything, as in this example.] ❖ Craigslist is ugly. It is ranks of pale-blue links on a field of gray. No pictures, no icons, no banner ads. Yet under the watchful eye of **demiurge** Craig Newmark, craigslist.org has become the single most useful commerce site on the Internet. (Daniel Torday, "Craig Newmark Set Out to Make a Useful and Humane Local Internet Site, and He Ended Up Building the Best and Most Efficient E-Commerce Site on the Web," *Esquire*, 12/1/2002.)

credulous *adj.*: **ultrafidian.** [Latin. "Ultra fidem" means "beyond faith."] ❖ On 1 April 1992, USA National Public Radio's programme *Talk of the Nation* had its phones jammed for hours with irate callers after announcing that [Richard Nixon] was, once again, running for the presidency. *Talk of the Nation* further inflamed its **ultrafidian** listeners by stating that the new candidate's campaign slogan was to be, "I didn't do anything wrong, and I won't do it again." (www.ssu.org.au/media/swine_2003/_ed09, "The Swine," 5/5/2003.)

(2) credulous (person) *n.*: **gobemouche** [French]. See *gullible*

creeky (as in decrepit) *adj.*: **spavined**. See *decrepit*

creeping *adj.*: **reptant**. See *crawling*

crestfallen *adj.*: **chapfallen**. See *dejected*

(2) crestfallen *adj.*: **heartsore**. See *heartbroken*

crevices (full of . . .) *adj.*: **rimose**. See *cracks*

crickets (of or relating to . . .) *adj.*: **orthopterous**. See *insects*

crime (a . . . because it is prohibited by statute rather than because the conduct is wrong by its own nature or by natural law) *n.*: **malum prohibitum**. [Latin. The counterpart to this term, *malum in se*, refers to an offense that is wrong or evil by its own nature or by natural law rather than because prohibited by statute. See *wrongdoing*.] ❖ Unable to state without equivocation that racial preferences are wrong, [Supreme Court Justice Sandra Day] O'Connor meanders about the fields of logic with backflips. . . . [She states that a] 16-seat quota [for minority admissions to law school] is **malum prohibitum**, but the Michigan admissions officers keeping a daily tally on the race makeup of their incoming class is hunky-dory. (Marianne Jennings, "O'Connor's an Idiotic Liberal Hand-Wringer," *Salt Lake City Desert News*, 7/7/2003.)

(2) crime (or wrongdoing in public office) *n.*: **malversation**. See *wrongdoing*

(3) crime (or wrongdoing in public office) *n.*: **misprision**. See *wrongdoing*

criminal (spec. an adult who instructs children how to steal) *n.*: **Fagin** [based on a character in the Charles Dickens novel *Oliver Twist*, who teaches children to be pickpockets]. See *thief*

(2) criminal *n.*: **malefactor**. See *wrongdoer*

crimson *adj.*: **incarnadine**. ❖ [In] *The Tale of the Body Thief*, the fourth entry in Anne Rice's enormously successful series, The Vampire Chronicles . . . [she writes] prose that is not so much purple as **incarnadine**. "Blood is warm, cherie. Come with me, and drink blood, as you and I know how to do." (Gene Lyons, review of *The Tale of the Body Thief*, by Anne Rice, *Entertainment Weekly*, 11/6/1992, p. 60.)

cringe (as in recoil, due to fear or intimidation) *v.t.*: **quail**. See *recoil*

(2) cringe *v.i.*: **blench**. See *flinch*

(3) cringe *v.i.*: **resile**. See *recoil*

crinkle *n.*, *v.t.*: **rimple**. See *wrinkle*

cripple (as in deprive of strength) *v.t.*: **enervate**. See *debilitate*

(2) cripple (as in deprive of strength) *v.t.*: **geld**. See *weaken*

crisis (as in combination of events or circumstances that creates a . . .) *n.*: **conjuncture**. ❖ [W]hether or not the United States will invade Iraq has temporarily drawn the attention of many from a deepening economic crisis that is shaping up to be the worst crisis of global capitalism since the Great Depression 70 years ago. What makes the current **conjuncture** particularly volatile and unique is the way the chronic crisis at the heart of the system of production is unfolding alongside a massive crisis of the system of reproduction of global capitalism. (Walden Bello, "The Multiple Crises of Global Capitalism," *Canadian Dimension*, 1/1/2003.)

(2) crisis (as in predicament, from which it is difficult to extricate onself): **tar baby**. See *predicament*

(3) crisis (stage or period) *n., adj.*: **climacteric**. See *critical*

(4) crisis *n.*: **Torschlusspanik** [German]. See *panic*

critic (severe . . .) *n.*: **aristarch**. ❖ [Rasikamani T. K. Chidambaranatha Mudaliar] was fond of saying that poetry must be rescued from the pundits, and that it was rarer to come across a genuine rasika than a good poet. [But] know that his ruthless trouncing of the spurious is in direct proportion to his passion for poetry. He was no grim **aristarch** out to censure, but [one who] identified himself with the creative mind in the niceties and nuances of expression. (Gowri Ramnarayan, "The Price of a Poet," *Hindu*, 4/8/2001.)

(2) critic (who is inferior or incompetent) *n.*: **criticaster**. ❖ [S]ince [book] awards are always with us, it is better to have writers, practitioners, people who ply the trade, taking a hand in the decisions made. The alternatives are clear and ghastly [i.e., those with no literary skill]. . . . In some distant studio sits the familiar panel [of judges] from hell: the rumpled iconoclast, the seething bard, and the pert **criticaster**. (Christopher Hope, "Bloomsday Schoomsday," *New Statesman*, 6/21/1996, p. 12.)

(3) critic (whose reviews are negative and sometimes unjust) *n.*: **Zoilus**. See *criticism*

critical (stage or period) *n., adj.*: **climacteric**. ❖ During the autumn of 1932, the state crisis of the Weimar Republic deepened. No resolution was in sight. In the first months of the winter of 1932–3, it entered its **climacteric** phase. (Ian Kershaw, *Hitler*, Norton [1998], p. 379.)

(2) critical (as in decisive remark, blow, or factor) *n.*: **sockdolager**. See *decisive*

(3) critical (as in faultfinding) *adj.*: **captious**. See *faultfinding*

(4) critical (as in faultfinding, person) *n.*: **smellfungus**. See *faultfinder*

(5) critical (as in urgent) *adj.*: **necessitous**. See *urgent*

criticism (hostile . . .) *n.*: **animadversion** (*v.t.*: **animadvert**). ❖ One of the most pressing challenges for the secretary of defense . . . is the proliferation of nuclear weaponry to North Korea; but here is the secretary of defense-designate [Bobby Ray Inman] fleeing government, and citing as a cause of his flight the **animadversions** of [journalist] Ellen Goodman. . . . A man who will not stand up to Ellen Goodman will not stand up to Kim Il Sung. (Leon Wieseltier, "Remembering Bobby," *New Republic*, 2/7/1994, p. 4.)

(2) criticism (which is negative and sometimes unjust) *n.*: **Zoilism**. [This is based on the fourth-century B.C. Greek critic Zoilus.] ❖ No one, as they say, ever built a statue to a critic. **Zoilism**—negative criticism—has always been resented by writers and artists. . . . It's painful (not to say ruinous) if you have spent two years writing a novel, a year making a film, or six months mounting a West End production, exhibition or concert, to have some swine devastate it in 500 words [but] everyone loves a hatchet job as long as it's not their own neck on the block. (John Sutherland, "Who Needs Critics?" *Independent* [London], 12/12/1998.)

(3) criticism (as in catching severe . . .) *idiom*: **(catching) unshirted hell**. ["Unshirted" by itself is a rare word meaning undisguised, naked, or plain. However, it is used almost exclusively as part of the phrase "catching (or caught) unshirted hell" in the sense of being criticized for doing something.] ❖ The biggest and most difficult decision in my life was the Nixon pardon. Of course, I caught **unshirted hell** for it. But I thought it was the right thing to do for the country, not for Mr. Nixon. I would have been paralyzed as president if I had not granted the pardon. (Gerald Ford, "What I've Learned," *Esquire*, 1/1/2003.)

(4) criticism (mania for . . . of others) *n.*: **cacoëthes carpendi** [Latin]. See *faultfinding*

(5) criticism (as in denunciation) *n.*: **commination**. See *denunciation*

(6) criticism (as in insult, which is clever or polite) *n.*: **asteism**. See *insult*

(7) criticism (delivered while leaving the scene) *n.*: **Parthian shot**. See *parting shot*

criticize (harshly) *v.t.*: **flay**. ❖ These young [tennis players] today. They are a favorite target for Jimmy Connors; he doesn't like their high-octane game, their monochromatic personalities, the fact that they're not . . . well, like him. . . . With soaring TV ratings to boost his case, Connors **flayed** the younger men mercilessly. (S. I. Price, Tennis, *Sports Illustrated*, 5/26/1997, p. 92.)

(2) criticize (harshly) *v.t.*: **fustigate**. ❖ France is at peace, prosperous, economically and socially dynamic after years of stagnation, firmly committed to the European Union in which it is perhaps the major player. . . . How paradoxical then that in this summer of 2000, a book that **fustigates** the French for their frenetic pursuit of a vague ideal of happiness and sharply criticizes French society and its values would be a runaway bestseller. (Thomas Bishop, Notebook: "France in Pursuit of Happiness," *Newsday*, 9/24/2000.)

(3) criticize (oneself) *v.t.*: **flagellate** (*n.*: **flagellation**). [This word means to whip or flog another, and is properly used in that sense, but is generally used figuratively, esp. as in of oneself, sometimes as in self-flagellation]. ❖ Journalists belong to the only profession whose members regularly get together to **flagellate** themselves in public. (Sheryl McCarthy, "Here's How We Cover the Blob," *Newsday*, 4/12/1995.)

(4) criticize (or scold or rebuke) *v.t.*: **objurgate**. ❖ The act about to be **objurgated** here calls on the Food and Drug Administration to oversee a broad revision of food labeling. . . . The agency must also Solomonically settle the age-old question of how large is a "serving," which Congress has unhelpfully defined as "an amount customarily consumed." . . . Who needs all this? Aside from the silliness the law will generate, the nutritional information has a cost. (Daniel Seligman, "Keeping Up," *Fortune*, 7/1/1991, p. 94.)

(5) criticize (sharply) *v.t.*: **scarify**. [This word means to cut or lacerate (see *cut*) and in this context means to make cutting remarks. It is sometimes wrongly thought to mean the same as to scare.] ❖ [C]horeographer [Mark Morris] is nothing if not honest. ("His dances are outrageously honest, like him," Mikhail Baryshnikov said recently.) And an interview with him is half-unprintable; he will often **scarify** some person or some place, and then say: "But please. Don't quote that." (Paul Montgomery, "A Bad Boy of Dance Scampers Off to Brooklyn," *New York Times*, 6/20/1990.)

(6) criticize (in a false way so as to humiliate or disgrace) *v.t.*: **traduce**. See *malign*

(7) criticize (a statement, opinion, or action) *v.t.*: **oppugn**. See *oppose*

(8) criticize (as in disparage) *v.t.*: **vilipend**. See *disparage*

(9) criticize (as in raise trivial objections) *v.t.*: **cavil**. See *quibble*

(10) criticize (by making false or malicious statements) *v.t.*: **calumniate**. See *malign*

(11) criticize (or attack in writing) *n.*: **coup de plume** [French; attack by pen]. See *attack*

(12) criticize (sharply) *v.t.*: **keelhaul**. See *rebuke*

criticizing (or expressing disapproval) *adj.*: **dyslogistic**. See *uncomplimentary*

critique *v.t.*: **assay**. See *evaluate*

crook (as in thief) *n.*: **gonif** or **ganef** or **goniff** [Yiddish]. See *thief*

(2) crook (as in thief, caught red-handed) *n.*: **backberend**. See *thief*

crooked (as in unscrupulous) *adj.*: **jackleg**. See *unscrupulous*

(2) crooked (behavior) *n.*: **knavery**. See *corruption*

(3) crooked (group of . . . politicians) *n.*: **plunderbund**. See *corrupt*

(4) crooked (politician) *n.*: **highbinder**. See *corrupt*

cross (a body of water, esp, in a shallow part) *v.t.*: **ford**. ❖ "In some places the lagoon is no more than 2 meters high," Sarunis had said. "Sabonis could walk across it!" By this he meant that a 7-footer could **ford** the lagoon, not literally walk across it. (Alexander Wolff, *Big Game, Small World*, Warner Books [2002], p. 24.)

(2) cross (as in cranky or testy) *adj.*: **querulous**. See *peevish*

(3) cross (as in grouchy, person) *n.*: **crosspatch**. See *grouch*

(4) cross (as in irritable) *adj.*: **liverish**. See *irritable*

(5) cross (as in irritable) *adj.*: **shirty**. See *irritable*

(6) cross (as in irritable) *adj.*: **waspish**. See *irritable*

(7) cross (as in surly) *adj.*: **atrabilious**. See *surly*

(8) cross (as in surly) *adj.*: **bilious**. See *surly*

(9) cross (mood) *n.pl.*: **mulligrubs**. See *grumpiness*

(10) cross *adj.*: **splenetic**. See *irritable*

(11) cross *adj.*: **tetchy**. See *grouchy*

cross-eyed *adj.*: **strabismic**. [Though a medical term for cross-eyed, it also refers figuratively to any failure to perceive something clearly or accurately or not being based on clear observation or analysis.] ❖ In the FDA's **strabismic** eyes, a product must be judged as either a food (in which case it must merely contain what it says it contains, and not be poisonous) or a drug (in which case it must meet tests of efficacy as well). But are dietary supplements drugs? Is a tablet of vitamin C a food, like rice, or a drug, like Prozac? . . . The reasons for the FDA's choice of targets are often hard to fathom. (Jeff Elliot, "Taking Vitamins: the FDA's Raids on Promoters of Dietary Supplements Seem Designed to Keep Consumers in the Dark," *National Review*, 11/21/1994.)

crosswise *prep., adv.*: **athwart**. See *across*

crossword puzzles (one who enjoys solving or creating . . .) *n.*: **cruciverbalist**. ❖ Despite the fact that thousands of people across the nation are hooked on crosswords and their seductive siblings, acrostics, no 12-step program has been developed to treat it. . . . In high school, I was a closet **cruciverbalist** [because] working crosswords seemed so uncool. (Kristin Tillotson, "The Life and Times of a Crossword Addict," *Minneapolis Star Tribune*, 3/13/1995.)

crotchety (old man) *n.*: **alter kocker** [Yiddish]. See *old man*

crow (hoarse, raucous sound of) *n.*: **caw**. ❖ [T]ens of thousands of crows . . . inexplicably flock to the treetops above downtown buildings and parks about this time every year. The birds call incessantly, with loud, grating, monotonous **caws**. (Susan Levine, "City Hopes Crows Respond to Distress Signal," *Dallas Morning News*, 12/22/1996.)

(2) crow (of, relating to, or resembling) *adj.*: **corvine**. ❖ A crow has primary school mums in a flap with its own terrifying version of Hitchcock's *The Birds*. The **corvine** pest sits in trees near St Margarets Roman Catholic Primary School in Dunfermline watching for approaching women. When it spots one it fancies, it swoops down and digs its claws into her hair and [starts] scratching. (*Daily Mirror* [London], "Bird Has Brunette Targets," 3/16/2007.)

crowd (of people, as in multitude or throng) *n.*: **ruck**. See *multitude*

(2) crowd (the . . . , as in the masses) *n.*: **vulgus** [Latin]. See *masses*

crowded (heavily . . . region or city) *n.*: **megalopolis**. ❖ Deng's plan envisions the **megalopolis** of 13 million inhabitants [Shanghai, China] as a booster engine, towing the country's midriff and north into the 21st century. (James Walsh, "Nothing in Wang Hon Gwen's Life Belittled Him So Much as . . . ," *Time* International, 10/5/1992, p. 18.)

(2) crowded (together, esp. in rows) *adj.*: **serried**. ❖ The crowd went wild at Hitler's entrance, standing on chairs and benches, waving, shouting "Heil," stamping their feet. Around 200 stormtroopers in **serried** ranks with banners filed past Hitler, greeting him with the fascist salute. (Ian Kershaw, *Hitler*, Norton [1998], p. 292.)

(3) crowded (with) *adj.*: **aswarm**. See *teeming*

crowd-pleasing (of an argument designed for . . .) *adj., adv.*: **ad captandum** (or **ad captandum vulgus**) [Latin]. See *argument*

crowd-pleasing (of an argument designed for . . . , as in appealing to prejudices or sentiments, rather than facts or logical reasoning) *adj., adv.*: **ad populum** [Latin]. See *argument*

crucial (as in urgent) *adj.*: **necessitous**. See *urgent*

(2) crucial (stage or period) *n., adj.*: **climacteric**. See *critical*

crude (or poorly put together, esp. with respect to a writing or speech) *adj.*: **incondite**. ❖ Suddenly I'm tired, despite the java fix, and resigned to the fact that come Monday, I'll have about enough free time—between diaper origami and learning the baby language of the day and getting the turkey loaf done before my wife comes home—to write an **incondite** self-pitying limerick: "There was an old pop in Seattle / Who was stuck between bottle and rattle." (R. W. Lucky, "What I Want to Be After My Child Grows Up," *Seattle Times*, 3/27/1994.)

(2) crude *n.*: **artless**. ❖ [For George Bush and Al Gore in campaign ads], clever is dangerous. You can inadvertently alienate important sectors of the electorate (for instance, the stupid) or come off as slick and dishonest. Since Watergate, ads have been much more straightforward—and **artless**. [With all the] ugly, blaring ads, perhaps every ad, regardless of its content, becomes a negative one. (James Poniewozik, Nation/Campaign 2000: "Campaign Ad Nauseam," *Time*, 11/13/2000, p. 40.)

(3) crude (as in rough) *adj.*: **scabrous**. See *rough*

(4) crude (person) *n.*: **grobian**. See *boor*

(5) crude (person) *n.*: **yahoo**. See *boor*

cruel *adj.*: **fell** (*n.*: **fellness**). ❖ [In this fairy tale (written in 2007), a brother and sister and trav-

eled away from home, and the brother decided not to return. Long after, she went to find him and asked why he had never returned. It was because of his hatred of their father.] "Our Lord Father" and he scowled and sneered at his words, "cared so much that he kept you against your will and could not even find it in him to make his way unto me. . . . No, I do not believe father has changed at all." She was much amazed at the **fellness** of his words. (www .calenathrim.com, "Aratakhina," 10/28/2007.)

(2) cruel (in the manner of an oppressive and despotic organization) *adj.*: **jackbooted**. See *oppressive*

(3) cruel (one who is . . .) *n.*: **tricoteuse**. See *knitter*. [See the note at "knitter" for why this word can be synonymous with cruel.]

crumble (away) *v.i.*: **molder**. ❖ Following its New York premiere at the Liberty Theater on Sept. 5, 1916, *Intolerance* was repeatedly cut and re-edited, at first by [D. W.] Griffith himself, in an effort to stimulate box-office activity. . . . During the years that followed, footage was lost, and butchered prints **moldered**. (Vincent Canby, "Seeing *Intolerance* Is Hard Work," *New York Times*, 10/29/1989.)

crumbly *adj.*: **friable**. ❖ But there is a much easier way to make these crumb-crowned desserts. You can make a pastry base and a crumbly topping from one mixture, instead of preparing two separate doughs. Simply blend the ingredients for a sweet dough in the food processor until it forms a **friable** mixture. (Faye Levy, "Crumb-Topped Treats," *Jerusalem Post*, 2/24/1995.)

(2) crumbly *adj.*: **pulverulent**. See *powdery*

crumple (or wrinkle) *n., v.t.*: **rimple**. See *wrinkle*

(2) crumple *n., v.t.*: **rimple**. See *wrinkle*

crusade (for an idea or principle) *n.*: **jihad**. ❖ Mr. Withey was convinced that electromagnetic fields cause cancer. And, at the time he was waging his courtroom **jihad** against Big Electric, he had at least two widely reported scientific papers to support his conclusion—to give him real hope that, one day, he just might extract an asbestos-like or breast-implantlike settlement from the nation's deep-pocket utilities. (Joseph Perkins, "Payoffs for Junk Science," *Washington Times*, 8/3/1999.)

crush (as in reduce to powder) *v.t.*: **comminute**. See *pulverize*

(2) crush (spec. the emotional thrill and excitement one feels when initially in love) *n.*: **limerence** (*adj.*: **limerent**). See *love*

crux (of a matter, as in the essence) *n.*: **quiddity**. See *essence*

cry (as in plea) *n.*: **cri de coeur** [French; lit. cry of the heart]. See *plea*

(2) cry (as in screech, like a cat in heat) *v.i.*: **caterwaul**. See *screech*

(3) cry (as in wail) *v.i.*: **ululate**. See *wail*

(4) cry (as in yelp, bark, or screech) *v.t., n.*: **yawp**. See *shriek*

(5) cry (in a whiny or whimpering way) *v.i.*: **pule**. See *whimper*

(6) cry (in lament for the dead) *v.i.*: **keen**. See *wail*

(7) cry (over, as in lament) *v.t.*: **bewail**. See *lament*

(8) cry (weakly) *v.i.*: **mewl**. See *whimper*

crying (given to . . .) *adj.*: **larmoyant**. See *tearful*

(2) crying (of or relating to) *adj.*: **lachrymal**. See *tears*

(3) crying *adj.*: **lachrymose**. See *tearful*

crypt (esp. under a church) *n.*: **undercroft**. ❖ There are also distortions that are simply silly. "Every Christmas night the entire population squeezes into the **undercroft** to hear read the passages of the Gospel of St. Luke," . . . he writes. It is not only ridiculous to imagine the entire population of 12,000 crowding into one little crypt on Christmas Eve; it is silly to expect all the Christians of Beit Sahour to attend any service together. (David Bar-Illan, "Fiction Which Passes as 'Respectable' Reportage," *Jerusalem Post*, 1/20/1995.)

cryptic (or ambiguous or equivocal) *adj.*: **sibylline** (or **sibilline**; often cap.) [This word derives from Sibyl (or Sybil), one of a number of women regarded as prophets by the ancient Greeks. It also means "prophetic."] ❖ It was

crucial, [Federal Reserve Board chairman Alan] Greenspan added, that the US continue to keep inflation in check. Although there were "some reasons for concern, at least with regard to the nearer term," prospects for achieving this were "fundamentally good." This typically **sibylline**, central bankerly language does nothing to reduce the likelihood that the policy-setting Federal Open Market Committee will raise rates at its meeting next Tuesday. (Rupert Cornwall, "Fed Chief Hints Any Interest Rate Rise Will Be Small," *Independent* [London], 1/26/1995.)

(2) cryptic (or obscure speech or writing, esp. deliberately) *adj.*: **elliptical**. ❖ "We're thinking of building out here—we'll have to if we're going to have kids," [Melanie Griffith] says offhandedly. "Excuse me?" Griffith's smile is as ambiguous as the Mona Lisa's. . . . Is she **elliptically** trying to confirm a persistent tabloid report? Not this day. (Peter Chandler, Features: "Melanie in Love," *InStyle*, 3/1/1996, p. 80.)

(3) cryptic (or obscure) *adj.*: **Delphic**. See *ambiguous*

cryptography *n.*: **steganography**. See *codes*

cuddle (as in caress or fondle) *v.i.*: **canoodle** (often "canoodle with"). See *caress*

cuddling *idiom*: **slap and tickle**. See *sex*

culmination (as in climax, of a drama) *n.*: **catastasis**. See *climax*

cultivated (person) *n.*: **bel esprit**. ❖ Momigliano [showed] that the "antiquarians" of the sixteenth and seventeenth centuries were neither maniacal collectors nor narrow specialists, but strong and disciplined minds, philosophically well-equipped scholars [and] Gibbon, who detested the **bel esprit** side of the Enlightenment, was the heir of these scholars, and he knew it. (Marc Fumaroli, "The Antiquarian as Hero," *New Republic*, 5/28/2001.)

cultivation (fit for . . .) *adj.*: **arable**. See *farming*

cultural (moral and/or intellectual spirit of an era) *n.*: **zeitgeist**. See *spirit*

culture (modification of one's . . . through living in another culture) *n.*: **acculturation**. ❖ He describes acculturatic as the process of exchange by which immigrants modify their attitudes, cultural norms and behaviors as a result of interaction within the United States culture. "**Acculturation** produces changes in sexual attitudes and behavior," Sabogal says. (Sandra Varner, "Demographics Help Explain Hispanic Sexual Behavior," *Oakland Post*, 10/29/1995.)

(2) culture (which is based on either strong interpersonal relationships and common values among its members [*n.*: **gemeinschaft**—see *community*] or impersonal such relationships [*n.*: **gesellschaft**—see *association*, which includes an example that uses both terms]) [German].

cultured (esp. those aspiring or pretending to be . . .) *adj.*: **lace-curtain**. See *well-bred*

culture wars *n.*: **Kulturkampf** [German]. ❖ Amid all the hubbub surrounding the defections of [two African American studies professors] from Harvard to Princeton recently, it went unmentioned that only thirty years ago, African-American studies as we know it today didn't even exist. Although the **Kulturkampf** of the 1960s touched many academic disciplines, it was the creation of black studies programs that led to the most rancorous debates on American campuses. (John McMillan, review of *White Boy: A Memoir,* by Mark D. Naison, *Nation*, 7/15/2002.)

cumbersome (and clumsy like an elephant) *adj.*: **elephantine**. See *clumsy*

cunning (artfully . . . or shrewd) *adj.*: **pawky**. See *shrewd*

(2) cunning (characterized by . . . conduct, esp. in regard to the pursuit and maintenance of political or other power) *adj.*: **Machiavellian**. See *deceitful*

(3) cunning (conduct) *n.*: **skullduggery**. See *deceitfulness*

(4) cunning (or crafty) *adj.*: **jesuitical** (sometimes cap.). See *crafty*

cup (shallow . . . or bowl with a handle) *n.*: **porringer**. See *bowl*

curative (as in having the power to cure or heal) *adj.*: **sanative**. See *healthful*

cure (alleged . . . that is untested or unproved) *n.*: **nostrum**. See *remedy*

cure-all *n.*: **catholicon**. See *remedy*

curing (of or relating to medicine or the art of . . . , as in healing) *adj.*: **Aesculpian**. See *healing*

currency (of or relating to . . . , including collecting) *adj.*: **numismatic**. See *coins*

current (being . . . with or informed about something) *adj.*: **au fait** [French]. See *familiar*

curse (as in put a . . . upon) *v.t.*: **imprecate**. ❖ [Chinese Premier Li Peng] has a gift for remorselessness. He has gone out of his way not merely to trounce human rights and crush democracy, but to do so in a way calculated to insult and to taunt the U.S. government. He is convinced, not without reason, that Washington will never do anything more than **imprecate**. Trade, he is sure, certainly will never become an instrument of American pressure. (Michael Kelly, "A Toast," *New Republic*, 4/14/1997.)

(2) curse *n.*: **malediction**. ❖ Almost everyone knows about Irish blessings: May the wind always be at your back, and may you be in heaven half an hour before the Devil knows you're dead. But there's a darker side to the coin: The Irish curse. The **malediction** is as Irish as cable-knit sweaters, soda bread and Guinness Stout. (Bill Marvel, "The Good Auld Curse: In the Spirit of St. Patrick's Day, We Look to the Art Form of the True Irish Curse," *Dallas Morning News*, 3/17/2000.)

(3) curse (as in detest) *v.t.*: **execrate**. See *hate*

(4) curse *n., adj.*: **hoodoo**. See *bad luck*

cursed (perpetually . . . , as in unlucky person) *n.*: **schlimazel** [Yiddish].

cursing (excessive, esp. involuntarily when mentally ill) *n.*: **coprolalia**. ❖ "I've always said that 15 percent of the people with Tourette's have **coprolalia**, but 100 percent of jazz musicians have it," Wolff jokes. "So I definitely swear, but not because of Tourette's." (Brett Anderson, "Playing It Backward; Musician's Medical Disorder May Be a Grace Note," *Washington Post*, 6/8/2001.)

(2) cursing (or dirty talk to relieve tension) *n.*: **lalochezia**. See *swearing*

cursory (as in possessing only superficial knowledge of a subject while pretending to be learned) *n.*: **sciolism**. See *superficial*

curtail (as in put an end to) *v.t.*: **quietus** (as in "put the quietus to"). See *termination*

(2) curtail (as in overly restrict or . . . , as to amount or share) *v.t.*: **scant**. See *stint*

curtailed (something . . . , as in abridged) *n.*: **bobtail**. See *abridged*

curve (slightly) *v.t., v.i.*: **camber**. ❖ Favourably **cambered** bends are great. Bikers love them, because they instill confidence and allow faster cornering. Off-**cambered** bends are horrible; they give less ground clearance and your bike can easily slide away from you, especially in the wet. (Olly Duke, Motoring: "Going Round the Bend," *Daily Telegraph* [London], 08/22/1998.)

(2) curve (away from a course or intended path) *v.t.*: **yaw**. See *veer*

(3) curve (in and out) *v.i.*: **sinuate**. See *wind*

curved (like a bow) *adj.*: **arcuate**. ❖ The [trademark infringement] complaint specified that Levi's is the owner of an "**arcuate** stitching design" trademark. . . . It described the offending Karl Kani pocket stitching design as one that "starts on the side seams of the pocket and curves downward toward the center of the pocket." Levi's said that the "[appearance] of the Karl Kani pocket stitching design [is] highly similar to the . . . appearance created" by Levi's **arcuate** trademark. (*WWD*, "Levi's Suit Charges Karl Kani with Trademark Infringement," 5/25/2000.)

curving (as in winding or waving) *adj.*: **flexuous**. See *waving*

custom (as in habit or practice) *n.*: **praxis**. ❖ Pot for the nausea and the heaviness of heart, vitamin C for cell structure, sugar for the depleted blood, caffiene to burn off the moral fog—the whole **praxis** of alcoholism and reckless living. (Michael Chabon, *Wonder Boys*, Villard [1995], p. 132.)

(2) custom (excessive reverence for . . . or forebears) *adj.*: **filiopietistic**. See *old-fashioned*

(3) custom (precise observance of . . .) *n.*: **punctilio**. See *etiquette*

customary *adj.*: **wonted**. ❖ Of course, the [CIA], with its **wonted** high-handedness, was trying to find a substitute for the democratically elected president, Jean-Bertrand Aristide, whom it slandered in one of its famous "psychological profiles." The CIA seems to feel that democracy is all very well and good, but it can be overdone. (Mary McGrory, "Resources Wasted on Costly CIA," *St. Louis Post-Dispatch*, 10/21/1994.)

customer (regular . . . of a place, esp. a place of entertainment) *n.*: **habitué** [French]. See *regular*

customs (of a person, people, or culture) *n.*: **ethos**. See *character*

cut (to make a small or shallow . . . in the skin) *v.t.*: **scarify**. [Note: This word is sometimes wrongly thought to mean the same as to scare.] ❖ At any rate, things happen to us, deep, profound, indelible things. That's how you know you're human. That's why we **scarify** ourselves—so we can share our scars and say, Here, look, that's where the knife went after it came out of the fire—it traced an arc across my cheek like a meteor across the night sky. (Cary Tennis, "Dreamy Obsession," *Salon.com*, 7/16/2003.)

cut down (with an ax) *v.t.*: **hew**. See *ax*

cute (affectedly or excessively . . . , quaint, or dainty) *adj.*: **twee**. See *quaint*

cutoff (in a sentence from one construction to a second, grammatically inconsistent construction) *n.*: **anacoluthon**. See *shift*

cut off (as in consider separately) *v.t.*: **prescind** (generally as in "prescind from"). See *isolate*

cutting (as in . . . remarks) *adj.*: **astringent**. See *harsh*

cycle (as in generation or era) *n.*: **saeculum**. See *generation*

cynic (as in pessimist who continually warns of a disastrous future) *n.*: **Jeremiah**. See *pessimist*

(2) cynic *n.*: **crepehanger**. See *pessimist*

cynical (as in skeptical) *adj.*: **zetetic**. See *skeptical*

dabbler (as in amateur) *n.*: **dilettante**. See *amateur*

daffy (informal as in daffy or loony) *adj.*: **doolally**. See *crazy*

daft (as in foolish) *adj.*: **barmy** [British]. See *foolish*

(2) daft (as in foolish) *adj.*: **balmy**. See *foolish*

daily *adj.*: **diurnal**. ❖ Wilt [Chamberlain] remains the most nocturnal of men; often, he will not call it a day before the sun comes up. Apart from the hours he sets aside for his exercise, there is no pattern to his existence. He does not even live a **diurnal** life as we know it. He will, for example, go on a complete fast, eat nothing at all for three days, and then suddenly, at 4:30 in the morning, devour five greasy pork chops. . . . He is as independent as anyone in the world. (Frank Deford, "Doing Just Fine, My Man," *Sports Illustrated*, 8/18/1986.)

dainty (in an affected manner) *adj.*: **niminy-piminy**. ❖ "Jo does use such slang words," observed Amy, with a reproving look at the long figure stretched on the rug. . . . "Don't, Jo; it's so boyish." "That's why I do it," [said Jo]. "I detest rude, unlady-like girls," [said Amy]. "I hate affected, **niminy-piminy** chits," [said Jo]. (Polly Frost, "The Woman in Winona," *Harper's Bazaar*, 12/1/1994, p. 162.)

(2) dainty (affectedly or excessively . . .) *adj.*: **twee**. See *quaint*

damages (awarded for injured feelings, as opposed to financial loss or physical suffering) *n.*: **solatium**. See *compensation*

damaging (as in harmful) *adj.*: **nocuous**. See *harmful*

(2) damaging (mutually . . . to both sides) *adj.*: **internecine**. See *destructive*

(3) damaging *adj.*: **nocent**. See *harmful*

damnation (as in loss of the soul) *n.*: **perdition**. ❖ The question is whether expanding the definition of marriage to include same-sex couples launches us on the path to **perdition** or merely heralds the shedding of another irrational prejudice. (William Raspberry, "Why Not Encourage Monogamy?" *Washington Post*, 5/1/2000.)

dampen (flax to separate fibers) *v.t.*: **ret**. See *moisten*

dance (in a leaping or frolicking manner) *v.i.*: **curvet**. ❖ [The Fiesta] is about to begin. . . . On a terrace above us looms Zozobra, a forty-foot-high, white-skirted monster. . . . Long white arms and hands flail helplessly at his sides as two high-crowned dancers leap and **curvet** up a stone stairway to the foot of the scaffold, brandishing torches. (Herb Greer, "American Shangri-la," *World & I*, 9/1/1995, p. 122.)

(2) dance (uncontrollable urge to . . .) *n.*: **tarantism**. ❖ [During the period roughly from the fifteenth to the seventeenth century in Italy, the victim] would react to the bite of the [tarantula] spider by developing uncontrollable urges to dance . . . until [he or she] died of poison or exhaustion. [L]ater medical historians . . . regarded **tarantism** as a mental disease, in other words, mass hysteria. (Simon Wessely, "Laughs on the Way to Salvation," *Times*, 6/28/1994.)

(3) dance (formal . . . esp. for debutantes) *n.*: **cotillion**. See *ball*

dance hall (in France) *n.*: **bal musette**. ❖ At first, while the audience is settling into its ad hoc cabaret in the chapel of Mount Vernon College on Friday, the "Encore Paris" show seems to be a dance program. A striking couple is putting old 78s on a phonograph and behaving as though the chapel were a Parisian **bal musette**. (*Washington Post*, Performing Arts, 5/2/2000.)

dancing (act of . . . , sometimes with leaping about) *n.*: **saltation**. ❖ Yes, folks, it's [the] sultan of sexy Broadway **saltation**. . . . Welcome back, Bob Fosse! You may have been in hoofer heaven/hell for 11 years now, but your snazzy steps are alive and kicking—and prancing and slithering and popping too. Not just in the hit revival of *Chicago*, but now in *Fosse: A Celebration in Song and Dance*. (Jan Breslauer, Theater Review: "Paying Homage the Best Way Hoofers Can," *Los Angeles Times*, 10/23/1998.)

(2) dancing (of or related to) *adj.*: **terpsichorean**. ❖ The real scandal in my working as a stripper is that I can't dance. It's just not a talent I've ever possessed. . . . But lacking **terp-sichorean** skills never hurt me that much. (Lily Burana, *Strip City*, Talk Miramax Books [2001], p. 33.)

dandruff (covered with . . .) *adj.*: **scurfy**. ❖ Q: I have a 10-year-old cat who has never been outside. . . . The only problem I see is that her fur has dandruff at the back. I groom her regularly and the fur on her paws and face is fine. Mrs. Ann Lyons, Glasgow. A: A dry and **scurfy** coat is not an uncommon problem in animals that live indoors. (*Sunday Mail* [London], "Can My Moggie Shake Off Her Dandruff Problem?" 10/1/2000.)

dandy *n.*: **fop**. See *vain*

dangerous (as in irresponsible or reckless) *adj.*: **harum-scarum**. See *reckless*

(2) dangerous (as in perilous) *adj.*: **parlous**. See *perilous*

(3) dangerous (as in reckless) *adj.*: **temerarious**. See *reckless*

(4) dangerous (as in expose to or put in a . . . situation (*v.t.*) or be in a . . . situation (*v.i.*): **periclitate**. See *imperil*

(5) dangerous (journey or passage, with dangers on both sides) *idiom*: **between Scylla and Charybdis**. See *precarious*

(6) dangerous (or harmful) *adj.*: **noisome**. See *harmful*

(7) dangerous (potentially . . . place or situation) *n.*: **tinderbox**. See *explosive*

(8) dangerous (very . . . , as in causing or portending death) *adj.*: **funest**. See *deadly*

dank (as in musty) *adj.*: **fusty**. See *musty*

dapper (as in elegant) *adj.*: **Chesterfieldian**. See *elegant*

daredevil (as in rash or impetuous person) *n.*: **Hotspur**. See *impetuous*

daring (as in creative and/or original) *adj.*: **Promethean**. See *creative*

(2) daring (as in gall or temerity) *n.*: **hardihood**. See *gall*

(3) daring (in a reckless way) *adj.*: **temerarious**. See *reckless*

(4) daring (or bold while under the influence of alcohol) *adj.*: **potvaliant**. See *courageous*

(5) daring (overly . . .) *adj.*: **Icarian**. See *overambitious*

(6) daring *n.*: **hardihood**. See *courage*

dark (and misty and gloomy) *adj.*: **caliginous**. ❖ But the . . . pervasive creepiness [of the television show *The X-Files*] is not for everyone. Even the look of the show is **caliginous**—much of the action takes place in the dark, with the agents' trademark flashlights beaming through the mist. (M. S. Mason, "Decoding *X-Files*: The Movie," *Christian Science Monitor*, 6/19/1998.)

(2) dark (esp. as to the ocean) *adj.*: **aphotic**. ❖ The depths [of the ocean] can be divided into three realms—sunlit, twilight and midnight where there is no light at all and temperatures are near freezing. The midnight zone, called the **aphotic** zone by oceanographers, makes up 90 percent of the ocean. It is the home of little-known creatures and blind fish that will never see day, never venture even into the twilight. (Linton Weeks, "Cosmic Relief," *Washington Post*, 1/2/2000.)

(3) dark (literary style that is . . . , gloomy, remote, and/or grotesque) *adj.*: **gothic**. ❖ Steeped in creepy **gothic** gloom, the narrative provides a series of mazes within mazes, dead ends and sudden tantalizing glimpses of a logical solution. It's pleasant enough entertainment for the sort of reader who likes spooky thrills mixed with serious edification. (Francine Prose, Picks & Pans: Pages, *People*, 5/12/1997, p. 28.)

(4) dark *adj.* (*adv.*: in the . . .) **darkling**. ❖ Not every competitive field has been surrendered to foreigners. Bright spots on the **darkling** plain include the computer industry, which 28% of bosses think is America's best world competitor. (Terence P. Pare, "CEO Poll/Cover Stories: Why Some Do It the Wrong Way," *Fortune*, 5/21/1990, p. 75.)

(5) dark *adj.*: **stygian** (sometimes cap.). ❖ Lasting over two and a half hours, featuring almost no dialogue and prone to lengthy contemplations of inanimate objects, *Into Great*

Silence offers scant pleasures for the impatient or easily bored. Indeed, even the most devout disciples of cinematic inertia may find their attention wandering during the **stygian** nocturnal sequences shot—all too obviously—without the use of artificial light in the monks' gloomy chapel. (Donald Clarke, "Sleepy Sounds of Silence," *Irish Times*, 1/5/2007.)

(6) dark (and dismal and gloomy) *adj.*: **acherontic**. See *gloomy*

(7) dark (and gloomy) *adj.*: **Cimmerian**. See *gloomy*

(8) dark (and gloomy) *adj.*: **tenebrous**. See *gloomy*

(9) dark (and gloomy, as in suggestive of a funeral) *adj.*: **sepulchral**. See *funereal*

darling (my . . .) *n.*: **mavourneen** [Irish]. ❖ "Come back to Erin, **mavourneen**, **mavourneen**, come back aroon to the land of my birth, come with the shamrock in the springtime, **mavourneen**." And [President Kennedy] continued, "This is not the land of my birth, but it is the land for which I hold the greatest affection, and I will certainly come back in the springtime." (Edythe Preet, "Presidents & First Ladies of Irish Ancestry," *Irish America*, 8/31/1994.)

(2) darling *n.*: **acushla** (my . . .) [Irish]. ❖ When St. Patrick offered to allow [the women to propose marriage] every seven years, St. Bridget threw her arms round his neck and said: "Arrah, Patrick, jewel, I daurn't go back to the girls wid such a proposal. Make it one year in four." St. Patrick replied: "Bridget, **acushla**, squeeze me that way agin, an' I'll give ye leap-year, the longest of the lot." (William Hartston, "Numbers a Giant Leap in Time," *Independent* [London], 2/29/1996.)

dash (as in small amount) *n.*: **soupçon** [French]. See *trace*

date (as in appointment, esp. for illicit sexual relations) *n.*: **assignation**. See *appointment*

dated (as in out of style) *adj.*: **démodé** [French]. See *outmoded*

(2) dated (as in outdated) *adj.*: **retardataire** [French]. See *outdated*

daughter (of or relating to a son or . . .) *adj.*: **filial**. See *offspring*

dawdle (as in idle or waste time) *v.i.*: **footle** (usu. as in "footle around"). ❖ [Hillman says] you can't use accidents as a measure of danger. . . . Name the safest form of transport, he commands. You **footle** around until he comes up with the answer, which is a heavy [truck], because if you're driving one you're unlikely to be killed in a crash. Now name the most dangerous. Answer: again a heavy [truck], because if one hits you, you're pretty sure to be killed. (Anne Karpf, "A Chain Reaction: For 30 Years Mayer Hillman Has Been Busily Turning Conventional Political Thinking on Its Head," *Guardian* [London], 11/2/2002.)

(2) dawdle (as in procrastinate or hesitate to act) *v.i.*: **shilly-shally**. See *procrastinate*

(3) dawdle (due to indecision) *v.i.*: **dither**. See *procrastinate*

dawn (of or relating to . . . or dusk, as in twilight) *adj.*: **crepuscular**. See *twilight*

(2) dawn (of or relating to . . . or morning) *adj.*: **matutinal**. See *morning*

daybreak (of or relating to . . .) *adj.*: **matinal**. See *morning*

(2) daybreak (of or relating to . . .) *adj.*: **matutinal**. See *morning*

daydreamer (as in an impractical, contemplative person with no clear occupation or income) *n.*: **luftmensch** [lit. man of air; German, Yiddish]. See *dreamer*

daze *v.t.*: **benumb**. ❖ The main flaw, though, is that he **benumbs** the reader with too many useless facts. At times, for instance, he seems more taken with minutiae about the yacht than with the passion of Callas and Onassis. And that sinks the story. (Linnea Lannon, Picks & Pans: Pages, *People*, 11/20/2000, p. 57.)

dazzling (in effect) *adj.*: **foudroyant** [French]. ❖ Heavy on élan and the damper pedal, pianists such as Simon, Earl Wild, Jorge Bolet and Byron Janis wow you with **foudroyant** playing. (Andrew Druckenbrod, "Pianist Abbey Simon Mixes Flashiness, Substance," *Minneapolis Star Tribune*, 7/7/1999.)

(2) dazzling (as in shining brightly) *adj.*: **effulgent**. See *bright*

(3) dazzling (as in shining brightly) *adj.*: **fulgurant**. See *bright*

(4) dazzling (as in shining brightly) *adj.*: **refulgent**. See *bright*

(5) dazzling (like a diamond) *adj.*: **diamantine**. See *diamonds*

dead (abnormal fear of . . . people) *n.*: **necrophobia**. See *fear*

(2) dead (actually or appearing . . .) *adj.*: **exanimate**. See *lifeless*

(3) dead (fascination with or erotic attraction to . . . people) *n.*: **necrophilia**. See *corpses*

(4) dead (list of recently . . . persons) *n.*: **necrology**. See *obituary*

(5) dead (repository for bones or bodies of the . . .) *n.*: **charnel**. See *repository*

(6) dead (worship of . . . people) *n.*: **necrolatry**. See *worship*

deaden *v.t.*: **narcotize**. ❖ Imagine being locked in a room with [Ontario's Premier Mike Harris]. How long do you think you could stay awake? Five minutes? . . . Harris was helped by the **narcotizing** drone of his voice and the way he walked as though someone had shot novocaine into both shoulders. (Paul Wells, "Canada/Election 2000," *Time* International, 11/20/2000, p. 64.)

(2) deaden *v.t.*: **obtund**. ❖ [He hoped he] would recover in time for their proposed [naval] action upon Boxing Day, or weather not permitting, upon the New Year's day. It seemed wise to attack when the better part of their foes, complacent with garrison duty, would be **obtunded** from holiday celebrations. (S. N. Dyer, "Resolve and Resistance," *Omni*, 4/1/1995, p. 66.)

deadly (as in causing or portending death) *adj.*: **funest**. ❖ Something that regularly clangs painfully on my ears is abuse of the word "fun" [as in:] "It's the funest thing I've ever done." That means the opposite of what is intended. If you take advantage of a deal and pay only $1 to bungee jump on a system designed and built by 12-year-olds, it could be the [most] **funest**

thing you ever did. (Dave Brown, "Case of the Disappearing Canadian Corpses Has Been Resolved," *Ottawa Citizen*, 11/21/2002.)

deal (as in pact) *n.*: **amicabilis concordia**. See *pact*

dealer (esp. a person who sells quack medicines) *n.*: **mountebank**. See *huckster*

dear (as in darling) *n.*: **acushla** [Irish]. See *darling*

(2) dear (my . . .) *n.*: **mavourneen** [Irish]. See *darling*

death (fascination with . . .) *n.*: **thanatophilia**. ❖ A worker in a palliative care unit in Paris, [Marie De Hennezzel has written a book] filled with honeyed words, New Age gimcrackery, and a fair amount of Mary Worth–style common sense, as is usual in self-help books. When she holds the dying or listens to their life-narratives, she can't help a bit of self-congratulatory preening. The clinical name for her malady might be **thanatophilia**. (Jon Newlin, "Death Prattle," *New Orleans Times-Picayune*, 7/13/1997.)

(2) death (after . . .) *adj.*: **post obitum** [Latin]. ❖ Dear Mr. Buckley: What do you make of this from *The New Yorker*?: "For the people waiting outside it, in a line to view Pope John Paul II's body which stretched for more than three miles, the arms of Bernini's great flanking colonnades were ahead . . . " Sayre Miller. Dear Mr. Miller: I take that to be *The New Yorker*'s idea of the **post obitum** indulgence of the late Holy Father. (William F. Buckley, Notes and Asides, *National Review*, 7/4/2005.)

(3) death (from overwork) *n.*: **karoshi**. [Japanese. This term came into use in Japan in the 1980s and is still in common use there. However, it would seem that there is no reason that the concept need be confined to Japan.] ❖ **Karoshi** lawsuits may . . . be what forces companies to try to meet their workers' mental-health needs. In March 2000, Japan's Supreme Court found Dentsu Inc., the nation's largest public-opinion and advertising agency, liable for the death of a 24-year-old employee who committed suicide in 1991 after reportedly working for 17 months without a single day off. (Deborah Hodgson, "Death by Conformity," *Newsweek*, 8/20/2001.)

(4) death (of, relating to, or resembling . . .) *adj.*: **thanatoid**. ❖ The Marquess of Bristol had been dying in public for many years [from drug abuse]. At first his audience was amused—they gathered in Deauville for grand house parties held at his expense. **Thanatoid** flamboyance commanded morbid respect until it became apparent that to be a member of Bristol's entourage was to experience the throes of his disorders. (Jessica Berens, obituary of the Marquess of Bristol, *Independent* [London], 1/12/1999.)

(5) death (reflection on . . .) *n.*: **thanatopsis**. ❖ Reacting to the 1996 death at age 49 of Harris Collins, brother of skating tour impresario Tom Collins, [figure skater Michelle] Kwan wrote a poetic meditation on death. Her **thanatopsis** reveals a mind that has ranged beyond the tunnel in which young elite athletes often live: "What is death? Death is a question to ask. There is no answer. It is impossible." (Philip Hersh, "Gather up the Kids, It's Their Story Time," *Chicago Tribune*, 8/21/1997.)

(6) death (abnormal fear of . . .) *n.*: **necrophobia**. See *fear*

(7) death (blow, as in put an end to) *n.*: **quietus** (esp. as in "put the quietus to"). See *termination*

(8) death (fascination with or erotic attraction to . . .) *n.*: **necrophilia**. See *corpses*

(9) death (notice of . . .) *n.*: **necrology**. See *obituary*

(10) death (object that reminds one of . . .) *n.*: **memento mori** [Latin]. See *mortality*

deathly (as in pale or corpselike) *adj.*: **cadaverous**. See *corpselike*

death sentence (for convicted persons, spec. burning of heretics at the stake) *n.*: **auto-da-fé**. See *execution*

debased (morally . . .) *v.t.*: **cankered**. See *corrupted*

debatable (as in controversial opinion or person who holds one) *n.*: **polemic**. See *controversy*

debate (about a philosophical or theological issue) *n.*: **quodlibet**. [See also the use of this word at *subtlety*.] ❖ Sir: Your [article] supporting the ordination of women, like other exponents of this bias, has its argument flawed by one simple fact. For the Christian, this **quodlibet** is not to be solved by worldly conjecture or current trends but by informed examination of biblical doctrine. The Bible is the basic text and first book of reference on Christianity and to depart from it when formulating doctrine will be eventually harmful to the Christian church. (Colin Poyner, letter to the editor, *Sydney Morning Herald*, 1/3/1992.)

(2) debate (as in dialogue, in which neither side hears or understands or pays attention to the other) *n.*: **dialogue de sourds** [French]. See *dialogue*

(3) debate (given to argument or . . .) *adj., n.*: **eristic**. ❖ Within the war room [of General Motors' strategy board], the atmosphere is informal, spirited, irreverent, **eristic**—and often openly critical of GM's past practices. (*Time*, "Inside GM's War Room," 12/13/1993, p. 70.)

(4) debate (person who hates rational . . . or enlightenment) *n.*: **misologist**. See *closed-minded*

debauched (person) *n.*: **rakehell**. See *libertine*

(2) debauched *adj.*: **scrofulous**. See *depraved*

debilitate (as in deprive of strength) *v.t.*: **enervate**. ❖ To some the [extension of credit to ex-slaves] was worse than crooked. It resembled an old-fashioned dole, a series of **enervating** handouts, although the tenants had earned their money through backbreaking work. (David Oshinsky, *Worse Than Slavery*, The Free Press [1996], p. 118.)

debilitated (from loss or lack of body strength) *adj.*: **asthenic** (*n.*: **asthenia**). See *weak*

debonair (as in elegant) *adj.*: **Chesterfieldian**. See *elegant*

(2) debonair (as in refined or elegant) *adj.*: **raffiné** (or **raffine**) [French]. See *refined*

debris *n.*: **detritus**. ❖ Either these beachgoers were unusually tidy or the French comb this beach regularly, because there was very little interesting **detritus**. (Katharine Weber, *Objects in Mirror Are Closer Than They Appear*, Crown [1995], p. 35.)

debutantes (formal ball for) *n.*: **cotillion**. See *ball*

decade *n.*: **decennium**. ❖ We'll call this the **decennium**-plus-five list. It's a compendium wrought from 15 years of covering state government and politics. Contemplating this list of Ohio's political bests and worsts since 1985 is bound to make you . . . listless. (Joe Hallett, "Best, Worst, Whatever: This List Tops Off 15 Years of Coverage," *Columbus Dispatch*, 12/26/1999.)

decadent (excessively . . . , esp. in a sensuous way) *adj.*: **sybaritic**. See *luxurious*

decay (causing or relating to . . .) *adj.*: **saprogenic**. ❖ Edward Platt certainly knows about the Londoners who linger against all expectations in **saprogenic** corners of the city. He has spent five years in Shepherd's Bush [where] the air is sugary, the noise appalling [and where he finds] squatters . . . (Christopher Hawtree, "On the Road to Nowhere in London's Wild West," review of *Leadville*, by Edward Platt, *Independent* [London], 6/8/2000).

(2) decay (of bone or teeth) *n.*: **caries** (*adj.*: **carious**). ❖ What are we to make of the success of the water fluoridation program? Initiated and endlessly encouraged by the U.S. Public Health Service and many local agencies, the program has dramatically reduced dental **caries**, just as its proponents predicted four decades ago. . . . Fifty years ago, 90% of American kids had some form of tooth decay. Today the country is close to eliminating decay. (Daniel Seligman, "Keeping Up: The Terrible News About Teeth," *Fortune*, 10/10/1988, p. 175.)

(3) decay (as in crumble away) *v.i.*; **molder**. See *crumble*

deceit (spec. the act of engaging in . . . under a false name or identity) *n.*: **imposture**. See *hoax*

(2) deceit *n.*: **legerdemain**. See *trickery*

deceitful (actions, spec. by trying to represent

something as being other than it is) *n.*: **false colors**. See *misrepresentations*

(2) deceitful (characterized by . . . and cunning conduct, esp. in regard to the pursuit and maintenance of political or other power) *adj.*: **Machiavellian**. [This word derives from *The Prince*, a short book written in 1513 by the Italian diplomat Niccolò di Bernardo dei Machiavelli (1469–1527), which decribes the means—some of which are unscrupulous—by which a prince may attain power.] ❖ Every drafting system leaves room for some **Machiavellian** stacking ploy. In leagues where managers rate their own players, several managers say one trick (which they've never tried themselves, of course) is to rate a good player lower than he deserves. That way other managers will leave the kid alone long enough for the same manager to draft him again. (Patrick Boyle, "Choosing Sides/Today's Little League Coaches Put Together Teams Through a Mix of Skill, Luck and, Sometimes, a Little Cunning," *Newsday*, 4/13/1997.)

(3) deceitful (as in hypocritical) *adj.*: **Janus-faced**. See *two-faced*

(4) deceitful (as in insincere) *adj.*: **crocodilian**. See *insincere*

(5) deceitful (as in unscrupulous) *adj.*: **jackleg**. See *unscrupulous*

(6) deceitful (behavior) *n.*: **knavery**. See *corruption*

(7) deceitful (scheming or trickery) *n.*: **jiggery-pokery**. See *trickery*

(8) deceitful *adj.*: **mendacious**. See *dishonest*

deceitfulness *n.*: **skullduggery**. ❖ Although no one knows exactly how much money is lost to financial planner fraud each year, a 30-state survey . . . estimated it totaled $400 million in 1988. . . . "Investments are the perfect vehicle for **skullduggery** because you don't expect to get a return for months or years. By the time you discover the fraud, the money is long gone." (Christine Dugas, "Fraud Warnings—You Can't Protect Yourself from Bad Advice Unless You Keep Some Control over Your Money," *Newsday*, 5/7/1995.)

deceive *v.t.:* **hornswoggle**. ❖ The JCC Holding Corp. says its Canal Street casino is "poised to do well in the future," and so many people believe it that the share price, though still modest, came close to doubling in the last few weeks. But experience tells us that it is not difficult to **hornswoggle** stock market investors, and that it is not wise to rely on the veracity of any pronouncement from the casino. (James Gill, "Jackpot for Harrah's? Don't Bet on It," *New Orleans Times-Picayune*, 3/24/2002.)

(2) deceive *v.t.:* **humbug**. ❖ [A] speechwriter for Dan Quayle declared that for the past decade and a half, the American people have been hypocrites, wanting smaller government, lower taxes and all the benefits of the welfare state, all at the same time. And that is the truth. Our people wanted to be **humbugged**, which is the reason they liked Ronald Reagan so much. He was a master at equivocation and hypocrisy. (William Brown, letter to the editor, *Pittsburgh Post-Gazette*, 1/27/1997.)

(3) deceive *v.t.:* **gull**. [This word is also a noun that refers to the person deceived or cheated.] ❖ The only authentic mystery behind who will come out on top each season on the UPN hit *America's Next Top Model* may be how Americans can be willingly **gulled** into thinking that the result of this deliciously kooky weekly confection is a cliffhanger. [The truth is that the winner] is Tyra Banks, the show's host and producer, a Victoria's Secret beauty with a snap queen's attitude. (Guy Trebay, "Who Is America's Next Top Model, Really?" *New York Times*, 11/6/2005.)

(4) deceive (and defraud in the process) *v.t., v.i.:* **cozen**. See *defraud*

(5) deceive (as in bluff) *v.t.:* **four-flush** (*n.:* **four-flusher**). See *bluff*

(6) deceive (as in defraud) *v.t.:* **mulct**. See *defraud*

(7) deceive (as in lie, through the intentional use of misleading, ambiguous or evasive language) *v.t.:* **prevaricate**. See *lie*

(8) deceive (as in swindle) *n., v.t.:* **thimblerig**. See *swindle*

(9) deceive (as in swindle) *v.t.:* **bunco**. See *swindle*

(10) deceive (as in trick or cheat) *v.t.:* **euchre**. See *cheat*

(11) deceive (or force someone into doing something, esp. by fraud or coercion) *v.t.:* **shanghai** (person who does so *n.:* **shanghaier**). See *coerce*

(12) deceive (specious reasoning intended to . . . or rationalize) *n.:* **casuistry**. See *fallacious*

deceiving (something that is . . . , as in delusion) *n.:* **ignis fatuus**. See *delusion*

decency (lit. humanity) *n.:* **menschlichkeit** [German, Yiddish]. ❖ [John Paul II] is a selfless figure in a me-first world. [When traveling, not once] did the pope ever ask where he was going to sleep, what he would eat or wear, or what his creature comforts would be. . . . A person may be liberal or conservative, avant garde or traditional, but let him or her be decent, and most of the time that's enough. This realm of **menschlichkeit**, authentic humanity is where John Paul's appeal comes from. (John L. Allen Jr., "Twenty-Five Years: In His Long, Polarizing Pontificate, John Paul II Has Defied Categorization," *National Catholic Reporter*, 10/10/2003.)

deception (as in swindle) *n., v.t.:* **thimblerig**. See *swindle*

(2) deception (spec. an intentional omission of something, so as to mislead) *n.:* **elision**. See *omission*

(3) deception (spec. the act of engaging in . . . under a false name or identity) *n.:* **imposture**. See *hoax*

(4) deception *n.:* **legerdemain**. See *trickery*

deceptive (actions, spec. by trying to represent something as being other than it is) *n.:* **false colors**. See *misrepresentations*

(2) deceptive (as in crafty) *adj.:* **jesuitical** (sometimes cap.). See *crafty*

(3) deceptive (conduct) *n.:* **skullduggery**. See *deceitfulness*

(4) deceptive (as in insincere) *adj.:* **crocodilian**. See *insincere*

(5) deceptive (something that is . . . , as in delusion) *n.:* **ignis fatuus**. See *delusion*

(6) deceptive (or meaningless words or language) *n.:* **flummery**. See *meaningless*

decision making (based on faith alone rather than reason, esp. in philosophical or religious matters) *n.:* **fideism**. See *faith*

decisive (remark, blow, or factor) *n.:* **sockdolager**. ❖ The American Council for the Arts [wanted to] show how much the American people love the arts. . . . [T]hey retained pollster Lou Harris [who knows that] 99% of a public opinion poll lies in framing the questions to be asked. . . . Lou asked them, "How important do you think it is to the quality of life in the community to have such things as museums, theater and concert halls in the community?" That was a **sockdolager**. [84% said very important or somewhat important.] (James J. Kilpatrick, "An Artfully Assembled Poll?" *St. Petersburg [FL] Times*, 4/29/1992.)

declaration (made without proof or support) *n.:* **ipse dixit** [Latin]. See *allegation*

(2) declaration (which is official, as in with the authority of one's office) *adv., adj.:* **ex cathedra**. See *official*

declare (publicly, solemnly, or formally) *v.t.:* **nuncupate**. [This verb is generally considered rare but it does appear in some dictionaries and finds its way into contemporary usage from time to time. The adjectival form of the word is "nuncupative." See *oral*.] ❖ President Musharraf estimates the number of extremists at "no more than 1 percent of the population." That's 1.5 million religious fanatics who are holding, according to Mr. Musharraf, "99 percent of the population hostage." But what happens when the moderates **nuncupate**— only to echo the extremists? [One of the supposed moderates had stated that terrorists are "freedom fighters" of a "Muslim world facing unprecedented oppression and injustice."] (Arnaud de Borchgrave, "Over the Cuckoo's Nest," *Washington Times*, 12/2/2003.)

(2) declare *v.t.:* **asseverate**. ❖ Nowhere do you even try to show why, under the U.S. Constitution, [the right of privacy] leads to [the right of abortion]. Instead, you simply **asseverate**: "This right of privacy . . . is broad enough to encompass a woman's decision whether or not to terminate her pregnancy." Harry [Blackmun], be reasonable. Your job is to prove it, not just say it. (Daniel Seligman, "Keeping Up: Big Applesauce," *Fortune*, 8/27/1990, p. 111.)

(3) declare *v.t.:* **annunciate**. See *announce*

decline (as in downward slope) *n.:* **declivity** (*adj.:* **declivitous**). ❖ People have been building houses and hotels atop ravines and steep slopes for years. . . . Environmental law actually forbids building on ravines with a certain **declivity**. But which official was up to upholding the law during the New Order regime? (Putu Wirata, "Digging of Steep Slopes Spells Disaster for Many," *Jakarta Post*, 3/2/1999.)

(2) decline (esp. extending down from a fortification) *n.:* **glacis**. ❖ Those who fought their way across the deadly **glacis** of Normandy's beaches had little time to reflect on the justice of their cause or the morality of their mission. (Christopher Redman, Special Report/D-Day, *Time* International, 6/6/1994, p. 39.)

(3) decline *n.:* **declension**. ❖ When Richard Nixon got into trouble, the cliché was that there was something Shakespearean about his crisis, and his fall, if it lacked Shakespearean poetry, had a Shakespearean subject: the slow **declension** of ambition into crime, and of crime into evil. But nobody would call Clinton's troubles Shakespearean; they're more bourgeois than that. (*Washington Times*, "Culture, et Cetera," 11/18/1998 [quoting from Adam Gopnik, writing on "American Studies" in the September 28, 1998, issue of *The New Yorker*].)

(4) decline (spec. past one's prime) *n.:* **paracme**. See *past one's prime*

(5) decline (esp. from a position of strength) *n.:* **dégringolade** [French]. See *downfall*

(6) decline (esp. of moral principles or civil order) *n.:* **labefaction**. See *weakening*

(7) decline (of or relating to a . . . , as in downfall, esp. after an innocent or carefree time) *adj.*: **postlapsarian**. See *downfall*

declining (as in worsening) *adj.*: **ingravescent**. See *worsening*

decompose (as in crumble away) *v.i.*: **molder**. See *crumble*

decorate (as in spruce up) *v.t.*: **titivate**. See *spruce up*

(2) decorate (or dress in a showy or excessive manner) *v.t.*: **bedeck**. See *adorn*

(3) decorate (or dress in a showy or excessive manner) *v.t.*: **bedizen**. See *adorn*

decoration *n.*: **garniture**. ❖ Q. I would like to know more about my pair of vases that I inherited from my grandparents. They're made of pink glass with painted flowers. . . . A. . . . Art glass vases such as these were purely decorative and often used as mantle **garniture**. (Jay Moore, "Hand-Blown Glass Vases Were Purely Decorative," *Tampa Tribune*, 8/31/2002.)

decorum (precise observance of . . . or etiquette) *n.*: **punctilio**. See *etiquette*

decrease *n.*: **declension**. See *decline*

decree *n.*: **diktat**. ❖ When [Coppola] brought up Brando's name [to play the lead in The Godfather], Stanley Jaffe . . . slammed his fist on the table, and announced that the actor would never play the Don as long as he was head of Paramount Pictures. Whereupon [Coppola] appeared to have an epileptic fit, and dramatically collapsed in a heap on the floor, as if rendered senseless by the stupidity of Jaffe's **diktat**. (Peter Biskind, *Easy Riders, Raging Bulls*, Simon & Schuster [1998], p. 153.)

(2) decree *n.*: **ukase**. ❖ Florida Secretary of State . . . Katherine Harris announced preemptively that she wouldn't honor any hand recounts in the [2000] presidential contest in Florida, no matter what they showed. . . . "For Bush's own sake, he should be more open to a recount," said Rep. Peter King (R-N.Y.), who spoke in an interview before Harris issued her **ukase**. (E. J. Dionne Jr., "Back to '84," *Washington Post*, 11/17/2000.)

decrepit (and sick elderly person) *n.*: **Struldbrug**. [This is based on a group of characters in Swift's *Gulliver's Travels* who never die but who, as they age, become ever sicker and more decrepit and live on wretchedly at the state's expense. The term is sometimes applied in connection with the challenges imposed on governments and society when people have outlived their actuarial tables.] ❖ In the end, all one can say to the food fascists is to leave well enough alone. For the government to reduce the joy of life that comes with eating and imbibing [by constantly publishing dietary guidelines] is not a good deal. Sometimes, it seems as if our social planners wish to make **Struldbrugs** of us all—those decrepit, shuffling human beings Gulliver met who could never die. (Barbara Amiel, "Food Police Cook Up More Nonsense," *Toronto Sun*, 8/21/1994.)

(2) decrepit *adj.*: **spavined**. ❖ I have patellar tendinitis in each knee . . . a "degenerative disk" . . . a chronically stiff neck . . . a budding hernia [etc.] . . . Here's the problem: I didn't play basketball yesterday. Nor the day before that. I played three days ago. When I was 25, I could play from sunup to sundown and feel nothing. And now 72 hours go by and I am still **spavined** and weak. Is this how God taps you on the shoulder, before he slaps you silly? (Michael Segell, "Over the Hill, My Ass!" *Esquire*, 3/1/1997.)

(3) decrepit (as in broken-down or worn-out) *adj.*: **raddled**. See *worn-out*

dedication (as in allegiance) *n.*: **vassalage**. See *allegiance*

deduce (as in analyze, logically) *v.i.*: **ratiocinate**. See *analyze*

(2) deduce (as in figure out) *v.t.*: **suss** (usually with "out"; slang). See *figure out*

deduction (as in inference) *n.*: **illation**. See *inference*

deductive (as in logical) *adj.*: **ratiocinative**. See *logical*

deeds *n.pl.*: **res gestae**. [Latin; lit. things done. This term can have a positive connotation when used in the sense of achievements, but it can be used in a neutral or negative sense as well. It is also a legal term, but is not being defined in that sense here.] ❖ [Despite the] avowed commitment [of academies] to the written word, few have left a paper trace sufficient to reconstruct their activities. . . . Those whose **res gestae** are recorded benefitted from greater longevity, closer links with printers, patrons more willing to fork out to preserve their memory, than the Accademia degli Oziosi. (Maurice Slawinski, review of *Una Quiete Operosa: Forme e Pratiche dell'Accademia Napoletana degli Oziosi, 1611–1645*, by Girolamo de Miranda, *Modern Language Review*, 4/1/2003.)

deep (as in difficult to understand) *adj.*: **recondite**. See *complicated*

deep-rooted (as in innate) *adj.*: **connate**. See *innate*

deer (of, relating to, or resembling) *adj.*: **cervine**. ❖ Deer and elk, especially, rely on this place, . . . to sustain them through the long and often brutal Colorado winters. . . . [But as a result of developing the land,] come the next killer winter (and come it will), this place, this wildlife "refuge," will become a place of suffering and horror, a **cervine** dying field. (David Petersen, "Searching for Common Ground," *Backpacker*, 12/1/1995, p. 46.)

defamation (as in the destroying of one's reputation) *n.*: **famicide**. ❖ **Famicide** Fatal / Defamation destroys / dignity / as riot-bombs attack / another's reputation / detonating. ("Tangled Angle," *Famicide Fatal,* allpoetry.com/poem/3145020, 7/2/2007.)

defame *v.t.*: **asperse**. ❖ The inquiry . . . has alleged that the military was either directly or indirectly involved in violence in East Timor. . . . "We have lost the territory (East Timor), lost our best sons, caused many to become orphans and widows, . . . and now we are still being **aspersed** with these groundless accusations," [the military officer] said. (*Jakarta Post*, "Military Men Deplore Comments Made by Rights Commission," 12/11/1999.)

(2) defame (by making false or malicious statements) *v.t.*: **calumniate**. See *malign*

(3) defame (so as to humiliate or disgrace) *v.t.*: **traduce**. See *malign*

defeat (by upsetting) *v.t.*: **unhorse**. ❖ Philippine Christian University came through with a big surprise yesterday, stunning highly-favored Letran, 67–56, to barge into the win column in the NCAA seniors basketball tournament at the Rizal Memorial Coliseum. (Jean Malandum, "Dolphins **Unhorse** Knights," *Manila Bulletin*, 7/5/2002).

defeated (capable of being . . .) *n.*: **vincible**. See *beaten*

defeatist (as in pessimist who continually warns of a disastrous future) *n.*: **Jeremiah**. See *pessimist*

(2) defeatist *n.*: **crepehanger**. See *pessimist*

defect (tragic . . . , esp. in a literary character) *n.*: **hamartia**. See *flaw*

defection (from one's religion, principles, or causes) *n.*: **apostasy**. See *abandonment*

defend (attempt to . . . seriousness of an offense) *v.t.*: **palliate**. See *downplay*

(2) defend (intended to . . . against evil) *adj.*: **apotropaic**. See *protect*

(3) defend *v.t.*: **forfend**. See *protect*

defender (of a cause) *n.*: **paladin**. See *proponent*

defense (line of . . . that is thought to be effective, but is not in reality) *n.*: **Maginot Line** [after André Maginot, French minister of war, who set up a line of defense along France's border with Germany prior to World War II, which proved ineffective when the Germans attacked through Belgium instead]. ❖ I am dismayed by the Bush administration's decision to scrap the Antiballistic Missile Treaty with Russia. The antimissile system for which President Bush would destroy this treaty will give us a false sense of security while draining our resources away from wiser defense measures. It will be a **Maginot Line** in space: an extraordinarily expensive and cumbersome system that cannot possibly work. (Richard Mullen, letter to the editor, *New York Times*, 12/14/2001.)

(2) defense (against attack or danger) *n.*: **bulwark**. See *protection*

(3) defense (formal . . . of one's acts or beliefs) *n.*: **apologia**. See *justification*

(4) defense (spec. a piece of armor) *n.*: **cuirass**. See *armor*

defenseless (person or thing): *n.*: **clay pigeon**. See *vulnerable*

(2) defenseless (when born) *adj.*: **altricial**. See *helpless*

defer (esp. a session of Parliament) *v.t.*: **prorogue**. See *discontinue*

deference (as in, with all . . . to) *prep.*: **pace** [Latin]. See *respectfully*

(2) deference (not necessarily sincere or unforced) *n.*: **obeisance**. See *homage*

deferential (as in subservient) *adj.*: **sequacious**. See *subservient*

(2) deferential (to behave toward in a . . . manner) *v.t.*: **bootlick**. See *kowtow*

(3) deferential *adj.*: **biddable**. See *obedient*

defiant (as in unrepentant) *adj.*: **impenitent**. See *unrepentant*

(2) defiant (person, spec. one who hates or mistrusts authority) *n.*: **misarchist**. See *rebel*

(3) defiant *adj.*: **contumacious**. See *obstinate*

deficiency (tragic . . . , esp. in a literary character) *n.*: **hamartia**. See *flaw*

deficient (psychiatric diagnosis for one who is mentally . . . , as in retarded) *adj.*: **oligophrenic**. See *retarded*

defining (as in distinctive shape or outline, often of a face) *adj.*: **lineament** (often **lineaments**). See *contour*

definite (as in sure-fire, esp. with respect to a plan, deal, or investment that can be trusted completely because it is supposedly safe and sure to succeed) *adj.*: **copper-bottomed** [British]. See *sure-fire*

(2) definite (necessarily or demonstrably . . . , as in incontrovertible) *adj.*: **apodictic**. See *incontrovertible*

definition (as in the word or phrase that is being defined in a dictionary or elsewhere) *n.*: **definiendum**. ❖ Still, it is noteworthy that this clause [i.e., the definition of "substandard or secondary cases of punishment"

in the textbook being analyzed] includes a puzzling circularity: The very term "punishment" is included in the **definiendum** of substandard or secondary cases of punishment. (Douglas Husak, "Philosophical Analysis and the Limits of the Substantive Criminal Law," *Criminal Justice Ethics*, 6/22/1999.)

(2) definition (having more than one . . .) *adj.*: **polysemous** (or **polysemic**). See *meaning*

(3) definition (of word or phrase in a dictionary or elsewhere) *n.*: **definiens**. ❖ By "evaluative" I assume he means a definition that includes in the **definiens** at least one term that either is or implies a normative concept. (Leon Rosenstein, "The End of Art Theory," *Humanitas*, 3/22/2002.)

(4) definition (using a . . . of a word other than in its customary sense) *adj.*: **Pickwickian**. [This word derives from the odd sense given to common words by certain characters in *The Pickwick Papers*, by Charles Dickens. It is often used in the phrase "in a Pickwickian sense," as in the example here]. ❖ Only by using the word in its most **Pickwickian** sense would I ever call myself a "young" theologian. Indeed, I belong, at least chronologically, to that post-fifty generation—so effectively dissected by Christopher Ruddy in his article "Young Theologians." (Edward T. Oakes, "Continuing the Conversation," *Commonweal*, 6/2/2000.)

(5) definition (inability to recall . . . of words or using them incorrectly) *n.*: **paramnesia**. See *amnesia*

definitions (study of subtle distinctions between . . . of similar words or synonyms) *n.*: **synonymy**. See *synonyms*

definitive (as in unambiguous) *adj.*: **univocal**. See *unambiguous*

defraud *v.t.*: **mulct**. [This word has three somewhat related definitions, including (1) to fine or penalize, (2) to extract money unfairly (but not necessarily illegally), and (3) to extract money illegally, esp. by fraud, extortion, or theft. This is an example of the third definition.] ❖ Like many others before her, Julia had fallen for a "matrimonial swindler," a con artist devoted exclusively to bilking the lovelorn of their hard-earned cash. Tales of these smooth operators—some of whom would marry and **mulct** 40 or 50 times—filled the newspapers from the early 1900s well into the 1940s. (Diane Mapes, "Some Bad Dates Go Down in History: Think Courtship Today Is Bad? It Used to Be Much, Much Worse," *Seattle Post-Intelligencer*, 3/1/2007.)

(2) defraud *v.t., v.i.*: **cozen**. ❖ Slack enforcement spells opportunity for crooks. Institutional Treasury Management, a registered investment advisory outfit in Irvine, California, managed to **cozen** investors out of $174 million in the late Eighties and early Nineties. Instead of putting his clients' money in conservative investments as he promised, ITM's owner, Steven D. Wymer, speculated in derivatives and used his customer's cash to buy toys for himself, including a Ferrari, a pair of Mercedes-Benzes, and a couple of boats. (Terence P. Pare, "Money & Markets: How to Find a Financial Planner: It's Easy to Spend Good Money on Bad Advice," *Fortune*, 5/16/1994, p. 103.)

(3) defraud (as in deceive) *v.t.*: **hornswoggle**. See *deceive*

(4) defraud (as in embezzle) *v.t., v.i.*: **peculate**. See *embezzle*

(5) defraud (as in swindle) *n., v.t.*: **thimblerig**. See *swindle*

(6) defraud (or force someone into doing something) *v.t.*: **shanghai** (person who does so *n.*: **shanghaier**). See *coerce*

deft (as in nimble) *adj.* **lightsome**. See *nimble*

deftness (or subtlety, esp. in political or business dealings) *n.*: **Italian hands** [often used in the phrase "fine Italian hands"]. See *subtlety*

degenerate (morally . . .) *adj.*: **scrofulous**. See *depraved*

(2) degenerate (sexual . . .) *n.*: **paraphiliac**. See *pervert*

(3) degenerate *n., v.i.*: **atrophy**. See *wither*

degenerating (as in worsening) *adj.*: **ingravescent**. See *worsening*

degradation (of a religious, national, or racial

group) *n.*: **helotism** (*v.t.*: **helotize**). See *oppression*

deification *n.*: **apotheosis** (*v.t.*: **apotheosize**). See *exaltation*

deign (as in bestow, by one with higher power) *v.t.*: **vouchsafe**. See *bestow*

deity (belief in one . . . without denying others) *n.*: **henotheism**. ❖ On the empirical side, Lind thinks he sees an accelerating pattern of religious indifferentism in this country; Americans, he argues, have adopted the **henotheism** of "one God and many equally true religions." (George Weigel, "The Next American Nation: The New Nationalism and the Fourth American Revolution," *Commentary*, 7/1/1995, p. 62.)

(2) deity (belief there is only one . . .) *n.*: **monotheism**. ❖ This myth—the belief in one God, creator of the heavens and the earth—constitutes "a system in which identity depends upon rejection of the Other and subjection of the Self." Sometimes Schwartz goes so far as to suggest that **monotheism** lies at the root of evil in the Western world. (Peter Berkowitz, "Thou Shalt Not Kill," *New Republic*, 6/23/1997.)

(3) deity (worship of or belief in more than one . . .) *n.*: **polytheism**. ❖ The Vikings believed in gods and goddesses, led by Odin, Frey and Thor. . . . With their tradition of **polytheism**, adding Jesus to the list was no problem. (Sharon Begley, "The Ancient Mariners," *Newsweek*, 4/3/2000, p. 48.)

(4) deity (guardian . . . of a place) *n.*: **genius loci** [Latin]. See *spirit*

déjà vu (false . . . , as in confusion of remembrance with actual fact) *n.*: **paramnesia**. See *misremember*

dejected *adj.*: **chapfallen**. ❖ Under the headline "Wielders of mass deception?" on the cover of this week's *Economist*, President Bush sits, stroking his chin, mouth covered by his right hand, his brow furrowed, with . . . a melancholy look that seems to say, "Now what?" Seated next to him is a **chapfallen** British Prime Minister Tony Blair, weary head propped up by his left hand, whose unspoken thought could easily be,

"I'm not his poodle, but no one believes me." (Arnaud de Borchgrave, "Loony Lucubrations," *Washington Times*, 10/10/2003.)

(2) dejected (chronically . . . , as in depressed) *adj., n.*: **dysthymic**. See *depressed*

(3) dejected *adj.*: **heartsore**. See *heartbroken*

dejection (as in depression) *n.*: **cafard** [French]. See *depression*

(2) dejection (as in depression) *n.*: **megrims** (pl. of **megrim**; also means migraine headache). See *headache*

(3) dejection (as in disappointment) *n.*: **Apples of Sodom**. See *disappointment*

(4) dejection (as in inability to experience pleasure or happiness) *n.*: **anhedonia**. See *unhappiness*

(5) dejection (general feeling of . . . , as form of depression) *n.*: **dysphoria**. See *depression*

(6) dejection (to fret or complain, including as a result of . . .) *v.i.*: **repine**. See *complain*

delay (intentional . . . or procrastination) *n.*: **cunctation**. ❖ [Vansittart] advocated a policy of **cunctation**: delay a confrontation with Nazi Germany, buy time for rearmament, and keep Germany guessing about British policy while being ready to negotiate. (Michael Carley, "Churchill," *Canadian Journal of History*, 8/1/1995.)

(2) delay (as in hesitate to act due to indecision) *v.i.*: **dither**. See *procrastinate*

(3) delay (as in procrastinate or hesitate to act) *v.i.*: **shilly-shally**. See *procrastinate*

(4) delay (engaging in . . . tactics, esp. as a means to wear out an opponent or avoid confrontation) *adj.*: **Fabian**. See *dilatory*

delectable *adj.*: **esculent**. See *edible*

(2) delectable *adj.*: **sapid**. See *tasty*

(3) delectable *adj.*: **toothsome**. See *tasty*

delegate (authority or duties to another) *v.t.*: **depute**. ❖ After a long eight years, the residents of Dhaka . . . will cast their vote today to choose their mayors and ward commissioners. Large contingents of army . . . have been deployed to maintain law and order so that the electorate can exercise their franchise freely without any fear or intimidation. . . . The Canadian High Commission in Dhaka has also **deputed** one observer to monitor the polls. (*Independent* [London], "All Set for Battle of Ballot in Three Cities," 4/25/2002.)

deleterious *adj.*: **nocent**. See *harmful*

deletion (as in omission) *n.*: **elision**. See *omission*

deliberation (of matters outside oneself, i.e., the outside world) *n.*: **extrospection** (*adj.*: **extrospective**). See *observation*

deliberate (as in contrived) *adj.*: **voulu** [French]. See *contrived*

(2) deliberate (as in premeditated) *adj.*: **prepense** (usually used as part of the phrase "malice prepense"). See *premeditated*

delicacy *n.*: **bonne bouche** [French]. ❖ Janine, who spent five years of her life in the lobster Valhalla that is Maine, USA, wondered for a moment if it was over-buttered, then decided it was the best she'd ever had in London. The portion she grudgingly allowed me to taste seemed the last word in succulent bliss, the kind of **bonne bouche** you imagine forking into Kim Basinger's blindfolded face, should they ever plan a sequel to *9-1/2 Weeks*. (John Walsh, "Rock Stars Wow a Sole Man," *Independent* [London], 9/23/1994.)

delicate (as in fragile) *adj.*: **frangible**. See *fragile*

(2) delicate (as in sheer or transparent) *adj.*: **diaphanous**. See *transparent*

(3) delicate (as in sheer or transparent) *adj.*: **gossamer**. See *transparent*

(4) delicate (as in slender and/or graceful) *adj.*: **gracile**. See *slender*

(5) delicate (in an affected manner) *adj.*: **niminy-piminy**. See *dainty*

(6) delicate (affectedly or excessively . . . , quaint, or dainty) *adj.*: **twee**. See *quaint*

delicious (said esp. of food or drink that is so good that one wants more) *adj.*: **moreish** [chiefly British]. See *addictive*

(2) delicious *adj.*: **esculent**. See *edible*

(3) delicious *adj.*: **sapid**. See *tasty*

(4) delicious *adj.*: **toothsome**. See *tasty*

delight (causing or tending to produce . . .) *adj.*: **felicific**. See *happiness*

(2) delight *n.*: **beatitude**. See *bliss*

(3) delight *n.*: **delectation**. See *pleasure*

(4) delight *n.*: **oblectation**. See *pleasure*

delighted (often in a boastful way) *adj.*: **cock-a-hoop**. See *elated*

delightful *adj.*: **Elysian**. See *blissful*

(2) delightful *adj.*: **frabjous** (often as in "Oh frabjous day!"). See *wonderful*

(3) delightful *adj.*: **galluptious** [slang]. See *wonderful*

(4) delightful *adj.*: **gladsome**. See *gladness*

delineate (as in describe, by painting or writing) *v.t.*: **limn**. See *describe*

delirium (emotional . . . , esp. as caused by something unattainable) *n.*: **nympholepsy**. [This word often, though not always, refers to an erotic frenzy.] See *frenzy*

deliver (from slavery, servitude, or bondage) *v.t.*: **manumit**. See *emancipate*

deliverance (having the power or intent to bring about . . .) *adj.*: **salvific**. See *salvation*

delivery (of or relating to . . . of a baby) *adj.*: **parturient**. See *childbirth*

(2) delivery (slow or difficult . . . of a baby) *n.*: **dystocia**. See *childbirth*

delude (as in deceive) *v.t.*: **humbug**. See *deceive*

deluge *n.*: **cataract**. See *downpour*

delusion *n.*: **ignis fatuus**. ❖ A trans-Atlantic labor charter, if not likely, is at least possible, unlike the **ignis fatuus** of a global labor-law regime. (Michael Lind, "A Plea for a New Global Strategy: Looking Past NATO," *New Leader*, 6/30/1997, p. 9.)

(2) delusion (that one possesses superior intelligence) *n.*: **sophomania** (person having this delusion *n.*: **sophomaniac**). [In this example, two bloggers, Tim and Nell, are quarreling about the merits of being a vegetarian.] ❖ Dear Timothy: you certainly sound as though you do have a "medical condition," the one known by specialists as . . . "talkin' through yir erse." Dear Nelly: If my "condition" is spreading throughout Canada it will raise the average IQ by at least 20 points. So, instead of being

130 or so it will be 150. Dear Timothy: I diagnose **sophomania** now too. You forgot to put the decimal point in your IQ, folks that "130" should read "13.0." (thescotsman.scotsman.com/ViewArticle.aspx?articleid=3285578, 5/14/2007.)

(3) delusion (held by two closely associated persons) *n.*: **folie à deux** [French]. ❖ Yet the [fire] ants were real enough or else [my dog] Lizbeth had become my partner in a **folie à deux**. (Lars Eighner, *Travels with Lizbeth*, St. Martin's Press [1993], p. 127.)

(4) delusion (as in opinion, belief, or doctrine that is false) *n.*: **pseudodoxy**. See *fallacy*

(5) delusion (esp. something that at first seems a wonderful discovery or development, but that turns to be a . . . or a hoax) *n.*: **mare's nest**. See *hoax*

(6) delusion (living in a world of . . . , with a glorified or romanticized conception of oneself, as a result of boredom in one's life) *n.*: **Bovarism**. See *self-delusion*

delusional (having . . . fantasies about having power, fame, omnipotence, etc.) *n.*: **megalomania**. ❖ After that, [David] Koresh took over [the Branch Davidian cult]. His **megalomania**, say former followers, quickly became evident. . . . One of his teachings was that he was the "Lamb," or the son of God—something most of his followers grew to accept without question. (Joe Treen, "On His Road to Armageddon, Would-be Messiah David Koresh Seduced His Followers into a Life of Paranoia, Violence and Sexual Abuse," *People*, 3/15/1993, p. 38.)

(2) delusional *adj.*: **fatuous**. ❖ After the 1992 election, I wrote [an article] on Bill Clinton. . . . I did express high, and in retrospect rather **fatuous**, hopes for the coming Clinton Administration. . . . I cherished, for a time, a kind of fresh-start, non-partisan, post-ideological, post–Cold War faith that a new-paradigm Clinton might lead the nation brilliantly toward . . . toward, well, the bridge to the twenty-first century! (Lance Morrow, "U.S. v. Clinton," *National Review*, 9/28/1998, p. 39.)

(3) delusional (spec. the tendency to see

things as more beautiful than they really are) *n*.: **kalopsia**. See *rose-colored glasses*

delusionary (hope or goal that is not realistically obtainable) *n*.: **will-o'-the-wisp**. See *pipe dream*

demanding (as in difficult situation or problem) *n*.: **nodus**. See *complication*

   (2) demanding (attention) *adj*.: **clamant**. See *urgent*

demarcate (as in set the boundaries of) *v.t.*: **delimit**. ❖ When viewed from above, some state boundaries make sense—they follow rivers, declivities, chain of hills—but the straight lines defining Wyoming are purely notional and basically **delimit** a mammoth sandbox. (Walter Kirn, *Up in the Air*, Doubleday [2001], p. 202.)

demean *v.t.*: **vilipend**. See *disparage*

demeanor *n*.: **mien**. ❖ When Roosevelt addressed [George Marshall] as "George," [Marshall] frowned. The president, who thereafter always called him "General," was taken aback at first by this plain-spoken soldier of serious **mien**. But in the end he concluded that Marshall was an anchorage of honesty in a sea of flattery and guile. (Gerald Parshall, "The Strategists of War," *U.S. News & World Report*, 3/16/1998.)

demented (slightly . . . , often used humorously) *adj*.: **tetched**. See *crazy*

demise (of or relating to a . . . , as in downfall, esp. after an innocent or carefree time) *adj*.: **postlapsarian**. See *downfall*

   (2) demise (as in downfall, esp. from a position of strength) *n*.: **dégringolade** [French]. See *downfall*

demon (female . . . who has sex with sleeping men) *n*.: **succubus**. ❖ Q: My best friend—who is a guy—told me that when his girlfriend went to see her parents over the holidays, he had a dream that he had sex with a ghost. . . . Dr. Judy: . . . Folklore would say he was visited by a **succubus** who seduces men in their sleep to take their spirit, or that a witch put a spell on him to make him succumb to her. (Fitness File/ Sex Q&A, *Newsday*, 1/11/1999.)

   (2) demon (who has sex with sleeping women) *n*.: **incubus**. ❖ Here's some good marketing advice: Never name women's footwear after a demon who in medieval lore had sex with sleeping women. Common sense? Well, Reebok International found out that it had done just that with its line of women's running shoes named after the mythically infamous **incubus**. (Betsy Streisand, "Whoops! Did the Devil Make Them Do It?" *U.S. News & World Report*, 3/3/1997.)

demonic *adj*.: **Mephistophelean**. See *devilish*

demure (as in prim or prudish) *adj*.: **missish**. See *prim*

denigrate (as in the destroying of one's reputation) *n*.: **famicide**. See *defamation*

   (2) denigrate (by making false or malicious statements) *v.t.*: **calumniate**. See *malign*

   (3) denigrate (oneself) *v.t.*: **flagellate** (*n*.: **flagellation**). See *criticize*

   (4) denigrate (sharply) *v.t.*: **scarify**. See *criticize*

   (5) denigrate (so as to humiliate or disgrace) *v.t.*: **traduce**. See *malign*

denouement (as in moment of recognition, often the point in the plot at which the protagonist recognizes his or her or some other character's true identity or discovers the true nature of his or her own situation) *n*.: **anagnorisis**. See *recognition*

denounce (harshly) *v.t.*: **fustigate**. See *criticize*

   (2) denounce (sharply) *v.t.*: **scarify**. See *criticize*

   (3) denounce *v.t.*: **execrate**. See *hate*

   (4) denounce *v.t.*: **flay**. See *criticize*

   (5) denounce *v.t.*: **objurgate**. See *criticize*

dense (as in region or city with . . . population) *n*.: **megalopolis**. See *crowded*

   (2) dense (as in slow to understand or perceive) *adj*.: **purblind**. See *obtuse*

denunciation *n*.: **commination**. ❖ The bellows of outrage by George Bush, Margaret Thatcher and other leaders against Iraq's seizure of Kuwait should not be allowed to obscure the less virtuous realities of the situation. . . . It's all the rage to say so, but one should be cautious amid these extravaganzas of **commination**. Saddam [Hussein] is a tyrant with gruesome abuses of civilized behavior on his record. In this he is egregious but not singular. (Alexander Cockburn, "Beat the Devil," *Nation*, 8/27/1990.)

(2) denunciation (as in criticism) *n.*: **animadversion** (*v.t.*: **animadvert***)*. See *criticism*

(3) denunciation (being subject to . . . , esp. public) *n.*: **obloquy**. See *abuse*

(4) denunciation *n.*: **philippic**. See *tirade*

denunciatory (language) *n.*: **vituperation** (*adj.*: **vituperative**). See *invective*

deny (as in disavow or recant) *v.t.*: **abjure**. See *disavow*

(2) deny (esp. responsibility or duty) *v.t.*: **abnegate**. See *renounce*

depart (hurriedly or secretly) *v.t.*: **absquatulate**. See *leave*

(2) depart (hurriedly or secretly) *v.t.*: **decamp**. See *leave*

departure (which is unannounced, abrupt, secret, or unceremonious) *n.*: **French leave** (or **French Leave**) [derives from eighteenth-century French custom of leaving a party without saying good-bye to the host or hostess]. ❖ [The New England Patriots training camp] hasn't even been in session for two weeks yet, but [coach] Belichick had already endured the . . . unauthorized defection of linebacker Andy Katzenmoyer. A day after Panos retired, Katzenmoyer took **French Leave**. ("I don't think he was kidnapped, but I don't know," Belichick cracked in reporting Katzenmoyer's absence.) (*Boston Herald*, 8/8/2001.)

(2) departure (act of . . . as in abandonment, from one's religion, principles, or causes) *n.*: **apostasy**. See *abandonment*

dependence (on faith alone rather than reason, esp. in philosophical or religious matters) *n.*: **fideism**. See *faith*

dependent (as in acting subservient as opposed to leading) *adj.*: **sequacious**. See *subservient*

(2) dependent (as in subjected to external controls and impositions; i.e., the opposite of autonomous) *adj.*: **heteronomous** (*n.*: **heteronomy**). See *subjugated*

depict (as in describe, by painting or writing) *v.t.*: **limn**. See *describe*

deplete (of strength) *v.t.*: **enervate**. See *debilitate*

deplorable (as in abominable) *adj.*: **execrable**. See *abominable*

deportment (appropriate . . . , as in propriety) *n.*: **correctitude**. See *propriety*

(2) deportment *n.*: **mien**. See *demeanor*

depose (as in unseat) *v.t.*: **unhorse**. See *unseat*

deposit (of mud or sand on a riverbank) *n.*: **alluvium**. See *mud*

depraved (morally . . .) *adj.*: **scrofulous**. ❖ In my opinion, we are not unlike those confused, **scrofulous** hippies of the late 1960s who finally showed up at the doors of the free clinics in Haight-Ashbury to get their dose of traditional medicine [after getting bizarre diseases resulting from not bathing]. . . . We need to take an active stand against the divisive unlearning that is corrupting the integrity of our society. (Christina Hoff Sommers, "Are We Living in a Moral Stone Age?" *USA Today Magazine*, 3/1/1999.)

(2) depraved (preference for . . . or unusual sexual practices) *n.*: **paraphilia**. See *deviant*

depravity (place of . . . , as in corruption) *n.*: **Augean stable**. See *corruption*

depressant (as in something that induces forgetfulness of or indifference to pain, suffering, or sorrow) *n.*: **nepenthe**. See *narcotic*

depressed (chronically . . .) *adj., n.*: **dysthymic**. ❖ "Before taking Prozac," recalls a middle-aged woman with **dysthymic** symptoms, "my first thought on waking up would be, 'Oh God, when can I go back to bed.' I felt ugly and stupid. I'd change my clothes fifty times before a party and then decide not to go because nobody would notice or care whether I was there." (Kathleen McAuliffe, "Prozac: What's in It for You?" *Cosmopolitan*, 3/1/1995, p. 208.)

(2) depressed (as in dismal and gloomy) *adj.*: **acherontic**. See *gloomy*

(3) depressed (or grumpy mood) *n.pl.*: **mulligrubs**. See *grumpiness*

(4) depressed *adj.*: **chapfallen**. See *dejected*

depressing *adj.*: **trustful**. See *sad*

depression (general feeling of . . .) *n.*: **dysphoria**. ❖ Let me be more detailed about those mood swings, because they bear directly on the question of whether Myrna was depressed when she killed herself. . . . In euphoria she never thought of suicide; in **dysphoria** she was wholly involved in fretting over relative trivia. In euphoria she was rash and impulsive. In **dysphoria** she could not make a decision and could not act. (Jamie Talan, "Deathbed Suicide—The Depression Factor," *Newsday*, 5/21/1996.)

(2) depression *n.* **cafard** [French]. ❖ This January was apparently the most light-starved since records began, preceded by the tenth coldest December this century and the chilliest February for two decades. All of which has a demoralising impact on the human psyche. The weather produced record levels of winter depression. Arctic countries have long had terms for the **cafard** of winter: "Cabin fever" and "Lapp sickness." (Andrew Brown, "After the Gloom, a Lighter Outlook," *Independent* [London], 4/1/1996.)

(3) depression (as in inability to experience pleasure or happiness) *n.*: **anhedonia**. See *unhappiness*

(4) depression (as in world-weariness or sentimental pessimism over the world's problems) *adj.*: **Weltschmerz** [German]. See *pessimism*

(5) depression *n.*: **megrims** (pl. of **megrim**; also means migraine headache). See *headache*

(6) depression (sometimes resulting from spiritual apathy) *n.*: **acedia**. See *apathy*

deprive (of strength) *v.t.*: **enervate**. See *debilitate*

deprived (of something, as in bereft or forlorn) *adj.*: **lorn**. See *forlorn*

depth (measurement of . . . of bodies of water) *n.*: **bathymetry**. ❖ The only way to obtain precise depths in the open ocean is with traditional **bathymetry**, in which a ship measures the distance to the ocean floor by bouncing sound waves off the bottom. Unfortunately, a ship can take soundings only in a narrow strip. (Dana Mackenzie, "Earth Science: Ocean Floor Is Laid Bare by New Satellite Data," *Science*, 9/26/1997.)

deranged (informal, as in daffy or loony) *adj.*: **doolally**. See *crazy*

(2) deranged (person) *n.*: **bedlamite**. See *lunatic*

(3) deranged (slightly . . . , often used humorously) *adj.*: **tetched**. See *crazy*

deride (esp. through the use of satire) *v.t.*: **pasquinade**. See *satirize*

derision (as in contempt) *n.*: **misprision** (*v.t.*: **misprize**). See *contempt*

(2) derision (express . . .) *idiom*: **cock a snook**. See *thumb one's nose*

derivation (as in source and origin) *n.*: **fons et origo** [Latin]. See *source and origin*

(2) derivation (principal . . . or source) *n.*: **wellhead**. See *source*

derogatory (as in faultfinding person) *n.*: **smellfungus**. See *faultfinder*

(2) derogatory (as in faultfinding) *adj.*: **captious**. See *faultfinding*

(3) derogatory (or expressing disapproval) *adj.*: **dyslogistic**. See *uncomplimentary*

derrière (a fat . . .) *n.*: **steatopygia** (having a fat . . . *adj.*: **steatopygic**). See *rear end*

(2) derrière (as in buttocks) *n.pl.*: **nates**. See *buttocks*

(3) derrière (having a hairy . . .) *adj.*: **dasypygal**. See *rear end*

(4) derrière (having a nicely proportioned . . .) *adj.*: **callipygian**. See *rear end*

descend (a mountain with a rope) *v.t.* (or noun when referring to the descent itself): **abseil** ❖ Somehow it seems beyond the call of parental duty. [For] the past two hours I have been at an indoor climbing centre [watching my children] scale artificial cliffs. The job involves gearing up in a climbing harness, securing each boy's safety line, pulling in the rope as he ascends and releasing it slowly as he **abseils** down. After a couple of hours I've developed a serious crick in my neck from looking up at a sharp angle. (Deborah Hope, "The Age of the Hyper Parent," *Weekend Australian*, 7/19/1997)

descent (esp., in Greek mythology, into the underworld) *n.*: **katabasis.** [The word also means a military retreat]. ❖ Like Western civilization itself, as his friend and chief critical promoter Harold Rosenberg sardonically remarked, De Kooning was always in decline. This **katabasis** is supposed to have begun in the early '50s, with the Woman series. (Robert Hughes, "Seeing the Face in the Fire," review of Willem de Kooning, National Gallery, Washington, D.C., *Time*, 5/30/1994.)

(2) descent (a . . . down an incline of a snowy mountain) *n.*: **glissade.** See *slide*

(3) descent (as in downward slope) *n.*: **declivity** (*adj.*: **declivitous**). See *decline*

(4) descent (esp. extending down from a fortification) *n.*: **glacis.** See *decline*

(5) descent (esp. from a position of strength) *n.*: **dégringolade** [French]. See *downfall*

(6) descent (of or relating to a . . . , as in downfall, esp. after an innocent or carefree time) *adj.*: **postlapsarian.** See *downfall*

(7) descent *n.*: **declension.** See *decline*

describe (by painting or writing) *v.t.*: **limn.** ❖ A few weeks ago, *Newsweek* ran a cover story on what it called "the new male dilemma," as **limned** by writer Susan Faludi in amusingly overcooked prose: "As the nation wobbled toward the millennium, its pulse-takers all seemed to agree that a domestic apocalypse was under way: American manhood was under siege." (William Powers, "Media: She-Male Nation," *National Journal*, 10/2/1999.)

(2) describe (as in set the boundaries of) *v.t.*: **delimit.** See *demarcate*

(3) describe (in a sketchy or incomplete way) *v.t.*: **adumbrate.** See *outline*

description (as in brief summary) *n.*: **précis** [French]. See *summary*

descriptive (word that is more . . . than another given word) *n.*: **hyponym.** See *word*

desensitize *v.t.*: **hyposensitize.** ❖ Allergy shots can **hyposensitize** your pet, making it less sensitive to whatever is causing the itchiness. (*Minneapolis Star Tribune*, Pet Talk: "Allergy May Cause Dog to Pull Out Hair," 7/16/1995.)

(2) desensitize *v.t.*: **narcotize.** See *deaden*

desertion (from one's religion, principles, or causes) *n.*: **apostasy.** See *abandonment*

deserved (esp. in reference to a punishment) *adj.*: **condign.** ❖ Those who had seen the Standard Oil dissolution as **condign** punishment for Rockefeller were in for a sad surprise: It proved to be the luckiest stroke of his career. (Ron Chernow, *Titan*, Random House [1998], p. 556.)

designate (as in classify) *v.t.*: **taxonomize.** See *classify*

designer (of women's fashions) *n.*: **modiste.** ❖ Trendsetting **modiste** Clare Potter, one of the designers credited with inventing American sportswear, died on Jan. 5 in Fort Ann, N.Y. She was 95. Her unconventional notions in the 1930s and '40s helped make trousers on women, for example, standard wear today. (David Cobb Craig, Passages, *People*, 1/25/1999, p. 81.)

desirable (said esp. of food or drink that is so good that one wants more) *adj.*: **moreish** [chiefly British]. See *addictive*

desire (as in greed) *n.*: **pleonexia.** See *greed*

(2) desire (as in hope for or want) *v.t.*: **desiderate.** See *want*

(3) desire (as in irresistible compulsion) *n.*: **cacoëthes.** See *compulsion*

(4) desire (as in worship of or devotion to money) *n.*: **plutolatry.** See *wealth*

(5) desire (condition involving . . . to eat nonfood items) *n.*: **pica.** See *craving*

(6) desire (esp. for something one once had but has no more) *n.*: **desiderium.** See *longing*

(7) desire (excessive . . . for wealth) *n.*: **cupidity.** See *greed*

(8) desire (excessive sexual . . . by a man) *n.*: **satyriasis.** See *horniness*

(9) desire (having a strong . . . , esp. sexual) *adj.*: **concupiscent** (*n.*: **concupiscence**). See *lustful*

(10) desire (hidden or ulterior . . .) *n*.: **arriere-pensee** (or **arrière-pensée**) [French]. See *motive*

(11) desire (mad or crazy . . . , as in love) *n*.: **amour fou** [French]. See *love*

(12) desire (mental process marked by . . . to do something) *n*.: **conation**. See *determination*

(13) desire (sexual . . . for the elderly) *n*.: **gerontophilia**. See *lust*

(14) desire (slight or faint . . .) *n*.: **velleity**. See *hope*

(15) desire (strong . . .) *n*.: **avidity**. See *craving*

(16) desire (which is delusive or not realistically obtainable) *n*.: **will-o'-the-wisp**. See *pipe dream*

(17) desire *n*.: **appetence**. See *craving*

desiring (esp. something one once had but has no more) *n*.: **desiderium**. See *longing*

desirous (strongly . . .) *adj*.: **appetent** (*n*.: **appetence**). ❖ [Knowing] that President-elect George W. Bush is an ardent advocate of closer US-Taiwanese military ties, the Chinese . . . have been deliberately avoiding any reciprocation to [the Taiwanese president's] overtures in a hope that Bush, who would be too **appetent** to register a political score in his early days . . . may try to convince the Taiwanese leadership to offer further concessions to seek headway with China. (Imran Khalid, "China Cool to Taiwan's Chen," *New Straits Times* [Malaysia], 1/5/2001.)

(2) desirous (as in lustful) *adj*.: **lickerish**. See *lustful*

(3) desirous *adj*.: **athirst**. See *eager*

desk *n*.: **escritoire**. ❖ Each room is furnished differently, with high-quality reproduction antiques in boudoir settings (a soft-blue "queen single," for instance, invites correspondence at a lovely **escritoire**). (*USA Today*, "Three Faces of NYC," 5/23/1997.)

despair (out of the depths of . . . or misery) *n*., *adv*.: **de profundis**. [This term is Latin for "out of the depths." It is the beginning of psalm 130 of the King James Version of the Bible ("Out of the depths have I cried unto thee, O Lord")

and is a liturgical prayer for the dead. It can be used as a noun, when referring to the expression of despair itself, or as an adverb.] ❖ The demise of the Honorable [Dan] Rostenkowski has provoked orgies of hand-wringing here in Washington. . . . Establishmentarians [gaze] sadly upon their fallen colleague, heads bowed, blinking back the tears. Their tears are not crocodile tears; the expressions of remorse are genuine, **de profundis**. (Andrew Ferguson, "The Rosty Man," *National Review*, 6/27/1994.)

(2) despair (as in depression) *n*.: **cafard** [French]. See *depression*

(3) despair (as in inability to experience pleasure or happiness) *n*.: **anhedonia**. See *unhappiness*

(4) despair (general feeling of . . . as form of depression) *n*.: **dysphoria**. See *depression*

(5) despair (over) *v.t*.: **bewail**. See *lament*

(6) despair (to fret or complain, including as a result of . . .) *v.i*.: **repine**. See *complain*

(7) despair *n*.: **dolor** (*adj*.: **dolorous**). See *sadness*

(8) despair *n*.: **megrims** (pl. of **megrim**; also means migraine headache). See *headache*

despicable (or treacherous) *adj*.: **reptilian**. ❖ A sad schoolgirl rejects a suitor, even though he's immensely wealthy and devoted. Not long afterward, she spurns a handsome admirer who crossed the Atlantic just to look at her. A few years later, having come into her own fortune (unexpectedly, from a rich uncle), the young woman agrees to marry a **reptilian** creep: a sneaky, shameless gold-digger without redeeming traits. (Bob Ross, "That Was No 'Lady,' That Was Her Life," *Tampa Tribune*, 1/17/1997.)

(2) despicable (person) *n*.: **caitiff**. ❖ [The purpose of the Black Liberation Army] was indiscriminate slaughter of whites to provoke a revolution and race war. Jacob John Dougan and four of his [fellow members] cruised Jacksonville searching for potential victims and decided on an 18-year-old hitchhiker. The gang of **caitiffs** stabbed the youth repeatedly, and the rebarbative Dougan ended the ordeal by shooting him in the chest and in the ear amid pleas for mercy. (Bruce Fein, "Justice's Views May Set Back War on Crime," *Insight on the News*, 11/22/1993.)

(3) despicable *adj.*: **ugsome**. See *loathsome*

despise (as in treat with contempt) *v.t.*: **contemn**. See *scorn*

(2) despise *v.t.*: **execrate**. See *hate*

(3) despise *v.t.*: **misprize**. See *hate*

despite (that) *adv.*: **withal**. See *nevertheless*

(2) despite (the views of, as in, with all respect to) *prep.*: **pace** [Latin]. See *respectfully*

despondency (general feeling of . . . as form of depression) *n.*: **dysphoria**. See *depression*

despondent (chronically . . . , as in depressed) *adj., n.*: **dysthymic**. See *depressed*

(2) despondent (or grumpy mood) *n.pl.*: **mulligrubs**. See *grumpiness*

despot (potential . . . , as in dictator) *n.*: **man on horseback**. See *dictator*

despotic (ruthlessly and violently . . .) *adj.*: **jackbooted**. See *oppressive*

dessert table *n.*: **Viennese table** (or **Viennese Table**). ❖ At my brother's wedding, I [sliced my finger]. Luckily, a handsome doctor with a great sense of humor came to my rescue, cleaning the wound with vanilla vodka and suturing it using frayed napkin strands. After cocktails and dancing, we hid from the crowd under the **Viennese Table** and he told me he loved me—that table of delicious pastries serving as chuppah to our love. (Esther Kustanowicz, "Wedding Bell Blues," *New York Jewish Week*, 9/1/2006.)

destination (as in final point) *n.*: **terminus**. See *end*

destiny *n.*: **kismet**. See *fate*

destitute *adj.*: **impecunious**. See *poor*

(2) destitute *adj.*: **necessitous**. See *poor*

destitution *n.*: **illth**. See *poverty*

(2) destitution *n.*: **penury**. See *poverty*

destroy *v.t.*: **extirpate**. See *abolish*

destruction (of ecology or environment by mankind) *n.*: **ecocide**. See *environment*

destructive (mutually . . . to both sides) *adj.*: **internecine**. ❖ What such worries suggest is that even if the airlines manage to avoid their usual **internecine** struggles over ticket prices, they will have to move gingerly in their effort to raise prices. Any sizable across-the-board increase would also bring squawks from business travelers, who account for about 60% of the industry's revenues. (Kenneth Labich, "Competition: What Will Save the U.S. Airlines," *Fortune*, 6/14/1993, p. 98.)

(2) destructive (as in harmful) *adj.*: **nocent**. See *harmful*

detach (as in consider separately) *v.t.*: **prescind** (generally as in "prescind from"). See *isolate*

detached (as in unemotional or even-tempered) *adj.*: **phlegmatic**. See *even-tempered*

(2) detached (as in neutral) *adj.*: **adiaphorous**. See *neutral*

detachment (a matter of . . . , as in indifference, esp. in matters of religion and theology; i.e., neither right nor wrong, beneficial nor harmful) *n.*: **adiaphoron** (*adj.*: **adiaphorous**). See *indifference*

detailed (as in particularized) *adj.*: **pointillistic**. See *particularized*

details (precise observance of . . . or etiquette) *n.*: **punctilio**. See *etiquette*

detect (as in discover, through careful or skillful examination or investigation) *v.t.*: **expiscate**. See *discover*

(2) detect (by careful observation or scrutiny) *v.t.*: **descry**. See *perceive*

deter *v.t.*: **forfend**. See *avert*

deteriorate (as in crumble away) *v.i.*: **molder**. See *crumble*

deteriorated (as in broken-down and/or worn-out) *adj.*: **raddled**. See *worn-out*

deteriorating (as in worsening) *adj.*: **ingravescent**. See *worsening*

deterioration (as in downfall, esp. from a position of strength) *n.*: **dégringolade** [French]. See *downfall*

(2) deterioration (esp. of moral principles or civil order) *n.*: **labefaction**. See *weakening*

(3) deterioration (movement toward or degree of . . . or disorder in a system or society) *n.*: **entropy**. See *disorder*

(4) deterioration (of a group or social structure as a result of lack of standards or values) *n.*: **anomie**. See *breakdown*

(5) deterioration *n., v.i.*: **atrophy**. See *wither*

(6) deterioration *n.*: **declension**. See *decline*

(7) deterioration (of or relating to a . . . , as in downfall, esp. after an innocent or carefree time) *adj.*: **postlapsarian**. See *downfall*

determination (mental process marked by . . . to do something) *n.*: **conation**. ❖ [Bill Clinton] is unique as an instance of pure **conation**. He will do whatever is required to hold himself together. No principles or ideals or moral scruples are allowed to get in the way of this self-protective impulse. (Loren Lomasky, "Piling on the Prez," *Reason*, 12/1/1998.)

(2) determination (as in decree) *n.*: **diktat**. See *decree*

(3) determination (as in courage) *n.*: **hardihood**. See *courage*

determinative (remark, blow, or factor) *n.*: **sockdolager**. See *decisive*

determined (but obstinate) *adj.*: **contumacious**. See *obstinate*

detest *v.t.*: **execrate**. See *hate*

(2) detest *v.t.*: **misprize**. See *hate*

detestable (or treacherous) *adj.*: **reptilian**. See *despicable*

dethrone *v.t.*: **unhorse**. See *unseat*

detrimental (as in harmful) *adj.*: **nocuous**. See *harmful*

(2) detrimental (mutually . . . to both sides) *adj.*: **internecine**. See *destructive*

(3) detrimental *adj.*: **nocent**. See *harmful*

develop (as in result) *v.i.*: **eventuate**. See *result*

developing (as in coming into being) *adj.*: **nascent**. See *emerging*

deviant (preference for . . . sexual practices) *n.*: **paraphilia**. ❖ There are many **paraphilias**, ranging from frotteurism (compulsively rubbing up against strangers) to acrotomophilia (an attraction to amputees). Their most striking feature is that they are an almost exclusively male phenomenon. (Michael Segell, "Meet the Kinks," *Esquire*, 5/1/1996, p. 40.)

(2) deviant (sexual . . .) *n.*: **paraphiliac**. See *pervert*

deviate (from a course or intended path) *v.t.*: **yaw**. See *veer*

(2) deviate (from the subject) *v.i.*: **divagate**. See *digress*

deviation (as in digression) *n.*: **excursus**. See *digression*

(2) deviation (as in passing comment) *n.*: **obiter dictum** [Latin]. See *passing comment*

devil (as in scoundrel or rascal) *n.*: **scapegrace**. See *scoundrel*

(2) devil (as in scoundrel or unprincipled person) *n.*: **blackguard**. See *scoundrel*

(3) devil (female . . . who has sex with sleeping men) *n.*: **succubus**. See *demon*

(4) devil (who has sex with sleeping women) *n.*: **incubus**. See *demon*

(5) devil *n.*: **Beelzebub**. See *Satan*

devilish *adj.*: **Mephistophelean** [after the devil in the Faust legend to whom Faust sold his soul]. ❖ The question now is "Who is the real John McCain?" For the sake of victory, he sold his soul to the devil, to the **Mephistophelean** tactics of Karl Rove, which consist mainly of throwing mud until it sticks. (Anna Quindlen, "Obama the Unruffled," *Newsweek*, 10/27/2008.)

devilry *n.*: **diablerie**. ❖ [Ian] McKellen . . . took the part of the fugitive Nazi, Kurt Dussander, in *Apt Pupil*. . . . "It's the fate of most middle-aged actors, particularly with my background, that you get asked to play Nazis or villains or oddball characters," Mr. McKellen noted. . . . So he enjoyed playing this personification of **diablerie**? "It was great fun," he said with a laugh. (Alan Riding, "Go Hollywood? Sir Ian Rather Likes the Idea," *New York Times*, 10/19/1998).

devious (actions, spec. by trying to represent something as being other than it is) *n.*: **false colors**. See *misrepresentations*

(2) devious (as in crafty) *adj.*: **jesuitical** (sometimes cap.). See *crafty*

(3) devious (behavior) *n.*: **knavery**. See *corruption*

(4) devious (characterized by . . . and cunning conduct, esp. in regard to the pursuit and maintenance of political or other power) *adj.*: **Machiavellian**. See *deceitful*

(5) devious (conduct) *n.*: **skullduggery**. See *deceitfulness*

(6) devious (scheming or trickery) *n.*: **jiggery-pokery**. See *trickery*

devise (an idea, plan, theory, or explanation after careful thought) *v.t.*: **excogitate**. ❖ You have agreed and the majority and minority have agreed to several changes that have, in my judgment, greatly improved the [anti-terrorism] bill, left it a very effective law enforcement effort. . . . And we have been able to do that by working together between Thursday and today. Another week would make it do even better. It's no criticism of your work product to note that no one can **excogitate** the perfect [antiterrorism] bill here, and working together helped. (Rep. Barney Frank [speaker], Media Coverage of Activities Regarding Government Response to Terrorism, *Talk of the Nation*, NPR, 9/24/2001.)

devitalize (as in deprive of strength) *v.t.*: **geld**. See *weaken*

devoted (overly . . . or submissive to one's wife) *adj.*: **uxorious**. ❖ [See also the next entry for the female counterpart to this word.] ❖ [Jay Leno's wife, Mavis,] was an aspiring writer who read far more than she wrote; she still devours 10 books a week. "I don't make wife jokes," Leno points out. He may be the first comedian since George Burns who could be described as **uxorious**. (Richard Stengel, "Jay Leno, Succeeding Johnny Carson as Late-Night Host to Millions, Has Already Won the Office of Most Popular Regular Guy in America," *Time*, 3/16/1992, p. 58.)

(2) devoted (overly . . . to one's husband) *adj.*: **maritorious** [This is the much rarer counterpart to "uxorious," above. Also, whereas "uxorious" can mean either excessive devotion or submissiveness, "maritorious" refers to excessive devotion only. In 1607, in *Tragedy of Bussy D'Ambois*, George Chapman wrote. "Dames **maritorious** ne'er were meritorious." The

example of the word given here—all of four words—comes from an online response to the following description of a couple who owned a noted house in Orange County, CA: "Nellie didn't take [her husband's] demise all that well, giving a go at suicide on a few occasions. While none of those attempts was successful, the poor woman grew to be an eccentric kook who, among other things, preserved her home in a museum-like fashion as kind of a shrine to her late husband."] ❖ The poor **maritorious** Nellie. (bigorangelandmarks.blogspot .com/2009/04/no-230-villa-maria, 4/28/2009.)

(3) devoted (and unquestioning assistant) *n.*: **myrmidon**. See *assistant*

devotee (of a place, esp. a place of entertainment) *n.*: **habitué** [French]. See *regular*

(2) devotee (strong . . . of a cause, religion, or activity) *n.*: **votary**. See *supporter*

devotion (as in allegiance) *n.*: **vassalage**. See *allegiance*

(2) devotion (as in loyalty) *n.*: **fealty** See *loyalty*

devotional (tacky or kitschy . . . or religious ornament) *n.*: **bondieuserie** [French]. See *ornament*

devour (food like a glutton) *v.t.*: **gormandize**. ❖ The problem is that matzo—unless it's of the whole wheat variety—has little fiber and often is eaten to excess [on Passover]. . . . "People say, 'I love matzo,' and it's addictive. It's like trying to eat one potato chip," said Harriet Roth. . . . "They look forward to this all year and when Passover comes they **gormandize** and they overindulge." (*Arlington Morning News*, "Jews Share Joys of Passover, Pain of 'Matzo Stomach,'" 4/18/1998.)

(2) devour *v.t.*: **guttle**. ❖ Best of all, gastronomes have the option of lounging at a bar-stool bolted elegantly to a raised green cement podium or taking advantage of generous car parking facilities to **guttle** foot-long hotdogs without leaving the comfort of their shaggin' wagons. (Emma Tom, "Here's a Tip for All You Food Lovers," *Sydney Morning Herald*, 6/27/1998.)

(3) devour (as in ingest) *v.t.*: **incept**. See *ingest*

(4) devour (greedily) *v.t.*: **englut**. See *swallow*

devouring *adj.*: **edacious**. See *voracious*

devout (in terms of strictness of one's religious practices) *n.*: **orthopraxy**. See *orthodoxy*

dexterity (or subtlety, esp. in political or business dealings) *n.*: **Italian hands** [often used in the phrase "fine Italian hands"]. See *subtlety*

diabolic *adj.*: **iniquitous**. See *wicked*

(2) diabolic *adj.*: **malefic**. See *evil*

(3) diabolic *adj.*: **malevolent**. See *evil*

diabolical *adj.*: **Mephistophelean**. See *devilish*

diagnose (as in analyze, that which has already occurred; i.e., to project into the past) *v.t.*: **retroject**. See *analyze*

dialect (regional . . .) *n.*: **patois**. ❖ George Broomfield, a Hempstead resident who grew up speaking a lilting **patois** in his native Jamaica, said he knows from experience how hard it can be for black children to learn the tongue of white America. (Martin C. Evans, "Locally, Few Favor Movement," *Newsday*, 1/13/1997.)

dialogue (in which neither side hears or understands or pays attention to the other) *n.*: **dialogue de sourds** [French; dialogue of the deaf]. ❖ The transatlantic debate on multiculturalism has many aspects of a **dialogue de sourds**. Both sides end up sounding like right wingers to the other. . . . When some French intellectuals hear "multiculturalism," they think . . . "globalization" and "threat to the Republic." When US multiculturalists hear French anti-multiculturalism, it sounds to them like the discredited "color blind" and "integrationist" discourse of 1950s white liberals. (Ella Shohat, "French Intellectuals and the U.S. Culture Wars," *Black Renaissance*, 3/22/2001.)

(2) dialogue (between two people) *n.*: **duologue**. See *conversation*

(3) dialogue (informal . . . , as in chat or discussion) *n.*: **causerie**. See *chat*

(4) dialogue (one skilled at dinner . . .) *n.*: **deipnosophist**. See *conversation*

(5) dialogue *n.*: **interlocution**. See *discussion*

diamonds (made of, resembling, or reminiscent of) *adj.*: **diamantine**. [This word is often used in reference to something that sparkles like a diamond, whether literally or figuratively, as in the example given.] ❖ With her speedy leaps and turns and her unshakable balances, Nina Ananiashvili was a confident Princess Aurora whose movements possessed such clarity that they shone with **diamantine** brilliance. (Jack Anderson, "Appealing to the Imagination," review of *Sleeping Beauty* [ballet], *New York Times*, 6/2/1998.)

diatribe *n.*: **jeremiad**. See *complaint*

(2) diatribe *n.*: **philippic**. See *tirade*

dictate (as in order or direct) *v.t.*: **adjure**. See *order*

dictation (one who takes . . .) *n.*: **amanuensis**. See *secretary*

dictator (esp. in Spanish-speaking countries) *n.*: **caudillo**. ❖ [Mexican presidential candidate Vicente Fox] speaks of himself in the third person, seems to have all the answers and sometimes sounds messianic. It is not impossible that he would be tempted to overstep the limits of a democratic presidency and follow the traditional Mexican role of the populist **caudillo**, the strongman who . . . imposes his personal decisions by fiat. (Enrique Krauze, Latin America: "The Psychology of Power," *Time* International, 5/29/2000, p. 20.)

(2) dictator (potential . . .) *n.*: **man on horseback**. [This term refers to a man (often but not necessarily a military figure) whose ambitions, popularity, and influence may afford him, or seem to afford him, the position of a dictator, often during a period of crisis. It derives from General Georges Boulanger, who often rode on a black horse, and who was picked by a group of royalists to lead a coup against the Third Republic in France in the late nineteenth century] ❖ The name of the [Ross] Perot danger is fascism. . . . Take away the anti-Semitism of Adolf Hitler and Benito Mussolini and the Marxist ideology of Fidel Castro, and

Ross Perot fits the model of the fascist dictator perfectly. . . . In his own image and that of those who mindlessly support him, he is the savior of America, not a big **man on horseback** but a little man on a billion dollars. (Andrew Greeley, "Mindless Populism Boosts Perot—and Fascist Specter," *Chicago Sun-Times*, 5/31/1992.)

dictionary (process of writing or compiling) *n.*: **lexicography**. ❖ Even the **lexicographers** in their rarified world are aware of the pressures of an increasingly cut-throat market [to sell dictionaries]. Judy Pearsall, who compiles for Oxford University Press, says research shows that clarity of entries is of pivotal importance. (Kathy Marks, "Dictionaries Try Every Trick in the Book as They Battle for Sales," *Independent* [London], 8/14/1998.)

(2) dictionary *n.*: **lexicon**. ❖ Though Noah Webster produced his first American dictionary in 1806, his name never appeared in the title of his editions until after his death. Webster's has since passed into generic usage, and any publisher can slap the word into the titles of its own **lexicons**. (Jesse Birnbaum, Language: Defining Womyn [and Others]—Random House's New Dictionary Is Gender Neutral, Politically Correct—and an English-Lover's Disappointment," *Time*, 6/24/1991, p. 51.)

(3) dictionary (entry that defines a word or phrase) *n.*: **definiendum**. See *definition*

(4) dictionary (or word list) *n.*: **onomasticon**. See *word list*

difference (as in diversity) *n.*: **variegation** *v.t.*: **variegate**. See *diversity*

(2) difference (as in that quality which makes one thing different from any other) *n.*: **haecceity** (or **haeccity**). See *individuality*

(3) difference (of opinion) *n.*: **divarication**. See *disagreement*

different (state or quality of being . . . from others) *n.*: **alterity**. ❖ [The novel *Le Divorce*] wants to appeal to our latent Francophobia. The French eat vile things. They are still very much into fur and hide. They are ridiculously involved with their cheese and wine, their old plates and antique chairs. They retain a formi-

dable **alterity**. (Neil Schmitz, "The Toast of France Meets the White Bread of American Women," *Buffalo News*, 2/9/1997.)

(2) different (as in not homogeneous) *adj.*: **heterogeneous** (*n.*: **heterogeneity**). See *dissimilar*

(3) different (holding . . . opinions or having a . . . perspective) *adj.*: **heterodox** (*n.*: **heterodoxy**). See *unconventional*

(4) different (love of or enthusiasm for anything new and . . .) *n.*: **neophilia**. See *novelty*

differentiate *v.t.*, *v.i.*: **secern**. ❖ We are so egoistic that we care more about what Brad [Pitt] and Angelina [Jolie] are making than . . . what those who wish to [destroy] our nation are making. We can no more **secern** between enemies and friends. We turn our [backs] on those who [have] supported and stood by us [while] we indulge countries [that have made] it clear that they wish to [destroy] this state. (emphysemaucwg.spaces.live.com/Blog/cns!A2C044604D322DED!106, "The Bubble Syndrome," 3/12/2009.)

(2) differentiate (as in separate) *v.i.*: **disaggregate**. See *separate*

differentiating *adj.*: **diacritical**. See *distinguishing*

differentiation (as in diversity) *n.*: **variegation** (*v.t.*: **variegate**). See *diversity*

(2) differentiation (spec. the study of the subtle distinctions or nuances between words that are synonyms or otherwise similar) *n.*: **synonymy**. See *synonyms*

differing (esp. from majority view) *adj.*: **dissentient**. See *dissentient*

difficult (to understand, sometimes due to being obscure) *adj.*: **abstruse**. ❖ Roger Penrose is hardly the sort of man who would normally excite much popular interest, let alone controversy. The shy, somewhat rumpled and unfailingly polite Oxford professor, 58, has spent most of his career spinning theories in the most **abstruse** areas of mathematics and physics. (Michael D. Lemonick, Ideas: "Those Computers Are Dummies," *Time*, 6/25/1990, p. 74.)

(2) difficult (as in intricate or complex) *adj.*: **involute**. See *intricate*

(3) difficult (as in painful journey or experience) *n.*: **via dolorosa**. See *ordeal*

(4) difficult (situation or problem) *n.*: **nodus**. See *complication*

(5) difficult (to understand) *adj.*: **recondite**. See *complicated*

difficulty (as in intricacy) *n.*: **cat's cradle**. See *intricacy*

(2) difficulty (as in predicament, from which it is difficult to extricate oneself) *n.*: **tar baby**. See *predicament*

(3) difficulty (period of . . . , sometimes, but not necessarily, economic) *n.*: **locust years**. See *hardship*

(4) difficulty (spec. a problem that is difficult for a beginner or one who is inexperienced) *n.*: **pons asinorum** [Latin]. See *problem*

diffusion (as in diversity) *n.*: **variegation**. See *diversity*

dig (as in insult, delivered while leaving the scene) *n.*: **Parthian shot**. See *parting shot*

digging (adapted for . . .) *adj.*: **fossorial**. ❖ Some reptiles from Mozambique, northern Botswana and northern Namibia had proved particularly evasive. "The **fossorial** snakes and lizards are extremely difficult to photograph as they just want to go underground. So you see a bit of body with the head in sand," [said professor John Marais]. (Myrtle Ryan, "Adventures with Creepy-Crawlies, *Sunday Tribune* [South Africa], 11/18/2007.)

digest (as in brief summary) *n.*: **précis** [French]. See *summary*

digestion (of or relating to) *adj.*: **peptic**. ❖ Dear Reader: Air in the stomach often has a fetid odor when it is mixed with stomach contents and digested food, and expelled through the mouth. This perception suggests the possibility of **peptic** disease or a common condition called reflux, when stomach contents with or without air are inappropriately released and travel upward into the esophagus. (Dr. Peter Gott, "Jaw Pain Could Be Angina Sign," *Ottawa Sun*, 9/23/2000.)

dignified (as in elegant) *adj.*: **Chesterfieldian**. See *elegant*

dignified (as in lordly) *adj.*: **seigneurial**. See *lordly*

dignity (an insult to another's . . .) *n.*: **lese majesty**. See *insult*

(2) dignity (beneath one's . . .) *adj.*: **infra dig**. See *undignified*

(3) dignity (personal . . .) *n.*: **izzat** [Hindi]. See *honor*

digress *v.i.*: **divagate**. ❖ The story **divagates**, exfoliates, crumbles and reconstitutes itself. It can move simultaneously in two or three different time frames, so that we get someone recounting a story in which someone recounts another story. (Richard Eder, "An Act of Omission," *Newsday*, 2/12/1995.)

digression *n.*: **excursus**. ❖ [Pragmatism is,] in its bare bones, the view that the meaning of ideas is simply to be found in terms of their consequences. . . . The pragmatists were only interested in results. It was their distinctive feature and their proudest boast. That, therefore, is how they must be judged. To do so in detail here would require an unwarranted **excursus**. (Robin Harris, "Post-Civil War Thought; Four American Thinkers Who Made America Modern," *Washington Times*, 5/27/2001.)

(2) digression (as in passing comment) *n.*: **obiter dictum** [Latin]. See *passing comment*

digressive *adj.*: **excursive**. ❖ Those who came expecting a stroll down memory lane to the tune of a Santana jukebox set may have been disappointed—the show was largely defined by **excursive** marathon jams, some of which wandered mazes of polyrhythms for as long as 10 or 15 minutes before resolving. (Robin Vaughn, "Santana's Jamfest Flows Like Honey," *Boston Herald*, 7/26/1997).

(2) digressive *adj.*: **discursive**. See *rambling*

dig up (through careful or skillful examination or investigation) *v.t.*: **expiscate**. See *discover*

dilapidated (and worn-out) *adj.*: **raddled**. See *worn-out*

(2) dilapidated *adj.*: **tatterdemalion**. See *ragged*

dilatory (engaging in . . . tactics, esp. as a means to wear out an opponent or avoid confrontation) *adj.*: **Fabian**. [This adjective derives from Roman general Quinton Fabius Maximus, who, through caution, avoidance of direct confrontation, and harassment, defeated Hannibal in the Second Punic War. Today, it has become synonymous with caution or conservativeness, delay or dilatoriness, or guerrilla warfare, and is often used in the phrase "Fabian tactics."] ❖ Last Thursday, Senate Judiciary Committee Chairman Patrick Leahy, Vermont Democrat, and Subcommittee Chairman Charles Schumer, New York Democrat . . . ardently defended the committee's **Fabian** tactics (i.e., refusing hearings or committee votes) to thwart a bevy of President George Bush's glittering judicial nominees. (Bruce Fein, "Confirmation Equivocations," *Washington Times*, 5/14/2002.)

dilemma (where there are three options, all of which are or seem to be unsatisfactory) *n.*: **trilemma**. ❖ [The Fifth Amendment privilege against self-incrimination] often permits people to stonewall investigators or otherwise frustrate important social interests. Yet [its value] is immense. It prevents government from coercing confessions from people, and it relieves people of the so-called "cruel **trilemma**": the choice between confessing to crimes, lying under oath and defying lawful authorities. (*Washington Post*, "A Right When It Counts," 6/15/2002.)

(2) dilemma (which is difficult to solve) *n.*: **Gordian knot.** [This term derives from an exceedingly complicated knot tied by King Gordius of Phrygia, with the promise that whoever could undo it would be the next ruler of Asia. The problem was solved by Alexander the Great, who cut through it with his sword, thus leading to the expression "cutting the Gordian knot."] ❖ [The first sign came with the collapse of Digital Entertainment Network], considered an early pioneer in the convergence of Hollywood and the Internet. . . . The company blithely burned through $3 million a month [and filed for bankruptcy]. . . . Despite this object lesson, other Internet companies in Hollywood hoped to cut the **Gordian knot**— finding ways to make money from free Web entertainment. (Sharon Waxman, "The Film Industry's Dot-Combustion," *Washington Post*, 9/17/2000.)

(3) dilemma (as in choice of taking what is offered or nothing; i.e., no real choice at all) *n.*: **Hobson's choice**. See *predicament*

(4) dilemma (as in combination of events or circumstances that creates a crisis) *n.*: **conjuncture**. See *crisis*

(5) dilemma (as in dangers on both sides) *idiom*: **between Scylla and Charybdis**. See *precarious*

(6) dilemma (as in the situation of having to make a move where any move made will weaken the existing position) *n.*: **zugzwang** [German]. See *predicament*

(7) dilemma (from which it is difficult to extricate oneself) *n.*: **tar baby**. See *predicament*

(8) dilemma (resulting from an inopportune occurrence) *n.*: **contretemps**. See *mishap*

diligent (in effort or application) *adj.*: **sedulous**. ❖ Much of the public worries about school names [renaming a school in honor of Congresswoman Barbara Jordan instead of Jefferson Davis] because, for ease and convenience, it beats worrying about, or doing anything about, academic standards and achievement. And here is what we should find truly sad: That same portion of the public pretends this **sedulous** attention is for the sake of low-income kids, largely black and Hispanic. (William Murchison, "School Names Irrelevant to Real Problem," *Dallas Morning News*, 6/30/1999.)

(2) diligent (appearing . . . only when the boss is watching) *n.*: **eyeservice**. See *work*

dilute (as in deprive of strength) *v.t.*: **geld**. See *weaken*

dim (as in dark, misty, or gloomy) *adj.*: **caliginous**. See *dark*

(2) dim (as in dark or in the dark) *adj., adv.*: **darkling**. See *dark*

diminish (as in deprive of strength) *v.t.*: **geld**. See *weaken*

   (2) diminish (as in to deal with or treat inadequately or neglectfully) *v.t.*: **scant**. See *slight*

   (3) diminish *v.t.*: **minify**. See *minimize*

diminutive (person) *n.*: **homunculus**. See *midget*

   (2) diminutive (person) *n.*: **hop-o'-my-thumb**. See *midget*

   (3) diminutive *adj., n.*: **Lilliputian**. See *tiny*

   (4) diminutive *adj.*: **bantam**. See *tiny*

   (5) diminutive *adj.*: **minikin**. See *tiny*

dim-witted (as in slow to understand or perceive) *adj.*: **purblind**. See *obtuse*

   (2) dim-witted (esp. used of a person, as in . . . and confused) *adj.*: **addlepated**. See *confused*

   (3) dim-witted *adj.*: **gormless** [British]. See *unintelligent*

din *n.*: **bruit**. ❖ I believe that, to many, noise exaggerates—and, sadly, heightens—the experience of dining. . . . Thought is impossible. We are, as it were, poleaxed by the **bruit**. (It's the roar of the lion, remember, that freezes its victim.) (Alexander Theroux, "The Din of Dining Out," *Cosmopolitan*, 6/1/1996, p. 36.)

   (2) din (and confusion, esp. from simultaneous voices) *n.*: **babel**. See *noise*

   (3) din (as in hubbub) *n.*: **charivari**. See *hubbub*

dining (of or relating to . . . with others) *adj.*: **commensal**. ❖ A close examination of our everyday lives will reveal that they are permeated with rituals . . . such as how we greet each other, how we make introductions, how we conduct ourselves at **commensal** gatherings, and the like. . . . The structures of a shared meal can simultaneously be expressing sociologic, psychologic, and religious functions. (Joseph Keenan, "The Japanese Tea Ceremony and Stress Management," *Holistic Nursing Practice*, 1/1/1996, p. 30.)

   (2) dining (science of . . .) *n.*: **aristology**. ❖ At a glance, [the cookbook written by former baseball pitcher Catfish Hunter] wouldn't get him inducted into the Hot Stove League, but everybody's doing it these days, so why not a nice old pitcher? Way to go, Cat. . . . It does not pretend to be history, sociology, literature or, even, **aristology**. . . . He says he likes to eat and these are his favorite dishes. (Robert Sherill, "An Unsavory South/These Cookbooks Offer a Sadly 'Nonexpert' View of Southern Food," *St. Petersburg [FL] Times*, 10/11/1987.)

   (3) dining (art or science of good . . .) *n.*: **gastronomy**. See *eating*

   (4) dining (practice of . . . together) *n.*: **commensality**. See *eating*

diplomat (or ambassador who is fully authorized to represent a government) *n.*: **plenipotentiary**. [This word is also used as an adjective to describe being invested with such powers.] ❖ [U]ltimately, the Arab leaders respect raw power. [Outgoing British Prime Minster Tony] Blair will be arriving this time [as Middle East envoy], not as the leader of a second-rate power but as the **plenipotentiary** of the world's only superpower. No other envoy, not even some of the US's own ambassadors and secretaries of state, ha[s] had such implicit backing from the White House. (Anshel Pfeffer, "Four Reasons Why Blair Is the Perfect Envoy," *Jerusalem Post*, 6/27/2007.)

dipping (outward from the center in all directions, as if from a dome) *adj.*: **quaquaversal**. ❖ I was reminded in places of the many harrowing scenes in Ford's *The Good Soldier*, that casebook on love triangles. It is also about how we delude, unfairly accuse ourselves. Gillian quite convincingly loves both men, at least in the **quaquaversal** way she comes to see she does, and, though vain to a degree, she does examine her conscience. (Alexander Theroux, "Was It Something They Said?" *Washington Post*, 10/13/1991.)

dire (as in causing or portending death) *adj.*: **funest**. See *deadly*

direct (as in channel) *v.t.*: **canalize**. See *channel*

   (2) direct (as in give an order to) *v.t.*: **adjure**. See *order*

direction (relating to the giving of . . . , as in advice) *adj.*: **paraenetic** (*n.*: **paraenesis**). See *advice*

directive (as in decree) *n*.: **diktat**. See *decree*

director (as in manager or overseer) *n*.: **gerent**. See *manager*

dirge *n*.: **threnody**. See *requiem*

dirt (abnormal fear of) *n*.: **mysophobia**. See *fear*

dirty (to make . . .) *v.t.*: **begrime**. ❖ All told, diesel emissions—from tailpipes, at ground level —expose New Yorkers to the risks of lung cancer, pneumonia, pleurisy, asthma, bronchitis, chronic coughs and mutant genes. Plus they smell bad and **begrime** the city's buildings. (Joanna D. Underwood, "New York Forum About Transit—The TA's Route to Pollution," *Newsday*, 8/6/1993.)

(2) dirty (full of . . . or impure matter) *adj*.: **feculent**. See *filthy*

(3) dirty (as in sooty) *adj*.: **fuliginous**. See *sooty*

(4) dirty (as in unkempt or slovenly) *adj*.: **frowzy**. See *messy*

(5) dirty (or impure) *adj., v.t.*: **maculate**. See *impure*

(6) dirty (to make . . .) *v.t.*: **besmirch**. See *tarnish*

dirty talk (or swearing to relieve tension) *n*.: **lalochezia**. See *swearing*

disabled (as in out of action) *adj., adv*.: **hors de combat** [French]. ❖ [Fashion designer] Oscar de la Renta was **hors de combat** for a moment there after a model accidentally stabbed him with her 5-foot stiletto heel on a fashion runway. Ah, the perils of haute couture! (Liz Smith, "How Oscar Partied," *Newsday*, 3/26/1998.)

disadvantage (or drawback) *n*.: **disamenity**. [This word is used primarily with respect to real estate issues and land use.] ❖ Highly educated, professional workers—the economic gold of these times—gravitate to places with high quality of life, parks and recreation included. Indeed, firms in less attractive places have to struggle with "**disamenity** compensation"—premium pay to draw talent. (Neil Pierce, "Green Alchemy," *Nation's Cities Weekly*, 5/29/2006.)

disaffirmance (as in retraction) *n*.: **palinode**. See *retraction*

disagree (with, as in oppose, a statement, opinion, or action) *v.t.*: **oppugn**. See *oppose*

disagreeable (as in bothersome) *adj*.: **pestiferous**. See *bothersome*

(2) disagreeable (as in grouchy person) *n*.: **crosspatch**. See *grouch*

(3) disagreeable (as in irritable) *adj*.: **liverish**. See *irritable*

(4) disagreeable (as in irritable) *adj*.: **shirty**. See *irritable*

(5) disagreeable (as in irritable) *adj*.: **waspish**. See irritable

(6) disagreeable (as in repellent or irritating) *adj*.: **rebarbative**. See *repellent*

(7) disagreeable (as in surly) *adj*.: **atrabilious**. See *surly*

(8) disagreeable (as in surly) *adj*.: **bilious**. See *surly*

disagreeing (esp. with majority view) *adj*.: **dissentient**. See *dissentient*

disagreement (as in difference of opinion) *n*.: **divarication**. ❖ The *Jerusalem Post* report said Israeli Prime Minister Ehud Olmert had initially barred [Israeli Foreign Minister Tzipi Livni from meeting with UN Secretary-General Kofi Annan in New York], which was considered as a result of the **divarication** between the two in military operations in Lebanon. Livni had opposed the decision to bomb Hezbollah's headquarters in Beirut at the start of the war, the report said. (Xinhua News Agency [China], "Israeli FM to Meet with Annan on Lebanon Following Ceasefire," 8/15/2006.)

(2) disagreement (characterized by internal . . .) *adj*.: **factious**. See *dispute*

(3) disagreement (heated . . . or friction between groups) *n*.: **ruction**. See *dissension*

(4) disagreement (relating to or attempting to create . . . , separation or a breach of union, esp. within the Christian church) *adj*.: **schismatic**. See *disunity*

disappear *v.t.*: **evanesce**. ❖ It used to be that people had to be famous for a reasonably long time before anyone would want to read a book by them. But in the go-go '90s, the period between appearing on TV and getting a fat book deal is **evanescing**. (Belinda Luscombe, People, *Time*, 2/10/1997, p. 85.)

(2) disappear (as if by melting away) *v.i.*: **deliquesce**. See *melt*

(3) disappear (as in a departure that is unannounced, abrupt, secret, or unceremonious) *n.*: **French leave** (or **French Leave**). See *departure*

disappearance (as in state of being absent from view, lost to notice, or concealed) *n.*: **occultation**. ❖ Is there, moreover, a single underlying viewpoint in these texts [Genesis and Samuel]? . . . [I]n the former God walks the earth and looks like a man, whereas in the latter He is almost entirely absent from the human stage. Friedman invokes his thesis of the progressive **occultation** of God . . . to explain the disparity, but it seems a bit implausible that a single author would have shifted grounds so drastically. (Robert Alter, "The Genius of J," *New York Times*, 11/15/1998.)

disappearing (as in lasting only briefly) *adj.*: **evanescent**. See *transient*

disappointed (as in dejected) *adj.*: **chapfallen**. See *dejected*

disappointment *n.*: **Apples of Sodom** [This term derives from a fruit, described by ancient writers, that is externally appealing but dissolves into smoke and ashes when plucked; also referred to as "Dead Sea fruit."] ❖ Old [Alfa Romeos] often used to be like the **Apples of Sodom**, tragic disappointments, but quality has now radically improved. (Stephen Bayley, "A Juliet for Alfa Romeos," *Daily Telegraph* [London], 10/16/2004.)

(2) disappointment *n.*: **Dead Sea fruit.** [This term derives from a fruit, described by ancient writers, that is externally appealing but dissolves into smoke and ashes when plucked.] ❖ Harold Macmillan, whose elevation [to British prime minister] was achieved by a brutality, cunning and greed for power normally met only in conclaves of Mafia capi, said, after

he had climbed the greasy pole and pushed all his rivals off . . . that the whole thing was **Dead Sea fruit**. Even he, who had revelled in the post more than any other prime minister since Disraeli, found that the glittering prizes were made not of diamonds, nor even convincing paste, but glass. (Bernard Levin, "Frittering Away Their Lives for a Little Sham Authority," *Times* [London], 11/20/1990.)

(3) disappointment (as in anticlimax) *n.*: **bathos**. See *anticlimax*

disapproval (as in criticism) *n.*: **animadversion** (*v.t.*: **animadvert**). See *criticism*

(2) disapproval (as in denunciation) *n.*: **commination**. See *denunciation*

(3) disapproval (develop a strong . . . of) *n.*: **scunner** (esp. as in "take a scunner") [British]. See *dislike*

(4) disapproval (mania for . . . , as in criticism, of others) *n.*: **cacoëthes carpendi** [Latin]. See *faultfinding*

(5) disapproval (as in receiving severe . . .) *idiom*: **(catching) unshirted hell**. See *criticism*

disapprove (as in criticize, sharply) *v.t.*: **scarify**. See *criticize*

(2) disapprove (of, as in scold or rebuke) *v.t.*: **objurgate**. See *criticize*

(3) disapprove (or reject or condemn) *v.t., n.*: **discountenance**. See *reject*

disapproving (as in faultfinding) *adj.*: **captious**. See *faultfinding*

(2) disapproving (as in faultfinding, person) *n.*: **smellfungus**. See *faultfinder*

(3) disapproving *adj.*: **dyslogistic**. See *uncomplimentary*.

disarray (in a state of . . . or confusion) *idiom*: **at sixes and sevens**. [There are various theories for where this phrase comes from, including the Bible, Geoffrey Chaucer, and a dice game called Hazard.] ❖ Republican candidates for this autumn's elections speak with a single voice. Defend the tax cut; pump up spending on the war on terror; praise the president; and—sotto voce—question the patriotism of anyone who criticises him. The Democrats, by contrast, are **at sixes and sevens** over everything from who should lead them to what they should stand for. (*Economist*, "Don't Drop the Dead Donkey," 4/13/2002.)

(2) disarray *n., adj.*: **hugger-mugger**. See *confusion*

disarrayed *adj., adv.*: **higgledy-piggledy**. See *haphazard*

disaster (as in combination of events or circumstances that creates a crisis) *n.*: **conjuncture**. See *crisis*

(2) disaster (as in episode having the quality of a nightmare) *n.*: **Walpurgis Night**. See *nightmare*

(3) disaster (one who is always predicting . . .) *n.*: **catastrophist**. See *pessimist*

disastrous (as in causing or portending death) *adj.*: **funest**. See *deadly*

disavow (esp. responsibility or duty) *v.t.*: **abnegate**. See *renounce*

(2) disavow *v.t.*: **abjure**. See *renounce*

disavowal (as in retraction) *n.*: **palinode**. See *retraction*

disbeliever (as in one with no faith or religion) *n., adj.*: **nullifidian**. See *nonbeliever*

discard (as in shed, a skin or covering) *v.t., v.i.*: **exuviate**. See *shed*

discern *v.t.*: **descry**. See *perceive*

discernible (barely . . .) *adj.*: **liminal**. See *invisible*

discerning (as in having a penetrating quality) *adj.*: **gimlet** (esp. as in "gimlet eye"). See *penetrating*

(2) discerning (as in wise) *adj.*: **sapient**. See *wise*

(3) discerning *adj.*: **perspicacious**. See *astute*

discernment *n.*: **aperçu** [French]. See *insight*

discharge (contents, as if flowing water) *v.i.*: **disembogue**. [Playwright Greg Motton offers an alternative version of the last day of the Conservative Party conference.] ❖ Dissatisfied man of denigrated intelligence in lower hall: "Oi Baby! what abaht this bloomin' country then? It's overrun with foreigners." . . . The royal guards swoop down and beat the man

senseless. They squeeze him into Baby Ubu's gauntlet and urge the [baby] to **disembogue** upon him, a request to which he readily complies. (Greg Motton, "Baby Ubu: An Absurd Play with Real Lives," *Guardian* [London], 10/13/1992.)

(2) discharge (as in dismiss, from a position of command or authority—often military—and especially for disciplinary reasons) *v.t.*: **cashier**. See *dismiss*

(3) discharge (as in outflow) *n.*: **efflux**. See *outflow*

(4) discharge (as in termination) *n.*: **quietus**. See *termination*

(5) discharge (waste from the body) *v.t.*: **egest**. See *excrete*

(6) discharge (as in force out or cause to escape from proper channels, esp. a liquid or something that flows) *v.t., v.i.*: **extravasate**. See *exude*

disciple (strong . . . of a cause, religion, or activity) *n.*: **votary**. See *supporter*

(2) disciple *adj.*: **acolyte**. See *follower*

disciplinarian (strict . . .) *n.*: **martinet**. ❖ Certainly, Wolfgang Schmidt did not fit the mold of the model East German sports hero—sober, stoic, obedient. In recent years he had sometimes seemed to go out of his way to irritate the **martinets** and party hardliners who ran [the East German athletic governing body]. He had flouted the rules that forbade him to befriend athletes from the West. (William Oscar Johnson, "Wolfgang Schmidt, the Discus Thrower," *Sports Illustrated*, 1/21/1991, p. 50.)

discipline (as in marked by simplicity, frugality, self-restraint, and/or . . .) *adj.*: **Lacedaemonian**. See *spartan*

disciplined (strictly . . .) *adj.*: **monastic**. See *strict*

disclaim (esp. responsibility or duty) *v.t.*: **abnegate**.

(2) disclaim *v.t.*: **abjure**. See *renounce*

disclose (one's thoughts or feelings) *v.t., v.i.*: **unbosom**. See *confide*

(2) disclose *v.t.*: **disinter**. ❖ Most mortifying of all to Rockefeller, [reporter Ida] Tarbell

disinterred his oldest and deepest shame: [his father] Big Bill's rape indictment in Moravia in the late 1840's. (Ron Chernow, *Titan*, Random House [1998], p. 459.)

discomfort (as in bother or inconvenience) *v.t.*: **incommode**. See *inconvenience*

disconcert *v.t.*: **discomfit**. ❖ The agonies he must have suffered in those terrible asylum nights have granted us all a benefit. He was mad, and for that, we have reason to be glad. A truly savage irony, on which it is **discomfiting** to dwell. (Simon Winchester, *The Professor and the Madman*, HarperCollins [1998], p. 214.)

disconnected (talk or act in a . . . or incoherent fashion) *v.i.*: **maunder**. See *ramble*

disconnection (as in a fallacious argument where one proves or disproves a point that is not at issue) *n.*: **ignoratio elenchi** [Latin]. See *irrelevancy*

(2) disconnection (into two parts, esp. by tearing apart or violent separation) *n.*: **diremption**. See *separation*

discontent (to fret or complain, including as a result of . . .) *v.i.*: **repine**. See *complain*

discontentment (as in disappointment) *n.* **Apples of Sodom**. See *disappointment*

(2) discontentment (as in disappointment) *n.*: **Dead Sea fruit**. See *disappointment*

discontinuance (state of inactivity or . . .) *n.*: **desuetude**. See *disuse*

discontinuation (as in termination) *n.*: **quietus**. See *termination*

discontinue (temporarily . . . esp. a session of Parliament) *v.t.*: **prorogue**. ❖ While the government introduced an Ontarians with Disabilities Act last November, the proposed legislation died on the order paper in December, when the Legislature **prorogued**. . . . Citizenship Minister Isabel Bassett has promised to reintroduce the act when the Legislature resumes this spring. (Caroline Mallan, "Group Seeks Barrier-Free Election Polls," *Toronto Star*, 4/15/1999.)

discord (as in difference of opinion) *n.*: **divarication**. See *disagreement*

(2) discord (as in heated disagreement or friction between groups) *n.*: **ruction**. See *dissension*

(3) discord (of or relating to . . . within a group or country) *adj.*: **internecine**. See *dissension*

(4) discord (relating to or attempting to create . . . , separation or a breach of union, esp. within the Christian church) *adj.*: **schismatic**. See *disunity*

discordant (or contrary) *adj.*: **absonant**. ❖ [The *New York Times* states] that the nation's economic tides move [inversely to] Federal taxation and [directly with] Federal expenditures. There are substantial indications that . . . the use of this theory in determining policy will produce outcomes for Federal finances that are incongruous, **absonant**, extravagant and preposterous. (Ward Harrington, "Economic Theories Allergic to Practice," *New York Times*, 2/14/1983.)

(2) discordant (sounds) *adj.*: **scrannel**. See *cacophonous*

discount (as in to deal with or treat inadequately or neglectfully) *v.t.*: **scant**. See *slight*

discouraged (as in dejected) *adj.*: **chapfallen**. See *dejected*

(2) discouraged (chronically . . . , as in depressed) *adj., n.*: **dysthymic**. See *depressed*

discourse (about in a scholarly manner, often used in a derogatory fashion) *v.i.*: **lucubrate**. [Occasionally defined as limited to writing only, but in actual usage it refers to writing or speech.] ❖ The Westminster world endlessly **lucubrates** on the horrors of a politics without vision, of a leader without a streak of grandeur, of the mesmerising bitterness at large in the Conservative Party. But even in politics, talk can sometimes be taken for what it is: no more than talk. (Hugo Young, Commentary: "It Will Be Surprising If John Major Doesn't Face a Leadership Challenge After Three Years," *Guardian* [London], 4/8/1993.)

(2) discourse (as in formal analysis or discussion of a subject) *n.*: **disquisition**. [A disquisition tends to be a discussion that is more exploratory or investigative than one that lends itself to a definitive answer. It can be oral or written.] ❖ It was a solemn judicial **disquisition** on the true meaning and intent of the term "horse's ass." As in whether Tim Eyman, the anti-tax initiative guru, is or is not one. . . . Thurston County Superior Court Judge Gary Tabor heard arguments over the proper ballot summary for a proposed Initiative 831, proclaiming Eyman to be a horse's ass. The issue was whether the summary should contain that phrase, as the initiative does, or an almost comically bland substitute drafted by the state Attorney General's Office. (Neil Modie, "High-Minded Discussion Mulls Lowbrow Initiative on Eyman," *Seattle Post-Intelligencer*, 2/14/2003.)

(3) discourse *v.i., n.*: **descant**. See *talk*

discover (or find through careful or skillful examination or investigation) *v.t.*: **expiscate**. ❖ There are many vestiges of authors not in his library whom [satirist Jonathan] Swift can be shown to have read. From his works one can **expiscate** some 464 authors or anonymous texts, of whom some loom large while others are merely represented by a marginal note. (Dirk Friedrich Passmann, *The Library and Reading of Jonathan Swift: A Bio-bibliographical Handbook*, Peter Lang Publishing [2004], p. xii.)

(2) discover (as in figure out) *v.t.*: **suss** (usually with "out"; slang). See *figure out*

(3) discover (by careful observation or scrutiny) *v.t.*: **descry**. See *perceive*

(4) discover (wonderful to . . . , as in behold) *adv.*: **mirabile visu** [Latin]. See *behold*

discovery (a lucky . . . , as in find) *n.*: **trouvaille** [French]. See *find*

(2) discovery (moment of . . . , often the point in the plot at which the protagonist recognizes his or her or some other character's true identity or discovers the true nature of his or her own situation) *n.*: **anagnorisis**. See *recognition*

(3) discovery (of fortunate things by accident) *n.*: **serendipity** (*adj.*: **serendipitous**). See *fortuitous*

discredit (being subject to . . . , esp. public) *n.*: **obloquy**. See *abuse*

(2) discredit (by making false or malicious statements) *v.t.*: **calumniate**. See *malign*

(3) discredit (by making false statements) *v.t.*: **traduce**. See *malign*

discrepancy (in terms or ideas) *n.*: **antilogy**. See *contradiction*

discretion (as in moderation) *n.*: **sophrosyne**. See *moderation*

discretionary (as in optional) *adj.*: **facultative**. See *optional*

discriminating (as in discerning and astute) *adj.*: **perspicacious**. See *astute*

discrimination (against homosexuals) *n.*: **heterosexism**. See *homosexuals*

discriminatory (unjustly . . . in matters of distinguishing between groups) *adj.*: **invidious**. ❖ Of course only a lunatic would believe that the predominance of black males on NBA rosters was a product of **invidious** discrimination against white males, let alone against, say, Asian females. (Paul Campos, "The Lies We Tell About Diversity," *Denver Rocky Mountain News*, 10/24/2000.)

discuss (a subject at length in speech or writing) *v.i.*: **expatiate**. See *expound*

(2) discuss (casually) *n.*: **chinwag** [slang]. See *chat*

(3) discuss (casually) *v.i.*: **confabulate**. See *chat*

(4) discuss (esp. at length) *v.i., n.*: **descant**. See *talk*

(5) discuss (esp. in a long-winded or pompous manner) *v.i.*: **bloviate**. See *speak*

(6) discuss (in a scholarly manner, often used in a derogatory fashion) *v.i.*: **lucubrate**. See *discourse*

discussion *n.*: **interlocution**. ❖ [The movie *Chasing Amy* is] a boy-meets-lesbian, boy-loses-lesbian romantic comedy loaded with wit, charm, and unbelievably filthy dialogue, including an epic **interlocution** on the perils of oral sex. (Benjamin Svetkey, News & Notes/Behind the Scenes: "Getting the Girl: *Clerks* Creator Kevin Smith Comes Out from Behind the Counter with *Amy,*" *Entertainment Weekly,* 4/11/1997, p. 25.)

(2) discussion (esp. at the start of negotiations) *n.:* **pourparler** [French]. ❖ [The Swiss publishers trying to sign up French authors] calculated how they could undercut the Parisian publishers by shaving costs and profits and then set out to steal the best authors. . . . They entered into **pourparlers** with d'Alembert, Raynal, Beaumarchais, Mably, Marmontel, and Morellet. They even approached Benjamin Franklin with a scheme to peddle French books in the New World. (Robert Darnton, "The Forgotten Middlemen," The Perils of Publishing, Part 4, *New Republic,* 9/15/1986.)

(3) discussion (esp. with an enemy or adversary) *n., v.t.:* **parley**. ❖ America cannot deal with [its potential enemies] all on its own . . . especially as new threats—cyberwar, biological war, economic instability, cults and disease—now jostle with the more familiar ones of ethnic hatred and religious rivalry. [The instruments to deal with such threats] range from diplomatic **parley** through economic sanctions to military support to armed attack. (*Seattle Post-Intelligencer,* editorial, "Dubya's World," 1/11/2001.)

(4) discussion (as in formal analysis or . . . of a subject) *n.:* **disquisition**. See *discourse*

(5) discussion (about a philosophical or theological issue) *n.:* **quodlibet**. See *debate*

(6) discussion (between three people) *n.:* **trialogue**. See *conversation*

(7) discussion (between two people) *n.:* **duologue**. See *conversation*

(8) discussion (esp. about art or literature) *n.:* **conversazione** [Italian]. See *conversation*

(9) discussion (idle . . .) *n.:* **palaver**. See *small talk*

(10) discussion (in which neither side hears or understands or pays attention to the other) *n.:* **dialogue de sourds** [French]. See *dialogue*

(11) discussion (informal . . .) *n.:* **causerie**. See *chat*

(12) discussion (light or playful back and forth . . .) *n.:* **badinage**. See *banter*

(13) discussion (of a subject in a light-hearted way, as in chitchat) *n.:* **persiflage**. See *chitchat*

(14) discussion (one skilled at dinner . . .) *n.:* **deipnosophist**. See *conversation*

(15) discussion (spec. a final effort made by architectural students to complete a solution to a problem within an allotted time, but sometimes used to refer to any kind of workshop or brainstorming session). *n.:* **charette** (or **charrette**). See *workshop*

disdain *n.:* **misprision** (to hold in . . .) *v.t.:* **misprize**. ❖ The Government does, of course, support the countryside in theory. [Prime Minister Blair has said that] there is a great "tourism industry" [*sic*] out there that needs our support. That, however, is at the root of Labour's **misprision** of rural matters. To them, it is a theme park, where "their people" play at weekends. What they fail to understand is that the theme park is only kept open by the people who farm it and the millions who live in it and sustain it. (Simon Heffer, "This Election Is Between Town and Country: Simon Heffer Says That Labour's Ignorance of Rural Affairs Has Split Britain," *Sunday Telegraph* [London], 5/6/2001.)

(2) disdain *v.t.:* **contemn**. See *scorn*

disdainful (as in haughty or condescending) *adj.:* **toplofty**. See *haughty*

(2) disdainful (as in haughty) *adj.:* **fastuous**. See *haughty*

(3) disdainful (as in lordly) *adj.:* **seigneurial**. See *lordly*

(4) disdainful (toward another, often by being insulting or through humiliation) *adj.:* **contumelious**. See *contemptuous*

disease (carrier) *n.:* **vector**. ❖ Having a pesky new mosquito is bad enough, but the real danger lies in the tiger mosquito's ability to carry some truly awful viral diseases, including dengue and yellow fever. "The tiger mosquito is a competent **vector** for both viruses," as well as others. (Robert Cooke, "A Plague on All Our Houses," *Popular Science,* 1/1/1996, p. 50.)

(2) disease (caused by a physician) *adj.*: **iatrogenic**. ❖ While medical technology and knowledge of diseases have leapt forward over the past two decades, the rate of **iatrogenic** diseases has remained the same—especially from prescribed drugs. (*Medical Post*, "Hospital Deaths Linked to Drug Errors," 2/9/1999, p. 8.)

(3) disease (causing) *adj.*: **morbific**. ❖ June 7, 1998: CNN airs [a false story that U.S. forces dropped lethal nerve gas in Laos in 1970]. The Tailwind reporting, in fact, was a chain reaction of three firecrackers sequenced to trigger a mega-explosion [i.e., overzealous producers, unsupervised reporters, and ratings pressure]. Taken alone, each could have been containable [and] could have spared CNN . . . the misfortune it suffered. But all three together created a **morbific** cocktail. (Neil Hickey, "Ten Mistakes That Led to the Great CNN/*Time* Fiasco," *Columbia Journalism Review*, 9/1/1998).

(4) disease (causing) *adj.*: **pathogenic**. ❖ There is growing evidence that preventing diseases in infancy may be a mixed blessing. Can intervening in an illness sometimes be worse than doing nothing at all? . . . It is, of course, well known that preventing or treating an infectious disease can have profound effects on the **pathogenic** organism that causes it. (*Economist*, "Plagued by Cures," 11/22/1997.)

(5) disease (fear of) *n.*: **nosophobia**. ❖ What this country needs right now is a national psychiatrist to determine why Americans are discarding wholesome food in a mindless effort to reduce the risk of cancer. It's a good bet that the professional 50-state diagnosis would be acute **nosophobia**. (Elizabeth M. Whelan, "A Morbid Fear of Illness Makes America Trash Good Food and Common Sense," *Los Angeles Times*, 3/20/1989.)

(6) disease (showing no evidence of) *n.*: **asymptomatic**. ❖ Some HIV-positive people have remained **asymptomatic** for extensive periods. Moreover, several studies indicate that exercise and diet can help an individual remain **asymptomatic**. (Jack McCallum,

"There He Stood, 24 Feet from the Basket," *Sports Illustrated*, 2/17/1992, p. 18.)

(7) disease (which is widespread) *n.*: **pandemic**. ❖ Our world has been swept by three influenza **pandemics** in this century. The most devastating by far was the so-called Spanish flu in 1918: virtually every person on Earth was infected, and an estimated 30 million died, many more than those killed in World War I. (Patricia Gadsby, "There Was a Fear of Flu," *Discover* 1/1/1999.)

(8) disease (of or relating to a . . . developed by a patient while in a hospital) *adj.*: **nosocomial**. See *hospital*

(9) disease (of a . . . that has no known cause) *adj.*: **idiopathic** (*n.*: **idiopathy**). See *illness*

(10) disease (early sign of . . .) *n.*: **prodrome**. See *symptom*

disfavor (or reject or disapprove) *v.t., n.*: **discountenance**. See *reject*

disgrace (as in the destroying of one's reputation) *n.*: **famicide**. See *defamation*

(2) disgrace (being subject to . . . , esp. public) *n.*: **obloquy**. See *abuse*

(3) disgrace (by making false statements) *v.t.*: **traduce**. See *malign*

(4) disgrace (to one's reputation) *n.*: **blot (or stain) on one's escutcheon** *idiom*. See *dishonor*

disgraceful (as in indecent) *adj.*: **ostrobogulous**. See *indecent*

(2) disgraceful *adj.*: **opprobrious** (*n.*: **opprobrium**). See *contemptuous*

disguise (or mask) *n., v.t.*: **vizard**. ❖ In the old days it was the baddies who hid their faces. Now it's just as likely to be the good guys in disguise. But why this need for anonymity? And why do celebrities such as [Jacqueline Onassis and Princess Diana] feel the need to cover up? Henry Porter [writes] on the transformation of the **vizard**, from executioner's helm to badge of courage to fashion accessory. (*Guardian* [London], "Going Behind the Mask," 6/10/1996.)

(2) disguise (as in something that is impressive-looking on the outside but which hides or covers up undesirable conditions or facts) *n*.: **Potemkin village**. See *facade*

disgust (develop a . . . about) *n*.: **scunner** (esp. as in "take a scunner") [British]. See *dislike*

disgusting *adj*.: **ugsome**. See *loathsome*

disharmony (relating to or attempting to create . . . , separation, or a breach of union, esp. within the Christian church) *adj*.: **schismatic**. See *disunity*

disheartened *adj*.: **chapfallen**. See *dejected*

disheveled (or bloated in appearance) *adj*.: **blowsy** (or **blowzy**). "I'd rather stay home and watch the soaps," a big, **blowsy** woman in curlers said, and they all laughed. (Joe Klein, *Primary Colors*, Random House [1996], p. 160.)

(2) disheveled *adj*.: **frowzy**. See *messy*

dishonest *adj*.: **mendacious**. ❖ Clinton continues to injure himself with optional nonsense like his bragging about his agricultural knowledge. Voters know nonsense when they hear it. And they may be concluding that although Clinton is not consciously **mendacious** when he says things such as he said in Iowa, he thinks that whatever makes him feel good when he blurts it out must be true. (George Will, "Clinton Attempts to Reap Farm Vote," *St. Louis Post-Dispatch*, 5/4/1995.)

(2) dishonest (as in crafty) *adj*.: **jesuitical** (sometimes cap.). See *crafty*

(3) dishonest (as in unscrupulous) *adj*.: **jackleg**. See *unscrupulous*

(4) dishonest (characterized by . . . and cunning conduct, esp. in regard to the pursuit and maintenance of political or other power) *adj*.: **Machiavellian**. See *deceitful*

(5) dishonest (conduct) *n*.: **skullduggery**. See *deceitfulness*

(6) dishonest (group of . . . politicians) *n*.: **plunderbund**. See *corrupt*

(7) dishonest (person or scoundrel) *n*.: **blackguard**. See *scoundrel*

(8) dishonest (person, spec. one who accepts bribes) *n*.: **boodler**. See *corrupt*

(9) dishonest (politician) *n*.: **highbinder**. See *corrupt*

(10) dishonest (scheming or trickery) *n*.: **jiggery-pokery**. See *trickery*

dishonesty *n*.: **improbity**. ❖ Governor Ryan [commissioned a report that] examined how driver's license programs are run in Illinois. . . . The report describes a too-trusting attitude for validating an applicant's identity and residence, a situation that ripens the potential for **improbity**. (*Chicago Sun-Times*, "Good Start, but More Is Needed," 11/30/2000.)

(2) dishonesty (spec. an intentional omission of something, so as to mislead) *n*.: **elision**. See *omission*

(3) dishonesty *n*.: **knavery**. See *corruption*

dishonor (to one's reputation) *n*.: **blot (or stain) on one's escutcheon** *idiom*. ❖ Women fleeing bondage to fathers, husbands, or male relatives are denied eligibility for asylum in the United States despite the moral abomination that their plights present. This **stain on** the nation's **escutcheon** should be removed. Holding females in servitude is every bit as morally repugnant as are the outrages that qualify for asylum. (Watson, "A Stain on Our Asylum Law?" *Washington Times*, 6/8/2003.)

(2) dishonor (as in insult another's dignity) *n*.: **lese majesty**. See *insult*

(3) dishonor (as in the destroying of one's reputation) *n*.: **famicide**. See *defamation*

dishonorable (and unprincipled person) *n*.: **reprobate**. See *unprincipled*

(2) dishonorable (as in shameful) *adj*.: **opprobrious** (*n*.: **opprobrium**). See *contemptuous*

dishwasher (at a hotel or restaurant) *n*.: **plongeur** [French]. ❖ [At the Green Room Restaurant,] pans sizzle on the burners, bread rolls appear from ovens, salads whisk from fridge to plate, desserts magically materialise from nowhere. The flick of a wrist and plates levitate for that short journey to the table, where the magic begins for diners. The **plongeur** takes the used pans, swiftly washes and dries them for the next shift and the whole thing starts again. (Geoff Laws, "Schedule in a Stop at the

Green Room," *Journal* [Newcastle, England], 2/18/2005.)

disillusionment (as in disappointment) *n.*: **Apples of Sodom**. See *disappointment*

(2) disillusionment (as in disappointment) *n.*: **Dead Sea fruit**. See *disappointment*

disinclination *n.*: **nolition**. See *unwillingness*

disingenuous (as in false or insincere showing of naive or simplistic behavior) *adj.*: **faux-naïf** [French]. See *naive*

(2) disingenuous (as in hypocritical) *adj.*: **Janus-faced**. See *two-faced*

disintegrate (tending to . . . or break up) *adj.*: **fissiparous**. See *break up*

(2) disintegrate *v.i.*: **molder**. See *crumble*

disinterest (sexual . . .) *n.*: **anaphrodisia**. See *sex*

disinterested (as in neutral) *adj.*: **adiaphorous**. See *neutral*

disinterestedness (esp. on matters of politics or religion) *n.*: **Laodiceanism**. See *indifference*

disjunction (into two parts, esp. by tearing apart or violent separation) *n.*: **diremption**. See *separation*

dislike (strong . . .) *n.*: **scunner** (esp. as in "take a scunner") [British]. ❖ [M]ost recent evidence suggests that the great British public has at last taken a **scunner** [to the proposed British lottery]. For although most people are happy enough to have a flutter on the Lottery, they don't like the scale of the profits being made by the contractors who run it, and have been disappointed by how little of their ticket money is reaching charities. (Ian Aitken, "Chocolate-Bar Politics," *New Statesman & Society*, 6/9/1995, p. 12.)

(2) dislike (intense . . . , such as toward an enemy) *n.*: **enmity**. See *hatred*

(3) dislike (of children) *n.*: **misopedia**. See *children*

(4) dislike (of strangers or foreigners) *n.*: **xenophobia**. See *distrust*

(5) dislike (person who has . . . for all people) *n.*: **misanthrope**. See *hatred*

(6) dislike (strongly . . .) *v.t.*: **execrate**. See *hate*

(7) dislike (strongly) *v.t.*: **misprize**. See *hate*

disliked (something that is . . . , dreaded, or to be avoided) *n.*: **bête noire** [French]. See *dreaded*

dislodge (as in unseat) *v.t.*: **unhorse**. See *unseat*

(2) dislodge (as in extract or pry or force out, whether from a place or position, or information) *v.t.*: **winkle** (usually used with *out*). See *extract*

disloyal (man married to . . . wife) *n.*: **cuckold** (*v.t.*: to make a . . . of). See *adulterous*

(2) disloyal (to a belief, duty, or cause) *adj.*: **recreant**. See *unfaithful*

(3) disloyal *adj.*: **perfidious**. See *unfaithful*

dismal (and dark and gloomy) *adj.*: **acherontic**. See *gloomy*

dismay (as in disappointment) *n.*: **Apples of Sodom**. See *disappointment*

dismiss (from a position of command or authority—often military—and especially for disciplinary reasons) *v.t.*: **cashier**. ❖ As the British and German troops approached . . . General Roche-Fermoy abandoned his command and did not return until [the Battle of Trenton] was over. . . . [Later] he managed to set fire to his quarters and revealed the entire American position just as the British approached. He was **cashiered** from the army. (David Fisher, *Washington's Crossing*, Oxford University Press [2004], p. 296.)

(2) dismiss (as in to deal with or treat inadequately or neglectfully) *v.t.*: **scant**. See *slight*

disobedient (as in resistant to control or authority) *adj.*: **refractory**. See *stubborn*

(2) disobedient (or contrary in a stubborn way) *adj.*: **froward**. See *contrary*

(3) disobedient *adj.*: **contumacious**. See *obstinate*

disorder (movement toward or degree of . . . in a system or society) *n.*: **entropy**. ❖ This basic tenet of modern physics, you may recall, maintains that the universe tends to move from order to disorder. But if this [new theory of] emerging science is right, then **entropy** may not be the final answer. (Suneel Ratan, Books & Ideas: "It's Not That Simple," *Fortune*, 3/8/1993, p.137.)

(2) disorder (and confusion) *n., adj.*: **hugger-mugger**. See *confusion*

(3) disorder (as in chaos) *n.*: **tohubuhu**. See *chaos*

(4) disorder (as in commotion) *n.*: **bobbery**. See *commotion*

(5) disorder (as in commotion) *n.*: **kerfuffle**. See *commotion*

(6) disorder (as in commotion) *n.*: **maelstrom**. See *commotion*

(7) disorder (as in confused or disarrayed mess) *n.*: **welter**. See *jumble*

(8) disorder (in a state of . . . or confusion) *idiom*: **at sixes and sevens**. See *disarray*

disorderly (in a . . . and hasty manner) *adv.*: **pell-mell**. ❖ [L]ike many of her neighbors, she has heard City Hall's promises of renewal before. They worry that the city has rushed **pell-mell** into demolition [of abandoned buildings in Philadelphia] without knowing what will rise upon the rubble. (Michael Powell, "Raze of Sunshine in Philadelphia? City Pins Renewal Hopes on Clearing Vast Areas of Blight, Seeking Development," *Washington Post*, 3/19/2002.)

(2) disorderly (as in haphazard) *adj., adv.*: **higgledy-piggledy**. See *haphazard*

(3) disorderly (as in unruly) *adj.*: **indocile**. See *unruly*

(4) disorderly (situation that is . . . or confused or complicated) *n.*: **mare's nest**. See *chaotic*

disorganization (and confusion) *n., adj.* **hugger-mugger**. See *confusion*

(2) disorganization (of a person or group as a result of lack of standards or values) *n.*: **anomie**. See *breakdown*

disorganized (situation that is . . . or chaotic or complicated) *n.*: **mare's nest**. See *chaotic*

(2) disorganized (talk or act in a . . . or incoherent fashion) *v.i.*: **maunder**. See *ramble*

(3) disorganized *adj., adv.*: **higgledy-piggledy**. See *haphazard*

disparage *v.t.*: **vilipend**. ❖ He began by yelling [at the mules] in a coarse, strident voice, "Arre! arre!" (Get up!) [He then] proceeded to **vilipend** the galloping beasts separately, beginning with the leader. He informed him, still in this wild, jerking scream, that he was a dog, that his mother's character was far from that of Caesar's wife. (John Hay, "Castilian Days: A Castle in the Air," *History of the World*, 1/1/1992.)

(2) disparage (by making false or malicious statements) *v.t.*: **calumniate**. See *malign*

(3) disparage (in a false way so as to humiliate or disgrace) *v.t.*: **traduce**. See *malign*

disparagement (as in disdain) *n.*: **misprision** (*v.t.*: **misprize**). See *disdain*

(2) disparagement (mania for . . . of others) *n.*: **cacoëthes carpendi** [Latin]. See *faultfinding*

disparaging (another, often by being insulting or through humiliation) *adj.*: **contumelious**. See *contemptuous*

(2) disparaging (as in faultfinding) *adj.*: **captious**. See *faultfinding*

(3) disparaging (as in faultfinding, person) *n.*: **smellfungus**. See *faultfinder*

(4) disparaging (language) *n.*: **vituperation** (*adj.*: **vituperative**). See *invective*

(5) disparaging (or expressing disapproval) *adj.*: **dyslogistic**. See *uncomplimentary*

disparate (as in not homogeneous) *adj.*: **heterogeneous** (*n.*: **heterogeneity**). See *dissimilar*

(2) disparate (as in things that do not mix together) *adj.*: **immiscible**. See *incompatible*

disperse (able to . . . freely in a given environment; used of species) *adj.*: **vagile**. See *move*

(2) disperse (as in branch out) *v.i.*: **ramify**. See *branch out*

dispersion (as in diversity) *n.*: **variegation** (*v.t.*: **variegate**). See *diversity*

dispirited *adj.*: **chapfallen**. See *dejected*

displace (esp. from one's accustomed environment) *v.t.*: **deracinate**. See *uproot*

displaced (of . . . people having lost class status) *adj.*: **lumpen**. ❖ The University of Phoenix is a for-profit [on-line] enterprise. . . . [A typical] faculty member is part time and earns only $2,000 a course, teaching from a standardized curriculum. Is Phoenix then an academic sweatshop where underpaid **lumpen** intellectuals slave for a pittance? No way. . . . Most of the profs hold down full-time jobs in the professions they teach. (Lisa Gubernick, "I Got My Degree Through E-mail," *Forbes*, 6/16/1997, p. 84.)

display (glass . . . case) *n*.: **vitrine**. See *showcase*

(2) display (violent . . . in which shame, degradation, or harm is inflicted on a person, often for the enjoyment of onlookers) *n*.: **Roman holiday**. See *spectacle*

disposition (of a person, people, or culture) *n*.: **ethos**. See *character*

dispossessed (of . . . people having lost class status) *adj*.: **lumpen**. See *displaced*

disprove (convincingly) *v.t*.: **confute**. See *refute*

disputable (as in controversial, opinion or person who holds one) *n*.: **polemic**. See *controversy*

disputatious *adj., n*.: **eristic**. See *debate*

dispute (characterized by internal . . .) *adj*.: **factious**. ❖ Before this switch from anti-government to pro-government, the most conspicuous feature of Democratic conventions was divisiveness. In the 1800s, for example, the Democrats were notoriously **factious** because their roots were Southern. . . . These factions made resolution of the slavery issue difficult and ultimately led to the party's division in 1860. (Thomas V. DiBacco, "Nothing Conventional About Democrats' History," *Washington Times*, 8/13/2000.)

(2) dispute (a statement, opinion, or action) *v.t*.: **oppugn**. See *oppose*

(3) dispute (about words) *n*.: **logomachy**. See *words*

(4) dispute (engaging in frequent and possibly specious . . .) *adj., n*.: **eristic**. See *specious* and *debate*

(5) dispute (minor . . . as in skirmish) *n*.: **velitation**. See *skirmish*

disputing (esp. majority view) *adj*.: **dissentient**. See *dissenting*

disregard (as in to deal with or treat inadequately or neglectfully) *v.t*.: **scant**. See *slight*

(2) disregard (intentionally) *v.t*.: **pretermit**. See *omit*

disregarding (or omitting or passing over) *n*.: **preterition**. See *omitting*

disrespect (as in disdain) *n*.: **misprision** (*v.t*.: **misprize**). See *disdain*

(2) disrespect (as in insult, which is clever or polite) *n*.: **asteism**. See *insult*

(3) disrespect (religious . . .) *n*.: **impiety** (*adj*.: **impious**). See *irreverence*

disrespectful (as in being presumptuous; venturing beyond one's province) *adj*.: **ultracrepidarian**. See *presumptuous*

dissatisfaction (as in disappointment) *n*.: **Apples of Sodom**. See *disappointment*

(2) dissatisfaction (as in disappointment) *n*.: **Dead Sea fruit**. See *disappointment*

dissect (as in analyze closely) *v.t*.: **anatomize**. See *analyze*

dissension (as in heated disagreement or friction between groups) *n*.: **ruction**. ❖ The OSP [Office of Special Plans] is the brainchild of Defense Secretary Donald Rumsfeld [to show] that the CIA had overlooked the threat posed [by Saddam Hussein and Iraq]. But its rise has caused massive **ructions** in the normally secretive world of intelligence gathering. . . . Former CIA officials are caustic about the OSP. Unreliable and politically motivated, they say it has undermined decades of work by the CIA's trained spies. (Paul Harris, "Iraq after Saddam: US Rivals Turn on Each Other as Weapons Search Draws a Blank," *Observer*, 5/11/2003.)

(2) dissension (of or relating to . . . within a group or country) *adj*.: **internecine**. ❖ In a dangerous new trend in the Muslim world—one that has already blossomed into brutal **internecine** violence—the most militant among these groups also look down on more moderate Islamic groups, such as the 70-year-old Muslim Brotherhood, that seek power through the ballot box. (Susan Sachs, "Roots of the Jihad," *Newsday*, 9/24/1996.)

dissent (as in difference of opinion) *n*.: **divarication**. See *disagreement*

(2) dissent (characterized by internal . . .) *adj*.: **factious**. See *dispute*

(3) dissent (from, as in oppose a statement, opinion, or action) *v.t.*: **oppugn**. See *oppose*

dissenter (orig. Catholics who did not follow Church of England) *n.*: **recusant**. ❖ Rehnquist, in his book, also expressed doubts about the validity of most of the articles of impeachment against [Republican President Andrew] Johnson. . . . The "**recusant** Republican senators" who defied their party and "tipped the balance in favor of Johnson" won praise from Rehnquist for putting principle above politics. (Gaylord Shaw, "Portrait of a Trial," *Newsday*, 1/5/1999.)

dissenting (esp. from majority view) *adj.*: **dissentient**. ❖ Politicised by chronic underfunding, [younger composers in Great Britain] can be dangerously critical of the status quo, so much so that serious contemporary music is often classified as **dissentient**. (Marc Bridle, "Unacknowledged Notation," *New Statesman & Society*, 4/12/1996, p. 32.)

dissertation (or discussion of a subject) *n.*: **disquisition**. See *discourse*

dissident (as in rebel) *n.*: **frondeur** [French]. See *rebel*

dissimilar (as in not homogeneous) *adj.*: **heterogeneous** (*n.*: **heterogeneity**). ❖ [T]he starting point for [the change to the euro] is that Europe currently has **heterogeneous** customers who largely buy **heterogeneous** products with different ingredients, labels and packages. Much else will need to converge before prices do. (*Economist*, "Survey: Borders and Barriers," 12/1/2001, p. 18.)

dissimilar (state or quality of being . . . from others) *n.*: **alterity**. See *different*

dissolute (morally . . .) *adj.*: **scrofulous**. See *depraved*

(2) dissolute (person) *n.*: **rakehell**. See *libertine*

dissolve (by melting away) *v.i.*: **deliquesce**. See *melt*

dissuade (as in argue against) *v.t.*: **expostulate**. See *object*

distant (or remote destination or goal) *n.*: **ultima Thule** [Latin; derives from Thule, thought by ancient geographers to be the northernmost point of the habitable world]. ❖ High in those mountains [of the Provençal Alps], Meailles, a remote, deserted and windblown depot, was the **ultima Thule** of my journey—about as far in style and spirit as you can get from the modern station at Paris' Charles de Gaulle Airport, where our trip had begun last March. (Karl Zimmerman, "France; Two Rail Ways, Swift and Scenic," *Los Angeles Times*, 6/23/2002.)

distaste (develop a strong . . . for) *n.*: **scunner** (esp. as in "take a scunner") [British]. See *dislike*

distasteful (as in repellent) *adj.*: **rebarbative**. See *repellent*

(2) distasteful (as in unpalatable) *adj.*: **brackish**. See *unpalatable*

distended (as in swollen) *adj.*: **dropsical**. See *swollen*

(2) distended (as in swollen, used often of body parts such as the penis) *adj.*: **tumescent**. See *swollen*

(3) distended *adj.*: **tumid**. See *swollen*

distinct (from, as in separable) *adj.*: **dissociable**. See *separable*

(2) distinct (state or quality of being . . . from others) *n.*: **alterity**. See *different*

distinction (marking a . . .) *adj.*: **diacritical**. See *distinguishing*

distinctive (shape or outline, often of a face) *adj.*: **lineament** (often **lineaments**). See *contour*

distinctness (as in that quality which makes one thing different from any other) *n.*: **haecceity** (or **haeccity**). See *individuality*

distinguished (as in select or excellent) *adj.*: **eximious**. See *excellent*

distinguish (as in differentiate) *v.t.*, *v.i.*: **secern**. See *differentiate*

distinguishing (between) *adj.*: **diacritical**. ❖ My husband's Eastern European surname ["Ode," pronounced OH-dee] is consistently mispronounced. Our sixth-grader no longer wants to call attention to himself by correcting people, while our third-grader has taken matters in the opposite direction by reverting to the Old World pronunciation, complete with **diacritical** embellishments. (Kim Ode, "You Can Call Me Anything, but . . . Don't Ever Think That a Name Doesn't Influence Who We Are, How We Got There," *Minneapolis Star Tribune*, 5/21/2000.)

(2) distinguishing (shape or outline, often of a face) *adj.*: **lineament** (often **lineaments**). See *contour*

distortion (of words or of language) *n.*: **verbicide**. ❖ One manager, Rep. Steve Buyer of Indiana, said the president [Clinton] really is guilty of **verbicide** for his linguistic gymnastics and personal definitions. "He murdered the plain-spoken English language," Mr. Buyer said. (Frank J. Murray, "Prosecutors Demand Removal, Not Censure; Managers End Round of Arguments," *Washington Times*, 1/17/1999.)

(2) distortion (spec. an intentional omission of something, so as to mislead) *n.*: **elision**. See *omission*

distracted (esp. because of worries or fears) *adj.*: **distrait**. ❖ As it looks to the start of the 21st century [France] is **distrait** and irresolute. At home, the nation is racked by a 12.3% unemployment rate; a growing gap between rich and poor; festering urban problems; and a tide of social unrest that has seen tens of thousands of protesting students, workers, homeless and AIDS activists take to the streets over the past few weeks. (Thomas Sancton, France: "If at First You Don't Succeed; Jacques Chirac Has Come from Behind to Lead the Race for the Presidency, but Polls Suggest It Will Be a Fight to the Finish," *Time* International, 4/24/1995, p. 46.)

distracting (as in bothersome) *adj.*: **pestiferous**. See *bothersome*

distress (state of extreme . . .) *n.*: **swivet** (as in "in a swivet") *informal*. ❖ Gosh, silly us, getting in a **swivet** over war and peace. The president is on vacation! He's giving interviews to *Runner's World*, not *Meet the Press*. . . . We don't have to worry, so party hearty, and try not to make a big deal out of the fact that Bush's lawyers are now claiming he can launch an attack on Iraq without congressional approval. (Molly

Ivins, "Can Bush Look Himself in Either of His Faces?" *Denver Rocky Mountain News*, 8/28/2002.)

(2) distress (as in a state of nervous tension) *n.*: **fantod**. See *tension*

(3) distress (as in trouble) *n.*: **tsuris** [Yiddish]. See *trouble*

(4) distress (as in worry) *v.t.*, *v.i.*, *n.*: **cark**. See *worry*

(5) distress (experience of intense . . . , as in suffering) *n.*: **Calvary** [based on hill near Jerusalem where Jesus was crucified]. See *suffering*

(6) distress (period of . . . , sometimes, but not necessarily, economic) *n.*: **locust years**. See *hardship*

distressed (as if by a witch or by unfounded fears) *adj.*: **hagridden**. See *tormented*

distribute (proportionately) *v.t.*: **admeasure**. See *apportion*

district (surrounding . . . served by an institution, such as a school or hospital) *n.*: **catchment area**. ❖ The periodic eruption of unruly, and even criminal behavior in our student body would seem to be a fact of school life for the foreseeable future. Given the socioeconomic profile of our **catchment area**, only a fool would imagine otherwise. (Zoë Heller, *What Was She Thinking?* Henry Holt [2003], p. 63.)

(2) district (Spanish-speaking . . .) *n.*: **barrio**. See *Spanish*

distrust (of strangers or foreigners) *n.*: **xenophobia**. ❖ It is widely known that the word for enemy and stranger are often the same in many cultures. **Xenophobia** is tearing our country apart. There are a lot of black people that have never had a white friend and vice versa. (*Minneapolis Star Tribune*, "Sample of Readers' Opinions on the State of the Union," 2/5/1997.)

(2) distrust (person who has . . . for humankind) *n.*: **misanthrope**. See *mistrust*

disturb (as in agitate) *v.t.*: **commove**. See *agitate*

(2) disturb (as in bother or inconvenience) *v.t.*: **discommode**. See *inconvenience*

(3) disturb (as in bother or inconvenience) *v.t.*: **incommode**. See *inconvenience*

disturbance (as in commotion) *n.*: **bobbery**. See *commotion*

(2) disturbance (as in commotion) *n.*: **kerfuffle**. See *commotion*

(3) disturbance (as in commotion) *n.*: **maelstrom**. See *commotion*

(4) disturbance (as in commotion) *n.*: **pother**. See *commotion*

(5) disturbance (over a trifling matter) *n.*: **foofaraw**. See *fuss*

disturbing (as in bothersome) *adj.*: **pestiferous**. See *bothersome*

disunity (relating to or attempting to create . . . , separation, or a breach of union, esp. within the Christian church) *adj.*: **schismatic**. ❖ Some of the cardinals [meeting with Pope Benedict XVI] raised concerns, thereby encouraging the pope to slow down about reconciliation with the **schismatic** group, called Lefebvrites, who are followers of the late Marcel Lefebvre, an ultraconservative archbishop who opposed Vatican II and was excommunicated. (Michael Paulson, "Pope Sees Expanded Role for Cardinals," *Boston Globe*, 3/26/2006.)

disuse (state of inactivity or . . .) *n.*: **desuetude**. ❖ Since Vietnam, members of Congress have tried to prevent administrations from sneaking the country into a war. The first effort, the War Powers Act, fell into **desuetude**. It was designed to give Congress a mechanism for disapproving incremental escalations, but Congress hesitated to invoke it when troops were in peril. (Michael Barone, "A Question of Going to War," *U.S. News & World Report*, 11/1/1993.)

ditzy (person) *n.*: **featherhead**. See *flighty*

diver *n.*: **urinator**. ❖ It's a safe bet that Aristotle, an advocate of reason and moderation, would not have become a **urinator** for all the tea in China. To go underwater simply defies the natural order. [W]ater is a hostile element where the most basic life-fuel, air, cannot be guaranteed. (Stuart Wavell, "Artists of the Floating World," *Sunday Times* [London], 8/5/2001.)

diverge (from a course or intended path) *v.t.*: **yaw**. See *veer*

diverse (often used of a performer or artist) *adj.*: **protean**. See *versatile*

(2) diverse *adj.*: **multifarious**. See *versatile*

(3) diverse (as in dissimilar) *adj.*: **heterogeneous** (*n.*: **heterogeneity**). See *dissimilar*

diversion (as in digression) *n.*: **excursus**. See *digression*

diversity (as in region populated by people from a . . . of countries or backgrounds) *n.*: **cosmopolis**. ❖ The subway, I find, is also oddly liberating. It takes you not only to your destination, but along the way to another world. . . . Your fellow riders are a jostling microcosm of a teeming **cosmopolis**: men, women and children from every stratum of society, of every imaginable color, sporting all kinds of dress (or undress) and chattering in most of the languages of the planet. (Shashi Tharoor, Letter from America: "Notes from the Underground," *Newsweek* International, 8/27/2001, p. 41.)

(2) diversity *n.*: **variegation** (*v.t.*: **variegate**). ❖ A typical sentence as heard coming out of our TV set might be: "Mah fellow Ah Mare Cuns. This country is in whore-bull shape. . . ." [But] we ought to rejoice that in an age dominated by trite, homogenized media English, so much heterogeneity of speech survives, even thrives. The great diversity of tongues in America . . . give texture and **variegation** to our common nationhood. It would be whore-bull if we all talked alike. (Robert Reno, Reno at Large: "Just Whose English Do We Declare Our Official Language?" *Newsday*, 9/27/1995, p. A43.)

divert (oneself in a light, frolicsome manner) *v.t.*, *v.i.*: **disport**. See *frolic*

divide (esp. into districts or geographic regions) *v.t.*: **cantonize**. ❖ The Palestinian Press countered National Infrastructure Minister Ariel Sharon's warning that the Palestinians were about to declare statehood, by accusing him of trying to **cantonize** the West Bank. Israel was accused of surrounding autonomous Palestinian areas with Jewish settlements and roads. (Michael Sela, "Palestinian Press Review," *Jerusalem Post*, 12/1/1997.)

(2) divide (from others, as in isolate) *v.t.*: **enisle**. See *isolate*

(3) divide (into parts) *v.i.*: **disaggregate**. See *separate*

(4) divide (into thin layers) *v.i.*: **delaminate**. See *separate*

(5) divide (proportionately) *v.t.*: **admeasure**. See *apportion*

(6) divide (tending to . . . into parts or break up) *adj.*: **fissiparous**. See *break up*

divided *adj.*: **cloven**. See *split*

dividing (act of . . . into parts) *n.*: **fission**. See splitting

divination (by picking random Bible passages) *n.*: **bibliomancy**. ❖ We sat cross-legged on the floor in front of her modest library of religious books. . . . [S]he gave advice over the phone on questions concerning religious precepts and a suitable marriage alliance. She also . . . performed a **bibliomancy** for the husband of a member of her gatherings concerning whether he should embark on a new business venture. (Azam Torab, "Piety as Gendered Agency," *Journal of the Royal Anthropological Institute*, 6/1/1996.)

divination (by communing with the dead) *n.*: **necromancy**. ❖ The great escapologist, Houdini, was briefly obsessed with **necromancy** and set out to disprove that the dead could communicate with the living. (Patrick Gale, Books: "Final Escape—Into Death," *Daily Telegraph* [London], 3/27/1999.)

(2) divination (by fire) *n.*: **pyromancy**. ❖ [A]n Abenaqui female shaman, a convert to Christianity, explaining to her mission priest why she continued to practice **pyromancy**: "Listen, God has given men different gifts. To the Frenchmen, he has given the Scriptures by which you learn the things that take place far from you as if they were in front of you; to us he has given the art of knowing, by fire, things remote in time or place." (Gordon Sayre, "Native Signification and Communication," *Early American Literature*, 9/22/2003.)

(3) divination (by touching or proximity to an object) *n.*: **psychometry**. ❖ The **Psy-**chometry Test. Anita: "This is where I hold a personal object belonging to you [that] can tell me other things about you and your past." (Jane hands over a Russian wedding ring and Anita twists it around her finger). "It takes a couple of seconds for me to tune into it." . . . Anita: "I'm also getting something else. . . . Do you drive?" Jane: "Yes!"Anita: "But you failed your test the first time you took it." Jane: "Yes!" (*People* [London], "So What's on the Cards for Leanne?" 1/16/2000.)

(4) divination (relating to the art of . . .) *adj.*: **mantic**. See *prophetic*

(5) divination (relating to the art of . . .) *adj.*: **sibylline** (or **sybilline**; often cap.). See *prophetic*

divine (as in angelic) *adj.*: **seraphic**. See *angelic*

(2) divine (having both human and . . . [as in godlike] attributes) *adj.*: **theanthropic**. See *godlike*

diviner (by using lightning or animal innards) *n.*: **haruspex**. See *fortune-teller*

division (into three parts) *n.*: **trichotomy**. ❖ [The film *Cowboys and Angels*] examines the apparent social **trichotomy** of modern Ireland, where you're . . . a fashion designer, a drug dealer, or a complete square. (Akiva Gottlieb, "Cowboys and Angels," *Village Voice*, 9/15/2004.)

(2) division (into two parts, esp. by tearing apart or violent separation) *n.*: **diremption**. See *separation*

(3) division (often from or within a group or union) *n.*: **scission**. See *split*

(4) division (relating to or attempting to create . . . , or a breach of union, esp. within the Christian church) *adj.*: **schismatic**. See *disunity*

divulge (one's thoughts or feelings) *v.t., v.i.*: **unbosom**. See *confide*

(2) divulge *v.t.*: **disinter**. See *disclose*

dizzy *adj.*: **vertiginous**. ❖ More than anything, however, I felt positively giddy—that sort of **vertiginous** wooziness which I usually associate with the third Martini or the second bottle of Champagne. But it wasn't just the high altitude—and the hyperpure mountain air—

that was making me feel more than a little light headed. (Douglas Kennedy, Essay: "A Walking Miracle," *Independent* [London], 9/15/2001.)

docile *adj.*: **biddable**. See *obedient*

doctor (equipment, including supplies and instruments, used by a . . .) *n.*: **armamentarium**. ❖ In the Latin phrases that get tossed about by physicians, "primum non nocere" ("first, do no harm") . . . is a Hippocratic albatross that today's physicians have come to understand subconsciously in its appropriate context. Every weapon in the physician's **armamentarium** is double-edged; every cure has a potential harm. (Kenneth LeCroy, letter to the editor, *American Family Physician*, 12/15/2001.)

(2) **doctor** (disease caused by a . . .) *adj.*: **iatrogenic**. See *disease*

(3) **doctor** (replacement . . .) *n.*: **locum tenens**. See *temporary*

doctrinaire *adj.*: **bien-pensant**. See *right-thinking*

doctrine (which is false) *n.*: **pseudodoxy**. See *fallacy*

(2) **doctrine** *n.*: **shibboleth**. See *principle*

doctrines (to be believed; articles of faith) *n.pl.*: **credenda**. See *beliefs*

dodge (as in avoid a straight answer) *v.t.*: **tergiversate**. See *evade*

dog days (of or relating to . . . of summer) *adj.*: **canicular**. ❖ What happens in Venice, Rome, Positano, and San Gimignano is appalling: witless, crudely contrived, blatantly preposterous, and desperately sweaty under the collar—and I am not referring to the **canicular** Italian climate. (John Simon, review of *Only You*, *National Review*, 11/7/1994.)

dogged (as in stubborn) *adj.*: **pervicacious**. See *stubborn*

(2) **dogged** (in effort or application) *adj.*: **sedulous**. See *diligent*

(3) **dogged** (in holding to a belief or opinion) *adj.*: **pertinacious**. See *stubborn*

doldrums (as in depression) *n.*: **cafard** [French]. See *depression*

dole out (proportionately) *v.t.*: **admeasure**. See *apportion*

dolt *n.*: **jobbernowl** [British]. See *idiot*

(2) **dolt** *n.*: **mooncalf**. See *fool*

domain (as in area of activity or interest) *n.*: **purlieu**. ❖ In fact, [Stanley] Dance regarded Swing as the **purlieu** of white musicians like Benny Goodman and Artie Shaw. Mainstream was to encompass the work of black musicians including Duke Ellington, Earl Hines, Count Basie, Coleman Hawkins and Buck Clayton. (Steve Voce, obituary of Stanley Dance, *Independent* [London], 3/2/1999.)

dominance (of one political state over others) *n.*: **hegemony**. ❖ Now, however, the United States has claimed authority to hold sovereign nations accountable, in American courts, for failing to honor American laws in their dealings with Cuba. Even for the United States, that's carrying **hegemony** too far. (*Minneapolis Star Tribune*, "Cuba/The United States Is Out of Step," 10/16/1998.)

(2) **dominance** (as in superiority or state of being better) *n.*: **meliority**. See *superiority*

dominant *adj.*: **regnant**. See *predominant*

dominate *v.t.*: **bestride** (past tense: **bestrode**). ❖ Napoleon III ruled France as emperor during the American Civil War. . . . Yet the specter of another Napoleon, the first, haunted Civil War battlefields. Bonaparte died at St. Helena about 40 years before the war, but his figure **bestrode** the 19th century. In art and legend, he incarnated martial glory. In military theory, he was celebrated as the model genius of the times. (Tom O'Brien, "Napoleon's Shadow over American Warriors," *Washington Times*, 9/9/2000.)

dominated (as in subjected to external controls and impositions; i.e., the opposite of autonomous) *adj.*: **heteronomous** (*n.*: **heteronomy**). See *subjugated*

domination (of a nation or group over another) *n.*: **suzerainty**. ❖ No doubt, not everyone in the German leadership saw their **suzerainty** over so many Jews purely in terms of "opportunity," for the disposal of so many Jews posed enormous practical problems and created day-to-day difficulties for those charged with Jewish affairs. (Daniel Goldhagen, *Hitler's Willing Executioners*, Knopf [1996], p. 144.)

(2) domination (of a religious, national, or racial group) *n.*: **helotism** (*v.t.*: **helotize**). See *oppression*

domineering (as in haughty) *adj.*: **fastuous**. See *haughty*

(2) domineering (woman who is overbearing and . . .) *n.*: **virago**. See *shrew*

(3) domineering (phenomenon of a . . . mother who is overprotective and controlling of her sons, thus hindering their maturation and emotional development) *n.*: **momism**. See *mother*

donation (as in offering) *n.*: **oblation**. See *offering*

(2) donation (which is all one can afford) *n.*: **widow's mite**. ❖ "The true measure of philanthropy lies in giving, even when it hurts. And then a **widow's mite** trumps the rich man's might." Owen Willis, Tantallon, N.S. (Unsigned letter to the editor, *Time*, 8/14/2000, p. 9.)

donor (generous . . . , esp. to the arts) *n.*: **Maecenas**. See *benefactor*

doom (as in damnation) *n.*: **perdition**. See *damnation*

doomsayer *n.*: **catastrophist**. See *pessimist*

(2) doomsayer *n.*: **crepehanger**. See *pessimist*

doomsday (branch of theology concerned with) *n.*: **eschatology**. See *Judgment Day*

dope *n.*: **jobbernowl** [British]. See *idiot*

(2) dope *n.*: **mooncalf**. See *fool*

(3) dope (or fool or loser or idiot or anyone generally not worthy of respect) *n.*: **schmendrick** or **shmendrik** [Yiddish]. See *fool*

dormant (as in inanimate) *adj.*: **insensate**. See *inanimate*

(2) dormant (as in not moving or temporarily inactive) *adj.*: **quiescent**. See *inactive*

(3) dormant *adj.*: **torpid**. See *lethargic*

dote (on, as in treat with excessive concern) *n.*, *v.t.*: **wet-nurse**. See *coddle*

doting (overly . . . on, or submissive to, one's wife) *adj.*: **uxorious**. See *devoted*

doting (overly . . . on one's husband) *adj.*: **maritorious**. See *devoted*

dotted (with a darker color) *adj.*: **brindled** (or **brindle**). See *spotted*

double (ghostly . . . of a living person) *n.*: **doppelgänger**. See *twin*

double-crosser (esp. who aids an invading enemy) *n.*: **quisling**. See *traitor*

(2) double-crosser (esp. who betrays under guise of friendship) *n.*: **Judas**. See *betrayer*

double-crossers (as in traitors or group of . . . working within a country to support an enemy and who may engage in espionage, sabotage, or other subversive activities) *n.*: **fifth column**. See *traitors*

double meaning (as in subject to two different interpretations) *n.*: **amphibiology**. See *ambiguity*

(2) double meaning (as in subject to two different interpretations) *adj.*: **amphibolous**. See *ambiguous*

double-sided *adj.*: **Janus-faced**. See *two-faced*

doubt (esp. as in beyond . . .) *n.*: **peradventure**. ❖ According to an NBC/*Wall Street Journal* survey, the lying cheating hound [President Clinton] has risen in his job approval ratings from 64 per cent to 67 per cent. Prove to the American people beyond **peradventure** that he's a Grade A philanderer and fraud—and they conclude that he's even better at doing his job! (Boris Johnson, "How Clinton Gets Off: Reach Out and Touch," *Daily Telegraph* [London], 9/15/1998.)

(2) doubt (expression of . . . as to one's opinion on an issue, esp. arising from awareness of an opposing viewpoint) *n.*: **aporia**. ❖ [Several scenes in the movie *Do the Right Thing*] all suggest that [director Spike] Lee advocates violence. Or is there an honest uncertainty, a true **aporia**, expressed in the two quotations Lee appends to the film: one from Dr. King, decrying violence as a solution, followed by another from Malcolm X, saying that it is stupid not to resort to violence in "self-defense," i.e., in righting social inequity. (James Gardner, "A Star Is Reborn," *National Review*, 8/4/1989.)

(3) doubt (as in oppose, a statement, opinion, or action) *v.t.*: **oppugn**. See *oppose*

doubter *n.*: **crepehanger**. See *pessimist*

doubtful (as in skeptical) *adj.*: **zetetic**. See *skeptical*

(2) doubtful (morality or taste) *adj.*: **louche**. See *questionable*

doubtfulness *n.*: **dubiety**. ❖ Republicans now calling for revival of the [independent counsel] law are ignoring its constitutional **dubiety**. But today the word "Watergate" still serves as an argument for the law. That is absurd. (George Will, "Let the Voters Be the Judge," *Newsday*, 1/9/1994.)

(2) doubtfulness (statement of . . . , as in unlikelihood, expressed in the form of an exaggerated comparison with a more obvious impossibility; for example, "the sky will fall before I get married") *n.*: **adynaton**. See *unlikelihood*

dour (as in dark and gloomy) *adj.*: **acherontic**. See *gloomy*

(2) dour (as in person who never laughs) *n.*: **agelast**. See *humorless*

(3) dour (as in sullen or morose) *adj.*: **saturnine**. See *sullen*

(4) dour (or grumpy mood) *n.pl.*: **mulligrubs**. See *grumpiness*

douse (as in soak) *v.t.*: **imbrue**. See *soak*

downcast (as in sullen or morose) *adj.*: **saturnine**. See *sullen*

(2) downcast (or grumpy mood) *n.pl.*: **mulligrubs**. See *grumpiness*

(3) downcast *adj.*: **chapfallen**. See *dejected*

downfall (esp. from a position of strength) *n.*: **dégringolade** [French]. ❖ *Time's* greatest influence was exerted in forming the nation's attitudes, its political opinions and social conscience—especially in the decades after World War II. In the '60s, during Vietnam, *Time* was caught in a general American **dégringolade**, a deconstruction of established authority from the President on down. (Lance Morrow, "The Time of Our Lives," *Time*, 3/9/1998.)

(2) downfall (of or relating to a . . . , esp. after an innocent or carefree time) *adj.*: **postlapsarian**. [This word literally means "after the Fall," referring to that period in the Garden of Eden after Adam and Eve lost their innocence after eating from the Tree of Knowledge. It is used more generally to refer to a downfall or collapse, especially after an innocent or carefree time. Its opposite is prelapsarian. See *innocent.*]

❖ [In a dot-com hurricane, says Mead,] "people lose touch with reality." Not Foveon, which resisted a quick IPO before nailing down a path to profits. It wasn't easy. "You couldn't get suppliers." . . . The ones who took billion-dollar bites from the apple are [now] suffering **postlapsarian** blues. But Foveon is only beginning its ride. "Now," Mead says proudly, "we have lasting value." (Steven Levy, "The Film of Tomorrow: Foveon: It's the Technology," *Newsweek*, 3/25/2002.)

(3) downfall (esp. of moral principles or civil order) *n.*: **labefaction**. See *weakening*

(4) downfall (violent or turbulent . . . of a society or regime) *n.*: **Götterdämmerung** [German]. See *collapse*

downplay (attempt to . . . seriousness of an offense) *v.t.*: **palliate**. ❖ Every civilization needs its self-justifying myths. . . . America's great national myth of the settlement and taming of the frontier grew out of the slaughter of indigenous peoples, which it was meant to explain and **palliate**. (James Bowman, "Alien Menace: Lt. Ripley Is Hollywood's Mythical Woman—Butch and Ready to Kill," *National Review*, 1/26/1998, p. 35.)

downpour *n.*: **cataract**. ❖ It takes a bit more than a downpour to ruffle his demeanour. Let there be a deluge of Biblical proportions, let the winds crack their cheeks and **cataracts** and hurricanes spout on the Wimbledon Park Road and Des would glance out of the window, raise an eyebrow and murmur: "Nasty out." (Andrew Baker, "Wimbledon 1997: Golden Days Brighten the Grey Afternoons," *Independent on Sunday*, 6/29/1997.)

downturn *n.*: **declension**. See *decline*

downward (slope) *n.*: **declivity** (*adj.*: **declivitous**). See *decline*

(2) downward (slope, esp. extending down from a fortification) *n.*: **glacis**. See *decline*

downy (as in velvety) *adj.*: **velutinous**. See *velvety*

draft (as in compose or write) *v.t.*: **indite**. See *compose*

drag (a person or group from one place to another, whether literally or figuratively) *v.t.*: **frogmarch**. See *march*

drain (of strength) *v.t.*: **enervate**. See *debilitate*

drained (as in appearing lifeless) *adj.*: **exanimate**. See *lifeless*

drama (of or relating to . . . or the art of the theater, esp. the writing of plays) *adj.*: **dramaturgic**. See *theater*

dramatic (or artistic piece imitating previous pieces) *n.*: **pastiche**. See *imitation*

(2) dramatic (overly . . . behavior) *n., adj.*: **operatics**. See *melodramatic*

(3) dramatic (relating to speech that is designed for . . . effect) *adj.*: **epideictic**. See *impress*

draw (as in describe, by painting or writing) *v.t.*: **limn**. See *describe*

drawback (or disadvantage) *n.*: **disamenity**. See *disadvantage*

drawing (dealing with evening or night) *n.*: **nocturne**. See *painting*

(2) drawing (which looks like a photograph or something real) *n.*: **trompe l'oeil** [French]. See *illusion*

dread (as in panic) *n.*: **Torschlusspanik** [German]. See *panic*

(2) dread (source or object of . . . or fear) *n.*: **hobgoblin**. See *fear*

dreaded (something that is . . . , disliked or to be avoided) *n.*: **bête noire** [French]. ❖ Line drives [hit back at the pitcher] are the **bête noire** of this glittering season. And as the season moves into its final month, come-backers are an unpredictable "X" factor nobody wants to think about. If, say, Padres ace [pitcher] Kevin Brown went down, San Diego's World Series dreams virtually would vanish. (Steve Marantz, "Duck!" *Sporting News*, 8/31/1998, p. 14.)

dream (bad . . . , or episode having the quality of one) *n.*: **Walpurgis Night**. See *nightmare*

dreamer (as in an impractical contemplative person with no clear occupation or income) *n.*: **luftmensch** [lit. man of air; German, Yiddish]. ❖ Humor analysts trying to explain [Seinfeld's] popularity have overlooked the Jewish connection . . . : George is the "schlemiel," the born loser; Elaine plays the lovable "yenta." Kramer is the proverbial "**luftmensch**." His head in the clouds; he is forever involved in impractical schemes to make money. And Jerry Seinfeld? He's the rabbi, of course. (Robert Menchin, "*Seinfeld* Explained," *Chicago Tribune*, 1/2/1998.)

(2) dreamer *n.*: **fantast**. ❖ In his dreams, Boris Yeltsin believes he is president of Russia. Similarly, Ryutaro Hashimoto likes to imagine he is the actual leader of Japan. The two **fantasts** got together on April 18th in Kawana, a resort south-west of Tokyo, for a weekend of mutual make-believe. (*Economist*, "Dreams Among the Cherry Blossom," 4/25/1998.)

dreamland (living in a . . . , with a glorified or romanticized conception of oneself, as a result of boredom in one's life) *n.*: **Bovarism**. See *self-delusion*

dreams (of, relating to, or suggestive of) *adj.*: **oneiric**. ❖ I bet Stanley Kubrick never had a nightmare while shooting a movie. Oh, I'm sure he had budgetary and logistic nightmares as any filmmaker must, but no **oneiric**, forehead-dampening visitations. (Richard Alleva, "Stanley Kubrick," *Commonweal*, 4/23/1999.)

dreamworld (as in paradise) *n.*: **Xanadu**. See *paradise*

(2) dreamworld (as in place of extreme luxury and ease where physical comforts and pleasures are always at hand) *n.*: **Cockaigne**. See *paradise*

(3) dreamworld (spec. a place of fabulous wealth or opportunity) *n.*: **El Dorado**. See *paradise*

(4) dreamworld (usually invented by children, which can involve its own history, geography, and language) *n.*: **paracosm**. See *fantasy*

dreary (as in dismal and gloomy) *adj.*: **acherontic**. See *gloomy*

drench (as in soak) *v.t.*: **imbrue**. See *soak*

dress (as in clothes) *n.*: **habiliment(s)**. See *clothing*

(2) dress (as in outfit or equip) *v.t.*: **accouter**. See *outfit*

(3) dress (in a showy or excessive manner) *v.t.*: **bedeck**. See *adorn*

(4) dress (or adorn in a showy or excessive manner) *v.t.*: **bedizen**. See *adorn*

(5) dress (showy article of . . .) *n.*: **frippery**. See *finery*

(6) dress (showy article of . . .) *n.*: **froufrou**. See *clothing*

dressed (inappropriately . . .) *adj.*: **misclad**. ❖ [In the Battle of Manila Bay in 1898], the Spanish fleet offered no contest, but Filipinos themselves did, mounting a bitter 2 1/2-year resistance to American conquest. At the war's peak, 70,000 US troops, **misclad** in hot felt hats and canvas breeches, fought Filipinos through the steaming tropics. (Tom Ashbrook, "An Absorbing Look at US-Filipino Relations," *Boston Globe*, 5/8/1989.)

(2) dressed (being partially, carelessly, or casually . . .) *n.*: **dishabille** [French]. See *attired*

drift (aimlessly) *v.i.*: **maunder**. See *roam*

(2) drift (from the subject) *v.i.*: **divagate**. See *digress*

drifter *n.*: **clochard** [French]. See *vagrant*

drill *v.t.*: **catechize**. See *teach*

drink (final . . . before leaving) *n.*: **doch-an-dorris** See *nightcap*

drinking (of or related to) *adj.*: **potatory**. ❖ [You] arrive in Upper Woodford for a thirst-quenching pint at The Bridge. Beyond the pub, turn right down a track and back to the river. Follow the track beside the river and up again, cross the road and down through the woods opposite. . . . [T]his is a good place for a post-**potatory** snooze. (*Guardian* [London], "Time Off: Romancing the Stones," 6/20/1996.)

(2) drinking (as in given to or marked by consumption of alcohol) *adj.*: **bibulous**. See *imbibing*

(3) drinking (or eating in moderation) *adj.*: **abstemious**. See *restrained*

drip (as in light splash) *n.*: **plash**. See *splash*

drive (as in energy coupled with a will to succeed) *n.*: **spizzerinctum**. See *energy*

drivel (as in meaningless talk or nonsense) *n.*: **galimatias**. See *gibberish*

(2) drivel (as in nonsense) *n.*: **codswallop** [British]. See *nonsense*

(3) drivel (as in nonsense) *n.*: **folderol** (or **falderal**). See *nonsense*

(4) drivel (as in nonsense) *n.*: **piffle**. See *nonsense*

(5) drivel (as in nonsense) *n.*: **trumpery**. See *nonsense*

drone (as in speaker or writer who is dull and boring) *n.*: **dryasdust**. See *boring*

droning (a . . . hum) *n.*: **bombilation**. See *buzzing*

drool *v.i., n.*: **slaver**. ❖ OK, I admit it. When the rhino stuck her head in the van and drooled on my lap—I flat-out flinched. I also fumbled the apple I was supposed to feed her. . . . The rhinoceros **slavered**, blinked and dropped her lower lip farther open; it looked like a wet, fleshy trapdoor the size of a shoe box. (Catherine Watson, "Going Wild in San Diego/Braving Rhino Slobber," *Minneapolis Star Tribune*, 9/27/1998.)

drop (as in downward slope) *n.*: **declivity** (*adj.*: **declivitous**). See *decline*

(2) drop (as in light splash) *n.*: **plash**. See *splash*

(3) drop (as in shed, a skin or covering) *v.t., v.i.*: **exuviate**. See *shed*

(4) drop (to the bottom of the ocean) *v.i.*: **go to Davy Jones's locker**. See *ocean*

drops (having or resembling . . . on the skin) *adj.*: **guttate**. ❖ Yet fully a third of psoriasis patients encounter it in the first two decades of life. Your daughter seems to have the **guttate** form, marked by small raindrop-like lesions amid the familiar white-scaled red patches. (Dr. Paul Donohue, "There Are Several Heartburn Options: Choose from Medical or Surgical," *St. Louis Post-Dispatch*, 1/3/1996.)

drowning (mass . . . as a form of execution) *n.*: **noyade**. ❖ The ghastly events [of the French Revolution] prove Dostoyevsky's words: "If there is no God, everything is permitted." . . . Equally hideous were the **noyades**, the drownings in the Loire . . . of naked men and women coupled and fettered in pairs. (Erik von Kuehnelt-Leddihn, "Reflections on the Terror," *National Review*, 7/14/1989.)

drowsiness (relating to period of . . . just before falling asleep) *adj.*: **hypnagogic**. ❖ Sometimes, between sleeping and waking, I suddenly glimpse the shadowy forms [standing nearby]. . . . As the **hypnagogic** state deepens into sleep, they merge into the background of panelled wall and moulded ceiling and are lost to view. (Peter Simple, "Hypnagogic Days," *Daily Telegraph* [London], 8/2/2002.)

(2) drowsiness *n.*: **somnolence**. See *sleepiness*

(3) drowsiness (as in condition of stupor or unconsciousness resulting from narcotic drugs) *n.*: **narcosis**. See *stupor*

drowsy (as in sluggish or lethargic) *adj.*: **torpid**. See *lethargic*

(2) drowsy (pertaining to . . . , as in semiconscious, state just before waking) *adj.*: **hypnopompic**. See *semi-conscious*

drudge *v.i.*: **moil**. See *toil*

drug (as in something that induces forgetfulness of or indifference to pain, suffering, or sorrow) *n.*: **nepenthe**. See *narcotic*

drum (relating to or resembling) *adj.*: **tympanic**. ❖ The hammering of her compressed heart against her breastbone echoed **tympanically** within her, and it seemed to fill the claustrophobic confines of her hiding place to such an extent that the intruder was certain to hear. (Dean Koontz, *Intensity*, Knopf [1995], p. 20.)

drumbeat (or other repeating noise such as machine-gun fire or hoofs of a galloping horse) *n.*: **rataplan**. See *noise*

drum roll *n.*: **paradiddle**. ❖ I never wanted to be a guitar hero. When I was 8, I wanted to play drums like my best friend John Priestley, but a few klutzy **paradiddles** set me straight about that. (Ty Burr, "Rock & Roll Fantasy," *Entertainment Weekly*, 2/3/1995, p. 57.)

drunk (as in given to or marked by consumption of alcohol) *adj.*: **bibulous**. See *imbibing*

drunkard *n.*: **dipsomaniac** (*adj.*: **dipsomaniacal**). See *alcoholic*

drunken *adj.*: **bacchic**. [Brazilian soccer star Garrincha's] career had a depressingly familiar structure: dazzling success, **bacchic** excess, swift decline. . . . His performances in [the World Cups of] 1958 and 1962 turned him into an international star and a revered symbol throughout Brazil. By 1966, drink and injuries had ruined him. While more self-disciplined players had been training their bodies and expanding their bank balances, Garrincha just played, drank and screwed until he collapsed. (Josh Lacey, "Garrincha: The Triumph and Tragedy of Brazil's Forgotten Hero," *Guardian* [London], 8/14/2004.)

dry (of or adapted to a very . . . habitat) *adj.*: **xeric**. ❖ In 1886, he was asked to design the campus for a university to be built in Palo Alto, California. Here the landscaping challenge was to convince Leland Stanford to forgo his dream of lush lawns and trees—characteristic of New England—in favor of a drought-resistant **xeric** landscape more suited to the western climate. (Norma Jane Langford, "A Place to Unbend," *World & I*, 3/1/1995.)

(2) dry (out thoroughly) *v.t.*, *v.i.*: **desiccate**. ❖ With summertime temperatures in the shade—if you can find any—exceeding [120 degrees], **desiccating** winds and no water, surviving a day in the Arabian desert is hot work. (*Economist*, "How to Be Cool in the Desert," 12/18/1999.)

(3) dry (as in uninteresting) *adj.*: **jejune**. See *uninteresting*

dry up (and shrivel) *v.i.*: **wizen**. See *shrivel*

dubious (as in skeptical) *adj.*: **zetetic**. See *skeptical*

duck (of or relating to the domestic fowl, including . . .) *adj.*: **gallinaceous**. See *fowl*

duel (as in hostile meeting) *n.*: **rencontre** [French]. ❖ [A] young Frenchman named Georges d'Anthès started paying increasingly indiscreet attention to Pushkin's beautiful wife. Rumors, probably untrue, began to circulate. Then one day Pushkin received an anonymous note enrolling him in a society of cuckolds. He immediately issued a challenge to d'Anthès, but their **rencontre** was averted through the machinations of friends. (Michael Dirda, "Russia's Greatest Poet Was Also a Rake, a Gambler and a Hot-Tempered Aristocrat," *Washington Post*, 11/16/2003.)

dull (or ignorant, stupid, obtuse, or uncultured) *adj.*: **Boeotian** [derives from ancient Greek region of Boeotia, noted for the dullness and stupidity of its inhabitants]. ❖ [As a writer,] Violeta is no García Márquez. She refers to herself as a writer [but] left alone, she writes lines like, "I am ever vigilant about feelings that alight on my subconscious carrying a concealed pain." No wonder the C.I.A. ghosted her Op-Ed. . . . [This is a] repetitive, fuddled, **Boeotian** and dispiriting autobiography. (H. Aram Vesser, review of *Dreams of the Heart: The Autobiography of President Violeta Barrios de Chamorro of Nicaragua, Nation*, 9/30/1996.)

(2) dull (as in bland, though wanting to appear grandiose or having pretensions of grandeur) *adj.*: **blandiose**. See *bland*

(3) dull (as in daze) *v.t.*: **benumb**. See *daze*

(4) dull (as in desensitize) *v.t.*: **hyposensitize**. See *desensitize*

(5) dull (as in insipid, intellectual nourishment, like baby food) *n.*: **pabulum** (also **pablum**). See *insipid*

(6) dull (as in sluggish) *adj.*: **bovine**. See *sluggish*

(7) dull (as in uninspired) *adj.*: **invita Minerva** [Latin]. See *uninspired*

(8) dull (passage or section in a book or work of performing art) *n.*: **longueur**. See *tedious*

(9) dull (to make . . . , as in deaden) *v.t.*: **obtund**. See *deaden*

(10) dull (writer or speaker) *n.*: **dryasdust**. See *boring*

(11) dull *adj.*: **anodyne**. See *bland*

(12) dull *adj.*: **jejune**. See *uninteresting*

(13) dull *v.t.*: **narcotize**. See *deaden*

dullness (as in lethargy) *n.*: **hebetude**. See *lethargy*

(2) dullness (as in condition of stupor or unconsciousness resulting from narcotic drugs) *n.*: **narcosis**. See *stupor*

dull-witted (as in slow to understand or perceive) *adj.*: **purblind**. See *obtuse*

dumb (as in foolish) *adj.*: **barmy** [British]. See *foolish*

(2) dumb (as in slow to understand or perceive) *adj.*: **purblind**. See *obtuse*

(3) dumb (class of people regarded as . . . or unenlightened) *n.*: **booboisie**. See *unsophisticated*

(4) dumb (esp. used of a person, as in . . . and confused) *adj.*: **addlepated**. See *confused*

(5) dumb (lit. brainless) *adj.*: **excerebrose**. See *brainless*

(6) dumb (or dull or ignorant or obtuse or uncultured) *adj.*: **Boeotian**. See *dull*

(7) dumb (person or loser or idiot or anyone generally not worthy of respect) *n.*: **schmendrick** or **shmendrik** [Yiddish]. See *fool*

(8) dumb (equally . . .) *adj.*: **unasinous**. See *stupid*

(9) dumb (person) *n.*: **dullard**. See *stupid*

(10) dumb (person) *n.*: **dummkopf** [German]. See *stupid*

(11) dumb *adj.*: **gormless** [British]. See *unintelligent*

dummy (or fool or loser or idiot or anyone generally not worthy of respect) *n.*: **schmendrick** or **shmendrik** [Yiddish]. See *fool*

dunce *n.*: **jobbernowl** [British]. See *idiot*

(2) dunce *n.*: **mooncalf**. See *fool*

dung (eating) *adj.*: **scatophagous**. See *excrement*

(2) dung (esp. that of sea birds) *n.*: **guano**. See *bird dung*

(3) dung (feeding on) *n.*: **coprophagous**. See *excrement*

(4) dung (interest in . . . , often sexual) *n.*: **coprophilia**. See *excrement*

(5) dung (obsession with) *n.*: **coprology**. See *excrement*

(6) dung (of or relating to) *adj.*: **stercoraceous**. See *excrement*

(7) dung (study of or obsession with) *n.*: **scatology**. See *excrement*

(8) dung *n.*: **egesta**. See *excrement*

(9) dung *n.*: **ordure**. See *excrement*

dungeon *n.*: **oubliette**. [This term refers to a secret place of imprisonment, such as a dungeon, usually with only one opening and that at the top, as found in some medieval castles. It is often used generally or metaphorically to refer to any kind of prison or place of involuntary confinement, as in the following example.] ❖ [For one of the best airlines,] my sleeper award goes to Air France. . . . Having sampled economy class to India, Mali and Egypt during the past couple of years, I've been impressed each time by the free wine, unlimited baguettes, entertainment options and amenities packets. . . . If the airline faces one hugely damaging liability, it's the concrete **oubliette** that is Charles de Gaulle airport. (Patrick Smith, "Ask the Pilot: What Is Salon Readers' Favorite Airline?" *Salon.com*, 5/7/2004.)

duo (arranged in or forming a . . .) *adj.*: **jugate**. See *pair*

   (2) duo (two individuals or units regarded as a . . .) *n.*: **dyad**. See *pair*

   (3) duo *n.*: **duumvirate**. ❖ [Abstract painter Cy] Twombly . . . is the Third Man, a shadowy figure, beside that vivid **duumvirate** of his friends Jasper Johns and Robert Rauschenberg. (Robert Hughes, Arts & Media: "The Grafitti of Loss in Nuanced Abstractions," *Time*, 10/17/1994, p. 72.)

dupe (as in one easily deceived) *n.*: **gudgeon**. See *sucker*

   (2) dupe (as in to deceive or cheat or the person being cheated or deceived) *n.*: **gull**. See *deceive*

duplicate (ghostly . . . of a living person) *n.*: **doppelgänger**. See *twin*

duplicating (a particular act over and over, often after initial stimulus has ceased) *n.*: **perseveration** (*v.i.*: **perseverate**). See *repeating*

duplicitous (characterized by . . . and cunning conduct, esp. in regard to the pursuit and maintenance of political or other power) *adj.*: **Machiavellian**. See *deceitful*

   (2) duplicitous (conduct) *n.*: **skullduggery**. See *deceitfulness*

durable (extremely . . .) *adj.*: **perdurable**.

❖ Reinventing James Bond as a kind of Navy SEAL with an attitude problem, *Casino Royale* turns out to be cracking good entertainment, as well as a fresh start for the **perdurable** 21-picture franchise. Daniel Craig kicks major maximus as a Bond who'd never use a computer where a punch will do. (Stephen Hunter, "An Agent of Change; With *Casino Royale*, Blond Bond Hits the Ground Running," *Washington Post*, 11/17/2006.)

duration (of or over the same . . . period) *adj.*: **coetaneous**. See *contemporaneous*

dusk (of or relating to . . . or dawn, as in twilight) *adj.*: **crepuscular**. See *twilight*

   (2) dusk (of, relating to, or occurring in . . . or evening) *adj.*: **vespertine**. See *evening*

   (3) dusk *n.*: **gloaming**. See *twilight*

dust storm (esp. in Arabia and Africa) *n.*: **haboob**. See *sandstorm*

dwarf (like a . . .) *n.*, *adj.*: **Lilliputian**. See *tiny*

   (2) dwarf *n.*: **homunculus**. See *midget*

   (3) dwarf *n.*: **hop-o'-my-thumb**. See *midget*

dwelling (on a height) *n.*: **aerie**. ❖ For six years [the couple] had a million-dollar view of Atlanta's skyline. . . . Their 22nd floor **aerie** at Buckhead's posh Park Place was far above the din. But slowly the din has come up to meet them and other residents on the south side of the 40-floor condominium complex, whose most famous resident is rock star Elton John. (Tinah Saunders, "Buckhead Condo Now More Noisy, Less Scenic," *Atlanta Journal-Constitution*, 10/19/2001.)

dwell on (as in repeating, a particular act over and over, often after initial stimulus has ceased) *n.*: **perseveration** (*v.i.*: **perseverate**). See *repeating*

dyeing (of or relating to) *adj.*: **tinctorial**. ❖ Pantone adheres to rigorous standards in producing the swatches in a miniature dye pilot plant. It analyzes each batch of reactive dye for purity and **tinctorial** value. (Edward J Elliott, "Chemical Treatment & Finishing: How Textiles Is Perfecting Color," *Textile World*, 1/1/2000.)

eager *adj.*: **athirst**. ❖ From its inception the Whitney was obviously an artist-oriented institution, in contrast with the major art museums of the time, which addressed aesthetic consumers **athirst** for the beauty and spiritual meaning attributed to the fine arts. (Arthur C. Danto, Books & the Arts: "Of Time and the Artist," *Nation*, 6/7/1999, p. 27.)

(2) eager (extremely . . .) *adj.*: **perfervid**. See *impassioned*

(3) eager (strongly . . . , as in desirous) *adj.*: **appetent** (*n.*: **appetence**). See *desirous*

eagerness *n.*: **avidity**. See *craving*

(2) eagerness (excessive or unbridled . . . , as in enthusiasm) *n.*: **schwarmerei** (or **schwärmerei**) [German]. See *enthusiasm*

eagle (pertaining to or similar to) *adj.*: **aquiline** (esp. as in aquiline nose). ❖ This 53-year-old CEO, who with a bald head and **aquiline** nose looks himself a bit like an eagle, sets back-breaking standards and raises them methodically each year. (Brian Dumaine, "Managing: Those Highflying PepsiCo Managers," *Fortune*, 4/10/1989, p. 78.)

ear (of a sound that is pleasing to the . . .) *adj.*: **euphonious** (*n.*: **euphony**). See *melodious*

(2) ear (pleasing to the . . .) *adj.*: **dulcet**. See *melodious*

earlier (as in antecedent) *adj.*: **prevenient** (often as in "prevenient grace"). See *antecedent*

earliest (stage of growth or development) *adj.*: **germinal**. ❖ In due course, the Cold War would be waged through proxy armies across every continent, would stretch out over nearly five decades, and would threaten the planet with nuclear annihilation. But [in 1945], in its **germinal** stages, it was fought [in the form of a long-distance chess match] between a brainy American businessman and [a Soviet] electrical engineer marshaling the Semi-Slav Defense. (David Shenk, *The Immortal Game*, Doubleday [2006], p. 167.)

(2) earliest (version of a text or version of a musical score or literary work) *n.*: **urtext** [German]. See *original*

early *adv.*: **betimes**. ❖ It would be hard to say who was more excited—us or the [Finnish sleigh] dogs. . . . The younger huskies had been so keen to get going that they'd whined and barked at the imperturbable older dogs who headed the team and placidly prevented them from setting off **betimes**. (Danuta Brooke, "Santa Really Does Wear a Red Coat," *Independent on Sunday*, 11/16/1997.)

(2) early (as in relating to morning) *adj.*: **matutinal**. See *morning*

earnest (but in a smug or false manner) *adj.*: **oleaginous**. See *unctuous*

earnings (as in payment or wages) *n.*: **emolument**. See *wages*

Earth (of, relating to, or inhabiting) *adj.*: **tellurian** [also used as a noun for earthling]. ❖ Thus, the once integrated earthly being, whose relationship with both **tellurian** and heavenly realms had been fluid and balanced, was transformed into a strictly celestial force. (Bettina Knapp, "The Archetypal Woman Fulfilled," *Symposium*, 3/1/1996, p. 28.)

earthly *adj.*: **sublunary**. [This word literally means "beneath the moon" and is sometimes used in the more literal sense of "of the earth" and sometimes in the sense of "mundane." The example used here conveys both senses of the word.] ❖ Can it really be two decades since Neil Armstrong set foot on the moon? It seems like only last summer. . . . The moment was genuinely unique, absolutely unrepeatable. Its symbolism dwarfed the landings of Columbus and Lindbergh: for the first time, man had walked on a heavenly body other than this one. The nation returned to its **sublunary** concerns refreshed, inspired, somehow strengthened. (*National Review*, "Getting High," 8/18/1989.)

earthquake *n.*: **temblor**. ❖ Registering 6.6 on the moment-magnitude scale, a measure of earthquake energy that among scientists has largely replaced the Richter scale, the Northridge **temblor** didn't qualify as a Big One. (J. Madeleine Nash, "The Next Big One," *Time*, 1/31/1994, p. 45.)

easy (as in elementary or basic) *adj.*: **abecedarian**. See *basic*

easygoing *adj.*: **dégagé** [French]. ❖ Rather than emphasize her feminine fragility, Katharine Hepburn preferred to play up her "one of the boys" personality with turtleneck sweaters, fluid men's trousers and sneakers. . . . Whether on-duty at state dinners or off-duty and swimming in Long Island Sound, [women like Hepburn] had a wonderful **dégagé** attitude toward dressing, as if they just ran out the door. (Jennifer Alfano, "The Best of American Fashion," *Harper's Bazaar*, 5/1/2003.)

(2) easygoing (or carefree behavior) *n.*: **rhathymia**. See *carefree*

eat (as in ingest) *v.t.*: **incept**. See *ingest*

(2) eat (excessive desire to . . .) *n.*: **polyphagia**. See *appetite*

(3) eat (greedily) *v.t.*: **guttle**. See *devour*

(4) eat (like a glutton) *v.i.*: **gormandize**. See *devour*

eater (hearty . . .) *n.*: **trencherman**. See *glutton*

eating (art or science of good . . .) *n.*: **gastronomy**. ❖ You'd think that moving into the premises of Gordon—one of Chicago's most beloved and sorely missed dining rooms—would anger the gods of **gastronomy**, but the spirits have been smiling on Naha [restaurant] and chef Carrie Nahabedian. (John Mariani, The Best New Restaurants [2001], *Esquire*, 12/1/2001, p. 90.)

(2) eating (practice of . . . together) *n.*: **commensality**. ❖ In essence through his miracles and **commensality**, Jesus is providing unbrokered access to God to all, a notion foreign and radical to the culture in which he lived. (Graydon Royce, "And on the Third Day . . . ," *Minneapolis Star Tribune*, 4/5/1996.)

(3) eating (of or relating to . . . with others) *adj.*: **commensal**. See *dining*

(4) eating (or drinking in moderation) *adj.*: **abstemious**. See *restrained*

(5) eating (science of . . . , spec. dining) *n.*: **aristology**. See *dining*

eavesdrop *v.t.*: **earwig**. ❖ There's a downside to being Harvey Weinstein's favourite South American. After a preview screening at Bafta of Walter Salles's new film, *Behind the Sun*, I **earwigged** on the post-credits conversations. "He's such a sentimentalist!" whooped a voice behind me. "He's so bloody Miramax!" [Weinstein was the head of Miramax Films.] (Matthew Sweet, Film: "Everything under the Sun?" *Independent* [London], 1/25/2002.)

ebullient (as in exuberant) *adj.*: **yeasty**. See *exuberant*

eccentric *adj.*: **pixilated**. ❖ In a bizarre encounter with a man seeking employment, [Steve] Jobs demands to know if the guy is "a virgin" and then insults him before stomping off in a huff and a half. . . . "I need artists!" he screams in regard to his **pixilated** personnel practices, denouncing employees who are "clock-punching losers." (Tom Shales, "TNT's Pirates: The Geek Tycoons; Tale of Computer Icons Gates & Jobs a Net Loss," *Washington Post*, 6/20/1999.)

(2) eccentric (as in departing from the standard or norm) *adj.*: **heteroclite**. See *abnormal*

(3) eccentric (as in unconventional) *adj.*: **outré** [French]. See *unconventional*

echo (mindlessly . . . ideas that have been drilled into the speaker or repeat things that reflect the opinions of the powers-that-be) *v.t., v.i., n.*: **duckspeak**. See *recite*

echoing (as in reverberating) *adj.*: **reboant**. See *reverberating*

(2) echoing (pathological or uncontrollable or a child's . . . of another's words) *n.*: **echolalia**. See *repeating*

eclipse (of a star or planet by the moon) *n.*: **occultation**. ❖ On Dec. 7, the crescent moon passes in front of the planet Jupiter between 3:50 and 5 a.m. in a rare **occultation** of the planet by the moon. (Tom Burns, "Another Total Lunar Eclipse Awaits Astronomer's Telescope," *Columbus [OH] Dispatch*, 1/20/2004.)

economical (speech or writing being very . . .) *adj.*: **elliptical**. See *terse*

ecstatic (often in a boastful way) *adj.*: **cock-a-hoop**. See *elated*

Eden (spec., having the characteristics of a mythical romantic place) *adj.*: **Ruritanian**. See *paradise*

edge *n.*: **selvage**. ❖ One Midtown Kitchen. Located on a ragged **selvage** of Piedmont Park, this restaurant is all about buzz, . . . commerce and its own sure vision of comfort chic. (John Kessler, 2003 Guide Book: Dining: "Dig In: You'll Find All Kinds of Tastes," *Atlanta Journal-Constitution*, 7/24/2003.)

edible *adj.*: **esculent**. [Though this word, generally applied to roots and vegetables, is simply a synonym for "edible," it is often used as a synonym for "delicious," as in the first example here. In the second example given, it means edible.] ❖ Great cooking is a time-consuming art form, creating **esculent** masterpieces that can only be savoured and appreciated in a restaurant, and many of the greatest names in gastronomy are virtually unknown outside their own profession because they refuse to fritter away their time and talent for the benefit of TV cameras. (Victor Lewis-Smith, "Too High in Fatuousness," *Evening Standard* [London], 1/17/2003.)

(2) edible *adj.*: **esculent**. ❖ America's Founding Fathers, Washington, Jefferson, Madison and Monroe, had long urged Congress to "collect, cultivate and distribute the various vegetable productions of this and other countries, whether medicinal, **esculent**, or for the promotion of arts and manufactures." (Suzanne Richardson, "Lush Growth at the New Botanic Garden," *Washington Post*, 12/21/2001.)

(3) edible *n.*: **comestible**. ❖ Over the years, the cramped, crowded and congenial Cleveland Park Safeway often ran out of ketchup or cauliflower or some other **comestible**. Now—to the distress of loyal patrons—the Safeway has run out of time. (Anne Simpson, "Cleveland Park Losing Neighbor with Closing of 'Soviet Safeway,'" *Washington Post*, 9/10/1987.)

edict *n.*: **diktat**. See *decree*

(2) edict *n.*: **ukase**. See *decree*

edification *n.*: **éclaircissement** [French]. See *clarification*

edit (a book or a writing in a prudish manner) *v.t.*: **bowdlerize** [after Thomas Bowdler (1754–1825), who published a sanitized edition of Shakespeare in 1818]. ❖ Today the robust words [of the "Marseillaise"], which . . . enjoin the children of revolutionary France to "drench our fields" with the "tainted blood" of the enemy, are under siege by those who feel the piece smacks of political incorrectness. The idea of **bowdlerizing** the ferocious lyrics . . . first surfaced three years ago. (Kevin Fedarko, "France Meddling with the 'Marseillaise'; A Proposal to Bowdlerize France's Barn-Burning Anthem Provokes an Indignant Mon Dieu! from Traditionalists," *Time*, 3/16/1992, p. 42.)

(2) edit (text or language by removing errors or flaws) *v.t.*: **blue-pencil**. ❖ [S]he went looking for a magazine job—but ended up as an editor at Random House, where she has **blue-penciled** the prose of Julia Phillips, David Mamet, and Sandra Cisneros for the Turtle Bay Books division. (*Entertainment Weekly*, "Features That Deal with More Than One Media," 2/26/1993, p. 26.)

(3) edit (text or language by removing errors or flaws) *v.t.*: **emend**. ❖ As it turned out, the opinion written by Justice Anthony Kennedy showed considerable understanding of how speech is translated into print. Kennedy condoned the widespread journalistic practice of **emending** quotations in the areas of grammar and syntax. (Paul Gray, Press: "Justice Comes in Quotes: Journalists Can Tinker with the Words of Interview Subjects—But Reckless Falsity Can Be Libelous," *Time*, 7/1/1991, p. 68.)

educate *v.t.*: **catechize**. See *teach*

educated (people as a group) *n.*: **clerisy**. ❖ Adorno was . . . heir to a German romantic tradition, according to which intellectuals form a secular **clerisy** guarding the moral and intellectual health of the nation. (Ian Buruma, "Real Wounds, Unreal Wounds," *New Republic*, 2/12/2001.)

(2) educated (person who is . . . , as in knowledgeable, in many areas) *n.*: **polyhistor**. See *knowledgeable*

(3) educated (person who is . . . , as in knowledgeable, in many areas) *n.*: **polymath**. See *scholar*

(4) educated (person, as in lover of learning) *n.*: **philomath**. See *scholar*

education (excess striving for or preoccupation with . . . , as in knowledge) *n.*: **epistemophilia**. See *knowledge*

(2) education (of adults) *n.*: **andragogy**. See *adult education*

(3) education (person who acquires . . . late in life) *n.*: **opsimath**. See *learning*

(4) education (universal . . . , as in knowledge) *n.*: **pansophy** (*adj.*: **pansophic**). See *knowledge*

educator *n.*: **pedagogue**. See *teacher*

eerie *adj.*: **eldritch**. ❖ Many things go into the making of a movie classic, but Alfred Hitchcock's timeless thriller is inseparable in our memory from Bernard Hermann's [*sic*] **eldritch**, bump-in-the-night score [in *Psycho*]. (Michael Walsh, The Arts & Media/Music, *Time*, 9/11/1995, p. 77.)

effect (as in aftereffect) *n.*: **sequela** (pl. **sequelae**). See *aftereffect*

(2) effect (as in outgrowth) *n.*: **excrescence**. See *outgrowth*

effeminate *adj.*: **epicene**. ❖ The world will be poorer without Quentin Crisp. He stood apart from the rest of us, not so much because of his lilac hair and **epicene** manners as because of his genuine individualism. Homosexuality, like other alternative life-styles, can impose a conformity of its own; but Mr. Crisp was having none of it. (*Daily Telegraph* [London], "Crisp and Courteous," 11/22/1999.)

(2) effeminate (person) *n.*: **pantywaist**. See *sissy*

effort (mental process marked by . . . to do something) *n.*: **conation**. See *determination*

(2) effort (the . . . to achieve a particular goal or desire) *n.*: **nisus**. See *goal*

(3) effort (which is laborious but futile) *adj.*: **Sisyphean**. See *futile*

effortlessness (appearance of . . .) *n.*: **sprezzatura** [Italian; taken from a 1528 book by Baldassare Castiglione, who stated: "Practice in all things a certain sprezzatura . . . so as to conceal art, and make whatever is done or said appear to be without effort and almost without any thought about it"]. ❖ Anthony Blunt, when principal of the Courtauld—where [National Museum Director Neil] MacGregor trained after giving up on the law—called him "the most brilliant student I ever had." His tutor, Anita Brookner, said: "He was brilliant then and he's brilliant now." He epitomises the Renaissance ideal of **sprezzatura**—the studied nonchalance that makes achievement seem effortless. (Alice Thomson, "Britain's Paintings," *Daily Telegraph* [London], 2/1/2002.)

effrontery *n.*: **hardihood**. See *gall*

effusive (as in characterized by a ready and easy flow of words) *adj.*: **voluble**. See *talkative*

egg (-shaped) *adj.*: **ovoid**. ❖ [I]n the corner [was a] wooden egg shaped like Boris Yeltsin that holds successively tinier **ovoid** representations of the leaders of the Soviet Union, from Lenin to Gorbachev. (Stanley Bing, "While You Were Out. . .," *Fortune*, 7/19/1999, p. 49.)

eggplant *n.*: **aubergine** (used as an adjective when referring to color, as in the example given). Denis made no sound at all because there was no air getting in or out of his lungs. Instead he steadily turned the color surrounding his injured eye, which had passed indigo and was entering **aubergine**. (Larry Doyle, *I Love You, Beth Cooper*, Ecco [2007], pp. 93–94.)

ego (as in self-esteem) *n.*: **amour-propre** [French]. See *self-esteem*

egotist (esp. a little man) *n.*: **cockalorum**. See *boastful*

(2) egotist (spec. someone in love with his own opinions) *n.*: **philodox**. See *narcissist*

egotistical (and vain person) *n.*: **coxcomb**. See *conceited*

(2) egotistical (and vain) *adj.*: **vainglorious**. See *boastful*

(3) egotistical (person) *n.*: **Gascon** (act of being . . . *n.*: **Gasconade**). See *braggart*

eject (contents, as if flowing water) *v.i.*: **disembogue**. See *discharge*

(2) eject (as in force out or cause to escape

from proper channels, esp. a liquid or something that flows) *v.t.*: **extravasate**. See *exude*

elaborate (as in intricate or complex) *adj.*: **involute**. See *intricate*

(2) elaborate (on a subject at length in speech or writing) *v.i.*: **expatiate**. See *expound*

(3) elaborate *adj.*: **rococo**. See *ornate*

(4) elaborate (as in overly complicated) *adj.*: **Rube Goldberg**. See *complicated*

elated (often in a boastful way) *adj.*: **cock-a-hoop**. ❖ Forced onto the [auction] market by death duties, [the collection of paintings] was exactly the sort of property that would once have gone to Christie's as a matter of course, and Sotheby's was **cock-a-hoop** that their competitive commission cuts had secured such prestigious business so soon after their move. (Robert Lacey, *Sotheby's—Bidding for Class*, Little, Brown [1998], p. 68.)

elderliness *n.*: **senectitude**. ❖ British fiction has been besieged by a heaving regiment of late-adolescent thirty somethings, visibly clinging to their youth. . . . With his second novel James Hawes is the first to break away from this . . . and admit his age. . . . Hawes' comfortable submersion into **senectitude** is daring in its honesty. But this initial bravery is about the only thing he deserves credit for. (Ra Page, review of *Rancid Aluminium*, by James Hawkes, *New Statesman*, 8/8/1997, p. 52.)

elderly (branch of science dealing with) *adj.*: **gerontology**. ❖ To Dr. Barbara Stancil, age was nothing but a number, one that should not be ignored, but celebrated. As founder and longtime director of the **Gerontology** Center at Georgia State University, a nationally recognized research center, Dr. Stancil devoted her professional life to studying older Americans and advocating on their behalf. (Stephania H. Davis, obituary of Barbara Stancil, *Atlanta Journal-Constitution*, 7/23/2001.)

(2) elderly (of or relating to . . . people, esp. women) *adj.*: **blue-rinse**. ❖ As for elderly drivers, sorry, but [my thesis is] that slow drivers cause accidents. From my observation, and here I will anger the **blue-rinse** crowd, if I

have a problem with a driver, it's often a small, elderly woman who appears to be observing the road through her steering wheel. (John Downing, "Life in the Slow Lane; Speed Limits Don't Make Us Safer, Just More Regulated," *Toronto Sun*, 8/13/2003.)

(3) elderly (and sick person) *n.*: **Struldbrug**. See *decrepit*

(4) elderly (government by the . . .) *adj.*: **gerontocracy**. See *government*

(5) elderly (growing . . .) *adj.*: **senescent**. See *aging*

(6) elderly (of or like an . . . woman) *adj.*: **anile**. See *old woman*

(7) elderly (of or relating to the . . .) *adj.*: **gerontic**. See *old age*

(8) elderly (sexual attraction toward the . . .) *n.*: **gerontophilia**. See *lust*

eldest (child) *n.*: **primogeniture**. See *first-born*

election (direct . . . where electorate exercises right of self-determination) *n.*: **plebiscite**. ❖ It is precisely because direct democracy is such a manipulatable sham that every two-bit Mussolini adopts it as his own. Pomp and **plebiscites**. The Duce and the people. No need for the messy stuff in between. Not for nothing did the Founders abhor direct democracy. They knew it to be a highway to tyranny. (Charles Krauthammer, Essay: "Ross Perot and the Call-In Presidency," *Time*, 7/13/1992, p. 84.)

elections (study of) *n.*: **psephology**. ❖ Pippa Norris . . . surveys what has been found out about voters and their motivations in Britain since 1945, and in particular since David Butler and Donald Stokes, doyens of **psephology** in Britain and in America respectively, published their first numerical analyses of political change in the 1960s. (*Economist*, British Political Books: "Division Time," 3/22/1997.)

elective (as in optional) *adj.*: **facultative**. See *optional*

elegant *adj.*: **Chesterfieldian**. [This word derives from the fourth Earl of Chesterfield (1694–1773), known for his elegant manner.] ❖ Another trial [at the dog training school] was a set of steps. . . . The steps sound easy—but almost all of the puppies spread their hind legs and braced themselves as if for a tug of war. The dogs between 7 and 11 months old did much better. . . . The older dogs walked up the steps, posed and gazed grandly at the crowd from the top, and walked with a casual **Chesterfieldian** air down the other side. (Zan Thompson, "Tiny Paws That Will Lead and Protect," *Los Angeles Times*, 5/28/1989.)

(2) elegant *adj.*: **nobby** [British]. ❖ According to a recent survey by the slightly oxymoronic British Hospitality Association, increasing numbers of three- and four-star hotels are insisting on dress codes. A few **nobby** five-star joints tried to give the impression that they were above such vulgar requirements, but my experience suggests that they're just as bad. (*Independent* [London], "The Weasel," 10/5/1996.)

(3) elegant *adj.*: **soigné** [French]. ❖ A description was provided, suggesting that . . . the Baron had survived his prison experience without obvious damage to his **soigné** airs: "Always well-dressed. Has a distinguished appearance because of his polished manners. Speaks very courteously. Always stays at the best hotels." (Ben Macintyre, *The Napoleon of Crime*, Farrar, Straus and Giroux [1997], p. 204.)

(4) elegant *adj.*: **raffiné** (or **raffine**) [French]. See *refined*

(5) elegant (and stately, as befitting a baron) *adj.*: **baronial**. See *stately*

elegy *n.*: **threnody**. See *requiem*

elemental (as in essential) *adj.*: **constitutive**. See *essential*

elementary *adj.*: **abecedarian**. See *basic*

elephant (of, relating to, or resembling; sometimes as in big like an . . .) *adj.*: **pachydermatous**. ❖ The agenda [for a demolition derby] was—and is—breathtakingly basic: a mess of very big, very old cars slam into one another until just one, the winner, is still running. "Boys must wreck cars," summarized Tommy Walkowiak, 24, a boiler repairman who brought a **pachydermatous** Ford, a 1976 Country Squire station wagon, to Riverhead Raceway here this Saturday night. (Douglas Martin, "It Destroys, It Brings Chaos and It Just Won't Die," *New York Times*, 9/13/1996.)

elevated (as in of or related to the sky or heavens) *adj.*: **empyreal**. See *celestial*

(2) elevated (as in of or related to the sky or heavens) *adj.*: **supernal**. See *celestial*

elicit (as in extract or pry or force out, whether from a place or position, or information) *v.t.*: **winkle** (usually used with "out"). See *extract*

eliminate (as in put an end to) *v.t.*: **quietus** (as in "put the quietus to"). See *termination*

(2) eliminate *v.t.*: **extirpate**. See *abolish*

elite (person, esp. in intellectual or literary circles) *n.*: **mandarin**. See *influential*

elixir (supposed . . . which is untested or unproved) *n.*: **nostrum**. See *remedy*

(2) elixir *n.*: **catholicon**. See *remedy*

eloquent (of or relating to . . . speech) *adj.*: **Ciceronian**. See *speech*

elsewhere (as in originating from . . . ; not endemic) *adj.*: **ecdemic**. See *foreign*

elusive (lit. soapy) *adj.*: **saponaceous**. See *slippery*

emaciated (esp. as to children as a result of malnutrition) *adj.*: **marasmic** (*n.*: **marasmus**). ❖ As a widespread drought worsens North Korea's famine, South Korea agreed yesterday to send another massive food shipment to its rival. . . . But the food aid may come too late for children who are already malnourished. . . . Dr. Milton Amayun examined 52 children who were 2 years old or younger. He found that 60 percent were moderately or severely malnourished. Half of the children were **marasmic**— just skin and bones. (Alison Beard, "South Korea Agrees to Send More Relief to Famished North," *Washington Times*, 7/26/1997.)

(2) emaciated (esp. in a pale or corpselike way) *adj.*: **cadaverous**. See *corpselike*

emaciation (due to chronic disease) *n.*: **cachexia**. See *wasting*

emanation *n.*: **effluence**. ❖ Look at her. She has the same lizard-lidded eyes, the same cute little drop-seat mouth that marred and made her daddy's famous face. Like her old man, Lisa Marie Presley exudes a none-too-subtle **effluence** of brat and sings, it's said, with instinctive ease and wooing charm. (*People*, The 25 Most Intriguing People: "Lisa Marie Presley," 12/26/1988, p. 59.)

(2) emanation (as in outflow) *n.*: **efflux**. See *outflow*

(3) emanation (impalpable . . . as in aura) *n.*: **effluvium**. See *aura*

(4) emanation (which is thick and vaporous or noxious) *n.*: **miasma**. See *noxious*

emancipate (from slavery, servitude, or bondage) *v.t.*: **manumit**. ❖ As President, Lincoln tried for years to exclude slavery from his war aims, and actually reimposed slavery after two of his generals **manumitted** slaves in Southern areas they held. (Garry Wills, "Dishonest Abe—America's Most Revered Politician Dissembled, Waffled, Told Racist Stories and Consorted with Corrupt Politicians," *Time*, 10/5/1992, p. 41.)

(2) emancipate (from slavery, servitude, or bondage) *v.t.*: **disenthrall**. See *liberate*

emasculate *v.t.*: **geld**. See *castrate*

embarrass (by making false statements) *v.t.*: **traduce**. See *malign*

(2) embarrass (to . . . , as in disconcert) *v.t.*: **discomfit**. See *disconcert*

embarrassing (as in inappropriate or tasteless comments) *n.*: **dontopedalogy**. See *foot-in-mouth*

embarrassment (as in dishonor to one's reputation) *n.*: **blot (or stain) on one's escutcheon** *idiom*. See *dishonor*

(2) embarrassment (resulting from an inopportune occurrence) *n.*: **contretemps**. See *mishap*

embellish (as in exaggerate) *v.t.*: **overegg**. See *exaggerate*

(2) embellish (as in exaggerate) *v.t.*: **aggrandize**. See *exaggerate*

embellishment (abnormal propensity for . . .) *n.*: **mythomania**. ❖ [Victor Hugo's conception] took place in a forest 3,000 ft. up on the flank of Mount Donon, overlooking the Rhineland, in May 1801, though it's typical of Hugo's own **mythomania** that in adult life he claimed it happened 3,000 ft. higher still, and on Mont Blanc. (Robert Hughes, Art: "Sublime Windbag Writer, Lover, National Hero, Victor Hugo Was Also a Brilliant Draftsman of the Unconscious," *Time*, 4/27/1998, p. 71.)

(2) embellishment (which is showy or superfluous or frilly) *n.*: **furbelow**. See *ornamentation*

(3) embellishment (false . . . , as in boast, esp. one that is designed to harm or prejudice another) *n.*: **jactitation**. See *boast*

embezzle *v.i.*: **defalcate**. ❖ According to local reports, some government institutions and non-governmental organizations (NGOs) **defalcate** special funds donated by foreign countries, draining precious resources from the fight on AIDS. (Cheng Zhiliang, Roundup: "HIV/AIDS Keeps on Spreading in Africa," Xinhua News Agency [China], 9/20/2003.)

(2) embezzle *v.t.*, *v.i.*: **peculate**. ❖ [The Mazda] Miata gets passersby smiling and talking. . . . Other conspicuous cars are costly and imposing and draw hate waves, as they are intended to. Decent householders glare, knowing you couldn't own the thing unless you were a drug dealer or a **peculating** [bureaucrat]. (John Skow, Living: "Miatific Bliss in Five Gears, This Is Definitely Not Your Father's Hupmobile," *Time*, 10/2/1989, p. 91.)

embitter *v.t.*: **envenom**. ❖ The idea is to convince both sides [in the Arab-Israeli peace talks] that neither is a demon and that however **envenomed** the territorial disputes become, they can still reach accommodation on other issues. (George J. Church, World: "Middle East—Must We Talk? Now?" *Time*, 10/21/1991, p. 67.)

embodiment *n.*: **avatar**. ❖ Today, [Susan Sarandon] is a certified member of Hollywood's coveted A-list, and the **avatar** of a maturing era of cinematic sexy women who are intelligent, self-assured, sensual, and, gasp, in their 40s. (Hilary de Vries, "Late Bloomer Susan Sarandon's Career Didn't Really Catch Fire Until *Bull Durham*," *Newsday*, 2/23/1993.)

(2) embodiment (spec. the perfect or beautiful example of something) *n.*: **beau ideal**. See *ideal*

embody (as in making an abstract concept seem real) *v.t.*: **reify**. See *materialize*

embolden (as in encourage) *v.t.*: **inspirit**. See *encourage*

embrace (as in caress or fondle) *v.i.*: **canoodle** (often "canoodle with"). See *caress*

embracing *adj.*: **osculant**. See *hugging*

embroil (as in entangle) *v.t.*: **embrangle**. See *entangle*

embryo (of or relating to malformations in) *adj.*: **teratogenic**. See *fetus*

emerge *v.i.*: **debouch**. ❖ [In 1914,] Princeton played many of its [hockey] games in big-city arenas, notably the St. Nicholas in Manhattan, where the socially prominent **debouched** in evening finery from limousines and carriages as if attending a cotillion. (Ron Fimrite, Bonus Piece, *Sports Illustrated*, 3/18/1991, p. 78.)

emergency (as in combination of events or circumstances that creates a crisis) *n.*: **conjuncture**. See *crisis*

(2) emergency (as in critical, stage or period) *n., adj.*: **climacteric**. See *critical*

emerging (as in coming into being) *adj.*: **nascent**. ❖ Out of a thousand **nascent** business plans, maybe 100 will have enough merit to justify a few hundred thousand dollars of angel investment. (Gary Hamel, "Innovation's New Math," *Fortune*, 7/9/2001, p. 130.)

(2) emerging (as in bursting forth or through) *adj.*: **erumpent**. See *bursting*

emissary (such as a diplomatic agent or an ambassador who is fully authorized to represent a government) *n.*: **plenipotentiary**. See *diplomat*

emit (contents, as if flowing water) *v.i.*: **disembogue**. See *discharge*

emitting (out or forth) *n.*: **effluence**. See *emanation*

emoting (behavior) *n., adj.*: **operatics**. See *melodramatic*

emotional (overly . . . and sentimental) *adj.*: **mawkish**. See *sentimental*

emperor (or monarch or sultan or shah or the like; also used to refer to a powerful or important person generally) *n.*: **padishah**. ❖ From the rum punch put in your hand for the two-mile boat ride from Antigua to the resort's private dock to the fluffy towels and robes in your room, the aura bespeaks elegance. Rooms in the four-bedroom villas are palatial. . . . Bicycles are offered for circling the grounds; tennis courts are on the island. Otherwise, life's simply relaxing. Sure, prices would appeal only to a **padishah**, but what do you expect for paradise? (Margaret Zellers, Island Hideaways: "Where the Footprints in the Sand Are Your Own," *Chicago Tribune*, 9/27/1992.)

employee (as in aide or assistant) *n.*: **factotum**. See *assistant*

(2) employee (who works solely for a fee, esp. one hired to perform tasks that are dangerous, offensive, or menial) *n.*: **hireling**. See *mercenary*

employees (who are salaried, as opposed to lower class wage-earners) *n.*: **salariat**. [The salariat is generally considered the middle class or upper middle class of society, as contrasted with the wage earners, or proletariat.] ❖ Big American corporations responded to the 1982 recession by [subcontracting] many of their previous in-house departments (computers, clerical, humble) which weren't really working full-time. This subcontracting has put several million Americans out on a limb. . . . During the subcontracting, the **salariat** in big Fortune 500 companies felt less job-secure than small-town soda jerkers, whose jobs multiplied. (*Economist*, "America's Next Jobless (Employees of Small Businesses)," 2/6/1988).

employer (as in boss or owner) *n.*: **padrone**. See *boss*

employment (requiring little work but paying an income) *n.*: **sinecure**. See *occupation*

empty (or discharge waste from the body) *v.t.*: **egest**. See *excrete*

encapsulate (the flavor or essence of something, as if by boiling down) *v.t.*: **decoct**. See *boil down*

enchant *v.t.*: **ensorcell** (or **ensorcel**). ❖ Trying to soften his military image and lure more female voters in New Hampshire, Gen. Wesley Clark switched from navy suits to argyle sweaters. It's an odd strategy. It's also a little alarming that he thinks the way to **ensorcell** women is to swaddle himself in woolly geometric shapes that conjure up images of Bing Crosby on the links or Fred MacMurray at the kitchen table. (Maureen Dowd, "The General Is Sweating His Image," *New York Times*, 1/13/2004.)

enchanting (as in alluring) *adj.*: **illecebrous**. See *alluring*

enchantress *n.*: **Circe** [based on a goddess in Greek mythology who turns men into swine]. ❖ Having honed her characterization of Morticia [Addams] to larger-than-large eyes, a curl of a mouth, and a whisper of a voice, [Angelica] Huston floats through the scenes, underplaying remarkably. . . . Whether delighting in her labor pains, consoling her husband, or commiserating with Debbie's unhappy childhood, Morticia is "the serene center of the film . . . almost mythical," a **Circe** without the attitude problem, according to the *Baltimore Sun*. (*Magill's Survey of Cinema*, "Addams Family Values," 6/15/1995.)

encircle (often protectively) *v.t.*: **embosom**. See *surround*

(2) **encircle** *v.t.*: **girdle**. See *surround*

encircling (as in surrounding) *adj.*: **ambient**. See *surrounding*

(2) **encircling** (as in surrounding) *adj.*: **circumambient**. See *surrounding*

(3) **encircling** (as in surrounding) *adj.*: **circumjacent**. See *surrounding*

enclose (as in confine) *v.t.*: **immure**. See *confine*

(2) **enclose** (as in surround, often protectively) *v.t.*: **embosom**. See *surround*

enclosed (completely . . . , as in sealed) *adj.*: **hermetic**. See *sealed*

encompass (as in surround) *v.t.*: **girdle**. See *surround*

(2) **encompass** (as in surround, often protectively) *v.t.*: **embosom**. See *surround*

encompassing (as in surrounding) *adj.*: **ambient**.

(2) **encompassing** (as in surrounding) *adj.*: **circumambient**. See *surrounding*

encounter (as in hostile meeting) *n.*: **rencontre** [French]. See *duel*

encountering (fortunate things by accident) *n.*: **serendipity** (*adj.*: **serendipitous**). See *fortuitous*

encourage *v.t.*: **inspirit**. ❖ A party convention is supposed to **inspirit** the faithful, prompting them to stiffen their sinews, summon up their blood and sally forth to fight for the nominee. But Wednesday's platform compromise on abortion language did not entirely lay to rest the danger that this convention could be the cemetery of Bob Dole's hopes . . . (*Seattle Post-Intelligencer*, "GOP Convention: Politicians vs. Prophets," 8/11/1996.)

encouragement (as in stimulus) *n.*: **fillip**. See *stimulus*

encouraging (or inciting or inspiring to action) *adj.*: **proceleusmatic**. See *exhorting*

(2) **encouraging** (as in urging someone to take a course of action) *adj.*: **hortatory**. See *urging*

encumbrances (spec. baggage, equipment, supplies, or any object that hinders progress or movement) *n.pl.*: **impedimenta**. See *baggage*

encyclopedic (person with . . . knowledge) *n.*: **polyhistor**. See *knowledgeable*

(2) **encyclopedic** (person with . . . knowledge) *n.*: **polymath**. See *scholar*

end (point or destination) *n.*: **terminus**. ❖ Michalak's attitude was understandable, given that his baseball life had been an eight-season, five-organization odyssey, but now his traveling days may be over . . . after his 2000 season at Albuquerque (the **terminus** of that cross-country haul), where he went 11–3 with a 4.26 ERA. (Daniel G. Habib, "The Truck Stops Here," *Sports Illustrated*, 6/4/2001, p. 94.)

(2) **end** (as in the thing that is being looked for; also the answer to a problem) *n.*: **quaesitum**. See *objective*

(3) **end** (as in put an end to) *v.t.*: **quietus** (as in "put the quietus to"). See *termination*

endanger (as in expose to or put in a perilous situation (*v.t.*) or be in a perilous situation (*v.i.*): **periclitate**. See *imperil*

endangered (journey or passage, with dangers on both sides) *idiom*: **between Scylla and Charybdis**. See *precarious*

endeavor (the . . . to achieve a particular goal or desire) *n.*: **nisus**. See *goal*

(2) endeavor (which is fruitless or hopeless) *n.*: **fool's errand**. See *hopeless*

endemic (as in indigenous) *adj.*: **authochthonous**. See *indigenous*

ending *n.*: **desinence**. ❖ It seems a great pity to me as I feel it does to hundreds of other South Australians that we should just stand by and tolerate the decline and ultimately the **desinence** of a unique institution like the band of the SA Police. No other State in Australia has a band with military instrumentation as talented and professional as the SA Police Band. (Ian Drinkwater, "Band Decision Could Lead to Demise of One of SA's Best Assets," *Advertiser*, 2/19/1996.)

(2) ending (violent or turbulent . . . to a society or regime) *n.*: **Götterdämmerung** [German]. See *collapse*

endless (as in everlasting) *adj.*: **sempiternal**. See *everlasting*

(2) endless *adj., adv.* (endlessly): **ad infinitum**. See *forever*

(3) endless *adj.*: **aeonian** (or **eonian**). See *eternal*

endlessly *adv.*: **in aeternum** [Latin]. See *forever*

end of the world (branch of theology concerned with) *n.*: **eschatology**. See *Judgment Day*

endorsement (as in giving one's stamp of approval) *n.*: **nihil obstat** [Latin]. See *approval*

endure (ability to . . .) *n.*: **sitzfleisch**. [German. This word, which literally means seat-flesh, refers to the ability to sit still for long periods of time, or more generally, the ability to endure or persevere at an activity. The example given here is somewhat more literal than others, which have nothing to do with literally sitting in a seat, though this usage of the word is not uncommon.] ❖ Some prominent seats [at the State of the Union address] go to those with prominence. Others go to those with **sitzfleisch**, like Representative Eliot L. Engel. Every year since 1989, the Bronx Democrat has won a prime spot at the . . . Address simply by showing up early and sitting in it. [He and others] grab a seat along the aisle, the ones whose occupants get to shake hands with the President—and are shown on national TV doing so. (Elizabeth Kolbert, "An Aisle Seat in the House or the *Titanic*," *New York Times*, 1/30/1998.)

(2) endure *v.i.*: **perdure**. ❖ [The James Beard Award for best cook will be won by someone] who did not receive the same nod last year, nor the year before, nor the year before that. . . . But chefs (or writers, musicians, teachers, moms and dads—all regular recipients of "bests") **perdure** in their skill beyond a year's time. Why isn't this year's "best teacher" the same person from last year? Because we'd like everyone to get a medal. (Bill St. John, "Not Quite the Best," *Denver Rocky Mountain News*, 1/6/1996.)

enduring (forever) *adj.*: **sempiternal**. See *everlasting*

enema *n.*: **clyster**. ❖ I had imagined liposuction as a slow, precise, dignified art; it isn't. A huge needle, the diameter of a turkey baster or **clyster** pipe, is shoved around blind inside the patient's body like roughly vacuum-cleaning the inside of a cushion cover while in a premenstrual bad mood; meanwhile, at the end of a tube, blood and yellow fat splash into a jar. (Lynne Truss, "Vanity Galore, Almost Enough for a Bonfire," *Times* [London], 10/21/1994.)

energetic (not . . .) *adj.*: **bovine**. See *sluggish*

(2) energetic (not . . .) *adj.*: **logy**. See *sluggish*

energize (as in enliven) *v.t.*: **vivify**. See *enliven*

energizer (as in something which invigorates) *adj., n.*: **roborant**. See *invigorating*

energy (coupled with a will to succeed) *n.*: **spizzerinctum**. ❖ [In the 1950s, its] super-salesman mayor, M. E. Sensenbrenner, laid the foundation for Columbus to become one of the nation's largest cities in area. [After losing the mayoral election in 1959,] Sensenbrenner came back to win in 1963 and again in 1967, enlivening the city with his trademark **spizzerinctum**—an optimistic, slogan-filled brand of politicking and governing. (Michael Curtin, "In Politics, a Century of Reform Corruption Abates," *Columbus [OH] Dispatch,* 10/31/1999.)

(2) energy (full of . . .) *n.:* **brio**. ❖ What [Woody Allen and his band] communicate is a rowdy, loose, primitive sensibility that has less to do with re-creating Dixieland jazz and more to do with projecting a modern Manhattan form of New Orleans jazz (the rhythm is more Times Square than Congo Square), played with emotional **brio**. (Norman Weinstein, "Woody Allen Takes Manhattan," *Christian Science Monitor,* 2/20/1998.)

(3) energy (lack of . . . from having no energy or nourishment) *n.:* **inanition**. See *exhaustion*

(4) energy (lacking . . .) *adj.:* **bovine**. See *sluggish*

(5) energy (lacking . . .) *adj.:* **logy**. See *sluggish*

(6) energy (as in life force inherent in all things) *n.:* **Qi** [Chinese]. See *life force*

(7) energy *n.:* **élan** [French]. See *spirit*

enfeeble (as in deprive of strength) *v.t.:* **enervate**. See *debilitate*

(2) enfeeble (as in deprive of strength) *v.t.:* **geld**. See *weaken*

enfeebled *adj.:* **etiolated**. See *weakened*

engaged (to be . . .) *v.t.:* **affianced**. See *marriage*

engagement (as in appointment, esp. for illicit sexual relations) *n.:* **assignation**. See *appointment*

engaging *adj.:* **piquant**. See *appealing*

English (admiration of . . . manners, customs, styles, etc.) *n.:* **Anglophilia**. See *British*

(2) English (exaggerated fondness for . . . manners, customs, styles, etc.) *n.:* **Anglomania**. See *British*

(3) English (fear, distrust, or dislike of . . . manners, customs, styles, etc.) *n.:* **Anglophobia**. See *British*

engraving (esp. of gemstones) *n., adj.:* **glyptic**. See *carving*

enigmatic (as in cryptic or ambiguous) *adj.:* **Delphic**. See *ambiguous*

(2) enigmatic (as in cryptic or obscure speech or writing, esp. deliberately) *adj.:* **elliptical**. See *cryptic*

enjoy (the taste of) *v.t.:* **degust**. See *savor*

enjoyment (as in pleasure) *n.:* **delectation**. See *pleasure*

(2) enjoyment (as in well-being) *n.:* **weal** (usu. as in "weal or woe" or "weal and woe"). See *well-being*

(3) enjoyment (from other's misfortunes) *n.:* **schadenfreude** [German]. See *sadism*

(4) enjoyment (from witnessing other's misfortunes) *n.:* **Roman holiday**. See *sadism*

(5) enjoyment (solely devoted to the seeking of . . .) *adj.:* **apolaustic**. See *hedonistic*

(6) enjoyment (spec. someone excessively devoted to luxury or sensual pleasures) *n.:* **voluptuary**. See *hedonist* and *sensualist*

(7) enjoyment *n.:* **oblectation**. See *pleasure*

enlarge (in scope) *v.t.:* **aggrandize**. See *expand*

enlarged (as in swollen or distended) *adj.:* **tumid**. See *swollen*

(2) enlarged (as in swollen) *adj.:* **dropsical**. See *swollen*

(3) enlarged (as in swollen, used often of body parts such as the penis) *adj.:* **tumescent**. See *swollen*

enlargement (abnormal . . . of the bones, hands, or feet) *n.:* **acromegaly**. ❖ I knew hGH was expensive, but I'd read in a muscle magazine that it was safer than steroids, and I wanted to believe that. I also knew that hGH could cause **acromegaly**—the enlargement of the brow, hands and feet that's sometimes called "Frankenstein's syndrome." (Tommy Chaikin, Bonus Piece: "The Nightmare of Steroids," *Sports Illustrated,* 10/24/1988, p. 82.)

enlightened (self-proclaimed . . . people) *n.pl.:* **illuminati**. ❖ [The premise of contemporary liberals] is that most Americans, particularly

African-Americans, are pathologically incapable of controlling atavistic urges to gratify their every sexual desire. Among these self-proclaimed **illuminati**, it is considered unfashionable to suggest that this basic instinct would best be channeled toward the goal of creating long-term, loving relationships between men and women in a traditional family mode. (Gerald Ortbals, "Who Lost America?" *St. Louis Post-Dispatch*, 6/16/1992.)

enlightenment (as in clarification or clearing up) *n.*: **éclaircissement** [French]. See *clarification*

(2) enlightenment (person who hates . . . or reasoning) *n.*: **misologist**. See *closed-minded*

enliven *v.t.*: **vivify**. ❖ [Sara M. Evans's] depictions [in *Tidal Wave—How Women Changed America At Century's End*] of a broad spectrum of activity in the 1970s and '80s—countercultural music festivals, Emily's List, campaigns against forced sterilization, feminist-inspired labor organizing—**vivify**, as no generalizations could, the extraordinary creative reach of the movement. (Christine Stansell, "After the Revolution," *Washington Post*, 3/23/2003.)

ennui (sometimes in matters spiritual, and sometimes leading to depression) *n.*: **acedia**. See *apathy*

enormous (like an elephant) *adj.*: **elephantine**. ❖ My crusade started when I turned 13. A chubbette-size five-foot-two-inch preadolescent tipping the scales at more than 160, I was determined not to spend my teen years feeling **elephantine**. (Paula M. Siegel, "How I Lost 45 Pounds . . . and Never Gained Them Back," *Redbook*, 8/1/1996, p. 53.)

(2) enormous *adj.*: **Bunyanesque**. ❖ Clamping a bear hug on the appliance, the 6-ft. 3-in, 286-lb. Russian hoisted it off the floor. "It was a huge fridge," he recalls, "and I carried it to my apartment up eight flights of stairs." . . . This **Bunyanesque** figure is a husband and the father of three children, including a daughter who was born this year. (John Greenwald, The Summer Olympics: "The Ones to Beat: Alexander Kareli," *Time*, 9/11/2000, p. 80.)

(3) enormous (like an elephant) *adj.*: **pachydermatous**. See *elephant*

(4) enormous (object) *n.*: **leviathan**. See *huge*

(5) enormous *adj.*: **cyclopean**. See *big*

(6) enormous *adj.*: **brobdingnagian** (often cap.). See *huge*

(7) enormous *adj.*: **Pantagruelian**. See *gigantic*

(8) enormous *adj.*: **pythonic**. See *huge*

(9) enormous *adj.*: **mastodonic**. See *big*

enraged *adj.*: **apoplectic**. See *angry*

(2) enraged *adj.*: **furibund**. See *furious*

(3) enraged *adj.*: **wroth**. See *angry*

enslavement *n.*: **thralldom**. See *bondage*

ensnared (capable of being . . .) *adj.*: **illaqueable**. [This word is usually considered rare or obsolete, but it is legitimate and has been used in the *New York Times* and thus is included here.] ❖ [In *Alien Empire*, a TV special on bugs, the narrator plays] a haunted-house host evoking "monstrous body snatchers." . . . The background music changes to suit the mood as the program celebrates both the [alluring] and the **illaqueable** of bugdom. Walter Goodman, "Sex, Beauty, Home and Travel Tips on Bugs," *New York Times*, 2/9/1996.

ensue (as in happen or occur) *v.t.*: **betide**. See *happen*

(2) ensue (as in result) *v.i.*: **eventuate**. See *result*

entangle *v.t.*: **embrangle**. ❖ There are so many petty annoyances that **embrangle** everyday life in England today [one of which is voice mail. When I call] *The Journal* . . . a nice lady answers and most efficiently puts me through to nice Mr Patterson, or, to be more correct, his voice mail. Now I know that nice Mr Patterson exists because I have met him, but I can rarely get to speak to him first time. (Willy Poole, *Journal* [Newcastle, England], 9/22/2005.)

entangled (capable of being . . . , as in ensnared) *adj.*: **illaqueable**. See *ensnared*

enter (suddenly or forcibly, as in burst in) *v.i.*: **irrupt**. See *burst in*

entertain (oneself in a light, frolicsome manner) *v.t., v.i.*: **disport**. See *frolic*

entertainer (street . . .) *n.*: **busker**. See *performer*

entertainment (as in pleasure) *n.*: **delectation**. See *pleasure*

enthusiasm (excessive or unbridled . . .) *n.*: **schwarmerei** (or **schwärmerei**) [German]. ❖ We [now] have America's new, all-volunteer military, [George W. Bush's] administration's sacred cow, repeatedly used to quell all criticism of the war. "Support our troops" is the teary-eyed mantra that resonates from the West Wing through every lunch counter, bowling alley, saloon and church in middle America. Lost in the ceaseless flag-waving and patriotic **schwarmerei** is the fact that America is becoming the most militarized nation on Earth. (Theodore Roszak, Open Letter to George W. Bush, *News Internationalist*, 3/1/2005.)

(2) enthusiasm (as in full of energy) *n.*: **brio**. See *energy*

(3) enthusiasm (undue . . . for one subject or idea) *n.*: **monomania**. See *obsession*

(4) enthusiasm *n.*: **élan** [French]. See *spirit*

enthusiast (as in fanatic) *n.*: **energumen**. See *fanatic*

(2) enthusiast (strong . . . for a cause, religion, or activity) *n.*: **votary**. See *supporter*

enthusiastic (as in exuberant) *adj.*: **yeasty**. See *exuberant*

(2) enthusiastic (speech or writing) *n.*: **dithyramb**. ❖ Your correspondent has not pinpointed the recent epiphanic moment when he suddenly got it all together in his head about yuppies and realized that he was feeling quite affirmative about them. And has had it up to Ronald Reagan's keister with yuppie-bashing. Warning: You are about to read a **dithyramb**, or at least a few kind words, about the controversial species in question. (Daniel Seligman, "Hurray for Yuppies," *Fortune*, 8/13/1990, p. 119.)

entice (as in bewitch or enchant) *v.t.*: **ensorcell** (or **ensorcel**). See *enchant*

(2) entice *v.t.*: **inveigle**. See *lure*

enticement (as in incentive) *n.*: **fillip**. See *incentive*

(2) enticement (as in lure or temptation) *n.*: **Lorelei call**. See *lure*

(3) enticement (by flattery) *n.*: **blandishment** (*v.t.*: **blandish**). See *flattery*

enticing *adj.*: **sirenic**. [See also the nouns *siren call* and *Lorelei call* under *lure*.] See *alluring*

(2) enticing (but in a way that is solely based on deception or pretense or gaudiness) *adj.*: **meretricious**. See *attractive*

(3) enticing *adj.*: **illecebrous**. See *alluring*

entire (as in complete or unlimited, esp as in . . . power) *adj.*: **plenary**. See *complete*

entirely (as in, in the entirety) *adv.*: **holus-bolus**. See *entirety*

entirety (in the . . .) *adv.*: **holus-bolus**. [This word is used in two related but slightly distinct ways, although they are sometimes interchangeable. One is "in the entirety," which is the sense given here. The other is "all at once" or "simultaneously"; see *simultaneously*.] ❖ In subsequent years, [the Israeli group] Peace Now (which in 1984 was nominated for the Nobel Peace Prize) remained formally outside of the Knesset as a non-governmental organization. It supported the peace moves of the Rabin government virtually **holus-bolus** from 1992, and it was equally . . . active in opposition, from 1996, to the Netanyahu government policies. (*Chicago Jewish Star*, "Peace Now + 25 Years," 3/13/2003.)

(2) entirety (in the . . .) *adv.*: **in extenso** [Latin]. ❖ Oddly, [Soviet spy Kim] Philby's comments on world politics and on his colorful past seem wan and trite. It is almost as if this supermole wanted to demystify his own legend, making double agentry seem as banal as bartending. The impression of ordinariness is reinforced by his chatty letters to Knightley, which are cited **in extenso**. (John Elson, review of *The Master Spy*, by Phillip Knightley, *Time*, 4/24/1989, p. 86.)

(3) entirety (viewed in the . . .) *adv.*: **sub specie aeternitatis** [Latin]. See *big picture*

entitlement (spec. one presumed arrogantly or asserted involuntarily against others) *n.*: **droit du seigneur** [French for "right of the lord." This term originally referred to an alleged right, reputedly claimed by some medieval feudal lords, to have sexual relations with a vassal's bride on her wedding night. Today it is used both with respect to sexual relations and, more generally, to denote an abuse of power by virtue of one's rank or status. The following passage contains two examples of the term.] ❖ "I did something for the worst possible reason," [Bill Clinton] told Dan Rather about his march of folly with Monica [Lewinsky]. "Just because I could." . . . What a world of meaning is packed into that simple phrase. His "could" reflects a selfish "Who's gonna stop me?" power move, stemming from a **droit du seigneur** attitude, as opposed to "should," signifying obligation, or "must," indicating compulsion. . . . In his memoirs, Clinton complains about Republican **droit du seigneur**, writing that impeachment was driven neither by "morality" nor "the rule of law" but, as Newt Gingrich said: "Because we can." (Maureen Dowd, "Clinton and Bush: They Did It Because They Could," *New York Times*, 6/21/2004.)

entrance (as in bewitch or enchant) *v.t.*: **ensorcell** (or **ensorcel**). See *enchant*

(2) entrance (spec. the corridor in a stadium that connects the outer concourse to the interior of the stadium itself) *n.*: **vomitory**. See *corridor*

entrancing *adj.*: **piquant**. See *appealing*

entrapped (capable of being . . . , as in ensnared) *adj.*: **illaqueable**. See *ensnared*

entreat (earnestly) *v.t.*: **adjure**. See *plead*

entreating (someone to take a course of action) *adj.*: **hortatory**. See *urging*

entreaty (spec. a prayer mentioning things held to be sacred) *n.*: **obsecration**. ❖ Cardinal Law's **obsecrations** against *The Last Temptation of Christ* stirred memories for Dick Sinnott, censor from 1960 to 1982, when Boston had a reputation for purity, if not probity, and "Banned in Boston" was a badge of honor and promise

of profits elsewhere. . . . "Producers would bait you, add nudity, lewdity or offensive dialogue that had nothing to do with the story, hoping Boston would ban it. (Jack Thomas, "Streetcar Named Nostalgia," *Boston Globe*, 8/22/1988.)

entrust (authority or duties to another) *v.t.*: **depute**. See *delegate*

envelop (as in surround, often protectively) *v.t.*: **embosom**. See *surround*

enveloping (as in surrounding) *adj.*: **ambient**. See *surrounding*

(2) enveloping (as in surrounding) *adj.*: **circumambient**. See *surrounding*

envious *adj.*: **emulous**. [This word is used in a number of different ways, including, variously, (1) competitive, (2) ambitious (as in ambitious to equal or surpass another), (3) jealous/envious. The following is an example of the third definition.] ❖ [*Twilight on the Lawn* involves] Gus, the wraith-like narrator; Tony and Josie, the "golden couple" on whom the story turns; and . . . Josie's father, a rapacious insolvency accountant named Geoffrey Pagan-Jones. Desperately **emulous** of Tony's dapper ways and presumed destinies (he seems booked to take on Pagan-Jones's . . . daughter), Gus is pulled up short when the relationship breaks apart and Pagan-Jones turns nasty. (*Independent* [London], review of *Twilight on the Lawn*, 10/28/1995.)

environment (destruction of . . . by mankind) *n.*: **ecocide**. ❖ [I]n their new book, *Ecocide in the U.S.S.R.* (Basic Books, $24), [the authors contend that] no other great industrial civilization so systematically and so long poisoned its air, land, water and people. (Douglas Stanglin, "Toxic Wasteland," *U.S. News & World Report*, 4/13/1992.)

(2) environment (physical . . . or setting) *n.*: **mise-en-scène** [French; putting on stage]. See *setting*

environs *n.pl.*: **purlieus**. See *outskirts*

envision (as in to conceive of or form an image of) *v.t.*: **ideate**. See *visualize*

envoy (such as a diplomatic agent or an ambassador who is fully authorized to represent a government) *n.*: **plenipotentiary**. See *diplomat*

ephemeral *adj.*: **fugacious**. See *fleeting*

epicenter (as in nerve center) *n.*: **ganglion** (pl. **ganglia**). See *nerve center*

epidemic *adj.*: **pandemic**. See *widespread*

epithet (substitution of an . . . for a person's proper name) *n.*: **antonomasia**. [Examples would be calling someone a Casanova or a Scrooge.] ❖ We've heard much about "Bubba" recently, but in the vast storied realms of Southern **antonomasia**, Bubba is not terribly important. What Americans should contemplate is the South's sobriquet for a certain type of woman. We call her a "luhvly puhson." (Florence King, "The Lovely Person," *National Review*, 12/28/1992.)

epitome (spec. the perfect or beautiful example of something) *n.*: **beau ideal**. See *ideal*

equal (in strength, power, or effectiveness) *adj.*: **equipollent**. ❖ We should live in a world of **equipollent** continents. African civilisation would have contended on equal terms with those of Eurasia and the Americas. White abuse of black slavery would have been impossible, modern racism unthinkable. (Felipe Fernandez-Armesto, "What if the Armada Had Landed . . . ?" *New Statesman*, 12/20/1999.)

(2) equal (to be or to make . . . in weight) *v.t.*, *v.i.*: **equiponderate**. [When used in the sense of being equal in weight, as in the example given, the verb is intransitive. When used in the sense of making equal in weight, it is transitive.] ❖ The "true doubt" rule provided that "[w]hen there is conflicting, but equally probative, evidence for and against the existence of a particular fact in the benefits inquiry, or, ultimately, when the evidence for and against entitlement to black lung benefits is **equiponderate** . . . the benefit of the doubt [must] be given to the claimant." [Citing] *Grizzle v. Pickands Mather & Co.*, 994 F.2d 1093, 1096 (4th Cir. 1993). (The Honorable Karen Williams, *Milburn v. Hicks*, 138 F.3d 524, 528 [4th Cir.1998]).

(3) equal (person or thing without . . .) *n.*: **nonesuch**. See *paragon*

equality (of rights, laws, or privileges) *n.*: **ison-omy**. ❖ Hannah Arendt . . . wrestled with the psychic impact of totalitarianism, and . . . recommended steps toward recovering civil society. [She] spoke of **isonomy** chastened by authority . . . (Joseph McKenna, "Civil Society, Civil Religion," *Theological Studies*, 6/1/1997.)

equanimity (esp. under pressure or trying circumstances) *n.*: **sang-froid** [French]. See *composure*

equestrian *n.*: **caballero**. ❖ He was raised riding horses, learning at the knee of his **caballero** grandfather. (William Nack, "Only Way That Horses Will Win Is if You Sit There and Spend Time . . . ," *Sports Illustrated*, 6/10/1991, p. 66.)

equilibrium *n.*: **equipoise**. ❖ "Peace," insists this book again and again, "does not keep itself," but must be maintained both by substantial forces in being and a credited willingness to use them. Take the Peloponnesian War, which broke out in a bipolar world like that of the Cold War. Sea-power Athens and its empire were in uneasy **equipoise** with land-power Sparta and its allies. (Donald Lyons, review of *On the Origins of War: And the Preservation of Peace*, by Donald Kagan, *National Review*, 3/6/1995, p. 65.)

equip (as in outfit or clothe) *v.t.*: **accouter**. See *outfit*

equipment (or baggage or supplies or any object which hinders progress or movement) *n.pl.*: **impedimenta**. See *baggage*

equitable (uncompromisingly . . . , as in just) *n.*: **Rhadamanthine**. See *just*

equivalent (in strength, power, or effectiveness) *adj.*: **equipollent**. See *equal*

equivocal (word, phrase, or expression) *n.*: **equivoque**. [The equivocation is generally intentional, such as a double meaning. The word is therefore also a synonym for double entendre or pun.] ❖ "The Faith Zone of the Dome" [has been] renamed plain "Faith Zone" [because] the definite article ["the" was] potentially offensive to non-Christians. . . . [This] suggests that much of the energy going into the [Millennium] Dome's completion is [based on] doubt and hypersensitivity, rather than into boundless seas of national self-confidence and healthy contempt for the **equivoque**. (Cal McCrystal, "First Lady of the Dome," *Evening Standard* [London], 12/9/1999.)

(2) equivocal (as in having multiple interpretations or signifying different things) *adj.*: **multivocal**. See *multivocal*

(3) equivocal (as in subject to two different interpretations) *adj.*: **amphibolous**. See *ambiguous*

(4) equivocal (or cryptic or ambiguous) *adj.*: **sibylline** (or **sybilline**; often cap.). See *cryptic*

(5) equivocal (use of . . . , as in ambiguous, words) *n.*: **parisology**. See *ambiguous*

equivocate (as in avoid a straight answer) *v.i.*: **tergiversate**. See *evade*

(2) equivocate (as in lie, through the intentional use of misleading, ambiguous, or evasive language) *v.t.*: **prevaricate**. See *lie*

era (of or over the same . . .) *adj.*: **coetaneous**. See *contemporaneous*

(2) era (of the same . . . ; contemporary) *adj., n.*: **coeval**. See *contemporary*

(3) era *n.*: **saeculum**. See *generation*

eradicate (as in abolish) *v.t.*: **extirpate**. See *abolish*

(2) eradicate (as in put an end to) *v.t.*: **quietus** (as in "put the quietus to"). See *termination*

erase (as in abolish) *v.t.*: **extirpate**. See *abolish*

erect (having a persistently . . . penis) *adj.*: **priapic**. See *phallic*

(2) erect (having an . . . penis) *adj.*: **ithyphallic**. See *penis*

erectile dysfunction *n.*: **impotentia coeundi** [Latin]. ❖ In many respects archivists in presidential libraries aren't very different from home field announcers; they want to see the local boy (or girl) do good. They certainly don't want potential troublemakers writing about congested colons, irritated bowels, or, god forbid, **impotentia coeundi** or some other Latinate cover for not being able to sport wood post–Inaugural Ball. (David Houck, Forum:

"The Politics of Archival Research," *Rhetoric and Public Affairs*, 4/1/2006.)

erection (inability to sustain an . . .) *n.*: **impotentia coeundi** [Latin]. See *erectile dysfunction*

(2) erection (loss of . . .) *n.*: **detumescence**. See *shrinkage*

erode *v.t.*: **abrade**. See *chafe*

erogenous (relating to or exhibiting . . . behavior in many forms) *adj.*: **pansexual**. See *sexual*

erotic (study of . . . material) *n.*: **erotology**.
❖ The mother lode of pornography isn't stashed in Al Goldstein's basement. It's in San Francisco, at a scholarly place called the Institute for Advanced Study of Human Sexuality (IASHS). Composed of more than three million pieces of cataloged ribaldry, this hoard of naughtiness qualifies as the largest **erotology** library in the world, dwarfing the combined porn holdings of both the Kinsey Institute and the Library of Congress. (Rene Chun, "Notes from a Nasty Ebert," *Esquire*, 11/1/1997.)

(2) erotic (as in lustful) *adj.*: **concupiscent** (*n.*: **concupiscence**). See *lustful*

(3) erotic (as in sexual lovemaking) *adj.*: **amatory**. See *lovemaking*

(4) erotic (attraction to animals) *n.*: **zoophilia** (person attracted: **zoophile**). See *bestiality*

(5) erotic (desire to look at . . . scenes or images) *n.*: **scopophilia**. See *voyeurism*

(6) erotic (relating to or exhibiting . . . behavior in many forms) *adj.*: **pansexual**. See *sexual*

erring (as in sinful) *adj.*: **peccant**. See *sinful*

erroneous (and/or illogical argument) *n.*: **choplogic**. See *fallacy*

(2) erroneous (argument, spec. where one argues that because event B followed event A, then event A must have caused event B) *n.*: **post hoc, ergo propter hoc** [Latin for "after this, therefore, because of this"]. See *fallacy*

(3) erroneous (as in relating to reasoning that sounds plausible but is false or insincere) *adj.*: **meretricious**. See *specious*

(4) erroneous (engaging in argument that may be . . . , as in specious) *adj., n.*: **eristic**. See *specious*

(5) erroneous (argument, usually, but not necessarily related to philosophy) *n*.: **philosophism**. See *argument*

(6) erroneous (reasoning in logic in which a false conclusion is drawn from two premises, neither of which conveys information about all members of the designated class) *n*.: **undistributed middle**. See *fallacy*

(7) erroneous (reasoning intended to mislead or rationalize) *n*.: **casuistry**. See *fallacious*

(8) erroneous (reasoning that is fallacious or specious) *n*.: **syllogism**. See *specious*

error (with regard to where an event or thing occurred) *n*.: **anachorism** [This word is the geographical equivalent of "anachronism," which has as one definition "an error in time."] ❖ Before getting on with this article, let me point out that I am not having a problem with **anachorism** when I refer to towns like Athens and Decatur. The two towns really do exist but in Alabama, not in Georgia. (D. L. Stanley, "No 'Right Place, Right Time' for Brody Horton," *Atlanta Inquirer*, 11/2/1996.)

(2) error (grammatical . . . in speaking or writing because of trying too hard to be grammatically correct) *n*.: **hypercorrection**. ❖ The attempt to teach "It is I" often results in the **hypercorrection** "She gave it to Jane and I" or in avoidance of the pronoun even where it would occur in normal speech, as in "Harry and George and myself went to the game." (Daniel Suits, letter to the editor, *New York Times*, 9/1/1996.)

(3) error (confession of . . . , as in sin) *n*.: **peccavi**. See *confession*

(4) error (correction of . . . , esp. in printed material) *n*.: **corrigendum**. See *correction*

(5) error (in grammar) *n*.: **solecism**. See *misuse*

(6) error (in speech) *n*.: **lapsus linguae** [Latin]. See *slip of the tongue*

(7) error (in writing) *n*.: **lapsus calami** [Latin]. See *slip of the pen*

(8) error (small or trifling . . .) *n*.: **peccadillo**. See *infraction*

(9) error (tragic . . . , as in flaw, esp. by a literary character) *n*.: **hamartia**. See *flaw*

(10) error (verbal . . . such as a slip of the tongue or malapropism) *n*.: **parapraxis**. See *blunder*

erupting (as in bursting forth or through) *adj*.: **erumpent**. See *bursting*

eruption (of emotion, feeling, or action) *n*.: **paroxysm**. See *outburst*

(2) eruption (volcanic . . .) *adj*.: **pelean** (or **Pelean**). See *volcanic*

escape (as in a departure that is unannounced, abrupt, secret, or unceremonious) *n*.: **French leave** (or **French Leave**). See *departure*

(2) escape (from danger) *n*.: **hegira**. ❖ The Lindberghs rose early on December 31, 1935, in Liverpool's harbor [having fled to England to escape from the pressures of living in America and because of threats on their lives]. It suddenly seemed as though this **hegira** might be for naught, as a frenzied gauntlet of photographers gathered at the gangplank. (Scott Berg, *Lindbergh*, Putnam [1998], p. 346.)

(3) escape (desperate . . . , as in retreat) *n*.: **Dunkirk**. See *retreat*

essay (as in formal analysis or discussion of a subject) *n*.: **disquisition**. See *discourse*

esoteric (as in difficult to understand) *adj*.: **recondite**. See *complicated*

essence (the . . . of a matter, as in the bottom line, the main point, the substance, etc.) *n*.: **tachlis** (esp. as in "talk tachlis") [Yiddish]. ❖ My current cookbook bible is *How to Cook Everything* by Mark Bittman. The author writes for the *New York Times* . . . and he's written several other good-read cookbooks. Yes he's opinionated, very. But this guy talks **tachlis**, he gets right to the point and tells you what you need to know in a clear, down to earth manner. (Ann Kleinberg, *Books for Cooks*, *Jerusalem Post*, 6/18/2004.)

(2) essence *n*.: **quiddity**. ❖ Baker reminds us that the entire microfilm process is thoroughly riven with shoddiness. Whole pages might be skipped, images darkened to invisibility, text rendered blurry and illegible, the film itself liable to chemical degradation and, not least, the historical **quiddity** of the original book or periodical utterly lost—in the case of unique items, irrevocably so. (*Washington Post*, "Double Fold," 4/15/2001.)

(3) essence (as in embodiment) *n*.: **avatar**. See *embodiment*

(4) essence (of two things having an identical . . .) *adj*.: **consubstantial**. See *identical*

(5) essence (spec. the perfect or beautiful example of something) *n*.: **beau ideal**. See *ideal*

essential *adj*.: **constitutive**. ❖ [Homophobia] brings together into a new configuration beliefs and attitudes that evolved at different times and in different contexts. Fone chronicles the successive appearance, in Western philosophy, literature, theology and law, of the **constitutive** elements of homophobia as we know it. (Laurent Cartayrade, "With Prejudice," *Washington Post*, 10/8/2000.)

(2) essential (element or condition) *n*.: **sine qua non** [Latin]. See *indispensable*

essentially *adv*.: **au fond** [French]. See *basically*

establishment (again, as in renewal or restoration of something after decay, lapse of time, or dilapidation) *n*.: **instauration**. See *restoration*

estate (grounds belonging to an . . .) *n*.: **demesne**. ❖ The two houses I own, side by side, are on a quiet, well-treed street in the established black neighborhood known as Wallace Hill, snugged in between our small [central business district] and the richer white **demesnes** on the west side, more or less behind the hospital. (Richard Ford, *Independence Day*, Knopf [1995], p. 24.)

esteem (as in homage, not necessarily sincere or unforced) *n*.: **obeisance**. See *homage*

etched (into rock) *adj*.: **rupestrian**. See *carved*

eternal *adj*.: **aeonian** (or **eonian**). ❖ During **aeonian** stretches of oppressive silence, interspersed with "All of our customer service representatives are currently . . . ," my ear got that familiar numb sensation against the receiver. (Anne R. Lawrence, "Voting Virgin: An Ardent Alien's Confounding Quest for Citizenship," *World & I*, 9/1/2001, p. 282.)

(2) eternal (as in everlasting or immortal) *adj*.: **amaranthine**. See *immortal*

(3) eternal *adj*.: **sempiternal**. See *everlasting*

eternity (for . . .) *adv*.: **in aeternum** [Latin]. See *forever*

ethics (deciding right and wrong by applying . . .) *n*.: **casuistry** ❖ P. is particularly critical of **casuistry** and the traditional moral manuals, asserting that together they misled the whole discipline of Christian ethics into an improper preoccupation with law and obligation, rather than centering reflection on the moral life in terms of beatitude and the virtues. (James T. Bretzke, review of *The Sources of Christian Ethics*, by Servais Pinckaers, *Theological Studies*, 6/1/1996, p. 371.)

(2) ethics (study of) *n*.: **deontology**. ❖ **Deontology** concentrates on the righteousness of the human action itself, while teleology focuses on the rightness of the consequences of that action (Hunt and Vitell, 1986). (*Journal of Consumer Affairs*, "Spousal Ethical Justifications of Casino Gambling: A Psychometric Analysis," 6/1/1991.)

etiquette (precise observance of . . .) *n*.: **punctilio**. ❖ Have you ever wondered whether you should invite the boss home for dinner, or what to say when you're late to an important business meeting? If you have, you may need help from Miss Manners, [the] high priestess of **punctilio**. (Judith Martin [Miss Manners], Executive Life: "Miss Manners on Office Etiquette," *Fortune*, 11/6/1989, p. 155.)

(2) etiquette (appropriate . . . , as in propriety) *n*.: **correctitude**. See *propriety*

eulogy (as in giving praise or tribute) *n*.: **encomium** (one who delivers praise or tribute *n*.: **encomiast**). See *praise* and *tribute*

euphemism (opposite of . . .) *n*.: **dysphemism**. ❖ Most of us know euphemism, substitution of a kinder, gentler word for one that might be thought harsh. Have you run in to its antonym, **dysphemism**? Examples include shrink for psychiatrist; pencil pusher for superbly skilled print-media communicator. (Alden Wood, "Lawyerly Phrase of 'Counsel' Finds Itself Hitched to a Hip New Communicause," *Communication World*, 12/1/1997, p. 43.)

evade (a straight answer) *v.t.:* **tergiversate.** ❖ The proceedings were short, confusing and often hilarious, as Worth **tergiversated** [on the witness stand], trying to throw [the prosecutor] off with a combination of charm, equivocation, calculated self-incrimination, and straightforward perjury. (Ben Macintyre, *The Napoleon of Crime*, Farrar, Straus and Giroux [1997], p. 195.)

(2) evade (as in avert or ward off) *v.t.:* **forfend.** See *avert*

evaluate (under a new standard, esp. one that differs from conventional norms) *v.t.:* **transvaluate.** ❖ After all, in the **transvaluated** world of Germany during the Nazi period, ordinary Germans deemed the killing of Jews to be a beneficent act for humanity. (Daniel Goldhagen, *Hitler's Willing Executioners*, Knopf [1996], p. 452.)

(2) evaluate *v.t.:* **assay.** ❖ "Right now Jackie Robinson doesn't shape up as a first baseman," wrote Pat Lynch of the *New York Journal American*. "His weak hitting is something the shrewd **assayers** of baseball talent have been on to all along." (William Nack, "Baseball: The Breakthrough Fifty Years Ago," *Sports Illustrated*, 5/5/1997, p. 56.)

(3) evaluate (as in analyze, that which has already occurred; i.e., to project into the past) *v.t.:* **retroject.** See *analyze*

evaluating (act or process of . . . , as in measuring) *n.:* **mensuration.** See *measuring*

evaporate (as in vanish or disappear) *v.t.:* **evanesce.** See *disappear*

evasive (engaging in . . . tactics, esp. as a means to wear out an opponent or avoid confrontation) *adj.:* **Fabian.** See *dilatory, guerrilla,* and *cautious*

evasiveness (in speech or writing) *n.:* **circumlocution.** ❖ To do that—to break the memoir curse—a full treatment of [Bill Clinton's] mistakes should include at least: . . . 5) His failure in using preposterous **circumlocutions** and flimsy legalisms to try to escape the consequences of his affair with Monica Lewinsky. (Jonathan Alter, "Writing the Book of Bill," *Newsweek*, 8/20/2001, p. 22.)

evening (of, relating to, or occurring in) *adj.:* **vespertine.** ❖ For television sets should be like theatres, concert halls, owls, bats and vampires: they are **vespertine** creatures, and may properly emerge only in the evening from their daytime slumbers. It upsets television's natural biorhythms to be hauling it out of its bed and bestirring it to work at dawn. (Kevin Myers, Comment: "Breakfast TV Is a Dog's Dinner," *Sunday Telegraph* [London], 10/11/1998.)

(2) evening (as in twilight) *n.:* **gloaming.** See *twilight*

event (secondary . . . that accompanies or results from another) *n.:* **epiphenomenon** (*adj.:* **epiphenomenal**). See *phenomenon*

even-tempered *adj.:* **phlegmatic.** ❖ Outwardly, [Vancouver Grizzlies coach Brian] Winters has remained composed; volcanic eruptions are not his style. "Really, what would be the point?" he says. However, at halftime of the Grizzlies' 86–75 defeat on March 26 in Detroit, the **phlegmatic** Winters threw what for him is a tantrum. (Austin Murphy, Pro Basketball: "Down . . . but Not Out as Their NBA Record Losing Streak Hits 22," *Sports Illustrated*, 4/8/1996, p. 54.)

everlasting *adj.:* **sempiternal.** ❖ [Will] private colleges . . . be utterly priced out of the market[?] That's unlikely for the really high-priced institutions. Princeton is nowhere near setting a "market clearing price" (the price that is so high that it exhausts the number of potential buyers). This is a **sempiternal** truth for institutions of high prestige. Someone will pay (almost) anything for Ivy-ish credentials. (Dennis O'Brien, "A 'Necessary' of Modern Life? A Very Expensive College Education," *Commonweal*, 3/28/1997, p. 9.)

(2) everlasting *adj.:* **aeonian** (or **eonian**). See *eternal*

(3) everlasting *adj.:* **amaranthine.** See *immortal*

everlastingly *adv.:* **in aeternum** [Latin]. See *forever*

everyday (as in mundane) *adj.:* **sublunary.** See *earthly*

(2) everyday (as in routine or mechanical) *adj.*: **banausic**. See *routine*

(3) everyday (of or relating to the . . . people) *adj.*: **plebian**. See *common*

(4) everyday (people, as in the masses) *n.*: **canaille**. See *masses*

(5) everyday (people, as in the masses) *n.*: **hoi polloi**. See *commoners*

(6) everyday *adj.*: **quotidian**. See *mundane*

evident (as in easily understood or seen through, like motives) *adj.*: **transpicuous**. See *transparent*

evil *adj.*: **malefic**. ❖ It is not remarkable that celluloid Russians would change from villains to heroes and back over time. Yet, I never expected them to prove so volatile, or to move so consistently with fluctuations in U.S. policy toward the Soviets. Nor could I have conceived how overly angelic would be the good Russians and how utterly **malefic** the bad ones. (Michael J. Strada, "Politics and the Movies: Art Anticipating Life," *USA Today Magazine*, 11/1/1998.)

(2) evil *adj.*: **malevolent**. ❖ The [tobacco] companies' threat is simple. Without their agreement, it may be hard to get rid of advertising to kids. When Bill Clinton heard they were walking, he asked disparagingly, "What are they going to do? Say, we're going to go back to advertising to children?" Well, bless their **malevolent** hearts, yes. (Ellen Goodman, "The Bluster and Bluff of Big Tobacco," *St. Louis Post-Dispatch*, 4/15/1998.)

(3) evil (and scheming woman) *n.*: **jezebel** (sometimes cap.). See *woman*

(4) evil (as in cruel) *adj.*: **fell** (*n.*: fellness). See *cruel*

(5) evil (as in devilish) *adj.*: **Mephistophelean**. See *devilish*

(6) evil (as in wicked) *adj.*: **flagitious**. See *wicked*

(7) evil (female spirit who has sex with sleeping men) *n.*: **succubus**. See *demon*

(8) evil (intended to ward off . . .) *adj.*: **apotropaic**. See *protect*

(9) evil (person) *n.*: **caitiff**. See *despicable*

(10) evil (portending . . .) *adj.*: **baleful**. See *sinister*

(11) evil (spirit who has sex with sleeping women) *n.* **incubus**. See *demon*

(12) evil *adj.*: **facinorous**. See *wicked*

(13) evil *adj.*: **iniquitous**. See *wicked*

(14) evil (or wrongdoing by its own nature or natural law rather than because prohibited by statute) *n.*: **malum in se** [Latin]. See *wrongdoing*

evildoer *n.*: **malefactor**. See *wrongdoer*

(2) evildoer *n.*: **miscreant**. See *wrongdoer*

evil vs. good (conflict in the soul between . . .) *n.*: **psychomachia**. See *good vs. evil*

(2) evil vs. good (philosophy that divides the world into . . .) *n.*: **Manichaeism or Manicheism** (*adj.*: **Manichaean** or **Manichean**) [sometimes not cap.]. See *good vs. evil*

evolution (spec. a fundamental transformation of mind or character, esp. a spiritual conversion) *n.*: **metanoia**. See *conversion*

exact (translation) *n.*: **metaphrase**. See *translation*

(2) exact (word that is more . . . than another given word) *n.*: **hyponym**. See *word*

exacting (overly . . .) *adj.*: **persnickety**. See *picky*

exaggerate *v.t.*: **overegg**. Many celebrity memoirs **overegg** the rotten aspects of a childhood in order to flatter the achievements which follow it, but [Julie] Andrews resists this. (Emma Brockes, "Climb Every Mountain," *New York Times*, 3/30/2008.)

(2) exaggerate *v.t.*: **aggrandize**. ❖ It is hardly an act of heroism to reject neo-Nazism. Hasselbach exaggerates the importance of his former life so as to **aggrandize** the importance of his present life. Though no longer a fascist, he is still peddling the fascination of fascism. (Noah Isenberg, review of *Fuhrer-Ex: Memoirs of a Former Neo-Nazi*, by Ingo Hasselbach and Tom Reiss, *New Republic*, 4/8/1996, p. 28.)

exaggerated (behavior) *n.*, *adj.*: **operatics**. See *melodramatic*

exaggeration (abnormal propensity toward . . .) *n.*: **mythomania**. See *embellishment*

(2) exaggeration (false . . . , as in boast, esp. one that is designed to harm or prejudice another) *n.*: **jactitation**. See *boast*

exalt (as in idealize) *v.t.*: **platonize**. See *idealize*

exaltation (to divine rank or stature) *n.*: **apotheosis** (*v.t.*: **apotheosize**). ❖ Mother [Theresa] would probably have recoiled at the extravagance. A state funeral televised around the world. A military guard bearing her coffin to a ceremony attended by the powerful and the famous. Billboards proclaiming her **apotheosis**. (*Time*, World: "For the Poor, an Immortal," 9/22/1997, p. 42.)

exalted (as in lordly) *adj.*: **seigneurial**. See *lordly*

(2) exalted (as in of or related to the sky or heavens) *adj.*: **empyreal**. See *celestial*

(3) exalted (as in of or related to the sky or heavens) *adj.*: **supernal**. See *celestial*

examination (of a subject, as in survey) *n.*: **conspectus**. See *survey*

(2) examination (detailed . . . of a literary work) *n.*: **explication de texte** [French]. See *analysis*

(3) examination (of matters outside oneself—i.e., the outside world) *n.*: **extrospection** (*adj.*: **extrospective**). See *observation*

examine (closely, esp. for purposes of surveillance) *v.t.*: **perlustrate**. [A separate but related definition of this word is to travel through an area or building for purposes of inspecting it, as if doing a survey.] ❖ To get even approximately accurate intelligence on the mood and attitudes of the population, the Soviet leaders would have had to resort to sources which tapped private communications, by **perlustrating** personal letters and building networks of informers. (en.wikipedia.org/wiki/People's_Correspondent.)

(2) examine (as in analyze closely) *v.t.*: **anatomize**. See *analyze*

(3) examine (as in analyze, that which has already occurred; i.e., to project into the past) *v.t.*: **retroject**. See *analyze*

(4) examine (as in touch, esp. for medical reasons) *v.t.*: **palpate**. See *touch*

(5) examine (closely) *v.t.*: **catechize**. See *question*

examiner (or investigator) *n.*: **scrutator**. ❖ What gives any member of the legal profession the right to blame local graduates for the poor quality of lawyers? Was any research conducted? Has a **scrutator** been appointed to provide statistics to prove that foreign law graduates are nonpareil? (Mariette Peters-Goh, "Drop Blame Game, Focus on Solution," *New Straits Times*, 7/2/2007.)

example *n.*: **exemplum**. ❖ His thesis . . . was that white male America was praising Asians as the "ideal minority." He made use of revisionist history by citing examples from the 19th century, when white planters in Mississippi brought in Chinese workers as an **exemplum** for the black sharecroppers, thereby driving home his propaganda that Asians and blacks are at odds because of whites. (W. J. Reeves, "Will Zealots Spell the Doom of Great Literature?" *USA Today Magazine*, 9/1/1996.)

(2) example (spec. the perfect or beautiful . . . of something) *n.*: **beau ideal**. See *ideal*

(3) example (original . . .) *n.*: **archetype**. See *model*

exceed (the limits, resources, or capabilities of) *v.t.*: **beggar**. See *surpass*

exceeding (as in going above and beyond the call of duty or what is required) *adj.*: **supererogatory**. [This word has both a positive meaning (as given above) and a negative meaning. In the negative sense (which is more common), it means superfluous or unnecessary. See *superfluous*. The following is an example of the positive sense.] ❖ [J]udgment is passed on [differences from the norm]. . . . A person is put to shame whenever he is regarded as having fallen below the standards. It follows from this structure that even if someone is approved because she has performed something extraordinary—perhaps she performed a **supererogatory** deed, or simply because she is so much above the standards in beauty, intelligence, athletics, piano playing—she will also feel ashamed if praised by a community. . . . (Agnes

Heller, "Five Approaches to the Phenomenon of Shame," *Social Research*, 12/22/2003.)

excellence (as in superiority or state of being better) *n.*: **meliority**. See *superiority*

excellent (generally used in the sense of select, choice, or distinguished) *adj.*: **eximious** [sometimes considered obscure, but recent uses are not uncommon]. ❖ One claim not to be made for Edouard Vuillard is that he is "one of the great modern masters of his generation." . . . That [such a claim is] made by the President of the Royal Academy in a foreword to the catalogue of that **eximious** institution's latest exhibition is, however, excusable in that it is his duty to whip us in to see it, and the lash of hyperbole is far more ready and at his hand than the carrot of simple truth. (Brian Sewell, "The Minor Master of Domestic Detail," *Evening Standard* [London], 1/30/2004.)

(2) excellent *adj.*: **galumptious** [slang]. ❖ [The] Ford F-150 pickup moves with lightning speed and scares the devil out of anyone who gets in its way. It's a big, muscular truck with a 240-horsepower V-8 that'll thump lesser vehicles. . . . Add 17-inch cast-aluminum wheels, performance shock absorbers and that **galumptious** V-8, and you've got something that really hauls . . . fast. (Warren Brown, "Lightning Hot Rod," *Washington Post*, 12/2/1994.)

(3) excellent *adj.*: **palmary**. ❖ This [the Middle Ages] is the very age of Universities; it is the classical period of the schoolmen; it is the splendid and **palmary** instance of the wise policy and large liberality of the Church, as regards philosophical inquiry. When was there ever a more curious, more meddling, bolder, keener, more penetrating, more rationalistic exercise of the reason than at that time? (William Hoye, "The Religious Roots of Academic Freedom," *Theological Studies*, 9/1/1997, p. 409.)

(4) excellent *adj.*: **skookum**. ❖ Yes, the boys of Alien Ant Farm are cheekier than Adam Ant in red leather pants, but we admire their foolhardy spirit and infamous reverse mohawks. On Sunday night, the band that took on the king of pop with a **skookum** cover of

"Smooth Criminal" stops by Axis at 8; $10. (Christopher Muther, Go! Weekend, *Boston Globe*, 7/25/1993.)

(5) excellent (as in first-class) *adj.*: **pukka**. See *first-class*

(6) excellent (as in of the highest quality) *n.*: **first water** (usu. as in "of the first water"). See *quality*

(7) excellent *adj.*: **frabjous** (often as in "Oh frabjous day!"). See *wonderful*

(8) excellent *adj.*: **mirific**. See *wonderful*

excerpt (esp. from the Bible) *n.*: **pericope**. ❖ Wittingly or unwittingly, when President George W Bush claimed, "Either you are with us or you are with the terrorists," he was excerpting from and paraphrasing the words attributed to Jesus in the **pericope** about collusion with Satan in the Gospel according to Matthew. The full quotation is, "He who is not with me is against me, and he who does not gather with me scatters" (Matt 12:30). (Brian Finch, "Channel Anger and Energy into Intelligence," *Herald* [Glasgow], 9/22/2001.)

excess *n.*: **nimiety**. ❖ Just as daily life contains all the comforts of what one owns, there is also a natural shedding or forgetting and a natural dulling, otherwise one becomes burdened with a sense of **nimiety**, a sense (as Kenneth Clark put it in his autobiography) of the "too-muchness" of life. Of course, this **nimiety** is also just tiredness, to be expected in an old man, and Prince registers that on seeing the Caravaggios: "By this time I have been / too long on my feet, / seen too much and am tiring." (Nicholas Poburko, "Poetry, Past and Present: F. T. Prince's Walks in Rome," *Renascence: Essays on Values in Literature*, 1/1/1999.)

excessive *adj.*: **de trop** [French]. ❖ [The CEO of Starbucks Coffee] is the perfect spokesman for an era when "decaf latte" has entered the upper-middle-class lexicon as shorthand for a little self-indulgence. Indulgence? Once, we knew the true meaning of that word. Indulgences should be decadent, degenerate, altogether **de trop**. They should not be decaffeinated. (Andrew Stuttaford, Food & Drink:

"Mug's Game," *National Review*, 12/7/1998, p. 71.)

(2) excessive (as in superfluous) *adj.*: **excrescent**. See *superfluous*

(3) excessive (as in superfluous) *adj.*: **super-erogatory**. See *superfluous*

exchange (as in dialogue, in which neither side hears or understands or pays attention to the other) *n.*: **dialogue de sourds** [French]. See *dialogue*

excited (nervously . . .) *adj.*: **atwitter**. ❖ Left, right, left, right . . . forward, backward . . . hop, hop, hop. Pardon me, but I'm in training for the 2000 Olympics. In case you missed the big news that has set the Olympic world **atwitter**, on April 3 the International Olympic Committee granted provisional recognition to ballroom dancing and surfing. (E. M. Swift, "Point After: Calling Arthur Murray: Ballroom Dancing Has as Much Right to Be in the Olympics As, Say, Rhythmic Gymnastics," *Sports Illustrated*, 4/24/1995, p. 72.)

excited (or enthusiastic speech or writing) *n.*: **dithyramb**. See *enthusiastic*

excitement (moment of intense . . .) *n.*: **frisson** [French]. See *shudder*

(2) excitement (sexual . . . from rubbing against something or someone) *n.*: **frottage**. See *rubbing*

(3) excitement (excessive or unbridled . . . , as in enthusiasm) *n.*: **schwarmerei** (or **schwärmerei**) [German]. See *enthusiasm*

exciting (wildly . . . as in frenzied) *adj.*: **corybantic**. See *frenzied*

exclamation *n.*: **ecphonesis**. ❖ Meantime the hellish tattoo of the heart increased. It grew quicker and quicker, and louder and louder every instant. The old man's terror must have been extreme! It grew louder, I say, louder every moment! ("The Tell-Tale Heart") Poe's frequent use of **ecphonesis** is surely responsible to a large degree for the charge that he wrote in such an overwrought style. (Brett Zimmerman, "A Catalogue of Rhetorical and Other Literary Terms from American Literature and Oratory," *Style*, 12/22/1997.)

exclude (as in consider separately) *v.t.*: **prescind** (generally as in "prescind from"). See *isolate*

(2) exclude (as in omit intentionally) *v.t.*: **pretermit**. See *omit*

excluded (as in ostracized or exiled) *v.t.*: **sent to Coventry**. [British]. See *ostracized*

exclusion (as in omission) *n.*: **elision**. See *omission*

exclusive (person, esp. in intellectual or literary circles) *n.*: **mandarin**. See *influential*

exclusively *adv.*: **ex professo** [Latin]. See *expressly*

excrement (eating) *adj.*: **scatophagous**. ❖ [In India], I ordered a local fish dish with an unfamiliar name. William, a fellow traveler, leaned across the table to tell me, "That fish is called **Scatophagous** Argos, the keen-eyed shit-eater." I took a mouthful; it tasted divine. (Colin Barraclough, "Oil and Herbs Blend Well with Sun and Sea Breeze," *Insight on the News*, 9/30/1996.)

(2) excrement (feeding on) *adj.*: **coprophagous**. ❖ Some dogs are **coprophagous**, says Gerba. That means they eat feces. When Scruffy laps your face, he can transmit E. coli, salmonella, or Pasteurella multocida, possibly giving you the trots. (Tom Zoellner, "Where the Germs Are," *Men's Health*, 9/1/1999, p. 119.)

(3) excrement (interest in . . . , often sexual) *n.*: **coprophilia**. ❖ My "Ugh" column really struck a nerve. So many of you sent me examples of offensive ads and clippings that I must now be in possession of the largest collection of pictures of toilets outside the ranks of the National Association for the Advancement of **Coprophilia**. (Florence King, "The Misanthrope's Corner," *National Review*, 8/12/2002.)

(4) excrement (obsession with) *n.*: **coprology**. ❖ TMP: How did your interest in fecal matter develop? Lewin: I noted differences in the shape and size of various kinds of deer pellets and wondered what made them so different. . . . That led me in turn to consider the wider subject of what we might call comparative **coprology** in general, and begin this survey of what seems to be a fascinating if neglected topic. (Elaine McNinch, "Merde!" *Medical Post*, 10/12/1999.)

(5) excrement (of or relating to) *adj.*: **stercoraceous**. ❖ [In the movie *Goldmember*,] there are . . . more than a few shit jokes, and I don't mean jokes that aren't funny. Indeed, there are times in *Goldmember* when Myers's vision is hilariously . . . **stercoraceous**. . . . It's tasteless and vulgar, offensive and utterly puerile. I loved every minute of it. (Philip Kerr, "Hitting the Base Notes," *New Statesman*, 8/5/2002.)

(6) excrement (study of or obsession with) *n.*: **scatology**. ❖ Eliminated matter is something of a theme for Frewer. . . . Ask him about proposing to Amanda, 32: " . . . I almost stepped in a pile of dog poo," he says. "And instead of going 'Whoooa!' I said, 'Will you marry me?' I can actually thank a dog with bowel problems for my being married." Psychiatrists would have to listen for hours to find an explanation for Frewer's **scatology**. (Margot Dougherty, Tube: "With Max Headroom Behind Him, Matt Frewer Mad-libs Through *Doctor, Doctor* and a Smash Film," *People*, 7/17/1989, p. 111.)

(7) excrement *n.*: **egesta**. ❖ [The novel] *Bridget Jones's Diary* has a lot to answer for. It's not just literary diarrhea, it's the thin bowel water which tells you that your session of diarrhea is at an end, and (although PR hype has turned this diluted **egesta** into an international bestseller) we all know that a series of fragmented testimonials does not a novel make. (Victor Lewis-Smith, "The World of Hump It and Hop It," *Evening Standard* [London], 2/4/1999.)

(8) excrement *n.*: **ordure**. I loved seeing the hoi polloi—the great California populace who voted Arnold Schwarzenegger into office but who weren't allowed in for the inauguration— pressing by the hundreds against the cyclone fence like spuds against a potato masher, all just for an eyeful or earful of the new governor. . . . I loved the **ordure** the Capitol's mounted

police's mounts left behind, lending a whiff of the circus to the circus. (Patt Morrison, "There Was Much to Love About the Inauguration," *Los Angeles Times*, 11/18/2003.)

(9) excrement (esp. that of sea birds) *n.*: **guano**. See *bird dung*

excrete (or discharge waste from the body) *v.t.*: **egest**. ❖ The correlation between [fossilized excrement] dimensions and animal size is not absolute, however. Although the quantity of **egested** waste is proportional to body size, the entire fecal mass may not be recovered because of the fragmentary nature of fecal material. (Karen Chin, "On the Elusive Trail of Fossil Dung," *National Forum*, 6/22/1998, p. 36.)

excusable *adj.*: **venial**. See *forgivable*

excuse (attempt to . . . an offense or crime) *v.t.*: **palliate**. See *downplay*

(2) excuse (formal . . . , as in justification, for one's acts or beliefs) *n.*: **apologia**. See *justification*

(3) excuse (as in act or event that is used as a justification to provoke battle, literally or figuratively) *n.*: **casus belli** [Latin: occasion of war]. See *provocation*

execute (by strangling or cutting the throat) *v.t.*: **garrote**. See *strangle*

execution (of convicted persons, spec. burning of heretics at the stake) *n.*: **auto-da-fé**. ❖ In theory, Bill Clinton should have been nervous. It had been nearly a year since he'd held a full-scale press conference—a year in which he'd been exposed, impeached, humiliated and nearly convicted for lying under oath. The networks were going live for the **auto-da-fé**. (Howard Fineman, "In the Line of Fire," *Newsweek*, 3/29/1999, p. 28.)

(2) execution (mass . . . by drowning) *n.*: **noyade**. See *drowning*

exemplary *adj.*: **palmary**. See *excellent*

exhaust (as in deprive of strength) *v.t.*: **geld**. See *weaken*

exhausted (as in weakened) *adj.*: **etiolated**. See *weakened*

(2) exhausted (chronically . . .) *adj.*: **neurasthenic**. See *fatigued*

exhausting (as in laborious) *adj.*: **operose**. See *laborious*

exhaustion (from lack of energy or nourishment) *n.*: **inanition**. ❖ But why should we assume that divorce is always preceded by open conflict? Some marriages die a quiet death, preceded by boredom, silent contempt, or sheer **inanition**. (Joseph Adelson, "Splitting Up," *Commentary*, 9/1/1996, p. 63.)

exhilarated (often in a boastful way) *adj.*: **cock-a-hoop**. See *elated*

exhilarating (as in exuberant) *adj.*: **yeasty**. See *exuberant*

exhorting (or inciting or inspiring to action) *adj.*: **proceleusmatic** (pros-uh-loos-MAT-ik). ❖ [While rock climbing with Dad and me, Doug loses his balance.] Dad is there, takes hold of the line and together we stop his fall but he's over the edge and we can't see him. From behind us we hear Liz's **proceleusmatic** words over the din of the storm, "Way to go you guys! You saved him from falling!" (Richard Ellis, *Round Rock Rolls*, members .cox.net/2dellis/sylvia/sylvia_main.html?412, 5/16/2006.)

(2) exhorting (as in . . . someone to take a course of action) *adj.*: **hortatory**. See *urging*

exiled (as in against the world) *adv., adj.*: **contra mundum** [Latin]. See *against the world*

exiled (or ostracized) *v.t.*: **sent to Coventry** [British]. See *ostracized*

existence (while coming into . . .) *adv.*: **aborning**. See *born*

exit (as in a departure that is unannounced, abrupt, secret, or unceremonious) *n.*: **French leave** (or **French Leave**). See *departure*

(2) exit (hurriedly or secretly) *v.t.*: **absquatulate**. See *leave*

(3) exit (hurriedly or secretly) *v.t.*: **decamp**. See *leave*

exodus (from danger) *n.*: **hegira**. See *escape*

exoneration (obtaining . . . through testimony of others) *n.*: **compurgation**. See *acquittal*

exotic (as in unusual or rare) *adj.*: **recherché** [French]. See *rare*

expand (in scope) *v.t.*: **aggrandize**. ❖ Thus, where the old history took place primarily in the political arena, the new history focuses on the home, family, community, workplace—in short, on civil society. The effect of the new history has been not only to depoliticize history but to de-**aggrandize** it as well, to shift attention from great, public, historic events and personages to the daily lives of the "anonymous masses." (Gertrude Himmelfarb, "For the Love of Country" *Commentary*, 5/1/1997, p. 34.)

(2) expand (as in burgeon; lit. bear fruit) *v.i.*: **fructify**. See *burgeon*

expectant (nervously . . . and excited) *adj.*: **atwitter**. See *excited*

(2) expectant (as in anticipatory) *adj.*: **prevenient**. See *anticipatory*

expectation (that something is going to occur) *n.*: **presentiment**. See *premonition*

expecting (as in pregnant) *adj.*: **enceinte** [French]. See *pregnant*

(2) expecting (as in pregnant) *adj.*: **gravid**. See *pregnant*

expedition (to a sacred place or shrine, esp. to Mecca) *n.*: **hadj**. See *pilgrimage*

expel (as in unseat) *v.t.*: **unhorse**. See *unseat*

experience (difficult or painful . . .) *n.*: **via dolorosa**. See *ordeal*

experiment (with) *v.t.*: **assay**. ❖ Jazz and blues have been inseparable since the birth of the former; indeed, the dividing line between some barrelhouse piano and jazz keyboard pyrotechnics can be hard to find. And virtually every jazz personage has **assayed** the blues at least once. (*Philadelphia Tribune*, "New CDs Prove the Significance of Blues," 1/8/1999.)

expert *n.*: **cognoscente**. See *connoisseur*

(2) expert (as in skillful) *adj.*: **habile**. See *skillful*

(3) expert (as in skillful) *adj.* **au fait** [French]. See *skillful*

expertise (area of . . .) *n.*: **bailiwick**. ❖ The law, after all, can do very little to prevent espionage—or even the score. Such a task would seem to be the **bailiwick** of the CIA, which . . . could in theory spy on foreign corporations and steal their secrets. (Jamie Malanowski, Features: "Silicon Bond Looking to Become a Superspy?" *Time*, 6/1/1997, p. 36.)

(2) expertise (area of . . .) *n.*: **métier** [French]. See *forte*

(3) expertise (of an argument based on the supposed . . . or say-so of another, but in an area that is outside his or her field; i.e., improperly trading on the reverence and respect of another) *adj., adv.*: **ad verecundiam** (*n.*: **argumentum ad verecundiam**) [Latin]. See *argument*

expiatory *adj.*: **piacular**. See *atoning*

explain (a subject at length in speech or writing) *v.i.*: **expatiate**. See *expound*

(2) explain (attempt to . . . an offense with excuses) *v.t.*: **palliate**. See *downplay*

explanation (additional . . . or clarification) *n.*: **epexegesis** (*adj.*: **epexegetic**). ❖ How does minimalism [i.e., saying as little as possible to justify an outcome] play out in the current Supreme Court? . . . While Justice [Antonin] Scalia always preaches judicial restraint, his opinions range far and wide over the legal countryside. When he has a majority, he will take the Court as far as it is willing to go, restrained only by how much he worries about losing the majority if he gets too **epexegetic**. (Abner Mikva, "One Case at a Time," *Washington Monthly*, 5/1/1999.)

(2) explanation (as in clarification or clearing up) *n.*: **éclaircissement** [French]. See *clarification*

(3) explanation (esp. of a text) *n.*: **exegesis**. See *interpretation*

(4) explanation (formal . . . of one's acts or beliefs) *n.*: **apologia**. See *justification*

(5) explanation (having more than one . . . or signifying different things) *adj.*: **multivocal**. See *ambiguous*

(6) explanation (of a text by adding one's own ideas) *n.*: **eisegesis**. See *interpretation*

explanatory (as in interpretative, often regarding a document or text, such as scripture) *n.*: **hermeneutic**. See *interpretation*

exploding (as in bursting forth or through) *adj.*: **erumpent**. See *bursting*

exploitation (of a religious, national, or racial group) *n.*: **helotism** (*v.t.*: **helotize**). See *oppression*

exploration (of a subject, as in survey) *n.*: **conspectus**. See *survey*

explore (as in analyze, that which has already occurred; i.e., to project into the past) *v.t.*: **retroject**. See *analyze*

explosion (causing intense heat and light) *n.*: **deflagration**. ❖ Grove claims that the Bismarck's shell ignited the 100 tons of cordite propellant in the aft magazines [of HMS *Hood*], which created "a massive **deflagration** that burnt its way like a blowlamp through the ship." (Simon Crerar, "The Riddle of the Hood," *Sunday Times* [London], 12/16/1.)

explosive (potentially . . . or volatile place or situation) *n.*: **tinderbox**. ❖ The Serbian province of Kosovo is a **tinderbox** that poses the biggest threat to Europe and the Balkan region since the Bosnian war ended in 1995. (Lee Michael Katz, "Kosovo Has the Potential to be Another Bosnia," *USA Today*, 3/10/1998.)

expose (as in disclose) *v.t.*: **disinter**. See *disclose*

(2) expose (as in disprove convincingly) *v.t.*: **confute**. See *refute*

exposed (as in vulnerable, person or thing) *n.*: **clay pigeon**. See *vulnerable*

exposition (as in formal analysis or discussion of a subject) *n.*: **disquisition**. See *discourse*

expound (on a subject at length in speech or writing) *v.i.*: **expatiate**. ❖ In interviews, [French President François Mitterrand] **expatiated** on his attitude [about] death. He paraded a highly intellectual agnosticism, logically not able to believe in a God but emotionally unable to embrace atheism. (Mary Dejevsky, "A Long Dying Ends with a Vicious Irony," *Independent* [London], 1/9/1996.)

(2) expound *v.i., n.*: **descant**. See *talk*

express (as in send a signal) *v.t., v.i.*: **semaphore**. See *signal*

expressed (not capable of being) *adj.*: **ineffable**. See *indescribable*

expression (or phrase or comment that is elegant, concise, witty, and/or well-put) *n.*: **atti-**

cism. ❖ Can a former adviser to [former British Prime Minster Margaret] Thatcher, an establishmentarian and literary grandee, make you laugh? Step forward Ferdinand Mount, in whose confident, brilliant comedy *Of Love and Asthma* witty **atticisms** flop like cream oozing from a sponge cake. (Brendan O'Keefe, Books: "Fostering Love out of Failure," *Observer*, 9/15/1991.)

(2) expression (as in demeanor) *n.*: **mien**. See *demeanor*

(3) expression (as in figure of speech) *n.*: **trope**. See *figure of speech*

(4) expression (as in manner of speaking) *n.*: **façon de parler** [French]. See *way of speaking*

(5) expression (as in using one word or phrase in . . . for something with which it is usually associated, such as using "city hall" to refer to city government) *n.*: **metonymy**. See *figure of speech*

(6) expression (facial . . . in the form of a grimace due to pain or disgust) *n.*: **rictus**. See *grimace*

(7) expression (in which one makes only passing mention of something in order to emphasize rhetorically the significance of what is being omitted; often preceded by the phrase "not to mention") *n.*: **paraleipsis**. See *figure of speech*

(8) expression (in which one makes reference to an issue by saying that one will not discuss it; e.g., "I'm not even going to get into the character issue.") *n.*: **apophasis**. See *figure of speech*

(9) expression (just the right . . . or word) *n.*: **mot juste** [French]. See *word*

(10) expression (new . . . , phrase, or word) *n.*: **neologism**. See *word*

(11) expression (pithy . . .) *n.*: **gnome** (*adj.*: **gnomic**). See *catchphrase*

(12) expression (written . . . that is concise, precise, or refined; lit. "as if engraved in a precious stone") *adj.*: **lapidary**. See *writing*

(13) expression *n.*: **locution**. See *phrase*

expressly *adv.*: **ex professo** [Latin]. ❖ Although the subtitle advertises the Jewish/Christian dialogue, not all the essays deal **ex professo** with that subject; indeed, only one essay in the book is by a Jew (Jacob Petuchowski's study of the Lord's Prayer from the perspective of Jewish prayer) and some of the essays are not about Judaism at all. (Lawrence Cunningham, "New Visions: Historical and Theological Perspectives on the Jewish-Christian Dialogue," *Commonweal*, 11/1/1994.)

expunge (a book or a writing in a prudish manner) *v.t.*: **bowdlerize**. See *edit*

extemporaneous *adj.*: **autoschediastic**. See *unrehearsed*

extend (as in branch out) *v.i.*: **ramify**. See *branch out*

extensive (as in widespread) *adj.*: **pandemic**. See *widespread*

extenuate (as in attempt to minimize seriousness of an offense) *v.t.*: **palliate**. See *downplay*

exterminate (as in put an end to) *v.t.*: **quietus** (as in "put the quietus to"). See *termination*

(2) exterminate *v.t.*: **extirpate**. See *abolish*

external (as in originating from the outside; extrinsic) *adj.*: **adscititious**. See *extrinsic*

(2) external (appearance, as opposed to the substance that lies beneath) *n.*, *n.pl.*: **superficies**. See *appearance*

externally *adv.*: **ab extra** [Latin]. ❖ Surely . . . the two Tory finance ministers on the bridge during fiscal 1992-93 did not sit with their pencils in hand working out their very own budget estimates. In fact, the estimates would come from the best minds in the treasury department, aided by those at the bank and abetted **ab extra** by some of [the 200 economists whom Finance Minster Paul Martin convened to meet]. (Dalton Camp, "We Need Good Forecasting, Not Ottawa Gamesmanship," *Toronto Star*, 12/12/1993.)

extort (money unfairly and in excessive amounts) *v.t.*: **mulct**. See *extract*

extortion *n.*: **chantage** [French]. ❖ [A woman hired a witch doctor to put a hex on another woman having an affair with her husband. She said:] "Soon after [that, the witch doctor] started blackmailing me. It was **chantage**, I tell you. **Chantage**." "What could she blackmail you with?" . . . "[S]he said if I did not give her what she wanted, she would take away the hex." (Manfred Wolf, "The Two Witch Doctors," *Literary Review*, 3/22/2001.)

(2) extortion (bribe or protection money) *n.*: **Danegeld** (or **Danegelt**). See *protection money*

extra (as in originating from the outside; extrinsic) *adj.*: **adscititious**. See *extrinsic*

(2) extra (or unexpected gift or benefit, sometimes as thanks for a purchase) *n.*: **lagniappe**. See *gift*

extract (money unfairly and in excessive amounts) *v.t.*: **mulct**. [This word has three somewhat related definitions, including (1) to fine or penalize, (2) to extract money unfairly (but not necessarily illegally), and (3) to extract money illegally, esp. by fraud, extortion, or theft. This is an example of the second definition.] ❖ Since 1999, when Vietnamese forces withdrew from the country, the Cambodian people, largely rice farmers and fisherman, have been ill-served by their government. The tourist concession at Angkor Wat has been sold to a Japanese consortium, including several public officials, who **mulct** millions annually from the high admission fees charged visiting tourists. (James Zirin, "Cambodia's Glimmer of Hope," *Washington Times*, 2/26/2006.)

(2) extract (or pry or force out, whether from a place or position, or information) *v.t.*: **winkle** (usually used with *out*). ❖ [Monica Lewinsky] came to see [President Clinton] that Saturday morning, Jan. 6; as a frequent visitor, she **winkled out** of a guard the infuriating fact that her Handsome was not with his lawyers, as claimed, but was seeing a woman she took to be a romantic rival. After she raised a rumpus, an angry President wanted an officer fired for letting Monica know the identity of his visitor. (William Safire, "Beyond Monica," *New York Times*, 9/24/1998.)

(3) extract (as in excerpt, esp. from the Bible) *n.*: **pericope**. See *excerpt*

(4) extract (the flavor or essence of something, as if by boiling down) *v.t.*: **decoct**. See *boil down*

extramarital (sex or relations) *n.*: **hetaerism**. See *affair*

extraneous (as in argument where one proves or disproves a point that is not at issue) *n.*: **ignoratio elenchi** [Latin]. See *irrelevancy*

(2) extraneous (as in originating from the outside; extrinsic) *adj.*: **adscititious**. See *extrinsic*

(3) extraneous (as in superfluous) *adj.*: **excrescent**. See *superfluous*

(4) extraneous (as in superfluous) *adj.*: **supererogatory**. See *superfluous*

(5) extraneous (word or phrase) *n.*: **pleonasm**. See *redundancy*

(6) extraneous (words) *n.*: **macrology**. See *verbosity*

extraordinary (as in supernatural) *adj.*: **preternatural**. See *supernatural*

(2) extraordinary (as in wonderful) *adj.*: **mirific**. See *wonderful*

(3) extraordinary (state of being . . . , as in superior or state of being better) *n.*: **meliority**. See *superiority*

extravagant (as in lavish) *adj.*: **Lucullan**. See *lavish*

extreme (as in the ultimate degree, as of a condition or quality, or the highest point that can be attained) *n.*: **ne plus ultra**. See *ultimate*

(2) extreme (to the . . .) *adv.*: **à l'outrance** [French]. See *utmost*

extremism (esp. in political matters) *n.*: **ultraism**. ❖ In the final week of the last general election, [Scottish National Party head] Alex Salmond posed awkwardly for one last photocall. The slogan [he was] advertising proclaimed that no-one ever celebrated devolution day. It was the height of SNP **ultraism**, the "independence, nothing less" approach. [The issue was whether Scotland should become independent of the United Kingdom with devolution being the alternate choice.] (*Scotsman*, "Salmond Still Pushing for Power over Purity," 9/25/1995.)

(2) extremism (of or relating to political . . .) *adj.*: **Jacobinical**. [Jacobins were members of a society of extremist democrats in France during the Revolution of 1789, so called because they used a former Jacobin friary as their headquarters in Paris. It generally, though not always, refers to left-wing political extremism.] ❖ [The complaint that the affluent class is self-perpetuating] is a very old complaint [causing those not in it to favor a higher estate tax.] The avoidance of taxes is a primal urge, like sex and patriotism and religion . . . though when the **Jacobinical** fever rages, people don't care whether they are stifling production with their taxes. All that they care about is that the Haves shall have less. (William F. Buckley, "What About the 'Overclass'?" *National Review*, 9/11/1995.)

extremist (a political . . . , who often believes in violence to attain an end) *n.*: **sans-culotte**. [French; derives from name given in the first French Revolution to members of the extreme Republican Party, who rejected breeches as an emblem peculiar to the upper classes or aristocracy.] ❖ The second revolutionary redistribution of Russian property in this century [which created a new upper and middle class] now seems likely to last [as a result of Yeltsin's victory]. Yet, while Russia's **sans-culotte** did not storm the red walls of the Kremlin, they did register a powerful protest that the nation's triumphant masters will ignore at their peril. Nearly 40 million Russians backed Yeltsin, but more than 29 million supported his Communist rival. (Chrystia Freeland, "A Foothold for Democracy; Yeltsin's Election Indicates Russia Is on Track, but Now It Needs to Share the Wealth," *Denver Rocky Mountain News*, 7/7/1996.)

extrinsic (as in originating from the outside) *adj.*: **adscititious**. ❖ [In the movie *Dick Tracy*, Warren Beatty and Madonna] are allowed to look like themselves; similarly pristine, but for a few **adscititious** freckles, is Charlie Korsmo, the child actor who plays the Kid, that immaculately conceived (because adopted) offspring of Dick and Tess's. (John Simon, review of *Dick Tracy*, *National Review*, 7/23/1990.)

extrovert (someone who is halfway between an . . . and an introvert) *n.*: **ambivert**. ❖ [Bob] Woodward affords us a glimpse behind the veil. Here, a recurring image is [of Fed Chairman Alan] Greenspan as the borderline **ambivert**—inherently a shy man, he feasts on the politicking of Beltway parties, but only as an anthology of intimate tête-à-têtes, not as a gather-round-the-piano stage show. (David Guo, "Greenspan Bio Gives Readers Their Money's Worth," *Pittsburgh Post-Gazette*, 1/7/2001.)

extroverted (young woman who is attractive and . . .) *n.*: **frippet** [British; informal]. See *woman*

exuberant *adj.*: **yeasty**. ❖ [*The Beggar's Opera* is] an exuberant celebration of London low life [in the 1720s.] . . . [It's] still fun to watch as performed by British actors who have the style in their blood, approach the job with affection, and share an infectious feeling of ensemble zest. It's no star vehicle; it's a mass excursion into **yeasty** pleasure. (Jay Carr, "Last Call for an Overlooked Gem," *Boston Globe*, 6/8/1987.)

exude (as in ooze out or cause to escape from proper channels, esp. a liquid or something that flows) *v.t.*, *v.i.*: **extravasate**. [This is a word from pathology which means to force out (as blood) or cause to escape from a proper channel or vessel. In a transitive sense, it is sometimes used as a synonym for force out or squeeze out or the like. In an intransitive sense, it is sometimes used as a synonym for ooze or seep or the like.] ❖ Here several hundred gay men and women had commandeered an unprepossessing uptown intersection. They lit candles. They shouted, with no talent for etymology, "Homophobia has to go." They wore T-shirts that said ACT UP. It was an out-take from 1968. I would've ignored them: let sparse Broadway traffic **extravasate** around on West End Avenue or Amsterdam. (D. Keith Mano, "Arresting Gays," *National Review*, 10/28/1988.)

exult (in, or boast, esp. about the accomplishments of a relative) *v.t.*, *n.*: **kvell** [Yiddish]. See *boast*

(2) exult (with boisterous public demonstrations) *v.i.*: **maffick** [British]. See *celebrate*

exultant (often in a boastful way) *adj.*: **cock-a-hoop**. See *elated*

eye (of or relating to) *adj.*: **ocular**. ❖ With the National Hockey League (NHL) season in full swing, *Ophthalmology Times* continues its ongoing series on sports-related eye injuries. In interviews with team eyecare physicians throughout the league, OT found that serious **ocular** injuries—while they do happen—are few and far between. (Sheryl Stevenson, "Ophthalmologists Help Put NHL Eye Injuries on Ice," *Ophthalmology Times*, 11/15/1997, p. 1.)

eyebrows (of or relating to) *adj.*: **superciliary**. ❖ Hail, Tweezer! . . . Juut Salonspa in Wayzata [, Minnesota, is] bringing to town none other than "BEVERLY HILL'S EYEBROW KING TO THE STARS." His **Superciliary** Highness, King Damone Roberts, paid an official visit Monday to share state secrets on "the art of creating flawless eyebrows." (Rachel Blount, "Item World," *Minneapolis Star Tribune*, 2/25/2003.)

(2) eyebrows (smooth area between . . . and above the nose) *n.*: **glabella**. ❖ Injecting Botox into the **glabella**, the area between the brows, releases the vertical lines and lifts the outer brow. The result: You appear more relaxed and less angry. Makes a nice gift for Charles Bronson. (Lucinda Chriss, Looks: "The End of the Lines," *Men's Health*, 10/1/1999, p. 94.)

eye for an eye *n.*: **lex talionis** [Latin. See also *talionic*, under *revenge*.] ❖ The Golden Rule ["do unto others as you would have them do unto you"] was not submitted to systematic analysis until Albrecht Dihle's classic work in 1962. Dihle rooted it in the oldest norm of human conduct, the principle of retribution. . . . The most severe form of this principle, found in primitive law and primitive morality, was the **lex talionis**. (John Topel, "The Tarnished Golden Rule (Luke 6:31): The Inescapable Radicalness of Christian Ethics," *Theological Studies*, 9/1/1998, p. 475.)

eyeglasses (clipped to the bridge of the nose) *n.*: **pince-nez**. ❖ Tammany Hall Democrats, however, weren't swooning [over Frankin Roosevelt]. They noted the freshman's habit of tossing his head back and peering down his nose (on which he wore **pince-nez** like Theodore Roosevelt, a fifth cousin) and read in it a squire's disdain for grubby city boys. (Gerald Parshall, "A Monumental Man," *U.S. News & World Report*, 4/28/1997.)

(2) eyeglasses (with a short handle like opera glasses) *n.*: **lorgnette**. ❖ David McVicar's new production of Massenet's opera at the London Coliseum is in the style of a modern thing in old clothes. The company, bepowdered and bewigged, eye the audience critically through **lorgnettes** as we take our seats. (Dermot Clinch, review of *Manon Lescaut*, *New Statesman*, 5/22/1998.)

eyelids (spasmodic blinking of) *n.*: **blepharospasm**. See *blinking*

eyes (having watery . . .) *adj.*: **rheumy**. See *watery*

eyesight (having poor . . . , as in nearly blind) *adj.*: **purblind**. See *blind*

(2) eyesight (loss of) *n.*: **amaurosis**. See *blindness*

eyewitness (based on . . . observation) *adj.*: **autoptic**. ❖ To enlarge the market share in China . . . Dell adopts peculiar sales strategy according to the characteristics of China market. Most of Chinese consumers believe in what they see. Thus it's very difficult for them to accept direct marketing. Then Dell holds **autoptic** sales promotion activities in shopping centers. (AsiaInfo Services, "Foreign PC Magnates Challenge China PC Market," 3/29/2002.)

fable (moral . . .) *n*.: **apologue**. ❖ [D]espite a known history of mental illness and suicide attempts . . . repeated requests for anti-psychotic medication by the inmate and a social worker were ignored, and he was soon found hanging in his cell, "cold to the touch." The report describing this incident reads like a series of all-too-truthful **apologues** illustrating how detainees with mental illnesses slip through the cracks, wither, and die behind bars. (Spencer P. M. Harrington, "New Bedlam: Jails—Not Psychiatric Hospitals—Now Care for the Indigent Mentally Ill," *Humanist*, 5/1/1999, p. 9.)

fabrication (petty or minor . . .) *n*.: **taradiddle** (or **tarradiddle**). See *lie*
  (2) fabrication (which is defamatory and published for political gain right before an election) *n*.: **roorback**. See *falsehood*

fabulous *adj*.: **mirific**. See *wonderful*

facade (as in something that is impressive-looking on the outside but which hides or covers up undesirable conditions or facts) *n*.: **Potemkin village** [derives from Grigori Potemkin, a Russian statesman, who had impressive fake villages erected along the route that Catherine the Great was to travel.] ❖ [M]any people thought the show of diversity [at the 2000 Republican Convention] was too over-the-top to be taken as sincere. . . . Alan Brinkley [stated:] "The level of artificiality in this is so palpable that it's hard to imagine that many people believe this is the true Republican Party on display. It's a **Potemkin village**." In fact, he said, Republicans have not attracted sizeable number of black voters in many decades. (Nita Lelyveld, "Skepticism Remains on GOP Efforts to Woo Minorities," Knight Ridder/Tribune News Service, 8/4/2000.)

face (appearance of . . .) *n*.: **physiognomy**. See *facial features*

facial (expression in the form of a grimace due to pain or disgust) *n*.: **rictus**. See *grimace*

facial features *n*.: **physiognomy**. ❖ The realistic depictions of the ancestors' countenances don't merely show the influence of European draftsmanship, however. . . . Chinese tradition held that character and destiny were revealed by **physiognomy**, so the contours of an individual's face told a story that shouldn't be ignored. (Mark Jenkins, "Haunting, Hallowed Portraits," *Washington Post*, 6/29/2001.)

facility (as in appearance of effortlessness) *n*.: **sprezzatura** [Italian]. See *effortlessness*

fact (historical . . .) *n*.: **historicity**. See *authenticity*
  (2) fact (in . . .) *adj*., *adv*.: **de facto** (as contrasted with de jure: legally or by law) [Latin]. See *in fact*
  (3) fact (invented . . . believed true due to repetition) *n*.: **factoid**. See *inaccuracy*
  (4) fact (relating to a story in which . . . and fiction are mixed together) *adj*.: **Pirandellian**. See *reality*

factions (tending to break into . . . or disintegrate) *adj*.: **fissiparous**. See *break up*

factual (as in reflecting reality) *adj*.: **veridical**. See *realistic*
  (2) factual (necessarily . . .) *adj*.: **apodictic**. See *incontrovertible*

fad (the latest . . .) *n*.: **dernier cri** [French]. See *trend*

fade (as in vanish or disappear) *v.t.*: **evanesce**. See *disappear*

faded (as in pale, and often sickly) *adj*.: **etiolated**. See *pale*

fading (away quickly) *adj*.: **fugacious**. See *fleeting*

failed (as in unsuccessful) *adj*.: **abortive**. See *unsuccessful*

faint (as in lightheaded or dizzy) *adj*.: **vertiginous**. See *dizzy*

fainthearted *adj*.: **pusillanimous**. See *cowardly*

fainting *n*.: **syncope**. ❖ Her pulse was close to stopping. Was it the drugs she was taking? . . . She had been sent from her cardiologist's office, the first stop after a fainting episode at home. His note read, "67 y.o. with **syncope** and bradycardia." . . . [T]his is the United States in the late 1990s, where bradycardia is more likely to be inflicted by a doctor than nature. (Tony Dajer, "When Pills Kill," *Discover*, 8/1/1999.)

fair (uncompromisingly . . .) *n.*: **Rhadaman-thine**. See *just*

fairylike (as in otherwordly) *adj.*: **fey**. See *otherwordly*

faith (reliance on . . . alone rather than reason, esp. in philosophical or religious matters) *n.*: **fideism**. ❖ In the middle is Father Sirico, who warns against two predominant and equally wrongheaded decision-making tendencies: to rely purely on reason on the one hand and **fideism** on the other, which he calls the "I'm just trusting on the Lord and I'm not going to think about it" approach. He suggests depending on reason but recognizing that reason alone doesn't explain all the mysteries of life. (Steven Greenhut, "Decisions, Decisions; Here's How to Think About How to Make Up Your Mind," *Orange County [CA] Register*, 6/20/1999.)

(2) faith (articles of . . . ; doctrines to be believed) *n.pl.*: **credenda**. See *beliefs*

faithful (and unquestioning assistant) *n.*: **myrmidon**. See *assistant*

faithfulness (as in allegiance) *n.*: **vassalage**. See *allegiance*

(2) faithfulness *n.*: **fealty**. See *loyalty*

faithless (man married to . . . wife) *n.*: **cuckold** (*v.t.*: to make a . . . of). See *adulterous*

(2) faithless (spouse) *n.*: **bedswerver**. See *unfaithful*

(3) faithless (to a belief, duty, or cause) *adj.*: **recreant**. See *unfaithful*

(4) faithless *adj.*: **perfidious**. See *unfaithful*

fake (as in artificial) *adj.*: **factitious**. See *artificial*

(2) fake (as in contrived) *adj.*: **voulu** [French]. See *contrived*

(3) fake (as in insincere) *adj.*: **crocodilian**. See *insincere*

(4) fake (as in invented or substituted with fraudulent intent) *adj.*: **supposititious**. See *supposed*

(5) fake (as in sham) *n.*: **postiche**. See *sham*

(6) fake (esp. a person who sells quack medicines) *n.*: **mountebank**. See *huckster*

(7) fake (out, as in bluff) *v.t.*: **four-flush** (*n.*: **four-flusher**). See *bluff*

(8) fake (sickness or other incapacity to avoid work) *v.i.*: **malinger**. See *shirk*

(9) fake *adj.*: **pinchbeck**. See *counterfeit*

fake front (as in something that is impressive-looking on the outside but which hides or covers up undesirable conditions or facts) *n.*: **Potemkin village**. See *facade*

faker (as in hypocrite, esp. one who acts humbly) *n.*: **Uriah Heep**. See *hypocrite*

(2) faker (as in hypocrite, esp. one who affects religious peity) *n.*: **Tartuffe** (or **tartuffe**). See *hypocrite*

fall (downward . . .) *n.*: **declension**. See *decline*

(2) fall (esp. from a position of strength or condition) *n.*: **dégringolade** [French]. See *downfall*

(3) fall (to the bottom of the ocean) *v.i.*: **go to Davy Jones' locker**. See *ocean*

(4) fall (of or relating to a . . . , as in downfall, esp. after an innocent or carefree time) *adj.*: **postlapsarian**. See *downfall*

fallacious (argument where one proves or disproves a point that is not at issue) *n.*: **ignoratio elenchi** [Latin]. See *irrelevancy*

(2) fallacious (argument, usually, but not necessarily, related to philosophy) *n.*: **philosophism**. See *argument*

(3) fallacious (argument, where one begs the question) *n.*: **petitio principii** [Latin]. See *begging the question*

(4) fallacious (as in relating to reasoning that sounds plausible but is false or insincere) *adj.*: **meretricious**. See *specious*

(5) fallacious (engaging in argument that may be . . . , as in specious) *adj.*, *n.*: **eristic**. See *specious*

(6) fallacious (reasoning) *n.*: **syllogism**. See *specious*

fallacy (and/or illogical argument) *n.*: **choplogic**. ❖ Anything that makes Quebec's separatists so mad can't be all bad. So, yes, partition does have something to be said for it. . . . They have had it all their own way far too long. Now, their lies about painless secession are being challenged. The puck has been shot into their end for a change, and the separatists are getting tangled in their own **choplogic**. Good. (Norman Webster, "If Quebec Is Divisible, So Is Federalism," *Maclean's*, 3/11/1996, p. 64.)

(2) fallacy (as in opinion, belief, or doctrine that is false) *n.*: **pseudodoxy**. ❖ [With respect to Sadaam Hussein's Baathist regime,] we can only hope that . . . whole baseless structure will come crashing down into the waters, not of the Rhine, but of the Tigris. Surely the spectacle of stupidity on so massive a scale is deeply saddening to anyone touched by the philosophic mood. What percentage of Iraqis are true believers in the Baathist **pseudodoxy** is not yet known, though it soon may be. (James Gardner, "One with Nineveh and Tyre," *National Review*, 5/13/1991.)

(3) fallacy (as in reasoning that is intended to rationalize or mislead) *n.*: **casuistry**. ❖ [Attorney Alan] Dershowitz continued: "[The jury's finding of liability against O. J. Simpson in his civil trial] doesn't in any way undercut the correctness of the first case at all." Of course not. Simpson did it but Simpson didn't do it, Simpson is guiltless but Simpson is liable. This is the **casuistry** of a man who is correctly worried about his reputation. (*New Republic*, "Mr. Guilty Is Liable," 2/24/1997.)

(4) fallacy (logical . . . in which a false conclusion is drawn from two premises, neither of which conveys information about all members of the designated class) *n.*: **undistributed middle**. [For example: "All oaks are trees and all elms are trees, and therefore, all oaks are elms"; neither of the first two premises says anything about all trees]. ❖ [Even my] buddy Bill Maher ha[s] hopped on the Bush bandwagon. "I've been supportive of President Bush," Maher told Wolf Blitzer this week, "now that I think Iraq is turning around. . . ." How did this cozy unanimity come to pass? Is it something in the water, a byproduct of Bush's gutting the EPA? [This is] the fallacy of the **undistributed middle**. . . . We invaded Iraq. Change is afoot in the Middle East. Therefore, the Middle East is changing because we invaded Iraq. (Arianna Huffington, "The Washington Establishment Fails Logic 101," *Salon.com*, 3/17/2005.)

(5) fallacy (logical . . . where one argues that because event B followed event A, then event A must have caused event B) *n.*: **post hoc, ergo propter hoc** [Latin for "after this, therefore, because of this"]. ❖ Despite how compelling they look on-screen, I must admit to finding that the "January Barometer," the "Super Bowl Effect" (linking NFC wins with bull markets), and other such indicators are based on the worst kind of "**post hoc ergo propter hoc**" thinking. (Charles Zehren, "'January Barometer'/Predicting Market Is Art, Not Science," *Newsday*, 2/2/2000.)

(6) fallacy (or illogical argument) *n.*: **paralogism** (*adj.*: **paralogical**). ❖ Yes, it is silly to bring up, as though they had a bearing on one another, increased executive salaries and diminished work forces. But that **paralogism** doesn't authorize scornful inattention to the implications of preposterous salaries. (William F. Buckley Jr., "Rich-Baiting Time," *National Review*, 5/6/1996, p. 62.)

(7) fallacy (accepted as fact due to repetition in print) *n.*: **factoid**. See *inaccuracy*

(8) fallacy (that if something cannot be proven false, then it must be true) *n.*: **argumentum ad ignorantiam** [Latin]. See *argument*

falling (outward from the center in all directions, as if from a dome) *adj.*: **quaquaversal**. See *dipping*

falling apart (of a group or social structure as a result of lack of standards or values) *n.*: **anomie**. See *breakdown*

false (and/or illogical argument) *n.*: **choplogic**. See *fallacy*

(2) false (as in artificial) *adj.*: **factitious**. See *artificial*

(3) false (as in relating to reasoning that sounds plausible but is . . . or insincere) *adj.*: **meretricious**. See *specious*

(4) false (as in untruthful or dishonest) *adj.*: **mendacious**. See *dishonest*

(5) false (make . . . or malicious statements about) *v.t.*: **calumniate** (*n.*: **calumny**). See *malign*

(6) false (make . . . statements about, so as to humiliate or disgrace) *v.t.*: **traduce**. See *malign*

(7) false (reasoning as in fallacious or specious) *n.*: **syllogism**. See *specious*

(8) false (reasoning intended to . . . rationalize or mislead) *n.*: **casuistry**. See *fallacious*

(9) false (something . . . , as in a sham) *n.*: **postiche**. See *sham*

(10) false (argument, usually, but not necessarily, related to philosophy) *n.*: **philosophism**. See *argument*

(11) false (story, report, or rumor, often deliberately) *n.*: **canard**. See *hoax*

false front (as in something that is impressive-looking on the outside but which hides or covers up undesirable conditions or facts) *n.*: **Potemkin village**. See *facade*

falsehood (which is defamatory and published for political gain right before an election) *n.*: **roorback** [derives from an incident in the election of 1844, when backers of Whig Party candidate Henry Clay circulated a false report by a fictional "Baron Roorback" claiming that Democratic candidate James K. Polk branded slaves with an iron. Polk won anyway]. ❖ For the next day or so, [don't] believe everything you read. Especially if it's about politics [and] if it's in a campaign brochure. . . . Because there's a good chance it might be a **roorback**. . . . [For example,] fliers with a grainy black-and-white photo of a candidate standing behind superimposed jail bars, under a headline that screams, "Candidate Bob Schmedlap Guilty of Drunk Driving!" (Gordon Dillow, "Beware the Wily Ghost of Roorback," *Orange County [CA] Register* 11/1/1998.)

(2) falsehood (accepted as fact due to repetition in print) *n.*: **factoid**. See *inaccuracy*

(3) falsehood (as in lie) *n.*: **fabulation** (one who does so: **fabulist**). See *lie*

(4) falsehood (as in opinion, belief, or doctrine that is false) *n.*: **pseudodoxy**. See *fallacy*

(5) falsehood (petty or minor . . .) *n.*: **taradiddle** (or **tarradiddle**). See *lie*

falsification (deliberate . . . or concealment of facts to gain an advantage) *n.*: **subreption**. See *misrepresentation*

falter (as in hesitate to act) *v.i.*: **shilly-shally**. See *procrastinate*

(2) falter (as in hesitate to act, due to indecision) *v.i.*: **dither**. See *procrastinate*

fame (one obsessed with one's own greatness or . . .) *n.*: **megalomania**. See *obsession*

(2) fame (or a taste or flair for being in the spotlight) *n.*: **réclame** [French]. See *publicity*

familiar (being . . . with, including being informed or up-to-date about something) *adj.*: **au fait**. [French; lit. to the fact. This term also means skillful or accomplished. See *skillful*.] ❖ Mr. McCain has delayed the formal announcement of his presidential bid until the end of the month. He is making room for three "major" policy speeches, and is revamping his fund-raising apparatus to make it more like the Bush machine that crushed him in the 2000 presidential campaign. He has also made room for a "blogger conference call," to give the impression that he is both accessible and **au fait** with modern technology. (*Economist*, "The Comeback Grandpa?" 4/14/2007.)

family *n.pl.*: **kith and kin**. See *relatives*

family ties *n.*: **propinquity**. See *kinship*

famished *adj.*: **esurient**. See *hungry*

fan out (as in branch out) *v.i.*: **ramify**. See *branch out*

fanatic *n.*: **energumen**. ❖ So Pat Buchanan comes along and argues that Great Britain would have been better off, in 1939, letting Hitler take Poland—and go on to take Moscow. Critics are justified in disagreeing, but it hardly follows from the conjecture that Buchanan is moved by the anti-Semitic **energumen**. (William F. Buckley Jr., "On the Right," *National Review*, 10/25/1999.)

fanaticism (of or relating to political . . . , as in extremism) *adj.*: **Jacobinical**. See *extremism*

fanciful (as in idealistic but likely impractical or unrealistic) *adj.*: **quixotic**. See *idealistic*

(2) fanciful (as in idealistic conduct without regard to practicality) *n.*: **knight-errantry**. See *idealistic*

(3) fanciful *adj.*: **chimerical**. See *unrealistic*

fancy (as in ornate) *adj.*: **rococo**. See *ornate*

(2) fancy *adj.*: **nobby** [British]. See *elegant*

fanfare *n.*: **éclat**. See *acclaim*

fans (group of . . . , as in fawning admirers) *n.*: **claque**. See *admirers*

fantasies (having delusional . . . about power, fame, omnipotence, etc.) *n.*: **megalomania**. See *delusional*

fantasized (or glorified conception of oneself, as a result of boredom in one's life) *n.*: **Bovarism**. See *self-delusion*

fantastic *adj.*: **frabjous** (often as in "Oh frabjous day!"). See *wonderful*

(2) fantastic *adj.*: **galluptious** [slang]. See *wonderful*

(3) fantastic *adj.*: **mirific**. See *wonderful*

(4) fantastic *adj.*: **palmary**. See *excellent*

(5) fantastic *adj.*: **skookum**. See *excellent*

fantasy (world, usually invented by children, which can involve its own history, geography, and language) *n.*: **paracosm**. ❖ [Walt Disney] had created the studio; then the studio, with his complicity, created him, making him, he fully understood, as much a commodity as a man—the very sort of diffident, genial, plainspoken, unprepossessing and childishly enthusiastic character who would have produced Walt Disney movies. Essentially, he had become his own **paracosm**. (Neal Gabler, *Walt Disney*, Knopf [2006], p. xix.) [Gabler actually used the word "parcosm," but the correct word is "paracosm."]

(2) fantasy (as in delusion held by two closely associated persons) *n.*: **folie à deux** [French]. See *delusion*

(3) fantasy (as in delusion) *n.*: **ignis fatuus**. See *delusion*

(4) fantasy (as in hope or goal that is not realistically obtainable) *n.*: **will-o'-the-wisp**. See *pipe dream*

(5) fantasy (esp. something that at first seems a wonderful discovery or development but that turns to be a . . . or a hoax) *n.*: **mare's nest**. See *hoax*

(6) fantasy (living in a world of . . . , with a glorified or romanticized conception of oneself, as a result of boredom in one's life) *n.*: **Bovarism**. See *self-delusion*

(7) fantasy (relating to a story in which . . . and reality are mixed together) *adj.*: **Pirandellian**. See *reality*

(8) fantasy (spec. the tendency to see things as more beautiful than they really are) *n.*: **kalopsia**. See *rose-colored glasses*

farewell (act of bidding . . .) *n.*: **valediction**. ❖ And yet, how many times had I flown into Newark International Airport (EWR) and heard that hoary **valediction** from the flight attendant, "If Newark is your final destination, we hope your stay is a pleasant one," without realizing its profound implications. One can chuckle at the comic dimension of the line—the number of fliers who consider Newark their destination is few indeed. (Mark Leyner, "Xmas in Newark," *Esquire*, 12/01/1997, p. 52.)

(2) farewell (as in parting words) *n.*: **envoi** [French]. See *parting words*

farming (fit for . . .) *adj.*: **arable**. ❖ Since Asia will be nine times as densely populated per acre of **arable** land, farm exports from the Western Hemisphere should be the salvation of that continent's already scarce environmental resources. (Dennis Avery, "What Does the Future Hold for Agriculture?" *USA Today Magazine*, 05/01/1995.)

farsightedness (as in unable to see close objects) *n.*: **presbyopia**. ❖ There's even a surgical solution in the works for **presbyopia**, or aging-eye syndrome—the affliction that drives nearly all middle-aged people into reading glasses. "Bad vision no longer has to be a disability," says Soloway. "It can be fixed, permanently." (Mary Murray, "Laser Eye Surgery: Should You Have Your Eyes Lasered?" *Fortune*, 9/27/1999, p. 194.)

farthest (as in most distant, or remote, destination or goal) *n.*: **ultima Thule**. See *distant*

farting (of or relating to reducing . . .) *adj.*: **carminative**. ❖ Good for treating bad breath and digestive problems, parsley has diuretic properties that help the body get rid of excessive water. It is also a **carminative**, easing flatulence and colic. (Batsheva Mink, "A Bouquet of Herbs," *Jerusalem Post*, 8/15/2001.)

(2) farting (of or relating to) *adj.*: **borborygmic**. See *passing gas*

fascinate (as in bewitch or enchant) *v.t.*: **ensorcell** (or **ensorcel**). See *enchant*

fascinating (woman) *n.*: **intrigante**. See *woman*

(2) fascinating (person) *n.*: **intrigant**. See *intriguing*

fashion (out of . . .) *adj.*: **démodé** [French]. See *outmoded*

(2) fashion (the latest . . .) *n.*: **dernier cri** [French]. See *trend*

fashionable (and wealthy young people) *n.*: **jeunesse dorée** [French]. ❖ One of the most popular topics of conversation among the **jeunesse dorée** of Plettenberg Bay this past vacation season was who had brought their maids down from Johannesburg for the holidays. One blond, bejeweled young mother had worried about taking her "girl" so far from home. "But she's having a super time," she chirped. "She's just yakking away with all her other little friends," that is, the other Johannesburg maids. (Richard Stengel, "Whites," *New Republic*, 4/22/1996, p. 13.)

(2) fashionable (as in well-bred, esp. those aspiring or pretending to be well-bred) *adj.*: **lace-curtain**. See *well-bred*

(3) fashionable (society) *n.*: **beau monde** [French]. See *high society*

(4) fashionable (society) *n.*: **bon ton** [French]. See *high society*

(5) fashionable *adj.*: **nobby** [British]. See *elegant*

(6) fashionable *adj.*: **soigné** [French]. See *elegant*

fast *adj.*: **velocious**. ❖ Fasten your seatbelt. Select your course; day or night, novice or expert. Will it be manual or automatic? Get ready. . . . Five, four, three, two, one GO!! The car begins to vibrate, humming and jerking, whipping your body around at a **velocious** pace. . . . Welcome to GameWorks. (*Yolk*, "GameWorks," 9/30/1998, p. 28.)

(2) fast (as in at top speed) *adv.*: **tantivy**. See *top speed*

(3) fast (as in hasty) *adj.*: **festinate**. See *hasty*

(4) fast (very . . . , as in, in an instant) *n.*: **trice** (as in "in a trice"). See *quickly*

fastidious *adj.*: **governessy**. ❖ [M]aria and Christina were **governessy** types whose interior lives were a good deal more intense than their buttoned-up appearance would suggest. (Kathryn Hughes, "Christina Rossetti," *New Statesman & Society*, 1/6/1995, p. 40.)

(2) fastidious (overly . . .) *adj.*: **persnickety**. See *picky*

fat *adj.*: **adipose**. ❖ Bank shot Fast Eddie Felson is back and director Martin Scorsese's got him. Fast Eddie, of course, is the pool shark played by Paul Newman in 1961's *The Hustler*. Jackie Gleason played his **adipose** rival Minnesota Fats. (*People*, Screen Preview, 9/1/1986, p. 101.)

(2) fat *adj.*: **Pickwickian** [after the heavyset Samuel Pickwick in Charles Dickens's 1870 novel *The Pickwick Papers*]. ❖ Appearances did not greatly help. No one, least of all Mr. Pitt, ever doubted his intelligence and erudition. But regulators should have a lean and hungry look. The rotund Mr. Pitt has a **Pickwickian** air. Hard worker though he is, he more easily imagined departing Le Cirque restaurant in New York after a decent lunch than drafting lawsuits against transgressors. (Robert Cornwell, "Business Analysis: How the Pendulum Finally Swung Against [Harvey] Pitt after Series of Gaffes; Heavyweight SEC Chairman Undone by Controversial Hiring of Accounting Watchdog," *Independent* [London], 11/7/2002.)

(3) fat (or perpetually short-winded as a result of being fat) *adj.*: **pursy**. [The rap star referred to in this example weighed well over 300 pounds. Note too the double entendre in the headline.] ❖ *Notorious* gives the Hollywood superhero treatment to the rapper Notorious B.I.G. [a/k/a] Biggie Smalls. . . . Biggie's hard-knock life and premature death (he was shot in 1997 at age 24) have been repackaged into an enjoyably ridiculous entertainment about a **pursy** young man with mysterious sex appeal who turns the rap world on its ear. (Wesley Morris, "Living Large, Dying Young: *Notorious* Recalls Rap Heavyweight," *Boston Globe*, 1/16/2009.)

(4) fat (and squat) *adj.*: **fubsy**. See *squat*

(5) fat (as in beer-bellied) *adj.*: **abdominous**. See *beer-bellied*

(6) fat (as in paunchy) *adj.*: **stomachy**. See *paunchy*

(7) fat (branch of medicine concerning . . . people) *n.*: **bariatrics**. See *obesity*

(8) fat (condition of being) *n.*: **embonpoint**. See *plump*

(9) fat (having a short, . . . physique) *adj.*: **pyknic**. See *stocky*

(10) fat (person, esp. with a large abdomen) *n.*: **endomorph** (*adj.*: **endomorphic**). See *pot-bellied*

(11) fat (state of being . . .) *n.*: **avoirdupois**. See *weight*

(12) fat (woman, as in plump or full-figured) *adj.*: **zaftig** [Yiddish]. See *full-figured*

fatal (as in causing or portending death) *adj.*: **funest**. See *deadly*

fat ass *n.*: **steatopygia** (having a . . .) *adj.*: **steatopygic**. See *rear end*

fate *n.*: **kismet** ❖ Edley . . . thought it **kismet** when he won his first U.S. [Scrabble] championship in 1980, but the suspicion that he was nothing but a tool for fate left him depressed— "like a higher power was leading me, and I didn't have much to do with it," Edley says. (S. I. Price, "Scrabble: Your Words Against Mine," *Sports Illustrated*, 12/18/1995, p. 106.)

father (biological . . .) *n.*: **genitor**. ❖ All cultures try to ensure that children have fathers who assume full responsibility for them— as providers, protectors and moral examples. Among the Nayar of India, a woman weds several men. Any one of them can be a **genitor**, a biological father, but only one can be a pater, one who fulfills all the functions and social duties of a father. Merely having a **genitor** in society is not enough. (David Murray, "Illegitimacy Fosters Social Disaster," *Chicago Tribune*, 6/25/1994.)

(2) father (legally and/or socially recognized . . . , as opposed to biological) *n.*: **pater** [Latin]. See *father*, above, for example.

(3) father (biological . . . or mother) *n.*: **genitor**. See *parent*

(4) father (of a family) *n.*: **paterfamilias**. See *head of household*

(5) father (of, relating to or derived from name of) *adj.*: **patronymic**. See *paternal*

fathom (difficult to . . .) *adj.*: **recondite**. See *complicated*

fatigue (in the muscles) *n.*: **myasthenia** (or **myasthenia gravis**). ❖ In **myasthenia**, the immune system barricades muscle receptors with antibodies, preventing acetylcholine attachment. That results in a feeble muscle contraction. The cardinal symptom of **myasthenia**, therefore, is muscle weakness. (Dr. Paul Donohue, Advice, *St. Louis Post-Dispatch*, 8/20/2001.)

(2) fatigue (as in tedium, of life) *n.*: **tedium vitae** [Latin]. See *tedium*

(3) fatigue (from lack of energy or nourishment) *n.*: **inanition**. See *exhaustion*

fatigued (chronically . . .) *adj.*: **neurasthenic**. [This word is the adjectival form of neurasthenia, a psychological disorder characterized by chronic fatigue and weakness, loss of memory, generalized aches and pains, and/or depression. It was thought to result from exhaustion of the nervous system. Though no longer in use as a scientific or medical term, it nevertheless remains in fairly frequent usage today.] ❖ It started when a friend mentioned that her boss, an editor for a well-known national magazine, had called in "depressed" on the day he knew a hostile profile was about to run in a rival publication. Intrigued, I started thinking of other legitimate reasons why a person might want to stay in bed on a workday morning. If you could call in depressed, I thought, what about calling in lonely? Or **neurasthenic**? Or inexplicably sad? (Liza Mundy, "Workable Excuses," *Washington Post*, 10/31/1999.)

(2) fatigued (as in weakened) *adj.*: **etiolated**. See *weakened*

fault (find . . . with on trivial grounds) *v.t.*: **cavil**. See *quibble*

(2) fault (oneself) *v.t.*: **flagellate** (*n.*: **flagellation**). See *criticize*

(3) fault (small or trifling . . .) *n.*: **peccadillo**. See *infraction*

(4) fault (tragic . . . , esp. in a literary character) *n.*: **hamartia**. See *flaw*

faultfinder *n.*: **smellfungus** [derives from Smellfungus, a hypercritical traveler in the Laurence Sterne novel *A Sentimental Journey Through France and Italy* (1768)]. ❖ The players used [the resignation of Denver Nuggets coach Dan Issel] as a convenient excuse for their own overweening, underachieving ineptitude. "Issel quit on us," the players wailed and whined when they weren't sucking on their thumbs. And a . . . **smellfungus** from the [*Denver Rocky Mountain News*] carped that Issel chose to jump when the schedule reached its toughest stretch. (Woody Paige, "Issel Is the Wrong Scapegoat in Nuggets' Mess," *Denver Post*, 02/13/1995.)

faultfinding (mania for . . .) *n.*: **cacoëthes carpendi** [Latin]. ❖ To aid their struggle, the Senate Democrats will hold brutal oversight hearings, which they have not had the power to do in six and a half years. In those hearings, the Democrats will display **cacoëthes carpendi**—a mania for finding fault. Pity the poor administration witnesses who must abide the fabricated outrage of their Democratic inquisitors. (Tony Blankley, "The Jeffords Effect," *Washington Times*, 5/30/2001.)

(2) faultfinding *adj.*: **captious**. ❖ [E]very time Cal [Ripken's] hitting went south, those hard workin' airwaves were filled with **captious** comment. People said Cal ought to sit down. Take a rest. Stop acting like Superman.

Stop putting his own streak ahead of the team! (Richard Ben Cramer, Baseball: "A Native Son's Thoughts [Many of Them Heretical] About Baltimore [Which Isn't What It Used to Be]," *Sports Illustrated*, 9/11/1995, p. 56.)

(3) faultfinding (as in criticism) *n.*: **animadversion** (*v.t.*: **animadvert**). See *criticism*

faultless *adj.*: **impeccable**. ❖ William C. Dawson Jr.'s attempt to [put a dent in] *National Review's* **impeccable** reputation fell short. He claims his life was ruined when *National Review* used "hung" rather than "hanged" in reference to an execution. Perhaps he can be assuaged by understanding that "hanged" is the capital aspect of the punishment, and comes into being only at the terminus of this impressive procedure. It's the destination, not the journey: A person is hung by the neck until hanged. (Julian Schmidt, letter to the editor, *National Review*, 10/15/2001.)

faulty (and/or illogical argument) *n.*: **choplogic**. See *fallacy*

(2) faulty (argument in which a false conclusion is drawn from two premises, neither of which conveys information about all members of the designated class) *n.*: **undistributed middle**. See *fallacy*

(3) faulty (argument, spec. where one argues that because event B followed event A, then event A must have caused event B) *n.*: **post hoc, ergo propter hoc** [Latin for "after this, therefore, because of this"]. See *fallacy*

(4) faulty (as in fallacious or illogical argument) *n.*: **paralogism** (*adj.*: **paralogical**). See *fallacy*

(5) faulty (as in relating to reasoning that sounds plausible but is false or insincere) *adj.*: **meretricious**. See *specious*

(6) faulty (reasoning as in fallacious or specious) *n.*: **syllogism**. See *specious*

(7) faulty (reasoning intended to rationalize or mislead) *n.*: **casuistry**. See *fallacious*

favoring (a particular point of view) *adj.*: **tendentious**. See *biased*

fawn *v.i.*: **truckle**. See *kowtow*

fawner (esp. someone who seeks to associate with

or flatter persons of rank or high social status) *n.*: **tufthunter**. See *hanger-on*

(2) fawner *n.*: **lickspittle**. See *sycophant*

fawning (admirers) *n.*: **claque**. See *admirers*

(2) fawning (as in sycophantic) *adj.*: **gnathonic**. See *sycophantic*

(3) fawning (one who seeks favor through . . . , esp. of one in power) *n.*: **courtier**. See *flattery*

(4) fawning (or worshipful biography) *n.*: **hagiography** (*adj.*: **hagiographic**). See *biography*

(5) fawning (to behave toward in a . . . manner) *v.t.*: **bootlick**. See *kowtow*

fear (abnormal . . . of death or corpses) *n.*: **necrophobia**. ❖ The Governor, who favors [building a stadium], recently told the people of Minnesota, who do not, that without major league sports the Twin Cities would be like Des Moines, "absolutely dead," which caused some consternation in Iowa and not much in Minnesota, where the fear of being like Des Moines, or **necrophobia**, is not so potent, except in Minneapolis, of course. (Garrison Keillor, Essay: "Sweet Home, Minnesota," *Time*, 03/24/1997, p. 108.)

(2) fear (abnormal . . . of or sensitivity to light) *adj.*: **photophobic**. ❖ Unlike largemouths or sunnies, smallmouths are difficult to keep. Simply turning on the aquarium lights can frighten them because they are **photophobic** and avoid light whenever possible. (Robert H. Boyle, First Person: "I Forget Why I Overimbibed One Night Some 14 Years Ago," *Sports Illustrated*, 4/22/1991, p. 102.)

(3) fear (of air or drafts or flying) *n.*: **aerophobia**. ❖ The horrific terrorist attacks [on the World Trade Center] in New York have meant that even those who were quite happy to fly before are now developing "**aerophobia**." (Caroline Green, Health: "How to Beat Your Fear of Flying," *Mirror* [London], 11/3/2001.)

(4) fear (of being buried alive) *n.*: **taphephobia**. ❖ [My mother had] bosoms so large she brought about my **taphephobia** every time we embraced. (Cornelious Biggins,

"My Thoughts," www.aledrjones.me.uk/blog_biggins/, 5/17/2003.)

(5) fear (of dirt or contamination) *n.*: **mysophobia**. ❖ Dear Ann: My wife has developed an obsession for clean hands and wears cotton gloves constantly, even at mealtimes. She is also afraid to shake hands with anyone or even hold my hand. . . . Dear Concerned: Your wife has **mysophobia**, which is an obsessive-compulsive disorder. This condition is not all that rare. (Ann Landers, *Newsday*, 11/16/1993.)

(6) fear (of heights) *n.*: **acrophobia**. ❖ As someone who had **acrophobia**, I understand how a person can be afraid of things that most others don't find threatening. I beat my **acrophobia** by riding on roller coasters and going to the top of the Eiffel Tower. (Unsigned letter to the editor, *Time*, 4/23/2001, p. 14.)

(7) fear (of noises, voices, or speaking aloud) *n.*: **phonophobia**. ❖ [K]arnau's auditory reception is also marked by a love/hate relationship toward the voice, which can turn abruptly from phonomania to **phonophobia**. (Ulrich Schonherr, "Topophony of Fascism: On Marcel Beyer's *The Karnau Tapes*," *Germanic Review*, 9/22/1998, p. 328.)

(8) fear (of open spaces or public places) *n.*: **agoraphobia**. ❖ [S]he suffered a bout of **agoraphobia** in college. It happened during her sophomore year as a drama major at Rutgers University. . . . [She] returned home—and spent most of the next eight months on a couch in the den watching TV. The thought of venturing almost anywhere else, she says, would provoke panic attacks that took the form of severe stomachaches. (Michael A. Lipton, Tube: "Phobic No More: Once Overwhelmed by Fear, Leila Kenzle Lets Loose on *Mad About You*," *People*, 12/11/1995, p. 107.)

(9) fear (source or object of . . . or dread) *n.*: **hobgoblin**. ❖ Global warming may turn out to be a reality, but right now there are enough reasons to conclude that what is masquerading as the most serious of environmental threats may be just another **hobgoblin** being used to advance agendas that can't survive on their own merits. (William F. O'Keefe, "It's Time to Reconsider Global Climate Change Policy," *USA Today Magazine*, 3/1/1997.)

(10) fear (as in anxiety or worry) *n.*: **inquietude**. See *anxiety*

(11) fear (as in panic) *n.*: **Torschlusspanik** [German]. See *panic*

(12) fear (as in worry) *v.t.*, *v.i.*, *n.*: **cark**. See *worry*

(13) fear (deliberate use of . . . and terror as a military tactic used by the Germans to break the will of the enemy) *n.*: **Schrecklichkeit** [German]. See *terror*

(14) fear (of God or God's wrath) *n.*: **theophobia**. See *God*

(15) fear (of water) *n.*: **hydrophobia**. ❖ It takes Truman until his thirties to overcome his **hydrophobia** and cross the road-bridge to the mainland. (Matthew Sweet, Cinema: "The Truman Doctrine," *Independent on Sunday*, 10/11/1998.)

(16) fear (of women) *n.*: **gynophobia**.

(17) fear (or distrust of strangers or foreigners) *n.*: **xenophobia**. See *distrust*

(18) fear (positive form of . . . , as in stress, brought on, for example, by a job promotion or a new baby) *n.*: **eustress**. See *stress*

(19) fear (that something is going to occur) *n.*: **presentiment**. See *premonition*

feared (something that is . . . , disliked, or to be avoided) *n.*: **bête noire** [French]. See *dreaded*

fearful *adj.*: **tremulous**. ❖ The Gaullist tradition from which Mr. Chirac springs still makes him nervous of the market and **tremulous** at the word "globalisation." . . . But ducking the challenge facing France is not the way to recovery. Mr. Chirac and his friends need to win the election—and then find the courage to succeed in a brave new world. (*Economist*, "The Chance for France," 5/24/1997.)

(2) fearful (and cautious and indecisive) *adj.*: **Prufrockian**. See *timid*

(3) fearful (as if of a witch or without reason) *adj.*: **hagridden**. See *tormented*

(4) fearful (as in cowardly) *adj.*: **pusillanimous**. See *cowardly*

(5) fearful (as in cowardly) *adj.*: **retromingent**. See *cowardly*

fearless *adj.*: **doughty**. See *brave*

fearlessness *n.*: **hardihood**. See *courage*

fears (as in nervousness) *n.pl.* but sing. or pl. in construction: **collywobbles**. See *bellyache*

feasible (as in appearing to be true or accurate) *adj.*: **verisimilar**. See *plausible*

feats *n.pl.*: **res gestae**. See *deeds*

February 29 (of or relating to) *adj.*: **bisextile**. See *leap year*

fecal (full of . . . matter) *adj.*: **feculent**. ❖ The Hon. Joe Knollenberg, Michigan Republican, is moving to repeal the hateful toilet law passed before the Revolution of 1994 that limits toilets to using 1.6 gallons of water, about half the amount used previously. The Hon. Knollenberg has noted that the new toilets are becoming **feculent** swamps. (*American Spectator*, "The Continuing Crisis: The Big Sleep; Soho Dog Show; Gorby Fails Detector Test," 6/1/1997.)

feces (eating) *adj.*: **scatophagous**. See *excrement*

(2) feces (feeding on) *n.*: **coprophagous**. See *excrement*

(3) feces (interest in . . . , often sexual) *n.*: **coprophilia**. See *excrement*

(4) feces (obsession with) *n.*: **coprology**. See *excrement*

(5) feces (of or relating to) *adj.*: **stercoraceous**. See *excrement*

(6) feces (study of or obsession with) *n.*: **scatology**. See *excrement*

(7) feces *n.*: **egesta**. See *excrement*

feeble (and ineffective) *adj.*: **feckless**. See *ineffective*

(2) feeble (as in decrepit) *adj.*: **spavined**. See *decrepit*

(3) feeble (as in pale) *adj.*: **etiolated**. See *pale*

(4) feeble (as in powerless) *adj.*: **impuissant**. See *powerless*

(5) feeble (as in weakened) *adj.*: **etiolated**. See *weakened*

(6) feeble (elderly person) *n.*: **Struldbrug**. See *decrepit*

feebleminded (condition of being . . . , as in weak-willed) *n.*: **akrasia** [Greek]. See *weak-willed*

(2) feebleminded (psychiatric diagnosis for one who is . . . , as in retarded) *adj.*: **oligophrenic**. See *retarded*

feebleness (that comes with old age) *n.*: **caducity**. See *old age*

feed (excessive desire to . . . oneself) *n.*: **polyphagia**. See *appetite*

feel (having . . . through the senses) *adj.*: **sensate**. ❖ [The candidate] was running on sheer willpower now; he was not entirely **sensate**, and the ceremonies of the stump—meeting, greeting, talking, walking—were performed reflexively. (Joe Klein, *Primary Colors*, Random House [1996], p. 167.)

(2) feel (around with one's hands) *v.i.*: **grabble**. See *grope*

(3) feel (as in of or relating to sense of touch) *adj.*: **haptic**. See *touch*

(4) feel (as in touch, esp. for medical reasons) *v.t.*: **palpate**. See *touch*

feeling (as in aura or impalpable emantion) *n.*: **effluvium**. See *aura*

(2) feeling (medical examination by . . . the body) *n.*: **palpation**. See *touching*

(3) feeling (that something is going to occur) *n.*: **presentiment**. See *premonition*

feet (having two . . .) *n., adj.*: **biped** (also *adj.*: **bipedal**). ❖ I blame my plight [being short] on my ancestors. Protoancestors, to be precise. If they hadn't risen to the challenge of evolution, abandoned their tails, and stood upright on two feet, I wouldn't be so downcast. Within an eon or two, nature seemed to favor the fastest, strongest, and tallest **bipeds**. (Melissa Rossi, "A Shorty Speaks Up," *Cosmopolitan*, 8/1/1994, p. 106.)

feign (sickness or other incapacity to avoid work) *v.i.*: **malinger**. See *shirk*

fell (with an ax) *v.t.*: **hew**. See *ax*

fellowship *n.*: **sodality**. ❖ For someone as social as Walt Disney, someone who loved **sodality**, loneliness was a curse, and he would have done anything to avoid it. (Neal Gabler, *Walt Disney*, Knopf [2006], p. 62.)

felon *n.*: **malefactor**. See *wrongdoer*

female See *woman*

females (fear of) *n.*: **gynophobia**. See *women*

femininity *n.*: **muliebrity**. ❖ Even more than shunning make-up, women felt that (in the U.S. at least) hair on our legs, under our arms, and on our face indisputably affronts the narrow boundaries of patriarchally-constructed **muliebrity**. Only one of us could recall an instance in which the mainstream media has featured a woman with body hair (Susan Sarandon in *White Palace*). (Contemporary Women's Issues Database, "Exploration of Issues—Women's Bodies," 1/1/1992.)

fence (made of stakes, used esp. for defensive purposes) *n.*: **palisade**. ❖ Archaeologists have discovered . . . that a defensive line of wooden **stakes** sprang up within a few centuries of the . . . founding [of Oaxaca, Mexico]. [Around 1500 B.C.,] villagers built a **palisade**, two alternating rows of pine posts [which is] the oldest defensive structure in Mexico . . . (Alexandra Witze, "Mexican Town May Hold Key to the Origins of American Warfare," *Dallas Morning News*, 9/15/2003.)

fence-sitter (esp. regarding political issues) *n.*: **mugwump**. See *undecided*

ferret (out) *v.t.*: **fossick** [Australian]. See *rummage*

fertile (in producing offspring) *adj.*: **philoprogenitive**. ❖ Vavasour was supposed to be an illegitimate son of the late **philoprogenitive** Sir Thomas, and thus Francis Tresham's half-brother. (Antonia Fraser, *Faith & Treason*, Doubleday [1996], p. 200.)

(2) fertile *adj.*: **fecund**. ❖ The manatee population continues to grow despite the few that are killed in boating accidents, just as our deer populations continue to thrive despite the deer that are struck on the highways. Manatees are not particularly **fecund** animals, but they have no natural predators. (Frank Sargeant, "Manatees Are Not Endangered Species," *Tampa Tribune*, 9/13/2000.)

fervor (excessive or unbridled . . . , as in enthusiasm) *n.* **schwarmerei** (or **schwärmerei**) [German]. See *enthusiasm*

festive (and social) *adj.*: **Anacreontic**. See *convivial*

fetus (of or relating to malformations in) *adj.*: **teratogenic**. ❖ McBride noticed that a disturbing number of women who had been taking the anti-morning-sickness drug thalidomide gave birth to children with terrible limb deformities. After he outlined his concerns in a 1961 letter to the British medical journal *The Lancet*, the drug's **teratogenic** effects were confirmed and it was withdrawn from sale. (Lisa Clausen, Time 100: "Pioneers of Medicine," *Time* International, 10/25/1999, p. 65.)

(2) fetus (destruction of) *n.*: **feticide**. See *abortion*

fever (of or relating to) *n.*: **pyretic**. ❖ Fever, however, makes people feel awful. So, it's all right to use **antipyretics** for comfort during ubiquitous illnesses, such as colds and flu. (Dr. Peter Gott, "Let Body's Defenses Kick In," *Ottawa Sun*, 10/30/2001.)

(2) fever (alternating with chills) *n.*: **ague**. See *chills*

feverish *adj.*: **febrile**. ❖ My mind is like a fly; it buzzes around in a . . . **febrile** fashion, and when it alights on some crumb or fragment of an idea, it's off again before I can apprehend a thing. (Will Self, "Inclusion," short story, *Esquire*, 2/1/1995, p. 108.)

fib (petty or minor . . .) *n.*: **taradiddle** (or **tarradiddle**). See *lie*

(2) fib *n.*: **fabulation** (one who does so: **fabulist**). See *lie*

fickle (one who is . . . or varies with trends) *n.*: **weathercock**. ❖ Far from being a unifier, Mr. Chirac is seen increasingly as a man of few convictions or ideas; power alone is his compass. Indeed, he looks like one of the great **weathercocks** of French politics. Once an outright Europhobe, now a lukewarm "pro-European." (*Economist*, "Jacques Chirac, Out of Steam," 7/31/1999.)

(2) fickle (person, whose opinion is always changing as the wind blows, like a weathervane) *n.*: **girouette** [French]. See *weathervane*

(3) fickle *adj.*: **labile**. See *changeable*

fiction (relating to a story in which . . . and reality are mixed together) *adj.*: **Pirandellian**. See *reality*

(2) fiction (which is dark, gloomy, remote, and/or grotesque) *adj.*: **gothic**. See *dark*

(3) fiction (work of . . . published in installments) *n.*: **feuilleton** [French]. See *novel*

fidelity (as in allegiance) *n.*: **vassalage**. See *allegiance*

(2) fidelity (as in loyalty) *n.*: **fealty** See *loyalty*

fidgeting (as in a state of nervous tension, often with irritability) *n.*: **fantod**. See *tension*

field (as in area of activity or interest) *n.*: **purlieu**. See *domain*

fiendish *adj.*: **Mephistophelean**. See *devilish*

fierce (as in wild or untamed) *adj.*: **farouche** [French]. See *untamed*

fiery (and infernal) *adj.*: **sulfurous** (or **sulphurous**). See *infernal*

fifty (years or a person who is . . . or in his fifties) *n., adj.*: **quinquagenarian**. ❖ DiMaggio was lucky to garner a [single] or better in 56 straight games in 1941, a feat you will be hearing a lot about in the **quinquagenarian** year of this astounding feat. (Daniel Seligman, "Keeping Up: Luck in the Batter's Box," *Fortune*, 5/6/1991, p. 115.)

fight (initiate a . . . or violence) *v.i.*: **aggress**. ❖ There are some, such as Joshua Andrews, who need special help in learning not to **aggress**. By the time Joshua had reached the age of 2, says his mother, Susan Andrews, he . . . kicked and head-butted relatives and friends. He poked the family hamster with a pencil and tried to strangle it. (Constance Holden, "The Violence of the Lambs," *Science*, 7/28/2000.)

(2) fight (people who . . . as if to the death) *n.*: **Kilkenny cats** (esp. as in "fight like Kilkenny cats"). [British; after an 1846 cartoon entitled "Kilkenny cats." The caption reads, "Oh, leave them alone, / They'll fight to the bone, / And leave naught but their tails behind 'em."] ❖ While many Liberals [in the Australian Labor Party] talk of a "union bloc," many unions are in different and opposing factions.

They agree on some issues, but often disagree and fight like **Kilkenny cats**—particularly when they are competing for members. (Mark Skulley, "Battle of the Networks," *Australian Financial Review*, 9/27/2002.)

(3) fight (minor . . . as in skirmish) *n*.: **velitation**. See *skirmish*

(4) fight (as in heated disagreement or friction between groups) *n*.: **ruction**. See *dissension*

(5) fight (as in hostile meeting) *n*.: **rencontre** [French]. See *duel*

(6) fight (engaged in a . . . , as in struggle) *adj*.: **agonistes**. See *struggle*

(7) fight (esp. public) *n*.: **affray**. See *brawl*

(8) fight (for an idea or principle) *n*.: **jihad**. See *crusade*

(9) fight (ready to . . . or pugnacious) *adj*.: **bellicose**. See *belligerent*

fighting (or conflict among the gods) *n*.: **theomachy**. See *gods*

(2) fighting (with a shadow or imaginary foe) *n*.: **sciamachy**. See *shadow-boxing*

figure (as in physique) *n*.: **somatotype**. See *physique*

figure of speech (as in using one word or phrase in place of something with which it is usually associated, such as using "city hall" to refer to city government) *n*.: **metonymy**. ❖ You thank Defense Secretary Donald H. Rumsfeld for scolding reporters who repeatedly say "The White House says" and pointing out that "White Houses do not talk . . . buildings can't speak." Not to be overly pedantic, but aren't reporters merely engaging in the time-honored use of **metonymy**? (Tim Toner, letter to the editor, *Chicago Sun-Times*, 2/10/2002.)

(2) figure of speech (in which one makes only passing mention of something in order to emphasize rhetorically the significance of what is being omitted; often preceded by the phrase "not to mention") *n*.: **paraleipsis**. ❖ The trick in playing the [blame game] is to play to win by denouncing the playing of it by the other side, thus associating oneself with a voter's self-deluding self-image as a reasonable and non-partisan person who hates bickering. The astute player of the blame game thereby avoids the easily seen-through **paraleipsis** of "I refuse to get down in the gutter with my opponent by reminding you of his prior convictions—" etc. (William Safire, "The Blame Game," *New York Times*, 6/2/2002.)

(3) figure of speech (in which one makes reference to an issue by saying that one will not discuss it; e.g., "I'm not even going to get into the character issue.") *n*.: **apophasis**. ❖ [A friend told me that] Bush used . . . **apophasis** [in his debate with Michael Dukakis]. . . . Mr. Bush began a rebuttal with "There's so many things [to challenge] there I don't quite know where to begin," that disarming pretense of being at a loss for words. (William Safire, On Language, *New York Times*, 10/9/1988.) [Safire's friend's use of this word in this context is correct if we assume that Bush did not in fact start challenging whatever he found wrong with Dukakis's statement and had no intention of doing so.]

(4) figure of speech (where a part is used to stand for the whole or vice versa) *n*.: **synecdoche**. ❖ Auschwitz has indeed come to serve as a **synecdoche** for the Nazis' deliberate, systematic destruction of the European Jews. (D. D. Guttenplan, *The Holocaust on Trial*, Norton [2001], p. 21.)

(5) figure of speech *n*.: **trope**. ❖ In the most general terms, a key **trope** has been Thabo Mbeki's evocation of the "African Renaissance" to describe the moment, continental and national, that he and his [African National Congress] now embrace. (John S. Saul, "Cry for the Beloved Country: The Post-Apartheid Denouement," *Monthly Review*, 1/1/2001, p. 1.)

(6) figure of speech *n*.: **façon de parler** [French]. See *way of speaking*

figure out *v.t*.: **suss** (usually with "out"; slang). ❖ So how do you **suss out** whether your mediocre man is really a James Bond in the rough? We went to sex experts and real women and found the five biggest clues that your Plain Wayne has potential in the passion department.

(Isabel Burton, "Suss Out His Sexual Potential: Can He Go from So-So to Oh, Oh, Oh?" *Cosmopolitan*, 9/1/1998.)

fill (to the point of excess, esp. with things sweet) *v.t.*: **cloy**. See *satiate*

filled (with) *adj.*: **aswarm**. See *teeming*

filler (words such as *um, uh, you know,* etc.) *n.*: **embolalia** (or **embololalia**). See *stammering*

film (lover) *n.*: **cineaste**. See *movie*

   (2) film (lover) *n.*: **cinephile**. See *movie*

filth (abnormal fear of) *n.*: **mysophobia**. See *fear*

   (2) filth (place of . . . , as in corruption) *n.*: **Augean stable**. See *corruption*

filthy (full of . . . or impure matter) *adj.*: **feculent**. [See also *fecal*.] ❖ They periodically make the news, uncomfortably reminding us of a tragedy it's easier to ignore, of the uncounted lives all around us lived in misery. They're animal collectors—usually women, usually lacking in human companionship—who take in dozens, sometimes hundreds, of homeless animals. Yet in the guise of "rescuing" animals from the misery of the streets, they actually hold the poor creatures captive in crowded, **feculent** conditions, oblivious to their distress, hostile to intervention. (Rebecca Jones, "In Misery's Company—Addicted to Adopting Stray Animals," *Denver Rocky Mountain News*, 5/4/1997.)

final (as in decisive remark, blow, or factor) *n.*: **sockdolager**. See *decisive*

   (2) final (point or destination) *n.*: **terminus**. See *end*

   (3) final (stroke or blow) *n.*: **quietus**. See *termination*

final analysis (in the . . .) *adv.*: **sub specie aeternitatis** [Latin]. See *big picture*

final resort *n.*: **pis aller** [French]. See *last resort*

final words (as in parting words) *n.*: **envoi** [French]. See *parting words*

financial *adj.*: **pecuniary**. See *monetary*

find (lucky . . .) *n.*: **trouvaille.** [French. This word is also defined as a windfall, which is not necessarily synonymous with a lucky find, in that it doesn't require a "find" at all. In practice, it is normally used in the sense of a lucky find, and not a windfall.] ❖ There's a refreshing lack of preciousness about St Leu [a district in the French town of Amiens]. Ordinary locals live side-by-side with students and there's not a tacky souvenir shop in sight. There are, however, a number of antiques shops where your chances of stumbling upon some genuine . . . **trouvaille** is far greater than in most French towns. (Paul Mansfield, "Buoyant in Amiens," *Evening Standard* [London], 10/9/2000.)

   (2) find (through careful or skillful examination or investigation) *v.t.*: **expiscate**. See *discover*

finding (fortunate things by accident) *n.*: **serendipity** (*adj.*: **serendipitous**). See *fortuitous*

find out (as in figure out) *v.t.*: **suss** (usually with "out"; slang). See *figure out*

fine (impose a monetary . . .) *v.t.*: **amerce**. ❖ On December 15, 2003, Tianjin Municipality announced that [it] would start banning any company or individual from making, selling, and using undegraded super thin plastic bags. Otherwise law enforcement officials will **amerce** a lawbreaking seller [$3,625]. (AsiaInfo Services, "Tianjin to Stop Using Undegraded Plastic Bags," 12/23/2003.)

   (2) fine (as in first-class) *adj.*: **pukka**. See *first-class*

   (3) fine (as in penalty) *n., v.t.*: **mulct**. See *penalize*

   (4) fine (very . . .) *adj.*: **frabjous** (often as in "Oh frabjous day!"). See *wonderful*

   (5) fine (very . . .) *adj.*: **galumptious**. See *excellent*

   (6) fine (very . . .) *adj.*: **skookum**. See *excellent*

fine points (precise observance of . . . of etiquette) *n.*: **punctilio**. See *etiquette*

finery (showy article of . . .) *n.*: **frippery**. ❖ [Designer Vera Wang] first forged her reputation with bridal dresses that banished the lacy **fripperies** adorning wedding-cake dolls in favor of the glowing sheen of modern romance. (Hal Rubenstein, "The Look of Vera Wang," *In Style*, 12/1/2000, p. 142.)

(2) finery *n.*: **caparison**. ❖ There are art lovers, after all, who are mainly in it for a touch of the high life, elegance, opulence, pageantry. Pisanello is certainly their man. His work shows a keen delight in costumes, accessories and ornaments, regalia and **caparisons**. (Tom Lubbock, "The Case of the Missing Master," *Independent* [London], 10/23/2001.)

(3) finery (showy article of . . . or attire) *n.*: **froufrou**. See *clothing*

fingers (having more than normal number of . . . or toes) *adj.*: **polydactyl**. See *toes*

finicky (overly . . .) *adj.*: **persnickety**. See *picky*

finish (as in put an end to) *v.t.*: **quietus** (as in "put the quietus to"). See *termination*

finisher (as in decisive remark, blow, or factor) *n.*: **sockdolager**. See *decisive*

fire (as in dismiss, from a position of command or authority—often military—and especially for disciplinary reasons) *v.t.*: **cashier**. See *dismiss*

fireball (meteoric . . .) *n.*: **bolide**. ❖ Once scientists had used the Apollo trove to learn the geological signature of meteorite impacts on the moon, Spudis said, they were then able to recognize signs of similar events on Earth—notably the Yucatan imprint of the huge **bolide** that wiped out the dinosaurs 65 million years ago. (Kathy Sawyer, "After Apollo 11; What's Happened Since," *Washington Post*, 7/14/1999.)

firebrand (as in inciter) *n.*: **stormy petrel**. See *inciter*

firework *n.*: **Catherine wheel**. [British; spec. a pinwheel that forms a rotating wheel of colored flames. The term derives from Saint Catherine of Alexandria, who was condemned to be tortured on a wheel. It is often used figuratively, as in the following example.] ❖ Fireworks bursting over the White House during the week of Bill Clinton's inauguration as the next American president are nothing compared to the potential pyrotechnic power of the problems awaiting him in the world. The **Catherine wheel** of Iraq, Iran and the Middle East, the rockets of the Balkans, a box full of big bangers

in Russia all are primed, their touchpapers presenting the new administration with the threat of getting burnt. (Roger Boyes, "Time to Put the Lid on Global Fireworks," *Times* [London], 1/20/1993.)

firm (as in hardened) *adj.*: **sclerotic**. See *hardened*

(2) firm (as in stubborn) *adj.*: **pervicacious**. See *stubborn*

(3) firm (in holding to a belief or opinion) *adj.*: **pertinacious**. See *stubborn*

firmness (as in rigidity, esp. with respect to moral or ethical principles or practices) *n.*: **rigorism**. See *rigidity*

first (among equals) *n.*: **primus inter pares** [Latin]. ❖ Sudarsono is one of many who think that the void after Suharto will initially be filled by the armed forces. There is simply no one else with enough clout. What is likely to take over, he expects, is a "military collective" from which a new leader will emerge as **primus inter pares**, much as Suharto did 30 years ago. (*Economist*, "The Army Can Control the Political Opposition, but May Itself Be Divided," 7/26/1997.)

(2) first (in sequence or time) *adj.*: **primordial**. ❖ The [Indian] rishis believed that, just as each animal has its signature call, the universe also generates a unique "sound" that changes every eight hours in a lunar cycle. At the time of your birth, the universe had a particular sound—this is your **primordial** mantra. (Rita Silvan, "Roots Music," *Flare*, 4/1/2000, p. 88.)

(3) first (stage of growth or development) *adj.*: **germinal**. See *earliest*

firstborn (child) *n.*: **primogeniture**. ❖ Nepotism rules at Brown-Forman, a meritocratic sort of nepotism for the most part, but one that still allows **primogeniture** to determine who becomes CEO. (Brett Duval Fromson, "Dynasties: Keeping It All in the Family," *Fortune*, 9/25/1989, p. 86.)

first-class *adj.*: **pukka**. ❖ The one I drink is Lille[t] Blanc. Buy a bottle for around pounds 9.50 if you can find it at Threshers, or at superior independents such as La Vigneronne (0171 589 6113) and **pukka** outlets such as Selfridges and Harrods. (Richard Ehrlich, "Richard Ehrlich's Beverage Report: Rebranding for Britain," *Independent on Sunday*, 8/30/1998.)

first-rate (as in of the highest quality) *n.*: **first water** (usu. as in "of the first water"). See *quality*

(2) first-rate *adj.*: **galumptious**. See *excellent*

(3) first-rate *adj.*: **palmary**. See *excellent*

(4) first-rate *adj.*: **pukka**. See *first-class*

(5) first-rate *adj.*: **skookum**. See *excellent*

fish (eating or feeding on) *adj.*: **ichthyophagous**. ❖ Though most often seen fishing, the great blue [heron] is not entirely **ichthyophagous**. It also eats frogs, snakes, insects, and small mammals. In fact, it will even eat small birds. (Ian de Silva, "A Feathered Friend Stands Tall," *The World & I*, 4/1/1996, p. 192.)

(2) fish (eating or feeding on) *adj.*: **piscivorous**. ❖ Unlike the entrepreneurs who took American fast food to Europe and Canada, Fujita had to induce his customers [in Japan] to try a new diet [McDonald's food]. Had he failed, the Japanese might still be a **piscivorous** people; he argues that eating fish leaves people looking "pale-faced and undignified." (Frederick Hiroshi Katayama, Profile: "Japan's Big Mac—In the Land of Sushi, Den Fujita Operates McDonald's Biggest Overseas Venture," *Fortune*, 9/15/1986, p. 114.)

(3) fish (of . . . that swim upstream) *adj.*: **anadromous**. ❖ Fishermen, boaters, and others who ply the waters and walk along the banks of the Saugus River and its tributaries planned to gather at Camp Nihan in Saugus yesterday to learn how to identify different species of **anadromous** fish that will begin swimming upstream to spawning grounds later this month. (*Boston Globe*, "Group to Identify Saugus River Fish," 3/10/2002.)

(4) fish (of or relating to) *adj.*: **piscatorial**. ❖ Host of the syndicated TV show *Good Fishing*, which appears in 89 markets, Babe is America's hottest video angler. Each week some 2 to 3 million armchair anglers tune in for 30 minutes of easy-to-follow advice from the perfect master of things **piscatorial**. (Jack Friedman, "Jocks: Playing All the Anglers, TV's Babe Winkelman Hooks a Huge Piscatorial Audience," *People*, 9/11/1989, p. 132.)

(5) fish (of or relating to) *adj.*: **piscine**. ❖ [At Le Bernardin], the late Gilbert Le Coze revolutionized seafood cookery and forever changed the way we eat it. . . . Le Coze's influence is reflected in the growing number of superb chefs . . . who have developed their own distinctive styles. Le Bernardin may still reign as the great **piscine** paragon, but these chefs aren't just pretenders to the throne; they're its legitimate heirs. (John Mariani, "Who's the Biggest Fish Now?" *Esquire*, 9/1/1997, p. 146.)

(6) fish (study of) *n.*: **ichthyology**. ❖ [T]he group was playing the biggest trivia game in America—Showdown on the National Trivia Network (NTN). Questions rolled up with multiple choice answers. Players scrambled to log in the right one in a matter of seconds: . . . "Which fish can grow over 500 pounds?" "The striped marlin!" chimed several who knew their **ichthyology**. (Walt Belcher, "Bar Wars," *Tampa Tribune*, 8/31/2001.)

(7) fish (with a net) *v.t.*, *v.i.*: **seine**. ❖ His hands were raised in front of him, stretched as high as he could reach [for the spider], and his fingers languorously combed the air. . . . His **seining** fingers, stained with blood, looked crushingly strong. (Dean Koontz, *Intensity*, Knopf [1995], p. 32.)

fishing (of or related to . . .) *adj.*: **halieutic**. ❖ In two volumes—A History of Flyfishing (1992) and The Dry Fly [1996]—he evoked with relish and gentle erudition the deep pleasure he found in the origins and traditions of his passionate pursuit, and his pages were free of that claptrap and mumbo-jumbo from which much **halieutic** prose frequently suffers. (Tam Dalyell, obituary of Conrad Voss Bark, *Independent* [London], 11/28/2000.)

fit (as in temper tantrum) *n.*: **boutade** [French]. See *temper tantrum*

(2) fit (of emotion, feeling, or action) *n.*: **paroxysm**. See *outburst*

fit out (as in outfit or equip) *v.t.*: **accouter**. See *outfit*

fitting (as in appropriate) *adj.*: **comme il faut** [French]. See *proper*

(2) fitting (as in appropriate) *adj.*: **felicitous**. See *appropriate*

(3) fitting (esp. in reference to a punishment) *adj.*: **condign**. See *deserved*

(4) fitting *adj.*: **apposite**. See *relevant*

five (group of) *n.*: **pentad**. ❖ Rigsbee says the success of partnering is based on the partnering **pentad**, the five key areas of every business. (*Trailer/Body Builders*, "Building a Better Business Through Partnering," 1/1/1998.)

(2) five (occurring once every . . . years) *n.*: **quinquennial**. ❖ In this study we investigate male and female age-specific suicide rates in Quebec for every five-year interval from 1931 to 1986. Five-year intervals are observed because many of the data in this analysis are derived from the **quinquennial** censuses of Canada and the provinces, including Quebec. (Catherine Krull, "The Quiet Revolution and the Sex Differential in Quebec's Suicide Rates: 1931–1986," *Social Forces*, 6/1/1994, p. 1121.)

fix (as in predicament, from which it is difficult to extricate oneself) *n.*: **tar baby**. See *predicament*

fix (text or language by removing errors or flaws) *v.t.*: **blue-pencil**. See *edit*

(2) fix (text or language by removing errors or flaws) *v.t.*: **emend**. See *edit*

(3) fix (up, as in spruce up) *v.t.*: **titivate**. See *spruce up*

fixation (on an idea or concept) *n.*: **idée fixe** [French]. See *obsession*

(2) fixation (undue . . . on one subject or idea) *n.*: **monomania**. See *obsession*

(3) fixation (with shopping) *n.*: **oniomania**. See *shopping*

fixed (as in incapable of being overthrown, driven out, or subdued by force) *adj.*: **inexpugnable**. See *impregnable*

fixing (as in atoning for) *adj.*: **piacular**. See *atoning*

flag (an inspiring . . .) *n.*: **oriflamme**. See *banner*

(2) flag (suspended from a crossbar, as opposed to on a flagstaff) *n.*: **gonfalon**. See *banner*

flagrant (as in infamous, esp. as to a crime or evil deed) *adj.*: **flagitious**. See *scandalous*

flags (of or relating to) *adj.*: **vexillary**. The city of Portland's flag leaves something to be desired. . . . [It's] pretty busy by flag-fancier standards. It has words on it, for one thing, and that means the letters will be backwards on one side. It's got a seal, and reliance on seals and crests is also considered a **vexillary** no-no. (*Portland [ME] Press Herald*, "Maybe It's Time to Redesign the Banner Flying over Portland," 10/21/2004.)

(2) flags (study of . . .) *n.*: **vexillology**. ❖ Artist Dread Scott's work, "What Is the Proper Way to Display the U.S. Flag?" involves placing the flag on the floor and inviting visitors to walk over it to sign the artist's book. . . . Despite the furor, college officials said there are no plans to remove the Exhibit, "**Vexillology**: The American Symbol in Art," which features a dozen artists' work scheduled to run through Oct. 1 at the college. (Olivia Winslow, "Flag Art Exhibit Raises Objections; Despite Furor, College Has No Plans to Remove Work," *Newsday*, 9/11/2003.)

flair (having . . . as magnetism or charm) *n.*: **duende**. See *charisma*

flamboyant (as in affected and high-flown, use of language) *adj.*: **euphuistic.** See *affected*

(2) flamboyant (as in ornate) *adj.*: **baroque**. See *ornate*

(3) flamboyant (as in ornate) *adj.*: **florid**. See *ornate*

(4) flamboyant (as in showy) *adj.*: **orchidaceous**. See *showy*

(5) flamboyant (young woman who is attractive and . . .) *n.*: **frippet** [British; informal]. See *woman*

flammable *adj.*: **tindery**. ❖ The worst of it came shortly after 1 a.m. last Thursday when firefighters were hosing down the **tindery** brush on the western edge of the Los Alamos National Laboratory. The wind was gusting to 60 miles an hour, and suddenly they were fighting two fires at once . . . (*Newsweek*, "Los Alamos under Siege: A Fire's Dangerous Cost," 5/22/2000.)

flap (on airplane wing) *n.*: **aileron**. ❖ Ideally, rubber de-icer boots expand and contract to break off ice as it forms on leading edge. Air flows smoothly over the wing, maintaining pressure over the **aileron**. *(*Stephen J. Hedges, "Fear of Flying: One Plane's Story," *U.S. News & World Report*, 3/6/1995.)

flash-forward (spec. acting as if or threatening that a future event [usually unwanted] has already occurred by reference to an event that precedes it; e.g., "If you look at my diary, you're dead") *n.*: **prolepsis**. See *prediction*

flashing (as in emitting flashes of light) *adj.*: **coruscant**. See *glittering*

flashy (as in ornate) *adj.*: **baroque**. See *ornate*

(2) flashy (as in ornate) *adj.*: **florid**. See *ornate*

(3) flashy (but cheap or tasteless, or such an object) *adj., n.*: **gimcrack**. See *showy*

(4) flashy (but cheap, or such an object) *adj., n.*: **brummagem**. See *showy*

(5) flashy (in a gaudy way) *adj.*: **meretricious**. See *gaudy*

(6) flashy *adj.*: **orchidaceous**. See *showy*

flat (and broad, like a spatula) *adj.*: **spatulate**. ❖ [Herman Kamen] was a large, shapeless, ungainly man with a **spatulate** nose and thick pop-bottle-bottomed glasses, and he parted his black hair unfashionably down the middle of his scalp, only adding to the impression of his gaucheness. (Neal Gabler, *Walt Disney*, Knopf [2007], p. 196.)

flatterer (esp. someone who seeks to associate with or flatter persons of rank or high social status) *n.*: **tuft-hunter**. See *hanger-on*

(2) flatterer *n.*: **lickspittle**. See *sycophant*

flattering (as in sycophantic) *adj.*: **gnathonic**. See *sycophantic*

(2) flattering (insincerely . . .) *adj.*: **fulsome**. See *insincere*

flattery (coaxing by . . .) *n.*: **blandishment** (*v.t.*: **blandish**). ❖ But why would a woman mature enough to vote, have an abortion, or pilot a nuclear bomber be too fragile to resist the **blandishments** of a male, however "powerful"? In Lewinsky's case it isn't even a question of **blandishments**; she made the first move, on her own story. (George Jonas, "Bill and the Big Lie," *Toronto Sun*, 12/17/1998.)

(2) flattery (one who seeks favor through . . . , esp. of one in power) *n.*: **courtier**. ❖ Sometimes it is a sense that pomposity or flattery cries out to be pricked. Even Louis XIV, not famous for his humility, felt that a **courtier** had gone too far when he compared, "not the king to God, but God to the king." "Too much, monsieur," was the monarch's murmured rebuke, "is always too much." (Godfrey Hodgson, "Moments of Truth," *Independent* [London], 3/9/1996.)

(3) flattery (empty, meaningless, or insincere . . .) *n.*: **flummery**. See *compliment*

(4) flattery (to win over or obtain by . . . or coaxing) *v.t.*: **inveigle**. See *lure*

(5) flattery *n.*: **palaver**. See *sweet talk*

flatulence (of or relating to reducing . . .) *adj.*: **carminative**. See *farting*

flavor (which is delicious) *n.*: **ambrosia** (*adj.*: **ambrosial**). ❖ Tropical Shrimp Salad—For a refreshing lunch on a steamy summer day, try this **ambrosial** mix of coconut milk, orange juice, and jalapeno pepper sauce splashed over cooked shrimp, Boston lettuce, and Texmati rice. (*Redbook*, "Salads That Really Satisfy," 8/1/1996, p. 123.)

flavorful *adj.*: **esculent**. See *edible*

(2) flavorful *adj.*: **sapid**. See *tasty*

flaw (tragic . . . , esp. in a literary character) *n.*: **hamartia**. ❖ [For director Oliver Stone] Nixon [was] undercut by his strict puritanical upbringing, his lack of charm especially vis-à-vis Kennedy, and his not having the right school tie and social background. These minuses are meant to add up to the **hamartia**, the tragic flaw in Nixon's potentially heroic stature. (John Simon, review of *Nixon*, *National Review*, 2/12/1996, p. 57.)

flawed *adj.*: **peccable**. ❖ "I understand the politics of this country better than anyone else in it," Hawke thundered. "My judgment on major political events has been impeccable." Most Australians, however, consider him **peccable** indeed. In the face of a deepening recession and a 10.5% unemployment rate, Hawke's approval rating in opinion polls has sunk to its lowest level ever. (Damien Murphy, Asia/Pacific, *Time* International, 12/23/1991, p. 22.)

(2) flawed (and/or illogical argument) *n.*: **choplogic**. See *fallacy*

(3) flawed (argument, spec. where one argues that because event B followed event A, then event A must have caused event B) *n.*: **post hoc, ergo propter hoc** [Latin for "after this, therefore, because of this"]. See *fallacy*

(4) flawed (as in fallacious or illogical, argument) *n.*: **paralogism** (*adj.*: **paralogical**). See *fallacy*

(5) flawed (as in relating to reasoning that sounds plausible but is false or insincere) *adj.*: **meretricious**. See *specious*

(6) flawed (engaging in argument that may be . . . , as in specious) *adj., n.*: **eristic**. See *specious*

(7) flawed (reasoning, as in fallacious or specious) *n.*: **syllogism**. See *specious*

(8) flawed (reasoning in logic in which a false conclusion is drawn from two premises, neither of which conveys information about all members of the designated class) *n.*: **undistributed middle**. See *fallacy*

(9) flawed (reasoning intended to rationalize or mislead) *n.*: **casuistry**. See *fallacious*

flawless (as in faultless or sinless) *adj.*: **impeccant**. See *faultless*

flecked (with a darker color) *adj.*: **brindled**. See *spotted*

flee (as in a departure that is unannounced, abrupt, secret, or unceremonious) *n.*: **French leave** (or **French Leave**). See *departure*

fleece (as in deceive) *v.t.*: **hornswoggle**. See *deceive*

(2) fleece (as in defraud) *v.t.*: **mulct**. See *defraud*

(3) fleece (as in swindle) *n., v.t.*: **thimblerig**. See *swindle*

fleeing (desperate . . . , as in retreat) *n.*: **Dunkirk**. See *retreat*

fleeting *adj.*: **fugacious**. ❖ On Sunday mornings I get up early and [go to a] café, . . . nurse a doppio espresso and consider my options. Between making a living, barely, and parenting, an occupation that keeps me fully employed in an emotional economy with its own recessions and surges, considering my options is a luxury, **fugacious** though it is. (R. W. Lucky, "What I Want to Be After My Child Grows Up," *Seattle Times*, 3/27/1994.)

(2) fleeting *adj.*: **evanescent**. See *transient*

fleshy (condition of having a . . . physique) *n.*: **embonpoint**. See *plump*

(2) fleshy (person, esp. with a large abdomen) *n.*: **endomorph** (*adj.*: **endomorphic**). See *pot-bellied*

flexible (as in persuadable) *adj.*: **exorable**. See *persuadable*

(2) flexible (as in pliable) *adj.*: **ductile**. See *pliable*

flickering (light . . . softly over a surface) *adj.*: **lambent**. See *shimmering*

flight (desperate . . . , as in retreat) *n.*: **Dunkirk**. See *retreat*

(2) flight (from danger) *n.*: **hegira**. See *escape*

flighty (person) *n.*: **featherhead**. ❖ If Oprah Winfrey can get huge numbers of women usually dismissed as romance-reading **featherheads** to tackle challenging novels by Toni Morrison and Ursula Hegi by talking her audience through them in a warm, enthusiastic, unscary, we're-all-in this-together way, think what the government could do if it was willing to spend a little money to enlarge our minds and broaden our tastes a bit. (Katha Pollitt, "Right-Wing Attack on Art Playing to Small Audience," *Chicago Tribune*, 8/7/1997.)

(2) flighty (person) *n.*: **flibbertigibbet**. ❖ Ultimately, Siggins concludes, a plethora of such triumphs must signal the end of "those demoralizing and demeaning stereotypes that have shadowed women like an ugly, black cloud since time immemorial . . . the ridiculous point of view that posits women as morally weak, intellectually inferior, the **flibbertigibbets** of the ages, is finally being exposed for what it is: a lie." (Elizabeth Abbott, "A Class Act," *Toronto Star*, 4/23/2000.)

(3) flighty (young woman who is attractive and flamboyant) *n.*: **frippet** [British; informal.]. See *woman*

(4) flighty (as in fickle, person whose opinion is always changing as the wind blows; like a weathervane) *n.*: **girouette** [French]. See *weathervane*

flimsy (as in sheer or transparent) *adj.*: **diaphanous**. See *transparent*

(2) flimsy (as in sheer or transparent) *adj.*: **gossamer**. See *transparent* and *tenuous*

flinch (as in draw back from or shy away from) *v.i.*: **blench**. ❖ [Russian] strongman Alexander Lebed . . . hawks law and order in a way that would make any redneck sheriff **blench**. (Josef Joffe, Viewpoint: "Embracing Mr. Wonderful: The West's Problems with Russia Haven't Been Resolved by Yeltsin's Victory," *Time* International, 7/15/1996, p. 26.)

(2) flinch (as in recoil, due to fear or intimidation) *v.t.*: **quail**. See *recoil*

(3) flinch *v.i.*: **resile**. See *recoil*

fling (as in love affair) *n.*: **amourette** [French]. See *love affair*

flirtatious (glance at in a . . . way) *idiom*: **make sheep's eyes**. Our always interesting EU trade commissioner Peter Mandelson, 53, is said to have parted from his dance partner of ten years, handsome Brazilian Reinaldo da Silva, 34. Mandy is **making sheep's eyes** at 32-year-old Italian fashion designer Marco Coretti, who owns a smart boutique close to Rome's Spanish steps. (Peter McKay, "Browned Off Already by Gordon," *Daily Mail* [London], 5/14/2007.)

(2) flirtatious (glance) *n.*: **oeillade** [French]. See *glance*

float (dancer's seeming ability to . . .) *n.*: **ballon** [French]. ❖ An impossible consummation may be the definition of all ballet: the great dancer's yearning to become totally airborne and never to touch ground. Ballet is **ballon** writ large: the defeat of the force of gravity. (John Simon, "The Master and the Muse" [choreographer George Balanchine and dancer Suzanne Farrell], *New Leader*, 2/10/1997, p. 21.)

(2) float (along swiftly and easily, used esp. of clouds) *v.i.*: **scud**. See *move*

(3) float (as in glide, through the air like glider) *n., v.i.*: **volplane**. See *glide*

flock (as in parish or congregation) *n.*: **laity**. See *parish*

(2) flock (of geese) *n.*: **gaggle** (generally as in . . . of geese). See *geese*

flog (generally used figuratively) *v.t.*: **larrup**. See *whip*

(2) flog (oneself) *v.t.*: **flagellate** (*n.*: **flagellation**). See *criticize*

flogging (the soles of the feet with a stick as a form of punishment or torture) *n., v.t.*: **bastinado**. See *beating*

flood (of, relating to, or produced by) *adj.*: **diluvial**. ❖ A storm broke out as we entered Tetema in late afternoon. **Diluvial** rain clattered on corrugated zinc roofs and cascaded into buckets. (Victor Englebert, "A Joyful Funeral: Ghana's Rite of Eternal Rest," *World & I*, 5/1/2000, p. 198.)

floral (arrangement) *n.*: **nosegay**. See *bouquet*

flounce (so as to attract attention) *v.i.*: **tittup**. See *strut*

flounder (around with one's hands) *v.i.*: **grabble**. See *grope*

flourish (often at another's expense) *v.i.*: **batten**. See *thrive*

flourished (as in the period during which a person worked or was most active, especially set forth in parentheses after the person's name) *n.*: **floruit** [Latin]. ❖ Gilgamesh, a king in historical reality (**floruit** 2800 BCE) is, when first we meet him in [the *Epic of Gilgamesh*, written in 1200 BCE], a youthful tyrant; his strength and energy are employed in contests against young male subjects and in seductions of young female ones. (Paul Binding, "Still a Thriller," *Independent* [London], 3/7/1999.)

flow (as in outflow) *n*.: **efflux**. See *outflow*

(2) **flow** (out or away from proper channels, esp. a liquid or something that flows) *v.t.*: **extravasate**. See *exude*

flower (cluster) *n*.: **inflorescence**. ❖ The most aggressive of the male bushes is *Skimmia japonica* "Rubella." Its flowers may be tiny, but they are produced in huge conical heads, several hundreds packed tightly together in one **inflorescence** that can be 9 in. tall and 3-4 in. across at the base. (Fred Whitsey, Gardening: "Fortune's Favourite *Skimmia* Sex Wars," *Daily Telegraph* [London], 2/5/2000.)

(2) **flower** (petals of a . . . , taken separately or as a whole) *n*.: **corolla**. See *petals*

flowering (as in blooming) *n*.: **efflorescence** (*v.i.*: effloresce). See *blooming*

(2) **flowering** (as in blooming) *n*.: **florescence**. See *blooming*

(3) **flowering** (more than once per season) *adj*.: **remontant**. See *blooming*

flowers (bearing . . .) *adj*.: **floriferous**. ❖ In February 2002 garden centres will be full of hebe "Pink Pixie"—a very disease-resistant variety. A good compact shrub, it's hugely **floriferous** and is better than hebe "Rosie." (Howard Drury, Living: "All Change!" *Sunday Mercury*, 9/16/2001.)

(2) **flowers** (bunch of . . .) *n*.: **nosegay**. See *bouquet*

flowery (as in ornate) *adj*.: **florid**. See *ornate*

flowing (of, relating to, or living in . . . water systems, such as rivers and streams) *adj*.: **lotic**. See *water*

(2) **flowing** (smoothly or copiously, like a stream) *adj*.: **profluent**. ❖ In *Untitled (Cosmetics)*, 1997, [artist Claude] Closky collaged the ubiquitous flow and spills of beauty products into a **profluent** maze of turquoise squirts. (Dike Blair, Openings: Claude Closky, *Artforum*, 11/1/2003.)

(3) **flowing** (out or forth) *n*.: **effluence**. See *emanation*

fluffy (having a . . . appearance) *adj*.: **flocculent**. ❖ Today, however, the glass (which is populated by cherubs, a celestial mother figure, a harp or two, ethereal blue sky and sunlit, **flocculent** clouds) isn't restored so much as reborn. (James B. Meadow, "Great Panes Restoring, Creating Stained Glass Is Precision Work," *Denver Rocky Mountain News*, 10/10/1998.)

fluid (as in like liquid or tending to become liquid) *adj*.: **liquescent**. See *liquid*

fluke (as in random) *adj*.: **stochastic**. See *random*

flunky *n*.: **running dog**. See *lackey*

flustered *adj*.: **in a dither**. ❖ She had never been away from her puppyhood home and the separation from me and the presence of all the other dogs left her **in a dither**. (Lars Eighner, *Travels with Lizbeth*, St. Martin's Press [1993], p. 10.)

flutter (one's eyes) *v.i.*: **nictitate**. See *blink*

fly (through the air like an airplane with its engine shut off) *n., v.i.*: **volplane**. See *glide*

flying (or capable of . . .) *adj*.: **volant**. ❖ Penguins travel slowly in comparison to **volant** seabirds (Wilson 1985), which means that prey densities may easily become depleted around the islands . . . (K. Putz, "Foraging Strategy of King Penguins During Summer at the Crozet Islands," *Ecology*, 9/1/1998.)

(2) **flying** (esp. too high for safety) *adj*.: **Icarian**. See *soaring*

(3) **flying** (fear of . . .) *n*.: **aerophobia**. See *fear*

foamy *adj*.: **spumescent** (*n*.: **spumescence**). ❖ In [the wake of the tidal wave] follow a cavalcade of hump-backed waves; they're not river waves, but frothing, **spumescent** seaish waves. (Penelope Bennet, "Waiting for the Bore [Tidal Wave up a River]," *Contemporary Review*, 9/1/1996.)

focal point (as in nerve center) *n*.: **ganglion** (pl. **ganglia**). See *nerve center*

(2) **focal point** (of attention) *n*.: **cynosure**. See *center of attention*

(3) **focal point** *n*.: **omphalos**. See *center*

focus (emotional energy on an object, idea, or person) *v.t.*: **cathect** (*n*.: **cathexis**). ❖ The real problem, in other words, is that there is no strong male within the prison with whom Marie Allen, the protagonist, can **cathect**. She is thus thrown to the mercy of "the boys" who run a shoplifting syndicate, which eventually recruits her for a life of continued crime. (Anne Morey, "The Judge Called Me an Accessory [Women's Prison Films]," *Journal of Popular Film and Television*, 6/1/1995, p. 80.)

(2) focus (point of . . . or area of concentration, esp. in a military attack) *n.*: **schwerpunkt** [German]. Bush, the stable family man with his pert and decent wife, has all along made the **schwerpunkt**, the strategic direction of his political attack, his contrast with the personal and alleged financial scandals of Clinton. (United Press International, Analysis: "Bush Shows Political Brains," 8/11/2000.)

(3) focus (as in channel) *v.t.*: **canalize**. See *channel*

(4) focus (of attention) *n.*: **cynosure**. See *center of attention*

(5) focus (undue . . . on one subject or idea) *n.*: **monomania**. See *obsession*

fog *n.*: **brume**. ❖ Whiteness: the perfect whiteness of an enveloping fog. Muted sounds: voices, the creak of sails and rigging. Very slowly, the outlines of a 19th century sailing ship begin to take shape through the **brume**. (Richard Schickel, Cinema: "Hail the Epic-Size Hero," *Time*, 1/2/1989, p. 94.)

(2) fog (over one's vision) *v.t.*: **obnubilate**. See *obscure*

foggy (as in a failure to perceive something clearly or accurately based on clear observation or analysis as a result of being cross-eyed, literally or figuratively) *adj.*: **strabismic**. See *cross-eyed*

foil (as in person who serves as a . . . to another) *n.*: **deuteragonist**. See *secondary*

foist (oneself or one's ideas in an unwelcome way) *v.t.*: **obtrude**. See *impose*

fold (of loose skin hanging from neck, esp. of cattle, but also of people) *n.*: **dewlap**. See *jowl*

(2) fold (or wrinkle) *n.*, *v.t.*: **rimple**. See *wrinkle*

follow (slowly) *v.i.*: **draggle**. ❖ A year ago, when Carolina Herrera showed bustles and

a few other [dress] designers showed trains, it seemed like a joke. Then trains **draggled** across the stage after several movie stars at the Oscars. (Patricia McLaughlin, "The Train Chugs into the Future," *St. Louis Post-Dispatch*, 10/13/1994.)

(2) follow (apt to . . . as opposed to leading) *adj.*: **sequacious**. See *subservient*

(3) follow (as in happen or occur) *v.t.*: **betide**. See *happen*

(4) follow (as in result) *v.i.*: **eventuate**. See *result*

(5) follow (closely to a line, rule, or principle) *v.i.*: **hew**. See *conform*

follower (devoted) *adj.*: **acolyte**. ❖ Observes Kristol, a senior Bush Administration official: "Newt [Gingrich is] a complicated man; there's a lot of ego there, and there's a little bit of susceptibility to grandiose promises. He can sort of invent this giant scheme for the future, and his **acolytes** tell him that it's great." (Julie Johnson, Congress: "In the Eyes of Newt— The Minority Whip Has His Sights on a G.O.P. Takeover of the House," *Time*, 10/10/1994, p. 35.)

(2) follower (devout . . . of a cause, religion, or activity) *n.*: **votary**. See *supporter*

(3) follower (servile . . .) *n.*: **running dog**. See *lackey*

(4) follower (who is loyal and unquestioning) *n.*: **myrmidon**. See *assistant*

(5) follower (as in one who conforms, often self-righteously) *adj.*: **bien-pensant**. See *right-thinking*

following (a meal, esp. dinner) *adj.*: **postprandial**. See *meal*

folly *n.*: **bêtise** [French]. See *stupidity*

fondle *v.i.*: **canoodle** (often "canoodle with"). See *caress*

fondling *idiom*: **slap and tickle**. See *sex*

food (item of) *n.*: **viand**. ❖ The chic Chicagoan now turns his eye on what can be done with exotic as well as more familiar **viands** with *Charlie Trotter's Meat and Game* (Oct., $50). (*Publishers Weekly*, Ten Speed Press, 7/23/2001.)

(2) food (item of) *n.*: **victual**. ❖ Tables inside his studio hold a variable smorgasbord of [fake] **victuals**, enough fake baked hams, plum puddings, cookies, cakes, plump walnuts, boiled beef, artichokes and pastry-topped stews to make a hungry reporter weep. (Melissa Stoeltje, Fee Fi Faux Fare: Henri Gadbois Is a Giant in the Field of Fake Food," *Houston Chronicle*, 12/23/1994.)

(3) food (lover of good . . .) *n.*: **gourmandise**. ❖ During his first winter in Virginia, Captain John Smith, known more for his love life than his **gourmandise**, extolled the virtues of native American foods introduced to him by the Powhatan Indians. (Annette Stramesi, "Final Take," *Colonial Homes*, 11/1/1997, p. 112.)

(4) food (which is genetically modified) *n.*: **Frankenfood**. ❖ Over the last 10 years or so there has been a maelstrom of claims and counter-claims about the use of bioengineered, or gene-spliced crops. . . . Detractors have railed that **Frankenfood** will cause lethal allergies, decimate beneficial fauna, pollute the genomes of traditional crops, create "super-weeds," and not profit anyone but the industry giants that produce them. (Ruth Kava, "Giving Green Light to Frankenfood," *Washington Times*, 7/13/2003.)

(5) food (abnormally increased appetite for) *n.*: **hyperphagia**. See *appetite*

(6) food (as in nourishment) *n.*: **alimentation**. See *nourishment*

(7) food (esp. insipid, like baby food) *n.*: **pabulum** (also **pablum**). See *insipid*

(8) food (excessive desire or craving for) *n.*: **polyphagia**. See *appetite*

(9) food (lover of good . . .) *n.*: **epicure**. See *gourmet*

(10) food (lover of good . . .) *n.*: **gastronome**. See *gourmet*

(11) food *n.*: **comestible**. See *edible*

fool (or loser or dope or idiot or anyone generally not worthy of respect) *n.*: **schmendrick** or **shmendrik** [Yiddish]. ❖ "And number three, we have on our schedule next a private tour [of] the gas chamber, which is a very special treat that doesn't happen every day to any old **schmendrik**. Come on, gang. (Tova Reich, *My Holocaust*, HarperCollins [2007], p. 53.)

(2) fool *n.*: **mooncalf**. ❖ The *Buckley vs. Valeo* case, decided in 1976, says that money is equal to speech. As a result, any limits on how much politicians collect or spend is a violation of free speech rights under the Constitution. Any **mooncalf** knows money is not equal to speech. If a man standing next to me has a million dollars to donate to a senator, I can yell as loudly as he can, but he'll get a meeting with the senator to discuss his legislative needs a lot more quickly than will I. (Bonnie Erbe, "It Looks Hopeless on the Reform Front," *Denver Rocky Mountain News*, 10/18/1997.)

(3) fool (as in buffoon, who is sometimes boastful) *n.*: **Scaramouch**. See *buffoon*

(4) fool (as in deceive) *v.t.*: **humbug**. See *deceive*

(5) fool (as in swindle) *v.t.*: **bunco**. See *swindle*

(6) fool (or force someone into doing something, esp. by fraud or coercion) *v.t.*: **shanghai** (person who does so *n.*: **shanghaier**). See *coerce*

(7) fool *n.*: **balatron**. See *buffoon*

(8) fool *n.*: **jobbernowl** [British]. See *idiot*

(9) fool *v.t.*: **hornswoggle**. See *deceive*

(10) fool (as in deceive) *v.t.*: **gull**. See *deceive*

fool around (as in idle or waste time) *v.i.*: **footle** (usu. as in "footle around"). See *dawdle*

foolhardy (as in irresponsible or reckless) *adj.*: **harum-scarum**. See *reckless*

(2) foolhardy *adj.*: **Icarian**. See *overambitious*

(3) foolhardy *adj.*: **temerarious**. See *reckless*

foolish (in a smug or complacent manner) *adj.*: **fatuous**. ❖ "Jerry Garcia destroyed his life on drugs," Rush Limbaugh fearlessly proclaimed. You don't have to advocate heroin addiction or alcoholism to feel that all this moralistic fury is inanely misdirected. Nothing is more **fatuous** than to indict some performer for his failure to conform to the prescribed virtues of the "role model." Smug, self-satisfied, sanctimonious, this line of thinking fails first of all to acknowledge the true complexities of human existence. (John Taylor, "Live and Let Die: In Praise of Mickey [Mantle], Jerry, and the Reckless Life," *Esquire*, 12/1/1995, p. 120.)

(2) foolish *adj.*: **barmy** [British]. ❖ The web page called "The American Taliban" is a particularly rich source of obnoxiously **barmy** quotations, beginning with a prize one from somebody called Ann Coulter who, American colleagues have persuaded me, is not a spoof: "We should invade their countries, kill their leaders and convert them to Christianity." (Richard Dawkins, *The God Delusion*, Houghton-Mifflin [2006], p. 288.)

(3) foolish *adj.*: **balmy**. ❖ [As Dr. Moreau, Marlon Brando is] perched aloft in a parody of the Popemobile, an appropriate vehicle for this mad-scientist demigod who reigns over a tropical island populated by half-human animals he's created by genetic engineering. . . . Brando's Moreau is a cracked idealist—you can't help but think of his Kurtz in *Apocalypse Now*, gone **balmy** up Coppola's Vietnamese river. (David Ansen, review of *The Island of Dr. Moreau*, *Newsweek*, 9/2/1996.)

(4) foolish (person) *n.* **dullard**. See *stupid*

(5) foolish (as in futile activity) *n.*: **mug's game** [British; informal]. See *futile*

foolishness *n.*: **flapdoodle**. See *nonsense*

(2) foolishness (or talk . . .) *v.i.*, *n.*: **piffle**. See *nonsense*

(3) foolishness *n.*: **bêtise** [French]. See *stupidity*

(4) foolishness *n.*: **codswallop** [British]. See *nonsense*

(5) foolishness *n.*: **folderol** (or **falderal**). See *nonsense*

(6) foolishness *n.*: **trumpery**. See *nonsense*

foot (on . . .) *idiom*: **shank's mare** (or **shank's pony**). See *walking*

foot-in-mouth (disease) *n.*: **dontopedalogy**. [This word was coined by Prince Philip to describe his own frequent tendency in this

regard, and in this example is being applied to him]. ❖ Brickbats—For chronic **dontopedalogy**, to Prince Philip. The prince has often suffered from foot-in-mouth disease and last week he displayed serious symptoms. . . . Speaking on BBC radio [about a school shooting, he said that] handguns are no more lethal than . . . cricket bats [and that "if somebody] decided to go into a school and batter a lot of people to death with a cricket bat . . . I mean, are you going to ban cricket bats?" (*Gazette* [Montreal], "Bouquets & Brickbats," 12/21/1996.)

forage (about or through) *v.t.*: **fossick** [Australian]. See *rummage*

forbearance (in the face of adversity) *n.*: **longanimity**. See *patience*

force (a person or group to go from one place to another, whether literally or figuratively) *v.t.*: **frogmarch**. See *march*

(2) force (as in power or might) *n.*: **puissance**. See *power*

(3) force (initial . . . , as in prime mover) *n.*: **primum mobile** [Latin]. See *prime mover*

(4) force (oneself or one's ideas in an unwelcome way) *v.t.*: **obtrude**. See *impose*

(5) force (or trick someone into doing something, esp. by fraud or coercion) *v.t.*: **shanghai** (person who does so *n.*: **shanghaier**). See *coerce*

(6) force (to act, esp. by violent measures or threats) *v.t.*: **dragoon**. See *coerce*

(7) force (out or extract, whether from a place or position, or information) *v.t.*: **winkle** (usu. used with "out"). See *extract*

(8) force (out) *v.t.*: **extrude**. See *push out*

forebears (excessive reverence for . . . or tradition) *adj.*: **filiopietistic**. See *old-fashioned*

foreboding (that something is going to occur) *n.*: **presentiment**. See *premonition*

forecast (the future by gazing into a crystal ball) *v.t.*: **scry**. See *predict*

forecaster (as in one who makes correct predictions of misfortune that are ignored) *n.*: **Cassandra**. See *predictor*

forefathers (excessive reverence for . . . or tradition) *adj.*: **filiopietistic**. See *old-fashioned*

foreign (as in originating elsewhere; non-native) *adj.*: **allochthonous**. ❖ At 7 p.m., a horticulturist leads an evening walk to point out both native and **allochthonous** plants, including roses, that thrive in early summer. (Adrian Higgins, "Coming Up . . . ," *Washington Post*, 6/11/1998.)

(2) foreign (as in originating from elsewhere; not endemic) *adj.*: **ecdemic**. ❖ In recent years, while Shanghai was trying to fetch in foreign capital, they drew up a system of favorable policy to attract **ecdemic** investment. . . . The favorable policy included special service of industrial and commercial registration, non-retesting of registration capital. Until now, over 1500 **ecdemic** enterprises have settled in Shanghai. (AsiaInfo Services, "Domestic Investors Think Highly of Shanghai," 8/31/2001.)

(3) foreign (person who appreciates . . . customs and manners) *n.*: **xenophile**. ❖ Today's global society demands that we become **xenophiles**, respecting and appreciating people, things, and customs from cultures other than our own. Nursing and health care are culturally defined, so you need to understand the systems and beliefs important to patients from other cultures. (Edwina McConnell, "26 Words Toward a Successful Nursing Career," *Nursing*, 6/1/1997, p. 41.)

foreigner (from another country or place) *n.*: **outlander**. ❖ The Middle American Dream, circa the mid-1950s and '60s, a time when Washington became what Manhattan had been a generation before: a magnet for young **outlanders** with yearning sensations to go East and make a mark for themselves. (Victor Gold, "Fitzwater's Wit and Charm Come Out in *Call the Briefing*," *Washington Times*, 11/6/1995.)

(2) foreigner (in Japan) *n.*: **gaijin**. ❖ But over the last decade, that facade of virtue [in the Japanese sport of sumo wrestling] has crumbled in the face of new temptations—dope, fast cars, girls—as much as from the **gaijin** invasion [into the sport]. In 1986, baseball replaced sumo as the most popular sport on Japanese television. (Velisarios Kattoulas, "Selling Sumo," *Newsweek* International, 6/21/1999, p. 84.)

(3) foreigner *n.*: **auslander**. ❖ The result is that more and more U.S. managers are learning what it's like to have a boss from abroad. While the experience varies from employer to employer, veterans say a few lessons should be borne in mind by anyone thinking of working for an **auslander**. First, be sure your prospective employer knows what it's doing in coming to America. (Faye Rice, "Executive Life: Should You Work for a Foreigner?" *Fortune*, 8/1/1988, p. 123.)

foreigners (fear or distrust of) *n.*: **xenophobia**. See *distrust*

forerunner *n.*: **progenitor**. See *predecessor*

foreshadow *v.t.*: **adumbrate**. ❖ Some America Firsters [argued that the Nuremburg trials] were inevitably tainted by the involvement of the Soviets, who were "just as bad [as the Nazis]." In this, the old right isolationists **adumbrated** Buchanan's own later fixation [on the Justice Department's pursuit of Nazi war criminals, which he believed] was delegitimated by its reliance on Soviet sources. (Charles Lane, "Daddy's Boy: The Roots of Pat Buchanan's Authoritarianism," *New Republic*, 1/22/1996, p. 15.)

(2) foreshadow *v.t.*: **betoken**. See *portend*

foreshadowing *adj.*: **fatidic**. See *prophetic*

forest (of or relating to woods or . . . , or having many trees) *adj.*: **bosky**. See *trees*

forestall (as in avert or ward off) *v.t.*: **forfend**. See *avert*

foretell (as in one who makes correct predictions of misfortune that are ignored) *n.*: **Cassandra**. See *predictor*

(2) foretell *v.t.*: **adumbrate**. See *foreshadow*

(3) foretell *v.t.*: **betoken**. See *portend*

(4) foretell *v.t.*: **vaticinate**. See *predict*

foretelling *adj.*: **fatidic**. See *prophetic*

forever *adv.*: **in aeternum** [Latin]. ❖ *The Brady Bunch*, which ran from 1969 to 1974, but which will live in syndication **in aeternum**, may be one of the worst sitcoms of all times. (*Washington Times*, "Generation X Digs Their Story;

Brady Bunch Film Is a Surprise Hit," 3/13/95.)

(2) forever (lasting . . .) *adj.*: **aeonian** (or **eonian**). See *eternal*

(3) forever (lasting . . .) *adj.*: **sempiternal**. See *everlasting*

forget (to . . . the meaning of words or to use them incorrectly) *n.*: **paramnesia**. See *amnesia*

forgetfulness *n.*: **Lethe**. [In Greek mythology, Lethe (pronounced LEE-thee) was one of the several rivers of Hades. Those who drank from it experienced complete forgetfulness. Today it is used to refer to one in an oblivious or forgetful state. The word is also sometimes used in the phrase "drinking from the River Lethe." See also *oblivion*.] ❖ Gang warfare ebbs in Brighton, but the council's Mike Middleton strikes new fear in residents' hearts. To him, playground sandpits are not innocent fun; they are "lethal," to be closed down forthwith—and a few bob saved. Have the waters of **Lethe** made him forget that fatalities are more likely in scaffolders such as himself than at any sandpit? (Christopher Hawtree, Pursuits: "Words—Lethal, adj.," *Independent* [London], 6/20/2001.)

forgetting (condition of . . . words or the right one) *n.*: **lethologica**. See *lethologica*

forgivable *adj.*: **venial**. ❖ Many Americans regard the denial of a sexual affair as a **venial** sin. Most people have lied about their sex lives at one time or another. You lie to protect yourself, your spouse, your lover, your children. (Arthur Schlesinger Jr., "Starr Pursues Clinton as Ahab Did the Whale," *Minneapolis Star Tribune*, 8/10/1998.)

forgiveness (as in place or occasion of humiliation and seeking . . .) *n.*: **Canossa**. See *penance*

forgiving (as in compassionate) *adj.*: **ruthful**. See *compassionate*

forlorn *adj.*: **lorn**. ❖ If every melodrama needs a poor, **lorn** widow, cheated by a scheming cad, then Mrs. Backus perfectly fitted Tarbell's description of Rockefeller. (Ron Chernow, *Titan*, Random House [1998], p. 445.)

form (take . . . , as in making an abstract concept seem real) *v.t.*: **reify**. See *materialize*

formal (act, declaration, or statement, issued with the authority of one's office) *adv., adj.*: **ex cathedra**. See *official*

formalities (precise observance of . . . or etiquette) *n.*: **punctilio**. See *etiquette*

formality (one who demands adherence to . . .) *n.*: **martinet**. See *disciplinarian*

former *adj.*: **ci-devant** [French]. ❖ Having read so much about recession-torn New Hampshire, I half expected, at the border crossing from Vermont near Lebanon, to encounter scenes reminiscent of the **ci-devant** Soviet Union: throngs clamoring for bread, [etc.]. (Alexander Cockburn, "Sex, Clinton and Contras," *Nation*, 2/10/1992.)

(2) former *adj.*: **quondam**. ❖ The most extraordinary detail at Nell's is its ever-present namesake, Nell Campbell. A **quondam** actress whose best credit is her role as the tap-dancing groupie Columbia in *The Rocky Horror Picture Show*, Nell, 33, presides over the club as if it were "my own drawing room." (Michael Small, "Host: If You Want to Lounge on a Love Seat in New York's Hippest Club, You'll Have to Get Nell Campbell's Okay," *People*, 2/2/1987, p. 117.)

(3) former (or "formerly," when used as an adverb) *adj.*: **whilom**. [This word, pronounced hwī'-lum, is usually considered archaic, although the editors at *Merriam-Webster's Collegiate Dictionary* argue that it is not, while acknowledging that its "strange look" gives it "an archaic quality." In any event, current usages are not particularly hard to come by.] ❖ In the interests of electoral gain, especially in the **whilom** one-party South, [the Republican Party] has welcomed the votes of racists and other occupants of the margins, deluding itself into believing that it could retain its imagined purity while riding those votes to triumph after triumph; it has convinced itself, in other words, that it could lie down with dogs without rising with fleas. (Jonathan Yardley, "The GOP's Self-Inflicted Wound," *Washington Post*, 2/26/1996.)

formulate (an idea, plan, theory, or explanation

after careful thought) *v.t.:* **excogitate**. See *devise*

fornication *n.:* **houghmagandy** (Scottish). See *intercourse*

(2) fornication *n.:* **venery**. See *intercourse*

forsake (esp. responsibility or duty) *v.t.:* **abnegate**. See *renounce*

forsaken (as in forlorn) *adj.:* **lorn**. See *forlorn*

forswear *v.t.:* **abjure**. See *renounce*

forte *n.:* **métier** [French]. ❖ Within a few years of his arrival at Paramount, [Hal Wallis] signed Kirk Douglas, Burt Lancaster, Anna Magnani, Lizabeth Scott and Charlton Heston. As his résumé indicates, comedy wasn't Wallis' **métier**. (Shawn Levy, *The King of Comedy*, St. Martin's Press [1996], p. 89.)

(2) forte (as in favorite topic or activity) *n.:* **cheval de bataille** [French for "battle-horse"]. See *hobby*

fortification (esp. a low, temporary, quickly built . . .) *n.* **breastwork**. ❖ Armed with a mountain of blotting material and crouched behind a **breastwork** of floating vinyl booms, a small army of biologists and fishermen here is waging the most dramatic battle of the oil spill in Prince William Sound. Their mission: To save more than 200 million inch-long, squiggling salmon so sensitive to oil that even a few dozen gallons from the millions in the sound could be deadly. (Cass Peterson, "Millions of Salmon at Stake In 'Battle of Sawmill Bay,'" *Washington Post*, 4/4/1989.)

(2) fortification *n.:* **barbican**. ❖ These magnificent 13th- and 14th-century walls surround the city centre in a three-mile circuit. . . . It costs nothing to climb these sentinel towers with their commanding gates . . . and **barbicans**—they provide good reference points for lost tourists looking for the "big church."(Anna Melville-James, "Between You, Me and the Gatehouse," *Sunday Telegraph* [London], 12/17/2000.)

(3) fortification *n.:* **bulwark**. See *protection*

fortitude *n.:* **hardihood**. See *courage*

fortuitous (occurrence) *n.:* **serendipity** (*adj.:* **serendipitous**). ❖ Then **serendipity** struck again. . . . [I] read a story that caught my eye. It was about a bear incident in Anchorage. There were no injuries, but I recognized the name of the Fish and Game trooper who was quoted. I'd roomed with him for a year during college. I hadn't heard from him in a decade, so I called him up, and we arranged to meet. (Jim Buchta, "In Alaska, Only Thing Predictable Is Its Unpredictability," *Minneapolis Star Tribune*, 3/10/1996.)

fortunate (discovering . . . things by accident) *n.:* **serendipity** (*adj.:* **serendipitous**). See *fortuitous*

fortunately (to behold) *adv.:* **mirabile visu** [Latin]. See *behold*

(2) fortunately (to relate) *adv.:* **mirabile dictu** [Latin]. See *wonderful*

fortune (as in destiny or fate) *n.:* **kismet**. See *fate*

(2) fortune (devotion to the pursuit of . . . , as in wealth) *n.:* **mammonism**. See *wealth*

fortune-teller (by using lightning or animal innards) *n.:* **haruspex**. ❖ The **haruspex** who cast Rome's future from the examination of sheep entrails was no less a scientist than those of us who scour for significant portent in the results of the Iowa straw poll. (Murray Kempton, "GOP Is Showing Democrat-like Fissures," *Newsday*, 8/23/1995.)

fortune-telling (by fire) *n.:* **pyromancy**. See *divination*

(2) fortune-telling (by picking random biblical passages) *n.:* **bibliomancy**. See *divination*

(3) fortune-telling (by reading palms) *n.:* **chiromancy**. See *palm-reading*

(4) fortune-telling (by touching or proximity to an object) *n.:* **psychometry**. See *divination*

for want of (anything better) *adv.:* **faute de mieux** [French]. See *lacking*

forward (as in assertive, in an obnoxious or loud way) *adj.:* **bumptious**. See *pushy*

foul (full of . . . matter, such as feces) *adj.:* **feculent**. See *fecal* and *filthy*

(2) foul (language) *n.:* **billingsgate**. See *language*

(3) foul (odor) *adj.:* **fetid**. See *smelly*

(4) foul (odor) *adj.*: **graveolent**. See *smelly*

(5) foul (odor) *adj.*: **mephitic** (*n.*: **mephitis**). See *smelly*

(6) foul (odor) *adj.*: **noisome**. See *smelly*

foul up (esp. a golf shot) *v.t., n.*: **foozle**. See *botch*

foundation (on which something is built) *n.*: **warp and woof**. ❖ Corporations will have to decide whether and how to use the [Internet] in manufacturing, distributing, advertising, and recruiting—whether to make it part of the **warp and woof** of American business. (Andrew Kupfer, "Fortune's Information Technology: 4 Forces That Will Shape the Internet," *Fortune*, 7/6/1998, p. 92.)

(2) foundation (as in root) *n.*: **taproot**. See *root*

(3) foundation (as in source and origin) *n.*: **fons et origo** [Latin]. See *source and origin*

(4) foundation (as in that which set the standard or established the model from which others followed or on which others are based) *n.*: **locus classicus** [Latin]. See *model*

(5) foundation (as in assumption or set of assumptions) *n.*: **donnée** [French]. See *assumption*

four (-year period) *n.*: **quadrennium**. ❖ Of the [United States Olympic Committee's] operating budget of $149.9 million for the current (1985–88) **quadrennium**, only $2.2 million has gone directly to prospective Olympians, via a program called Operation Gold. (E. M. Swift, "An Olympian Quagmire," *Sports Illustrated*, 9/12/1988, p. 38.)

fowl (of or relating to the domestic . . .) *adj.*: **gallinaceous**. ❖ Chickens are **gallinaceous** birds like pheasants and quail—and their young hatch out able to walk, feed, and drink for themselves. (Buff Orpingtons, "Save the Chickens!" *Mother Earth News*, 12/10/1996, p. 26.)

fox (killing of a . . . by means other than by hunting with hounds) *n.*: **vulpicide**. ❖ Although I have taken great pleasure and satisfaction in watching hounds hunt and catch foxes, I have never even considered killing a fox. I consider

the sin of **vulpicide** to be Mortal. (Willie Poole, *Journal* [Newcastle, England], 6/9/2005.)

(2) fox (of, relating to, or characteristic of) *adj.*: **vulpine**. ❖ Eli Broad has all the appearances of a fox. His **vulpine** cunning is evident in everything he does, from becoming one of the luminaries of Los Angeles' high society to accumulating one of the world's best collections of modern art. (*Economist*, "The Cunning of the Hedgehog," 9/27/1997.)

fracas (esp. public) *n.*: **affray**. See *brawl*

fraction (as in portion) *n.*: **moiety**. See *portion*

fragile *adj.*: **frangible**. ❖ As with so many two-night "miniseries," its soul is thin as March ice and just as **frangible**. But the movie's zeal for unearthing an obscure fragment of American history [escorting Jewish refugees from Europe to America in 1944] partly counteracts the poetical shortcomings, and within its fragile framework lie some striking performances. (*Seattle Post-Intelligencer*, "Big Names in Small Roles Ultimately Save *Haven*," 2/9/2001.) See *breakable*

fragments (usually, but not necessarily, in reference to literary . . . or to disjointed quotations) *n.pl.*: **disjecta membra** [Latin]. See *bits and pieces*

(2) fragments *n.*: **flinders**. See *bits and pieces*

frail (and sickly person, esp. one morbidly concerned with his own health) *n., adj.*: **valetudinarian**. See *sickly*

(2) frail (as in powerless) *adj.*: **impuissant**. See *powerless*

(3) frail (from loss or lack of body strength) *adj.*: **asthenic** (*n.*: **asthenia**). See *weak*

frailty (that comes with old age) *n.*: **caducity**. See *old age*

France (one who dislikes . . . or its people) *n.*: **Francophobe**. ❖ If business in Germany is hard work, it is even tougher in France: across Europe, French companies came top of the list of those with whom their fellow Europeans think it is hardest to do business. The Dutch were most **Francophobe**: 59% put French firms top of the list. (*Economist*, "There

Was a German, a Belgian and a Spaniard . . . ,"
1/23/1999.)

(2) France (one who is fond of . . . or its people) *n*.: **Francophile**. ❖ Most [home] buyers are die-hard **Francophiles** who love the
slow pace and country comforts—hearty cuisine and cheap and plentiful wine—of rural
France. (Thomas K. Grose, "Once More
onto the Beach!" *U.S. News & World Report*,
1/12/1998.)

frantic (and frenzied woman) *n*.: **maenad**. See
woman

(2) frantic (as in frenzied) *adj*.: **corybantic**.
See *frenzied*

fraternity (as in fellowship or association) *n*.:
sodality. See *fellowship*

fraud (as in deliberate misrepresentation of facts
to gain an advantage) *n*.: **subreption**. See
misrepresentation

(2) fraud (as in hypocrite, esp. one who acts
humbly) *n*.: **Uriah Heep**. See *hypocrite*

(3) fraud (as in hypocrite, esp. one who affects
religious piety) *n*.: **Tartuffe** (or **tartuffe**). See
hypocrite

(4) fraud (as in sham) *n*.: **postiche**. See *sham*

(5) fraud (as in swindle) *n., v.t*.: **thimblerig**.
See *swindle*

(6) fraud (esp. a person who sells quack medicines) *n*.: **mountebank**. See *huckster*

(7) fraud (esp. something that at first seems
a wonderful discovery or development, but
that turns to be a . . . or a delusion) *n*.: **mare's
nest**. See *hoax*

(8) fraud (spec. the act of engaging in deception under a false name or identity) *n*.: **imposture**. See *hoax*

fraudulent (as in invented or substituted with . . .
intent) *adj*.: **supposititious**. See *supposed*

frayed (in appearance) *adj*.: **tatterdemalion**.
See *ragged*

freak (as in someone or something which deviates from the norm) *n*.: **lusus** [Latin; almost
always used as part of the term "lusus naturae,"
or freak of nature]. ❖ There is a long tradition
of fiction in which animals talk, and you can
break it down into [several] categories. [One

of them is] the realistic narrative in which animal speech is a freak, a **lusus naturae**, and
the fact that an animal talks is the linchpin of
the narrative. In this class we can place Francis the talking mule, Mr. Ed the talking horse
and now *Seymour the Fractal Cat*. (Robert
Franks, Radio Review, *Independent* [London],
4/11/1996.)

freckled *adj*.: **lentiginous**. ❖ My own addiction [to makeup] started young, when I realised
that my freckly Celtic complexion wasn't a
curse I had to endure for life, and my offensively **lentiginous** skin could be smoothed
into picture-perfect ivory. (Simon Price, "Slap-
Happy: Cover-Up, Powder and Eyeliner,"
Guardian [London], 12/14/2002.)

free (from slavery, servitude, or bondage) *v.t*.:
manumit. See *emancipate*

(2) free (from slavery, servitude, or bondage)
v.t.: **disenthrall**. See *liberate*

freedom (new period of . . . , esp. as a contrast
to, and sandwiched between periods of oppression or lack of rights) *n*.: **Prague Spring**. See
liberalization

freely *adv., adj*.: **ad libitum** [Latin]. See *at will*

free speech (or frank speech) *n*.: **parrhesia**.
❖ [O]ne of the functions of poetry is, to tell
the truth, to exercise **parrhesia**, to engage in
frank and plain speech about a very delicate
and difficult situation [i.e., the war in Iraq].
(Cornel West, Analysis: War Poems, *The Tavis
Smiley Show*, NPR, 2/26/2003.)

freethinker (esp. on matters of morals and religion) *n*.: **libertine**. ❖ Henri urges the driver
to return to his senses, to be "reasonable." He
reasserts the most conventional sort of order-
liness in the Western tradition. . . . The driver
. . . accuses Henri of being "only the most banal
and predictable of poets. No **libertine**, no
man of vision and hence suffering, but a banal
moralist." The driver's disregard for order as
safe haven is easily surpassed by his contempt
for the pretensions, the presumptions that
the orderly man displays. (Joseph M. Conte,
"Design and Debris: John Hawkes's 'Travesty,'
Chaos Theory, and the Swerve," *Critique: Stud-*

ies in *Contemporary Fiction*, 1/1/1996, p. 120.)

freewheeling (as in uninhibited, in exhibiting emotion or celebration) *adj.*: **saturnalian**. ❖ The young New Yorker [Zia Jaffrey, author of *The Invisibles: A Tale of the Eunuchs of India*] perceived that the Hijra, lower in caste even than the Untouchable dung-cleaners, somehow cut to the heart of the paradox of India. They were clownish and **saturnalian** in spirit: "I thought of them almost like Shakespearian fools, being given permission to comment on society and speak their mind in the way that no one else could." (*Independent* [London], "Caste Aside," 7/29/1997.)

(2) freewheeling (and reckless person) *n.*: **rantipole**. See *wild*

freeze *v.t.*: **glaciate**. ❖ Schwarzenegger, meanwhile, masticates freeze-dried one-liners, from "the Iceman cometh" to "Let's kick some ice." He plays a scientist who has caught a permanent chill while trying to cryogenically preserve his wife. Wearing refrigerated armor, he is a Teutonic Tin Man, crashing around with giant guns that **glaciate** all comers. (Brian D. Johnson, Films: "A Bat out of Hell: The Latest Batman Movie Is an Infernal Mess," *Maclean's*, 7/1/1997, p.106.)

freeze-frame (esp. by costumed performers sustaining a . . . , as if in a picture) *n.*: **tableau vivant** [French]. See *pose*

freezing (and storing of deceased body) *n.*: **cryonics**. ❖ Two Southern California **cryonics** companies have shut down in recent years, and a third is said to be seeking alternative storage facilities for a dozen "patients" still on ice. (Davis Lazarus, "Cryonics Suffers from Freezer Burn," *San Francisco Chronicle*, 8/26/2001.)

(2) freezing *adj.*: **hyperborean**. [This word also means the Arctic or far north region, and in the following example, both meanings would be appropriate.] ❖ [If there were drilling in the Arctic National Wildlife Refuge,] how many drilling rigs, it's fair to ask, would cause postpartum psychosis among caribou? . . . Would oil pipes and pumps in just 2,000 acres of the 9 million-acre refuge seriously harm ani-

mals and migrating birds? And if it does, is that the overriding consideration? Certainly no tourist jobs are at stake in that desolate, **hyperborean** plain. (Edwin A. Roberts Jr., "Ruminations on Oil and Its Origins," *Tampa Tribune*, 11/18/2001.)

(3) freezing (as in of, like, or occurring in winter) *adj.*: **brumal**. See *winter*

(4) freezing (of or relating to . . . temperatures) *adj.*: **cryogenic**. See *cold*

(5) freezing *adj.*: **algid**. See *cold*

(6) freezing *adj.*: **gelid**. See *cold*

French (become . . . in character or custom) *v.t., v.i.*: **Gallicize**. ❖ Tunisia was occupied by France in 1881 and remained a French protectorate for 75 years. The French impact on Tunisia was profound, imposing French institutions, leaving the imprint of French culture and technology, and creating a **gallicized** elite to whom leadership passed when the protectorate was ended in 1956. (Robert Rinehart, "Tunisia: Chapter 1A. Historical Setting," *Countries of the World*, 1/1/1991.)

(2) French (word, phrase, or idiom used in another language) *n.*: **Gallicism**. ❖ I am not a native French speaker, but do speak the language and learned some French words directly in context without being sure of the English. I've sat under many more Francophone pergolas than Anglophone pergolas, and would have said "trellis," not being sure of the English term and fearing that "pergola" was a **Gallicism**. (Unsigned letter to the editor, *Washington Post*, 7/19/2001.)

(3) French *adj.*: **Gallic**. ❖ On a hot summer evening, dozens of limousines and SUVs ferrying the cream of Parisian society pull up in front of the Pompidou Center, the city's contemporary art complex. . . . The luminaries are gathered to applaud Jean-Marie Messier as he accepts that most **Gallic** of awards, the insignia of the Chevalier of the Legion of Honor. (Devin Leonard, "Mr. Messier Is Ready for His Close-Up," *Fortune*, 9/3/2001, p. 136.)

frenzied *adj.*: **corybantic**. ❖ Activision's Quake II, a first-person shooter for the Macintosh, was worth the wait and is one of the best multi-player games ever developed. [It provides] fast, **corybantic**, and brutal game action. The single player version consists of many levels of gothic corridors, hideous villains, and destructive weapons. Fighting is furious and bloody, and the gamer gets to wield many revamped Quake I weapons. (Rick Sanchez, "Quake II," *SoftBase*, 9/30/2001.)

(2) frenzied (as in raging or furious) *adj.*: **furibund**. See *furious*

(3) frenzied (woman) *n.*: **maenad**. See *woman*

frenzy (emotional . . . , esp. as caused by something unattainable) *n.*: **nympholepsy**. [This word often, though not always, refers to an erotic frenzy.] ❖ The night before last [the young woman took] a shower in the main bathroom, and left the door open. I looked right in, right through the transparent shower door, and saw her, a full-bodied [woman] oiled with water. And saw myself as well, in the fogged mirror, amid the steam, a peeping old [man] in a silken gown in the throes of **nympholepsy**. (Alfred Acorn, "Chapter 9: Wednesday, Oct. 18," *Salon.com*, 7/18/2001.)

(2) frenzy (as in panic) *n.*: **Torschlusspanik** [German]. See *panic*

(3) frenzy (in a . . . , as in distress) *n.*: **swivet** (as in "in a swivet") *informal*. See *distress*

(4) frenzy (of emotion, feeling, or action) *n.*: **paroxysm**. See *outburst*

frequenter (of a place, esp. a place of entertainment) *n.*: **habitué** [French]. See *regular*

fresh (love of or enthusiasm for anything . . .) *n.*: **neophilia**. See *novelty*

fret (or complain) *v.i.*: **repine**. See *complain*

(2) fret *v.t., v.i., n.*: **cark**. See *worry*

fretting (as in a state of nervous tension, often with irritability) *n.*: **fantod**. See *tension*

friction (as in heated disagreement or . . . between groups) *n.*: **ruction**. See *dissension*

(2) friction (of or relating to . . . within a group or country) *adj.*: **internecine**. See *dissension*

friend (as in comrade) *n.*: **tovarich** [Russian]. See *comrade*

(2) friend (faithful . . . , as in companion) *n.*: **Achates**. See *companion*

friendliness (as in affability) *n.*: **bonhomie**. See *affability*

(2) friendliness (as in cordiality) *n.*: **empressement** [French]. See *cordiality*

friendly (and pleasant) *adj.*: **sympathique** [French]. See *genial*

friendship (as in fellowship or association) *n.*: **sodality**. See *fellowship*

fright (as in panic) *n.*: **Torschlusspanik** [German]. See *panic*

(2) fright (deliberate use of . . . and terror as a military tactic used by the Germans to break the will of the enemy) *n.*: **Schrecklichkeit** [German]. See *terror*

frighten *v.t.*: **affright**. See *scare*

frightened *adj.*: **tremulous**. See *fearful*

frigid *adj.*: **algid**. See *cold*

(2) frigid *adj.*: **hyperborean**. See *freezing*

frilly (ornamentation that is . . . or superfluous or showy) *n.*: **furbelow**. See *ornamentation*

fringe benefit (sometimes as thanks for a purchase) *n.*: **lagniappe**. See *gift*

fritter (. . . something away) *v.t.*: **fribble**. See *squander*

frivolous (and flighty person) *n.*: **flibbertigibbet**. See *flighty*

(2) frivolous (as in trivial) *adj.*: **nugacious**. See *trivial*

frog (of, relating to, or resembling) *adj.*: **ranine**. ❖ [I] began writing for newspapers in the Far East. . . . [E]very night [while writing] a large frog came and called "Waah!" so loudly that I could not concentrate. After periods of deep breathing I would explode, racing out to the jungle's edge to hurl rocks and anti-**ranine** abuse. The frog would fall politely silent, allow my breathing to recover, allow me to reseat myself and return to the story. Then he would start again. "Waaah!" (Kevin Rushby, "Small Is Beautiful," *Guardian* [London], 10/26/2002.)

frolic *v.i.*: **gambol**. ❖ Soon [the lions and cubs] walked off, leaping, pouncing on each other, wrestling, dancing, seemingly as benign as Disney lions. . . . Suddenly the **gamboling**

ceased and the pride swung into single file and turned into the bush, making not a sound, not even that of a breaking twig. (R. W. Apple Jr., "Rebirth of a Nation," *Town & Country*, 5/1/1996, p. 92.)

(2) frolic *v.t., v.i.*: **disport**. ❖ Late in the ballet, [Tinkerbell's] fairy cohorts add to the merriment, stumbling across stage tipsy from revels, preening goofily and in general **disporting** themselves as a wild parody of every classical ballet fairy who ever bourreed gracefully. (Margaret Putnam, "Flight of Fancy: FWDB's *Peter Pan* Swoops in and Soars," *Dallas Morning News*, 4/22/2000.)

(3) frolic *v.i.*: **curvet**. See *dance*

frolicsome (as in playful) *adj.*: **gamesome**. See *playful*

frostbite (or inflamation of skin due to exposure to cold) *n.*: **chilblains**. See *inflammation*

frosted (as in streaked with or partly gray) *adj.*: **griseous**. See *grizzled*

frosty *adj.*: **gelid**. See *cold*

frothy *adj.*: **spumescent**. See *foamy*

frown (as in pout) *n.*: **moue** [French]. See *pout*

frowner (as in person who never laughs) *n.*: **agelast**. See *humorless*

frozen *adj., v.t.* (past participle of freeze): **glaciated**. ❖ The success of lawsuits against once-invincible Big Tobacco . . . may have won me over. Couldn't lots of stalled issues use a bit of legal spurring? . . . When powerful interests, money or inertia thwart progress, courts look mighty tempting. Some issues have simply **glaciated** in Congress, all frozen over, no movement, only a pretense of debate. One is gun control. (Geneva Overholser, " . . . See You in Court," *Washington Post*, 5/20/1999.)

frugal (as in stingy) *adj.*: **cheeseparing**. See *stingy*

(2) frugal (excessively . . .) *adj.*: **costive**. See *stingy*

(3) frugal (excessively . . .) *adj.*: **niggardly**. See *stingy*

(4) frugal (excessively . . .) *adj.*: **penurious**. See *stingy*

frugality (as in marked by simplicity, self-discipline, self-restraint, and/or . . .) *adj.*: **Lacedaemonian**. See *spartan*

(2) frugality (person who practices extreme . . . , esp. for spiritual improvement) *n., adj.*: **ascetic**. See *austerity*

fruit (bearing . . .) *adj.*: **fructiferous**. ❖ A 401(k) contribution invested in assets earning 9% a year will return a whopping 63.5% annually, after tax benefits and a 50% company match are taken into account. . . . So be thankful for the **fructiferous** 401(k), but water it well. (Elizabeth Fenner, "Retirement Planning: How to Grow a Lush 401[k]," *Money*, 11/1/1992, p. 92.)

(2) fruit (eating) *adj.*: **frugivorous**. ❖ The Society for the Protection of Nature in Israel is trying to help local authorities cope with a problem that is driving some people batty. **Frugivorous** bat season is here again, the time of year when the little nocturnal flying mammals are particularly drawn to the fruit ripening on trees with very little respect to the fact that they might be fouling private property. (Liat Collins, "SPNI Offers Advice for Battling Seasonal Invaders," *Jerusalem Post*, 4/12/2001.)

(3) fruit (study of . . .) *n.*: **pomology**. ❖ I'll try a lecture on **pomology** aimed at the state of Washington, whence come these beautiful but tasteless Red Delicious apples. (*Christian Science Monitor*, "A Thing or Two About Apples," 2/2/2001.)

(4) fruit (with one stone, such as peach, plum, or cherry) *n.*: **drupe**. ❖ Plums are more varied in size, color, flavor, and texture than other stone, or **drupe**, fruits, including apricots and peaches. (Lucy Wing, "A Passion for Plums," *Country Living*, 7/1/1995, p. 120.)

fruitful (make . . .) *v.i.*: **fructify**. ❖ Sex, associated with procreation, had always been recognized as the principle of life; but for these liberators, the orgiastic energy of the sexual act takes precedence over the fate of the seed, whether **fructified** or wasted. (Ruth Wisse, review of *Sabbath's Theater*, by Philip Roth, *Commentary*, 12/1/1995, p. 61.)

(2) fruitful (or productive) *adj.*: **fructuous**.

❖ [Karl] Lagerfeld is talking about reducing his mighty Chanel shows to more intimate experiences. And this collection proved that such a **fructuous** collaboration with the couture hands deserves to be played out on a quieter note. (Suzy Menkes, "Chanel Plays the Pipes," *International Herald Tribune*, 7/3/2008.)

(3) fruitful (esp. as in fertile) *adj.*: **fecund**. See *fertile*

fruition (while coming into . . .) *adj.*: **aborning**. See *born*

fruitless (as in unsuccessful) *adj.*: **abortive**. See *unsuccessful*

(2) fruitless (mission or project) *n.*: **fool's errand**. See *hopeless*

fruits (mixture of . . . and/or vegetables) *n.*: **macédoine** [French]. See *mixture*

frustrated (in realizing one's goals) *adj.*: **manque** (esp. as in artist . . .). ❖ Scowling from a sofa, Martin Amis declares that: "Any biographer is likely to be some sort of artist **manque**. It's second or third best to what you want to be." (Peter Parker, "Literary Lifers: The Good, the Bad and the Nosey," *Independent* [London], 3/9/1996.)

frustration (as in disappointment) *n.*: **Apples of Sodom**. See *disappointment*

(2) frustration (as in disappointment) *n.*: **Dead Sea fruit**. See *disappointment*

full (as in complete or unlimited, esp as in . . . power) *adj.*: **plenary**. See *complete*

(2) full (sound or voice) *adj.*: **orotund**. See *sonorous*

full-bosomed *adj.*: **bathycolpian**. See *busty*

full-bosomed *adj.*: **hypermammiferous**. See *busty*

full-figured (woman) *adj.*: **zaftig** [Yiddish]. ❖ Amber soon finds she has a **zaftig** rival: Tracy Turnblad (Ricki Lake), who is plump, perky and, pound for bouffanted pound, the snappiest Caucasian dancer in town. (Richard Corliss, Cinema: "Buxom Belles in Baltimore *Hairspray*," *Time*, 2/29/1988, p. 101.)

full speed (at . . .) *adv.*: **tantivy**. See *top speed*

fully (as in, in the entirety) *adv.*: **holus-bolus**. See *entirety*

(2) fully (as in, in the entirety) *adv.*: **in extenso** [Latin]. See *entirety*

fumble (around with one's hands) *v.i.*: **grabble**. See *grope*

fumes (malodorous . . . from waste or decayed matter) *n.*: **effluvium**. See *odor*

fun (as in playful) *adj.*: **ludic**. See *playful*

functional *adj.*: **utile**. See *useful*

functionary (as in bureaucrat) *n.*: **satrap**. See *bureaucrat*

fundamental (as in essential) *adj.*: **constitutive**. See *essential*

fundamentalist (in terms of strictness of one's religious practices) *n.*: **orthopraxy**. See *orthodoxy*

fundamentally *adv.*: **au fond** [French]. See *basically*

funeral (rite or ceremony) *n.*: **obsequy** (often pl., **obsequies**). ❖ In all the words spent on Strom Thurmond's life and times since his death, I saw no acknowledgment of the most interesting of his sundry racial legacies. She is Essie Mae Washington Williams, a widowed former school teacher in her 70s, living in Los Angeles. Presumably she did not show up for any of the **obsequies** even though Strom Thurmond was almost certainly her father. Williams is black. (Diane McWhorter, "Strom's Race Against His Past," *Philadelphia Daily News*, 12/27/2003.)

(2) funeral (rites or ceremony) *n.*: **exequy**. [This word is usually expressed in the plural, exequies, as in the following example.] ❖ The [elaborate funeral of] 22-year-old pop singer and actress Aaliyah . . . struck Rod Dreher, a columnist for the *New York Post*, as a little much. "The family of Aaliyah," he wrote, "does the poor woman's memory no favors with this tasteless gesture." . . . [He] compared the singer's **exequies** with those of Princess Diana— "a ghoulish saturnalia of sentimentality . . . the epitome of modern celebrity worship." (*National Review*, "Culture Watch: The Rev. Thug" [Al Sharpton], 10/1/2001.)

(3) funeral (procession at a . . .) *n.*: **cortege**. See *procession*

funereal *adj.*: **sepulchral**. ❖ In a David Fincher movie a house is never a home. Take a peek inside the dank Gothic asylum of *Alien 3*, the **sepulchral** gloom of apartment . . . forbidding, underlit and about as friendly as a funeral parlour. You wouldn't want to live there. Bela Lugosi wouldn't want to live there. (Anthony Quinn, Film: "They Know Where You Live," *Independent* [London], 5/3/2002.)

fungus (expert) *n.*: **mycologist**. ❖ Note to budding **mycologists** . . . : "The Fungus Among Us" comes to Sterling Nature Center at 1 p.m. Sunday. (Jim Reilly, "Sterling Program Looks at the World of Mushrooms," *Syracuse [NY] Post-Standard*, 3/8/2002.)

fun-loving (as in lazy person devoted to seeking pleasure and luxury) *n.*: **lotus-eater**. See *hedonist*

(2) **fun-loving** (as in playful) *adj.*: **gamesome**. See *playful*

funnel (as in channel) *v.t.*: **canalize**. See *channel*

funniness *n.*: **jocosity**. See *humor*

funny (as in witty) *adj.*: **waggish**. See *witty*

(2) **funny** (finding things . . . , as in ability or tendency to laugh) *n.*: **risibility**. See *laugh*

(3) **funny** (in a sarcastic or biting way) *adj.*: **mordant**. See *sarcastic*

(4) **funny** (line) *n.*: **bon mot** [French]. See *quip*

(5) **funny** (line) *n.*: **epigram**. See *quip*

(6) **funny** (person who tries to be . . . but is not) *n.*: **witling**. See *humorless*

(7) **funny** *adj.*: **gelastic**. See *laughable*

(8) **funny** *adj.*: **risible**. See *laughable*

(9) **funny** (sayings) *n.pl.*: **facetiae**. See *witty*

fur (of a rabbit) *n.*: **lapin** [French]. See *rabbit fur*

(2) **fur** (or hair or wool that covers the body of a mammal) *n.*: **pelage**. See *hair*

furious *adj.*: **furibund**. ❖ [Actor John] Turturro, with his common, indeed coarse, face and ability to go from bewildered to **furibund** in a twinkling, has been a perfect interpreter of the—generally Italo-American—everyman, sometimes put-upon and pathetic, more often defiant and even vicious. (John Simon, review of *Sommersby*, *National Review*, 329/1993.)

(2) **furious** *adj.*: **apoplectic**. See *angry*

(3) **furious** *adj.*: **vesuvian** (esp. as in . . . temper). See *temper*

(4) **furious** *adj.*: **wroth**. See *angry*

furnish (as in outfit or equip) *v.t.*: **accouter**. See *outfit*

furnishings (as in trappings) *n.*: **habiliment(s)**. See *trappings*

furrowed (as in grooved) *adj.*: **striated**. See *grooved*

furthermore *adv.*: **withal**. See *moreover*

furthest (as in most distant, or remote, destination or goal) *n.*: **ultima Thule**. See *distant*

fuse (as in bring together) *v.t.*: **conflate**. See *combine*

fused (of things that cannot be . . .) *adj.*: **immiscible**. See *incompatible*

fuss (over a trifling matter) *n.*: **foofaraw**. ❖ As political plums go, it was not particularly juicy: the establishment of a minor international agency with 30 jobs attached. Even so, Environment Minister Sheila Copps managed to turn what should have been a straightforward decision and a routine announcement last week into a familiar Canadian **foofaraw**. At issue was Copps's choice of Montreal over 24 other Canadian cities in competition for a $5-million-a-year environmental watchdog agency. (E. Kaye Fulton, "The Sound and the Fury: A Regional Dogfight Explodes after a NAFTA Agency Goes to Montreal," *Maclean's*, 4/11/1994, p. 16.)

(2) **fuss** (about petty matters) *v.i.*: **pettifog**. See *quibble*

(3) **fuss** (as in commotion) *n.*: **bobbery**. See *commotion*

(4) **fuss** (as in commotion) *n.*: **kerfuffle**. See *commotion*

(5) **fuss** (as in commotion) *n.*: **maelstrom**. See *commotion*

(6) **fuss** (as in commotion) *n.*: **pother**. See *commotion*

(7) **fuss** (as in fret or complain) *v.i.*: **repine**. See *complain*

(8) **fuss** (in a state of . . . , as in distress) *n.*: **swivet** (as in "in a swivet") *informal*. See *distress*

fussy (overly . . .) *adj*.: **persnickety**. See *picky*

futile (efforts that are laborious but . . .) *adj*.: **Sisyphean**. [In Greek mythology, Sisyphus was a king who was punished by the gods for various misdeeds. His punishment was to roll a boulder up a hill, only to watch it roll down near the top, forcing him to roll it up again, and repeating this throughout eternity.] ❖ Medical studies and painful individual experiences have shown dieting is too often a **Sisyphean** nightmare. At least two-thirds of people who shed weight will gain back the lost pounds—and often more—in a few years. (Anastasia Toufexis, "Forget About Losing Those Last 10 Pounds: The Pursuit of Sylphlike Thinness Is Not Only Futile for Most Men and Women, It Can Be Downright Unhealthy," *Time*, 7/8/1991, p. 50.)

(2) futile (relating to the view that all human striving and aspiration is . . . , or people who hold such a view) *adj*., *n*.: **futilitarian**. ❖ Some medical ethicists and health care cost utilitarians uphold the belief that it is unethical for a hopelessly ill person to demand any medical intervention just to gain you a few extra weeks of life. . . . Welcome to the surrealistic world of biomedical ethics, where **futilitarians** are actively redefining the role of doctors, the ethics of health care, the perceived moral worth of sick and disabled people, and the power of patients over their own bodies. (Wesley J. Smith, "The Discardable People," *Human Life Review*, 6/22/1998.)

(3) futile *adj*.: **bootless**. ❖ A subpoena to Mr. Clinton to testify would not be a **bootless** exercise, even if he declined by asserting his Fifth Amendment privilege. An impeachment trial is a non-criminal proceeding. In such cases, the Supreme Court held in *Baxter vs. Palmigiano* (1976), the trier of fact may consider as evidence of wrongdoing a party's Fifth Amendment silence. (Bruce Fein, "The Power, but Not the Will?" *Washington Times*, 1/19/1999.)

(4) futile (or unprofitable activity) *n*.: **mug's game** [British; informal]. ❖ The **mug's game** of the day is predicting interest rates. Even quoting forecasts for longer-term interest rates can be embarrassing. (Jonathan Fuerbringer, "A Drumroll, Again, for Interest Rates," *New York Times*, 9/26/2004.)

(5) futile (as in unsuccessful) *adj*.: **abortive**. See *unsuccessful*

(6) futile (mission or project) *n*.: **fool's errand**. See *hopeless*

(7) futile *adj*.: **nugatory**. See *worthless*

(8) futile *adj*.: **otiose**. See *useless*

fuzzy (as in a failure to perceive something clearly or accurately based on clear observation or analysis as a result of being cross-eyed, literally or figuratively) *adj*.: **strabismic**. See *cross-eyed*

gabby (and flighty or scatterbrained person) *n.*: **flibbertigibbet**. See *flighty*

gadget (odd or fanciful . . .) *n.*: **whigmaleerie**. ❖ For baubles and knickknacks, **whigmaleeries** and rattletraps, trinkets and whatnots, look no farther than Bouckville next week. Beginning Monday, thousands of antique dealers will set up the best of their wares for New York State's largest antique show along a 1.5-mile stretch of Route 20. (Emily Kulkus, "Days of Old; People Come from Around the East to Hunt for Antiques in Bouckville," *Syracuse Post-Standard*, 8/7/2003.)

gain (as in "to whose . . . ?") *n.*: **cui bono** [Latin]. See *advantage*

gall *n.*: **hardihood**. ❖ [Louis Marshall stated: "Henry Ford] had the **hardihood** to say to me through his agents that he knew nothing of the [anti-Semitic] articles published in his paper." (Neil Baldwin, *Henry Ford and the Jews*, Public Affairs [2001], p. 236.)

galloping (as in at top speed) *adv.*: **tantivy**. See *top speed*

gambling (pertaining to . . .) *adj.*: **aleatory**. ❖ Las Vegas, Nevada, the fastest growing city in the U.S. . . . (Wagers are available on everything from the Big Game's winner to whether Dennis Rodman's combined points and rebounds will number higher than Denver's points.) To the casual visitor, it's a good time. To the addicted sports bettor, it's **aleatory** bliss. (Ken Kurson, "Las Vegas Rules: Sports Betting Isn't Like the Market, It Is the Market," *Esquire*, 4/1/1998, p. 138.)

gap (between teeth) *n.*: **diastema**. ❖ Brown just beams when he looks at his [sculpture of former mayor Sharon Sayles Belton]. He was not receptive to any critiques. I didn't think the sculpture's **diastema** was wide enough. "I don't want any big gap in her teeth," Brown said. I wasn't proposing a Dave Letterman gap. (Cheryl Johnson, "Sculptor Brown Proud of Bust of Ex-Mayor," *Minneapolis Star Tribune*, 7/14/2002.)

(2) gap (esp. small . . . between things or events) *n.*: **interstice**. ❖ I subscribe to the belief that we live most fully in the **interstices**—en route, in between, on hiatus. My whole desperate life has been an effort to find some kind of perpetual interstice to inhabit, however paradoxical and ultimately futile that may be. (Mark Leyner, "Xmas in Newark [Perspectives on Little Moments That Make Up Life]," *Esquire*, 12/1/1997, p. 52.)

(3) gap *n.*: **lacuna**. ❖ For the biographer of John D. Rockefeller, the most exasperating **lacuna** in his story is [his wife] Cettie's transformation from a bright, witty girl into a rather humorless woman, prone to a rather nunlike religiosity. (Ron Chernow, *Titan*, Random House [1998], p. 233.)

(4) gap (as in omission) *n.* **elision**. See *omission*

(5) gap (in continuity, esp. between the end of a sovereign's reign and the ascension of a successor) *n.*: **interregnum**. See *interval*

garb (as in clothes) *n.*: **habiliment(s)**. See *clothing*

garbage (study of a culture by examining its . . .) *n.*: **garbology**. ❖ During a recent speech to the Society of Forensic Toxicologists, Rathje said, "Every bag of garbage tells a story. If archaeologists learn important things about ancient societies by looking at old garbage, then we should be able to learn important things about ourselves by looking at fresh garbage." Rathje pioneered **garbology**. (Lee Siegel, "Trash Talks to Top Garbologist," *Denver Rocky Mountain News*, 11/3/1997.)

(2) garbage *n.*: **spilth**. [The primary meaning of this word is the act of spilling or the amount spilled but a secondary meaning is garbage or trash.] ❖ [The Skymall in flight] catalog goes on for 235 pages. Not everything in it is astonishing **spilth**. Here and there are items that can be justified by their utility or their beauty. But is it any wonder that other cultures look at us and gasp at our superfluous commerce, our schlock? They imagine this stuff reflects our core values. Some days I think they're right. (Bill Tammeus, "Sky's the Limit in Catalog for Airline Passengers," *Kansas City Star*, 12/7/2002.)

(3) garbage (accumulation of . . . , esp. prehistoric) *n.*: **midden**. See *trash*

(4) garbage (as in printed material which is trivial) *n.*: **bumf** [British]. See *junk*

(5) garbage *n.*: **dross**. See *trash*

(6) garbage *n.*: **offal**. See *trash*

garish *adj.*: **meretricious**. See *gaudy*

garland (for the head) *n.*: **chaplet**. ❖ In the middle of it were three poles decorated with coils of cloth, a sort of maypole arrangement around which women wearing **chaplets** of limes and fantastic, heavy jewellery were dancing to drums. (Harriet O'Brien, "New Year's Day of the Dead," *Independent* [London], 12/27/1997.)

garlic (characteristic of . . . or onion) *adj.*: **alliaceous**. See *onion*

garment *n.*: **raiment**. See *clothing*

gas (of or relating to reducing passing . . .) *adj.*: **carminative**. See *farting*

gatekeeper (as in watchdog) *n.*: **Cerberus**. See *watchdog*

gaudy *adj.*: **meretricious**. ❖ Working for wealthy clients in Europe and America, he managed to take large and imposing sites and bestow on them a design that was typically balanced, matching the majesty of the property without becoming **meretricious**. (Adrian Higgins, "Expert's Picks: Gardening," *Washington Post*, 5/2/1999.)

(2) gaudy *adj.*: **orchidaceous**. See *showy*

gaunt (esp. in a pale or corpselike way) *adj.*: **cadaverous**. See *corpselike*

gawky (and clumsy boy) *n.*: **hobbledehoy**. See *clumsy*

gay (as in cheerful) *adj.*: **riant**. See *cheerful*

(2) gay (as in exuberant) *adj.*: **yeasty**. See *exuberant*

(3) gay (as in lesbian) *adj.*: **sapphic**. See *lesbian*

(4) gay (as in lesbian) *n.*: **tribade**. See *lesbian*

(5) gay (as in merry and social) *adj.*: **Anacreontic**. See *convivial*

(6) gay (discrimination against . . . people) *n.*: **heterosexism**. See *homosexuals*

(7) gay (person or one concerned with gay rights) *n., adj.*: **homophile**. See *homosexual*

geese (flock of) *n.*: **gaggle** (generally as in . . . of geese). ❖ Geese toting M-16s? Well, not quite, but after a successful trial run, **gaggles** of geese will soon begin guard duty at American military installations in West Germany. (*Time*, World Notes—West Germany: "Enter the Goose Patrol," 5/26/1986, p. 42.)

gel (esp. used to groom hair) *n.*: **pomade**. See *hair gel*

gem (which is highly polished and unfaceted) *n.*: **cabochon**. See *jewel*

gems (one who cuts and polishes . . .) *n.*: **lapidary**. See *jeweler*

gender (one having characteristics or reproductive organs of each . . .) *n.*: **hermaphrodite**. See *bisexual*

general (as in widespread) *adj.*: **pandemic**. See *widespread*

(2) general (as in widespread) *adj.*: **regnant**. See *widespread*

(3) general (in scope or applicability) *adj.*: **ecumenical**. See *universal*

generality (as in breadth of inclusiveness) *n.*: **catholicity** (*adj.*: **catholic**). See *universality*

generation (or era) *n.*: **saeculum** (pl. **saecula**). [Latin. In this example, the author is discussing the state of America in a post-9/11 world.] ❖ Classic virtues that didn't necessarily pay off in an Unraveling (like loyalty, reliability, patience, perseverance, thrift, and selflessness) will become hard currency in Crisis. Were history not seasonal, these virtues would have long since atrophied, vanished from memory as useless to humanity. They remain in our tradition because, once every **saeculum**, they are reaffirmed in full glory, rewarding those who embrace them and penalizing those who do not. (William Strauss, *The Fourth Turning: An American Prophecy*, Broadway [1997], quoted in an article by Joel Garreau, "Hinges of Opportunity; When the World Moves, The Important Thing to Figure

Out Is What's Being Born," *Washington Post*, 10/14/2001.)

generic (of or relating to a word that is more . . . than another given word) *adj*.: **superordinate**. ❖ "World English" originally meant "standard English." . . . More recently, however, the term has expanded to mean "English around the world." As McArthur puts it, "world English is both shorthand for English as a world language and a **superordinate** term for Australian English, British English, Irish English, Nigerian English and the like." It enforces the idea that English is diverse, not confined to one country or continent. (Nathan Bierma, "English Has Won over the World, Globe and Universe," *Chicago Tribune*, 9/16/2004.)

generous (as in charitable) *adj*.: **caritative**. See *charitable*

genial (and pleasant) *adj*.: **sympathique**. [French. While the similar sounding word "sympathetic" is sometimes listed as one of the synonyms for this word, its more frequent usage is in the sense given. This word sounds like, but is not synonymous with, sympathetic. When referencing the "pleasant" sense of the word, it can also be used to refer to places or things.] ❖ According to the opinion polls, [French president Jacques Chirac] is better liked than ever, across the political spectrum. He seems big-hearted, tolerant, easy-going, altogether **sympathique**—quite different from his cold, haughty, scheming Socialist predecessor, François Mitterrand. (*Economist*, "Jacques Chirac, Out of Steam," 7/31/1999.)

geniality *n*.: **bonhomie**. See *affability*

(2) geniality *n*.: **empressement** [French]. See *cordiality*

genitalia (male . . .) *n*.: **virilia**. ❖ In this memoir, Nigel Slater recalls . . . his dad in the greenhouse with his penis looking larger than it did in the bath; a jolly gardener who was sportingly unashamed of showing his **virilia** to a young boy. (Murrough O'Brien, Paperbacks, *Independent on Sunday*, 5/23/2004.)

genteel (esp. those aspiring or pretending to be . . .) *adj*.: **lace-curtain**. See *well-bred*

gentle (esp. with respect to the wind) *adj*.: **favonian**. See *mild*

gentleness *n*.: **mansuetude**. ❖ Jem wisely surrounds the lovely sadness of her voice with buoyant beats and chipper melodies, and it's this contrast that fuels her music. And while her voice may have an air of **mansuetude**, she proved that she could easily cut above the din of the boys in her band, particularly when she launched into a vibrant interpretation of "They." (Christopher Muther, "Vibrant Jem Proves a Cut Above," *Boston Globe*, 6/24/2004.)

genuine *adj*.: **pukka**. ❖ A quasi-particle is, as its name suggests, not exactly real. But it is real enough to be detectable—it is a stable excitation state of some of the atoms in the helium that behaves enough like a **pukka** particle to be detected like one. (*Economist*, "Hearts of Darkness; Artificial Black Holes," 1/26/2002, p. 83.)

(2) genuine *adj*.: **echt** [German]. ❖ Andy Warhol must be chuckling in his grave over a report in *Vanity Fair* that as many as one in six Warhol works is a fake. . . . [Warhol] craved immortality, but he loved trash and produced tons of it. We may never be able to tell **echt** Andy from [fake Andy]. . . . As Warhol might have said: everyone will have a fake for 15 minutes. (Andrew Renton, "Spot the Warhol: A Row over Which of the Factory Works Are Genuine Is Raising Serious Questions about the Real Value of the Artist's Hand," *Evening Standard* [London], 11/4/2003.)

(3) genuine (appearing to be . . . or accurate) *adj*.: **verisimilar**. See *realistic*

gesture (esp. while speaking) *v.t., v.i*.: **gesticulate**. ❖ [A] driver and a female passenger were **gesticulating** heatedly, indicating a marital-type disagreement. (Carl Hiaasen, *Stormy Weather*, Knopf [1995], p. 254.)

(2) gesture (gracious . . .) *n*.: **beau geste**. ❖ [After the fire, company owner Aaron Feuerstein] made a stunning announcement to several hundred employees: Not only would he rebuild his factory, he would also continue paying their salaries and benefits for at least another month—at a cost of $1.5 million a week. . . . Feuerstein's **beau geste** made him America's newest overnight folk hero. (Richard Jerome, "Angels: Holding the Line After Fire Wrecked His Mill, Aaron Feuerstein Didn't Let His Workers Down," *People*, 2/5/1996, p. 122.)

gestures (spec. the study and analysis of signs and symbols as part of communication) *n.*: **semiotics**. See *communication*

get (by mooching or sponging off of) *v.t.*: **cadge**. See *mooch*

getaway (as in a departure that is unannounced, abrupt, secret, or unceremonious) *n.*: **French leave** (or **French Leave**). See *departure*

(2) getaway (desperate . . . , as in retreat) *n.*: **Dunkirk**. See *retreat*

ghetto (as in shantytown) *n.*: **bidonville**. See *shantytown*

(2) ghetto (esp. in Brazil) *n.*: **favela**. See *slum*

ghettolike *adj.*: **Dickensian.** [This adjective derives from the harsh portrayal of Victorian England in Charles Dickens's works, and refers generally to any situation in which one may find conditions of squalor such as poverty, crime, slums, grime, and/or worker exploitation.] ❖ [Director John] Woo tells of a poverty-stricken, **Dickensian** childhood in a Hong Kong slum full of prostitutes, gangsters and drug dealers, [and] says he abhors violence. (Desson Howe, "Target: American," *Washington Post*, 8/20/1993.)

ghost (that manifests itself by making various noises) *n.*: **poltergeist**. ❖ We are stopped, yet the can of Mountain Dew in the cup holder is doing the watusi. The windows are closed, yet my hair is doing a scene from *Twister*. The truck roof is bouncing up and down like popcorn in a pan. **Poltergeist?** No, just Shaquille O'Neal turning up the 3,700-watt stereo system in his blue Ford Expedition. (Rick Reilly, Pro Basketball, *Sports Illustrated*, 4/21/1997, p. 82.)

(2) ghost *n.*: **phantasm**. See *apparition*

(3) ghost *n.*: **wraith**. See *apparition*

ghostly (as in pale or corpselike) *adj.*: **cadaverous**. See *corpselike*

(2) ghostly (as in pale, and often sickly) *adj.*: **etiolated**. See *pale*

(3) ghostly (as in pale, as from absence of sunlight) *adj.*: **etiolated**. See *pale*

giant (like an elephant) *adj.*: **elephantine**. See *enormous*

(2) giant (like an elephant) *adj.*: **pachydermatous**. See *elephant*

(3) giant *adj.*: **cyclopean**. See *big*

(4) giant *adj.*: **brobdingnagian** (often cap.). See *huge*

(5) giant *adj.*: **Bunyanesque**. See *enormous*

(6) giant *adj.*: **Pantagruelian**. See *gigantic*

(7) giant *adj.*: **pythonic**. See *huge*

(8) giant *n.*: **leviathan**. See *huge*

(9) giant *adj.*: **mastodonic**. See *big*

gibberish *n.*: **galimatias**. ❖ [M]ost of the television I've reviewed this year has struck me as utter cack. I can't recall—off hand—a single documentary that's taught me anything much. . . . I think that many documentaries would be considerably more informative, for me, if I had a pre-frontal lobotomy. [The new documentary] *Position Impossible* [is] a peculiar example of televisual **galimatias**. (Will Self, Television: "Bad Enough to Make Your Lingam Shrivel Up," *Independent on Sunday*, 2/18/2001.)

(2) gibberish (as in unintelligible baby talk) *n.*: **lallation**. See *baby talk*

giddy (as in lightheaded or dizzy) *adj.*: **vertiginous**. See *dizzy*

gift (extra or unexpected . . . sometimes given with customer's purchase) *n.*: **lagniappe**. ❖ *Forbes FYI* is the magazine that *GQ* and *Esquire* want to be. Under the editorship of Christopher Buckley, the magazine is consistently humorous, crisply written and slightly, but not obnoxiously, tongue in cheek. . . . Unfortunately, you can't find the magazine on newsstands. It's the quarterly **lagniappe** sent to devoted subscribers of *Forbes* magazine. (Cathy Hainer, "Dreaming of a Martha Stewart Christmas—*Forbes FYI* Gives the Funny Bone a Good Workout," *USA Today*, 11/29/1994.)

(2) gift (as in blessing) *n.*: **benison**. See *blessing*

(3) gift (as in donation, which is all one can afford) *n.*: **widow's mite**. See *donation*

(4) gift (as in offering) *n.*: **oblation**. See *offering*

(5) gift (such as flowers, to a wife from a guilty husband) *n.*: **drachenfutter** [German; lit. dragon fodder]. See *peace offering*

gigantic *adj.*: **Pantagruelian**. [This word is generally defined as "marked by coarse satire," a definition with which this example does not match. However, the word derives from Pantagruel, the gigantic son of Gargantua in Rabelais's 1532 novel *Pantagruel*, and this use of "gigantic" is the far more common one]. ❖ [At Voilà! restaurant,] portions are sensible, not **Pantagruelian**. (Patricia Brooks, Dining Out, *New York Times*, 1/11/1998.)

(2) gigantic (like an elephant) *adj.*: **elephantine**. See *enormous*

(3) gigantic (object) *n.*: **leviathan**. See *huge*

(4) gigantic *adj.*: **brobdingnagian** (often cap.). See *huge*

(5) gigantic *adj.*: **Bunyanesque**. See *enormous*

(6) gigantic *adj.*: **pythonic**. See *huge*

G.I. Joe (British equivalent of . . .) *n.*: **Tommy Atkins**. See *soldier*

gilded (as in golden) *adj.*: **aureate**. See *golden*

girl (French working-class . . .) *n.*: **grisette** [French]. ❖ Some [women who eventually became prostitutes] were upper-class girls, down on their luck, who chose to service rich men rather than serve as governesses to their children. . . . Many more were born into a life of poverty, earning paltry livings as **grisettes**, or seamstresses, before emerging like glittering butterflies from the grey muslin dresses that gave them their name. (Lucy Moore, "How to Get Ahead in Bed," *Sunday Times* [London], 2/24/2002.)

(2) girl (who is playful or impish) *n.*: **gamine** [French]. ❖ Though just 4 ft. 6-1/2 in. and a slight 72 lbs., [gymnast Dominique] Moceanu is a fetching **gamine** who can ignite an arena

with her Audrey Hepburn–like looks and contagious ebullience. (Jill Smolowe, "Altius: Flexible Flyer; Big Things Are Expected from the Small Package of Teenybopper Dominique Moceanu," *Time*, 6/28/1996, p. 64.)

(3) girl (who is high-spirited and boisterous) *n.*: **hoyden**. See *tomboy*

girlfriend (or woman with whom one is in love or has an intimate relationship) *n.*: **inamorata**. ❖ One of the few people who was close to both of the Waleses, Hoare invited [Prince] Charles and his **inamorata** Camilla Parker Bowles to discreet dinners at his home and served as an ad hoc counselor for [Princess Diana]. (Michelle Green, "A Princess in Peril—Accused of Harassing a Married Friend with Silent Phone Calls, a Troubled Diana Seems to Be Spinning Out of Control," *People*, 9/5/1994, p. 70.)

gist (of a matter, as in the essence) *n.*: **quiddity**. See *essence*

(2) gist (the . . . of a matter, as in the bottom line, the main point, the substance, etc.) *n.*: **tachlis** (esp. as in "talk tachlis") [Yiddish]. See *essence*

give (a prize to) *v.t.*: **premiate**. See *award*

give back (often a territory) *v.t.*: **retrocede**. See *return*

give up (as in renounce or disavow) *v.t.*: **abjure**. See *renounce*

(2) give up (esp. responsibility or duty) *v.t.*: **abnegate**. See *renounce*

glad *adj.*: **eupeptic**. See *cheerful*

gladly (to behold) *adv.*: **mirabile visu** [Latin]. See *behold*

(2) gladly (to relate) *adv.*: **mirabile dictu** [Latin]. See *wonderful*

gladness (causing or showing . . .) *adj.*: **gladsome**. ❖ In this year's White House Christmas card, George W. Bush and his wife, Laura, wish us "love and peace." Both items are in short supply at the onset of the **gladsome** season. Take love. It took an awful beating from Senate Republican leader Trent Lott, who at Strom Thurmond's 100th birthday party spoke hateful and hurtful words to African Americans. (Mary McGrory, "Cruel Yule," *Washington Post*, 12/15/2002)

(2) gladness (causing or tending to produce . . .) *adj.*: **felicific**. See *happiness*

glamorize (as in idealize) *v.t.*: **platonize**. See *idealize*

glamorized (or romanticized conception of oneself, as a result of boredom in one's life) *n.*: **Bovarism**. See *self-delusion*

glance (which is flirtatious) *n.*: **oeillade** [French]. ❖ [In the movie *Witness*, Captain Book] exchang[es] loving glances with Rachel . . . especially during a barn raising at which he carpenters and she waits on the communal tables. The two swap so many **oeillades** that it is a miracle the milk doesn't end up in a Lapp's lap, and Book's finger nailed to the roof beam. (John Simon, review of *Witness*, *National Review*, 4/5/1985.)

(2) glance (with a sideways . . .) *adv.*: **asquint**. ❖ Over a weakish chin, [Cleveland Indians pitcher Paul Assenmacher] sports a sparse salt-and-pepper beard that appears to be fashioned after Yasir Arafat's. Peering in for the sign with mild eyes **asquint** and lips parted slightly, he could not cow a Cub Scout. (Scott Raab, "The Face of Baseball," *Esquire*, 5/1/1998, p. 108.)

(3) glance *n.*: **dekko** [British; informal]. ❖ Alas, eBay is the too-perfect distraction for a writer stuck at home. Here I am, just now, finishing this, and it occurs to me that my wastepaper basket is falling apart. Let's just take a quick **dekko** at rattan baskets. Hmm, here's a Chinese reed basket, supposedly Qing dynasty. (Kate Jennings, "Something for Kate," *Australian Financial Review*, 12/12/2003.)

(4) glance (quick . . .) *n.*: **coup d'oeil** [French]. ❖ "Remember that . . . it is only at length that I can hope to please, and then only if there is in those who regard me a grain of indulgence; but for the passerby, the **coup d'oeil** is too hasty, he sees only the surface, he who does not have the time, moves on" [written by French painter Camille Pissarro to his son in 1883]. (Rachael Ziady DeLue, "Pissarro, Landscape, Vision, and Tradition," *Art Bulletin*, 12/1/1998, p. 718.)

(5) glance (a quick cursory . . .) *n.*: **Cook's tour**. See *scan*

glass (of, resembling, or relating to) *adj.*: **vitreous**. [To change or make into glass is to vitrify.] ❖ Women have made tremendous progress in the labor market except for the area of management, where the glass ceiling still exists. . . . American research has also found that some of the few women who do crack the **vitreous** barrier feel so unsatisfied and undervalued that they leave early—and in proportionately greater numbers than their male rivals. (*Economist*, "Breaking the Glass Ceiling," 8/10/1996.)

(2) glass (display case) *n.*: **vitrine**. See *showcase*

(3) glass (of, relating to, or resembling . . .) *adj.*: **hyaline**. See *glassy*

glasses (clipped to the bridge of the nose) *n.*: **pince-nez**. See *eyeglasses*

(2) glasses (with a short handle like opera . . .) *n.*: **lorgnette**. See *eyeglasses*

glassy *adj.*: **hyaline**. ❖ Graham and Rorem also share the ability to balance elegantly on the rim of sentimentality. "Early in the Morning," a deceptively simple setting of a genuinely simple poem by Robert Hillyer, captures the **hyaline** clarity that comes from mixing memories of Paris and youth. (Justin Davidson, On the Record/Classical Music, *Newsday*, 4/28/2000.)

gleaming (esp. with gold or tinsel) *adj.*: **clinquant**. See *glittering*

(2) gleaming *adj.*: **coruscant**. See *glittering*

(3) gleaming *adj.*: **effulgent**. See *bright*

(4) gleaming *adj.*: **fulgurant**. See *bright*

(5) gleaming *adj.*: **refulgent**. See *bright*

(6) gleaming *adj.*: **scintillescent**. See *sparkling*

(7) gleaming (like a diamond) *adj.*: **diamantine**. See *diamonds*

glee (from other's misfortunes) *n.*: **schadenfreude** [German]. See *sadism*

(2) glee (from witnessing others' misfortunes) *n.*: **Roman holiday**. See *sadism*

gleeful *adj.*: **Falstaffian**. See *jovial*

glide (through the air like a glider) *n., v.i.*: **volplane**. ❖ At a signal, the boy runs off into the field, little legs pumping, dove-white cheeks flushed, and the shadow of the hawk swells on the grass as it closes in on the child at a brisk **volplane**, then strikes the fake bunny. (Jay Kirk, "Fool at War: A Mirthful and Tragic Tale of Kester, the English Jester," *Harper's*, 10/1/2005.)

glimmer (as in trace or small amount of) *n.*: **tincture**. See *trace*

glimpse (quick . . .) *n.*: **coup d'oeil** [French]. See *glance*

(2) glimpse (with a sideways . . .) *adv.*: **asquint**. See *glance*

(3) glimpse *n.*: **dekko** [British; informal]. See *glance*

glistening (esp. with gold or tinsel) *adj.*: **clinquant**. See *glittering*

(2) glistening *adj.*: **scintillescent**. See *sparkling*

glittering (esp. with gold or tinsel) *adj.*: **clinquant**. ❖ [Harford city officials believe] that no residential owner could possibly object to having his land "upgraded" to commercial or industrial zoning. . . . Left unchallenged, however, is the assumption that business activity is the higher, more valuable use of the land. It's a judgment often packaged in such **clinquant** wrappings as jobs, tax revenues, economic growth, net return to the county. (Mike Burns, "What Constitutes Best and Highest Use of Land?" *Baltimore Sun*, 11/5/1995.)

(2) glittering *adj.*: **coruscant**. ❖ Not since Joan Sutherland used to dazzle us from the Met's stage with the bravura of "Ah! Non giunge" from *La Sonnambula* has a Met audience heard quite such **coruscant** pyrotechnics [as from Italian mezzo-soprano Cecilia Bartoli in *La Cenerentola*]. (John Ardoin, "Love Match: In *Cenerentola*, Glitter Is More Bartoli Than Glass," *Dallas Morning News*, 11/13/1997.)

(3) glittering *adj.*: **refulgent**. See *bright*

(4) glittering *adj.*: **scintillescent**. See *sparkling*

global (in scope or applicability) *adj.*: **ecumenical**. See *universal*

gloominess (as in depression) *n.*: **cafard** [French]. See *depression*

(2) gloominess (as in world-weariness or sentimental pessimism over the world's problems) *adj.* **Weltschmerz** [German]. See *pessimism*

gloomy *adj.*: **Cimmerian**. ❖ There is still the semblance of an independent judiciary [in Zimbabwe], though probably not for long. . . . And a free press still operates under heroic circumstances, although journalists in Harare see a **Cimmerian** darkness descending on them. (Tony Leon, "South Africa's Defining Moment—Why Mbeki Should Offer Zimbabwe More Sticks and Fewer Carrots," *Time International*, 4/23/2001, p. 48.)

(2) gloomy (and dark) *adj.*: **tenebrous**. ❖ [In 1944, Alfred Kazin wrote an article] that will live long in the annals of that **tenebrous** time [i.e., the era of Nazi Germany]. "In Every Voice, in Every Ban" was a cry of outrage at the suicide of Shmuel Ziegelboim, the representative of the Bund who killed himself in London to protest the world's indifference to the extermination of the Jews. (*New Republic*, "Alfred Kazin," 6/29/1998.)

(3) gloomy (and dark and dismal) *adj.*: **acherontic**. ❖ [This word derives from Acheron, which is one of the five rivers of Hades, the river of woe or sorrow.] ❖ [Presidential candidate Bob Dole] is trying his darndest to be nice. [Often,] however, inhibition shows: the mien is, yes, doleful, the image verges on the **acherontic**, the look of souls confronting hell. Never mind. If he should actually win the nomination and the election, he will probably cheer up. (Walter Goodman, "Never Mind His Politics, Is the Man Telegenic?" *New York Times*, 2/20/1996.)

(4) gloomy (and dark and misty) *adj.*: **caliginous**. See *dark*

(5) gloomy (as in dark; hellish) *adj.*: **stygian** (sometimes cap.). See *dark* and *hellish*

(6) gloomy (as in sad or melancholy) *adj.*: **tristful**. See *sad*

(7) gloomy (as in suggestive of a funeral) *adj.*: **sepulchral**. See *funereal*

(8) gloomy (as in sullen or morose) *adj.*: **saturnine**. See *sullen*

(9) gloomy (or grumpy mood) *n.pl.*: **mulligrubs**. See *grumpiness*

glorification *n.*: **apotheosis** (*v.t.*: **apotheosize**). See *exaltation*

glorified (or romanticized conception of oneself, as a result of boredom in one's life) *n.*: **Bovarism**. See *self-delusion*

glorify (as in idealize) *v.t.*: **platonize**. See *idealize*

glory (in, or boast, esp. about the accomplishments of a relative) *v.t., n.*: **kvell** [Yiddish]. See *boast*

gloss (over, as in make pleasant or less harsh) *v.t.*: **edulcorate**. See *sweeten*

gloss over (try to . . . an offense with excuses) *v.t.*: **palliate**. See *downplay*

glowing *adj.*: **lucent**. ❖ The Postman, however, is strangely rib-tickling and heart-melting, strange even in what went on behind the scenes, which, in this case, is not irrelevant, and further irradiates an already **lucent** movie. (John Simon, review of *The Postman*, *National Review*, 7/31/1995, p. 64.)

(2) glowing (softly . . .) *adj.*: **lambent**. See *shimmering*

(3) glowing *adj.*: **effulgent**. See *bright*

(4) glowing *adj.*: **fulgurant**. See *bright*

(5) glowing *adj.*: **refulgent**. See *bright*

glue (or bond together) *v.t.*: **agglutinate**. See *adhere*

gluey *adj.*: **viscid**. See *sticky*

glum (as in sullen or morose) *adj.*: **saturnine**. See *sullen*

(2) glum (or grumpy mood) *n.pl.*: **mulligrubs**. See *grumpiness*

(3) glum (and/or shy and/or socially withdrawn or inexperienced) *adj.*: **farouche** [French]. See *shy*

glutton *n.*: **trencherman**. ❖ "Deeelicious!" says [Tommy Lasorda], the 59-year-old manager of the Los Angeles Dodgers, an epic **trencherman** who claims that he "never met a meal I didn't like." In fact he carries a spare fork in his back pocket, just in case he runs into a dish he can't resist. (Todd Gold, "Host: Next to His Family and His Beloved Dodger Blue, Tommy Lasorda Lives for Food—and His Restaurant," *People*, 7/13/1987, p. 103.)

(2) glutton (as in anyone who behaves like a pig, whether in his or her personal habits or by being greedy) **chazzer** [Yiddish]. See *pig*

(3) glutton (to eat like a . . .) *v.t.*: **gormandize**. See *devour*

gluttony *n.*: **gulosity**. ❖ But humans, especially Americans, scarf up whatever's shoved in their face. . . . The result of my holiday **gulosity** impacted upon me one night at a Santa Monica restaurant called Rix. The owner had stopped by to chat and was discussing a live jellyfish he planned on placing in a tank as part of the restaurant's decor. I was in a comatose state and when I heard jellyfish I said, "Sure, I'll try it, just a small bite." (Al Martinez, "Eat, Eat, Eat, Drink, Eat, Chat, Drink, Eat, Eat," *Los Angeles Times*, 12/22/1999.)

gnashing (of teeth during sleep) *n.*: **bruxism**. See *grinding*

goal (esp. of life) *n.*: **telos** [Greek; derives from Aristotle's inquiry into our goal and purpose in life; our reason for being]. ❖ [The preamble to the constitution of the European Union] presents a picture of Europe's past in terms that suggest the EU is the . . . Aristotelian **telos**, toward which Europe has been enthusiastically striving over thousands of years. . . . The implication is that the European constitution represents the consummation of this dream. (Peter Jones, "Perverted View of History in EU Preamble: Bureaucrat-Written Constitution Says a Lot About EU's Mentality," *Gazette* [Montreal], 1/11/2004.)

(2) goal *n.*: **nisus**. ❖ "Shufflin'" is more like it. However Morris "Magic Slim" Holt wishes to title his latest effort, his **nisus** is shuffling the blues along a well-worn path, inviting you to stomp your feet and clap your hands. (Paul Hampel, review of *Scufflin'*, by Magic Slim & the Teardrops, *St. Louis Post-Dispatch*, 2/6/1997.)

(3) goal (as in the thing that is being looked for; also the answer to a problem) *n.*: **quaesitum**. See *objective*

(4) goal (directed toward a . . .) *adj.*: **telic**. See *purposeful*

(5) goal (hidden or ulterior . . .) *n.*: **arrierepensee** (or **arrière-pensée**) [French]. See *motive*

(6) goal (highest . . . to be attained, lit. the greatest or highest good) *n.*: **summum bonum** [Latin]. See *ideal*

(7) goal (which is delusive or not realistically obtainable) *n.*: **will-o'-the-wisp**. See *pipe dream*

goat (of or relating to, esp. as to smell) *adj.*: **hircine**. ❖ Did I do something to deserve to be called a goat? Was I employing the best of conflict resolution skills by bellowing in reply, "No, pal, you're the goat"? Yet after some thought, I have a clear conscience about my near fisticuffs last Friday. There are times when one must take a stand, even at the risk of being outed as an ill-tempered **hircine** ruminant. I fought my fight for my own self-respect as a man among Russian men. (*Moscow Times* [Russia], "Sorry, Pal, You're the Goat!" 4/23/2001.)

gobble (food like a glutton) *v.t.*: **gormandize**. See *devour*

gobbledygook *n.*: **galimatias**. See *gibberish*

go-between *n.*: **comprador**. See *intermediary*

go beyond (or exceed the limits, resources, or capabilities of) *v.t.*: **beggar**. See *surpass*

God (appearance of . . . to a person) *n.*: **theophany**. ❖ Leaders can hope to influence, not by majestic miracles and thunderous **theophanies**, but rather by silent sensitivity and loving outreach. (Shlomo Riskin, "Judaism's Silent Thunder," *Jerusalem Post*, 3/12/2004.)

(2) God (belief in the existence of . . . , esp. one . . .) *n.*: **theism**. ❖ "Abortion is a matter between a woman, her doctor and God."—Premier Ralph Klein of Alberta. . . . By referring to such an entity he has at least taken a stand for **theism**. Whether atheists like it or not, he says, "God" is a factor in the abortion question. (Virginia Ted-Byfield, "What Exactly Does Ralph Klein Mean When He Brings 'God' into the Abortion Issue?" Alberta Report/Western Report, 10/16/1995, p. 41.)

(3) God (centering on . . . as the primary concern) *adj.*: **theocentric**. ❖ The concept that "man is the measure of all things," as Protagoras put it, confronted the church's **theocentric** portrait of the universe. (John Elson, "Looking Back: The Millennium of Discovery," *Time*, 10/15/1992, p. 16.)

(4) God (controlled or governed by . . .) *n.*: **theonomous**. ❖ Cinema, especially in mythic form, is concerned with the depth dimension of the human situation. It is concerned with ultimates, which most people call God. God is in us, closer to us than we are to ourselves. Yet God flows beyond us in every way. This means that the human situation is **theonomous**. In its depths, it can be transparent to the God who lives there. (Ellwood Keiser, "Why I Make Movies," *National Catholic Reporter*, 4/9/1999.)

(5) God (fear of . . . or God's wrath) *n.*: **theophobia**. ❖ School officials at a public high school in Hampton, Va., have ordered a student Christian club to eliminate "Easter" from the title of an annual canned food drive because it may offend students of other faiths. . . . "This sets a terrible precedent," said [the students' lawyer]. "This smacks of **theophobia** where now the schools are nitpicking at names. This is simply a result of being overzealous and being overly cautious on the issue of the separation of church and state." (Ellen Sorokin, "School Tells Club 'Easter' Must Be Off Food-Drive Title; Christians Told Use 'Spring' Instead," *Washington Times*, 3/14/2002.)

(6) God (having an animal form) *adj.*: **theriomorphic**. ❖ In the myth Yeluri personifies evil. . . . With the help of several **theriomorphic** goddesses such as the hedgehog goddess, the rat goddess, and the eagle goddess, to mention only the most important ones, the good goddesses finally succeed in beating back the attacks of the demon Yeluri and ban him to live under the surface of the earth. (Georg Heyne, review of *Mandschurische Göttinnen und Iranis-*

che Teufel, edited by Bäcker Jörg, *Asian Folklore Studies*, 6/1/2001.)

(7) God (vindication of the justice of . . . , esp. in permitting or ordaining natural or moral evil) *n*.: **theodicy**. ❖ [The novel *Hey Nostradamus!* by Douglas Coupland chronicles the aftermath of a shooting spree at a Vancouver high school in 1988. It contains] a more serious (if glancingly handled) treatment of **theodicy**: If you believe in God, how do you answer the question "Why does God allow these horrific things to happen?" (Meghan O'Rourke, "Ambitious Novel Leaves Unanswered Questions," *Chicago Sun-Times*, 8/17/2003.)

(8) god (worshiping one . . . only) *n*.: **monolatry**. ❖ [Hector] Avalos's main goal is to contrast the complexities of therapies in the Greco-Roman systems with the simplicity of those offered by Christianity. Avalos argues that this was due, principally, to the difference between polytheism and the "**monolatry**" of Christianity. The very fact that people had so many different gods and therapies to choose from in the polytheistic systems rendered those systems more complicated and expensive. (Dale Martin, "Health Care and the Rise of Christianity," *Church History*, 3/1/2001.)

(9) god (belief in one . . . without denying others) *n*.: **henotheism**. See *deity*

(10) God (belief there is only one . . .) *n*.: **monotheism**. See *deity*

(11) God (government by . . . or a divine being) *n*.: **theocracy**. See *government*

(12) god (worship of or belief in more than one . . .) *n*.: **polytheism**. See *deity*

godlike (having both human and . . . attributes) *adj*.: **theanthropic**. ❖ [After September 11, 2001,] our government should order the CIA to air drop to the Mullahs and their angry young men millions of pages from the Victoria's Secret catalogues. Anyone familiar with the September 11 atrocities knows that these fellows are sexually repressed. . . . Pursuing the **theanthropic** [Victoria's Secret model Laetitia Casta] through Google-space, they will be lured toward the pages of *The American Spec-*

tator, where they will enjoy the health benefits of cultural diversity. (R. Emmett Tyrell Jr., "The Continuing Crisis," *American Spectator*, 1/1/2002.)

gods (battle or conflict among . . .) *n*.: **theomachy**. ❖ Kuhn's thesis is that . . . science is all theoretical talk and negotiation, which never really establishes anything. . . . [His theory] is also an instance of the enduring appeal of **theomachy**, [namely that] what was previously thought to be a continuous and uninteresting succession of random events is discovered to be a conflict of a finite number of hidden gods (classes, complexes, paradigms, as the case may be), who manipulate the flux of appearances to their own advantage. (James Franklin, review of *Thomas Kuhn: A Philosophical History for Our Times*, by Steve Fuller, *New Criterion*, 6/1/2000.)

God willing *phr*.: **Deo volente** [Latin]. ❖ It is supposed to be part of the rite of passage, cutting your hair short because you have reached a certain age. [Are you] some chiffon-clad nymph grooving at a pop festival with daisies in her flowing tresses? No, you say to yourself, the summer of love is over and you are a successful woman, the mother of a flowing-tressed nymph and one day, **Deo volente**, even a grandmother. Long hair is not for you any longer. It's time for the chop. (Celia Brayfield, "A Lifestyle Haircut," *Times* [London], 7/20/2004.)

going above and beyond (the call of duty or what is required) *adj*.: **supererogatory**. See *exceeding*

gold (of, pertaining to, or containing) *adj*.: **auric**. ❖ [From the movie *Goldfinger*:] **Auric** Goldfinger: This is gold, Mr. Bond. All my life I've been in love with its color, its brilliance, its divine heaviness. I welcome any enterprise that will increase my stock, which is considerable. [James Bond:] I think you've made your point, Goldfinger. Thank you for the demonstration. (Scott Simon, interview with Professor James Chapman, Weekend Edition, NPR, 9/9/2000.)

golden *adj*.: **aureate**. ❖ In the second quarter of '86, he lost $100 million. "We took too much risk. I should have been fired," he says. Suddenly First Boston's California golden boy wasn't looking so **aureate**. (Andy Serwer, "The Hidden Beauty of Bonds," *Fortune*, 3/19/2001, p. 118.)

gondolier (song of) *n*.: **barcarole**. See *song*

good (greatest or highest . . .) *n*.: **summum bonum**. [Latin]. See *ideal*

(2) good (said esp. of food or drink that is so good that one wants more) *adj*.: **moreish** [chiefly British]. See *addictive*

(3) good (very . . .) *adj*.: **palmary**. See *excellent*

(4) good (very . . . , as in excellent) *adj*.: **galumptious**. See *excellent*

(4) good (very . . . , as in excellent) *adj*.: **skookum**.

(5) good (very . . . as in first-class) *adj*.: **pukka**. See *first-class*

(6) good (very . . . as in of the highest quality) *n*.: **first water** (usu. as in "of the first water"). See *quality*

(7) good (very . . . , as in wonderful) *adj*.: **frabjous** (often as in "Oh frabjous day!"). See *wonderful*

(8) good (very . . . , as in excellent) *adj*.: **mirific**. See *wonderful*

good-bye (act of saying . . .) *n*.: **valediction**. See *farewell*

(2) good-bye (as in parting words) *n*.: **envoi** [French]. See *parting words*

good-looking (esp. sexually) *adj*.: **toothsome**. See *sexy*

(2) good-looking (in an unconventional way) *adj*.: **jolie laide** (or **belle laide**) [French]. See *pretty* or *handsome* or *beautiful*

good-natured (and pleasant) *adj*.: **sympathique** [French]. See *genial*

good-naturedness *n*.: **bonhomie**. See *affability*

goodness (as in virtue or integrity) *n*.: **probity**. See *integrity*

(2) goodness (lit. humanity; often used in the sense of decency) *n*.: **menschlichkeit** [German, Yiddish]. See *decency*

good vs. evil (conflict in the soul between . . .) *n*.: **psychomachia**. ❖ [Boxer Sonny] Liston was seen, by black as well as white, as the Bad Nigger. Of course, if the NAACP had any faith that the Good Nigger [Floyd Patterson] had a shot in hell at vanquishing the Bad Nigger, they would have supported the fight. . . . How had boxing become **psychomachia**? (Nick Tosches, *The Devil and Sonny Liston,* Little, Brown [2000], p. 160.)

(2) good vs. evil (philosophy that divides the world into . . .) *n*.: **Manichaeism** or **Manicheism** (*adj*.: **Manichaean** or **Manichean**) [sometimes not cap.]. ❖ Lanz and his followers were obsessed by homoerotic notions of a **manichean** struggle between the heroic and creative "blond" race and a race of predatory "beast-men" who preyed on the "blond" women with animal lust and bestial instincts that were corrupting and destroying mankind and its culture. (Ian Kershaw, *Hitler*, Norton [1998], p. 50.)

goody-goody (as in prim or prudish) *adj*.: **missish**. See *prim*

(2) goody-goody (or anyone who is a prude or hostile to minor vices or forms of popular entertainment) *n*.: **wowser** [Australian slang]. See *killjoy*

gooey *adj*.: **viscid**. See *sticky*

goof-off *n*.: **wastrel**. See *slacker*

goose (of, relating to, or resembling) *adj*.: **anserine**. ❖ Brian was aiming to expand the circle of my **anserine** acquaintances and he was given the chance when he discovered six White-fronted geese in a flock of 30 Greylags at the tail-end of the year. (James O'Hagan, "Wind and Sun Cook Watcher's Goose Country Diary," *Scotsman* [Edinburgh], 1/9/1999.)

(2) goose (of or relating to the domestic fowl, including . . .) *adj*.: **gallinaceous**. See *fowl*

goose bumps (get . . . from fear, anxiety, or cold) *v.t*.: **horripilate** (*n*.: **horripilation**). ❖ Tessa [a flirtatious, attractive student] extricated herself from the seat-and-desk contraption she was in and came over to [the professor]. He felt himself **horripilating**. What was expected of him now? (Erik Tarloff, *The Man Who Wrote the Book*, Crown [2000], p. 137.)

gorge (on food) *v.i.*: **gormandize**. See *devour*

(2) gorge (to the point of excess, esp. things sweet) *v.t.*: **cloy**. See *satiate*

gorgeous (in an unconventional way) *adj.*: **jolie laide** (or **belle laide**) [French]. See *pretty* or *handsome* or *beautiful*

gorilla (of or relating to, or resembling) *adj.*: **anthropoid**. See *ape*

gory (as in bloody) *adj.*: **sanguinary**. See *bloody*

gossip (as in spread news or a rumor about) *v.t.*: **bruit**. See *rumor*

(2) gossip (idle . . . , as in small talk) *n.*: **palaver**. See *small talk*

(3) gossip (person who is a . . .) *n.*: **quidnunc**. See *busybody*

gourmet *n.*: **epicure**. ❖ In my last column, I reviewed the best new entrants on London's revived restaurant scene, but it would be a shame to overlook some of the city's long-established gems—restaurants that have been seducing international **epicures** for many years. (James Villas, "London's Classics, Updated: Our Critic Discovers That Britain's Grand Old Restaurants Haven't Lost Their Savor," *Town & Country*, 8/1/1996, p. 54.)

(2) gourmet *n.*: **gastronome**. ❖ The growing diversity of foods available in the U.S. is enough to make even the most picky **gastronome** swoon. (James Villas, "The Genuine Article," *Town & Country*, 2/1/1996, p. 56.)

government (by a few persons or factions) *n.*: **oligarchy**. ❖ Atlanta in 1964 was run by an **oligarchy** of conservative white businessmen and lawyers, most of whom hung around the crusty old Piedmont Driving Club or the Capital City Club, and virtually all of whom had no use for the civil rights movement. (John Huey, "The Atlanta Game Against All Odds: This Sunbelt Hustler Snagged the Olympics by Selling Itself as a Third World City; The Biggest Lie It Ever Told Turns Out to Be True," *Fortune*, 7/22/1996, p. 42.)

(2) government (by clergy) *n.*: **hierocracy**. ❖ When asked which existing regime most closely approximates an ideal Islamic order, fundamentalists most often cite the governments of the Sudan or Iran—the first a military regime, the second a **hierocracy** ruled by an increasingly autocratic cleric, and both first-order violators of human rights. (Martin Kramer, "Islam vs. Democracy," *Commentary*, 1/1/1993.)

(3) government (by God or a divine being) *n.*: **theocracy**. ❖ The essay, "God as a Running Mate," reminded readers that the Constitution decrees the separation of church and state, and worried—scornfully—that Republican and Democratic presidential candidates have been making speeches in which they "sound as if they would not be uncomfortable in an evangelical **theocracy**." (Michael Joseph Gross, Books & the Arts: "Mourning and America," *Nation*, 11/1/1999, p. 29.)

(4) government (by old people) *n.*: **gerontocracy**. ❖ Ezra Taft Benson [was] the supreme authority of the Mormon Church until his death last week at the age of 94. [His successor may be 86-year-old Howard Hunter,] who had open-heart surgery eight years ago and a gall-bladder operation last year. . . . In spite of this **gerontocracy**, the Church of Jesus Christ of Latter-day Saints remains vibrant. (Sophfronia Scott Gregory, Religion: "Saints Preserve Us—The Mormons Are Likely to Choose Another Aged, Ailing Leader, but Nevertheless Their Church Is Thriving," *Time*, 6/13/1994, p. 65.)

(5) government (by prostitutes) *n.*: **pornocracy** [The example gives the historical derivation of the word]. ❖ Between 914 and 963 AD, the landed aristocracy under the leadership of a Roman senator Theophylact, his wife Theodora and their daughter Marozia came increasingly to dominate the Curia. Marozia, mistress of Pope Sergius III and mother of his son, the future Pope John XI, took control of Rome. . . . This period is known as the "**Pornocracy**." Whether Theodora and Marozia were whores in the true sense of the word is a moot point. (Colin Andrew, "Notes and Queries: A Bridge

Not Quite Far Enough," *Guardian* [London], 10/16/1992.)

(6) government (by the least qualified or least principled people) *n.*: **kakistocracy**. ❖ Cannon: Well, we couldn't convict [Bill Clinton]. But I think the American people understand what [the Clinton] administration is all about. . . . And we have the greatest system on earth, a system strong enough to withstand the assaults over the last six years of this **kakistocracy**. (Sean Hannity and Alan Colmes, Ken Starr Investigation, Hannity & Colmes, Fox News Network, 6/24/1999.)

(7) government (by the military) *n.*: **stratocracy**. [For] nineteen-plus years . . . the (P)NDC ruled Ghana by military fiat. . . . The (P)NDC was a **stratocracy** that deployed a culture of wanton and extra-judicial assassinations in the specious guise of revolutionary house-cleaning. (Kwame Okoampa Ahoofe, "Question of Kettle Calling the Pot Black," *New York Beacon*, 10/9/2003.)

(8) government (by the mob or the masses) *n.*: **mobocracy**. ❖ The spasm of communal violence [by Hindu militants] has almost brought down the 11-month-old government of Prime Minister V. P. Singh. . . . Said [one politician]: "The country is at a crossroads. We have to choose between secularism and religious fundamentalism, between democracy and **mobocracy**, between unity and disintegration." (Guy D. Garcia, India: "The Awesome Wrath of Rama Religious Nationalism Threatens to Bring Down the Government and Splinter the Country," *Time*, 11/12/1990, p. 47.)

(9) government (by the mob or the masses) *n.*: **ochlocracy**. ❖ [There are] ominous signs of how unrest is taking hold all across the U.S.S.R. . . . Discontent is everywhere. . . . "Intellectuals have mostly withdrawn to their homes, and it is **ochlocracy** that now reigns in the streets in the absence of either a strong hand or democracy," [said one journalist]. (Yuri Zarakhovich, "It Was Just What the Other Republics Fear," *Time* International, 1/29/1990, p. 13.)

(10) government (by the wealthy) *n.*: **plu-** **tocracy**. ❖ One of the biggest problems of modern US politics, he said, is wealthy individuals from the business world bumping veterans who've worked their way up. "You don't want a **plutocracy** running your government," he said. (Tim Cornwell, "Wealth Talks Loudest in Race for California Governor," *Independent* [London], 2/16/1998.)

(11) government (by three entities) *n.*: **triarchy**. ❖ For international financial negotiations, Grant suggests a new G8. This would consist of the US, Russia, China, Euroland, Canada, Brazil, India, and Japan, and he sees the world economy as being dominated by a **triarchy**—the US, the enlarged EU, and a new East Asian grouping, including China, Japan, Korea, and the ASEAN countries. (Leonard Dick, "Eye on the EU: Forecasting the EU's Far Future" *Europe*, 11/1/2000.)

(12) government (by women, or political or social dominance by women) *n.*: **gynocracy**. ❖ All my working life, there have been women. This newspaper is edited by a woman; I send in this column to a woman. The publisher I am down here writing a book for is a woman. Most of my editors have been women. The odd thing is that working, as I do, in a delightful, intelligent, staunch, humane **gynocracy** is an experience that simply wasn't available to this house's founder. (Michael Bywater, "It's a Man's Man's Man's World," *Independent on Sunday*, 3/16/1997.)

(13) government (by women) *n.*: **gynarchy**. ❖ By far the philosopher's most-favoured correspondent was his mother, Maude, for whom he confessed "an Oedipal complex the size of a house." She appears in these letters as a formidable matriarch in the family tradition of strong females, which her approval-seeking son called "the **gynarchy**." (Chris Champion, "And Now, the Real George Grant Emerges," Alberta Report/Western Report, 11/18/1996, p. 45.)

(14) government (by young people) *n.*: **neocracy**. ❖ A little more **neocracy** may be exactly what Greece needs. In quasi-capitalist Greece . . . many occupations—from medicine to politics, from academia to the civil service—are dominated by an elderly establishment which has made sure that long service is well rewarded and kept pesky young high-fliers in their place. (*Economist*, "A Bit More Neocracy, Please [Younger Generation Needs to Play More Active Role in Greece]," 10/10/2002.)

(15) government (characterized by greed and corruption) *n.*: **kleptocracy**. ❖ Conversely, when narrow elites establish a chokehold on foreign trade, and also steal most of the foreign aid and foreign loans coming into the country, then the country will become even poorer—just what's happening in sub-Saharan Africa, where almost every government is a **kleptocracy**. (Dave Kopel, "Police Shootings Need Closer Look," *Denver Rocky Mountain News*, 7/29/2001.)

(16) government (dominated by military rather than civilian personnel, esp. one whose military preparations threaten to turn it into a totalitarian state) *n.*: **garrison state**. [This term derives from a 1941 article by Harold Lasswell in which he stated that "under conditions of continual crisis and perpetual preparedness for total war, every aspect of life would eventually come under state control."] ❖ Defining our national stance as "war" [in the wake of September 11] takes us more in the direction of the **garrison state**. We are already one of the most heavily armed societies in history. Need we go further in that direction—killing innocent foreigners and restricting our own freedoms—before we realize it is the wrong direction for our country? (Kevin Danaher, "Justice, Not War," *Washington Post*, 9/29/2001.)

(17) government (in proportion to wealth or property ownership) *n.*: **timocracy**. ❖ The battle for Seattle over the World Trade Organization's meetings was the embryonic stage of the struggle against global "**timocracy**," . . . Aristotle's idea of a state in which political power is in direct proportion to property ownership. To the uninitiated in the globalism phenomenon, **timocracy** appears to be rearing its

ugly head. The three executives at the top of the Microsoft ladder are now worth more than 170 million Americans. (Arnaud De Borchgrave, "Warm-up for the Long Haul," *Washington Times*, 12/6/1999.)

(18) government (of or relating to an industry owned or partly controlled by . . .) *adj.*: **parastatal**. ❖ Nigeria's **parastatal** organisations illustrate the point nicely. Set up to run everything from telephones to electricity, insurance and paper-making, these state enterprises now number over 1,000, their board members over 4,000. The grants and write-offs they receive each year from the government are bigger than the rest of the national budget. (*Economist*, "Nigeria in Civvy Street," 6/19/1999.)

(19) government (or political dominance of men) *n.*: **androcracy**. ❖ All the varieties of Christianity in Africa are riddled with androcentrism and misogyny. For women to be at home in Christianity, they suspend belief that it is **androcracy** that dominates them and not the will of God or their own special innate sinfulness arising out of being women. (Mercy Amba Oduyoye, "Christianity and African Culture," *International Review of Mission*, 1/1/1995.)

(20) government (utopian . . . where everyone rules equally) *n.*: **pantisocracy**. ❖ Utopia has never existed. . . . [W]henever it fails, there is always someone around to tell you the wrong reasons for it and propose another model, which in turn proves equally unworkable. This is as true of nutty little proposals by discontented geniuses—like the idea of communalist, rural "**pantisocracy**" put forward by Shelley, Coleridge and others in their youth. (Robert Hughes, The Arts/Ideas: "The Phantom of Utopia Geniuses," *Time*, 11/6/2000, p. 120.)

(21) government (which is dependent on revenue from oil exports) *n.*: **petrocracy**. ❖ Nothing drives global governments crazy like oil. Oil money is the fuel on which today's corridors of power are run. Oil is to nations what blood is to the human being. Democracy? Away with it! Give us **petrocracy** and we shall live! (Fisayo Adejuyigbe, "The Blood Is Oil," University Wire, 10/29/2002.)

(22) government (actions of pompous but inefficient . . . officials) *n.*: **bumbledom**. See *bureaucracy*

grab (money unfairly and in excessive amounts) *v.t.*: **mulct**. See *extract*

(2) grab (property to compel payment of debts) *v.t.*: **distrain**. See *confiscate*

grabbing (adapted for . . . , esp. a tail) *adj.*: **prehensile**. See *grasping*

graceful (and slender woman) *n.*: **sylph**. See *woman*

(2) graceful (and/or slender) *adj.*: **gracile**. See *slender*

(3) graceful (as in nimble) *adj.* **lightsome**. See *nimble*

graceless (as in clumsy) *adj.*: **lumpish**. See *clumsy*

graduate (student about to . . .) *n.*: **graduand** [chiefly British]. ❖ [I]t may be argued that [honorary degrees] are an anachronism. But, as graduating students appreciate, they have another function: they enliven the proceedings of a graduation ceremony at which each attending **graduand** has otherwise to sit through several hundred other awards of degrees. (*Independent* [London], "Time to Honour a Degree of Openness," 5/6/1999).

grafter *n.*: **boodler**. ❖ You'd think we might catch a break from the **boodlers** and influence peddlers, if only out of a wartime sense of patriotic duty. Won't happen. [Chicago] can continue to revel in the stink of its corruption and greed. Just when we need it, along comes the news that we still are in the boodle playoffs. Through it all, Chicago still is Chicago. (Dennis Byrne, "Disgraceful Behavior Not a Problem," *Chicago Tribune*, 10/29/2001.)

grammarian (who is petty or pedantic) *n.*: **grammaticaster**. See *pedantic*

grand (and stately, as befitting a baron) *adj.*: **baronial**. See *stately*

grandeur (delusions of . . . or obsession with . . .) *n.*: **folie de grandeur** [French]. ❖ A weak person tends to make himself look strong by putting on a show. [The Shah of Iran] concentrated authority in his own hands, thinking he would make Iran a world power. . . . He was encouraged in his **folie de grandeur** by the steep rise in the price of oil during Opec's heyday, enriching his coffers with petro-dollars. (David Krivine, "The Fall of the Peacock Throne," *Jerusalem Post*, 1/30/1990.)

(2) grandeur (having a delusional fantasy that one has . . .) *n.*: **megalomania**. See *delusional*

grandiose (as in affected and high-flown, use of language) *adj.*: **euphuistic.** See *affected*

(2) grandiose (esp. regarding speaking or writing style) *adj.*: **magniloquent**. See *pompous*

(3) grandiose (esp. regarding speaking or writing style) *adj.*: **orotund**. See *pompous*

grant (as in bestow, by one with higher power) *v.t.*: **vouchsafe**. See *bestow*

grapes (of or relating to) *adj.*: **vineal**. ❖ [In the coming fall, harvests] will produce boulder-size cabbages for that home-made slaw or sauerkraut. . . . Grapes . . . will fulfill their **vineal** destiny in old wooden tubs and stainless steel vats as grappa or slivovitz. (Jon Hahn, "Sing Your Swan Song, Sweet September," *Seattle Post-Intelligencer*, 9/9/1997.)

grasp (as in understand thoroughly and/or intuitively) *v.t.*: **grok**. See *understand*

(2) grasp (as in figure out) *v.t.*: **suss** (usually with "out"; slang). See *figure out*

(3) grasp (person or thing that maintains a tenacious . . . on something, whether literally or figuratively) *n.*: **limpet**. See *clinger*

(4) grasp (person or thing that maintains a tenacious . . . on something, whether literally or figuratively) *n.*: **remora**. See *clinger*

grasping (adapted for . . . , esp. a tail) *adj.*: **prehensile**. ❖ Kinkajous and spider monkeys grasp branches with wraparound **prehensile** tails. (Mary Roach, "Aliens in the Treetops," *International Wildlife*, 11/1/1994, p. 4.)

grass-eating *adj.*: **graminivorous**. ❖ If a computer program were asked to define a "horse," it would respond with an updated, animated version of Mr. Gradgrind's answer in *Hard Times*—"Quadruped. **Graminivorous**. Forty teeth," etc. (James Fallows, review of *The Cult of Information: The Folklore of Computers and the True Art of Thinking*, by Theodore Roszak, *New Republic*, 7/14/1986.)

grasshoppers (of or relating to . . .) *adj.*: **orthopterous**. See *insects*

gratification (sexual . . . from rubbing against something or someone) *n.*: **frottage**. See *rubbing*

(2) gratification (solely devoted to the seeking of . . .) *adj.*: **apolaustic**. See *hedonistic*

(3) gratification (spec. someone excessively devoted to luxury or sensual pleasures) *n.*: **voluptuary**. See *hedonist* and *sensualist*

gratified (often in a boastful way) *adj.*: **cock-a-hoop**. See *elated*

grating (of a sound or noise that is . . . , harsh, shrill, or otherwise unpleasant) *adj.*: **stridulous**. ❖ [While riding, the bobsled's] centrifugal force slams my arms against the sled's sides. My neck jerks forward and back, and I hunch my shoulders to defend against whiplash. . . . The sled vibrates with the **stridulous** notes of scraping ice, and G-forces pound our faces like thick, relentless wind. (Sam Harrison, "Hold the Ether; 53.16 Seconds of Terror and Joy in a Bobsled," *Chicago Tribune*, 10/8/2000.)

(2) grating (on the ears) *adj.*: **scrannel**. See *cacophonous*

gratuity (in Near Eastern countries, esp. to expedite service) *n.*: **baksheesh**. ❖ **Baksheesh** is to Egypt as oil is to engines: It makes things work. It probably greased the palms of the process that built the pyramids. (Catherine Watson, "In Egypt, the Extended Palm Is Found Almost Everywhere," *Minneapolis Star Tribune*, 3/9/1997.)

(2) gratuity *n.*: **pourboire** [French]. ❖ Simply uncorking the bottle early is practically useless. It will expose an amount of wine in the neck of the bottle equal to the size of the bottom of the cork. In other words, almost no wine at all. Mostly it gives the waiter or wine steward a bit of stage business to help inflate the **pourboire**. (Frank J. Prial, "Liquid Assets/Wine Has to Breathe, You Say? Put a Cork in It," *Minneapolis Star Tribune*, 12/2/1999.)

(3) gratuity (as in extra or unexpected gift or benefit, sometimes as thanks for a purchase) *n.*: **lagniappe**. See *gift*

grave (suggestive of a . . . , as in a funeral) *adj.*: **sepulchral**. See *funereal*

graveyard *n.*: **necropolis**. ❖ French researchers . . . were called in to examine a stash of mummies unearthed by the Egyptians in a **necropolis** at Ain Labakha, a village within the oasis inhabited by 500 to 1,000 people around the time of Christ. Because working-class graves are of little interest to treasure hunters, the mummies were virtually undisturbed. (Michael D. Lemonick, Archaeology: "Working Stiffs Mummies from a Rural Oasis Provide a Rare Window onto the Brief, Back-breaking Lives of Ordinary Egyptians 2,000 Years Ago," *Time*, 4/6/1998, p. 60.)

graveyards (one who loves . . .) *n.*: **taphophile**. See *cemeteries*

gray (covered with . . . or white hair as if with age) *adj.*: **hoary**. ❖ We live in an age where old age is scorned; rather than honoring a **hoary** head, we lock it away behind closed doors in an institution commonly called a nursing home. (Rabbi Shlomo Riskin, "Beauty That Lasts," *Jerusalem Post*, 9/24/1999.)

(2) gray (streaked with or partly . . .) *adj.*: **griseous**. See *grizzled*

greasy (as in slippery) *adj.*: **lubricious**. See *slippery*

(2) greasy (oily, or unctuous) *adj.*: **pinguid**. See *oily*

great (as in excellent) *adj.*: **galumptious**. See *excellent*

(2) great (as in excellent) *adj.*: **palmary**. See *excellent*

(3) great (as in of the highest quality) *n.*: **first water** (usu. as in "of the first water"). See *quality*

(4) great (as in wonderful) *adj.*: **frabjous** (often as in "Oh frabjous day!"). See *wonderful*

(5) great (as in wonderful) *adj.*: **galluptious** [slang]. See *wonderful*

(6) great *adj.*: **mirific**. See *wonderful*

(7) great *adj.*: **skookum**. See *excellent*

greatest (good) *n.*: **summum bonum**. [Latin]. See *ideal*

greatness (delusions of . . . or obsession with . . .) *n.*: **folie de grandeur** [French]. See *grandeur*

(2) greatness (having a delusional fantasy that one has . . .) *n.*: **megalomania**. See *delusional* and *obsession*

Greece (one who admires or is interested in) *n.*: **philhellene**. ❖ Much of Mr. Hanson's book will definitely please the **philhellene**. As the military might of ancient civilizations ebbed and flowed, the emergence of the Greek polis permanently changed the geopolitical balance of power. . . . In every Western victory, Mr. Hanson sees a road leading back to classical Greece. (*Washington Times*, "2,500 Years of Military Supremacy?" 9/16/2001.)

greed (esp. for wealth) *n.*: **cupidity**. ❖ Europe's past keeps sending awful bonbons to its present. In recent months, we have learned that Swiss banks piled up millions of dollars in assets stolen from Jewish victims of the Nazis. . . . No one would argue that German evil absolves Swiss **cupidity** or French collaboration. (John Marks, "Swiss Cupidity, but German Evil," *U.S. News & World Report*, 12/15/1997.)

(2) greed (insatiable . . .) *n.*: **pleonexia**. ❖ The [Malaysian National Vision Plan goes] beyond the bare necessities of life to the good life, a life in which growth and consumption will still see justice and happiness flourish. [It pays] heed to the dangers of the idolatry of materialism and **pleonexia** . . . and[,] thus, formulate[s] special efforts to instill positive social and spiritual values. The result? Capitalism with a humane face. (*New Straits Times*, "A Way to Move Forward," 4/5/2001.)

(3) greed (as in worship of or devotion to money) *n.*: **plutolatry**. See *wealth*

greedy (person; lit. a large, fish-eating sea bird) *n.*: **cormorant**. ❖ Bleeding from the most savage political bites in its twenty-five-year history,

the National Endowment for the Arts—that profoundly underfunded government agency devoted to the development of culture and the needs of artists—is now foundering in the water with its belly up for all the **cormorants** to feed on [including various pressure groups and constituencies]. (Robert Brustein, "The NEA Belly Up," *New Republic*, 6/18/1990.)

(2) greedy *adj.*: **banausic**. See *materialistic*

green (or somewhat . . .) *adj.*: **viridescent**. ❖ It's time to head [to Desert Hot Springs, CA]. What draws us isn't the shimmering resort cities of Palm Springs, Rancho Mirage, Indian Wells, or La Quinta, with their **viridescent** golf courses, designer stores and general fabulousness. What we want from the desert (besides the stellar winter weather) is the steaming-hot mineral water that's the hallmark of Desert Hot Springs . . . (Deborah Caulfield Rybak, "At a Desert Hot Springs Hotel That's More Retro Than Chic, the Hottest Attraction Is the Water," *Minneapolis Star Tribune*, 2/13/2005.)

greeting (relating to a . . . or other speech where the purpose is to establish a mood of sociability rather than to communicate information or ideas, such as "have a nice day") *adj.*: **phatic**. See *pleasantries*

gregarious (and social) *adj.*: **Anacreontic**. See *convivial*

grief (as in world-weariness or sentimental pessimism over the world's problems) *adj.*: **Weltschmerz** [German]. See *pessimism*

(2) grief (expressing . . . , often regarding something gone) *adj.*: **elegiac**. See *sorrowful*

(3) grief *n.*: **dolor** (*adj.*: **dolorous**). See *sadness*

(4) grief (out of the depths of . . . or despair) *n., adv.*: **de profundis**. See *despair*

(5) grief (as in receiving severe . . . or criticism) *idiom*: **(catching) unshirted hell**. See *criticism*

grieve (over) *v.t.*: **bewail**. See *lament*

grieved (easily . . . , as in offended) *adj.*: **umbrageous**. See *offended*

grim (as in dismal and gloomy) *adj.*: **acherontic**. See *gloomy*

grimace (gaping . . .) *n*.: **rictus**. ❖ [After a horse-racing accident,] the flesh of his leg had been ripped away, exposing the bone. Pollard's face was a **rictus** of agony, his lips peeled back over his teeth, and gusts of pain were rolling through his body. (Laura Hillenbrand, *Seabiscuit*, Random House [2001], p. 218.)

(2) grimace *v.i.*: **girn** [Scottish]. ❖ Warwick Castle will be teeming with terrible trolls, ginormous giants and frightful fairies during Halloween half-term week. . . . Top tips on being scary and pulling ugly faces will culminate in a gruesome **girning** competition. (Ann Evans, "Frightfully Good Fun," *Coventry Evening Telegraph*, 10/14/2006.)

grime (abnormal fear of) *n*.: **mysophobia**. See *fear*

grin (in a silly, self-conscious, or affected manner, or to say something in such a fashion) *v.i., n.*: **simper**. See *smirk*

grind (as in crush or reduce to powder) *v.t.*: **comminute**. See *pulverize*

(2) grind (as in toil) *v.i.*: **moil**. See *toil*

grinding (of teeth during sleep) *n*.: **bruxism**. ❖ The findings suggest that **bruxism** is not only a serious medical condition but also extremely common. About 8% of those surveyed reported grinding their teeth at least once a week, suggesting that 27 million Americans may be afflicted. (Mitch Nelin, "Developments to Watch: Bad News for Teeth Grinders," *Business Week*, 2/12/2001, p. 97.)

grip (person or thing that maintains a tenacious . . . on something, whether literally or figuratively) *n*.: **limpet**. See *clinger*

(2) grip (person or thing that maintains a tenacious . . . on something, whether literally or figuratively) *n*.: **remora**. See *clinger*

gripe (as in fret or complain) *v.i.*: **repine**. See *complain*

grizzled *adj*.: **griseous**. ❖ Indeed, the whole Clinton team shows [the effect of 67-year old MIT economist Robert Solow]. There is nothing **griseous** about the eminence here except the hair and the shadowy effect: Solow is about as well loved a man as any person on the planet. (David Warsh, "The Best and Brightest," *Boston Globe*, 1/17/1993.)

grogginess (relating to period of . . . just before falling asleep) *adj*.: **hypnagogic**. See *drowsiness*

grooved *adj*.: **striated**. ❖ You have to spend the whole day outside in this miserable, steamy summer heat surrounded by people with **striated** fat rolls that look like Hostess Ho-Hos. (Tony Kornheiser, *Pumping Irony*, Times Books [1995], p. 37.)

grope *v.i.*: **grabble**. ❖ The concept is simple: breaking down divisions between formal eating and informal drinking. But blaring bar music and a steady traipse of drinkers wobbling past to the loo, as you **grabble** with your lobster crackers, isn't conducive to a restful evening out. (Adrian Turpin, Food & Drink: "Eating Out—As Time Goes By," *Independent on Sunday*, 6/10/2001.)

(2) grope (literally, fish with a net) *v.t., v.i.*: **seine**. See *fish*

grouch *n*.: **crosspatch**. ❖ This collection of [Charlie] LeDuff's journalism and street vignettes for *The New York Times* portrays a city of a thousand faltering dreams, hard work and that special camaraderie at the Yankee Tavern, where old-timers deride the postponement of opening day and where sits "Paulie Peterson, the 75-year-old **crosspatch** who lives alone and is delighted when he is able to tell somebody, anybody, to go to hell." (Tyler D. Johnson, "Work and Other Sins—Life in New York City and Thereabouts," *New York Times*, 3/28/2004.)

grouchy *adj*.: **tetchy**. ❖ He estimated that the first volume of the dictionary would be available to the world within two years. "And were it not for the dilatoriness of many contributors," he wrote, clearly in a **tetchy** mood, "I should not hesitate to name an earlier period." (Simon Winchester, *The Professor and the Madman*, HarperCollins [1998], p. 108.)

(2) grouchy (mood) *n.pl.*: **mulligrubs**. See *grumpiness*

(3) grouchy (old man) *n*.: **alter kocker** [Yiddish]. See *old man*

(4) grouchy *adj.*: **atrabilious**. See *surly*

(5) grouchy *adj.*: **bilious**. See *surly*

(6) grouchy *adj.*: **liverish**. See *irritable*

(7) grouchy *adj.*: **querulous**. See *peevish*

(8) grouchy *adj.*: **shirty**. See *irritable*

(9) grouchy *adj.*: **splenetic**. See *irritable*

(10) grouchy *adj.*: **waspish**. See *irritable*

groundless (and/or illogical argument) *n.*: **choplogic**. See *fallacy*

(2) groundless (as in relating to reasoning that sounds plausible but is false or insincere) *adj.*: **meretricious**. See *specious*

(3) groundless (reasoning, as in fallacious or specious) *n.*: **syllogism**. See *specious*

group *n.*: **gaggle**. ❖ On most Saturday nights Barry Bowman and a **gaggle** of his Southwestern Louisiana teammates gather around a television set to watch American Gladiators. (Tim Crothers, Inside College Basketball, *Sports Illustrated*, 1/23/1995, p. 87.)

(2) group (of objects, people, or ideas) *n.*: **congeries**. See *collection*

(3) group (of riders in a bike race) *n.*: **peloton** [French]. See *cluster*

(4) group (together) *v.t.*: **colligate**. See *unite*

(5) group (united by close personal bonds) *n.*: **gemeinschaft** (sometimes cap.) [German]. See *community*

(6) group (which is based on either strong interpersonal relationships and common values among its members [**gemeinschaft**—see *community*] or impersonal such relationships [**gesellschaft**—see *association*, which includes an example that uses both terms]) [German].

(7) group (as in classify) *v.t.*: **taxonomize**. See *classify*

grovel *v.i.*: **genuflect**. See *kneel*

(2) grovel *v.i.*: **truckle**. See *kowtow*

groveling (person) *n.*: **lickspittle**. See *sycophant*

(2) groveling (to behave toward in a . . . manner) *v.t.*: **bootlick**. See *kowtow*

grow (as in burgeon or expand; lit. bear fruit) *v.i.*: **fructify**. See *burgeon*

growing (in rubbish, poor land, or waste, such as weeds along the highway) *adj.*: **ruderal** (*n.*: a plant that grows in such conditions). ❖ R. E. Frenkel, *Ruderal* Vegetation along Some California Roadsides, University of California Press (1977).

growth (as in outgrowth) *n.*: **excrescence**. See *outgrowth*

grueling (as in difficult or painful, journey or experience) *n.*: **via dolorosa**. See *ordeal*

grumble (as in fret or complain) *v.i.*: **repine**. See *complain*

(2) grumble (as in sulk) *v.t.*: **mump** [British]. See *sulk*

grumbling (as in complaining) *adj.*: **querulous**. See *ordeal*

grumpiness (or despondency) *n.pl.*: **mulligrubs**. [This word is not common but does appear in the *OED* and other comprehensive dictionaries, including *Webster's Third New International Dictionary*. Contemporary uses can be found, such as the example given here. It is sometimes preceded by the word "the."] ❖ TC announced one evening last week that we were having an all-vegetable dinner. Her announcement threw me into deep-blue **mulligrubs.** I prayed for guidance and strength. Dinner has to have meat and potatoes (or rice, at least). A meal of all vegetables won't support life, I told her. She proceeded merrily as I sulked. (Richard Allin, Our Town: "Hush Puppy, Here's a Donut," *Arkansas Democrat-Gazette*, 4/13/2000.)

grumpy *adj.*: **liverish**. See *irritable*

(2) grumpy *adj.*: **shirty**. See *irritable*

(3) grumpy (person) *n.*: **crosspatch**. See *grouch*

(4) grumpy *adj.*: **atrabilious**. See *surly*

(5) grumpy *adj.*: **bilious**. See *surly*

(6) grumpy *adj.*: **splenetic**. See *irritable*

(7) grumpy *adj.*: **tetchy**. See *grouchy*

(8) grumpy *adj.*: **waspish**. See *irritable*

guaranteed (esp. with respect to a plan, deal, or investment that can be trusted completely because it is supposedly safe and sure to succeed) *adj.*: **copper-bottomed** [British]. See *sure-fire*

guardian (or protector) *n.*, *adj.*: **tutelary**. ❖ Hall of fame jockey Johnny Longden has always thought he had a guardian angel, one that perched precariously on his shoulder whenever he rode. "There he is now," the 87-year-old gnome rasps, pointing his cane toward the shimmering California sky. . . . Longden believes the **tutelary** started looking out for him one day in the spring of 1912, in his native England. (Stephanie Diaz, "Back on Track," *Sports Illustrated*, 7/11/1994.)

(2) guardian (as in watchdog) *n.*: **Cerberus**. See *watchdog*

(3) guardian (of a place) *n.*: **genius loci** [Latin]. See *spirit*

guard(s) (esp. who protect a leader) *n.*: **Praetorian guard**. [The Praetorian Guard was a special force of guards used by Roman emperors, created by the emperor Augustus in 27 B.C. The Guard lasted until 312 A.D. Because the Guard propped up a number of ruthless regimes in its later years, the term today generally refers to any person or group who provides protection—bodily or otherwise—to a political leader, especially dictators or those considered evil. The word "praetorian" is also an adjective for politically corruptible, as were those members of the original Guard. See *corruptible*.] ❖ [Vice President Dick] Cheney has been so well protected by his **Praetorian guard** all these years that it's been hard for the public to see his dastardly deeds and petty schemes. But now, because of Patrick Fitzgerald's investigation . . . he's been flushed out as the heart of darkness: All sulfurous strands lead back to the man W. aptly nicknamed Vice. (Maureen Dowd, "Cheney Malarkey," *International Herald Tribune*, 10/27/2005.)

guerrilla (warfare or tactics, esp. as a means to wear out an opponent) *adj.*: **Fabian** [This adjective derives from Roman general Quintus Fabius Maximus, who, through caution, avoidance of direct confrontation, and harassment, defeated Hannibal in the Second Punic War. Today, it has become synonymous with, alternately, caution or conservativeness, delay or dilatoriness, or guerrilla tactics, and is often used in the phrase "Fabian tactics."] ❖ **Fabian** tactics also were employed by the Confederacy at times. . . . The South sometimes resorted to such strategy because it did not have the manpower or the industrial might of the North and could ill afford the head-on clashes that sapped its strength much more quickly than its enemy's. But guerrilla tactics and avoidance of battle were not congenial to the Southern temperament. (Edward Colimore, "Could South Have Won with Other Strategy?" *Charlotte [NC] Observer*, 7/9/2001.)

guffaw *v.i.*: **cachinnate** (*n.*: **cachinnation**). See *laugh*

guidance (relating to the giving of . . .) *adj.*: **paraenetic** (*n.*: **paraenesis**). See *advice*

guide (and interpreter for travelers, esp. where Arabic, Turkish, or Persian is spoken) *n.*: **dragoman**. ❖ Sometimes during our journey across eastern Afghanistan, the threat of violence has been more obvious. A group of bandits fired shots in the general direction of our two vehicles as we drove through a river valley. It was their way of showing they wanted a lift. Our Afghan **dragoman**, a delightfully piratical character, ran over to head them off. (John Simpson, International: "How I Was Robbed by Afghan Bandits," *Sunday Telegraph* [London], 10/5/1997.)

(2) guide (as in channel) *v.t.*: **canalize**. See *channel*

(3) guide (as in tour . . .) *n.*: **cicerone**. See *tour guide*

guidebook (to a country) *n.*: **Baedeker** (or **baedeker**). ❖ This income, supplemented by royalties from his books on Italian painting (carried by superior tourists along with their **Baedekers**), allowed him gradually to form his own exquisite collection, still to be seen in the villa. (William Weaver, "The Renaissance of I Tatti," *Town & Country*, 8/1/1994, p. 94.)

(2) guidebook *n.*: **vade mecum**. ❖ Since, unlike most curators, the writers [of the program accompanying the Edward Hopper exhibit at the Whitney Museum] can write, one can read this **vade mecum** with pleasure after the show. (Robert Hughes, "Under the Crack of Reality—Edward Hopper Saw an America That No Other Painter Had Got Right," *Time*, 7/17/1995, p. 54.)

(3) guidebook *n.*: **enchiridion**. See *handbook*

(4) guidebook (as in primer) *n.*: **hornbook**. See *primer*

guileless *n.*: **artless**. ❖ [H]e presents a Cleopatra who likes to put on an artfully **artless** show of guileless girlishness.... [In the all-male production of *Antony and Cleopatra*] Rylance skips about barefoot, like some innocent heroine. (Paul Taylor, Theatre: "Everything but the Girl," *Independent* [London], 8/3/1999.)

guilt (caused by murder or bloodshed) *n.*: **bloodguilt**. ❖ The Roman triumph served three crucial purposes. First, and most venerable, the ceremony not only acknowledged military success but also purified the city of Rome and its soldiers contaminated by the **bloodguilt** of war. (Peter Holliday, "Roman Triumphal Painting: Its Function, Development, and Reception," *Art Bulletin*, 3/1/1997, p. 130.)

guilty (as in sinful) *adj.*: **peccant**. See *sinful*

gullible (person) *n.*: **gobemouch** [French]. ❖ A "gobemouche" is "one who believes everything he hears." This word derives from the French gober, "to swallow," and mouche, "a fly." (Howard Richler, English Is Rich in Rare but Useful Words," *Gazette* [Montreal] 3/13/1999.)

(2) gullible (person) *n.*: **gudgeon**. See *sucker*

(3) gullible *adj.*: **ultrafidian** [Latin]. See *credulous*

gulp (as in guzzle) *v.t.*, *v.i.*: **ingurgitate**. See *guzzle*

(2) gulp (down greedily) *v.t.*: **englut**. See *swallow*

gummy (as in sticky) *adj.*: **mucilaginous**. See *sticky*

(2) gummy *adj.*: **glutinous**. See *sticky*

gunfire (directed along a sweeping target) *n.*: **enfilade**. ❖ For more than a year, White and fellow Seattle-area freshman, Randy Tate, have

been subjected to an **enfilade** of ads from the AFL-CIO and other liberal groups that has been continuous, massive, and damaging. (Rich Lowry, "Surviving in Seattle?" *National Review*, 11/11/1996, p. 21.)

gurgle *v.t.*: **plash**. ❖ They burble, they babble, they **plash**.... No matter how you describe the calm-down sound of water trickling over polished stones into a serene pool, Zen-inspired tabletop relaxation fountains—now available just about everywhere—are making a big splash this holiday shopping season. (Don Oldenburg, Focus: "A Cash Niagara from Desktop Waterfalls," *Washington Post*, 12/21/1999.)

gush (as in speak quickly and excitedly) *v.t.*: **burble**. ❖ On Tuesday night, . . . a host of celebrities worshipped at the altar of Michael Flatley, self-anointed Lord of the Dance. By Wednesday, we were down to the more humble disciples but their faith was absolute. "Ooh look: 'Video available October,'" **burbled** the folk behind me excitedly as they devoured their souvenir programme—and they hadn't even seen the show yet. (Louise Levene, "Lord of the Dance—Coliseum, London," *Independent* [London], 7/26/1996.)

(2) gush (as in excessive or contrived sentimentality) *n.*: **bathos**. See *sentimentality*

(3) gush (of emotion, feeling, or action) *n.*: **paroxysm**. See *outburst*

gushiness (as in excessive or contrived sentimentality) *adj.*: **bathetic**. See *sentimental*

gushy (as in overly sentimental) *adj.*: **mawkish**. See *sentimental*

gust (sudden violent . . . of wind) *n.*: **williwaw**. ❖ With the bad weather approaching, Phil and Linda rowed the short distance across to Fallado from where Windora was anchored in a calm spot on the island's western coast. In the time it took to look at the "chart," the sea had become choppy and **williwaws** had begun slamming into the bay from the hilltops above. (Tracy Neal, "Storm Story," *Nelson Mail* [New Zealand], 5/5/2004.)

gutless (as in cowardly) *adj.*: **pusillanimous**. See *cowardly*

(2) gutless (as in cowardly) *adj.*: **retromingent**. See *cowardly*

(3) gutless (condition of being . . . , as in weak-willed) *n.*: **akrasia** [Greek]. See *weak-willed*

guts *n.*: **hardihood**. See *courage*

gutsy (or bold while under the influence of alcohol) *adj.*: **potvaliant**. See *courageous*

guzzle *v.t., v.i.*: **ingurgitate**. ❖ [T]he French cling patriotically to their contrariness, buoyed no doubt by their recent defiance of all Western, Eastern and alternative medicine in being the one country that can laugh at heart disease as its people **ingurgitate** the red wine, triple-cream cheeses and foie gras that kill everyone else. (Jonathan Reynolds, "The Death of French Food," *New York Times*, 7/23/2000.)

gymnastics (club) *n.*: **turnverein** [German]. ❖ [Lou] Gehrig loved all sports: football, baseball, soccer, swimming, ice skating, gymnastics (his father used to take him to the local German **turnverein**, or gym club). (Robert W. Creamer, "Lou Gehrig: The Original Iron Man," *Sports Illustrated*, 9/15/1995, p. 24.)

gyp (as in swindle) *n., v.t.*: **thimblerig**. See *swindle*

gyrating (as in whirling) *adj.*: **vortical**. See *whirling*

habit (or custom) *n.*: **praxis**. See *custom*

habitation (right of use and . . . of property belonging to another) *n.*: **usufruct**. See *use*

habitual (frequenter of a place, esp. a place of entertainment) *n.*: **habitué**. See *regular*

hackneyed (one who utters . . . remarks, as in platitudes) *n.*: **platitudinarian**. See *platitudes*

(2) hackneyed (remark or statement) *n.*: **platitude**. See *cliche*

hag *n.*: **beldam**. ❖ Re: Police say man near airport was practicing satanic ritual, Jan. 17. We see by the papers that a witch has been arrested by police in Tampa, who suspect him of practicing a religion. Mr. Richard Lee Mullins, who is an unusual witch in that he carries no broom and is not the ordinary **beldam** one associates with the faith, has been charged with trespassing on Aviation Authority land. (Earl Irey, letter to the editor, *St. Petersburg [FL] Times*, 1/28/1989.)

(2) hag *n.*: **crone**. ❖ As Magda, the over-tanned **crone** who kisses her dog with a touch too much enthusiasm, Shaye had a central role in the gross-out comedy of 1998 [*There's Something About Mary*]. In one spectacularly tasteless scene, Shaye undresses in front of a window, revealing what appears to be her leather-skinned, over-tanned, sagging and cronish bosom. (Liz Braun, "Shaye It Ain't So: *Mary* Actor Real Ugly Hag at Times," *Ottawa Sun*, 12/24/1998, p. 33.)

haggardly (of or like a . . . old woman) *adj.*: **anile**. See *old woman*

hair (desire to pull out one's . . .) *n.*: **trichotillomania**. ❖ Thank you for printing the letter from the woman whose daughter has **trichotillomania**. I, too, pull my hair out compulsively and didn't even know there was a name for it. (Joseph and Teresa Graedon, "The People's Pharmacy/Does Alcohol Increase Risk of Breast Cancer?" *Newsday*, 6/11/2001.)

(2) hair (having or producing) *adj.*: **piliferous**. ❖ It is "manscaping," the *Queer Eye for the Straight Guy* buzzword that means landscaping the male body. . . . "It's important to have a clean look," said 25-year-old Charlie,

who . . . unfortunately, has a bit of a monkey on his back. As in, it's pretty **piliferous**. So guess what? Instead of embracing his hirsute self, he heads to the salon for a big ol' back wax. (Lauren Falcone, "Hitting the Salons for All the Trimmings: Isn't Just a Girl Thing," *Boston Herald*, 4/8/2004.)

(3) hair (having straight . . .) *adj.*: **lissotrichous**. ❖ Madonna's Blond Ambition tour notwithstanding, women really aspire to be **lissotrichous** brunettes, since sleekness and shine—the season's chief criteria—show much better on dark hair. (Pamela Swanigan, "Blondness: It's Probably Not the Real Thing," *Vancouver Sun*, 6/16/2001).

(4) hair (head of . . .) *n.*: **chevelure**. ❖ [T]he current show has to do with the social and psychological meaning of hair. . . . In one giant image, the lines [of hair] flail like snakes, perhaps on the unseen head of Medusa. The viewer does not turn to stone, but the unruly **chevelure**, unframed and held only by pins, could at any minute break loose. (Henry Lehmann, "Good Hair, Bad Hair Days at the Saidye Bronfman Centre," *Gazette* [Montreal], 3/15/1997.)

(5) hair (of, relating to, or covered with) *adj.*: **capillary**. ❖ Embracing research that fortifies the **capillary** with nutrients like a soy protein known as guar, Erilia offers a range of hair products that nourish the keratin fibers, thereby leaving hair healthier and easier to maintain. (Amy Barone, "Hair Care in Italy: Untapped Potential," *Drug & Cosmetic Industry*, 4/1/1997, p. 12.)

(6) hair (or fur or wool that covers the body of a mammal) *n.*: **pelage**. ❖ [A]s for *Desperate Housewives* star Eva Longoria's penchant for animal **pelage**, PETA [People for the Ethical Treatment of Animals] quipped: "You'd think she'd be more sympathetic to the plight of rabbits considering the way she (bleeps) around like one on Wisteria Lane." (*Boston Herald*, "PETA Bares Fangs at Fur-wearing Waifs," 11/29/2006.)

(7) hair (remove one's own . . . from the head or body) *v.t.*: **auto-depilation**. ❖ A computer could quickly examine all of these graphs, but most people would tear their hair out long before finishing. With the help of a little logic such **auto-depilation** can be avoided. (Bruce Schecter, *My Brain Is Open*, Simon & Schuster [1998], p. 84.)

(8) hair (study of) *n*.: **trichology**. ❖ Philip Kingsley, the man who coined the phrase "bad hair day" back in the 1950s, is celebrating 50 years at the forefront of **trichology**. Kingsley . . . said he has a new project in the works. "I want to fill the huge dearth of proper hair treatment centres in spas and salons," he revealed. (*Cosmetics International*, "Happy Hair Day," 12/14/2007).

(9) hair (covered with . . .) *adj*.: **pilose**. See *hairy*

hair gel (esp. used to groom hair) *n*.: **pomade**. ❖ The anti-frizz product is the hottest hair item of the nineties, and there are literally hundreds to choose from. . . . Dan Sharp, a hairstylist to Marisa Tomei . . . adds a generous amount of **pomade** to sopping-wet hair, then combs it through from root to ends. (Rachael Combe, Beauty Report: "Frizzies, Split Ends, Bad Bangs, Creeping Gray? Hair Masters Reveal 30 Great Fixes for the Trickiest Problems," *InStyle*, 10/1/1998, p. 244.)

hairiness (extreme . . .) *n*.: **hypertrichosis**. ❖ Choices, choices. On one channel: Hidden Lives: It's Not Easy Being a Wolf Boy, a sensitively titled documentary about a young man suffering from **hypertrichosis**. (Thomas Sutcliffe, "Keeping Up Observances," *Independent* [London], 10/4/2005.)

hairless *adj*.: **glabrous**. See *bald*

(2) hairless *n*.: **alopecia**. See *baldness*

hairpiece *n*. **postiche**. ❖ [Photo caption:] Maxine Kroll constructs a classic French twist with two bobby pins and attaches a 10-inch waved **postiche** at the top of the twist. (Paul Glick, "Dramatic Upswing/'Up' Hairdo Upbraids Short Style," *Chicago Sun-Times*, 6/22/1986.)

(2) hairpiece (esp. worn by men in the seventeenth and eighteenth centuries) *n*.: **peruke**. See *wig*

hairstyle (with deep waves made by a curling iron) *n*.: **marcel**. ❖ Style secret: Barnard created thirties-era **marcels** using a curling iron and hairpins. (Joseph V. Amodio, Beauty Report: "Sheared Perfection," *InStyle*, 8/1/2000, p. 194.)

hairy *adj*.: **pilose**. ❖ So, who is this year's hair apparent? According to the Hair Club for Men, a company that knows a thing or two about the importance of a **pilose** head, it's [George W.] Bush—with his fluffier, let's-touch-it-and-see kind of hair. In contrast, Gore's bald spot, or "sandtrap" as some have taken to calling it, almost gleams when lighted from the back. (Saeed Ahmed, "Hair Vote Goes to Bush; Height Favors Gore: Creative Ways to Pick Winner Abound [in 2000 Campaign]," *Atlanta Journal-Constitution*, 11/7/2000.)

halcyon (and carefree time) *adj*.: **prelapsarian**. See *innocent*

half *n*.: **moiety**. See *portion*

half-joking (and half-serious) *adj*.: **jocoserious**. See *semiserious*

half-truth (considered true due to printed repetition) *n*.: **factoid**. See *inaccuracy*

halfway (as in intermediate or transitional state, phase, or condition) *adj*.: **liminal**. See *transitional*

hallucination (as in mirage) *n*.: **fata morgana**. See *mirage*

hallway (spec. the hallway in a stadium that connects the outer concourse to the interior of the stadium itself) *n*.: **vomitory**. See *corridor*

halo *n*.: **aureole**. ❖ There are five versions of Christ on the Sea of Galilee in the Philadelphia show, in two of which Christ's sleeping head is surrounded by an **aureole**. (Arthur C. Danto, Books & the Arts: "Art: The Late Works of Delacroix," *Nation*, 11/9/1998, p. 30.)

halt (as in put an end to) *v.t*.: **quietus** (as in "put the quietus to"). See *termination*

handbag (women's drawstring . . .) *n*.: **reticule**. ❖ But there is an actual **reticule** also associated with Iago. In the opening lines of the play Roderigo says, "I take it much unkindly that thou, Iago, who hast had my purse, as though the strings were thine, shouldst know of this." From the beginning, then, Shakespeare represents Iago as the one who holds the purse strings. (*Studies in the Literary Imagination*, "'Prophetic Fury': Othello and the Economy of Shakespearean Reception," 4/1/1993.)

handbook *n*.: **enchiridion**. ❖ The writer-director, Alan Rudolph, has learned only one thing in the 15 films he has churned out: how to make each worse than the one before. . . . [His movie] *Afterglow* is an **enchiridion** of every known literary and cinematic cliché. (John Simon, "The Sweet Hereafter," *National Review*, 2/9/1998, p. 59.)

(2) handbook (for ready reference like a guidebook) *n*.: **vade mecum**. See *guidebook*

handkerchief *n*.: **mouchoir** [French]. ❖ She is interviewed about her abstinence [and] declares with a **mouchoir** held to her deep tragic eyes that she only drank because her heart broke when Hartley Manners passed away, however she will have a little medicinal triple Scotch if the reporter can get the waiter fast enough because she is so emotionally upset now over the possibility of Hartley's coming to life again. (Tim Page, "Letters by Dawn Powell to Edmund Wilson," *New Criterion*, 9/1/1999.)

handrail (and supports for) *n*.: **balustrade**. ❖ Descending the staircase—its **balustrade** laced with ivy and white orchids—she tossed handfuls of red rose petals from a basket. (Jill Smolowe, "Kilt By Association—Amid Tears, Tiaras and Scottish Tartan, Madonna and Guy Ritchie Baptize Baby Rocco and Tie the Knot, *People*, 1/8/2001, p. 44.)

hands (requiring or using both . . .) *adj*.: **bimanual**. ❖ The **bimanual** examination comes next. In this procedure, the doctor inserts one or two lubricated fingers into your vagina and uses the other hand to press down on your abdomen. This helps detect abnormalities of the internal organs, such as the ovaries and the uterus. (*Good Housekeeping*, "10 Ways to Take Charge of Your Health," 3/1/1995, p. 173.)

handsome (in an unconventional way) *adj*.: **joli laid** (or **joli-laid**). [French, for "pretty-ugly." This term refers to being attractive in an unconventional or unusual way, or more literally, pretty and ugly at the same time. (The feminine form would be "jolie laide." See *pretty*.) It can also be applied to inanimate objects, and can be used as a noun to refer to the person or thing being described. See *man* for an example, since that is the noun most commonly used. Finally, a related (but rare) word meaning the state of being unattractive but sexy at the same time is "cacocallia."] ❖ "[Actor Pete Postlethwaite] is no different from Jack Nicholson. He's no great beauty, but he has great charisma. It's not about classic good looks, but presence," [said one movie producer]. "He's not the sort of person I'd normally find attractive, but on screen it doesn't matter who he's with, you just can't stop looking at him," [said another.] . . . He does possess an uncanny, **joli-laid** screen magnetism. (James Rampton, "Pete Postlethwaite Is a Terrific Actor Who Gives Great Face," *Independent* [London], 12/22/1998.)

(2) handsome (or pretty) *adj*.: **toothsome**. See *sexy*

handwriting (bad . . .) *n*.: **cacography**. ❖ Every young kid suffers through the loop-de-loop of cursive handwriting, a bumpy and sometimes traumatizing ride. By adulthood, though, most people have abandoned the torturous exercise for a slapdash mishmash of printing and script that ranges from barely legible to completely incomprehensible. "We have a national affliction, and it's called **cacography**," . . . says Barbara Getty, handwriting expert. (Lisa Ryckman, "Rewriting Handwriting—Some Say Italic Is the Answer to America's Illegibility, *Denver Rocky Mountain News*, 3/13/2006.)

(2) handwriting (study of . . . , esp. to study character) *n*.: **graphology**. ❖ Because everyone's handwriting, like DNA, is different, and because your loops and squiggles are the windows to your identity, **graphology** is even being used by companies to screen out potential crooks and incompetents. (Nadia Lerner, "Handwriting Reveals Your Soul, Expert Says," *Dallas Morning News*, 2/3/1999.)

handwritten (document entirely . . . by signatory) *n.*: **holograph**. ❖ Abraham Lincoln **holographs** appearing on the auction block these days are likely to be routine memos from the 16th President—a postmaster's appointment or some such. Much rarer is a Lincoln paper in his own hand on a key political issue. (*Time*, Society: "A $50,000 Fragment: Part of Lincoln's Pivotal "House Divided" Speech Will be Auctioned," 8/31/1992, p. 20.)

hanger-on (esp. someone who seeks to associate with or flatter persons of rank or high social status) *n.*: **tuft-hunter**. [Tuft-hunters often flatter those with whom they are trying to curry favor, and, thus, "sycophant," "flatterer," and their synonyms are, in most instances, perfectly proper synonyms for this word. However, to be precise, the essence of the word is in the first instance simply the attempt to associate with those persons, which may well (and in the example given here, does) include acting like a sycophant, but not always.] ❖ [Attorney General Janet] Reno has demonstrated pretty convincingly that she is no fawning courtier who hovers nearby eagerly waiting to clean up the messes that [President Clinton] leaves behind. [S]he possesses the quality that is indispensable in the nation's premier law enforcement officer: integrity. And if her critics attempt to paint her as a pliant **tuft-hunter** trying to ingratiate herself with the man who appointed her, they will disgrace themselves. (Ross Baker, "A Commendable Woman in Unenviable Job," *Los Angeles Times*, 12/8/1997.)

hangout (as in a place one frequents) *n.*: **purlieu**. ❖ The gym of the Holy Family Boxing Club, their former **purlieu**, has been converted into a community center; group photos of young boxers, now scattered or killed, incongruously bedeck the walls. (John Simon, review of *The Boxer*, *National Review*, 3/9/1998, p. 67.)

hangover (remedy) *n.*: **hair of the dog** (or **hair-of-the-dog**). [This phrase refers to the (erroneous) remedy of drinking more alcohol as a cure for a hangover. It is a shortening of the phrase "hair of the dog that bit you," which refers to the (also erroneous) remedy of placing the hair of a rabid dog in the bite wound.] ❖ It was **hair-of-the-dog** time yesterday afternoon, when bleary-eyed survivors of Saturday's White House Correspondents' Dinner dragged into the Willard Hotel for John and Christina McLaughlin's annual VIP brunch. One more chance to schmooze with celebrities and dish about Washington's annual political prom . . . (Roxanne Roberts, Out & About, *Washington Post*, 5/6/2002.)

(2) hangover *n.*: **katzenjammer**. ❖ Peebles, in his rejoinder, compared the intense activity in cosmology over the last few years to "a really good party." But he also listed open questions that, he said, left him with an "uneasy feeling"—a kind of cosmic **katzenjammer**—about whether the concordance will survive new and more precise tests. (James Glanz, "Cosmology: Does Science Know the Vital Statistics of the Cosmos?" *Science*, 11/13/1998.)

(3) hangover (or eating too much) *n.*: **crapulence**. See *indulgence*

hankering (esp. for something one once had but has no more) *n.*: **desiderium**. See *longing*

haphazard *adj.*, *adv.*: **higgledy-piggledy**. ❖ [The Thai city of] Thon Buri remains much as it was in the old days, a **higgledy-piggledy** confusion of cramped urbanity bound together by a maze of canals . . . so bound by canals, in fact, that to explore it, you need never leave the water. (David Yeadon, "Lessons of Life Among the Klongs of Bangkok," *Washington Post*, 1/10/1988.)

(2) haphazard (as in actions taken or statements made which are broader than necessary to hit their target or accomplish their goal) *adj.*, *n.*: **blunderbuss**. See *scattershot*

hapless (perpetually . . . , as in unlucky, person) *n.*: **schlimazel** [Yiddish]. See *unlucky*

happen (as in result) *v.i.*: **eventuate**. See *result*

(2) happen *v.t.*: **betide**. ❖ (*Forbes*, "Whatever **Betides**, Think Stocks," 7/6/1998, p. 282.)

happening (secondary . . . that accompanies or results from another) *n.*: **epiphenomenon** (*adj.*: **epiphenomenal**). See *phenomenon*

happenstance (as in by chance) *adj.:* **adventitious**. See *chance*

happily (to behold) *adv.:* **mirabile visu** [Latin]. See *behold*

(2) happily (to relate) *adv.:* **mirabile dictu** [Latin]. See *wonderful*

happiness *n.:* **eudemonia** (or **eudaemonia**) [based on a concept of Aristotle that the goal of life is happiness, but which is to be achieved through reaching one's full potential, as opposed to through the hedonistic pursuit of pleasure]. ❖ [The] objective is a good life, an Aristotelian **eudemonia**, which embraces a substantial dose of self-interest, but also incorporates concern for others, fulfillment at work, and the respect earned from others by participating in activities, including economic activities, which they value. (John Kay, "Staking a Moral Claim," *New Statesman*, 10/11/1996.)

(2) happiness *n.:* **felicity** (causing or tending to produce . . .) *adj.:* **felicific**. ❖ If the only purpose of a marriage is for two persons to make each other happy, then that marriage is bound to fail. First of all, no one can give happiness as a gift to another, and no couple can experience unending and uninterrupted **felicity**. (Michael Medved, "Skip the Honeymoon, Save Your Marriage," *Washington Times*, 6/9/1996.) ❖ The hedonistic argument that [the poet John] Donne will be found a better **felicific** investment than Agatha Christie is often used dishonestly by teachers, I think. The number of those for whom it is true must be small, and many people read Agatha Christie over and over again with the greatest of pleasure. (A. D. Nuttall, "Why Scholarship Matters," *Wilson Quarterly*, 9/22/2003.)

(3) happiness (as in pleasure) *n.:* **delectation**. See *pleasure*

(4) happiness (delusive or illusory . . .) *n.:* **fool's paradise**. See *illusion*

(5) happiness (from other's misfortunes) *n.:* **schadenfreude** [German]. See *sadism*

(6) happiness (from witnessing other's misfortunes) *n.:* **Roman holiday**. See *sadism*

(7) happiness (solely devoted to the seeking of . . .) *adj.:* **apolaustic**. See *hedonistic*

(8) happiness (spec. someone excessively devoted to luxury or sensual pleasures) *n.:* **voluptuary**. See *hedonist* and *sensualist*

(9) happiness (supreme . . .) *n.:* **beatitude**. See *bliss*

(10) happiness *n.:* **oblectation**. See *pleasure*

(11) happiness *n.:* **weal** (usu. as in "weal or woe" or "weal and woe"). See *well-being*

happy (as in delightful or blissful) *adj.:* **Elysian**. See *blissful*

(2) happy (blissfully . . .) *adj.:* **beatific** (to make . . . *v.t.:* **beatify**). See *joyful*

(3) happy (very . . . , often in a boastful way) *adj.:* **cock-a-hoop**. See *elated*

(4) happy *adj.:* **eupeptic**. See *cheerful*

(5) happy *adj.:* **gladsome**. See *gladness*

(6) happy *adj.:* **riant**. See *cheerful*

happy-go-lucky (behavior) *n.:* **rhathymia**. See *carefree*

happy medium *n.:* **juste milieu** [French]. ❖ [T]here is a sneaking suspicion that maybe the French have got it right, that they have located the **juste milieu**, and that their particular blend of artistic modishness and cultural conservatism, of welfare-statism and intense individualism, of clear-eyed realism and sappy romanticism—that these proportions are wise, time-tested and as indisputable as they are subtle. (Jeff Baker [quoting Edmund White in *The Flâneur*], "Lucky Novelists Wander through Paris, Sydney and Florence," *Sunday Oregonian*, 6/23/2002.)

harangue *n.:* **philippic**. See *tirade*

harass *v.t.:* **chivvy**. See *pester*

(2) harass *v.t.:* **hector**. See *bully*

harassed (as if by a witch or by unfounded fears) *adj.:* **hagridden**. See *tormented*

harden *v.t., adj.:* **indurate**. ❖ Years of adroit propaganda by the religious right have convinced many [in Congress] that a vote for preserving the [National Endowment for the Arts] in any form is a vote for sodomy, blasphemy and child abuse. This has become a matter of **indurated** faith, resistant to any insert of mere fact. (Robert Hughes, The Arts & Media: "Pulling the Fuse on Culture—The Conservatives' All-Out Assault on Federal Funding Is Unenlightened, Uneconomic and Undemocratic," *Time*, 8/7/1995, p. 60.)

(2) harden *v.t.*: **anneal**. See *strengthen*

hardened *adj.*: **sclerotic**. [The noun to which this word relates, sclerosis, refers to the hardening of a body part, such as an artery. The adjective is sometimes used to refer to anything that is rigid or inflexible, including a mindset.] ❖ [In 1941] the Red Army was well equipped, but its **sclerotic** command structures deprived it of flexibility in field conditions. (Catherine Merridale, *Ivan's Army*, Metropolitan Books [2006], p. 103.)

hard-hearted (as in unfeeling, person, as in one who is interested only in cold, hard facts, with little concern for emotion or human needs) *n.*: **Gradgrind**. See *unfeeling*

hardship (period of . . . , sometimes economic) *n.*: **locust years** [coined by British Prime Minister Winston Churchill to refer to the mid-1930s in Britain, after "the years that the locust hath eaten" from the Bible, Joel 2:25]. ❖ The 1850's were the **locust years** for [Ulysses] Grant. The peacetime army assigned him to dull postings far from Julia, where he took to drink. After one bout of intemperance, he was forced to resign his commission. He moved to the Midwest, where he failed at various commercial ventures. "He was too tenderhearted to be a rent collector," Smith notes, "and too candid to sell real estate." (Richard Brookheiser, "Who's Buried in Grant's Tomb?" *New York Times*, 4/22/1991.)

(2) hardship (as in burden) *n.*: **incubus**. See *burden*

(3) hardship (spec. a problem that is difficult for a beginner or one who is inexperienced) *n.*: **pons asinorum** [Latin]. See *problem*

hardworking (appearing . . . only when the boss is watching) *n.*: **eyeservice**. See *work*

(2) hardworking (person) *n.*: **Stakhanovite**. See *workaholic*

hare (of or relating to . . . or rabbit) *adj.*: **leporine** (or **leporid**). See *rabbit*

harem *n.*: **seraglio**. ❖ The title [of the movie *8½ Women*], at least, is precise. A financier, rich and recently widowed, transforms his stately country home into a **seraglio** for eight-point-five mistresses. The fraction is a mute, legless Japanese woman. Cute touch. (Leah Rozen, Picks & Pans: Screen, *People*, 6/12/2000, p. 39.)

harm (portending . . .) *adj.*: **baleful**. See *sinister*

harmful (or dangerous) *adj.*: **noisome**. ❖ The [2000 summer] Olympics that Americans ignored in large numbers . . . was nothing less than sensational. The food in Sydney was fine, the weather mostly fine, the hosts the finest. Even a **noisome** appearance by that menace of modern Olympics, performance-enhancing drugs, couldn't spoil this party. (*Time*, "Field of Dreams: Did Americans Just Sleep Through the Most Dazzling Olympic Games in Decades?" 10/9/2000.)

(2) harmful *adj.*: **nocent**. ❖ [W]ith respect to the disastrous imbalance in trade between the U.S. and the rest of the world, I would urge the administration and Congress to consider alternatives to import limitations. Besides the **nocent** effects on world trade that such limitations would cause, there is the very real threat of imposing exports of capital back to Europe, thus completely upsetting the American capital markets. (John Murphy, "Fighting the Trade Imbalance," *Chicago Tribune*, 10/31/1985.)

(3) harmful *adj.*: **nocuous**. ❖ Since late April, the city's authorities have made four large-scale inspections to crack down on the crimes of making counterfeit and poor quality food. . . . The inspections were aimed at checking for **nocuous** chemicals and heavy-metal additives in food. (Xinhua News Agency [China], "Tianjin Destroys Counterfeit Food," 6/22/2001.)

(4) harmful (atmosphere or influence) *n.*: **miasma**. See *noxious*

(5) harmful (in matters of discrimination between groups) *adj.*: **invidious**. See *discriminatory*

(6) harmful (mutually . . . to both sides) *adj.*: **internecine**. See *destructive*

harmonious (sound) *adj.*: **euphonious** (*n.*: **euphony**). See *melodious*

(2) harmonious (voice or sound) *adj.*: **mellifluous**. See *melodious*

(3) harmonious (voice or sound) *adj.*: **mellisonant**. See *melodious*

(4) harmonious *adj.*: **simpatico**. See *compatible*

harmonizing (a statement . . . conflicting ideas, esp. to make peace) *n.*: **eirenicon**. See *peace offering*

(2) harmonizing (or uniting of opposing viewpoints or beliefs) *adj.*: **syncretic** (or **syncretistic**). See *reconciling*

harmony (in . . .) *adj.*: **consonant**. ❖ "The early work [of photographer Ansel Adams] is more **consonant** with his experience of being in those woods alone; it's quieter and more private. The later work is more public and declamatory," says Szarkowski, director emeritus of the New York Museum of Modern Art's photography department. (Marco R. della Cava, "Ansel Adams at 100 Refocuses Artist's Legacy," *USA Today*, 8/27/2001.)

(2) harmony (in the arrangement of parts with respect to a whole) *n.*: **concinnity**. ❖ [A]n amendment that would absolutely forbid abortions has the same chance an amendment to abolish slavery would have had in 1850. [Senator Dole] knows this [and thus his] contribution to Republican **concinnity** was his idea that the platform should also profess "tolerance" for positions different from the Pro-Life position. (William F. Buckley Jr., "Tolerate Dole?" *National Review*, 7/15/1996, p. 58.)

(3) harmony (concerned with establishing . . . among churches or religions) *adj.*: **ecumenical**. See *churches*

harp on (as in repeating a particular act over and over, often after initial stimulus has ceased) *n.*: **perseveration** (*v.i.*: **perseverate**). See *repeating*

harsh (as in . . . remarks) *adj.*: **astringent**. ❖ [S]ome of his most **astringent** remarks are directed at figures such as Ronald Reagan, whose "macho talk around the White

House" concerning aid to the Nicaraguan contras prompts Jacobs to observe: "President Reagan, though sometimes confused about it, spent World War II in California making training films for the government and regular ones (with pretty ladies) for himself." (Scott Sherman, Politics, *Washington Post*, 11/21/1999.)

(2) harsh (as in rough) *adj.*: **scabrous**. See *rough*

(3) harsh (as in sharp or bitter to taste or smell) *adj.*: **acrid**. See *pungent*

(4) harsh (of a sound or noise that is . . . , grating, shrill, or otherwise unpleasant) *adj.*: **stridulous**. See *grating*

(5) harsh (on the ears) *adj.*: **scrannel**. See *cacophonous*

harshness *n.*: **asperity**. See *acrimony*

haste *n.*: **celerity**. See *speed*

hasty *adj.*: **festinate**. ❖ In October 1997, Eric Schmidt told us he was giving himself two to three years to turn Novell around. . . . Even [Novell's] successes like GroupWise, ManageWise and ZENworks are vestiges of 1990s thinking. They may halt a **festinate** death, but you don't build a company around them. (Fritz Nelson, "Faith or Wraith?" *Network Computing*, 8/21/2000.)

(2) hasty (as in impetuous) *adj.*: **gadarene**. See *impetuous*

(3) hasty (as in sudden, or unexpected) *adj.*: **subitaneous**. See *sudden*

hat (bell-shaped woman's . . .) *n.*: **cloche**. ❖ **Cloche** hats, named after the French word for "bell" because of their distinctive shape, have become a staple this season for women who want to shut out unpleasant weather or unwanted stares. (Julie K. L. Dam, Style Watch: "Cloche Encounters," *People*, 3/29/1999, p. 127.)

hate *v.t.*: **execrate**. ❖ [June O'Leary states:] "I **execrate** and loathe the way TV stations speed up and obliterate the credits and cast list at the end of movies or previews." (George Gamestar, "Cell Phone Abusers Belong in a Cell," *Toronto Star*, 11/11/96.)

(2) hate *v.t.*: **misprize**. ❖ Like jaded millionaires, we [Floridians] see all our water wealth as a damnable nuisance. Cloudbursts slow our suntans, cut short our golf games, ruin our picnics, rot our citrus crops, back up our drains, mildew our bathroom tiles and spawn algae in our swimming pools. We cannot wait for the rain to stop. We **misprize** every drop. . . . Then, once the water is gone [we want it back], for showers, dishwashers, Jacuzzis and miniature golf waterfalls. (Michael Browning, "Whatever Happened to Florida's Water?" *Miami Herald*, 5/24/1998.)

(3) hate (as in treat with contempt) *v.t.*: **contemn**. See *scorn*

(4) hate (person who has . . . for reason and logic) *n.*: **misologist**. See *closed-minded*

hateful (as in despicable, or treacherous) *adj.*: **reptilian**. See *despicable*

(2) hateful (one who is . . .) *n.*: **tricoteuse**. See *knitter* [See the note at "knitter" for why this word can be synonymous with hateful.]

(3) hateful *adj.*: **ugsome**. See *loathsome*

hatred (man who feels . . . toward women) *n.*: **misogynist**. ❖ Q [to the author]: In your novel *Less Than Zero*, a 12-year-old girl is raped. In *The Rules of Attraction*, a college girl has a violent sexual experience. Do you see yourself as a completely demented **misogynist**? A. Yes. Yes I am. I am a completely demented **misogynist**. (Roger Friedman, "Bret Speaks," *Entertainment Weekly*, 3/8/1991, p. 33.)

(2) hatred (of children) *n.*: **misopedia**. ❖ [T]he subject of the meeting—to ensure that America's 15 million young people have access to resources "that can help them lead healthy, fulfilling and productive lives"—might not appeal to [W. C.] Fields, who was infamous for his . . . **misopedia** (as in, "Children should neither be seen nor heard from—ever again"). (*Minneapolis Star Tribune*, "Volunteering/Do It for Your Own Sake, Too," 4/16/1997.)

(3) hatred (of men) *n.*: **misandry** (one who hates men *n.*: **misandrist**.). ❖ I was shocked and horrified by your cover story, not only because of the recent rash of wife and child murders, but also by the strong suggestion that

it is in the biological nature of males to be violent and abusive. . . . I suppose we can now expect another wave of **misandry** in this country such as the one that followed the Montreal Massacre by Marc Lépine. (*Maclean's*, unsigned letter to the editor, 8/28/2000, p. 4.)

(4) hatred (person who feels . . . toward all people) *n.*: **misanthrope**. ❖ Thomas Bernhard—dramatist, novelist, warped genius and **misanthrope**—despised his fellow Austrians with such ferocious thoroughness that, when he died of a heart attack in 1989, he left a will expressly forbidding the performance of any of his plays there. (Paul Taylor, "Fear and Loathing," *Independent* [London], 8/20/1997.)

(5) hatred (towards an enemy) *n.*: **enmity**. ❖ Dr. Baruch Goldstein was so blinded by **enmity** toward Arabs as to seem "batty" even to some of his fellow ultranationalist, fervently religious neighbors in the Jewish settlement of Kiryat Arba, near Hebron in the West Bank. (George J. Church, Middle East, *Time* International, 3/7/1994, p. 16.)

(6) hatred (and ill-will that occurs when disputes about religion arise) *n.*: **odium theologicum**. See *intolerance*

(7) hatred (develop a . . . for) *n.*: **scunner** (esp. as in "take a scunner") [British]. See *dislike*

haughty (or arrogant) *adj.*: **fastuous**. Sunday's *Journal* [stated:] "When the hostages had been released and their alleged captor arrested, a regal-looking Hillary Rodham Clinton strolled out of her Washington home, the picture of calm in the face of crisis." I submit that Hillary wouldn't appear regal were she wearing a diamond tiara on her head and sporting an orb and scepter. Haughty or **fastuous**, perhaps, but never regal. (F. D. Petree, letter to the editor, journal-news.net/page/content.detail/id/501648.html?nav=5061, 12/11/2007.)

(2) haughty *adj.*: **orgulous**. ❖ Long may Gill and Michael Winner . . . prosecute their quest to deride and deflate the **orgulous** arrogance of that most pretentious, patronising and pompous person—The Celebrity (sic) Cook.

(Ian Liversedge, "Gill Gets Kebabed," *Sunday Times* [London], 10/25/1998.)

(3) haughty *adj.*: **toplofty**. ❖ This absence of emotional engagement [in the memoir *Burning the Days*, by James Salter] is paired with an exceedingly **toplofty** manner that does not wear well. Critics have praised Salter's chiseled sentences, but one often wishes he would pick up a more prosaic instrument. . . . At its worst, in an embarrassingly gushy section on Irwin Shaw, his style devolves into a sort of advertising copy for a way of life you'll never afford. (Gerald Howard, "Burning the Days: Recollection," *Nation*, 10/6/1997.)

(4) haughty (as in condescending) *adj.*, *adv.*: **de haut en bas** [French]. See *condescending*

(5) haughty (as in pedantic) *adj.*: **donnish**. See *pedantic*

(6) haughty *adj.*: **hoity-toity**. See *pompous*

haunt (as in place one frequents) *n.*: **purlieu**. See *hangout*

haunted (as if by a witch or by unfounded fears) *adj.*: **hagridden**. See *tormented*

hawk (with long tail) *n.*: **accipiter**. ❖ An **accipiter**, the Cooper's [hawk]'s short, powerful, rounded wings and long tail are designed for quick pursuit of medium-sized forest mammals and birds. (George Harrison, "A Raptor's Return: The Increasingly Common Cooper's Hawk Is No Chicken," *Sports Afield*, 11/1/1997, p. 28.)

hawker (esp. who sells quack medicines) *n.*: **mountebank**. See *huckster*

haze (over one's vision) *v.t.*: **obnubilate**. See *obscure*

hazy (as in a failure to perceive something clearly or accurately, or not being based on clear observation or analysis as a result of being cross-eyed, literally or figuratively) *adj.*: **strabismic**. See *cross-eyed*

head (abnormally small . . .) *n.*: **microcephaly**. ❖ Other parents, though, feel certain that the Gulf War somehow left their children deformed. One-year-old Amanda Miedona of Chicago Ridge, Ill., suffers from **microcephaly**. Her head, which measures about 12 1/4 inches in circumference, is about one-third smaller than normal. (Richard Jerome, "An Enemy Within—Gulf War Vets Face a Medical Mystery: The Birth Defects Threatening Many of Their Children," *People*, 1/30/1995, p. 32.)

(2) head (back of the . . .) *n.*: **occiput**. ❖ All you have to do is watch TV commercials to know that real people have headaches. Real people are intimate with Excedrin, Tylenol, Advil, Aleve and Alka-Seltzer. Real people have felt that jackhammer in the temples, the stiletto stab in the **occiput**. (Mary Schmich, "Headache-Free People Are Alien Even to the Pros," *Chicago Tribune*, 9/12/2003.)

(3) head (of, relating to, located on, in, or near) *adj.*: **cephalic**. ❖ The British in 1901 decided that Hafeez's forefathers fit into the category of Arab or Pathan conquerors, not local converts. They reached the conclusion by applying the **cephalic** index: measuring the proportion of the breadth of the head to its length, as well as of the breadth of the nose to its length. (Parthasarathi Swami, "Serving God and Mammon—India's Religious Crisis Has More to Do with Economics Than Faith," *Time International*, 2/15/1999, p. 19.)

(4) head (as in commander) *n.*: **imperator**. See *commander*

(5) head (as in ruler, of the universe) *n.*: **kosmokrator** [Greek]. See *ruler*

(6) head (male . . . of a household) *n.*: **paterfamilias**. See *head of household*

(7) head (of a group, esp. one who is overbearing or domineering) *n.*: **cock of the walk**. See *leader*

(8) head (of a party, school of thought, or group of persons) *n.*: **coryphaeus**. See *leader*

(9) head (study of shape of) *n.*: **phrenology**. See *skull*

(10) head (as in leader) *n.*: **bell cow**. See *leader*

headache (as in migraine) *n.*: **megrims** (pl. of **megrim**). ❖ Barich ages another 25 years and his marriage takes sick, as the state suffers severe economic **megrims** and rattles with real earthquakes, not toy ones, and realists among its population head for Oregon, where

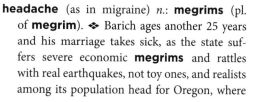

they are cordially requested to go away. (John Skow, Arts & Media/Books: "Lotus Land No More," *Time*, 7/4/1994, p. 74.)

(2) headache (as in hangover) *n.*: **katzenjammer**. See *hangover*

(3) headache (as in trouble) *n.*: **tsuris** [Yiddish]. See *trouble*

head-in-the-sand (as in complacent person who ignores any unpleasant facts) *n.*: **Podsnap** (*adj.*: **Podsnappian**). See *ostrich*

headless *n.*: **acephalous** [lit. without a head, but often used in the sense of leaderless]. See *leaderless*

headlong (as in at top speed) *adv.*: **tantivy**. See *top speed*

(2) headlong (as in impetuous) *adj.*: **gadarene**. See *impetuous*

(3) headlong (as in rash or impetuous person) *n.*: **Hotspur**. See *impetuous*

(4) headlong *adv.*: **pell-mell**. See *disorderly*

head of household (female . . .) *n.*: **materfamilias** [Latin]. ❖ As one physician noted in 1884: The time has passed when paterfamilias can complacently congratulate himself upon having disinfected his house with a bottle of carbolic acid, which he has brought in his vest pocket from the corner drug store. Indeed, it was now time for **materfamilias** to take charge. The democratization of the indoor toilet brought the responsibility of scrubbing the bowls to ever greater numbers of women. (Janet Golden, "Germ Warfare," *Women's Review of Books*, 10/1/1998, p. 9.)

(2) head of household (male . . .) *n.*: **paterfamilias** [Latin]. ❖ Another traveling companion remembered the Rockefellers sitting at a private dining room in a Roman hotel as the **paterfamilias** [John D. Rockefeller] dissected the weekly bill, trying to ascertain whether they had really consumed two whole chickens, as these slippery foreigners alleged. (Ron Chernow, *Titan*, Random House [1998], p. 236.)

head of state (acting either as a representative or under the dominion and control of a foreign power) *n.*: **satrap**. See *ruler*

headstrong (as in one who clings to an opinion or belief even after being shown that it is wrong) *n.*: **mumpsimus**. See *stubborn*

(2) headstrong (as in practice of refusing to consider a change in one's beliefs or opinions, esp. in politics) *n.*: **standpatism**. See *stubbornness*

(3) headstrong (as in stubborn) *adj.*: **pervicacious**. See *stubborn*

(4) headstrong (in holding to a belief or opinion) *adj.*: **pertinacious**. See *stubborn*

(5) headstrong *adj.*: **contumacious**. See *obstinate*

healing (of or relating to medicine or the art of . . .) *adj.*: **Aesculapian** [after Aesculapius, the Greco-Roman god of medicine]. Professor Andrew announced . . . that, once, all that stood between me and a career in medicine was him. . . . [T]o present himself as the sole bastion of decency and good sense between me and a subsequent epidemic of slaughtered, maimed, molested patients, malpractice suits, strikings . . . is disingenuous. Firstly, there were other reasons for my stepping off the **Aesculapian** path. Indolence, for one. (Michael Bywater, The Lost World of Michael Bywater—With an Arse Like This, Who Needs Elbows?" *Independent* [London], 3/18/2001.)

(2) healing (used often of a medicinal treatment) *adj.*: **balsamic**. See *soothing*

health (as in condition) *n.*: **fettle**. See *condition*

healthful (as in having the power to cure or heal) *adj.*: **sanative**. ❖ Americans sometimes think the benefits from this relationship flow only one direction—toward Tokyo. But that's short-sighted. [T]he challenge Japanese economic strength poses may turn out to be more **sanative** than harmful. The Japanese example has helped force issues like the low American savings rate to the fore. Japanese management theories have sparked useful reform in American industry. (*Christian Science Monitor*, "Ties to Tokyo," 10/31/1989.)

heap *n.*: **cumulus**. ❖ Oceanaire is the only restaurant I've been to where a waiter has volunteered to "break down" my Key lime pie (hidden under a **cumulus** of whipped cream, the wedge is served with a steak knife). (Tom Sietsema, "Big Fish; Bigger Fish," *Washington Post*, 11/19/2000.)

(2) heap (confused or jumbled . . .) *n.*: **agglomeration**. See *jumble*

hearing (of or pertaining to sense of . . .) *adj.*: **auricular**. ❖ **Auricularly**, after thirty, you gradually lose sensitivity to high-frequency noises as sound-receptor cells in the inner ear decrease. (Michael Segell, "How Your Body Ages," *Cosmopolitan*, 4/1/1994, p. 172.)

(2) hearing (act of . . . , often with a stethoscope) *n.*: **auscultation**. See *listening*

hearsay (as in paraphrase) *n.*: **oratio obliqua** [Latin for "indirect speech"]. See *paraphrase*

heart (by . . .) *adv.*: **memoriter**. See *memory*

(2) heart (of a matter, as in the essence) *n.*: **quiddity**. See *essence*

(3) heart (the . . . of a matter, as in the bottom line, the main point, the essence, etc.) *n.*: **tachlis** (esp. as in "talk tachlis") [Yiddish]. See *essence*

heartbeat (abnormally slow . . .) *n.*: **bradycardia**. ❖ Arrhythmias may develop because of abnormalities in how impulses are conducted. Delays in the spreading of impulses can occur anywhere in the conduction system. When the transmission of impulses is blocked intermittently or completely, **bradycardia** may result. (*USA Today Magazine*, "Arrhythmias," 2/1/1997.)

heartbroken *adj.*: **heartsore**. ❖ "You don't want to be a burden to your children, do you?" This is the coup de grace [of the funeral preplanner]. . . . I see them now—my darling sons, my fierce daughter—**heartsore** and vulnerable at the news of my untimely and possibly heroic death. I think of them with their cell phones and gold cards and higher educations and inheritance. And it occurs to me: why shouldn't I be a burden to my children? My children have been a burden to me. (Thomas Lynch, "Calling the Undertaker," *Newsweek*, 12/14/1998.)

hearten (as in encourage) *v.t.*: **inspirit**. See *encourage*

heartless (as in cruel) *adj.*: **fell** (*n.*: **fellness**). See *cruel*

(2) heartless (as in unfeeling, person, as in one who is interested only in cold, hard facts, with little concern for emotion or human needs) *n.*: **Gradgrind**. See *unfeeling*

heat (-releasing) *adj.*: **exothermic**. ❖ Washington is by nature **exothermic**. Let us take you to the hot zones. You want hot? Fine. Try stem cells. See if that heats ya up. Stem cell research is the hottest science going. It's so hot, President Bush interrupted his month-long vacation in Texas (where, we might note, it's hot) on Thursday night to tell the nation his policy on stem cell funding. (Frank Ahrens, "Sizzling City; Even When the Temperature Cools, You Can Feel the Heat," *Washington Post*, 8/11/2001.)

(2) heat (subject person or thing to intense . . . , often to create sweat) *v.t.*: **parboil**. ❖ He also dreamed up a particularly foul-smelling recipe for self-**parboiling** that required [jockeys] to steep for up to 35 minutes . . . in piping-hot water mixed with 3 to 5 pounds of Epsom salts, one quart white vinegar, 2 ounces of household ammonia and a mystery lather he called Hawley's cream. (Laura Hillenbrand, *Seabiscuit*, Random House [2001], p. 68.)

(3) heat (as in of or relating to dog days of summer) *adj.*: **canicular**. See *dog days*

heave (as in making an effort to vomit) *v.i.*: **keck**. See *vomit*

heaven *n.*: **Abraham's bosom**. ❖ An exception to this rule is his chilling parable of Lazarus and Dives: The rich master, consigned to hell, lifts up his eyes to the beggar, who has been "carried by angels into **Abraham's bosom**," requesting that Lazarus dip a finger in some water to cool him. (David Van Biema, Religion: "Does Heaven Exist? It Used to Be That the Hereafter Was Virtually Palpable, but American Religion Now Seems Almost Allergic to Imagining It," *Time*, 3/241997, p. 70.)

(2) heaven (highest reaches of . . .) *n.*: **empyrean**. ❖ The celestial being who would become Satan had many names in heaven. Most of Western tradition identifies him as Lucifer, the Morning Star, the most brilliant of all the denizens of the **empyrean**. (Howard Chua-Eoan, "Angels Among Us," *Time*, 12/27/1993.)

(3) heaven (as in paradise) *n.*: **Xanadu**. See *paradise*

(4) heaven (spec. a place of fabulous wealth or opportunity) *n.*: **El Dorado**. See *paradise*

(5) heaven (as in place of extreme luxury and ease where physical comforts and pleasures are always at hand) *n.*: **Cockaigne**. See *paradise*

heavenly (as in celestial) *adj.*: **ethereal**. ❖ Anyone who has ever wondered what a heavenly chorus might sound like need only listen to the opening track, "Love Letters from Old Mexico," on this performing debut by one of Nashville's most successful songwriters. On that lovely tune, Emmylou Harris and Alison Krauss provide backing vocals, helping [Leslie] Satcher create an angelic, **ethereal** sound. (Nick Charles, Song, *People*, 4/16/2001, p. 41.)

(2) heavenly (as in angelic) *adj.*: **seraphic**. See *angelic*

(3) heavenly (as in of or related to the sky or heavens) *adj.*: **empyreal**. See *celestial*

(4) heavenly (as in of or related to the sky or heavens) *adj.*: **supernal**. See *celestial*

(5) heavenly (spec. having the characteristics of a mythical romantic place) *adj.*: **Ruritanian**. See *paradise*

heavens (the . . .) *n.*: **welkin**. ❖ Liza Gennaro's choreography is entry-level but diverting, Bruce Coughlin's deft orchestrations make the **welkin** ring. (Stefan Kanfer, review of *Once Upon a Mattress* [Broadhurst Theater, New York], *New Leader*, 1/13/1997, p. 22.)

heavy (as in state of being overweight) *n.*: **avoirdupois**. See *weight*

(2) heavy (as in beer-bellied) *adj.*: **abdominous**. See *beer-bellied*

(3) heavy (as in fat) *adj.*: **adipose**. See *fat*

(4) heavy (as in fat) *adj.*: **pursy**. See *fat*

(5) heavy (as in overweight, and squat) *adj.*: **fubsy**. See *squat*

(6) heavy (as in paunchy) *adj.*: **stomachy**. See *paunchy*

(7) heavy (person, esp. with a large abdomen) *n.*: **endomorph** (*adj.*: **endomorphic**). See *pot-bellied*

(8) heavy *adj.*: **Pickwickian**. See *fat*

hedge (as in avoid a straight answer) *v.t.*: **tergiversate**. See *evade*

hedonist (as in lazy person devoted to seeking pleasure and luxury) *n.*: **lotus-eater** [derives from the Lotophagi, a group of people described in Homer's *Odyssey* who eat lotuses and live in a state of lazy contentment]. ❖ All the ingredients are here: the innocent/not-so-innocent celebration of sensual pleasure; the mix of locals with wannabe locals from Europe and Latin America [and the] sense that just about any law can be ignored or manipulated. The South Beach cocktail. I've been here for less than 24 hours and part of me is already seduced, like a **lotus-eater**, by the manifold pleasures of this place. (Don George, Travel Essay: "South Beach's Manifold Pleasures," *Newsday*, 1/26/2001.)

(2) hedonist (spec. someone excessively devoted to luxury or sensual pleasures) *n.*: **voluptuary**. [See also *sensualist*.] ❖ [Marlon Brando] was an enormously self-indulgent man. I mean, he famously slept with many, many, many, many women. You know, he bought an island. He was—you know, I always pictured him as this sort of Gauguin-like **voluptuary** who sat on a hammock in his island, you know, consuming, you know, not a piece of pie, but whole pies at a time, you know? (David Edelstein, "Life and Death of Marlon Brando," NPR Special, 7/2/2004.)

(3) hedonist (as in man about town) *n.*: **boulevardier**. See *man about town*

hedonistic *adj.*: **apolaustic**. ❖ Turn to the theatre advertisements in this paper and you enter a parallel world of terminal ecstasy suggested by the critics' quotes. "Sheer, unadulterated joy," cries the *Daily Express* of *The Producers*. . . . "Heart-wrenching perfection," gasps *The Telegraph*. . . . Such remarks spring from an ancient tradition of **apolaustic** reviews. Harold Hobson [blamed Bernard Levin] for praising Camelot "in terms that would have been extravagant for the Resurrection." (Nicholas De Jongh, "Ecstasy! Heaven! Critics Should Stop Gushing," *Evening Standard* [London], 6/3/2005.)

(2) hedonistic *adj.*, *n.*: **libertine**. See *promiscuous*

heed (as in attention) *n.*: **advertence**. See *attention*

heedless (as in impetuous) *adj.*: **gadarene**. See *impetuous*

(2) heedless (as in rash or impetuous person) *n.*: **Hotspur**. See *impetuous*

(3) heedless (as in reckless) *adj.*: **temerarious**. See *reckless*

(4) heedless *adj.*: **harum-scarum**. See *reckless*

height (as in "the . . . of") *n.*: **apogee**. ❖ Is animation a market that will always expand? Or was the Simba spectacular [Disney's *The Lion King*] the **apogee** of a trend? Or a glorious fluke? (Richard Corliss, "There's Tumult in Toon Town—For 60 Years, the Animated Feature Was a Disney Monopoly; Now Rival Studios Are Muscling In, Led by Fox with a Winsome Anastasia," *Time*, 11/17/1997, p. 88.)

(2) height (as in highest point that can be attained or the ultimate degree, as of a condition or quality) *n.*: **ne plus ultra**. See *ultimate*

(3) height (fear of . . .) *n.*: **acrophobia**. See *fear*

(4) height (the . . . , lit. the greatest or highest good) *n.*: **summum bonum** [Latin]. See *ideal*

(5) height (as in climax, of a drama) *n.*: **catastatis**. See *climax*

heights (the . . . , as in the pinnacle) *n.*: **Parnassus**. See *pinnacle*

heir (as in inheritor) *n.*: **heritor**. See *inheritor*

hell (as in opposite of utopia) *n.*: **dystopia**. ❖ In this optimistic season, two thoughtful writers warn that we are stumbling toward **dystopia**. . . . In this **dystopia**, the affluent would most likely live as they do in Latin America—behind walls topped with shards of glass and with riflemen patrolling their lawns. And the great mass of people would live as many of our

poorest citizens do today—in a society where violent males kill other men and abuse women. (Michael Barone, "Slouching Toward Dystopia," *U.S. News & World Report*, 12/20/1993.)

(2) hell (as in place or occasion of great suffering) *n.*: **Gethsemane** [derived from garden east of Jerusalem on the Mount of Olives where Jesus was arrested]. ❖ The Japanese suffered most, of course [at Okinawa in 1945]. About 76,000 perished, as did 24,000 Okinawan conscripts. But the GIs and Marines lost 7,631 killed . . . and 39,000 wounded. . . . For all the gore, the Japanese saw dead GIs and Marines as a mere bonus. Their true target was the American fleet—and off Okinawa, the United States Navy would endure its own **Gethsemane**. (Harry Levins, "Hell and Glory in the Pacific—Japanese Exact Bloody Toll in Fierce Battles for Iwo Jima and Okinawa," *St. Louis Post-Dispatch*, 2/19/1995.)

(3) hell (as in place or occasion of great suffering) *n.*: **Golgotha** [derives from hill near Jerusalem where Jesus was crucified]. ❖ Auschwitz is a place that was once described as "having scared God," and which Pope John Paul has called "the **Golgotha** of our century." (Stephen C. Feinstein, "A Chilling Story of Extreme Manifestation of Evil/Brilliant Work Puts Auschwitz into Context of Romanticism, Political Defeat, Racism That Led to Resettlement, Genocide," *Minneapolis Star Tribune*, 2/9/1997.)

(4) hell *n.*: **Gehenna**. ❖ There has been little pretense in [Russian President] Boris Yeltsin's war against the Chechens. . . . "We have been told to fire and fire again. There are no other choices," said a brigade commander. Grozny was a free-fire zone. For the moment, however, the tides of war may have shifted. Hundreds of Russian soldiers have been killed, trapped in the **Gehenna** of their burning tanks. (*New Republic*, "The Chechen Adventure," 1/23/1995, p. 7.)

(5) hell (as in damnation, as in loss of the soul) *n.*: **perdition**. See *damnation*

hellish *adj.*: **stygian** (sometimes cap.). ❖ Meanwhile, older and older fossils have all but proved that life did not evolve at the leisurely pace Darwin envisioned. Perhaps most intriguing of all, the discovery of organisms living in oceanic hot springs has provided a **Stygian** alternative to Darwin's peaceful picture. Life . . . may not have formed in a nice, warm pond, but in "a hot pressure cooker." (Madeleine Nash, Science: "How Did Life Begin? In Bubbles? On Comets? Along Ocean Vents? Scientists Find Some Surprising Answers to the Greatest Mystery on Earth," *Time*, 10/11/1993, p. 68.)

(2) hellish *adj.*: **sulfurous** (or **sulphurous**). See *infernal*

helper (as in aide or assistant) *n.*: **factotum**. See *assistant*

(2) helper (as in assistant, esp. to a scholar or magician) *n.*: **famulus**. See *assistant*

(3) helper (who is loyal and unquestioning) *n.*: **myrmidon**. See *assistant*

(4) helper *n.*: **adjutant**. See *assistant*

helpless (when born) *adj.*: **altricial**. ❖ Those bare-naked, helpless-type babies, and they include all the songbirds, are **altricial**. The other kind—ducks, geese, Easter chicks, killdeers and so on—are precocial. Think of "precocious." It is as if human children arrived asking to borrow the car. (Joey Slinger, "Birding for Cynics" [excerpts from *Down & Dirty Birding*, by Joey Slinger], *Maclean's*, 5/20/1996, p. 58.)

(2) helpless (as in powerless) *adj.*: **impuissant**. See *powerless*

(3) helpless (as in vulnerable, person or thing): *n.*: **clay pigeon**. See *vulnerable*

helpmate *n.*: **helpmeet**. [It would be difficult not to list *helpmate* as the closest synonym to *helpmeet*, and in fact a helpmeet can be male or female. However, the word is frequently used as a synonym for *wife*, and specifically a traditional wife who may, for example, stay at home and raise the children, as in the example used here]. ❖ Maureen Dowd writes that "[presidential candidate Howard Dean's wife] Judith Steinberg has shunned the role of **helpmeet**." Reporters who itch to ride campaign roller coasters do not approve that a spouse would

prefer to keep the home fires burning and tend her own business. (Annlinn Grossman, letter to the editor, *New York Times*, 1/16/2004.)

helter-skelter *adv.*: **pell-mell**. See *disorderly*

henchman *n.*: **satrap**. [This word has various definitions, including (1) a leader or ruler generally (see *leader*), (2) a prominent or notable person generally (see *bigwig*), (3) a henchman, (4) a bureaucrat (see *bureaucrat*), and (5) the head of a state acting either as a representative or under the dominion and control of a foreign power (see *ruler*). This is an example of the third definition.] ❖ [M]any of the killings [of ex-Baathists loyal to Saddam Hussein] are being carried out systematically—and with the same cruelty Saddam's own henchmen once used against the regime's opponents. . . . [T]he Western authorities in Baghdad have shown no concern about the murders. It is, of course, hard to show pity for **satraps** of the former regime whose own victims are still being dug up in their thousands from the mass graves of southern Iraq. (Robert Fisk, "Hooded Men Executing Saddam Officials," www.derechos.org/nizkor/iraq/doc/saddam3.html, 12/28/2003.)

Herculean (task, esp. of cleaning up or remedying bad situations) *n.*: **Augean task** [after Augeas, a legendary Greek king who did not clean out his stable for thirty years, until it was cleaned by Hercules]. ❖ Gorbachev came to realize several years ago that the apparatus of Soviet power both at home and abroad was expensive, wasteful, cumbersome, distracting and provocative. . . . All those missiles in their silos, all those troops in foreign lands, all those rubles and cheap oil flowing to Cuba, represented resources that he desperately needed for the **Augean task** of cleaning up the mess that stretches from Vilnius to Vladivostok. (Strobe Talbott, "Goodfellas: How Mikhail Gorbachev and George Bush Developed One of the Most Extraordinary Yet Subtle Collaborations in History," *Time*, 8/5/1991.)

herediatary (as in innate) *adj.*: **ingenerate**. See *innate*

heretic (orig. Catholics who did not follow the Church of England) *n.*: **recusant**. See *dissenter*

hermit (as in recluse, esp. for religious reasons) *n.*: **anchorite**. See *recluse*

(2) hermit (as in recluse, esp. for religious reasons) *n.*: **eremite**. See *recluse*

heroic (task, esp. of cleaning up or remedying bad situations) *n.*: **Augean task**. See *Herculean*

hesitancy (as in chronic inability to make decisions) *n.*: **abulia** (also spelled **aboulia**). See *indecisiveness*

(2) hesitancy (as in the dilemma of being given a choice between two equally appealing alternatives and thus being able to choose neither one) *n.*: **Buridan's ass**. See *paralysis*

(3) hesitancy (as in unwillingness) *n.*: **nolition**. See *unwillingness*

hesitant (and timid and cautious) *adj.*: **Prufrockian**. See *timid*

(2) hesitant (as in spineless or indecisive, or such a person) *adj.*, *n.*: **namby-pamby**. See *spineless*

hesitate (as in vacillate) *v.i.*: **shilly-shally**. See *vacillate* and *procrastinate*

(2) hesitate (to act due to indecision) *v.i.*: **dither**. See *procrastinate*

hesitation (words such as *um, uh, you know,* etc.) *n.*: **embolalia** (or **embololalia**). See *stammering*

hex (as in put a . . . upon) *v.t.*: **imprecate**. See *curse*

(2) hex *n.*: **malediction**. See *curse*

hibernate (in the summertime, esp. used of animals) *v.t.*: **aestivate** (or **estivate**). ❖ Snails are remarkable in that they are extremely resistant to climatic conditions. They can hibernate, that is become dormant in winter. . . . They can also **estivate** in summer, sealing themselves in their shells with a sort of glue that keeps their vital fluids inside, and only wakening when the rains come and the moisture dissolves their gluey seal. (D'vora Ben Shaul, "Creatures Close to the Ground," *Jerusalem Post*, 8/11/1995.)

hibernating (as in dormant or motionless) *adj.*: **torpid**. See *lethargic*

hickey *n.*: **passion purpura**. ❖ Delivering or submitting to a **passion purpura** . . . lets you live out your vampire fantasies after catching a particularly saucy episode of Buffy. And if you're on the receiving end of someone's suction cup, the hickey serves as a happy, albeit surprising, reminder of what you got up to the night before. (Emma Taylor, "Sex Myths: Love Bites Are for 14-Year-Olds," *Guardian* [London], 5/24/2003.)

hidden *adj.*: **delitescent**. ❖ [The TV hostess, Marla] had just begun to chat it up with Brevard Commissioner Sue Schmitt. Well, sort of. . . . Commissioner Sue was nowhere to be seen. Not on my screen anyway. [Marla] was looking off toward someone or some mystery thing the rest of us could not see. . . . The hostess kept referring to this **delitescent** entity as "Sue" or "Commissioner." I tell you, it was eerie. (Allen Rose, "Unseen TV Guest Pulls Off Interview," *Orlando Sentinel*, 1/15/1994.)

(2) hidden (as in state of being . . . from view, lost to notice, or concealed) *n.*: **occultation**. See *disappearance*

hiding (as in lying in wait for prey, often used of insects) *adj.*: **lochetic**. See *ambushing*

(2) hiding (as in, in concealment) *adv.*: **doggo** (esp. as in "lying doggo"; slang). See *concealment*

(3) hiding (deliberate . . . or misrepresentation of facts to gain an advantage) *n.*: **subreption**. See *misrepresentation*

(4) hiding (social . . .) *n.*: **purdah**. See *seclusion*

(5) hiding *n.*: **hugger-mugger**. See *secrecy*

hiding place (esp. for valuables or goods) *n.*: **cache**. ❖ Days after a Freemen militia sympathizer was seriously injured in an explosion at his home, a powerful **cache** of explosives was seized at the motor home of two of his associates. (Associated Press, "Friends of Injured Freemen Sympathizer Are Arrested; Cache of Explosives Found," as printed in *Denver Rocky Mountain News*, 5/2/1997.)

highbrow (as in haughty or condescending) *adj.*: **toplofty**. See *haughty*

(2) highbrow (as in pedantic) *adj.*: **donnish**. See *pedantic*

(3) highbrow (as in scholarly or bookish) *adj.*: **donnish**. See *bookish*

high-class *adj.*: **nobby** [British]. See *elegant*

higher (in rank, class, status, or value) *adj.*: **superordinate**. See *superior*

highest (point that can be attained or the ultimate degree, as of a condition or quality) *n.*: **ne plus ultra**. See *ultimate*

(2) highest (point) *n.*: **apogee**. See *height*

(3) highest (the . . . point, as in the pinnacle) *n.*: **Parnassus**. See *pinnacle*

highlight (as in climax, of a drama) *n.*: **catastatis**. See *climax*

high-pitched (sound made by bagpipes) *n.*: **skirl**. See *bagpipes*

high society *n.*: **beau monde** [French]. ❖ New York's **beau monde** is currently up in arms about a ghastly new threat to its continued well-being: stealth paparazzi. These are apparently normal kids who frequent Manhattan's trendy nightspots and fashionable parties armed with hidden video cameras. (T. Young, "New York Confidential: Titanic Sequel Sinks without a Trace," *Independent* [London], 7/3/1998.)

(2) high society *n.*: **bon ton** [French]. ❖ Nick Truelocke can't wait to see it happen—to see the champagne corks popping, the love affairs blossoming, the song and dance and romance. And he need wait only a few hours now, because tomorrow night the doors of his club, the Cafe de Paris, will open once more, to admit the **bon ton** of the Nineties. (James Style, "Come to the Cafe: Chill Out in Style," *Independent* [London], 10/2/1996.)

high-spirited (as in exuberant) *adj.*: **yeasty**. See *exuberant*

(2) high-spirited (as in jolly) *adj.*: **Falstaffian**. See *jovial*

(3) high-spirited (girl) *n., adj.*: **hoyden**. See *tomboy*

(4) high-spirited *adj.*: **mettlesome**. See *spirited*

high wire (walker, or one who balances things) *n.*: **equilibrist**. See *balancer*

(2) high wire (walker) *n.*: **funambulist**. See *tightrope walker*

hill (as in upward slope) *n.*: **acclivity** (*adj.*: **acclivitous**). See *incline*

hindrances (spec. baggage, equipment, supplies, or any object that hinders progress or movement) *n.pl.*: **impedimenta**. See *baggage*

hint (as in clue to solving a puzzle or deciphering a code that has not previously been solved or deciphered) *n.*: **Rosetta stone**. See *clue*

(2) hint (as in small amount) *n.*: **soupçon** [French]. See *trace*

(3) hint (as in trace or small amount of) *n.*: **tincture**. See *trace*

hissing (pronounce with . . . sounds) *v.t.*: **assibilate**. ❖ In fact, some American gay men do pronounce sibilants (s, z, sh, and so on) distinctively, but not with a lisp. They hiss—adding more sibilation—a phenomenon phonologists call assibilation. Gay men are not the only group prone to **assibilate**. (*Economist*, "Boy George, I Think He's Got It," 7/15/1995, p. 63.)

historian (or chronicler) *n.*: **annalist**. See *chronicler*

historic (of an event or period that is . . .) *adj.*: **epochal**. See *momentous*

histrionic (behavior) *n., adj.*: **operatics**. See *melodramatic*

hit (repeatedly, often used figuratively) *v.t.*: **buffet**. ❖ The administration acknowledged this week that Ickes improperly used a White House fax machine, telephone and possibly a computer in communicating with an intermediary about the donation. Ickes' actions could pose a more serious problem for the White House, already **buffeted** by the widening fund-raising furor. (*Minneapolis Star Tribune*, "Agency Opens Inquiry into Claims of Illegal Fund-Raising by Ickes," 2/6/1997.)

(2) hit (with a club) *v.t.*: **cudgel**. See *club*

(3) hit (with the critics but not the public) *n.*: **succès d'estime** [French]. See *success*

hoarseness (causing inability to speak) *n.*: **dysphonia**. ❖ It may seem like a case of laryngitis you just can't shake. Your voice remains hoarse and sounds weak, even after you clear your throat. . . . "Chronic **dysphonia** can occur in people such as teachers who use their voices a lot, and in people who have experienced trauma or surgery that affects the larynx," says Nicolas E. Maragos, M.D. (The Mayo Clinic Health Letter, "Finding Your Voice: New Procedure Offers Hope to Chronically Hoarse," *St. Louis Post-Dispatch*, 5/2/1993.)

hoax (as in false story, often deliberately) *n.*: **canard**. ❖ . . . exposes a number of influential hoaxes, meticulously tracking the way they have been mindlessly repeated by the media until they have come to seem part of received wisdom. These include the Super Bowl **canard** holding that wife beating increases 40 percent during the game (utterly baseless, but TV stations ran ads urging men to remain calm). (Tama Starr, review of *Who Stole Feminism: How Women Have Betrayed Women*, by Christina Hoff Sommers, *Reason*, 10/1/1994, p. 62.)

(2) hoax (esp. something that at first seems a wonderful discovery or development but which turns out to be a . . .) *n.*: **mare's nest**. ❖ [As part of the Ponzi scheme,] Wallenbrock officials admitted to the SEC and Donell that the company took in $230.1 million from investors, gave back $102.6 million in interest and principal, and then passed more than $124 million to Citadel Capital, a company in the same office that funds corporate start-ups. Donell found that the books and records of Wallenbrock and Citadel were essentially a **mare's nest**. Osaki and his compatriots have taken the Fifth Amendment. (Don Bauder, "Appeals Court Upholds Ruling against San Diego–Area Investment Scam," *San Diego Union-Tribune*, 12/28/2002.)

(3) hoax (spec. the act of engaging in deception under a false name or identity) *n.*: **imposture**. ❖ Recently, a suicide bomber, masquerading as an Israeli soldier, blew himself up in Netanya, killing three Israelis. How easy would it be for a terrorist here to carry out a similar **imposture**? At left is a photograph of one of New York's finest. Only it's not.

[Everything he is wearing was] bought over the Internet with no identification required. (Dean Murphy, "Dressing Just Like the Boys in Blue," *New York Times*, 6/2/2002.)

hobbling (as in limping, from lack of blood flow to leg muscles) *n.*: **claudication**. See *limping*

hobby (as in favorite topic or activity) *n.*: **cheval de bataille** [French for "battle-horse"]. ❖ "Though I studied everything [said Podles], Rossini was my **cheval de bataille**. I would finish every exam with some Rossini, and later a Rossini aria would be my finale in every competition." Nevertheless, while Rossini arias were her staple, she had yet to tackle complete roles. (Barrymore Laurence Scherer, "Alto Rhapsody," [Poland's Ewa Podles, contralto], *Opera News*, 6/1/1997.)

hobo *n.*: **clochard** [French]. See *vagrant*

hodgepodge (as in assortment) *n.*: **farrago**. See *assortment*

(2) hodgepodge (as in assortment) *n.*: **gallimaufry**. See *assortment*

(3) hodgepodge (as in assortment) *n.*: **olla podrida** [Spanish]. See *assortment*

(4) hodgepodge (as in assortment) *n.*: **omnium-gatherum** [Latin]. See *assortment*

(5) hodgepodge (as in assortment) *n.*: **salmagundi**. See *assortment*

(6) hodgepodge (as in assortment) *n.*: **welter**. See *jumble*

(7) hodgepodge (composed of a . . . of items) *adj.*: **farraginous**. See *mixed*

hog (as in anyone who behaves like a pig, whether in his or her personal habits or by being greedy) **chazzer** [Yiddish]. See *pig*

(2) hog (as in hearty eater) *n.*: **trencherman**. See *glutton*

hogs (give birth to a litter of . . .) *v.t.*: **farrow**. See *pigs*

(2) hogs (of or relating to) *adj.*: **porcine**. See *pigs*

hold (closely to a line, rule, or principle) *v.i.*: **hew**. See *conform*

holding (adapted for . . . , esp. a tail) *adj.*: **prehensile**. See *grasping*

hole (as in gap) *n.*: **lacuna**. See *gap*

holes (full of . . . , as in cracks) *adj.*: **rimose**. See *cracks*

holier-than-thou (in a hypocritical way) *adj.*: **pharisaical**. See *self-righteous*

(2) holier-than-thou (persons who are . . . and critical of others) *n.pl.*: **unco guid** (preceded by "the"). See *self-righteous*

(3) holier-than-thou *adj.*: **Pecksniffian**. See *self-righteous*

holy (having both human and . . . [as in godlike] attributes) *adj.*: **theanthropic**. See *godlike*

holy oil (often used at baptisms and confirmations) *n.*: **chrism**. ❖ [On Joe DiMaggio Day in 1998, he rode around the warning track and he] held both hands above his head—half a wave, half a blessing, like the Pope does. He'd part his hands, throw them open towards the crowd, both at once, [so that] a whiff of his **chrism**, some glint of his godhood would fly from him back to the crowd. (Richard Ben Cramer, *Joe DiMaggio: The Hero's Life*, Simon & Schuster [2001], p. v.)

holy place (or sanctum) *n.*: **adytum**. See *sanctum*

holy water (sprinkle with . . .) *v.t.*: **asperse**. See *sprinkle*

homage (not necessarily sincere) *n.*: **obeisance**. ❖ Given that throughout history those who did not find their culture's gods credible have suffered for it, simple self-preservation explains [why people pretend to have religious beliefs]. The early Christians (along with everyone else) were required to give token **obeisance** to the Roman gods once a year. . . . Those who refused even that option were considered unpatriotic and punished. (*Minneapolis Star Tribune*, unsigned letter to the editor, 10/30/1999.)

(2) homage (as in allegiance) *n.*: **vassalage**. See *allegiance*

(3) homage (as in tribute) *n.*: **panegyric** (one who does so, *n.*: **panegyrist**). See *tribute*

home (on a height) *n.*: **aerie**. See *dwelling*

homebuilder (spec. a carpenter) *n.*: **housewright**. See *carpenter*

homeless (child who roams the streets) *n.*: **gamine** (or **gamin** for masculine) [French]. ❖ In Cali, ragged-looking Black youth between six and 14-years-old form protective bands that roam city blocks in search of food and shelter. The **gamins** (street urchins) live on the streets and face constant harassment from police and businesses. (Michael J. Franklin, "Colombian Blacks Face Heart-Wrenching Racism: State Denies They Even Exist," *Chicago Citizen*, 2/13/1994.)

homesickness (extreme . . .) *n.*: **nostomania**. [The Woodville football team] is suffering all the symptoms [of] **nostomania**. Take Woodville away from its familiar surroundings and it becomes bewildered, disoriented—something to be pitied and plundered. Two weeks ago it left the safety of Woodville Oval, went to Football Park to play North Adelaide and was humiliated by 69 points. (Geoff Kingston, "Woodville Proving a Poor Traveller," *Advertiser*, 6/13/1987.)

homogeneous (of things that cannot be made . . .) *adj.*: **immiscible**. See *incompatible*

homosexual (person or one concerned with gay rights) *n.*, *adj.*: **homophile**. ❖ In 1971, Hislop cofounded one of the earliest gay support groups in the country, the Community **Homophile** Association of Toronto. (Scott Steele, Coming Out: The State Is Out of the Bedroom, but after 25 Years, Old Attitudes Still Linger," *Maclean's*, 5/16/1994, p. 40.)

(2) homosexual (as in lesbian) *adj.*: **sapphic**. See *lesbian*

homosexuals (discrimination against . . .) *n.*: **heterosexism**. ❖ Growing acceptance of gays is part of a movement more concerned with democratic integration and individual rights than with nationalistic separatism and collective responsibilities, he writes. As this consensus gains power, legal discrimination and cultural **heterosexism** wither. (Wayne Hoffman, "The Gay Israelis," *Washington Post Book World*, 7/26/2000.)

honest (as in truthful) *adj.*: **veridical**. See *truthful*

honesty (as in integrity) *n.*: **probity**. See *integrity*

honey (producing or yielding . . .) *adj.*: **melliferous**. ❖ Syria—the birthplace of farming—is a dream place for those interested in bee-keeping. There you can find a specific race of honey bees, large **melliferous** areas and traditions that have remained unchanged from long ago; all these contribute to make this desert land buzz with life. (Gilles Fert, "Beekeeping in Syria," www.apiservices.com/articles/us/fert/syria.htm.)

honeyed (voice or sound) *adj.*: **mellifluous**. See *melodious*

(2) honeyed (voice or sound) *adj.*: **mellisonant**. See *melodious*

honor (personal . . .) *n.*: **izzat** [Hindi]. ❖ Mateen's life is not easy. He wants to donate sufficient funds to the building of a new mosque to keep his dignity and his family's **izzat**, but he has little money to spare. (Sushil Jain, review of *The Song of the Loom*, by Abdul Bismillah, *World Literature Today*, 3/22/1997, p. 454.)

(2) honor (as in give a prize to) *v.t.*: **premiate**. See *award*

(3) honor (as in integrity) *n.*: **probity**. See *integrity*

(4) honor (as in tribute) *n.*: **panegyric** (one who does so *n.*: **panegyrist**). See *tribute*

(5) honor (or to bestow . . . upon, as in an accolade) *n., v.t.*: **garland**. See *accolade*

(6) honor (to pay . . . to, not necessarily sincere or unforced) *n.*: **obeisance**. See *homage*

honorableness *n.*: **honorificabilitudinity**. ❖ **Honorificabilitudinity** and the requirements of Scrabble fans dictated that the *New Shorter* [*Oxford English Dictionary*]'s makers be open-minded enough to include dweeb (a boringly conventional person), droob (an unprepossessing or contemptible person, esp. a man) and droog (a member of a gang: a young ruffian). (Jennifer Fisher, "Droobs and Dweebs," *U.S. News & World Report*, 10/11/1993.)

hood (woolen . . . that covers head and neck) *n.*: **balaclava**. ❖ The **balaclava** fits tight around my face and extends well into my turtleneck undershirt to prevent air leaks. (Ed Pavelka, "Dress for Duress: Toasty Tips for Safe and Comfortable Winter Cycling," *Bicycling*, 2/1/1995, p. 86.)

hoofs (an animal having . . .) *n., adj.*: **ungulate**. ❖ It takes clout to be a good elk tracker. Sorry, the pun was irresistible. Clout is the name of half a cloven hoof, one toe, if you will, of a deer, elk, moose or any other two-toed **ungulate**. (Ed Dentry, "Tracking Video Turns Hunters into Sleuths," *Denver Rocky Mountain News*, 10/27/1999.)

hooker (as in prostitute) *n.*: **fancy woman**. See *prostitute*

(2) hooker (of or relating to being a . . .) *adj.*: **meretricious**. See *prostitute*

(3) hooker *n.*: **bawd**. See *prostitute*

(4) hooker *n.*: **demimondaine**. See *prostitute*

(5) hooker *n.*: **doxy**. See *prostitute*

(6) hooker *n.*: **trollop**. See *prostitute*

hookers (as a group) *n.*: **bawd**. See *prostitutes*

hope (slight or faint . . .) *n.*: **velleity**. ❖ *Out of the Depths* contains private, not communal, women's prayers, more than half of which pertain (as if they were indeed one lifelong prayer) to childbirth: from a woman's first preconception **velleity** through (many months or years later) her last post-delivery beatitude. (Susan Schnur, review of *Out of the Depths I Call to You: A Book of Prayers for the Married Jewish Woman*, by Nina Beth Cardin, *Lilith*, 4/30/1993.)

(2) hope (as in reliance on . . . alone [as in faith] rather than reason, esp. in philosophical or religious matters) *n.*: **fideism**. See *faith*

(3) hope (for) *v.t.*: **desiderate**. See *want*

(4) hope (which is delusive or not realistically obtainable) *n.*: **will-o'-the-wisp**. See *pipe dream*

hopeful (as in one habitually expecting an upturn in one's fortunes, sometimes without justification) *adj.*: **Micawberish** (*n.*: **Micawber**). See *optimistic*

(2) hopeful (esp. blindly or naively . . .) *adj.*: **Panglossian**. See *optimistic*

(3) hopeful (excessively or unrealistically . . . person) *n.*: **Pollyanna**. See *optimistic*

hopeless (mission or project) *n.*: **fool's errand**. ❖ Just how likely is it that the United States will sustain an attack with biological weapons? In one sense . . . the quest for a clear threat assessment is essentially a **fool's errand**. No attack has ever been registered in the United States, and accordingly there is no way to assign degrees of probability. (Helle Bering, "A Plague of Chad? It Could Be Biological Terrorism," *Washington Times*, 11/29/2000.)

(2) hopeless (relating to the view that all human striving and aspiration is . . . , or people who hold such a view) *adj., n.*: **futilitarian**. See *futile*

(3) hopeless (as in unrealistic) *adj.*: **chimerical**. See *unrealistic*

(4) hopeless (esp. as to poverty) *adj.*: **abject**. See *wretched*

hopelessness (as in world-weariness or sentimental pessimism over the world's problems) *adj.*: **Weltschmerz** [German]. See *pessimism*

horniness (male . . .) *n.*: **satyriasis**. ❖ [T]hose who are angry over the Clinton scene are angry not with [Hillary] but with [Bill]. They might be tangentially angry with her for putting up with his **satyriasis**, but almost certainly not in critical numbers. (William F. Buckley Jr., "Senator Hillary?" *National Review*, 1/25/1999.)

horny *adj.*: **ithyphallic**. See *lustful*

horrible (person) *n.*: **caitiff**. See *despicable*

(2) horrible *adj.*: **ugsome**. See *loathsome*

horror (deliberate use of . . . and terror as a military tactic used by the Germans during World War I to break the will of the enemy) *n.*: **Schrecklichkeit** [German]. See *terror*

horse (lover) *n.*: **hippophile**. ❖ Horse lovers love horses, for sure, but liking is a different matter. Just as people, horses have their different characters and although no genuine **hippophile** would be wilfully bad to an animal under his or her care, there are certainly some with whom you'd be happier to go for a beer, a curry and a chat about David Beckham's foot than others. (Sue Montgomery, Racing: "Quitte La France Is Happy to Have the Last Laugh," *Independent* [London], 4/13/2002.)

horseback riding (of or relating to) *adj.*: **equitational**. ❖ [At Club Med,] I signed up for the intermediate class and discovered that I could learn a whole range of **equitational** skills, including jumping, dressage, "trick riding" and, if I really felt like playing Prince Philip for a week, carriage-driving. (Rosie Millard, "Saddle Up for Club Med with a Difference," *Independent* [London], 5/31/1997.)

horseman *n.*: **caballero**. See *equestrian*

horses (study of) *n.*: **hippology**. ❖ The Rock County team was the grand champion in the recent state 4-H horse judging championship. Another team with nearly the same membership won reserve grand championship in **hippology**, which tests their knowledge in everything and anything to do with horses. (*Janesville [WI] Gazette*, "4-H Teens Show Some Real Horse Sense," 9/23/2006.)

hospital (originating in) *adj.*: **nosocomial**. [This term is used with respect to infections, sicknesses, or diseases contracted by patients while in hospitals.] ❖ Under fire for failing to safeguard patients' health, the nation's most influential hospital regulator said Wednesday that it will step up its oversight of facilities to cut down on fatal infections contracted there. [The president of the group stated that] "prevention of **nosocomial** infections must be a high priority . . . for the leaders of, and health-care professionals who work in, America's health-care organizations." (Bruce Japsen, "Hospital Regulator to Step Up Oversight of Infections," *Chicago Tribune*, 1/22/2003.)

hostile *adj.*: **bellicose**. See *belligerent*

(2) hostile *adj.*: **oppugnant**. See *antagonistic*

hostility (develop a strong . . . toward) *n.*: **scunner** (esp. as in "take a scunner") [British]. See *dislike*

(2) hostility (initiate . . . or violence) *v.i.*: **aggress**. See *fight*

(3) hostility (intense . . . , such as toward an enemy) *n.*: **enmity**. See *hatred*

(4) hostility (minor . . . , as in skirmish) *n.*: **velitation**. See *skirmish*

hot (as in of or relating to dog days of summer) *adj.*: **canicular**. See *dog days*

    (2) hot (white-. . .) *adj.*: **candescent**. See *white-hot*

hotel (actually an inn, but generally used as synonym for . . . as well) *n.*: **caravansary**. See *inn*

    (2) hotel (proprietor or innkeeper) *n.*: **boniface**. See *innkeeper*

hotheaded (as in rash or impetuous person) *n.*: **Hotspur**. See *impetuous*

hot water (of or relating to . . .) *adj.*: **hydrothermal**. ❖ Very hot (greater than 400 degrees C) water is still found today in underground geothermal and undersea **hydrothermal** areas, where the pressure is supplied by the overlying rock or water. (Gary Olsen, "Origins of Life," *National Forum*, 1/1/1996, p. 20.)

house (on a height) *n.*: **aerie**. See *dwelling*

    (2) house (very large . . .) *n.*: **manse**. See *mansion*

housekeeper (hired to do cleaning work) *n.*: **charwoman**. See *maid*

    (2) housekeeper (in India and Asia, often serving as a wet nurse) *n.*: **amah**. See *maid*

howl (as in wail) *v.i.*: **ululate**. See *wail*

    (2) howl (like a cat in heat) *v.i.*: **caterwaul**. See *screech*

    (3) howl (or yelp, bark, or screech) *v.t., n.*: **yawp**. See *shriek*

hub (as in nerve center) *n.*: **ganglion** (pl. **ganglia**). See *nerve center*

    (2) hub (person or object that is the focal point of a . . .) *n.*: **cynosure**. See *center of attention*

hubbub *n.*: **charivari**. ❖ Amid the **charivari** of huzzahs and cagey praise that greets Bill Gass's prose, there is always the slur that he remains unapologetically highbrow. (Paul West, "At-Swim Among the Noble Gasses," *Review of Contemporary Fiction*, 9/22/2004.)

    (2) hubbub (and confusion, esp. from simultaneous voices) *n.*: **babel**. See *noise*

huckster (esp. who sells quack medicines) *n.*: **mountebank**. ❖ As a traveling **mountebank**, selling dubious cures to credulous rural folk, [John D. Rockefeller's father] Bill took a dim view of people's intelligence and didn't

hesitate to exploit their naive trust. (Ron Chernow, *Titan*, Random House [1998], p. 25.)

hue *n.*: **tincture**. ❖ The morning light had broadened, gained greater depth, and lay in a clean sheet across the bay, giving it a silver **tincture**. (David Guterson, *Snow Falling on Cedars*, Harcourt Brace [1994], p. 12.)

    (2) hue (having only one . . .) *adj.*: **monochromatic**. See *color*

hug (as in caress or fondle) *v.i.*: **canoodle** (often "canoodle with"). See *caress*

huge (object) *n.*: **leviathan**. ❖ One of the largest industrial machines in existence, [papermaking machine] No. 35 took two years to build and cost $395 million. It is higher than a five-story building and a third longer than a football field. . . . Every 60 seconds, this **leviathan** generates a stream of office paper more than half a mile long and 29 feet wide. (Alex Taylor III, Competition: "Why an Industry That Was Up a Tree Is on a Big Roll—Everything Is Monumental in the Paper Game," *Fortune*, 4/17/1995, p. 134.)

    (2) huge *adj.*: **brobdingnagian** (often cap.) [derives from Brobdingnag, an imaginary land inhabited by giants in Jonathan Swift's *Gulliver's Travels* (1745)]. ❖ Target isn't Wal-Mart, the giant that wooed suburbia with its acres of guns and gummy bears. And it definitely isn't Kmart, which still seems downscale despite its Martha Stewart tea-towel sets. [Target] may have been founded in 1962, the same year as those other **Brobdingnagian** outlets, but it has developed its own distinct interpretation of the big box format. (Shelly Branch, Features/Retailing: "How Target Got Hot Hip: Goods and Hipper Ads Are Luring the MTV and BMW Crowds into the Big Box," *Fortune*, 5/24/1999, p. 169.)

    (3) huge *adj.*: **pythonic**. ❖ There are more than 120 courses [near Myrtle Beach, SC], with more being added all the time, and I suspect that as America turns into the world's largest amusement park, with fairways replacing wetlands, the entire Carolina coast will become one **pythonic** links with 25,000 holes. . . . A lunatic golfer may one day be able to play almost continuously from Wilmington to Hilton Head Island, S.C. (William Nack, "Shoving Off . . . on an Unscripted Golfing Adventure," *Sports Illustrated*, 3/23/2004.)

(4) huge (like an elephant) *adj.*: **elephantine**. See *enormous*

(5) huge (like an elephant) *adj.*: **pachydermatous**. See *elephant*

(6) huge *adj.*: **cyclopean**. See *big*

(7) huge *adj.*: **Bunyanesque**. See *enormous*

(8) huge *adj.*: **Pantagruelian**. See *gigantic*

(9) huge *adj.*: **mastodonic**. See *big*

hugging *adj.*: **osculant**. ❖ Timkul and Chung remove each other's filmy, linen nightshirts and kiss each other's bodies. Then they pour it on—warm, succulent, **osculant**, shadowy love. (Stephen Short, "*Pride & Passion* Director Nonzee Nimibutr Makes Movies That Set Thailand's Box-Office Alight," *Time* International, 4/16/2001, p. 54.)

human (ascribe . . . characteristics to) *v.t.*: **anthropomorphize**. ❖ [To make the movie *Cats & Dogs*,] the canine and feline stars had to take on the facial expressions, emotions and eccentricities of humans, but still look as if they were exhibiting natural animal behavior. **Anthropomorphizing** the animals, though cute and cuddly, was no walk in the park. (Claudia Puig, "*Cats & Dogs* Unleashes a Host of Effects Treats—Painstaking Movements Took Time," *USA Today*, 7/9/2001.)

(2) human (resembling a . . . being) *adj.*: **hominoid**. ❖ Human evolution comes alive—or nearly so—in a permanent exhibition at the American Museum of Natural History that is one of the city's most popular current attractions. . . . [T]he display traces human history from early **hominoids** to "Lucy," who lived in Ethiopia 3.2 million years ago, to 15,000-year-old Cro-Magnon fossils found in France. (Jeffery C. Rubin, Traveler's Advisory: North America, *Time* International, 5/10/1993, p. 6.)

(3) human (resembling or characteristic of a . . . being) *n.*: **anthropoid**. ❖ So far, Hawass's team has explored four tombs, with a total of 105 mummies laid on top of one another in neat stacks. All told, the remains were interred in four distinct ways. One type was . . . placed in so-called **anthropoid** coffins—pottery sarcophagi with human faces—and a few were only wrapped in linen. (Andrea Dorfman, Archaeology: "Valley of the Lost Tombs—A Cache of Pristine Mummies Offers a Look at Egyptian Life and Death Around the Time of Jesus," *Time*, 9/6/1999, p. 62.)

(4) human (having both godlike and . . . attributes) *adj.*: **theanthropic**. See *godlike*

human body (or a representation of same, with the skin removed so as to show the bones and musculature underneath) *n.*: **écorché** [French]. See *body*

humanity (lit. meaning, often used in the sense of decency) *n.*: **menschlichkeit** [German, Yiddish]. See *decency*

humble (condition of being . . .) *n.*: **pudency**. See *modesty*

humid (as in of or relating to dog days of summer) *adj.*: **canicular**. See *dog days*

humiliate (by making false statements) *v.t.*: **traduce**. See *malign*

humiliating (or insulting another) *adj.*: **contumelious**. See *contemptuous*

humiliation (as in place or occasion of . . . and seeking forgiveness) *n.*: **Canossa**. See *penance*

humility *n.*: **pudency**. See *modesty*

humming (and droning sound) *n.*: **bombilation**. See *buzzing*

humor *n.*: **jocosity**. ❖ "I was an accountant from when I was 20 until I was 30. What a waste of 14 years," says Fred MacAulay, who clearly never had a natural head for figures. But [he] is a natural born funny man, and this looks like being his year. MacAulay was an accountant until March 1991, then worked part-time as a consultant for the firm while doing stand-up gigs until January last year, when he threw the suit away and became a full-time purveyor of **jocosity**. (Ian Black, "Adding Up Laughs," *Sunday Times* [London], 8/7/1994.)

(2) humor (having a sense of . . . , as in ability or tendency to laugh) *n.*: **risibility**. See *laugh*

humorless (as in person who never laughs) *n.*: **agelast**. ❖ [Comedian Sandi Toksvig has to go off] to do her bit for the literary festival, which, it turns out, is less a book plug, more an hour of stand-up, which the audience absolutely loves. I don't spot a single **agelast**. (Deborah Ross, "For a National Treasure, the Comedian and Author Sandi Toksvig Is Not Terribly Conventional," *Independent* [London], 7/16/2001.)

(2) humorless (as in person who tries to be funny but is not) *n.*: **witling**. ❖ The Woman Author on the Market: "'She is an authoress!' has long been the sneering remark among ignorant **witlings**, of both sexes," the *Ladies Magazine* observed. . . . [In the nineteenth century,] women's authorship was still the exception . . . , and certainly no American woman could dream of sustaining a living from her pen. The author was male. (Michael J. Everton, "The Courtesies of Authorship: Hannah Adams and Authorial Ethics in the Early Republic," *Legacy: A Journal of American Women Writers*, 1/1/2003.)

humorous (in a coarse or robust way or marked by bold caricature) *adj.*: **Rabelaisian** [after François Rabelais (1494–1553), a French writer of satirical attacks on medieval philosophy and superstition]. ❖ [Artist Red] Grooms captures the brawly, filthy, exciting, open-at-all-hours-of-the-year, disorganized nature of New York with a startling immediacy—and with an attention to detail that renders the subject virtually sacred and an affection that brings tears to the eyes. [His art turns] the city into a raucous, tumultuous, **Rabelaisian** world of wonder. (Thomas Hoving, "The Man Who Makes a Ruckus of New York," *New York Times*, 7/11/2004.)

(2) humorous *adj.*: **gelastic**. See *laughable*

(3) humorous *adj.*: **risible**. See *laughable*

(4) humorous (sayings) *n.pl.*: **facetiae**. See *witty*

hunch (that something is going to occur) *n.*: **presentiment**. See *premonition*

hundred (person who lives to be 100) *n.*: **centurion**. ❖ "I want a real headstone, rising from real turf, with an appropriate inscription. Not just 'Chuck Ramkissoon, Born 1950, Died' whenever—2050." He looked at me as if he'd just had a brainstorm. "Why not? Why not die a **centurion**?" (Joseph O'Neill, *Netherland*, Pantheon [2008], p. 160.)

hunger (as in craving) *n.*: **appetence**. See *craving*

(2) hunger (as in craving) *n.*: **avidity**. See *craving*

(3) hunger (as in longing, esp. for something one once had but has no more) *n.*: **desiderium**. See *longing*

(4) hunger (condition involving . . . for non-food items) *n.*: **pica**. See *craving*

(5) hunger (excessive or pathological . . .) *n.*: **polyphagia**. See *appetite*

hungry *adj.*: **esurient**. ❖ These new censors, the deconstructionists, take the most luscious and delicious apple and show it to a hungry person. They then seal the fruit with plastic wrap and demand that the **esurient** victim enjoy its flavour. (Michael Coren, "Behold the Deconstructionist, Who Liberates Literature by Confining It to a Cult," *Alberta Report/Western Report*, 4/10/1995, p. 36.)

(2) hungry (as in voracious) *adj.*: **edacious**. See *voracious*

hunt (about or through) *v.t.*: **fossick** [Australian]. See *rummage*

hunter *n.*: **nimrod** [based on a hunter in the Book of Genesis]. ❖ [If my readers want their trophy photos published in the paper,] I will give preferential treatment to firearms hunters who have the good sense to wear a hunter orange hat, coat or vest for photographic purposes. State research shows the wearing of hunter orange dramatically reduces a person's chances of being involved in a hunting accident, and [sets] a good example for young **nimrods**. (J. Michael Kelly, "Hunters Should Think Safety First," *Syracuse [NY] Post-Standard*, 11/18/2001.)

hunting (act of . . .) *n.*: **venery**. ❖ His lawyers argued that, as owner of 900 acres in Wyoming, he had a preferential right to hunt wildlife on it without state interference. . . . This legal concept, called the "right of **venery**," is more appropriate to medieval Europe than to the twentieth-century American West. (*National Wildlife*, "How NWF Is Defending Our Natural Heritage," 10/20/1995, p. 50.)

(2) hunting (of or relating to . . .) *adj.*: **cynegetic**. ❖ The best summation of [the relationship a hunter has to his prey] is to be found in the title of author Paul Shepard's 1973 **cynegetic** classic, *The Tender Carnivore and the Sacred Game*. (Thomas McIntyre, "The Most Serious Act of All," *Sports Afield*, 10/1/1994, p. 13.)

hurl (something or someone out of a window) *v.t.*: **defenestrate** (*n.*: **defenestration**). See *throw*

hurried (as in hasty) *adj.*: **festinate**. See *hasty*

hurriedly (as in, in a disorderly and hasty manner) *adv.*: **pell-mell**. See *disorderly*

hurry (as in, in a . . . , as in very shortly) *n.*: **trice** (as in "in a trice"). See *quickly*

hurt (as in bother or inconvenience) *v.t.*: **discommode**. See *inconvenience*

(2) hurt (as in bother or inconvenience) *v.t.*: **incommode**. See *inconvenience*

hurtful (as in harmful) *adj.*: **nocent**. See *harmful*

husband (having more than one . . . at a time) *n.*: **polyandry**. ❖ In Bhutan, many women practice **polyandry** because in the poor valleys of the Himalayas a lone husband cannot support a family. (Sharon Begley, "Sex and the Single Fly," *Newsweek*, 8/14/2000, p. 44.)

(2) husband (or wife who is unfaithful) *n.*: **bedswerver**. See *unfaithful*

(3) husband (who is overly devoted to or submissive to his wife) *adj.*: **uxorious**. See *devoted*

hushed (as in quiet) *adj., adv., n.*: **pianissimo**. See *quiet*

(2) hushed (said in . . . tones, not to be overheard) *adv., adj.*: **sotto voce**. See *whispered*

husky (having a . . . body build) *adj.*: **mesomorphic**. See *muscular*

hymn (short . . . expressing praise and glory to God) *n.*: **doxology**. [This word is included here not for its literal religious meaning but because it is sometimes used more generally in a nonreligious sense of paying homage to principle or a set of beliefs, as in the example given here.] ❖ The first and most obvious [reality of the 2002 midterm elections] is that our government has never before been taken over by an extremist group of ideologues. Some remember when Eisenhower was president and both houses were Republican. But they forget we had a Supreme Court that was in no way subservient to Republican **doxology**, and the Republicans in control were more Jim Jeffords than Trent Lott. (Ed Garvey, "Elections Confirm Shift Toward Devout Plutocracy," *Capital Times*, 11/12/2002.)

hyperactive *adj.*: **hyperthyroid**. [Though this word technically refers to an overactive thyroid gland, it is frequently used as a synonym for hyperactive.] ❖ Whereas the **hyperthyroid** [Alexander] Hamilton jumped at his assignment [as Treasury Secretary, Thomas] Jefferson dithered through the winter about taking the State Department job and did not accept until mid-February, 1790. (Ron Chernow, *Alexander Hamilton*, Penguin [2004], p. 310.)

hyperbole (abnormal propensity toward . . .) *n.*: **mythomania**. See *embellishment*

hypercritical (person) *n.*: **smellfungus**. See *faultfinder*

(2) hypercritical *adj.*: **captious**. See *faultfinding*

hypnotize (as in bewitch or enchant) *v.t.*: **ensorcell** (or **ensorcel**). See *enchant*

hypocrite (esp. one who acts humbly) *n.*: **Uriah Heep** [based on the villainous character of the same name, from the Charles Dickens novel *David Copperfield*, who always effected false humility]. ❖ More than any presidential campaign in memory, [Senator John] Edwards's crusade against "special interests" is beholden to an interest group—his fellow trial lawyers—whose lucrative rapacity depends on thwarting reforms from Washington. He uses their millions to advertise his hardscrabble origins and oneness with the masses. His **Uriah Heep** candidacy should pay royalties to Charles Dickens. (George F. Will, "The Politics of Manliness," *Washington Post*, 1/29/2004.)

(2) hypocrite (esp. one who affects religious piety) *n.*: **Tartuffe** (or **tartuffe**) [after the protagonist in the play *Tartuffe* by Molière]. ❖ Add to this melange the pathetic figure of Al Gore's nominee for Vice-President, Senator Joe Lieberman. He is the American **Tartuffe**, the consummate hypocrite. Lieberman, an orthodox Jew, suddenly discovered on his way to wooing black voters that he had a great deal of respect for American black Muslim leader Louis Farrakhan, author of some of America's nastiest anti-Semitic quotes. (Barbara Amiel, "The Empty-Headed Myths That America's Voters Laid to Rest," *Daily Telegraph* [London], 12/18/2000.)

hypocritical (as in insincere) *adj.*: **crocodilian**. See *insincere*

(2) hypocritical (in a self-righteous or sanctimonious way) *adj.*: **Pecksniffian**. See *self-righteous*

(3) hypocritical (or sanctimonious, pious, and/or insincere speech) *n.*: **cant**. See *pious*

(4) hypocritical *adj.*: **Janus-faced**. See *two-faced*

hysteria (emotional . . . , esp. as caused by something unattainable) *n.*: **nympholepsy**. [This word often, though not always, refers to an erotic frenzy.] See *frenzy*

hysterical (woman) *n.*: **maenad**. See *woman*

(2) hysterical (as in laughable) *adj.*: **gelastic**. See *laughable*

(3) hysterical (as in laughable) *adj.*: **risible**. See *laughable*

ice (coating of . . .) *n.*: **rime**. ❖ Even the . . . ice storm [in the movie *The Ice Storm*] is made to look preposterous, what with **rime** covering everything in bluish silvery splendor, like a Disney wonderland. (John Simon, review of *The Ice Storm*, *National Review*, 11/24/1997, p. 61.)

(2) ice (from a storm or floating . . . chunks) *n.*: **tiddledies**. ❖ Dear Sharon: I can't seem to ever be warm when the temperature dips. No matter what I wear, I'm always the one who's chilled to the bone. What can I do to avoid my death of cold?—Fashion Freeze-out. Dear Fashion Freeze-out: Brrrr, those jarring Siberian blues. But, my glacial princess, besides a case of the sniffles and surfing the **tiddledies** of an ice storm, there are real dangers of hypothermia and frostbite when the mercury plummets below the freezing level. (Sharon Haver, "Potions Leave No Excuse for Damaged Skin," *Denver Rocky Mountain News*, 1/22/1998.)

(3) ice (thin coating of . . . , as on a rock) *n.*: **verglas**. ❖ The scene was magnificent—[there was] pure white [snow] across the loch and, above us, tiny figures moved in and out of the mist on the ridge. My, we felt smug, even when it became clear that the obvious way back up [the ski mountain] consisted of nasty shiny **verglas**! (Donald Shiach, "Tour Party," *Scotsman*, 3/6/1999.)

iciness (often in relations between people) *n.*: **froideur** [French]. See *chilliness*

iconoclast (orig. Catholics who did not follow Church of England) *n.*: **recusant**. See *dissenter*

icy (as in of, like, or occurring in winter) *adj.*: **brumal**. See *winter*

(2) icy *adj.*: **gelid**. See *cold*

(3) icy *adj.*: **hyperborean**. See *freezing*

idea (or concept that can be expressed in one word) *n.*: **holophrasis** (*adj.*: **holophrastic**). ❖ [We] looked at the term *Thomson*, as the market leader [in the London travel agent business]. Where was its magic? They might have called themselves Lord Thomson, but self-effacingly stayed plain Thomson, like the bloke next door. . . . Thomson . . . has hardly any sub-

text. Despite this mild heritage, Thomson sells [travel] packages easy as shooting fish in a barrel. Thomson is **holophrastic**. (Trader Horn, Travel: "Agents of Change," *Guardian* [London], 9/17/1994.)

(2) idea (about which one is obsessed) *n.*: **idée fixe** [French]. See *obsession*

(3) idea (as in creative inspiration) *n.*: **afflatus**. See *inspiration*

(4) idea (to form an . . . of or about) *v.t.*: **ideate**. See *visualize*

(5) idea (which is controversial or person who holds a controversial opinion) *n.*: **polemic**. See *controversy*

(6) idea (which is odd, stubborn, or whimsical) *n.*: **crotchet**. See *notion*

ideal (the . . . , lit. greatest or highest good) *n.*: **summum bonum** [Latin]. ❖ Over and over, I hear parents complain that their kids don't like to read, that the boys are obsessed with sports and the girls are already superconscious—at 8—of their looks and their weight and their clothes. But where do children get a different message about what's important? In *Hercules*, being strong and destructive is the **summum bonum** for all the men and, being beautiful, thin and sexy is the basic requirement for all the female characters. (Katha Pollitt, "Get Thee Behind Me, Disney," *Nation*, 7/21/1997.)

(2) ideal (spec. the perfect or beautiful example of something) *n.*: **beau ideal**. [While obviously similar to "ideal," this term, meaning "beautiful ideal" in French, is in a sense more emphatic and refers to the perfect type or model, or the concept of perfect beauty.] ❖ He's handsome and dresses with care, and he's what Joe Biden might call "clean and articulate." Women love him. He's the new **beau ideal** of the popular culture. But we're not talking about Barack Obama. . . . He's a vampire. At a theater near you, virginal young girls, anxious young women and lots of mothers are lining up for the opening of *Twilight*. (Suzanne Fields, "Present Day Vampires; What You See Is Not Always What You Get," *Washington Times*, 11/20/2008.)

idealist (as in dreamer) *n.*: **fantast**. See *dreamer*

idealistic (but likely impractical or unrealistic) *adj.*: **quixotic**. ❖ Few serious candidates are **quixotic** enough to refuse to descend to the level of their opponents' demeaning and deceptive attacks. The best hope remains the classic free-market solution: a voter rebellion against candidates whose [negative campaigning] tactics are an embarrassment to democracy. (Walter Shapiro, Ethics: "Voters vs. the Negative Nineties—What to Do When Campaigns Are as Nasty as a David Lynch Film," *Time*, 10/15/1990, p. 98.)

(2) idealistic (conduct, spec. idealistic conduct without regard to practicality) *n.*: **knight-errantry**. [This term derives from knights, as portrayed in medieval romances, who wandered in search of challenges to prove their chivalry or military prowess.] ❖ George W. Bush's presidential campaign in 2000 featured criticism of nation-building as **knight-errantry** run amok. But President Bush is attempting to build democracies in Afghanistan and Iraq with no democratic building blocks, a first cousin of alchemy. (Bruce Fein, "The Spirit of America," *Washington Times*, 4/22/2008.)

(3) idealistic (as in one habitually expecting an upturn in one's fortunes, sometimes without justification) *adj.*: **Micawberish** (*n.*: **Micawber**). See *optimistic*

(4) idealistic (esp. blindly or naively . . . , as in optimistic) *adj.*: **Panglossian**. See *optimistic*

(5) idealistic (person, as in an impractical, contemplative person with no clear occupation or income) *n.*: **luftmensch** [lit. man of air; German, Yiddish]. See *dreamer*

idealize *v.t.*: platonize. ❖ [D]espite the inclination to **platonize** the effort and yield of what has managed in the last year to find its way between covers [in regard to nineteenth-century British literature], there is little doubt that . . . it is impossible to issue this report without recognizing that it is (and to some extent always has been) an essay about books in a more fundamental sense: namely, what is being published and by whom. (William Galperin, "Recent Studies in the Nineteenth Century," *Studies in English Literature*, 9/22/1997.)

idealized (or romanticized conception of oneself, as a result of boredom in one's life) *n.*: **Bovarism**. See *self-delusion*

(2) idealized (or worshipful biography) *n.*: **hagiography** (*adj.*: **hagiographic**). See *biography*

ideas (source of . . . , as in inspiration) *n.*: **Pierian spring**. See *inspiration*

identical (having an . . . nature, substance, or essence) *adj.*: **consubstantial**. ❖ Contiguous they may be, **consubstantial** they are not. The countries of central Europe . . . are growing tired of being lumped together in generalizations of all kinds. . . . Not every country in central Europe is a poor, small place with bad roads, corrupt officials, a rackety Russian-built nuclear-power plant and a squabbling coalition government. (Economist, "Happy Hotch-Potch; Central Europe," 1/31/2004.)

(2) identical (in strength, power, or effectiveness) *adj.*: **equipollent**. See *equal*

identify (as in classify) *v.t.*: **taxonomize**. See *classify*

identity (as in self-identity) *n.*: **ipseity**. See *self-identity*

ideology (spec. doctrines to be believed; articles of faith) *n.pl.*: **credenda**. See *beliefs*

idiom (as in phrase or expression) *n.*: **locution**. See *phrase*

idiot *n.*: **jobbernowl** [British]. ❖ There's no point beating a dead horse, or commenting sensibly on a **jobbernowl**, and in his defense I should say this about [Reagan's Secretary of the Interior, James Watt]: there is no asinine statement he can make that would surprise a single soul. (Henry Mitchell, "Of Being Born Dumb and Standing Fast," *Washington Post*, 4/8/1983.)

(2) idiot *n.*: **balatron**. See *buffoon*

(3) idiot (as in one mentally deficient from birth) *n.*: **ament**. See *moron*

(4) idiot *n.*: **dullard**. See *stupid*

(5) idiot *n.*: **mooncalf**. See *fool*

(6) idiot (or fool or dope or loser or anyone generally not worthy of respect) *n.*: **schmendrick** or **shmendrik** [Yiddish]. See *fool*

idiotic (as in foolish) *adj.*: **barmy** [British]. See *foolish*

(2) idiotic (as in foolish) *adj.*: **balmy**. See *foolish*

(3) idiotic (lit. brainless) *adj.*: **excerebrose**. See *brainless*

idle (. . . during the summer) *v.i.*: **aestivate** (or **estivate**). See *laze*

(2) idle (as in lazy) *adj.*: **fainéant** [French]. See *lazy*

(3) idle (as in not moving or temporarily inactive) *adj.*: **quiescent**. See *inactive*

(4) idle (person, who stays in bed out of laziness) *n.*: **slugabed**. See *lazy*

(5) idle (to waste time) *v.i.*: **footle** (usu. as in footle around). See *dawdle*

idleness (as in disuse) *n.*: **desuetude**. See *disuse*

(2) idleness (as in lethargy) *n.*: **hebetude**. See *lethargy*

(3) idleness *n.*: **torpor**. See *lethargy*

idler (as in work avoider) *n.*: **embusque** [French]. See *slacker*

(2) idler *n.*: **wastrel**. See *slacker*

idyllic (as in a place that is rustic, peaceful, and simple) *adj.*: **Arcadian**. See *pastoral*

iffy (as in tenuous) *adj.*: **gossamer**. See *tenuous*

(2) iffy (morality or taste) *adj.*: **louche**. See *questionable*

ignoble (state of being . . . , as in small-minded) *n.*: **parvanimity**. See *small-minded*

ignominious *adj.*: **opprobrious** (*n.*: **opprobrium**). See *contemptuous*

ignorant *adj.*: **nescient** (*n.*: **nescience**). ❖ Occasionally, I am invited to share my thoughts about my life as a lesbian with college classes—Alternative Lifestyles 101. After being asked the **nescient**, yet well-meaning, question, "When did you know you were a lesbian?" I'm usually asked, "How do you know you're a lesbian?" Oh, seekers of knowledge, let me count the ways. (Amy Adams, "Too Much Emphasis on Sex," *St. Louis Post-Dispatch*, 6/9/1998.)

(2) ignorant (class of people regarded as . . . , as in unsophisticated) *n.*: **booboisie**. See *unsophisticated*

(3) ignorant (intellectually or morally . . .) *adj.*: **benighted**. See *unenlightened*

(4) ignorant (or dull, stupid, obtuse, or uncultured) *adj.*: **Boeotian**. See *dull*

(5) ignorant (person with respect to artistic or cultural values) *adj.*: **philistine**. See *uncultured*

ignore (as in to deal with or treat inadequately or neglectfully) *v.t.*: **scant**. See *slight*

ill (and sickly person, esp. one morbidly concerned with his own health) *n.*, *adj.*: **valetudinarian**. See *sickly*

ill-bred (person) *n.*: **grobian**. See *boor*

illiterate *adj.*: **analphabetic**. ❖ It is not so surprising when one reflects that all cultures possess a literature. In an **analphabetic** culture, the literature will be an oral one. (Scott Herring, "Du Bois and the Minstrels," *Melus*, 6/22/1997, p. 3.)

illness (of an . . . or disease that has no known cause) *adj.*: **idiopathic** (*n.*: **idiopathy**). ❖ The male reproductive system has so many mysterious foes, the cause of infertility is often listed as **idiopathic**—unknown. (Michael Krantz, "Dealing with Male Infertility," *Cosmopolitan*, 1/1/1996, p. 102.)

(2) illness (caused by a physician) *adj.*: **iatrogenic**. See *disease*

(3) illness (causing, as in disease-causing) *adj.*: **morbific**. See *disease*

(4) illness (pretend to have an . . . or other incapacity to avoid work) *v.i.*: **malinger**. See *shirk*

(5) illness (early symptom of . . . , esp. migraines, herpes, or depression) *n.*: **prodrome**. See *symptom*

illogical (something that is . . .) *n.*: **alogism**. ❖ Concurrent works [in the show] dubbed "alogic compositions," or "**alogisms**," depict illogical combinations of unrelated elements such as a bar of music, a serpentine ladder and a cone or trapezoid. (Janet Kutner, "Exhibit Expands Our Understanding of Kazimir

Malevich's Spare Vision," *Dallas Morning News*, 12/31/2003.)

(2) illogical (argument, where one begs the question) *n.*: **petitio principii** [Latin]. See *begging the question*

(3) illogical (or fallacious argument) *n.*: **choplogic**. See *fallacy*

(4) illogical (or fallacious argument) *n.*: **paralogism** (*adj.*: **paralogical**). See *fallacy*

(5) illogical (argument in which a false conclusion is drawn from two premises, neither of which conveys information about all members of the designated class) *n.*: **undistributed middle**. See *fallacy*

(6) illogical (argument where one proves or disproves a point that is not at issue) *n.*: **ignoratio elenchi** [Latin]. See *irrelevancy*

(7) illogical (argument, spec. where one argues that because event B followed event A, then event A must have caused event B) *n.*: **post hoc, ergo propter hoc** [Latin for "after this, therefore, because of this"]. See *fallacy*

(8) illogical (as in relating to reasoning that sounds plausible but is false or insincere) *adj.*: **meretricious**. See *specious*

(9) illogical (or specious reasoning) *n.*: **syllogism**. See *specious*

(10) illogical (statement that is . . . , as in logically impossible; usually not recognized by the speaker) *n.*: **Irish bull**. See *incongruity*

ill temper (as in acrimony) *n.*: **asperity**. See *acrimony*

(2) ill temper *n.*: **bile**. See *bitterness*

(3) ill temper *n.*: **choler** (*adj.*: **choleric**). See *anger*

ill-tempered (as in grouchy, person) *n.*: **crosspatch**. See *grouch*

(2) ill-tempered (as in grumpy, mood) *n.pl.*: **mulligrubs**. See *grumpiness*

(3) ill-tempered (as in irritable) *adj.*: **liverish**. See *irritable*

(4) ill-tempered (as in irritable) *adj.*: **shirty**. See *irritable*

(5) ill-tempered (as in irritable) *adj.*: **waspish**. See *irritable*

(6) ill-tempered *adj.*: **atrabilious**. See *surly*

(7) ill-tempered *adj.*: **bilious**. See *surly*

(8) ill-tempered *adj.*: **querulous**. See *peevish*

(9) ill-tempered *adj.*: **splenetic**. See *irritable*

illusion (of plenty when in fact there is little) *adj.*: **Barmecidal** (esp. as in "Barmecidal feast") [after Barmecide, a character in *The Arabian Nights*, who served an imaginary feast to a beggar]. ❖ Here is an English manor house with a rather unusual staff. Alan Bates is the butler, Helen Mirren the housekeeper, and Eileen Atkins the head cook. . . . [Upstairs,] too, are unusual folk: Michael Gambon, the manorial master, Kristin Scott Thomas, his wife, and such guests as Maggie Smith, a countess. . . . What a promising feast. But it turns out to be **Barmecidal**. *Gosford Park* runs 137 minutes and spends two-thirds of that time introducing the many characters. (Stanley Kauffman, review of *Gosford Park*, *New Republic*, 12/31/2001.)

(2) illusion (of contentment or happiness) *n.*: **fool's paradise**. ❖ No one denies that the upsurge in energy prices is causing pain. It clearly is. But we have been living in something of a **fool's paradise** over much of the past 10 to 12 years, counting on cheap energy supplies as though they would last forever. (Toronto Star, "Cutting Fuel Taxes Panders to Gas Guzzlers," 9/21/2000.)

(3) illusion (painting or drawing that gives . . . of being a photograph or something real) *n.*: **trompe l'oeil** [French; deceive the eye]. ❖ "Of course it's a hoax!" says Melamid later in the van. "But, you see, all art is a hoax. C'mon! Like the idea of three-dimensionality in paintings, the creation of illusion." He assumes the voice of an amazed museumgoer looking at, say, Flemish **trompe l'oeil**: "It's a window! No, it's a painting! Oh my God, what a master!" (David Eggers, "Portrait of Artist with Trunk [Teaching Elephants to Paint]," *Esquire*, 12/01/1998, p. 65.)

(4) illusion (as in delusion) *n.*: **ignis fatuus**. See *delusion*

(5) illusion (as in hope or goal that is not

realistically obtainable) *n*.: **will-o'-the-wisp**. See *pipe dream*

(6) illusion (as in something that is impressive-looking on the outside but which hides or covers up undesirable conditions or facts) *n*.: **Potemkin village**. See *facade*

(7) illusion (esp. something that at first seems a wonderful discovery or development, but that turns to be an . . . or a hoax) *n*.: **mare's nest**. See *hoax*

(8) illusion (relating to a story in which . . . and reality are mixed together) *adj*.: **Pirandellian**. See *reality*

(9) illusion *n*.: **fata morgana**. See *mirage*

illusory (as in delusional) *adj*.: **fatuous**. See *delusional*

(2) illusory (as in idealistic but likely impractical or unrealistic) *adj*.: **quixotic**. See *idealistic*

(3) illusory (as in unrealistic) *adj*.: **chimerical**. See *unrealistic*

ill will (and intolerance that occurs when disputes about religion arise) *n*.: **odium theologicum**. See *intolerance*

image (as in representation) *n*.: **simulacrum**. See *representation*

imaginary (as in delusional) *adj*.: **fatuous**. See *delusional*

(2) imaginary (as in invented or substituted with fraudulent intent) *adj*.: **supposititious**. See *supposed*

(3) imaginary (as in unrealistic) *adj*.: **chimerical**. See *unrealistic*

imagination (source of . . . , as in inspiration) *n*.: **Pierian spring**. See *inspiration*

imaginative (and/or original) *adj*.: **Promethean**. See *creative*

(2) imaginative (as in resourceful, person) *n*.: **debrouillard** (or **débrouillard**) [French]. See *resourceful*

imagine *v.t*.: **ideate**. See *visualize*

imbecile (as in one mentally deficient from birth) *n*.: **ament**. See *moron*

(2) imbecile *n*.: **jobbernowl** [British]. See *idiot*

(3) imbecile *n*.: **mooncalf**. See *fool*

imbibing (as in given to or marked by consump-

tion of alcohol) *adj*.: **bibulous**. ❖ Sometimes the course of history is dictated by obscure forces at work beneath the surface. One theory, for example, suggests that Rome declined and fell because the lead content in the wine cups of the **bibulous** power elite made them weak and stupid. (Lance Morrow, Essay: "Guerrillas in Our Midst," *Time*, 3/18/1996, p. 102.)

imitation (of a previous artistic, musical, or literary piece) *n*.: **pastiche**. ❖ [P]astiches can be more attractive than authentic works. Those who make them have only one goal: to seduce viewers. For that reason, they tend to exaggerate an already forceful manner, or to sweeten an already gentle style. In the case of the Milkmaid, I believe the work can only be understood as by the hand of a follower of Goya. (Juliet Wilson-Bareau, letter to the editor, *Independent* [London], 4/14/2001.)

(2) imitation (of the real world in art or literature) *n*.: **mimesis** (*adj*.: **mimetic**). ❖ Still, the fact is I *would* like to see more marital equity in the pages of our fiction. And I'd be willing to honor the principle of **mimesis** and settle for a straight 50 percent success/failure rate. (Penny Kaganoff, *Women on Divorce*, Harcourt Brace [1995].)

(3) imitation (as in counterfeit) *adj*.: **pinchbeck**. See *counterfeit*

imitator (inferior . . . of artist, writer, or painter) *n*.: **epigone**. ❖ [L]ike Japan itself, [Takeshi] has grown into a bloated, entertainment superpower, still funny, still possessing formidable hidden powers, but an **epigone** of what he once was and, in many ways, the embodiment of the rigid patriarchy he used to despise. (Tim Larimer, The Arts/Cinema: "The Beat Goes On," *Time* International, 2/12/2001, p. 46.)

immaterial (as in intangible; lacking material form or substance) *adj*.: **incorporeal**. See *intangible*

(2) immaterial (as in superfluous) *adj*.: **excrescent**. See *superfluous*

(3) immaterial (as in superfluous) *adj*.: **supererogatory**. See *superfluous*

(4) immaterial *adj.*: **nugatory**. See *unimportant*

(5) immaterial *adj.*: **picayune**. See *trivial*

(6) immaterial *adj.*: **piffling**. See *trivial*

immateriality (as in argument where one proves or disproves a point that is not at issue) *n.*: **ignoratio elenchi** [Latin]. See *irrelevancy*

immature (retention of . . . , as in infantile, characteristics into adulthood) *n.*: **paedomorphism** (person who retains these characteristics *n.*: **paedomorph**). See *infantile*

(2) immature *adj.*: **jejune**. See *juvenile*

(3) immature *adj.*: **puerile**. See *juvenile*

immaturity (period of . . .) *n.*: **nonage**. See *youth*

immense (like an elephant) *adj.*: **elephantine**. See *enormous*

(2) immense (object) *n.*: **leviathan**. See *huge*

(3) immense *adj.*: **cyclopean**. See *big*

(4) immense *adj.*: **brobdingnagian** (often cap.). See *huge*

(5) immense *adj.*: **Bunyanesque**. See *enormous*

(6) immense *adj.*: **Pantagruelian**. See *gigantic*

(7) immense *adj.*: **pythonic**. See *huge*

(8) immense *adj.* **mastodonic**. See *big*

immerse *v.t.*: **imbrue**. See *soak*

immigration (of Jews into Israel) *n.*: **aliyah**. ❖ Making **aliyah** is made possible by the "Law of Return," passed by the Israeli parliament in 1950. It grants the right to Israeli citizenship to anyone with a Jewish grandparent. . . . Over the last half-century, Jews from around the world have taken advantage of the law to go to Israel. American Jews who make **aliyah** can also keep their U.S. citizenship. (Miranda Leitsinger, "Move to Israel Stirs Fear of Violence; Jewish Couple's Friends, Relatives Cite Dangers in 'Aliyah,'" *Washington Times*, 6/16/2001.)

immobilize (a person by holding down his arms) *v.t.*: **pinion**. ❖ [The Tibetan king wanted to build a temple] but the site he chose was directly over the heart of a demoness who was reputed to sleep deep beneath Tibet. In order to keep the demoness at rest, [he] built 12 other temples at vast distances to **pinion** her arms, feet and hips. Only when these were complete could construction on the main temple begin. (Thomas Dunn, "Detour," *Time International*, 2/19/2001, p. 8.)

immoral (as in of questionable morality) *adj.*: **louche**. See *questionable*

(2) immoral (government by the most . . . people) *n.*: **kakistocracy**. See *government*

(3) immoral (person) *n.*: **rakehell**. See *libertine*

(4) immoral (person) *n.*: **reprobate**. See *unprincipled*

immorality (place of . . . , as in corruption) *n.*: **Augean stable**. See *corruption*

immortal (or everlasting) *adj.*: **amaranthine**. ❖ The novel [*Quicksilver*] begins in 1713, with the apparently **amaranthine** Enoch Root (a mysterious figure who appears also in the twentieth-century world of Cryptonomicon). (Deborah Friedell, "Tap Tap Tap," *New Republic*, 10/27/2003.)

(2) immortal (as in everlasting) *adj.*: **sempiternal**. See *everlasting*

(3) immortal (having a delusional fantasy that one is . . .) *n.*: **megalomania**. See *delusional*

immortality (one obsessed with one's own greatness, fame, or . . .) *n.*: **megalomania**. See *obsession*

immovable (as in incapable of being overthrown, driven out, or subdued by force) *adj.*: **inexpugnable**. See *impregnable*

(2) immovable (person or thing clinging to something tenaciously, whether literally or figuratively) *n.*: **limpet**. See *clinger*

immune (as in thick-skinned) *adj.*: **pachydermatous**. See *thick-skinned*

impairment (esp. of moral principles or civil order) *n.*: **labefaction**. See *weakening*

impale *v.t.*: **lancinate**. See *pierce*

impart (as in send a signal) *v.t.*, *v.i.*: **semaphore**. See *signal*

impartial (uncompromisingly . . . , as in just) *n.*: **Rhadamanthine**. See *just*

(2) impartial (as in neutral) *adj.*: **adiaphorous**. See *neutral*

impartiality (a matter of . . . or indifference, esp. in matters of religion and theology; i.e., neither right nor wrong, beneficial nor harmful) *n*.: **adiaphoron** (*adj*.: **adiaphorous**). See *indifference*

impassioned (or enthusiastic speech or writing) *n*.: **dithyramb**. See *enthusiastic*

    (2) impassioned *adj*.: **perfervid**. ❖ It is spring, always a time when an NFL general manager's fancy turns to quarterbacks. But in this first season of true free agency, the courting has been especially **perfervid**. (Peter King, Pro Football, *Sports Illustrated*, 4/25/1994, p. 26.)

impassive (as in unemotional or even-tempered) *adj*.: **phlegmatic**. See *even-tempered*

impede (as in block up) *v.t*.: **occlude**. See *block*

impediments (spec. baggage, equipment, supplies, or any object that hinders progress or movement) *n.pl*.: **impedimenta**. See *baggage*

impenetrable (as in difficult to fathom through investigation or scrutiny) *adj*.: **inscrutable**. See *mysterious*

imperative (as in urgent) *adj*.: **necessitous**. See *urgent*

    (2) imperative *adj*.: **clamant**. See *urgent*

imperceptive (as in slow to understand or perceive) *adj*.: **purblind**. See *obtuse*

imperfect (or impure) *adj*.: **maculate**. See *impure*

    (2) imperfect *adj*.: **peccable**. See *flawed*

imperil (as in expose to or put in a perilous situation (*v.t*.) or be in a perilous situation (*v.i*.): **periclitate**. ❖ A recent spate of Christmas-related shopping has somewhat **periclitated** the state of my finances. The two rather cute shop boys persuading me to buy a pair of expensive leather boots did not help things, either. (intergalacticrigamarole.blogspot.com, "Bedecked with Debt," 12/18/2006.)

imperiled (journey or passage, with dangers on both sides) *idiom*: **between Scylla and Charybdis**. See *vulnerable*

imperious (as in lordly) *adj*.: **seigneurial**. See *lordly*

impermanent *adj*.: **evanescent**. See *transient*

impersonation (of a male role by a female actress) *n*.: **breeches part**. [The term derives from breeches, knee-length trousers formerly worn by men.] ❖ Arlene Rolph's Cherubino is a disturbingly androgynous joy, not least when this female singer taking on a **breeches part** then pretends to be a young girl. (Christopher Morley, "*Marriage* Remains Fresh Second Time Around," *Birmingham Post*, 3/17/2006.)

impertinent (as in being presumptuous; venturing beyond one's province) *adj*.: **ultracrepidarian**. See *presumptuous*

imperturbability (esp. under pressure or trying circumstances) *n*.: **sang-froid** [French]. See *composure*

    (2) imperturbability *n*.: **ataraxy** (or **ataraxia**). See *calmness*

imperturbable (as in unemotional or even-tempered) *adj*.: **phlegmatic**. See *even-tempered*

impervious (to outside influences) *adj*.: **hermetic**. See *sealed*

impetuous (or rash person) *n*.: **Hotspur** [after Henry Percy, a/k/a Harry Hotspur, an English soldier killed in a rebellion against Henry IV (1364–1403).] ❖ [On Thursday, Joseph P. Kennedy II] pulled out of the governor's race. It was a mature and sober decision by a man, still relatively young, whose reputation has been that of the headstrong Kennedy, the hard-charging and impetuous **Hotspur** of the sprawling, brawling Irish clan that has dominated the state's politics for decades. (David Nyhan, "Kennedy Machine a Matter of Myth," *Boston Globe*, 8/31/1997.)

    (2) impetuous *adj*.: **gadarene** [often cap.; derives from the Gadarene swine (Matthew 8:28) who rushed into the sea and drowned after Jesus sent into them demons exorcised from a demoniac person]. ❖ [Quoting] Ross Mackenzie, of the *Richmond (VA) Times-Dispatch*: [Why did George Bush win the election? Partly because voters] fear the culture is tracking in the wrong direction—perhaps even has reached the chasm's edge. They draw their fears from today's horrific tugs at the young.

They fear the drift—the **gadarene** rush—aided by Hollywood, television, and rock "artists"; they fear a corresponding collapse of education. (Jane Pope, Observations, *Charlotte [NC] Observer,* 11/14/2004.)

impetuously (as in, in a disorderly and hasty manner) *adv.*: **pell-mell**. See *disorderly*

impetus *n.*: **fillip**. See *stimulus*

impish (and magical) *adj.*: **elfin**. See *sprightly*

(2) impish (girl with . . . or playful appeal) *n.*: **gamine** [French]. See *girl*

(3) impish (or playful young woman) *n.*: **hoyden**. See *tomboy*

implication (as in inference) *n.*: **illation**. See *inference*

implicit *adj.*: **immanent**. See *inherent*

implore *v.t.*: **adjure**. See *plead*

impolite (person who makes . . . comments that seem to be offering sympathy but instead make the person feel worse, either intentionally or unintentionally) *n.*: **Job's comforter**. See *comforter*

(2) impolite (or tasteless comments) *n.*: **dontopedalogy**. See *foot-in-mouth*

impoliteness (in behavior or speech due to arrogance or contempt) *n.*: **contumely**. See *contempt*

importance (of equal . . .) *n.*: **equiponderance**. ❖ Such linkages go far toward explaining both the sheer abundance of apparent musical digression in the opera and its strange **equiponderance** with the terse main line of the action. They are not digressions at all—or only digressions at first hearing. (Richard Taruskin, "Another World: Why *The Queen of Spades* Is the Great Symbolist Opera," *Opera News,* 12/23/1995.)

important (as in critical stage or period) *n., adj.*: **climacteric**. See *critical*

(2) important (of an event or period that is . . .) *adj.*: **epochal**. See *momentous*

(3) important (or self-important person or official) *n.*: **high muck-a-muck** (or **high-muck-a-muck**). See *bigwig*

(4) important (or self-important person or official) *n.*: **panjandrum**. See *bigwig*

(5) important (person in a field or organization) *n.*: **wallah**. See *notable*

(6) important (person) *n.*: **satrap**. See *bigwig*

(7) important (things) *n.pl.*: **notabilia**. See *noteworthy*

(8) important (person, esp. in intellectual or literary circles) *n.*: **mandarin**. See *influential*

impose (oneself or one's ideas in an unwelcome way) *v.t.*: **obtrude**. [This word is subtly distinct from the more common verb "intrude." To intrude is to thrust oneself into a place without permission or welcome, and often suggests violation of privacy. To obtrude is to unjustifiably force oneself, one's remarks, opinions, etc., into consideration or sight. The example given here illustrates the distinction well because intrude could not be used interchangeably with obtrude.] ❖ In these dark times, when war threatens to engulf a considerable portion of the globe, I hesitate to **obtrude** upon the public a merely personal problem; but the fact is that we in France—I mean my wife and I—have a border problem. Our neighbors' goats stray onto our land continually and cause us a great deal of irritation. (Anthony Daniels, "The Menace in France: In Which Our Correspondent Talks Goats," *National Review,* 8/28/2006.)

impossible (as in not mutually possible; incapable of coexisting) *adj.*: **incompossible**. See *incompatible*

impossibility (statement of . . . , as in unlikelihood, expressed in the form of an exaggerated comparison with a more obvious impossibility; for example, "the sky will fall before I get married.") *n.*: **adynaton**. See *unlikelihood*

(2) impossibility (statement contains a logical . . . , usually not recognized by the speaker) *n.*: **Irish bull**. See *incongruity*

impostor (as in hypocrite, esp. one who acts humbly) *n.*: **Uriah Heep**. See *hypocrite*

(2) impostor (esp. one who sells quack medicines) *n.*: **mountebank**. See *huckster*

(3) impostor (as in hypocrite, esp. one who affects religious peity) *n.*: **Tartuffe** (or **tartuffe**). See *hypocrite*

impotent (as in ineffective) *adj.*: **feckless**. See *ineffective*

(2) impotent (as in powerless) *adj.*: **impuissant**. See *powerless*

impoverished *adj.*: **Dickensian**. See *ghettolike*

(2) impoverished *adj.*: **impecunious**. See *poor*

(3) impoverished *adj.*: **necessitous**. See *poor*

impoverishment *n.*: **illth**. See *poverty*

impractical (and contemplative person with no clear occupation or income) *n.*: **luftmensch** [lit. man of air; German, Yiddish]. See *dreamer*

(2) impractical (and idealistic conduct) *n.*: **knight-errantry**. See *idealistic*

(3) impractical (as in idealistic but likely unrealistic or . . .) *adj.*: **quixotic**. See *idealistic*

imprecise (as in equivocal, word, phrase, or expression) *n.*: **equivoque**. See *equivocal*

(2) imprecise (as in having multiple interpretations or signifying different things) *adj.*: **multivocal**. See *multivocal*

(3) imprecise (in terms of the effect that one action or activity will have on another) *adj.*: **Heisenbergian**. See *uncertain*

(4) imprecise (as in actions taken or statements made that are broader than necessary to hit their target or accomplish their goal) *adj.*, *n.*: **blunderbuss**. See *scattershot*

impregnable (as in incapable of being overthrown, driven out, or subdued by force) *adj.*: **inexpugnable**. [This word sounds like, but is distinct from, "inexpungible," which means incapable of being erased or eliminated.] ❖ [A]fter World War I this once so promising cohabitation [between Jewish and non-Jewish Hungarians] became deeply, at times tragically, damaged. Now, three or four generations later, disturbing symptoms still exist, but their frequency and their echoes may be diminishing, while the "Hungarianness" of Jewish Hungarians remains **inexpugnable**—it goes on and on. (John Lukacs, "A People of Extraordinary Contradictions," *National Interest*, 9/22/2003.)

impregnate *v.t.*: **fecundate**. ❖ China now has about 1,000 giant pandas, including 70 artificially **fecundated** ones, according to a national survey recently. (Xinhua News Agency [China], "Survey: China Has about 1,000 Pandas," 4/22/2001.)

impress (relating to speech that is designed to . . .) *adj.*: **epideictic**. [The Greek *epideictic* means "fit for display." Thus, this branch of oratory is sometimes called "ceremonial" or "demonstrative" oratory, and is often applied to orations of praise or blame. Funeral orations are a typical example of epideictic oratory. In recent times, it has been used more broadly to refer to speech that is intended to impress or for dramatic effect.] ❖ [I]n one of my radio interviews with [William F. Buckley], in 1983, I sought to parody his legendary vocabulary . . . , to wit: "Mr. Buckley, your supporters regard your style as **epideictic**. . . . How do you feel about that?" (Mike Rosen, "Two Irreplaceable Minds," *Denver Rocky Mountain News*, 3/28/2008.)

impressing (favorably) *adj.*: **prepossessing**. See *pleasing*

impressive (very . . . in effect, as in dazzling) *adj.*: **foudroyant** [French]. See *dazzling*

imprimatur (as in giving one's stamp of approval) *n.*: **nihil obstat** [Latin]. See *approval*

imprison (as in confine) *v.t.*: **immure**. See *confine*

imprisonment *n.*: **durance vile**. See *jail*

improbability (statement of . . . , expressed in the form of an exaggerated comparison with a more obvious impossibility; for example, "the sky will fall before I get married") *n.*: **adynaton**. See *unlikelihood*

improbable (as in idealistic but likely impractical or unrealistic) *adj.*: **quixotic**. See *idealistic*

(2) improbable (as in unrealistic) *adj.*: **chimerical**. See *unrealistic*

impromptu *adj.*: **autoschediastic**. See *unrehearsed*

improper (as in inappropriate or out of place) *adj.*: **malapropos**. See *inappropriate*

(2) improper (as in inappropriate, comments) *n.*: **dontopedalogy**. See *foot-in-mouth*

impropriety (in public office) *n.:* **malversation**. See *wrongdoing*

improve (text or language by removing errors or flaws) *v.t.:* **blue-pencil**. See *edit*

(2) improve (text or language by removing errors or flaws) *v.t.:* **emend**. See *edit*

improvised (as in unrehearsed) *adj.:* **autoschediastic**. See *unrehearsed*

impudence *n.:* **hardihood**. See *gall*

impudent (and conceited person) *n.:* **jackanapes**. See *conceited*

impugn (by making false or malicious statements) *v.t.:* **calumniate**. See *malign*

(2) impugn (so as to humiliate or disgrace) *v.t.:* **traduce**. See *malign*

impulse (as in creative inspiration) *n.:* **afflatus**. See *inspiration*

(2) impulse (mental process marked by . . . to do something) *n.:* **conation**. See *determination*

impulsive (as in impetuous) *adj.:* **gadarene**. See *impetuous*

(2) impulsive (as in irresponsible or reckless) *adj.:* **harum-scarum**. See *reckless*

(3) impulsive (as in reckless) *adj.:* **temerarious**. See *reckless*

(4) impulsive (or rash person) *n.:* **Hotspur**. See *impetuous*

impure *adj.:* **maculate**. ❖ Rabbi Halivni endeavors to show that a Jew can accept, along with the Bible's critics, that the Torah is a **maculate** text, full of "bumps and fissures" and still remain an observant, believing Jew. (*Forward*, "When Perfect Faith Meets Imperfect Text," 6/26/1998.)

inability (statement of . . . to do something) *n.:* **non possumus** [Latin]. ❖ [French president Jacques Chirac stated:] "[O]ur ambitions [to form a constitution for the European Union] have been reduced on tax and social questions." . . . [He blamed "the] '**non possumus**' clearly and strongly put forward by the United Kingdom"—in essence, a plea of inability by Britain's government to cede any power to Brussels on these questions in the face of fierce opposition among voters at home. (Thomas

Fuller, "EU Waters Down Charter to Save It," *International Herald Tribune*, 6/18/2004.)

inaccuracy (accepted as fact due to repetition in print) *n.:* **factoid**. ❖ What better time [than now] to dispose of some of the persistent myths that impede sound public policy? 1. "Guns in the home are 43 times more likely to kill a family member or friend than an intruder." Ellen Goodman wrote that in 1993, but let's not pick on her. This **factoid** is endlessly repeated by congressmen, by Handgun Control, Inc. by TV crime shows, and even sitcoms. (Ramesh Ponnuru, "The New Myths," *National Review*, 11/9/1998, p. 42.)

(2) inaccuracy (as in opinion, belief, or doctrine that is false) *n.:* **pseudodoxy**. See *fallacy*

inactive (temporarily . . .) *adj.:* **quiescent**. ❖ The People Power revolution that brought down Philippine dictator Ferdinand Marcos in 1986 wrote a script almost too perfect: a nation **quiescent** for more than a decade would rise and, relatively peacefully, replace their leader with his assassinated rival's widow. (Nisid Hajari, Time 100: "Asians of the Century—A Combination of Towering Individuals and Societies That Played Down Individualism Helped Liberate, Ravage and Resurrect the Vast Protean Region," *Time* International, 8/23/1999, p. 32.)

(2) inactive (as in lazy) *adj.:* **fainéant** [French]. See *lazy*

(3) inactive *adj.:* **torpid**. See *lethargic*

inactivity (as in disuse) *n.:* **desuetude**. See *disuse*

(2) inactivity (spend the summer in a state of relative . . .) *v.i.:* **aestivate** (or **estivate**). See *laze*

(3) inactivity *n.:* **torpor**. See *lethargy*

inadequate (as in meager) *n.:* **exiguous**. See *meager*

inalienable (as in inviolable) *adj.:* **infrangible**. See *inviolable*

inane (as in foolish) *adj.:* **barmy** [British]. See *foolish*

(2) inane (as in foolish) *adj.:* **balmy**. See *foolish*

(3) inane (in a smug or complacent manner) *adj.*: **fatuous**. See *foolish*

inanimate *adj.*: **insensate**. ❖ When the guys who wrote the Bible made lust one of the seven deadly sins, they were talking about bad lust. You know, the kind that hoots at and objectifies women, that stupid, grunting, hubba-hubba kind of lust. I'm talking about good lust, the kind that might even be described as zest or vitality. . . . A man without good lust is an **insensate** mass, a lump. (Hugh O'Neill, "Your Honey or Your Wife," *Men's Health*, 1/11/1996, p. 72.)

inapplicability (as in argument where one proves or disproves a point that is not at issue) *n.*: **ignoratio elenchi** [Latin]. See *irrelevancy*

inappropriate *adj.*: **malapropos**. ❖ After Lot's wife turns back to look at the destruction of Sodom and Gomorrah and is transformed into a pillar of salt as a result, Lot tells Noah, "She always said she was the salt of the earth, and suddenly, she was." Such **malapropos** wise cracks are driven home with a relentlessly upbeat soundtrack which serenades scenes of human tragedy with bouncy, Disneyesque melodies. (Steve Rabey, "Noah's Ark" Hits Bottom: Miniseries Suffers from Lack of Accuracy, *Arlington Morning News*, 5/2/1999.)

(2) inappropriate (as in being presumptuous; venturing beyond one's province) *adj.*: **ultracrepidarian**. See *presumptuous*

(3) inappropriate (as in indecent) *adj.*: **ostrobogulous**. See *indecent*

(4) inappropriate (person who makes . . . comments that seem to be offering sympathy but instead make the person feel worse, either intentionally or unintentionally) *n.*: **Job's comforter**. See *comforter*

(5) inappropriate (comments) *n.*: **dontopedalogy**. See *foot-in-mouth*

inapt (as in inappropriate or out-of-place) *adj.*: **malapropos**. See *inappropriate*

inattentive (or preoccupied, esp. because of worries or fears) *adj.*: **distrait**. See *distracted*

in-between (as in intermediate or transitional state, phase, or condition) *adj.*: **liminal**. See *transitional*

inborn (as in inherent) *adj.*: **immanent**. See *inherent*

inbred (as in innate) *adj.*: **ingenerate**. See *innate*

(2) inbred (as in innate) *adj.*: **connate**. See *innate*

inbreeding (esp. as the result of isolation) *n.*: **homogamy**. ❖ The inbreeding of the populations observed in our study can be related to various causes: (i) positive assortative matings between individuals (**homogamy**) . . . (M. Frisch, "Genetic Diversity," *Crop Science*, 1/1/2004.)

incapable (as in powerless) *adj.*: **impuissant**. See *powerless*

incapacitated (as in out of action) *adj., adv.*: **hors de combat** [French]. See *disabled*

(2) incapacitated (pretend to be . . . to avoid work) *v.i.*: **malinger**. See *shirk*

incarcerate (as in confine) *v.t.*: **immure**. See *confine*

incarceration *n.*: **durance vile**. See *jail*

incendiary (as in inciter) *n.*: **stormy petrel**. See *inciter*

incensed *adj.*: **wroth**. See *angry*

(2) incensed (as in indignant) *n.*: **dudgeon** (often expressed as "in high dudgeon"). See *indignant*

(3) incensed *adj.*: **furibund**. See *furious*

incentive (as in stimulus) *n.*: **fillip**. See *stimulus*

incident (to) *adj.*: **appurtenant**. See *pertaining*

incidental (as in by chance) *adj.*: **adventitious**. See *chance*

incisive *adj.*: **trenchant**. ❖ [In] this rewarding six-hour documentary series [about Australia] writer-host Robert Hughes . . . provides the TV reviewer with enough witty, **trenchant** observations to fill three notebooks. (Terry Kelleher, Picks & Pans: Tube, *People*, 9/4/2000, p. 39.)

incisiveness *n.*: **acuity**. See *keenness*

inciter *n.*: **stormy petrel**. [A storm petrel is a small seabird of the north Atlantic Ocean. Early sailors thought that they foreshadowed coming storms. Today, the term "stormy petrel" is used to refer to one who is an inciter or troublemaker or a harbinger of trouble.] ❖ British Labour MP Clare Short has always been a **stormy petrel**. Throughout her political career, most of which had been spent on the opposition benches, Ms Short has made no effort to mince her words or dress them in diplomatic niceties. She has also refused to be hypocritical—"I say what I mean and if other people don't like it, that's their problem." Her bluntness has outraged her opponents as often as it has made her own colleagues squirm. (*African Business*, "Watch Out for Clare Short," 12/1/1997.)

inciting (or exhorting or inspiring to action) *adj.*: **proceleusmatic**. See *exhorting*

incivility (in behavior or speech, due to arrogance or contempt) *n.*: **contumely**. See *contempt*

inclement (as in stormy) *adj.*: **procellous**. See *stormy*

inclination (mental process marked by . . . to do something) *n.*: **conation**. See *determination*

(2) inclination (slight or faint . . .) *n.*: **velleity**. See *hope*

incline (as in upward slope) *n.*: **acclivity** (*adj.*: **acclivitous**). ❖ Nearby is Mummy Mountain, where every Saturday at sunrise a large pack heads out for runs of 10 to 20 miles over paved, rolling terrain—with a few monster **acclivities**—through some of Phoenix's poshest neighborhoods. (Doug Rennie, "Phoenix and Scottsdale," *Runner's World*, 8/1/1994, p. 40.)

(2) incline (downward . . . , esp. extending down from a fortification) *n.*: **glacis**. See *decline*

inclusion (as in insertion, of something between existing things) *n.*: **intercalation**. See *insertion*

inclusive (state of being . . . of everything) *n.*: **omneity**. See *all-inclusive*

inclusiveness (breadth of . . .) *n.*: **catholicity** [*adj.*: **catholic**]. See *universality*

incoherent (speech, esp. heard in certain Christian congregations) *n.*: **glossolalia**. See *unintelligible*

(2) incoherent (talk or act in an aimless or . . . fashion) *v.i.*: **maunder**. See *ramble*

incomparable (state of being . . . , as in superior, or state of being better) *n.*: **meliority**. See *superiority*

incompatible (as in things that do not mix together) *adj.*: **immiscible**. ❖ [T]o put it in high-tech terms, the Israelis and the Palestinians seem like different computer systems—say, IBM and Apple. Each system makes elaborate and perfect sense within its own universe, but . . . is utterly incapable of communicating with the other. . . . The two sides seem **immiscible** systems of culture and thought and history. (Lance Morrow, World: "Israel—At 40, the Dream Confronts Palestinian Fury and a Crisis of Identity," *Time*, 4/4/1988, p. 36.)

(2) incompatible (as in not mutually possible; incapable of coexisting) *adj.*: **incompossible**. ❖ Hershman would go further with her follow-up effort, Deep Contact (1984), in attempting to suture the **incompossible** spaces of the virtual and the actual with an installation where the interface consisted principally of a female figure in which portions of her fragmented body act as navigational tools or portals toward increasing interactivity. (Kevin Wynter, "Towards a Theory of Virtual Pornography," *CineAction*, 3/22/2007.)

incompetent (as in ineffective) *adj.*: **feckless**. See *ineffective*

(2) incompetent (mentally . . .) *adj.*: **non compos mentis** [Latin]. See *insane*

incomprehensible (as in involving factors not to be comprehended based on reason alone) *adj.*: **suprarational**. ❖ The miracle which is at the heart of the Christian incomprehensibility: . . . It is irrational. Science cannot explain it; science cannot conduct an experiment; it cannot formulate any equation about it. It therefore cannot exist. [In response:] A miracle is assuredly irrational (or **suprarational**) in that it escapes from the ordinary nexus of cause and effect. (Phillippe Beneton, "Pascalian Suite," *Perspectives on Political Science*, 1/1/2002.)

(2) incomprehensible (as in difficult to fathom through investigation or scrutiny) *adj.*: **inscrutable**. See *mysterious*

(3) incomprehensible (speech, esp. heard in certain Christian congregations) *n.*: **glossolalia**. See *unintelligible*

incongruity (statement that contains an . . . or is logically impossible; usually not recognized by the speaker) *n.*: **Irish bull**. ❖ "After the stewardess made the announcement," he told us, "nobody said a word! We just kept right on talking." [For another] **Irish Bull** . . . I'm indebted to my wife. At dinner, while cautioning one of the children about stuffing his mouth, she said, "Don't you put another thing in your mouth until you've swallowed it first." (Will Stanton, "Watch Out for the Wollypops," *Saturday Evening Post*, 5/1/1991.)

incongruous (as in things that do not mix together) *adj.*: **immiscible**. See *incompatible*

inconsequential (as in unimportant or insignificant) *adj.*: **nugatory**. See *unimportant* and *worthless*

(2) inconsequential (as in unimportant or trivial) *adj.*: **piffling**. See *trivial*

(3) inconsequential *adj.*: **picayune**. See *trivial*

inconsiderate (person who makes . . . comments that seem to be offering sympathy but instead make the person feel worse, either intentionally or unintentionally) *n.*: **Job's comforter**. See *comforter*

inconsistency (in terms or ideas) *n.*: **antilogy**. See *contradiction*

(2) inconsistency (statement that contains a logical . . . , usually not recognized by the speaker) *n.*: **Irish bull**. See *incongruity*

(3) inconsistency (between laws, rules, or principles) *n.*: **antinomy**. See *conflict*

inconsistent (as in not mutually possible; incapable of coexisting) *adj.* **incompossible**. See *incompatible*

(2) inconsistent (as in fickle, person whose opinion is always changing as the wind blows, like a weathervane) *n.*: **girouette** [French]. See *weathervane*

(3) inconsistent (as in hypocritical) *adj.*: **Janus-faced**. See *two-faced*

incontestable (necessarily or demonstrably . . .) *adj.*: **apodictic**. See *incontrovertible*

(2) incontestable *adj.*: **irrefragable**. See *unquestionable*

incontrovertible (as in an . . . truth) *adj.*: **apodictic**. [In the precise use of the term, for something to be apodictic it must necessarily be true, such as a mathematical equation. However, it is frequently used as a rhetorical device, such as in expressing a matter of opinion that something must be true in the opinion of the writer, or sarcastically, such as accusing another of treating something as being apodictic, when it obviously is not.] ❖ A number of letters in response to your excellent June 27 editorial "The Disaster of Failed Policy" reveal that many still do not accept the **apodictic** fact that Hussein had no hand in the 9/11 outrage. Bush's "great courage" was perfectly justified in the invasion of Afghanistan but totally served a personal vendetta . . . in the case of the war and occupation of Iraq. (Paul McCaig, "Surveying Iraq with Allawi at the Helm," *Los Angeles Times*, 7/2/2004.)

(2) incontrovertible *adj.*: **irrefragable**. See *unquestionable*

inconvenience *v.t.*: **discommode**. ❖ You kept quiet when they made air bags compulsory. When they passed laws to keep adults from owning guns. When they tried to censor the Internet. Yes, all of these eroded Americans' freedom to make decisions for themselves. . . . But none of them **discommoded** you personally, so you didn't see any reason to speak out. (Jeff Jacoby, "Posse Poised to Ambush Junk Food," *Washington Times*, 11/27/1998.)

(2) inconvenience *v.t.*: **incommode**. ❖ [G]iven that the National Gallery's "Johannes Vermeer" show had scarcely opened on Nov. 12 before it was shut down—first by budget politics, then by weather—none of the art pilgrims on the train felt at all **incommoded** by the cost or effort of the journey. (Sylviane Gold, "On Track to Vermeer," *Newsday*, 1/22/1996.)

incorporate (the ideas or attitudes of others, esp. parents, into one's own personality) *v.t.*: **introject**. ❖ Michael Friedrich . . . believes the origin for [people's] phobia[s] probably lies in their experience of how anxiety was dealt with by their parents when they were very young. . . . "If within a family there is a culture of saying, even in distressing situations, 'I can cope with this,' then the child will **introject** that feeling. Conversely, if the parents fail to give this impression, the child will absorb the idea that . . . stressful or difficult situations can't be dealt with." (Penny Hancock, Health: "Living with Fear," *Independent* [London], 3/5/2003.)

incorrigible (person) *n.*: **scapegrace**. See *scoundrel*

increase (as in burgeon or expand; lit. bear fruit) *v.i.*: **fructify**. See *burgeon*

incriminate *v.t.*: **inculpate**. See *blame*

incumbent (as in reigning) *adj.*: **regnant**. See *reigning*

in debt (to be heavily . . . or have financial instability) *n.*: **queer street** [sometimes cap.; British]

indecent *adj.*: **ostrobogulous**. ❖ The problem with CompuServe is cost. CompuServe's basic fees are only $9.95 per month. But many of the services listed in [the book] *Using CompuServe to Make You Rich* cost upwards of $22.80 per hour. So $22.80 per hour is an **ostrobogulous** amount to add to the cost of investing. Have a care, would-be rich people—the less you use CompuServe, the richer you will be. (Michael Finley, Knight Ridder/Tribune Business News, 3/5/1995.)

(2) indecent (as in lewd or obscene) *adj.*: **fescennine**. See *obscene*

(3) indecent (as in vulgar) *adj.*: **meretricious**. See *vulgar*

(4) indecent (compulsive . . . behavior) *n.*: **corpropraxia**. See *obscene*

indecision (as in doubt) *n.*: **peradventure**. See *doubt*

(2) indecision *adj.*, *v.i.*; *n.*: **shilly-shally**. See *vacillate*

indecisive (and timid and cautious) *adj.*: **Prufrockian**. See *timid*

(2) indecisive (as in fickle, person whose opinion is always changing as the wind blows, like a weathervane) *n.*: **girouette** [French]. See *weathervane*

(3) indecisive (or such a person) *adj.*, *n.*: **namby-pamby**. See *spineless*

(4) indecisive (to be . . .) *v.i.*: **dither**. See *procrastinate*

indecisiveness (as in chronic inability to make decisions) *n.*: **abulia** (or **aboulia**). [Another related definition of this word is a lack of willpower. See *willpower*.] ❖ When the rebellion came, in his first engagement as commander of the U.S. Army [in the Civil War, General Grant] lost 17,000 men by nightfall. The survivors, accustomed to McClellan's chronic **abulia** at such moments, assumed he would call retreat. But after a night during which he is said to have wept, Grant gave the signal for pursuit. A soldier wrote: "For the first time, we felt the boss had arrived." (Matthew Scully, review of *Ulysses S. Grant: Memoirs and Selected Letters, 1839–1865*, edited by Mary Drake McFeely et al., *National Review*, 12/17/1990.)

(2) indecisiveness (as in the dilemma of being given a choice between two equally appealing alternatives and thus being able to choose neither one) *n.*: **Buridan's ass**. See *paralysis*

indecorous (as in inappropriate or out of place) *adj.*: **malapropos**. See *inappropriate*

indefensible (as in unpardonable) *adj.*: **irremissible**. See *unpardonable*

indefinite (as in equivocal, word, phrase, or expression) *n.*: **equivoque**. See *equivocal*

(2) indefinite (as in having multiple interpretations or signifying different things) *adj.*: **multivocal**. See *multivocal*

(3) indefinite (in terms of the effect that one action or activity will have on another) *adj.*: **Heisenbergian**. See *uncertain*

indefinitely *adv.*: **sine die** [Latin; generally used with respect to an adjournment of a meeting or of a political session]. ❖ Both chambers adjourned **sine die** Sunday, ending the Legislature's third special session of the year. (Peggy

Fikac, "Legislature OKs New Map," *San Antonio Express-News*, 10/13/2003.)

indelible *adj.*: **ineffaceable**. ❖ Censure [of President Clinton] is not meaningless, it will not subvert the Constitution, and it will be indelibly seared into the **ineffaceable** record of history for all future generations to see and to ponder. For those who fear that it can be expunged from the record, be assured that it can never be erased from the history books. Like the mark that was set upon Cain, it will follow even beyond the grave. (Robert Byrd, "Don't Tinker with Impeachment," *Washington Post*, 2/3/1999.)

(2) indelible (as in incapable of being overthrown, driven out, or subdued by force) *adj.*: **inexpugnable**. See *impregnable*

independence (new period of . . . , esp. as a contrast to, and sandwiched between, periods of oppression or lack of rights) *n.*: **Prague Spring**. See *liberalization*

independent (as in neutral) *adj.*: **adiaphorous**. See *neutral*

(2) independent (of or relating to events that occur close in time but which are . . . of each other) *adj.*: **acausal**. See *unconnected*

(3) independent (thinker, esp. on matters of morals and religion) *n.*: **libertine**. See *freethinker*

indescribable *adj.*: **ineffable**. ❖ There's no question that Charles Schulz' characters tap into an **ineffable** quality of the human spirit. (Mary Voboril, "Importance of *Peanuts*," *Newsday*, 12/29/1999.)

indestructible (as in incapable of being overthrown, driven out, or subdued by force) *adj.*: **inexpugnable**. See *impregnable*

(2) indestructible *adj.*: **irrefrangible**. See *unbreakable*

indeterminate (in depth, meaning, or significance) *adj.*: **unplumbable**. See *unexplorable*

(2) indeterminate (in terms of the effect that one action or activity will have on another) *adj.*: **Heisenbergian**. See *uncertain*

indicate (as in send a signal) *v.t.*, *v.i.*: **semaphore**. See *signal*

(2) indicate *v.t.*: **adumbrate**. See *foreshadow*

(3) indicate *v.t.*: **betoken**. See *portend*

indication (audio . . .) *n.*: **klaxon**. See *signal*

indifference (a matter of . . . , esp. in matters of religion and theology; i.e., neither right nor wrong, beneficial nor harmful) *n.*: **adiaphoron** (*adj.*: **adiaphorous**). ❖ The 14 contributors to this book, all claiming to be Christian . . . are convinced that the Holocaust is not an **adiaphoron**, a matter of no direct significance to the substance of Christian theology and faith. All are steeped in the history of the Church's anti-Judaism, of the Western world's antisemitism, and . . . how utterly deeply the Holocaust . . . has compromised, if not irreparably distorted, Christianity itself . . . (Martin Rumscheidt, review of *"Good News" after Auschwitz? Christian Faith within a Post-Holocaust World*, edited by Carol Rittner and John K. Roth, *Shofar*, 1/1/2003.)

(2) indifference (esp. on matters of politics or religion) *n.*: **Laodiceanism**. [This term derives from the Laodiceans, a Christian community in the ancient city of Laodicea. They were criticized for their perceived indifference or neutrality on religious and political issues.] ❖ As Kevin Myers wrote in *The Irish Times* in 1991 [describing Bishop] Walton Empey: the accent is broad, the manner genial, the figure ample, the laughter ready, and most important of all, the opinion strong and free and forthright. All the political timidity, the [pretense] at **Laodiceanism** lest opinion on all but traffic accidents and dog licences be taken as disloyalty to Ireland, . . . all are absent from Walton Empey. (Patsy McGarry, "Archbishop Walton Empey to Retire in July," *Irish Times*, 5/1/2002.)

(3) indifference (sometimes in matters spiritual, and sometimes leading to depression) *n.*: **acedia**. See *apathy*

indifferent (esp. neither right nor wrong, beneficial nor harmful) *adj.*: **adiaphorous**. See *neutral*

(2) indifferent *adj.*: **pococurante**. See *apathetic*

indigence *n.*: **penury**. See *poverty*

indigenous *adj.*: **autochthonous**. ❖ Just as the Japanese can adjust to being the world leaders in information technology without ceasing to be Japanese, so the Inuit can adjust to the snowmobile and the rifle without losing touch with whatever it is that binds them together. For cultures are not monoliths. They are fragmentary, patchworks of **autochthonous** and foreign elements. (Anthony Pagden, "Culture Wars," *New Republic*, 11/16/1998.)

(2) indigenous *adj.*: **aboriginal**. See *native*

indigent *adj.*: **impecunious**. See *poor*

(2) indigent *adj.*: **necessitous**. See *poor*

indigestion *n.*: **dyspepsia** (*adj.*: **dyspeptic**). ❖ Now that she was so close to what she wanted all her life [a high tennis ranking], Willy's stomach didn't yowl with appetite, but clenched in clammy, **dyspeptic** fear. (Lionel Shriver, *Double Fault*, Doubleday [1997], p. 162.)

indignant (mood) *n.*: **dudgeon** (often expressed as "in high dudgeon"). ❖ The American College of Obstetricians and Gynecologists was in high **dudgeon** last week over the difference some private health insurers see between Viagra, the new impotency pill, and birth control pills. Some insurers will pay for Viagra prescriptions but will not cover prescription birth control. That, the doctors said, constitutes a clear case of gender discrimination. (*Minneapolis Star Tribune*, "Viagra & the Pill: A Silly Attempt to Find Gender Bias," 5/18/1998.)

indignity (being subject to . . . , esp. public) *n.*: **obloquy**. See *abuse*

indirectly (proceeding . . . esp. in a cautious or furtive manner) *adv.*: **crabwise**. [This word, often seen in the phrase "moving crabwise," can be used both figuratively, as in the example here, and literally. See *sideways*.] Britain's Official Secrets Act . . . makes it a crime to disclose any Government information without official approval, even if the purpose is to expose wrongdoing. . . . [T]he Reagan Administration is now trying to impose on the United States a replica of the Official Secrets Act. Few have noticed, because the Administration is moving **crabwise** toward that objective. It is not asking Congress to pass a law: Congress would say no. Instead it is seeking silence by an ingenious lawsuit. (Anthony Lewis, "Abroad at Home; Silence by Lawsuit," *New York Times*, 2/17/1985.)

indiscriminate (as in actions taken or statements made that are broader than necessary to hit their target or accomplish their goal) *adj.*, *n.*: **blunderbuss**. See *scattershot*

indispensable (element or condition) *n.*: **sine qua non** [Latin]. ❖ A lean physique is a **sine qua non** of physical attractiveness in girls and women alike. In the words of a Bloomingdale's ad, the current ideal womanly shape is "being lean, slender as the night, narrow as an arrow, pencil thin," get the point? (Debra Lynn Stephens, "The Beauty Myth and Female Consumers: The Controversial Role of Advertising," *Journal of Consumer Affairs*, 6/22/1994, p. 137.)

indisputable (necessarily or demonstrably . . .) *adj.*: **apodictic**. See *incontrovertible*

(2) indisputable *adj.*: **irrefragable**. See *unquestionable*

individual (as in specific to one person or thing) *adj.*: **idiographic**. See *unique*

individualist (esp. on matters of morals and religion) *n.*: **libertine**. See *freethinker*

individuality (as in that quality that makes one thing different from any other) *n.*: **haecceity** (or **haeccity**). ❖ [Author Nicholson Baker has] an ability to evoke the sensual **haecceity** of ordinary things. [He] notices a Franklin Library edition of [John Updike's] *Rabbit, Run*, which he pulls from the shelf: "The padded, bright red binding was somewhat more reminiscent of a comfortable corner booth at an all-night, all-vinyl coffee shop than one might have thought fitting for so aggressively 'classic' an enterprise." (Michael Dirda, "Rabbit Pursuit: A Passion for Updike," *Washington Post Book World*, 5/6/1991.)

(2) individuality (as in self-identity) *n.*: **ipseity**. See *self-identity*

indivisible (or unbreakable) *adj.*: **infrangible**. See *unbreakable*

indolent (as in lazy) *adj.*: **fainéant** [French]. See *lazy*

inducement (as in stimulus) *n.*: **fillip**. See *stimulus*

indulge (as in placate) *v.t.*: **propitiate**. See *placate*

(2) indulge (as in treat with excessive concern) *n., v.t.*: **wet-nurse**. See *coddle*

(3) indulge (in a pampering or overprotective way) *v.t.*: **mollycoddle**. See *overprotect*

(4) indulge *v.t.*: **cosset**. See *pamper*

indulgence (excessive . . . , esp. with respect to eating or drinking) *n.*: **crapulence**. ❖ What better way is there to shrug off your Yuletide **crapulence** than by slumping on the sofa and ogling . . . a game of darts? The world championships have arrived. . . . Some participants will no doubt look like they, too, have been overdoing the grub and grog, but the game is trying determinedly to rid itself of a slovenly image. (Travers, "Botham and Lloyd: A Partnership Founded on Expertise," *Scotland on Sunday*, 12/26/1999.)

(2) indulgence (in the face of adversity) *n.*: **longanimity**. See *patience*

indulgent (in exhibiting emotion or celebration) *adj.*: **saturnalian**. See *uninhibited*

(2) indulgent (person, spec. someone excessively devoted to luxury or sensual pleasures) *n.*: **voluptuary**. See *hedonist* and *sensualist*

(3) indulgent *adj.*: **apolaustic**. See *hedonistic*

industrious (person) *n.*: **Stakhanovite**. See *workaholic*

ineffective *adj.*: **feckless**. ❖ The Rangers, often defensively **feckless** during a season in which they finished with 86 points—18 fewer than the Devils—have been airtight since the start of the playoffs, yielding 15 goals in 10 games. Why hadn't they played this way all season? (Austin Murphy, NHL Playoffs: "Crunch Time—The Pursuit of the Stanley Cup Raises the Level of Intensity," *Sports Illustrated*, 5/19/1997, p. 36.)

(2) ineffective (as in powerless) *adj.*: **impuissant**. See *powerless*

(3) ineffective (as in vain or worthless) *adj.*: **nugatory**. See *worthless*

(4) ineffective (efforts that are laborious but . . .) *adj.*: **Sisyphean**. See *futile*

(5) ineffective *adj.*: **inutile**. See *useless*

(6) ineffective *adj.*: **otiose**. See *useless*

inefficient (actions of pompous but . . . government officials) *n.*: **bumbledom**. See *bureaucracy*

inept (actions of pompous but . . . government officials) *n.*: **bumbledom**. See *bureaucracy*

(2) inept (habitually . . . person) *n.*: **schlemiel** [Yiddish]. See *bumbler*

(3) inept (as in clumsy) *adj.*: **bunglesome**

(4) inept (as in clumsy) *adj.*: **ambisinister**. See *clumsy*

inescapable *adj.*: **ineluctable**. See *unavoidable*

inescapably (as in whether or not willingly or desired) *adv.*: **nolens volens** [Latin]. See *unavoidably*

inevitable (as in unavoidable) *adj.*: **ineluctable**. See *unavoidable*

inevitably (as in whether or not willingly or desired) *adv.*: **nolens volens** [Latin]. See *unavoidably*

inexact (as in equivocal, word, phrase, or expression) *n.*: **equivoque**. See *equivocal*

(2) inexact (as in having multiple interpretations or signifying different things) *adj.*: **multivocal**. See *multivocal*

(3) inexact (as in actions taken or statements made that are broader than necessary to hit their target or accomplish their goal) *adj., n.*: **blunderbuss**. See *scattershot*

inexplicable (as in perplexing) *adj.*: **quisquous**. See *perplexing*

inexcusable (as in unpardonable) *adj.*: **irremissible** See *unpardonable*

inexpressible *adj.*: **ineffable**. See *indescribable*

in fact *adj., adv.*: **de facto** (as contrasted with de jure: legally or by law) [Latin]. ❖ While ultra-Orthodox leaders [in Israel] regularly bluster against the courts, they comply with court rulings. Even more telling, they regularly turn to the courts when they think that doing so will protect their interests. The ultra-Orthodox oppose the courts de jure, but they do not **de facto**. (Noah Efron, *Real Jews,* Basic Books [2003], p. 218.)

infallibility *n.*: **inerrancy**. ❖ "A wife is to submit graciously to the servant leadership of her husband, even as the church willingly submits to the headship of Christ."—New 18th Article of the Baptist Faith and Message. The Southern Baptists, who have always believed in biblical **inerrancy**, set off an uproar this week when they lifted their language on family life straight into the headlines. (Cathy Lynn Grossman, "Baptists Explain the Moral Tone," *USA Today,* 6/11/1998.)

infallible (necessarily or demonstrably . . . , as in indisputable) *adj.*: **apodictic**. See *incontrovertible*

infamous *adj.*: **flagitious**. See *scandalous*

infant (collection of clothing and equipment for newborn . . .) *n.*: **layette**. See *newborn*

(2) infant (newborn . . . , esp. younger than four weeks old) *n.*: **neonate**. See *newborn*

(3) infant (who is deserted or abandoned) *n.*: **foundling**. See *orphan*

infantile (retention of . . . characteristics into adulthood) *n.*: **paedomorphism** (person who retains these characteristics, *n.*: **paedomorph**). ❖ Who was [Adolf Hitler]? He was, primarily, a child, a paedomorph. He retained infantile characteristics into adulthood. . . . Human **paedomorphism** stunts the development of the normal adult instincts of compassion, fear and rational contemplation of the consequences of one's deeds. The **paedomorph** is like a small, spoilt child, incapable of generosity. (Kevin Myers, "The Hatred of Hitler," *Irish Times,* 4/29/1995.)

(2) infantile *adj.*: **jejune**. See *juvenile*

(3) infantile *adj.*: **puerile**. See *juvenile*

infatuation (mad or crazy . . . , as in love) *n.*: **amour fou** [French]. See *love*

(2) infatuation (spec. the emotional thrill and excitement one feels when initially in love) *n.*: **limerence** (*adj.*: **limerent**). See *love*

infected (morally . . .) *v.t.*: **cankered**. See *corrupted*

infection (of or relating to an . . . developed by a patient while in a hospital) *adj.*: **nosocomial**. See *hospital*

inference *n.*: **illation**. ❖ Whatever the future of campaign financing, its consequence on the millennial presidency and congressional elections will be immense. The current rules of engagement narrowly restrict campaign fund raising, courting sharp practice and abuse. The **illation** that elected office can be bought screams reform. Nonetheless, failure to underwrite the high cost of political campaigns spells defeat. (Rotan E. Lee, "Democratic President Means Advances for Community," *Philadelphia Tribune,* 5/5/2000.)

inferior (as in made without regard to quality) *adj.*: **catchpenny**. ❖ Nothing in *Gladiator* or *The Patriot* proved as engrossing as Mike Figgis' *Time Code,* a split-screen, real-time movie that applied *Blair Witch* economics to a grown-up storyline. This, not the **catchpenny** *Blair Witch 2,* was the true sequel to last year's most striking cinematic invention [i.e., the original *Blair Witch Project*]. (Thomas Sutcliffe, Review of the Year: Arts—Cultural Overview, *Independent* [London], 12/29/2000.)

(2) inferior (rank, esp. in the military) *n.*: **subaltern**. See *subordinate*

(3) inferior (as in acting subservient as opposed to leading) *adj.*: **sequacious**. See *subservient*

infernal (and fiery) *adj.*: **sulfurous** (or **sulphurous**). ❖ Any man who becomes Senate majority leader [like Trent Lott is] someone who instinctively knows that opening his raincoat to flash a little nostalgia for the segregation era—the obvious interpretation of his testimonial to Mr. Thurmond's segregationist presidential candidacy—will induce sudden political death, not to mention a **sulfurous** afterlife. How could Mr. Lott have meant what he seemed to say? It had to be a dopey mistake. . . . (Diana West, "The Lott Parable: America Must Be Colorblind," *Washington Times,* 12/20/2002.)

(2) infernal (as in dark, dismal, or gloomy) *adj.*: **acherontic**. See *gloomy*

(3) infernal (relating to gods and spirits of the . . . regions) *adj.*: **chthonic**. See *underworld*

(4) infernal *adj.*: **Stygian** (sometimes cap.). See *hellish*

infinite (as in everlasting) *adj.*: **sempiternal**. See *everlasting*

infinitely *adv.*: **in aeternum** [Latin]. See *forever*

infirm (and sickly person, esp. one morbidly concerned with his own health) *n., adj.*: **valetudinarian**. See *sickly*

(2) infirm (elderly person) *n.*: **Struldbrug**. See *decrepit*

inflamer *n.*: **stormy petrel**. See *inciter*

inflammable *adj.*: **tindery**. See *flammable*

inflammation (of skin due to exposure to cold) *n.*: **chilblains**. ❖ Metropolitan smokers are a forlorn lot these days. As more cities ban cigarettes in public places, smokers are altering every daily habit but the one they most crave. . . . Shivering in shirt-sleeves outside their office complexes, they increase the risk that they will succumb not to emphysema but to **chilblains**. (Richard Corliss, Marketing: "Chuff Chuff, Puff Puff, All Aboard the *Marlboro Unlimited*, a High-Tech Train Where You Can Smoke in Nearly Every Car," *Time*, 1/8/1996, p. 51.)

inflate (as in exaggerate) *v.t.*: **overegg**. See *exaggerate*

inflated (as in pompous) *adj.*: **flatulent**. See *pompous*

(2) inflated (as in pompous) *adj.*: **turgid**. See *pompous*

(3) inflated (as in swollen or distended) *adj.*: **tumid**. See *swollen* and *bombastic*

(4) inflated (as in swollen) *adj.*: **dropsical**. See *swollen*

(5) inflated (as in swollen, used often of body parts such as the penis) *adj.*: **tumescent**. See *swollen*

inflexibility (as in rigidity, esp. with respect to moral or ethical principles or practices) *n.*: **rigorism**. See *rigidity*

inflexible (and stern) *adj.*: **flinty**. See *stern*

(2) inflexible (as in hardened) *adj.*: **sclerotic**. See *hardened*

(3) inflexible (as in narrow-minded) *adj.*: **hidebound**. See *narrow-minded*

(4) inflexible (as in one who clings to an opinion or belief even after being shown that it is wrong) *n.*: **mumpsimus**. See *stubborn*

(5) inflexible (as in practice of refusing to consider a change in one's beliefs or opinions, esp. in politics) *n.*: **standpatism**. See *stubbornness*

(6) inflexible (as in stubborn) *adj.*: **pervicacious**. See *stubborn*

(7) inflexible (in holding to a belief or opinion) *adj.*: **pertinacious**. See *stubborn*

(8) inflexible (to make or become . . .) *v.t., adj.*: **indurate**. See *harden*

inflict (oneself or one's ideas in an unwelcome way) *v.t.*: **obtrude**. See *impose*

influence (of one political state over others) *n.*: **hegemony**. See *dominance*

influential (person, esp. in intellectual or literary circles) *n.*: **mandarin**. ❖ [*New York Post* reporter Murray] Kempton was a **mandarin** among the street columnists, schooled in subjects as various as Etruscan mosaics and the internal politics of the Five Families. (David Remnick, *King of the World*, Random House [1999], p. 45.)

inform (on, as in tattle) *v.i.*: **peach**. See *tattle*

informal (language of the people) *n.*: **vulgate**. See *vernacular*

information (false . . . accepted as fact due to repetition in print) *n.*: **factoid**. See *inaccuracy*

informed (person who is very . . . in many areas) *n.*: **polyhistor**. See *knowledgeable*

(2) informed (person who is very . . . in many areas) *n.*: **polymath**. See *scholar*

(3) informed (self-proclaimed . . . people) *n.pl.*: **illuminati**. See *enlightened*

(4) informed (being . . . with or familiar with something) *adj.*: **au fait** [French]. See *familiar*

informer (esp. who betrays under guise of friendship) *n.*: **Judas**. See *betrayer*

(2) informer *n.*: **delator**. See *accuser*

infraction (small or trifling . . .) *n.*: **peccadillo**.

❖ They got their baseball uniforms dirty, chugged booze, chased women, ate slabs of red meat, smoked unfiltered cigarettes and busted up the Copacabana night club every now and then. And the sports heroes never had to say they were sorry, because the newspapers godded them up and never told us about their **peccadilloes**. (Bernie Miklasz, "Life in a Bottle Over, The Mick Has New Fight," *St. Louis Post-Dispatch*, 6/9/1995.)

ingenious (as in creative and/or original) *adj.*: **Promethean**. See *creative*

(2) ingenious (as in resourceful, person) *n.*: **debrouillard** (or **débrouillard**) [French]. See *resourceful*

ingenuous (as in guileless) *n.*: **artless**. See *guileless*

(2) ingenuous (false or insincere show of . . . or naive behavior) *adj.*: **faux-naïf** [French]. See *naive*

ingest *v.t.*: **incept**. ❖ With the improvement of living level and the change of meal structure that means people **incept** more fat than ever, the obesity patients are more and more in China, which will introduce easily many kinds of diseases, especially the cardiovascular diseases. (Chinese Markets for Weight Control/Loss Products, "Weight Loss/Diet Products Industry Assessments," 1/1/2003.)

ingesting (act or process of) *n.*: **deglutition**. See *swallowing*

ingratiating (in a smug or false manner) *adj.*: **oleaginous**. See *unctuous*

inhabitant (of a town) *n.*: **burgher**. See *resident*

inhale *v.t.*: **aspirate**. ❖ Dr. Austin went on to explain that my mother might need the help of a respirator. Already, he said, he had contacted the intensive care unit (ICU) on the assumption that she had pneumonia, a typical result of **aspirating** foreign matter into the lung. (Leslie Goerner, "You Do Understand About DNR? Don't You? Don't You?" *Commonweal*, 11/21/1997, p. 20.)

inherent *adj.*: **immanent**. ❖ For the first time in my young life, I glimpsed something [Sophia Loren] sublime and preternatural and irrevocable and everlasting—at once an aura, a presence, an **immanent** beauty and elegance, a luminous charisma of sensuality and serenity, maternal light and darkest passion— that imbues certain women. (Jimmy Breslin, Women We Love: The Definitive Selection, 1994, *Esquire*, 8/1/1994, p. 58.)

(2) inherent (as in innate) *adj.*: **connate**. See *innate*

(3) inherent (as in inviolable) *adj.*: **infrangible**. See *inviolable*

inheritor *n.*: **heritor**. ❖ The [Massachusetts Bay Colony] thrived for 40 years or so, before economic downturn and the horrors of King Philip's War made the inhabitants less sure of God's favor. By then the original migrants had mostly died out and their social and religious discipline was greatly diluted in their **heritors**. (David Mehegan, "The Strength and Struggle of the Settlers," *Boston Globe*, 11/28/1991.)

initial (in sequence or time) *adj.*: **primordial**. See *first*

initiative (as in energy coupled with a will to succeed) *n.*: **spizzerinctum**. See *energy*

injection (as in insertion, of something between existing things) *n.*: **intercalation**. See *insertion*

injudicious (comments) *n.*: **dontopedalogy**. See *foot-in-mouth*

injured (as in out of action) *adj., adv.*: **hors de combat** [French]. See *disabled*

injurious (mutually . . . to both sides) *adj.*: **internecine**. See *destructive*

(2) injurious *adj.*: **nocent**. See *harmful*

(3) injurious *adj.*: **nocuous**. See *harmful*

inn (large . . .) *n.*: **caravansary**. ❖ Because L. A. is the endless-summer beach city, you might as well enjoy a room with a view, an ocean view, especially since the pink grande dame, the Beverly Hills Hotel, has been closed for a three-year renovation. The **caravansary** of the moment is Shutters on the Beach. (William Stadiem, "L.A. When It Settles," *Esquire*, 3/1/1994, p. 37.)

innate *adj.*: **ingenerate** [This word is occasionally dictionary-recognized but is rare.] ❖ [In visiting Grand Forks, ND, my sister found that] human beings, faced by the reality of our littleness, impotence and radically mutual need, were washed clean of the pathetic and patently artificial barriers of religion, race, ethnicity, maleness and femaleness, and woefully stupid economic and social status whose **ingenerate** emptiness all collapsed in the face of equal opportunity destruction. (Glif Marouis, Perspective: "Garbage In—Garbage Out," *Los Angeles Sentinel*, 5/28/1997.)

(2) innate *adj.*: **connate**. ❖ Was this the first time these two members of the Palestinian Army showed any propensity for blowing themselves up in the vicinity of Jews? . . . If there was a conspiracy, did their superiors know about it? . . . These and similar questions would be easy to pose to Yasser Arafat, but his **connate** predilection for lying would probably prevent our getting any serious answers. (Yehiel Leiter, "Cost & Consequence," *Jerusalem Post*, 4/4/1997.)

(3) innate *adj.*: **immanent**. See *inherent*

(4) innate (reaction, as in reflex) *n.*: **tropism**. See *reflex*

inner circle (as in advisors, often scheming or plotting) *n.*: **camarilla**. See *advisors*

innermost (as in secret parts, thoughts, or places) *n.*: **penetralia**. See *secret*

inner self (as in soul) *n.*: **anima**. See *soul*

innkeeper *n.*: **boniface**. ❖ Else Barth's Seventh Inn in the Seven Trails subdivision is marking its 30th anniversary. The Copenhagen-born **boniface** recently visited her hometown and caught song stylist Clinton Gallagher at that city's premiere hotel lounge. (Jerry Berger, "Newspaper Recalls 'Gentlemen's Agreement' That Casts Mizzou in Bad Light," *St. Louis Post-Dispatch*, 5/6/2001.)

innocence (determining . . . or determination of . . . through testimony of others) *n.*: **compurgation**. See *acquittal*

innocent (and carefree time) *adj.*: **prelapsarian**. [This word literally means "before the Fall," referring to that period in the Garden of Eden before Adam and Eve lost their innocence by eating from the Tree of Knowledge. It is used more generally to refer to any innocent and carefree time, especially before dire events that follow. Its opposite is postlapsarian. See *downfall*.] ❖ Cyberspace, to its early denizens, was supposed to be a **prelapsarian** world, free from the taint of commerce . . . full of sweetness and light and universal siblinghood. . . . Well, have you visited cyberspace lately? . . . There is commerce aplenty, but that's not the problem. . . . The nasty parts of the Web are where people are doing what the Founding Surfers intended: expressing themselves and forming communities. (Michael Kinsley, "Cybercreeps Run Amok; Internet Libertarians Should Learn Civil Discourse," *Washington Post*, 7/24/2005.)

(2) innocent (as in guileless) *n.*: **artless**. See *guileless*

(3) innocent (false or insincere showing of childlike or . . . behavior) *adj.*: **faux-naïf** [French]. See *naive*

innovative (as in creative, and/or original) *adj.*: **Promethean**. See *creative*

(2) innovative (love of or enthusiasm for anything . . .) *n.*: **neophilia**. See *novelty*

inopportune (occurrence, leading to an awkward or embarrassing situation) *n.*: **contretemps**. See *mishap*

inquire (closely) *v.t.*: **catechize**. See *question*

(2) inquire (formally about governmental policy or action) *v.t.*: **interpellate**. See *interrogate*

inquirer (of an astrologer) *n.*: **querent**. See *questioner*

(2) inquirer *n.*: **querist**. See *questioner*

inquiry (as in formal . . . into or discussion of a subject) *n.*: **disquisition**. See *discourse*

insane (as in not of sound mind) *adj.*: **non compos mentis** [Latin]. ❖ Three years ago, when Spargur, a retired Indianapolis beautician, attended the tapdance recital of one of her 11 great-great-grandchildren, she declared her intention to sign up for lessons. Hearing the news, her family wanted to have her declared **non compos mentis**. (*People*, "On the Move:

When Octogenarian Dance Queen Ruth Spargur First Put on Taps Three Years Ago, Something Clicked," 6/20/1988, p. 75.)

(2) insane (informal as in daffy or loony) *adj.*: **doolally**. See *crazy*

(3) insane (person) *n.*: **bedlamite**. See *lunatic*

(4) insane (slightly . . . , often used humorously) *adj.*: **tetched**. See *crazy*

insatiable *adj.*: **edacious**. See *voracious*

inscribed (on rock) *adj.*: **rupestrian**. See *carved*

insect (of or relating to the . . . order that includes grasshoppers, crickets, and praying mantises) *adj.*: **orthopterous**. [The *News & Record* asked its readers to critique "Grasshoppers" as the new name for Greensboro's minor-league baseball team. One reader stated: "It makes sense to me. Greensboro has long been known for its abundance of plant-eating **orthopterous** insects. However, I would've preferred a name that conveys a message on environmental issues. But I guess the 'Greensboro Holes in the Ozone' would be too much of a mouthful." (Jeff Curley, letter to the editor, *Piedmont Triad [NC] News & Record*, 10/5/2004.)

insects (of or relating to . . .) *adj.*: **entomic**. The creatures on display in [*Alien Empire*] are real, although some seem improbable, and the science has nothing fictional about it. What we have here, courtesy of Nature and the BBC, is an **entomic** universe of busy bees, battling beetles, beautiful butterflies and other of the billions of bugs that share the globe with human-come-latelys. (Walter Goodman, "Sex, Beauty, Home and Travel Tips on Bugs," *New York Times*, 2/9/1996.)

(2) insects (study of) *n.*: **entomology**. ❖ "We have 450,000 bugs and spiders that all have to go to the new building intact, so we'll hand-carry the specimen drawers," said Virginia Scott, manager of the museum's **entomology** collection. (Jim Erickson, "Bugging Out: 450,000 Fragile Insects Being Packed up for Trip to New Lodgings in CU's Natural History Museum," *Denver Rocky Mountain News*, 5/14/2001.)

(3) insects (prickling or tingling or itching sensation that . . . are crawling on you) *n.*: **formication**. See *prickling*

(4) insects (feeding on) *adj.*: **entomophagous**. See *bugs*

insecure (and/or sullen and/or socially withdrawn or inexperienced) *adj.*: **farouche** [French]. See *shy*

inseminate *v.t.*: **fecundate**. See *impregnate*

insensitive (as in cruel) *adj.*: **fell** (*n.*: **fellness**). See *cruel*

(2) insensitive (as in thick-skinned) *adj.*: **pachydermatous**. See *thick-skinned*

inseparable (or unbreakable) *adj.*: **infrangible**. See *unbreakable*

insertion (of something between existing things) *n.*: **intercalation**. ❖ [In the employment process for low-wage jobs, there is no bargaining stage for the employee because] first you are an applicant and then suddenly you are an orientee. . . . The **intercalation** of the drug test between application and hiring tilts the playing field even further, establishing that you, and not the employer, are the one who has something to prove. (Barbara Ehrenreich, *Nickel & Dimed*, Metropolitan Books [2001], p. 149.)

(2) insertion (esp. of penis into vagina) *n.*: **intromission** (*v.t.*: **intromit**). See *penetration*

inside out (to turn . . .) *v.t.*: **evaginate**. ❖ [Lynn Barber, author of *Mostly Men: Interviews*] should be locked up for preternatural deployment of lethal armaments. She does nothing as vulgar as assassinate character. Rather, she deftly **evaginates** her subject and displays the remains skewered on a pike at the city gates. Surrounding her victims' masochism there lurks mystery almost as deep as her incisions. . . . Devoured collectively [her interviews] cruelly expose the petty vanity which must be typical of us all. (Patricia Morris, Books: "Demon Barber's Cut-Throat Razor," *Observer*, 4/28/1991.)

insight *n.*: **aperçu** [French]. ❖ He lights another cigarette and gives me another **aperçu**: "You don't drink and drive in Russia, and you don't pick a fight. They're all in the military. They like

Schwarzenegger. They love Chuck Norris. They like to kill." (Patric Kuh, "Comrade, Your Table Is Ready [Restaurants in Moscow, Russia]," *Esquire*, 3/1/1997, p. 96.)

(2) insight (sudden . . .) *n.*: **epiphany**. See *realization*

insightful *adj.*: **trenchant**. See *incisive*

insignificant (as in excusable fault, offense, or sin) *adj.*: **venial**. See *forgivable*

(2) insignificant (or worthless matter) *n.*: **dross**. See *worthless*

(3) insignificant (thing or matter) *n.*: **bagatelle**. See *trifling*

(4) insignificant *adj.*: **footling** [chiefly British]. See *unimportant*

(5) insignificant *adj.*: **nugacious**. See *trivial*

(6) insignificant *adj.*: **nugatory**. See *unimportant*

(7) insignificant *adj.*: **picayune**. See *trivial*

(8) insignificant *adj.*: **piffling**. See *trivial*

insincere (esp. praise or flattery) *adj.*: **fulsome**. ❖ One of the Chicago Cubs, third baseman Tyler Houston, had reached first. . . . "Tell you what," Houston said [to the opposing Phillies first baseman]. "You guys got a good club." The numbers the game produces are ruthlessly truthful, but baseball conversation is often false or **fulsome**. What is honest stands out, and Houston was telling the truth. (Michael Bamberger, Baseball: "No Sitting Still: Throwing an Impressive Combination of Pitching and Muscle at the Hapless Cubs, the Phillies Showed Why They Might Soon Blossom into a Contender," *Sports Illustrated*, 7/12/1999, p. 42.)

(2) insincere *adj.*: **crocodilian**. ❖ I made a toll call to NWL's policyholder department and got one of those unctuous, **crocodilian** recordings telling me to make a selection from a menu of confusing choices. I did, and—eureka!—was slickly transferred to a second oily voice offering a second menu of choices. I bit my tongue and pressed No. 1. Then a third sleek, insincere recording responded: "Thank you for calling NWL. We will be with you as soon as possible." (*Joliet [IL] Herald News*,

"Insurance Company Isn't User-Friendly," 2/6/1997.)

(3) insincere *adj.*: **oleaginous**.

(4) insincere (or hypocritical, sanctimonious, and/or pious speech) *n.*: **cant**. See *pious*

(5) insincere (as in excessive or contrived sentimentality) *adj.*: **bathetic** (*n.*: **bathos**). See *sentimental*

insipid (intellectual nourishment, like baby food) *n.*: **pabulum** (also **pablum**). ❖ Idealist or Egotist? The only infraction that Greco-Roman silver medalist Matt Ghaffari is guilty of is accepting all the invitations extended to him and not having an agent to spoon-feed him noble **pabulum** to regurgitate for the media. (*Sports Illustrated*, unsigned letter to the editor, 10/21/1996, p. 8.)

(2) insipid (as in bland, though wanting to appear grandiose or having pretensions of grandeur) *adj.*: **blandiose**. See *bland*

(3) insipid (as in uninteresting or dull) *adj.*: **jejune**. See *uninteresting*

(4) insipid *adj.*: **anodyne**. See *bland*

insistent (as in one who clings to an opinion or belief even after being shown that it is wrong) *n.*: **mumpsimus**. See *stubborn*

(2) insistent (as in practice of refusing to consider a change in one's beliefs or opinions, esp. in politics) *n.*: **standpatism**. See *stubbornness*

(3) insistent (as in stubborn) *adj.*: **pervicacious**. See *stubborn*

(4) insistent (but obstinate) *adj.*: **contumacious**. See *obstinate*

(5) insistent (in holding to a belief or opinion) *adj.*: **pertinacious**. See *stubborn*

insolence (in behavior or speech) *n.*: **contumely**. See *contempt*

(2) insolence *n.*: **hardihood**. See *gall*

insolent (as in being presumptuous; venturing beyond one's province) *adj.*: **ultracrepidarian**. See *presumptuous*

inspect (closely, esp. for purposes of surveillance) *v.t.*: **perlustrate**. See *examine*

inspector (as in investigator or examiner) *n.*: **scrutator**. See *examiner*

inspiration (creative . . .) *n.*: **afflatus**. ❖ As for the world of high intellect, that is where my doubts about the claims for the genome begin. There are all kinds of intellect. Some types of intellect, for instance the artistic, are distinguished by aesthetic **afflatus**. Only a person far gone on the scientific method would believe an artist's genius can be explained by genes. (R. Emmett Tyrrell Jr., "Miracles . . . and Misgivings," *Washington Times*, 6/30/2000.)

(2) inspiration (source of . . .) *n*.: **Pierian spring** [drives from spring in Macedonia that was sacred to the Muses in Greek mythology]. ❖ By 1918, aged 30, [Giorgio] de Chirico was already past his peak and about to spend the next 60 years in deliberate decline, but . . . no old enthusiast should neglect this opportunity, sad though it is, to witness his flawed genius unfulfilled. He took too shallow a [drink] of the **Pierian spring**. (Brian Sewell, "Flawed Genius and a Haunting Obsession; His Work Influenced Ernst, Dalí and Magritte. Now a Brave New Show Celebrates the Best—and Worst—of Giorgio De Chirico," *Evening Standard* [London], 1/24/2003.)

inspiring (or inciting or exhorting to action) *adj*.: **proceleusmatic**. See *exhorting*

instability (financial . . . or to be heavily in debt) *n*.: **queer street** [sometimes cap.; British] ❖ Procter & Gamble, the tough and respected consumer brands powerhouse which sells everything from soap powder to Pringles crisps, has an amazingly consistent long-term record. The last 30 years are depicted in the chart above. But this week its directors decided their company could be heading up **queer street**, and sacked the man they appointed 18 months ago. (Durk Jager, Equity Markets, *Financial Times* [London], 6/10/2000.)

instance (as in example) *n*.: **exemplum**. See *example*

instant (as in, in an . . .) *n*.: **trice** (as in "in a trice"). See *quickly*

instigation (as in event that causes or provokes war, literally or figuratively) *n*.: **casus belli** [Latin; occasion of war]. See *provocation*

instigator *n*.: **stormy petrel**. See *inciter*

instinctive (reaction, as in reflex) *n*.: **tropism**. See *reflex*

instruct *v.t*.: **catechize**. See *teach*

instruction (providing introductory . . .) *n., adj*.: **propaedeutic**. See *introduction*

instruction book *n*.: **enchiridion**. See *handbook*

instructor *n*.: **pedagogue**. See *teacher*

insubordinate *adj*.: **contumacious**. See *obstinate*

insubstantial (as in tenuous) *adj*.: **gossamer**. See *tenuous* and *transparent*

(2) insubstantial *adj*.: **diaphanous**. See *transparent*

insult (an . . . to another's dignity) *n*.: **lese majesty**. ❖ Mr. Clinton is an honorable man, at least as honorable as Brutus and Cassius in Shakespeare's *Julius Caesar*. To suggest that he might economize on the truth would smack of **lese majesty**. (Bruce Fein, "Vintage Clinton," *Washington Times*, 12/28/1999.)

(2) insult (clever or polite . . .) *n*.: **asteism**. ❖ When my boss has insulted my mom, / And I need to respond with aplomb, / I disdain to use nasty-isms, / Favoring **asteisms**: / Polite ways of dropping a bomb. (Mark Mironer, *The Omnificent English Dictionary in Limerick Form* [oedilf.com], 3/22/2006.)

(3) insult (delivered while leaving the scene) *n*.: **Parthian shot**. See *parting shot*

(4) insult (ethnic . . .) *n*.: **ethnophaulism**. See *slur*

insulted (easily . . . , as in offended) *adj*.: **umbrageous**. See *offended*

insulting (in behavior or speech due to arrogance or contempt) *n*.: **contumely**. See *contempt*

(2) insulting (or humiliating another) *adj*.: **contumelious**. See *contemptuous*

insurgent (as in rebel) *n*.: **frondeur** [French]. See *rebel*

(2) insurgent (spec. one who hates or mistrusts authority) *n*.: **misarchist**. See *rebel*

insurrection (peasant's . . .) *n*.: **jacquerie**. See *revolt*

(2) insurrection *n*.: **émeute** [French]. See *rebellion*

(3) insurrection (against existing social or

artistic conventions) *n.*: **titanism** (often cap.). See *revolt*

intangible (as in lacking material form or substance) *adj.*: **incorporeal**. ❖ As the passage of time removes from the scene more and more of the accused wrongdoers, and more and more of their possible victims, it makes less and less moral or economic sense—and ultimately no sense at all—for the law to exact monetary redress from **incorporeal** institutions such as corporations or governments. (Stuart Taylor Jr., "Legal Affairs: Paying Reparations for Ancient Wrongs Is Not Right," *National Journal*, 4/7/2001.)

integral (as in essential) *adj.*: **constitutive**. See *essential*

(2) integral (as in innate) *adj.*: **connate**. See *innate*

integrate (as in incorporate, the ideas or attitudes of others, esp. parents, into one's own personality) *v.t.*: **introject**. See *incorporate*

integrity *n.*: **probity**. ❖ [Special prosecutor Kenneth] Starr's indifference to polls is a facet of the **probity** that makes him unintelligible to Clinton, and surely there are Democrats of **probity** who are unwilling to ratify by passivity any more of his defining political deviancy down. (George Will, "Moments of Truth—a Half-Century Apart—Over Issues Great and Small," *St. Louis Post-Dispatch*, 8/6/1998.)

(2) integrity (personal . . . , as in honor) *n.*: **izzat** [Hindi]. See *honor*

intellect (of, relating to, or understood by the . . .) *adj.*: **noetic**. ❖ The mental ego, according to Wilber, is "the first structure that can not only think about the world but think about thinking; hence, it is the first structure that is clearly self-reflexive and introspective. . . . It is also the first structure capable of . . . propositional reasoning ('if a, then b'), which allows it to apprehend higher or purely **noetic** relationships." (Sean M. Kelly, "Revisioning the Mandala of Consciousness," *ReVision*, 4/1/1996, p. 19.)

intellectual (as in literary, community) *n.*: **republic of letters**. See *literary*

(2) intellectual (as in pedantic, scholarly, or bookish) *adj.*: **donnish**. See *pedantic* and *bookish*

(3) intellectual (moral and/or cultural spirit of an era) *n.*: **zeitgeist**. See *spirit*

(4) intellectual (people as a group) *n.*: **clerisy**. See *educated*

(5) intellectual (person who is prominent in . . . or literary circles) *n.*: **mandarin**. See *influential*

(6) intellectual (pertaining to knowledge of . . . or spritual things) *adj.*: **gnostic**. See *spiritual*

(7) intellectual (self-proclaimed . . . , as in enlightened, people) *n.pl.*: **illuminati**. See *enlightened*

intelligent (as in wise) *adj.*: **sapient**. See *wise*

(2) intelligent (person who is cultivated) *n.*: **bel esprit**. See *cultivated*

intelligible (as in clear, in thought or expression) *adj.*: **luculent**. See *clear*

(2) intelligible (as in clear, in thought or expression) *adj.*: **pellucid**. See *clear*

(3) intelligible *adj.*: **limpid**. See *understandable*

(4) intelligible *adj.*: **perspicuous**. See *understandable*

intense *adj.*: **perfervid**. See *impassioned*

intent (as in goal, esp. of life) *n.*: **telos** [Greek]. See *goal*

(2) intent (hidden or ulterior . . .) *n.*: **arriere-pensee** (or **arrière-pensée**) [French]. See *motive*

(3) intent (to achieve a particular goal or desire) *n.*: **nisus**. See *goal*

intention (as in the thing that is being looked for; also the answer to a problem) *n.*: **quaesitum**. See *objective*

intentional (as in premeditated) *adj.*: **prepense** (usually used as part of the phrase "malice prepense"). See *premeditated*

intercourse (sexual . . .) *n.*: **houghmagandy** [Scottish]. ❖ [A Penn State University] major study of sexual activity involving 10,000 Americans has just been completed. [It showed that those] with doctorates manage less

houghmagandy than those with first degrees only, jazz enthusiasts more than rock music lovers, Catholics a weeny bit more than Protestants but 20 per cent less than agnostics or Jews. (David Aaronovitch, "If Only I Were a Hard-Working, Hard-Drinking Jewish Agnostic," *Independent* [London], 1/17/1998.)

(2) intercourse (sexual . . .) *n.*: **venery**. ❖ Among the Major government's other recent disasters in the **venery** department have been headlines about (a) the environment minister who was forced to resign for impregnating a local government legislatress established to be not his wife. (Daniel Seligman, "Keeping Up: Depravity Among Conservatives," *Fortune*, 5/2/1994, p. 129.)

(3) intercourse (sexual . . . , spec. insertion of penis into vagina) *n.*: **intromission** (*v.t.* **intromit**). See *penetration*

(4) intercourse (sexual . . .) *idiom*: **slap and tickle**. See *sex*

interdenominational *adj.*: **intercredal**. ❖ From [cave] 4Q has come not one complete [Dead Sea] scroll, but, according to the official report, "at least 15,000 fragments . . ." These fragments were brought to the "scrollery" of the Palestine Archaeological Museum in East Jerusalem. . . . Then began the giant jigsaw puzzle. An international and **intercredal** team of seven scholars was set up to work on the puzzle and prepare the texts for publication. (Joseph Fitzmyer, "What They Found in the Caves: Let's Go to the Scrolls," *Commonweal*, 12/18/1992)

interest (undue . . . over one subject or idea) *n.*: **monomania**. See *obsession*

interesting (as in lively or stimulating) *adj.*: **piquant**. See *stimulating* and *provocative*

interferer (officious . . . who frustrates the success of a plan by stupidly getting in the way) *n.*: **marplot**. See *meddler*

interim (esp. between the end of a sovereign's reign and the ascension of a successor) *n.*: **interregnum**. See *interval*

(2) interim (esp. short . . . between things or events) *n.*: **interstice**. See *gap*

interlock (like the fingers of one's hands) *v.i.*:

interdigitate. ❖ "Some protein structures, when you see them, prompt an instant 'Aha!'" says [Lawrence] Shapiro. "The cadherin structure was like that—the structural basis for how cadherins function was immediately apparent. They **interdigitate** like the teeth of a zipper." (Josie Glausiusz, "The All-Important Zipper," *discovermagazine.com*, 9/1/1995.)

interlude (esp. short . . . between things or events) *n.*: **interstice**. See *gap*

intermeddler (officious . . . who frustrates the success of a plan by stupidly getting in the way) *n.*: **marplot**. See *meddler*

intermediary *n.*: **comprador**. ❖ Foreigners doing business in Asia have long relied on middlemen—**compradors**, as they are known in the region—to cut through red tape, hook up with the right people, get deals done, and occasionally take a small piece of the action. (Louis Kraar, Global: "Need a Friend in Asia? Try the Singapore Connection," *Fortune*, 3/4/1996, p. 172.)

intermediate (as in lying or placed between or among others) *adj.*: **interjacent**. See *intervening*

(2) intermediate (or transitional state, phase, or condition) *adj.*: **liminal**. See *transitional*

internalize (as in incorporate, the ideas or attitudes of others, esp. parents, into one's own personality) *v.t.*: **introject**. See *incorporate*

interpretation (esp. of a text) *n.*: **exegesis**. ❖ For nearly 40 years, Bob Dylan has tantalized us with inscrutable images. Most have been of the verbal variety—phrases such as "the geometry of innocence," "darkness at the break of noon," "the ghost of electricity," and hundreds of others that continue to pique our collective id and defy easy **exegesis**. (Tom Sinclair, "His Back Pages—The Times May Have Changed, but Early Dylan . . . Revisits His Evolution from a Dusty Young Folkie to a Plugged-in Rock & Roller," *Entertainment Weekly*, 10/22/1999, p. 44.)

(2) interpretation (of a text by adding one's own ideas) *n.*: **eisegesis**. ❖ "In this approach, you place yourself in the text and basically use your imagination to decide what the text says," Pfizenmaier said. . . . "Now people want to understand scripture by **eisegesis**— putting themselves into Scripture," he said. (Patricia Rice, "Presbyterians Here Discuss Question of Ordaining Gays, Lesbians: Regional Legislatures Will Vote on Whether to Allow Such Ordinations," *St. Louis Post-Dispatch*, 6/18/2001.)

(3) interpretation (having more than one . . .) *adj.*: **polysemous** (or **polysemic**). See *meaning*

(4) interpretation (having more than one . . . or signifying different things) *adj.*: **multivocal**. See *ambiguous*

(5) interpretation (additional . . . , as in explanation) *n.* **epexegesis** (*adj.*: **epexegetic**). See *explanation*

(6) interpretation (as in translation, which is literal) *n.*: **metaphrase**. See *translation*

interpretative (often regarding a document or text, such as scripture) *n.*: **hermeneutic**. ❖ Longerich quickly demonstrates that he is . . . perfectly at ease with **hermeneutic** considerations. . . . "What a historian has to do . . . is look at each document and look at the context and then try to reconstruct from the context what actually the meaning of this passage might be." (D. D. Guttenplan, *The Holocaust on Trial*, Norton [2001], p. 236.)

interpreter (and guide for travelers, esp. where Arabic, Turkish, or Persian is spoken) *n.*: **dragoman**. See *guide*

(2) interpreter (spec. one who provides comments, explanation, or interpretation of a text) *n.*: **glossator**. See *commentator*

interrogate (as in question formally about governmental policy or action) *v.t.*: **interpellate**. ❖ [At the upcoming meeting of political parties] opposition parties plan to **interpellate** the government on the alleged bribery case involving former Construction Minister Eiichi Nakao and on other issues such as the bankruptcy of major department store operator Sogo Co. (*Daily Yomiuri* [Tokyo], "Opposition Parties Set to Grill Coalition," 7/28/2000.)

(2) interrogate (closely) *v.t.*: **catechize**. See *question*

interruption (as in pause) *n.*: **caesura**. See *pause*

(2) interruption (in a sentence from one construction to a second, grammatically inconsistent construction) *n.*: **anacoluthon**. See *shift*

interspersed *v.t.*: **interleaved**. See *interwoven*

intertwine (like the fingers of one's hands) *v.i.*: **interdigitate**. See *interlock*

intertwined *v.t.*: **interleaved**. See *interwoven*

interval (in continuity, esp. between the end of a sovereign's reign and the ascension of a successor) *n.*: **interregnum**. ❖ During the **interregnum** between [Jack] Parr and [Johnny] Carson, various guest hosts were used to keep *The Tonight Show* in the public eye. (Shawn Levy, *The King of Comedy*, St. Martin's Press [1996], p. 278.)

(2) interval (esp. short . . . between things or events) *n.*: **interstice**. See *gap*

intervening (as in lying or placed between or among others) *adj.*: **interjacent**. ❖ *The White Stuff* is a classic Bloke Book, an instant new entry for the gender studies reading lists. [Author] Simon Armitage is also a bloke, clearly, and his account of blokehood is sensitive and sympathetic. In **interjacent**, italicised chapters of reverie . . . Armitage uses his protagonist to meditate on the lot and the role of the modern bloke. (Colin Greenland, "Men Trying to Behave Well," *Guardian* [London], 3/13/2004.)

interwoven *v.t.*: **interleaved**. [This verb is a printing term that technically refers to the insertion of blank leafs, or interleaves, into the pages of a book, as for example to protect color plates. It is also more generally used in the sense of interweaving things together, as in the example here. The past-tense usage is more common than the present-tense usage.] ❖ The radiant core of the whole thing is a 124-page chronology of Diane Arbus' life from 1923 until its sudden end in 1971. That section represents what seems to me a most important breakthrough in biographical technique. It gives the bare facts, **interleaved** with lots and lots of eloquently surprising quotes from Diane's own letters and notebooks. (Alexander Eliot, "Looking Again Through Dark, Avid Lens of Diane Arbus," *Washington Times*, 1/4/2004.)

in the act (esp. of committing an offense or a sexual act) *adv.*: **in flagrante delicto**. ❖ Of Worth's inner circle, Ned Wynert . . . had suffered the traditional adulterer's fate, gunned down **in flagrante delicto** by an enraged husband. (Ben Macintyre, *The Napoleon of Crime*, Farrar, Straus and Giroux [1997], p. 175.)

in the first place *adv.*: **imprimis**. ❖ Elton (1999) argues that considerable empirical evidence exists to question whether historical returns should be used to estimate expected returns **imprimis**. (Gregory Nagel, "The Effect of Risk Factors on Cost of Equity Estimation," *Quarterly Journal of Business and Economics*, 1/1/2007.)

in-the-know (being . . . or informed about something) *adj.*: **au fait** [French]. See *familiar*

intimacy (sexual . . .) *idiom*: **slap and tickle**. See *sex*

intimidate *v.t.*: **Bogart** [slang, after roles played by Humphrey Bogart]. ❖ Here are some tips to help avoid getting drawn into a road-rage situation. . . . Do not glare at other drivers, or try to "**Bogart**"—i.e., intimidate them with scowls, frowns, and rude gestures, such as giving the "bird." You have no way of knowing whether the other motorist you're making faces at is near the end of his rope on this particular day and just looking for someone to go off on. (Eric Peters, "Dealing with 'Road Rage' Safely and Effectively," *Consumers' Research*, 5/1/2003.)

intimidation (as in suggesting the use of force to settle an issue or argument) *n.*: **argumentum ad baculum** [Latin]. See *threat*

intolerable (as in unpardonable) *adj.*: **irremissible**. See *unpardonable*

intolerance (and ill will that occurs when disputes about religion arise) *n.*: **odium theologicum** [lit. theological hatred]. ❖ [There exists an] **odium theologicum** of the sci-

entific attacks on religious belief even where it doesn't seek to trespass on scientific territory. . . . Professor Steven Weinberg, a Nobel Prize–winning physicist from the University of Texas, said, "I think one of the great historical contributions of science is to weaken the hold of religion. That's a good thing." (James Bowman, "Manicheanism a la Mode," *New Criterion*, 11/1/2005.) [Note: Manicheanism, or Manichaeism, is the philosophy that divides the world into good vs. evil. See *good vs. evil*.]

intolerant (as in narrow-minded) *adj.*: **hidebound**. See *narrow-minded*

(2) intolerant (insistence on conventionality) *n.*: **Grundyism**. See *puritanical*

into the middle *adv.*: **in medias res**. [Latin. This term means into the midst or the heart of things and is often used to refer to jumping directly into the course of a story or plot without any preliminaries, as in the example given. A related term is "in media res," into the middle of things.] ❖ Viewers, beware. *The Two Towers*, the dazzling second installment of the *Lord of the Rings* trilogy, picks up exactly where the first one left off. No Star Wars–style scroll to bring you up to speed, no quick compilation of scenes from the first film, no opening Cate Blanchett narration—nothing. It begins **in medias res**, as though you had just stepped out for a few seconds to get more popcorn. (Jess Cagle, "Lure of the Rings," *Time*, 12/2/2002.)

intoxicated (as in given to or marked by consumption of alcohol) *adj.*: **bibulous**. See *imbibing*

(2) intoxicated *adj.*: **bacchic**. See *drunken*

intrepid *adj.*: **doughty**. See *brave*

intricacy *n.*: **cat's cradle**. [This term derives from the children's game in which a string looped over the fingers is transferred back and forth on the hands of the players so as to form different designs]. ❖ Scientists investigating the **cat's cradle** of faults underlying Southern California believe the Jan. 17 earthquake, the costliest in U.S. history, measurably increased the quake potential in areas of metropolitan

Los Angeles in a pattern that seems to have shaped major quakes there since 1933. (*Washington Post*, "Seismology: Looking for Linkage in Quakes," 9/5/1994.)

intricate (or skillful in design or function) *adj.*: **daedal**. ❖ He gathered toward the end of his life a very extensive collection of illustrated books and illuminated manuscripts, and took heightened pleasure in their **daedal** patterns as his own strength declined. (Florence Boos, review of *The Collected Letters of William Morris*, *Victorian Studies*, 6/22/1997, p. 730.)

(2) intricate *adj.*: **involute** (*n.*: **involution**). ❖ Told mostly in flashback, the film purports to track the torrid relationship between waitress Lucia and novelist Lorenzo, but [the director] weaves in a parallel reality drawn from the book that Lorenzo is working on. . . . Daringly **involute** in construction, *Sex and Lucia* replicates the intoxicating, and often disorienting, sensation of being in love. (Michael O'Sullivan, Film Capsules, *Washington Post*, 10/18/2002.)

(3) intricate (as in complicated) *adj.*: **byzantine**. See *complicated*

(4) intricate (as in overly complicated) *adj.*: **Rube Goldberg**. See *complicated*

intriguing (person) *n.*: **intrigant**. [The example is in the headline.] ❖ Dzhaba Ioseliani, a former paramilitary leader at the crossroads of Georgia's rough-and-tumble political and criminal worlds, died Tuesday. . . . He was equally comfortable in battle fatigues and formal wear, sometimes making public appearances in a white suit and white bow tie, an outfit he topped off with a white cane. He was known as a [scholar] and writer, as well as a gifted politician. (Misha Dzhindzhikhashvili, "Dzhaba Ioseliani, Former Georgian Paramilitary Leader and Political **Intrigant**, Dies at 76," AP Worldstream, 3/4/2003.)

(2) intriguing (as in alluring) *adj.*: **sirenic**. [See also the nouns *siren call* and *Lorelei call* under *lure*.] See *alluring*

(3) intriguing *adj.*: **piquant**. See *provocative*

(4) intriguing (woman) *n.*: **intrigante**. See *woman*

intrinsic (as in innate) *adj.*: **connate**. See *innate*

(2) intrinsic *adj.*: **immanent**. See *inherent*

introduction (often to a speech or writing) *n.*: **exordium**. ❖ Women who successfully conceive [after age 40] know, of course, that giving birth isn't the end of the story. It's really a new beginning, an **exordium** to the challenges and rewards of midlife motherhood. (Leslie Laurence, "Pregnancy After Forty," *Town & Country*, 8/1/1995, p. 86.)

(2) introduction (to a lengthy or complex work) *n.*: **prolegomenon**. ❖ All this, however, is by way of a **prolegomenon** to the book's real work, which is to show what feminist thought has to contribute to bioethics. (Hilde Lindemann Nelson, review of *Feminist Approaches to Bioethics: Theoretical Reflections and Practical Applications*, by Rosemarie Tong, *Hypatia*, 9/22/1998, p. 112.)

(3) introduction *n.*, *adj.*: **propaedeutic**. ❖ A 50-page **propaedeutic** locates Schelling in his cultural, philosophical, and religious times, while a lengthy retrospect discusses the meaning and value of this philosophy of religion for today. (Thomas F. O'Meara, review of *Schelling's Philosophy of Mythology and Revelation*, by Friedrich Wilhelm Joseph von Schelling, *Theological Studies*, 3/1/1997, p. 192.)

(4) introduction (as in insertion of something between existing things) *n.*: **intercalation**. See *insertion*

(5) introduction *n.*: **proem**. See *preface*

introductory (as in basic) *adj.*: **abecedarian**. See *basic*

introvert (someone who is halfway between an . . . and extrovert) *n.*: **ambivert**. See *extrovert*

introverted (and/or sullen and/or socially withdrawn or inexperienced) *adj.*: **farouche** [French]. See *shy*

intrude (as in burst in, suddenly or forcibly) *v.i.*: **irrupt**. See *burst in*

(2) intrude (as in impose oneself or one's ideas in an unwelcome way) *v.t.*: **obtrude**. See *impose*

intrusive (as in bothersome) *adj.*: **pestiferous**. See *bothersome*

intuition (as in premonition, that something is going to occur) *n.*: **presentiment**. See *premonition*

invade (as in burst in, suddenly or forcibly) *v.i.*: **irrupt**. See *burst in*

invalidate (as in refute convincingly) *v.t.*: **confute**. See *refute*

invective *n.*: **vituperation** (*adj.*: **vituperative**). ❖ And when the wave [of antisemitic expression] subsides, the diminution of antisemitic **vituperation** is understood to have been caused by a decrease in, or the passing of, antisemitic belief and writing. This account of antisemitism is wrong. (Daniel Goldhagen, *Hitler's Willing Executioners*, Knopf [1996], p. 43.)

invent (an idea, plan, theory, or explanation after careful thought) *v.t.*: **excogitate**. See *devise*

invented (or substituted with fraudulent intent) *adj.*: **supposititious**. See *supposed*

inventive (as in creative and/or original) *adj.*: **Promethean**. See *creative*

(2) inventive (as in resourceful, person) *n.*: **debrouillard** (or **débrouillard**) [French]. See *resourceful*

(3) inventive (love of or enthusiasm for anything . . .) *n.*: **neophilia**. See *novelty*

inventor (as in creator) *n.*: **demiurge**. See *creator*

inversion (of words or phrases) *n.*: **chiasmus**. See *reversal*

investigate (as in analyze, that which has already occurred; i.e., to project into the past) *v.t.*: **retroject**. See *analyze*

(2) investigate (through formal questioning about governmental policy or action) *v.t.*: **interpellate**. See *interrogate*

investigator (or examiner) *n.*: **scrutator**. See *examiner*

invigorate (as in enliven) *v.t.*: **vivify**. See *enliven*

invigorating (or something that is . . .) *adj., n.*: **roborant**. ❖ Ginseng root is a valuable herb in oriental medicine and has long been used as a remedy for a number of disorders. The root of ginseng has been utilized for over 2,000 years, in the belief that it is a panacea, tonic, **roborant**, and promotes longevity. (C. S. Yuan, "Anti-hyperglycemic Effect of . . . American Ginseng Berry Extract," *Phytomedicine*, 2/1/2004.)

inviolable *adj.*: **infrangible**. ❖ Like banks, marbled and colonnaded to instill confidence in their investors, orchestras have only approximate control over the stuff they deal with every day. Consequently, opening night at the New York Philharmonic arrives every year with certain **infrangible** guarantees: a marquee soloist, a pair of blue-chip scores and plenty of vigorous applause. (Justin Davidson, "Routine Opener with a Special Flair," *Newsday*, 9/25/1999.)

invisible (nearly . . .) *adj.*: **liminal**. ❖ [David Shipler's book *The Working Poor* shows] that even those who hold steady, minimum-wage jobs in the sweatshops, bakeries, canning factories, and other unseen venues that make our economy run are not saints. Shipler clearly humanizes this **liminal** army of workers who clean up our tables, stitch our clothes, and care for our elderly. (Dalton Conley, "Labor Intensive," *Boston Globe*, 4/4/2004.)

(2) invisible (as in hidden) *adj.*: **delitescent**. See *hidden*

inviting (as in alluring) *adj.*: **siren**. [See also the nouns *siren call* and *Lorelei call* under *lure*.] See *alluring*

(2) inviting (as in warm and cozy) *adj.*: **gemütlich** [German]. See *cozy*

involuntary (as in subjected to external controls and impositions; i.e., the opposite of autonomous) *adj.*: **heteronomous** (*n.*: **heteronomy**). See *subjugated*

invulnerable (as in incapable of being overthrown, driven out, or subdued by force) *adj.*: **inexpugnable**. See *impregnable*

irate (as in indignant) *n.*: **dudgeon** (often expressed as "in high dudgeon"). See *indignant*

(2) irate *adj.*: **apoplectic**. See *angry*

(3) irate *adj.*: **furibund**. See *furious*

(4) irate *adj.*: **vesuvian** (esp. as in . . . temper). See *temper*

(5) irate *adj.*: **wroth**. See *angry*

ire *n.*: **bile**. See *bitterness*

(2) ire *n.*: **choler** (*adj.*: **choleric**). See *anger*

iridescent (like a pearl) *adj.*: **nacreous**. ❖ Asked to name their personal favorites in the [pearl] show, the curators bristle, as if required to choose a favorite child. However, Mr. Landman concedes that he feels particularly fond of the "fossil pearls from 40 million years ago, which still retain their **nacreous** luster. . . . [I]t is important to recognize that pearls have been around probably as long as mollusks have, some 530 million years." (Benjamin Ivy, "The Luster of "Pearls" Is Focus of New Exhibition: Two Museums String Together a Dazzling Story," *Christian Science Monitor*, 10/19/2001.)

(2) iridescent *adj.*: **opalescent**. ❖ The future of cosmetics is glossy and bright. Vibrant hues of pink, coral, orange, purple, lime, aqua and gold are key players in spring and summer beauty palettes. . . . [M]ost new products are sheer and **opalescent**, giving a translucent, glowing finish. Sheer formulas allow women of all ages to experiment with brighter looks and shimmery eye, lip and cheek colours. (Heather Toskan, "Sheer & Shimmery/Colour Is Key, with Co-ordinated Eyes, Cheeks, Lips and Nails the Order of the Day," *London Free Press*, 5/8/2001.)

Irish (of or relating to Ireland or the . . .) *adj.*: **Hibernian**. ❖ "Notre Dame has nothing to do with the rest of Indiana," I argued [to my son who was resisting considering it because it is in Indiana]. . . . "Notre Dame is the mystical cradle of the Irish-American dream, the repository of our Celtic hopes, the spawning ground of our **Hibernian** reveries, the incubator of our most fiercely beloved stereotypes." (Joe Queenan, Endpaper: "The Age of Reasons," *New York Times*, 11/9/2003.)

irksome *adj.*: **pestiferous**. See *bothersome*

irony (spec. the use of a word or phrase that is contrary to its normal meaning, such as "a seven-foot midget") *n.*: **antiphrasis**. ❖ Then there are the titles that work by irony or "**antiphrasis**." *Far From the Madding Crowd* is about passion and violence, not rural calm. *Ulysses* does not have any epic hero. (John Mullan, "What's in a Name? John Mullan on a Compendium of Titles," *Guardian* [London], 1/11/2003.)

irrational (as in involving factors not to be comprehended based on reason alone) *adj.*: **supra-rational**. See *incomprehensible*

(2) irrational (as in not of sound mind) *adj.*: **non compos mentis** [Latin]. See *insane*

(3) irrational (something that is . . . , as in illogical) *n.*: **alogism**. See *illogical*

irrefutable (necessarily or demonstrably . . .) *adj.*: **apodictic**. See *incontrovertible*

(2) irrefutable *adj.*: **irrefragable**. See *unquestionable*

irregular (as in departing from the standard or norm) *adj.*: **heteroclite**. See *abnormal*

irrelevancy (as in a fallacious argument where one proves or disproves a point that is not at issue) *n.*: **ignoratio elenchi** [Latin]. ❖ [In his argument in favor of immigration, he] will occasionally indulge in the logical fallacy of **ignoratio elenchi**, more popularly known as creating a straw man. Thus, to counter the valid claim that many of our immigrants are ill-educated and low-skilled, he argues that they are more educated than the natives on average. This is interesting, but it is not the issue. (Jagdish Bhagwati, review of *The Economic Consequences of Immigration*, by Julian L. Simon, *New Republic*, 5/14/1990.)

irrelevant (as in superfluous) *adj.*: **excrescent**. See *superfluous*

(2) irrelevant (as in superfluous) *adj.*: **supererogatory**. See *superfluous*

irresolute (as in fickle, person whose opinion is always changing as the wind blows, like a weathervane) *n.*: **girouette** [French]. See *weathervane*

(2) irresolute *adj.*, *v.i.*, *n.*: **shilly-shally**. See *vacillate*

irresponsible *adj.*: **feckless**. ❖ We hear an awful lot about teenagers these days. According to the tabloids, they are lazy, **feckless** and ignorant. According to just about everyone, including the Office of National Statistics, they are having too much sex. (Maureen Freely, "They Never Tell Us the Things We

Really Want to Know," *Independent* [London], 11/1/1999.)

(2) irresponsible (as in reckless) *adj.*: **harum-scarum**. See *reckless*

(3) irresponsible (as in reckless) *adj.*: **temerarious**. See *reckless*

irreverence (religious . . .) *n.*: **impiety** (*adj.*: **impious**). ❖ Jewish **impiety**, unlike the impiety of other non-Christians, was understood by John Chrysostom and those who thought as he did to be not just mere **impiety**, born of ignorance or the inability to recognize the true path, but a sort of madness. (Daniel Goldhagen. *Hitler's Willing Executioners*, Knopf [1996], p. 51.)

irreversibility *n.*: **Rubicon** (esp. as in "cross the Rubicon"). [This word (and term} derives from the name of a river in Italy that Julius Caesar crossed in 49 B.C. to start a civil war, stating en route, "The die is cast."]. ❖ The growing fear [is that] North Korea has already made the fundamental decision to develop a nuclear arsenal and no longer intends to treat its nuclear program as a bargaining chip to be bartered away in exchange for money and pacts. "It's possible North Korea has **crossed the Rubicon**," says Prof. Ashton Carter of Harvard University. "The regime may now believe it has to have nuclear weapons for its own security." (B. J. Lee, "Driving a Hard Bargain," *Newsweek* International, 4/21/2003.)

irreversible (as in offering no possibility of return) *adj.*: **irremeable**. [This word is generally considered archaic but is still sometimes found in current usage.] ❖ The economic losses from the S&L's misadventures are **irremeable**. Rather than spending the next decade parceling out blame, Washington should make sure it doesn't happen again. (Sylvia Nasar, "That Lollapaloozan S&L Tab," *U.S. News & World Report*, 7/9/1990.)

irrevocability *n.*: **Rubicon**. See *irreversibility*

irrevocable (as in offering no possibility of return) *adj.*: **irremeable**. See *irreversible*

irritability (as in a state of tense and nervous . . .) *n.*: **fantod**. See *tension*

(2) irritability (as in acrimony) *n.*: **asperity**. See *acrimony*

(3) irritability *n.*: **bile**. See *bitterness*

(4) irritability *n.*: **choler** (*adj.*: **choleric**). See *anger*

irritable *adj.*: **liverish**. ❖ Oh, shut up: Actor Jason Patric sounds a bit **liverish** about the movies he saw this summer: "Take Angelina Jolie. It doesn't matter that everyone hates *Tomb Raider II*," he told the British *Glamour* magazine. "She looks great and so everyone says how wonderful it is. It's like Charlie's Angels—everyone pretending it's empowering. It's pure crap." (Doug Camilli, "Diaz's Nose Out of Joint: Surfing Accident Has Her 'Bummed Out,'" *Gazette* [Montreal], 9/4/2003.)

(2) irritable *adj.*: **shirty**. ❖ At a press conference, an American reporter asked French President Jacques Chirac a question in French, and Bush got all **shirty**. "Very good," he snapped sarcastically. "The [reporter] memorizes four words and he plays like he's intercontinental. I'm impressed. Que bueno. Now I'm literate in two languages." (Patt Morrison, "In Plain English, the Big Enchilada Got French Fried," *Los Angeles Times*, 6/19/2002.)

(3) irritable *adj.*: **splenetic**. ❖ "I'd like to see us piss people off occasionally," said Gatehouse. "I think a lot of people out there think they know the kind of thing they are going to read in *Maclean's*. I think it's time to throw them some curves. I think we can be grumpier, argumentative, even **splenetic** sometimes. That's where I fit in." (Murray Whyte, "Can *Maclean's* Leave It to Beaver to Survive?" *Toronto Star*, 8/22/2002.)

(4) irritable *adj.*: **waspish**. ❖ [You try] to talk to someone in Atlanta, for example. It's [area code] 404, of course. But then you're treated to a **waspish** recorded message explaining that the area code for the area formerly served by 404 has been changed but not what it's been changed to. And then, when you find out what it's changed to, it's some hideous, non-melodious jumble with no number-vowel in the middle, something like 873. (Jacquelyn Mitchard, "Code Red over

Numbers without Nuance," *Milwaukee Journal-Sentinel*, 2/1/1998.)

(5) irritable *adj.*: **querulous**. See *peevish*

(6) irritable (as in grumpy, mood) *n.pl.*: **mulligrubs**. See *grumpiness*

(7) irritable *adj.*: **tetchy**. See *grouchy*

irritate *v.t.*: **chivvy**. See *pester*

irritating (as in repellent) *adj.*: **rebarbative**. See *repellent*

(2) irritating *adj.*: **pestiferous**. See *bothersome*

isolate (as in consider separately) *v.t.*: **prescind** (generally as in "prescind from"). ❖ The Internet is fast becoming a . . . universal library of books in print. Millions of books are available almost immediately, through a simple click of the mouse. But even if we **prescind** from the conservative complaint that books aren't as good as they used to be, it's still statistically improbable that the best books in any given field will happen to be the most recent ones. That's why it's so important that worthy old titles be restored to print. (Mike Potemra, Book Shelf, *National Review*, 10/9/2000.)

(2) isolate (from others) *v.t.*: **enisle**. ❖ Meryle Secrest, the biographer of the fraudulent art connoisseur Bernard Berenson, records that, when depressed, he referred to himself as feeling **enisled** in the sea of life. (Christopher Hawtree, Words, *Independent* [London], 9/22/1998.)

(3) isolate (esp. from one's accustomed environment) *v.t.*: **deracinate**. See *uproot*

isolated (and stagnant or backward place or situation) *n.*: **backwater**. See *stagnant*

(2) isolated (as in against the world) *adv., adj.*: **contra mundum** [Latin]. See *against the world*

(3) isolated (from outside influences) *adj.*: **hermetic**. See *sealed*

isolation (social . . .) *n.*: **purdah**. See *seclusion*

issue (as in problem, which is difficult for a beginner or one who is inexperienced) *n.*: **pons asinorum** [Latin]. See *problem*

itch (as in irresistible compulsion) *n.*: **cacoëthes**. See *compulsion*

itching (skin condition characterized by . . . or stinging; hives) *n.*: **urticaria** (causing itching or stinging *adj.*: **urticant**). ❖ Q. I am an aerobics dance instructor. About halfway into a class my face and legs turn red and itch. . . . What can be done? A. I think you can narrow the possibilities to two—cholinergic **urticaria** or exercise-induced **urticaria**. Either causes skin reddening, hives and itching. (Paul Donohue, "Extensive Testing May Be Needed to Find Cause of Fatigue," *Chicago Sun-Times*, 8/19/1993.)

(2) itching (as in longing, esp. for something one once had but has no more) *n.*: **desiderium**. See *longing*

(3) itching (of skin with prickling sensation) *n.*: **paresthesia**. See *prickling*

(4) itching (or prickling or tingling sensation that insects are crawling on you) *n.*: **formication**. See *prickling*

jagged (as in irregularly notched, toothed, or indented) *adj.*: **erose**. See *uneven*

jail *n.*: **durance vile** [This term is almost always used as part of the phrase "in durance vile," as in the example given.]. ❖ We know quite definitely that Mr. Clinton did lie to a grand jury, and then to the electorate, and then to Congress. For an ordinary citizen the first of the lies on that list is a clearly indictable offense for which you can be landed **in durance vile** and/or heavily fined. (Herb Greer, "Bill Clinton and John Profumo," *Washington Times*, 12/29/1998.)

(2) jail *n.*: **hoosegow**. ❖ A 46-year-old Florida man is in the **hoosegow** today, charged with aggravated assault with a deadly weapon after he allegedly tried to run down Rep. Katherine Harris (R-Fla.) with his Cadillac. While Harris campaigned at a Sarasota intersection Tuesday evening, Barry Seltzer, a registered Democrat, aimed his car "straight at Ms. Harris" but "swerved at the last minute," police said. . . . "I was exercising my political expression. . . . I scared them a little." (Richard Leiby, The Reliable Source, *Washington Post*, 10/28/2004.)

(3) jail (as in confine) *v.t.*: **immure**. See *confine*

(4) jail (as in dungeon) *n.*: **oubliette**. See *dungeon*

(5) jail (study of . . . management) *n.*: **penology**. See *prison*

(6) jail (where a guard can see all prisoners) *n.*: **panopticon**. See *prison*

(7) jail *n.*: **bastille**. See *prison*

jam (as in predicament, from which it is difficult to extricate oneself) *n.*: **tar baby**. See *predicament*

jammed (together, esp. in rows) *adj.*: **serried**. See *crowded*

jargon (regional . . .) *n.*: **patois**. See *dialect*

jaunt (a slow, leisurely . . .) *n.*: **paseo**. See *stroll*

javelin (or spear) *n.*: **assegai**. See *spear*

jaw (having a prominent . . .) *adj.*: **prognathous**. ❖ Bolt, though, was a cartoon. Tall (5′11″), with Marine Corps–erect posture, he had a swagger. He stood with his head cocked, which accentuated his **prognathous** jaw. (Al Barkow, "All the Rage with the U.S. Open: Returning to the Scene of His Greatest Win, Terrible Tommy Bolt Is Suddenly Hot Again," *Sports Illustrated*, 5/21/2001, p. G15.)

(2) jaw (protruding lower . . .) *n.*: **lantern jaw**. ❖ [Coach Bill Cowher] takes no notice of a copy of *Steeler Digest* with his face on the cover, that pronounced **lantern jaw** jutting out from the surface of the coffee table in the living room. . . . [H]e has the jawbone of a blue whale. (Tim Crothers, "The Face: Bill Cowher's Mug—Like His Steelers—Is Beloved in Pittsburgh," *Sports Illustrated*, 1/9/1995, p. 52.)

jawbone (lower) *n.*: **mandible**. ❖ [Poem by George Foreman's trainer Archie Moore before Foreman's fight against Muhammad Ali in 1974:] Foreman's left will make you dance; / Turkey in the straw; / When his right connects with your **mandible**; / Goodbye jaw! (George Plimpton, Scorecard, *Sports Illustrated*, 12/21/1998, p. 29.)

jaws (or mouth or stomach of a carnivorous animal) *n.*: **maw**. See *mouth*

jealous *adj.*: **emulous**. See *envious*

Jell-O (as in relating to or resembling gelatin) *adj.*: **gelatinous**. ❖ In her mind's athletic eye, she was trotting the length of the corridors, shoving open every door that was ajar, calling [out for her missing son] in a clear, Doris Day voice, welcoming him. In fact, her legs were **gelatinous**, she could not stand. (Jacqueline Mitchard, *The Deep End of the Ocean*, Viking [1996], p. 30.)

jellyfish (a . . . , or relating to or resembling a . . .) *n., adj.*: **medusoid**. ❖ "Almost no one [here] would ever consider eating a jellyfish," the *Darien News* reported two years ago. "It has certainly never been on any local restaurant's menu." Yet [Yao-Wen Huang, a seafood expert at the University of Georgia,] feels duty-bound to introduce the maligned **medusoid** to the palates of the American public. (Dan Chapman, "Georgia Shrimpers Cash in on Asian Delicacy: Jellyfish," *Atlanta Journal-Constitution*, 2/26/2003.)

jeopardize (as in expose to or put in a perilous situation (*v.t.*) or be in a perilous situation (*v.i.*): **periclitate**. See *imperil*

jerk (or loser or dope or idiot or anyone generally not worthy of respect) *n.*: **schmendrick** (or **shmendrik**) [Yiddish]. See *fool*

jest *v.i.*, *n.*: **jape**. See *joke*

Jesus (belief in the Second Coming of . . . , spec. that He will return in visible form, set up a theocratic kingdom, and reign for 1,000 years) *n.*: **chiliasm**. ❖ As the millennium limps to a close . . . some of the most astute scientific minds are turning again to speculations on the existence of God, or at least of a God, that is, a controlling being of some supreme kind. Whether they are just indulging in self-deluding **chiliasm**, or turning to the Beyond out of despair of the Here, it is evidence that even if God is dead, we shall continue to insist on re-inventing Him. (John Banville, "Pushed from the Centre of Creation," *Irish Times*, 12/31/1999.)

(2) Jesus (depiction of . . . wearing crown of thorns) *n.*: **ecce homo** [Latin]. ❖ Taxi drivers still reminisce fondly about Mark Wallinger's statue for the Fourth Plinth in Trafalgar Square. They know what they like, and even if they don't know the artist's name, they loved **Ecce Homo**, the life-size figure of a diminutive Christ wearing a crown of thorns that topped the vacant plinth last year. (Rose Aidin, Profile: "Mark Wallinger—Race, Class and Sex," *Independent* [London], 6/2/2001.)

jet set *n.*: **beau monde** [French]. See *high society*

(2) jet set *n.*: **bon ton** [French]. See *high society*

jewel (which is highly polished and unfaceted) *n.*: **cabochon**. ❖ Terms of Adornment: . . . Retro: 1935–1950; big and bold American, often in 14K gold; stones are both **cabochon** and faceted. (Jennifer Jackson, "Treasure Map," *Harper's Bazaar*, 12/1/1996, p. 60.)

(2) jewel (or trinket) *n.*: **bijou**. See *trinket*

jeweler (or jewels) *n.*: **lapidary**. ❖ Of the town's 38,000 inhabitants . . . there are some 600 **lapidary** workshops, studios, and factories, which purvey to gem buyers, collectors, and whole-

sale and retail jewelers around the globe. (John Dornberg, "Idar-Oberstein: The Gemstone Capital," *German Life*, 11/30/ 1995.)

jiffy (as in, in a . . .) *n.*: **trice** (as in "in a trice"). See *quickly*

jingling (of bells) *n.*: **tintinnabulation**. See *ringing*

jingoism (as in patriotism) *n.*: **amor patriae** [Latin]. See *patriotism*

jinx (as in put a . . . upon) *v.t.*: **imprecate**. See *curse*

(2) jinx *n.*, *adj.*: **hoodoo**. See *bad luck*

jinxed (perpetually . . . , as in unlucky, person) *n.*: **schlimazel** [Yiddish]. See *unlucky*

jitters *n.pl.* but sing. or pl. in construction: **collywobbles**. See *bellyache*

job (as in profession) *n.*: **métier** [French]. See *profession*

(2) job (requiring little work but paying an income) *n.*: **sinecure**. See *occupation*

join (as in blend) *v.t.*, *v.i.*: **inosculate**. See *blend*

(2) join (as in bring together) *v.t.*: **conflate**. See *combine*

(3) join (in a series or chain) *v.t.*, *adj.*: **concatenate** (*n.*: **concatenation**). See *connect*

(4) join (together) *v.t.*: **colligate**. See *unite*

(5) join (together, as with glue) *v.t.*: **agglutinate**. See *adhere*

joined (closely . . .) *adj.*: **coadunate**. ❖ [Samuel Coleridge] shows a consistent desire to see the many diverse parts of a scene in relationship to the whole of the scene. In projecting his **coadunating** imagination into nature, he follows his own basic principle of the reconciliation of the many into one, the establishing of unity in the presence of variety. (Monarch Notes, *Works of Samuel T. Coleridge: Interpretation—The Main Theme Of "Kubla Khan,"* 1/1/1963.)

(2) joined (of things that cannot be . . .) *adj.*: **immiscible**. See *incompatible*

(2) joined (by a close relationship) *adj.*: **affined**. See *connected*

jointly (as in simultaneously or all at once) *adv.*: **holus-bolus**. See *simultaneously*

joints (pain in . . .) *n.*: **arthralgia**. See *arthritis*

joke *v.i.*, *n.*: **jape**. ❖ Posing as "Tweeds" Bush

(a takeoff on Tammany Hall's Boss Tweed) in a top hat and shades, [George W. Bush while in high school] could get 800 sullen teenage boys laughing and roaring with his **japes** and riffs. (Evan Thomas, "A Son's Restless Journey," *Newsweek*, 8/7/2000, p. 32.)

(2) joke (as in quip) *n.*: **bon mot** [French]. See *quip*

(3) joke (as in quip) *n.*: **epigram**. See *quip*

joker (as in buffoon, who is sometimes boastful) *n.*: **Scaramouch**. See *buffoon*

joking (as in good-natured teasing) *n.*: **raillery**. See *teasing*

(2) joking (partly . . . and partly serious) *adj.*: **jocoserious**. See *semiserious*

jolly *adj.*: **eupeptic**. See *cheerful*

(2) jolly *adj.*: **Falstaffian**. See *jovial*

(3) jolly *adj.*: **riant**. See *cheerful*

josh (playfully) *v.t., v.i., n.*: **chaff**. See *teasing*

journey (about, esp. on foot, and esp. as in roam or wander) *v.t., v.i.*: **peregrinate**. See *roam*

(2) journey (about, esp. on foot, and esp. as in roam or wander) *v.t., v.i.*: **perambulate**. See *roam*

(3) journey (difficult or painful . . .) *n.*: **via dolorosa**. See *ordeal*

(4) journey (from danger) *n.*: **hegira**. See *escape*

(5) journey (to a sacred place or shrine, esp. to Mecca) *n.*: **hadj**. See *pilgrimage*

jovial *adj.*: **Falstaffian** [based on Sir John Falstaff, a character in *Henry IV* and *The Merry Wives of Windsor* by William Shakespeare]. ❖ From the time [Don King] arrived full-bore on the boxing landscape as the promoter of the "Rumble in the Jungle" between Muhammad Ali and George Foreman in Zaire in 1974, followed a year later by the epic "Thrilla in Manila" between Ali and Joe Frazier, King has manipulated the pieces of his sport with **Falstaffian** flamboyance. (Leigh Montville, "He Is a Storm on the Horizon as He Approaches," *Sports Illustrated*, 9/19/1994, p. 136.)

(2) jovial *adj.*: **riant**. See *cheerful*

(3) jovial (and social) *adj.*: **Anacreontic**. See *convivial*

jowl (esp. of cattle, but also of people) *n.*: **dewlap**. ❖ "You have to wonder" said Nels Gudmundsson, and he began to massage his throat again and pull at the **dewlaps** of skin there. (David Guterson, *Snow Falling on Cedars*, Harcourt Brace [1994], p. 17.)

joy (as in pleasure) *n.*: **delectation**. See *pleasure*

(2) joy (causing or tending to produce . . .) *adj.*: **felicific**. See *happiness*

(3) joy *n.*: **beatitude**. See *bliss*

(4) joy *n.*: **felicity**. See *happiness*

joyful *adj.*: **beatific** (to make . . . *v.t.*: **beatify**). ❖ Six months later I was signing books at a Barnes & Noble, half a continent away from my office. A lovely woman dressed in bright purple-and-blue silk floated up to me like Glinda the Good Witch, her face transformed by a **beatific** smile. (Martha Beck, "How to Find Your Happiest Self," *Redbook*, 4/1/2001, p. 96.)

(2) joyful *adj.*: **eupeptic**. See *cheerful*

(3) joyful *adj.*: **riant**. See *cheerful*

joyous (as in exuberant) *adj.*: **yeasty**. See *exuberant*

(2) joyous *adj.*: **gladsome**. See *gladness*

jubilant (often in a boastful way) *adj.*: **cock-a-hoop**. See *elated*

judge (under a new standard, esp. one that differs from conventional norms) *v.t.*: **transvaluate**. See *evaluate*

(2) judge *v.t.*: **assay**. See *evaluate*

(3) judge (on matters of taste, fashion, style, protocol, etc.) *n.*: **arbiter elegantiae** [Latin]. See *arbiter*

Judgment Day (branch of theology concerned with) *n.*: **eschatology**. ❖ The Jews, the central demonic figures in Nazi **eschatolgy**, inevitably fared badly when Germans gave free rein to their eliminationist sensibilities, to their dreams of reconstructing the social landscape and "human substance" of Europe, and to their "problem"-solving inventiveness. (Daniel Goldhagen, *Hitler's Willing Executioners*, Knopf [1996], p. 144.)

jumble (as in confused or disarrayed mass) *n.*: **welter**. ❖ Now, as [Japan's ruling Liberal

Democratic Party] crumbles—57 members of parliament already have resigned—and a **welter** of splinter parties and reform groups pop up promising change, Japanese voters have a real choice for the first time in a generation. (Steven Butler, "Peddling a New Line," *U.S. News & World Report*, 7/12/1993.)

(2) jumble *n*.: **agglomeration**. ❖ *Ranting Mophead* [1995] presents a mop and a rant. The mop stands upright beside a lectern. Attached to its handle is a mechanized **agglomeration** of valves, pipes, clothes pins, screw-top plastic water bottles, garbage bag twist-ties, gears and paper clips, which, when operating properly, babbles. It says: "I am a blabbermouth." And "Ow Ow Ow Wow." And "I am a man." (Paul Richard, "Bodily Charm; Tim Hawkinson Really Puts Himself into His Art," Truly, *Washington Post*, 4/15/2001.)

(3) jumble (and confusion) *n., adj*.: **huggermugger**. See *confusion*

(4) jumble (as in assortment) *n*.: **farrago**. See *assortment*

(5) jumble (as in assortment) *n*.: **gallimaufry**. See *assortment*

(6) jumble (as in assortment) *n*.: **olla podrida** [Spanish]. See *assortment*

(7) jumble (as in assortment) *n*.: **omnium-gatherum** [Latin]. See *assortment*

(8) jumble (as in assortment) *n*.: **salmagundi**. See *assortment*

jumbled (as in haphazard) *adj., adv*.: **higgledy-piggledy**. See *haphazard*

(2) jumbled (situation that is . . . or chaotic or complicated) *n*.: **mare's nest**. See *chaotic*

jump (esp. by a horse) *n*.: **capriole**. ❖ And the **capriole**, in which the horse leaps into the air and kicks out its hind legs, could be used to extricate horse and rider from nasty combat situations. (Susan Davis, Equestrian: "Operation Cowboy—In 1945 a Group of U.S. Soldiers Liberated 375 Lipizzans from Nazi Captivity," *Sports Illustrated*, 10/16/1995, p. R4.)

junior (rank, esp. in the military) *n*.: **subaltern**. See *subordinate*

junk (as in printed material that is trivial) *n*.:

bumf [British]. ❖ Teachers these days are used to receiving a barrage of official **bumf** telling them how to do their jobs. Never before, however, have they been given a step-by-step guide on how to eat carrots. . . . Teachers yesterday said the guidelines were patronising and "bureaucracy gone mad." (Laura Clark, "How to Eat a Carrot; Munch from the Bottom and Discard the Top, the Health Police Tell Primary School Pupils," *Daily Mail* [London], 9/25/2003.)

(2) junk *n*.: **trumpery**. ❖ Trump's **Trumpery**. A Mara-Lago garage sale was held in West Palm Beach Tuesday. About 100 treasure hunters picked through truckloads of Trump junk purchased by a salvage dealer who emptied out the garage and pump house at the famed estate in Florida. Among the trashy treasures, an arched window that went for $90 and a 3-1/2-foot plastic Santa Claus that sold for $110. (Tom Collins, "You Can't Make This Stuff Up," *Newsday*, 4/20/1995.)

(3) junk (as in garbage) *n*.: **spilth**. See *garbage*

juror *n*.: **venireman**. ❖ [In one case, a woman was sentenced to life in prison] in the shooting death of her allegedly abusive husband. The defendant unsuccessfully sought to have her conviction overturned because she had not been allowed to strike one white male juror, who she said was "smirking" during [jury selection]. . . . The judge rejected [this argument] because he did not see the **venireman** smirk. (Susan Hightower, "Sex and the Peremptory Strike: An Empirical Analysis," *Stanford Law Review*, 4/1/2000.)

just (uncompromisingly . . . , as in fair) *n*.: **Rhadamanthine** [after Rhadamanthus, son of Zeus and Europa, who, in reward for his exemplary justice, was made one of the judges of the souls of the underworld]. ❖ A governor must behave with . . . **Rhadamanthine** impartiality. Even overtly political appointees have been able to do so. . . . By contrast, when governors or governors-general descend into the political fray, they forgo their nonpartisan position, they demean the office and undermine our system. (Janet Albrechtson, "Butler's Duty to Serve the People, Not to Play Politics," *Australian*, 8/27/1993.)

(2) just (as in deserved, esp. in reference to a punishment) *adj.*: **condign**. See *deserved*

justification (formal . . . of one's acts or beliefs) *n.*: **apologia**. ❖ In October, *The Washington Post* . . . tried to explain why the belief is widely held in black neighborhoods that the CIA was behind the crack epidemic in the inner city of Los Angeles. "Conspiracy theories can often ring true; history feeds blacks' mistrust," read the *Post's* headline. This **apologia** for African American credulity ran alongside a story that proved that the allegation about the CIA and crack was utterly unfounded. (Jeffrey Rosen, "The Bloods and the Crips: O. J. Simpson, Critical Race Theory, the Law, and the Triumph of Color in America," *New Republic*, 12/9/1996, p. 27.)

(2) justification (as in act or event that is used as a . . . to provoke battle, literally or figuratively) *n.*: **casus belli** [Latin; occasion of war]. See *provocation*

(3) justification (additional . . . , as in explanation) *n.*: **epexegesis** (*adj.*: **epexegetic**). See *explanation*

justify (attempt to . . . an offense with excuses) *v.t.*: **palliate**. See *downplay*

juvenile (as in childish) *adj.*: **jejune**. ❖ [The TV show] *Mad TV* has turned out to be a formidable opponent [to *Saturday Night Live*]. . . . It has also developed a following among teenagers who can be readily found on the Internet proclaiming its superiority with appropriately **jejune** postings like "Mad TV blows SNL away." (Ginia Bellafante, "The Battle for Saturday Night Comedy Isn't Pretty, and *SNL* Is Losing Its Outrageous Edge to a Hot New Rival on Fox," *Time*, 2/12/1996, p. 70.)

(2) juvenile (as in childish) *adj.*: **puerile**. ❖ [In the TV comedy *Arli$$*] a session with another owner . . . ends when [a sports agent's] client (a pitcher demanding $2 million a year after a one-win season) emits an impossibly powerful stream of urine across the owner's desk. Not all the humor is that **puerile**, though neither is it exactly highbrow. (Richard O'Brien, Scorecard: "Medalists Hit the Talk Shows," *Sports Illustrated*, 8/19/1996, p. 31.)

(3) juvenile (retention of . . . , as in infantile, characteristics into adulthood) *n.*: **paedomorphism** (person who retains these characteristics *n.*: **paedomorph**). See *infantile*

keen (as in having a penetrating quality) *adj.*: **gimlet** (esp. as in "gimlet eye"). See *penetrating*

    (2) keen (as in incisive or perceptive) *adj.*: **trenchant**. See *incisive*

keenness *n.*: **acuity**. ❖ [T]here has always been a nagging suspicion that the subtle changes in personality and lapses in mental **acuity** that are sometimes seen after bypass surgery might be the result of brain damage caused by the operation itself. (Christine Gorman, Medicine: "Hearts and Minds," *Time*, 2/19/2001, p. 58.)

key (something such as a master . . . or passkey, which permits one to gain access or pass at will) *n.*: **passe-partout**. See *passkey*

    (2) key (to solving a puzzle or deciphering a code that has not previously been solved or deciphered) *n.*: **Rosetta stone**. See *clue*

kid (as in young child) *n.*: **moppet**. See *child*

    (2) kid (playfully) *v.t., v.i., n.*: **chaff**. See *teasing*

kidding (as in good-natured teasing) *n.*: **raillery**. See *teasing*

kidnap (often to perform compulsory service abroad) *v.t.*: **shanghai**. ❖ Chinese cooking obviously isn't an American franchise. But what about fate, encapsulated in that bivalved wafer known as the Chinese fortune cookie? Made in U.S.A. Legend suggests it was invented in San Francisco by coolies **shanghaied** to build the first transcontinental railroads. (Adam Piore, "The Meaning of Life," *Newsweek* International, 7/8/2002, p. 37.)

kids (hatred of) *n.*: **misopedia**. See *hatred*

kill (by strangling or cutting the throat) *v.t.*: **garrote**. See *strangle*

    (2) kill (by strangling or cutting the throat) *v.t.*: **jugulate**. See *strangle*

    (3) kill (as in put an end to) *v.t.*: **quietus** (as in "put the quietus to"). See *termination*

    (4) kill (oneself by fire) *v.t.*: **immolate**. See *suicide* and *sacrifice*

killer (of one wife after another) *n.*: **bluebeard** (or **Bluebeard**). See *murderer*

killing (mass . . . of unresisting persons) *n.*: **battue** [French]. ❖ Historians agree that police fired into the crowd at a mid-afternoon football match in Dublin, killing about a dozen people. . . . The plan really was to stop the match and search the crowd. Once they reached the Park, however, the police began shooting without provocation. There were no rebel gunmen outside the park, and there was no return fire from the crowd. The Croke Park massacre was a **battue**, not a battle. (David Leeson, "Death in the Afternoon: The Croke Park Massacre, 21 November 1920," *Canadian Journal of History*, 4/1/2003.)

    (2) killing (of a king) *n.*: **regicide**. ❖ An unidentified man in a mask severs the royal head; another waves it aloft: the scene . . . might have been expressly designed to drive home to those who witnessed it the enormity of the act of **regicide**. Any nation that separates the head of its lawful king from his body had better be sure that it did so with good cause. (*Economist*, "Bagehot: The End of the King—and Kings: 1649," 12/31/1999.)

    (3) killing (of one's father) *n.*: **patricide**. ❖ By the time he was sixteen, however, John [D. Rockefeller] was sufficiently embittered against his father to commit metaphorical **patricide**. . . . He would publicly deny his father's existence for thirty years. (Jackson Lears, "Capitalism, Corrected and Uncorrected: The Lobster and the Squid," *New Republic*, 2/15/1999.)

    (4) killing (of one's mother) *n.*: **matricide**. ❖ A Brooklyn man accused of **matricide** told detectives he has multiple personalities and claimed one of his alter egos stabbed his mother to death Friday morning, according to police sources. (Sean Gardiner, "Cops: Man Admits Killing His Mother," *Newsday*, 4/14/2001.)

    (5) killing (of parent or close relative) *n.*: **parricide**. ❖ Pierson is one of the 300 or so children each year across the U.S. who murder one or both of their parents. . . . Says Paul Mones, a Los Angeles attorney and **parricide** expert: "Courts are finally waking up to the problem. Kids just don't take these actions unless something is very, very wrong." (Jon D. Hull, Behavior: "Brutal Treatment, Vicious Deeds," *Time*, 10/19/1987, p. 68.)

(6) killing (of wife by her husband) *adj.*: **uxoricide**. ❖ We can think badly enough of O. J. Simpson if we recognize that he misgoverned himself by the logical standards of the wife-beater, and wait to find out whether he finally compounded his infamies with **uxoricide** plus stranger murder. The puzzle of why this man beat this woman is quite tough enough as it is. (Murray Kempton, "A Wife-Beater Starts Small," *Newsday*, 6/26/1994.)

(7) killing (of a female) *n.*: **femicide**. See *murder*

(8) killing (large-scale . . . or sacrifice) *n.*: **hecatomb**. See *slaughter*

(9) killing (of one's brother or sister) *n.*: **fratricide**. See *murder*

(10) killing (of one's own children) *n.*: **filicide**. See *murder*

killjoy (or anyone who is puritanical, prudish, or hostile with respect to minor vices or forms of popular entertainment) *n.*: **wowser** [Australian slang]. ❖ The Fourth of July was once, from the American boy's point of view, [a great holiday]. [F]athers set up Roman candles and nailed Catherine wheels to trees in the front yard, lighting thrilling displays that children rushed to from up and down the street. But the **wowsers** are always among us in America and helped by the annual casualty rate—fingers gone here and there, the occasional eye—they managed to stamp out all of that. (William Pfaff, "When Patriotism Turns into Paranoia," *International Herald Tribune*, 7/4/2002.)

(2) killjoy (as in pessimist who continually warns of a disastrous future) *n.*: **Jeremiah**. See *pessimist*

(3) killjoy *n.*: **crepehanger**. See *pessimist*

kill time (as in idle or waste time) *v.i.*: **footle** (usu. as in "footle around"). See *dawdle*

kind (original . . . or example) *n.*: **archetype**. See *model*

kindly (and pleasant) *adj.*: **sympathique** [French]. See *genial*

kinds (of all . . .) *adj.*: **omnifarious**. See *varied*

king (as in commander) *n.*: **imperator**. See *commander*

(2) king (as in ruler, of the universe) *n.*: **kosmokrator** [Greek]. See *ruler*

(3) king (killing of . . .) *n.*: **regicide**. See *killing*

(4) king (or emperor or sultan or shah or the like; also used to refer to a powerful or important person generally) *n.*: **padishah**. See *emperor*

(5) king (or other ruler who holds great power or sway) *n.*: **potentate**. See *ruler*

kingly (as in lordly) *adj.*: **seigneurial**. See *lordly*

kinship *n.*: **propinquity**. ❖ For individuals, kin ties through one's parents and by marriage to a wide range of persons define rights, obligations, and opportunities. . . . But kinship rights and obligations are not immutably fixed: an individual often has a choice as to which links he will seek to shore up or, looked at in another way, take advantage of. Sometimes this will be governed by **propinquity**. (Margarita Dobert, "Tanzania: Chapter 3B, Ethnic Groups," *Countries of the World*, 1/1/1991.)

kiss *v.t.*: **osculate**. ❖ To judge from the kiss, they like wedded bliss. In fact Charles and Diana were **osculating** all over the British tabloids last week. (Guy D. Garcia, "People," *Time*, 7/15/1985, p. 67.)

kissing (of the hand) *n.*: **baisemain** [French]. ❖ . . . *Voyage en Grande Bourgeoisie*, which is a sociological self-help book for those who wish to [act like the upper crust]. . . . [W]hile it doesn't exactly give etiquette lessons it does invoke the problems of balancing a full glass and a petit four while chatting at a crowded reception and warns of such tribal customs as hand kissing or the **baisemain**. "The **baisemain** surprises and even aggresses those who are not accustomed to its use," they write. (Mary Blume, "Classes in Class: Studying a Gilded Ghetto," *International Herald Tribune*, 8/2/1997.)

(2) kissing *idiom*: **slap and tickle**. See *sex*

kitschy (or tacky religious or devotional ornament) *n., adj.*: **bondieuserie** [French]. See *ornament*

klutzy (habitually . . . person) *n.*: **schlemiel** [Yiddish]. See *bumbler*

(2) klutzy *adj.*: **lumpish**. See *clumsy*

kneel (in worship, often in a servile manner) *v.i.*: **genuflect**. ❖ "Why do people want to be on TV?" asks author Neal Gabler. . . . Because of the fame, the power, the money, the glory, the women, everything. We live in a society that absolutely extols and worships and **genuflects** before celebrity." (Verne Gay, "Look at Me! I'm on TV!/Who Wants to Be on Television? Maybe You Should Ask Who Doesn't," *Newsday*, 6/30/2000.)

knickknack *n.*: **bibelot**. See *trinket*

(2) knickknack *n.*: **gewgaw**. See *trinket*

(3) knickknack *n.*: **whigmaleerie**. See *gadget*

knitter (female . . .) *n.*: **tricoteuse**. [French. Translated literally, this word is simply French for a woman who knits. However, its history is far more interesting. It frequently refers to the women who knitted while attending beheadings during the Reign of Terror in France in the eighteenth century, indicating their lack of sympathy for those about to be executed. Today, it is used synonymously (for either sex) with words such as bloodthirsty, vengeful, vindictive, and the like. The example below is a good use of the word.] ❖ Once we decided Saddam [Hussein] was a "monster"—a monster whom, let's not forget, the West [supported,] we gave ourselves permission to indulge the basest, most voyeuristic atavism. Cloaked in this murderous sanctimony, we join as one with the crowds who gather weekly in Teheran to enjoy watching criminals swing from a crane. The rhetoric of a war launched in the name of civilisation has degenerated into the cackling of a **tricoteuse** at the foot of the guillotine. We should be bloody ashamed. (Sam Leith, "The Shame of Punishment as Pornography," 1/1/2007.)

knockout (blow, as in punch that ends a bout) *n.*: **quietus**. See *termination*

knotty (situation or problem) *n.*: **nodus**. See *complication*

know (as in understand, thoroughly and/or intuitively) *v.t.*: **grok**. See *understand*

(2) know (as in figure out) *v.t.*: **suss** (usu. with "out"; slang). See *figure out*

know-it-all (as in one who clings to an opinion or belief even after being shown that it is wrong) *n.*: **mumpsimus**. See *stubborn*

(2) know-it-all (as in smart aleck or wise guy) *n.*: **wisenheimer**. See *smart aleck*

knowledge (branch of philosophy dealing with the nature, extent, and validity of . . .) *n.*: **epistemology**. ❖ I challenged the theologians to answer the point that a God capable of designing a universe, or anything else, would have to be complex and statistically improbable. I heard that I was brutally foisting a scientific **epistemology** upon an unwilling theology. (Richard Dawkins, *The God Delusion*, Houghton Mifflin [2006], p. 153.)

(2) knowledge (excess striving for or preoccupation with . . .) *n.*: **epistemophilia**. ❖ [Sigmund Freud] hinted at the ease with which scholarship can spill over into psychosis. . . . Nowhere is this state of what he termed "**epistemophilia**" more in evidence than in the spectral silence of the public library. In its peculiar role of providing open access to private worlds, it both allows and denies us possession of those mysteries that feed our pathology. Libraries make us consumers who lack the power of purchase, bibliophiles doomed to eternal browsing. (Graham Caveney, Books: "When Too Much Learning Can Be a Fatally Dangerous Thing," *Independent* [London], 3/23/2002.)

(3) knowledge (show of . . . of a subject that is actually superficial) *n.*: **sciolism**. See *superficial*

(4) knowledge (person who acquires . . . late in life) *n.*: **opsimath**. See *learning*

(5) knowledge (pertaining to . . . of spiritual or intellectual things) *adj.*: **gnostic**. See *spiritual*

(6) knowledge (universal . . .) *n.*: **pansophy** (*adj.*: **pansophic**). ❖ Comenius was most famous for his **pansophic** plan to universalize knowledge, holding that if an educational idea or method was good for one group of people in one place, it must be good for all people in all places. (Diederik C. D. De Jong, "Krček: Jan Amos Comenius [Symphony 3]," *American Record Guide*, 5/1/1997.)

(7) knowledge (as in perception or awareness) *n*.: **ken**. See *perception*

knowledgeable (person who is very . . . in many areas) *n*.: **polymath**. See *scholar*

(2) knowledgeable (person who is . . . in many areas) *n*.: **polyhistor**. ❖ At the weekly salon [Srenus] Zeitblom encounters Dr. Chaim Breisacher. A Jew, he was also [according to Zeitblom] "a **polyhistor**, who could talk about anything and everything, a philosopher of culture, whose opinions, however, were directed against culture insofar as he affected to see all of history as nothing but a process of decline." (Stephen Goode, "The Conscience of a Composer, and a Nation," *Washington Times*, 4/5/1998.)

(3) knowledgeable (being . . . about, as in familiar with something) *adj*.: **au fait** [French]. See *familiar*

kowtow *v.i.*: **truckle**. ❖ Missouri is the nation's second-biggest auto-producing state, but [Senator John] Danforth doesn't **truckle** to the carmakers. He calls the industry's seat-belt proposals a sham and wants to require air bags in all new U.S. cars by 1989. (Craig C. Carter, Politics & Policy: "Voice of Commerce Committee—Chairman Danforth Makes Himself Heard on Issues from Autos to Beer Ads," *Fortune*, 6/24/1985, p. 87.)

(2) kowtow *v.t.*: **bootlick**. ❖ A risk for humorists brought into close contact with their prey is that they'll get an attack of politeness. But Maher doesn't observe the prevailing TV conventions about what you can't say to guests; he doesn't **bootlick** "important" panelists as (the otherwise contemptuous) Letterman and (the always jovial) Leno tend to do. (Scott Shuger, "Comic Relief," *U.S. News & World Report*, 1/20/1997.)

kowtower (esp. someone who seeks to associate with or flatter persons of rank or high social status) *n*.: **tuft-hunter**. See *hanger-on*

label (as in classify) *v.t.*: **taxonomize**. See *classify*

labor (as in toil) *v.i.*: **moil**. See *toil*

   (2) labor (avoider) *n.*: **embusque** [French]. See *slacker*

   (3) labor (doing . . . only when the boss is watching) *n.*: **eyeservice**. See *work*

   (4) labor (forced . . . for little or no pay) *n.*: **corvée**. See *servitude*

   (5) labor (of or relating to . . . before childbirth) *adj.*: **parturient**. See *childbirth*

   (6) labor (slow or difficult . . . regarding a pregnancy) *n.*: **dystocia**. See *childbirth*

laborer (Mexican . . . allowed to work in United States) *n.*: **bracero**. ❖ For two decades until 1964, the United States had such an arrangement, the **bracero** program, which brought seasonal farmworkers from Mexico to California. While on paper "guestworkers" are guaranteed labor rights, they depend on a job's continuation to remain in the country. (David Bacon, "INS Declares War on Labor," *Nation*, 10/25/1999.)

laborious *adj.*: **operose**. ❖ Computers and the Internet offer unprecedented access to a world of information. Rather than becoming obsolete, basic skills such as spelling, referencing source material and typing are vital in maneuvering one's way efficiently through the electronic multimedia landscape. With three splendiferous CD-ROMs, users can complete these **operose** tasks expediently and efficiently. (Donald Liebenson, "Fact Finders: With These Reference Works, a World of Knowledge Is Only a Few Keystrokes Away," *Chicago Tribune*, 5/8/1997.)

   (2) laborious (as in hardworking, person) *n.*: **Stakhanovite**. See *workaholic*

   (3) laborious (task, esp. of cleaning up or remedying bad situations) *n.*: **Augean task**. See *Herculean*

lacerate (as in to make a small or shallow cut in the skin) *v.t.*: **scarify**. See *cut*

lackadaisical (as in moving like a slug) *adj.*: **limacine**. See *slug*

lackey (as in willing tool or servant of another)

n.: **âme damnée** [French; lit. damned soul]. ❖ Eugene McCarthy once remarked of a Democratic senatorial colleague whom he considered an opportunist that he'd "cut off his mother's head and take bets on which way it would fall." That crack leaps to mind as one considers the case of Dick Morris [who was] the **âme damnée** of Bill Clinton in his 1996 reelection campaign until Morris's spectacular fall from power in a tawdry sex scandal. (Doug Ireland, "Behind the Oval Office: Winning the Presidency in the Nineties," *Nation*, 3/3/1997.)

   (2) lackey *n.*: **running dog**. ❖ Today some South Koreans worry that [Lee Hoi-chang] may be too close to a Bush administration that many see as unnecessarily hard-line toward the North. Case in point: when the *Washington Post* ran a story last week alleging that Lee had "endorsed Bush's 'axis of evil' remarks," he found himself under immediate attack. His aides now worry that he'll be painted as Washington's **running dog** for months. (B. J. Lee, "Seoul's Stiff Reed," *Newsweek* International, 2/25/2002.)

lacking (anything better) *adv.*: **faute de mieux** [French]. ❖ [T]here is probably no alternative to Mr. Buchanan [as the Reform Party candidate], unless [Jesse] Ventura changes his mind and agrees to run himself. The governor of Minnesota seems unprepared to stand in his way. . . . So if Mr. Buchanan [decides to] leave the Republican Party, he stands a good chance of winning the Reform Party nomination, **faute de mieux**. (*Economist*, "Pat Buchanan's Reforming Moment," 9/18/1999.)

ladies' man (as in man who seduces women) *n.*: **Lothario**. See *playboy*

   (2) ladies' man *n.*: **roué** [French]. See *playboy*

lake (of or relating to) *adj.*: **lacustrine**. ❖ When Cortes and his men entered the Valley of Mexico almost 500 years ago they found mostly water: a vast lake, actually five interlocking lakes, stretched across the basin. . . . For years this final outpost of a **lacustrine** empire seemed destined for landfill. (Michael Ybarra,

L

"Cruising on an Aztec Lake," *New York Times*, 5/12/1996.)

lakes (of or relating to still water, such as . . .) *adj.*: **lentic**. See *water*

(2) lakes (of or occurring in . . . or ponds) *adj.*: **limnetic**. See *water*

lamb (of, relating to, or characteristic of sheep or . . .) *adj.*: **ovine**. See *sheep*

lame (as in decrepit) *adj.*: **spavined**. See *decrepit*

(2) lame (as in limping, from lack of blood flow to leg muscles) *n.*: **claudication**. See *limping*

lament (over) *v.t.*: **bewail**. ❖ Hamed Essafi, the U.N. disaster-relief coordinator, could only **bewail** the extent to which lifesaving measures fell short in Bangladesh. (James Walsh, "And No Bells Tolled," *Time* International, 5/20/1991, p. 56.)

(2) lament (as in wail) *v.i.*: **ululate**. See *wail*

(3) lament (bitter . . .) *n.*: **jeremiad**. See *complaint*

(4) lament (expressing . . . often regarding something gone) *adj.*: **elegiac**. See *sorrowful*

(5) lament (poem or song of . . . , esp. for a dead person) *n.*: **threnody**. See *requiem*

(6) lament (wail in . . . for the dead) *v.i.*: **keen**. See *wail*

lampoon (esp. by ridiculing or making fun of someone) *n., v.t.*: **pasquinade**. See *satirize*

lance (or spear) *n.*: **assegai**. See *spear*

land (consisting of . . . and water) *adj.*: **terraqueous**. ❖ I'm certain that in recent days Bill Esrey and Bernie Ebbers, the chief players in the proposed merger of Sprint and MCI WorldCom, have felt at times that they could cup-cushion this entire **terraqueous** globe in the palms of their hands. (George Gurley, "The Sprint Deal Proves That No Matter How Big You Get, There's Always Room to Get a Little Bigger," *Kansas City Star*, 10/31/1999.)

(2) land (of, relating to, containing, or possessing . . .) *adj.*: **praedial**. ❖ Norma believes she was born to be a farmer, smelling the soil. She recognizes the problems of **praedial** larceny but says that [while] much depends on what you have on your farms, goats are prime targets for thieves. (Marie Gregory, "Problems of Jamaican Women Farmers," *Caribbean Today*, 11/30/1994.)

land of opportunity (spec. a place of fabulous wealth or opportunity) *n.*: **El Dorado**. See *paradise*

landslide (from mudslide or a volcano) *n.*: **lahar**. ❖ "If you have a big eruption, you're going to have a long lead time. Mount St. Helens was rumbling and shaking for almost a year" before it erupted in May 1980, Finn said. "But with small eruptions, you don't get that much lead time, and that's the thing you have to worry about with these **lahars**," she said. "They're dangerous because they travel pretty fast." (Jim Erickson, "Scientists Peer into Heart of Giant," *Denver Rocky Mountain News*, 2/1/2001.)

language (coarse, offensive, or abusive . . .) *n.*: **billingsgate**. ❖ The remarks were what I later came to know as anti-Semitic clichés: about money, noses, ambition, slyness, and all the rest. The tone of this suburban **billingsgate** was chummy, almost chortling, as if passwords or signs of mutual recognition were being exchanged. (Herb Greer, "An Amateur Jew," *Commentary*, 3/1/1995, p. 52.)

(2) language (common . . . between people who speak different languages) *n.*: **lingua franca**. ❖ [Chambers] was an adept linguist, with idiomatic German—still communism's **lingua franca**—and so could easily communicate with agents sent from overseas. (Sam Tanenhaus, *Whittaker Chambers*, Random House [1997], p. 80.)

(3) language (person who knows only one . . .) *n.*: **monoglot**. ❖ [M]odern English-speakers [have] a taste for foreign writers—Colombian, Japanese, German, as well as Latin and Greek. But, since English-speakers themselves are notoriously **monoglot**, they rely on translation to import into the language the international output of books. (*Economist*, "Back to the Basics," 5/18/1996, p. 85.)

(4) language (having a good feel for what is appropriate in the use of spoken or written . . .)

n.: **sprachgefühl** [German]. ❖ [Michael] Avallone had major problems with his raw material: words, and the uses to which they can be put. He had problems with sentences, syntax, subordinate clauses, alliteration, assonance, dialogue, indeed virtually anything that was not simply subject-verb-object—and he could sometimes be uneasy with those. He was not, in short, a man with an innate **sprachgefühl**. (Jack Adrian, obituary of Michael Avallone, *Independent* [London], 3/20/1999.)

(5) language (obsession with . . . , as in words) *n.*: **logomania**. See *words*

(6) language (one who studies . . . and words) *n.*: **philologist**. See *linguist*

(7) language (common . . . of the people) *n.*: **vulgate**. See *vernacular*

(8) language (distortion or destruction of sense of . . .) *n.*: **verbicide**. See *distortion*

(9) language (pattern that is unique to each person) *n.*: **idiolect**. See *speech*

(10) language (spec. the study and analysis of signs and symbols as part of communication) *n.*: **semiotics**. See *communication*

(11) language (specialized . . . or speech used by a particular group) *n.*: **argot**. See *vernacular*

(12) language (used by members of the underworld or a particular group) *n.*: **cant**. See *vernacular*

(13) language (which is meaningless or deceptive) *n.*: **flummery**. See *meaningless*

(14) language (as in vocabulary) *n.*: **lexicon**. See *vocabulary*

languages (mixture of two or more . . .) *adj.*: **macaronic**. ❖ Mikhalkov charges in. . . . He gives Mastroianni a hearty hug, then shouts, "Hokay!" and dashes about the pseudo-stage like a Cossack, interpreting nine roles at once with magical expressiveness—but in Russian, which his aide, Alla Garrubba, translates into Italian. It's a **macaronic** ramble-scramble but it works. (Brad Darrach, Bio: "Marcello Mastroianni: He Lives for Art, He Lives for Love—at 63, He's the Old Wild King of the Movies," *People*, 12/7/1987, p. 98.)

(2) languages (speaking or writing in many different . . .) *adj.*: **polyglot**. See *multilingual*

large (like an elephant) *adj.*: **pachydermatous**. See *elephant*

(2) large (very . . . object) *n.*: **leviathan**. See *huge*

(3) large (very . . .) *adj.*: **cyclopean**. See *big*

(4) large (very . . .) *adj.*: **brobdingnagian** (often cap.). See *huge*

(5) large (very . . .) *adj.*: **Bunyanesque**. See *enormous*

(6) large (very . . .) *adj.*: **Pantagruelian**. See *gigantic*

(7) large (very . . .) *adj.*: **pythonic**. See *huge*

(8) large (very . . . , like an elephant) *adj.*: **elephantine**. See *enormous*

(9) large (very . . .) *adj.*: **mastodonic**. See *big*

large-chested (condition of having overly large breasts) *n.*: **macromastia**. See *breasts*

(2) large-chested *adj.*: **bathycolpian**. See *busty*

(3) large-chested *adj.*: **hypermammiferous**. See *busty*

laryngitis (as in loss of voice due to disease, injury, or psychological causes) *n.*: **aphonia**. ❖ So strong was Schnitzler's faith in hypnosis, in fact, that in the conclusion of his article on **aphonia** he proposed that hypnosis might be used to treat the more general neurotic conditions responsible for loss of voice. (Laura Otis, "The Language of Infection: Disease and Identity in Schnitzler's *Reigen*," *Germanic Review*, 3/1/1995, p. 65.)

lascivious (man or playboy) *n.*: **roué** [French]. See *playboy*

(2) lascivious *adj.*: **fescennine**. See *obscene*

(3) lascivious *adj.*: **ithyphallic**. See *lustful*

(4) lascivious *adj.*: **lickerish**. See *lustful*

(5) lascivious *adj.*: **lubricious**. See *lewd*

lash (generally at oneself) *v.t.*: **flagellate** (*n.*: **flagellation**). See *criticize*

(2) lash (generally used figuratively) *v.t.*: **larrup**. See *whip*

(3) lash *n.* (to flog with a . . .) *v.t.*: **knout**. See *whip*

lashing (the soles of the feet with a stick as a form of punishment or torture) *n.*, *v.t.*: **bastinado**. See *beating*

last (ability to . . . , as in endure) *n.*: **sitzfleisch**. See *endure*

(2) last (as in endure) *v.i.*: **perdure**. See *endure*

lasting (extremely . . .) *adj.*: **perdurable**. See *durable*

(2) lasting (forever or immortal) *adj.*: **amaranthine**. See *immortal*

(3) lasting (forever) *adj.*: **sempiternal**. See *everlasting*

(4) lasting (only a brief time) *adj.*: **fugacious**. See *fleeting*

Last Judgment (branch of theology concerned with) *n.*: **eschatology**. See *Judgment Day*

last resort *n.*: **pis aller** [French]. ❖ Like Warhol and Harvey, Rodchenko was a commercial as well as a fine artist. Unlike Warhol, he began as fine, but unlike Harvey, his downshift into visual rhetoric was not a **pis aller**—a matter of having to make a living. (Arthur C. Danto, Books & the Arts: "'Art into Life': Rodchenko," *Nation*, 9/21/1998.)

last stop *n.*: **terminus**. See *end*

last words (as in parting words) *n.*: **envoi** [French]. See *parting words*

late (as in overdue) *adj.*, *adv.*: **behindhand**. See *late*

(2) late (too . . . , as in a statement, thought, knowledge, or action that comes to mind or occurs after the fact when it is too late to act on it, such as locking the barn door after the cows have left) *n.*: **afterwit**. See *belated*

latent (as in temporarily inactive) *adj.*: **quiescent**. See *inactive*

latest (the . . . thing) *n.*: **dernier cri** [French]. See *trend*

latrine *n.*: **cloaca**. ❖ "Pecunia non olet," replied the Emperor Vespasian when it was suggested to him that it might be unseemly to put a tax on public toilets. A piece of gold, after all, can emerge even from a **cloaca**. (Richard Klein, "Get a Whiff of This: Breaking the Smell Barrier," *New Republic*, 2/6/1995, p. 18.)

lauding (insincerely . . .) *adj.*: **fulsome**. See *insincere*

laugh (having an ability or tendency to . . .) *n.*: **risibility**. ❖ In the early '60s, hiding a TV camera was a fresh idea, and Allen Funt's sly use of hidden cameras touched the nation's **risibility**. "Smile," his befuddled victims were told, "you're on Candid Camera." Funt died last week. The humor predeceased him by years. Today, few public spaces are without a camera. Surveillance cameras, both hidden and obvious, are ubiquitous—and unfunny. (*Newsday*, "It's No Longer Funny to Be Caught on Camera," 9/13/1999.)

(2) laugh (loud and hard) *v.i.*: **cachinnate** (*n.*: **cachinnation**). ❖ In "The Animal Ridens: Laughter as Metaphor in Modem American Literature," Del Kehl contrasts [Nathaniel] Hawthorne's "sharp, dry **cachinnation**" and [Mark] Twain's laughter that can "blow the colossal humbug to rags and atoms at a blast" with [Saul] Bellow's "animal ridens, the laughing creature, forever rising up." (Don Nilsen, "Humorous Contemporary Jewish-American Authors: An Overview of the Criticism," *Melus*, 12/1/1996, p. 71.)

laughable *adj.*: **gelastic**. [This word is synonymous with "risible" (see next entry) but is not used nearly as frequently. In fact, its most common usage is in reference to the medical condition gelastic epilepsy, which is a form of epilepsy producing uncontrollable laughter. Thus, while "gelastic," like "laughable" and "risible," could presumably be meant in both a straightforward sense and pejoratively (see the example accompanying "risible"), one does not often see it used in the pejorative sense.] ❖ [In the TV show *Men Behaving Badly*], curiously, the word "lager" is considered hilarious, and the drinking of it to excess positively **gelastic**. Supplementing this, tonight's episode also relies on telegraphed sight gags and a well-rehearsed studio audience with the lowest laugh threshold in the northern hemisphere. (Mike Harris, Tube, *Australian*, 10/31/1996.)

(2) laughable *adj.*: **risible**. [As with the

word "laughable" itself, this word is sometimes used in the straightforward sense, but is more frequently used pejoratively, as in "his argument was so ridiculous, it was laughable."]
❖ By endorsing Howard Dean before a single vote has been cast [in the primaries], Al Gore has done Democrats hoping for a victory next November a true disservice. . . . [I]t's hard to say what was more **risible** about Gore's remarks: His claim that he respected the prerogative of caucus and primary voters or his suggestion to the other candidates that they should "keep their eyes on the prize" and eschew attacks on the front-runner. (Scott Lehigh, "Gore Hurts Democrats with Premature Nod," *Boston Globe*, 12/12/2003.)

laughing *adj.*: **riant**. See *cheerful*

lavish *adj.*: **Lucullan**. ❖ [Christina] Whited, a . . . psychic experimenter [swears that she has been getting recipes from the late noted chef James Beard]. . . . [A]nybody could lose weight following the recipes Whited says Beard has been dictating to her. Far from the **Lucullan** feasts for which he was renowned, they include such prim nibbles as tofu pudding pie, rye sesame sticks and carob cookies. (Mary Huzinec, "The New Soup-to-Nuts Cookbook: A Channeler Says She's Getting Recipes from the Late James Beard," *People*, 3/7/1988.)
(2) lavish (excessively . . . , esp. in a sensuous way) *adj.*: **sybaritic**. See *luxurious*

law (as a matter of . . .) *adj.*, *adv.*: **de jure** (lit. by law, as contrasted with de facto: in reality or in fact) [Latin]. See *legally*

lawbreaker *n.*: **malefactor**. See *wrongdoer*

lawful *adj.*: **licit**. See *legal*

lawless (as in unruly) *adj.*: **indocile**. See *unruly*

lawlessness (as in government by the mob or the masses) *n.*: **mobocracy**. See *government*
(2) lawlessness (as in government by the mob or the masses) *n.*: **ochlocracy**. See *government*

lawmaker *n.*: **solon**. See *legislator*

lawsuits (persistent instigation of . . . , esp. groundless ones) *n.*: **barratry**. ❖ Why is jurisprudence suddenly the hot new pop read? . . . [T]his year lawyers, next year civil engineers or professional bowlers. . . . In any case, the entire, ever wistful publishing industry now chases riches through **barratry**, the offense of excessive litigation. There is a cranked-out feel to most legal thrillers. (John Skow, Books: "Burden of Turow," *Time*, 1/11/1993, p. 51.)

lawyer (who may be petty, dishonest, or disreputable) *n.*: **pettifogger**. ❖ For 27 years, Nolo has thrived on unrestrained hostility to **pettifoggers**. The desks of some Nolo executives contain treats of shark-shaped gummy lawyers, and the company's award-winning Web site features a running list of lawyer jokes classified in 20 categories ranging from "Outrageous Fees" to "Lawyers as Crooks, Cheats and Felons." (Doreen Carvajal, "Legal Publisher Under Fire: Texas Lawyers Challenge Firm's Do-It-Yourself Guides," *Atlanta Journal-Constitution*, 8/26/1998.)

laying low (as in, in concealment) *adv.*: **doggo** (esp. as in "lying doggo"; slang). See *concealment*

laypersons (as in parish or congregation) *n.*: **laity**. See *parish*

laze (around during the summer) *v.i.*: **aestivate** (or **estivate**). ❖ Above all, my children **aestivate**. From May to September their life is a langorous stroll from pool to hammock to beach to barbecue. Their biggest challenges are ice creams that melt before the first lick, and fireflies that resist capture in jam jars. (Gerald Baker, "The Long Hot Summer," *Financial Times* [London], 7/12/2003.)

laziness (as in lethargy) *n.*: **hebetude**. See *lethargy*

lazy (person, who stays in bed out of laziness) *n.*: **slugabed**. ❖ If the Patriots win the Super Bowl, Bill Parcells will finally get a good night's sleep. It seems the least the franchise could do for him. "I was up at 3:30 and my mind started racing with all the things I had to do," Parcells said the morning after New England's 20–6 win over Jacksonville in the AFC Championship game. It's a safe bet the coach hasn't been a **slugabed** since that morning, either.

(Michael Gee, "10 Reasons the New England Patriots Should Win the Super Bowl; Reason 2: It's a Great Farewell Present for Bill Parcells," *Boston Herald*, 1/22/1997.)

(2) lazy *adj.*: **fainéant** [French]. ❖ [I]f non-hunters ever knew how many properly dressed, entirely palatable big-game carcasses wind up in dumpsters because someone was simply too **fainéant** to butcher and cook and eat an animal he could find the time and energy to shoot and kill, hunting would be in even greater jeopardy than it is today. (Thomas McIntyre, "The Meaning of Meat [A Hunter's View]," *Sports Afield*, 8/1/1997, p. 18.)

(3) lazy (person devoted to seeking pleasure and luxury) *n.*: **lotus-eater**. See *hedonist*

(4) lazy (person) *n.*: **wastrel**. See *slacker*

(5) lazy (person, as in work avoider) *n.*: **embusque** [French]. See *slacker*

leader (of a group, esp. one who is overbearing or domineering) *n.*: **cock of the walk**. [The "walk" is where barn-door fowls are fed, and if there is more than one cock, they will fight for supremacy in the area.] ❖ Like the **cock of the walk**, Senator Mitch McConnell strutted across the Senate floor, preening his new First Amendment feathers and pecking to death the latest (and most modest) of campaign finance reforms set before that body. For four days of debate he tended to his flock of grateful Republican colleagues, commending them on how well they followed his script. (Ellen Miller, "Free Speech & Campaign Myth: How Was Campaign-Finance Reform Killed?" *Nation*, 4/27/1998.)

(2) leader (of a party, school of thought, or group of persons) *n.*: **coryphaeus**. ❖ The official titles for Stalin used in Pravda and the official histories: Leader and Teacher of the Workers of the World, Father of the Peoples, Wise and Intelligent Chief of the Soviet People, the Greatest Genius of All Times and Peoples, the Greatest Military Leader of All Times and Peoples, **Coryphaeus** of the Sciences, Faithful Comrade-In-Arms of Lenin, Devoted Continuer of Lenin's Cause, the Lenin of Today, the

Mountain Eagle and Best Friend of All Children. (David Remnick, "Standing by Stalin; In the Glasnot Era, a Cadre of Loyalists Stuck in Time," *Washington Post*, 11/15/89.)

(3) leader (or spokesman, esp. for a political cause) *n.*: **fugleman**. ❖ [Arthur M. Schlesinger Jr.:] "The battles of the Thirties shaped my politics. . . . I remain to this day a New Dealer, unreconstructed and unrepentant." . . . In that context it is interesting to learn that the "particular hero" of this **fugleman** for the New Deal was H. L. Mencken . . . for whom he retains affection and admiration even in the face of Mencken's "virulent attacks on Franklin D. Roosevelt and the New Deal" and the "mean-spirited" tone of his posthumously published diaries. (Jonathan Yardley, review of *A Life in the 20th Century*, by Arthur M. Schlesinger Jr., *Washington Post*, 11/12/2000.)

(4) leader (political . . .) *n.*: **sachem**. ❖ The Republican presidential field has something for everyone (and comedy tonight?). But no matchup of the contenders provides a more vivid contrast than social conservative **sachem** Gary Bauer and "capitalist tool" Steve Forbes. (Don Feder, "Bauer & Forbes: Main St. vs. Wall St.," *Boston Herald*, 4//7/1999.)

(5) leader *n.*: **bell cow**. ❖ Starbucks' megawatt reputation could help attract other similarly upscale tenants [to the new shopping mall, Ralph] Megna said. "Part of this issue has to do with chemistry. . . . Starbucks is being given very strong consideration because it is a **bell cow** for other retailers," he said. (Teena Hammond, "Starbucks, Local Coffeehouse at Standoff in Riverside, California," Knight Ridder/Tribune Business News, 6/24/1996)

(6) leader (or ruler generally) *n.*: **satrap**. [This word has various definitions, including (1) a leader or ruler generally, (2) a prominent or notable person generally (see *bigwig*), (3) a henchman (see *henchman*), (4) a bureaucrat (see *bureaucrat*), and (5) the head of a state acting either as a representative or under the dominion and control of a foreign power (see *ruler*). This is an example of the first definition. Often—but not always—it has a negative connotation, as it does in this example.]

❖ Matthew Crosson directs the Long Island Association as if he were a petty **satrap** and Long Island his fief. Over the past few years, Mr. Crosson has frozen many important initiatives begun by others outside of the L.I.A. sphere. If the initiative didn't line the greedy pockets of the small, select private club of investors who actually control the L.I.A., then it simply did not matter. (Richard Arfin, letter to the editor, *New York Times*, 7/29/2001.)

(7) leader (or proponent of a cause) *n.*: **paladin**. See *proponent*

(8) leader (or ruler who holds great power or sway) *n.*: **potentate**. See *ruler*

(9) leader (acting either as a representative or under the dominion and control of a foreign power) *n.*: **satrap**. See *ruler*

(10) leader (as in commander) *n.*: **imperator**. See *commander*

(11) leader (as in dictator, esp. in Spanish-speaking countries) *n.*: **caudillo**. See *dictator*

(12) leader (as in ruler, of the universe) *n.*: **kosmokrator** [Greek]. See *ruler*

(13) leader (esp. hereditary) *n.*: **dynast**. See *ruler*

(14) leader *n.*: **duce** [Italian]. See *commander*

leaderless *n.*: **acephalous** (lit. without a head).

❖ Since the Umuofians are **acephalous**, their central political power is invested in the ndichie, council of elders, and in the egwugwu, masked spirits of the ancestors who come to sit in judgment over civil and criminal disputes. (Ato Quayson, "Realism, Criticism, and the Disguises of Both: A Reading of Chinua Achebe's *Things Fall Apart* with an Evaluation of the Criticism Relating to It," *Research in African Literatures*, 12/22/1994, p. 117.)

leaf (of or relating to a . . .) *adj.*: **foliar**. ❖ Thirty years ago, Smith was assigned to work with and breed red clover. His success is evident in the breeding he performed to make red clover plants resistant to root rots such as Fusarium and to **foliar** diseases such as anthracnose . . . a disease that causes plants to lose their leaves,

weaken, and die. (Linda Cooke, "New Red Clover Puts Pastures in the Pink," *Agricultural Research*, 12/1/1996, p. 9.)

leafy *adj.*: **frondescent**. ❖ *White Interior* (1932) [by Pierre Bonnard greets] the viewer upon arrival. . . . A fiery sky peeks in over the Mediterranean Sea and above a coastal town, through a cluster of **frondescent** trees, through a window and its windowpane, shimmering in reflection. (James Panero, "Bonnard's 'Butterflies,'" *New Criterion*, 12/1/2002.)

leak (as in escape from proper channels, esp. a liquid or something that flows) *v.i.*: **extravasate**. See *exude*

lean (body type) *adj.*: **ectomorphic**. ❖ Tina Gaudoin writes in the July issue of *Bazaar* that the magazine has received "stacks and stacks of angry letters, newspaper articles and phone calls decrying our use of 'stick figure, prepubescent, anorexic-looking models who represent an unattainable ideal for most females.'" Yet she goes on to say, "This is an **ectomorphic** body type. It's in fashion. You'll be seeing more of it." (Anne Tumlinson, "Strong Women Are Not in Fashion," *St. Louis Post-Dispatch*, 9/17/1993.)

(2) lean (and/or graceful) *adj.*: **gracile**. See *slender*

leap (esp. by a horse) *n.*: **capriole**. See *jump*

leap year (of or relating to) *adj.*: **bisextile**. ❖ Officially called "**bisextile**" year because of its placement in the Julian calendar, it became known as "leap" year because English courts did not recognize Feb. 29, so it was "leapt" over. (PR Newswire, "Four Million People Worldwide Celebrate Leap Year Birthdays," 4/7/2000.)

learn (about, as in discover, through careful or skillful examination or investigation) *v.t.*: **expiscate**. See *discover*

(2) learn (as in figure out) *v.t.*: **suss** (usually with "out"; slang). See *figure out*

learned (as in pedantic) *adj.*: **donnish**. See *pedantic*

(2) learned (as in scholarly or bookish) *adj.*: **donnish**. See *bookish*

(3) learned (of a . . . , but pedantic, word or term) *adj.*: **inkhorn**. See *pedantic*

(4) learned (people as a group) *n.*: **clerisy**. See *educated*

(5) learned (person who is . . . in many areas) *n.*: **polyhistor**. See *knowledgeable*

(6) learned (person who is . . . in many areas) *n.*: **polymath**. See *scholar*

(7) learned (person, as in lover of learning) *n.*: **philomath**. See *scholar*

learning (person who acquires . . . late in life) *n.*: **opsimath**. ❖ Dear Mr. Buckley: Having recently celebrated my 90th birthday, am I too young to be an **opsimath**? Sincerely, David L. Soper, San Diego, Calif. Dear Mr. Soper: No no no, you are perfect to be an **opsimath**! (David L. Soper, letter to the editor, *National Review*, 11/21/2005.)

(2) learning (as in branch of philosophy dealing with nature, extent, and validity of knowledge) *n.*: **epistemology**. See *knowledge*

(3) learning (excess striving for or preoccupation with . . .) *n.*: **epistemophilia**. See *knowledge*

(4) learning (on a subject that is superficial but appears to be deep) *n.*: **sciolism**. See *superficial*

(5) learning (from one's errors, and a return to a sane, sound, or correct position and the wisdom gained from the experience) *n.*: **resipiscence**. See *reformation*

(6) learning (pertaining to . . . of spiritual or intellectual things) *adj.*: **gnostic**. See *spiritual*

(7) learning (universal . . .) *n.*: **pansophy** (*adj.*: **pansophic**). See *knowledge*

leave (hurriedly or secretly) *v.t.*: **absquatulate**. ❖ [Jackie Gleason's m]other Mae was a rosary addict. Father Herb worked in the death claims department of a small insurance firm, drank like a culvert and **absquatulated** when Jackie was 9, leaving Mae on her uppers. ("He was as good a father," Jackie later quipped, "as I've ever known.") (Brad Darrach, A Fond Goodbye to the Great One," *People*, 7/13/1987, p. 94.)

(2) leave (hurriedly or secretly) *v.t.*: **decamp**. ❖ She had deliberately packed for only four days, so she would have an excuse for a short visit. When her clothes ran out, she would have to go home. . . . She was glad that she had had the foresight to arrange an unbreakable excuse for **decamping** soon. She had no intention of getting stuck in a very small town. (Aaron Latham, "The Ballad of Gussie & Clyde: A True Story of True Love," *Good Housekeeping*, 8/1/1997, p. 149.)

leave out (intentionally) *v.t.*: **pretermit**. See *omit*

leaves (having many . . .) *adj.*: **frondescent**. See *leafy*

(2) leaves (of or relating to . . .) *adj.*: **foliar**. See *leaf*

leaving (as in a departure that is unannounced, abrupt, secret, or unceremonious) *n.*: **French leave** (or **French Leave**). See *departure*

leaving out (or omitting or passing over) *n.*: **preterition**. See *omitting*

lecher *n.*: **rakehell**. See *libertine*

lecherous (man or playboy) *n.*: **roué** [French]. See *playboy*

(2) lecherous *adj.*: **concupiscent** (*n.*: **concupiscence**). See *lustful*

(3) lecherous *adj.*: **ithyphallic**. See *lustful*

(4) lecherous *adj.*: **lickerish**. See *lustful*

(5) lecherous *adj.*: **lubricious**. See *lewd*

lecture (as in formal analysis or discussion of a subject) *n.*: **disquisition**. See *discourse*

(2) lecture (about, esp. at length) *v.i.*, *n.*: **descant**. See *talk*

(3) lecture (as in complaint) *n.*: **jeremiad**. See *complaint*

(4) lecture (at length) *v.i.*: **perorate** (*n.*: **peroration**). See *monologue*

(5) lecture (on a topic, esp. in a long-winded or pompous manner) *v.i.*: **bloviate**. See *speak*

(6) lecture (pompously, loudly, or theatrically) *v.i.*: **declaim**. See *proclaim*

(7) lecture (scolding . . .) *n.*: **philippic**. See *tirade*

(8) lecture (very enthusiastic or excited . . . or writing) *n.*: **dithyramb**. See *enthusiastic*

leech (as in one who mooches) *n.*: **schnorrer** [Yiddish; slang]. See *moocher*

left (on the . . . side or left-handed) *adj.*: **sinistral**. See *left-handed*

left-handed *adj.*: **sinistral**. ❖ The model predicts that today everyone has genes which confer a basic predisposition of 78% to be right-handed. How children actually turn out, however, can be influenced by whether their parents are dextral [right-handed] or **sinistral**. (*Economist*, "Sinister Evolution: Population Genetics," 8/26/1995, p. 69.)

leftover (as in warmed over, food or old material) *n., adj.*: **rechauffé** [French]. See *warmed-over*

left to right (moving from . . .) *adj.*: **sinistro-dextral**. See *right to left*

legal *adj.*: **licit**. ❖ Diane's liaison with "The Weasel," as her cyber-Romeo signed his E-mail, may not meet the legal definition of adultery—which implies physical, not virtual, coupling. But there's no doubt that cyberromances, whether **licit** or not, generate genuine feelings. (Anastasia Toufexis, "Romancing the Computer: The First Cyberadultery Suit Shows the Risks of Looking for Love Online," *Time*, 2/19/1996, p. 53.)

legally *adj., adv.*: **de jure** (lit. by law, as contrasted with de facto: in reality or in fact) [Latin]. ❖ While ultra-Orthodox leaders [in Israel] regularly bluster against the courts, they comply with court rulings. Even more telling, they regularly turn to the courts when they think that doing so will protect their interests. The ultra-Orthodox oppose the courts **de jure**, but they do not de facto. (Noah Efron, *Real Jews*, Basic Books [2003], p. 218.)

legislator *n.*: **solon**. ❖ Who were these **solons** rhapsodized by Benjamin Franklin as "the most August and respectable assembly he was ever in in his life?" The 55 delegates [at the Constitutional Convention] representing 12 states . . . scarcely constituted a cross-section of America. They were white, educated males and mostly affluent property owners. (Ron Chernow, *Alexander Hamilton*, Penguin [2004], p. 229.)

legitimate *adj.*: **cromulent**. [This word is not yet dictionary-recognized but it is increasing in popularity. It comes from an episode of *The Simpsons* in which Lisa's teacher, Miss Hoover, in discussing another invented word, "embiggens," remarks that "it's a perfectly cromulent word." Because of the original context in which the word arose (i.e., "embiggens" not being a real word), there are some who maintain that the word should only be used ironically, as in "not acceptable," but this is not a majority view.] ❖ In the New Year's Honours list for 2000, it was declared that, in recognition of his distinguished services to Arts Education, Professor Christopher John Frayling[,] "historian, critic, broadcaster, Rector of the Royal College of Art and one of the very Greatest and Goodest (yes, goodest: a perfectly **cromulent** superlative) of our nation's Great and Good[,]" had been granted the title of Knight. (Christopher Frayling, "How the West Was Won," *Independent on Sunday*, 4/10/2005.)

(2) legitimate (as in genuine) *adj.*: **echt** [German]. See *genuine*

legs (one's own . . .) *idiom*: **shank's mare** (or **shank's pony**). See *walking*

lender (who charges high interest) *n.*: **shylock**. [This derives from the moneylender of the same name in Shakespeare's *The Merchant of Venice*.] ❖ Chili—so named for his infinite cool—has spent the past dozen or so years as the laid-back enforcer for a mob-connected loan-sharking operation in Miami. . . . He quickly masters the latest Hollywood jargon. ("There were a lot of terms you had to learn, as opposed to the **shylock** business where all you had to know how to say was 'Give me the f*** money.'") (Josh Rubins, review of *Get Shorty*, by Elmore Leonard, *Entertainment Weekly*, 8/17/1990, p. 24.)

lengthy (as in rambling) *adj.*: **discursive**. See *rambling*

lesbian *adj.*: **sapphic**. ❖ Sheba and I were a bit *too* fond of one another, she told people; a bit *too* close. The implication was that Sheba and I were involved in some sort of **sapphic** love affair. . . . I am quite accustomed to [this] by now. Vulgar speculation about sexual proclivity would seem to be an occupational hazard for a single woman like myself [i.e., in her sixties], particularly one who insists on maintaining a certain discretion about her private life. (Zoë Heller, *What Was She Thinking?* Henry Holt [2003], p. 147.)

(2) lesbian *n.*: **tribade**. ❖ The tough "queer-core" [girl] band Tribe 8—the name plays on **tribade**—is not for the timid. (Margaret Saraco, "Where Feminism Rocks," *On the Issues*, 3/1/1996, p. 26.)

lessen (in value, amount or degree) *v.t.*: **attenuate**. ❖ We must . . . sometimes **attenuate** perfect freedom so as to ensure safety and security for all. To reasonably ensure the safety of jurors so as further to provide a fair and evenhanded trial for [Timothy] McVeigh, the trial judge is correct in modestly curtailing the right of open court to the public. (Peter J. Riga, "Judge Right to Close Trial," *USA Today*, 4/24/1997.)

(2) lessen *v.t.*: **minify**. See *minimize*

lesson (used to make a point) *n.*: **exemplum**. See *example*

let (as in bestow, by one with higher power) *v.t.*: **vouchsafe**. See *bestow*

letdown (as in anticlimax) *n.*: **bathos**. See *anticlimax*

(2) letdown (as in disappointment) *n.*: **Apples of Sodom**. See *disappointment*

(3) letdown (as in disappointment) *n.*: **Dead Sea fruit**. See *disappointment*

lethal (as in causing or portending death) *adj.*: **funest**. See *deadly*

lethargic *adj.*: **torpid**. ❖ One reason nerds are nerds is that parents don't make them play sports. They wile away the hours at Dungeons and Dragons while other boys are outside playing sports. They park in front of video games, gobble potato chips and Cokes, and pretend to wreak retribution on the world. Yet for all their electronic bravado, they are fat, soft, **torpid** and complacent. Whose fault is that? (R. Cort Kirkwood, "Blame Isn't Sporting," *Ottawa Sun*, 5/9/1999.)

(2) lethargic (as in appearing lifeless) *adj.*: **exanimate**. See *lifeless*

(3) lethargic (as in moving like a slug) *adj.*: **limacine**. See *slug*

(4) lethargic *adj.*: **bovine**. See *sluggish*

(5) lethargic *adj.*: **logy**. See *sluggish*

lethargy *n.*: **hebetude**. ❖ [Bend, Oregon, is] a city with a bike rack on every car, a canoe in every garage and a restless heart in every chest. While too many Americans slouch toward a terminal funk of **hebetude** and sloth, Bendians race ahead with toned muscles, wide eyes and brains perpetually wired on adrenaline. (*Washington Times*, "Wild Rides in the Heart of Central Oregon—Bent Out of Shape in Bend," 8/11/2001.)

(2) lethargy *n.*: **torpor**. ❖ Eliza Mowry . . . awoke many atheists from ineffectual complaining and **torpor** to become an effective force against the social evils they observed resulting from organized religion. Unfortunately, today we find much the same sluggishness and inactivity among freethinkers that Eliza found in her day. Groups meet only to complain about religion. (Carole Gray, "Atheism and Activism: The Life and Work of Eliza Mowry Bliven," *Humanist*, 1/11/1996, p. 18.)

(3) lethargy (as in condition of stupor or unconsciousness resulting from narcotic drugs) *n.*: **narcosis**. See *stupor*

(4) lethargy (sometimes in matters spiritual, and sometimes leading to depression) *n.*: **acedia**. See *apathy*

letter (capital . . .) *n.*: **majuscule**. See *uppercase*

(2) letter (lowercase . . .) *n.*: **minuscule**. See *lowercase*

(3) letter (love . . .) *n.*: **billet-doux** [French]. See *love letter*

letters (of or relating to . . . or the writing of . . .) *adj.*: **epistolary**. ❖ [I received a letter from Sanjay Krishnaswamy, who was aware] that I was a big fan of Elvis Costello and was wondering if I might have in my possession an extremely rare recording [by] Costello. . . . Mr. Krishnaswamy would soon find out that his **epistolary** endeavors were to pay off in spades [because I found the recording and mailed it to him.] (Joe Queenan, *My Goodness*, Hyperion [2000], p. 64.)

(2) letters (one who is learning the . . . of the alphabet) *n.*: **abecedarian**. See *alphabet*

lewd *adj.*: **lubricious**. ❖ On some of the desert visits, police allege, [Coach] Pearson took along two boys and played a **lubricious** game with them. Everyone would flip a quarter simultaneously, after which, depending on how the coins landed, the players would either have to touch Pearson's genitals or let him touch theirs. (William Nack, "Every Parent's Nightmare," *Sports Illustrated*, 9/13/1999, p. 40.)

(2) lewd (as in lustful) *adj.*: **ithyphallic**. See *lustful*

(3) lewd (compulsive . . . behavior) *n.*: **corpropraxia**. See *obscene*

(4) lewd *adj.*: **fescennine**. See *obscene*

(5) lewd *adj.*: **lickerish**. See *lustful*

lexicon (or word list) *n.*: **onomasticon**. See *word list*

liar *n.*: **Ananias** [based on an early Christian, who, according to Acts, dropped dead when he lied to the Apostle Peter]. ❖ [Twelve women] are subjects of Claudia Roth Pierpont's *Passionate Minds*. . . . [T]he consummate liar Anaïs Nin (whose name, perhaps, should have been **Ananias**) [emerges] as the most loathsome. Although trenchant in her criticisms, Pierpont shows sympathy for all her subjects. (Only Nin's pathological dishonesty and narcissism seem to exhaust her tolerance.) (Merle Rubin, "Essays Take Critical Look at Female Icons," *Los Angeles Times*, 3/27/2000.)

libel (as in the destroying of one's reputation) *n.*: **famicide**. See *defamation*

(2) libel (which is published for political gain right before an election) *n.*: **roorback**. See *falsehood*

liberal (person in beliefs and conduct) *n.*: **latitudinarian**. See *open-minded*

liberalization (new period of . . . of rights, esp. as a contrast to, and sandwiched between, periods of oppression or lack of rights) *n.*: **Prague Spring**. ["Prague Spring" refers to a period of political liberalization in Czechoslovakia in 1968, during which various political reforms were introduced, such as increased freedom of the press. This displeased the Soviets, who invaded the country later that year. The term is now used to refer to any short-lived period of increased liberty or freedom, often within a repressive environment.] ❖ Lord Woolf believed that maintaining family links would help prisoners to rebuild their lives. So warders were required to stop reading all prisoners' letters, telephones were installed and more home leave allowed. . . . "It was like the **Prague Spring** for [prisoners]," says Stephen Shaw. . . . [After some escapes,] Derek Lewis, then director-general of the prison service, told governors that their first three priorities were "security, security and security." (*Economist*, "[UK Home Secretary Michael] Howard's Rubbish: Prisons," 5/25/1996.)

liberate (from slavery, servitude, or bondage) *v.t.*: **disenthrall**. [This word, while certainly legitimate today, was famously used by Abraham Lincoln in 1862 in reference to the Civil War: "As our case is new, so we must think anew, and act anew. We must **disenthrall** ourselves, and then we shall save our country."] ❖ It's not just investment banks that have fallen by the wayside in the recent carnage; it's the ideology of unregulated capitalism—of Reaganism. And if Republicans cannot find a way to **disenthrall** themselves from their faith in their old gods, they may ensure that the GOP itself becomes one more casualty in the collapse of laissez faire. (Harold Myerson, "Slow Rise for a New Era," *Washington Post*, 10/1/2008.)

(2) liberate (from slavery, servitude, or bondage) *v.t.*: **manumit**. See *emancipate*

libertine (as in one acting without moral restraint) *n.*: **rakehell**. [While this word can theoretically be applied to either sex, it is usually applied to men and usually (though not necessarily) in connection with their relations with women.] ❖ [Who persuaded state Senator Bob Schaffer not to campaign on Sundays? He said it was the wife of a] Democratic senator who is "notorious for his, uh, extracurricular activities." . . . "No," Schaffer said, "not Ted Kennedy." While we were mentally reviewing the other known **rakehells** among the U.S. Senate's Democratic contingent, and giving up in despair, Schaffer told the story. (Peter Blake, "On Seventh Day, Schaffer Rests," *Denver Rocky Mountain News*, 2/28/1996.)

liberty (new period of . . . , esp. as a contrast to, and sandwiched between, periods of oppression or lack of rights) *n.*: **Prague Spring**. See *liberalization*

library *n.*: **athenaeum**. ❖ Whole wings of libraries could be built around the literature of loss. A person dies, and if a novelist is nearby there's a pretty good chance a book will be born. . . . *The Summer After June*, Ashley Warlick's second novel, belongs in that vast annex of the **athenaeum** reserved solely for stories of mourning. (Chris Bohjalian, "Starting Over," *Washington Post*, 4/2/2000.)

license (as in entitlement, spec. one presumed arrogantly or asserted involuntarily against others) *n.*: **droit du seigneur** [French]. See *entitlement*

(2) license (as in giving one's stamp of approval) *n.*: **nihil obstat** [Latin]. See *approval*

licentious *adj.*: **fescennine**. See *obscene*

(2) licentious *adj.*: **lickerish**. See *lustful*

(3) licentious *adj.*: **lubricious**. See *lewd*

lie (esp. through the intentional use of misleading, ambiguous, or evasive language) *v.t.*: **prevaricate**. ❖ More and more, with Bush administration pronouncements about the Iraq war, it depends on what the meaning of the word "is" is. W. built his political identity on the idea that he was not Bill Clinton. He didn't parse words or **prevaricate**. He was the Texas straight shooter. So why is he now presiding over a completely Clintonian environment, turning the White House into a Waffle House, where truth is camouflaged by word games . . .? (Maureen Dowd, "National House of Waffles," *New York Times*, 7/13/2003.)

(2) lie (petty or minor . . .) *n.*: **taradiddle** (or

tarradiddle). ❖ The Bosnian war has produced its own crop of nonsense. [Two Serbs] uncloak[ed] Bosnia's president as a closet Muslim fundamentalist, with a pre-war membership video put out by his party to prove it. Alas, the pair also rashly offered a translation, which proved exactly the opposite. . . . That sort of **taradiddle** is old stuff, though. (*Economist*, "The Injuries of War," 7/29/1995, p. 64.)

(3) lie *n.*: **fabulation** (one who does so: **fabulist**). ❖ Given that no one had witnessed their altercation, [the defendant] was clearly at liberty to give any answer he wished. . . . [He] could have asserted [self-defense] or, at the very least, that [the victim] threatened his life. These would have been the obvious **fabulations** of a defendant seeking sympathy, a savvy criminal trying to confect a safe story. (Graham Burnett, *A Trial by Jury*, Knopf [2001], p. 144.)

(4) lie (which is defamatory and published for political gain right before an election) *n.*: **roorback**. See *falsehood*

(5) lie (accepted as fact due to repetition in print) *n.*: **factoid**. See *inaccuracy*

(6) lie (as in a false story, often deliberately told) *n.*: **canard**. See *hoax*

(7) lie (as in something that is impressive-looking on the outside but which hides or covers up undesirable conditions or facts) *n.*: **Potemkin village**. See *facade*

lies (abnormal propensity toward telling . . . , esp. by embellishing) *n.*: **mythomania**. See *embellishment*

life (as in soul or inner self) *n.*: **anima**. See *soul*

life force (as in vital spirit or soul) *n.*: **pneuma** [Greek]. See *soul*

(2) life force (inherent in all things) *n.*: **Qi** [Chinese]. ❖ Acupuncture is the insertion of needles into specific points along the body's meridians, or energy pathways, to help stimulate the flow and balance of **Qi**, the invisible life force that flows through all living organisms. . . . When **Qi**, pronounced "chee," is balanced and flowing smoothly, health is good. When **Qi** is blocked, disease can occur, especially if the condition goes untreated. (Ellen Anderson, "On Campus—Stick with Alternative Medicine," *Boston Herald*, 3/12/1998.)

lifeless (actually or appearing . . .) *adj.*: **exanimate**. ❖ The Wild Women, one of only three all-female teams in a 57-team field, had shoved off from Fan Pier at 6:45 in the morning for Nantasket Beach and after 20 miles of kayaking, 22 miles of mountain biking, and 19 miles of trekking, with a stop at the quarries for a little rappelling, they were exhilarated, exhausted, nearly **exanimate**. (Barbara Matson, "Adventure Story for Three Women," *Boston Globe*, 8/28/2002.)

(2) lifeless (as in sluggish or lethargic) *adj.*: **torpid**. See *lethargic*

(3) lifeless (as in sluggish) *adj.*: **bovine**. See *sluggish*

(4) lifeless (as in sluggish) *adj.*: **logy**. See *sluggish*

lifestyle *n.*: **modus vivendi** [Latin]. ❖ Under normal conditions they would grow to hate each other, but their strange **modus vivendi** inadvertently keeps the dew on the rose. Claude lives with Maggie in Brooklyn during the cold months and takes off as soon as the weather turns warm. She doesn't know where he goes but he always comes back, and when he does it's like a honeymoon again. (Florence King, "The Joys of Re-reading," *National Review*, 12/23/1996, p. 52.)

light (interplay of . . . and shadows, often in a pictorial representation) *n.*: **chiaroscuro**. ❖ The clearing he emerged into was a **chiaroscuro** of torchlight and strangely elongated shadows. (Val McDermid, *A Place of Execution*, St. Martin's Press [2000], p. 36.)

(2) light (abnormal fear of or sensitivity to) *adj.*: **photophobic**. See *fear*

(3) light (and delicate, sheer, or transparent) *adj.*: **diaphanous**. See *transparent*

(4) light (and delicate, sheer, or transparent) *adj.*: **gossamer**. See *transparent*

(5) light (without . . . , esp. as to the ocean) *adj.*: **aphotic**. See *dark*

light-headed *adj.*: **vertiginous**. See *dizzy*

lighthearted (as in playful) *adj.*: **ludic**. See *playful*

(2) lighthearted (discussion of a subject, as in chitchat) *n.*: **persiflage**. See *chitchat*

(3) lighthearted (or carefree behavior) *n.*: **rhathymia**. See *carefree*

lightning (as in thunderbolt) *n.*: **coup de foudre** [French; though literally meaning "thunderbolt," this is almost always used in the sense of "love at first sight"]. See *love at first sight*

likable (and pleasant) *adj.*: **sympathique** [French]. See *genial*

likely (as in appearing to be true or accurate) *adj.*: **verisimilar**. See *plausible*

like-minded *adj.*: **simpatico**. See *compatible*

likeness (as in representation) *n.*: **simulacrum**. See *representation*

(2) likeness (of sounds to each other) *n.*: **assonance**. See *similarity*

likes (as in personal preference) *n.*: **de gustibus** [Latin]. See *taste*

limelight (as in publicity or a taste or flair for being in the . . .) *n.*: **réclame** [French]. See *publicity*

limit (as in overly restrict or . . . , as to amount or share) *v.t.*: **scant**. See *stint*

(2) limit (as in set the boundaries of) *v.t.*: **delimit**. See *demarcate*

(3) limit (as in to deal with or treat inadequately or neglectfully) *v.t.*: **scant**. See *slight*

limitless (limitlessly) *adj.*, *adv.*: **ad infinitum**. See *forever*

limping (from lack of blood flow to leg muscles) *n.*: **claudication**. ❖ [T]he 53-year-old couldn't walk more than 100 yards without some pain; he was unable to prowl the mall or go on strolls with his wife. Specialists had told him he'd just have to live with it. The little pills changed all that. "Now I can walk as much as I want," he says happily. Yet intermittent **claudication** is often linked to bad habits—smoking, lack of exercise, obesity. (Scott Woolley, "The Quest for Youth," *Forbes*, 5/3/1999, p. 146.)

line (witty or clever . . .) *n.*: **bon mot**. ❖ Here are some of Mae West's most memorable **bon**

mots: "It's not the men in my life that counts—it's the life in my men." "A man in the house is worth two in the street." "Too much of a good thing can be wonderful." "He who hesitates is last." (Kevin Thomas, "Mae West—She Helped Make Sex Into a Laughing Matter," *St. Louis Post-Dispatch*, 8/15/1993.)

linen (household . . . , esp. table . . . , such as napkins) *n.*: **napery**. ❖ On Aug. 30, the last night she had fended off those advances, Diana sat with Dodi inside Paris's Ritz Hotel. Amid the starched **napery** of L'Espadon restaurant, the 36-year-old princess . . . seemed happy. (J. D. Reed, "Goodbye England's Rose," *People*, 9/1/1997, p. 78.)

linguist *n.*: **philologist**. ❖ American wordsmiths are a quiet bunch, rarely shaking the beehive of lexicography. But not the late Frederic Cassidy. He broke out his **philologist** shovel and set to work unearthing the buried gems of American regional English. (Lane Hartill, "Let's Hit the 'Flang Dang' and 'Honeyfuggle' the Chaperones," *Christian Science Monitor*, 4/17/2001, p. 14.)

link (as in bond or tie) *n.*: **vinculum**. See *bond*
(2) link (in a series or chain) *v.t.*, *adj.*: **concatenate** (*n.*: **concatenation**). See *connect*
(3) link *n.*: **catenation** (*v.t.*: **catenate**). See *chain*

linked (by a close relationship) *adj.*: **affined**. See *connected*

lions (of, relating to, or characteristic of) *adj.*: **leonine**. ❖ [The TV show *Lions* is] nowhere near the scope of the Disney classic *The African Lion* but includes some intriguing familial disputes!—like an episode of a **leonine** soap opera. (Susan Reed, Picks & Pans: Video, *People*, 5/29/1989, p. 20.)

lip reader *n.*: **oralist**. ❖ Kisor, 49, has been totally deaf since he was struck by meningitis at the age of 3. Through the work of his parents and a remarkable teacher, and possibly because he had some memory of words, he became part of a minority among the deaf—an "**oralist**" who communicates by speech and lipreading rather than sign language. Among the deaf, there is considerable controversy between advocates of "signing" and the **oralists**. (Bob Dart, "Challenge Henry Kisor to 'Read My Lips,' and He'll Do Exactly That," *St. Louis Post-Dispatch*, 7/3/1990.)

lips (of or relating to both . . .) *adj.*: **bilabial**. ❖ The raspberry—that goofy noise created by vibrating upper and lower lips and tongue—is what phoneticians call **bilabial** trills. (Laura Flynn McCarthy, Infants: "Why Babies Do What They Do," *Parenting*, 3/1/1998, p. 88.)

liquid (like . . . or tending to become . . .) *adj.*: **liquescent**. ❖ Several observers have noted that [Florence] Pierce's works have the look of ice on a pond, at once liquid and solid. It is the **liquescent** feel of her images that has led the artist herself to say that "no matter what I say about light, I feel like I'm working with water. . . . It's alive." (Jan Ernst Adlmann, "Eye on the Transcendent: New Mexico Artist Florence Pierce," *Art in America*, 12/1/2006.)

liquor (given to or marked by consumption of . . .) *adj.*: **bibulous**. See *imbibing*
(2) liquor (one having an insatiable craving for . . .) *n.*: **dipsomaniac** (*adj.*: **dipsomaniacal**). See *alcoholic*

listen in (as in eavesdrop) *v.t.*: **earwig**. See *eavesdrop*

listening (act of . . . , often with a stethoscope) *n.*: **auscultation**. ❖ **Auscultation** requires extremely focused listening and counting of each fetal heart beat as it is heard. (Linda Goodwin, "Intermittent Auscultation of the Fetal Heart Rate: A Review of General Principles," *Journal of Perinatal & Neonatal Nursing*, 12/1/2000, p. 53.)

listless (as in appearing lifeless) *adj.*: **exanimate**. See *lifeless*
(2) listless (as in moving like a slug) *adj.*: **limacine**. See *slug*
(3) listless (as in sluggish or lethargic) *adj.*: **torpid**. See *lethargic*
(4) listless (as in weakened) *adj.*: **etiolated**. See *weakened*
(5) listless *adj.*: **bovine**. See *sluggish*
(6) listless *adj.*: **logy**. See *sluggish*

listlessness (as in lethargy) *n*.: **hebetude**. See *lethargy*

(2) listlessness (as in condition of stupor or unconsciousness resulting from narcotic drugs) *n*.: **narcosis**. See *stupor*

literal (as in the very words used by a writer or speaker) *phr*.: **ipsissima verba** [Latin.] See *words*

(2) literal (translation) *n*.: **metaphrase**. See *translation*

literally *adv*.: **literatim**. ❖ It was Friday, April 13, 1900, the first year of the new century or last of the old, depending on your point of view. It was Eastertide, too, and Good Friday. But at the old Railroad Exchange Saloon in Port Newton, California, we always remembered it as the night Jack Dobbs floated into town. And I mean that **literatim**: the son of a bitch floated right on into town. (George Jansen, *The Fade-Away*, Pocol Press [2007], p. 1.)

literary (community) *n*.: **republic of letters** [This term, *res publica* (sometimes *respublica*) *litterarum*, possibly coined by the humanist Francesco Barbaro in 1417, was first intended to designate the community of early modern scholars. Today it refers to the literary community generally.] ❖ Jonathan Franzen is one of the most nuanced minds at work in the dwindling **republic of letters**. It's easy to tell that from *How to Be Alone* . . . a collection of lucid, saturnine essays that have appeared in various magazines since 1994. Franzen is not the first serious writer to mourn the slow death of serious reading. (Richard Lacayo, "Total Eclipse of the Heart," *Time*, 11/25/2002.)

(2) literary (piece imitating previous pieces) *n*.: **pastiche**. See *imitation*

(3) literary (style that is dark, gloomy, remote, and/or grotesque) *adj*.: **gothic**. See *dark*

(4) literary (woman with . . . or scholarly interests) *n*.: **bluestocking**. See *woman*

literate (people as a group) *n*.: **clerisy**. See *educated*

(2) literate (person who chooses not to read) *n*.: **alliterate**. See *reader*

literature (such as poetry or certain works of fiction, valued for their aesthetic qualities rather than to provide information or instruction) *n.pl*. but sing. in construction: **belles lettres** [French for "beautiful" or "fine letters" or "writing"]. ❖ [In his novel *Northline*, Willy] Vlautin shows us people who, if they have jobs at all, do the dirty work, scratching out livings in the depths of society. . . . What redeems Vlautin's work is that his objective isn't to produce **belles lettres**, but to tell the stories of America's underclass, as he did in his first novel, *The Motel Life*. The brutal events that are so frequent for his characters are rendered with chilling nonchalance. (Eric Williamson, "Down but Not Out," *Washington Post*, 7/27/2008.)

litigation (persistent instigation of . . . , esp. groundless suits) *n*.: **barratry**. See *lawsuits*

litter (as in garbage) *n*.: **spilth**. See *garbage*

(2) litter *n*.: **detritus**. See *debris*

(3) litter *n*.: **offal**. See *trash*

little (person) *n*.: **homunculus**. See *midget*

(2) little (person) *n*.: **hop-o'-my-thumb**. See *midget*

(3) little (very . . .) *adj., n*.: **Lilliputian**. See *tiny*

(4) little (very . . .) *adj*.: **bantam**. See *tiny*

(5) little (very . . .) *adj*.: **minikin**. See *tiny*

liveliness *n*.: **brio**. See *energy*

(2) liveliness *n*.: **élan** [French]. See *spirit*

lively (as in stimulating) *adj*.: **piquant**. See *stimulating*

livid *adj*.: **furibund**. See *furious*

living (way of . . .) *n*.: **modus vivendi** [Latin]. See *lifestyle*

lizard (of, relating to, or resembling) *adj*.: **lacertilian**. ❖ Lizards are the real-world inspiration for the dragons of medieval fantasies, for reasons that will become obvious to readers of *Lizards: Windows to the Evolution of Diversity*. . . . This engaging, well-researched volume depicts an amazing variety of **lacertilian** beasts in its lavish illustrations and deftly examines their bizarre lifestyles and behaviors. (Michael Szpir, "Slithy Toves," *American Scientist*, 11/1/2003.)

(2) lizard (of, relating to, or resembling) *adj.*: **saurian**. ❖ Billie, 55, hadn't tangled seriously with gators for 10 years, so he was a bit rusty. One of the surly **saurians** promptly chomped a digit off the chief's right hand. "He bit me, so I gave him the finger," Billie joked in the emergency room. (Carl Hiaasen, "A Few Tips for Aspiring Gator Wrestlers," *Miami Herald*, 9/10/2000.)

(3) lizard (of, relating to, or resembling) *adj.*: **saurian**. ❖ Danny Vines knew he was hunting for a big alligator, but he wasn't fully prepared for the reptile that surfaced from the murky Trinity River slough. In all its **saurian** splendor, the gator resembled an aquatic dinosaur from a prehistoric waterway. (Ray Sasser, "Trinity River in Texas Is Alligator Alley for Monsters," *Dallas Morning News*, 5/16/2007.)

loaf (around during the summer) *v.i.*: **aestivate** (or **estivate**). See *laze*

(2) loaf (by pretending to be sick or incapacitated) *v.i.*: **malinger**. See *shirk*

(3) loaf (or waste time) *v.i.*: **footle** (usu. as in footle around). See *dawdle*

loafer (as in one who avoids work or assigned duties) *n., v.i.*: **goldbrick**. See *goldbrick*

(2) loafer (as in one who strolls through city streets idly) *n.*: **flâneur** [French] (**loafing** *n.*: **flânerie**). See *wanderer*

(3) loafer (as in work avoider) *n.*: **embusque** [French]. See *slacker*

(4) loafer *n.*: **wastrel**. See *slacker*

loathe *v.t.*: **execrate**. See *hate*

(2) loathe *v.t.*: **misprize**. See *hate*

loathsome *adj.*: **ugsome**. ❖ War makes deep and longstanding hatred and prejudices temporarily dissolve. During World War II, for example, the United States transformed the **ugsome** Josef Stalin, co-villain with Adolf Hitler in the Ribbentrop-Molotov pact, into a fetching "Uncle Joe" after an alliance was struck with the Soviet Union to defeat the Third Reich. (*Washington Times*, "Looming Afghan Shipwreck," 1/1/2002.)

(2) loathsome (as in repellent) *adj.*: **rebarbative**. See *repellent*

(3) loathsome (or treacherous) *adj.*: **reptilian**. See *despicable*

(4) loathsome (person) *n.*: **caitiff**. See *despicable*

local (as in parochial) *adj.*: **parish pump** [British]. See *parochial*

locality (name that foreigners, but not locals, give to a . . .) *n.*: **exonym**. See *name*

location (as in condition of being located in a particular place) *n.*: **ubiety**. See *place*

(2) location (surrounding . . . served by an institution, such as a school or hospital) *n.*: **catchment area**. See *district*

lock up (as in confine) *v.t.*: **immure**. See *confine*

loft (or attic or room on top floor) *n.*: **garret**. ❖ Two years ago I sought out Levy to see what was happening to the embattled species [i.e., the inventor] in its natural habitat: the **garret**. As it happens, Levy's is the top floor of an old three-story house in Cambridge, Mass. Clumping up to his cluttered loft from time to time, I've had a chance to observe the magic of intellectual property aborning. (David Stipp, "Inventor," *Fortune*, 3/29/1999, p. 104.)

lofty (as in of or related to the sky or heavens) *adj.*: **empyreal**. See *celestial*

(2) lofty (as in of or related to the sky or heavens) *adj.*: **supernal**. See *celestial*

logic (in which one of the propositions— usually the premise [which may or may not be accurate]—is omitted, leading listeners to fill in the premise themselves) *n.*: **enthymeme**. See *argument*

(2) logic (person who hates . . . or enlightenment) *n.*: **misologist**. See *closed-minded*

(3) logic (that if something cannot be proven false, then it must be true) *n.*: **argumentum ad ignorantiam** [Latin]. See *argument*

(4) logic (which is complicated and often illogical) *n.*: **choplogic**. See *fallacy*

logical *adj.*: **ratiocinative**. ❖ "What do you say to folks who play with snakes in church?" Lester asked. "You can't appeal to their **ratiocinative** capacities." His reference to playing with snakes in church alluded to a bizarre form of Christian worship practiced by certain Pentecostal congregations, where the handling of poisonous serpents is, like speaking in tongues, regarded as a sign of salvation. (Darcy O'Brien, "Crime and Politics in Appalachia," *The World & I*, 1/1/1995, p. 300.)

logrolling *v.t., v.i.*: **birl**. ❖ Her legs are corded with muscles, and she **birls** like a bucking horse, in spasms of bobs, reverses, runs and kicks. "I'm a total powerhouse," says Salzman, who is 5′6″ and weighs 148 pounds. "The other women hang on [to the log] for dear life." (Michael Finkel, Birling: "The World Logrolling Championships Make a Splash Every Summer in Wisconsin," *Sports Illustrated*, 11/27/1995, p. R2.)

loner (as in relating to one who may be socially withdrawn or inexperienced and/or shy and/or sullen) *adj.*: **farouche** [French]. See *shy*

(2) loner (as in recluse, esp. for religious reasons) *n.*: **anchorite**. See recluse

(3) loner (as in recluse, esp. for religious reasons) *n.*: **eremite**. See *recluse*

long (for) *v.t.*: **desiderate**. See *want*

longevity (having . . .) *adj.*: **macrobian**. See *long-lived*

longing *n.*: **desiderium**. [This word refers especially to a longing for something one once had but has no more, such as a past love, though it is not used as such in this example.] ❖ I spent last week looking for Woody, and I wasn't alone. In department stores, toy warehouses and catalogue shops throughout the land a desperate posse is on the trail of the lanky star of Toy Story. . . . But the cupboard was bare . . . no Woody, no Buzz Lightyear—just a few disconsolate Mr Potato Heads, a mere wallflower, it seems, in the childish **desiderium**. (Thomas Sutcliffe, "*Toy Story* and Christmas . . . All the Vital Ingredients for a Full-on Crisis of Conscience," *Independent* [London], 12/5/1996.)

(2) longing *n.*: **avidity**. See *craving*

long-lasting (extremely . . .) *adj.*: **perdurable**. See *durable*

long-lived *adj.*: **macrobian**. ❖ A **macrobian** female giant panda passed away at the age of 36, equivalent to a human being aged 108, on

Tuesday afternoon in Guilin City of south China's Guangxi Zhuang Autonomous Region. Meimei, the oldest panda, had been suffering from eating difficulties and gradual failure of varied organs. (Xinhua News Agency [China], "World's Oldest Panda in Pen Dead in S. China Zoo," 7/12/2005.)

long shot (statement of being a . . . , expressed in the form of an exaggerated comparison with a more obvious impossibility; for example, "the sky will fall before I get married") *n.*: **adynaton**. See *unlikelihood*

long-winded (as in characterized by a ready and easy flow of words) *adj.*: **voluble**. See *talkative*

(2) long-winded (as in rambling) *adj.*: **discursive**. See *rambling*

(3) long-winded (mania for being . . . in speech) *n.*: **cacoëthes loquendi** [Latin]. See *talking*

(4) long-winded *adj.*: **inaniloquent**. See *verbose*

look (a quick cursory . . . , as in scan) *n.* **Cook's tour**. See *scan*

(2) look (as in demeanor) *n.*: **mien**. See *demeanor*

(3) look (as in glance) *n.*: **dekko** [British; informal]. See *glance*

(4) look (quick . . . , as in glance) *n.*: **coup d'oeil** [French]. See *glance*

(5) look (with a sideways . . .) *adv.*: **asquint**. See *glance*

lookout (esp. for changes in trends) *n.*: **weather eye** (esp. as in "keep a weather eye"). [The term derives from being watchful for changes in the weather, but is also used more broadly to refer to other kinds of changes.] ❖ For 3 1/2 decades my working days and not a few nights and weekends—have been spent keeping a **weather eye** on American culture. [O]ne question remains . . . mysterious to me . . . : Why it is that some writers and artists find large and remunerative followings while others, equally gifted if not more so, spend their lives neglected and unknown? (Jonathan Yardley, "Steve Forbert, Unsung Singer," *Washington Post*, 9/6/1999.)

(2) lookout (on the . . .) *idiom*: **on the qui vive**. ❖ It was [Desi Arnaz] who saw dollar signs upon reading *The Untouchables* by retired G-man Eliot Ness. . . . Warner Brothers had taken an option on the book, but never got around to developing it. Desi ordered his legal department to stay **on the qui vive**: the day Warner dropped its option they were to grab the project for Desilu. (Stefan Kanfer, *Ball of Fire*, Knopf [2003], p. 192.)

loony (slightly . . . , often used humorously) *adj.*: **tetched**. See *crazy*

(2) loony *adj.*: **doolally**. See *crazy*

loose (as in of questionable morality) *adj.*: **louche**. See *questionable*

(2) loose (sexually . . . woman) *n.*: **round-heel**. See *slut*

(3) loose (sexually) *adj., n.*: **libertine**. See *promiscuous*

loosen (as in extract or pry or force out, whether from a place or position, or information) *v.t.*: **winkle** (usu. used with "out"). See *extract*

loot (as in plunder) *v.t., v.i.*: **depredate** (*n.*: **depredation**). See *plunder*

looting *n.*: **rapine**. ❖ This being the age of image enhancement, descendants of the Vikings would like it understood that their fierce, sea-scouring, village-slaughtering, monastery-looting, town-burning ancestors also had a kinder, gentler side. . . . Obscured by all this **rapine** and slaughter, the show's 15 curators note, is the earth-girdling significance of the Vikings' westward voyaging. (Hank Burchard, "The Civilized Side of Viking Life," *Washington Post*, 7/14/2000.)

loquacious *adj.*: **inaniloquent**. See *verbose*

lord (as in ruler, of the universe) *n.*: **kosmokrator** [Greek]. See *ruler*

lordly *adj.*: **seigneurial**. [In the feudal system of landholding in Canada, seigneurs were lords granted land by the king in return for their oath of loyalty and promise to support him in time of war. Like "lordly" itself, the word can have connotations that are either positive (such as dignified, noble, or exalted) or negative (such as arrogant, overbearing, or imperi-

ous). Examples of both are presented here, first the positive and then the negative.] ❖ *Vanity Fair*'s front cover is one of the prime slots in American show business, making [editor Graydon] Carter a Very Powerful Person. Everyone wants to stay sweet with him. He accepts his grandeur with **seigneurial** benevolence and drops the name of Robert De Niro as casually as a boy playing a yo-yo. (Quenton Letts, "Tinseltown, Tina and Me; Graydon Carter, the Editor of Vanity Fair," *Evening Standard* [London], 11/13/2002.) ❖ The guy was driving his cream-colored Rolls-Royce Corniche along West Broadway in SoHo. Actually, to call it driving is giving him too much credit. Bobbing and weaving is more like it. Several times, he nearly hit parked cars. Once, he almost veered into oncoming traffic. Naturally, he was gabbing on a cell phone the whole time, with a **seigneurial** indifference to anything in his path. (Clyde Haberman, "We Need More Tickets, Not Fewer," *New York Times*, 6/13/2003.)

loser (or fool or dope or idiot or anyone generally not worthy of respect) *n.*: **schmendrick** (or **shmendrik**) [Yiddish]. See *fool*

losing (capable of . . .) *n.*: **vincible**. See *beaten*

lot (as in destiny or fate) *n.*: **kismet**. See *fate*

lotion (or balm which is soothing) *n.*: **demulcent**. See *soothing*

loud (and boisterous) *adj.*: **strepitous**. ❖ From shortly after noon to six o'clock [Londoners] filled Drury Lane with a riot of enthusiasm, a torrent of emotion, a hurly-burly of hysteria, and sang "Auld Lang Syne" in chorus, not without tears. For in our experience we have seen nothing quite like [it], nothing so crowded with hearty and demonstrative citizens, nothing so "rich and varied," nothing so lengthy, and nothing so **strepitous**. (*Times* [London], "Ellen Terry Celebration," 6/13/1991.)

(2) loud *adj., adv., n.*: **fortissimo**. [Italian. This word, a musical direction, can be used as an adverb (the band played fortissimo), an adjective, or a noun, meaning a note or passage delivered loudly, as in the example here. Its opposite—pianissimo—is listed under *quiet*.]

❖ [The] pointed observations and stark declarations from [Senator Bob Kerrey] come in staccato barks of rising volume—rising, rising—to a **fortissimo** of incredulity and horror in the hushed Senate hearing room. "The bottom line for me is, it just pains me to have to say that on the 11th of September that 19 men and less than half a million dollars defeated every single defensive mechanism we had in place—utterly." (David Montgomery, "On 9/11 Panel, Bob Kerrey Seconds the Emotion," *Washington Post*, 3/25/2004.)

(3) loud *adj.*: **clamant**. ❖ [Patrick] Buchanan has been the most **clamant** anti-war voice of the 1990s; he is also the only prominent politician of either party who addresses the appalling maldistribution of wealth in our erstwhile republic—all of which makes him the nation's leading leftist. (Bill Kauffman, "The Americans Who Won't Be Celebrating NATO's 50th," *Independent on Sunday*, 4/25/1999.)

(4) loud *adj.*: **clangorous**. ❖ [Living in a Swiss apartment in the 1970s was very limited.] Often, no showers are permitted between 10 P.M. and 7 A.M. No toilets may be flushed during those hours, either. When relieving themselves, men are expected to sit. (Is it the likelihood of an errant drop that so offends? Or the **clangorous** tinkle?) (Alexander Wolff, *Big Game, Small World*, Warner Books [2002], p. 54.)

(5) loud (as in gaudy) *adj.*: **meretricious**. See *gaudy*

loudmouth (who often talks foolishness) *adj.*: **blatherskite**. See *babbler*

lout (person) *n.*: **grobian**. See *boor*

love (mad or crazy . . .) *n.*: **amour fou** [French]. ❖ It has been a torrid romance lasting almost 10 years. Some thought that the longer it continued the more it looked like madness, an **amour fou** which would end in pain and grief. . . . Whatever their motivations, the infatuation of foreign investors with the US dollar has seen them pump almost $2 trillion into US assets since 1992. . . . But now the affair is over. (Stewart Fleming, "End of the Great

American Affair," *Evening Standard* [London], 5/30/2002.)

(2) love (spec. the emotional thrill and excitement one feels when initially in . . .) *n.*: **limerence** (*adj.*: **limerent**). [This term was coined by Dorothy Tennov in her 1979 book *Love and Limerence: The Experience of Being in Love*. Though not yet universally recognized in print dictionaries, it can be commonly found in online dictionaries.] ❖ I have been shopping for beauty products and underwear in a fever. I read cookbooks now. I spend an embarrassing amount of time looking at myself naked. My classic symptoms—involuntary preoccupation, mood swings, emotional sensitivity enhanced sensual awareness—are what tip the diagnosis. I am **limerent**. In the throes of **limerence**. It is both a psychological and physiological state. It is also the state I wish to call home. (Valerie Frankel, "The Love Drug: What a Feeling! But Can That First Flash-Dancing, Knee-Buckling Sensation of Falling in Love Endure?" *O, The Oprah Magazine*, 9/1/2002.)

(3) love (of or relating to illicit . . .) *adj.*: **paphian** (or **Paphian**). See *sexual*

(4) love (of women) *n.*: **philogyny**. See *women*

(5) love (pertaining to . . . , esp. in the sexual sense) *adj.*: **amatory**. See *lovemaking*

love affair *n.*: **amourette** [French]. ❖ [A sociology professor] is trying to test the notion that the baby boom generation, the cohort that began "the sexual revolution," came into adulthood with different cultural and moral values from their parents'. Using data from other studies and some 300 interviews she plans to conduct, she hopes to chart the details of baby boom love, sex and marriage, including extramarital **amourettes**. (Michael Norman, "Getting Serious About Adultery; Who Does It and Why They Risk It," *New York Times*, 7/4/1998.)

love at first sight *n.*: **coup de foudre** [French; lit. thunderbolt]. ❖ [In Marianne Wiggins's novel *Eveless Eden*] Lilith caromed around the world, recording its atrocities on film, and minding her motto to "live like a man and love like a woman." Noah, a cautious Southern boy made good who knew all along that "**coups de foudre** lead straightaway to broken hearts and crimes of passion," lost his heart to her. But their tempestuous relationship is cut brutally short. (Frances Stead Sellers, "After the Fall," *Washington Post*, 12/3/1995.)

love letter *n*.: **billet-doux** [French]. ❖ Hyped as a treasury of tidbits from the 120 **billets-doux** [Princess] Diana had sent [Major James Hewitt] during their five-year affair, Hewitt's *Love and War* in fact reveals little: Copyright laws prevented him from quoting the princess's letters. (Kim Hubbard, "Royals: A Cad's Lament," *People*, 11/1/1999, p. 163.)

loveliness (physical) *n*.: **pulchritude**. See *beauty*

(2) loveliness (facetious way of measuring . . . by units) *n*.: **millihelen**. See *beauty*

lovely (in an unconventional way) *adj*.: **jolie laide** (or **belle laide**) [French]. See *pretty* or *beautiful*

lovemaking (of or relating to) *adj*.: **amatory**. ❖ *Harris's List of Covent-Garden Ladies* [was] an annual publication that made "frequent use of nautical expressions in describing the physical accomplishments of some of the [prostitutes]," among them Miss Devonshire of Queen Anne Street; this being a family newspaper, we cannot quote Harris's delicious account of Miss Devonshire's **amatory** skills. (Jonathan Yardley, "Women Sailors and Sailors' Women," *Washington Post*, 3/4/2001.)

(2) lovemaking *n*.: **houghmagandy** [Scottish]. See *intercourse*

(3) lovemaking *n*.: **venery**. See *intercourse*

love potion *n*.: **philter**. See *potion*

lover (female) *n*.: **inamorata**. See *girlfriend*

(2) lover (male . . . of a married woman) *n*.: **cicisbeo**. See *boyfriend*

(3) lover (male . . .) *n*.: **inamorato**. See *boyfriend*

(4) lover (male . . .) *n*.: **swain**. See *suitor*

loving (as in amorous) *adj*.: **amative**. See *amorous*

lower (rank, esp. in the military) *n*.: **subaltern**. See *subordinate*

lowercase letter *n*.: **minuscule**. ❖ A had its bomb, B its movie, C its section and D its day. Now E is having its era. . . . You must have seen its amazing breakthrough performance in e-mail. Soon there were EStamps, Etrade, eToys.com, e-etc. Now, E's got capital status; as we like to say, E is "E-biquitous!" . . . What versions does E come in? You can get E in a manly, three-pronged [capital letter] or a dainty, curly **minuscule** that almost looks like a smiley face! (Jesse Green, "E-nough Already," *Washington Post*, 11/21/1999.)

loyal (and unquestioning assistant) *n*.: **myrmidon**. See *assistant*

(2) loyal (subordinate, esp. of a political leader) *n*.: **apparatchik**. See *underling*

loyalist (esp. who supports or protects a political leader) *n*.: **Janissary**. See *supporter*

(2) loyalist (strong . . . for a cause, religion, or activity) *n*.: **votary**. See *supporter*

loyalty *n*.: **fealty**. ❖ The revenues from black crude—which reached a high of $113 billion in 1981 and this year are expected to top $60 billion—have enabled the House of Saud to create a modern state almost overnight and, in the process, buy the continued **fealty** of its subjects. (Lisa Beyer, "The Gulf: Lifting the Veil," *Time*, 9/24/1990, p. 38.)

(2) loyalty *n*.: **vassalage**. See *allegiance*

lucid *adj*.: **limpid**. See *understandable*

(2) lucid *adj*.: **perspicuous**. See *understandable*

luck (as in unpredictable outcome) *adj*.: **aleatory**. See *unpredictable*

(2) luck (bad . . .) *n*., *adj*.: **hoodoo**. See *bad luck*

(3) luck (of finding good things by accident) *n*.: **serendipity** (*adj*.: **serendipitous**). See *fortuitous*

luckless (perpetually . . . person) *n*.: **schlimazel** [Yiddish]. See *unlucky*

ludicrous (as in laughable) *adj*.: **gelastic**. See *laughable*

(2) ludicrous (as in laughable) *adj*.: **risible**. See *laughable*

luggage (or equipment or supplies or any object

that hinders progress or movement) *n.pl.*: **impedimenta**

lull (as in pause) *n.*: **caesura**. See *pause*

lullaby *n.*: **cradlesong**. ❖ She closed the set of songs with Wolf's "Schlafendes Jesuskind"—a meditation on a painting that depicts a sleeping Christ child. The mezzo's voice opened into a sweet, prayerful timbre that matched the gently swaying **cradlesong**. (Verena Dobnik, "Kirtschlager, Orpheus Ensemble Shine," AP Worldstream, 2/10/2002.)

luminous (softly . . .) *adj.*: **lambent**. See *shimmering*

(2) luminous *adj.*: **lucent**. See *glowing*

lump sum (in a . . . , as in, in the entirety) *adv.*: **holus-bolus**. See *entirety*

lunatic *n.*: **bedlamite**. ❖ Night is theater. . . . No wonder it's "Hallowe'en" and not "Hallow-mornin." The nighttime is the right time to dress up like somebody else, to laugh like a **bedlamite** and be scared half to death by your own shadow. (David Kirby, Books: "Searching Souls Find Each Other in This 'Night,'" *Atlanta Journal-Constitution*, 4/15/2001.)

lung disease (suffered by coal miners resulting from inhalation of very fine quartz dust) *n.*: **pneumonoultramicroscopicsilicovol-canoconiosis**. [This word is included solely because, at 45 letters and 19 syllables, it is considered the longest word in the English language. Finding usages of the word is not particularly difficult, only because the word is invariably used to point out this distinction. Finding an example where the word is actually used for its intended purpose is just about impossible. In any event, a humorous usage follows, and is in response to a contest in which readers were asked to provide amusing definitions of long words or phrases.] ❖ **Pneumonoultrami-croscopicsilicovolcanoconiosis** tourette: A rare disease where you never know what's going to come out of your lungs next. (Bruce Alter, letter to the editor, *Washington Post*, 8/8/2004.)

lure *n.*: **Lorelei call**. [This term derives from Lorelei, who was a siren of Germanic legend.]

❖ As media scholar Richard D. Heffner said: I don't like [cameras in the courts]. . . . [I believe] that what happens in the view of courtroom cameras will inevitably and increasingly be molded by trial participants' awareness of what will "play" on the 6 or the 11 o'clock news! Can we realistically expect that they alone in American life will resist the **Lorelei call** of mass media? (Christo Lassiter, "TV or Not TV— That Is the Question," *Journal of Criminal Law and Criminology*, 3/22/1996.)

(2) lure *n.*: **siren call**. [In Greek mythology, the sirens were three bird-women who, through their beautiful singing, lured mariners to destruction on the rocks and cliffs surrounding their island. Today, the word often suggests something that is alluring, but dangerous if heeded (as in the example given here). Just as frequently, it refers to something simply alluring. It is also referred to as a "siren song." See also the adjective *sirenic* under *alluring*.] ❖ [T]o eliminate the **siren call** of the Ben & Jerry's [ice cream] from your freezer at home, bypass the ice cream aisle at the supermarket. (Patricia Kitchen, "Willpower/May the Force Be with You," *Newsday*, 8/20/1996.)

(3) lure *v.t.*: **inveigle**. ❖ Forty-three-inch-tall Eddie Gaedel, who was **inveigled** by Bill Veeck into stepping to the plate in a major league game with the promise of baseball immortality, would probably have given the shirt off his back to be ensconced in the Baseball Hall of Fame. [Now his jersey is.] (John Walters, Scorecard: "Forty-three-Inch-Tall Eddie Gaedel," *Sports Illustrated*, 7/15/1991, p. 17.)

(4) lure (as in bewitch or enchant) *v.t.*: **ensor-cell** (or **ensorcel**). See *enchant*

(5) lure (as in extract or pry or force out, whether from a place or position, or information) *v.t.*: **winkle** (usu. used with "out"). See *extract*

luring (by flattery) *n.*: **blandishment** (*v.t.*: **blandish**). See *flattery*

luscious *adj.*: **toothsome**. See *tasty*

lush *n.*: **dipsomaniac** (*adj.*: **dipsomaniacal**). See *alcoholic*

lust (sexual . . . for the elderly) *n*.: **gerontophilia**. ❖ The reader must also be warned that this reviewer is subject to a passion many might consider warped or queer, what Havelock Ellis might have called **gerontophilia** rosacea. That is, I have this thing for old unrepentant Reds. There is something about that handful of octogenarian men and women I cannot resist. (John Mage, "Unrepentant Leftist: A Lawyer's Memoir," *Monthly Review*, 11/1/1996, p. 43.)

(2) lust (as in greed) *n*.: **pleonexia**. See *greed*

(3) lust (as in worship of or devotion to money) *n*.: **plutolatry**. See *wealth*

(4) lust (excessive . . . for wealth) *n*.: **cupidity**. See *greed*

(5) lust (mad or crazy . . . , as in love) *n*.: **amour fou** [French]. See *love*

lustful *adj*.: **concupiscent** (*n*.: **concupiscence**). ❖ The name is Klein and the subject is underwear. But it's the designer's wife, Kelly, who's behind *Underworld*, published by Knopf, and hers is a curatorial rather than **concupiscent** approach to the subject. So keep your pants on. (E. Jean Carroll, "How Not to Buy a Woman Lingerie," *Esquire*, 12/1/1995, p. 54.)

(2) lustful *adj*.: **ithyphallic**. ❖ [T]he women testifying to the **ithyphallic** social ways of President Clinton brought fact and collateral details with them. Each came forward, some with dates and corroborating witnesses, to divulge a steamy encounter with Bill Clinton. . . . Ultimately their revelations contributed to a composite profile of a sex maniac, our forty-second president, a deviant in need of therapy. (R. Emmett Tyrell Jr., "The Worst Book of the Year; Prof. Dr. Anita Hill Undistinguishes Herself Again," *American Spectator*, 6/1/1998.)

(3) lustful *adj*.: **lickerish**. ❖ In [Richardson's] professedly moral work there is more descriptive lubricity by far than one finds in Fielding. When Pamela is brought to bed between Mrs. Jewkes and Mr. B_____, for example, Richardson's superficial horror cannot conceal a certain **lickerish** interest in physical detail. (Monarch Notes, *Works of Henry Fielding: Character Analyses*, 1/1/1963.)

(4) lustful *adj*.: **lubricious**. See *lewd*

(5) lustful (man or playboy) *n*.: **roué** [French]. See *playboy*

lustrous (like a pearl) *adj*.: **nacreous**. See *iridescent*

luxurious (excessively . . . , esp. in a sensuous way) *adj*.: **sybaritic**. ❖ When [Peter Guber] entertained a visitor for lunch in his private dining room, he served low-fat cuisine but extolled the **sybaritic** pleasures of lolling in his new at-home flotation tank— which included a television screen on which he could watch films. (Nancy Griffin and Kim Masters, *Hit and Run*, Simon & Schuster [1996], p. 389.)

(2) luxurious *adj*.: **Lucullan**. See *lavish*

luxury (someone excessively devoted to . . .) *n*.: **voluptuary**. See *hedonist*

lying (abnormal propensity for . . . , esp. by embellishing) *n*.: **mythomania**. See *embellishment*

(2) lying (above) *adj*.: **superjacent**. See *overlying*

(3) lying *adj*.: **mendacious**. See *dishonest*

(4) lying *n*.: **improbity**. See *dishonesty*

lying down *adj*.: **decumbent**. ❖ With much satisfaction, [William Least Heat-Moon] reports it was Thomas Jefferson who directed that all of the nation except the already mapped East be ruled into grids, never mind natural or political borders. "Chase County [, Kansas,] sleeps north-south or east-west . . . , the **decumbent** folk like an accountant's figures neatly between ruled lines, their slumber neatly compartmentalized in Tom's grand grid." (John Skow, review of *PrairyErth*, by William Least Heat-Moon, *Time*, 10/21/1991.)

machine (having the form or qualities of a . . .) *adj.*: **mechanomorphic**. ❖ The young [William] Roberts drew his subject matter largely from clubs, pubs and music halls, painting dancers and their audiences as if they were the idols of some primitive cult; or abstracting them into **mechanomorphic** shapes with pumping pistons for limbs; or depicting them like shards of some crystalline material. (*Sunday Telegraph* [London], "Caveman's Last Relic," 5/2/2004.)

(2) machine (self-operating . . .) *n.*: **automaton**. See *robot*

mad (as in indignant) *n.*: **dudgeon** (often expressed as "in high dudgeon"). See *indignant*

(2) mad (extremely . . .) *adj.*: **furibund**. See *furious*

(3) mad (informal as in daffy or loony) *adj.*: **doolally**. See *crazy*

(4) mad (slightly . . . , as in deranged, often used humorously) *adj.*: **tetched**. See *crazy*

madam (as in prostitute) *n.*: **bawd**. See *prostitute*

(2) madam (as in prostitute) *n.*: **fancy woman**. See *prostitute*

made (finely or skillfully . . . , as in intricate) *adj.*: **daedal**. See *intricate*

made-up (as in invented or substituted with fraudulent intent) *adj.*: **supposititious**. See *supposed*

madman *n.*: **bedlamite**. See *lunatic*

magic *n.*: **necromancy** [See also *black magic*]. ❖ But no one factors into the bizarre arrangement the measure of Tita's heartbreak, the power of her love and, more to the point, the extent of her culinary **necromancy**—a talent that is the catalyst for much of the novel [*Like Water for Chocolate*]'s drama. (Joanne Kaufman, Picks & Pans: Pages, *People*, 11/16/1992, p. 39.)

(2) magic (as in sleight of hand) *n.*: **prestidigitation**. See *sleight of hand*

(3) magic (as in supernatural) *adj.*: **numinous**. See *supernatural*

(4) magic (feat of . . . , sometimes in a deceitful way) *n.*: **legerdemain**. See *trickery*

magical *adj.*: **fey**. ❖ As Sallie Tisdale writes in *A Weight That Women Carry*, "The first **fey** days of a new diet would be colored with a sense of control—organization and planning, power over the self." But after those first few days (or hours or minutes) "the basic futile misery took over." (Leora Tanenbaum, "Mirror, Mirror on the Wall . . . ," *Women's Review of Books*, 11/1/1994, p. 14.)

(2) magical (having a . . . and sprightly quality) *adj.*: **elfin**. See *sprightly*

magician *n.*: **thaumaturgist**. See *miracle worker*

magic potion (or love potion) *n.*: **philter**. See *potion*

magnetism (personal . . .) *n.*: **duende**. See *charisma*

magnificent *adj.*: **mirific**. See *wonderful*

magnify (as in exaggerate) *v.t.*: **overegg**. See *exaggerate*

maid (esp. woman hired to do cleaning) *n.*: **charwoman**. ❖ *Mrs. Arris Goes to Paris* (CBS, Sun., Dec. 27, 9 P.M. ET) is a charming little fantasy in which Angela Lansbury plays a dowdy London **charwoman** whose dream is to have a Dior gown created just for her. (David Hiltbrand, Picks & Pans: Tube, *People*, 12/21/1992, p. 13.)

(2) maid (in India and Asia, often serving as a wet nurse) *n.*: **amah**. ❖ Sadly, my father died when I was just four. My mother had scarce means and almost no education. To survive, she took a job as a live-in **amah** for a wealthy Chinese family. (Emily Lau, "Reflections: A Passion for Politics," *Time* International, 5/15/1997, p. 36.)

majestic (and stately, as in befitting a baron) *adj.*: **baronial**. See *stately*

make (as in devise an idea, plan, theory, or explanation after careful thought) *v.t.*: **excogitate**. See *devise*

(2) make (cheaply and flimsily) *v.t.*: **jerrybuild**. See *build*

make known (as in send a signal) *v.t., v.i.*: **semaphore**. See *signal*

maker (as in creator) *n.*: **demiurge**. See *creator*

makeup (artist) *n.*: **visagiste**. ❖ "Men are definitely getting more vain," a **visagiste** from a French cosmetics house recently assured the press. "An enthusiasm for manicures and anti-wrinkle creams used to be the preserve of Italians and Frenchmen, but now the Americans and British have caught up. (Gillian Glover, "The New Vain of Manhood," *Scotsman*, 1/30/2002.)

(2) makeup (cosmetic or theatrical) *n.*: **maquillage** [French]. ❖ The world is learning what [the top models] already know about makeup artist Kevyn Aucoin. Wearing black boots and black Levi's, chains around his wrist and neck, a striped vest, a goatee, and a Caesar haircut, Kevyn Aucoin, 31, the Michelangelo of **maquillage**, stares intently at his canvas, brush in hand. The canvas is the delicate face of Kate Moss. (James Servin, "The Face Maker," *Harper's Bazaar*, 1/1/1994, p. 30.)

make up for *v.t., v.i.*: **expiate**. See *atone*

malaise (general feeling of . . . as form of depression) *n.*: **dysphoria**. See *depression*

malcontent (as in rebel) *n.*: **frondeur** [French]. See *rebel*

(2) malcontent *n.*: **crepehanger**. See *pessimist*

male (centered on point of view of a . . .) *adj.*: **androcentric**. ❖ Amy Agigian denies that [the use of "him or her"] is cumbersome . . . : "The charges of awkwardness are usually a thinly veiled cover for hostility toward treating women as equals. This is a pseudo-issue where those who are benefitting from male privilege and from an **androcentric** world try to accuse those who want change of frivolity [and] nitpicking. (Daniel Seligman, "Keeping Up: Where Henry Fonda Went Wrong," *Fortune*, 4/1/1996, p.163.)

(2) male (lover of a married woman) *n.*: **cicisbeo**. See *boyfriend*

(3) male (of or derived from name of . . . ancestor) *adj.*: **patronymic**. See *paternal*

(4) male (one having both . . . and female characteristics or reproductive organs of) *n.*: **hermaphrodite**. See *bisexual*

(5) male (with whom one is in love) *n.*: **inamorato**. See *boyfriend*

(6) male (young . . . just entering manhood) *n.*: **ephebe** (*adj.*: **ephebic**). See *boy*

male superiority (one who believes in . . .) *n.*: **phallocrat**. ❖ During the late 1960s, [author John Updike] was seen as both unacceptably right-wing (he supported America's presence in Vietnam) [and] dangerously libertarian. In the 1990s, it became fashionable to view him as a misogynist, a **phallocrat**, "a penis with a thesaurus" as one reader described him. . . . Perhaps it [was his derogatory decription of women in his "Rabbit" novels] to which some feminists objected. (Terence Blacker, "Updike Outsmarted His Critics," *Independent* [London], 1/30/2009.)

males (government by or political dominance of . . .) *n.*: **androcracy**. See *government*

malfeasance (confession of . . .) *n.*: **peccavi**. See *confession*

(2) malfeasance (in public office) *n.*: **malversation**. See *wrongdoing*

(3) malfeasance (in public office) *n.*: **misprision**. See *wrongdoing*

malicious (person who makes comments that seem to be offering sympathy but instead make the person feel worse, either intentionally or unintentionally) *n.*: **Job's comforter**. See *comforter*

(2) malicious (one who is . . .) *n.*: **tricoteuse**. See *knitter*. [See the note at "knitter" for why this word can be synonymous with malicious.]

(3) malicious *adj.*: **flagitious**. See *wicked*

(4) malicious *adj.*: **malefic**. See *evil*

(5) malicious *adj.*: **malevolent**. See *evil*

malign (by making false or malicious statements) *v.t.*: **calumniate**. ❖ [C]learly, the time has come for some argumentative character to utter a kind word about poor old trickle-down economics (hereafter TDE). Bill Clinton and Al Gore have combined to **calumniate** TDE 17 times in this year's titanic debates, and neither George Bush nor Dan Quayle has attempted to defend it. (Daniel Seligman, "Keeping Up, Tricklism," *Fortune*, 11/16/1992, p. 199.)

(2) malign (so as to humiliate or disgrace) *v.t.*: **traduce**. ❖ [S]ome [Britons] request that if their reputation is to be besmirched, the movie [*The Patriot*] should at least be worth seeing. "Failure to entertain is the supreme crime of [this] movie," chides Adam Mars-Jones. . . . "If you're going to **traduce** my ancestors—blacken their names—then at least give me a better time when you do it." (Kim Campbell, "Brits Take Brunt as Hollywood Rewrites History," *Christian Science Monitor*, 7/14/2000.)

(3) malign (as in the destroying of one's reputation) *n.*: **famicide**. See *defamation*

malleable (as in pliable) *adj.*: **ductile**. See *pliable*

malnourished (and thus emaciated, esp. as to children) *adj.*: **marasmic**. See *emaciated*

malnourishment (condition of . . . of a child) *n.*: **marasmus**. ❖ The UN team reached a shocking conclusion. Child mortality had risen five-fold since 1990. Diseases of malnutrition, like kwashshiorkor and **marasmus**, which had been virtually unknown in Iraq, were rampant. . . . Studies have shown that half a million Iraqi children have died because of the sanctions and 30% of the survivors are permanently maimed or stunted by malnutrition. (Deidre Griswold, "A Silent War: The Children Are Dying; The Impact of Sanctions on Iraq," *Atlanta Inquirer*, 6/22/1996.)

man (who is unconventionally attractive) *n.*: **joli laid** (or **joli-laid**). [French, for "pretty-ugly." This term refers to a man who is handsome in an unconventional or unusual way, or more literally, handsome and ugly at the same time. (The feminine form would be "jolie laide." See *pretty*.) It can also be applied to inanimate objects, and can be used as an adjective. See *handsome* for an example.] ❖ I read the books [about detective Bulldog Drummond] voraciously in my youth as I had seen Gerald du Maurier in a West End production of the original novel. He had transformed the chauvinistic, muscular hero with hands likened to "a leg of mutton" into a **joli-laid**, elegant man-about-

town. (Nonie Beerbohm, "Literary Essays and Reviews," *Contemporary Review*, 5/1/1994.)

(2) man (centered on point of view of a . . .) *adj.*: **androcentric**. See *male*

(3) man (cranky or stubborn old . . .) *n.*: **alter kocker** [Yiddish]. See *old man*

(4) man (who has sexual relations with a boy) *n.*: **pederast**. See *sodomizer*

(5) man (who hates women) *n.*: **misogynist**. See *hatred*

(6) man (who is a lover of a married woman) *n.*: **cicisbeo**. See *boyfriend*

(7) man (who seduces women) *n.*: **Lothario**. See *playboy*

(8) man (with whom one is in love or has an intimate relationship) *n.*: **inamorato**. See *boyfriend*

man about town *n.*: **boulevardier**. ❖ The Borgata, scheduled to open this summer, is the first blackjack emporium to incorporate "spa" into its name—the Borgata Hotel Casino & Spa. Imagine Sky Masterson getting a relaxing eye-contour treatment between rounds of craps. . . . Going "spa" is an attempt to attract more overnight guests rather than drive-by gamblers, to court the **boulevardier** and his Mrs. (Karen Heller, "Atlantic City Has a Mistaken Notion That People Will Visit for Its Calm," *Philadelphia Inquirer*, 4/4/2003.)

manager *n.*: **gerent**. ❖ [Henry VIII] appointed himself "supreme governor" of the English church. His chief minister, Thomas Cromwell, became "vice-**gerent**," overseeing it on his behalf. (*Economist*, "Church and State—Monastic Error: 1539," 12/31/1999.)

(2) manager (as in boss or owner) *n.*: **padrone**. See *boss*

mandate (as in decree) *n.*: **diktat**. See *decree*

man-eating *adj.*: **anthropophagous**. See *cannibalistic*

maneuver (as in course of action) *n.*: **démarche** [French]. See *course of action*

mania (as in irresistible compulsion) *n.*: **cacoëthes**. See *compulsion*

(2) mania (for shopping) *n.*: **oniomania**. See *shopping*

manic (as in frenzied) *adj.*: **corybantic**. See *frenzied*

manly (relating to or concerned with being . . .) *adj.*: **priapic**. ❖ Anthropologist Matthew Gutmann . . . wanted to find out how the realities of Mexican men's lives compared to the popular image of Mexican men as violent, harddrinking, **priapic** machos. (Michael Schwalbe, review of *The Meanings of Macho: Being a Man in Mexico City*, by Matthew C. Gutmann, *Social Forces*, 6/1/1997, p. 1488.)

man-made (as in artificial) *adj.*: **factitious**. See *artificial*

manner (as in demeanor) *n.*: **mien**. See *demeanor*

manner of speaking *n.*: **façon de parler** [French]. See *way of speaking*

manners (appropriate . . . , as in propriety) *n.*: **correctitude**. See *propriety*

(2) manners (precise observance of . . .) *n.*: **punctilio**. See *etiquette*

manor (grounds belonging to a . . .) *n.*: **demesne**. See *estate*

mansion *n.*: **manse**. ❖ [Michael Medavoy] and Patricia built a massive vanilla-colored house in Coldwater Canyon, which was displayed in a full-color spread in the November, 1992 issue of W magazine. . . . Patricia complained that decorating the **manse** had actually given her chronic fatigue syndrome. (Griffin and Masters, *Hit and Run*, Simon & Schuster [1996], p. 355.)

(2) mansion (grounds belonging to a . . .) *n.*: **demesne**. See *estate*

mantises (of or relating to . . .) *adj.*: **orthopterous**. See *insects*

mantra (as in hymn, expressing praise and glory to God) *n.*: **doxology**. See *hymn*

manual (as in primer) *n.*: **hornbook**. See *primer*

(2) manual *n.*: **enchiridion**. See *handbook*

manufacture (cheaply and flimsily) *v.t.*: **jerrybuild**. See *build*

many (and varied) *adj.*: **manifold**. See *numerous*

marble (of, relating to, or resembling) *adj.*: **marmoreal**. ❖ She, Bruce and Teddy hit the road together and drive to a Palladian dream-house in search of a sixth-century BC fragment of marble statuary, featuring the hips and bottom of a nameless Greek athlete. After a long wait, Bruce appears, his arms wrapped around the **marmoreal** bum, which he manhandles into his car—en route, not to Sotheby's, but to his own London flat. (*Independent* [London], The Books Interview: "Hopes and Anchors," 4/17/1999.)

march (a person or group from one place to another against their will) *v.t.*: **frogmarch** [spec. carrying a resisting prisoner facedown by the arms and legs, but more generally used in the sense of forcing a person or group from one place to another, whether literally or figuratively; chiefly British]. ❖ [O]h, the pleasure it gives to meet and greet children and hear the same old excuses I've made on behalf of my children being repeated back to me: "It's because he's not on his home turf,". . ."She's just exhausted, aren't you darling?" . . . And then my favourite . . . when one traditionally grips a child by the shoulders and **frogmarches** her up to the hostess to "say goodbye." (Rachel Johnson, "The Mummy Diaries—Negotiating the Maze of Modern Motherhood," *Daily Telegraph* [London], 5/3/2003.)

marionettes (or employing . . .) *n.pl.*: **fantoccini** [Italian]. ❖ Dennis Silk, [author of] *William the Wonder-Kid: Plays, Puppet Plays and Theater Writings* [is] like a traveling hurdy-gurdy player and **fantoccini** man. . . . [His book] is a collection of plays for puppets and actors, some of which have been performed successfully in Israel and will now reach a wider public of performers and spectators. (Zvi Jagendorf, "The Thing's the Play," *Jerusalem Post*, 3/20/1997.)

marriage (announcement of forthcoming . . . , esp. in a church) *n.*: **banns**. ❖ In a renewed attempt to circumvent laws that bar gay marriages, two same-sex couples exchanged wedding vows in a Toronto church after following the tradition of publishing marriage **banns** announcing their intention to wed. (*Time* International, Notebook/World Watch, 1/29/2001, p. 12.)

(2) marriage (hatred of . . .) *n*.: **misogamy**. ❖ In Jeremiah Johnson, Bear Claw says that his former Cheyenne wife of 10 years was "the meanest bitch that ever balled for beads." Such bleak hatred illuminates the misogyny and **misogamy** harbored by mountain veterans who prefer being alone or exclusively in the company of men. (Patrick McCarthy, "Westers, Not Westerns: Exteriorizing the 'Wild Man Within,'" *Journal of Popular Film and Television*, 9/1/1995, p. 116.)

(3) marriage (late in life) *n*.: **opsigamy**. ❖ [F]or those frequent exercises in **opsigamy**, the goal of the honeymoon shuffle (now a real shuffle) should not be Buffalo with its celebrated Niagara Falls, but rather Sunset City and Viagra Falls. (www.newenglishreview.org/blog_print_link.cfm?blog_id=3389, "Offer and Acceptance," 11/20/2006.)

(4) marriage (of or relating to . . . to a person of inferior rank where the rank of the inferior partner remains unchanged and children of the marriage do not succeed to the titles of the parent of higher rank) *adj*.: **morganatic**. ❖ Public opinion may forever stand in the way of Camilla Parker Bowles being crowned Queen, but couldn't she and Prince Charles enter into a "**morganatic** marriage"? . . . A **morganatic** marriage was also suggested as a way of solving Britain's abdication crisis in 1936, when Edward VIII chose to give up his throne rather than the woman he loved, twice-divorced Wallis Simpson. (*Birmingham Post*, "There Is a Way They Could Marry," 1/29/1999.)

(5) marriage (outside the clan or other social unit) *n*.: **exogamy**.❖ Not only was the ancient rabbinic standard [as to who was Jewish] universally accepted, the barriers to intermarriage created by internal Jewish taboos as well as by Gentile hostility saw to it that the standard was fairly easily maintained. But with today's massive increase in **exogamy**, some have been prompted to reconsider traditional definitions. (Jack Wertheimer, "Judaism without Limits," *Commentary*, 7/1/1997, p. 24.)

(6) marriage (pledge of . . .) *v.t*.: **affiance**.

❖ "It's the [sexual] tension that makes it interesting for an audience." Then it may be lucky that the **affianced** Catherine Zeta-Jones and Michael Douglas share no screen time in December's *Traffic*. "Once people are married, it's like, eh," says marketing analyst Tony Angellotti. "Married people know there's no more sexual tension when people are married—you're not going to fool them." (Gillian Flynn, News & Notes: "Love Is a Battlefield," *Entertainment Weekly*, 10/6/2000, p. 10.)

(7) marriage (to one of lower social status) *n*.: **mesalliance** [French]. ❖ Grand Duke Kirill married a divorcee, and was accordingly banished from Russia. . . . Grand Duke [Paul was] banished for marrying a divorced commoner. . . . But until at least 1907 Nicholas believed the succession still to be more or less safe. . . . [H]is brother, Grand Duke Michael, had yet to follow his cousins down the road of **mesalliance** and disgrace. (Anne Applebaum, review of *Michael and Natasha: The Life and Love of the Last Tsar of Russia*, by Donald and Rosemary Crawford, *New Statesman*, 10/17/1997, p. 54.)

(8) marriage (to someone dissimilar, esp. with regard to religion or ethnicity) *n*.: **heterogamy**. ❖ Indeed, age **heterogamy** is more common among low income than higher income groups. Young unwed mothers may be better able to compete against older single women in the marriage market for older men. (Leanna Mellott, "Out-of-Wedlock Childbearing, Marital Prospects and Mate Selection," *Social Forces*, 9/1/2005.)

(9) marriage (to someone of a higher social class, esp. by women) *n*.: **hypergamy**. ❖ The New York family of Auchincloss is of "recent arrival" (1803), as Sitting Bull used to say, but they have managed, through marriage, to become related to everyone who matters—to everyone in the United States who matters, that is. For idle **hypergamy** . . . there has not been a family like them since . . . the Hapsburgs. (Gore Vidal, "Reflections on Capital Glories," *Washington Post*, 7/7/1991.)

(10) marriage (to someone of a lower social

class, esp. by women) *n*.: **hypogamy**. ❖ [In India,] **hypogamy** is facilitated by the fact that the lower-caste man compensates with wealth, education, a well-paid government job, and a good family reputation, which are highly valued assets [to the higher-caste woman]. (Oddvar Hollup, "The Disintegration of Caste and Changing Concepts of Indian Ethnic Identity in Mauritius," *Ethnology*, 9/22/1994.)

(11) marriage (to someone similar, esp. with regard to religion, ethnicity, or socioeconomic status, but also including gender) *n*.: **homogamy**. ❖ A certain degree of **homogamy** . . . seems to be prevalent in all periods and all places. He concluded that there is a significant tendency towards religious **homogamy** in Christians (Protestants marry Protestants, and Catholics Catholics, and this goes beyond the ordinary "boy next door effect"), but that it is especially marked among Jews. (Richard Dawkins, *The God Delusion*, Houghton Mifflin [2006], p. 262.)

(12) marriage (within a group based on applicable custom) *n*.: **endogamy**. ❖ Thirty years ago, Jews were considered the most **endogamous** ethnic group in the United States; in the early 1960s, less than 11 percent of Jews who married chose non-Jewish spouses. (Rachel Altman, "The New Minority: Jews Who Choose Jews," *Lilith*, 6/30/1994.)

(13) marriage (as in absence, nonrecognition, or nonregulation of . . .) *n*.: **agamy**. See *unmarried*

(14) marriage (or sexual relations involving persons of different races) *n*.: **miscegenation**. See *sex*

(15) marriage (of or relating to . . .) *adj*.: **hymeneal**. See *wedding*

married (happily . . . elderly couple seldom seen apart) *n*.: **Darby and Joan** [British]. ❖ "It didn't cross my mind that something which is so old [i.e., having an affair with a married man whom she later married herself] could become an issue," she says. "I mean it all happened 20 or 30 years ago. Desmond and I thought we had turned into **Darby and Joan** and I didn't

expect it to become a priority." (Diane Parkes, interview with Esther Rantzen, *Evening Mail* [London], 3/17/2001.)

married (woman) *n*.: **feme covert** [French]. ❖ If, as J. Paul Hunter suggests, "novels are an easy place . . . to sort out the ways of the world, to crack the code of adulthood and social expectation," then what might have the young woman reader of [Mary Davys's 1724 novel *The Reform'd Coquet*] sorted out? Certainly a grim portent of what it means to be a **feme covert**, for whom a husband thinks, speaks, and acts. (Natasha Saje, "The Assurance to Write," *Essays in Literature*, 9/22/1996, p. 165.)

marsh *n*.: **fen**. See *swamp*

marshy *adj*.: **quaggy**. ❖ Checking a nest box [of a warbler] takes on average less than a minute, but paddling between nest boxes . . . takes considerably longer. The scientists can enter Presquile only at high tide. It is a race against the clock to check part of the line and get out before becoming stranded in the **quaggy** muck of tuckahoe and yellow swamp iris and negligently perched ash and gum and maple trees. (Diane Tennant, "A Bird in the Hand for 15 Years," *Virginian-Pilot*, 5/26/2002.)

(2) marshy (or full of puddles) *adj*.: **plashy**. See *puddles*

(3) marshy *adj*.: **paludal**. See *swampy*

marvelous (as in of the highest quality) *n*.: **first water** (usu. as in "of the first water"). See *quality*

(2) marvelous *adj*.: **frabjous** (often as in "Oh frabjous day!"). See *wonderful*

(3) marvelous *adj*.: **galluptious** [slang]. See *wonderful*

(4) marvelous *adj*.: **galumptious**. See *excellent*

(5) marvelous *adj*.: **mirific**. See *wonderful*

(6) marvelous *adj*.: **palmary**. See *excellent*

(7) marvelous *adj*.: **skookum**. See *excellent*

masculine (condition of a woman having supposedly . . . tendencies) *n*.: **viraginity** (*adj*.: **viraginous**). ❖ Krafft-Ebing . . . did equate the most degenerate forms of lesbianism with an inverted gender style. . . . In describing

viraginity, Krafft-Ebing focuses on the women's tomboyish childhood; their preference for playing with soldiers; and their inclination for male garments, science, smoking, drinking, and imagining themselves men in relation to women. (Cheshire Calhoun, "The Gender Closet: Lesbian Disappearance Under the Sign 'Women,'" *Feminist Studies*, 3/22/1995.)

(2) masculine (relating to or concerned with being . . .) *adj.*: **priapic**. See *manly*

mask (or disguise) *n., v.t.*: **vizard**. See *disguise*

masochism *n.*: **algolagnia** [this word includes both ends of the pain spectrum, pleasure from receiving pain and from giving it]. ❖ The French, and indeed almost all the rest of the world, have been amazed for centuries by the English habit, begun at school but continuing for ever, of hitting one another with sticks and suchlike; statistics must inevitably be difficult or impossible to acquire, but I would bet a lot that the English would demonstrate an addiction to **algolagnia** far greater than in any other country. (Bernard Levin, "Oh, to Slap the Jailer in the Jug," *Times* [London], 12/14/1989.)

mass (confused or jumbled . . .) *n.*: **agglomeration**. See *jumble*

(2) mass (of people) *n.*: **ruck**. See *multitude*

massacre (of unresisting persons) *n.*: **battue** [French]. See *killing*

massage (involving quick percussive strokes on the body) *n.*: **tapotement**. ❖ "Better than a bonus," Ms. Touhamy murmured as Ms. Valentino's fingers did a series of **tapotement**, or brisk and uniform percussion strokes, like karate chops, along her spine. This was certainly more fun than the free Wednesday breakfasts the company offers. (Marcelle Fischler, "Having a Bad Day? She Rubs It Away," *New York Times*, 5/10/1998.)

(2) massage (of the body with lotion) *n.*: **embrocation** (*v.t.*: **embrocate**). See *body rub*

(3) massage (spec. a gentle stroking used in . . .) *n.* **effleurage**. See *stroking*

masses (of common people) *n.*: **canaille**. ❖ "How I loved the game [of golf]," [P. G. Wodehouse] wrote in 1973. "I have sometimes wondered if we of the **canaille** don't get more pleasure out of it than the top-notchers. (Robert Sullivan, Golf: "Bard of the Links," *Sports Illustrated*, 5/29/1995, p. R10.)

(2) masses (pertaining to the . . .) *n.*: **demotic**. ❖ Unlike Jefferson, however, [Supreme Court Justice John] Marshall never acquired the cultivated elegance of his Randolph forebears. He never shed the rough but genial manners of his frontier father. He had simple tastes and a **demotic** temperament that Jefferson lacked, a common touch that Jefferson snidely attributed to "his lax lounging manners." (Gordon S. Wood, "The Father of the Court," *New Republic*, 2/17/1997.)

(3) masses (the . . .) *n.*: **vulgus**. [Latin. In this example, "profanum vulgus" refers to the profane or ignorant or uneducated masses.] ❖ The mass attitude has changed in recent decades: the profanum **vulgus** has discovered the virtues of empowerment and entitlement, and the vices of elitism and lookism. In movie-star terms, this translates into: the plainer the better, because the more like us. (John Simon, "The Mirror Has Two Faces," *National Review*, 12/23/1996.)

(4) masses (as in the common people) *n.*: **hoi polloi**. See *commoners*

(5) masses (government by the . . .) *n.*: **mobocracy**. See *government*

(6) masses (government by the . . .) *n.*: **ochlocracy**. See *government*

(7) masses (suitable for or comprehensible by the . . .) *adj.*: **exoteric**. See *accessible*

massive *adj.*: **cyclopean**. See *big*

(2) massive (like an elephant) *adj.*: **elephantine**. See *enormous*

(3) massive (like an elephant) *adj.*: **pachydermatous**. See *elephant*

(4) massive (object) *n.*: **leviathan**. See *huge*

(5) massive *adj.*: **brobdingnagian** (often cap.). See *huge*

(6) massive *adj.*: **Bunyanesque**. See *enormous*

(7) massive *adj.*: **Pantagruelian**. See *gigantic*

(8) massive *adj.*: **pythonic**. See *huge*

(9) massive *adj.*: **mastodonic**. See *big*

master (as in boss or owner) *n.*: **padrone**. See *boss*

  (2) master (as in ruler, of the universe) *n.*: **kosmokrator** [Greek]. See *ruler*

  (3) master (or ruler who holds great power or sway) *n.*: **potentate**. See *ruler*

master key (spec. something such as a . . . that allows one to gain access or pass at will) *n.*: **passe-partout** [French]. See *passkey*

masterpiece (esp. in art or literature) *n.*: **chef d'oeuvre** [French]. ❖ So, welcome to the High Museum's [art exhibition]. Only three paintings, but what stellar canvases they are, starring van Gogh's **chef d'oeuvre** and one of his most famous works, *The Starry Night*. (Catherine Fox, "Fans to Get Starry-Eyed View of Van Gogh Classic," *Atlanta Journal-Constitution*, 9/1/2000.)

master race *n.*: **herrenvolk** [German]. ❖ Virginia was a status society, whereas the Puritan colonies were caste societies, "**herrenvolk**" democracies in which a small group (the elect) had rights and the great majority had only the right to obey. These colonies were far more racist than Virginia. Virginia hanged no witches, did not burn African Americans at the stake (as colonial New York did) and did not pay for Indian scalps. (Patrick E. Kennon, "New England: No Model," *Washington Post*, 5/22/2007.)

masturbation *n.*: **autoeroticism**. ❖ More-recent studies indicate that the number of women who masturbate has risen to about half (15 percent do it "quite often"), while the proportion of men who do remains about the same. Unmarried women and college-educated women are more likely to indulge in **autoeroticism** than others. (Michael Segell, "Sexual Performance: A Hard Look at the Primal Urge," *Esquire*, 3/1/1994, p. 119.)

  (2) masturbation *n.*: **onanism**. ❖ Although sexual self-satisfaction is as old as the Bible . . . males have begun to rely on it heavily. The reason: As they get on with the great project of letting vanity rule every aspect of their lives,

they become less attractive as bed partners to women. The result is a burgeoning **onanism** industry, with the "Body Electric" masturbation school for men in Oakland. (Guy Martin, "The Encyclopedia of Male Vanity," *Esquire*, 3/1/1997, p. 82.)

matchless (person or thing) *n.*: **nonesuch**. See *paragon*

matchmaker (Jewish . . .) *n.*: **shadchan** [Yiddish]. ❖ Matchmaking is an ancient tradition, especially among small, isolated communities like those of the Eastern European shtetl, where the key to survival was tight social cohesion. In many ways, Hakimian is the modern-day inheritor of the generations-old role of the **shadchan**. (Jonathan Krashinsky, "Bringing People Together," *Jerusalem Post*, 2/2/2001.)

mate (or close partner, often, but not always, one in marriage) *n.*: **yokefellow**. See *partner*

materialism (as in greed) *n.*: **pleonexia**. See *greed*

  (2) materialism (as in worship of or devotion to money) *n.*: **plutolatry**. See *wealth*

materialistic *adj.*: **banausic**. ❖ Those [studying Latin will be asked,] "What on earth are you going to do with that?" The question is often intended to be merely rhetorical, because the assumption is that no justification could possibly exist. . . . Students of Latin typically subscribe to a different view, one in which people do not assume that everything must have a **banausic** purpose. (*Washington Times*, "Finding Beauty and Meaning in Latin Despite Modern History of Rejection," 7/29/2001.)

  (2) materialistic *adj.*: **bourgeois**. ❖ And what happened to romance? I grew up on images of struggling artists shacking up in Bohemian apartments, surviving mostly on love and thumbing their noses at shallow **bourgeois** values. The people I knew dreamed of passion and poetry rather than rocks on ring fingers or maid service. (Rekha Basu, "*Multimillionaire Show Pitted Marriage Values Against Money*," Gannett News Service, 2/24/2000.)

materialize (as in making an abstract concept seem real) *v.t.*: **reify**. ❖ [Ron Haskins] says that in returning over and over to the human stories, DeParle made a "constant attempt to **reify** the abstract principles of welfare reform. You could see what it meant to have a work requirement, when you have a mom in Milwaukee with six kids, and she has to get up at 6 in the morning to catch a bus or whatever." (William Powers, "Welfare: The Trickster," *National Journal*, 3/10/2001.)

(2) materialize (as in emerge) *v.i.*: **debouch**. See *emerge*

maternal (of or relating to name of . . . ancestor) *adj.*: **matronymic**. ❖ Although there are numerous variations, Spanish surnames usually consist of two parts: the patronymic name followed by the **matronymic**. In the case of President Luis Alberto Monge Álvarez, for example, Monge is his father's name; Álvarez, his mother's name. (Harold D. Nelson, "Costa Rica: Front Matter," *Countries of the World*, 1/1/1991.)

math (difficulty with or inability to do . . .) *n.*: **acalculia** (or **dyscalculia**) ❖ Whatever the reason for the lack of popularity of this kind of research, the topic of learning disabilities in mathematics requires serious attention. Many children receive diagnoses of mathematics learning disability, or the related **dyscalculia** and **acalculia**. (Herbert P. Ginsburg, "Mathematics Learning Disabilities: A View from Developmental Psychology," *Journal of Learning Disabilities*, 1/1/1997.)

mathematical (having . . . ability) *adj.*: **numerate**. ❖ Some of the most prominent chief executives, presidents, entrepreneurs, and inventors in the world are graduates of IIT, India's elite institution of higher learning. Its impossibly high standards, compelling the mostly male student body to average fewer than five hours of sleep a night, produce **numerate** graduates who are masters at problem-solving. (Manjeet Kripalani, Management: "Whiz Kids," *Business Week*, 12/7/1998.)

matrimony (of or relating to . . .) *adj.*: **hymeneal**. See *wedding*

mattress (straw-filled . . .) *n.*: **palliasse**.

❖ After lights out, on their beds of lumpy **palliasses** on wooden planks, [military] recruits moaned about their lot, their fag-ends glowing like agitated fireflies, but all shared the companionship of the temporarily oppressed; the enforced community living often leading to lasting friendships. (Albert Morris, "Last Post Sounds for the Barracks Dorm," *Scotsman* [Edinburgh], 3/17/2001.)

maudlin *adj.*: **bathetic**. See *sentimental*

maverick (orig. Catholics who did not follow Church of England) *n.*: **recusant**. See *dissenter*

(2) maverick (spec. one who hates or mistrusts authority) *n.*: **misarchist**. See *rebel*

mawkish (as in excessive or contrived sentimentality) *adj.*: **bathetic**. See *sentimental*

mawkishess (as in excessive or contrived sentimentality) *n.*: **bathos**. See *sentimentality*

maxim (pithy . . .) *n.*: **gnome** (*adj.*: **gnomic**). See *catchphrase*

(2) maxim (witty or clever . . . or line) *n.*: **bon mot**. See *line*

(3) maxim *n.*: **apothegm**. See *saying*

maxims (given to stating . . . , esp. in a moralizing way) *adj.*: **sententious**. See *aphoristic*

maximum (to the . . .) *adv.*: **à l'outrance** [French]. See *utmost*

maybe *adv.*: **perchance**. See *possibly*

meager *adj.*: **mingy**. [This is likely a blended word—also known as a portmanteau word—which combines "mean" and "stingy." However, in actual usage, it is generally used as a synonym for "stingy" or for the less pejorative "meager."] ❖ While overall retail sales — excluding the highly volatile auto sales—edged up a **mingy** 0.2 percent in February, sales in the nation's furniture and home furnishings outlets jumped up by 1.4 percent over January levels. (Don Hogsett, "Home Outpaces Overall Retail Sales," *Home Textiles Today*, 3/25/2002.)

(2) meager *n.*: **exiguous**. ❖ They became a "tightly knit unit," bound together by the effort to maintain the household on the **exiguous** sum Jay sent them—eight dollars a week by Vivian's recollection. (Sam Tanenhaus, *Whittaker Chambers, Random House [1997], p. 7.)

(3) meager (as in stingy) *adj*.: **cheeseparing**. See *stingy*

meal (before a . . . , esp. dinner) *adj*.: **preprandial**. ❖ Any fellow dinner guest reading [my dull résumé] could have been forgiven for sneaking up to the table for a quick squint during the **preprandial** stage and doing a quick shuffle of the placement cards. (Tony Rennell, "Why I Hate Dinner Parties Now," *New Statesman*, 6/28/1999.)

(2) meal (following a . . . , esp. dinner) *adj*.: **postprandial**. ❖ Even [Rockefeller's] daily breaks—the midmorning snack of crackers and milk and the **postprandial** nap—were designed to conserve energy and strike the ideal balance between the physical and mental forces. (Ron Chernow, *Titan*, Random House [1998], p. 174.)

mealy (as in startchy) *adj*.: **farinaceous**. See *starchy*

mean (as in lacking moral qualities) *adj*.: **ignoble**. ❖ We are, sadly, living in a rude, **ignoble** age in this country, and professional sports have become the living, seething proof. Our kids see pro athletes trash-talking, brawling, spitting, taunting, and retaliating —and being rewarded and admired for behavior that used to be the opposite of the American ideal of sportsmanship. (John Kehe, "Remember When Playing Kids' Sports Was Actually Fun?" *Christian Science Monitor*, 7/19/2000.)

(2) mean (as in cruel) *adj*.: **fell** (*n*.: **fellness**). See *cruel*

(3) mean (as in despicable, person) *n*.: **caitiff**. See *despicable*

(4) mean (as in portend) *v.t.*: **betoken**. See *portend*

(5) mean (as in wicked) *adj*.: **flagitious**. See *wicked*

meander (as in talk or act in an aimless or incoherent fashion) *v.i.*: **maunder**. See *ramble*

meaning (having more than one . . .) *adj*.: **polysemous** (or **polysemic**). [This word can refer to a word having literally more than one meaning, as in the example given, or can mean

a word that means different things to different people. For example, one writer stated: "We cannot control the meaning of such a slippery and **polysemic** concept as 'multiculturalism.'"] ❖ There is nothing like a game of Scrabble with non-native speakers to heighten your appreciation for your own native tongue. . . . Just take the word run: You can run up a bill, or you can run up a hill. You can be on the run—as in dodging the law—or you can have the runs. How versatile three little letters can be. (Genine Babakian, "Coming to Grips with **Polysemous** Vocabulary," *St. Petersburg Times* [Russia], 7/25/2000.)

(2) meaning (inability to recall . . . of words or using them incorrectly) *n*.: **paramnesia**. See *amnesia*

(3) meaning (using a . . . of a word other than in its customary sense) *adj*.: **Pickwickian**. See *definition*

(4) meaning (having more than one . . . or signifying different things) *adj*.: **multivocal**. See *ambiguous*

meaningless (or deceptive words or language) *n*.: **flummery**. ❖ A lot of the yammering about welfare "reform" is pure **flummery**. Politicians know there is a pent-up urge to drastically cut welfare and are calling their intention to try to do so "reform." (Linda Chavez, "The Welfare-Reform Fantasy," *USA Today*, 1/25/1995.)

meanings (study of subtle distinctions between . . . of similar words or synonyms) *n*.: **synonymy**. See *synonyms*

meanness (as in being small-minded) *n*.: **parvanimity**. See *small-minded*

measly (as in meager) *adj*.: **mingy**. See *meager*

(2) measly *n*.: **exiguous**. See *meager*

measuring (act or process of . . .) *n*.: **mensuration**. ❖ Yet [the issue of which is the world's tallest building is] hotly contested. One Randall Krause, for example . . . is lord of the International Superstructure **Mensuration** Alliance, the master of its Website, and something of a rebel among the edifice-measurement set. He's the one out there asking the hard questions. ("What is the meaning of high? How does it differ from tall?") (*Fortune*, "The World's Tallest Buildings: Too Big to Lose," 5/24/1999, p. 232.)

mechanical (as in having the form or qualities of a machine) *adj.*: **mechanomorphic**. See *machine*

(2) **mechanical** (as in routine) *adj.*: **banausic**. See *routine*

meddle (one who would . . . into other's affairs) *n.*: **quidnunc**. See *busybody*

meddler (officious . . . who frustrates the success of a plan by stupidly getting in the way) *n.*: **marplot** [after Marplot, a character in *The Busy Body*, a play by Susanna Centlivre (1669–1723)]. ❖ For Thanksgiving, [several George W. Bush supporters have] given a big fat turkey of an issue to Sen. John McCain in his campaign for the GOP presidential nomination [by allegedly] spreading rumors that McCain's imprisonment as a POW in Vietnam made him unstable, mentally unfit for the presidency. . . . [T]he chief **marplot** [is Senator Trent Lott, who denies the charge]. (Guy Friddell, "Rumors Rile Ex-POW McCain and His Supporters," *Virginian-Pilot*, 11/25/1999.)

medication (which is untested or unproved) *n.*: **nostrum**. See *remedy*

medicine (of or relating to . . . or the art of healing) *adj.*: **Aesculpian**. See *healing*

(2) **medicine** (which relieves pain) *n.*: **anodyne**. See *pain reliever*

mediocre (as in made without regard to quality) *adj.*: **catchpenny**. See *inferior*

meditate (on something, often used as a directive, as in "Consider this:") *v.t.*: **perpend**. See *consider*

meditation (staring at one's belly-button as an aid to . . .) *n.*: **omphaloskepsis**. ❖ The point [of Paul Goodman's philosophy], as near as I can make it out, is to achieve a kind of perpetual **omphaloskepsis**, repeatedly examining yourself and your motives and connections with the world around [you], and thus achieving health, or at least avoiding neurosis, by putting forth, as much and continuously as possible, the authentic self.

(Talk about the examined life!). (Kirkpatrick Sale, review of *Crazy Hope and Finite Experience: Final Essays of Paul Goodman*, *Nation*, 4/10/1995.)

medley (as in assortment) *n.*: **gallimaufry**. See *assortment*

(2) **medley** (as in assortment) *n.*: **olla podrida** [Spanish]. See *assortment*

(3) **medley** (as in assortment) *n.*: **omnium-gatherum** [Latin]. See *assortment*

(4) **medley** (as in assortment) *n.*: **salmagundi**. See *assortment*

(5) **medley** (as in mixture) *n.*: **farrago**. See *assortment*

(6) **medley** (esp. of fruits and vegetables) *n.*: **macédoine** [French]. See *mixture*

meek (and cautious and indecisive) *adj.*: **Prufrockian**. See *timid*

(2) **meek** (and unassertive person) *n.*: **milquetoast**. See *unassertive*

(3) **meek** (as in cowardly) *adj.*: **pusillanimous**. See *cowardly*

(4) **meek** (as in cowardly) *adj.*: **retromingent**. See *cowardly*

(5) **meek** (as in timid person) *n.*: **nebbish** [Yiddish]. See *timid*

(6) **meek** (esp. from lack of self-confidence) *adj.*: **diffident**. See *timid*

meeting (esp. for illicit sexual relations) *n.*: **assignation**. See *appointment*

(2) **meeting** (esp. with an enemy or adversary) *n., v.t.*: **parley**. See *discussion*

(3) **meeting** (spec. a final effort made by architectural students to complete a solution to a problem within an allotted time, but sometimes used to refer to any kind of workshop or brainstorming session) *n.*: **charette** (or **charrette**). See *workshop*

melancholy (as in depression) *n.*: **cafard** [French]. See *depression*

(2) **melancholy** (as in sullen or morose) *adj.*: **saturnine**. See *sullen*

(3) **melancholy** (as in world-weariness or sentimental pessimism over the world's problems) *adj.*: **Weltschmerz** [German]. See *pessimism*

(4) melancholy *adj*.: **tristful**. See *sad*

mélange (as in assortment) *n*.: **farrago**. See *assortment*

(2) mélange (as in assortment) *n*.: **gallimaufry**. See *assortment*

(3) mélange (as in assortment) *n*.: **olla podrida** [Spanish]. See *assortment*

(4) mélange (as in assortment) *n*.: **omnium-gatherum** [Latin]. See *assortment*

(5) mélange (of fruits or vegetables) *n*.: **macédoine** [French]. See *mixture*

meld (as in blend) *v.t.*, *v.i.*: **inosculate**. See *blend*

(2) meld (as in bring together) *v.t.*: **conflate**. See *combine*

melee *n*.: **affray**. See *brawl*

mellifluous (sound) *adj*.: **euphonious** (*n*.: **euphony**). See *melodious*

melodious (to the ear) *adj*.: **dulcet**. ❖ In the quirky world of National Public Radio, **dulcet**-toned commentators provide long, thoughtful analyses of issues both momentous and amusing, their reports bookended by tinkling music. (Elizabeth Gleick, Nation: "Static on Public Radio," *Time*, 4/7/1997, p. 55.)

(2) melodious (voice or sound) *adj*.: **euphonious** (*n*.: **euphony**). ❖ Moments after his death was disclosed Thursday night, Sinatra's silvery tone flowed into every communication channel, reclaiming the airwaves with a **euphony** and honesty that never goes out of fashion. (Edna Gundersen, "A Silvery Tone for a Lifetime, Sinatra Forever an Inspiration," *USA Today*, 5/18/1998.)

(3) melodious (voice or sound) *adj*.: **mellifluous**. ❖ Silence also puts us in tune with the extraordinary world around. . . . It is in silence that we often hear soothing, healing sounds: the **mellifluous** song of a bird, a gentle wind whispering through leaves, the scampering of a squirrel up the trunk of a tree or the voice of God. (Dayle Allen Shockley, "We Should Cherish the Sound of Silence," *Dallas Morning News*, 7/18/1999.)

(4) melodious (voice or sound) *adj*.: **mellisonant**. ❖ Playing the Quintet Op. 28, No. 4

[by Boccherini] is a lesson in proportion and perspective. With the intended Grave movement coming before the Rondo we immerse ourselves in a luxuriant, exotic sound-arama, a **mellisonant** world of beauty and perfection. (*Strings*, "Quintet in C Major," 2/1/2004.)

melodrama (as in excessive or contrived sentimentality) *n*.: **bathos**. See *sentimentality*

melodramatic (behavior) *n*., *adj*.: **operatics**. ❖ The conventional melodrama provides Fassbinder with his most powerful techniques for constructing his narrative. The earliest street melodramas were silent and depended on exaggerated posturings and prolonged stares. . . . Fassbinder also revives the theatrical, **operatic** posturings of the early melodramas. (*Magill's Survey of Cinema*, "Fox and His Friends; Faustrecht der Freiheit," 6/15/1995.)

(2) melodramatic (as in excessive or contrived sentimentality) *adj*.: **bathetic**. See *sentimental*

melt *v.i.*: **deliquesce**. ❖ [Sugar Ray] Robinson was hitting Maxim at will for 11 rounds, winning easily on all cards and about to take his third world title before **deliquescing** in the 104 degree heat. (William Nack, "The 20th Century," *Sports Illustrated*, 6/7/1999, p. 100.)

melting (as in like liquid or tending to become liquid) *adj*.: **liquescent**. See *liquid*

memorandum (which contains outline of an agreement or summary of diplomatic negotiations) *n*.: **aide-mémoire** [French]. ❖ Russia is pulling out of a 1995 arms agreement signed by Vice President Al Gore after portions of the pact were disclosed in the Washington Times, U.S. officials said yesterday. . . . The Times published sections of the **aide-mémoire** on Oct. 17. The agreement [was] signed by Mr. Gore and then-Russian Prime Minister Viktor Chernomyrdin. . . . The Gore campaign said the disclosures were politically motivated. (Bill Gertz, "Russia Will Not Honor Gore's Secret Arms Deal," *Washington Times*, 11/23/2000.)

memory (an aid to . . . , such as a mnemonic device) *n*.: **aide-mémoire**. ❖ Can't remember the name of a bird between *shrike* and *tern*?

In [a 1558 vocabulary book by John Withals], there is *swallow* and *swift*—and at a stroke, his book becomes, if little else, an **aide-mémoire**. (Simon Winchester, *The Meaning of Everything*, Oxford University Press [2003], p. 20.)

(2) memory (by or from . . .) *adv.* **memoriter**. ❖ It is by no means advisable that the whole of a speech should be committed to writing, and then committed to memory. Unless a man be an actor, he will not be able to speak with real freedom, point, or vigor, if he adopts the **memoriter** method. (George Murray, "Fame and Fortune from Public Speaking Through the Ages," *Canadian Speeches*, 11/1/1997.)

(3) memory (having an exact or vivid . . .) *n.:* **hypermnesia**. ❖ The story resembles the natural but morbid tendency for **hypermnesia** touched off when we know that we are about to die. Our memory plays out the details of important scenes from our lives. (Anthony Wall, "Chatter, Memory, and Mysticism in Louis-René des Forêts," *Romanic Review*, 5/1/1993.)

(4) memory (having detailed . . . of visual images) *adj.:* **eidetic**. ❖ His mind was **eidetic**—that is to say, it could hold and retrieve images with photographic accuracy, be they mid-game positions in chess, crossword puzzles or encoded German naval signals —and he was working with his eyes closed. (Robert Harris, *Enigma*, Random House [1995], p. 57.)

(5) memory (of or relating to) *adj.:* **mnesic** (or **mnestic**). ❖ PVM underwent cognitive testing in May 1998 and May 1999. During the first interview, he reported **mnesic** problems, such as remembering telephone numbers and the events of the previous day, but complained of no physical symptoms. (Francisco Laynez, "Two Cases of Acute Poisoning," *Environmental Health Perspectives*, 6/1/2005.)

(6) memory (confusion of one's . . . with fact) *n.:* **paramnesia** See *misremember*

(7) memory (recalling to . . .) *n.:* **anamnesis**. See *remembrance*

men (government by or political dominance of . . .) *n.:* **androcracy**. *See government*

(2) men (hatred of . . .) *n.:* **misandry**. *See hatred*

menacing *adj.:* **minatory**. ❖ Allied forces must win big enough to change Iraq's politics. It is not sufficient to drive Saddam from Kuwait, waggle a **minatory** finger at him, and say, "Be a good boy and don't ever do that again." (Thomas A. Stewart, "Winning the Peace," *Fortune*, 2/25/1991, p. 28.)

(2) menacing *adj.:* **baleful**. See *sinister*

ménage à trois *n.:* **troilism** (person engaged) *adj.:* **troilist**. [This word is defined in a number of different ways, though they all relate to a ménage à trois in one form or another. Sometimes it is defined as each participant. Sometimes it refers specifically to the third participant. Sometimes it refers to the person who is merely watching two other people engage in sexual activity. The word is also sometimes used in a nonsexual sense. See *threesome*.] ❖ [During the celibacy pledge, the pastor urged the congregants to] date God, not the cute guy with the wandering hands. But then things got more complicated. The pastor sandwiched one member of his flock between two young believers who had fallen from grace. They stood back-to-back and linked arms and then the pastor tied them all together with a length of yellow rope. It looked like a Sears catalogue version of **troilist** bondage but it turned out to be a theological argument. (Thomas Sutcliffe, review of a church service promoting celibacy, *Independent* [London], 7/5/1995.)

menopause (period culminating in . . .) *n.*, *adj.:* **climacteric** (usu. as in "the . . . "). ❖ Menopause is actually not a single event but a transition period during which a woman experiences changes in menstruation leading to the **climacteric**. (Dianne Kieren, "Women's Choicemaking About Menopause: Issues and Directions for Action," *Contemporary Women's Issues Database*, 9/1/1995, p. 143.)

menstruation (suppression of or absence of . . .) *n.*: **amenorrhea**. ❖ Women who train intensely—and who don't eat enough to keep up with the demands of that training—may stop having their periods. That, in and of itself, is not harmful, but the estrogen deficiency that causes **amenorrhea** also can cause bone loss and osteoporosis. (Bill Stump, "Don't Ignore These Symptoms," *Runner's World*, 6/1/1999, p. 66.)

(2) menstruation (woman's first . . .) *n.*: **menarche**. ❖ Full bosomed and womanly by her early teens, she obviously had started **menarche** at a young age. (Dorothy Herrmann, *Helen Keller*, Knopf [1998], p. 107.)

mental (activity) *n.*: **mentation**. See *thinking*

(2) mental (having . . . balance) *adj.*: **compos mentis**. See *sane*

mentally ill (person) *n.*: **bedlamite**. See *lunatic*

mercenary *n.*: **hireling**. ❖ [I]f basic American values are truly being tested around the world, one more question: Should we not deal with today's Army at least as honorably as our British overlords of 1776 did with the Hessian hirelings who were famously recruited to put down the Revolution? (Lionel Van Deerlin, "A Draft for Our Volunteer Military," *San Diego Union-Tribune*, 6/9/2004.)

merciful (as in compassionate) *adj.*: **ruthful**. See *compassionate*

merciless (as in cruel) *adj.*: **fell** (*n.*: **fellness**). See *cruel*

mere (as in meager) *adj.*: **mingy**. See *meager*

merged (of things that cannot be . . .) *adj.*: **immiscible**. See *incompatible*

merited (esp. in reference to a punishment) *adj.*: **condign**. See *deserved*

merry (and social) *adj.*: **Anacreontic**. See *convivial*

(2) merry *adj.*: **eupeptic**. See *cheerful*

(3) merry *adj.*: **Falstaffian**. See *jovial*

(4) merry *adj.*: **gladsome**. See *gladness*

(5) merry *adj.*: **riant**. See *cheerful*

merrymaker *n.*: **roisterer**. See *revel*

mesmerize (as in bewitch or enchant) *v.t.*: **ensorcell** (or **ensorcel**). See *enchant*

mess (as in disorderly confusion) *n., adj.*: **hugger-mugger**. See *confusion*

mess around (as in idle or waste time) *v.i.*: **footle** (usu. as in "footle around"). See *dawdle*

messenger (spec. a character in a book, play, or movie who appears to act as a mouthpiece for the opinions of the author) *n.*: **raisonneur** [French]. See *mouthpiece*

mess up (esp. a golf shot) *v.t., n.*: **foozle**. See *botch*

messy (as in unkempt or slovenly) *adj.*: **frowzy**. ❖ Beethoven's bad hair just got worse. Scientists analyzed eight strands of the composer's **frowzy** mane and found lead at more than 100 times the norm. Lead poisoning could explain his constant abdominal distress, irritability, and depression and may have led to his death. The lock behind it all is profiled in a new book, *Beethoven's Hair*. (*U.S. News & World Report*, Transitions, 10/30/2000.)

(2) messy (as in disheveled) *adj.*: **blowsy** (or **blowzy**). See *disheveled*

(3) messy (as in haphazard) *adj., adv.*: **higgledy-piggledy**. See *haphazard*

(4) messy (situation that is . . . or confused or complicated) *n.*: **mare's nest**. See *chaotic*

metamorphosis (complete . . .) *n.*: **permutation**. See *transformation*

(2) metamorphosis (spec. a fundamental transformation of mind or character, esp. a spiritual conversion) *n.*: **metanoia** [Greek for "repentance"]. See *conversion*

metaphor (misuse or strained use of a word, phrase, or . . . , sometimes deliberate) *n.*: **catachresis**. See *misuse*

(2) metaphor (or figure of speech) *n.*: **trope**. See *figure of speech*

meteor (exploding . . .) *n.*: **bolide**. See *fireball*

methodical (as in logical) *adj.*: **ratiocinative**. See *logical*

meticulous (as in fastidious) *adj.*: **governessy**. See *fastidious*

(2) meticulous (overly . . .) *adj.*: **persnickety**. See *picky*

metropolis *n.*: **conurbation**. ❖ London, said to be the largest city in Europe, was [in the early 1600s] a vast, sprawling **conurbation** of teeming tenements and slums, as well as palaces and mansions. (Antonia Fraser, *Faith & Treason*, Doubleday [1996], p. 100.)

mettle *n.*: **hardihood**. See *courage*

mezzanine *n.*: **entresol** [French]. ❖ Defining characteristics of this example of Creole-American style include the second-floor balcony with iron railing, and the **entresol**, a half-floor or mezzanine between the first and second floors, usually used for storage. (David Maurer, "Good for What Ails You [New Orleans Pharmacy Museum]," *Colonial Homes*, 4/1/1997, p. 76.)

mice (of or relating to . . . or rats) *adj.*: **murine**. See *rodents*

middle (as in central point) *n.*: **omphalos**. See *center*

    (2) middle (into the . . .) *adv.*: **in medias res** [Latin.] See *into the middle*

    (3) middle (moving, directed, or pulled toward the . . .) *adj.*: **centripetal**. See *center*

middle class (as a group, which is smug, narrow-minded, and conformist; also a group that recognizes material success but not artistic values) *n.*: **Babbitry**. ❖ We know no spectacle so ridiculous as the arts establishment in one of its periodic fits of immorality. It sets out boldly to shock the bourgeoisie, but when the bourgeoisie is shocked, [the arts establishment] starts back nervously and babbles about **Babbitry**. . . . For years now the arts establishment has repeated mantra-like that the purpose of art is to shock, to disturb, to challenge. (John O'Sullivan, "Philistines at the Gate," *National Review*, 6/11/1990.)

    (2) middle class (employees, as opposed to lower class wage-earners) *n.*: **salariat**. See *employees*

middle ground *n.*: **tertium quid** [Latin for "third thing"]. ❖ If you want to increase support for a tyrant, bomb his people. It's no skin off his nose. Something must be done about this genocide [in the Balkans]. But Cook and Blair have expressed a false opposition between non-intervention on the one hand, and the "bombing for peace" of a sovereign state on the other, as if there were no **tertium quid**. (Chris Maslanka, "Puzzle Master," *Independent* [London], 3/27/1999.)

    (2) middle ground (appropriate . . . , as in happy medium) *n.*: **juste milieu** [French]. See *happy medium*

middleman *n.*: **comprador**. See *intermediary*

middle way (or middle ground) *n.*: **via media.** [Latin. The traditional via media is the Anglican Church, which is considered a middle ground between Catholicism and Protestantism. However, it can also be used to refer to any kind of middle ground or compromise.] ❖ Designed to find a **via media** between the anarchy of states and a consolidated empire (the two great poles along the spectrum of possibilities), both creations [i.e., the Federal Constitution and creation of the system linking the United States with the advanced industrial democracies after the Second World War] nevertheless sought to safeguard . . . the liberty of states and the preservation of peace and order over an extended territory. (David Hendrikson, "In Our Own Image: The Sources of American Conduct in World Affairs," *National Interest*, 12/22/1997.)

midget *n.*: **homunculus**. ❖ How irredeemably bad is this latest version of the H. G. Wells novel [*The Island of Dr. Moreau*]? Start with the scene where Marlon Brando wears an ice bucket on his head for no discernible reason. Move on to the blender-size **homunculus** who accompanies him everywhere. (Ty Burr, Best & Worst/Video, *Entertainment Weekly*, 12/26/1997, p. 164.)

    (2) midget (like a . . .) *adj.*, *n.*: **Lilliputian**. See *tiny*

    (3) midget *n.*: **hop-o'-my-thumb**. ❖ *Joseph and the Amazing Technicolour Dreamcoat*—Stephen Gately is [a television personality]. I had only the vaguest idea who this little **hop-o'-my-thumb** was, but . . . I found him quite beguiling. . . . Gately posed in a variety of shiny outfits and gold pants and looked understandably terrified when Mrs. Potiphar, a giantess, flung one of her great gams over his shoulder. (*Independent on Sunday,* Theatre: Opening This Week, 3/16/2003.)

midlife crisis *n.*: **Torschlusspanik** [German]. See *panic*

midpoint (as in middle way) *n.*: **via media** [Latin]. See *middle way*

midway (as in intermediate or transitional state, phase or condition) *adj.*: **liminal.** See *transitional*

midwifery *n.*: **tokology** (or **tocology**). ❖ The catalog's offerings are eclectic, ranging from a 1902 copy of Douglas MacKenzie's *The Ethics of Gambling* to a medical treatise on turn-of-the-century—as in 1900—midwifing by Alice Stockham: *Tokology: A Book for Every Woman.* (O. K. Carter, "Collection of Oddities Awaits Visitors at Book Event," *Fort Worth [TX] Star Telegram*, 10/20/2003.)

might (as in power) *n.*: **puissance.** See *power*

migraine *n.*: **megrims** (pl. of **megrim**). See *headache*

mild (esp. with respect to the wind) *adj.*: **favonian.** ❖ Go! is feeling about as ornery as Donald Rumsfeld as we wait for spring to make a glorious return. After a week of **favonian** breezes, we're having a hard time enduring any air mass under 70 degrees. (Christopher Muther, Go! Wednesday: "Got to Be Real," *Boston Globe*, 4/2/2003.)

mildew (smelling of . . .) *adj.*: **fusty.** See *musty*

mildness *n.*: **mansuetude.** See *gentleness*

milieu (as in setting or physical environment) *n.*: **mise-en-scène** [French; putting on stage]. See *setting*

military (government) *n.*: **stratocracy.** See *government*

(2) military (or, relating to, or suggesting . . . life) *adj.*: **martial.** See *warlike*

milk (giving . . .) *adj.*: **milch** [German]. ❖ He even turned his stylish official colonial residence in New Delhi into the crude dwelling of a prosperous farmer from his home state of Haryana, complete with a string of **milch**

cows. . . . Irrespective of the hour it was mandatory for anyone visiting [him], including journalists, to drink enormous glasses of milk, thick with cream, in an acknowledgement of his hospitality. (Kuldip Singh, obituary of Devi Lal, *Independent* [London], 4/28/2001.)

(2) milk (producing, secreting, or conveying) *adj.*: **lactiferous.** ❖ If you're nursing, examine yourself immediately following a feeding, since it's easier to detect lumps when the breasts are empty. Be aware, though, that clogged **lactiferous** ducts can cause masses that feel suspicious, but are nothing to be alarmed about. (Daryn Eller, Your Health, *Parenting*, 8/1/1998, p. 45.)

millennium *n.*: **chiliad.** ❖ In a sense, the millennium is Bill Clinton's larger theater; for him there is a balm in the **chiliad.** . . . The millennium is a sort of hallucination—the calendar's neverland. . . . For three years after this week's Inauguration, Clinton will play variations on the great-expectations theme inherent (however artificially) in time's odometer, the rolling toward three zeroes. (Lance Morrow, "Will the Crescendo Toward 2000 Help Clinton Beat the Second-Term Jinx?" *Time*, 1/27/1997.)

mimicking (pathological or uncontrollable . . . of another's actions) *n.*: **echopraxia.** See *repeating*

(2) mimicking (pathological, uncontrollable or a child's . . . of another's words) *n.*: **echolalia.** See *repeating*

mimicry (of the real world in art or literature) *n.*: **mimesis** (*adj.*: **mimetic**). See *imitation*

mimimize *v.t.* **minify.** ❖ The patience, the intelligence, of [Condoleezza Rice and Colin Powell] had set [free a U.S. military crew that had been detained in China]. . . . [T]he best the black establishment and the national media could or would toss Dr. Condi and Colin was a collective shrug. A dismissive act, the effect of which was to **minify** the significance of their accomplishment. (John Ridley, "The Manifesto of Ascendancy," *Esquire*, 12/1/2006.)

mincing *adj.*: **niminy-piminy.** See *dainty*

mind (as a blank before receiving outside information) *n.*: **tabula rasa.** See *blank slate*

(2) mind (of, relating to, or understood by the . . .) *adj.*: **noetic**. See *intellect*

(3) mind (taking place entirely within the . . .) *adj.*: **immanent**. See *subjective*

mindfulness (as in attention) *n.*: **advertence**. See *attention*

mindless (repetition of ideas that have been drilled into the speaker or that reflect the opinions of the powers-that-be) *v.t.*, *v.i.*, *n.*: **duckspeak**. See *recite*

miniature *adj.*, *n.*: **Lilliputian**. See *tiny*

(2) miniature *adj.*: **bantam**. See *tiny*

minimize (attempt to . . . seriousness of an offense) *v.t.*: **palliate**. See *downplay*

minion (as in willing tool or servant of another) *n.*: **âme damnée** [French]. See *lackey*

minister (government by a . . . or other clergy members) *n.*: **hierocracy**. See *government*

minor (a fuss over a . . . matter) *n.*: **foofaraw**. See *fuss*

(2) minor (as in excusable fault, offense, or sin) *adj.*: **venial**. See *forgivable*

(3) minor (period when one is a . . .) *n.*: **nonage**. See *youth*

(4) minor *adj.*: **picayune**. See *trivial*

minute (as in, in a . . . , as in very shortly) *n.*: **trice** (as in "in a trice"). See *quickly*

(2) minute (in a . . .) *adv.*: **anon**. See *momentarily*

miracle (worker) *n.*: **thaumaturgist**. ❖ George Malley is a nice, smiling auto mechanic [who], amid mysterious circumstances, is visited with genius. This has the crowd-pleasing aspects of enabling him to make objects move without touching them. . . . This offensive concoction is well acted . . . but it would take a greater **thaumaturgist** than George Malley to make me stomach it. (John Simon, review of *Phenomenon*, *National Review*, 7/29/1996, p. 49.)

miracles (study of . . .) *n.*: **thaumatology**. ❖ Already built is a half-scale replica of the Eiffel Tower [where you can] look out on the skyline of New York City. Yes, that's a replica of the Statue of Liberty. . . . In clear view: pirate ships fighting, multistory lions watching and a pyramid sending a beam which can be seen in outer space. It's enough to prompt you to enroll in a course on **thaumatology**. (Jack Williams, "Forget It, Florida, and Hello, Vegas!" *Boston Herald*, 4/16/1999.)

miraculous (as in involving factors not to be comprehended based on reason alone) *adj.*: **suprarational**. See *incomprehensible*

mirage *n.*: **fata morgana**. [This term derives from a meteorological phenomenon. When there is temperature inversion—cold air lying beneath relatively warmer air—distant objects and features at the horizon appear as spikes, turrets, or towers, objects with great vertical exaggeration rising from the surface. This is known as a fata morgana.] ❖ Consensus texts and convergence documents culminate with references to the church unity for which Christ prayed, "so that the world may believe" (John 17:21). . . . [O]ne is entitled to ask whether the constant references to John 17:21 have not simply become an empty formula. . . . Invoking the "visible unity of the church," in my view, is simply chasing a mirage, a **fata morgana**. (Irmgard Kindt-Siegwalt, "Believing in Unity and Accepting Difference," *Ecumenical Review*, 4/1/1999.)

(2) mirage (esp. something that at first seems a wonderful discovery or development, but that turns to be a . . . or a hoax) *n.*: **mare's nest**. See *hoax*

mirror image *n.*: **enantiomorph**. ❖ The d- and l-tartaric acids are **enantiomorphs;** each molecule is asymmetrical and is the mirror image of the other. (*Columbia Encyclopedia*, Fifth Edition, "Isomer," 1/1/1993.)

mirthful *adj.*: **eupeptic**. See *cheerful*

(2) mirthful *adj.*: **riant**. See *cheerful*

mirthless (as in person who never laughs) *n.*: **agelast**. See *humorless*

misapprehension (spec. the delusion that one possesses superior intelligence) *n.*: **sophomania**. See *delusion*

misappropriate (as in embezzle) *v.t.*, *v.i.*: **peculate**. See *embezzle*

misbehavior (in public office) *n.*: **misprision**. See *wrongdoing*

(2) misbehavior (in public office) *n.*: **malversation**. See *wrongdoing*

(3) misbehavior (because it is prohibited by statute rather than because the conduct is wrong by its own nature or natural law) *n.*: **malum prohibitum**. See *crime*

(4) misbehavior (by its own nature or natural law rather than because prohibited by statute) *n.*: **malum in se** [Latin]. See *wrongdoing*

miscellaneous (composed of a group of . . . items) *adj.*: **farraginous**. See *mixed*

miscellany (as in assortment) *n.*: **farrago**. See *assortment*

(2) miscellany (as in assortment) *n.*: **gallimaufry**. See *assortment*

(3) miscellany (as in assortment) *n.*: **olla podrida** [Spanish]. See *assortment*

(4) miscellany (as in assortment) *n.*: **omnium-gatherum** [Latin]. See *assortment*

(5) miscellany (as in assortment) *n.*: **salmagundi**. See *assortment*

mischief *n.*: **doggery** [doglike behavior]. ❖ [Jerry Springer] is the closest I've ever seen to a male feminist. No matter what he does after the show (it is rumoured he frequently liaises with guests, especially if they are busty strippers), he is a man absolutely intent on depicting men in all their **doggery**. Especially himself. [When] asked if any of the guests were fake, "No," replied Jerry sadly. "They're all real. I'm the fake." (Emma Forrest, "Iconography: So His Show's Sleazy, but He Is a Feminist," *Guardian* [London], 4/6/1998.)

(2) mischief (as in prank) *n.*: **dido**. See *prank*

mischief-maker (as in inciter) *n.*: **stormy petrel**. See *inciter*

(2) mischief-maker (as in scoundrel) *n.*: **scapegrace**. See *scoundrel*

mischievous *adj.*: **elfin**. ❖ [Filmmaker Ken Russell] and Shirley [his first wife] were this sly, mischievous, way off-centre pair; hippy before hippies, maverick before mavericks. They were **elfin**, the two of them, very much a little republic. (Isabel Lloyd, "How We Met: Melvyn Bragg & Ken Russell," *Independent on Sunday*, 1/28/2001.)

(2) mischievous (girl who is high-spirited or boisterous) *n.*: **hoyden**. See *tomboy*

mischievousness (as in devilry) *n.*: **diablerie**. See *devilry*

misconception (accepted as fact due to repetition in print) *n.*: **factoid**. See *inaccuracy*

(2) misconception (as in delusion held by two closely associated persons) *n.*: **folie à deux** [French]. See *delusion*

(3) misconception (as in opinion, belief, or doctrine that is false) *n.*: **pseudodoxy**. See *fallacy*

(4) misconception (in which a false conclusion is drawn from two premises, neither of which conveys information about all members of the designated class) *n.*: **undistributed middle**. See *fallacy*

(5) misconception (spec. logical fallacy where one argues that because event B followed event A, then event A must have caused event B) *n.*: **post hoc, ergo propter hoc** [Latin for "after this, therefore, because of this"]. See *fallacy*

misconduct (confession of . . .) *n.*: **peccavi**. See *confession*

(2) misconduct (in public office) *n.*: **malversation**. See *wrongdoing*

(3) misconduct (in public office) *n.*: **misprision**. See *wrongdoing*

(4) misconduct (because it is prohibited by statute rather than because the conduct is wrong by its own nature or natural law) *n.*: **malum prohibitum**. See *crime*

(5) misconduct (by its own nature or natural law rather than because prohibited by statute) *n.*: **malum in se** [Latin]. See *wrongdoing*

misconstruing (of what you think you heard) *n.*: **mondegreen**. See *misunderstanding*

miser *n.*: **lickpenny**. ❖ In our politically correct, "caring is sharing" times, it takes bravery to be a cheapskate. These daring souls care not about "suggested donation" prices, aren't deterred by indignant looks, and completely ignore righteous huffing. So, you remorse-free **lickpennies**, test drive your miserly ways at these places. (Melanie McFarland, "Hey,

Cheapskate, Not Even a Donation?" *Seattle Times*, 6/3/1999.)

miserable (esp. as to poverty) *adj.*: **abject**. See *wretched*

miserly (as in stingy) *adj.*: **cheeseparing**. See *stingy*

(2) miserly *adj.*: **costive**. See *stingy*

(3) miserly *adj.*: **mingy**. See *stingy*

(4) miserly *adj.*: **niggardly**. See *stingy*

(5) miserly *adj.*: **penurious**. See *stingy*

misery (as in inability to experience pleasure or happiness) *n.*: **anhedonia**. See *unhappiness*

(2) misery (as in occasion or place of great suffering) *n.*: **Gethsemane**. See *hell*

(3) misery (as in occasion or place of great suffering) *n.*: **Golgotha**. See *hell*

(4) misery (as in place or occasion of great suffering, or hell) *n.*: **Gehenna**. See *hell*

(5) misery (as in place, condition, or society filled with . . . ; spec., opposite of utopia) *n.*: **dystopia**. See *hell*

(6) misery (experience of intense . . . , as in suffering) *n.*: **Calvary**. See *suffering*

(7) misery (out of the depths of . . . or despair) *n., adv.*: **de profundis**. See *despair*

misfortune (esp. involving an awkward or embarrassing situation) *n.*: **contretemps**. See *mishap*

(2) misfortune *n., adj.*: **hoodoo**. See *bad luck*

mishap (esp. involving an awkward or embarrassing situation) *n.*: **contretemps**. ❖ Another diplomatic **contretemps** flared up when U.S. troops briefly invaded the residence of Nicaragua's Ambassador to Panama Antenor Ferrey, apparently to search for a cache of weapons. They turned up five rifles, which were later returned with an apology. (George J. Church, Panama: "No Place to Run; With Noriega Cornered but Not Caught, Was the Pain of Invasion Worth the Gain?" *Time*, 1/8/1990, p. 38.)

mishearing (of what you think you heard) *n.*: **mondegreen**. See *misunderstanding*

mishmash (as in assortment) *n.*: **farrago**. See *assortment*

(2) mishmash (as in assortment) *n.*: **gallimaufry**. See *assortment*

(3) mishmash (as in assortment) *n.*: **olla podrida** [Spanish]. See *assortment*

(4) mishmash (as in assortment) *n.*: **omnium-gatherum** [Latin]. See *assortment*

(5) mishmash (as in assortment) *n.*: **salmagundi**. See *assortment*

(6) mishmash (as in assortment) *n.*: **welter**. See *jumble*

misinterpretation (of what you think you heard) *n.*: **mondegreen**. See *misunderstanding*

mislead (as in bluff) *v.t.*: **four-flush** (*n.*: **four-flusher**). See *bluff*

(2) mislead (as in deceive or defraud in the process) *v.t., v.i.*: **cozen**. See *defraud*

(3) mislead (as in deceive) *v.t.*: **humbug**. See *deceive*

(4) mislead (as in lie) *v.t.*: **prevaricate**. See *lie*

(5) mislead (spec. an intentional omission of something, so as to . . .) *n.*: **elision**. See *omission*

(6) mislead (specious reasoning intended to . . . or rationalize) *n.*: **casuistry**. See *fallacious*

(7) mislead (as in deceive) *v.t.*: **gull**. See *deceive*

misleading (actions, spec. by trying to represent something as being other than it is) *n.*: **false colors**. See *misrepresentations*

(2) misleading (appearance of plenty when in fact there is little) *adj.*: **Barmecidal** (esp. as in "Barmecidal feast"). See *illusion*

(3) misleading (speech or writing that is . . . , as in evasive) *n.*: **circumlocution**. See *evasiveness*

(4) misleading (story, report, or rumor, often deliberately) *n.*: **canard**. See *hoax*

misremember (as in confusion of one's memory with actual fact) *n.*: **paramnesia**. ❖ What causes déjà vu? Sixteen centuries ago Saint Augustine called this phenomenon false memory. It has also been called **paramnesia**, double perception, and false recognition. Charles Dickens's character David Copperfield called it "the strange feeling to which no one is quite a stranger." (Kaylan Pickford, "I Lost My Daughters to a Cult," *Redbook*, 3/1/1995, p. 54.)

misrepresent (as in bluff) *v.t.*: **four-flush** (*n.*: **four-flusher**). See *bluff*

(2) misrepresent (as in exaggerate) *v.t.*: **overegg**. See *exaggerate*

(3) misrepresent (as in exaggerate) *v.t.*: **aggrandize**. See *exaggerate*

misrepresentation (deliberate . . . or conceal-ment of facts to gain an advantage) *n.*: **subrep-tion**. ❖ [In *Farewell the Peaceful Kingdom: The Seduction and Rape of Canada*, author Joe C. W. Armstrong states:] "Most of our prime min-isters have been elected by **subreption**—they gain the job by concealing their true ambitions. . . . The citizens continue to be de-democratized by an entrenched autocracy. . . . Regardless of which party is in power, change however lim-ited is out of the question." (Barry Eastwood, "Analyzing 30 Years of National Destruction," Alberta Report/Western Report, 8/14/1995.)

(2) misrepresentation (spec. the act of engaging in deception under a false name or identity) *n.*: **imposture**. See *hoax*

misrepresentations (which are intended to deceive, spec. by trying to represent some-thing as being other than it is) *n.*: **false colors** (esp. as in "flying under false colors" or "sail-ing under false colors"). [The colors of a ship's flag identifies it. When a ship sails under false colors, it is trying to deceive an enemy as to its true nature.] ❖ Sometime next month, the new Bush economic team will propose another tax cut, probably labeled a "stimulus package." It will be sailing under **false colors**, says Rich-ard Kogan, an economist. [The tax cuts] won't give much of a boost to the sluggish economy in 2003, he says. Rather, the tax package will aim its benefits primarily at corporations and stockholders, Mr. Kogan says. (David R. Fran-cis, "Assessing the Form, Impact, of Loom-ing Tax Package," *Christian Science Monitor*, 12/16/2002.)

missing person *n.*: **Judge Crater**. [Joseph Cra-ter was a judge in New York City who suddenly disappeared on the night of August 6, 1930. He was never seen again and his case became national news and earned him the title of "The Missingest Man in New York." Today, his name is used to refer generally to a missing person, as in the example given. This would also be an example of a "metonymy," which is a figure of speech where the name of a person or thing is used for that with which it is associated. See *fig-ure of speech*.] ❖ It would seem Rep. Gus Sav-age reads the papers about as often as he shows up on the floor of Congress—probably even less. In the wake of recent reports that he made unwanted sexual overtures to a female Peace Corps worker during a trip to Zaire, the **Judge Crater** of Congress lashed out at reporters who wanted to ask him about the charges, "You don't ask white congressmen questions like that." (Ruth Daniel, "Savage's Short Memory," *Chicago Sun-Times*, 7/22/1989.)

mission (to achieve a particular goal or desire) *n.*: **nisus**. See *goal*

(2) mission (which is fruitless or hopeless) *n.*: **fool's errand**. See *hopeless*

misspeak (as in a transposition of letters or sounds, which creates a comic effect, usually unintentionally) *n.*: **spoonerism**. See *blooper*

misspeaking (spec. a grammatical error in speaking or writing because of trying too hard to be grammatically correct) *n.*: **hypercorrec-tion**. See *error*

misspelling (use of . . . to represent either an uneducated speaker or dialectical or collo-quial speech, such as "sez" for "says") *n.*: **eye dialect**. ❖ "Gotcha is not slang," insists Jesse Sheidlower, a senior editor in the reference division of Random House and a slang special-ist. "The **eye-dialect** spelling suggests infor-mality, but it's actually standard usage, and wouldn't be entered in any of the slang the-sauri." (So how come, Jesse, you can find it in the *Random House Historical Dictionary of American Slang*? Gotcha!) (William Safire, On Language: "Gotcha, Hobbes," *New York Times*, 4/13/1997.)

mist *n.*: **brume**. See *fog*

mistake (in grammar) *n.*: **solecism**. See *misuse*

(2) mistake (in speech) *n.*: **lapsus linguae** [Latin]. See *slip of the tongue*

(3) mistake (in writing) *n.*: **lapsus calami** [Latin]. See *slip of the pen*

(4) mistake (small or trifling . . .) *n.*: **peccadillo**. See *infraction*

(5) mistake (tragic . . . , as in flaw, esp. by a literary character) *n.*: **hamartia**. See *flaw*

(6) mistake (verbal . . . such as a slip of the tongue or malapropism) *n.*: **parapraxis**. See *blunder*

(7) mistake (with regard to the location of an event or thing) *n.*: **anachorism**. See *error*

(8) mistake (grammatical . . . in speaking or writing because of trying too hard to be grammatically correct) *n.*: **hypercorrection**. See *error*

mistranslation (of what you think you heard) *n.*: **mondegreen**. See *misunderstanding*

mistress *n.*: **fancy woman**. [An alternate definition for this term is prostitute. See *prostitute*.] ❖ Margaret's husband, Gavin, said it was like having a new wife when her bust went from 60 inches to 34, her waist from 54 inches to 27 and her hips from 64 inches to 36. She laughs: "Friends thought Gavin had a slim **fancy woman**. It was amazing the number of people who didn't recognise me. (Lorna Frame, "Weight to Go! Winning Losers," *Daily Mirror* [Glasgow], 1/21/1997.)

mistrust (person who has . . . of humankind) *n.*: **misanthrope**. ❖ Lofton and Nelson agree with Mancini that mistrust is a fundamental part of [baseball player Albert] Belle's personality. It wasn't always. Growing up in a middle-class section of Shreveport, Belle gave no signs of becoming the public **misanthrope** he is today. (Michael Bamberger, Baseball: "He Thrives on Anger," *Sports Illustrated*, 5/6/1996, p. 72.)

misty (and dark and gloomy) *adj.*: **caliginous**. See *dark*

misunderstanding (of what you think you heard) *n.*: **mondegreen.** [The term derives from Sylvia Wright, who as a child heard the Scottish ballad "The Bonny Earl of Murray" and believed that one stanza went: "Ye Highlands and Ye Lowlands, / Oh where hae you been? /

They hae slay the Earl of Murray, / And Lady Mondegreen." The last line is actually "And laid him on the green." Wright thought that Lady Mondegreen had been killed. as well.] ❖ It's easy to commit a **mondegreen**. You hear Glen Campbell sing, "Rhinestone Cowboy" and you think he's saying "Limestone Cowboy." . . . Or you think the song "Guantanamera" is about a "One Ton Tomato." . . . [Or that Paul Simon is singing:] "When I think back on all the crafts [as opposed to crap] I learned in high school." (David Chartrand, "Vote for Me if You Want Red Cologne!" *Kansas City Star*, 1/25/2004.)

(2) misunderstanding *n.*: **malentendu** [French]. ❖ [In the movie *Eurotrip*, Scotty] and his friend Cooper . . . head to Germany because of an amusing **malentendu**. It seems that Scotty has been e-mailing a German pen pal for years in the belief the pal was a boy named Mike. It turns out that it is someone named Mieke, which is (get this) a German girl's name! (Jay Stone, "Stupid, Vulgar and Proud of It: This Teen Sex Comedy Glories in Bad Taste, Cultural Bigotry and, of Course, Gratuitous Nudity," *Ottawa Citizen*, 2/20/2004.)

misuse (of word or phrase in grammar) *n.*: **solecism**. ❖ "If we pass this all-encompassing tax reform bill," he says, "it will be the hallmark of my career." He probably means to say capstone. **Solecisms** and malapropisms are a hallmark of Rostenkowski's 28 years in Congress. (Montgomery Brower, "Illinois Rep. Dan Rostenkowski Cut the Deals in Congress That May Cut Your Taxes," *People*, 9/1/1986, p. 38.)

(2) misuse (or strained use of words or phrases, sometimes deliberate) *n.*: **catachresis**. ❖ Cat scan: They call their party The Furball. And leading the band is a lady called Lily Wilde. This might lure a lesser columnist into wordplay, but—not willing to risk an outbreak of **catachresis**—I'm just going to say that the Feral Cat Coalition of Oregon will be feline groovy June 4 at the World Forestry Center. (Jonathan Nicholas, "Californians, Catastrophes and the Most Musselcular Man in Portland," *Oregonian*, 5/10/1999.)

(3) misuse (as in embezzle) *v.i.*: **defalcate**. See *embezzle*

(4) misuse (as in embezzle) *v.t., v.i.*: **peculate**. See *embezzle*

(5) misuse (of words or of language) *n.*: **verbicide**. See *distortion*

mites (study of . . . and ticks) *n.*: **acarology**. See *ticks*

mix (as in blend) *v.t., v.i.*: **inosculate**. See *blend*

(2) mix (as in bring together) *v.t.*: **conflate**. See *combine*

(3) mix *v.t.*: **amalgamate**. See *combine*

mixed (composed of a . . . group of items) *adj.*: **farraginous**. ❖ [The] linguine alla grana (whole wheat pasta) was a disaster, a **farraginous** mound with bits of filet mignon and mushrooms in a fatty brown sauce. (M. H. Reed, Dining Out: "Where the Appetizers Take Center Stage," *New York Times*, 11/5/1995.)

(2) mixed (as in interwoven) *v.t.* **interleaved**. See *interwoven*

(3) mixed (of things that cannot be . . .) *adj.*: **immiscible**. See *incompatible*

mixed-up (esp. used of a person, as in . . . and stupid) *adj.*: **addlepated**. See *confused*

mixture (esp. involving dissimilar elements) *n.*: **admixture**. ❖ The keys to certain attributes of [George W. Bush's] character—his irreverence, his disdain for "arrogant liberal intellectuals," his complex **admixture** of superficiality and self-discipline—lie half-hidden in Bush's formative years, in his schooling and especially in his loving but demanding relationship with his parents. (Evan Thomas, "A Son's Restless Journey," *Newsweek*, 8/7/2000, p. 32.)

(2) mixture (of fruits or vegetables) *n.*: **macédoine** [French]. ❖ At Chef Allen's in North Miami Beach, Allen Susser's most popular dishes include rock shrimp hash topped by a mustardy sabayon sauce, followed perhaps by seared citrus-crusted yellow-fin tuna with a **macédoine** of papaya, mango and yellow pepper. (Cathy Booth, "Food: A Taste of Miami's New Vice," *Time*, 8/19/1991, p. 60.)

(3) mixture (of two or more languages) *adj.*: **macaronic**. See *languages*

(4) mixture *n.*: **gallimaufry**. See *assortment*

(5) mixture *n.*: **olla podrida** [Spanish]. See *assortment*

(6) mixture *n.*: **omnium-gatherum** [Latin]. See *assortment*

(7) mixture (as in assortment) *n.*: **farrago**. See *assortment*

(8) mixture (as in assortment) *n.*: **salmagundi**. See *assortment*

mob (government by the . . .) *n.*: **mobocracy**. See *government*

(2) mob (government by the . . .) *n.*: **ochlocracy**. See *government*

(3) mob (the . . . , as in the masses) *n.*: **vulgus** [Latin]. See *masses*

mock (esp. through the use of satire) *v.t.*: **pasquinade**. See *satirize*

mockery (as in insult, which is clever or polite) *n.*: **asteism**. See *insult*

model (as in that which set the standard or established the foundation from which others followed or on which others are based) *n.*: **locus classicus**. [Latin. This term literally means "classical passage," but it is used in the broader sense given here.] ❖ The [media has] taken notice of apocalypticism as a trend within pop culture [evidenced by movies such as *End of Days* and *Reign of Fire*]. The **locus classicus** for this sort of thing is the early 1980s *Mad Max* series . . . , except that the apocalypticism of those movies lacked the lunatic religiosity implicit or explicit in the current wave of end-of-the-world narratives. (Christopher Sharrett, "Past Classics, Summer Rubbish," *USA Today Magazine*, 9/1/2002.)

(2) model (of an intended larger work, such as a building) *n.*: **maquette**. ❖ Before Graham started on [his 24-foot bronze sculpture called *Monument to Joe Louis*], he submitted a **maquette**, a two-foot-high model of the larger work, for approval. (Donald J. Barr, From the Publisher, *Sports Illustrated*, 10/27/1986, p. 4.)

(3) model (original . . . or example) *n.*: **archetype**. ❖ Slow and stagy, the [1993 remake of the movie *Frankenstein*] also suffers the fate that greets singers interpreting Beatles tunes: The original version with Boris Karloff is such an indelible **archetype** that any imitation is doomed. (David Hiltbrand, Picks & Pans: Tube, *People*, 6/14/1993, p. 13.)

(4) model (as in example) *n.*: **exemplum**. See *example*

(5) model (spec. the perfect or beautiful example of something) *n.*: **beau ideal**. See *ideal*

moderate (as in not indulgent) *adj.*: **abstemious**. See *restrained*

moderation (in all things) *n.*: **sophrosyne** [Greek]. ❖ [In Joseph Conrad's novel *Lord Jim*,] Jim's scale of human values is excessively romantic. . . . The fact is that he is too "noble" to accommodate real-life situations. . . . [H]is lofty conception of what is required of him in responsible leadership and duty, his high idealism, mar the supreme [Greek] virtue of **sophrosyne**. Jim's conduct dramatizes to an "unsafe" degree the extremes of arrogance, and of self-delusion and self-assertion. (George A. Panichas, "The Moral Sense in Joseph Conrad's Lord Jim," *Humanitas*, 3/22/2000.)

(2) moderation (appropriate . . . , as in happy medium) *n.*: **juste milieu** [French]. See *happy medium*

modern (as in of recent origin) *adj.*: **neoteric**. See *recent*

modernization (of an organization to meet contemporary conditions, esp. as proposed by Pope John XXIII with respect to the Catholic church after Vatican II) *n.*: **aggiornamento** [Italian]. See *updating*

modesty *n.*: **pudency**. ❖ "The most important thing is the ship, and the ship needed someone at the helm who knew better about the operational aspects of getting a business to grow than me," says Fields with typical **pudency**. (Melanie Warner, "A Singular Visionary: After Bumping Heads with One of the Software Industry's Bad Boys, Michael Fields Explored His Options—$1 Million of Them—and Scored," *Fortune*, 8/4/1997, p. 59.)

modification (esp. a scholarly critical . . . , as in revision) *n.*: **recension**. See *revision*

moisten (flax to separate fibers) *v.t.*: **ret**. ❖ Water **retting**, primarily used by the Belgians and Irish, **rets** the fibers by leaving them in running water and produces a classic, pale-yellow linen. (Tracy A. Keegan, "Flaxen Fantasy: The History of Linen," *Colonial Homes*, 8/1/1996, p. 62.)

moistener *n., adj.*: **humectant**. ❖ Tropical Fruit Masque/Smooths wrinkles, refreshes your skin. . . . Each [piece of fruit] contains a natural enzyme (bromelain in pineapple and papain in papaya) that sloughs off dead skin cells. When combined with honey, a natural **humectant** that hydrates your skin, the result is a soft, luminescent complexion. (Paula Hunt, "Look Younger Naturally!" *Prevention*, 6/1/1999, p. 128.)

mold (of body part often used in criminal investigation or disaster relief) *n.*: **moulage**. ❖ In some cases a husband would punish his wife for even suspected infidelities by slicing off her nose. . . . [My father was a plastic surgeon who cared for these victims.] Sometimes, using clay, he molded a nose directly on a woman's face, to see what shape might look good on her, or he made a mold of her face. Once, he tried a plastic **moulage** on my brother before applying it to a patient. (Mary Blocksma, "My Father and Other Good Guys: Plastic Surgeons Abroad [Practice in Third World Countries]," *Saturday Evening Post*, 3/1/1986.)

molded (capable of being . . . , such as with plastic, clay, or earth) *adj.*: **fictile**. ❖ Qahtan Al Amin's work is another creative approach towards artistic expression. He has used **fictile** material to form dimensional shapes where he carved various drawings and symbols as a manifestation of the pastoral life in Iraq. (Rasheed Al Roussan, "'Mercury 20'—The Quest for Identity," *Star* [Jordan], 3/4/1999.)

moldy (as in musty) *adj.*: **fusty**. See *musty*

mollify (as in placate) *v.t.*: **propitiate**. See *placate*

(2) mollify *v.t.*: **dulcify**. See *appease*

mollifying (as in peacemaking) *adj.*: **irenic**. See *peacemaking*

moment (as in, in a . . . , as in very shortly) *n.*: **trice** (as in "in a trice"). See *quickly*

momentarily *adv.*: **anon**. ❖ Most campuses are awash with talk about things racial (and sexual, and other categories indispensable for the practice of identity politics, more about which **anon**). (George F. Will, "Focus on Race Distracts Nation from Real Problem," *Minneapolis Star Tribune*, 6/20/1997.)

momentary *adj.*: **fugacious**. See *fleeting*

momentous (of an event or period that is . . .) *adj.*: **epochal**. ❖ Is the hunger for *Star Wars* so insatiable that the audience won't notice that this **epochal** event [*Star Wars: Episode I, The Phantom Menace*] is actually a little . . . dull? (David Ansen, "*Star Wars*: The Phantom Movie," *Newsweek*, 5/17/1999, p. 56.)

monarch (or emperor or sultan or shah or the like; also used to refer to a powerful or important person generally) *n.*: **padishah**. See *emperor*

(2) monarch (who holds great power or sway) *n.*: **potentate**. See *ruler*

monetary (of or relating to . . . gain) *adj.*: **chrematistic**. ❖ Work is still seen as productive transformation of nature, but with the conceptual divorce of production and consumption, all work is seen as **chrematistic** accumulation. (John Dupre, "A Brief History of Work," *Journal of Economic Issues*, 6/1/1996, p. 553.)

(2) monetary *adj.*: **pecuniary**. ❖ Obits. Write your own! Tony O'Brien did: . . . Preceded in death by most of the people who have ever lived. Known far and wide as a charitable man, Mr. O'Brien made his **pecuniary** contributions mainly to obscure organizations such as the IRS, of Washington, D.C., and Guido's Sports Parlor, located in the Graft Exchange Building in northeast Minneapolis. (James Lileks, "Change Isn't in the Wind—It's in the Pants/Those Coins Jingling in Men's Pockets Are All Part of a Long, Silly Tradition," *Minneapolis Star Tribune*, 9/28/1997.)

money (as in wealth) *n.*: **pelf**. See *wealth*

(2) money (devotion to the pursuit of . . .) *n.*: **mammonism**. See *wealth*

(3) money (source of . . .) *n.*: **Golconda**. See *wealth*

(4) money (worship of or devotion to . . .) *n.*: **plutolatry**. See *wealth*

moneylender (who charges high interest) *n.*: **shylock**. See *lender*

monk (who travels from one place to another) *n.*: **gyrovague**. ❖ He praises those [monks] who live in a community within a web of relationships and responsibilities, and he admires those who have become so advanced in their religious practice that they have withdrawn from society to be with God [but] he castigates the "**gyrovagues**," because they do nothing but wander from place to place, looking everywhere for new spiritual "experiences." (Robert Neralich, "Theme of Benedict's Way: Humans Hear God If They Listen Closely," *Arkansas Democrat-Gazette*, 5/20/2000.)

monk (person who lives as if a . . . , esp. for spiritual improvement) *n., adj.*: **ascetic**. See *austerity*

monkey (move by swinging with arms, like a . . .) *v.i.*: **brachiate**. See *swing*

(2) monkey (of, relating to, or resembling) *adj.*: **simian**. See *ape*

monologue (as in lengthy speech) *n.*: **peroration**. ❖ The monologues went on and on, taking on a form, or formlessness, of their own, sometimes almost crowding out the music. On the last night he delivered what amounted to a kind of extended **peroration**, with Priscilla and Lisa Marie sitting with Sheila in the booth. (Peter Guralnick, *Careless Love: The Unmaking of Elvis Presley*, Little, Brown [1999], p. 541.)

monotonous (as in uninteresting or dull) *adj.*: **jejune**. See *uninteresting*

(2) monotonous (speaker or writer, as in one who is dull and boring) *n.*: **dryasdust**. See *boring*

monster (as in freak of nature) *n.*: **lusus naturae** [Latin]. See *freak*

monument (honoring a dead person buried elsewhere) *n.*: **cenotaph**. ❖ Congressional Cemetery also features great diversity in stone styles. Its name, incidentally, comes from the **cenotaphs**, sandstone monuments erected to memorialize senators and members of Congress buried elsewhere. (Lisa Rauschart, "Now the Memorials Are in Neighborhoods," *Washington Times*, 5/25/2001.)

mooch (or sponge off of) *v.t.*: **cadge**. ❖ None of the adulation, though, quieted a deep insecurity that Nicholas Gage, author of *Greek Fire*, a new biography of Callas and Onassis, says began with an unstable mother who alternately criticized Callas and **cadged** money from her. A fed-up Callas finally told her mother to get a job or, failing that, "jump out of the window or drown yourself," *Time* once reported. (Christina Cheakalos, "Auction: Diva's Delight," *People*, 12/4/2000, p. 131.)

moocher *n.*: **schnorrer** [Yiddish; slang]. ❖ For the fourth year in a row, your intrepid reporter has slogged her way down to Miami Beach to attend the sizzling Art Basel Festival. . . . At the opening "press conference," dozens of media poseurs and perennial **schnorrers** sucked up the free champagne, Perrier and fried artichokes. (Laura Washington, "Sadly, Diversity Isn't the State of the Arts," *Chicago Sun-Times*, 12/5/2005.)

mood (normal . . .) *n.*: **euthymia**. Among women [with bipolar disorder] who choose to continue a mood stabilizer during pregnancy to minimize the risk of recurrence, lithium appears to be the safest option. . . . "The goal is to maintain **euthymia** by reintroducing the mood stabilizer early," [said Dr. Adele Viguera, M.D.]. (Diana Mahoney, "Navigating Tx of Bipolar Disorder in Pregnancy," *Ob Gyn News*, 11/1/2005.)

(2) mood (of an era) *n.*: **zeitgeist**. See *spirit*

moody (as in sullen or morose) *adj.*: **saturnine**. See *sullen*

(2) moody (or grumpy mood) *n.pl.*: **mulligrubs**. See *grumpiness*

mope (as in pout) *n.*: **moue** [French]. See *pout*

(2) mope *v.t.*: **mump** [British]. See *sulk*

moral (intellectual and/or cultural spirit of an era) *n.*: **zeitgeist**. See *spirit*

moralistic (and self-righteous) *adj.*: **pharisaical**. See *self-righteous*

(2) moralistic (hypocritically . . .) *adj.*: **Pecksniffian**. See *self-righteous*

(3) moralistic (persons who are . . . and critical of others) *n.pl.*: **unco guid** (preceded by "the"). See *self-righteous*

morality (as in integrity) *n.*: **probity**. See *integrity*

(2) morality (of questionable . . .) *adj.*: **louche**. See *questionable*

moralizing (given to . . . , by using aphorisms and maxims) *adj.*: **sententious**. See *aphoristic*

morals (deciding right and wrong by applying . . .) *n.*: **casuistry**. See *ethics*

(2) morals (study of) *n.*: **deontology**. See *ethics*

moreover *adv.*: **withal**. ❖ [Joe DiMaggio] excelled and continued to excel, against injury and age, against the mounting "natural" odds. He exceeded, **withal**, the cruelest expectations: He was expected to lead and to win—and he did. (Richard Ben Cramer, "The DiMaggio Nobody Knew," *Newsweek*, 3/22/1999, p. 52.)

morning (of or relating to . . .) *adj.*: **matinal**. ❖ [As a gesture of goodwill, I decided to deliver Krispy Kreme doughnuts to protesters in Lafayette Square.] The person I found protesting in Lafayette Square shortly after daybreak was a relatively handsome bearded man. . . . "How do you feel about some Krispy Kremes this morning?" I asked. . . . The beneficiary of my **matinal** munificence now identified himself as Troy. (Joe Queenan, *My Goodness*, Hyperion [2000], p. 108.)

(2) morning (of or relating to . . .) *adj.*: **matutinal**. ❖ Margaret Roythorne's **matutinal** stroll through her local park in Hastings turned to nightmare when her tiny Cairn terrier Flynn dashed out from some bushes and was sucked up and killed by a mobile "pooperscooper." (Paul Sieveking, "It Was a Very Bad Year. . . ," *Independent* [London], 12/31/1994.)

moron (as in one mentally deficient from birth) *n.*: **ament**. [Note: The writer of the example uses an adjectival version of the word ("amentic") that does not appear in dictionaries (and in fact was unnecessary for the writer's purpose anyway), although the meaning is clear. However, the adjectival form of "moron" and its synonyms "imbecile" and "idiot" do end in "ic."] ❖ In Ottawa, Canada, a close aide of Prime Minister Jean Chretien, Françoise Ducros, paid dearly for her . . . abusiveness: her job. When President Bush called on member states to increase defense spending at the NATO summit in Prague, Françoise muttered within earshot of reporters: "What a moron." [She] should have said . . . "**amentic**" instead. (*Manila Bulletin*, "Casualties in the War on Terror," 12/16/2002.)

(2) moron *n*.: **jobbernowl** [British]. See *idiot*

(3) moron *n*.: **mooncalf**. See *fool*

moronic (as in foolish) *adj*.: **barmy** [British]. See *foolish*

(2) moronic (as in foolish) *adj*.: **balmy**. See *foolish*

(3) moronic (lit. brainless) *adj*.: **excerebrose**. See *brainless*

morose (and/or shy and/or socially withdrawn or inexperienced) *adj*.: **farouche** [French]. See *shy*

(2) morose (as in person who never laughs) *n*.: **agelast**. See *humorless*

(3) morose *adj*.: **saturnine**. See *sullen*

mortality (reminder[s] of our . . .) *n., sing. and pl*.: **memento mori** [Latin]. ❖ [T]he show [of Paul Cézanne's work] includes dozens of lesser-known works in less familiar genres: portraits, interiors, tableaux of card players, and perhaps most unexpected, several paintings of skulls, **memento mori** that he composed in the decade preceding his own death, in 1906. (Jim Lewis, "Cézanne," *Harper's Bazaar*, 3/1/1996, p. 334.)

mother (biological . . .) *n*.: **genetrix** (*pl*. **genetrices**). ❖ [In the book] *I've Always Meant to Tell You: Letters to Our Mothers—An Anthology of Contemporary Women Writers* . . . writers from Joyce Carol Oates to Judith Ortiz Cofer to Rita Dove gather here to address their **genetrices**—the living and the dead—as well as to be pictured with them in touching por-

traits and telling little biographies. (*Washington Post*, Hardcovers in Brief, 5/11/1997.)

(2) mother (legally and/or socially recognized . . . , as opposed to biological) *n*.: **mater** [Latin]. ❖ Features generally associated with patriarchy include . . . sociological paternity: pater and **mater** as socially recognized parents as opposed to genitor and genetrix as physiological parents—cf. the father adopting of children as his own; primogeniture of males; inheritance limited to or dominated by males; cult dominated by males. (John H. Elliott, "Jesus Was Not an Egalitarian," *Biblical Theology Bulletin*, 6/22/2002.)

(3) mother (phenomenon of a . . . who is overprotective and controlling of her sons, thus hindering their maturation and emotional development) *n*.: **momism**. ❖ [This word was coined by Philip Wylie in his 1942 novel *Generation of Vipers*. He felt that these mothers destroyed their sons' masculinity, which in turn threatened America's security during World War II. Today, the term is sometimes extended to domineering mothers generally.] In the original [version of *The Manchurian Candidate*], Shaw's overbearing mother (Angela Lansbury), who is also his hypnotic controller, stands for **momism** [the concept of] American sons being unmanned by their controlling, seductive mothers—a menace that Lansbury positively nailed. (Cliff Doerksen, "The Right Kind of Remake," *Chicago Reader*, 8/4/2004.)

(4) mother (attitude or policy that encourages becoming a . . .) *n*.: **pronatalism**. See *childbearing*

(5) mother (biological . . . or father) *n*.: **genitor**. See *parent*

(6) mother (of or derived from name of . . . or maternal ancestor) *adj*.: **matronymic**. See *maternal*

(7) mother (who is head of a household) *n*.: **mater familias** [Latin]. See *head of household*

motion (of, relating to, or produced by) *adj*.: **kinetic**. ❖ The **kinetic** art movement . . . began around 1914—when artists felt the urge to incorporate the illusion, and ultimately the reality, of motion into their work. (*Economist*, "The Biology of Art," 4/3/1999.)

motionless (as in not moving or temporarily inactive) *adj.*: **quiescent**. See *inactive*

(2) motionless *adj.*: **torpid**. See *lethargic*

motivation (mental process marked by . . . to do something) *n.*: **conation**. See *determination*

motive (hidden or ulterior . . .) *n.*: **arriere-pensee** (or **arrière-pensée**). [French. This derives from the French for "behind" (or "back") plus "thought." It is sometimes used in the sense of having mental reservations about something and sometimes in the sense of having a hidden or ulterior motive, as in the example given here.] ❖ The vast majority of French men and women, including the less viscerally anti-American, supported President Jacques Chirac's opposition to the Iraq war. But so did [the Tour de France favorite, American Lance] Armstrong. . . . "I'm no fan of war," he said. . . . It would be unkind to suspect any **arriere-pensee**—but he might have had an inkling that his fifth appearance on the winner's podium would be sticky enough this year without any Stars-and-Stripes triumphalism. (Geoffrey Wheatcroft, "Lance Armstrong: The Texan Rider's Four Consecutive Victories Against All Odds in the Tour De France: He Still Has to Capture the Hearts of the French," *Financial Times* [London], 7/26/2003.)

mottled *adj.*: **dappled**. See *spotted*

motto (at the start of a literary piece setting forth a theme or message) *n.*: **epigraph**. See *quotation*

(2) motto (pithy . . .) *n.*: **gnome** (*adj.*: **gnomic**). See *catchphrase*

(3) motto *n.*: **shibboleth**. See *catchword*

mound *n.*: **cumulus**. See *heap*

mountain (as in heap or pile) *n.*: **cumulus**. See *heap*

mournful (often regarding something gone) *adj.*: **elegiac**. See *sorrowful*

(2) mournful (sounds) *adj.*: **plangent**. ❖ Her songs catalog every sin a man can commit, every pain a woman can bear. If you turn on the radio and hear a strong heart breaking, chances are it's the one in that **plangent** [Patty] Loveless voice. (Richard Corliss, "She Can Handle the Truth: In Her Gorgeous, Pulverizing New Album, Country Torch Artist Patty Loveless Sings About the Aftershock of Betrayal," *Time*, 3/11/1996, p. 71.)

(3) mournful *adj.*: **tristful**. See *sad*

mournfulness *n.*: **dolor** (*adj.*: **dolorous**). See *sadness*

mourning (poem or song of . . . esp. for a dead person) *n.*: **threnody**. See *requiem*

mouth (or jaws or stomach of a carniverous animal) *n.*: **maw**. ❖ All in a day's work for the most famous alligator wrestler in America. Kenny Cypress likes being famous, even if it came at the expense of half his head of hair, a trip to the hospital, a fractured jaw and 30 unpleasant seconds with his head stuck in the **maw** of one of the creatures he regularly plays with. (Mike Williams, "Crazy About Gators: Wrestlemania," *Atlanta Journal-Constitution*, 3/22/1998.)

mouthpiece (spec. a character in a book, play, or movie who appears to act as a . . . for the opinions of the author) *n.*: **raisonneur** [French].❖ [Tre] thrives under the guidance of Furious, who in one disturbing scene lectures him on the need to avoid the gunfights among black "brothers" that the whites, he says, encourage in order to decimate the black population. This is the only overtly white-hating speech, but as it is delivered by Furious, the film's **raisonneur**, one suspects that it issues from the filmmaker's mouth as well. (John Simon, review of *Boyz N the Hood*, *National Review*, 9/23/1991.)

move (able to . . . freely in a given environment; used of species) *adj.*: **vagile**. ❖ [Two experts] propose that most families of birds common to the two continents arrived in South America by long-distance dispersal. According to [two other experts], less **vagile** mammals, such as primates and caviomorph rodents, likewise arrived considerably after the separation, in these cases via island hopping. (Robert

A. Voeks, "Biological Relationships Between Africa and South America," *Geographical Review*, 1/1/1995, p. 115.)

(2) move (as in course of action) *n.*: **démarche** [French]. See *course of action*

(3) move (heavily or clumsily) *v.i.*: **galumph**. See *tromp*

(4) move (swiftly and easily, used esp. of clouds) *v.i.*: **scud**. ❖ It was windy. Thunderclouds **scudded** by overhead, and hawks swooped and circled. (Ellen Ficklen, "An Unexpected Kind of Family Foresight," *Newsweek*, 3/25/2002.)

movement (for an idea or principle) *n.*: **jihad**. See *crusade*

(2) movement (of, relating to, or produced by) *adj.*: **kinetic**. See *motion*

movie (lover) *n.*: **cineaste**. ❖ Quinlan's updated guide to the stars is a treasure chest for anyone who loves movies—the experienced viewer and the budding **cineaste** alike. (Dan Kincaid, "Starring Lineup: 'Ultimate' Bios for Movie Lovers," *Arizona Republic*, 1/21/2001.)

(2) movie (lover) *n.*: **cinephile**. ❖ A quiet **cinephile** meets a smart-mouthed party girl in a genial comic valentine from Ireland. . . . The introverted hero of *When Brendan Met Trudy* is not merely an obsessive movie nerd, he seems particularly enamored of films, such as *Sunset Boulevard* and *Breathless*, whose chief reference point are other movies. (Jan Stuart, "This Time, Reel Love Conquers All," *Newsday*, 3/8/2001.)

moving (about) *adj.*: **ambulant,** (*v.i.*: **ambulate**, *adj.*: **ambulatory**). ❖ Thinly clad **ambulant** hospital patients shelter under scant eaves in winter on a rainy day [to smoke]. (*Waikato Times* [New Zealand], "Tunnel Vision," 5/25/2000.)

(2) moving (smoothly or copiously, like a stream) *adj.*: **profluent**. See *flowing*

(3) moving (with soles of feet entirely on the ground, as humans and bears do) *adj.*: **plantigrade**. See *walking*

moving force *n.*: **primum mobile** [Latin]. See *prime mover*

much (too . . . , as in excessive) *adj.*: **de trop** [French]. See *excessive*

mud (deposited from flowing water on a riverbank) *n.*: **alluvium**. ❖ The resulting tidal drop, at times approaching 25 feet, exposes hundreds of acres of mud flats: the foreshore of the Thames. In that unassuming mud lies treasure. . . . **Alluvium** beachcombers, whether dedicated scholars or afternoon idlers, are called "mudlarks"—persons who grub in the mud. (John J. Ronan, "Down & Dirty: When the Tide's Away, Treasure Hunters Scour Thames Banks at London," *Dallas Morning News*, 1/9/2000.)

(2) mud (living in . . .) *adj.*: **limicolous**. ❖ Terry Teachout lives by a different creed [than critics of high culture only]. He has applied his formidable critical acumen not only to string quartets, ballets, and novels, but also to movies, TV shows, cartoons, and musicals. Unlike more radical critics, however, whose **limicolous** pop-culture wallowing subverts all sense of propriety, he tirelessly upholds the existence of standards. (Austin Bramwell**,** review of *A Terry Teachout Reader*, by Terry Teachout, *National Review*, 5/3/2004.)

(3) mud (prepared for therapeutic purposes) *n.*: **peloid**. ❖ A number of thermal muds can offer therapeutic benefits . . . but only the **peloid** variety employ the particular ripening process which allows them to be used in home treatments. (Dr. Pierfrancesco Morganti, "Glorious Mud," *Soap, Perfumery & Cosmetics*, 6/1/1998, p. 56.)

(4) mud (soil with or cause to sink into . . .) *v.t.*: **bemire**. ❖ On the 4th of July, seas started to moderate and by 6 July they were calm, but the heavens were not. "The second week of occupation brought torrential downpours that **bemired** virtually all mobile equipment, rendering doubly difficult the task of unloading the landing craft as they beached." (George C. Dyer, "The Amphibians Came to Conquer," *U.S. History*, 9/1/1990.)

muddle *v.t.*: **befog**. ❖ And it is clear that [the debate over tax cuts] is going to be politics of a broader band than we are accustomed to, which will help clarify things, which is good. Without such clarification, the tax debate gets **befogged** by claims about lock boxes, the reliability of 10-year forecasts, [and] goody-two-shoes bidding wars about who is more "fiscally responsible." (Ben J. Wattenberg, "Defining the Stakes," *Washington Times*, 3/1/2001.)

(2) muddle (as in disorderly confusion) *n.*, *adj.*: **hugger-mugger**. See *confusion*

(3) muddle (as in entangle) *v.t.*: **embrangle**. See *entangle*

muddled (esp. used of a person, as in . . . and stupid) *adj.*: **addlepated**. See *confused*

muddy (as in a failure to perceive something clearly or accurately or not being based on clear observation or analysis as a result of being cross-eyed, literally or figuratively) *adj.*: **strabismic**. See *cross-eyed*

(2) muddy (as in marshy) *adj.*: **quaggy**. See *marshy*

(3) muddy (as in swampy) *adj.*: **paludal**. See *swampy*

(4) muddy *adj.*: **turbid**. ❖ The influx of sediment from rain or swollen streams can make water so **turbid** you can't see your lure, even if it's just inches below the surface. (Homer Circle, "Muddy Waters," *Sports Afield*, 4/1/1995, p. 53.)

mudslide (or landslide from a volcano) *n.*: **lahar**. See *landslide* and *volcano*

mull (over something, often used as a directive, as in "Consider this:") *v.t.*: **perpend**. See *consider*

multicolored (as in having different colors) *n.*: **heterochromatic**. ❖ [Phillies pitcher] Jamie Moyer doesn't throw 95 mph . . . and doesn't have two different colored eyes. So it's understandable that the veteran lefthander wasn't the marquee attraction in last night's series opener against the Diamondbacks who sent highly touted—and **heretochromatic**—rookie Max Scherzer to the mound for his first big league start. (David Murphy, "Jamie Still Slows How to Get Things Done," *Philadelphia Daily News*, 5/6/2008.)

(2) multicolored (as in having many colors) *n.*: **polychromatic**. ❖ Here are some of the more glaring design problems: . . . Too many colors, or colors that clash. Like an excess of materials, too many colors can spoil the look of a house. . . . Making a house monochromatic may not be desirable, but making it overly **polychromatic** is equally undesirable. (Roger K. Lewis, "Blossoming Trees Can Hide a Multitude of 'Grammatical Errors' in Design," *Washington Post*, 4/7/2001.)

(3) multicolored (esp. iridescent) *adj.*: **opalescent**. See *iridescent*

multidirectional (as in dipping outward from the center in all directions, as if from a dome) *adj.*: **quaquaversal**. See *dipping*

multifaceted (as in two-faced) *adj.*: **Janus-faced**. See *two-faced*

(2) multifaceted (often used of a performer or artist) *adj.*: **protean**. See *versatile*

(3) multifaceted *adj.*: **multifarious**. See *versatile*

multilingual (as in speaking or writing in many different languages) *adj.*: **polyglot**. ❖ Passports were essential for traveling Communist agents and American passports were preferred above all others because anyone, even non-English speakers, could travel on them without arousing suspicion, thanks to the country's vast **polyglot** population, with its many immigrants. (Sam Tanenhaus, *Whittaker Chambers*, Random House [1997], p. 99.)

multiple (and varied) *adj.*: **manifold**. See *numerous*

multitude (of people) *n.*: **ruck**. ❖ He might have watched a game show on television, read a couple of chapters in a romance novel by Robert James Waller, and skimmed an issue of *People* to remind himself of those things that the desperate **ruck** of humanity uses to anesthetize itself against the awareness of its true animal nature and the inevitability of death. (Dean Koontz, *Intensity*, Knopf [1995], p. 207.)

mundane *adj.*: **quotidian**. ❖ Fed up with special effects, mega-stars and simulation, audiences seem to have turned to so-called reality.

Why are we so fascinated by this phenomenon that alternately, and sometimes even simultaneously, exposes the tediously **quotidian** and threatens the sanctity of privacy? (Marshall Blonsky, "'Real' Has Appeal But It's Not Reality; What We See in Voyeur TV," *Washington Post*, 7/30/2000.)

(2) mundane (as in routine or mechanical) *adj.*: **banausic**. See *routine*

(3) mundane (as in uninteresting or dull) *adj.*: **jejune**. See *uninteresting*

(4) mundane *adj.*: **sublunary**. See *earthly*

murder (of a female) *n.*: **femicide**. ❖ Only about 10 percent of the 360 Minnesota women and children killed by domestic violence during the past 12 years had obtained court orders for protection before being fatally attacked, according to a new study. . . . The latest annual report . . . showed that 34 women and children died from domestic abuse in 1999. "These numbers are appalling, almost obscene," said Char Thompson, a coalition researcher who prepared the **femicide** report. (Heron Estrada, "Few Protection Orders Are Sought Before Slayings," *Minneapolis Star Tribune*, 10/27/2000.

(2) murder (of one's brother or sister) *n.*: **fratricide**. ❖ [T]he filmed-in-Hamilton drama profiles the turbulent lives of Jim and Artie Mitchell, the San Francisco siblings who shot the breakthrough XXX-rated classic *Behind the Green Door* in 1971. The Mitchells' quick wealth and subsequent descent into a world of drugs, sex and booze ended in **fratricide**. (*London Free Press*, Entertainment Buzz, 6/29/2000.)

(3) murder (of one's own children) *n.*: **filicide**. ❖ Many mothers who kill their children do so out of desperation, "either economic or social or because of some mental instability," says Dick DeGuerin. . . . Surprisingly, mothers are the perpetrators in a majority of cases of **filicide**. While men are more violent overall . . . experts agree that mothers are to blame in child murders more than two-thirds of the time. (Kris Axtman, "Why Juries Often Spare Mothers Who Kill," *Christian Science Monitor*, 7/9/2001.)

(4) murder (by strangling or cutting the throat) *v.t.*: **garrote**. See *strangle*

(5) murder (by strangling or cutting the throat) *v.t.*: **jugulate**. See *strangle*

(6) murder (large-scale . . . or sacrifice) *n.*: **hecatomb**. See *slaughter*

(7) murder (mass . . . of unresisting persons) *n.*: **battue** [French]. See *killing*

(8) murder (of a king) *n.*: **regicide**. See *killing*

(9) murder (of one's father) *n.*: **patricide**. See *killing*

(10) murder (of one's mother) *n.*: **matricide**. See *killing*

(11) murder (of parent or close relative) *n.*: **parricide**. See *killing*

(12) murder (of wife by her husband) *adj.*: **uxoricide**. See *killing*

murderer (of one wife after another) *n.*: **bluebeard** (or **Bluebeard**). ❖ Henri Verdoux is a contemporary **Bluebeard** who makes a career out of marrying wealthy women and then murdering them for their fortunes. *Monsieur Verdoux* is Chaplin's most controversial film, as well as one of his personal favorites. (*Magill's Survey of Cinema*, "Monsieur Verdoux," 6/15/1995.)

murky (as in a failure to perceive something clearly or accurately or not being based on clear observation or analysis as a result of being cross-eyed, literally or figuratively) *adj.*: **strabismic**. See *cross-eyed*

murmured (said in . . . tones, not to be overheard) *adv., adj.*: **sotto voce**. See *whispered*

murmuring (as in to make a soft rustling sound) *v.i.*: **soughing**. See *rustling*

(2) murmuring (or whispering sound) *n.*: **susurrous**. See *whispering*

muscle (loss resulting from chronic disease) *n.*: **cachexia**. See *wasting*

muscles (loss of coordination of) *n.*: **ataxia**. ❖ She was diagnosed with a form of hereditary **ataxia**, a neuromuscular disease. By her mid-20s, she no longer had enough control over her throat muscles to continue singing. (Heidi Mulik, "An Essay on Familial Discovery; Winner Learns Mom's History," *Washington Times*, 3/3/2001.)

(2) muscles (weakness or fatigue in) *n.*: **myasthenia** (or **myasthenia gravis**). See *fatigue*

muscle tone (loss of . . . due to extreme emotional stimulus) *n.*: **cataplexy**. ❖ "The patient with this symptom may fall face forward into his soup," McCutcheon said. "This is something over which he has little control. **Cataplexy** is very disabling and very embarrassing." (Madelyn Birdzell, "New Clue, New Treatment for Narcolepsy; Chronic Sleep Disorder Can Be Terrifying and Dangerous," *Washington Post*, 8/31/1999.)

muscular (having a . . . body build) *adj.*: **mesomorphic**. ❖ The cartoonist, as is so often the case, captured the point of India testing its nuclear bomb. Ann Telnaes, published in *Newsday* last week, depicted a bespectacled Indian with atomic biceps and **mesomorphic** upper body attached to a frail torso and scrawny legs. (Les Payne, "From the Begging Bowl to the Big Time," *Newsday*, 5/17/1998.)

mush (as in excessive or contrived sentimentality) *n.*: **bathos**. See *sentimentality*

mushroom (eater) *n.*: **mycophagist**. ❖ Victoria Chansamone Mountha is the first to admit she failed to heed sage advice for novice **mycophagists**: When it comes to wild mushrooms, stick to what you know. She didn't, and she's paying for it. (Charles E. Brown, "Ill Mushroom Picker Strayed from Familiar," *Seattle Times*, 11/13/1997.)

mushy (as in overly sentimental) *adj.*: **mawkish**. See *sentimental*

(2) mushy *adj.*: **bathetic**. See *sentimental*

music (characterized by trills and runs) *n.*: **coloratura**. ❖ The voice you are hearing is fresh and juicy. This singer can make the trills tease, the roulades flirt. . . . "I have a natural facility for the **coloratura**," she says. "It was born in here," she adds, pointing to her chest. (Martha Duffy, Music: "Opera's Roman Candle—

Newcomer Cecilia Bartoli Lights Up the Stage," *Time*, 12/14/1992, p. 63.)

(2) music (inability to produce or understand) *n.*: **amusia**. ❖ "This goes way beyond an inability to carry a tune," observes psychologist Isabelle Peretz of the University of Montreal. . . . "They all appear to have been born without the wiring necessary to process music." Intriguingly, people with **amusia** show no overt signs of brain damage. (Michael D. Lemonick, "Music on the Brain: Experts Still Don't Know How and Why Tunes Tickle Our Fancy—but New Research Offers Intriguing Clues," *Time*, 6/5/2000, p. 74.)

musical (piece imitating previous pieces) *n.*: **pastiche**. See *imitation*

musician (street . . . or performer) *n.*: **busker**. See *performer*

music-lover *n.*: **melomaniac**. ❖ It may be protested, with some reason, that because of the omnipresence of radio and recordings, the 50 famous pieces are now worn out. Familiarity can breed, at least, indifference. . . . That unquestionably is true for the compulsive music listener, the **melomaniac** who must be tuned to radio, cassette or CD while showering, driving and working. (Donal Henahan, Music View: "The Basic Repertory," *New York Times*, 6/3/1990.)

musty (atmosphere of crowded or poorly ventilated area) *n.*: **fug**. ❖ What would he have made of the top deck of a corporation bus on a wet November evening, that warm **fug** of damp wool and thick smoke? (Kim Fletcher, Comment: "Smoking: There Is a Third Way," *Sunday Telegraph* [London], 3/15/1998.)

(2) musty *adj.*: **fusty**. ❖ Like a homeowner airing out a **fusty** basement, Huntington officials recently made a deliberate effort to open the town's timid, slow and dilatory planning procedures to new ideas and outside advice. (*Newsday*, "Lesson for Huntington and LI: Fight NIMBYitis," 6/9/1998.)

mutant (as in freak of nature) *n.*: **lusus naturae** [Latin]. See *freak*

mute (lit. loss of voice due to disease, injury,

or psychological causes) *n.*: **aphonia**. See *laryngitis*

muttered (said in . . . tones, not to be overheard) *adv.*, *adj.*: **sotto voce**. See *whispered*

mysterious (as in difficult to fathom through investigation or scrutiny) *adj.*: **inscrutable**. ❖ A lifeguard sat on his chair, surveying the bathers **inscrutably** from behind his dark glasses. (Anne Tyler, *Ladder of Years*, Knopf [1995], p. 75.)

(2) mysterious (as in perplexing) *adj.*: **quisquous**. See *perplexing*

(3) mysterious (as in eerie) *adj.*: **eldritch**. See *eerie*

(4) mysterious (as in involving factors not to be comprehended based on reason alone) *adj.*: **suprarational**. See *incomprehensible*

(5) mysterious (or cryptic or ambiguous) *adj.*: **sibylline** (or **sybilline**; often cap.). See *cryptic*

mystical (as in supernatural) *adj.*: **numinous**. See *supernatural*

mystifying (as in perplexing) *adj.*: **quisquous**. See *perplexing*

nabbed (as in . . . in the act, esp. of committing an offense or a sexual act) *adv.*: **in flagrante delicto**. See *in the act*

nag (as in shrew) *n.*: **Xanthippe**. See *shrew*

(2) nag (female . . . , as in shrew) *n.*: **harridan**. See *shrew*

(3) nag (female . . . , as in shrew) *n.*: **termagant**. See *shrew*

(4) nag (female . . . , as in shrew) *n.*: **virago**. See *shrew*

(5) nag (female . . . , as in shrew) *n.*: **vixen**. See *shrew*

(6) nag *v.t.*: **chivvy**. See *pester*

nail-biting *n.*: **onychophagia**. ❖ Confession: I've been afflicted with **onychophagia** for half a century. . . . I'm increasingly embarrassed by it. I've always been baffled by it. . . . These days, onychophagia is known as a grooming disorder or repetitive behavior disorder. In extreme cases, it's called obsessive-compulsive behavior. It turns out that it's a guy thing, too. More men than women are nail biters. (Jay Weiner, "Biting the Hand That Feeds Him," *Minneapolis Star Tribune*, 6/14/2006.)

naive (in a false or insincere way) *adj., n.*: **faux-naïf**. ❖ Much of the fault of *The Language of Life* lies with [Bill] Moyers' decision to "go soft"—to play the genial, wide-eyed interviewer who encounters a revelation at every turn. He's fond of **faux-naïf** questions (at least one hopes the faux is genuine) such as, "So politics is not only a matter of revolution?" (Brad Leithauser, The Arts & Media/Television: "'I'm Ed, and I'm a Poet'; In His Earnest Series *The Language of Life*, Bill Moyers Turns Poetry into a Mixture of Therapy Session and A.A. Meeting," *Time*, 7/3/1995, p. 54.)

(2) naive (as in guileless) *n.*: **artless**. See *guileless*

name (having the same . . . , or same sounding . . .) *adj.*: **homonymous**. ❖ Their **homonymous** designs to the contrary, Ralph Lauren, Gloria Vanderbilt and Calvin Klein aren't Dr. Ruth Kavenoff's competition. They make jeans; she makes genes. Well, sort of. [She makes clothing] decorated with stunning copies of magnified pictures of chromosomes, genes and RNA and DNA molecules from the common intestinal bacteria called E. coli. (*People*, Style: "Ruth Kavenoff Liked What She Saw in Her Microscope, So She's Putting Genes and Germs on Her T-shirts," 11/9/1987, p. 133.)

(2) name (of a . . . or term consisting of one word) *adj.*: **monomial**. ❖ The attractive cast also includes the **monomial** Polish actress Tess, as a ski-patrol exchange student. (Ralph Novak, review of *Ski Patrol*, *People*, 2/5/1990.)

(3) name (of a person well suited to its owner) *n.*: **aptronym**. ❖ Viewers apparently haven't minded that they already knew the ending [to the World Series of Poker]. The well-publicized competition, held in May, was won by Tennessee amateur Chris Moneymaker (talk about **aptronyms**!), whose only previous poker tournaments were on the Internet. (Jack Broom, "A Sure Bet: Poker Is Hot, Televised Games Spur Local Players to Up the Ante," *Seattle Times*, 9/14/2003.)

(4) name (of, relating to, or explaining a . . .) *adj.*: **onomastic**. ❖ The greengage's **onomastic** originator was Sir William Gage, who in 1725 gave his name to a newly imported yellow-green plum. He also marketed the blue gage and the purple gage, but those names did not survive. (Christopher Howse, Comment: "Nice Name, Pity About the Image," *Sunday Telegraph* [London], 9/5/1999.)

(5) name (or term consisting of one word) *n.*: **mononym**. ❖ No one else projects romantic anguish amid such lush upholstery as Seal. Like Sade, another celebrated English **mononym**, he has become a global soul-soother by evoking not ache's desolation but its multi-hued cornucopia of emotion, its limitless swank. (Steve Dollar, Weekend at Home—Music: Mini Reviews, *Atlanta Journal-Constitution*, 11/19/1998.)

(6) name (that foreigners, but not locals, give to a place) *n.*: **exonym**. ❖ Roger Payne: Your example of Wien vs. Vienna is a good example of . . . an **exonym**, which is a name that other people use, but the German or Austrian form is Wien. (Interview: Roger Payne Discusses an International Conference to Standardize Geographic Names, NPR Morning Edition, 9/2/2002.)

(7) name (last . . .) *n.*: **cognomen**. See *surname*

nameless (as in anonymous) *adj.*: **innominate**. See *anonymous*

namely *adv.*: **scilicet**. ❖ ["Millennium"] was the M-word, that was. Y1K has gone. Let her go. I do not care if this year I have to read "millennium" as often as the word occurs in the Bible. **Scilicet**, NEVER. (Philip Howard, Philip Howard Column, *Times* [London], 1/7/2000.)

(2) namely *adv.*: **videlicet**. ❖ PRIVATE PROPERTY. No skateboarding. No bicycling. No loitering. There is a certain kind of person to which a sign like that is directed, **videlicet**, [fourteen-year-old] Cliff Howard, who is mounted on a $1,300 blue BMX bicycle and who passes the sign going maybe 25 mph. His bike is not equipped with brakes, nor is his skull with a helmet, and he is a few moments away from a crash. (*Milwaukee Journal Sentinel*, "Skidding on the Edge of Injury and Trouble," 5/10/2002.)

napkins (linen . . .) *n.*: **napery**. See *linen*

narcissist (spec. someone in love with his own opinions) *n.*: **philodox**. ❖ I was not at all surprised to read that Simone de Beauvoir thought Jean-Paul Sartre a lousy lay. . . . Mind you, for the father of existentialism to be lousy in the sack is pretty ridiculous. . . . Sartre was a **philodox**, someone in love with his own opinions. A **philodox** is by nature an unmitigated disaster [in bed]. As they say, it takes two to tango, but according to Simone, Sartre went at it all by his little own self. (Taki, "In the Sack with Sartre," *Spectator*, 3/1/1997.)

narcotic (as in something that induces forgetfulness of or indifference to pain, suffering, or sorrow) *n.*: **nepenthe**. ❖ "If suffering has no value, Jesus wasted all his pain and agony," wrote Gerald W. Potkay, suggesting that Dr. Jack Kevorkian by assisting suicides is depriving sufferers of their heavenly reward. . . . Pot-

kay wrote that self-inflicted death may bring an even more unpleasant suffering from which there is never hope of escape. Perhaps so. But if my death entails prolonged terminal agony, I wonder which person I would like to find at my beside—Potkay with his dire alternative, or Kevorkian with his **nepenthe**? (Lou Houston, "If Agony Has Value, Why Did Jesus Relieve It?" *Greensboro [NC] News & Record*, 1/3/1997.)

narrow-minded *adj.*: **hidebound**. ❖ [The right to watch the trial of accused Sept. 11 terrorist-conspirator Zacarias Moussaoui on television will not] be extended to . . . Americans who watched in horror as 110-story buildings collapsed and the nation's defense headquarters burned. Thanks to the outdated policies of the federal judiciary, the televising of federal trials is forbidden. That **hidebound** attitude will be challenged at a hearing Wednesday before the judge who will preside over the trial. (*USA Today*, "Televise Terrorist Trial; War Effort Will Benefit," 1/7/2002.)

(2) narrow-minded (as in practice of refusing to consider a change in one's beliefs or opinions, esp. in politics) *n.*: **standpatism**. See *stubbornness*

(3) narrow-minded (state of being . . . , as in small-minded) *n.*: **parvanimity**. See *small-minded*

nasal *adj.*: **adenoidal**. ❖ B-Real, the lead rapper for L.A.'s Cypress Hill, has an **adenoidal** squall that makes him sound as if he has overdosed on helium, but his cartoonish delivery has served him well. (Billy Altman, Picks: Song, *People*, 8/30/1993, p. 20.)

nationalism (as in patriotism) *n.*: **amor patriae** [Latin]. See *patriotism*

native *adj.*: **aboriginal**. ❖ If Ottawa had any hope **aboriginal** people would register their guns in droves, that was dashed by an Alberta chief and Alberta's Indian Association head. Neither of them are complying with the legislation. (Rachel Evans, "Natives Won't Register Guns/Chiefs Say They Oppose Idea," *Edmonton Sun*, 4/13/2001.)

(2) native (as in indigenous) *adj.*: **authochthonous**. See *indigenous*

nature (of a person, people, or culture) *n.*: **ethos**. See *character*

(2) nature (true . . . of something, as in its essence) *n.*: **quiddity**. See *essence*

(3) nature (of two things having an identical . . .) *adj.*: **consubstantial**. See *identical*

naughty (as in mischiveous) *adj.*: **elfin**. See *mischievous*

(2) naughty (as in scandalous) *adj.*: **scabrous**. See *scandalous*

(3) naughty (behavior, as in mischief) *n.*: **doggery** [i.e., doglike behavior]. See *mischief*

nauseating (as in overly sentimental) *adj.*: **mawkish**. See *sentimental*

naval (supremacy) *n.*: **thalassocracy**. See *supremacy*

Neanderthal *n.*: **troglodyte**. ❖ Most [executive recruiters] try to keep the identity of their client secret in the early stages, but they still want to know how computer-literate you are. Expect questions like "How do you write your letters and memos?" One **troglodyte** killed his chances forever by replying, "I call my gal in to dictate." (Marshall Loeb, "What to Do If a Headhunter Calls," *Fortune*, 8/7/1995, p. 266.)

near (as in approach) *v.t.*: **appropinquate**. See *approach*

nearer (spec. getting closer and closer to a goal but never quite reaching it) *adv.*: **asymptotically**. See *closer*

nearness (in place, time, or relation) *n.*: **propinquity**. See *closeness*

neat (as in clean and tidy) *adj.*: **in Bristol fashion** [British]. See *tidy*

necessarily (due to force of circumstance) *adv.*: **perforce**. ❖ [In defending his decision to speak to the media about the Microsoft antitrust case where he was the judge, District Judge Thomas stated:] "The ostensible reason [there should be no public commentary about a case] is that anything said informally, but publicly, about a case must **perforce** detract from the court's 'appearance of impartiality.' " (James Grimaldi, "Microsoft Judge Takes His Case to the Public," *Washington Post*, 10/7/2002.)

(2) necessarily (as in whether willingly or desired or not) *adv.*: **nolens volens** [Latin]. See *unavoidably*

necessary (element or condition) *n.*: **sine qua non** [Latin]. See *indispensable*

necessity (as in irresistible compulsion) *n.*: **cacoëthes**. See *compulsion*

neck (twisted or sprained . . .) *n.*: **torticollis**. ❖ In 1984, one of my patients attended a chiropractor for the treatment of headaches, was given neck manipulation, and developed painful **torticollis** which persisted for several months. (*Medical Post*, unsigned letter to the editor, 2/16/2000.)

(2) neck (as in kiss) *v.t.*: **osculate**. See *kiss*

need (as in irresistible compulsion) *n.*: **cacoëthes**. See *compulsion*

(2) need (mental process marked by . . . to do something) *n.*: **conation**. See *determination*

needless (as in superfluous) *adj.*: **excrescent**. See *superfluous*

(2) needless (word or phrase) *n.*: **pleonasm**. See *redundancy*

(3) needless (words) *n.*: **macrology**. See *verbosity*

needy (as in poor) *adj.*: **impecunious**. See *poor*

(2) needy (as in poor) *adj.*: **necessitous**. See *poor*

ne'er-do-well *n.*: **scapegrace**. See *scoundrel*

(2) ne'er-do-well (as in scoundrel or unprincipled person) *n.*: **blackguard**. See *scoundrel*

negative (as in faultfinding person) *n.*: **smellfungus**. See *faultfinder*

(2) negative (as in faultfinding) *adj.*: **captious**. See *faultfinding*

(3) negative (as in uncomplimentary or expressing disapproval) *adj.*: **dyslogistic**. See *uncomplimentary*

negative attribute (or disadvantage) *n.*: **disamenity**. See *disadvantage*

negativist (as in pessimist who continually warns of a disastrous future) *n.*: **Jeremiah**. See *pessimist*

negativity (as in criticism) *n.*: **animadversion** (*v.t.*: **animadvert**). See *criticism*

neglect (as in to deal with or treat inadequately or with . . .) *v.t.*: **scant**. See *slight*

(2) neglect (intentionally) *v.t.*: **pretermit**. See *omit*

neglecting (or omitting or passing over) *n.*: **preterition**. See *omitting*

negligible *adj.*: **nugatory**. See *unimportant*

(2) negligible *adj.*: **picayune**. See *trivial*

(3) negligible *adj.*: **piffling**. See *trivial*

negotiation (the start of . . .) *n.*: **pourparler** [French]. See *discussion*

Negro (admirer of . . . persons) *n.*: **Negrophile**. See *black*

(2) Negro (one who fears or dislikes black persons) *n.*: **Negrophobe**. See *black*

(3) Negro (person who is one-quarter . . .) *n.*: **quadroon**. See *black*

(4) Negro (person who is one-eighth . . .) *n.*: **octoroon**. See *black*

neighborhood (physical . . . , as in vicinity) *n.*: **vicinage**. See *vicinity*

(2) neighborhood (Spanish-speaking) *n.*: **barrio**. See *Spanish*

(3) neighborhood *n.*: **purlieu**. See *vicinity*

neighborhoods (as in outskirts) *n.pl.*: **purlieus**. See *outskirts*

neophyte *n.*: **dilettante**. See *amateur*

nerve (as in gall or temerity) *n.*: **hardihood**. See *gall*

nerve center *n.*: **ganglion** (*pl.* **ganglia**). ❖ [T]he power of [Mario Cuomo's] delivery was real enough. He also took aim at targets that liberals really wanted to hit. At the height of Reaganism, Cuomo attacked the pernicious new orthodoxy far more effectively than Tip O'Neill or Walter Mondale. The media **ganglia** of Washington, D.C., and New York City took note. Cuomo was rewarded by being considered a long-shot presidential candidate during the next two election cycles. (Richard Brookheiser, "Super Mario," *National Review*, 10/10/1994.)

nervous (excitement) *adj.*: **atwitter**. See *excited*

nervousness (as in a state of tense . . . , often with irritability) *n.*: **fantod**. See *tension*

(2) nervousness (as in panic) *n.*: **Torschlusspanik** [German]. See *panic*

(3) nervousness (positive form of . . . , as in stress, brought on, for example, by a job promotion or a new baby) *n.*: **eustress**. See *stress*

(4) nervousness *n.pl.* but sing. or pl. in construction: **collywobbles**. See *bellyache*

nest (esp. in a high place) *n.*: **aerie**. ❖ [In] the Snake River Canyon . . . cliffs drop 700 feet to the narrow canyon floor; ledges, cracks, and crevices along the cliff walls provide shelter for birds to nest and raise their young. Some eagle **aeries**—thick fortresses of interwoven branches and twigs—weigh 2,000 pounds and measure seven feet across. (Guy Hand, "Sagebrush and Time: Wide-Eyed in the Idaho Desert," *Sierra*, 3/13/1998, p. 24.)

neutral (esp. neither right nor wrong, beneficial nor harmful) *adj.*: **adiaphorous**. ❖ Much thanks for the marvelous profile on the great US radio talk host, Larry Elder. Unlike the anemic, **adiaphorous**, lightweight, thumb-suckingly dull and crude "shock jocks" on air in this country, Larry Elder is brilliant in using the genre for telling not the story of the day, but the "real" story of the day. (Chuck Brooks, letter to the editor, *Australian*, 1/20/2003.)

(2) neutral (or undecided person, esp. regarding political issues) *n.*: **mugwump**. See *undecided*

neutrality (a matter of . . . or indifference, esp. in matters of religion and theology; i.e., neither right nor wrong, beneficial nor harmful) *n.*: **adiaphoron** (*adj.*: **adiaphorous**). See *indifference*

never (as in a time that will never come) *n.*: **Greek calends** (or **Greek kalends**). [This term, usually used in the phrase "until the Greek calends" (or kalends), derives from the fact that calends did not exist on the ancient Greek calendar. In the Roman calendar, they corresponded to the first day of each month.] ❖ [W]e could justify sending Marines and USAID officials into about 50 countries that have anti-American oppressive [governments]. That really would be "imperial overstretch." . . . Obviously we need some criteria to decide which states pose the most dangerous threats requiring prompt American action—and which can be postponed until the **Greek kalends**. (John O'Sullivan, "Safety in Numbers: The Limits of Unilateralism," *National Review*, 3/22/2004.)

nevertheless *adv.*: **withal**. ❖ [T]raffic is considerably less in Havana than in U.S. cities its size (approximately 2 million people). This may be due to a shortage of petroleum, only a portion of which is produced by the island itself. **Withal**, life seems to move on, in many ways normally, despite politics and shortages. (Benjamin P. Tyree, "Calling on Communist Cuba," *Washington Times*, 3/9/2001.)

new (as in of recent origin) *adj.*: **neoteric**. See *recent*

(2) new (love of or enthusiasm for anything . . .) *n.*: **neophilia**. See *novelty*

newborn (baby, esp. less than four weeks old) *n.*: **neonate**. ❖ Systems should be in place so that nurses respond quickly and appropriately when a fetus or **neonate** is in jeopardy. (Camille D. DiCostanzo, "Legal Issues in Neonatal Nursing," *Journal of Perinatal & Neonatal Nursing*, 12/1/1996, p. 47.)

(2) newborn (collection of clothing and equipment for the . . .) *n.*: **layette**. ❖ If you know someone who is expecting a baby, chances are you've been browsing baby shops for the perfect little gift to welcome home both Mom and child. While anything to add to the **layette** or to outfit the nursery is sure to be appreciated, there's really nothing like a gift you make, assemble or dream up on your own. (Martha Stewart, "Homemade Presents for Baby—and the Parents," *Newsday*, 3/27/2002.)

newest (the . . . thing) *n.*: **dernier cri** [French]. See *trend*

next-to-last *adj.*: **penultimate**. ❖ Level with Woods and Flesch after 16 holes, Els . . . went to the top of the leaderboard when he knocked a drive and six-iron to three feet at the **penultimate** hole. (Lewine Mair, Open Championship: "Els Steals in on Wind to Snatch Lead," *Daily Telegraph* [London], 7/21/2000.)

nice (as in genial, and pleasant) *adj.*: **sympathique** [French]. See *genial*

(2) nice (as in pleasing) *adj.*: **prepossessing**. See *pleasing*

nickname (as a term of endearment) *n.*: **hypocorism** (*adj.*: **hypocoristic**). ❖ The nicknames occurring in the sagas [in Icelandic literature], rude and demeaning beyond description, were, as far as we can judge, not looked upon as offensive. . . . Finnur Jonsson . . . explained about everything there was to collect in Icelandic literature: . . . **hypocoristic** names [such] as fiss (weak farter) and Pambarskelfir (belly shaker). (Anatoly Liberman, "Gone with the Wind: More Thoughts on Medieval Farting," *Scandinavian Studies*, 1/1/1996.)

(2) nickname *n.*: **agnomen**. ❖ The son of a NASA engineer father and a "very sweet" mother named George and Sylvia Zupp, Chicken George got his **agnomen** from the demented chicken paintings he started doing in West Texas, where he grew up. (Donna Alvis-Banks, "Chicken George on Life, Art and Poultry," *Roanoke Times*, 7/17/2003.)

(3) nickname *n.*: **sobriquet**. ❖ The [Connecticut women's basketball freshmen] arrived in the summer of 1998 with high expectations and a slick **sobriquet**. Dubbed the T.A.S.S.K. Force, the quintet of high school All-Americas included [Tamika Williams, Asjha Jones, Swin Cash, Sue Bird, and Keirsten Walters]. (Richard Deitsch, Big East Tournament: "Up to the T.A.S.S.K.," *Sports Illustrated*, 4/19/2000, p. 40.)

(4) nickname (spec. the substitution of an epithet for a person's proper name) *n.*: **antonomasia**. See *epithet*

niggle *v.i.*: **pettifog**. See *quibble*

night blindness *n.*: **nyctalopia**. ❖ Medical science now recognizes a pathological condition called Carsonoge-neous Monocular **Nyctalopia**: temporary blindness in one eye caused by watching the Carson show with one visual organ buried in the pillow and the other on the box. (*People*, Top 25 Stars: "Johnny Carson: H-e-e-e-r-r-e's TV's Top Gun," 5/4/1989, p. 20.)

nightcap *n*.: **doch-an-dorris** [Scottish Gaelic] ❖ [W]hen the boozed, kilted MacBryde leads a halting Court audience in a chorus of "Just a wee **doch-an-dorris**," Byrne encourages the music-hall notion that the Scots are a race of drunken comics. (Michael Billington, Theatre: "Shrouded in Scotch Myths; Michael Billington on John Byrne's Sorry Parade of Stereotypes at the Royal Court," *Guardian* [London], 9/24/1992.)

nightclub *n*.: **boîte** [French]. ❖ The Dynasty Nightclub had been open for only a week, but the tables in the rooftop **boîte** were packed with affluent customers drinking imported beer and applauding the performance of a sultry chanteuse. (Richard Hornik Rangoon, Burma, *Time* International, 11/9/1992, p. 20.)

nightfall (as in twilight) *n*.: **gloaming**. See *twilight*

(2) nightfall (of or relating to) *adj*.: **vespertine**. See *evening*

nightmare (or episode having the quality of a . . .) *n*.: **Walpurgis Night**. [Derives from the evening before May Day, believed during medieval times to be the night that witches celebrate Sabbath. The German word "Walpurgisnacht" is sometimes used instead.] ❖ I love New York . . . but I have thoroughly lost patience with the self-congratulatory myth, trumpeted ad nauseam since the recent blackout, that New York is a changed city since 9/11. . . . The latest piece of "evidence" offered on behalf of the city's transformation is the near-absence of looting in comparison to the 1977 blackout— a **Walpurgis Night** that produced more than 3,700 arrests, 1,600 ransacked stores and 1,000 fires. (Susan Jacoby, "I Want to Wake Up in the City That Can Get Over Itself," *Washington Post*, 8/24/2003.)

nimble *adj*. **lightsome**. ❖ The expectant mother (Cherry Jones) is a lesbian who wants to have a child, but without the complications of questions of paternity. . . . [Ms. Jones has] a flourishing fantasy life, in which [she] becomes a proper English schoolboy. . . . The fact that she can be so **lightsome** while playing a preg-

nant woman pretending to be a schoolboy is testimony to her theatrical alchemy. (Mel Gussow, "Parents-to-Be Regress to Childhood," *New York Times*, 5/7/1993.)

nine (group or set of . . .) *n*.: **ennead**. ❖ [At Disney's Animal Kingdom] an **ennead** of gorillas—four bachelors on one side of a waterfall, a family of five safely on the other—scuff their knuckles as they proudly prowl. (Richard Corliss, The Arts/Leisure: "Beauty and the Beasts," *Time*, 4/20/1998, p. 66.)

(2) nine (of or relating to the number . . .) *adj*.: **novenary**. ❖ No. 9 Park proprietor Barbara Lynch and French chef Julia Child traded kitchen secrets at No. 9's big 9/9/99 bash the other night. Which was a 10. But across town, at the Boston maggie hoe-down, the **novenary** night was far less memorable. (Gayle Fee, "Boston Mag Gala Dials C for Chaos," *Boston Herald-American*, 9/12/1999.)

nitpick *v.i.*: **pettifog**. See *quibble*

(2) nitpick *v.t.*: **cavil**. See *quibble*

nitpicker (on issues of grammar) *n*.: **grammaticaster**. See *pedantic*

(2) nitpicker (person who is a . . . in observing established rules or customs, esp. with regard to religious observances) *n*.: **precisian**. See *stickler*

noble (as in lordly) *adj*.: **seigneurial**. See *lordly*

noise (and confusion, esp. from simultaneous voices) *n*.: **babel**. ❖ Homer Explosion—Hot Bats, Hot Air—At times it seems everyone but Jim Garrison has chimed in with reasons for baseball's offensive explosion. But might the **babel** emanating from purists and conspiracy theorists be drowning out the reasoned voice of science? (Richard Hoffer, Scorecard, *Sports Illustrated*, 5/15/2000, p. 31.)

(2) noise (which is repeating, such as a drumbeat, machine-gun fire or hooves of a galloping horse) *n*.: **rataplan**. ❖ Gore accused Dukakis of being "absurdly timid" in criticizing [Jesse] Jackson, declared that "we're not choosing a preacher, we're choosing a president," and finally, after garnering what he thought was the coveted endorsement of Ed Koch, stood by as the irascible mayor delivered a **rataplan** of one-liners about [Jackson]. (Ellen Nakashima, "13 Ways of Looking at Al Gore and Race," *Washington Post*, 4/23/2000.)

(3) noise (as in hubbub) *n.*: **charivari**. See *hubbub*

(4) noise (fear of) *n.*: **phonophobia**. See *fear*

(5) noise (which is pleasant) *adj.*: **euphonious** (*n.*: **euphony**). See *melodious*

(6) noise (which is unpleasant or incongruous) *n.*: **dissonance**. See *sound*

(7) noise *n.*: **bruit**. See *din*

noisy *adj.*: **clangorous** (*n.*: **clangor**). ❖ My freedom [living in a Swiss apartment in the 1970s was limited.] Often, no showers are permitted between 10 P.M. and 7 A.M. No toilets may be flushed during those hours, either. When relieving themselves, men are expected to sit. (Is it the likelihood of an errant drop that so offends? Or the **clangorous** tinkle?) (Alexander Wolff, *Big Game, Small World*, Warner Books [2002], p. 54.)

(2) noisy *adj.*, *adv.*, *n.*: **fortissimo** [Italian]. See *loud*

(3) noisy *adj.*: **clamant**. See *loud*

(4) noisy *adj.*: **strepitous**. See *loud*

no matter what (as in whether willingly or desired or not) *adv.*: **nolens volens** [Latin]. See *unavoidably*

nonbeliever (as in one with no faith or religion) *n.*, *adj.*: **nullifidian**. ❖ Down with the infidels of multiculturalism . . . condoms for kiddies . . . [and] two mommies. . . . Religion arms the faithful with a comprehensive strategy for living; denying religion leaves the **nullifidians** in a personal void, which they try to fill with the litany of their moral confusion, composed in the cords of dissonance. (Paul Heusinger, letter to the editor, *Fort Lauderdale Sun-Sentinel*, 1/14/1994.)

nonchalance (as in appearance of effortlessness) *n.*: **sprezzatura** [Italian]. See *effortlessness*

(2) nonchalance (esp. on matters of politics or religion) *n.*: **Laodiceanism**. See *indifference*

nonchalant *adj.*: **dégagé** [French]. See *easygoing*

nonconformist (orig. Catholics who did not follow Church of England) *n.*: **recusant**. See *dissenter*

(2) nonconformist (spec. one who hates or mistrusts authority) *n.*: **misarchist**. See *rebel*

nonessential (as in superfluous) *adj.*: **excrescent**. See *superfluous*

(2) nonessential (as in superfluous) *adj.*: **supererogatory**. See *superfluous*

nonetheless *adv.*: **withal**. See *nevertheless*

nonpariel (person or thing) *n.*: **nonesuch**. See *paragon*

nonpartisan *adj.*: **adiaphorous**. See *neutral*

nonrecognition (spec. a condition where one cannot recognize familiar faces) *n.*: **prosopagnosia**. ❖ To people with **prosopagnosia**, the instant someone leaves their sight the memory of that person's face is blank— or, at best, a palette of muddled features. . . . [D]istinguishing between different tones or faces is nearly impossible. The effects of **prosopagnosia** can be so bad that people with severe cases cannot recognise their own parents or children. (*Economist*, "About Face," 12/4/2004.)

nonreliance (on imports or economic aid) *n.*: **autarky**. See *self-sufficient*

nonsense (or talk . . .) *v.i.*, *n.*: **piffle**. ❖ [British Prime Minister Tony] Blair denied he was seeking to impose a candidate and insisted it was up to the party in Wales to elect its candidate for the leadership of the Welsh Assembly. But, he said, it was "nonsense" and "**piffle**" that the leadership contest was a fight between Wales and London. (Auslan Cramb, "Scots and Welsh Inflict Double Misery on Blair," *Daily Telegraph* [London], 11/28/1998.)

(2) nonsense (as in foolish talk or writing or opinions) *n.*: **flapdoodle** [informal]. ❖ How strange it is to describe someone in the context of the controversial things they have said, as though all of their lives were spent babbling nonsense or offensive gibberish or inflammatory **flapdoodle**. It may well be the one characteristic that links the disgraced radio icon Don Imus to the late media preacher who was behind the Moral Majority, the Rev. Jerry Falwell. (*Chicago Tribune*, "Falwell, Imus and Words," 5/22/2007.)

(3) nonsense (writing or verse, especially that which seems to have meaning but is meaningless) *n.*: **amphigory**. [In this example, the author is parodying the overuse of metaphors in the aftermath of a recent political election.] ❖ In the days that followed, we . . . witnessed the slaughtering of sacred cows and the somewhat safe traversing of the third rail. My favourite, by far, was "electoral earthquake." . . . I am all metaphored out. . . . By accepting metaphor as analysis, we have mistaken it for reason and explanation, when it is, in fact, nothing more than **amphigory**. (Umapagan Ampikaipakan, "Metaphors of Change the Order of the Day," *New Straits Times* [Malaysia], 3/25/2008.)

(4) nonsense *n.*: **codswallop** [British]. ❖ Mr. Brierley suggests that horses' immune systems have been "irreparably damaged by constant exposure to vaccines" [and] that humans today are less healthy and more prone to problems like cancer, heart disease and asthma due to the "jabs" they are subjected to. Utter **codswallop**. I can only assume he, like me, is too young to remember the days of whooping cough, polio and diphtheria. (Mark Johnston, "Coughs and Codswallop," *Racing Post*, 7/22/2000.)

(5) nonsense *n.*: **folderol** (or **falderal**). ❖ The conservative **folderol** that legalizing drugs will tell impressionable youngsters it's OK to snort up is foolishness so perfect that even liberals should be impressed. (Thomas W. Hazlett, "Guns, Drugs, and Rock 'n' Roll: Weeding Out the Root Causes of Violence," *Reason*, 3/1/1994, p. 66.)

(6) nonsense *n.*: **trumpery**. ❖ We have been told since the moment bin Laden's name was mentioned in connection with the horrible events of Sept. 11 that America's military would face dire consequences and overwhelming difficulty in any action taken in Afghanistan. This

trumpery is fed to us [by the same] ninnies who told us the "elite" Republican Guard in Iraq was a well-trained, well-supplied force that was to be feared by the U.S. military. (Robert Stewart, "Why the United States Can Succeed in Afghanistan," *Buffalo News*, 11/11/2001.)

(7) nonsense (spec. meaningless or deceptive words or language) *n.*: **flummery**. See *meaningless*

(8) nonsense (as in meaningless talk) *n.*: **galimatias**. See *gibberish*

(9) nonsense (as in unintelligible baby talk) *n.*: **lallation**. See *baby talk*

nonsensical (as in fallacious or illogical argument) *n.*: **paralogism** (*adj.*: **paralogical**). See *fallacy*

nonviolence (Buddhist and Hindu doctrine of . . . , which expresses belief in sacredness of all living creatures) *n.*: **ahimsa**. ❖ The word Jainism conjures up images of ascetics who cover their mouths and sweep the ground before them with small brushes to avoid injuring the most minuscule forms of life. . . . These overt manifestations of an ancient faith challenge the comfortable—and near-universal—assumption of human precedence over other creatures. They dramatise for us the doctrine of **ahimsa**: non-violence or, more literally, the avoidance of anything that causes harm. (Aidan Rankin, "Face to Faith: The 'Many-Sidedness' of Jainism Could Inoculate Us Against Fundamentalist Rigidity," *Guardian* [London], 1/27/2007.)

nonviolent resistance *n.*: **satyagraha**. [Sanskrit. This word, coined by Mahatma Gandhi and meaning truth-force or soul-force, refers to nonviolent resistance as a philosophy and practice to convert (but not coerce) the wrongdoer. It is rarely used without reference to Gandhi himself. In the example given, the writer is criticizing a court decision that awarded damages to an abortion clinic against a right-to-life group that passively interfered with access to the clinics.] ❖ Indeed, the decision below erases any distinction between peaceable, nonviolent protest, such as a sit-in, and physical violence against persons or property. Jury findings of "extortion" therefore reflected NOW's theory that using your body to block access is "forcible" so long as you don't move aside when asked. Gandhian **satyagraha**—"truth force" generated by sit-ins—is "extortionate." (U.S. Newswire, "Supreme Court Will Address Whether Acts of Peaceful Civil Disobedience Are Federal Felony Crimes of 'Extortion,'" 12/3/2002.)

normal (as in usual or customary) *adj.*: **wonted**. See *customary*

  (2) normal (the act of becoming . . . , as in routine) *n.*: **routinization**. See *routinization*

north (of or pertaining to) *adj.*: **boreal**. ❖ There is reason, but not rhyme, to the travels of **boreal** seedeaters. Contrary to popular belief, hard winters do not drive the birds south. . . . Immune to winter's worst, then, immense flocks of **boreal** birds wander the Canadian forest year-round. (Les Line, "Staying the Winter," *National Wildlife*, 2/12/1995, p. 52.)

  (2) north (of or relating to the far . . .) *adj.*: **hyperborean**. See *Arctic*

northern lights *n.*: **aurora borealis**. ❖ SCI-ENTISTS FIND SPACE CATALYST FOR **AURORA BOREALIS**. . . . The Northern Lights will be just as mystical the next time you see them, but slightly less mysterious. (Peter Calamai, "Weird Waves Help Light Night Sky," *Toronto Star*, 3/29/2001.)

nose (which is turned up) *adj.*: **retroussé**. [French. Although the word is an adjective meaning "turned up," it is almost always used in reference to a nose.] ❖ He just looked so undistinguished. Medium height. Medium build. Medium-brown hair—a small nose, positively **retroussé**—the photo had been a very flattering one. What a dud, I thought. (Tiffany Trott, The Back Page: "Did Any of the 11 Men I Met Last Night Ask for My Number? Dating Diary," *Daily Telegraph* [London], 9/27/1997.)

  (2) nose (within the . . .) *adj.*: **intranasal**. ❖ What is jammed up nostrils, supposedly provides a jolt, and isn't cocaine? Presenting Ener-B, an **intranasal** gel loaded with vitamin B12 and sold in health stores for $12 a twelve-

dose box. (*Time*, Health & Fitness: "New Nostril Nostrum," 3/30/1987, p. 74.)

  (3) nose (having a runny . . . or watery eyes) *adj.*: **rheumy**. See *watery*

nose job *n.*: **rhinoplasty**. ❖ During Andrea's consultation, Dr. Glasgold suggested not only a nose job but an implant to improve her receding chin. . . . According to Glasgold, 25 percent of all **rhinoplasty** patients also have receding chins. (Marjorie Rosen, "New Face, New Body, New Self—Five Teens Talk About the Trials and Triumphs of Plastic Surgery," *People*, 4/26/1993, p. 8.)

nose-picking *n.*: **rhinotillexomania**. ❖ Advancing science: University of Wisconsin-Madison researchers, fighting ignorance, have done a study on **rhinotillexomania**. And not a moment too soon, either. . . . [They] gave a questionnaire to 1,200 people, with questions like, "What finger do you use?" and "How often do you find yourself looking at what you have removed?" And thus man's knowledge advances, a booger at a time. (Doug Robarchek, "Alcohol May Cause Brain Damage," *Charlotte [NC] Observer*, 10/19/2000.)

nostalgic (of or relating to something that is pretty in a superficially . . . way) *adj.*: **chocolate-box**. See *pretty*

nosy (person) *n.*: **quidnunc**. See *busybody*

notable (person in a field or organization) *n.*: **wallah** ❖ Shaw got a computer science Ph.D. from Stanford in 1980. . . . He wasn't the only **wallah**-in-training at Stanford in those days. Leonard Bosack and Andreas Bechtolsheim, co-founders of Cisco Systems and Sun Microsystems, respectively, and Jim Clark, founder of Silicon Graphics and now chairman of Netscape—all were either faculty members or fellow students. (James Aley, Extreme Investing: "Wall Street's King Quant David Shaw's Secret Formulas Pile Up Money; Now He Wants a Piece of the Net," *Fortune*, 2/5/1996, p. 108.)

  (2) notable (of an event or period that is . . .) *adj.*: **epochal**. See *momentous*

  (3) notable (person) *n.*: **satrap**. See *bigwig*

noteworthy (things) *n.pl.*: **notabilia**. ❖ [W]hen

the 26-member board of directors of the New York Shakespeare Festival summarily dismissed JoAnne Akalaitis from her job as the festival's artistic director on March 15, [she] packed away 20 months' worth of **notabilia**, issued a polite but unequivocal statement to the press, [and] talked with characteristic frankness to friends and colleagues about how and why she was fired. (Jim O'Quinn, "Change of Will," *American Theatre*, 5/1/1993.)

nothing (from or out of . . .) *adj., adv.*: **ex nihilo** [Latin]. ❖ Planning a city **ex nihilo** is an awesome undertaking, but it is easier to build roads, homes and schools than to create the ineffable feeling of community one finds in the best towns. (Noah Efron, *Real Jews,* Basic Books [2003], p. 115.)

noticable (barely . . .) *adj.*: **liminal**. See *invisible*

notice (as in attention) *n.*: **advertence**. See *attention*

(2) notice (something that may be difficult to discern) *v.t.*: **descry**. See *perceive*

(3) notice (wonderful to . . . , as in behold) *adv.*: **mirabile visu** [Latin]. See *behold*

notion (which is odd, stubborn, or whimsical) *n.*: **crotchet**. ❖ But [presidential candidate Pat] Buchanan's **crotchets**—Wall Street bankers, immigration (legal as well as illegal), trade and the New World Order (whatever that is)—are idiosyncratic enough to keep his following to a minority. (Mona Charen, "Republicans Need Candidate Who Can Lead on Moral Issues," *St. Louis Post-Dispatch*, 10/16/1995.)

(2) notion (about which one is obsessed) *n.*: **idée fixe** [French]. See *obsession*

notorious *adj.*: **flagitious**. See *scandalous*

notwithstanding (that) *adv.*: **withal**. See *nevertheless*

(2) notwithstanding (the views of, as in, with all respect to) *prep.*: **pace** [Latin]. See *respectfully*

noun (which used to stand alone but then requires a modifier due to changes in technology or other new developments) *n.*: **retronym**. See *word*

nourishment *n.*: **alimentation**. ❖ Aside from computer management designed to select out the most productive cows, Mr. Blumstein hopes to implement new **alimentation** methods and erect an Israeli-engineered payload that requires fewer workers and provides detailed milk-related data on each cow. (Masha Leon, "Israeli Milkman Mooooving into New Territory," *Forward*, 11/4/1994.)

(2) nourishment (esp. insipid, like baby food) *n.*: **pabulum** (also **pablum**). See *insipid*

nouveau riche *n.*: **parvenu**. See *upstart*

novel (in which real people, places, or events are portrayed in fictional guise) *n.*: **roman à clef** [French; lit. novel with a key]. ❖ [Joe] Klein used the pen name "Anonymous" when he wrote *Primary Colors*, the scandalous 1996 **roman à clef** about the '92 presidential campaign. His womanizing Southern governor was widely believed to be based on Bill Clinton. (*Cincinnati Post*, "'Anonymous' Klein Delivers 2nd Novel," 1/21/2000.)

(2) novel (published in installments) *n.*: **feuilleton** [French]. ❖ Policarpo Quaresma, who gives name to the third book in the list, is a tragicomic ultranationalist hero. Lima Barreto (1881–1922) initially published the story in 1911 in installments in Rio's *Jornal do Commercio*, as a **feuilleton**. The book would only appear four years later. (*Brazzil*, Literature: "The Great Brazilian Novel," 9/30/1998, p. 12.)

(3) novel (style that is dark, gloomy, remote, and/or grotesque) *adj.*: **gothic**. See *dark*

(4) novel (as in of recent origin) *adj.*: **neoteric**. See *recent*

(5) novel (which follows the development of its main character over time, as in a coming-of-age story) *n.*: **bildungsroman** [German]. See *coming-of-age*

novelist (esp. who writes in quantity) *n.*: **fictioneer**. ❖ If you're looking for a critique and celebration of capitalism, for a discussion of ethics or ethnicity, for a distillation of democracy and its discontents, you'd do at least as well to heed [*The Simpsons*] as you would to ponder similarly prolific prose **fictioneers**, from Norman Mailer to Stephen King. (Ken Tucker, "At 300 Episodes and Counting, *The Simpsons*—TV's

Answer to the Great American Novel—Continues to Be a Show About Everything," *Entertainment Weekly*, 2/7/2003.)

novelty (love of or enthusiasm for . . .) *n.*: **neophilia**. ❖ Sensation, the present Saatchi exhibition at the Royal Academy, makes the point: the big, flashy, headline gesture is all that counts. These people are inspired by the intrinsic **neophilia** of technology. The technocrat and the machine require no past, only the thin film of the present. The artist similarly bows to the imperative of now. (Bryan Appleyard, "Oasis Are Criticised, Even by Their Heroes the Beatles, for Being Derivative," *New Statesman*, 10/10/1997, p. 34.)

novice *n.*: **abecedarian**. See *beginner*

(2) **novice** *n.*: **catechumen**. See *beginner*

(3) **novice** *n.*: **dilettante**. See *amateur*

now (for . . .) *n.*: **nonce** (used as "for the nonce"). See *time being*

now and then *adv.*: **betimes**. See *sometimes*

noxious (atmosphere or influence) *n.*: **miasma**. ❖ Air pollution—the gray **miasma**—from coal, industry ash and leaded fuel—that smothers most of China's cities is barely breathable. The World Bank estimates that air pollution causes nearly 300,000 deaths nationwide every year. (Nisid Hajari, "A Litany of Ills: China's 10 Top Ecological Problems," *Time* International, 3/1/1999, p. 21.)

(2) **noxious** (fumes from waste or decayed matter) *n.*: **effluvium**. See *odor*

(3) **noxious** (or harmful) *adj.*: **noisome**. See *harmful* and *smelly*

(4) **noxious** (smell) *adj.*: **mephitic** (*n.*: **mephitis**). See *smelly*

nuance (as in a subtle point raised within the context of a philosophical or theological debate; also refers to such a debate itself) *n.*: **quodlibet**. See *subtlety*

nuances (study of the . . . between similar words or synonyms) *n.*: **synonymy**. See *synonyms*

numb *v.t.*: **narcotize**. See *deaden*

numbers (having ability with . . .) *adj.*: **numerate**. See *mathematical*

numbness (as in medication causing inability to feel pain) *n.*: **analgesia**. ❖ Administering pain medication prior to surgery helps patients long after they return home from the hospital. The idea behind preemptive **analgesia** is to head off pain by blocking the central nervous system's response before the surgery occurs. (*USA Today Magazine*, "A Preemptive Strike Before Surgery," 10/1/1997.)

numbskull *n.*: **jobbernowl** [British]. See *idiot*

(2) **numbskull** *n.*: **mooncalf**. See *fool*

numerous (and varied) *adj.*: **manifold**. ❖ For all his **manifold** talents, [Steve] Martin is simply the wrong man for the role [of Sergeant Bilko]. (*People*, Picks & Pans, 4/15/1996, p. 19.)

nuptials (of or relating to . . .) *adj.*: **hymeneal**. See *wedding*

nurse (or housekeeper in India and Orient, often serving as a wet nurse) *n.*: **amah**. See *maid*

nuts (as in crazy) *adj.*: **doolally**. See *crazy*

nuzzling *idiom*: **slap and tickle**. See *sex*

nymphomaniac *n.*: **roundheel**. See *slut*

oaf (habitual . . . , as in bumbler) *n.*: **schlemiel** [Yiddish]. See *bumbler*

oafish (person) *n.*: **yahoo**. See *boor*

obdurate (as in one who clings to an opinion or belief even after being shown that it is wrong) *n.*: **mumpsimus**. See *stubborn*

(2) obdurate *adj.*: **pertinacious**. See *stubborn*

obedience (as in allegiance) *n.*: **vassalage**. See *allegiance*

(2) obedience (as in marked by insistence on rigid conformity to a belief, system, or course of action without regard to individual differences) *adj.*: **Procrustean** (*n.*: **Procrustean bed**). See *conformity*

obedient *adj.*: **biddable**. ❖ America likes its neighbours **biddable** and quiet; Cuba, with wars, coups and corrupt governments, has always made a nuisance of itself. (*Economist*, "Dances with Wolves," 4/6/1996.)

(2) obedient (as in subservient) *adj.*: **sequacious**. See *subservient*

obese *adj.*: **Pickwickian**. See *fat*

(2) obese *adj.*: **pursy**. See *fat*

(3) obese (person, esp. with a large abdomen) *n.*: **endomorph** (*adj.*: **endomorphic**). See *pot-bellied*

(4) obese *adj.*: **adipose**. See *fat*

obesity (branch of medicine dealing with . . .) *n.*: **bariatrics**. ❖ As director of a **bariatrics** clinic providing medical treatment of obesity and related conditions, I am often confronted with people who think they can't afford treatment simply because they don't have the proper information. (*People*, unsigned letter to the editor, 5/3/1999, p. 1.)

(2) obesity *n.*: **avoirdupois**. See *weight*

obey (as in acting subservient as opposed to leading) *adj.*: **sequacious**. See *subservient*

obfuscate (one's vision as if by clouds, fog, or vapor) *v.t.*: **obnubilate**. See *obscure*

obituary *n.*: **necrology**. ❖ I was lucky that none of my closest friends perished [on September 11, 2001], but still, I think of those people, and I sometimes think of how they died. And I try to remember to forget. But then I open a newsletter from my college and in a **necrology** there's a startling cluster of three or four names with the date of death: Sept. 11, 2001. (Andy Serwer, "Terrorists Are Ruining My Middle Age," *Fortune*, 12/24/2001, p. 135.)

object *v.t.*: **expostulate**. ❖ [When some overweight American Airlines flight attendants were fired], a group of women went to the [Equal Employment Opportunity Commission] claiming discrimination, and the commission turned around and sued American. But wait—[our] readers are **expostulating** in unison—there is no federal ban on weight bias. How could the EEOC launch such a suit? (Daniel Seligman, "Fat Chances—A Case for Putting on Weight, a Weird Job Application, and Other Matters," *Fortune*, 5/20/1991, p. 155.)

(2) object (as in goal, esp. of life) *n.*: **telos** [Greek]. See *goal*

(3) object (esp. in the form of pleading with) *v.t.*: **remonstrate**. See *plead*

(4) object (on trivial grounds) *v.t.*: **cavil**. See *quibble*

(5) object (to, as in oppose, a statement, opinion, or action) *v.t.*: **oppugn**. See *oppose*

objectionable (in matters of discrimination between groups) *adj.*: **invidious**. See *discriminatory*

objective (as in the thing that is being looked for; also the answer to a problem) *n.*: **quaesitum**. ❖ [Economist John Maynard] Keynes maintains the vision of an economy moving through time: an economy that is complex and difficult to analyze because organizations change, unexplored opportunities arise, and new choices are made. New factors could come into the picture and the main determinants of analysts' **quaesitum** may change. Furthermore, the **quaesitum** itself may change as new problems develop. (Giuseppe Fontana, "Keynes on the 'Nature of Economic Thinking,'" *American Journal of Economics and Sociology*, 10/1/2001.)

(2) objective (directed toward an . . .) *adj.*: **telic**. See *purposeful*

(3) objective (hidden or ulterior . . .) *n.*: **arriere-pensee** (or **arrière-pensée**) [French]. See *motive*

(4) objective (uncompromisingly . . . , as in just) *n.*: **Rhadamanthine**. See *just*

(5) objective (as in neutral) *adj.*: **adiaphorous**. See *neutral*

objects (everyday . . . , esp. those that show the lifestyle of a people) *n.pl.*: **realia**. ❖ Victorians, Moderns and Beats: New in the Berg Collection, 1994–2001 [is] an exhibition that opens today at the New York Public Library. The title is a little misleading: among the manuscripts, letters, books, juvenilia and **realia** on display, Victorian material is modest, modern prolific, Beat largely weighted toward Jack Kerouac. (Michael Frank, "Writings That Defy Time's Toll," *New York Times*, 4/26/2002.)

oblivion *n.*: **Lethe**. [In Greek mythology, Lethe (pronounced LEE-thee) is one of the several rivers of Hades. Those who drink from it experience complete forgetfulness. Today it is used to refer to one in an oblivious or forgetful state. The word is also sometimes used in the phrase "drinking from the River Lethe." See also *forgetfulness*.] ❖ En route to work today, I heard an ad for an alarm clock with soothing sounds to help you sleep. It had the usual sounds to lull you off to **Lethe**—pounding surf, waterfalls, crickets, a C-SPAN hearing. The announcer was pleased to introduce two new sounds: birds and New York traffic. (James Lileks, "Soothing Sounds—from New York?" *Minneapolis Star Tribune*, 11/19/2002.)

oblivious (as in ignorant) *adj.*: **nescient** (*n.*: **nescience**). See *ignorant*

obscene (compulsive . . . behavior) *n.*: **copropraxia**. ❖ In one painfully hilarious moment, an expert witness for the prosecution, Dr. Rampling, suffers from three neurological conditions, coprolalia, **copropraxia** and echopraxia, which make her shout obscenities [i.e., coprolalia], grab her own breasts and mimic her questioners [i.e., echopraxia] as she testifies, all unconsciously. (Richard Bernstein, "Just a Couple of All-American Orphans on Trial," *New York Times*, 8/6/1997.)

(2) obscene *adj.*: **fescennine**. ❖ Nurses minister to people's bodies. Consequently, they invade private and personal territory in ways that other kinds of workers do not. Arguably, **fescennine** comments made by patients to nurses who are doing their jobs may arise from the embarrassment of feeling exposed and vulnerable. (Patricia M. Hanrahan, "'How Do I Know If I'm Being Harassed or If This Is Part of My Job?' Nurses and Definitions of Sexual Harassment," Contemporary Women's Issues Database, 6/1/1997.)

(3) obscene *adj.*: **ostrobogulous**. See *indecent*

(4) obscene (as in vulgar) *adj.*: **meretricious**. See *vulgar*

obscenity (excessive use of . . . , esp. involuntarily when mentally ill) *n.*: **coprolalia**. See *cursing*

obscure (vision, as if by clouds, fog, or vapor) *v.t.*: **obnubilate**. ❖ The usual, if unarticulated, thinking is that knowing occurs by the mind's getting its version of 20/20 vision—"the view from nowhere," with nothing allowed to **obnubilate** the mental looks. But notice this stark fact: the mind that asks no questions, reaches no answers. In other words, gaping at the Rosetta stone gets you nowhere. Without asking, "What does this mean?" . . . I shall not know. (Patrick McKinley Brennan, review of *The Edge of Meaning*, by James Boyd White, *Michigan Law Review*, 5/1/2003.)

(2) obscure (as in a failure to perceive something clearly or accurately or not being based on clear observation or analysis as a result of being cross-eyed, literally or figuratively) *adj.*: **strabismic**. See *cross-eyed*

(3) obscure (as in cryptic or ambiguous) *adj.*: **Delphic**. See *ambiguous*

(4) obscure (as in dark, misty, and gloomy) *adj.*: **caliginous**. See *dark*

(5) obscure (as in difficult to understand) *adj.*: **recondite**. See *complicated*

(6) obscure (as in muddle or confuse) *v.t.*: **befog**. See *muddle*

(7) obscure (or cryptic speech or writing, esp. deliberately) *adj.*: **elliptical**. See *cryptic*

obsequious (person) *n.*: **lickspittle**. See *sycophant*

(2) obsequious (to behave toward in an . . . manner) *v.t.*: **bootlick**. See *kowtow*

observance (or ceremony that is pretentious) *n.*: **mummery**. See *ceremony*

(2) observance (precise . . . of formalities or etiquette) *n.*: **punctilio**. See *etiquette*

observant (in terms of strictness of one's religious practices) *n.*: **orthopraxy**. See *orthodoxy*

(2) observant (person) *n.*: **Argus**. See *watchful*

observation (and analysis of matters outside oneself, i.e., of the outside world) *n.*: **extrospection** (*adj.*: **extrospective**). [This word is the less common, but legitimate, opposite of introspection. A photographer's work is sometimes said to be extrospective. The word is not to be confused with an extrovert, a person who has more interest in his environment and others than in himself. An extrovert participates, while an extrospective person observes. In the example given, the author appears to be suggesting that, for the reason given, Los Angeles almost considers itself to be outside of the United States, or vice versa.] ❖ It's not surprising that, in films, LA figures in so many criminal masterplans, or that so many aliens from outer space decide to land there—it is the centre of the movie-making universe, after all, and its extreme parochialism makes the rest of the United States seem almost **extrospective**. (Anne Bilson, The Arts: "Stop That Magma Cinema," *Sunday Telegraph* [London], 10/5/1997.)

(2) observation (additional . . . , as in explanation) *n.*: **epexegesis** (*adj.*: **epexegetic**). See *explanation*

(3) observation (as in insight) *n.*: **aperçu** [French]. See *insight*

(4) observation (based on eyewitness . . .) *adj.*: **autoptic**. See *eyewitness*

(5) observation (esp. for changes in trends) *n.*: **weather eye** (esp. as in "keep a weather eye"). See *lookout*

(6) observation (or expression or phrase that is elegant, concise, witty, and/or well put) *n.*: **atticism**. See *expression*

(7) observation (or line that is witty) *n.*: **epigram**. See *quip*

observe (wonderful to . . . , as in behold) *adv.*: **mirabile visu** [Latin]. See *behold*

observer (as in investigator or examiner) *n.*: **scrutator**. See *examiner*

obsession (over one subject or idea) *n.*: **monomania**. ❖ [S]tay tuned for a replay of the poisonous psychodrama where race is used as a cynical cover for the real liberal **monomania**, abortion—as if the entire universe revolves around a single issue affecting the private conduct and personal convenience of heterosexual Western women. (*Washington Times*, Culture, etc., 1/19/2001.)

(2) obsession (with an idea or concept) *n.*: **idée fixe** [French]. ❖ For those who doubted it before, the book depicts in detail just how completely the company [Volkswagen] was a creature of Nazism. Soon after his rise to power, Hitler began to pester the leaders of Germany's automobile industry with an **idée fixe**. He wanted them to create a mass-produced "people's car" that would be affordable to average Germans. (Christian Caryl, "A Beetle Faces Up to Its Past," *U.S. News & World Report*, 12/2/1996.)

(3) obsession (with power, wealth, fame, immortality, etc.) *n.*: **megalomania**. ❖ In his 60s, [Wilt Chamberlain] was boldly declaring himself the greatest player ever to walk on the hardwood. In a sports world in which we allow our heroes to spend only so much time in the rarefied air before we bring them crashing back to earth, Chamberlain's **megalomania** always begged for its comeuppance. (Jeff Ryan, "Remembering Wilt: A Bum Rap," *Sporting News*, 10/25/1999.)

(4) obsession (as in focus of emotional energy on an object or idea) *n.*: **cathexis**. See *focus*

(5) obsession (mad or crazy . . . , as in love) *n.*: **amour fou** [French]. See *love*

(6) obsession (with shopping) *n.*: **oniomania**. See *shopping*

obsessive (person who is . . . about work) *n.*: **Stakhanovite**. See *workaholic*

obsolete *adj.*: **superannuated**. ❖ [Even if a four-day political] convention is nothing more than a speech, [politicians still] see their conventions as opportunities to put their best foot forward and gain a lot of free television exposure. So, many Democrats continue to cherish the picture—**superannuated** though it may be—of the stirring acceptance speech that will draw a huge television audience and send the party faithful out of the Fleet Center presumably brimming with optimism. (Jack W. Germond, "I'll Still Show Up for This Non-Show," *Washington Post*, 5/30/2004.)

(2) obsolete (as in outdated) *adj.*: **retardataire** [French]. See *outdated*

(3) obsolete *adj.*: **antediluvian**. See *outdated*

obstacle (as in predicament, from which it is difficult to extricate oneself) *n.*: **tar baby**. See *predicament*

obstacles (spec. baggage, equipment, supplies, or any object that hinders progress or movement) *n.pl.*: **impedimenta**. See *baggage*

obstetrics (as in midwifery) *n.*: **tokology** (or **tocology**). See *midwifery*

obstinate *adj.*: **contumacious**. ❖ In a final swipe, the judge derides [President Clinton's] "**contumacious** conduct" [in the Monica Lewinsky matter]. . . . All of which raises some interesting questions, given our current state of affairs: Can we really have a **contumacious** commander in chief? Can the leader of the nation's armed forces obstinately resist authority? (And whose authority would he resist, anyway?) (Gloria Borger, "Considering Contempt," *U.S. News & World Report*, 04/26/1999.)

(2) obstinate (as in one who clings to an opinion or belief even after being shown that it is wrong) *n.*: **mumpsimus**. See *stubborn*

(3) obstinate (as in practice of refusing to consider a change in one's beliefs or opinions, esp. in politics) *n.*: **standpatism**. See *stubbornness*

(4) obstinate (as in resisting constraint or compulsion) *adj.*: **renitent**. See *resistant*

(5) obstinate (as in stubborn) *adj.*: **pervicacious**. See *stubborn*

(6) obstinate (in a contrary or disobedient way) *adj.*: **froward**. See *contrary*

(7) obstinate (to make or become . . .) *v.t.*, *adj.*: **indurate**. See *harden*

(8) obstinate *adj.*: **pertinacious**. See *stubborn*

obstruct *v.t.*: **occlude**. See *block*

obtain (by mooching or sponging off of) *v.t.*: **cadge**. See *mooch*

(2) obtain (money unfairly and in excessive amounts) *v.t.*: **mulct**. See *extract*

obtuse (as in slow to understand or perceive) *adj.*: **purblind**. ❖ Only the naive think [Martin Luther] King's murder begins and ends with [James Earl] Ray. Only the **purblind** ignore FBI Director J. Edgar Hoover's vendetta against King. (Greg Boeck, "Ray Doesn't Need Trial," *USA Today*, 2/18/1997.)

(2) obtuse (or dull, ignorant, stupid, or uncultured) *adj.*: **Boeotian**. See *dull*

obvious (esp. as in easily understood or seen through, likes motives) *adj.*: **transpicuous**. See *transparent*

occasion (secondary . . . that accompanies or results from another) *n.*: **epiphenomenon**. See *phenomenon*

occasionally *adv.*: **betimes**. See *sometimes*

occupant (of a town) *n.*: **burgher**. See *resident*

occupation (requiring little work but paying an income) *n.*: **sinecure**. ❖ [After] nearly ten years in government service, where everything is geared to the lowest common denominator, I find it refreshing to have work that rewards initiative and effort. Certainly I would be happy to have a **sinecure** again, but I am no longer brokenhearted that I left one. (Lars Eighner, *Travels with Lizbeth*, St. Martin's Press [1993], p. 124.)

(2) occupation (right of use and . . . of property belonging to another) *n.*: **usufruct**. See *use*

(3) occupation (as in profession) *n.*: **métier** [French]. See *profession*

occupy (oneself in a light, frolicsome manner) *v.t.*, *v.i.*: **disport**. See *frolic*

occur (as in result) *v.i.*: **eventuate**. See *result*

(2) occur *v.t.*: **betide**. See *happen*

occurrence (secondary . . . that accompanies or results from another) *n.*: **epiphenomenon**. See *phenomenon*

ocean (bottom of the . . .) *n.*: **Davy Jones's locker** [origin unknown]. ❖ In the spring of 1990, Pat Kane, a golfer and inventor from San Diego, hopped aboard a cruise ship, eagerly looking forward to sending a few buckets of balls off the practice tee on the fantail and down into **Davy Jones's locker**. But to Kane's disappointment, he discovered that maritime golfing was no longer possible [because it was made illegal]. (Steve Wulf, "Fore and Aft," *Sports Illustrated*, 4/27/1992.)

(2) ocean (of or pertaining to . . . or sea) *adj.*: **pelagic**. See *sea*

(3) ocean (of or relating to the . . . or sea) *adj.*: **thalassic**. See *sea*

(4) ocean (across or beyond the . . . ; coming from across or beyond the . . .) *adj.*: **transmarine**. See *sea*

odd (as in departing from the standard or norm) *adj.*: **heteroclite**. See *abnormal*

(2) odd (as in eccentric) *adj.*: **pixilated**. See *eccentric*

(3) odd (as in unconventional) *adj.*: **outré** [French]. See *unconventional*

(4) odd (as in perplexing) *adj.*: **quisquous**. See *perplexing*

(5) odd (as in unusual) *adj.*: **selcouth**. See *unusual*

oddball (as in someone or something that deviates from the norm) *n.*: **lusus** [Latin; almost always used as part of the term "lusus naturae," or freak of nature]. See *freak*

oddity (as in notion that is odd, stubborn, or whimsical) *n.*: **crotchet**. See *notion*

ode (in the form of a song or poem in honor of a bride or bridegroom) *n.*: **epithalamium**. See *toast*

odor (bad . . . from waste or decayed matter) *n.*: **effluvium**. ❖ This deathliness generates its own momentum. Nobody in Ladysmith can flee the overpowering stink of enteric and dysentery; the local water becomes fouled by animal waste; the **effluvium** given off by corpses both stings the eyes and causes nausea, bringing more typhus-laden flies into town in a self-renewing cycle of woe. (Peter Wolfe, "The Horrors of Boer War Have the Ring of Truth," *St. Louis Post-Dispatch*, 5/21/2000.)

(2) odor (bad . . . from foul-smelling sweat) *n.*: **bromidrosis**. See *sweat*

(3) odor (foul . . .) *adj.*: **noisome**. See *smelly*

(4) odor (foul) *n.*: **fetor**. See *stench*

(5) odor (foul) *n.*: **mephitic** (*n.*: **mephitis**). See *smelly*

(6) odor (having a smelly . . .) *adj.*: **graveolent**. See *smelly*

offbeat (holding . . . opinions or having an . . . perspective) *adj.*: **heterodox** (*n.*: **heterodoxy**). See *unconventional*

offend (as in insult another's dignity) *n.*: **lese majesty**. See *insult*

offended (easily . . .) *adj.*: **umbrageous**. ❖ [In criticizing] the Programme of the Communist Party of the Soviet Union . . . we realize full well that they will doubtless think we are just being **umbrageous** over the Programme's view of Western journalism. ("Evermore baleful is the role of the bourgeois mass media which befuddles people in the interests of the ruling class.") (Daniel Seligman, "Sulfur from Sunkist, Tass Vs. Microsoft, Herblock's Hysterics, and Other Matters," *Fortune*, 12/23/1985, p. 131.)

offender (as in wrongdoer) *n.*: **miscreant**. See *wrongdoer*

(2) offender (criminal . . . , or wrongdoer) *n.*: **malefactor**. See *wrongdoer*

offense (small or trifling . . .) *n.*: **peccadillo**. See *infraction*

(2) offense (surprise . . . , as in attack) *n.*: **coup de main** [French; attack by hand]. See *attack*

(3) offense (an . . . , as in wrongdoing, by its own nature or by natural law rather than because prohibited by statute) *n.*: **malum in se** [Latin]. See *wrongdoing*

(4) offense (an . . . because it is prohibited by statute rather than because the conduct is wrong by its own nature or by natural law) *n.*: **malum prohibitum**. See *crime*

offensive (to the taste or sensibilities, esp. due to insincere praise) *adj.*: **fulsome**. ❖ Working for a Republican is the "ultimate sacrifice"? Voting for one makes you brave? . . . [This strategy of Republicans pandering to conservative blacks,] while indisputably brilliant, is laced with equal parts contempt and condescension. How else to interpret such **fulsome** bootlicking except that with blacks there is always danger, even for deviating from the party line? (Debra Dickerson, "The GOP's 'Good' Blacks," *Washington Post*, 3/13/2001.)

(2) offensive (as in being presumptuous; venturing beyond one's province) *adj.*: **ultracrepidarian**. See *presumptuous*

(3) offensive (as in indecent) *adj.*: **ostrobogulous**. See *indecent*

(4) offensive (as in repellent) *adj.*: **rebarbative**. See *repellent*

(5) offensive (as in vulgar) *adj.*: **meretricious**. See *vulgar*

(6) offensive (in matters of discrimination between groups) *adj.*: **invidious**. See *discriminatory*

(7) offensive (language) *n.*: **billingsgate**. See *language*

offering *n.*: **oblation**. ❖ PGA Tour Inc. (PGA) deserves Scrooge-like infamy for its heartless treatment of disabled golfer Casey Martin [who has a disease that makes it difficult to walk the golf course]. . . . Do its petrified forest of nabobs [i.e., the PGA executives] envision Casey Martin as their **oblation** to social Darwinism? (Bruce Fein, "PGA's Heartless Hazard," *Washington Times*, 1/30/2001.)

(2) offering (which is all one can afford) *n.*: **widow's mite**. See *donation*

offhand (as in unrehearsed) *adj.*: **autoschediastic**. See *unrehearsed*

offhandedness (appearance of . . .) *n.*: **sprezzatura** [Italian]. See *effortlessness*

official (act, declaration, or statement, as in with the authority of one's office) *adv., adj.*: **ex cathedra**. [Latin for "from the chair." This term is often, but not necessarily, used with reference to papal declarations.] ❖ Rather than support their conclusion [with] a close analysis of the founders' text, the justices declared **ex cathedra** that the Constitution no longer permits the execution of mentally retarded inmates simply because "a national consensus has developed against it." This declaration ought to frighten every friend of freedom. (Andy Brehm, letter to the editor, *Washington Times*, 6/23/2002.)

(2) official (as in bureaucrat) *n.*: **satrap**. See *bureaucrat*

offset (spec. to be or to make equal in weight) *v.t., v.i.*: **equiponderate**. See *equal*

offshoot (as in outgrowth) *n.*: **excrescence**. See *outgrowth*

offspring (of or relating to) *adj.*: **filial**. ❖ Because families often live with three generations under one roof, parents can find themselves awkwardly positioned between their children and their own parents. Dr. Vo calls them "sandwich parents." If parents side with their Americanized children, she says, they worry that they are not paying "**filial** duty" to the grandparents. (Marilyn Gardner, "New Country, Old Customs," *Christian Science Monitor*, 8/9/2000.)

(2) offspring (having had one or more . . .) *n.*: **parous**. See *birth*

oil painting (dealing with evening or night) *n.*: **nocturne** [can also refer to a musical piece, esp. for piano]. See *painting*

oily (greasy, or unctuous) *adj.*: **pinguid**. ❖ [Radio Authority Chairman] Lord Chalfont [took away the license of] Britain's first commercial radio broadcaster. And the reason why, your Lordship? With that **pinguid** charm which has made this peer so popular an appointment with his Tory overseers, Chalfont loftily explained to a press conference that the Radio Authority was not obliged to give its reasons. (Mike Carlton, "Waves of Discomfort . . . and Joy," *Guardian* [London], 9/6/1993.)

(2) oily *adj.*: **lubricious**. See *slippery*

(3) oily *adj.*: **oleaginous**. See *unctuous*

ointment (esp. used to groom hair) *n.*: **pomade**. See *hair gel*

okay (as in legitimate; acceptable) *adj.*: **cromulent**. See *legitimate*

(2) okay (as in approve, esp. to confirm officially) *v.t.*: **homologate**. See *approve*

(3) okay (as in giving one's stamp of approval) *n.*: **nihil obstat** [Latin]. See *approval*

old (extremely . . .) *adj.*: **hoary**. ❖ [M]any Jews are alarmed by what they see as a worldwide blaze of anti-Semitism: torched synagogues in France, a resurgence of malevolent myths about Jews in the Arab world, sweeping anti-Israel diatribes in European newspapers and a measurable swell in the acceptance of **hoary** stereotypes in the United States. (Justin Davidson, "Bonding in Troubled Times/Fear of a Growing Anti-Semitism and Concerns over Israel Are Making American Jews Put Aside Their Differences," *Newsday*, 7/15/2002.)

(2) old (and sick person) *n.*: **Struldbrug**. See *decrepit*

(3) old (as in decrepit) *adj.*: **spavined**. See *decrepit*

(4) old (as in obsolete) *adj.*: **superannuated**. See *obsolete*

(5) old (branch of science dealing with . . . people) *adj.*: **gerontology**. See *elderly*

(6) old (esp. as in outdated) *adj.*: **antediluvian**. See *outdated*

(7) old (government by . . . people) *adj.*: **gerontocracy**. See *government*

(8) old (growing . . .) *adj.*: **senescent**. See *aging*

(9) old (of or relating to . . . people, esp. women) *adj.*: **blue-rinse**. See *elderly*

(10) old (sexual attraction to . . . people) *n.*: **gerontophilia**. See *lust*

(11) old (woman who is ugly) *n.*: **crone**. See *hag*

old age (of or relating to . . .) *adj.*: **gerontic**. ❖ [In Gertrude Atherton's novel, Agnes the spinster's] sex-repression results in a middle-aged mania. . . . [Mary] urges the spinster to have the "Steinach Treatment" and then have sex. . . . Mary is unsympathetic to Agnes's plight, that of a "debauched **gerontic** virgin." (Dale Bauer, "Refusing Middle Age," *ANQ*, 1/1/2002.)

(2) old age (often with accompanying senility) *n.*: **caducity**. ❖ Aged care in Australia is teetering on the edge of a crisis, as nurses leave in droves and baby boomers creep closer to **caducity**. (AAP General News [Australia], Fed: "Nursing Homes Caught in Catch-22 as Crisis Looms," 8/8/2003.)

(3) old age (living to an . . .) *adj.*: **macrobian**. See *long-lived*

(4) old age *n.*: **senectitude**. See *elderliness*

oldest (child) *n.*: **primogeniture**. See *firstborn*

old-fashioned (as in excessive reverence for tradition) *adj.*: **filiopietistic**. ❖ The controversy over what should be taught in American history classes reveals a deep fissure between today's dominant school of historians and mainstream public opinion. This is not entirely new. University historians have long disdained the study of great men and what one historian calls the "**filiopietistic**" history of popular imagination. (Robert Lerner, "Gendering American History," *The World & I*, 4/1/1996, p. 326.)

(2) old-fashioned (person, spec. a person who is opposed to advancements in technology) *n.*: **Luddite**. See *traditionalist*

(3) old-fashioned (spec. a person who is opposed to individual or political reform or enlightenment) *n.*: **obscurant** (doctrine of such opposition: **obscurantism**). See *traditionalist*

old-line (person, spec. a person who is opposed to advancements in technology) *n.*: **Luddite**. See *traditionalist*

(2) old-line (spec. a person who is opposed to individual or political reform or enlightenment) *n.*: **obscurant** (doctrine of such opposition: **obscurantism**). See *traditionalist*

old man (cranky or stubborn . . .) *n.*: **alter kocker** [Yiddish]. ❖ Benny [is] a character whom Corduner, drawing on his Jewish upbringing, invented to entertain his friends. "Benny is an old bigoted English Jew, an **alter kocker**, who could be running an antique store on the Portobello Road. . . . And what did Benny have to say about Venice? "It's all crumbling," says Benny . . . "They call it distressed; I call it disgusting.

It needs a paint job." (Howard Feinstein, "His Topsy-Turvy Life," *Advocate*, 2/15/2000.)

old woman (of or like an . . .) *adj.*: **anile**. ❖ But when the camera closed in on [Jane] Fonda . . . you could see that she'd let herself go and that the promise of old ladyhood wasn't far off. She was persistently beautiful but the ravages of time were unmistakable, her features having become pointed, sharp, furrowed and **anile**. She'd done nothing to avert the terrible tragedy of age, which pays its cruel visit to us all every minute. (Lloyd Dykk, "Cher and Cher Alike," *Vancouver Sun*, 1/25/1997.)

ominous *adj.*: **baleful**. See *sinister*

omission *n.* **elision**. [One definition of elision is an omission of something, such as text or facts. The word can have either a neutral meaning or a pejorative connotation, especially if the omission is used for the purpose of being misleading.] ❖ Carl Bernstein, a sometimes admiring Hillary Clinton biographer, has called the Bosnia debacle [in which Ms. Clinton wrongly claimed that she landed there under "sniper fire"] "a watershed event" for her campaign because it revives her long history of balancing good works with "misstatements and **elisions**," from the health-care task force fiasco onward. (Frank Rich, "Hillary's St. Patrick's Day Massacre," *New York Times*, 3/30/2008.)

omit (intentionally) *v.t.*: **pretermit**. ❖ [In one case, police included] Davis's name and mug shot in a list of "active shoplifters," even though Davis had been accused but not convicted of that offense. [However,] the Supreme Court construed the "life, liberty, or property" protected by due process to exclude reputation. The effect of this ruling was not merely to preclude money damages, but to **pretermit** any federal constitutional scrutiny of official condemnation of identified individuals. (John Jeffries, "Disaggregating Constitutional Torts," *Yale Law Journal*, 11/1/2000.)

omitting (or passing over or neglecting) *n.*: **preterition**. ❖ Singer-guitarist Thalia Zedek of Boston used to play in an arty blues-punk band called Come, but she's put all that behind her now. . . . Though some of it might be gaining ground. For her first solo [recording] Zedek seems alternately obsessed with and haunted by her past, its lost loves, its missed opportunities and her own tragic **preterition**. (Rommie Johnson, "Spin This," *Tampa Tribune*, 12/14/2001.)

omnipotence (one obsessed with one's own greatness, fame, or . . .) *n.*: **megalomania**. See *obsession*

once (as in former) *adj.*: **quondam**. See *former*

(2) once (as in former) *adj.*: **whilom**. See *former*

oneness (as in that quality which makes one thing different from any other) *n.*: **haecceity** (or **haeccity**). See *individuality*

one-time (as in occurring only once) *adj.*: **one-off** [British]. ❖ The creationist completely misses the point because he (women should not for once mind being excluded by the pronoun) insists on treating the genesis of statistical improbability [i.e., the creation of the world] as a single, **one-off** event. (Richard Dawkins, *The God Delusion*, Houghton Mifflin [2006], p. 121.)

(2) one-time (as in former) *adj.*: **ci-devant** [French]. See *former*

(3) one-time (as in former) *adj.*: **quondam**. See *former*

(4) one-time (as in former) *adj.*: **whilom**. See *former*

one-trick pony (as in having only one talent or power) *adj.*: **monodynamic**. ❖ [Singer Cassandra Wilson has] proved that you didn't have to make a lot of noise to keep an audience riveted. Influenced also by Nina Simone's minimalist approach, Wilson favors an intense, mesmerizing vocal attack. Yet where Simone is merely **monodynamic** (sometimes annoyingly so), Wilson . . . instead of just holding back [is] actually saving a carefully calculated outburst of feeling just so she can let you have it when you least expect it. (Will Friewald, "Miles Tone," *Village Voice*, 12/16/1997.)

onion (characteristic of . . . or garlic) *adj.*: **alliaceous**. ❖ Mom was severely allergic to [onions and garlic], and so the onion that was somehow thought essential to the Thanksgiving turkey stuffing was the only **alliaceous** substance that entered her kitchen from year's end to year's end. (Linda Bridges, "Late Discoveries," *National Review*, 12/22/1997, p. 72.)

on purpose (as in premeditated) *adj.*: **prepense** (usually used as part of the phrase "malice prepense"). See *premeditated*

onset (from the . . .) *adv.*: **ab initio** [Latin]. See *beginning*

(2) onset (from the . . .) *adv.*: **ab ovo** [Latin]. See *beginning*

ooze (as in escape from proper channels, esp. a liquid or something that flows) *v.i.*: **extravasate**. See *exude*

open (as in guileless) *n.*: **artless**. See *guileless*

(2) open (split . . . or crack . . .) *v.t., v.i., n.*: **fissure**. See *crack*

open air (in the . . .) *adv.*: **en plein air** [French]. See *outdoors*

opening (as in preface) *n.*: **proem**. See *preface*

(2) opening (as in space or gap) *n.*: **lacuna**. See *gap*

(3) opening (narrow . . . , as in slit) *n.*: **aperture**. See *slit*

(4) opening (to a lengthy or complex work) *n.*: **prolegomenon**. See *introduction*

open-minded *adj.*: **latitudinarian**. ❖ Homosexuals are famously **latitudinarian** on matters sexual. Materials distributed by the Gay Men's Health Crisis include advice on "fisting," "water sports" and "mutilation." (Mona Charen, "The Two Faces of Gay Activism," *Baltimore Sun*, 6/10/1996.)

open spaces (fear of . . . or public places) *n.*: **agoraphobia**. See *fear*

opera glasses (with a short handle) *n.*: **lorgnette**. See *eyeglasses*

opinion (as in personal preference) *n.*: **de gustibus** [Latin]. See *taste*

(2) opinion (of the world) *n.*: **weltanschauung** [German]. See *worldview*

(3) opinion (preconceived . . . on an issue) *n.*: **parti pris** [French]. See *preconception*

(4) opinion (which is controversial, or person who holds one) *n.*: **polemic**. See *controversy*

(5) opinion (which is false) *n.*: **pseudodoxy**. See *fallacy*

(6) opinion (which is odd, stubborn, or whimsical) *n.*: **crotchet**. See *notion*

opinions (spec. doctrines to be believed; articles of faith) *n.pl.*: **credenda**. See *beliefs*

oppose (a statement, opinion, or action) *v.t.*: **oppugn**. ❖ Newspaper editors and columnists who **oppugn** the *Daily Trust* editorial on the grounds that the paper was hawking a military takeover either do not understand the English language or didn't read the said editorial at all. (Africa News Service, "If This Is Democracy," 12/8/2003.)

(2) oppose (as in argue against) *v.t.*: **expostulate**. See *object*

(3) oppose (as in reject or disapprove) *v.t., n.*: **discountenance**. See *reject*

opposing (as in resisting constraint or compulsion) *adj.*: **renitent**. See *resistant*

(2) opposing (esp. majority view) *adj.*: **dissentient**. See *dissenting*

(3) opposing *adj.*: **oppugnant**. See *antagonistic*

opposite (having . . . ideas or qualities) *adj.*: **bipolar**. ❖ Liquidity. It's at the center of the current debate about [Amazon.com's] viability, a debate that keeps growing sharper. "There are a lot of **bipolar** opinions about this company," Bezos said. (David Streitfeld, "Analysts, Vendors Increasingly Wary About Amazon," *Washington Post*, 2/21/2001.)

opposition (as in conflict, between laws, rules, or principles) *n.*: **antinomy**. See *conflict*

(2) opposition (to set in . . .) *v.t.*: **counterpose**. See *contrast*

oppression (of a religious, national, or racial group) *n.*: **helotism** (*v.t.*: **helotize**). ❖ Since the Germans were **helotizing** the denizens of the [concentration] camp world, they, not surprisingly, took many measures to dehumanize them. (Daniel Goldhagen, *Hitler's Willing Executioners*, Knopf [1996], p. 175.)

(2) oppression (as in burden) *n.*: **incubus**. See *burden*

oppressive (ruthlessly and violently . . .) *adj.*: **jackbooted**. ❖ The bureau [of Alcohol, Tobacco and Firearms] is not the **jackbooted** monolith of N.R.A. lore, however. Far from it: court documents and internal reports uncovered in a two-month *Time* investigation reveal ATF as a divided and troubled agency far more likely to abuse the rights of its own employees than those of law-abiding citizens. (Erik Larson, "ATF Under Siege—Demon Agency? Far from It; Torn by Internal Strife, the Bureau Has Lost Its Sense of Mission," *Time*, 7/24/1995, p. 20.)

optimist (as in one habitually expecting an upturn in one's fortunes, sometimes without justification) *n.*: **Micawber** (*adj.*: **Micawberish**) [based on the character Wilkins Micawber in the Charles Dickens novel *David Copperfield*, who always says that "something will turn up"]. ❖ By their nature Americans are optimistic. But none of their leaders, not even FDR, has exhibited the quality like Mr. Reagan. It was **Micawberish** at times, a seemingly blind conviction that even the darkest events had a silver lining; but no other politician could summon that politically priceless "feel-good factor." (Rupert Cornwell, "Ronald Reagan 1911–2004: A President Whose Optimism Earned Him a Place in History," *Independent* [London], 6/7/2004.)

(2) optimist (or person with a confidently affirmative attitude) *n.*: **yeasayer**. [This word is the less common, though equally legitimate, counterpart to its opposite word, "naysayer."] ❖ [Harvard Professor of Religion Harvey] Cox is an inveterate **yeasayer** who has always spied the workings of God's grace . . . in one cultural movement after another, from the pragmatic secularism of the Kennedy era to the carnival spirit of the counterculture and the worldwide growth of Pentecostalism. . . . He responded to Ms. Pollitt's onslaught with characteristic good humor. . . . Ms. Pollitt, on the other hand, is a born naysayer. (Peter Steinfels, Beliefs, *New York Times*, 1/27/1996.)

optimistic (esp. blindly or naively . . .) *adj.*:

Panglossian [based on Dr. Pangloss, the optimistic tutor of Candide in the novel of the same name, by Voltaire]. ❖ Although overall holiday-sales forecasts range from **Panglossian** to Scroogesque, analysts agree that online shopping is booming. (Paul Andrews, "Christmas Clicking," *U.S. News & World Report*, 12/15/2003.)

(2) optimistic (excessively or unrealistically . . . person) *n.*: **Pollyanna**. ❖ "[W]e will win games this year. I'm very confident of that" [said Chicago Bears coach Dave Wannstedt]. . . . He is talking Super Bowl—and he insists he is serious. Apparently, he hasn't looked at the schedule. . . . It's no wonder Bears fans are confused: Do they have a great coach needing more time to develop or a **Pollyanna**, who is in over his head? (T. J. Simers, "Bullish on Chicago? Bad News, Bears Fans," *Sporting News*, 8/18/1997.)

option (bad . . . , as in the situation of having to make a move where any move made will weaken the position) *n.*: **zugzwang** [German]. See *predicament*

(2) option (of taking what is offered or nothing; i.e., no real option at all) *n.*: **Hobson's choice**. See *predicament*

optional *adj.*: **facultative**. ❖ The Soviet map was transformed yesterday with such devastating effect that it can never be undone. . . . The new proposal grants by implication the right for any republic to secede. It appears to be an entirely **facultative** exercise in which only those republics "which wish to" will sign the Union Treaty. . . . It is up to each signing republic to decide for itself the form of participation in the Union. (*Guardian* [London], "Mikhail Signs, but Boris Calls the Shots," 9/3/1991.)

opulent (excessively . . . , esp. in a sensuous way) *adj.*: **sybaritic**. See *luxurious*

oracular *adj.*: **vatic**. See *prophetic*

oral *adj.*: **nuncupative**. [This word is usually used as part of the phrase "nuncupative will," referring to a will delivered by one in imminent fear of death orally to witnesses rather than written. A nuncupative statement is usually delivered publicly, solemnly, or formally. The verb form of the word—which is rarely used—is "nuncupate." See *declare*.] ❖ How Al Michaels—the play-by-play man I want for my next wedding—retains his sanity [during NFL Monday Night Football], I don't know. Maybe he wears a Walkman for three hours. Actually, the elegant Michaels has upped his **nuncupative** game this season. Here is a list of actual words he has used during Monday broadcasts: "propitious," "amortizing," "preparatory," "alacrity," [and] "punitive." (Norman Chad, "Monday Night Fever Has Evolved into Insipid Virus," *Boston Globe*, 10/16/1998.)

(2) oral *adj.*, *adv.*: **viva voce** [Latin]. See *verbal*

orate (on a topic, esp. in a long-winded or pompous manner) *v.i.*: **bloviate**. See *speak*

(2) orate (pompously, loudly, or theatrically) *v.i.*: **declaim**. See *proclaim*

oration (enthusiastic or excited . . . or writing) *n.*: **dithyramb**. See *enthusiastic*

oratory (of or relating to . . . that is ornate, flowery, forceful, and/or eloquent) *adj.*: **Ciceronian**. See *speech*

ordeal (as in painful journey or experience) *n.*: **via dolorosa** [derives from Jesus' route from Pontius Pilate's judgment hall to Calvary to be crucified]. ❖ From the Nazi occupation and the liquidation of Lidice, to the Communist show trials and the persecution of Charter 77, Czech history in the past century has been—apart from two periods of independence under Masaryk and Havel—a **via dolorosa**. (Daniel Johnson, "The Dwarves Who Posture on the Shoulders of Giants," *Daily Telegraph* [London], 9/28/2000.)

(2) ordeal (a great . . . , as in experience of intense suffering) *n.*: **Calvary** [based on hill near Jerusalem where Jesus was crucified]. See *suffering*

(3) ordeal (as in burden) *n.*: **incubus**. See *burden*

(4) ordeal (period of . . . , sometimes, but not necessarily, economic) *n.*: **locust years**. See *hardship*

order *v.t.*: **adjure**. ❖ Ho Chi Minh is a wispy man (100 lbs.), mild and slow-spoken, and disarmingly forthright. . . . "You must give the people an example of poverty, misery and denial," he sometimes **adjures** his disciples, and off he plods, ostentatiously, through the villages, with a knapsack on his back. (*Time* International, "1946–1960: Independence—A Tidal Wave of Nationalist Fervor Washed Away Centuries of Colonial Rule, Transforming the Physical and Political Map," 5/4/1998, p. 70.)

(2) order (as in decree) *n.*: **diktat**. See *decree*

(3) order (as in sequence or progression) *n.*: **consecution**. See *sequence*

(4) order *n.*: **ukase**. See *decree*

orderly (as in clean and tidy) *adj.*: **in Bristol fashion** [British]. See *tidy*

ordinary (as in mundane; everyday) *adj.*: **sublunary**. See *earthly*

(2) ordinary (as in routine or mechanical) *adj.*: **banausic**. See *routine*

(3) ordinary (in tastes and ideas and culture) *adj.*: **philistine**. See *uncultured*

(4) ordinary (of or relating to the . . . people) *adj.*: **plebian**. See *common*

(5) ordinary (people, as in the masses) *n.*: **canaille**. See *masses*

(6) ordinary (people, as in the masses) *n.*: **hoi polloi**. See *commoners*

(7) ordinary *adj.*: **quotidian**. See *mundane*

organization (which is based on either strong interpersonal relationships and common values among its members [**gemeinschaft**—see *community*] or impersonal such relationships [**gesellschaft**—see *association*, which includes an example that uses both terms]) [German].

orgasm (failure or inability to achieve . . .) *adj.*: **anorgasmic**. ❖ This approach is a basic step in treatment programs for sexual dysfunction. For example, a majority of **anorgasmic** women discover that their mother either never talked about sex with her mother, or grew up thinking sex was sinful or dirty and similarly warned her daughter. (Dr. Judy, Fitness File/Sex/Q&A, *Newsday*, 7/5/1999.)

origin (and source) *n.*: **fons et origo** [Latin]. See *source and origin*

(2) origin (as in prime mover) *n.*: **primum mobile** [Latin]. See *prime mover*

(3) origin (as in root) *n.*: **taproot**. See *root*

(4) origin (existing from the . . . , as in innate) *adj.*: **connate**. See *innate*

(5) origin (principal . . .) *n.*: **wellhead**. See *source*

original (text or version of a musical score or literary work) *n.*: **urtext** [German]. [The notebook of synonyms created by Peter Roget when he was a boy] is clearly the **urtext** . . . of *Roget's Thesaurus*. (Joshua Kendall, *The Man Who Made Lists*, Putnam [2008], p. 42.)

(2) original (and/or creative) *adj.*: **Promethean**. See *creative*

(3) original (as in first) *adj.*: **primordial**. See *first*

(4) original (as in genuine) *adj.*: **echt** [German]. See *genuine*

(5) original (as in of recent origin) *adj.*: **neoteric**. See *recent*

(6) original (as in that which set the standard or established the model from which others followed or on which others are based) *n.*: **locus classicus** [Latin]. See *model*

(7) original (in the . . . position) *adj.*, *adv.*: **in situ** [Latin]. See *unmoved*

(8) original (model or example) *n.*: **archetype**. See *model*

(9) original (stage of growth or development) *adj.*: **germinal**. See *earliest*

originator (as in creator) *n.*: **demiurge**. See *creator*

origins (study of . . . , esp. relating to medical conditions) *n.*: **etiology**. See *causes*

ornament (esp. resembling a tuft of plumes) *n.*: **aigrette**. ❖ But despotic rule can produce great art. That of the Ottomans is now seen in Washington in the Corcoran Gallery of Art's Palace of Gold & Light: Treasures from the Topkapi, Istanbul. . . . Other trappings of power appear in the show. Jeweled **aigrettes** for decorating turbans exuded wealth. They took their name from the egret feathers embellishing them. (Joanna Shaw-Eagle, "Turkish Treasures; 'Gold, Light' from Topkapi Palace in Istanbul," *Washington Times*, 3/4/2000.)

(2) ornament (tacky or kitschy religious or devotional . . .) *n.*: **bondieuserie** [French]. ❖ Harry Bartlett ran the Art and Book Company, publishers and church furnishers. The shop, opposite the main door of Westminster Cathedral, was known for its good taste, and disdain for **bondieuserie**. (Peter Howell, obituary of Aelred Bartlett, *Independent* [London], 7/16/2004.)

(3) ornament (in a showy or excessive manner) *v.t.*: **bedeck**. See *adorn*

(4) ornament (or dress in a showy or excessive manner) *v.t.*: **bedizen**. See *adorn*

(5) ornament (small . . . or trinket) *n.*: **bibelot**. See *trinket*

(6) ornament (small . . . or trinket) *n.*: **bijou** See *trinket*

(7) ornament (small . . . or trinket) *n.*: **gewgaw**. See *trinket*

(8) ornament *n.*: **garniture**. See *decoration*

ornamentation (which is showy or superfluous or frilly) *n.*: **furbelow**. [The primary definition of this word is a ruffle or flounce on a woman's garment. This leads to the secondary broader definition of the word, which is anything with the above characteristics. It is often, though not always, used in a disparaging manner.] ❖ [In designing his "System-Built Houses," architect Frank Lloyd] Wright has eliminated the ugly, meaningless **furbelows**. He has done away with the hideous twists and scrolls and other "fancy" work that has done more than anything else to make our house building so universally bad. (Lori Rotenberk, quoting Sherwood Anderson, "A 'Brave and Direct' Design," *Chicago Sun-Times*, 3/19/1991.)

ornate *adj.*: **baroque**. ❖ The **baroque** style, which originated in Rome during the 1600s, is art in the grandest manner. Florid, ornate and luxurious, baroque art was designed to dazzle the eye and reflect the owner's importance and wealth. (Mary Abbe, "Institute Lends Artifacts to New York Show," *Minneapolis Star Tribune*, 4/25/1999.)

(2) ornate *adj.*: **florid**. ❖ Overwriting [is] so common and so ridiculous that a national contest [exists for the worst writing]. . . . The contest is named for [the] novelist who first penned the words "It was a dark and stormy night" and whose work was so **florid** that it inspired guffaws. We see ornate and affected prose everywhere, from the modest workplace memo to the ambitious academic report. (Paula LaRocque, "Poor Writing Often Tries Too Hard to Impress," *Dallas Morning News*, 3/13/2000.)

(3) ornate *adj.*: **rococo**. ❖ He grew portly and his mustache evolved in shapes ever more luxurious and **rococo**, for he had become what Pinkerton called a "silk glove man." (Ben Macintyre, *The Napoleon of Crime*, Farrar, Straus and Giroux [1997], p. 158.)

ornery (person) *n.*: **crosspatch**. See *grouch*

(2) ornery *adj.*: **atrabilious**. See *surly*

(3) ornery *adj.*: **bilious**. See *surly*

(4) ornery *adj.*: **liverish**. See *irritable*

(5) ornery *adj.*: **querulous**. See *peevish*

(6) ornery *adj.*: **shirty**. See *irritable*

(7) ornery *adj.*: **waspish**. See *irritable*

orphan (as in baby who is deserted or abandoned) *n.*: **foundling**. ❖ At ten days old, Dave, now 30, was dumped in a London tube station toilet. He is one of Britain's **foundling** babies—last year there were five—whose mothers are never traced. (*Daily Mirror* [London], "Anguish of the Foundling Babies," 2/28/1996.)

orthodox *adj.*: **bien-pensant**. See *right-thinking*

orthodoxy *n.*: **orthopraxy**. [Although "orthodoxy" may be a logical base word for "orthopraxy," the two words are not synonymous. The former refers to the strictness or correctness of one's belief in a certain religion, while the latter refers to the strictness or correctness of its practices, rather than its beliefs.] ❖ [T]wo themes [are] readily apparent: orthodoxy and **orthopraxy**. In Judaism, as in other religions, there is a tradition of ideology and a

tradition of practice. . . . Is it possible for someone to identify himself as an Orthodox Jew if he believes in a certain ideological tradition but does not observe ritual law? Conversely, can one identify himself similarly if he strictly observes the rituals but follows the ideological path of another Judaic denomination? (Seth Wikas, "Joseph Lieberman: Too Much Media Hype, Too Little Orthodoxy," University Wire, 9/26/2000.)

ostentatious (object) *n.*: **frippery**. ❖ The indictment [against Harry and Leona Helmsley] claimed that they listed as business expenses such personal **fripperies** as a $130,000 indoor-outdoor stereo system for their home. (Joyce Wadler, "For the Love of Money—They Have Each Other and More Than a Billion Dollars, but, Charges the Government, Harry and Leona Helmsley Wanted More and Broke the Law to Get It," *People*, 5/2/1988, p. 90.)

(2) ostentatious (but actually superficial knowledge of a subject) *n.*: **sciolism**. See *superficial*

(3) ostentatious (speech or writing) *adj.*: **fustian**. See *pompous*

(4) ostentatious *adj.*: **orchidaceous**. See *showy*

ostracized (or exiled) *v.t.*: **sent to Coventry**. [British. There are conflicting explanations for the derivation of this term, which refers to a city in the West Midlands, England.] ❖ Our host was David Petrie, a Scottish lecturer of English at the university [in Verona, Italy]. David is currently suing the Italian state for discriminating against foreign lecturers, and naturally this course of action hasn't endeared him to his hosts. He's been **sent to Coventry**. He's been given a smaller office, then given no office at all. He's been sacked. . . . He's received death threats via the telephone. (Jeremy Clarke, "In Coventry, in Verona," *Spectator*, 11/29/2003.)

ostrich (as in complacent person who ignores any unpleasant facts) *n.*: **Podsnap** (*adj.*: **Podsnappian**). ❖ Attorney General Edwin Meese's committee . . . pushed for a "common sense" rationale for prosecution of pornographers when scientific evidence inconveniently suggested nonintervention. . . . Meese is rendered as a modern-day Mr. **Podsnap**, that pathetic character in Dickens's *Our Mutual Friend* who would haughtily dismiss any inconvenient fact, saying, "I don't want to know about it; I don't choose to discuss it; I don't admit it!" (Michael S. Kimmel, review of *The Secret Museum: Pornography in Modern Culture*, by Walter Kendrick, *Psychology Today*, 2/1/1988.)

(2) ostrich (of, relating to, or resembling) *adj.*: **struthious** [a word used figuratively as often as not]. ❧ It rankles me whenever I see a reference to "reluctant allies" or "the opposition of our allies." These **struthious** populations of France and Germany are not our allies [any longer. They] try to ennoble their own dishonest motives by describing war as the ultimate failure of diplomacy, something to be avoided at all costs, claiming the moral high ground by virtue of their having experienced the horrors of war. If they would get their heads out of the sand, they might avoid repeating those experiences. (*Orlando Sentinel*, "Another Word for 'Allies,'" 1/26/2003.)

otherworldly *adj.*: **fey**. ❧ The greatest mystery of [Arthur Conan] Doyle's life is how the creator of Sherlock Holmes—that "perfect reasoning and observing machine"—would eventually champion **fey** phenomena like séances and fairies, so that by his 1930 death at age 71 he was considered "hopelessly crazy." (Kristen Baldwin, Books/The Week, *Entertainment Weekly*, 4/23/1999, p. 58.)

oust (as in unseat) *v.t.*: **unhorse**. See *unseat*

outbreak (of violence or disorder) *n.*: **émeute** [French]. See *rebellion*

outburst (of emotion, feeling, or action) *n.*: **paroxysm**. ❧ [A]fter the 1970 ouster of Prince Norodom Sihanouk, Cambodia suffered **paroxysms** of violence that battered the entire populace and the country's infrastructure, including its roads. (Kay Johnson, "From Sapporo to Surabaya/Taheng, Cambodia: The Road to Riches—After Three Decades of Turmoil, Cambodia Is Trying to Repave Its Way

Back to Peace and Prosperity," *Time* International, 8/21/2000, p. 80.)

(2) outburst (as in temper tantrum) *n.*: **boutade** [French]. See *temper tantrum*

(3) outburst (marked by a sudden or violent . . .) *adj.*: **vesuvian** (esp. as in . . . temper). See *temper*

outcast *n.*: **Ishmael** [after the son of Abraham in the Old Testament, who was conceived in adultery with Sarah's handmaid, Hagar, and was cast out after Sarah gave birth to Isaac]. ❧ Hardie . . . chairman of the Parliamentary Labour Party [viewed] his role within Parliament, as an agitator rather than an administrator or organiser. [His proposals in favor of the working man] had little expectation of success in a Conservative-dominated Parliament but every hope of maximum publicity. Hardie seemed to relish the role of lone rebel and once described himself as "an **Ishmael** in public life." (Roger Spalding, "Keir Hardie: Socializing the World for the Workers—One of the Key Figures in the History of the Labour Party," *History Review*, 12/1/2001.)

outcry (as in plea; lit. cry of the heart) *n.*: **cri de coeur** [French]. See *plea*

outdated *adj.*: **antediluvian**. ❧ Take me out to the ball game, / Take me out to the Diamond View Suites. / Buy me some Dijon-marinated jumbo shrimp and Grgich Hills Chardonnay, / I don't care 'cause the company will pay. . . . Given the current state of pro sports economics, "Take Me Out to the Ball Game" needs a little updating. And so does the **antediluvian** notion that fan support is the key to franchise success. (Steve Wulf, Business: "How Suite It Isn't—Cities Are Winning and Losing Teams Based on How Many Luxury Boxes They Can Offer Greedy Owners," *Time*, 7/10/1995, p. 52.)

(2) outdated *adj.*: **retardataire**. [French. This adjective is often applied to artistic styles, by suggesting that they are behind the times or belonging to an earlier period.] ❧ Beautifully crafted as [Mr. Youngerman's wood sculptures are], the forms seem uninspired, even **retardataire** in light of more inventive contemporary sculpture. And, sad to say, they lack the vitality of Mr. Youngerman's sprightly earlier pieces. (Grace Glueck, Art in Review, *New York Times*, 12/3/1997.)

(3) outdated *adj.*: **superannuated**. See *obsolete*

(4) outdated *adj.*: **démodé** [French]. See *outmoded*

outdoors *adv.*: **en plein air**. [French. This term, meaning "in the open air," applies specifically to painting outdoors, as opposed to in a studio, notably by the Impressionists. However, it is also more generally used as a synonym for "outdoors."] ❖ I found myself at a coffee-house on Beverly to do a little sightseeing of another ilk. After all, it wouldn't be L.A. without the paper, a good bagel and a sweet vantage point of the "colorful" foot traffic. I'd hoped for sunshine and seating **en plein air**. Naturally, it was gray, moist and chilly. (Marji Davis-Williams, "Only in L.A.: Los Angeles, the Uncontested and Proverbial Land of Opportunity," *Los Angeles Sentinel*, 6/21/2000.)

(2) outdoors *adv., adj.*: **alfresco**. ❖ [The forty-two-year-old teacher and her fifteen-year-old student] returned to Hampstead Heath many times. . . . at least twenty [to carry out their affair.] The **alfresco** aspect of their sexual relations has greatly exercised the press but, contrary to all the reporters' salacious innuendo, [they] did not feel that there was any erotic bonus to their trysting outdoors. (Zoë Heller, *What Was She Thinking?* Henry Holt [2003], p. 122.)

(3) outdoors (fear of being . . .) *n.*: **agoraphobia**. See *fear*

outfit *v.t.*: **accouter**. ❖ [Dennis] Rodman claims that just as he visits gay bars without caring what people think, so he **accouters** himself regardless of others. So what the hell, when Rodman hits the road, he always packs some women's clothes. (Evan Gahr, review of *Bad As I Wanna Be*, by Dennis Rodman, *National Review*, 7/1/1996, p. 53.)

outfitter (for men's clothing) *n.*: **haberdasher**. See *clothier*

outflow *n.*: **efflux**. ❖ [In the early days of baseball,] spacious center fields provided a place for the well-heeled cranks to park their carriages. In all ballyards in those days, overflow crowds were allowed into the outfield, roped off. Hits popped into this human **efflux** were marked as doubles or triples; better to sell more tickets than to keep the games pristine. (Frank Deford, *The Old Ball Game*, Atlantic Monthly Press [2005], p. 104.)

outgrowth *n.*: **excrescence**. [This word is often used literally, such as to describe an abnormal growth on the body or of a bodily part, such as a wart, but just as often it is used in the sense of being an offshoot or consequence of a prior event or circumstance.] ❖ [In *Ceasefire!* author Cathy Young's intention] is to unmask the false claims of these "thought police," especially as they concern the supposed continued inequality of women in the United States. [C]ourt cases involving gender violence and sex crimes, child abuse and domestic violence, child custody and school curricula [are] **excrescences** of a cultural agenda that has been put in place to support spurious feminist claims and provide employment for enforcers. (Elizabeth Powers, "What Our Mothers Didn't Tell Us: Why Happiness Eludes the Modern Woman," *Commentary*, 3/1/1999.)

outlaw (as in outcast) *n.*: **Ishmael**. See *outcast*

outline (in a sketchy or incomplete way) *v.t.*: **adumbrate**. ❖ Nikolai Gogol was nineteenth-century Russia's greatest writer of prose. Not its greatest prose writer: Dostoyevsky, [Tolstoy] and others, framed complexities that have no counterpart in their odd predecessor, and they wrote on a scale that dwarfed his. They explored ideas; he, at best, **adumbrated** them. (Donald Fanger, "The Unrealist," *New Republic*, 11/2/1998.)

(2) outline (as in set the boundaries of) *v.t.*: **delimit**. See *demarcate*

(3) outline (as in summary) *n.*: **conspectus**. See *survey*

(4) outline (distinctive . . . , often of a face) *adj.*: **lineament** (often **lineaments**). See *contour*

(5) outline (spec. a memorandum containing . . . or summary of an agreement or diplomatic negotiations) *n.*: **aide-mémoire** [French]. See *memorandum*

outlying (area of a city) *n.*: **banlieu** [French]. See *suburb*

(2) outlying (area) *n.*: **purlieus**. See *outskirts*

(3) outlying (as in surrounding) *adj.*: **circumjacent**. See *surrounding*

outmoded *adj.*: **démodé** [French]. ❖ Remember when popular movies had women in them? In 1994's top films, the ladies were lucky if the guys let them even drive a bus. Affirmative action is **démodé** these days, but Hollywood needs some spur to bring women into full partnership with the Tom [Hank]s and Arnold [Schwarzenegger]s and Simba [the lion]s. (*Time*, The Best Cinema of 1994, 12/26/1994, p. 132.)

(2) outmoded *adj.*: **superannuated**. See *obsolete*

(3) outmoded *adj.*: **antediluvian**. See *outdated*

out-of-control (and undisciplined person) *n.*: **bashi-bazouk** [Turkish]. See *undisciplined*

out of sight (as in, in concealment) *adv.*: **doggo** (esp. as in "lying doggo"; slang). See *concealment*

outpour (as in outflow) *n.*: **efflux**. See *outflow*

outrageous (and reckless person) *n.*: **rantipole**. See *wild*

(2) outrageous (as in infamous, esp. as to a crime or evil deed) *adj.*: **flagitious**. See *scandalous*

outset (existing from the . . . , as in innate) *adj.*: **connate**. See *innate*

(2) outset (from the) *adv.*: **ab initio** [Latin]. See *beginning*

(3) outset (from the) *adv.*: **ab ovio** [Latin]. See *beginning*

outside (as in originating from elsewhere; not endemic) *adj.*: **ecdemic**. See *foreign*

(2) outside (as in outdoors) *adv., adj.*: **alfresco**. See *outdoors*

(3) outside (fear of being . . .) *n.*: **agoraphobia**. See *fear*

(4) outside (from the . . .) *adv.*: **ab extra** [Latin]. See *externally*

(5) outside *adv.*: **en plein air** [French]. See *outdoors*

outsider (as in foreigner) *n.*: **auslander**. See *foreigner*

(2) outsider *n.*: **Ishmael**. See *outcast*

outskirt *n.*: **banlieu** [French]. See *suburb*

outskirts *n.pl.*: **purlieus**. ❖ Some guys will do anything for a laugh. Michael Smith has donned fake eyeglasses that make him look Japanese—in a room full of Japanese people. In the laid-back **purlieus** of Silicon Valley such idiosyncratic behavior might go unnoticed. But [Smith is] the government's chief trade negotiator, and that makes him a maverick in an unfunny business. (Andrew Kupfer, The Year's 25 Most Fascinating Business People: "Smith to Japan—Here's the Beef," *Fortune*, 1/2/1989, p. 53.)

outstanding (as in of the highest quality) *n.*: **first water** (usu. as in "of the first water"). See *quality*

(2) outstanding *adj.*: **frabjous** (often as in "Oh frabjous day!"). See *wonderful*

(3) outstanding *adj.*: **galumptious**. See *excellent*

(4) outstanding *adj.*: **mirific**. See *wonderful*

(5) outstanding *adj.*: **palmary**. See *excellent*

(6) outstanding *adj.*: **skookum**. See *excellent*

outward (appearance, as opposed to the substance that lies beneath) *n., n.pl.*: **superficies**. See *appearance*

overabundance *n.*: **nimiety**. See *excess*

overactive *adj.*: **hyperthyroid**. See *hyperactive*

overactive *adj.*: **sthenic**. See *overstimulated*

overall (as in predominant) *adj.*: **regnant**. See *predominant*

overambitious *adj.*: **Icarian**. [This word is based on the Greek mythological character Icarus, who flew so high on man-made wings that the sun melted them.] ❖ Edward O. Wilson's book is audacious, prophetic, and bound to become a recurrent touchstone to test intellectual progress in the twenty-first century. . . . E. O. Wilson boldly seeks no less than a unification of all knowledge so that we might "know who we are and why we are here." He acknowledges that this **Icarian** reaching for the sun is dangerous but asks to "see how high we can fly before the sun melts the wax in our wings." [Note: The author of this passage is using "Icarian" in the sense of "daring" (as opposed to "overly daring"), and the word is sometimes used in this sense. However, for something to be truly "Icarian," it must be overambitious and not merely ambitious, because the latter implies possible success and the former does not. Moreover, Mr. Wilson aspires to "see how high we can fly *before* the sun melts the wax in our wings," not "until" the sun melts the wax. Thus, in this example, since it is clear that the author feels that Mr. Wilson's venture was ultimately successful, it might have been more precise to call it "potential" Icarian reaching.] (Michael Werner, review of *Consilience: The Unity of Knowledge*, by Edward O. Wilson, *Humanist*, 3/1/1999.)

overbearing (as in condescending) *adj., adv.*: **de haut en bas** [French]. See *condescending*

(2) overbearing (as in haughty or condescending) *adj.*: **toplofty**. See *haughty*

(3) overbearing (as in haughty) *adj.*: **fastuous**. See *haughty*

(4) overbearing (woman who is domineering and . . .) *n.*: **virago**. See *shrew*

overblown (as in affected and high-flown, use of language) *adj.*: **euphuistic**. See *affected*

(2) overblown (as in pompous) *adj.*: **tumid**. See *bombastic*

(3) overblown (as in pompous) *adj.*: **turgid**. See *pompous*

overcast *adj.*: **lowering**. [This adjective means dark, threatening, and/or ominous, and is almost always used with respect to weather conditions, as in the example given.] ❧ April contains one day for fooling, but fickle February fools us repeatedly, teasing us with pleasant days and then tormenting us with icy rains and spitting, **lowering** skies. February is a drama of hope and despair. (B. J. Atkinson, "Cure the February Blues with a Taste of the Caribbean," *Virginian-Pilot*, 2/16/2000.)

overbroad (as in actions taken or statements made that are broader than necessary to hit their target or accomplish their goal) *adj., n.*: **blunderbuss**. See *scattershot*

overcritical (person) *n.*: **smellfungus**. See *faultfinder*

(2) overcritical *adj.*: **captious**. See *faultfinding*

overdone (as in gaudy) *adj.*: **meretricious**. See *gaudy*

(2) overdone (behavior) *n., adj.*: **operatics**. See *melodramatic*

overdue *adj., adv.*: **behindhand**. ❧ [Question to Julie Andrews:] I've heard you have an autobiography coming out? [Answer:] It's commissioned, but it's a little **behindhand** because I have a wonderful imprint of children's books and I've been very busy getting the first four ready for its debut in the fall. (Sean Smith, Newsmakers, *Newsweek*, 4/28/2003.)

overeat *v.t.*: **gormandize**. See *devour*

overeating (or drinking too much) *n.*: **crapulence**. See *indulgence*

overexcited *adj.*: **sthenic**. See *overstimulated*

overflowing (with) *adj.*: **aswarm**. See *teeming*

overhead *adj.*: **superjacent**. See *overlying*

overhear (as in eavesdrop) *v.t.*: **earwig**. See *eavesdrop*

overheat (a person or thing, often to create sweat) *v.t.*: **parboil**. See *heat*

overindulge (on food) *v.t.*: **gormandize**. See *devour*

overindulgence (esp. from eating or drinking too much) *n.*: **crapulence**. See *indulgence*

overlap (like roof shingles or fish scales) *v.t.*: **imbricate**. ❧ There is almost no English surname, however ancient and dignified, that cannot be instantly improved by the prefix "Spanker." So deeply is the habit and culture of corporal punishment **imbricated** with the national psyche that whole shelves of specialist literature . . . are regularly devoted to the subject. (Christopher Hitchens, Minority Report: Johnson & Johnson, *Nation*, 6/29/1998, p. 8.)

overlook (as in to deal with or treat inadequately or neglectfully) *v.t.*: **scant**. See *slight*

overlying *adj.*: **superjacent**. ❖ [L]et me say that under section 44 of the National Land Code 1965, a landowner is guaranteed his right to the use and enjoyment of his land, the **superjacent** air space and the subsoil (Salleh Buang, "Onus on Local Authority to Act Against Illegal Factories," *New Straits Times* [Malaysia], 1/20/2001.)

overprotect (or overly indulge) *v.t.*: **molly-coddle**. ❖ A series of arrests, and the perception [Nebraska coach Tom Osborne] was **mollycoddling** his players, brought torrents of criticism, none creating more than the case of Lawrence Phillips. Phillips . . . pleaded no contest to charges of assaulting a former girlfriend. Osborne initially announced he was kicked off the team but reinstated him in time for Nebraska's Fiesta Bowl victory over Florida. (Vahe Gregorian, "Osborne Will Retire; Orange Bowl Game Will Be His Farewell," *St. Louis Post-Dispatch*, 12/11/1997.)

overprotective (phenomenon of an . . . mother who is smothering and controlling of her sons, thus hindering their maturation and emotional development) *n.*: **momism**. See *mother*

overreaching (as in overambitious) *adj.*: **Icarian**. See *overambitious*

overrun (with) *adj.*: **aswarm**. See *teeming*

oversee (students taking an examination) *v.i.*: **invigilate**. See *proctor*

overseer (as in boss or owner) *n.*: **padrone**. See *boss*

   (2) overseer (brutal . . . , as in taskmaster) *n.*: **Simon Legree**. See *taskmaster*

   (3) overseer *n.*: **gerent**. See *manager*

overstate (as in exaggerate) *v.t.*: **aggrandize**. See *exaggerate*

   (2) overstate *v.t.*: **overegg**. See *exaggerate*

overstatement (abnormal propensity for . . .) *n.*: **mythomania**. See *embellishment*

   (2) overstatement (false . . . , as in boast, esp. one that is designed to harm or prejudice another) *n.*: **jactitation**. See *boast*

overstimulated *adj.*: **sthenic**. ❖ [Sexual disease] was conceived as an imbalance in the fundamental life force of the body, taking the form of either overexcitement (**sthenic** illness, as in nymphomania) or underexcitement (aesthenia). (Ann Goldberg, "The Eberbach Asylum and the Practice(s) of Nymphomania in Germany, 1815–1849," *Journal of Women's History*, 1/1/1998.)

over the hill (as in past one's prime) *n.*: **paracme**. See *past one's prime*

over the top (as in excessive) *adj.*: **de trop** [French]. See *excessive*

overthrow (as in unseat) *v.t.*: **unhorse**. See *unseat*

   (2) overthrow (sudden attempt to . . . a government) *n.*: **putsch**. See *coup*

overturning (an . . . regarding one's beliefs, causes, or policies) *n.*: **tergiversation** (*v.i.*: **tergiversate**). See *change of mind*

   (2) overturning (as in abandonment, from one's religion, principles, or causes) *n.*: **apostasy**. See *abandonment*

   (3) overturning (esp. regarding one's beliefs, causes, or policies) *n.*: **bouleversement** [French]. See *change of mind*

overused (remark or statement) *n.*: **platitude**. See *cliché*

overview (of a subject, as in survey) *n.*: **conspectus**. See *survey*

overweight (and squat) *adj.*: **fubsy**. See *squat*

   (2) overweight (as in beer-bellied) *adj.*: **abdominous**. See *beer-bellied*

   (3) overweight *adj.*: **pursy**. See *fat*

   (4) overweight (as in paunchy) *adj.*: **stomachy**. See *paunchy*

   (5) overweight (medical branch concerning . . . people) *n.*: **bariatrics**. See *obesity*

   (6) overweight *adj.*: **Pickwickian**. See *fat*

   (7) overweight (state of being . . .) *n.*: **avoirdupois**. See *weight*

overwork (death from . . .) *n.*: **karoshi** [Japanese]. See *death*

owner *n.*: **padrone**. See *boss*

ox (of, relating to, or resembling) *adj.*: **bovine**. ❖ Worldwide, most of the 400,000,000 animals trained for draft are of the **bovine** persuasion, according to Richard Roosenberg, director of Tillers International, an organization that promotes the use of draft animals in general and ox power in particular. (Gail Damerow, "Is There a Draft Animal in Your Future?" *Countryside & Small Stock Journal*, 11/21/1996, p. 37.)

oxygen (absence or deficiency of . . .) *n*.: **anoxia**. ❖ It seems to me that in about one-quarter of twin labors, the area of uterus overlying the second baby's placenta shrinks drastically enough to cut off the oxygen supply to that placenta, and consequently to the baby still in the uterus. When that happens, I believe the baby still has about 30 minutes before it will run into serious anoxia. (John Stevenson, "What If Something Goes Wrong?" Contemporary Women's Issues Database, 3/1/1994, p. 6.)

oysters (of or relating to) *adj*.: **ostreal**. ❖ The peninsula side of Shoalwater Bay, he confided, was lined with mountainous reefs of oysters— oysters far tastier and fatter than those currently making fortunes for the Bruce boys. If grandpa would agree to hire Nahcati's tribe as a crew, Nahcati would personally guide him to this **ostreal** treasure. (Willard Espy, "Oysterville: Roads to Grandpa's Village," books .google.com/books?isbn=0295972254 [1992].)

pacificism (as in nonviolence; Buddhist and Hindu doctrine of . . . , which expresses belief in sacredness of all living creatures). *n.*: **ahimsa**. See *nonviolence*

pacify (as in appease) *v.t.*: **dulcify**. See *appease*

(2) pacify *v.t.*: **propitiate**. See *placate*

pacifying (as in peacemaking) *adj.*: **irenic**. See *peacemaking*

pack (as in group) *n.*: **gaggle**. See *group*

(2) pack (of riders in a bike race) *n.*: **peloton** [French]. See *cluster*

packed (together, esp. in rows) *adj.*: **serried**. See *crowded*

pact *n.*: **amicabilis concordia**. [Latin for "friendly agreement." This term refers to a 1444 document signed by four colleges in England that pledged to cooperate with the others in various ways. The following example uses the term somewhat more in the sense of a treaty or truce.] ❖ [Stephen Jay Gould coined the term "NOMA" as an acronym for "nonoverlapping magisteria," meaning that religion and science should not overlap with each other.] The whole point of NOMA is that it is a two-way bargain. The moment religion steps on science's turf and starts to meddle in the real world with miracles, [Gould's] **amicabilis concordia** is broken. (Richard Dawkins, *The God Delusion*, Houghton Mifflin [2006], p. 60.)

paddle (instrument such as a . . . for punishing children) *n.*: **ferule**. ❖ [His] warmth did not affect what I judged the extreme severity of the punishment I was twice sentenced to, for whatever social infraction. The first time it was a single **ferule** stroke, smacked down on my open hand. (William F. Buckley Jr., "A Spiritual Autobiography," adapted from *Nearer, My God: An Autobiography of Faith*, National Review, 10/13/1997, p. 33.)

pain (as in occasion or place of great suffering) *n.*: **Gethsemane**. See *hell*

(2) pain (as in occasion or place of great suffering) *n.*: **Golgotha**. See *hell*

(3) pain (as in place or occasion of great suffering, or hell) *n.*: **Gehenna**. See *hell*

(4) pain (as in place, condition, or society filled with . . . ; spec., opposite of utopia) *n.*: **dystopia**. See *hell*

(5) pain (in joints) *n.*: **arthralgia**. See *arthritis*

(6) pain (medication causing inability to feel) *n.*: **analgesia**. See *numbness*

painful (journey or experience) *n.*: **via dolorosa**. See *ordeal*

pain in the ass *n.*: **proctalgia**. [Of course, this is technically a medical term (often used as part of the phrase "proctalgia fugax"), but it obviously has other uses.] ❖ I'm predicting that the ass falls out of that whole celebrity-worship thing. It's really been taken to an excruciating level, and I think there has to be some sort of a backlash. It's not like in the '60s, when [celebrities] were celebrities because they were creating new and original work. Now it's that whole red-carpet celebrity adulation. It's just so **proctalgia** inducing. Of course, it's a cyclical thing. (Simon Doonan, Forecast: Culture, *Esquire*, 3/1/2001.)

pain reliever *n.*: **anodyne**. ❖ As a boy, Rick had found in basketball his **anodyne**, his escape from loneliness, and he had spent hours on the courts of Queens, losing himself in the game. (William Nack, College Basketball: "Full-Court Pressure—The Kentucky Wildcats' Relentless Attack Reflects the Ferocious Drive of Their Coach, Rick Pitino," *Sports Illustrated*, 2/26/1996, p. 80.)

(2) pain reliever (as in something that induces forgetfulness of or indifference to pain, suffering, or sorrow) *n.*: **nepenthe**. See *narcotic*

pain-relieving (as in comforting and soothing) *adj.*: **anodyne**. See *soothing*

painting (dealing with evening or night) *n.*: **nocturne**. ❖ Making art outdoors on misty autumn evenings and brisk winter nights has its ups and downs for painter Mike Lynch and photographer Chris Faust, whose serene show of poetic nightscapes opens today at the Minneapolis Institute of Arts. [Faust] had admired Lynch's **nocturnes** for nearly 30 years, having first seen them when he was still in high

P

school. (Mary Abbe, "Night Moves/Photographer Chris Faust and Painter Mike Lynch Do Their Best Work on the Third Shift," *Minneapolis Star Tribune*, 12/15/2000.)

(2) painting (living, esp. by costumed performers sustaining a pose as if in a . . .) *n.*: **tableau vivant** [French]. See *pose*

(3) painting (which looks like a photograph or something real) *n.*: **trompe l'oeil** [French]. See *illusion*

paintings (produced in the artist's youth) *n.*: **juvenilia**. See *compositions*

pair (arranged in or forming a . . .) *adj.*: **jugate**. ❖ Political buttons come in all sizes, shapes, and classifications. . . . Picture buttons are the most popular, especially the **jugates** that picture both running mates on the same button. (Jesse Palmer, "Button Up Your Social Studies Classroom," *Social Studies*, 3/13/1996, p. 52.)

(2) pair (two individuals or units regarded as a . . .) *n.*: **dyad**. ❖ She also shows how a commitment to the ideal of a mother-child **dyad** has created the conditions in which mother and child can only function as a **dyad**. (Rebecca Abrams, review of *Mother of All Myths: How Society Molds and Constrains Motherhood*, by Aminatta Forna, *New Statesman*, 7/31/1998.)

(3) pair (of people, as in partnership) *n.*: **duumvirate**. See *duo*

pal (faithful . . . , as in companion) *n.*: **Achates**. See *companion*

palatable (as in edible) *adj.* **esculent**. See *edible*

(2) palatable (as in tasty) *adj.*: **sapid**. See *tasty*

pale (and often sickly) *adj.*: **etiolated**. [This term specifically refers to plants becoming whitened due to lack of exposure to sunlight, but it is also used more generally to describe a pale and sickly appearance or condition.] ❖ [After the concentration camp in Berga, Germany, was discovered in May 1945,] the **etiolated** bodies were exhumed—eloquent of malnutrition, sickness, abuse, and suffering—and later many more bodies of GIs were found scattered on the route of the death march southward as the investigators retraced it. (Roger Cohen, *Soldiers and Slaves*, Knopf [2005], p. 221.)

(2) pale (as from absence of sunlight) *adj.*: **etiolated**. ❖ I've been re-acquainting myself with parts of my body I have not seen since last summer. Such as my legs. And quite a shock it has been, to wiggle out of my boots and tights and see them in all their **etiolated** glory. They're so pale they're practically luminous. So I start a process of leg rehabilitation: the fake tan goes on, the drying position is assumed. (Hermione Eyr, Beauty Spot—Hermione Eyre Takes It All Off, *Independent on Sunday*, 5/9/2004.)

(3) pale (or corpselike) *adj.*: **cadaverous**. See *corpselike*

palm-reading *n.*: **chiromancy**. ❖ [A new ordinance] bans "the practice of foretelling events and the prophecy of the future." Since [the ban], business has been slow for the [fortune-tellers,] with tarot cards unturned and palms unread. . . . Certainly, **chiromancy** and tarot readings are no more absurd than the horoscopes published in this and other newspapers that circulate in Terrebonne Parish. (James Gill, "Crystal Ball Says Law Must Go," *New Orleans Times-Picayune*, 10/8/2000.)

paltry (as in meager) *adj.*: **mingy**. See *meager*

(2) paltry *n.*: **exiguous**. See *meager*

pamper *v.t.*: **cosset**. ❖ Let's start by defining terms. The "nanny state" is the phrase conservatives have long used to disparage liberal programs that they believe **cosset** the poor with entitlements and nitpick everyone else with meddlesome rules and regulations. (Ronald Brownstein, "When Daddy Is a Nag," *U.S. News & World Report*, 6/1/1998.)

(2) pamper (as in treat with excessive concern) *n.*, *v.t.*: **wet-nurse**. See *coddle*

(3) pamper (in an overprotective way or indulge) *v.t.*: **mollycoddle**. See *overprotect*

panacea (alleged . . . which is untested or unproved) *n.*: **nostrum**. See *remedy*

(2) panacea *n.*: **catholicon**. See *remedy*

pandemonium (as in chaos) *n.*: **tohubuhu**. See *chaos*

panhandler *n*.: **mendicant**. See *beggar*

panic *n*.: **Torschlusspanik**. [German. This word means literally "gate-closing panic," as in not wanting to be the last one left before the gate closes, or having the feeling that life's opportunities may be passing one by, and is used in a myriad of figurative ways, including: (1) a midlife crisis; (2) for women, the sense that one's biological clock is ticking; (3) at an auction, the sense that one must have one of the last pieces of a collection being sold; (4) and in a financial panic, such as when there is a run on a bank. The example used here is somewhat more literal, but the concept is clear.] ❖ The idea for the [Berlin] Wall is credited to Walter Ulbricht, leader of the GDR, who had told a press conference in June 1961: "No one intends to build a wall." No one took the hint. But with so many East Germans gripped with **Torschlusspanik**—the rush to escape before the door was finally shut (30,415 arrived in West Berlin in July 1961)—the authorities had to do something drastic. (Alan Taylor, "The Wall to End All Walls," *Scotland on Sunday*, 10/31/1999.)

(2) panic (state of . . . , as in distress) *n*.: **swivet** (as in "in a swivet") *informal*. See *distress*

panting *adj*.: **suspirious** (*v.t*.: **suspire**). ❖ If you missed the first episode [of the TV movie *Anna Karenina*] you've missed most of the excitement, such as it was. Anna and Vronsky . . . had at each other after about two chats and three glances—one of those blurry, **suspirious** TV fumbles where both parties seem to go from nought to orgasm in 10 seconds flat, and that's not easy with all those Victorian layers to remove. (James Hall, "Screenwatch—Passion at a Price," *Australian*, 7/6/2000.)

paradigm (as in that which set the standard or established the model from which others followed or on which others are based) *n*.: **locus classicus** [Latin]. See *model*

paradise (as in place of extreme luxury and ease where physical comforts and pleasures are always at hand) *n*.: **Cockaigne**. ❖ Imag-

ine a country where whole cooked chickens fall from the sky, rivers of ricotta cheese flow freely, and laziness is rewarded. In fact, working will get you arrested. This is the Land of **Cockaigne**, a fabled place longed for by the overworked, underfed peasants of the Middle Ages. It was their idea of paradise. Each age has had its visions of an ideal society. (*Christian Science Monitor*, "From Ancient Eden to the Hippie Era—Searching for Utopia: New York Public Library Launches a New Exhibition on the Perfect Place," 10/19/2000.)

(2) paradise (like . . . ; spec., having the characteristics of a mythical romantic place) *adj*.: **Ruritanian**. [This term derives from Ruritania, which was the fictional kingdom in the 1894 novel *The Prisoner of Zenda*, by Anthony Hope.] ❖ The most ancient city in the South Tirol, Bressanone is the most beautiful and best preserved of the larger towns in the province. In a glorious mountain setting at an altitude of more than 1,800 feet (560 meters), it is pleasantly cool in summer, and has an average of three times as many sunny days as Vienna. [The town] maintains a timeless, almost **Ruritanian** air. (Roderick Morris, "History on View," *International Herald Tribune*, 10/16/1998.)

(3) paradise (spec. a place of fabulous wealth or opportunity) *n*.: **El Dorado** [derives from legendary place in South America thought to exist by sixteenth-century explorers]. ❖ If there is an **El Dorado**, it may look like this. . . . Outside [of the Boca Raton Resort & Club], conjuring up a modern vision of the legendary city of fabulous wealth, yachts bob at pristine docks, exotic birds flit through manicured tropical foliage, and golfers purr around a lush course in motorized pink carts. (Susan Harrigan, "A White Man's World: Diversity in Management," *Newsday*, 4/13/2000.)

(4) paradise *n*.: **Xanadu** [after a place in *Kubla Kahn*, a poem by Samuel Taylor Coleridge]. ❖ [From the plane,] a stunning landscape glides into view: jagged fjords, ice-capped peaks, a green carpet of ancient cedars. [Douglas Tompkins] has spent four years and

$15 million quietly buying up this 667,000-acre swath in remote southern Chile. The . . . committed environmentalist wants to turn his pristine **Xanadu** into a national park, protecting this fragile land forever. There is only one problem. The locals think he is crazy. (David Schrieberg, "Firestorm in Paradise," *Newsweek*, 5/22/1995.)

paragon *n.*: **nonesuch**. ❖ *Parade* magazine asks Priscilla Presley if she believed daughter Lisa Marie Presley was behaving responsibly when she wed pop **nonesuch** Michael Jackson. The reply: "I don't think she thought she was irresponsible. Then she took responsibility and got out of it." (Harry Levins, People, *St. Louis Post-Dispatch*, 2/8/1997.)

paralysis (as in the dilemma of being given a choice between two equally appealing alternatives and thus being able to choose neither one) *n.*: **Buridan's ass** [attributed to fourth-century French philosopher Jean Buridan, who presented a situation where an ass is given the option of two equally wonderful piles of hay, and starves to death because it cannot choose]. ❖ Sarah Jessica Parker has . . . **Buridan's ass**. Poor girl. . . . In the issue of *Newsweek* that commemorates the anniversary of September 11, Little Miss Zeitgeist is asked to choose between "a pair of Manolos and a Kelly bag," and she replies, "Oh, well, that's like *Sophie's Choice*. That's an impossible situation." This is what passes for smart in Manhattan now. (Leon Wieseltier, Washington Diarist, *New Republic*, 9/22/2003.)

paraphernalia (esp. trivial or worthless . . .) *n.*: **trumpery**. See *junk*

paraphrase *n.*: **oratio obliqua** [Latin for "indirect speech"]. ❖ [H]ow did it come about that Mrs. Thatcher [was never told] the truth about the man at the heart of the Westland leak? . . . [T]hat can only be answered by those who were there in the thick of it. Which is why even two and a half hours of Sir Robert Armstrong's courtly **oratio obliqua** were not, in the end, any adequate substitute [for the actual] witnesses it had sent for but been denied. (David McKie, Parliamentary Commentary: "A Little Light Shines Wanly," *Guardian* [London], 2/6/1986.)

parasite (esp. someone who seeks to associate with or flatter persons of high rank or social status) *n.*: **tuft-hunter**. See *hanger-on*

pardon (as in place or occasion of humiliation or to seek forgiveness) *n.*: **Canossa**. See *penance*

pardonable *adj.*: **venial**. See *forgivable*

parent (biological . . .) *n.*: **genitor**. ❖ Among the Nayar of India, a woman weds several men. Any one of them can be a **genitor**, a biological father, but only one can be a pater, one who fulfills all the functions and social duties of a father. (David Murray, "Disappearance of Marriage Threatens to Destroy Our Culture," *National Minority Politics*, 8/31/1994.)

parents (in place of) *adv.*: **in loco parentis** [Latin]. ❖ Not so long ago, administrators acted **in loco parentis**, trying to protect the welfare of their students by setting down rules of conduct, ethics, even dress. But in the aftermath of the '60s rebellion, all that changed. Students demanded to be treated as autonomous adults, and administrators obliged. (Naomi Schaefer, "Campus Crackdown," *National Review*, 4/5/1999.)

pariah (as in outcast) *n.*: **Ishmael**. See *outcast*

parish (as in church congregation) *n.*: **ecclesia**. See *congregation*

(2) parish *n.*: **laity**. ❖ Abbott claims that Episcopal ordination "does not raise priests to some superior status above the **laity**." But it does. The proof is in the practice: No Episcopal lay person can preside at the Lord's Supper because **laity** lack the special grace given in ordination. (Unsigned letter to the editor, *Minneapolis Star Tribune*, 5/27/2000.)

parochial *adj.*: **parish-pump** [British]. ❖ It is TV . . . that gives a voice to smaller communities. Topics for discussion will include not only the national or international issues of the day—but also local **parish pump** issues from that particular town. (*Evening Post* [Wellington, New Zealand], "Small Towns Hit Big Time," 6/12/2000.)

parody (esp. by ridiculing or making fun of someone) *n.*, *v.t.*: **pasquinade**. See *satirize*

parrot (of, relating to, or resembling) *adj.*: **psittacine**. ❖ [W]hen Polly wants more than a cracker, there's www.parrot.com/birdhealth/recipes.htm. Among the **psittacine**-friendly recipes: popcorn pizza, sweet potato balls and tropical rice pudding. (Denise Flaim, "Just for Pets," *Newsday*, 3/28/2004.)

(2) parrot (as in repeat, mindlessly, ideas that have been drilled into the speaker, or repeat things that reflect the opinions of the powers that be) *v.t.*, *v.i.*, *n.*: **duckspeak**. See *recite*

part (as in portion) *n.*: **moiety**. See *portion*

partial (to a particular point of view) *adj.*: **tendentious**. See *biased*

particular (overly . . .) *adj.*: **persnickety**. See *picky*

particularity (as in that quality which makes one thing different from any other) *n.*: **haecceity** (or **haeccity**). See *individuality*

particularized *adj.*: **pointillistic**. [This word derives from pointillism, the style of painting popularized by French neoimpressionist Georges Seurat in which tiny dots are applied to a canvas which create images that can only be seen from a distance.] ❖ [On the eve of the 1996 elections, voters have] fundamentally local concerns. . . . It is an era of **pointillistic** politics, which Clinton has matched by creating a **pointillistic** presidency, brimming with discrete, specific initiatives rather than some national crusade for renewal or reform. One reason is that Americans increasingly prefer local and state solutions to inflexible programs imposed by Washington. (Kenneth T. Walsh, "On the Brink," *U.S. News and World Report*, 11/4/1996).

parting shot *n.*: **Parthian shot** [derives from the custom of horsemen from Parthia, an ancient kingdom in West Asia, of firing arrows back at the enemy while retreating, or pretending to be retreating]. ❖ [F]ormer Bush aide John Dilulio . . . complained in his **Parthian shot** that the Bush White House paid far more attention to politics and message management than policy. "In eight months, I heard many, many staff discussions, but not three meaningful, substantive policy discussions," he wrote in a memo published by *Esquire* magazine. (Ron Hutcheson, "Insiders Portray President as Deaf to Outside Voices,"*Miami Herald*, 3/28/2004.)

parting words *n.*: **envoi**. [French. The primary definition of *envoi* is the explanatory or concluding remarks to a poem, essay, or book. However, it is also defined as any kind of parting word or farewell generally.] ❖ To my deep regret, I didn't get to see the perfect **envoi** to the '96 campaign—ABC's ancient marinator David Brinkley fulminating late on election night about "more goddamned nonsense" while . . . Peter Jennings shushed him. Just my luck: Brinkley has long been TV's greatest unwitting surrealist this side of Shari Lewis, and after all these years I'm MIA for his swan song. (Tom Carson, "Not Daffy?" *Village Voice*, 11/19/2006.)

partisan (as in fanatic) *n.*: **energumen**. See *fanatic*

(2) partisan *adj.*: **tendentious**. See *biased*

partition (esp. into districts or geographic regions) *v.t.*: **cantonize**. See *divide*

(2) partition (into two parts, esp. by tearing apart or violent separation) *n.*: **diremption**. See *separation*

partner (close . . . or associate, often, but not always, one in marriage) *n.*: **yokefellow**. ❖ Submission [in marriage] does not symbolize weakness. Submission is the epitome of strength because marriage is, or at least should be, a lifetime proposition. Marriage requires both the husband and the wife to practice submission. It requires a lifetime of fine-tuning to keep the two **yokefellows** pulling together, loving, serving and enjoying each other. (Sonya Toler, "There's Strength in Submission," *New Pittsburgh Courier*, 6/17/1998.)

(2) partner (as in comrade) *n.*: **tovarich** [Russian]. See *comrade*

partnership (of two people) *n.*: **duumvirate**. See *duo*

party (with boisterous public demonstrations) *v.i.*: **maffick** [British]. See *celebrate*

(2) party (as in engaging in noisy revelry or merrymaking) *v.i.*: **roister**. See *revel*

partyer (female . . .) *n.*: **bacchante** (male . . . : **bacchant**). See *reveler*

(2) partyer *n.*: **roisterer**. See *revel*

partying (riotous . . .) *n., adj.*: **bacchanal** (reveler *n.*: **bacchant**). See *revelry*

passage (as in excerpt, esp. from the Bible) *n.*: **pericope**. See *excerpt*

(2) passage (difficult or painful . . .) *n.*: **via dolorosa**. See *ordeal*

passé (as in outdated, obselete) *adj.*: **antediluvian**. See *outdated*

(2) passé *adj.*: **démodé** [French]. See *outmoded*

(3) passé *adj.*: **retardataire** [French]. See *outdated*

(4) passé *adj.*: **superannuated**. See *obsolete*

passing (as in brief or fleeting) *adj.*: **evanescent**. See *transient*

(2) passing (away quickly) *adj.*: **fugacious**. See *fleeting*

passing comment *n.*: **obiter dictum** [Latin]. ❖ I am in error about "an economic writer" and need to get out of error fast. In a recent **obiter dictum**, I parenthesized: "An 'economic writer' is a writer who uses as few words as possible." . . . "Didn't you really mean 'economical writer'?" [correctly] comments George Kelley. (William Safire, On Language: "Let Freedom Love," *New York Times*, 5/16/1982.)

passing gas (of or relating to) *adj.*: **borborygmic**. ❖ Cows, as it turns out, are highly **borborygmic**, though their gas does not pass through the anus but rather through the mouth. Indeed, cows produce 60 million tons of methane gas a year from their ruminative digestive practices and burp it into the atmosphere, producing more than 15% of the world's methane each year. (Adam Bresnick, "Baedeker for the Bowels," *Los Angeles Times*, 11/14/1999.)

(2) passing gas (of or relating to reducing . . .) *adj.*: **carminative**. See *farting*

passing over (or omitting or neglecting) *n.*: **preterition**. See *omitting*

passion (mad or crazy . . .) *n.*: **amour fou** [French]. See *love*

(2) passion (sexual . . . for the elderly) *n.*: **gerontophilia**. See *lust*

(3) passion (spec. the emotional thrill and excitement one feels when initially in love) *n.*: **limerence** (*adj.*: **limerent**). See *love*

(4) passion (excessive or unbridled . . . , as in enthusiasm) *n.* **schwarmerei** (or **schwärmerei**) [German]. See *enthusiasm*

passionate (as in rash or impetuous person) *n.*: **Hotspur**. See *impetuous*

(2) passionate (as in sexual lovemaking) *adj.*: **amatory**. See *lovemaking*

passive (as in sluggish or lethargic) *adj.*: **torpid**. See *lethargic*

passivity (as in lethargy) *n.*: **hebetude**. See *lethargy*

(2) passivity (as in condition of stupor or unconsciousness resulting from narcotic drugs) *n.*: **narcosis**. See *stupor*

passkey (spec. something such as a . . . that allows one to gain access or pass at will) *n.*: **passe-partout** [French for "pass everywhere"]. ❖ [In the 1991 movie *Cape Fear*, Max Cady,] it seems, can enter the Bowden residence at will, terrorizing the family with sundry small mementos, such as poisoning the beloved pooch. . . . Even more extraordinary than his **passe-partout** gift is the education Max has acquired in his 14 years' imprisonment, seven of them brought on by his murdering a fellow inmate: "I needed vice in the joint to remind me that I'm human." (John Simon, review of *Cape Fear*, *National Review*, 12/16/1991.)

pass out *n.*: **syncope**. See *fainting*

pass over (intentionally) *v.t.*: **pretermit**. See *omit*

past (as in former) *adj.*: **quondam**. See *former*

(2) past (as in former) *adj.*: **whilom**. See *former*

(3) past (of or relating to the . . . , spec. yesterday) *adj.*: **hesternal**. See *yesterday*

pastime (as in favorite topic or activity) *n.*:

cheval de bataille [French for "battle-horse"]. See *hobby*

past one's prime *n.*: **paracme**. [This uncommon but legitimate word derives from the Greek, para + acme, or past the height. It is used to refer to that period in a person's life when he is past his prime, which, in the view of the writer of this example, is not necessarily a bad thing.] ❖ **Paracme** brings wisdom and the understanding that each day is to be savored. It could be argued that you really do not start to live fully until you reach **paracme**; everything before that is preparation for the life you were destined to live. (Stephen Bales, "Nature Calling," stephenlynbales.blogspot.com/2008_08_01_archive.html, 8/11/2008)

pastoral (as in a place that is peaceful, rustic, and simple) *adj.*: **Arcadian**. ❖ [T]he festival's **Arcadian** home [is] nestled in the foothills of the Green Mountains in southern Vermont, . . . far from the stresses of urban life. . . . Being at Marlboro, says [a musician], "is like being in a kind of idyllic paradise where your purpose for all this practicing that you've done in your life is realized." (Jeremy Eichler, "The Marlboro Music Festival Celebrates 50 Years of Artistic Freedom and Determination," *Newsday*, 11/3/2000.)

pasty (as in pale, and often sickly) *adj.*: **etiolated**. See *pale*

paternal (of or relating to name of . . . ancestor) *adj.*: **patronymic**. ❖ [I]n the societal shifts of the past 40 years, women have repeatedly won the legal right to give their children their surnames. This has been a change from the **patronymic**, male-dominant norm handed down through several hundred years of European law that formed the basis for U.S. legal codes and social customs. (Neely Tucker, "Alexander's Last Name Is Illegal; Parents Seeking a Birth Certificate Fight D.C. Regulation," *Washington Post*, 5/15/2002.)

pathetic (or pitiful) *adj.*: **ruthful**. See *pitiful*

patience (in the face of adversity) *n.*: **longanimity**. ❖ What my Christian experience teaches me [is that] forgiveness does ideally come first and can, with . . . **longanimity**, yield a rich harvest of justice and peace in the way it facilitates the righting of wrongs and the reconciliation of the estranged. (Michael Hurley, "A Sober Truth Must Be Faced About Lack of Forgiveness," *Irish Times*, 10/24/1995.)

patriotism *n.*: **amor patriae** [Latin; lit. love of country]. ❖ My hope is that those history books of tomorrow will accord not shame but praise and honor to those American citizens who wanted to see justice prevail [in the Clinton impeachment proceedings] and who refused to allow reasonable outrage to die. Who hold within them a noble and ennobling sentiment: **amor patriae**. Love of country. (William Bennett, "Clinton Will 'Continue to Tarnish the Highest Office,'" *Washington Times*, 8/21/1998.)

patron (generous . . . , esp. of the arts) *n.*: **Maecenas**. See *benefactor*

(2) patron (regular . . . of a place, esp. a place of entertainment) *n.*: **habitué** [French]. See *regular*

patronizing (as in condescending) *adj.*, *adv.*: **de haut en bas** [French]. See *condescending*

(2) patronizing (as in haughty) *adj.*: **fastuous**. See *haughty*

pattern (as in that which set the standard or established the model from which others followed or on which others are based) *n.*: **locus classicus** [Latin]. See *model*

paunchy *adj.*: **stomachy**. ❖ Why does Baltimore deserve an NFL franchise? Because you've got a pricey aquarium? You want pricey? We've got pricey. Try parking at USAir Arena. Because of Boog Powell's barbecued ribs? You want a **stomachy** former athlete hawking food? . . . Because of the Colts test in *Diner*? . . . I'll take the back of the limo scene in *No Way Out*. (Tony Kornheiser, "Cheese for Their Whine," *Washington Post*, 10/28/1993.)

(2) paunchy (as in beer-bellied) *adj.*: **abdominous**. See *beer-bellied*

pause *n.*: **caesura**. ❖ Many of [the best moments in the novel *Battle Creek*] have to do with baseball, a subject Lasser knows his way around; he captures the game's interludes, its breaths and **caesuras**, with subtlety and grace. (David L. Ulin, "Baseball's Sweet Song," *Newsday*, 5/2/1999.)

(2) pause (as in hesitate to act due to indecision) *v.i.*: **dither**. See *procrastinate*

(3) pause (as in procrastinate or hesitate to act) *v.i.*: **shilly-shally**. See *procrastinate*

(4) pause (words such as um, uh, you know, etc.) *n.*: **embolalia** (or **embololalia**). See *stammering*

pawn (as in willing tool or servant of another) *n.*: **âme damnée** [French]. See *lackey*

payback (for damage or loss) *n.*: **quittance**. See *recompense*

(2) payback (in kind) *n.*: **lex talionis** [Latin]. See *eye for an eye*

(3) payback (of or relating to . . . in kind) *n.*: **talionic**. See *revenge*

payment (or wages) *n.*: **emolument**. See *wages*

peace (long period of . . . resulting from domination of one country—thus peace sustained by force) *n.*: **Pax Romana** [lit. Roman peace—referring to period of peace from 30 B.C. to 200 A.D. enforced by the Roman Empire]. ❖The United States has a vital interest in helping the United Nations to develop a competent and respected peace-keeping capability, especially since we will never again possess the hegemony conferred by the cold war. The end of the U.S.-Soviet "**Pax Romana**" will certainly encourage the eruption of many more local wars. It is in our national interest that they be contained and resolved quickly. (*Commonweal*, "Why Bosnia Matters," 7/14/1995.)

(2) peace (Buddhist and Hindu doctrine of . . . , as in nonviolence) *n.*: **ahimsa**. See *nonviolence*

peace of mind *n.*: **heartsease**. ❖ The players . . . one by one sought [golfer Greg Norman] out to [tell him] that they were proud of him and thoroughly impressed by the way he handled his defeat at the Masters. Everywhere, the galleries stood and cheered. The goodwill was **heartsease** to Norman, and more than his cynicism could take. On Wednesday he

declared himself a changed man. (Robinson Holloway, "Lovable Loser—A Funny Thing Happened to Greg Norman After His Disaster at the Masters," *Sports Illustrated*, 4/29/1996, p. G6.)

(2) peace of mind (as in calmness) *n.*: **ataraxy** (or **ataraxia**). See *calmness*

peaceful (and carefree time) *adj.*: **prelapsarian**. See *innocent*

(2) peaceful (as in a place that is . . . , rustic and simple) *adj.*: **Arcadian**. See *pastoral*

peacefulness (as in gentleness) *n.*: **mansuetude**. See *gentleness*

(2) peacefulness (Buddhist and Hindu doctrine of . . . , which expresses belief in sacredness of all living creatures) *n.*: **ahimsa**. See *nonviolence*

(3) peacefulness (as in tranquillity) *n.*: **quietude**. See *tranquillity*

peaceful resistance *n.*: **satyagraha** [Sanskrit]. See *nonviolent resistance*

peacemaking *adj.*: **irenic**. ❖ Peace is not exciting. . . . It is a rare society that tells exemplary stories of peacemaking—except, say, for the Gospels of Christ, whose **irenic** grace may be admired from a distance, without much effect on daily behavior. (Lance Morrow, Men of the Year: "The Peacemakers to Conquer the Past," *Time*, 1/3/1994, p. 32.)

peace offering (such as flowers, to a wife from a guilty husband) *n.*: **drachenfutter** [German; lit. dragon fodder.] ❖ It used to be common practice for German men working on a katzenjammer (a monumentally severe hangover) to go out carousing with their **drachenfutter** already bought and wrapped in anticipation of the harangue ahead. (Sam Orbaum, "Korinthenkacker," *Jerusalem Post*, 1/20/1989.)

(2) peace offering *n.*: **eirenicon**. ❖ [Martin Luther King's "I have a dream"] speech can be appreciated as an **eirenicon**—a thing of peace—which even today brings disparate people together more than the civil rights leader could ever have dreamed. (Jonathan Keats, "The Power of the Pulpit," *Christian Science Monitor*, 7/10/2003.)

peace treaty (which is so severe that it leads to the virtual destruction of the defeated party) *n.*: **Carthaginian peace**. [This term derives from the uneasy peace from 201 B.C. to 150 B.C. when Carthage, having lost two wars against Rome between 264 B.C. and 201 B.C., was forced to acknowledge the political hegemony of Rome. It is often used to refer to the peace imposed on Germany after World War I.] ❖ [Margaret MacMillan's] assessment does not include the common notion that the greatest failure of the [1919 Paris Peace] Conference was that it imposed an unjust and **Carthaginian peace** on Germany and thereby inevitably gave rise to World War II. "Hitler did not wage war because of the Treaty of Versailles," Ms. MacMillan writes. . . . Even if Germany had retained everything that was taken from it at Versailles, he would have wanted more. (Richard Bernstein, "Guide to How Not to Alter the World," *New York Times*, 11/27/2002.)

peacock (of or resembling) *adj.*: **pavonine**. ❖ We wish Russia would issue new ruble denominations to bridge the rather expansive gaps between 10 rubles and 50 rubles, or 100 and 500. This lack of "inbetweenies" puts a strain on consumers and retailers alike. . . . Russia has shown almost **pavonine** vanity in the past when it comes to revamping its currency—let that spirit rise again, this time in a way that will truly be useful. Give the people their 25-ruble notes! (*Moscow Times* [Russia], "Best Wishes for Russia in New Year," 12/23/2000.)

(2) peacock (man who is vain like a . . .) *n.*: **fop**. See *vain*

(3) peacock (man who is vain like a . . .) *n.*: **popinjay**. See *vain*

peak (as in highest point that can be attained or the ultimate degree, as of a condition or quality) *n.*: **ne plus ultra**. See *ultimate*

(2) peak (the . . . , as in the pinnacle) *n.* **Parnassus**. See *pinnacle*

(3) peak (as in climax, of a drama) *n.*: **catastatis**. See *climax*

pear (shaped) *adj.*: **pyriform**. ❖ Like many of my sex I am **pyriform**, pear-shaped. (Diane White, "Words Worth a Thousand Pictures," *Boston Globe*, 8/1/1996.)

pearly *adj.*: **nacreous**. See *iridescent*

(2) pearly *adj.*: **opalescent**. See *iridescent*

peculiar (as in unusual) *adj.*: **selcouth**. See *unusual*

(2) peculiar *adj.*: **outré** [French]. See *unconventional*

(3) peculiar *adj.*: **pixilated**. See *eccentric*

peculiarity (as in notion that is odd, stubborn, or whimsical) *n.*: **crotchet**. See *notion*

(2) peculiarity (as in someone or something that deviates from the norm) *n.*: **lusus** [Latin; almost always used as part of the term "lusus naturae," or freak of nature]. See *freak*

pedantic (of a . . . word or term) *adj.*: **inkhorn**. ❖ Mariani adds an academic, contemporary slant to his assessment of Crane's life and poetry. In his Prolegomenon (an **inkhorn** term for an introduction), he says: "It would be difficult to find a serious poet or reader of poetry in the U.S. today who has not been touched by something in Hart Crane's music." (*Toronto Star*, "Each Desperate Choice," 5/16/1999.)

(2) pedantic *adj.*: **donnish**. [This word, which means characteristic of a university don (the equivalent of a university professor), can have either a positive or a neutral connotation, as when used to mean scholarly or bookish, or a negative connotation, as when used to mean pedantic. An example of the latter is used here. An example of the former is found under "bookish."] ❖ Lawrence doesn't wear his academic credentials lightly. His **donnish** prattle has all the charm of a nine o'clock lecture in a [drafty], badly-lit room. Visiting a lady-friend who likes him more than he likes her, he observes: "In deferring to her sense of what existed between us, I appeared to have put myself in a position of paradoxical power." No wonder he has trouble getting dates. (*Economist*, "Getting the Horn," 2/2/2002)

(3) pedantic (person on issues of grammar) *n.*: **grammaticaster**. ❖ [Peter Prescott, an editor at *Newsweek* magazine, wrote to me to say:] "I shouldn't have used a word [fulsome] that is so often misused that its correct use will set the **grammaticasters** to fluttering." (William Safire, On Language, *New York Times*, 1/30/1983.)

(4) pedantic (speaker or writer who is dull and boring) *n.*: **dryasdust**. See *boring*

(5) pedantic (but actually possessing only superficial knowledge of a subject) *n.*: **sciolism**. See *superficial*

pee *v.i.*: **micturate**. See *urinate*

peeing (backwards, or animals that do so) *adj.*, *n.*: **retromingent**. See *urinating*

peek (quick . . . , as in glance) *n.*: **coup d'oeil** [French]. See *glance*

(2) peek (with a sideways . . .) *adv.*: **asquint**. See *glance*

(3) peek *n.*: **dekko** [British; informal]. See *glance*

peephole (esp. on a prison door) *n.*: **judas hole** (or **judas window**; sometimes cap.) ❖ Privacy is unheard of in prisons like Strangeways. Every hour of every day, you are being watched. The cell door has a **judas hole** and eyes without faces peer in at you. Male eyes, female eyes, whilst you try to eat, sleep, read, and take care of nature's functions. (John Sutton, "Grassroots: Loose Screws," *Guardian* [London], 6/8/1990.)

peerless (person or thing) *n.*: **nonesuch**. See *paragon*

peevish *adj.*: **querulous**. ❖ For now, [Ross] Perot's jousts with the press pay off for him. Each time reporters try to rough him up on television, scores, if not hundreds, of new campaign volunteers step forward. Over time, however, a series of confrontations could make him seem **querulous** and diminish his appeal. (David Gergen, "Riding the Perot Wave," *U.S. News & World Report*, 6/15/1992.)

(2) peevish (person) *n.*: **crosspatch**. See *grouch*

(3) peevish *adj.*: **atrabilious**. See *surly*

(4) peevish *adj.*: **bilious**. See *surly*

(5) peevish *adj.*: **liverish**. See *irritable*

(6) peevish *adj.*: **shirty**. See *irritable*

(7) peevish *adj.*: **splenetic**. See *irritable*

(8) peevish *adj.*: **tetchy**. See *grouchy*

(9) peevish *adj.*: **waspish**. See *irritable*

pejorative (or expressing disapproval) *adj.*: **dyslogistic**. See *uncomplimentary*

penalize *v.t.*: **mulct**. ❖ [O]ne doesn't have to look [far] to find examples of courts willing to soak foreign companies. . . . A North Carolina jury recently **mulcted** the Meineke muffler chain for an estimated $400 million to $600 million, more than the annual profits of its large British parent company, after a lawyer invited jurors to "send a message to foreign companies." (Walter Olson, "Their Own Petard," *Reason*, 1/1/1998, p. 42.)

(2) penalize (as in impose a monetary fine) *v.t.*: **amerce**. See *fine*

penalty *n.*: **mulct**. See *penalize*

penance (place or occasion of . . . or humiliation or hoped-for forgiveness) *n.*: **Canossa** (often as in "go to Canossa") [derives from town in Italy to which Emperor Henry IV traveled in 1077 to seek penance (and revocation of his excommunication) from Pope Gregory VII for appointing his own bishops]. ❖ This was . . . Donald Rumsfeld's **Canossa**. At Munich's annual security policy conference the American defense secretary . . . kept his mouth shut . . . which was itself so dramatic a change from his abrasive performance last year. . . . The reason for his change is that the occupation and democratic reinvention of Iraq is going rather badly, and the United States wants Europe's help, even the help of those European governments that opposed Washington on the war. (William Pfaff, "In Munich, Rumsfeld's Silence Speaks Volumes: Seeking Help for Iraq," *International Herald Tribune*, 2/13/2004.)

(2) penance (spec. the opportunity to withdraw from, or decide not to commit, an intended crime) *n.*: **locus poenitentiae** [Latin]. See *repentance*

penetrate (as in pass through) *v.t.*: **transpierce**. ❖ [Fall foliage] leaf images that seem to be inhabited by sunlight were [in fact often] made indoors. . . . In the studio, the [picked] leaves were laid in a [computer] cassette. . . . In turn, the cassette with its slim cargo was placed in a computer and scanned by a light source. [If] the object in the cassette is too thick, the scanner will obediently record its outlines, but not **transpierce** it. The sense of life within will be missing. (Florence Shinkle, "True Colors," *St. Louis Post-Dispatch*, 10/30/1991.)

(2) penetrate (as in pierce) *v.t.*: **lancinate**. See *pierce*

penetrating (having a . . . quality) *adj.*: **gimlet** (esp. as in "gimlet eye") [based on a gimlet tool, which is used for boring holes]. ❖ "I'm on a very lucky streak, and I can't believe there's any real reason for it," says [Wayne Knight—the character Newman in *Seinfeld*], who off-camera is smart, funny and quick to turn a **gimlet** eye on the unreality that surrounds his business. ["When people ask me], 'Where's Jerry?' I want to tell to them, 'I don't know, get out of your pitiful fantasy world and come back to Earth.'" (Drew Jubera, "Seinfeld's Wiseguy," *Atlanta Journal-Constitution*, 8/8/1993.)

(2) penetrating (as in keen or incisive) *adj.*: **trenchant**. See *incisive*

penetration (esp. of penis into vagina) *n.*: **intromission** (*v.t.*: **intromit**). ❖ One way [that a person with Peyronie's disease can become sexually disabled] is that the penis becomes distorted so that, mechanically, **intromission** cannot be achieved. Some innovative patients manage to remain sexually active, but it is a matter of acrobatics and, for most couples, is not very enjoyable. (*Urology Times*, "Charting Reconstruction's Present, Future," 1/1/1995, p. 2.)

penis (having an abnormally large . . .) *adj.*: **macrophallic**. ❖ The Large Penis Support Group claims to be [an online] support group for people (well, probably men) with abnormally large male genitals. . . . Topics on the site include fashion, sports, events and other things that would genuinely be of interest to those naturally drawn to this online oasis of **macrophallic** torment. (James Norton, "Large Penis Support Group," *flakmagazine.com*, 11/10/2000.)

(2) penis (having an erect . . .) *adj.*: **ithyphallic**. ❖ Min was an **ithyphallic** god, with a very pronounced penis on the early statutes, and the vajra in Tibet had a mystic connection with male power. (*Parabola*, "The Meaning of the Thunderbolt," 1/1/92.)

(3) penis (of an animal, esp. a bull or deer) *n.*: **pizzle**. ❖ The New Zealand deer **pizzle** trade is facing its stiffest test—the growing use of a Viagra substitute by Chinese men. About 200,000 of the deer penises, complete with testicles, are sent to China from New Zealand each year. . . . The **pizzles** were generally served in a soup, after being boiled for hours with herbs. Sometimes, a three-pizzle soup was made, from deer, snake and seal pizzles and served in slices. (Jon Morgan, "China's Pizzle Market Begins to Fizzle," *Press* [Christchurch, New Zealand], 10/5/2004.

(4) penis (removal of one's own) *n.*: **autopeotomy**. ❖ It is a brave, foolhardy, and desperate man who will perform an **autopeotomy**, in which one removes one's own organ—the more so when the operation is done in an unsterile environment and with a pen knife. (Simon Winchester, *The Professor and the Madman*, HarperCollins [1998], p. 193.)

(5) penis (small . . .) *n.*: **microphallus**. ❖ In a 1997 *Men's Health* article entitled "An Inch Too Far," I'd stated categorically that the only people who should even think of getting penis extensions were "men cursed with **microphalluses**, victims of car accidents, or editors at *Vanity Fair*. (Joe Queenan, *My Goodness*, Hyperion [2000], p. 158.)

(6) penis *n.*: **membrum virile** [Latin]. ❖ [In *The Golden Ass*, written in the second century,] the randy young intellectual finds himself transformed not into the wise owl he had hoped to become, but an ass. He's captured by robbers, turned into a freak show, humiliated and beaten, but there is one bonus. Society ladies find his impressive **membrum virile** irresitible—and don't seem at all deterred by the fact that it is attached to a donkey. (Charles Spencer, "A Thoroughly Enchanting Ass," *Daily Telegraph* [London], 8/17/2002.)

(7) penis (of, relating to, or resembling a . . .) *adj.*: **priapic**. See *phallic*

(8) penis (insertion of . . . into vagina) *n.*: **intromission** (*v.t.*: **intromit**). See *penetration*

penitence (as in place or occasion to show . . . and to seek forgiveness) *n.*: **Canossa**. See *penance*

(2) penitence *n.*: **metanoia**. [This Greek word, meaning change of mind or heart, refers specifically to a fundamental transformation of one's character or way of thinking, and is often used to refer to a spiritual conversion. It is often said to translate as "repentance" as well as change of mind (and thus it is a possible, though somewhat narrow, synonym for "penitence"), though as one writer has said, "**metanoia** is not simply repentance, nor even penitence: it is transformation (metamorphosis), regeneration, new birth." (Leandro Bosch, "The Assembly Theme," *Ecumenical Review*, 7/1/2005.) See *conversion* for the example.]

(3) penitence (spec. the opportunity to withdraw from, or decide not to commit, an intended crime) *n.*: **locus poenitentiae** [Latin]. See *repentance*

(4) penitence (spec. a recognition of one's errors, and a return to a sane, sound, or correct position) *n.*: **resipiscence**. See *reformation*

penmanship (study of . . . esp. to study character) *n.*: **graphology**. See *handwriting*

pen name (spec. woman's use of a man's name) *n.*: **pseudandry**. See *pseudonym*

pennant (suspended from a crossbar, as opposed to on a flagstaff) *n.*: **gonfalon**. See *banner*

penniless *adj.*: **impecunious**. See *poor*

(2) penniless *adj.*: **necessitous**. See *poor*

penny pincher (as in miser) *n.*: **lickpenny**. See *miser*

perceive (by careful observation or scrutiny) *v.t.*: **descry**. ❖ Dear Oddist: As a lifelong devotee of the weird, outre, and paranormal, I was naturally all aquiver on August 1 when the Dow Jones industrials rose by 33.67, a figure that "eerily matched" the gains of the previous trad-ing day. . . . I was wondering if you might conceivably **descry** significance in the fact that it happened soon after those comets started banging into my favorite planet, Jupiter. (Daniel Seligman, "Strange Days on Wall Street," *Fortune*, 9/5/1994, p. 113.)

(2) perceive (based on past experience) *v.t.*: **apperceive**. See *comprehend*

(3) perceive (through the senses) *adj.*: **sensate**. See *feel*

perceptible (barely . . .) *adj.*: **liminal**. See *invisible*

perception *adj.*: **ken**. ❖ There are limits, however, to how well the e-noses can be educated. Wine connoisseurs, for example, can distinguish fragrances beyond the **ken** of any chip. (Unmesh Kher, Science: "Electronic Noses Sniff Out a Market or Two: Chemical Sensing Just Got Sexy, Can't You Smell It?" *Time*, 3/20/2000, p. 64.)

(2) perception (high degree of . . .) *adj.*: **acuity**. See *keenness*

(3) perception *n.*: **aperçu** [French]. See *insight*

perceptive (as in wise) *adj.*: **sapient**. See *wise*

(2) perceptive *adj.*: **perspicacious**. See *astute*

(3) perceptive *adj.*: **trenchant**. See *incisive*

perfect (as in faultless or sinless) *adj.*: **impeccant**. See *faultless*

perfect example (of something) *n.*: **beau ideal**. See *ideal*

perfectionist (person who is a . . . , as in stickler, in observing established rules or customs, esp. with regard to religious belief) *n.*: **precisian**. See *stickler*

performer (street . . .) *n.*: **busker**. ❖ Separately, around 50 **buskers** urged the City Council to let them work the streets and earn a living amidst a mounting official crackdown aimed at restoring order in the city. "We only want to sing. We don't want to cause trouble," 23-year-old Adji Kusuma, one of the street singers, told Commission E on public welfare. (*Jakarta Post*, "Mayors Postpone Crackdown on Street Vendors," 7/18/2000.)

perfume bottle (giant . . . usually used for display purposes) *n.*: **factice**. ❖ "Perfume giants of the auction black [*sic*]," the first annual silent **factice** audition at Sephora, New York, NY, raised more than $10,000. More than 60 giant perfume bottles donated by the Fragrance Foundation and leading perfume bottle collectors were auctioned at Sephora in Rockefeller Center in January. (*Household & Personal Products Industry*, "Sephora Holds First Silent Factice Auction," 3/1/2002.)

perhaps *adv.*: **perchance**. See *possibly*

perilous *adj.*: **parlous**. ❖ [Columbia Pictures executive David] Begelman made an extremely sweet offer, almost twice as much as Warner's, way more than was prudent, given Columbia's **parlous** financial condition, and given the fact that Begelman hated the script [for the movie *Shampoo*], thought it was cynical and offensive. (Peter Biskind, *Easy Riders, Raging Bulls*, Simon & Schuster [1998], p. 191.)

(2) perilous (as in expose to or put in a . . . situation [*v.t.*] or be in a . . . situation [*v.i.*]): **periclitate**. See *imperil*

(3) perilous (journey or passage, with dangers on both sides) *idiom*: **between Scylla and Charybdis**. See *precarious*

period (of or over the same . . .) *adj.*: **coetaneous**. See *contemporaneous*

(2) period (of the same time . . .) *adj.*: **coeval**. See *contemporaneous*

(3) period (suppression of or absence of a woman's monthly . . .) *n.*: **amenorrhea**. See *menstruation*

(4) period (a woman's first . . .) *n.*: **menarche**. See *menstruation*

periodically *adv.*: **betimes**. See *sometimes*

perk (as in extra or unexpected gift or benefit, sometimes as thanks for a purchase) *n.*: **lagniappe**. See *gift*

permanent (as in extremely durable) *adj.*: **perdurable**. See *durable*

(2) permanent (as in indelible) *adj.*: **ineffaceable**. See *indelible*

permissible (as in legal) *adj.*: **licit**. See *legal*

(2) permissible (as in legitimate; acceptable) *adj.*: **cromulent**. See *legitimate*

permission (as in giving one's stamp of approval) *n.*: **nihil obstat** [Latin]. See *approval*

permit (as in approve, esp. to confirm officially) *v.t.*: **homologate**. See *approve*

(2) permit (as in bestow, by one with higher power) *v.t.*: **vouchsafe**. See *bestow*

pernicious *adj.*: **baleful**. See *sinister*

perplexing *adj.*: **quisquous**. [The usage is in the headline.] ❖ **Quisquous** Indeed—The Mystery of the Irate Savant. Well, it's been several months since the enervating and fascinating blog of the cranky undiscovered genius, The Irate Savant, has been updated, and I fear that foul play may have befallen him. He was getting into some weird stuff if his last few entries were any indication, and now months of silence. I figure it's either kidnapping and death or a book deal. (Scott Standridge, www.scottstandridge.com/?q=blog&page=4, 3/16/2006.)

perquisite (as in extra or unexpected gift or benefit, sometimes as thanks for a purchase) *n.*: **lagniappe**. See *gift*

persecution (of a religious, national, or racial group) *n.*: **helotism** (*v.t.*: **helotize**). See *oppression*

persevere (ability to . . .) *n.*: **sitzfleisch**. See *endure*

persevering (in effort or application) *adj.*: **sedulous**. See *diligent*

(2) persevering (in holding to a belief or opinion) *adj.*: **pertinacious**. See *stubborn*

persist (ability to . . .) *n.*: **sitzfleisch**. See *endure*

persistent (as in one who clings to an opinion or belief even after being shown that it is wrong) *n.*: **mumpsimus**. See *stubborn*

(2) persistent (as in practice of refusing to consider a change in one's beliefs or opinions, esp. in politics) *n.*: **standpatism**. See *stubbornness*

(3) persistent (in effort or application) *adj.*: **sedulous**. See *diligent*

(4) persistent (in holding to a belief or opinion) *adj.*: **pertinacious**. See *stubborn*

personable (and pleasant) *adj.*: **sympathique** [French]. See *genial*

personification (as in embodiment) *n.*: **avatar**. See *embodiment*

(2) personification (spec. the perfect or beautiful example of something) *n.*: **beau ideal**. See *ideal*

perspective (centered on male . . .) *adj.*: **androcentric**. See *male*

(2) perspective (which is controversial, or person who holds one) *n.*: **polemic**. See *controversy*

perspiration (an agent that causes . . . , or having the power to cause . . .) *n., adj.*: **diaphoretic**. See *sweat*

(2) perspiration (cause . . . by subjecting person or thing to intense heat) *v.t.*: **parboil**. See *heat*

(3) perspiration (foul-smelling . . .) *n.*: **bromidrosis**. See *sweat*

(4) perspiration (inducing . . .) *adj.*: **sudatory**. See *sweat*

persuadable *adj.*: **exorable**. [This word is the less common, though equally legitimate, counterpart to its opposite, "inexorable," which means not subject to persuasion or entreaty.] ❖ [T]hroughout last year, George W. Bush's nomination had the aura of inevitability because polls showed him trouncing Al Gore, his likely opponent in November. Now that Senator John McCain crushed Bush by a historic margin in the Republican primary in New Hampshire, we see the end of the inevitability of the former front-runner's nomination. A coronation at the G.O.P. Philadelphia convention has become both evitable and **exorable**. (William Safire, "Bush Can't Win," *New York Times*, 2/3/2000.)

persuading (as in urging someone to take a course of action) *adj.*: **hortatory**. ❖ [Writer Meg Greenfield] loved argument and continued a tradition under which [*Washington*] *Post* editorials avoided **hortatory** calls to action in favor of making points by marshaling facts. (J. Y. Smith, obituary of Meg Greenfield, *Washington Post*, 5/14/1999.)

persuasion (of another by flattery) *n.*: **blandishment** (*v.t.*: **blandish**). See *flattery*

pertaining *adj.*: **appurtenant**. ❖ Not very long ago the path to class glory was clear. You landed in a management-training program at some large company [and] eventually found yourself battling it out with a few others for one of the top positions. . . . There was absolutely no confusion about your class status; you were an Executive, with all the perks and status **appurtenant** thereto. (Kenneth Labich, "Class in America—Old Socioeconomic Rankings Have Given Way to the Increasing Segmentation of the U.S. Population, and More Americans Are Unsure Where They Stand," *Fortune*, 2/7/1994, p. 114.)

pertinent *n.*: **apposite**. See *relevant*

perusal (a quick, cursory . . .) *n.*: **Cook's tour**. See *scan*

pervasive *adj.*: **regnant**. See *predominant* and *widespread*

perversion (place of . . . , as in corruption) *n.*: **Augean stable**. See *corruption*

pervert (sexual . . .) *n.*: **paraphiliac**. ❖ In households with fundamentalist Christian convictions . . . punishment [for sexual urges] was often the surest route, not to the suppression of those urges, but to their redirection. [Mark's mother told him] that touching girls was a terrible sin and would make [him] grow up to be a crazy man. . . . He didn't. Instead, he climbed into fields late at night and did it to horses. . . . I don't mean to suggest that Christianity is doomed to turn us all into hardcore **paraphiliacs**. (Simon Andreae, "Desire: It Starts in Your Genes, Not in Your Jeans," *Independent* [London], 11/15/1998.)

perverted (morally . . .) *adj.*: **scrofulous**. See *depraved*

(2) perverted (preference for . . . or unusual sexual practices) *n.*: **paraphilia**. See *deviant*

pesky (as in bothersome) *adj.*: **pestiferous**. See *bothersome*

pessimism (world-weariness or sentimental . . . over the world's problems) *adj.*: **Weltschmerz** [German]. ❖ [There appears to be] an unprecedented prevalence of pessimism about the future. The nation appears to be trudging gloomily on its daily round burdened with mental sandwich-boards bearing the doomiest of legends. On cursory inspection, there is little unusual in this nationwide outbreak of **Weltschmerz**: it is the business of polls to point up dissatisfactions and the business of political parties to promise to put them right. (*Scotsman* [Edinburgh], "A Fearful Look to the Future," 6/13/1995.)

pessimist (as in one always predicting catastrophe) *n*.: **catastrophist**. ❖ Lester Brown . . . has been warning since the '60s of a soon-to-emerge food deficit and preaching the gospel of birth suppression. Mr. Peron thinks the **catastrophist** mindset was best illustrated in *The Problem Is Us*, a government-sponsored travelling exhibit warning American school children in the 1970s that "the birth rate must decrease and/or the death rate must increase." It showed them a picture of a rat on a dinner plate, and warned that when starvation overtakes the earth their parents might eat them. (Link Byfield, "A Good News Bulletin on the Population Crisis: There Isn't One," Alberta Report/Western Report, 11/20/1995.)

(2) pessimist (as in one who continually warns of a disastrous future) *n*.: **Jeremiah**. [Jeremiah was a Hebrew prophet who warned of the fall of the kingdom of Judah and whose writings are collected in the Book of Jeremiah.] ❖ [According to Colorado governor Richard Lamm,] the United States has become a modern-day Athens, lethargic and self-satisfied, sowing the seeds of its own demise. His message is constant: Every institution in the nation must be reformed if the country is to reverse what he sees as a steady and long-term decline. . . . His heretical views won him such appellations as "The High Plains **Jeremiah**." (Richard Stewart, "What Makes Richard Lamm Worry," *Boston Globe*, 2/10/1987.)

(3) pessimist (spec. one who believes that the world is getting worse) *n*.: **pejorist**. ❖ At one extreme stood the optimism of Leibnitz or Browning: this was the best of all possible worlds. Then there [are those] for whom the world was good but in danger of degeneration. [Then there are those like] George Eliot [who] took the view that the world was bad but capable, in some respects, of improvement. A **pejorist** like Housman believed that the world was both bad and deteriorating. (Nicholas Shrimpton, "'Lane, You're a Perfect Pessimist': Pessimism and the English Fin de Siècle," *Yearbook of English Studies*, 1/1/2007.)

(4) pessimist *n*.: **crepehanger**. ❖ Steve Forbes, Republican Presidential Candidate: America does not have to fear the world, America does not have to fear the future. Unlock the genius of the American people, and we'll once again prove wrong the critics and the skeptics and the **crepehangers** and the doubters and the isolationists and the wall-builders. (NPR Morning Edition, "Pat Buchanan Narrowly Leads the Pack in New Hampshire," 2/21/1996.)

pester *v.t*.: **chivvy**. ❖ Changing patent law is a job for politicians, and they can hardly complain if [private] genomics companies are taking advantage of their inertia. Nor should they be **chivvying** firms to give up hard-won and costly information just because public researchers have not been able to find it first. (*Minneapolis Star Tribune*, "Business Forum—In Genomics, the U.S. and British Governments Are Meddling in Things That Do Not Concern Them," 4/2/2000.)

(2) pester *v.t*.: **hector**. See *bully*

pet (as in caress or fondle) *v.i*.: **canoodle** (often "canoodle with"). See *caress*

petals (of a flower taken separately or as a whole) *n*.: **corolla**. ❖ Flowers may be as large as a wine cork or smaller than a pencil eraser, slim or chubby, with upturned or down-hanging sepals and tightly cupped or flared **corollas**. These **corollas** may be sublimely single, with only four petals; semidouble, with eight; or double, with heaven knows how many. (Wayne Winterrowd, "A Fancy for Fuchsias," *Horticulture*, 2/1/1998, p. 54.)

petite *adj.*: **minikin**. See *tiny*

pet name (as a term of endearment) *n.*: **hypocorism** (*adj.*: **hypocoristic**). See *nickname*

petty (person on issues of grammar) *n.*: **grammaticaster**. See *pedantic*

(2) petty (state of being . . . , as in smallminded) *n.*: **parvanimity**. See *small-minded*

(3) petty *adj.*: **picayune**. See *trivial*

petulant (as in grouchy, person) *n.*: **crosspatch**. See *grouch*

(2) petulant (as in irritable) *adj.*: **liverish**. See *irritable*

(3) petulant (as in irritable) *adj.*: **shirty**. See *irritable*

(4) petulant (as in surly) *adj.*: **atrabilious**. See *surly*

(5) petulant (as in surly) *adj.*: **bilious**. See *surly*

(6) petulant *adj.*: **querulous**. See *peevish*

(7) petulant *adj.*: **waspish**. See *irritable*

phallic *adj.*: **priapic**. ❖ To state the obvious first: Crimson Tide is a submarine movie and therefore entirely about penises. The USS *Alabama* and its Russian counterpart surge through the depths in a way that can only be called **priapic**, discharging manfully streamlined torpedoes at each other. (Jonathan Romney, review of *Crimson Tide*, *New Statesman & Society*, 11/3/1995, p. 32.)

phantom *n.*: **wraith**. See *apparition*

phenomenon (secondary . . . that accompanies or results from another) *n.*: **epiphenomenon** (*adj.*: **epiphenomenal**). ❖ He argued that the study of everyday life shows how normal life was for most Germans, most of whom were absorbed by the routine tasks of daily life. They were uninvolved in, and even unaware of, the regime's crimes. The racist, oppressive, inhuman aspects of Nazism were **epiphenomenal** to the texture of the quotidian in Hitler's Germany. (Daniel Goldhagen, "Pride and Prejudice," *New Republic*, 3/29/1999.)

philanderer *n.*: **rakehell**. See *libertine*

philanthropic (as in charitable) *adj.*: **caritative**. See *charitable*

(2) philanthropic *adj.*: **eleemosynary**. See *charitable*

philanthropist (female . . .) *n.*: **Lady Bountiful**. [This term derives from a character in George Farquhar's 1707 play *Beaux' Stratagem*. It is sometimes used pejoratively when the charitable giving is done for publicity or in an ostentatious way.] ❖ For many years, Brooke Astor was New York City's seemingly ageless **Lady Bountiful**. "Money is like manure," she liked to say in her disarming way. "It should be spread around." She gave away nearly $200 million, inherited from her late husband, Vincent Astor, to libraries, museums and charities large and small. (Evan Thomas, "A Blue-Blood Battle Royale," *Newsweek*, 8/7/2006.)

(2) philanthropist (esp. who gives to the arts) *n.*: **Maecenas**. See *benefactor*

philosopher (bad . . . , or one who pretends to be a . . .) *n.*: **philosophaster**. ❖ Reagan won the 1980 and 1984 debates and elections because he spoke plain sense to the American people. Simple phrases. Common words. Plainstuff. Broken sentences. So what? That's how normal people speak. . . . In contrast, Carter and Mondale spoke more in the highfalutin' lingo our professors and other **philosophasters** love. (*Orange County Register*, "Silliness about Senility," 12/27/1987.)

philosophical (fallacious . . . argument) *n.*: **philosophism**. See *argument*

philosophy (spec. doctrines to be believed; articles of faith) *n.pl.*: **credenda**. See *beliefs*

phony (as in artificial) *adj.*: **factitious**. See *artificial*

(2) phony (as in contrived) *adj.*: **voulu** [French]. See *contrived*

(3) phony (as in hypocrite, esp. one who acts humbly) *n.*: **Uriah Heep**. See *hypocrite*

(4) phony (as in hypocrite, esp. one who affects religious piety) *n.*: **Tartuffe** (or **tartuffe**). See *hypocrite*

(5) phony (as in insincere) *adj.*: **crocodilian**. See *insincere*

(6) phony (esp. a person who sells quack medicines) *n.*: **mountebank**. See *huckster*

(7) phony (something . . . , as in sham) *n.*: **postiche**. See *sham*

photograph (living, esp. by costumed performers sustaining a pose as if in a . . .) *n.*: **tableau vivant** [French]. See *pose*

phrase *n.*: **locution**. ❖ "As the child of Holocaust survivors. . . ." This is the exemplary **locution** of multicultural America, the highest rank that you can pull in a culture of victimhood. But what special authority, really, do the sons and daughters of the wretched possess? We are not victims. Our parents were victims. We are merely American Jews, the brats of Jewish history. (*New Republic*, Washington Diarist: "Shrunken," 11/9/1998.)

(2) phrase (as in saying or adage) *n.*: **apothegm**. See *saying*

(3) phrase (just the right . . . or word) *n.*: **mot juste** [French]. See *word*

(4) phrase (misuse or strained use of word or . . . , sometimes deliberate) *n.*: **catachresis**. See *misuse*

(5) phrase (new . . . , expression, or word) *n.*: **neologism**. See *word*

(6) phrase (of a . . . or word that is pedantic) *adj.*: **inkhorn**. See *pedantic*

(7) phrase (or expression or comment that is elegant, concise, witty, and/or well put) *n.*: **atticism**. See *expression*

(8) phrase (or word that used to stand alone but requires a modifier due to changes in technology or other new developments) *n.*: **retronym**. See *word*

(9) phrase (which is brand-new and created in the hope that others will use it and make it recognized) *n.*: **protologism**. See *word*

(10) phrase (witty or clever . . . or line) *n.*: **bon mot**. See *line*

physician (disease caused by a . . .) *adj.*: **iatrogenic**. See *disease*

(2) physician (equipment, including supplies and instruments, used by a . . .) *n.*: **armamentarium**. See *doctor*

(3) physician (replacement . . .) *n.*: **locum tenens**. See *temporary*

physique (esp. as reflecting characteristics of an endomorph, mesomorph, or ectomorph) *n.*: **somatotype**. ❖ Back in the 1940s, psychologist William Sheldon developed the theory of **somatotypes** from a study of 4,000 photographs of college-age men. Dr. Sheldon suggested that all bodies could be classified into one of three categories: endomorph, mesomorph and ectomorph. . . . If you're an endomorph, for example, it's wide hips. For an ectomorph, it's skinny limbs. And a mesomorph will have a stocky appearance. (Bridgette Williams, "Don't Fight Your Body Type—Fit It to Your Workout," *Dallas Morning News*, 9/7/2004.

(2) physique (of a person esp. as relating to tendency to develop disease) *n.*: **habitus**. ❖ Other variables affecting cardiac hypertrophy in athletes include body **habitus**, height, age, and gender. (Gordon Huie, "Cardiomyopathy in Athletes," *Physician Assistant*, 5/1/1997, p. 136.)

pick-me-up (as in something that invigorates) *adj., n.*: **roborant**. See *invigorating*

pickpocket (spec. an adult who instructs children how to be a . . .) *n.*: **Fagin**. See *thief*

picky (overly . . .) *adj.*: **persnickety**. ❖ RU 486, the so-called French abortion pill, would probably sail through the **persnickety** approval process at the Food and Drug Administration—if someone would put in an application. (*Time*, "Rethinking RU 486–With Clinton In, the French Abortion Pill May Finally Make It to the U.S.," 3/8/1993, p. 21.)

(2) picky (as in pedantic person on issues of grammar) *n.*: **grammaticaster**. See *pedantic*

picture (as in to conceive of or form an image of) *v.t.*: **ideate**. See *visualize*

(2) picture (living, esp. by costumed performers sustaining a pose as if in a . . .) *n.*: **tableau vivant** [French]. See *pose*

piece (as in excerpt, esp. from the Bible) *n.*: **pericope**. See *excerpt*

pieces (as in bits and . . .) *n.*: **flinders**. See *bits and pieces*

(2) pieces (usually, but not necessarily, in reference to literary . . . , as in fragments, or to disjointed quotations) *n.pl.*: **disjecta membra** [Latin]. See *bits and pieces*

pierce *v.t.*: **lancinate**. ❖ Then with a splash, one of the whalers cast the harpoon through the water, where it **lancinated** the fleshy back of the whale. (www.ambrosiasw.com-forums/lofiversion, 5/19/2002.)

piercing (having a . . . quality) *adj.*: **gimlet** (esp. as in "gimlet eye"). See *penetrating*

pig (or anyone who behaves like one, whether in his or her personal habits or by being greedy) **chazzer** [Yiddish]. ❖ [Maurice's son Norman wants to be appointed to the board of directors of the Holocaust Memorial Museum run by Maurice.] "Why are you being such a **chazzer**?" Maurice had demanded harshly. "Why should you not be satisfied mit what you have? It's not enough for you to be the big boss from our business Holocaust Connections, Inc.? What's wrong with you? You never heard from nepotism?" (Tova Reich, *My Holocaust*, HarperCollins [2007], p. 70.)

(2) pig (as in hearty eater) *n.*: **trencherman**. See *glutton*

piggish (as in greedy person) *n.*: **cormorant**. See *greedy*

pig-headed (as in one who clings to an opinion or belief even after being shown that it is wrong) *n.*: **mumpsimus**. See *stubborn*

(2) pig-headed (in holding to a belief or opinion) *adj.*: **pertinacious**. See *stubborn*

pig out *v.t.*: **gormandize**. See *devour*

pigs (give birth to a litter of . . .) *v.t.*: **farrow**. ❖ I have always found them to be idle, companionable, greedy and clean. The occasional boar is irritable, and sows, understandably, are wary of strangers visiting them soon after they have **farrowed**. But on the whole, particularly if you spend time with them, pigs are docile and sociable. (Lord Cranborne, "Pig Is Beautiful," *Sunday Telegraph* [London], 4/18/1999.)

(2) pigs (of or relating to) *adj.*: **porcine**. ❖ "They're destroying everything, those beasts," grumbled Jeannot Romana, a farmer in Provence. . . . "It's a plague of pigs." From the Luberon to the Riviera, in Southern France, homeowners report uninvited **porcine** families happily lounging by their swimming pools. Deep holes like bomb craters mar vegetable patches and flower beds. (Mort Rosenblum, "Pigs Have French Farmers Squealing; Wild Ones Gobble Treasured Truffles," *Washington Times*, 2/23/1999.)

pile (confused or jumbled . . .) *n.*: **agglomeration**. See *jumble*

(2) pile *n.*: **cumulus**. See *heap*

pilgrimage (to a sacred place or shrine, esp. to Mecca) *n.*: **hadj**. ❖ Visiting the [Scrabble] Archives, which I do first on a gloriously early summer's day, becomes a personal **hadj**: Mecca, the Louvre, and Cooperstown rolled into one. (Stefan Fatsis, *Word Freak*, Houghton Mifflin [2001], p. 90.)

pillage *n.*: **rapine**. See *looting*

(2) pillage *v.t., v.i.*: **depredate** (*n.*: **depredation**). See *plunder*

pimp *n.*: **souteneur** [French]. ❖ One of Bruant's most popular and harshly evocative songs was "À Montparnasse," which tells the gruesome story of an ageing prostitute whose **souteneur** murders her after he finds out she had been stealing from him in order to purchase liquor. (Nicolas Kenny, "Je Cherche Fortune," *Urban History Review*, 3/22/2004.)

pimping *n.*: **procuration**. ❖ Lawyer Daniel Zeeman says under current laws it is still an offence to live off the earnings of prostitution in Tasmania. But it is a more serious offence to procure a person to become a prostitute, he says. **Procuration** is a more serious offence under the Tasmanian Criminal Code. (*Mercury* [Australia], "Turning a New Leaf on Old Laws," 11/19/2004.)

pining (as in longing, esp. for something one once had but has no more) *n.*: **desiderium**. See *longing*

pink (as in ruddy) *adj.*: **florid**. See *ruddy*

pinnacle (the . . .) *n.*: **Parnassus**. [Mount Parnassus is a mountain peak in central Greece. In ancient times, it was considered sacred to Apollo, Dionysus, and the Muses. Today, it is sometimes used as a synonym for a pinnacle.] ❖ David Boren yielded the power and perks he amassed in the U.S. Senate to become president of the academically [quiet] University of Oklahoma three years ago. The Beltway Bunch scratched their heads in disbelief or wonderment at this descent from **Parnassus** to Podunk. (*Seattle Post-Intelligencer,* "Boren Finds Life Exists Outside Washington," 9/28/1997.)

(2) pinnacle (as in climax, of a drama) *n.*: **catastatis**. See *climax*

pins and needles (as in, in a state of suspense) *idiom*: **on tenterhooks**. See *suspense*

pious (or hypocritical and/or insincere speech) *n.*: **cant**. ❖ For all their sanctimonious **cant**, I find that [Jerry] Falwell and the "Christian" folk in the athletic department at Liberty University are really no different from their win-at-all-cost brethren at our more established football factories. (Gay Flood, letter to the editor, *Sports Illustrated,* 12/11/1989, p. 6.)

(2) pious (hypocritically . . .) *adj.*: **Pecksniffian**. See *self-righteous*

(3) pious (hypocritically . . .) *adj.*: **pharisaical**. See *self-righteous*

(4) pious (persons who are . . .and critical of others) *n.pl.*: **unco guid** (preceded by "the"). See *self-righteous*

pipe dream (as in hope or goal that is not realistically obtainable) *n.*: **will-o'-the-wisp**. ❖ [S]ince the **will-o'-the-wisp** of bipartisanship was likely to evaporate anyway, a fight to the finish could provide the President with an opportunity to charge that it was the Democrats who spoiled the atmosphere first. (Richard Lacayo, Nation: "So Much for Bipartisanship—If the Republicans Cannot Save Tower, They Are Determined to Tar the Democrats," *Time,* 3/13/1989, p. 20.)

(2) pipe dream (spec. the tendency to see things as more beautiful than they really are) *n.*: **kalopsia**. See *rose-colored glasses*

piss *v.i.*: **micturate**. See *urinate*

pissing (backwards, or animals that do so) *adj., n.*: **retromingent**. See *urinating*

pitchman (esp. a person who sells quack medicines) *n.*: **mountebank**. See *huckster*

pithy (saying) *n.*: **gnome** (*adj.*: **gnomic**). See *catchphrase*

pitiful (or compassionate or merciful) *adj.*: **ruthful**. [While "ruthless" is of course a common word, most people are not aware that "ruth" is a noun meaning pity or mercy or compassion and that "ruthful" is the adjectival form of that word. When used in the sense of pity, it can imply contempt or scorn for the person being pitied (as in the example given), as does the word "pity" itself. However, when not used in that sense, it can mean genuine sympathy or compassion. See *compassionate*.] ❖ [When telling the clerk it's hard to quit smoking because I enjoy cigarettes,] I find myself at the receiving end of a uniformly bemused, pitying and faintly disgusted stare. . . . Allan M. Brandt's *Cigarette Century* . . . delivers that same **ruthful** stare. Brandt . . . canvasses giant chunks of terrain here . . . without ever pausing to examine the central, vexing paradox of smoking: that in return for death, cigarettes give pleasure. (Jonathan Miles, review of *The Cigarette Century, New York Times Book Review,* 5/6/2007.)

pitiless (as in cruel) *adj.*: **fell** (*n.*: **fellness**). See *cruel*

pity (of an argument appealing to one's sense of . . .) *adv., adj.*: **ad misericordiam** [Latin]. See *argument*

placate *v.t.*: **propitiate**. ❖ [Historian Arthur Schlesinger wrote, "President Clinton] lacks self-discipline. . . . His political resilience strikes many as flagrant opportunism. His reactions are instinctively placatory. He rushes to **propitiate** the audience before him, often at his own expense." (Godfrey Sperling, "How Will History Rate Clinton?" *Christian Science Monitor,* 5/25/1999.)

placate *v.t.*: **dulcify**. See *appease*

place (as in condition of being located in a particular . . .) *n.*: **ubiety**. ❖ [T]he global merchant and investor community is defined not by spatial location governed by a spatially located sovereign, but by professional activity, commercial interest, and various social ties. [T]he global merchant and investment community has no "**ubiety**." It does not depend on a particular place. (Marc R. Poirier, "The NAFTA Chapter 11 Expropriation Debate Through the Eyes of a Property Theorist," *Environmental Law*, 9/22/2003.)

(2) place (close together, side by side, or in proper order) *v.t.*: **collocate**. ❖ East of Los Angeles, the San Andreas fault crosses Cajon Pass where many vital lifelines (highway; railroad; natural gas, water, and petroleum pipelines; fiber optic lines, and electric power transmission lines) are **collocated** in a very narrow pass subject to fault rupture. (Unattributed congressional testimony, "Earthquakes," 10/20/1999.)

(3) place (name that foreigners, but not locals, give to a . . .) *n.*: **exonym**. See *name*

(4) place (one frequents) *n.*: **purlieu**. See *hangout*

placebo (opposite of . . . effect, as in administering something producing harmful effects because it is believed to be harmful, but which in reality is harmless) *n.*: **nocebo** [Latin for "I will harm"]. ❖ The **nocebo** effect has been demonstrated among psychology students at the University of California in Los Angeles. When warned they might get a headache from a mild electric current being passed through their heads, two-thirds reported they felt pain. Even after the students were told that, in fact, there had been no current, none declared that the headache, too, hadn't been real. (Nicholas Wade, "Method & Madness: The Spin Doctors," *New York Times*, 1/7/1996.)

place-name *n.*: **toponym**. ❖ Many foreign visitors confuse "Newark" with "New York." To the foreign ear, the two **toponyms** are almost interchangeable. So it's not unusual to find sightseers from other countries wandering the streets of Newark, believing they are actually in New York City. During my last trip . . . in Newark's Central Ward, I encountered a group of . . . Belgian tourists who were looking for the St. Regis Hotel. (Mark Leyner, "Xmas in Newark," *Esquire*, 12/1/1997.)

plain (as in clear, in thought or expression) *adj.*: **luculent**. See *clear*

(2) plain (as in easily understood or seen through, likes motives) *adj.*: **transpicuous**. See *transparent*

(3) plain (esp. as in uncoded, language) *adj.*: **en clair** [French]. See *uncoded*

plaintive (often regarding something gone) *adj.*: **elegiac**. See *sorrowful*

(2) plaintive (sounds) *adj.*: **plangent**. See *mournful*

plan (as in course of action) *n.*: **démarche** [French]. See *course of action*

plane (tail assembly of) *n.*: **empennage** [French]. See *airplane*

plants (animal that feeds mainly on . . .) *n.*: **herbivore** (*adj.*: **herbivorous**). ❖ Consumers like deer can eat plants directly, or consumers such as mountain lions can eat plants indirectly when they eat the deer that ate the plant. **Herbivores** are known as primary consumers. (Ted Kerasote, "Hunters, Gatherers, and the Cycle of Life," *Sports Afield*, 5/1/1998, p. 36.)

platitudes (one who utters . . .) *n.*: **platitudinarian**. ❖ Her successor, Livingston Biddle, was a **platitudinarian**, who to this day likes to expatiate on his slogan that "the arts mean excellence"; one need only listen to him for two minutes to cease believing in art and excellence both. (Joseph Epstein, "What to Do About the Arts," *Commentary*, 4/1/1995).

plausible (as in appearing to be true or accurate) *adj.*: **verisimilar**. ❖ One of the most illuminating, sympathetic passages in his book deals with the Garden of Gethsemane, where Christ lingered and prayed the night he was betrayed and arrested. . . . [The author] looks at the actual ground. The result is a strikingly **verisimilar** explanation of the whole night, in very human terms, based on topography that still exists here. (Michael Browning, "Where Jesus Walked," *Palm Beach Post*, 12/8/2000.)

play (as in frolic) *v.t.*, *v.i.*: **disport**. See *frolic*

(2) play (of, relating to, or connoting) *adj*.: **ludic**. See *playful*

(3) play (on words) *n*.: **paronomasia**. See *word play*

(4) play *v.i.*: **gambol**. See *frolic*

playboy (as in man who seduces women) *n*.: **Lothario**. ❖ Of Worth's inner circle, Ned Wynert, a **Lothario** to the last, had suffered the traditional adulterer's fate, gunned down [in the act] by an enraged husband. (Ben Macintyre, *The Napoleon of Crime*, Farrar, Straus and Giroux [1997], p. 175.)

(2) playboy *n*.: **roué** [French]. ❖ Though a newlywed, [Jerry Lewis's father] Danny was still a dashing young man; in his bearing and wardrobe there would always be a hint of the **roué**, and [Jerry Lewis's mother,] Rae[,] more than anyone knew he could lay on the charm. (Shawn Levy, *The King of Comedy*, St. Martin's Press [1996], p. 9.)

playful *adj*.: **gamesome**. ❖ The attractive design [in this book of letters of the alphabet] skillfully blends illustrations and type to create many **gamesome** touches, such as a dolphin diving through the letter D and the letter R getting stuck in a reindeer's antlers. (*Publishers Weekly*, "From Albatross to Zoo: An Alphabet Book in Five Languages," 9/28/1992.)

(2) playful *adj*.: **ludic**. ❖ **Ludic** language . . . should be at the heart of any thinking we do about language, for it is closely bound up with our ability to be creative. . . . When partners cease to enjoy each other's language play—their Monty Python voices, made-up words, or nonsense noises—they will not be partners for much longer. (David Crystal, "From Scrabble to Drabble via Babble," *Independent* [London], 8/13/1998.)

(3) playful (as in witty) *adj*.: **waggish**. See *witty*

(4) playful (girl with . . . or impish appeal) *n*.: **gamine** [French]. See *girl*

(5) playful (young woman) *n*.: **hoyden**. See *tomboy*

playwriting (of or relating to . . . or the art of the theater) *adj*.: **dramaturgic**. See *theater*

plea (of a . . . to one's sense of pity or compassion) *adv., adj*.: **ad misericordiam** [Latin]. See *argument*

(2) plea (spec. a prayer mentioning things held to be sacred) *n*.: **obsecration**. See *entreaty*

(3) plea *n*.: **cri de coeur** [French; lit. cry of the heart]. ❖ There is indeed a great unhappiness in the land, but the letters suggest the emotion is less of anger than of pain, a **cri de coeur** from people who grew up believing America was special and now see that quality under assault from within. Louis Weinstein of Glenside, PA, lamented a "moral corruption" that is eating away at the nation's innards. (David Gergen, "What Troubles Our Readers," *U.S. News & World Report*, 10/23/1995.)

plea bargain (in which a person pleads guilty while maintaining innocence) *n*.: **Alford plea**. [This term derives from a 1970 case in which the defendant pleaded guilty to second-degree murder because he might have received the death penalty if convicted of first-degree murder. With an Alford plea, the defendant does not admit to committing the crime but admits that the prosecution could likely prove the charge.] ❖ A 35-year-old man was transferred to federal custody Friday after he entered an **Alford plea** in connection to charges that he molested [six] girls between the ages of 12 and 14. On Friday, he withdrew his original plea and entered an **Alford plea** for two counts of third-degree child molestation. (Thomas Clouse, "Man Accused of Molestation Changes Plea," *Spokane [WA] Spokesman-Review*, 9/23/2006.)

plead (in protest or objection) *v.t.*: **remonstrate**. ❖ "Who else hasn't been [vaccinated]?" Amadou asks the gathering mothers, hands on hips as she begins **remonstrating** with one who volunteered only two of her three children. A few mothers push their reluctant children forward. (Simon Robinson, "Letter from Niamey: Two Drops of Salvation," *Time* International, 7/3/2000, p. 34.)

(2) plead (with earnestly) *v.t.*: **adjure**.

❖ "This [President Clinton impeachment plan] is turning against the Republicans," a senior House Democrat said last week, **adjuring** members to vote against the G.O.P. impeachment plan. (Romesh Ratnesar, "Clinton's Crisis: Why The Midterms Matter—Impeachment Isn't the Godsend the G.O.P. Hoped For, but the Election Outlook Is Still Bleak for Democrats," *Time*, 10/19/1998, p. 54.)

pleasant (and genial) *adj.*: **sympathique** [French]. See *genial*

(2) pleasant (as in warm and cozy) *adj.*: **gemütlich** [German]. See *cozy*

(3) pleasant (sound) *adj.*: **euphonious** (*n.*: **euphony**). See *melodious*

(4) pleasant (sounding) *adj.*: **dulcet**. See *melodious*

(5) pleasant (voice or sound) *adj.*: **mellifluous**. See *melodious*

(6) pleasant (voice or sound) *adj.*: **mellisonant**. See *melodious*

pleasantly (to behold) *adv.*: **mirabile visu** [Latin]. See *behold*

(2) pleasantly (to relate) *adv.*: **mirabile dictu** [Latin]. See *wonderful*

pleasantness (as in affability) *n.*: **bonhomie**. See *affability*

pleasantries (relating to . . . , where the purpose is to establish a mood of sociability rather than to communicate information or ideas, such as "have a nice day") *adj.*: **phatic**. ❖ "Cheers," small, unpretending [word] that it seems, is a strange modern gesture of fellowship, a formal declaration of informality. . . . There is no stopping it. . . . It is our word for all weathers, our **phatic** egalitarian gesture. (John Mullan, Word of the Week: "Cheers: Let Us Give Thanks," *Guardian* [London], 11/21/2001.)

pleased (to behold) *adv.*: **mirabile visu** [Latin]. See *behold*

(2) pleased (to relate) *adv.*: **mirabile dictu** [Latin]. See *wonderful*

(3) pleased (very . . . often in a boastful way) *adj.*: **cock-a-hoop**. See *elated*

pleasing *adj.*: **prepossessing**. ❖ "The appearance of the boy was **prepossessing**," Sam-

uel wrote years later. "His eyes were bright and unclouded, and above them was a massive forehead and a finely shaped head, which might have been chosen as a model for an artist." (Lawrence Striegel, Long Island: "Our Past/A Voice Raised for Freedom," *Newsday*, 1/1/2001.)

(2) pleasing (as in wonderful) *adj.*: **frabjous** (often as in "Oh frabjous day!"). See *wonderful*

(3) pleasing (as in wonderful) *adj.*: **galluptious** [slang]. See *wonderful*

(4) pleasing (but in a way that is solely based on deception or pretense or gaudiness) *adj.*: **meretricious**. See *attractive*

(5) pleasing (in appearance in an unconventional way) *adj.*: **jolie laide** (or **belle laide**) [French]. See *pretty* or *handsome* or *beautiful*

(6) pleasing (in appearance, esp. sexually) *adj.*: **toothsome**. See *sexy*

(7) pleasing (to the ear) *adj.*: **dulcet**. See *melodious*

pleasure *n.*: **delectation**. ❖ Members of the jury, for your **delectation**—sorry, deliberation—we have here Exhibit A, as in awfully attractive: one Benjamin Bratt, a k a suave homicide detective Rey Curtis of NBC's *Law & Order*. (*People*, The 50 Most Beautiful People in the World 1999: Benjamin Bratt, Actor, 5/10/1999, p. 96.)

(2) pleasure *n.*: **oblectation**. ❖ Don't look for profound significance in my pictures, or outstanding artistic merit. I'm just an old man with a camera, and these are simply images of places and events I've enjoyed or been moved by or for some reason have taken particular notice of. . . . They are put here to add to the sum total of human **oblectation** (including mine) in the world. (Paul Dudley, "Portrait of Paul Dudley," www.pbase.com/lambsfeathers/profile.)

(3) pleasure (as in happiness) *n.*: **felicity**. See *happiness*

(4) pleasure (causing or tending to produce . . .) *adj.*: **felicific**. See *happiness*

(5) pleasure (delusive or illusory . . .) *n.*: **fool's paradise**. See *illusion*

(6) pleasure (from other's misfortunes) *n.*: **schadenfreude** [German]. See *sadism*

(7) pleasure (from witnessing other's misfortunes) *n.*: **Roman holiday**. See *sadism*

(8) pleasure (sexual . . . from rubbing against something or someone) *n.*: **frottage**. See *rubbing*

(9) pleasure (solely devoted to the seeking of . . .) *adj.*: **apolaustic**. See *hedonistic*

pleasure-seeker (as in lazy person devoted to seeking pleasure and luxury) *n.*: **lotus-eater**. See *hedonist*

(2) pleasure-seeker (as in man about town) *n.*: **boulevardier**. See *man about town*

(3) pleasure-seeker (as in one excessively devoted to luxury or sensual pleasures) *n.*: **voluptuary**. See *hedonist* and *sensualist*

pledge (of marriage) *v.t.*: **affiance**. See *marriage*

plenty (illusion of . . . when in fact there is little) *adj.*: **Barmecidal** (esp. as in "Barmecidal feast"). See *illusion*

pliable *adj.*: **ductile**. ❖ Steel cars are made of "monocoque" metal shells. Their strength and ability to bear loads resides largely in pressed-steel structures. Key parts of these structures, such as the floor-pan and the door pillars, involve complicated pressings for which steel, a **ductile** alloy, is well suited. But aluminium is not so **ductile**, and cannot easily be pressed into strong monocoques. (*Economist*, "Aluminium Cars: Audi-Lite," 4/15/2000.)

plight (as in choice of taking what is offered or nothing; i.e., no real choice at all) *n.*: **Hobson's choice**. See *predicament*

(2) plight (as in dilemma, except where there are three options, all of which are or seem to be unsatisfactory) *n.*: **trilemma**. See *dilemma*

(3) plight (as in predicament, from which it is difficult to extricate oneself) *n.*: **tar baby**. See *predicament*

(4) plight (as in the situation of having to make a move where any move made will weaken the position) *n.*: **zugzwang** [German]. See *predicament*

plop (as in light splash) *n.*: **plash**. See *splash*

plot (secret . . . or group of plotters) *n.*: **cabal**. ❖ Founded in 1958, the Birch Society became famous in the 1960s for its crusade against the fluoridation of water and for its elaborate conspiracy theories, which include the notion that President Eisenhower and his brother Milton were agents of the international Communist **cabal**. (Peter Carlson, "Pat Buchanan's Far Right Hand; Ezola Foster Can Make Even the Reform Party Candidate Look Like a Liberal," *Washington Post*, 9/13/2000.)

plotters (group of . . .) *n.*: **camarilla**. See *advisors*

plotting (and evil or shameless woman) *n.*: **jezebel** (sometimes cap.). See *woman*

pluck *n.*: **hardihood**. See *courage*

plug (up) *v.t.*: **occlude**. See *block*

plump (condition of having a . . . physique) *n.*: **embonpoint**. ❖ Unlike his fellow moguls, [John D. Rockefeller] was "lean as a greyhound" in a time when the measure of a man's prosperity was his **embonpoint**. (David Walton, "*Titan* Gives Rockefeller His Balance Due," *Dallas Morning News*, 5/31/1998.)

(2) plump (as in beer-bellied) *adj.*: **abdominous**. See *beer-bellied*

(3) plump (as in fat) *adj.*: **Pickwickian**. See *fat*

(4) plump (as in paunchy) *adj.*: **stomachy**. See *paunchy*

(5) plump (having a short . . . physique) *adj.*: **pyknic**. See *stocky*

(6) plump (woman who is pleasingly . . .) *adj.*: **zaftig** [Yiddish]. See *full-figured*

plunder *v.t.*, *v.i.*: **depredate** (*n.*: **depredation**). ❖ In 1766 the Spanish explorer Nicolás de Lafora found the dunes "very troublesome" and that approaching the only water near them required moving cautiously, for the Apache Indians "are wont to surprise and kill passers-by." Plodding south with his wagon train in 1839, the American merchant Josiah Gregg found that Apaches "continue to lay waste the ranches in the vicinity, and to **depredate** at will." (Joseph Leach, "The Dunes of Samayaluca," *Americas*, 5/15/1996, p. 14.)

(2) plunder *n.*: **rapine**. See *looting*

poem (consisting of one line) *n.*: **monostich**. ❖ These [very short entries in Nabakov's collection of writings] reminded me of the quintessential American **monostich**: "You owe me $64." I read it in *Poetry* magazine about a quarter of a century ago and am still stumped by it. It's there on the page, but what is it in aid of? (Roy Sergei, "Nabokov's Butterflies," *Moscow Times* [Russia], 6/3/2000.)

(2) poem (or song in celebration of a pending marriage) *n.*: **prothalamion**. See *song*

(3) poem (or song in honor of a bride or bridegroom) *n.*: **epithalamium**. See *toast*

(4) poem (or song of mourning, esp. for a dead person) *n.*: **threnody**. See *requiem*

poet (bad . . .) *n.*: **poetaster**. ❖ And now her first book of poems, *Yesterday I Saw the Sun*, has become a cause for further hiding. Just before the book's publication last month, a *New York Post* gossip item ridiculed her as a **poetaster**, contributing to her latest headache. "Ally Sheedy from bad to verse," chortled the headline on the item. ("Heartbreak—Ally Sheedy Says She Wrote Her Poems to Heal Her Wounds, but Their Publication Has Only Made Them Another Source of Pain," *Entertainment Weekly*, 3/29/1991, p. 28.)

poetry (of or relating to) *adj.*: **Parnassian**. [The word derives from Parnassus, a mountain in Greece sacred to Apollo and the Muses in Greek mythology.] ❖ The sterile narratives [Child Protective Services specialist Michael Guinn] had to write for courts and supervisors about the things he saw left no release for the things he felt. Thoughts of quitting entered his mind, and he jotted them down on a piece of paper. Guinn organized those thoughts into a little poem, which ignited a **Parnassian** spark and refocused his work. "One day I just picked up a pen and started writing," said Guinn, who has had two books of poetry published. (Ray Khirallah, "Work Release; Child Protective Services Specialist Finds Relief in Poetry," *Fort Worth Star-Telegram*, 5/27/2001.)

point (the . . . of a matter, as in the bottom line, the essence, etc.) *n.*: **tachlis** (esp. as in "talk tachlis") [Yiddish]. See *essence*

pointed (or coming to a point) *adj.*: **acuminate**. ❖ In the early medieval period the lives of countless peasants were defined by their relation to the castle. From the stern keep of the Norman overlord issued forth decrees and exactions; in a world of wood, wheat and water, its high stone walls were the most adamantine confirmation of the temporal order, just as the **acuminate** spire of the church pricked the oppressive heavens. (Will Self, "Psychogeography: #52: I'm the King of the Bouncy Castle," *Independent*, 9/25/2004.)

pointing (outward from the center in all directions, as if from a dome) *adj.*: **quaquaversal**. See *dipping*

pointless (mission or project) *n.*: **fool's errand**. See *hopeless*

(2) pointless (relating to the view that all human striving and aspiration is . . . , or people who hold such a view) *adj., n.*: **futilitarian**. See *futile*

(3) pointless (something that is . . . , as in useless) *n.*: **vermiform appendix**. See *useless*

(4) pointless *adj.*: **bootless**. See *futile*

(5) pointless (as in futile activity) *n.*: **mug's game** [British; informal]. See *futile*

point of no return *n.*: **Rubicon**. See *irreversibility*

point of view (centered on male . . .) *adj.*: **androcentric**. See *male*

(2) point of view (which is controversial, or person who holds one) *n.*: **polemic**. See *controversy*

poise (and confidence) *n.*: **aplomb**. See *confidence*

(2) poise (esp. under pressure or trying circumstances) *n.*: **sang-froid** [French]. See *composure*

poised *adj.*: **equable**. See *serene*

poisonous (or noxious atmosphere or influence) *n.*: **miasma**. See *noxious*

polemic *adj., n.*: **eristic**. See *debate*

police (member of French . . . organization, which is a branch of the armed forces) *n.*:

gendarme. ❖ Some 300 elite French troops and **gendarmes** had launched an operation to rescue 23 Frenchmen from a cave where they had been held by Melanesian separatists. In the 7 1/2-hour gun battle that ensued, two **gendarmes** and 19 militants died. (Michael S. Serrill, "Hostages—By Negotiation and by the Sword: Controversy Rages After Two Sets of French Captives Are Freed, *Time*, 5/16/1988, p. 55.)

policeman (Italian) *n.*: **carabiniere**. ❖ Patrolling the island [of Sardinia for a soccer game] will be 3,200 police and paramilitary commandos, some with dogs, others in camera-equipped helicopters, and all of them armed with pistols and rifles. Says a **carabiniere** commander: "If the hooligans see officers with rifles, they will be a little more afraid than of just a police stick." (*Time* International, "Sport: The Last Bit of English Hooliganism on Sardinia," 6/11/1990, p. 42.)

polished (and intelligent person) *n.*: **bel esprit**. See *cultivated*

(2) polished (as in elegant) *adj.*: **Chesterfieldian**. See *elegant*

(3) polished (as in refined or elegant) *adj.*: **raffiné** (or **raffine**) [French]. See *refined*

(4) polished (as in well bred, esp. those aspiring or pretending to be well bred) *adj.*: **lace-curtain**. See *well bred*

(5) polished (in an affected manner) *adj.*: **niminy-piminy**. See *dainty*

(6) polished *adj.*: **soigné** [French]. See *elegant*

politically correct *adj.*: **bien-pensant**. See *right-thinking*

politician (inept . . .) *n.*: **Throttlebottom** [after Alexander Throttlebottom, the name of a character who is the inept vice president in the musical comedy *Of Thee I Sing* (1932)]. ❖ Wednesday night's [televised vice-presidential debate] Donnybrook between Lloyd Bentsen and Dan Quayle—that might be called The Revenge of the Second Bananas. Bentsen was solid, senatorial and soothingly statesmanlike. Quayle, who often seemed as lost as an actor missing half the pages of his script, struggled to overcome his own **Throttlebottom** image—and lost. (Walter Shapiro, "How It Plays in Toledo; The Debate and the Campaign as Seen Through the Eyes of a Key Rustbelt City," *Time*, 10/17/1988.)

(2) politician (who is petty, unstatesmanlike, or generally contemptible) *n.*: **politicaster**. [The word also has a secondary meaning of one who dabbles in politics and is a kind of political wannabe. The example used here appears to reference the latter definition, insofar as the author uses the phrase "politicians and politicasters," but it is clear from the context that he would consider the subject to be a "politicaster" in the primary sense as well even if he were an actual politician]. ❖ Are there not in all those places, politicians and **politicasters** as demagogic and unscrupulous as the former Soviet pilot Dudayev, capable of stirring up an entire population with nationalist or religious rhetoric, and precipitating it into the most reckless adventures? (Mario Vargas Llosa, "Insights into the World; Russia Fueling Chechen Nationalism," *Daily Yomiuri*, 4/17/1995.)

(3) politician (spec. a legislator) *n.*: **solon**. See *legislator*

(4) politician (who is corrupt) *n.*: **highbinder**. See *corrupt*

(5) politician (who is or aims to be a reformer) *n.*: **goo-goo**. See *reformer*

politicians (as in actions of government officials who are pompous but inefficient) *n.*: **bumbledom**. See *bureaucracy*

politics (based on political realities as opposed to ethical, moral, or theological considerations) *n.*: **realpolitik** [German]. ❖ Chinese Premier Wen Jiabao [and] President George W. Bush [will discuss] Taiwan, trade and the North Korean nuclear impasse. What's encouraging is that both leaders seem willing to be pragmatic and flexible over these issues. It's refreshing Bush has accepted the need for diplomatic ambiguity in dealing with China over Taiwan, a **realpolitik** approach his former-president father would have approved and a welcome shift in his often-moralistic tone. (*Newsday*, "With Chinese Leader, Bush Shows He Can Be Pragmatic," 12/9/2003.)

(2) politics (of power . . . , as in belief that political power is best achieved through use of force) *n.*: **machtpolitik** [German]. ❖ When the lethal consequences of **machtpolitik** were stopped after two world wars that killed tens of millions of people, international institutions were created to obviate the use of war as an instrument of policy by a state or group of states invoking legal or political "necessity." The pertinent prohibitions are entrenched in the Charter of the United Nations. (Hugh MacDonald, "Playing Fast and Loose," *Jerusalem Post*, 4/5/1999.)

polluted (morally . . .) *v.t.*: **cankered**. See *corrupted*

polygamy (as in having more than one wife at a time) *n.*: **polygyny**. ❖ Polygyny is everywhere accompanied by the "bride price," a payment by the husband to the wife's family that, in effect, reflects the shortage of eligible brides. (The "dowry," a sum of money to make an eligible daughter more attractive, is strictly the product of monogamy.) (William Tucker, "All in the Family," *National Review*, 3/6/1995, p. 36.)

pomp (as in pretentious ceremony) *n.*: **mummery**. See *ceremony*

pomposity (in speech or writing) *n.*: **grandiloquence**. ❖ The politicians [in the 1868 impeachment trial of Andrew Johnson], untroubled by the absence of televised talk shows, missed no opportunity for **grandiloquence**. "This trial has developed, in the most remarkable manner, the insane love of speaking among public men," complained James Garfield, congressman and future president. (*Minneapolis Star Tribune*, "Temper of Times Was Much Nastier in 1868 Impeachment," 10/18/1998.)

pompous (esp. regarding speaking or writing style) *adj.*: **magniloquent**. ❖ From the plucking of the piano strings in *Hymn to a Celestial Musician* and the striking of the strings with percussion sticks in *Pastoral, No.*

1, to the use of ostinato techniques (not drone-like as the **magniloquent** and pretentious liner notes state) . . . Hovhaness has shown an understanding of many styles and a mastery of the vignette. (Michael H. Arshagouni, Music: "'Sacred Art' Remastered," *AIM*: Armenian International Magazine, 12/31/1991.)

(2) pompous (esp. regarding speaking or writing style) *adj.*: **orotund**. ❖ Damisch is repetitive, elliptical, pompous. He likes to end segments of argument not with conclusions, but with disingenuous and **orotund** questions. (Christopher S. Wood, review of *Le Jugement de Paris*, by Hubert Damisch, *Art Bulletin*, 12/1/1995, p. 677.)

(3) pompous (speech or writing) *adj.*: **fustian**. ❖ [*New Yorker* magazine editor Robert Gottlieb was] anxious to rid *The New Yorker* of its **fustian** ways, including such standard issue New Yorker language as "We betook ourselves." (Mary Vespa, Picks & Pans: Pages, *People*, 10/10/1988, p. 42.)

(4) pompous *adj.*: **flatulent**. ❖ Trudeau was a disaster as a prime minister. This arrogant, **flatulent** pseudointellectual is responsible for turning our parliamentary system into an elected dictatorship. (R. H. Nucich, letter to the editor, *Maclean's*, 4/7/1997, p. 9.)

(5) pompous *adj.*: **hoity-toity**. ❖ When is it socially acceptable for a snob to be snooty? When she has earned the right to be **hoity-toity**, of course. [Actress Patricia Routledge] has, through her portrayal of the embarrassingly haughty *Keeping Up Appearances* housewife . . . won the hearts, begrudgingly, of millions of television viewers worldwide. (AAP General News [Australia], "Popular British Actress Patricia Routledge in Australia," 7/11/2000.)

(6) pompous *adj.*: **turgid**. ❖ By their formidable intellect and persuasiveness as well as their personal charm, Rehnquist and Scalia stand at least a chance of making the [Supreme Court] more cohesive and coherent. Their judicial opinions will be more sprightly and readable than the **turgid** fare churned out by most of their brethren. (Evan Thomas, "Reagan's Mr. Right—Rehnquist Is Picked for the Court's Top Job," *Time*, 6/30/1986, p. 24.)

(7) pompous (and vain person) *n.*: **coxcomb**. See *conceited*

(8) pompous (as in affected and high-flown, use of language) *adj.*: **euphuistic.** See *affected*

(9) pompous (as in haughty or condescending) *adj.*: **toplofty.** See *haughty*

(10) pompous (as in haughty) *adj.*: **fastuous.** See *haughty*

(11) pompous (as in pedantic) *adj.*: **donnish.** See *pedantic*

(12) pompous (as in vain person) *n.*: **popinjay.** See *vain*

(13) pompous (but only superficial knowledge of a subject) *n.*: **sciolism.** See *superficial*

(14) pompous *adj.*: **tumid.** See *bombastic*

pompousness *n.*: **ampollosity.** ❖ By George, we think he's got it. A lot of those GIO shareholders feeling somewhat disenfranchised might say that the "it" was **AMPollosity**, and that George Trumpet had plenty. . . . Let's face it, we didn't like the Trumpet; he was too loud, too quickly rich, too disdaining of opposition. He wasn't like us at all. [AMP is a company in Australia that owns another company, GIO. The author was using a play on words.] (Chris Twyman, "T For 2—It's Our Cuppa," *Sydney Morning Herald*, 7/31/1999.)

ponder (as in think about) *v.t.*: **cerebrate.** See *think*

(2) ponder (as in think about) *v.t.*: **cogitate.** See *think*

(3) ponder (something, often used as a directive, as in "Consider this:") *v.t.*: **perpend.** See *consider*

ponderous (and clumsy like an elephant) *adj.*: **elephantine.** See *clumsy*

ponds (of or occurring in . . . or lakes) *adj.*: **limnetic.** See *water*

(2) ponds (of or relating to still water, such as . . .) *adj.*: **lentic.** See *water*

pontificate (on a topic, esp. in a long-winded or pompous manner) *v.i.*: **bloviate.** See *speak*

pool (esp. indoor swimming . . .) *n.*: **natato-**

rium. ❖ Plans for the tide-fed pool in Kapiolani Park remain in limbo, but the city is restoring the **natatorium's** imposing archway and public showers and changing rooms. (Laura Bly, "Constructing a New Image," *USA Today*, 5/12/2000.)

poop (eating) *adj.*: **scatophagous.** See *excrement*

(2) poop (esp. that of sea birds) *n.*: **guano.** See *bird dung*

(3) poop (feeding on) *n.*: **coprophagous.** See *excrement*

(4) poop (interest in . . . , often sexual) *n.*: **coprophilia.** See *excrement*

(5) poop (obsession with) *n.*: **coprology.** See *excrement*

(6) poop (of or relating to) *adj.*: **stercoraceous.** See *excrement*

(7) poop (study of or obsession with) *n.*: **scatology.** See *excrement*

(8) poop *n.*: **egesta.** See *excrement*

poor *adj.*: **impecunious.** ❖ Besides the 6.7 million Hong Kong people who are expected to saturate [the Disney park in Hong Kong] during its first year, most of the other visitors would be relatively **impecunious** mainlanders. (Until recently, many top hotels in the city discouraged mainland Chinese from booking rooms, worried they couldn't afford the bill.) (Mahlon Meyer, "Still Waiting for Mickey," *Newsweek* International, 7/12/1999, p. 67.)

(2) poor *adj.*: **necessitous.** ❖ In [Franklin Roosevelt's] last State of the Union Address in 1944, he said that: "**Necessitous** men are not free men. People who are hungry and out of a job are the stuff of which dictatorships are made." (*Backgrounder*, "Human Rights—Comment, Canada and the World," 5/1/1997.)

(3) poor (being . . .) *n.*: **illth.** See *poverty*

(4) poor (people, as in lowest class of society) *n.*: **lumpenproletariat.** See *underclass*

(5) poor *adj.*: **Dickensian.** See *ghettolike*

pope (qualified for or likely to become . . .) *adj.*: **papable.** ❖ When [Karol Wojtyła] was elected pope in 1978, practically everyone was surprised. It was his long years as a diocesan bishop that had rendered him **papable** to his fellow cardinals—he had shown he knew how to lead under difficult circumstances. (David Warsh, "Crucible of War: Exploring Capitalism's Global Triumph," *Boston Globe*, 4/30/2000.)

populace (pertaining to the . . . , as in the common people) *adj.*: **demotic**. See *masses*

(2) populace (suitable for or comprehensible by the . . .) *adj.*: **exoteric**. See *accessible*

popular opinion *n.*: **vox populi** [Latin; lit. voice of the people]. ❖ The **vox populi** has had its say in the nomination process and has said, with a continent-wide sigh, approximately this: "Oh well then all right—we'll settle for you two" [George H. W. Bush and Michael Dukakis]. [Republicans] have decorously nominated the consensus choice of most party leaders. . . . Democrats have done precisely what recent history warns against: They have nominated a Northeastern liberal. (George Will, "'Oh Well Then—We'll Settle for You Two,'" *Chicago Sun-Times*, 6/9/1988.)

(2) popular opinion (of an argument designed to appeal to . . .) *adj.*, *adv.*: **ad captandum** (or **ad captandum vulgus**) [Latin]. See *argument*

populated (by persons from many countries or backgrounds) *n.*: **cosmopolis**. See *diversity*

(2) populated (heavily . . . region or city) *n.*: **megalopolis**. See *crowded*

pore over (closely, esp. for purposes of surveillance) *v.t.*: **perlustrate**. See *examine*

pornographic (desire to look at . . . scenes) *n.*: **scopophilia**. See *voyeurism*

(2) pornographic (study of . . . material) *n.*: **erotology**. See *erotic*

portal (spec. the corridor in a stadium that connects the outer concourse to the interior of the stadium itself) *n.*: **vomitory**. See *corridor*

portend *v.t.*: **betoken**. ❖ The relatively high level of uninvested cash that mutual funds are holding **betokens** a ready source of funds to drive up the market when portfolio managers spot some bargains. (John Paul Newport Jr., "Believe It or Not, More Bull—There's a Growing Feeling Among Market Analysts That

Stocks Are Headed for a Rally in the Next Few Months," *Fortune*, 3/14/1988, p. 155.)

(2) portend *v.t.*: **adumbrate**. See *foreshadow*

portion *n.*: **moiety**. ❖ The original stand-up-turned novelist, Ben Elton, had a head start on the pack, thanks to his experience in sitcom writing, and because his stand-up voice was used to balancing mirth with belief, screams with themes, the tension demanded by the conflicting **moieties** of the novel: dialogue and plot on one side, reflection and issues on the other. (Ra Page, "Sit-Down Comics Lose Sight of the Audience," *New Statesman*, 6/12/1998, p. 49.)

portly (condition of having a . . . physique) *n.*: **embonpoint**. See *plump*

(2) portly (having a short . . . physique) *adj.*: **pyknic**. See *stocky*

(3) portly (person, esp. with a large abdomen) *n.*: **endomorph** (*adj.*: **endomorphic**). See *pot-bellied*

(4) portly *adj.*: **adipose**. See *fat*

(5) portly *adj.*: **Pickwickian**. See *fat*

(6) portly (or perpetually short-winded as a result of being fat) *adj.*: **pursy**. See *fat*

(7) portly (and squat) *adj.*: **fubsy**. See *squat*

(8) portly (as in beer-bellied) *adj.*: **abdominous**. See *beer-bellied*

(9) portly (as in paunchy) *adj.*: **stomachy**. See *paunchy*

(10) portly (state of being . . .) *n.*: **avoirdupois**. See *weight*

portray (as in describe, by painting or writing) *v.t.*: **limn**. See *describe*

pose (esp. by costumed performers sustaining a . . . as if in a picture) *n.*: **tableau vivant**. [French for "living picture." The term can also be used to apply to any situation where people appear to be motionless in a spot, thereby creating an image.] ❖ Marc Jacobs evidently enjoys making a scene—and we don't mean the backstage hissy fit variety. His fall 2007 New York runway show opened with a **tableau vivant** of 56 models posing in front of an enormous set of French doors. (Marc Karimzadeh, "Hitting the Marc," *W*, 5/1/2007.)

poser (or poseur, as in one striking an attitude) *n.*: **attitudinarian**. See *posturer*

posh *adj.*: **nobby** [British]. See *elegant*

position (as in condition of being located in a particular place) *n.*: **ubiety**. See *place*

(2) position (preconceived . . . on an issue) *n.*: **parti pris** [French]. See *preconception*

(3) position (which is controversial or person who holds one) *n.*: **polemic**. See *controversy*

possessions (personal . . .) *n.pl.*: **personalia**. See *belongings*

possible (as in appearing to be true or accurate) *adj.*: **verisimilar**. See *plausible*

possibly *adv.*: **perchance**. ❖ Those Republicans who will never forgive Mr. McCain for his stand on [campaign finance reform] are already lost to him (unless, **perchance**, he is the nominee, in which case everyone will forgive him). (Tod Lindberg, "Mr. McClean Campaign; McCain Ready, Willing and Available," *Washington Times*, 11/30/1999.)

posterior (toward or located near . . . or tail) *adj.*: **caudal**. See *tail*

postpartum (woman) *n.*: **puerperium**. ❖ Finally, offer the vaccine to these persons: women who are in the third trimester of pregnancy or early **puerperium** during the influenza season. (Martin M. Stevenson, "It's Just About Time to Start Giving the New Flu Vaccine," *Modern Medicine*, 9/1/1995, p. 47.)

(2) postpartum *adj.*: **puerperal**. ❖ An even more severe form of mental disease called **puerperal** psychosis may occur two days to three days after birth—and may last for three months to four months. This condition is associated with hallucinations and paranoid delusions and occurs in up to 1 percent of all pregnancies. (Paul L. Ogburn Jr., "Postpartum Depression Is Very Real," *Newsday*, 6/28/2001.)

postpone (as in avert or ward off) *v.t.*: **forfend**. See *avert*

(2) postpone (esp. a session of Parliament) *v.t.*: **prorogue**. See *discontinue*

postponement (as in procrastination or intentional delay) *n.*: **cunctation**. See *delay*

postponing (engaging in . . . tactics, esp. as a means to wear out an opponent or avoid confrontation) *adj.*: **Fabian**. See *dilatory*

posture (of or relating to erect . . .) *n.*: **orthostatic**. See *standing*

posturer (as in one striking an attitude) *n.*: **attitudinarian**. ❖ Odd new neckties are finding their way into the men's-wear stream. Short and stubby, they look as if Harpo Marx got to them with his scissors. These fat ties, as retailers call them, are wide at the business end—up to 5 inches—and very thin at the neck. In downtown Manhattan, fashion blades and other **attitudinarians** have been showing up in them. They represent the extreme of a trend toward wider men's ties in the last couple of years. (Woody Hochswender, "A 1990's Spin on the Neckwear of the 40's, *New York Times*, 12/31/1989.)

pot-bellied (person) *n.*: **endomorph** (*adj.*: **endomorphic**). ❖ When he showed up on campus weighing 344 pounds, he was, shall we say, roundly hailed. . . . Somewhat **endomorphic**—nobody would call him fat, exactly—his distinction was entirely physical. If he was going to terrorize anybody, it would be restaurateurs. (Richard Hoffer, "On the Wall of a University of Washington Hangout Called Shultzy's," *Sports Illustrated*, 9/21/1992, p. 40.)

(2) pot-bellied *adj.*: **abdominous**. See *beer-bellied*

(3) pot-bellied *adj.*: **stomachy**. See *paunchy*

potency (as in power or might) *n.*: **puissance**. See *power*

potion (as in magic . . . or love . . .) *n.*: **philter**. ❖ The herbalist is also the source for amulets, **philters**, and potions intended to further the intentions of the purchaser [such as one] seeking success as a lover. (Irving Kaplan, "South Africa: Indigenous Religions," *Countries of the World*, 1/1/1991.)

potpourri (as in assortment) *n.*: **farrago**. See *assortment*

(2) potpourri (as in assortment) *n.*: **gallimaufry**. See *assortment*

(3) potpourri (as in assortment) *n.*: **olla podrida** [Spanish]. See *assortment*

(4) potpourri (as in assortment) *n.*: **omnium-gatherum** [Latin]. See *assortment*

(5) potpourri (as in assortment) *n.*: **salmagundi**. See *assortment*

poultry (spec. of or relating to the domestic fowl) *adj.*: **gallinaceous**. See *fowl*

pour (forth, as if flowing water) *v.i.*: **disembogue**. See *discharge*

pout *n.*: **moue** [French]. ❖ His name was Stevie. She was eight years old. He broke her heart. "He was my brother's best friend," she says. "He was the love of my life, and he never loved me." [Whatever happened to Stevie?] "I don't know," she says, raising her eyebrows briefly, pursing her lips in a mock **moue**. "I think he's dead." And then she smiles, a smile that says, "Isn't it pretty to think so?" (Linda Darling, "Linda Fiorentino's Dirty Little Secret," *Esquire*, 11/1/1995, p. 108.)

(2) pout *v.t.*: **mump** [British]. See *sulk*

poverty *n.*: **illth**. [This is a term coined by the nineteenth-century philosopher John Ruskin in an essay called "The Illth of Nations" (written in response to Adam Smith's "The Wealth of Nations"), and it refers to the unintended and unwanted consequences of a prosperous society, including crime, pollution, corruption, and poverty. It is sometimes used as a synonym for poverty alone, but it should be understood that it is poverty in the above sense.] ❖ The Project evaluation results suggest that we need to move away from funding discrete, individual health projects around "**illth**" topics (e.g. drug use, injury, sedentary behaviour, poor diet) and move towards funding programs that support the "core business" already in existence in schools. (Shelley Maher, "Finding a Place for Health in the Schooling Process: A Challenge for Education," *Australian Journal of Education*, 6/1/2002.)

(2) poverty *n.*: **penury**. ❖ Beggary, **penury**, crime, alcoholism, stress, the horrible novelty of unemployment (now 9%, according to the International Labour Organisation) and

a male life expectancy of 58 years all help to keep the anger bubbling [in Russia after Communism]. (*Economist*, "Could It Lead to Fascism?" 7/11/1998.)

powder (reduce to . . . , as in pulverize) *v.t.*: **comminute**. See *pulverize*

powdery *adj.*: **pulverulent**. ❖ [T]he BMW *Tropical Beach Handbook* calls the 7 kilometers of Boracay's coast the "world's best stretch of sand." "Every **pulverulent** particle that clings to your sun-drenched body is a speckle of white coral and shell worn down by the powerful currents of the China and Sulu Seas on the southeastern edge of Asia." (Kyodo World News Service, "Travel Philippine —Philippine Gov't Frantically Woos Tourists," 12/28/2001.)

power *n.*: **puissance**. ❖ This summer Tiger [Woods] has disrupted countless weekend itineraries. Last month 28 million Americans, a 32% increase over last year, watched one of the least dramatic final rounds in the history of the British Open. They stayed for a glimpse of golfing **puissance**—and to see a reflection of themselves. (Romesh Ratnesar, "Tiger—How the Best Got Better: Changing Stripes Just as with His Golf Game," *Time*, 8/14/2000, p. 62.)

(2) power (as in domination of a nation or group over another) *n.*: **suzerainty**. See *domination*

(3) power (as in entitlement, spec. one presumed arrogantly or asserted involuntarily against others) *n.*: **droit du seigneur** [French]. See *entitlement*

(4) power (delusions of . . . or obsession with . . .) *n.*: **folie de grandeur** [French]. See *grandeur*

(5) power (one having delusional fantasies about . . . or omnipotence) *n.*: **megalomania**. See *delusional* and *obsession*

powerful (as in influential person, esp. in intellectual or literary circles) *n.*: **mandarin**. See *influential*

power grab (esp. sexual) *n.*: **droit de seigneur** [French]. See *entitlement*

power-hungry (esp. as in ambitious to equal or surpass another) *adj.*: **emulous**. See *ambitious*

powerless *adj.*: **impuissant**. ❖ When [the Greater Toronto Authority] flexes its planning muscle, local councils will simply become **impuissant** and impotent. Basic decision-making will be relegated to . . . recreational programs, library building, doling out parking and building permits, and maintaining our streets and back roads. Important decisions in the field of urban waste management, transportation, or trunk sanitary sewage lines will be made [by others]. (Frank Threlkeld Jr., "Municipalities Losing Autonomy," *Toronto Star*, 6/20/1989.)

(2) powerless (as in vulnerable, person or thing): *n.*: **clay pigeon**. See *vulnerable*

power politics (as in belief that political power is best achieved through use of force) *n.*: **machtpolitik** [German]. See *politics*

practical (politics, as in decisions based on political realities as opposed to ethical, moral, or theological considerations) *n.*: **realpolitik** [German]. See *politics*

practice (or custom) *n.*: **praxis**. See *custom*

pragmatic (politics, as in decisions based on political realities as opposed to ethical, moral, or theological considerations) *n.*: **realpolitik** [German]. See *politics*

praise *n.*: **approbation**. ❖ The series about Long Island judges was a great public service and the extensive research that went into it deserves **approbation**. (John V. Conti, letter to the editor, *Newsday*, 12/29/1999.)

(2) praise *n.*: **encomium** (one who delivers . . . or tribute; *n.*: **encomiast**). ❖ Mayor Richard Riordan jetted off to Asia to drum up business. [I would have liked to have gone with him.] Would that I were a first-class **encomiast** living off the gratuities of someone rich and powerful, traveling by his side, chronicling his every word and deed, scattering flowers at the feet of his entourage, laughing heroically at his witty cultural faux pas, wiping spittle from his chin. (Jane Robison, "Mayor's Costly Jaunt Leaves Asia in Wonder," *Daily News*, 3/8/1998.)

(3) praise (as in tribute) *n.*: **panegyric** (one who does so *n.*: **panegyrist**). See *tribute*

(4) praise (formal expression of . . .) *n.*: **encomium**. See *tribute*

(5) praise (one who seeks favor through . . . , esp. of one in power) *n.*: **courtier**. See *flattery*

(6) praise (or to bestow . . . upon) *n.*, *v.t.*: **garland**. See *accolade*

praiseworthy (as in of the highest quality) *n.*: **first water** (usu. as in "of the first water"). See *quality*

(2) praiseworthy *adj.*: **palmary**. See *excellent*

(3) praiseworthy *adj.*: **skookum**. See *excellent*

praising (insincerely. . .) *adj.*: **fulsome**. See *insincere*

prance (about so as to attract attention) *v.i.*: **tittup**. See *strut*

(2) prance (around) *v.i.*: **gambol**. See *frolic*

(3) prance *v.i.*: **curvet**. See *dance*

prank *n.*: **dido**. ❖ The most annoying vehicle is the water scooter. The scooter is noisier than most other craft, and that is annoying, but most concerning is that these things are high-speed, unstable toys, subject to no marine rules of the waterways, operated by youth seeking thrills and spills in erratic **didoes** in areas where sensible boat operators are traveling. (Burt Raughley, letter to the editor, *St. Petersburg [FL] Times*, 6/22/ 1990.)

praying mantises (of or relating to . . .) *adj.*: **orthopterous**. See *insects*

preaching (relating to or in the nature of . . . , esp. on a practical, rather than theological, matter) *adj.*: **homiletic**. ❖ [Rockefeller] especially enjoyed the company of ministers whose genial, **homiletic** style matched his own. (Ron Chernow, *Titan*, Random House [1998], p. 121.)

preachy (hypocritically . . .) *adj.*: **Pecksniffian**. See *self-righteous*

(2) preachy (hypocritically . . .) *adj.*: **pharisaical**. See *self-righteous*

(3) preachy (persons who are . . . and critical of others) *n.pl.*: **unco guid** (preceded by "the"). See *self-righteous*

preamble (to a lengthy or complex work) *n.*: **prolegomenon**. See *introduction*

(2) preamble *n.*: **proem**. See *preface*

precarious (as in a journey or passage with dangers on both sides) *idiom*: **between Scylla and Charybdis**. [This term derives from a formerly dangerous passage between Scylla, a rock on the Italian coast, which is opposite the whirlpool Charybdis, on the Sicilian coast; also represented as two female sea monsters in Greek mythology. It appears in two different ways, which are shown in the examples here.] ❖ [Federal Reserve chairman Alan Greenspan] is damned if he does and damned if he doesn't, trapped **between Scylla and Charybdis** [the risks of cutting or not cutting interest rates]. . . . For rate-cut enthusiasts, he allowed that the economy was still in a precarious state. For tax-cut enthusiasts, he averred that the economy's fundamentals were still so strong that the federal budget would likely produce big surpluses for several years. (Jodie T. Allen, "Is the Chairman Painted into a Corner?" *U.S. News & World Report*, 3/12/2001.) ❖ No subject needs the exercise of cool and critical intelligence more than that of child sexual abuse. We need to steer **between** the **Scylla** of indifference and denial, **and** the **Charybdis** of hysteria. In the present climate, Charybdis poses the greater danger. (*National Review*, "Salem in Newcastle: What a Recent Child-Abuse Scare in England Tells Us," 9/2/2002.)

(3) precarious (as in perilous) *adj.*: **parlous**. See *perilous*

precedent (as in that which set the standard or established the model from which others followed or on which others are based) *n.*: **locus classicus** [Latin]. See *model*

preceding (a meal, esp. dinner) *adj.*: **preprandial**. See *meal*

(2) preceding *adj.*: **prevenient** (often as in "prevenient grace"). See *antecedent*

precious (affectedly or excessively . . . , quaint, or dainty) *adj.*: **twee**. See *quaint*

precious stone (one who cuts and polishes a . . .) *n.*: **lapidary**. See *jeweler*

(2) precious stone (which is highly polished and unfaceted) *n.*: **cabochon**. See *jewel*

precipitous (as in impetuous) *adj.*: **gadarene**. See *impetuous*

(2) precipitous *adj.*: **declivitous** (*n.*: **declivity**). See *decline*

precise (word that is more . . . than another given word) *n.*: **hyponym**. See *word*

preconception *n.*: **parti pris** [French]. ❖ I began to follow his work attentively, and I noticed that, unlike some revered modern writers, [Polish poet Zbigniew] Herbert had no **parti pris**, no prior and axiomatic theory of the world. Instead of such dogma, I found in Herbert's work an unforced, flexible search for meaning. (Adam Zagajewski, "Is Literary Greatness Still Possible: The Shabby and the Sublime," *New Republic*, 4/5/1999.)

precursor *n.*: **progenitor**. See *predecessor*

predatory (person) *n.*: **harpy**. ❖ As chief instigator of [Rockefeller's] misery, he cited George Rice, an independent refiner, who would pursue him with the tenacity of a **harpy** for decades. (Ron Chernow, *Titan*, Random House [1998], p. 213.)

(2) predatory *adj.*: **lupine**. ❖ Some fishery biologists speculate that the presence of the predatory pike in the same drainage as brook trout may be responsible for the great size these Labrador trout achieve. . . . The brookies have to get big fast to evade the **lupine** jaws of the pitiless pike. (Robert F. Jones, "A Sojourn in Brobdingnag; In Labrador, Brook Trout Grow Big—but Dumb," *Sports Illustrated*, 9/10/1990, p. 146.)

predecessor *n.*: **progenitor**. ❖ Despite the size of the . . . [merger between Time Warner and America Online], it remains to be seen whether the new company can embrace the divergent backgrounds of its **progenitors**. The companies operate on different internal clocks, analysts said, and corporate harmony could become a merger casualty. (William Glanz, "Merger Boosts Case Legend; 'Positive Spinoffs' Seen from AOL-Time Warner Deal," *Washington Times*, 1/13/2000.)

predicament (as in choice of taking what is offered or nothing; i.e., no real choice at all) *n.*: **Hobson's choice** [derives from Thomas Hobson (1544–1630), English liveryman, who required his customers to take the horse nearest to the stable door or no horse]. ❖ Most of the land in Sumatra is not legally registered or titled, so the people working it often do not have rights of ownership. If a corporate bigwig can negotiate a land-use permit from the central government in Jakarta, the farmer faces a **Hobson's choice**: sell to the only available buyer, or try to stay and be harassed and forced to sell anyway. (*Economist*, "Sumptuous Sumatra: Indonesia," 9/24/1994, p. 33.)

(2) predicament (as in the situation of having to make a move where any move made will weaken the position) *n.*: **zugzwang**. [German. This word ordinarily refers to a chess situation where any particular move is disadvantageous to the player. It is occasionally used in a broader context, as in the example below.] ❖ Many in the GOP would like to take a pass on the abortion issue. . . . Stem cell [research, supported by some Republicans, offers] the hope of a cure for disease, everything from diabetes to Alzheimer's. But to right-to-lifers, each embryo, even if it is just a cluster of cells in a test tube, is an unborn child. . . . Bush and the GOP are caught in the middle. . . . But in politics, as in chess, **zugzwang** is not an option. (James P. Pinkerton, "Republicans Can't Evade Abortion Issue," *Newsday*, 1/22/2001.)

(3) predicament (from which it is difficult to extricate oneself) *n.*: **tar baby**. [Tar-Baby was a doll made of tar and turpentine, used by Br'er Fox and Br'er Bear to entrap Br'er Rabbit in the second of the Uncle Remus stories. He kicks the doll and then becomes stuck because of the tar. The term is often considered to be offensive to African Americans, although, as noted above, its genesis relates to the stickiness of the mixture rather than to the color of the tar.] ❖ Ever since President Bush took office he has been dancing nimbly to keep from being tarred in the S&L crisis, noting that it is a problem he inherited and that he is energetically fashioning a plan to make it go away. But last week, as the blame game raged on, the savings and loan **tar baby** began to stick to the one-time Texan. (*U.S. News & World Report*, "Where the Bucks Stop," 6/4/1990.)

(4) predicament (which is difficult to solve) *n.*: **Gordian knot**. See *dilemma*

(5) predicament (as in combination of events or circumstances that create a crisis) *n.*: **conjuncture**. See *crisis*

(6) predicament (as in dangers on both sides) *idiom*: **between Scylla and Charybdis**. See *precarious*

(7) predicament (as in dilemma, except where there are three options, all of which are or seem to be unsatisfactory) *n.*: **trilemma**. See *dilemma*

(8) predicament (resulting from an inopportune occurrence) *n.*: **contretemps**. See *mishap*

predict *v.t.*: **vaticinate**. ❖ Democracy, [the authors] **vaticinate**, will ultimately trump tyranny because most people believe legitimate government pivots on the consent of the governed, and most professional military officers believe in civilian supremacy (for example, in Nigeria, Bosnia, Somalia, or Burma). (Bruce Fein, Book Reviews, *Perspectives on Political Science*, 6/1/1994, p. 149.)

(2) predict *v.t.*: **adumbrate**. See *foreshadow*

(3) predict (the future by gazing into a crystal ball) *v.t.*: **scry**. ❖ It is in affairs of the heart that the psychic comes into her own. Whether it is by the turn of the tarot or through a glass darkly, the mystic can **scry** the features of the favoured son. Curiously, the man most will marry is never short, pallid and ugly and always possessed of a nice personality. (*Times* [London], "When Were You Born?" 8/14/1997.)

predictable (as in trained to show a conditioned response) *adj.*: **Pavlovian**. See *conditioned*

prediction (as in acting as if or threatening that a future event—usually unwanted—has already occurred by reference to an event that precedes it; for example, "if you look at my diary, you're dead") *n*.: **prolepsis**. ❖ The ragged-looking protestors say the planned highway is a violation of the earth. . . . [They] have an apocalyptic air, as if this is all that has been left of urban civilisation after some terrible eco-disaster [, as if] the population of Britain has been decimated by an awful laboratory-created virus, leaving everyone still alive in ragged Aran sweaters. . . . This is protest as **prolepsis**: an anticipation of what they seek to prevent. (Will Self, "Tree Surgery," *Observer* [London], 2/4/1996.)

(2) prediction (relating to the art of . . .) *adj*.: **mantic**. See *prophetic*

(3) prediction (relating to the art of . . .) *adj*.: **sybilline**. See *prophetic*

predictive *adj*.: **fatidic**. See *prophetic*

predictor (as in one who makes correct predictions of misfortune that are ignored) *n*.: **Cassandra.** [Note: There is some discrepancy among the dictionary definitions for this word as to (1) whether the predictions must prove to be correct, (2) whether the predictions must be of misfortune, doom, or disaster, and (3) whether the predictions must be ignored. For example, although the *OED* references all three, *Webster's Third* references only the second condition and neither of the other two. *The American Heritage Fourth* references only the third. However, the original Cassandra had the gift of prophecy bestowed upon her by Apollo, but when she spurned him, he converted the gift to a curse by decreeing that she would not be believed. Thus her fate was to know of future disasters and yet be powerless to prevent them. Accordingly, it is submitted that all three conditions must be met for a correct use of the word, which is the case in the following example.] ❖ Among the chorus of **Cassandras** prophesying the doom of financial markets if junk bond takeovers were not curbed was SEC Chairman Shad. Said he: "The more leveraged takeovers and buyouts today, the more bankruptcies tomorrow." (Brett Duval Fromson, Special Report: "The Last Days of Drexel Burnham," *Fortune*, 5/21/1990, p. 90.)

(2) predictor (by using lightning or animal innards) *n*.: **haruspex**. See *fortune-teller*

predilection (as in personal preference) *n*.: **de gustibus** [Latin]. See *taste*

predisposed (to a particular point of view) *adj*.: **tendentious**. See *biased*

predisposition *n*.: **parti pris** [French]. See *preconception*

predominant *adj*.: **regnant**. ❖ By the 1996 elections, American politics had come half-circle: Now you don't have to call yourself conservative to be one; it is simply the political air everyone, Democrats and Republicans alike, breathes. Once again an end of ideology has been proclaimed, only this time it disguises the fact that the **regnant** ideology is conservatism. (Rick Perlstein, "Ideas/Left Overtures for the Renewal of Liberalism," *Newsday*, 1/26/1997.)

preeminence (as in superiority or state of being better) *n*.: **meliority**. See *superiority*

preface *n*.: **proem**. ❖ Eugene Jolas's extraordinary memoir (he called it "my novel—autobiography—my fact and fiction book") opens with a rhapsodic **proem**. (Daniel Aaron, "A Child of the Century," *New Republic*, 11/9/1998.)

(2) preface (often to a speech or writing) *n*.: **exordium**. See *introduction*

(3) preface (to a lengthy or complex work) *n*.: **prolegomenon**. See *introduction*

preference (as in personal . . .) *n*.: **de gustibus** [Latin]. See *taste*

pregnancies (woman who has had two or more . . .) *n*.: **multigravida**. ❖ Ness et al. evaluated women from the Framingham cohort and found that the rates of coronary heart disease were higher among **multigravida** women than among women who had never been pregnant. (Mary Ann D'elio, "Are Life Stress and Social Support Related to Parity in Women?" *Behavioral Medicine*, 6/22/1997, p. 87.)

pregnancy (period of . . .) *n*.: **antepartum** [Latin]. ❖ **Antepartum** care encompasses the physical and psychosocial care of the family experiencing a pregnancy. (Virginia H. Kemo, "Perinatal Home Care," *Family and Community Health*, 1/1/1996, p. 40.)

(2) pregnancy (just after . . .) *adj.*: **puerperal**. See *postpartum*

(3) pregnancy (woman right after . . .) *n.*: **puerperium**. See *postpartum*

pregnant (woman who is . . . for the first time or has had only one child) *n.*: **primipara**. ❖ With breastfeeding, however, the "condition" does not really exist prior to hospital discharge; the mother's breasts have not yet begun to fill. The **primipara** has no experience of the condition, so it is unlikely that she will know if it becomes better or worse than it should be. (Marie Biancuzzo, "Breastfeeding Education for Early Discharge: A Three-Tiered Approach," *Journal of Perinatal & Neonatal Nursing*, 9/1/1997, p. 10.)

(2) pregnant *adj.*: **enceinte** [French]. ❖ It was probably only a matter of time. A British firm has unveiled what is believed to be the first line of maternity wedding gowns, in white and ivory, for today's **enceinte** bride. "Just because they're pregnant, there's no reason they shouldn't look beautiful," explains Jennie Andrews, designer for Ellis Bridals. (Thom Geier, "Eye on the '90s," *U.S. News & World Report*, 9/25/1995.)

(3) pregnant *adj.*: **gravid**. ❖ Should we take another look at those heatedly denied rumors about Julia Roberts being pregnant? . . . So, **gravid** or not? "Please, she's starting *Mary Reilly* in early May," says a Roberts spokeswoman, "and she's doing a cameo for Robert Altman's *Prêt-à-Porter* in March, so she can't be pregnant." (*Entertainment Weekly*, News and Notes, 11/19/1993, p. 14.)

(4) pregnant (cause to become . . .) *v.t.*: **fecundate**. See *impregnate*

prehistoric (person, as in Neanderthal) *n.*: **troglodyte**. See *Neanderthal*

prejudgment (as in preconception) *n.*: **parti pris** [French]. See *preconception*

prejudice (and ill will that develops when disputes about religion arise) *n.*: **odium theologicum**. See *intolerance*

(2) prejudice (preconceived . . . on an issue) *n.*: **parti pris** [French]. See *preconception*

prejudiced (as in advocating a particular point of view) *adj.*: **tendentious**. See *biased*

(2) prejudiced (as in narrow-minded) *adj.*: **hidebound**. See *narrow-minded*

prelude (to a lengthy or complex work) *n.*: **prolegomenon**. See *introduction*

(2) prelude *n.*: **proem**. See *preface*

premeditated *adj.*: **prepense** (usually used as part of the phrase "malice prepense"). ❖ In her original trial, there was ample testimony to Yvonne Sleightholme's gentle Christian qualities. Was such a woman capable of **malice prepense**? Was it conceivable that she had been driven to it? . . .Was [she] a professional killer, one who knew how to deliver expertly the fatal shot and then disappear without trace? (Alan Combes, "Blind Injustice?" *Guardian* [London], 2/27/1993.)

premise (as in assumption or set of assumptions) *n.*: **donnée** [French]. See *assumption*

premonition (that something is going to occur) *n.*: **presentiment**. [Usage note: Presentiment often, but not necessarily, refers to a premonition that something bad is going to occur.] ❖ The feeling that something could go very wrong [when the date becomes January 1, 2000] turns out to be hard to shake. . . . You can't criticize the decision to stay on the safe side. Who knows what lunatic or team of lunatics might turn a **presentiment** of doom into an active effort to usher it in? Maybe, just maybe, tonight will bring chaos. (Amy Schwartz, "New-Year Fears," *Washington Post*, 12/31/1999.)

preoccupation (undue . . . over one subject or idea) *n.*: **monomania**. See *obsession*

(2) preoccupation (with an idea or concept) *n.*: **idée fixe** [French]. See *obsession*

preoccupied (esp. because of worries or fears) *adj.*: **distrait**. See *distracted*

preposterous *adj.*: **fatuous** See *delusional*

presage *v.t.*: **adumbrate**. See *foreshadow*

(2) presage *v.t.*: **betoken**. See *portend*

presence (as in condition of being located in a particular place) *n.*: **ubiety**. See *place*

(2) presence (having . . . through magnetism or charm) *n.*: **duende**. See *charisma*

present (as in blessing) *n.*: **benison**. See *blessing*

(2) present (extra or unexpected . . . often given with customer's purchase) *n.*: **lagniappe**. See *gift*

(3) present (for the . . .) *n.*: **nonce** (used as "for the nonce"). See *time being*

(4) present (such as flowers, to a wife from a guilty husband) *n.*: **drachenfutter** [German; lit. dragon fodder]. See *peace offering*

presiding (as in lordly) *adj.*: **seigneurial**. See *lordly*

press (as in publicity or a taste or flair for being in the limelight) *n.*: réclame [French]. See *publicity*

pressed (together, esp. in rows) *adj.*: **serried**. See *crowded*

pressing *adj.*: **clamant**. See *urgent*

(2) pressing *adj.*: **necessitous**. See *urgent*

pressure (as in burden) *n.*: **incubus**. See *burden*

prestige (of an argument based on the . . . or say-so of another, but in an area that is outside his or her field of expertise; i.e., improperly trading on the reverence and respect of another) *adj.*, *adv.*: **ad verecundiam** (*n.*: **argumentum ad verecundiam**) [Latin]. See *argument*

presumptuous (as in venturing beyond one's province) *adj.*: **ultracrepidarian**. ❖ Bully a bully and you'll make him bullier. As you'd expect, the first thing Milosevic did after the bombing was to step up atrocities in Kosovo. . . . Denis Healey [a veteran of the invasion of Italy in 1944] was one of the few to seize upon these obvious and obstinate facts. [He] was told by Labour MP Ms Barbara Follett that he was wrong. . . . Ah! The arrogance of youth, condemned to repeat old mistakes but always in its own terms! [Hers were] **ultracrepidarian** remarks . . . (Chris Maslanka, "Puzzle Master," *Independent* [London], 3/27/1999.)

pretend (to be sick or incapacitated to avoid work) *v.i.*: **malinger**. See *shirk*

pretender (as in hypocrite, esp. one who acts humbly) *n.*: **Uriah Heep**. See *hypocrite*

(2) pretender (as in hypocrite, esp. one

who affects religious piety) *n.*: **Tartuffe** (or **tartuffe**). See *hypocrite*

pretense (as in something that is impressive-looking on the outside but which hides or covers up undesirable conditions or facts) *n.*: **Potemkin village**. See *facade*

pretentious (as in affected and high-flown, use of language) *adj.*: **euphuistic**. See *affected*

(2) pretentious (as in haughty or condescending) *adj.*: **toplofty**. See *haughty*

(3) pretentious (as in haughty) *adj.*: **fastuous**. See *haughty*

(4) pretentious (as in insincere) *adj.*: **crocodilian**. See *insincere*

(5) pretentious (as in pedantic) *adj.*: **donnish**. See *pedantic*

(6) pretentious (as in pompous) *adj.*: **flatulent**. See *pompous*

(7) pretentious (but only superficial knowledge of a subject) *n.*: **sciolism**. See *superficial*

(8) pretentious (esp. regarding speaking or writing style) *adj.*: **magniloquent**. See *pompous*

(9) pretentious (esp. regarding speaking or writing style) *adj.*: **orotund**. See *pompous*

(10) pretentious (or ostentatious object) *n.*: **frippery**. See *ostentatious*

(11) pretentious (or self-important person or official) *n.*: **high muck-a-muck** (or **high-muck-a-muck**). See *bigwig*

(12) pretentious (or self-important person or official) *n.*: **panjandrum**. See *bigwig*

(13) pretentious (person on issues of grammar) *n.*: **grammaticaster**. See *pedantic*

(14) pretentious (speech or writing) *adj.*: **fustian**. See *pompous*

(15) pretentious *adj.*: **hoity-toity**. See *pompous*

prettiness (facetious way of measuring . . . by units) *n.*: **millihelen**. See *beauty*

pretty (in a superficial, romanticized or sentimental way) *adj.*: **chocolate-box**. [The term is often, but not necessarily, applied to works of art.] ❖ In fact, in a sense, it is the corny art that makes the show since it best illustrates what [Parisian art in] 1900 was really like. For instance, Cézanne had already begun work on his revolutionary *Grandes Baigneuses* series, but the **chocolate-box** image of bathing maidens in Paul Chabas's *Joyous Frolics* (1899) was probably closer to public taste. (Alan Riding, Arts Abroad: "3 Shows on 1900, Not as a Landmark but as a Bridge," *New York Times*, 4/5/2000.)

(2) pretty (in an unconventional way) *adj.* **jolie laide** (or **jolie-laide**). [French, for "pretty-ugly." This term refers to being attractive in an unconventional or unusual way, or more literally, pretty and ugly at the same time. (The masculine form would be "joli laid." See *handsome*.) It can also be applied to inanimate objects, and can be used as a noun to refer to the person or thing being described. See *woman* for an example, since that is the noun most commonly used. A similar term is "belle laide," which is beautiful-ugly. See *beautiful*.] ❖ With her little snub nose and deep-set, dark-fringed hazel eyes, Jodie [Whittaker] has just the kind of **jolie-laide** looks needed to play this most unlikely leading lady opposite the patrician-looking Peter O'Toole. But it works. . . . I'm lucky that I'm not too beautiful. If you're stunning, which must be a wonderful thing to be, that can be limiting as an actor." (Maureen Paton, "Venus Rises," *Daily Mail* [London], 1/21/2007.)

(3) pretty (esp. in a sexual way) *adj.*: **toothsome**. See *sexy*

prevailing *adj.*: **regnant**. See *predominant*

prevalent *adj.*: **pandemic**. See *widespread*

(2) prevalent *adj.*: **regnant**. See *widespread*

prevent (a person's movement by holding down his arms) *v.t.*: **pinion**. See *immobilize*

(2) prevent (as in avert or ward off) *v.t.*: **forfend**. See *avert*

(3) prevent (intended to . . . against evil) *adj.*: **apotropaic**. See *protect*

previous (as in former) *adj.*: **ci-devant** [French]. See *former*

(2) previous (as in former) *adj.*: **quondam**. See *former*

(3) previous (as in former) *adj.*: **whilom**. See *former*

prickling (or tingling or itching sensation that insects are crawling on you) *n.*: **formication**. ❖ I can state with some confidence that I have experienced more than my fair share of **formication** this summer. Regrettably, that is not a spelling mistake. Rather, I am referring to the faintly more alarming sensation of ants crawling over my skin, courtesy of our insect-infatuated infants. When I was a child, "ants in your pants" was a turn of phrase; for our offspring it has now become a lifestyle choice. (Andrew Hoyle, "Daddy Cool," *Scotland on Sunday*, 7/27/2008.)

(2) prickling (of skin sensation) *n.*: **paresthesia**. ❖ [A] touch player with little or no sensation in her hands probably has a limited future, and [golfer Cathy] Gerring gets constant reminders of the odds stacked against her as a result of a burn accident]. . . . On cold days, her fingers ache. She also suffers from **paresthesia**, a pain she compares to being stabbed by needles. (Kevin Cook, Golf Plus/News & Notes, *Sports Illustrated*, 5/4/1998, p. G27.)

prickly *adj.*: **echinate**. ❖ Almost any fool should be discerning enough to recognize evil disguised as religion. . . . The harder issue is whether there's any eternal difference between and among religions followed by people of good will, [and] by people with a social conscience. . . . Joseph C. Hough Jr., president of Union Theological Seminary in New York, has been raising this **echinate** question in recent months. (Bill Tammeus, "Toward Theology in Dialogue," *Kansas City Star*, 3/30/2002.)

pride (as in self-esteem) *n.*: **amour-propre** [French]. See *self-esteem*

(2) pride (which is overbearing, as in arrogance) *adj.*: **hubris**. See *arrogance*

priest (government by a . . . or other clergy members) *n.*: **hierocracy**. See *government*

priestly *adj.*: **sacerdotal**. ❖ After [Cardinal-to-be John O'Connor] was ordained a priest in 1945, he followed the usual **sacerdotal** path, teaching high school and doing parish work. (Hanna Rosin, obituary of Cardinal John J. O'Connor, *Washington Post*, 5/4/2000.)

priests (of, used by, or relating to) *adj.*: **hieratic**. ❖ Antony Gormley's [sculpture] *Angel of the North* rears against the skyline of Gateshead like a crucifixion. . . . [T]his great winged figure looks more like an aeroplane than an angel. . . . The pose is **hieratic**, like a priest offering thanks to God, but the face, with its lack of features or expression, is vaguely menacing. (Andrew Lambirth, Visual Arts: Is It a Bird? Is It a Plane? No, It's a Gormley," *Independent* [London], 2/17/1998.)

prim (or prudish) *adj.*: **missish**. ❖ That men and women are different is an accepted tenet of popular culture. . . . Yet amble any great distance along the path of sex differences, and you will soon find yourself with Harvard President Larry Summers, tripping painfully on the [path]. Summers's crime, in this context, was to have the temerity to state what science has long known about men and women, and to do so without worrying about offending the **missish** sensibilities of some female academics. (Christine Rosen, "What (Most) Women Want," *Claremont Review of Books*, Spring 2005.)

(2) prim (in an affected manner) *adj.*: **niminy-piminy**. See *dainty*

(3) prim *adj.*: **governessy**. See *fastidious*

primarily (as in basically) *adv.*: **au fond** [French]. See *basically*

primary (as in basic) *adj.*: **abecedarian**. See *basic*

prime mover *n.*: **primum mobile** [Latin]. ❖ [Randall Robinson, who wrote *The Debt: What America Owes to Blacks*,] is hardly alone in his basic insistence that the growth of the black middle class is somehow "beside the point." . . . This sense of racism as rendering all black success "accidental" is ultimately the **primum mobile** of the reparations movement. . . . This belief that there is no path for blacks to the top accounts for Robinson's sour attitude toward blacks making progress. (John McWhorter, "Against Reparations: Why African Americans Can Believe in America," *New Republic*, 7/23/2001.)

primer *n.*: **hornbook**. ❖ The multicultural-

ists . . . grossly divide Americans into "oppressors" (all whites of European descent) and the "oppressed" (all persons of color from minority cultures). Howard Zinn's *A People's History of the United States*, a 750-page screed that depicts America as a continuing centuries-old conspiracy of rich white men to exploit minorities, is their **hornbook**. Many use it in their classrooms to demean America's Founders. (Robert Holland, "Multicultural Shaping of Teachers," *Washington Times*, 12/15/2004.)

primitive (as in crude, or poorly put together, esp. with respect to a piece of writing or speech) *adj.*: **incondite**. See *crude*

(2) primitive (person) *n.*: **troglodyte**. See *Neanderthal*

(3) primitive *n.*: **artless**. See *crude*

prince (or other ruler who holds great power or sway) *n.*: **potentate**. See *ruler*

principle *n.*: **shibboleth**. ❖ The Democrats had been out of power for 12 years when Clinton came on the scene as a "new Democrat" who defied some Democratic **shibboleths**, supporting welfare reform, free trade and the death penalty. (Susan Page, "GOP's New Face: 'W,' as in Win: Tired of Losing, Party Hands Bush the Reins; Will It Last?" *USA Today*, 8/3/2000.)

(2) principle (as in assumption or set of assumptions) *n.*: **donnée** [French]. See *assumption*

principles (spec. doctrines to be believed; articles of faith) *n.pl.*: **credenda**. See *beliefs*

printing (of secret or government-banned literature, or the literature produced by such a system) *n.*: **samizdat**. See *underground*

prior (as in former) *adj.*: **ci-devant** [French]. See *former*

(2) prior (as in former) *adj.*: **quondam**. See *former*

(3) prior (as in former) *adj.*: **whilom**. See *former*

(4) prior (to a meal, esp. dinner) *adj.*: **preprandial**. See *meal*

(5) prior *adj.*: **prevenient** (often as in "prevenient grace"). See *antecedent*

prison (study of . . . management) *n.*: **penology**. ❖ Formerly smooth-running, [Ottawa's Grande Cache prison] has since seen ceaseless trouble, and last month, a riot. The guards' union and a Reform MP say the incidents prove that Ottawa's liberal **penology** produces prisoners who are bored, irritable—and destructive. (Davis Sheremata, "The Results of Cherishing Prisoner Individuality," Alberta Report/Western Report, 12/9/1996, p. 30.)

(2) prison (where a guard can see all prisoners) *n.*: **panopticon**. ❖ Walk through the nearly completed seven-room house in Studio City, Calif., where 10 contestants will spend 89 days being filmed for edited, same-day broadcasts. . . . It is Martha Stewart's hell, a cold Bauhaus **panopticon** riddled with cameras. The decor, says creator Romer, is intentional. The hope is that the "houseguests" will decorate their prison themselves. (Benjamin Nugent, "We Like to Watch—Led by the Hit Survivor, Voyeurism Has Become TV's Hottest Genre," Time, 6/26/2000, p. 56.)

(3) prison *n.*: **bastille**. ❖ He has even lost the timbre of his voice. Facing him behind a sheet of perforated Plexiglas in the narrow visiting room of the prison—a **bastille** built in 1840 to entertain captured pirates—one has to press an ear against the barrier to hear him speak. (William Nack, "The Muscle Murders—When Bertil Fox, a Former Mr. Universe, Was Arrested for Double Homicide Last Year, He Became Only the Latest Accused Murderer Among Hard-Core Bodybuilders," Sports Illustrated, 5/18/1998, p. 96.)

(4) prison *n.*: **durance vile**. See *jail*

(5) prison *n.*: **hoosegow**. See *jail*

(6) prison *n.*: **oubliette**. See *dungeon*

prisoners (group of . . . or slaves chained together) *n.*: **coffle**. ❖ On his way to view the opening of a new session of the houses of Congress [in 1815], he was shocked to confront a slave **coffle** in the neighborhood of Capitol Hill. Nothing in his life had prepared him for the sight of men, women, and children being herded in chains through the streets of Washington.

(John Davis, "Eastman Johnson's 'Negro Life at the South' and Urban Slavery in Washington, D.C.," Art Bulletin, 3/1/1998, p. 67.)

prissy (as in prim or prudish) *adj.*: **missish**. See *prim*

private (as in, of or relating to a court, legislative body, or other group that meets in . . . , and often makes decisions that are harsh or arbitrary) *adj.*: **star chamber**. See *closed-door*

(2) private (most . . . parts, thoughts, or places) *n.*: **penetralia**. See *secret*

(3) private (as in shy and/or sullen and/or socially withdrawn or inexperienced) *adj.*: **farouche** [French]. See *shy*

privately *adj.*: **in petto** [Italian]. ❖ When she auditioned with Verdi and he explained to her that she would have no solos, she assured him she didn't mind, she was so honored to have been chosen by the maestro for the Falstaff premiere. Still, Verdi wrote afterward, he could tell that **in petto** she was disappointed, and he added the solo. (Joseph Kerman, review of Verdi: A Biography, by Mary Jane Phillips-Matz, New Republic, 1/10/1994, p. 42.)

(2) privately *adv., adj.*: **in camera**. [This term is well known to lawyers as referring to judicial proceedings that take place privately before a judge, but it is also used more generally to refer to any meetings that take place behind closed doors.] ❖ [A homeowner wanted to take down a catalpa tree on his property, but could not do so without approval.] The Tree Commission hearing on the catalpa took place May 13 in the city auditorium with a formality appropriate to serious judicial review. Then Chairman John Hartmann, 52, a professional gardener, ordered the witnesses and public (including a journalist) out so the commission could deliberate "**in camera**." The secret deliberation lasted 40 minutes. (Phil McCombs, "Up a Tree in Takoma Park," Washington Post, 7/19/2003.)

privilege (as in entitlement, spec. one presumed arrogantly or asserted involuntarily against others) *n.*: **droit du seigneur** [French]. See *entitlement*

prize (as in reward) *n.*: **guerdon**. See *reward*

(2) prize (give a . . . to) *v.t.*: **premiate**. See *award*

prized (household items) *n.pl.*: **lares and penates**. See *treasures*

probable (as in appearing to be true or accurate) *adj.*: **verisimilar**. See *plausible*

probe (as in touch, esp. for medical reasons) *v.t.*: **palpate**. See *touch*

(2) probe (closely) *v.t.*: **catechize**. See *question*

(3) probe (through formal questioning about governmental policy or action) *v.t.*: **interpellate**. See *interrogate*

(4) probe (closely, esp. for purposes of surveillance) *v.t.*: **perlustrate**. See *examine*

problem (which is difficult for a beginner or one who is inexperienced) *n.*: **pons asinorum** [Latin]. ❖ The minor characters are, as in the novel, preposterous caricatures; the once great Jeanne Moreau supplies the narration (in good English, the language of her mother, though even she trips up on the word recognize, a veritable **pons asinorum** for foreigners) . . . (John Simon, review of *The Lover*, *National Review*, 11/30/1992.)

(2) problem (as in combination of events or circumstances that create a crisis) *n.*: **conjuncture**. See *crisis*

(3) problem (as in dilemma, except where there are three options, all of which are or seem to be unsatisfactory) *n.*: **trilemma**. See *dilemma*

(4) problem (from which it is difficult to extricate onself) *n.*: **tar baby**. See *predicament*

(5) problem (which is difficult to solve) *n.*: **Gordian knot**. See *dilemma*

(6) problem (which is difficult to solve) *n.*: **nodus**. See *complication*

procedure (mode of . . . , as in course of action) *n.*: **démarche** [French]. See *course of action*

procession (of attendants, as for an important person) *n.*: **cortege**. ❖ These days one of the flashier **corteges** roaring around Moscow has a BMW out front, bodyguards in Mitsubishi jeeps on either side and a dark-blue, bulletproof Mercedes 60 in the center. It belongs

not to Boris Yeltsin but to the other Boris—the most influential new capitalist tycoon in Russia, Boris Berezovsky. (Fred Coleman, "Rich, the Russian Way," *U.S. News & World Report*, 1/13/1997.)

proclaim (pompously, loudly, or theatrically) *v.i.*: **declaim**. ❖ Sir James Goldsmith's Referendum Party . . . loudly opposes a federal Europe. At a recent rally, the tycoon **declaimed**, "If the only choice we have is to be part of a federal Europe, a superstate, then I would definitely get out." (James Walsh, "The Battle of Britain—A Nation Ruled by Conservatives for the Past 18 Years Prepares Itself for a New Era of Tony Blair's Gentler, Centrist 'New Labour,'" *Time* International, 4/28/1997, p. 22.)

(2) proclaim (as in declare, publicly, solemnly, or formally) *v.t.*: **nuncupate**. See *declare*

(3) proclaim *v.t.*: **annunciate**. See *announce*

proclamation *n.*: **ukase**. See *decree*

procrastinate (due to indecision) *v.i.*: **dither**. ❖ [BP Amoco head] Browne, 51, is not the kind of chief executive who **dithers**. He ordered up $2 billion of cost-cutting from BP Amoco by the end of 2000. Then, when oil prices tanked last year, he moved the target date up to the end of 1999. Boom. (Toni Mack, "Brass-Ring Time," *Forbes*, 5/3/1999, p. 56.)

(2) procrastinate *v.i.*: **shilly-shally**. ❖ Green had his staff pore over Victoria's Secret catalogs for days on end until they determined that the Secret people did not show enough minority models wearing their underwear. Green didn't **shilly-shally**. He cited them with a violation of city regulations—hell, right on the spot. (Michael Shain, Inside New York, *Newsday*, 6/20/1993.)

procrastinating (engaging in . . . tactics, esp. as a means to wear out an opponent or avoid confrontation) *adj.*: **Fabian**. See *dilatory*

procrastination (or delay) *n.*: **cunctation**. See *delay*

proctor (a school examination) *v.i.*: **invigilate**. ❖ A few weeks into my so-called teaching career, the dreaded four-letter word started appearing more and more often in the students' vocabulary. E-X-A-M. Preparing the question papers for the exam was no easy feat but being only a temporary teacher, I was spared that. Nonetheless, I still had to **invigilate** (which is an extremely tiresome and boring job) and yes, mark the exam papers. (Mark Hoew Han, "Teaching's Not for the Quitter," *New Straits Times*, 5/16/2003.)

prod (as in stimulus) *n.*: **fillip**. See *stimulus*

prodding (as in urging someone to take a course of action) *adj.*: **hortatory**. See *urging*

  (2) prodding (or inciting or inspiring to action) *adj.*: **proceleusmatic**. See *exhorting*

produce (as in build cheaply and flimsily) *v.t.*: **jerry-build**. See *build*

product (as in outgrowth) *n.*: **excrescence**. See *outgrowth*

productive (esp. as in fertile) *adj.*: **fecund**. See *fertile*

  (2) productive (in producing offspring) *adj.*: **philoprogenitive**. See *fertile*

  (3) productive (make . . .) *v.i.*: **fructify**. See *fruitful*

  (4) productive (or fruitful) *adj.*: **fructuous**. See *fruitful*

profess (as in confide, one's thoughts or feelings) *v.t., v.i.*: **unbosom**. See *confide*

profession *n.*: **métier** [French]. ❖ [Senator Joseph] McCarthy was in a business that permitted a certain latitude: it was politics, not physics. "McCarthy's record is . . . not only much better than his critics allege, but, given his **métier**, extremely good." Thus he "should not be remembered as the man who didn't produce 57 Communist Party cards but as the man who brought public pressure to bear . . . to eliminate from responsible positions flagrant security risks." (Elliott Abrams, review of *McCarthy and His Enemies*, by William F. Buckley Jr. and L. Brent Bozell, *National Review*, 2/26/1996, p. 57.)

professor (as in teacher) *n.*: **pedagogue**. See *teacher*

proficient (as in skillful) *adj.*: **habile**. See *skillful*

  (2) proficient (as in skillful) *adj.*: **au fait** [French]. See *skillful*

profile (distinctive . . . or outline, often of a face) *adj.*: **lineament** (often **lineaments**). See *contour*

profit (as in, "to whose . . . ?") *n.*: **cui bono** [Latin]. See *advantage*

profitable (as in fruitful; productive) *adj.*: **fructuous**. See *fruitful*

profligate *n.*: **wastrel**. See *slacker*

programmed (as in contrived) *adj.*: **voulu** [French]. See *contrived*

progression *n.*: **consecution**. See *sequence*

project (which is fruitless or hopeless) *n.*: **fool's errand**. See *hopeless*

proletariat *n.*: **canaille**. See *masses*

  (2) proletariat *n.*: **hoi polloi**. See *commoners*

proliferate (as in burgeon or expand; lit. bear fruit) *v.i.*: **fructify**. See *burgeon*

prolific (esp. as in fertile) *adj.*: **fecund** (*v.t.*: **fecundate**). ❖ The manatee population continues to grow despite the few that are killed in boating accidents, just as our deer populations continue to thrive despite the deer that are struck on the highways. Manatees are not particularly **fecund** animals, but they have no natural predators. (Frank Sargeant, "Manatees Are Not Endangered Species," *Tampa Tribune*, 9/13/2000.)

  (2) prolific (in producing offspring) *adj.*: **philoprogenitive**. See *fertile*

prominent (and/or wealthy person) *n.*: **nabob**. See *bigwig*

  (2) prominent (person) *n.*: **satrap**. See *bigwig*

promiscuous *adj., n.*: **libertine**. ❖ This drew on a plebeian morality in which the value placed on chastity was relatively low, and which allowed premarital sex upon promise of marriage and common-law marriage if a first marriage broke down. . . . For women the **libertine** ethic was perilous: pregnant sweethearts and abandoned wives and children paid for the freedoms of bachelor culture. (Anna Davin, "Before the Glass Ceiling," *Women's Review of Books*, 12/1/1995, p. 13.)

  (2) promiscuous (woman) *n.*: **roundheel**. See *slut*

promise (of marriage) *v.t.*: **affiance**. See *marriage*

promotion (of military officer without pay increase) *v.t., n.*: **brevet**. ❖ By the end of the year, though still nominally a lieutenant, he was **breveted** with the rank of captain as a reward for his services. (Simon Winchester, *The Professor and the Madman*, HarperCollins [1998], p. 67.)

pronounce (as in declare, publicly, solemnly, or formally) *v.t.*: **nuncupate**. See *declare*

(2) pronounce (study of how to . . . words) *n.*: **orthoepy**. See *pronunciation*

(3) pronounce (with hissing sounds) *v.t.*: **assibilate**. See *hissing*

pronouncement (made without proof or support) *n.*: **ipse dixit** [Latin]. See *allegation*

(2) pronouncement (which is official, as in with the authority of one's office) *adv., adj.*: **ex cathedra**. See *official*

(3) pronouncement *n.*: **ukase**. See *decree*

pronunciation (study of . . .) *n.*: **orthoepy**. [Ironically, a word meaning "study of pronunciation" not only does not lend itself to obvious pronunciation but in fact has different approved pronunciations. The most common one is probably or-THO-a-pee.] ❖ Don't be put off by the title of Ken Campbell's latest solo outing, *Macbed blong Wilum Sekspia*, as it's meant to be a simpler translation of Shakespeare . . . through exploring the possibilities of Pidgin, the [common language] of the South Pacific. . . . This is a comedy as well as an exercise in **orthoepy** . . . (*Independent* [London], "First Call, Last Call," 9/16/1998.)

(2) pronunciation (words having the same . . . but different meaning) *adj.*: **homophonic**. ❖ For no reason I can think of, the letter "P" provides the thickest file of **homophonic** pests. . . . [For example], to peak is to reach a maximum point. To peek is to look furtively or briefly. To pique is to arouse interest. Many writers have a terrible time with "pedal" and "peddle." (James Kilpatrick, "Helping the Homophonically Challenged to Help Themselves," *Denver Rocky Mountain News*, 3/30/1997.)

proofread (text or language by removing errors or flaws) *v.t.*: **emend**. See *edit*

propaganda *n.*: **agitprop**. ❖ If foodmakers can no longer count on the public's unquestioning acceptance of their products, it's not just because of activist theatrics and shrill **agitprop**. (Frederic Golden, "Trade Wars/Genetically Modified Food," *Time*, 11/29/1999, p. 49.)

proper *adj.*: **comme il faut** [French]. ❖ The French, on the other hand, think U.S. table manners are not **comme il faut**. "I have seen French dinner party hosts recoil in horror when their American guests have helped themselves to wine and gulped it down as if it was Coca-Cola," says Platt. "Another shocker would be to leave food on the plate. This is considered very impolite. Of course, the Americans do this all the time." (Barbara Wall, "Americans Still Bedeviled by Image as Yahoos Abroad," *USA Today*, 4/12/1996.)

(2) proper (a . . . thing to do) *n.*: **bon ton** [French]. See *appropriate*

(3) proper (as in legitimate; acceptable) *adj.*: **cromulent**. See *legitimate*

properly (as in "by the book") *idiom*: **according to Hoyle**. See *by the book*

proper name (of, relating to or explaining a . . .) *adj.*: **onomastic**. See *name*

property (personal . . . , as in belongings) *n.pl.*: **personalia**. See *belongings*

prophesier (as in one who makes correct predictions of misfortune that are ignored) *n.*: **Cassandra**. See *predictor*

prophesy (relating to the art of . . .) *adj.*: **mantic**. See *prophetic*

(2) prophesy (relating to the art of . . .) *adj.*: **sibylline** (or **sybilline**; often cap.). See *prophetic*

(3) prophesy (spec. acting as if or threatening that a future event [usually unwanted] has already occurred by reference to an event that precedes it; for example, "if you look at my diary, you're dead") *n.*: **prolepsis**. See *prediction*

(4) prophesy (the future by gazing into a crystal ball) *v.t.*: **scry**. See *predict*

(5) prophesy *v.t.*: **vaticinate**. See *predict*

prophet (as in predictor, by using lightning or animal innards) *n.*: **haruspex**. See *fortune-teller*

prophetic *adj.*: **fatidic**. ❖ [In Revelation, St. John the Divine predicted that Satan will stage] one final epic battle—Armageddon—but will be defeated and "thrown into the lake of fire" where he and all of his servants, including all false prophets, "will be tormented day and night for ever and ever." To some doomsday prophets, this **fatidic** vision will be played out at the end of human history. But how will we know when we are nearing it? (Michael Shermer, "The Fire That Will Cleanse," *Skeptic*, 6/22/1999.)

(2) prophetic *adj.*: **mantic**. ❖ Virgo—(Aug. 23–Sept. 22): Ability as character analyst surges to forefront. You will be asked to entertain by displaying your skill with the **mantic** arts, including astrology. Sagittarian involved. (Sydney Omarr, Today's Horoscope, *Washington Post*, 11/14/1999.)

(3) prophetic *adj.*: **sibylline** (or **sybilline**; often cap.) [This word derives from Sibyl (or Sybil), one of a number of women regarded as prophets by the ancient Greeks. It also means "cryptic," and an example is given under that word as well.] ❖ In fact, as my friends will testify, I turned out to be [cheerful,] though you'd never know it to look at me. . . . Mr Hunter, our Latin master, pained beyond endurance by my very presence, released this **sibylline** utterance: "Sinclair, one day they will hang you." This was not so far-fetched; the most famous alumnus of the secondary modern across the road was James Hanratty, who may or may not have been guilty of . . . murder, but was strung up anyway. (Clive Sinclair, "Cabbage Face; My Physiognomy and My Fortune," *Independent* [London], 8/5/1995.)

(4) prophetic *adj.*: **vatic**. ❖ It was, arguably, Rockefeller's supreme inspiration that he believed in the Ohio–Indiana [oil] fields—one of those flashes of **vatic** power that made him a business legend. (Ron Chernow, *Titan*, Random House [1998], p. 284.)

proponent (or leader of a cause) *n.*: **paladin**. ❖ In reality, Rockefeller voted for James G. Blaine, a **paladin** of business interests, and predicted the election would be "a great calamity" if [Grover] Cleveland won. (Ron Chernow, *Titan*, Random House [1998], p. 291.)

(2) proponent (strong . . . of a cause, religion, or activity) *n.*: **votary**. See *supporter*

proprieties (precise observance of . . . or etiquette) *n.*: **punctilio**. See *etiquette*

proprietor *n.*: **padrone**. See *boss*

propriety *n.*: **correctitude**. ❖ The [Church of England] is . . . liturgically corrupt, demonstrating in its appointment of women priests its subservience to political **correctitudes**. (Brian Sewell, "What This Country Needs Is . . . ," *New Statesman*, 4/11/1997, p. 29.)

prose (which is concise, precise, or refined; lit. "as if engraved in a precious stone") *adj.*: **lapidary**. See *writing*

prosper (often at another's expense) *v.i.*: **batten**. See *thrive*

prosperity *n.*: **weal** (usu. as in "weal or woe" or "weal and woe"). See *well-being*

prosperous (and/or prominent person) *n.*: **nabob**. See *bigwig*

prostitute *n.*: **bawd**. ❖ Outside the Clink, Londoners were frequently entertained by the "cartings" of topless whores being whipped to the prison where they were branded on the forehead with a B for **bawd**. (Alex Berlyne, "Richard the Cubhearted," *Jerusalem Post*, 1/8/1999.)

(2) prostitute *n.*: **demimondaine**. ❖ In one excerpt cited in the book, Trink describes the [prostitutes] as "meretricious, avaricious, mendacious and bone lazy. Never give your heart to a **demimondaine**: she'll chew it up and spit it out." (Robert Horn, "A Walk on the Wild Side—An Entertaining Biography Examines the Man Who Has Chronicled Bangkok and Its Sex Scene for 35 Years," *Time* International, 10/16/2000, p. 59.)

(3) prostitute *n.*: **doxy**. ❖ [Historically,] many prostitutes found the wages of sin to be death—dismal and early. The shameful sisterhood took heavy casualties but remained multitudinous. Since days of the republic, Texas was never without **doxies**. (Kent Biffle, "What Were Once Vices Still Are," *Dallas Morning News*, 2/9/2003.)

(4) prostitute *n*.: **fancy woman**. [An alternate definition for this term is mistress. See *mistress*.] ❖ [The movie] has to do with a trunk of gold rocks smuggled up to Harlem by a beautiful **fancy woman** from Natchez named Imabelle (Robin Givens). Miss Givens does particularly well as a [prostitute] with a heart of gold as well as a trunk full of it. (Vincent Canby, "Panning for Gold in 1950's Harlem," *New York Times*, 5/3/1991.)

(5) prostitute *n*.: **trollop**. ❖ From a men's room tucked into the corner of a scabrous press bullpen in a criminal-courts building, out walks a **trollop** and a policeman adjusting his clothes after what has obviously been a brief but close encounter. (William A. Henry III, Theater: "Hello, Sweetheart, Get Me Rethink," *Time*, 12/8/1986, p. 83.)

prostitutes (as a group) *n*.: **demimonde**. ❖ The nineties have not been kind to prostitution. Despite the superficial appeal of life as a Heidi Fleiss–style call girl—or even as a Sunset Boulevard streetwalker invited into Hugh Grant's BMW—denizens of the **demimonde** are in decline. (Ted Gup, "What's New with the World's Oldest Profession?" *Cosmopolitan*, 10/1/1995, p. 236.)

prostituting (as in pimping) *n*.: **procuration**. See *pimping*

prostitution (of or relating to) *adj*.: **meretricious**. ❖ Forced into **meretricious** traffic by drug addiction or harsh economic times, forced out of downtown by police sweeps or out-of-state pros traveling the national circuit, local [prostitutes] are now soliciting sex in heretofore virgin territories, or in communities experiencing a bold new wave of activity. (Ric Kahn, "This Old Cathouse," *Boston Globe*, 5/9/1993.)

(2) prostitution (house of . . .) *n*.: **bagnio**. See *brothel*

protect (intended to . . . against evil) *adj*.: **apotropaic**. ❖ [For Vincent van Gogh], it is as though the calmer color, the growing penchant for structuring his work as a process of sequential research into a given motif—a walled field near the asylum, the olive grove outside it, the pines in the asylum garden— had an **apotropaic** use for him, keeping at bay the demons of the unconscious. (Robert Hughes, Art: "Sanity Defense for a Genius— The Metropolitan Reveals Van Gogh's Shocking Freshness," *Time*, 12/1/1986, p. 80.)

(2) protect *v.t*.: **forfend**. ❖ Writes Seton, "Maybe that's one of the things that draws me to farming, the vast plain of unbudgeable routine. . . . In farming there is a rigid set of limitations governing one's versatility. Farmers can't move their land to a more desirable climate. They can't manipulate the rhythms of season nor **forfend** against freaky climatic extremes. (Kari Granville, "Read This," *Newsday*, 1/31/1995.)

(3) protect (in an overprotective way or indulge) *v.t*.: **mollycoddle**. See *overprotect*

protection (against attack or danger) *n*.: **bulwark**. ❖ Says Bill Martin: . . . "There's not great hope that GATT [General Agreement on Tariffs and Trade] can achieve much in the way of further trade liberalization. But GATT is a very important **bulwark** against galloping protectionism." (Barbara Rudolph, Business: "Bitter Standoff in Montreal—Hopes for a GATT Agreement Fade over Farm Subsidies, *Time*, 12/19/1988, p. 58.)

(2) protection (line of . . . that is thought to be effective, but is not in reality) *n*.: **Maginot Line**. See *defense*

(3) protection (place of . . . , as in small, usu. temporary defensive fortification) *n*.: **redoubt**. See *refuge*

(4) protection (spec. a piece of armor) *n*.: **cuirass**. See *armor*

(5) protection (area of . . . , as in safe haven) *n*.: **querencia**. See *safe haven*

protection money (or bribe) *n*.: **Danegeld** (or **Danegelt**). [Derives from a tax levied in

England in the tenth and eleventh centuries to pay off Viking raiders (usually led by the Danish king) to save the land from being ravaged by the raiders. Today it is generally used as a warning against, or criticism of, making coerced payments, whether in money or in kind, because the payments have to keep being made. As stated in the poem "Dane Geld," by Rudyard Kipling, "Once you have paid him the Danegeld, / You never get rid of the Dane."] ❖ [In attempting to prevent North Korea from developing nuclear weapons, the] **Danegeld** option is even more desperate [than economic sanctions]. This holds that a large enough collection of inducements—economic aid, diplomatic recognition, maybe a "guarantee" of North Korea's present political system—might persuade Kim Il Sung to give up his bomb-making plans. It seems unlikely. (*Economist*, "The Yongbyon Test," 6/4/1994.)

protective (covering like a turtle shell) *n.*: **carapace**. See *shell*

protector (or guardian) *n., adj.*: **tutelary**. See *guardian*

protector(s) (esp. who protect an evil leader or dictator) *n.*: **Praetorian guard**. See *guard*

protest (against existing social or artistic conventions) *n.*: **titanism** (often cap.). See *revolt*

(2) **protest** (against, as in oppose a statement, opinion, or action) *v.t.*: **oppugn**. See *oppose*

(3) **protest** (bitter . . .) *n.*: **jeremiad**. See *complaint*

(4) **protest** (esp. in the form of pleading with) *v.t.*: **remonstrate**. See *plead*

(5) **protest** (peasant's . . . , as in revolt) *n.*: **jacquerie**. See *revolt*

(6) **protest** *v.t.*: **expostulate**. See *object*

protocol (precise observance of . . .) *n.*: **punctilio**. See *etiquette*

prototype (as in original model or example) *n.*: **archetype**. See *model*

(2) **prototype** (as in that which set the standard or established the model from which others followed or on which others are based) *n.*: **locus classicus** [Latin]. See *model*

protrusion (as in outgrowth) *n.*: **excrescence**. See *outgrowth*

proud (as in haughty) *adj.*: **fastuous**. See *haughty*

(2) **proud** (like a peacock) *adj.*: **pavonine**. See *peacock*

(3) **proud** *adj.*: **orgulous**. See *haughty*

province (as in area of activity or interest) *n.*: **purlieu**. See *domain*

provincial (as in parochial) *adj.*: **parish pump** [British]. See *parochial*

provocation (as in event that causes or provokes [literally] war or [figuratively] conflict) *n.*: **casus belli**. [Latin; occasion of war. An example of both a figurative usage and a literal usage is provided.] ❖ Time now to suggest a new concept of "fought-over words," words that adversaries in national debate try to capture. . . . [N]otice that, for a majority of Americans, "equal opportunity" is in, "preferences" are out, and "affirmative action" is still a **casus belli**. (Daniel Schorr, "Good Words, Bad Words," *Christian Science Monitor*, 12/26/1997.) ❖ [T]he virtue [of] having a **casus belli** before going to war is so universally acknowledged that even Hitler paid homage to it. Immediately before Hitler attacked Poland, the SS staged a provocation—a "Polish" attack on a German radio station near Poland's border, a sham that included corpses of German "victims"—actually, concentration camp inmates shot by the SS. (George F. Will, "Improvised War Etiquette," *Washington Post*, 8/29/2002.)

provocative *adj.*: **piquant**. ❖ [Pauline] Kael was in her 40s before she became a fixture among cinephiles in Berkeley, California, where her criticism appeared in the form of program notes, radio reviews, screeds in the local film magazine. She couldn't have been further out of the [Hollywood] loop . . . so she devised a **piquant** strategy for being heard: she would go to a movie and review the audience. (Richard Corliss, The Arts & Media/Books, *Time* International, 11/28/1994, p. 68.)

provoke (as in agitate) *v.t.*: **commove**. See *agitate*

provoker *n.*: **stormy petrel**. See *inciter*

proximity (in place, time, or relation) *n.*: **propinquity**. See *closeness*

(2) **proximity** (physical . . . , as in vicinity) *n.*: **vicinage**. See *vicinity*

prude *n.*: **bluenose**. ❖ [W]henever **bluenoses** demand restraint against the porn and violence that are the staple of popular culture, they are met with "Who appointed you guardians of the public taste? Let the people decide." (Charles Krauthammer, "Casablanca in Color? I'm Shocked, Shocked!" *Time*, 1/12/1987, p. 82.)

(2) **prude** (person who is puritanical or hostile with respect to minor vices or forms of popular entertainment) *n.*: **wowser** [Australian slang]. See *killjoy*

prudence (as in moderation) *n.*: **sophrosyne**. See *moderation*

prudish (and intolerant conventionality) *n.*: **Grundyism**. See *puritanical*

(2) **prudish** (or prim) *adj.*: **missish**. See *prim*

pry (one who would . . . into other's affairs) *n.*: **quidnunc**. See *busybody*

(2) **pry** (out or extract or force out, whether from a place or position, or information) *v.t.*: **winkle** (usually used with "out"). See *extract*

pseudonym *n.*: **allonym**. ❖ Ibn al-Rawandi is the **allonym** of an English student of esotericism and world religions. (*Free Inquiry*, "Islam and Armageddon: Looking Behind the Myths" [the above sentence is referring to the author of the unsigned article cited], 3/22/2002.)

(2) **pseudonym** (spec. woman's use of a man's name) *n.*: **pseudandry**. ❖ The **pseudandry** of women authors like George Eliot let them reach a much larger Victorian readership. (www.usu.edu/markdamen/Wordpower/ PP/slides/31revoflat3, "Latin and Greek Elements in English.)

psychic *adj.*: **fey**. See *clairvoyant*

psychoanalysis (person undergoing . . .) *n.*: **analysand**. ❖ Psychoanalysis is the one form of therapy which leaves it to **analysands** to determine for themselves what their specific goals will be. (Jonathan Lear, "The Shrink Is In: A Counterblast in the War on Freud," *New Republic*, 12/25/1995, p. 18.)

psychotic (person) *n.*: **bedlamite**. See *lunatic*

puberty (onset of . . . for a woman, as in her first menstruation) *n.*: **menarche**. See *menstruation*

public (suitable for or comprehensible by the . . . at large) *adj.*: **exoteric**. See *accessible*

publication (of secret or government-banned literature, or the literature produced by such a system) *n.*: **samizdat**. See *underground*

publicity (or a taste or flair for being in the limelight) *n.*: **réclame** [French]. ❖ At 19, Fernando Bujones was dubbed the "Bad Boy of American Ballet," the result of the young dancer's outspoken views vis-à-vis the Russian defectors who had been given preferential treatment by American Ballet Theater. . . . Particularly incensed over the **réclame** attending Mikhail Baryshnikov's defection and subsequent appearances with ABT in 1974, Bujones [said] "Baryshnikov has the publicity but I have the talent!" (John Gruen, "Ballet's 'Bad Boy' Grows Up," *New York Times*, 6/15/1989.)

puddles (full of . . .) *adj.*: **plashy**. ❖ We gasped, then watched excitedly as [the snake] slithered through the brown, re-emerged a yard beyond, then disappeared down the bank. We approached the water's edge with caution, the ground **plashy** with black muck. Tip tossed his stick in and had to lean over to retrieve it. (Alma Giordan, "Autumnal Idyll of a 4 Year Old," *New York Times*, 10/5/1980.)

pudgy (condition of having a . . . physique) *n.*: **embonpoint**. See *plump*

(2) **pudgy** (having a short . . . physique) *adj.*: **pyknic**. See *stocky*

(3) **pudgy** (person, esp. with a large abdomen) *n.*: **endomorph** (*adj.*: **endomorphic**). See *pot-bellied*

(4) **pudgy** *adj.*: **adipose**. See *fat*

(5) **pudgy** *adj.*: **Pickwickian**. See *fat*

(6) **pudgy** (or perpetually short-winded as a result of being fat) *adj.*: **pursy**. See *fat*

(7) pudgy (and squat) *adj.*: **fubsy**. See *squat*

(8) pudgy (as in beer-bellied) *adj.*: **abdominous**. See *beer-bellied*

(9) pudgy (as in paunchy) *adj.*: **stomachy**. See *paunchy*

(10) pudgy (state of being . . .) *n.*: **avoirdupois**. See *weight*

puffy (as in swollen) *adj.* **dropsical**. See *swollen*

pugnacious *adj.*: **bellicose**. See *belligerent*

pull (used to . . .) *adj.*: **tractive**. ❖ Content to be just a normal family wagon the rest of the year, confining its **tractive** excellence to occasional pulls of the boat up algae-infested ramps, the Legacy becomes Super-Skimobile mid-year. (Paul Owen, "Subaru's Luxury Ride to Family Fun," *Evening Post*, 6/14/1996.)

(2) pull (out, as in extract or pry or force out, whether from a place or position, or information) *v.t.*: **winkle** (usually used with *out*). See *extract*

pullout (desperate . . . , as in retreat) *n.*: **Dunkirk**. See *retreat*

pulverize (or reduce to powder) *v.t.*: **comminute**. ❖ Other raw material animal foods such as **comminuted** foods (chopped, ground, flaked, or minced foods, such as ground beef, gyros, sausage, and fish) must be cooked to 155 [degrees] for at least 15 seconds. (Jorge Hernandez, Preparation and Cooking, *Restaurant Hospitality*, 5/1/1998, p. 162.)

pun *n.*: **paronomasia**. ❖ . . . [O]nce I was assured in my own mind that the outline of the story was not original to [Alexandre] Dumas, I continued with the [novel I was writing]. . . . I changed the names of my protagonists to anagrams of the originals in [*The Count of Monte Cristo*]. . . . Edmond's affianced Mercedes transforms herself (in an unforgivable example of automobile **paronomasia**) into Portia. (Stephen Fry, "Forget Ideas, Mr. Author. What Kind of Pen Do You Use?" *New York Times*, 7/29/2002.)

pungent *adj.*: **acrid**. ❖ The second-best known Mexican beverage might be tequila, the **acrid** and potent distillation of the yeasty home brew pulque, itself fermented from the agave cactus.

(Jack Robertiello, "Drinking in the Flavors of Mexico," 3/1/1994, p. 58.)

(2) pungent (agreeably . . . in taste or flavor) *adj.*: **piquant**. See *zesty*

punish (as in impose a monetary fine) *v.t.*: **amerce**. See *fine*

(2) punish (by imposing a fine or penalty) *v.t.*: **mulct**. See *penalize*

(3) punish (oneself) *v.t.*: **flagellate** (*n.*: **flagellation**). See *criticize*

punishing (journey or experience) *n.*: **via dolorosa**. See *ordeal*

(2) punishing (of convicted persons, spec. burning of heretics at the stake) *n.*: **auto-da-fé**. See *execution*

punishment (by beating the soles of the feet with a stick) *n., v.t.*: **bastinado**. See *beating*

puny (as in meager) *adj.*: **mingy**. See *meager*

puppets (or showing or employing . . . , as in marionettes) *n.pl.*: **fantoccini** [Italian]. See *marionettes*

purchasing (compulsion for . . . things) *n.*: **onomania**. See *shopping*

pure (and carefree time) *adj.*: **prelapsarian**. See *innocent*

(2) pure (as in angelic) *adj.*: **seraphic**. See *angelic*

(3) pure (as in chaste) *adj.*: **vestal**. See *chaste*

(4) pure (as in faultless or sinless) *adj.*: **impeccant**. See *faultless*

purge (spec. criminal prosecution of French and Italian officials considered to have been Nazi collaborators after World War II) *n.*: **epuration**. ❖ As part of the general process of **epuration** undertaken by the French government after the liberation of Paris, a number of collaborationist writers, critics, and political journalists were arrested, tried, and sentenced to death, primarily for the words they wrote. (David Carroll, review of *The Collaborator: The Trial and Execution of Robert Brasillach*, by Alice Kaplan, *American Scholar*, 6/22/2000.)

(2) purge (a book or a piece of writing in a prudish manner) *v.t.*: **bowdlerize**. See *edit*

purify (or cleanse) *v.t., v.i.*: **depurate**. See *cleanse*

purist (person who is a . . . , as in stickler, in observing established rules or customs, esp. with regard to religious practices) *n*.: **precisian**. See *stickler*

puritanical (and intolerant conventionality) *n*.: **Grundyism** [derives from Mrs. Grundy, a prudish character in Thomas Morton's 1798 play *Speed the Plow*]. ❖ His sexual investigations were brave and original. His unexpurgated translations of *The Thousand and One Nights* and other Eastern classics, defying all the **Grundyism** of the day, were great works of scholarship. (Jan Morris, Books: "10,001 Nights of Piety and Pornography," *Independent* [London], 10/31/1998.)

(2) puritanical (as in prim or prudish) *adj*.: **missish**. See *prim*

(3) puritanical (person who is prudish or hostile with respect to minor vices or forms of popular entertainment) *n*.: **wowser** [Australian slang]. See *killjoy*

(4) puritanical (person who is . . .) *n*.: **bluenose**. See *prude*

purple (as in eggplant in color) *adj*.: **aubergine**. See *eggplant*

purpose (esp. of life) *n*.: **telos** [Greek]. See *goal*

(2) purpose (hidden or ulterior . . .) *n*.: **arriere-pensee** (or **arrière-pensée**) [French]. See *motive*

purposeful *adj*.: **telic**. ❖ As there is a semblance to Orwell's *Animal Farm*, one might call the work an allegory, but where Orwell designed a **telic** action with specific goals set for well-defined characters, *A Book of Pigs* forces upon its hero too many purposeless meanderings. (Alfred Straumanis, "Cuku Gramata," *World Literature Today*, 9/1/1996, p. 999.)

purposelessness (of a person or group as a result of lack of standards or values) *n*.: **anomie**. See *breakdown*

purse (women's drawstring . . .) *n*.: **reticule**. See *handbag*

pus (containing, discharging, or causing the production of) *adj*.: **purulent**. ❖ [In the novel *Feed*, by M. T. Anderson], all the kids have unexplained skin lesions, assumed to be a result of environmental pollution, although no one seems concerned about the sores unless they occur in unattractive places. Then suddenly it's cool to have lesions, the more **purulent** the better. (Sonja Belle, "Teen Romance Off- and Online," *Newsday*, 2/16/2003.)

(2) pus (to form or discharge . . .) *v.i.*: **suppurate**. ❖ Pimples, zits or plain old spots, call them what you will, but you weren't really a proper teenager if you didn't have those angry red plooks. . . . [I still have acne at 44.] Friends congratulate me on my wrinkle-free skin, but I am beginning to think that I would prefer crow's-feet to **suppurating** pimples. And they could be around for a few decades yet. (Jennifer Veitch, "Black Spots on Your Landscape," *Evening News* [Edinburgh, Scotland], 2/26/2001.)

pushing (someone to take a course of action) *adj*.: **hortatory**. See *urging*

push out *v.t.*: **extrude**. ❖ If you're making 3,000 or even three dozen butter cookies, a cookie press is probably your best bet. Load the dough into the barrel, affix a disk with an appropriate stencil (Christmas tree, poinsettia, or star), and squeeze the trigger to **extrude** the desired shape. (Jane Dornbusch, "Getting Good Press on Baking Day," *Boston Globe*, 12/14/2005.)

pushover (female sexual . . .) *n*.: **roundheel**. See *slut*

pushy *adj*.: **bumptious**. ❖ When **bumptious** Donald Trump turned up in Palm Beach, Fla., in 1985, stuffy locals greeted him like a bad sunburn. "Too much, too soon, too lavish, too showy," complained one Old Guard resident of The Donald's arrival. (Cynthia Sanz, "Too Close for Comfort—When You've Got a Celebrity Residing Next Door, the Living May Be Far from Easy," *People*, 8/9/1993, p. 34.)

put (close together, side by side, or in proper order) *v.t.*: **collocate**. See *place*

putdown (as in insult, which is clever or polite) *n*.: **asteism**. See *insult*

(2) putdown (as in insult, delivered while leaving the scene) *n*.: **Parthian shot**. See *parting shot*

put off (or discontinue, esp. a session of Parliament) *v.t.*: **prorogue**. See *discontinue*

putrefying (or decaying) *adj.*: **saprogenic**. See *decay*

putrid *adj.*: **fetid**. See *smelly*

    (2) putrid *adj.*: **graveolent**. See *smelly*

    (3) putrid *adj.*: **mephitic** (*n.*: **mephitis**). See *smelly*

    (4) putrid *adj.*: **noisome**. See *smelly*

putting in (as in insertion, of something between existing things) *n.*: **intercalation**. See *insertion*

    (2) putting in (esp. penis into vagina) *n.*: **intromission** (*v.t.*: **intromit**). See *penetration*

put together (cheaply and flimsily) *v.t.*: **jerry-build**. See *build*

puzzling (as in perplexing) *adj.*: **quisquous**. See *perplexing*

Pyrrhic victory (as in a victory obtained only at great cost to the victor) *n.*: **Cadmean victory** [derives from Cadmus, a prince in Greek mythology, who killed a dragon but with only five of his men surviving]. ❖ The obscure poem of Lycophron enumerates many of these dispersed and expatriated heroes, whose conquest of Troy was indeed a **"Cadmean" victory** . . . , wherein the sufferings of the victor were little inferior to those of the vanquished. (George Grote, "Fall of Troy," *History of the World*, 1/1/1992.)

quack (as in a person who sells quack medicines) *n.*: **mountebank**. See *huckster*

quaint (affectedly or excessively . . . or dainty) *adj.*: **twee**. [This word is generally considered to be British but is being used more and more frequently outside Britain as well.] ❖ No American sporting event is more **twee** than the Masters, and the forced reverence in CBS's coverage can make even the most die-hard fans cringe. We're not saying don't watch it—just consider doing so with drinks in hand. When [announcer] Jim Nantz says "a tradition like none other," take a sip of fine cabernet. When he mentions loblolly pine, finish your glass of cabernet. (*Playboy*, "Masters Drinking Game," 4/1/2009)

quake (rapidly or spasmodically) *v.i.*: **judder**. See *shake*

quality (of outstanding . . .) *n.*: **first water** (usu. as in "of the first water"). ❖ [The book] *Dialect of the Southern Counties of Scotland* was to be published in 1873 and it fully confirmed for James Murray a reputation that had begun to grow as early as the 1860s: that he was a philologist **of the first water**. (Simon Winchester, *The Meaning of Everything*, Oxford University Press [2003], p. 78.)

(2) quality (as in aura or impalpable emanation) *n.*: **effluvium**. See *aura*

quandary (as in choice of taking what is offered or nothing; i.e., no real choice at all) *n.*: **Hobson's choice**. See *predicament*

(2) quandary (as in dangers on both sides) *idiom*: **between Scylla and Charybdis**. See *precarious*

(3) quandary (as in dilemma, except where there are three options, all of which are or seem to be unsatisfactory) *n.*: **trilemma**. See *dilemma*

(4) quandary (as in predicament, from which it is difficult to extricate oneself) *n.*: **tar baby**. See *predicament*

(5) quandary (as in the situation of having to make a move where any move made will weaken the position) *n.*: **zugzwang** [German]. See *predicament*

(6) quandary (which is difficult to solve) *n.*: **Gordian knot**. See *dilemma*

quantifying (act or process of . . . , as in measuring) *n.*: **mensuration**. See *measuring*

quantitative (having . . . ability) *adj.*: **numerate**. See *mathematical*

quantity (illusion of . . . when in fact there is little) *adj.*: **Barmecidal** (esp. as in "Barmecidal feast"). See *illusion*

quarrel (as in brawl, esp. public) *n.*: **affray**. See *brawl*

(2) quarrel (as in heated disagreement or friction between groups) *n.*: **ruction**. See *dissension*

(3) quarrel (initiate a . . . , fighting or violence) *v.i.*: **aggress**. See *fight*

quarrelsome *adj.*: **querulous**. See *peevish*

queen (reigning in her own right, as opposed to one having a royal title by marriage) *n.*: **queen regnant**. [Note: The example gives the term for queens who are married to reigning kings.] ❖ Q. If Prince Charles becomes king, will Princess Diana become queen or will she remain a princess? A. [She would be a] "queen consort"[;] she would not become queen in her own right in the event of her husband's death. . . . Only a "**queen regnant**," such as Britain's present queen, Elizabeth II, may rule as monarch. (*Boston Globe*, Ask the Globe, 12/5/1990.)

quest (as in crusade, for an idea or principle) *n.*: **jihad**. See *crusade*

question (closely) *v.t.*: **catechize**. ❖ Uma [Thurman] is beautiful, but if you bring it up, she is mildly cross, as I suppose we all would be if we were continually being **catechized** about our appearance, as Uma is. (Mim Udovitch, "An Alternate Umaverse," *Esquire*, 3/1/1998, p. 70.)

(2) question (as in oppose a statement, opinion, or action) *v.t.*: **oppugn**. See *oppose*

(3) question (as in problem, which is difficult for a beginner or one who is inexperienced) *n.*: **pons asinorum** [Latin]. See *problem*

(4) question (as to one's opinion on an issue, esp. arising from awareness of an opposing viewpoint) *n.*: **aporia**. See *doubt*

Q

(5) question (esp. as in beyond . . .) *n*.: **peradventure**. See *doubt*

(6) question (formally about governmental policy or action) *v.t.*: **interpellate**. See *interrogate*

questionable (morality or taste) *adj*.: **louche**. ❖ Some gay conservatives even blame the leftists for the enduring image of homosexual men—in the minds of some people—as effeminate, **louche** odd-balls who wear leather jockstraps. (*Economist*, "Now for a Queer Question About Gay Culture," 7/12/1997.)

questionableness *n*.: **dubiety**. See *doubtfulness*

questioner (of an astrologer) *n*.: **querent**. ❖ A Tarot deck has it all—the secret wisdom, the unexplained powers, the strange coincidences. . . . Why not [take a chance]? In one prediction, she [says,] "I see a lot of travel for you . . . [to Europe or South America or Africa or Asia]." Does this rule out Australia? The **querent** doesn't ask. Who can psych out the psychic? (Henry Allen, "The Tarot Psychic," *Washington Post*, 11/24/1980.)

(2) questioner *n*.: **querist**. ❖ [Isaac Newton] wanted to know the cause of gravity, not merely how it worked. His laws as stated did not satisfy the inward **querist** in Newton himself and his notes show him at his extended search. (Roger Sworder, "Gravity's Harmony," *Quadrant*, 7/1/1999.)

quibble *v.i.*: **pettifog**. ❖ In 1994, the United States, having been burned in Somalia, was desperate to stay out of Rwanda. How to manage that? By **pettifogging**. By arguing about semantics: the Clinton way. His Administration, pressed to honor the 1948 Genocide Convention (not to mention human decency) by intervening, quibbled at a furious rate about the meaning of the word genocide. (Lance Morrow, Essay: "Rwandan Tragedy, Lewinsky Farce," *Time*, 10/12/1998, p. 126.)

(2) quibble *v.t.*: **cavil**. ❖ Question: Why are drive through lines so long and service so slow at fast-food restaurants around here? Answer: Sir, we really must protest. You, apparently a newcomer, find yourself living in a desert paradise, a metropolitan area bursting with good weather, good health and good cheer, and you **cavil** at how long you must wait for a burger and fries. (Clay Thompson, "Sorry for the Wait, Sir, We're Flipping as Fast as We Can," *Arizona Republic*, 3/19/2000.)

quick (as in hasty) *adj*.: **festinate**. See *hasty*

(2) quick (as in nimble) *adj*.: **lightsome**. See *nimble*

quickly (very . . . , as in, in an instant) *n*.: **trice** (as in, in a trice). ❖ We were there [at the car dealership] for the taking. Armed, as we were, with a gratifyingly cheap loan from a nice man at the NatWest, any half-decent salesman would have had our signatures on the dotted line in a **trice**. (Neil Darbyshire, Motoring: "Wheel Life—All I Want Is a New Motor," *Daily Telegraph* [London], 4/8/2000.)

quickness (as in speed or haste) *n*.: **celerity**. See *speed*

(2) quickness *n*.: **alacrity**. See *speed*

quiet *adj., adv., n.*: **pianissimo**. [Italian. This word, often used as a musical direction, can be used as an adverb (the band played pianissimo), an adjective (such as in the example here), or a noun, meaning a note or passage delivered quietly. Its opposite—fortissimo—is listed under "loud."] ❖ [Hillary Clinton has] praised "that indispensable task of criticizing." But now Hillary's voice is often **pianissimo** on the current hot issue: how to get out of Iraq. . . . She knows if she wants to be the first woman president, she can't have love beads in her jewelry box. She has defended her vote to authorize the president to wage war . . . and she has argued for more troops in Iraq, knowing it sounds muscular. (Maureen Dowd, "A Lipstick President," *New York Times*, 8/31/2005.)

(2) quiet (as in not moving or temporarily inactive) *adj*.: **quiescent**. See *inactive*

(3) quiet (as in silence) *n*.: **harpocracy** (*adj*.: **harpocratic**). See *silence*

(4) quiet (as in silent) *v.i., adj., adv.*: **mumchance** [British]. See *silent*

(5) quiet (said in . . . tones, not to be overheard) *adv., adj.*: **sotto voce**. See *whispered*

quip *n*.: **bon mot** [French]. ❖ But his protestations notwithstanding, [basketball player Shaquille O'Neal] has never passed up an opportunity to deliver a **bon mot** on behalf of a corporate sponsor: . . . BROKAW: This is a serious question. What do you want to be when you grow up? SHAQ: I want to be a successful entrepreneur, such as yourself. I want to be happy. I want to always drink Pepsi. (*Sports Illustrated*, Scorecard, 4/24/1995, p. 13.)

(2) quip *n*.: **epigram**. ❖ The cafe has a colorful outdoor mural on its north wall and an **epigram** painted over the entrance that reads, "We are itching to get away from Portland, Oregon," a reference to a supposed "flea epidemic" of 1915, according to a cafe flier. (Paul Iorio, "The Howl Tour of San Francisco; For a Fresh View of the City by the Bay, Follow the Beat Path Forged by '50s Poet Allen Ginsberg," *Washington Post*, 5/7/2000.)

(3) quip *v.i.*, *n*.: **jape**. See *joke*

quit (an office or position) *v.i.*, *v.t.*: **demit** (as in demit office). See *resign*

quiver (from moment of intense excitement) *n*.: **frisson** [French]. See *shudder*

(2) quiver (rapidly or spasmodically) *v.i.*: **judder**. See *shake*

quivering *adj.*: **tremulous**. ❖ Near the end of the show [*Cabaret*], [Natasha] Richardson-as-Sally [Bowles] walks shakily onto the stage and reveals that she has had an abortion. She paints an unflinching portrait of denial, regret, and despair: the knocking knees, the **tremulous** voice, the vacant stare. (Steve Daly, "Don't Tell Mama," *Entertainment Weekly*, 7/31/1998, p. 32.)

quixotic (conduct without regard to practicality) *n*.: **knight-errantry**. See *idealistic*

quiz (closely) *v.t.*: **catechize**. See *question*

quotation (at the start of a literary piece setting forth a theme or message) *n*.: **epigraph**. ❖ The title page of E. L. Doctorow's wonderful 1975 novel, *Ragtime*, has a warning **epigraph** from rag master Scott Joplin himself: "Do not play this piece fast. It is never right to play Ragtime fast." (Linda Winer, Literary Notes: "Doctrow's *Ragtime*," *Newsday*, 12/9/1996.)

(2) quotation (as in excerpt, esp. from the Bible) *n*.: **pericope**. See *excerpts*

quotations (disjointed . . .) *n.pl.*: **disjecta membra** [Latin]. See *bits and pieces*

rabbit (of or relating to a . . .) *adj.*: **leporine**. ❖ Peter Rabbit, once a real English pet and now a worldwide licensing megabusiness, celebrates the 100th anniversary of his breaking into print this October. Three sites in England's Lake District can be visited to learn about the writer of the famous **leporine** tales, Beatrix Potter (1866–1943). (Martin Hollander, Itinerary Ideas, *Newsday*, 3/29/2002.)

rabbit fur *n.*: **lapin** [French]. ❖ Most of the play's comic relief comes from two sources. [One is] Wilson's portrayal of the annoying yet amusing Aunt Girlie who insists her *fur* coat is made of "**Lapin**, not rabbit!" (Noel Gallagher, "Heartfelt Play Done with Loving Care," *London Free Press*, 8/25/2001.)

rabbits (of or relating to . . . or hares) *adj.*: **leporid**. ❖ [In the British TV puppet show *Don't Eat the Neighbours*,] Fox was making futile attempts to trap his crafty **leporid** foe by developing a genetically modified cabbage "that no rabbit can resist." (Victor Lewis-Smith, "Puppets on a Wicked Spin," *Evening Standard* [London], 1/11/2002.)

rabble (as in the common people) *n.*: **hoi polloi**. See *commoners*

(2) rabble (the . . .) *n.*: **vulgus** [Latin]. See *masses*

(3) rabble *n.*: **canaille**. See *masses*

rabble-rouser *n.*: **stormy petrel**. See *inciter*

racket (as in din or clamor) *n.*: **bruit**. See *din*

(2) racket (as in hubbub) *n.*: **charivari**. See *hubbub*

(3) racket (as in noise, esp. from simultaneous voices, and confusion) *n.*: **babel**. See *noise*

raconteur (of or relating to being a great . . .) *adj.*: **Scheherazadean**. See *storytelling*

racy (as in scandalous) *adj.*: **scabrous**. See *scandalous*

radiant (esp. as to talent, wit, or ability) *adj.*: **lambent**. See *brilliant* and *shimmering*

(2) radiant *adj.*: **effulgent**. See *bright*

(3) radiant *adj.*: **fulgurant**. See *bright*

(4) radiant *adj.*: **lucent**. See *glowing*

(5) radiant *adj.*: **refulgent**. See *bright*

radical (a political . . . , who often believes in violence to attain an end) *n.*: **sans-culotte**. See *extremist*

(2) radical (as in dissenter, orig. Catholics who did not follow Church of England) *n.*: **radicalism** (of or relating to political . . .) *adj.*: **Jacobinical**. See *extremism*

recusant. See *dissenter*

radicalism (esp. in political matters) *n.*: **ultraism** See *extremism*

rage (as in temper tantrum) *n.*: **boutade** [French]. See *temper tantrum*

(2) rage (marked by a sudden or violent . . .) *adj.*: **vesuvian** (esp. as in . . . temper). See *temper*

ragged *adj.*: **tatterdemalion**. ❖ These days, [ex-Pittsburgh Steeler Joe] Gilliam roams the streets of Nashville panhandling for food, $12 for the flophouse and for whatever. . . . Bob Costas and the rest wanted to know how Gilliam felt about the Steelers' chances and how his life had collapsed to such a **tatterdemalion** state. (Les Payne, "The Benched Man Might Be the Best," *Newsday*, 2/4/1996.)

raging (woman) *n.*: **maenad**. See *woman*

(2) raging *adj.*: **furibund**. See *furious*

raid *v.t., v.i.*: **deprecate** (*n.*: **depredation**). See *plunder*

railing (and supports for) *n.*: **balustrade**. See *handrail*

rain (of or relating to) *adj.*: **pluvial, pluvious**. ❖ Lloyd's of London has always been synonymous with insurance underwriting expertise and the sober assessment of risk. . . . Lloyd's also issues what it calls **pluvious** policies to compensate sporting events, such as cricket matches, for losses caused by rain. (Barbara Rudolph, Business, *Time* International, 7/8/1991, p. 32.)

(2) rain (or other precipitation that evaporates before hitting the ground) *n.*: **virga**. ❖ Karen Carra, [a] hang glider pilot[, said,] "Last weekend, we were flying while watching snow showers off in the distance near Whitetail. I was ready to land if the snow came too close, but the only thing that happened was that ice **virga** fell within a few hundred feet of me and evaporated like thousands of strands of tiny crystals." (Matthew Graham, "Free Flight Fans Warm to Winter," *Washington Times*, 2/10/2000.)

rainstorm *n.*: **cataract**. See *downpour*

rake (as in lecherous man or playboy) *n.*: **roué** [French]. See *playboy*

raling (characterized by loud . . . sounds) *adj.*: **stertorous**. See *snoring*

ramble (aimlessly) *v.i.*: **maunder**. ❖ Gray thinly disguises his **maundering** narrator as "Brewster North," but the book has no fictional texture at all. It's a series of childhood memories, anecdotes, dreams, sexual fantasies, and feelings gotten in touch with. . . . [W]e get the aimless wanderings, transient enthusiasms, and permanent adolescent confusion of the narrator. (*Entertainment Weekly*, Print: Boy Talk, 7/17/1992, p. 50.)

(2) ramble *v.i.*: **divagate**. See *digress*

rambling *adj.*: **discursive**. ❖ [Poet Henry Wadsworth] Longfellow is **discursive**. He cannot resist adding description, lush and sometimes seemingly endless, to his narratives. (Paul O. Williams, "America's Favorite, Forgotten Poet," *Christian Science Monitor*, 10/26/2000.)

(2) rambling (as in digressive) *adj.*: **excursive**. See *digressive*

(3) rambling (as in verbose) *adj.*: **inaniloquent**. See *verbose*

ramming (spec. the act of one object . . . a stationary object, usually applied to ships) *n.*: **allision**. See *collision*

rampage (in speech) *n.*: **philippic**. See *tirade*

rampant *adj.*: **pandemic**. See *widespread*

(2) rampant *adj.*: **regnant**. See *widespread*

rancid *adj.*: **mephitic** (*n.*: **mephitis**). See *smelly*

(2) rancid *adj.*: **noisome**. See *smelly*

rancor *n.*: **asperity**. See *acrimony*

random *adj.*: **stochastic**. ❖ But the Christian too is without explanation for what happens at Lourdes, because we cannot reason to why [some people find] relief while so many others do not. But then this only reminds us that, what in the secular coinage we would think of as **stochastic** (Why the death-dealing volcanic eruption here? the pestilence there?), religion ascribes to a divine order that countenances extemporaneous afflictions, natural and personal. (William F. Buckley, "To Be a Pilgrim: A Visit to Lourdes," *National Review*, 8/9/1993.)

(2) random (as in by chance) *adj.*: **adventitious**. See *chance*

(3) random (as in haphazard) *adj., adv.*: **higgledy-piggledy**. See *haphazard*

(4) random (as in unpredictable outcome) *adj.*: **aleatory**. See *unpredictable*

range (as in sphere or realm) *n.*: **ambit**. See *realm*

rank (having a . . . smell) *adj.*: **graveolent**. See *smelly*

(2) rank (odor) *adj.*: **mephitic** (*n.*: **mephitis**). See *smelly*

(3) rank (odor) *adj.*: **noisome**. See *smelly*

ransack *v.t., v.i.*: **depredate** (*n.*: **depredation**). See *plunder*

rant *n.*: **jeremiad**. See *complaint*

(2) rant *n.*: **philippic**. See *tirade*

rapacious (as in predatory) *adj.*: **lupine**. See *predatory*

rapidity *n.*: **alacrity**. See *speed*

(2) rapidity *n.*: **celerity**. See *speed*

rapture *n.*: **beatitude**. See *bliss*

(2) rapture *n.*: **felicity**. See *happiness*

rapturous (as in delightful or blissful) *adj.*: **Elysian**. See *blissful*

(2) rapturous *adj.*: **beatific** (to make . . .) *v.t.*: **beatify**. See *joyful*

rare *adj.*: **recherché** [French]. ❖ When a city stakes a claim to sophistication and social significance, a few indispensable items had better be in its possession: a major-league sports franchise, a newspaper that has taken a few scalps among local politicians, restaurants offering ethnic cuisines more **recherché** than Italian and Chinese. (William A. Henry III, Theater: "Portland Offers a Calling Card in an Elegant Structure," *Time*, 12/12/1988, p. 88.)

(2) rare (as in unusual) *adj.*: **selcouth**. See *unusual*

rarity *n.*: **rara avis** [Latin]. ❖ John Feinstein is that **rara avis** of sports literature, a best-selling author. In fact, according to his publishers, his first book . . . , *A Season on the Brink*, which recounted the sometimes unseemly adventures of coach Bobby Knight and his Indiana University basketball team, is nothing less than the "best-selling sports book of all time." (Ron Fimrite, Books, *Sports Illustrated*, 10/14/1991, p. 6.)

rascal *n.*: **rapscallion**. ❖ In public, Southerners preach a hard gospel against sin and perdition, particularly sexual transgressions. But the South has a rich and storied lineage of silver-tongued political devils—most of them white males. And Southerners secretly celebrate their rogues and **rapscallions**. (Jim Nesbitt, "Bubba Factor—Overblown South's Distaste for Clinton 'Isn't About Sex, It's About Ideology,'" *Palm Beach Post*, 1/10/1999.)

(2) rascal (or unprincipled person) *n.*: **blackguard**. See *scoundrel*

(3) rascal *n.*: **scapegrace**. See *scoundrel*

rash (and irresponsible) *adj.*: **harum-scarum**. See *reckless*

(2) rash (as in impetuous) *adj.*: **gadarene**. See *impetuous*

(3) rash (as in overambitious) *adj.*: **Icarian**. See *overambitious*

(4) rash (as in reckless) *adj.*: **temerarious**. See *reckless*

(5) rash (or impetuous person) *n.*: **Hotspur**. See *impetuous*

rashly (as in, in a disorderly and hasty manner) *adv.*: **pell-mell**. See *disorderly*

rat (as in informer or accuser) *n.*: **delator**. See *accuser*

rational (as in right-thinking) *adj.*: **bien-pensant**. See *right-thinking*

rate (under a new standard, esp. one that differs from conventional norms) *v.t.*: **transvaluate**. See *evaluate*

(2) rate *v.t.*: **assay**. See *evaluate*

ratification (as in giving one's stamp of approval) *n.*: **nihil obstat** [Latin]. See *approval*

ratify (as in approve, esp. to confirm officially) *v.t.*: **homologate**. See *approve*

rational (as in logical) *adj.*: **ratiocinative**. See *logical*

(2) rational (as in sane) *adj.*: **compos mentis**. See *sane*

rationale (additional . . . , as in explanation) *n.*: **epexegesis** (*adj.*: **epexegetic**). See *explanation*

(2) rationale (formal . . . , as in justification, for one's acts or beliefs) *n.*: **apologia**. See *justification*

rationalize (specious reasoning intended to . . . or mislead) *n.*: **casuistry**. See *fallacious*

(2) rationalize (try to . . . an offense with excuses) *v.t.*: **palliate**. See *downplay*

rat out (as in tattle) *v.i.*: **peach**. See *tattle*

rats (of or relating to . . . or mice) *adj.*: **murine**. See *rodents*

rattle (rapidly or spasmodically) *v.i.*: **judder**. See *shake*

ravage *v.t.*, *v.i.*: **depredate** (*n.*: **depredation**). See *plunder*

ravenous (as in predatory) *adj.*: **lupine**. See *predatory*

(2) ravenous *adj.*: **edacious**. See *voracious*

(3) ravenous *adj.*: **esurient**. See *hungry*

raving (woman) *n.*: **maenad**. See *woman*

razz (playfully) *v.t.*, *v.i.*, *n.*: **chaff**. See *teasing*

reaction (as in reflex) *n.*: **tropism**. See *reflex*

reactionary (a political . . . , who often believes in violence to attain an end) *n.*: **sans-culotte**. See *extremist*

(2) reactionary (as in hatred or fear of anything new or different) *n.*: **misoneism** (person holding this view: **misoneist**). See *conservatism*

(3) reactionary (in beliefs and often stuffy, pompous, and/or elderly) *adj.*, *n.*: **Colonel Blimp**. See *conservative*

reactivate (as in revive) *v.t.*: **refocillate**. See *revive*

read (people who . . . too much) *n.*: **bibliobibuli**. ❖ Thomas Carlyle declared that "in books lies the soul of the whole past time," while Mencken complained about "**bibliobibuli**," those compulsive readers who are "constantly drunk on books, as other men are drunk on whisky or religion." (Michiko Kakutani, "*History of Reading* Rooted in Author's Own Passion for Books," *Seattle Post-Intelligencer*, 12/10/1996.)

(2) read (inability to) *adj.*: **analphabetic**. See *illiterate*

reader (who knows how to read but chooses not to) *n.*: **aliterate**. ❖ **Aliteracy** . . . like an invisible liquid, seeping through our culture, nigh impossible to pinpoint or defend against. It's the kid who spends hours and hours with video games instead of books. . . . There may be untold collateral damage in a society that can read but doesn't. "So much of our culture is embedded in literature," says Philip A. Thompsen, professor of communications at West Chester University in West Chester, Pa. He adds that . . . aliterate students are "missing out on our cultural heritage." (Linton Weeks, "Aliteracy: Read All About It, or Maybe Not; Millions of Americans Who Can Read Choose Not To," *Washington Post*, 5/14/2001.)

reading room *n.*: **athenaeum**. See *library*

real (as in genuine) *adj.*: **pukka**. See *genuine*

(2) real (as in legitimate; acceptable) *adj.*: **cromulent**. See *legitimate*

(3) real *adj.*: **echt** [German]. See *genuine*

realistic (appearing to be . . . or accurate) *adj.*: **verisimilar**. ❖ Tables inside his studio hold a variable smorgasbord of **verisimilar** victuals, enough fake baked hams, plum puddings, cookies, cakes, plump walnuts, boiled beef, artichokes and pastry-topped stews to make a hungry reporter weep. (Melissa Stoeltje, "Fee Fi Faux Fare: Herni Gadbois Is a Giant in the Field of Fake Food," *Houston Chronicle*, 12/23/1994.)

(2) realistic (as in reflecting reality) *adj.*: **veridical**. ❖ In an important and influential paper, Weinstein & Nicolich (1993) argued that empirical research on the relationship between perceptions of risk and behaviour has often confused two issues. The first is whether people's risk perceptions are **veridical** and accurately reflect their behaviour. (D. R. Rutter, "Perceptions of Risk in Motorcyclists: Unrealistic Optimism, Relative Realism and Predictions of Behaviour," *British Journal of Psychology*, 11/1/1998, p. 681.)

reality (relating to a story in which . . . and fiction are mixed together) *adj.*: **Pirandellian**. [This word derives from the Italian dramatist and novelist Luigi Piranedello (1867–1936), who is known for his plays and stories in which reality and fiction blend together and where there is intentional ambiguity as to which aspect the audience is watching at any one time. While not universally considered a common word, it is used frequently by movie, theater, and book critics.] ❖ Like Bill Cosby and Roseanne Arnold, Jerry Seinfeld has made the big and lucrative crossover from stand-up comedy to a weekly television series. But Mr. Seinfeld's transition has been considerably more **Pirandellian**. He plays a character named Jerry Seinfeld who makes a living as a stand-up comic. Each week, the sitcom portions of the show are punctuated with excerpts from the character's solo club routines, which are used as commentaries on the plots. Will the real Jerry Seinfeld stand up? (John O'Connor, Review/Television: "Seinfeld's Quirky Road to Reality," *New York Times*, 9/16/1992.)

(2) reality (historical . . .) *n.*: **historicity**. See *authenticity*

(3) reality (in . . .) *adj.*, *adv.*: **de facto** (as contrasted with de jure: legally or by law) [Latin]. See *in fact*

(4) reality (the . . . of something as it actually is, as opposed to how it is perceived by the senses) *n.* **noumenon**. See *thing-in-itself*

realization (sudden . . .) *n.*: **epiphany**. ❖ I have always loved tacky [Christmas] excesses. . . . But a couple of years ago, I had a midnight **epiphany** at Wal-Mart. Weighed down by sporting equipment and plastic toys, I realized that I had bought more gifts than anyone on my list could want or need and that it wasn't good for their spirits—or mine. (Amy Dickinson, Personal Time/Your Family, *Time*, 12/20/1999, p. 115.)

(2) realization (as in perception or awareness) *n.*: **ken**. See *perception*

(3) realization (as opposed to potentiality) *n.*: **entelechy**. See *actuality*

(4) realization (moment of . . . , often the point in the plot at which the protagonist recognizes his or her or some other character's true identity or discovers the true nature of his or her own situation) *n.*: **anagnorisis**. See *recognition*

(5) realization (while coming into . . .) *adv.*: **aborning**. See *born*

realize (as in understand, thoroughly and/or intuitively) *v.t.*: **grok**. See *understand*

(2) realize (as in figure out) *v.t.*: **suss** (usually with "out"; slang). See *figure out*

(3) realize (as in making an abstract concept seem real) *v.t.*: **reify**. See *materialize*

(4) realize (based on past experience) *v.t.*: **apperceive**. See *comprehend*

realm (as in area of activity or interest) *n.*: **purlieu**. See *domain*

(2) realm *n.*: **ambit**. ❖ Mexico is a comparative bright spot in the region, as are other countries directly in the **ambit** of U.S. foreign investment. (James Graff, Time Finance/World Economic Forum: "Of Risks and Rewards," *Time* International, 2/14/2000, p. 56.)

reappearance (of something after a period of dormancy or inactivity) *n.*: **recrudescence** (*v.i.*: **recrudesce**). ❖ In a country where female liberation posted one of the speediest, most far-reaching success stories of our time, a **recrudescence** of age-old prejudices is eating away the gains like acid rain at a monument's base. Women who grew up with remarkably fair job and schooling opportunities are under pressure to stay at home. (James Walsh, "Born to Be Second Class in China, Old Biases Against Women Have Emerged Once Again," *Time* International, 9/11/1995, p. 46.)

reappearing (spec. come back to life or revived) *adj.*: **redivivus**. See *revived*

rear (in or toward the . . .) *adv.*: **astern**. See *back*

rear end (a fat . . .) *n.*: **steatopygia** (having a fat . . .) *adj.*: **steatopygic**. ❖ The editorial content [of the magazine *Vibe* includes] a feminist critique of Sir Mix-a-Lot's salute to **steatopygia**, "Baby Got Back," [which includes the lyric: "I like big butts and I can not lie."] (David Mills, "The Corporate Hip-Hop Hope," *Washington Post*, 9/14/1992.)

(2) rear end (having a hairy . . .) *adj.*: **dasypygal**. ❖ This current generation [entering college] has emerged into a world with standards of health and wealth [but] do they count their blessings? Probably not. . . . [But if they go out and vote for] only those politicians who promise to take education seriously . . . and [turn] the volume of their in-car stereos down a bit, and pull their trousers up over their **dasypygal** features, there might be hope, yet. (Revel Barker, "Open Eye," *Independent* [London], 9/5/2000.)

(3) rear end (having a nicely proportioned . . .) *adj.*: **callipygian**. ❖ Are chopped-up celebrities worth more than whole regular people? You betcha. . . . **[C]allipygian** singer/actress Jennifer Lopez insured her bodacious back end for a tidy $300,000,000 (and her entire body for $1 billion). (Melissa August, Notebook: "The $400 Million Celebrity," *Time*, 12/20/1999, p. 32.)

(4) rear end (as in buttocks) *n.pl.*: **nates**. See *buttocks*

(5) rear end (as in buttocks) *n.*: **fundament**. See *buttocks*

reason (against) *v.t.*: **expostulate**. See *object*

(2) reason (as in source and origin) *n.*: **fons et origo** [Latin]. See *source and origin*

(3) reason (logically) *v.i.*: **ratiocinate**. See *analyze*

(4) reason (use the power of . . .) *v.t.*: **cerebrate**. See *think*

(5) reason (use the power of) *v.t.*: **cogitate**. See *think*

reasonable (as in logical) *adj.*: **ratiocinative**. See *logical*

(2) reasonable (as in right-thinking) *adj.*: **bien-pensant**. See *right-thinking*

reasoning (as in making an argument suggesting the use of force to settle an issue) *n.*: **argumentum ad baculum** [Latin]. See *threat*

(2) reasoning (given to . . . that may be specious, or one who is given to specious . . .) *adj.*, *n.*: **eristic**. See *specious*

(3) reasoning (in which one of the propositions, usually the premise—which may or may not be accurate—is omitted, leading listeners to fill in the premise themselves) *n.*: **enthymeme**. See *argument*

(4) reasoning (of . . . appealing to pity or compassion) *adv., adj.*: **ad misericordiam** [Latin]. See *argument*

(5) reasoning (person who hates . . . or enlightenment) *n.*: **misologist**. See *closed-minded*

(6) reasoning (specious . . . intended to mislead or rationalize) *n.*: **casuistry**. See *fallacious*

(7) reasoning (that if something cannot be proven false, then it must be true) *n.*: **argumentum ad ignorantiam** [Latin]. See *argument*

(8) reasoning (that silence from an opposing side or absence of evidence is itself indicative that the person making the argument must be correct) *n.*: **argumentum ex silentio** [Latin]. See *argument*

(9) reasoning (which is complicated and often illogical) *n.*: **choplogic**. See *fallacy*

(10) reasoning (which is fallacious) *n.*: **syllogism**. See *specious*

rebel (spec. one who hates or mistrusts authority) *n.*: **misarchist**. ❖ "I've always felt the nine most terrifying words in the English language are, 'I'm from the government and I'm here to help.'"—Ronald Reagan, 1986. . . . . [Reagan] perfected the role of the president as First **Misarchist**. [He] transformed the rhetoric of big government from the white-shoes laissez-faireism of Willkie and Dwight Eisenhower to a broader attack on the idea of government itself. "Government is not the solution to the problem," he said. "It is the problem." (Geoffrey Nunberg, "Thinking About the Government: Liberals Can't Compete with Conservatives on Government-Bashing," *American Prospect*, 5/1/2005.)

(2) rebel *n.*: **frondeur** [French]. ❖ Inevitably, the political resistance to Hitler and the Nazis within the Reich was fundamentally different from the paramilitary resistance to the Germans in occupied Europe. For the German **frondeurs** did not only confront a totalitarian state: they had also to wrestle with their consciences as German patriots. (Daniel Johnson, "All Delays Are Dangerous in War," *Times* [London], 7/21/1994.)

(3) rebel (orig. Catholics who did not follow Church of England) *n.*: **recusant**. See *dissenter*

rebellion *n.*: **émeute** [French]. ❖ [In *Les Misérables*, Victor] Hugo takes the time to comment upon the great **émeute** which he witnessed—that of 1848, which completely toppled the monarchy in France. (Monarch Notes, *Victor Hugo: Part V—Jean Valjean*, 1/1/1963.)

(2) rebellion (against existing social or artistic conventions) *n.*: **titanism** (often cap.). See *revolt*

(3) rebellion (peasant's . . .) *n.*: **jacquerie**. See *revolt*

rebellious *adj.*: **contumacious**. See *obstinate*

rebirth *n.*: **palingenesis**. ❖ Chapter 4 very helpfully expounds various conceptions of the end of the world: as successfully endured catastrophes, as cyclical **palingenesis**, as a one-time event, as annihilation and renewal, as destruction of the cosmos, as the decline of the West, as limits to growth, and as a nuclear holocaust. (Peter C. Phan, review of *The End of the World: A Theological Interpretation*, by Ulrich H. J. Körtner, *Theological Studies*, 3/1/1997, p. 175.)

(2) rebirth (spec. a fundamental transformation of mind or character, esp. a spiritual conversion) *n.*: **metanoia**. See *conversion*

reborn *adj.*: **renascent**. ❖ Last year, Alfred Lerner paid $530 million for the **renascent** Cleveland Browns franchise, which has revived the team's history, colors and fan base. (Richard Sandomir, "Pro Football; N.F.L. Goes Back to Houston for $700 Million," *New York Times*, 10/7/1999.)

(2) reborn (spec. come back to life or revived) *adj.*: **redivivus**. See *revived*

rebuke (sharply) *v.t.*: **keelhaul**. ❖ It would be a mistake for Clintonites to be complacent in the post-election period. While some Republicans sincerely want to work with Clinton, others are ready to **keelhaul** him when an opportunity arises. The press is also poised to turn against him, and the economy could cool off, too. (David Gergen, "Shoring Up a Second Term," *U.S. News & World Report*, 11/18/1996.)

(2) rebuke (as in criticism) *n.*: **animadversion** (*v.t.*: **animadvert***).* See *criticism*

(3) rebuke (as in criticize) *v.t.*: **flay**. See *criticize*

(4) rebuke (harshly) *v.t.*: **fustigate**. See *criticize*

(5) rebuke (sharply) *v.t.*: **scarify**. See *criticize*

(6) rebuke *v.t.*: **objurgate**. See *criticize*

rebut (as in refute convincingly) *v.t.*: **confute**. See *refute*

rebuttal (as in responding to an anticipated objection to an argument before that objection has been made) *n.*: **prolepsis**. ❖ Stephen Glass' [novel] . . . is a **prolepsis**, an extended, creepy one. . . . [He] disgraced himself at *The New Republic* by fabricating interviews. . . . [As a result, there was concern that the book wouldn't be reviewed at all or would be reviewed poorly.] The problem is that Mr. Glass has pre-empted both [arguments]. . . . He brings it up first thing in an author's note: "I was fired in 1998 from my job as a writer at *The New Republic*." (Jerome Weeks, "Glass' Repentance Highly Transparent; ex-*New Republic* Writer Seeks Forgiveness in *The Fabulist*," *Dallas Morning News*, 6/22/2003.)

recalcitrant (to yield or be swayed) *adj.*: **renitent**. See *resistant*

recall (having detailed . . . of visual images) *adj.*: **eidetic**. See *memory*

(2) recall (of or relating to) *adj.*: **mnesic**. See *memory*

recant *v.t.*: **abjure**. See *renounce*

recantation (as in retraction) *n.*: **palinode**. See *retraction*

recap *v.t.*: **précis** [French]. See *summarize*

recapitulation (of existing knowledge on a subject) *phr.*: **état present** [French]. See *summary*

(2) recapitulation *n.*: **précis** [French]. See *summary*

recent (of . . . origin) *adj.*: **neoteric**. ❖ As a final shot at Breyer, Thomas lectures that "ironically,

the **neoteric** Eighth Amendment claim proposed by Justice Breyer [i.e., that executing a prisoner after too lengthy a stay on death row is itself "cruel and unusual punishment"] would further prolong collateral review by giving virtually every capital prisoner yet another ground on which to challenge and delay his execution." (David C. Slade, "Decades on Death Row," *The World & I*, 4/1/2000, p. 80.)

receptacle (esp. as shrine for displaying relics) *n.*: **reliquary**. ❖ [T]he Constitution is not a delicate artifact. It sits in a helium-filled case over at the National Archives in one of those soundproof, heatproof and humidity-controlled **reliquaries** designed to protect its every word and wrinkle. (Nancy Gibbs, Nation/Election 2000: "Before Honor Comes Humility, Proverbs Says," *Time*, 12/18/2000, p. 28.)

receptive (to other views and opinions) *adj.*: **latitudinarian**. See *open-minded*

recess (as in gap) *n.*: **lacuna**. See *gap*

recite (as in mindlessly repeating ideas that have been drilled into the speaker or saying things that reflect the opinions of the powers that be) *v.t., v.i., n.*: **duckspeak**. [This is a word that is part of "Newspeak," the language of the monster state in George Orwell's *1984*. In "duckspeak," one repeats the orthodox opinions (thus, quacking like a duck) of the power structure, namely Big Brother.] ❖ The public school system is systematically destroying America by undermining our culture and destroying our understanding of the necessity of liberty, particularly in the minds of the common people and the working class. Though students are graduating from schools unable to read, no student is leaving school not knowing how to **duckspeak** the slogans of the liberal ruling class. (Bill White, letter to the editor, *Washington Post*, 3/2/2000.)

reckless (and irresponsible) *adj.*: **harum-scarum**. ❖ After [George W. Bush made fun of the phrase "risky tax scheme"], no Democrat is ever again going to be able to utter the phrase "risky tax scheme" without raising more guffaws than fears. . . . Next time Mr. Clinton and the Dems want to denounce GOP tax relief, they can call it a . . . "**harum-scarum** . . . tax contrivance." (Maggie Gallagher, "Lexicon That Taxes the Voting Class," *Washington Times*, 8/14/2000.)

(2) reckless *adj.*: **temerarious**. ❖ Back in the mid 1980s, [the idea of sailing] multihulls on the high seas simply meant madmen and mayhem. . . . Catamarans and trimarans were then in a very embryonic stage of development, and unfortunately many of the people designing, building and sailing them were **temerarious** by nature and lacked expertise, and as a result they did the concept few [favors]. (Rob Mundle, "Multihulls Revisited: Investigating the Latest Advances in Cruising Multihulls," *Offshore Yachting*, 4/1/2008.)

(3) reckless (and irresponsible) *adj.*: **feckless**. See *irresponsible*

(4) reckless (and wild person) *n.*: **rantipole**. See *wild*

(5) reckless (as in overambitious) *adj.*: **Icarian**. See *overambitious*

(6) reckless (as in rash or impetuous person) *n.*: **Hotspur**. See *impetuous*

reclamation (as in a claim by a nation to lands that formerly belonged to it) *n.*: **irredentism**. ❖ [John McCain] had accused Putin's regime of a . . . campaign to intimidate and reassert control over states [like Georgia] that our victory in the cold war had liberated from Soviet rule. . . . The first public inkling of U.S. concern with Putin's **irredentism** came in Secretary Colin Powell's trip last month to attend the inauguration of Georgia's new elected leader, signaling strong support for that nation's independence. (William Safire, "Putin's 'Creeping Coup,'" *New York Times*, 2/9/2004.)

reclining *adj.*: **decumbent**. See *lying down*

recluse (esp. for religious reasons) *n.*: **anchorite**. ❖ A judge is always the subject of public scrutiny. . . . That does not necessarily mean judges should live like **anchorites**. But the fact is that the public believes that distancing is a vital criterion in promoting confidence in their impartiality. Mingling with corporate figures, politicians, lawyers and prosecutors involved in cases before them may call their integrity into question. (*New Straits Times* [Malaysia], "Guaranteeing Impartiality," 4/30/2003.)

(2) recluse (esp. for religious reasons) *n.*: **eremite** (practice of living in such fashion, *n.*: **eremitism**). ❖ "The monks have to learn that everything changes. The world is not what it used to be," [said an Athens city official.] Even the monks would not deny that. Over the past year, the community has thrown **eremitism** to the winds, hooking up with the world through the Internet, computers and mobile phones. (Helena Smith, "Eve Demands Access to Garden of Eden," *Observer* [London], 4/12/1998.)

recognition (moment of . . . , often the point in the plot at which the protagonist recognizes his or her or some other character's true identity or discovers the true nature of his or her own situation) *n.*: **anagnorisis**. ❖ [Faced with his own] artistic doubts about [the quality of] his bird drawings . . . , it seems that the largely self-taught [John] Audubon experienced a wrenching creative **anagnorisis**, one that triggered a revised approach to the whole artistic ornithological oeuvre that we would come to know as the superb *Birds of America*. (Lee Gaillard, The Reader Replies, *American Scholar*, 9/22/1999.)

(2) recognition *n.*: **ken**. See *perception*

(3) recognition (of one's errors, and a return to a sane, sound, or correct position and the wisdom gained from the experience) *n.*: **resipiscence**. See *reformation*

recognize (based on past experience) *v.t.*: **apperceive**. See *comprehend*

(2) recognize (as in understand, thoroughly and/or intuitively) *v.t.*: **grok**. See *understand*

recoil (due to fear or intimidation) *v.t.*: **quail**. ❖ Arianne Cohen is a woman in a hurry. She **quailed** at the thought of spending months looking for an apartment, as she had seen friends and colleagues do. "They didn't seem upset that they were wasting years of their lives, languishing away on seemingly permanent hunts for apartments that would be somewhat transitory," she said. (Joyce Cohen, "With a Flashlight and a Stopwatch," *New York Times*, 3/22/2005.)

(2) recoil *v.i.*: **resile**. ❖ Ours is a principled policy based on upholding the rights of the oppressed people of Kashmir, and there can be no bargain or trading on it. We cannot **resile** from our moral and principled support to the Kashmiris, nor should the world. (Karamatullah Khan Ghori, "Trip to Washington Was for a Private Visit," *Washington Times*, 5/11/2000.)

(3) recoil (out of fear or shying away from) *v.i.*: **blench**. See *flinch*

recollection (confusion of . . . with fact) *n.*: **paramnesia**. See *misremember*

(2) recollection (having an exact or vivid . . .) *n.*: **hypermnesia**. See *memory*

(3) recollection (having detailed . . . of visual images) *adj.*: **eidetic**. See *memory*

(4) recollection (of or relating to) *adj.*: **mnesic**. See *memory*

(5) recollection *n.*: **anamnesis**. See *remembrance*

recompense (as compensation for damage or loss) *n.*: **quittance**. ❖ "It's horrendous," [World Jewish Congress secretary-general Israel] Singer said in an interview, before addressing a Jewish community dinner at a midtown hotel. The money [in Swiss banks belonging to Holocaust victims] was used by the Swiss "as a **quittance** to Poland for (return) of property that Swiss citizens had in Communist Poland." (Irwin Block, "Swiss to Identify Dormant Accounts," *Montreal Gazette*, 5/23/1997.)

(2) recompense (as in reward) *n.*: **guerdon**. See *reward*

reconciliation (of conflicting ideas, esp. to make peace) *n.*: **eirenicon**. See *peace offering*

reconciling (or uniting of opposing viewpoints or beliefs) *adj.*: **syncretic** (or **syncretistic**). [This word often, but not always, refers to the attempt to reconcile opposing religious views.] ❖ The **syncretic** tendencies of monotheism, and the common ancestry of the tales, mean in effect that a rebuttal to one is a rebuttal to all.

Horribly and hatefully though they may have fought with one another, [Judaism, Christianity and Islam] claim to share a descent at least from the Penateuch of Moses, and the Koran certifies Jews as "people of the book," Jesus as a prophet, and a virgin as his mother. (Christopher Hitchens, *God Is Not Great* [Twelve Books/Hachette [2007], p. 98.)

recovery (as in renewal or restoration of something after decay, lapse of time, or dilapidation) *n.*: **instauration**. See *restoration*.

recovery (as in a claim by a nation to lands that formerly belonged to it) *n.*: **irredentism**. See *reclamation*

rectify (as in atone for) *v.t.*, *v.i.*: **expiate**. See *atone*

recurrence (of a particular word, phrase, or sound) *n.* **repetend**. See *repetition*

recycled (as in warmed-over food or old material) *n.*, *adj.*: **rechauffé** [French]. See *warmed-over*

red (having a . . . glow) *adj.*: **rutilant**. ❖ If Joyce Jimenez does not show a **rutilant** face when asked about her rumored romantic relationship with television host TJ Manotoc, it's because (a) he is not her new beau, (b) she has gotten better at keeping private stuff to herself, (c) they're just in the getting-to-know-each-other stage and so there's nothing to divulge yet. (Walden Sadiri, "Joyce Jimenez: Single and a Woman of Substance in *Pinay Pie*," *Manila Bulletin*, 8/30/2003.)

(2) red (blood-. . .) *adj.*: **incarnadine**. See *crimson*

reddening (or blushing) *adj.*: **erubescent** (or **rubescent**). ❖ The president's high job approval rating has been a source of mystery to many pundits and to Republican Party stalwarts. Most (including this pundit) assumed the public release of the report by independent counsel Kenneth Starr and its **erubescent** details about his relationship with Monica Lewinsky would turn off voters and ultimately destroy Bill Clinton's presidency. (Bonnie Erbe, "Families Feel President's Pain," *Denver Rocky Mountain News*, 9/26/1998.)

reddish *adj.*: **rufous**. ❖ *Carex buchananii* [is a type of grass that] has a **rufous** quality, a foxy red cast to its twirling leaves that brings out the pumpkin shades hidden in many purple leaves. (*Seattle Post-Intelligencer*, "Reigning in Fall: There's Garden Glory Still to Behold," 11/7/1996.)

(2) reddish (as in ruddy) *adj.*: **florid**. See *ruddy*

reddish-brown *adj.*: **ferruginous**. See *rust*

(2) reddish-brown *adj.*: **rubiginous**. See *rust-colored*

red-handed (as in caught . . . , esp. of committing an offense or a sexual act) *adv.*: **in flagrante delicto**. See *in the act*

redressing (as in atoning for) *adj.*: **piacular**. See *atoning*

reduce (as in condense the flavor or essence of something, as if by boiling down) *v.t.*: **decoct**. See *boil down*

(2) reduce (in value, amount or degree) *v.t.*: **attenuate**. See *lessen*

(3) reduce *v.t.* **minify**. See *minimize*

redundancy *n.*: **pleonasm**. ❖ It was, after all, public officials who gave us "safe haven" during the Persian Gulf War. Someone apparently grafted the "safe" from "safe harbor" (not all harbors are safe) onto "haven" (by definition, a safe place). The creation of this obnoxious **pleonasm** . . . illustrates the bureaucrat's familiar combination of self-importance, pretension, and ignorance. (John E. McIntyre, "Words That Survive the Test of Time," *Christian Science Monitor*, 12/30/1999.)

(2) redundancy (as in obsessive repetition of meaningless words and phrases) *n.*: **verbigeration**. See *repetition*

(3) redundancy *n.*: **macrology**. See *verbosity*

red wine (having the color of . . .) *adj.*: **vinaceous**. ❖ Among [memoirs coming out] this year [is] *The Russian Tea Room: A Love Story*, about that **vinaceous** Manhattan establishment, by former owner Faith Stewart-Gordon. (Marie Arana, Fall Preview, *Washington Post*, 9/5/1999.) [Of course, to understand this word within the context of the example requires a familiarity with the Russian Tea Room, but suffice it to say that the primary color there is indeed a red wine color.]

reek *n.*: **fetor**. See *stench*

reeking *adj.*: **fetid**. See *smelly*

(2) reeking *adj.*: **graveolent**. See *smelly*

(3) reeking *adj.*: **mephitic** (*n.*: **mephitis**). See *smelly*

(4) reeking *adj.*: **noisome**. See *smelly*

reestablish (as in return to an original state or condition) *v.t.*: **repristinate**. See *restore*

reestablishment (as in renewal or restoration of something after decay, lapse of time, or dilapidation) *n.*: **instauration**. See *restoration*

reevaluation (spec. a fundamental transformation of one's character or way of thinking, often spiritual) *n.*: **metanoia**. See *conversion*

reference book *n.*: **vade mecum**. See *guidebook*

refined *adj.*: **raffiné** (or **raffine**) [French]. ❖ The [James Bond] formula remains stirring but not shaken. Bond still astonishes headwaiters with his **raffine** tastes, fondles weapons and women with equal ardor and moves with eerie confidence though a world of constant, cosmic peril. . . . The only evil talent his enemies lack is an ability to aim straight when shooting at him. "Do you lose as gracefully as you win?" one arch-scoundrel asks Bond. "I don't know," Bond shrugs elegantly. "I've never lost." (Franz Lidz, "007 Has Moved Smoothly through the Last 35 Years," *Dallas Morning News*, 12/30/1997.)

(2) refined *adj.*: **soigné** [French]. See *elegant*

(3) refined (and intelligent person) *n.*: **bel esprit**. See *cultivated*

(4) refined (affectedly or excessively . . . , quaint, or dainty) *adj.*: **twee**. See *quaint*

(5) refined (as in elegant) *adj.*: **Chesterfieldian**. See *elegant*

(6) refined (esp. those aspiring or pretending to be . . .) *adj.*: **lace-curtain**. See *well-bred*

(7) refined (in an affected manner) *adj.*: **niminy-piminy**. See *dainty*

reflect (as in think about) *v.t.*: **cerebrate**. See *think*

(2) reflect (as in think about) *v.t.*: **cogitate**. See *think*

(3) reflect (on something, often used as a directive, as in "Consider this:") *v.t.*: **perpend**. See *consider*

reflection (as in mirror image) *n.*: **enantio-morph**. See *mirror image*

(2) reflection (on matters outside oneself, i.e., on the outside world) *n.*: **extrospection** (*adj.*: **extrospective**). See *observation*

(3) reflection (staring at one's belly-button as an aid to . . .) *n.*: **omphaloskepsis**. See *meditation*

reflex *n.*: **tropism**. ❖ Over the year Amando Doronila, a columnist for the *Manila Chronicle*, has mused repeatedly on the unshakable Filipino attraction to basketball, even as that **tropism** always seemed to lead to disappointment [in international competition]. (Alexander Wolff, *Big Game, Small World*, Warner Books [2002], p. 225.)

reflexive (as in trained to show a conditioned response) *adj.*: **Pavlovian**. See *conditioned*

reformer (political . . .) *n.*: **goo-goo**. [The goo-goo movement (from the initials of "good government") was a reform movement, often associated with Theodore Roosevelt, aimed toward making government more honest. Today it is usually used in a disparaging way (though not in this example), as if to suggest that the effort is naive or will be unsuccessful. The noun form for the movement itself is "goo-gooism."] ❖ Before Mr. Obama can make government cool, however, he has to make it good. Indeed, he has to be a **goo-goo**. . . . Franklin Roosevelt was a **goo-goo** extraordinaire. He simultaneously made government much bigger and much cleaner. Mr. Obama needs to do the same thing. (Paul Krugman, "Barack Be Good," *New York Times*, 12/25/2008.)

reformation (spec. a recognition of one's errors, and a return to a sane, sound, or correct position) *n.*: **resipiscence**. [The Latin "resipiscere" means to recover one's senses. The word

is also defined as the wisdom gained from the experience. Although frequently used synonymously with "repentance," the sense of remorse implicit in that word is not required for resipiscence to occur. What is required is recognition and reformation.] ❖ The offender comes from a good family. He has shown character and substance on the sporting field. I am told that he has stopped abusing alcohol and taking drugs. . . . [He]has become a practising Christian. . . . The offender has acknowledged his error, is sorry for what he has done and appears to be determined not to re-offend. He has shown **resipiscence**. (J. Southwood, *The Queen v. Joseph Wesley*, www.supremecourt.nt.gov.au/archive/doc/sentencing_remarks/wesley.html, 8/8/2006.)

(2) reformation (road to . . . , as in rehabilitation or conversion) *n.*: **sawdust trail**. See *conversion*

refrain (as in hymn, expressing praise and glory to God) *n.*: **doxology**. See *hymn*

(2) refrain (as in repetition of a particular word, phrase, or sound) *n.* **repetend**. See *repetition*

refresh (as in revive) *v.t.*: **refocillate**. See *revive*

refresher (as in something that invigorates) *n.*, *adj.*: **roborant**. See *invigorating*

refreshing (as in restorative, esp. with respect to effect of certain drugs or medications) *adj.*: **analeptic**. See *restorative*

refuge (as in small, usu. temporary defensive fortification) *n.*: **redoubt**. [This word is sometimes used literally, as in the example given here, and sometimes figuratively, to suggest any sort of actual or metaphorical safe haven.] ❖ The last **redoubt** of the [Texan] defenders was the [Alamo] chapel. Its thick stone walls stood proof against the cannons the attackers leveled against it, but eventually its oaken doors were splintered by the 18-pound balls of the fort's large gun. (H. W. Brands, *Lone Star Nation*, Doubleday [2004], p. 373.)

(2) refuge (as in safe haven) *n.*: **querencia**. See *safe haven*

refuse (study of a culture by examining its . . .) *n.*: **garbology**. See *garbage*

(2) refuse *n*.: **offal**. See *trash*

refutation (as in responding to an anticipated objection to an argument before that objection has been made) *n*.: **prolepsis**. See *rebuttal*

refute (convincingly) *v.t.*: **confute**. ❖ In [the documentary *Sobibor*], Claude Lanzmann (*Shoah*) **confutes** two beliefs: that the Jews had no inkling of what awaited them in the gas chambers, and that they went to their deaths without resistance. (Heather M. Lajewski, Movies, *Chicago Tribune*, 3/8/2002.)

regal (as in lordly) *adj*.: **seigneurial**. See *lordly*

(2) regal (of a . . . and stately woman, often voluptuous) *adj*.: **Junoesque**. See *voluptuous*

regard (as in attention) *n*.: **advertence**. See *attention*

(2) regard (pay . . . to, as in homage, not necessarily sincere or unforced) *n*.: **obeisance**. See *homage*

regarding *prep*.: **anent**. ❖ Peter Stone's new version [of *Annie Get Your Gun*] called for vivisection of this fabulous musical, removing such Irving Berlin gems as "I'm a Bad, Bad Man," "I'm an Indian, Too" and "Colonel Buffalo Bill." Done, no doubt, in the name of political correctness **anent** intellectual Indians and liberated women—two groups apparently not around in 1946. (Richard Traubner, "It Was the Worst of Times," *American Record Guide*, 7/1/1999, p. 27.)

regardless *adv*.: **withal**. See *nevertheless*

regimented (strictly . . .) *adj*.: **monastic**. See *strict*

region (densely populated . . . or city) *n*.: **megalopolis**. See *crowded*

(2) region (populated by persons from many countries or backgrounds) *n*.: **cosmopolis**. See *diversity*

regret (as in disappointment) *n*. **Apples of Sodom**. See *disappointment*

(2) regret (as in disappointment) *n*.: **Dead Sea fruit**. See *disappointment*

regular (at a place, esp. a place of entertainment) *n*.: **habitué** [French]. ❖ Station Road's skillful manager, Carol Covell, will be familiar to **habitués** of Della Femina, both in East Hampton and New York. (Peter M. Gianotti, Dining Out: "Station Road," *Newsday*, 7/7/2000.)

(2) regular (as in mundane; everyday) *adj*.: **sublunary**. See *earthly*

(3) regular (of or relating to the . . . people) *adj*.: **plebian**. See *common*

(4) regular (people, as in the masses) *n*.: **canaille**. See *masses*

(5) regular (people, as in the masses) *n*.: **hoi polloi**. See *commoners*

regurgitation (act of . . .) *n*.: **emesis**. See *vomiting*

(2) regurgitation (an agent that causes . . .) *n., adj*.: **emetic**. See *vomiting*

rehabilitation (road to . . . or conversion) *n*.: **sawdust trail**. See *conversion*

(2) rehabilitation (study of . . . of criminals) *n*.: **penology**. See *prison*

rehashed (as in warmed-over food or old material) *n., adj*.: **rechauffé** [French]. See *warmed-over*

reigning *adj*.: **regnant**. ❖ Conventions for the incumbent are supposed to be ceremonial reaffirmations of the **regnant** leader. (Garry Wills, U.S. Campaign: "Unfriendly Skies: Faced with Its Own Explosive Issues, the G.O.P. Heads to Houston on a Wing and a Prayer," *Time*, 8/17/1992, p. 34.)

reimbursement (for damage or loss) *n*.: **quittance**. See *recompense*

reincarnation *n*.: **metempsychosis**. [This term specifically refers to the transmigration at death of the soul of a human being or animal into a new body.] ❖ Modern subscribers to the theory of **metempsychosis** might wish to return as a colt under Aidan O'Brien's care. For the elite of the elite at Ballydoyle now live in a sumptuous palace of a yard, the brand-new nerve centre of the most successful private racehorse training establishment in the annals of the turf. (Sue Montgomery, Racing: "the Mild-Mannered Look Is Not Quite a Lie, but the Brain Behind It Is a Steel Trap," interview with Aidan O'Brien, *Independent on Sunday*, 4/27/2003.)

reinstate (as in return to an original state or condition) *v.t.*: **repristinate**. See *restore*

reinterpretation (esp. a scholarly critical . . . , as in revision) *n.*: **recension**. See *revision*

reiterate (often for emphasis) *v.t.*: **ingeminate**. See *repeat*

reject (esp. responsibility or duty) *v.t.*: **abnegate**. See *renounce*

(2) reject (or condemn or disapprove) *v.t., n.*: **discountenance**. ❖ With such precedents of reparations to non-Black peoples in four continents, it would be sheer racism for the world to **discountenance** reparations claims from the Black world. (Conrad W. Worrill, "Plenty of Precedents Exist for Reparations," *Philadelphia Tribune*, 3/12/2002.)

rejection (as in disdain) *n.*: **misprision** (*v.t.*: **misprize**). See *disdain*

rejeuvenator (as in something that invigorates) *adj., n.*: **roborant**. See *invigorating*

rejoice (or boast, esp. about the accomplishments of a relative) *v.t., n.*: **kvell** [Yiddish]. See *boast*

(2) rejoice (with boisterous public demonstrations) *v.i.*: **maffick** [British]. See *celebrate*

rejoicing (often in a boastful way) *adj.*: **cock-a-hoop**. See *elated*

rejoinder (charging accuser with a similar offense) *n.*: **tu quoque** [Latin]. See *answer*

rekindled (as in revived or come back to life) *adj.*: **redivivus**. See *revived*

related *adj.*: **cognate**. ❖ His great theme is the decline, from its zenith at the turn of the century, of the "Anglo-American-Celtic" world dominance and of its **cognate** social expression, the ideal of the gentleman. (James Bowman, review of *A Thread of Years*, by John Lukacs, *National Review*, 5/18/1998, p. 52.)

relate to (tendency of people to . . . with, or be attracted to, others who they perceive are similar to them) *n.*: **homophily**. See *associate*

relating (to) *prep.*: **anent**. See *regarding*

(2) relating (to, as in associated with or incident to) *adj.*: **appurtenant**. See *pertaining*

relatives *n.pl.*: **kith and kin**. ❖ Authorities made clear that the testimony of strangers is not enough. It is a citizen's duty to betray his own **kith and kin**. The Zhou clan, willingly or by coercion, did its duty. [The sister of] Zhou

Fengsuo . . . explained that after seeing the wanted notices for her brother, she contacted security officials. (Jill Smolowe, "China: Deng's Big Lie—The Hard-liners Rewrite History to Justify Arrests and Bury Democracy," *Time*, 6/26/1989, p. 32.)

(2) relations (as in family ties) *n.*: **propinquity**. See *kinship*

relaxed (and carefree time) *adj.*: **prelapsarian**. See *innocent*

(2) relaxed *adj.*: **dégagé** [French]. See *easygoing*

(3) relaxed (or carefree behavior) *n.*: **rhathymia**. See *carefree*

relaxing (as in reducing stress or anxiety, often used with respect to medications) *adj.*: **anxiolytic** (*n.*: a product that has this effect). ❖ After a survey of anti-anxiety drugs, psychologist Ronald Lipman concluded there is little consistent evidence that they help patients with anxiety disorders: "Although it seems natural to assume that the **anxiolytic** medications would be the most effective . . . medications for the treatment of anxiety disorders, the evidence does not support this assumption." (Roger Greenberg, "Prescriptions for Happiness?" *Psychology Today*, 9/1/1995.)

(2) relaxing *adj.*: **calmative**. ❖ Mimieux practices neither [Buddhism nor Hinduism], but she says they made their mark on her mind as well as her exercise routine, which combines **calmative**, deep-breathing techniques with stretching and balancing routines. (Leah Rozen, Picks & Pans: Screen, *People*, 12/11/1995, p. 25.)

(3) relaxing (of pain, distress, or tension) *adj.*: **anodyne**. See *soothing*

release (from slavery, servitude, or bondage) *v.t.*: **manumit**. See *emancipate*

relevant *n.*: **apposite**. ❖ Oddly enough, H. D. Molesworth, explaining that the monarchy works at a powerful emotional rather than rational level, had once given a particularly **apposite** example. Many people—and this was common to various civilizations—he wrote, are convinced that the Blood Royal is "possessed of something special, like a petrol additive." (Alex Berlyne, "Homing Pidgin," *Jerusalem Post*, 12/30/1994.)

reliance (on faith alone rather than reason, esp. in philosophical or religious matters) *n.*: **fideism**. See *faith*

relief (medicine that offers . . . from pain) *n.*: **anodyne**. See *pain reliever*

relieving (as in reducing stress or anxiety, often used with respect to medications) *adj.*: **anxiolytic** (*n.*: a product that has this effect). See *relaxing*

relieving (of pain, distress, or tension) *adj.*: **anodyne**. See *soothing*

religions (concerned with establishing unity among . . .) *adj.*: **ecumenical**. See *churches*

religious (excessively . . .) *adj.*: **religiose**. ❖ Every Bush speech is richly encrypted with covert Biblical allusions and other secret handshakes with his fundamentalist listeners, but one need not be a fundamentalist to warm to this sort of **religiose** rhetoric, for it is every bit as much of an "American" thing as it is a "Christian" one. Rationalist liberals [are] tone-deaf to its appeal . . . (Jonathan Raban, "Pastor Bush: Why Do So Many Americans Dismiss the Evidence That the Occupation of Iraq Has Gone Disastrously Wrong?" *Guardian* [London], 10/6/2004.)

(2) religious (lacking . . . reverence) *n.*: **impiety** (*adj.*: **impious**). See *irreverence*

(3) religious (tacky or kitschy . . . or devotional ornament) *n.*: **bondieuserie** [French]. See *ornament*

relinquish (an office or position) *v.t.*: **demit** (as in demit office). See *resign*

(2) relinquish (esp. responsibility or duty) *v.t.*: **abnegate**. See *renounce*

relish (the taste of) *v.t.*: **degust**. See *savor*

reluctance (as in unwillingness) *n.*: **nolition**. See *unwillingness*

reluctant (and cautious and indecisive) *adj.*: **Prufrockian**. See *timid*

(2) reluctant (to yield or be swayed) *adj.*: **renitent**. See *resistant*

remains (fascination with or erotic attraction to human . . .) *n.*: **necrophilia**. See *corpses*

remark (as in insight or observation) *n.*: **aperçu** [French]. See *insight*

(2) remark (as in statement, which is left unfinished because the speaker is unwilling or unable to continue or because the rest of the message is implicit) *n.*: **aposiopesis**. See *statement*

(3) remark (in which one references an issue by saying that one will not discuss it; e.g., "I'm not even going to get into the character issue") *n.*: **apophasis**. See *figure of speech*

(4) remark (or line that is witty) *n.*: **epigram**. See *quip*

(5) remark (or phrase or comment that is elegant, concise, witty, and/or well put) *n.*: **atticism**. See *expression*

(6) remark (upon, esp. at length) *v.i.*, *n.*: **descant**. See *talk*

remarkable (as in wonderful) *adj.*: **mirific**. See *wonderful*

remedy (universal . . .) *n.*: **catholicon**. ❖ In the end, even the most intrusive measures [regarding verification of another country's nuclear capability] will not be foolproof: there is no verification **catholicon**. But perfect verification is as illusory as it is unnecessary. (Bruce Van Voorst, "Arms Control—An Exercise in Trust," *Time*, 7/31/1989, p. 24.)

(2) remedy (which is untested or unproved) *n.*: **nostrum**. ❖ Hypochondriacs that so many of us are, Americans are easily persuaded that we can improve our sex lives, avoid cancer and live longer by swallowing pills or nibbling on herbs. To clothe these largely unproved remedies in respectability, the sellers have come up with scientific-sounding terms for their **nostrums**: nutraceuticals or phytonutrients. (Paul Klebnikov, "A Healthy Business," *Forbes*, 9/21/1998, p. 89.)

remembrance *n.*: **anamnesis**. ❖ The finale of the novel is marked . . . by **anamnesis**. . . . Karnau's renewed listening to the children's voices almost fifty years after the end of the war leads to a repetition and retrieval of his own history. (Ulrich Schonherr, "Topophony of Fascism: On Marcel Beyer's *The Karnau Tapes*,"

Germanic Review, 9/22/1998, p. 328.)

(2) remembrance (confusion of . . . with fact) *n.*: **paramnesia**. See *misremember*

(3) remembrance (having an exact or vivid . . .) *n.*: **hypermnesia**. See *memory*

(4) remembrance (having detailed . . . of visual images) *adj.*: **eidetic**. See *memory*

reminiscence (as in memory) *n.*: **anamnesis**. See *remembrance*

reminiscent (of, or smelling like) *adj.*: **redolent**. ❖ As the sun rose, a tinny portable radio played and a powerful miasma enveloped the scene, the odor of unwashed bodies and open sewers **redolent** of a teeming, unruly refugee camp. (Warren P. Strobel, "Seeking Shelter," *U.S. News & World Report*, 4/19/1999.)

remorse (spec. a recognition of one's errors, and a return to a sane, sound, or correct position) *n.*: **resipiscence**. See *reformation*

remorseless *adj.*: **impenitent**. See *unrepentant*

remote (or most distant destination or goal) *n.*: **ultima Thule**. See *distant*

remove (as in shed, a skin or covering) *v.t.*, *v.i.*: **exuviate**. See *shed*

(2) remove (as in unseat) *v.t.* **unhorse**. See *unseat*

remuneration (as in wages) *n.*: **emolument**. See *wages*

renaissance (as in rebirth) *n.*: **palingenesis**. See *rebirth*

rendezvous (esp. for illicit sexual relations) *n.*: **assignation**. See *appointment*

rendition (as in translation, which is literal) *n.*: **metaphrase**. See *translation*

renew (as in revive) *v.t.*: **refocillate**. See *revive*

renewal (as in rebirth) *n.*: **palingenesis**. See *rebirth*

(2) renewal (as in updating of an organization to meet contemporary conditions, esp. as proposed by Pope John XXIII with respect to the Catholic church after Vatican II) *n.*: **aggiornamento** [Italian]. See *updating*

(3) renewal (of something after a period of dormancy or inactivity) *n.*: **recrudescence** (*v.i.*: **recrudesce**). See *reappearance*

(4) renewal (or restoration of something after decay, lapse of time, or dilapidation) *n.*: **instauration**. See *restoration*.

renewed (as in revived or come back to life) *adj.*: **redivivus**. See *revived*

renounce (esp. responsibility or duty) *v.t.*: **abnegate**. ❖ And while these Germans may have experienced personally the hatred and slights of others, they have never **abnegated** responsibility or understanding of that history. For these Germans this adopted voice poses the unspoken question: What is the statute of limitations on the Holocaust? (Ken Baron, "Opening and Closing the Wounds: A Young Jew Married to a German," *Jewish Week*, 2/3/1994.)

(2) renounce *v.t.*: **abjure**. ❖ Newly married to Henry Stanton, an antislavery pragmatist who had broken with Garrison, [Elizabeth Cady] Stanton refused to **abjure** her own loyalties to the women's rights wing of abolition. (*New Republic*, "The Feminism of the Mothers, the Feminism of the Daughters," 8/10/1998.)

renown *n.*: **réclame** [French]. See *publicity*

rent (exorbitant . . .) *n.*, *v.i.*, *adj.*: **rackrent**. [This word can be used as a noun (referring to the rackrent itself), a verb (referring to charging the rackrent), or an adjective (esp. when referring to a "rackrent landlord," as in this example)]. ❖ The book [*Dear Mama . . . An African Refugee Writes Home* is a tour] of the desperate fringes of the new Europe, a landscape peopled with pimps and prostitutes, **rackrent** landlords and forgers, drug couriers and mules, welfare scammers and bigamists. (*Irish Times*, "The Rules of the Asylum Game," 3/11/1999.)

reoccurrence (of something after a period of dormancy or inactivity) *n.*: **recrudescence** (*v.i.*: **recrudesce**). See *reappearance*

repartee (light or playful back and forth . . .) *n.*: **badinage**. See *banter*

(2) repartee *n.*: **persiflage**. See *chitchat*

repayment (for damage or loss) *n.*: **quittance**. See *recompense*

repeat (often for emphasis) *v.t.*: **ingeminate**.

❖ [The] Bob Woodward book of dubious reportage . . . claims to **ingeminate** actual events from behind closed doors and to **ingeminate** verbatim conversations—though no stenographer was present. (R. Emmett Tyrell Jr., "Artificial Ingemination," *American Spectator*, 1/1/2003.)

(2) repeat (as in to spread news or a rumor about) *v.t.*: **bruit**. See *rumor*

(3) repeat (mindlessly ideas that have been drilled into the speaker or that reflect the opinions of the powers that be) *v.t., v.i., n.*: **duck-speak**. See *recite*

repeating (a particular act over and over, often after initial stimulus has ceased) *n.*: **perseveration** (*v.i.*: **perseverate**). ❖ [A co-worker of the narrator has been falsely accused of sexual harassment in the workplace.] "This is all so degrading and atrocious," said [my wife. . . . My wife has a tremendous ability to be outraged at the common injustices society visits on its members. . . . At long last, she simply stopped **perseverating** on this subject and moved on to new ones. (Stanley Bing, *You Look Nice Today*, Bloomsbury [2003], p. 104.)

(2) repeating (pathological or uncontrollable or a child's . . . of another's words) *n.*: **echolalia**. ❖ Another symptom that "autistic-like" visually impaired children may share with autistic children is **echolalia**. There has been much speculation about what might cause some visually impaired children to echo in parrot-like fashion the words they hear spoken to them. (Charles Gourgey, "Music Therapy in the Treatment of Social Isolation in Visually Impaired Children," *Re:View*, 1/15/1998.)

(3) repeating (pathological or uncontrollable . . . of another's actions) *n.*: **echopraxia**. ❖ In one painfully hilarious moment, an expert witness for the prosecution, Dr. Rampling, suffers from three neurological conditions, coprolalia, copropraxia and **echopraxia**, which make her shout obscenities [coprolalia], grab her own breasts [copropraxia] and mimic her questioners as she testifies, all unconsciously. (Richard Bernstein, "Just a Couple of All-American Orphans on Trial," *New York Times*, 8/6/1997.)

(4) repeating (obsessive . . . of meaningless words and phrases) *n.*: **verbigeration**. See *repetition*

(5) repeating (of a particular word, phrase, or sound) *n.*: **repetend**. See *repetition*

(6) repeating (of words) *n.*: **macrology**. See *verbosity*

(7) repeating (unnecessary . . . of words) *n.*: **pleonasm**. See *redundancy*

repellent *adj.*: **rebarbative**. ❖ [Rudyard Kipling's] literary gifts were increasingly eclipsed in the public eye by his unpalatable politics. Which is not to deny that his views were often **rebarbative**: anti-feminist, chauvinist, racist, and anti-Semitic. (Martin Rubin, "English Writer Who Lost a Following," *Washington Times*, 4/30/2000.)

(2) repellent (as in despicable, or treacherous) *adj.*: **reptilian**. See *despicable*

repentance *n.*: **metanoia**. [This Greek word, meaning change of mind or heart, refers specifically to a fundamental transformation of one's character or way of thinking, and is often used to refer to a spiritual conversion. It is often said to translate as "repentance" as well as change of mind (and thus it is a possible, though somewhat narrow, synonym for repentance), though as one writer has said, "**metanoia** is not simply repentance, nor even penitence: it is transformation (metamorphosis), regeneration, new birth." (Leandro Bosch, "The Assembly Theme," *Ecumencial Review*, 7/1/2005.) See *conversion* for the example.]

(2) repentance (spec. the opportunity to withdraw from, or decide not to commit, an intended crime) *n.*: **locus poenitentiae**. [Latin; lit. place of repentance. Although technically the crime in question should not have been fully consummated for this term to apply, it is occasionally also used to refer to repentance after the fact as a means of mitigating the consequences, as in the example here.] ❖ [Former governor Mario Cuomo on how President Clinton might save his presidency after release of the Kenneth Starr report:] President Clinton should make Senator Joseph Lieberman his point man. . . . Mr. Lieberman criticized the President, but he also gave him a **locus poenitentiae**, a place for repentance under the law. The President should take advantage of that and say to the Senator: . . . "You have said that you can save my Presidency. Show me the way." (Mario Cuomo, "Can Clinton Find the Road Back?" *New York Times*, 9/13/1998.)

(3) repentance (spec. a change of mind or heart, a recognition of one's errors, and a resulting return to a sane, sound, or correct position) *n.*: **resipiscence** (*adj.*: **resipiscent**). See *reformation*

(4) repentance (road to . . . , as in rehabilitation, or conversion) *n.*: **sawdust trail**. See *conversion*

repetition (of a particular word, phrase, or sound) *n.*: **repetend**. ❖ Repetition is easily one of the foregrounded features of Poe's prose. . . . McElrath holds that Poe's prose sometimes embodies "a controlled repetition of words that appeal directly to the reader's audial and visual senses." Forrest also considers the devices of repetition that Poe and the Bible have in common: despite Poe's love of stylistic brevity, "outside the Bible it would be hard to find one who used the **repetend** more than he." (Brett Zimmerman, "Rhetoric and Style," quoting from William Forrest, *Biblical Allusions in Poe*, McGill-McQueens Press [2005], p. 122)

(2) repetition (of a phrase at the beginning of successive sentences or verses) *n.*: **anaphora**. ❖ The poetic quality in Marvin K. White's *Last Rights* . . . exists in his knowing that much can be achieved with the spare line and the riveting effects of **anaphora**. In "that thing," a poem about a man who has AIDS, [he writes]: "he still singing in the choir; / he still loving men; / he still kiki-ing at the club; / he still sometimes real still." (Jerry W. Ward Jr., Poetry, *Washington Post*, 8/1/1999.)

(3) repetition (of word or phrase at the end of sentences or clauses) *n.* **epistrophe**. ❖ [T]he headline for an Isuzu Trooper ad reads

"Cargo Ship." The ad uses a verbal metaphor to equate the Trooper to a cargo ship because it has the most cargo space in its class. . . . The headline [two pages later] reads "Kin Ship" and uses a pun to imply that the Rodeo is for families. In effect, the ad on page 17 layers onto the ad on page 15 to create a verbal **epistrophe** in which the word "ship" is repeated at the end of each headline. (Edward F. McQuarrie, "The Development, Change, and Transformation of Rhetorical Style in Magazine Advertisements, 1954–1999," *Journal of Advertising*, 12/22/2002.)

(4) repetition (obsessive . . . of meaningless words and phrases) *n.*: **verbigeration**. ❖ At the risk of adding superfluous **verbigeration** to the already overheated debate on affirmative action, it is perhaps time to get back to basics by bringing the focus to our constitution, where this practice originates. The Bill of Rights enshrines the right to equality before the law. (Paul Hoffman, "Redress Is a Lawful Act," *Cape Times* [South Africa], 5/25/2007.)

replacement (as in substitute) *n.*: **succedaneum**. See *substitute*

(2) replacement (esp. of a doctor or clergyman) *n.*: **locum tenens**. See *temporary*

reply (as in responding to an anticipated objection to an argument before that objection has been made) *n.*: **prolepsis**. See *rebuttal*

(2) reply (charging accuser with a similar offense) *n.*: **tu quoque** [Latin]. See *answer*

(3) reply (clever . . . that one thinks of after the moment has passed) *n.*: **esprit d'escalier** [French]. See *retort*

repose (in . . . , as in not moving or temporarily inactive) *adj.*: **quiescent**. See *inactive*

repossession (as in a claim by a nation to lands that formerly belonged to it) *n.*: **irredentism**. See *reclamation*

repository (for bones or bodies of the dead) *n.*: **charnel**. ❖ [The Nazi commandant] was ordered to open the mass graves and exhume the bodies of the thousands of Jews who were murdered during the liquidation of the ghetto in Krakow in 1943 . . . and to burn the bodies in pits. Anybody who has seen photographs or films of these fiery, open-air **charnels** knows that the camera has probably never recorded a sight more obscene. (Leon Wieseltier, review of *Schindler's List*, *New Republic*, 1/24/1994, p. 42.)

(2) repository (esp. as shrine for displaying relics) *n.*: **reliquary**. See *receptacle*

reprehensible *adj.*: **opprobrious** (*n.*: **opprobrium**). See *contemptuous*

represent (as in describe, by painting or writing) *v.t.*: **limn**. See *describe*

representation (or image) *n.*: **simulacrum**. ❖ Disneyland was another bet-the-farm risk, and Disney threw himself obsessively into the park's design, which anticipated many of the best features of modern urban planning, and into the "imagineering" by which the **simulacrums** of exotic, even dangerous creatures, places, fantasies could be unthreateningly reproduced. (Richard Schickel, Time 100: "Ruler of the Magic Kingdom: Walt Disney," *Time*, 12/7/1998, p. 124.)

representations (spec. the study and analysis of . . . and signs as part of communication, as for example in language, gesture, clothing, and behavior) *n.*: **semiotics**. See *communication*

representative (or leader esp. for a political cause) *n.*: **fugleman**. See *leader*

(2) representative (rather than a literal representation, esp. with respect to objects of worship) *adj.*: **aniconic**. See *symbolic*

(3) representative (spec. a character in a book, play, or movie who appears to act as a mouthpiece for the opinions of the author) *n.*: **raisonneur** [French]. See *mouthpiece*

(4) representative (such as a diplomatic agent or an ambassador who is fully authorized to represent a government) *n.*: **plenipotentiary**. See *diplomat*

repress (as in put an end to) *v.t.*: **quietus** (as in "put the quietus to"). See *termination*

reprimand (as in criticism) *n.*: **animadversion** (*v.t.*: **animadvert**). See *criticism*

(2) reprimand (as in criticize) *v.t.*: **flay**. See *criticize*

(3) reprimand (being subject to . . . , esp. public) *n.*: **obloquy**. See *abuse*

(4) reprimand (sharply) *v.t.*: **keelhaul**. See *rebuke*

(5) reprimand *v.t.*: **objurgate**. See *criticize*

(6) reprimand (as in receiving a severe . . . or criticism) *idiom*: **(catching) unshirted hell.** See *criticism*

reprisal (as in retaliation, esp. by one state against another, which is provoked by acts that may be lawful but are discourteous or inappropriate) *n.*: **retortion**. See *retaliation*

(2) reprisal (esp. to recover lost territory or political standing) *n.*: **revanche** [French]. See *revenge*

reproach (as in criticism) *n.*: **animadversion** (*v.t.*: **animadvert**). See *criticism*

(2) reproach (being subject to . . . , esp. public) *n.*: **obloquy**. See *abuse*

(3) reproach *v.t.*: **flay**. See *criticize*

(4) reproach *v.t.*: **objurgate**. See *criticize*

reproval (being subject to . . . , esp. public) *n.*: **obloquy**. See *abuse*

reprove *v.t.*: **objurgate**. See *criticize*

reptile (of, relating to, or resembling . . . , as in lizard) *adj.*: **lacertilian**. See *lizard*

(2) reptile (of, relating to, or resembling a . . . , as in lizard) *adj.*: **saurian**. See *lizard*

reptiles (study of) *n.*: **herpetology**. ❖ John L. Behler, a naturalist and curator of **herpetology** at the Bronx Zoo who became an influential and international voice for saving endangered turtles, snakes and other reptiles, died on Jan. 31 at his home in Amawalk, N.Y. (Jeremy Pearce, obituary of John L. Behler, *New York Times*, 2/5/2006.)

repudiate *v.t.*: **abjure**. See *renounce*

repugnant *adj.*: **rebarbative**. See *repellent*

repulsive (ugly, terrifying, or . . . woman) *n.*: **gorgon**. See *ugly*

(2) repulsive *adj.*: **ugsome**. See *loathsome*

reputation (of an argument based on the . . . or say-so of another, but in an area that is outside his or her field of expertise; i.e., improperly trading on the reverence and respect of another) *adj.*, *adv.*: **ad verecundiam** (*n.*:

argumentum ad verecundiam) [Latin]. See *argument*

reputed (as in supposed) *adj.*: **putative**. See *supposed*

request (earnestly) *v.t.*: **adjure**. See *plead*

requiem *n.*: **threnody**. ❖ [In] *The Perfect Storm*, Sebastian Junger describes the ominous siren song made by the wind during an apocalyptic ocean deluge: "Force 10 is a shriek. Force 11 is a moan. Over Force 11 is something fishermen don't want to hear . . . a deep tonal vibration like a church organ." I went [to see the movie version] hoping to hear, at least once, that otherworldly church-organ **threnody**. (Owen Gleiberman, review of *The Perfect Storm, Entertainment Weekly*, 7/14/2000, p. 51.)

require (a person or group to go from one place to another, whether literally or figuratively) *v.t.*: **frogmarch**. See *march*

(2) require (to act, esp. by violent measures or threats) *v.t.*: **dragoon**. See *coerce*

required (element or condition) *n.*: **sine qua non** [Latin]. See *indispensable*

reschedule (to an earlier date) *v.t.*: **prepone**. [This newer word is not yet dictionary-recognized but is becoming more common. It is used especially in India and some surrounding countries.] ❖ "The Miss Universe show is held in May and Miss Nepal in August," Dabur Nepal said. "So we used to miss out on the premier pageant. We had been planning to **prepone** our show so that eventually we could participate in Miss Universe. We will do that from next year." (*Hindustan Times*, "Miss Nepal Contest Falls Prey to Chaos," 7/9/2006.)

rescind *v.t.*: **abjure**. See *renounce*

rescission (as in retraction) *n.*: **palinode**. See *retraction*

rescue (having the power or intent to . . . , as in bring about salvation) *adj.*: **salvific**. See *salvation*

resemblance (as in representation) *n.*: **simulacrum**. See *representation*

(2) resemblance (of sounds to each other) *n.*: **assonance**. See *similarity*

resentful (easily made . . . , as in offended) *adj.*: **umbrageous**. See *offended*

resentment (spec. a negative attitude toward society or authority arising from repressed hostility or feelings of inadequacy, combined with a sense of powerlessness to express or act on those feelings) *n.*: **ressentiment**. [French. The term is particularly associated with the philosophy of Friedrich Nietzsche (1844–1900).] ❖ Instead of directly endorsing extermination, mass sterilization and selective breeding, [the authors of *The Bell Curve*] propose a world in which people will be slotted into places that fit their [ability]. The effect of this reform will be, as they see it, to end **ressentiment** from and against those who seek more than their just deserts or aspire beyond their natural capacities. (Adolph Reed Jr., review of *The Bell Curve: Intelligence and Class Structure in American Life*, by Richard J. Herrnstein and Charles Murray, *Nation*, 11/28/1994.)

(2) resentment (as in bitterness) *n.*: **bile**. See *bitterness*

reserved (being . . . , as in chilliness in relations between people) *n.*: **froideur** [French]. See *chilliness*

(2) reserved (as in shy and/or sullen and/or socially withdrawn or inexperienced) *adj.*: **farouche** [French]. See *shy*

residence (as in very large house) *n.*: **manse**. See *mansion*

resident (of a town) *n.*: **burgher**. ❖ [The Disney-designed town of Celebration, Florida] was full of people who so believed in human interaction that they'd bought closely clustered homes with porches. Still, I wasn't sure whether the **burghers** of Celebration really understood what a national 3-on-3 basketball championship would deliver [to their town]. (Alexander Wolff, *Big Game, Small World*, Warner Books [2002], p. 69.)

resign (from an office or position) *v.i.*: **demit** (as in demit office). ❖ Speaker Occah Seapaul last week rejected a no-confidence motion brought against her by the government. . . . In response to this unprecedented turn of events the government advanced a legislative proposal to change the country's constitution and require the speaker to **demit** office. (Elijah Charles, "Trinidad Military on Coup Alert: Security Has Been Stepped Up," *Weekly Journal*, 7/27/1995.)

resistance (as in unwillingness) *n.*: **nolition**. See *unwillingness*

resistant (to yield or be swayed) *adj.*: **renitent**. ❖ It is not that [poet Seamus Heaney] has lost his "guttural muse." He still, like a farmboy who stoops at the plough to grub out some shiny lump of quartz, picks up those **renitent** words that seem most resilient to language. (Rachel Campbell-Johnston, "Danger: High Voltage Poetry," *Times* [London], 4/4/2001.)

resolute *adj.*: **doughty**. See *brave*

resolve *n.*: **hardihood**. See *courage*

resonant (as in full and rich sound or voice) *adj.*: **orotund**. See *sonorous*

resounding (as in reverberating) *adj.*: **reboant**. See *reverberating*

resourceful (person) *n.*: **debrouillard** (or **débrouillard**) [French]. ❖ Adolphe Mulinowa . . . hustles to a roadside with a few plastic bottles of pink gasoline, which he hawks alongside dozens of other street vendors. . . . In a town of **debrouillards**, Mulinowa has learned to exploit tiny advantages. He has figured out that, because Goma has dozens of gasoline vendors, his chances are better two miles away at the Rwanda-Congo border. There, drivers have to slow down and are more likely to notice him. (Davan Maharaj, "When the Push for Survival Is a Full-Time Job; What Is It Like to Live on Less Than a Dollar a Day? Hundreds of Millions in Sub-Saharan Africa Know," *Los Angeles Times*, 7/11/2004.)

resourcefulness (or subtlety, esp. in political or business dealings) *n.*: **Italian hands** [often used in the phrase "fine Italian hands"]. See *subtlety*

respect (not necessarily sincere or unforced) *n.*: **obeisance**. See *homage*

(2) respect (personal . . . , as in honor) *n.*: **izzat** [Hindi]. See *honor*

(3) respect (with . . . to) *prep.*: **anent**. See *regarding*

(4) respect (paying . . . , lit. kissing of the hand) *n.*: **baisemain** [French]. See *kissing*

respectful (to be . . . in a servile way) *v.i.*: **genuflect**. See *kneel*

respectfully (to) *prep.*: **pace**. [This Latin word, meaning "peace" and pronounced pay-see, is used to express polite or ironically polite disagreement. In the example, Hitchens is referring to Dan Brown's novel *The Da Vinci Code*, which reaches a conclusion other than Hitchens's.] ❖ Jesus . . . [who] apparently undertook to return to earth very soon and who (**pace** the absurd Dan Brown) left no known descendants. (Christopher Hitchens, *God Is Not Great*, Twelve Books/Hachette [2007], p. 130.)

resplendent (as in shining brightly) *adj.*: **effulgent**. See *bright*

(2) resplendent (as in shining brightly) *adj.*: **fulgurant**. See *bright*

(3) resplendent (as in shining brightly) *adj.*: **refulgent**. See *bright*

response (as in . . . to an anticipated objection to an argument before that objection has been made) *n.*: **prolepsis**. See *rebuttal*

(2) response (charging accuser with a similar offense) *n.*: **tu quoque** [Latin]. See *answer*

(3) response (clever . . . that one thinks of after the moment has passed) *n.*: **esprit d'escalier** [French]. See *retort*

rest (as in pause) *n.*: **caesura**. See *pause*

restart (as in renewal or restoration of something after decay, lapse of time, or dilapidation) *n.*: **instauration**. See *restoration*

resting (as in not moving or temporarily inactive) *adj.*: **quiescent**. See *inactive*

restitution (for damage or loss) *n.*: **quittance**. See *recompense*

restlessness (as part of depressed state) *n.*: **dysphoria**. See *depression*

(2) restlessness *n.* **inquietude**. See *anxiety*

restoration (or renewal of something after decay, lapse of time, or dilapidation) *n.*: **instauration**. ❖ The anti-colonial struggles in the Third World were emancipatory too, but have not resulted in the **instauration** of the liberal order in Asia, Africa or the Caribbean. (G. M.

Tamas, "A Disquisition on Civil Society," *Social Research*, 6/1/1994.)

restorative (esp. with respect to effect of certain drugs or medications) *adj.*: **analeptic**. ❖ For since the turn of the century, . . . Irn-Bru has peddled a successful myth that the drink is in fact "a refreshing tonic beverage." . . . Of course, with the introduction of the all-new alcoholic . . . Irn-Bru into the equation, [who knows] whether the **analeptic** properties of the orange stuff are derived from the 32 secret ingredients in the pop or the proof alcohol? (*Herald* [Glasgow], "Pop Goes the Elixir," 12/30/1996.)

(2) restorative (as in having the power to cure or heal) *adj.*: **sanative**. See *healthful*

(3) restorative (as in something that invigorates) *adj., n.*: **roborant**. See *invigorating*

(4) restorative (used often of a medicinal treatment) *adj.*: **balsamic**. See *soothing*

restore (to an original state or condition) *v.t.*: **repristinate**. ❖ As the presidential team meets in Waco to **repristinate** the face of capitalism, signs of difficulty at a cultural level are everywhere. The *Wall Street Journal* informs us that defense attorneys are having a difficult time finding jurors who are unaffected by the desire to damage any defendant with a corporate background. [Recently over 50 percent of prospective jurors agreed with] the statement, "Corporate executives will lie to increase their profits." (William F. Buckley, Jr, "On the Right," *National Review*, 9/16/2002.)

restored (as in revived or come back to life) *adj.*: **redivivus**. See *revived*

restrain (a person by holding down his arms) *v.t.*: **pinion**. See *immobilize*

restrained (as in not indulgent) *adj.*: **abstemious**. ❖ The Jones[es] work at acquiring fine wines but are relatively **abstemious** in their own consumption. "Today, we are concentrating on acquiring fine wines in the birth years of our children," Dennis said. (Joan Foster Dames, "Wine Collectors—Know How to Put a Little Spirit into Their Lives," *St. Louis Post-Dispatch*, 7/11/1993.)

restraint (as in marked by simplicity, frugality, self-discipline, and/or . . .) *adj.*: **Lacedaemonian**. See *spartan*

(2) restraint (as in self-restraint) *n.*: **continence**. See *self-restraint*

restrict (a person's movement by holding down his arms) *v.t.*: **pinion**. See *immobilize*

(2) restrict (as in confine) *v.t.*: **immure**. See *confine*

(3) restrict (as in overly limit or . . . , as to amount or share) *v.t.* **scant**. See *stint*

result *v.i.*: **eventuate**. ❖ That May's lover happens to be a man half her age and the some-time-boyfriend of her grown daughter Paula (Cathryn Bradshaw) means Michell's film is equally an exploration of taboo and the consequences that **eventuate** when a mother, the sort who reliably takes care of everyone else, abruptly, selfishly, takes something for herself, something forbidden. (Deborah Hornblow, review of *The Mother*, *Hartford Courant*, 6/20/2004.)

(2) result (as in outgrowth) *n.*: **excrescence**. See *outgrowth*

(3) result (secondary . . . , as in aftereffect) *n.*: **sequela** (*pl.* **sequelae**). See *aftereffect*

resurrected (as in revived or come back to life) *adj.*: **redivivus**. See *revived*

resurrection (as in rebirth) *n.*: **palingenesis**. See *rebirth*

retaliation (esp. by one state against another, which is provoked by acts that may be lawful but are discourteous or inappropriate) *n.*: **retortion**. ❖ [During the Civil War.] U.S. Secretary of State Seward instructed the U.S. ambassador to London that should Great Britain recognize the Confederacy, he was to communicate to the British government "promptly and without reserve that all negotiations for treaties of whatever kind between the two governments will be discontinued." [This was an] act of **retortion**, aimed at adversely affecting British interests. (Guido Acquaviva, "Subjects of International Law: A Power-Based Analysis," *Vanderbilt Journal of Transnational Law*, 3/1/2005.)

retaliation (esp. to recover lost territory or political standing) *n.*: **revanche** [French]. See *revenge*

(2) retaliation (in kind) *n.*: **lex talionis** [Latin]. See *eye for an eye*

(3) retaliation (of or relating to . . . in kind) *n.*: **talionic**. See *revenge*

retaliatory (one who is . . .) *n.*: **tricoteuse**. See *knitter*. [See the note at "knitter" for why this word can be synonymous with retaliatory.]

retarded (psychiatric diagnosis for one who is . . .) *adj.*: **oligophrenic**. ❖ Children [in Russia] who show no signs of illness at birth but fall behind in school are sent off for further tests by child psychiatrists. They risk being found to be feebleminded, or **oligophrenic**—a catchall term for any form of mental problem, borrowed from 18th century French usage. . . . Any of these primitive diagnoses condemns the child to life in a home. (Vanora Bennett, "Russia's Forgotten Children; The Mentally Ill—and the Misdiagnosed—Are Kept in Bleak State Homes," *Los Angeles Times*, 2/22/1997.)

retch (making an effort to . . .) *v.i.*: **keck**. See *vomit*

retort (clever . . . that one thinks of after the moment has passed) *n.*: **esprit d'escalier** [French; roughly the "wit of the staircase," as in the thought that comes to mind on the staircase as one is leaving]. ❖ Proselytizing for Jehovah's Witnesses during last Sunday's Vikings game wasn't the smoothest call Prince has ever made. [He knocked on the door of a Jewish woman named Rochelle:] "It was so bizarre, you would have just laughed," she said. The perfect **esprit d'escalier** came to Rochelle after Prince left: "If I showed up at Paisley [Park], would you let me in your front door to talk about Judaism?" (Cheryl Johnson, "I-Witness News: Visit from Prince; Proselytizing Pop Star Knocks on Previously Committed Door," *Minneapolis Star Tribune*, 10/12/2003.)

(2) retort (charging accuser with a similar offense) *n.*: **tu quoque** [Latin]. See *answer*

retract *v.t.*: **abjure**. See *disavow*

retraction *n.*: **palinode**. ❖ According to this story, told by Plato in the Phaedrus, the poet wrote some verses insulting to Helen, for which she blinded him; to regain his sight, he composed an apologetic **palinode**. (Adam Kirsch, "All Mere Complexities," *New Republic*, 5/18/1998.)

retreat (desperate . . .) *n.*: **Dunkirk** [after city in northern France from whose beaches 330,000 Allied troops were evacuated in the face of enemy fire in May–June 1940]. ❖ It has become an unwritten law of TV journalism that CBS can't really do anything [right] in the morning. . . . Everything seems to fail. The new strategy is to . . . let local stations take over what they'd like to take over. . . . What we are seeing is really a disguised retreat. This is CBS News' **Dunkirk**. New owner Westinghouse has come in, surveyed the situation and said, "Hit the beaches, men." (Marvin Kitman, "Could *Capt. Kangaroo* Rescue CBS?" *Newsday*, 4/15/1996.)

(2) retreat (as in safe haven) *n.*: **querencia**. See *safe haven*

retribution (of or relating to . . . in kind) *n.*: **talionic**. See *revenge*

(2) retribution (in kind) *n.*: **lex talionis** [Latin]. See *eye for an eye*

return (property or territory) *v.i.*: **retrocede**. ❖ All that Americans knew in 1802 were rumors that Napoleon had induced Spain to **retrocede** Louisiana to France, including, as many thought, both East and West Florida. For Americans, and especially for President Jefferson, nothing could have been more alarming. (Gordon Wood, "Sale of the Century," *New Republic*, 5/26/2003.)

(2) return (as in renewal or restoration of something after decay, lapse of time, or dilapidation) *n.*: **instauration**. See *restoration*

(3) return (of something after a period of dormancy or inactivity) *n.*: **recrudescence** (*v.i.*: **recrudesce**). See *reappearance*

(4) return (to an original state or condition) *v.t.*: **repristinate**. See *restore*

returns (one who . . . after lengthy absence or

death) *n*.: **revenant**. ❖ [The clothing line] also underscored Versace's debt to the arrowy, tidy chic of André Courrèges, another '60s **revenant**. (Martha Duffy, "Classic Acts in the Established Bastions of High Fashion," *Time International*, 10/9/1995, p. 54.)

reused (as in warmed-over food or old material) *n*., *adj*.: **rechauffé** [French]. See *warmed-over*

reveal (as in confide, one's thoughts or feelings) *v.t.*, *v.i.*: **unbosom**. See *confide*

(2) reveal *v.t.*: **disinter**. See *disclose*

revel (as in have a noisy good time) *v.i.*: **roister** (*n*.: **roisterer**). ❖ For most of this century, New York has not been much of a beer town. At heart, it's a Champagne and martini kind of place. Beer is O.K. for Milwaukee or Chicago, but in New York what **roisterer** out for a night on the town would think of topping off dinner and a Broadway show with a pitcher of suds? Impossible. While taking Manhattan, I'll take a manhattan. (William Grimes, "The News of Brews: The Joints Are Hopping," *New York Times*, 9/1/1995.)

(2) revel (in, or boast, esp. about the accomplishments of a relative) *v.t.*, *n*.: **kvell** [Yiddish]. See *boast*

(3) revel (with boisterous public demonstrations) *v.i.*: **maffick** [British]. See *celebrate*

revelation (as in creative inspiration) *n*.: **afflatus**. See *inspiration*

(2) revelation (sudden . . .) *n*.: **epiphany**. See *realization*

reveler (female . . .) *n*.: **bacchante** (male . . . : **bacchant**) [derives from Bacchus, the Roman god of wine]. ❖ [*Aphrodite: A Memoir of the Senses*, by Isabel Allende, is] an unabashedly whimsical hodgepodge of memories [and lore. Allende] is by turns the sighing romantic ("The only true aphrodisiac is love") [and] the playful **bacchante** ("When you plan your orgy, you must count on it lasting all night, so a buffet isn't a good idea; after a few hours everything goes limp"). (Margaria Fichtner, "*Aphrodite* Seduces the Senses with its Phrasing, Imagery," *Miami Herald*, 3/22/1998.)

revelry (riotous . . .) *n*., *adj*.: **bacchanal**. ❖ The Oakland Athletics had decided against staging the riotous **bacchanal** that these days almost always accompanies world titles, sensing, quite rightly, that the sight of players pouring champagne over each other would have been inappropriate in the aftermath of the earthquake. (Steve Wulf, "Swept Away," *Sports Illustrated*, 11/6/1989, p. 24.)

revenge (esp. to recover lost territory or political standing) *n*.: **revanche** [French]. ❖ [Russian President Boris] Yeltsin had to maintain democratic illusions to keep his power, which he did by nurturing the Zyuganov-led "intransigent" opposition to scare Russians with the threat of a Red **revanche**. (Yuri Zarakhovich, "Forward into the Past: Russia Keeps Trading in One Group of Oppressors for Another," *Time* International, 10/12/1998, p. 41.)

(2) revenge (as in retaliation, esp. by one state against another, which is provoked by acts that may be lawful but are discourteous or inappropriate) *n*.: **retortion**. See *retaliation*

(3) revenge (of or relating to . . . in kind) *n*.: **talionic**. [See also *lex talionis* under *eye for an eye*.] ❖ The English system of wergild, for example, served as a framework for balancing scores. It was a way of totaling what price one should pay to be able to keep an eye, finger, or whatever body part was in question. Thus, the **talionic** sense of bodily equivalence remained fundamental for validating the means used for mitigating the wrongs done and rendering a sense of satisfaction to all parties involved. (Robert Heineman, review of *Eye for an Eye*, by William Ian Miller, *Perspectives on Political Science*, 3/22/2006.)

(4) revenge (one who is intent on . . .) *n*.: **tricoteuse**. See *knitter*. [See the note at "knitter" for why this word can be synonymous with revenge.]

reverberating *adj*.: **reboant**. ❖ The **reboant** thump of the kettledrum was matched with the nimble tabla-drum rhythms of Mr. Hussain; the airy bansuri flute melodies of Hariprasad Chaurasia were echoed by the orchestra's string section. (Neil Strauss, "Lush Odes to the Art of Two Film Makers," *New York Times*, 9/19/2006.)

revere (often in a servile manner) *v.i.*: **genuflect**. See *kneel*

reverence (not necessarily sincere or unforced) *n.*: **obeisance**. See *homage*

reversal (of words or phrases) *n.*: **chiasmus** (pronounced kī'azmus). ❖ It's not the men in my life, it's the life in my men.—Mae West. . . . A scout troop consists of twelve little kids dressed like schmucks following a big schmuck dressed like a kid.—Jack Benny. . . . This Week's Contest is to create an original **chiasmus**. We got this idea from a delightful new book edited by Mardy Grothe: *Never Let a Fool Kiss You or a Kiss Fool You*. (*Washington Post*, "The Style Invitational; Reverse Psychology," 4/25/1999.)

(2) reversal (a . . . regarding one's beliefs, causes, or policies) *n.*: **tergiversation** (*v.i.*: **tergiversate**). See *change of mind*

(3) reversal (as in abandonment, of one's religion, principles, or causes) *n.*: **apostasy** See *abandonment*

(4) reversal (esp. regarding one's beliefs, causes, or policies) *n.*: **bouleversement** [French]. See *change of mind*

(5) reversal (of policy or position) *n.*: **volte-face** [French]. See *about-face*

(6) reversal (sudden . . . of events, often in a literary work) *n.*: **peripeteia**. See *turnaround*

reverse (as in recoil) *v.i.*: **resile**. See *recoil*

(2) reverse (as in turn inside out) *v.t.*: **evaginate**. See *inside out*

review (a quick, cursory . . .) *n.* **Cook's tour**. See *scan*

(2) review (as in summarize) *v.t.*: **précis** [French]. See *summary*

(3) review (thorough . . . of existing knowledge on a subject) *phr.*: **état present** [French]. See *summary*

(4) review *v.t.*: **assay**. See *evaluate*

reviewer (as in investigator or examiner) *n.*: **scrutator**. See *examiner*

(2) reviewer (who is inferior or incompetent) *n.*: **criticaster**. See *critic*

(3) reviewer (who is given to negative and sometimes unjust criticism) *n.*: **Zoilus**. See *criticism*

revise (a book or piece of writing in a prudish manner) *v.t.*: **bowdlerize**. See *edit*

(2) revise (text or language by removing errors or flaws) *v.t.*: **blue-pencil**. See *edit*

(3) revise (text or language by removing errors or flaws) *v.t.*: **emend**. See *edit*

revision (esp. a scholarly critical . . .) *n.* **recension**. [This word refers specifically to the critical revision of a text, such as an ancient manuscript, in an effort to establish a definitive text. It is also used more generally to refer to any revision or updating or reinterpretation of an earlier work of literature, art, or music, as in the example here.] ❖ Just as every great work should be translated anew every generation (for translations date, if masterpieces never do), the lives of great writers should be retold, not only because new material becomes accessible, but because perspectives are more likely to be corrected, atmospheres clarified. Thus I recommend to English-speaking readers this industrious **recension** of the story of Proust and of his vast and forever indeterminate work. (Ronald Hayman, "Aspect of the Novelist," *Washington Post*, 12/30/1999.)

(2) revision (as in correction, esp. in printed material) *n.*: **corrigendum**. See *correction*

revitalization (as in updating, of an organization to meet contemporary conditions, esp. as proposed by Pope John XXIII with respect to the Catholic church after Vatican II) *n.*: **aggiornamento** [Italian]. See *updating*

revitalizer (as in something that invigorates) *adj., n.*: **roborant**. See *invigorating*

revival (as in rebirth) *n.*: **palingenesis**. See *rebirth*

revive *v.t.*: **refocillate**. ❖ [The TV show] *The National Lottery—In It to Win It*, which returned to BBC1 on Saturday night, [is unoriginal]. The [station's] plan was to **refocillate** its load of old balls by running a full-length quiz show ahead of the main draw, but the result will surely increase public apathy . . . because the lazy and derivative format smacks of desperation, not creativity. (Victor Lewis-Smith, "A Load of Old Balls and Dale," *Evening Standard* [London], 4/28/2003.)

(2) revival (as in renewal or restoration of something after decay, lapse of time, or dilapidation) *n.*: **instauration**. See *restoration*.

revive (as in return to an original state or condition) *v.t.*: **repristinate**. See *restore*

revived (spec. come back to life) *adj.*: **redivivus**. [This is a postpositive adjective, meaning that it follows the word being modified ("food aplenty," "bargains galore"). It is typically used figuratively to refer to a person who has made a comeback after being counted out or who has exhibited traits reminiscent of some other person, as in the example given. It can also be applied to places or things.] ❖ Midnight of the evening before Colonel North testifies. . . . I am perplexed and frightened. I am perplexed because I can't guess what course he will take in his testifying. . . . Will he brazen everything out, tell nothing and play Gordon Liddy **redivivus**? Will he show contrition and make an honest reporting of the whole affair? (James Michener, "Through Michener's Eyes," *Washington Post*, 7/10/1987.)

revocation (a . . . regarding one's beliefs, causes, or policies) *n.*: **tergiversation** (*v.i.*: **tergiversate**). See *change of mind*

(2) revocation (as in abandonment, of one's religion, principles, or causes) *n.*: **apostasy**. See *abandonment*

(3) revocation (esp. regarding one's beliefs, causes, or policies) *n.*: **bouleversement** [French]. See *change of mind*

revolt (against existing social or artistic conventions) *n.*: **titanism** (often cap.). ❖ The 60's attempted a return to nature that ended in disaster. The gentle nude bathing and playful sliding in the mud at Woodstock were a short-lived . . . dream. My generation, inspired by the Dionysian **titanism** of rock, attempted something more radical than anything since the French Revolution. We asked: why should I obey this law? And: why shouldn't I act on every sexual impulse? The result was a descent into barbarism. (Camille Paglia, "Ninnies, Pedants, Tyrants and Other Academics," *New York Times*, 5/5/1991.)

(2) revolt (peasant's . . .) *n.*: **jacquerie**. ❖ Do 1st Amendment rights apply to [people who work out of their homes, such as] therapists and masseurs? . . . Why should anyone who works at home pay city business tax, anyway? [This is] the war against the Los Angeles home-business tax. . . . The no home-business-tax **jacquerie** followed Los Angeles' well-meant attempt last year to legalize the increasing number of "nonintrusive" home businesses. (*Los Angeles Times*, "How a 1st Amendment Cause Could Become a Tax Dodge," 5/17/1998.)

revolutionary (a political . . . , who often believes in violence to attain an end) *n.*: **sans-culotte**. See *extremist*

(2) revolutionary (as in rebel) *n.*: **frondeur** [French]. See *rebel*

(3) revolutionary (spec. one who hates or mistrusts authority) *n.*: **misarchist**. See *rebel*

revolving (as in whirling) *adj.*: **vortical**. See *whirling*

(2) revolving (or spiraling motion, often an ocean current) *n.*: **gyre**. See *spiraling*

reward *n.*: **guerdon**. ❖ [Everyone] will be stirred by the sheer gotta-dance, gotta-sing energy of Telson's music [in] *The Gospel at Colonus* and the performances it receives from a stage brimming over with inspired musicians. Virtually everyone in the cast (the largest to appear on a Broadway stage in many years) merits his or her own **guerdon** of praise. (Peter Biskind, "The Manchurian Candidate," *Nation*, 5/14/1988.)

(2) reward (as in give a prize to) *v.t.*: **premiate**. See *award*

rewarmed (as in warmed-over food or old material) *n., adj.*: **rechauffé** [French]. See *warmed-over*

reworked (as in warmed-over old material) *n., adj.*: **rechauffé** [French]. See *warmed-over*

reworking (esp. a scholarly critical . . . , as in revision) *n.* **recension**. See *revision*

rhetorical (device in which one makes only passing mention of something in order to emphasize rhetorically the significance of what is being omitted; often preceded by the phrase "not to mention") *n*.: **paraleipsis**. See *figure of speech*

(2) rhetorical (device in which one references an issue by saying that one will not discuss it; e.g., "I'm not even going to get into the character issue.") *n*.: **apophasis**. See *figure of speech*

rhyme (as in similarity of sounds to each other) *n*.: **assonance**. See *similarity*

rib (playfully) *v.t., v.i., n*.: **chaff**. See *teasing*

rich (and/or prominent person) *n*.: **nabob**. See *bigwig*

(2) rich (government by the . . .) *n*.: **plutocracy**. See *government*

(3) rich (government by the . . . , i.e., in proportion to wealth or property ownership) *n*.: **timocracy**. See *government*

(4) rich (sound or voice) *adj*.: **orotund**. See *sonorous*

(5) rich (study of or focus on the . . . , esp. in artistic works) *n*.: **plutography**. See *wealth*

riches (devotion to the pursuit of . . .) *n*.: **mammonism**. See *wealth*

(2) riches (source of great . . .) *n*.: **Golconda**. See *wealth*

(3) riches *n*.: **pelf**. See *wealth*

rid (get . . . of) *v.t*.: **extirpate**. See *abolish*

(2) rid (oneself of, as in shed, a skin or covering) *v.t., v.i*.: **exuviate**. See *shed*

ridicule (as in good-natured teasing) *n*.: **raillery**. See *teasing*

(2) ridicule (esp. through the use of satire) *v.t*.: **pasquinade**. See *satirize*

(3) ridicule (to . . .) *idiom*: **cock a snook**. See *thumb one's nose*

(4) ridicule (which is clever or polite) *n*.: **asteism**. See *insult*

ridiculous (as in absurd or preposterous) *adj*.: **fatuous** See *foolish*

(2) ridiculous (as in laughable) *adj*.: **gelastic**. See *laughable*

(3) ridiculous (as in laughable) *adj*.: **risible**. See *laughable*

ridiculousness (as in nonsense) *n*.: **codswallop** [British]. See *nonsense*

(2) ridiculousness *n*.: **folderol** (or **falderal**). See *nonsense*

(3) ridiculousness *n*.: **piffle**. See *nonsense*

(4) ridiculousness *n*.: **trumpery**. See *nonsense*

riding (of or relating to horseback . . .) *adj*.: **equitational**. See *horseback riding*

riffraff (as in the common people) *n*.: **hoi polloi**. See *commoners*

(2) riffraff *n*.: **canaille**. See *masses*

right (as in entitlement, spec. one presumed arrogantly or asserted involuntarily against others) *n*.: **droit du seigneur** [French]. See *entitlement*

(2) right (necessarily . . .) *adj*.: **apodictic**. See *incontrovertible*

(3) right (on the . . . side or right-handed) *adj*.: **dextral**. See *right-handed*

right way (do things the . . . , as in "by the book") *idiom*: **according to Hoyle**. See *by the book*

right-angled *adj*.: **orthogonal**. ❖ In a Guastavino tile ceiling, the sum of a thousand right angles is a curve worthy of nature. . . . And what is astonishing about these great curving forms—the largest being the 135-foot-diameter dome of the Cathedral Church of St. John the Divine—is that they are made up of relentlessly **orthogonal** building blocks: flat clay tiles, typically 6 inches by 12 inches. (David Dunlap, "Sensuous Curves Ascend Around Hard-Edged City," *New York Times*, 3/3/2000.)

right-handed *adj*.: **dextral**. ❖ The researchers reckon that a child with two right-handed parents has a 91% probability of being right-handed . . . [but] . . . even if identical twins have parents who are both **dextral**, factors such as their position in the womb may result in the twins not preferring the same hands. (*Economist*, "Sinister Evolution: Population Genetics," 8/26/1995, p. 69.)

right-thinking *adj*.: **bien pensant**. [This French term, sometimes hyphenated, and literally meaning "well-thinking," has two very different usages. In the complimentary sense, it simply means right-minded or correct. In the derogatory sense (which is more common), it is used ironically, facetiously, or sarcastically to mean comformist or doctrinaire or politically correct, often self-righteously. Thus, though closer in definition to conservatism, when used in this latter sense, it is typically wielded by conservatives to criticize liberals. An example of each usage is presented here.] ❖ [In the French elections for president, the ability of seventy-three-year-old Jean-Marie Le Pen] to edge into the two-man run-off against incumbent Jacques Chirac . . . rightly made headlines. . . . Le Pen's good fortune provoked continental outrage. **Bien-pensant** Europeans vowed to turn back this candidate of the far-right fringe who—as almost every story on him points out—once called the Holocaust a "detail of history." (*National Review*, "Le Pen: Not So Mighty," 2/20/2002.) ❖ [With regard to the accusation of rape against three white Duke University lacrosse players by an African American woman, a *New York*] *Times* alumnus recently e-mailed me, "You couldn't invent a story so precisely tuned to the outrage frequency of the modern, metropolitan, **bien-pensant** journalist." . . . But real facts are stubborn things. And today, the preponderance of facts indicate that [the woman's accusation was false. Yet at the epicenter of **bien-pensant** journalism, the *New York Times*, reporters and editors . . . are declining to expose it. (Kurt Anderson, "Rape, Justice, and the *Times*," *New York*, 10/16/2006.)

right-to-left (moving from . . .) *adj.*: **dextrosinistral**. [The opposite word, for moving from left to right, is "sinistrodextral."] ❖ Dear Mr. Buckley: I am concerned about the subliminal campaign waged by left-leaning authorities. [For example:] A trained waiter/waitress serves from the left, takes from the right. . . . [This note] starts each line with reference to the left margin. We should list all such subliminal schemes so that our unconscious is not trained to accept that left is right. . . . [Buckley's answer:] Yes, it is certainly a swindle you've got your eyes on. Up [with] **dextrosinistral** reform! (William F. Buckley, Notes & Asides, *National Review*, 3/10/2003.)

right-wing (far . . . in beliefs and often stuffy, pompous, and/or elderly) *adj.*, *n.*: **Colonel Blimp**. See *conservative*

rigid (as in hardened) *adj.*: **sclerotic**. See *hardened*

(2) rigid (as in narrow-minded) *adj.*: **hidebound**. See *narrow-minded*

(3) rigid *adj.*: **monastic**. See *strict*

rigidity (condition characterized by muscular . . .) *n.*: **catalepsy**. ❖ Cannon proceeds to the next stage, "arm **catalepsy**." Your arm will become like a rod of steel. She lifts Valentyne's arm until it's thrust out at a right angle directly in front of her, tugs on the wrist to lock the elbow straight, then lets go. Valentyne's arm remains rigid. (Lily Nguyen, "Hypnosis," *Toronto Star*, 5/21/2000.)

(2) rigidity (esp. with respect to moral or ethical principles or practices) *n.*: **rigorism**. ❖ [T]o many critics, Pope John Paul's pro-life gospel comes with a few worms in the apple, a moral **rigorism** that seemingly subordinates human life to rigid rules: no artificial contraception regardless of danger to women's health, or evidence that abortions flourish when birth control is lacking, or life-threatening population explosions; no abortion, no matter how severe the medical urgency. (Edward Cuddy, "Searching for a Credible Pro-Life Philosophy," *Buffalo News*, 4/18/1999.)

rile up (as in agitate) *v.t.*: **commove**. See *agitate*

rim (as in edge) *n.*: **selvage**. See *edge*

ring (as in surround) *v.t.*: **girdle**. See *surround*

ringing (in one's ears) *n.*: **tinnitus**. ❖ Until six years ago, Dr. Stephen Nagler, 51, was a busy breast- and colon-cancer surgeon in Atlanta. But then he suddenly began suffering from **tinnitus**, which most people describe as a ringing in the ears. (Judy Foreman, "Learning to Tune Out Tinnitus," *Minneapolis Star Tribune*, 1/9/2000.)

(2) ringing (of bells) *n.*: **tintinnabulation**. ❖ Once again, love will redeem the beast, and Beauty's dancing clocks and singing teacups will blend marvelously with the **tintinnabulation** of bells this holiday season. (Mark Goodman, Picks & Pans: Screen, *People*, 11/18/1991, p. 21.)

ring-shaped *adj.*: **annular**. ❖ In an **annular** eclipse, the Moon's conical umbra, or shadow, doesn't quite reach the Earth—hence we have a broad, bright ring of light rather than a total eclipse, which is characterized by a darkened sky and a dramatic corona. (Cathy Johnson, "Celestial Occurrences," *Country Living*, 9/1/1994, p. 74.)

riot (or uprising) *n.*: **émeute** [French.] ❖ The revolt of June 1832, one of many between the two revolutions of 1830 and 1848, was by far the bloodiest. . . . Two decades later, in his *Misérables*, Hugo will distinguish this **émeute** from a full-fledged revolution by the very fact that it failed. (Isabelle Naginski, "Accidental Families," *Romanic Review*, 5/1/2005.)

(2) riot (as in commotion) *n.*: **bobbery**. See *commotion*

(3) riot (as in commotion) *n.*: **kerfuffle**. See *commotion*

(4) riot *n.*: **émeute** [French]. See *rebellion*

riotous (as in unruly) *adj.*: **indocile**. See *unruly*

(2) riotous (celebration) *n., adj.*: **bacchanal**. See *revelry*

rip (apart) *v.t.*: (past tense: **riven** or **rived**). See *tear*

RIP *abbreviation*: **requiescat in pace**. [Latin. Most people are aware that RIP is an abbreviation for "rest in peace." Less well known is the original Latin, which is itself not infrequently used in full, as in the example given.] ❖ In 1960, my parents surprised us with an artificial Christmas tree. . . . [I]n that pre-mod, pre-psychedelic interlude, with the "British invasion" building up steam in Hamburg night clubs (**requiescat in pace**, George and John!), the silver phantom trees whose needles shivered deliciously as they were fitted into their slots were the . . . triumphant flourish of a nation marching to the tune of Progress at all Costs. (*Washington Post*, "In 1960 My Parents Surprised Us," 12/16/2001.)

ripping (adapted for . . . apart flesh) *adj.*: **carnassial** (*n.*: a tooth so adapted). See *tooth*

rise (above) *v.t.*: **bestride**. See *dominate*

rising *adj.*: **assurgent**. ❖ At the time of the Russian revolution, a generation of artists, **assurgent** with hope for the future, liberated their imaginations to turn out a decade's worth of works that were both: a) masterpieces, and b) works in support of the state. It couldn't last; it didn't. Stalin and his apparatchiks took over. (Stephen Hunter, "Films Under Fire, Politicians Talk of a Perfect Past That Never Was," *Baltimore Sun*, 6/18/1995.)

(2) rising (esp. too high for safety) *adj.*: **Icarian**. See *soaring*

risky (and irresponsible) *adj.*: **harum-scarum**. See *reckless*

(2) risky (as in perilous) *adj.*: **parlous**. See *perilous*

(3) risky (as in reckless) *adj.*: **temerarious**. See *reckless*

(4) risky (journey or passage, with dangers on both sides) *idiom*: **between Scylla and Charybdis**. See *predicament*

risqué (slightly . . . or indecent) *adj.*: **ostrobogulous**. See *indecent*

(2) risqué *adj.*: **scabrous**. See *scandalous*

rite (funeral . . .) *n.*: **obsequy** (often pl.: **obsequies**). See *funeral*

ritual (which is pretentious) *n.*: **mummery**. See *ceremony*

ritzy *adj.*: **nobby** [British]. See *elegant*

rivalry (marked by a spirit of . . .) *adj.*: **emulous**. See *competitive*

river (of, relating to, or inhabiting) *adj.*: **fluvial**. ❖ "We have high standards for who we consider to be qualified to mess around with people's bodies in medicine," says Dave Montgomery, a **fluvial** geomorphologist at the University of Washington, "but we haven't hit that state of valuing rivers enough to require similar expertise." (Kathleen Wong, "Bringing Back the Logjams," *U.S. News & World Report*, 9/6/1999.)

(2) river (of, relating to, or resembling) *adj.*: **riverine**. ❖ The Rockefellers lived three miles east of town in an area of soft, bucolic meadows and **riverine** groves. (Ron Chernow, *Titan*, Random House [1998], p. 31.)

(3) river (of, relating to, or living in a moving water system, such as a stream or . . .) *adj.*: **lotic**. See *water*

river bank (of or relating to a . . .) *adj.*: **riparian**. See *water bank*

roam (about, esp. on foot) *v.t., v.i.*: **perambulate**. ❖ Over in the land of saints and scholars this is a notable day. June 16. Bloomsday. The occasion on which, in 1904, Leopold Bloom and Stephen Dedalus **perambulated** around Dublin in James Joyce's Ulysses, expeditions chronicled so exactly that Joyce believed Dublin, if ever razed by catastrophe, could have been reconstructed from his novel. (*Toronto Star*, "Tough Areas Get a Chance to Shine," 6/16/1998.)

(2) roam (about, esp. on foot) *v.t., v.i.*: **peregrinate**. ❖ The petty thieveries and lies of later childhood metastasized into a lunatic binge, in which our 17-year-old hero **peregrinated** around England on someone else's credit card. (Rod Dreher, "Moab Is My Washpot," *National Review*, 5/31/1999.)

(3) roam (aimlessly) *v.i.*: **maunder**. ❖ It's true, the Democrats have hired Terry McAuliffe. But aside from **maundering** around Florida upsetting the old folks with his constant whining, his primary function is as the imperator of importuning, the prince of beggars, the sultan of slush. He performs a coo for cash, not a coup for power. (Tony Blankley, "A Failing Grade; Dems' First 100 Days," *Washington Times*, 4/25/2001.)

(4) roam (compulsion to . . . or travel) *n.*: **dromomania**. See *travel*

(5) roam (able to . . . freely in a given environment; used of species) *adj.*: **vagile**. See *move*

(6) roam (from the subject) *v.i.*: **divagate**. See *digress*

roamer (as in one who strolls through city streets idly or aimlessly) *n.*: **flâneur** [French]; (strolling *n.*: **flânerie**). See *wanderer*

roaming (as in digressive) *adj.*: **excursive**. See *digressive*

rob (as in embezzle) *v.i.*: **defalcate**. See *embezzle*

(2) rob (as in embezzle) *v.t., v.i.*: **peculate**. See *embezzle*

(3) rob (as in plunder) *v.t., v.i.*: **depredate** (*n.*: **depredation**). See *plunder*

(4) rob (through swindling) *v.t.*: **bunco**. See *swindle*

robber (as in thief, caught red-handed) *n.*: **backberend**. See *thief*

robbery *n.*: **brigandage** (robber *n.*: **brigand**). ❖ His getaway was as flawed as his intended **brigandage**. (Tibor Fischer, *The Thought Gang*, The New Press [1994], p. 37.)

robbing (as in pillage or plunder) *n.*: **rapine**. See *looting*

robe (of a priest) *n.*: **alb**. ❖ Davis considered himself a Roman Catholic priest. [He] sometimes donned a long white **alb** and, all by himself outside the boma, performed services beside his Land Rover, chanting the Latin in a rich bass. (Lance Morrow, Essay: Africa, *Time*, 2/23/1987, p. 44.)

robot *n.*: **automaton**. ❖ Reggie, a 4-foot-tall wheeled **automaton**, may be coming to a hospital near you. . . . The hospital staff uses the robots, called HelpMates, to carry meal trays and deliver sterile supplies to nurses' stations. (Mark Alpert, News/Trends: "Sorry, No Bedpans," *Fortune*, 8/26/1991, p. 18.)

robotic (repetition of ideas that have been drilled into the speaker or that reflect the opinions of the powers that be) *v.t., v.i., n.*: **duckspeak**. See *recite*

robust (having a . . . and muscular body build) *adj.*: **mesomorphic**. See *muscular*

rock and a hard place (between a . . . , as in dangers on both sides) *idiom*: **between Scylla and Charybdis**. See *precarious*

rod (instrument such as a . . . for punishing children) *n.*: **ferule**. See *paddle*

rodents (of or relating to . . . , such as mice or rats) *adj.*: **murine**. ❖ But hormones aside, the stimulating role of motherhood itself would seem to play a role. When the investigators gave . . . rats [who had never given birth] another mother's pups to raise, the **murine** foster moms did almost as well in tests as their

. . . counterparts [who had given birth]. (*Medical Post*, "Does Mothering Make Females Smarter?" 2/9/1999, p. 37.)

rogue (or unprincipled person) *n*.: **blackguard**. See *scoundrel*

    (2) rogue *n*.: **rapscallion**. See *rascal*

    (3) rogue *n*.: **scapegrace**. See *scoundrel*

roll up *v.t*.: **furl**. ❖ The Rev. Jesse Jackson called Georgia's flag an "insult," adding that "the vanquished do not have the right to fly their flag." State Rep. Tyrone Brooks, an Atlanta Democrat, warned of "sanctions, boycotts and international embarrassment" if the General Assembly refuses to **furl** the flag. (Dan Chapman, "Behind the Scenes on the Flag Fight State," *Atlanta Journal-Constitution*, 1/7/2001.)

romantic (spec., having the characteristics of a mythical . . . place) *adj*.: **Ruritanian**. See *paradise*

romantic (as in amorous) *adj*.: **amative**. See *amorous*

romanticize (as in idealize) *v.t*.: **platonize**. See *idealize*

romanticized (of or relating to something that is pretty in a superficially . . . way) *adj*.: **chocolate-box**. See *pretty*

    (2) romanticized (or glamorized conception of oneself, as a result of boredom in one's life) *n*.: **Bovarism**. See *self-delusion*

Romeo (as in man who seduces women) *n*.: **Lothario**. See *playboy*

room (adequate . . . for living) *n*.: **lebensraum** [German]. See *breathing space*

rooster *n*.: **chanticleer**. ❖ Sunrise over the misty Mekong marks the beginning of the day in Vientiane. If not awakened by the crowing of the **chanticleers**, the beat of the drum at the Buddhist wat (monastery) across the street should do it. (Vern Harnapp, Laos: "Now Open for Tourist Business," *Focus*, 6/22/1998.)

root *n*.: **taproot**. [This word literally refers to the main root of a plant, thicker than the lateral roots and growing straight downward from the stem. It is also used more generally to refer to the basis or foundation of something.] ❖ Nearly 136 years after President Lincoln signed the Emancipation Proclamation, slavery remains the unhealed wound on the American soul. Every discussion of racial equality in America has its **taproot** in slavery. No wonder it is a subject regarded with trepidation and dread by whites and African-Americans alike. (Renee Graham, "Toward an Understanding of American Slavery," *Boston Globe*, 9/27/1998.)

    (2) root (about or through) *v.t*.: **fossick** [Australian]. See *rummage*

    (3) root (as in source and origin) *n*.: **fons et origo** [Latin]. See *source and origin*

rose-colored (or rosy) *adj*.: **roseate**. See *rosy*

rose-colored glasses (spec. the tendency to see things as more beautiful than they really are) *n*.: **kalopsia**. ❖ **Kalopsia** . . . has a positive benefit. I think it is essential to have a bit of blind optimism when painting instead of a heavy weight of critical skepticism which would only paralyze me and keep me from even trying to pick up a brush. I have noticed that **kalopsia** has it strongest influence right after the painting is finished as opposed to one year later when viewing the same painting. (Bob O'Brien, "Kalopsia Revisited," www.fineartviews.com/archives/nlarchive.asp?nl=700, 5/8/2008.)

rosy (esp. as in . . . cheeks) *adj*.: **rubicund**. ❖ Passing bills is an awful bore but it has to be done. Mary Mulligan, deputy health minister, is an awful bore about whom something should be done. . . . After ten minutes of her sugary, insubstantial voice, I'd made up my mind to swing down from the gallery, pinch her **rubicund** cheeks . . . and shout: "For God's sake, Mary, shut yir gob!" (Robert McNeil, "A Moderately Reflective Day to Be Passing Bills," *Scotsman* [Edinburgh], 2/7/2002.)

    (2) rosy *adj*.: **roseate**. ❖ Despite Rockefeller's **roseate** memories [of his childhood], early photos of him tell a much more somber tale. (Ron Chernow, *Titan*, Random House [1998], p. 17.)

    (3) rosy (as in ruddy) *adj*.: **florid**. See *ruddy*

rot (as in crumble away) *v.i*.; **molder**. See *crumble*

rotate (a log by spinning with the feet) *v.t*.: **birl**. See *logrolling*

rotating (as in whirling) *adj.*: **vortical**. See *whirling*

(2) rotating (or spiraling motion, often an ocean current) *n.*: **gyre**. See *spiraling*

rote (repetition of ideas that have been drilled into the speaker or that reflect the opinions of the powers that be) *v.t., v.i., n.*: **duckspeak**. See *recite*

rotting (or decaying) *adj.*: **saprogenic**. See *decay*

rotund (condition of having a . . . physique) *n.*: **embonpoint**. See *plump*

(2) rotund (having a short . . . physique) *adj.*: **pyknic**. See *stocky*

(3) rotund (person, esp. with a large abdomen) *n.*: **endomorph** (*adj.*: **endomorphic**). See *pot-bellied*

rough *adj.*: **scabrous**. ❖ The paganized, foultempered Mickey Sabbath is beyond all that. Some readers will find the material and language too **scabrous** for their taste. (R. Z. Sheppard, "Aging Disgracefully: Philip Roth's Latest Complainer Is Lecherous, Mean-Spirited, Politically Incorrect—And, After All These Years, Still Funny," *Time*, 9/11/1995, p. 82.)

(2) rough (as in crude, or poorly put together, esp. with respect to writing or speech) *adj.*: **incondite**. See *crude*

(3) rough (as in irregularly notched, toothed, or indented) *adj.*: **erose**. See *uneven*

roughness (as in acrimony or bitterness) *n.*: **asperity**. See *acrimony*

rough times (period of . . . , sometimes economic) *n.*: **locust years**. See *hardship*

roundabout (way of speaking or writing) *n.*: **circumlocution**. See *verbosity*

(2) roundabout (way of speaking or writing) *n.*: **periphrasis**. See *verbosity*

rounded *adj.*: **bulbous**. See *bulb-shaped*

roundness *n.*: **rondure**. ❖ [Certain] fetishes are nearly always a masculine phenomenon. Psychological and physiological reasons why some men are sexually aroused by fetish objects are discussed. When I feel a little low, I buy women's underwear. Lost amid a surfeit of sexy thingies, each one destined to trace a special **rondure** of breast, thigh, and buttock, I feel my spirits soar . . . (Michael Segell, "Meet the Kinks," *Esquire*, 5/1/1996.)

route (difficult or painful . . .) *n.*: **via dolorosa**. See *ordeal*

routine (or ordinary) *adj.*: **banausic**. ❖ Actually, when the question [of what do you do] comes, I quite often don't say "art critic." I say "commercial illustrator." That was once my living. It sounds a decent, **banausic** sort of trade. It causes no trouble. Whereas "art critic"— well, it's one of the very worst classes of person. (Tom Lubbock, "I'm No Artist but . . . ," *Independent* [London], 12/15/1998.)

(2) routine (the act of becoming . . .) *n.*: **routinization**. ❖ [P]olice officers nationwide are training for the once unimaginable nightmare scenario: a student on a killing spree. During the drills, students impersonate the dead and wounded while a mock maniac stalks the halls shooting blanks. . . . Across the United States, the organization has trained 3,000 officers. . . . As Draper admits, "It becomes like another day at the office." It's that **routinization** that's most disturbing. (Katherine Stroup, "The New Hall Monitors," *Newsweek*, 4/9/2001.)

(3) routine (as in habit or custom) *n.*: **praxis**. See *custom*

(4) routine (as in mundane; everyday) *adj.*: **sublunary**. See *earthly*

(5) routine (as in ordinary) *adj.*: **quotidian**. See *mundane*

rove (aimlessly) *v.i.*: **maunder**. See *roam*

(2) rove (from the subject) *v.i.*: **divagate**. See *digress*

rowdy (as in unruly) *adj.*: **indocile**. See *unruly*

royal (as in lordly) *adj.*: **seigneurial**. See *lordly*

rub (away or off by friction or scraping) *v.t.*: **abrade**. See *chafe*

(2) rub (of the body with lotion) *n.*: **embrocation** (*v.t.*: **embrocate**). See *body rub*

rubbing (against another something or someone for sexual pleasure) *n.*: **frottage**. ❖ To get a laugh, Tom Green has eaten human hair, slurped milk straight from a cow's udder and engaged in a bout of **frottage** with a dead moose. (Kendall Hamilton, "A Wild and Crazy Guy," *Newsweek*, 4/5/1999, p. 68.)

(2) rubbing (gentle . . . used in massage) *n.*: **effleurage**. See *stroking*

rubbish (accumulation of . . . , esp. prehistoric) *n.*: **midden**. See *trash*

(2) rubbish (study of a culture by examining its . . .) *n.*: **garbology**. See *garbage*

(3) rubbish *n.*: **detritus**. See *debris*

(4) rubbish *n.*: **dross**. See *trash*

(5) rubbish *n.*: **offal**. See *trash*

(6) rubbish *n.*: **spilth**. See *garbage*

ruddy (complexion) *adj.*: **blowzy**. ❖ While she had none of Christine's almost aristocratic delicacy, she was just as good-looking in a **blowzier** way. Even that young—perhaps twenty-five, twenty-six—her face was ruddy from drink, but the ruddiness became her like a rouge. (Karen Siegel, "The Year of the Glamorous Aunts," *Antioch Review*, 6/22/1994, p. 448.)

(2) ruddy *adj.*: **florid**. ❖ A short, plump man in a well-tailored suit approaches. He asks if he may help. . . . He is standing behind her. She looks at his smooth skin and prosperous, **florid** cheeks. (Sheila Kohler, "The Bride's Secret," short story, *Redbook*, 8/1/1996, p. 132.)

(3) ruddy (esp. as in . . . cheeks) *adj.*: **rubicund**. See *rosy*

rude (person who makes . . . comments that seem to be offering sympathy but instead makes the person feel worse, either intentionally or unintentionally) *n.*: **Job's comforter**. See *comforter*

(2) rude (toward another, often by being insulting or by trying to humiliate) *adj.*: **contumelious**. See *contemptuous*

rudeness (in behavior or speech due to arrogance or contempt) *n.*: **contumely**. See *contempt*

rudimentary *adj.*: **abecedarian**. See *basic*

rueful (or pitiful) *adj.*: **ruthful**. See *pitiful*

rugged (having a . . . and muscular body build) *adj.*: **mesomorphic**. See *muscular*

ruin (state of spiritual . . .) *n.*: **perdition**. See *damnation*

(2) ruin (of or relating to a . . . , as in downfall, esp. after an innocent or carefree time) *adj.*: **postlapsarian**. See *downfall*

(3) ruin (as in downfall, esp. from a position of strength) *n.*: **dégringolade** [French]. See *downfall*

ruinous (mutually . . . to both sides) *adj.*: **internecine**. See *destructive*

rule (as in tenet) *n.*: **shibboleth**. See *principle*

ruler (acting either as a representative or under the dominion and control of a foreign power) *n.*: **satrap**. [This word has various definitions, including: (1) a leader or ruler generally (see *leader*), (2) a prominent or notable person generally (see *bigwig*), (3) a henchman (see *henchman*), (4) a bureaucrat (see *bureaucrat*), and (5) the head of a state acting either as a representative or under the dominion and control of a foreign power. This is an example of the fifth definition. Often—but not always—it has a negative connotation.] ❖ The end [of the cold war] came in a private telephone call between Soviet President Mikhail Gorbachev and East German Communist leader Erich Honecker, in which the Russian told the German that further resistance was useless. . . . Honecker was a local **satrap** in a worldwide movement which held as an article of faith that the principal duty of its leaders was to seize and keep power by any means necessary. (John O'Sullivan, "James Burnham and the New World Order," *National Review*, 11/5/1990.)

(2) ruler (esp. hereditary) *n.*: **dynast**. ❖ By the 1950s expensive [Gucci] bags, shoes, belts, scarves, ties and watches had begun to adorn the svelte and wealthy around the world. [In 1995] its best known **dynast**, Maurizio Gucci, was shot in a Milan street. (*Economist*, "The Velvet Revolution," 12/14/1996, p. 70.)

(3) ruler (of the universe) *n.*: **kosmokrator** [Greek]. ❖ Jesus demonstrates his authority in many ways in the Gospel of Matthew. . . . 11:25–27 states that Jesus' Father is "Lord of heaven and earth." Now Jesus claims that he himself has lordship. He is the **kosmokrator**; resurrection has given him new status. This authority is total, extending throughout heaven and earth—that is, the universe. (Edgar Krentz, "'Make Disciples'—Matthew on Evangelism," *Currents in Theology and Mission*, 2/1/2006.)

(4) ruler (who holds great power or sway) *n.*: **potentate**. ❖ Their own way of ruling has a regal feel. The 55-year-old Pachakhan, Governor of three provinces, is an irascible **potentate** who holds court in the time-honored manner, seated on cushions at the far end of a long audience room. . . . In a far corner, his civil servants sit on the floor, leafing through papers. (Paul Quinn, "Standing Their Ground—A Family of Regional Royalist Potentates May Help Take Out Al-qaeda—But Isn't Too Keen on Ceding Power to Kabul," *Time* International, 1/28/2002, p. 25.)

(5) ruler (as in commander) *n.*: **imperator**. See *commander*

(6) ruler (or leader) *n.*: **satrap**. See *leader*

(7) ruler (as in dictator, esp. in Spanish-speaking countries) *n.*: **caudillo**. See *dictator*

(9) ruler (as in monarch or sultan or shah or the like; also used to refer to a powerful or important person generally) *n.*: **padishah**. See *emperor*

(10) ruler (potential . . . , as in dictator) *n.*: **man on horseback**. See *dictator*

(11) ruler *n.*: **duce** (Italian). See *commander*

(12) ruler *n.*: **gerent**. See *manager*

rules (one who demands rigid adherence to . . .) *n.*: **martinet**. See *disciplinarian*

ruling (as in lordly) *adj.*: **seigneurial**. See *lordly*

(2) ruling (as in reigning) *adj.*: **regnant**. See *reigning*

(3) ruling (by women) *n.*: **gynarchy**. See *government*

(4) ruling (or political dominance by women) *n.*: **gynocracy**. See *government*

(5) ruling (or political dominance of men) *n.*: **androcracy**. See *government*

rumination (staring at one's belly-button as an aid to . . .) *n.*: **omphaloskepsis**. See *meditation*

rummage (about or through) *v.t.*: **fossick** [Australian]. ❖ In a tale to gladden the hearts of all who **fossick** through local art fairs looking for forgotten gems, a work that Boston businessman Edward Puhl bought more than 30 years ago turned out to be *Little Regatta*, by Paul Klee. The bad news was that it had been stolen. (Belinda Luscombe, People, *Time*, 6/30/1997, p. 79.)

rumor (false . . .) *n.*: **furphy** [Australian]. ❖ [Will the Seven Network] change *Witness's* time slot from 9.30 pm Thursdays[?] There's a rough draft of Seven's post–Winter Olympics schedule doing the rounds which places the program at 7.30 pm Thursdays. However, those who have seen the schedule are sceptical. They wonder if it is a **furphy** to confuse the other networks about Seven's plans after the Winter Games. (Jacqueline Lee Lewis, "Wall-to-Wall Reality," *Daily Telegraph* [Sydney, Australia], 1/29/1998.)

(2) rumor *v.t.*: **bruit**. ❖ Yet [Rockefeller] remained extremely fussy about his food, taking small, sparing bites in a manner that spawned a thousand myths about his ruined system. For years it was **bruited** that he had a standing million-dollar offer for any doctor who could repair his stomach. (Ron Chernow, *Titan*, Random House [1998], p. 322.)

(3) rumor (or story that is false, often deliberately) *n.*: **canard**. See *hoax*

(4) rumor (spec. which is false, defamatory, and published for political gain right before an election) *n.*: **roorback**. See *falsehood*

rumormonger *n.*: **quidnunc**. See *busybody*

rumors (spread false . . .) *v.t.*: **asperse**. See *defame*

run (along swiftly and easily, used esp. of clouds) *v.i.*: **scud**. See *move*

(2) run (heavily or clumsily) *v.i.*: **galumph**. See *tromp*

rundown (and broken-down) *adj.*: **raddled**. See *worn-out*

(2) rundown (as in decrepit) *adj.*: **spavined**. See *decrepit*

(3) rundown *adj.*: **tatterdemalion**. See *ragged*

running (smoothly or copiously, like a stream) *adj.*: **profluent**. See *flowing*

runny (having a ,. . . nose) *adj.*: **rheumy**. See *watery*

run off (as in a departure that is unannounced, abrupt, secret, or unceremonious) *n.*: **French leave** (or **French Leave**). See *departure*

run-of-the-mill (as in routine or mechanical) *adj.*: **banausic**. See *routine*

rural *adj.*: **villatic**. ❖ According to [Richard Clarke], the Bush II administration was so dead-set on quenching Mr. Saddam Hussein, the former's father's inveterate enemy, that intelligence passed on by the preceding Clinton administration was simply ignored. Most likely, such intelligence was accorded the utmost contempt, since the elder George Bush was not particularly known to harbor any esteemed thoughts about the **villatic**, Hope, Arkansas, native [i.e., Bill Clinton]. (Kwame Okoampa-Ahoofe, "Crying Wolf and Living the Lie," *New York Beacon*, 4/7/2004.)

(2) rural (as in a place that is . . . peaceful and simple) *adj.*: **Arcadian**. See *pastoral*

(3) rural *adj.*: **agrestic**. See *rustic*

(4) rural *adj.*: **bucolic**. See *rustic*

rushed (as in hasty) *adj.*: **festinate**. See *hasty*

rush in (as in burst in, suddenly or forcibly) *v.i.*: **irrupt**. See *burst in*

rushing (as in at top speed) *adv.*: **tantivy**. See *top speed*

Russian (to make a language or culture more . . .) *v.t.*: **Russify**. ❖ The school was named after Yakub Kolas, one of [Belarus's] great poets and a leader in a 20th-century revival of Belarusian language and culture. Lukashenko, however, seems determined to **Russify** the country and has, at various times, proposed a union with Russia. "The Russian language will be in Belarus as long as I am president," he said this year. "The lack of the Russian language will be the death of the state." (Peter Finn, "School of 'Partisans' Goes Underground in Belarus," *Washington Post*, 10/17/2004.)

rust (colored) *adj.*: **ferruginous**. ❖ Crystal-bearing cavities . . . with the most **ferruginous** material contain the least amount of topaz, which might indicate that these cavities were breached during early stages of topaz crystallization. . . . Reddish-brown crystals are reported to fade upon long exposure to daylight. (Peter J. Modreski, "Colorado Topaz," *Rocks & Minerals*, 10/1/1996, p. 306.)

rust-colored *adj.*: **rubiginous**. ❖ New research carried out in the United States has suggested that redheads, such as the **rubiginous** television personality [Anne Robinson], need 20 per cent more anaesthesia than people with other hair colours. The unexpected finding not only suggests that gingers are more sensitive to pain, but offers insights into how anaesthesia works in humans. (Frank O'Donnell, "Why Having Red Hair Is a Pain," *Scotsman*, 10/16/2002.)

rustic *adj.*: **agrestic**. ❖ [Dubuffet's] attachment to rural images from earlier French art, particularly the earthy fields of Millet, is pervasive and obvious; the funniest and most **agrestic** of all his paintings were, undoubtedly, the cows—a snook cocked at Picasso's heroic Spanish bulls. (Robert Hughes, Art: "An Outlaw Who Loved Laws," *Time*, 7/26/1993, p. 62.)

(2) rustic *adj.*: **bucolic**. ❖ The N4 turned out to be an idyllic route to travel . . . that winds through quaint villages and **bucolic** farmland. (Sheila Rothenberg, "Irresistible Ireland," *USA Today Magazine*, 9/1/1996.)

(3) rustic (as in a place that is . . . peaceful and simple) *adj.*: **Arcadian**. See *pastoral*

rustling (to make a soft . . . sound) *v.i.*: **sough**. ❖ I wake to the **soughing** sound of my neighbour's wife sweeping the pavements of leaves outside our homes because cleanliness was ingrained in her as a small girl in Kashmir. (Maureen Messent, "Straight Talking: Muslims Not Our Enemies," *Birmingham Evening Mail*, 9/21/2001.)

(2) rustling (or whispering sound) *n.*: **susurrous**. See *whispering*

ruthless (as in cruel) *adj.*: **fell** (*n.*: **fellness**). See *cruel*

Sabbath (one who observes the . . .) *n.*: **Sabbatarian**. ❖ As a committed Christian and **Sabbatarian**, [Eric] Liddell refused to compete in the 100 metres at the Paris Olympics in 1924, because the heats would be run on a Sunday. Instead, he trained for the 200 and 400 metres—and took bronze in the 200 and gold in the 400. (Mary Lean, "Eric Liddell—Pure Gold," *For a Change*, 2/1/2002.)

sacred (as in inviolable) *adj.*: **infrangible**. See *inviolable*

sacred place *n.*: **adytum**. See *sanctum*

sacrifice (to kill as a . . .) *v.t.*: **immolate**. ❖ So might some Russian of the 3rd millennium A.D. rhapsodize about the ancient sacrificial rites of Stalinism, **immolating** its millions to the God of the Future. (Robert Hughes, Art: "Onward from Olmec: A Monumental Exhibit of Mexico's Art Redeems the 'Image Problem,'" *Time*, 10/15/1990, p. 80.)

(2) sacrifice (as in offering) *n.*: **oblation**. See *offering*

(3) sacrifice (large-scale . . . and slaughter) *n.*: **hecatomb**. See *slaughter*

sacrificial *adj.*: **piacular**. See *atoning*

sad *adj.*: **tristful**. ❖ Wilbur wittily denounces the so-called confessional poets in his poem, "Flippancies" (90): If fictive music fails your lyre, confess—Though not, of course, to any happiness. So it be **tristful,** tell us what you choose: Hangover, Nixon on the TV news, God's death, the memory of your rocking-horse, Entropy, housework, Buchenwald, divorce, Those damned flamingoes in your neighbor's yard. (Isabella Wai, "Wilbur's Cottage Street, 1953," analysis of a Richard Wilbur poem, *Explicator*, 3/1/1996, p. 183.)

(2) sad (as in dejected) *adj.*: **chapfallen**. See *dejected*

(3) sad (as in dismal and gloomy) *adj.*: **acherontic**. See *gloomy*

(4) sad (as in sullen or morose) *adj.*: **saturnine**. See *sullen*

(5) sad (chronically . . . , as in depressed) *adj.*, *n.*: **dysthymic**. See *depressed*

(6) sad (often regarding something gone) *adj.*: **elegiac**. See *sorrowful*

(7) sad (or grumpy mood) *n.pl.*: **mulligrubs**. See *grumpiness*

(8) sad (sounds) *adj.*: **plangent**. See *mournful*

(9) sad *adj.*: **heartsore**. See *heartbroken*

sadism (as in pleasure derived from others' misfortunes, although it does not require one's own infliction of the misfortune, as sadism implies) *n.*: **schadenfreude**. [German. A rare English equivalent for this word is "epicaricacy."] ❖ For **schadenfreude** buffs, 1998 has turned out to be one of the most enjoyable of recent years. . . . People who actually like to see the tallest poppies chopped down . . . have been beside themselves with joy as Bill Gates, Warren Buffett and hundreds of other billionaires have taken their lumps during the recent stock market collapse. (Joe Queenan, "Don't Worry, Be Happy," *Forbes*, 10/12/1998, p. 42.)

(2) sadism (as in pleasure derived from witnessing others' misfortunes or suffering) *n.*: **Roman holiday**. [This term—which does not require one's own infliction of the misfortune, as sadism implies—derives from gladiatorial combats of the ancient Roman circus staged for the entertainment of the audience. "Roman holiday" is distinguished from the German word "schadenfreude" in that one is presumed to be witnessing the event in question. The phrase also refers to both one's enjoyment of the event and the event itself. See *spectacle*.] ❖ [A] videotape of [former Tyco International CEO Dennis Kozlowski's] wife's Sardinian birthday party was screened for jurors in New York. Kozlowski was on trial for allegedly looting Tyco of millions, and the video depicts toga-clad models on a lavish set reeking of indulgence at shareholder expense. [C]olumnist Rachel Beck had a **Roman holiday** with the story: . . . "[T]he Tyco video was momentous. It had executives live on tape surrounded by such excess." [One presumes that her Roman holiday refers to watching Kozlowski's reaction to the video in the courtroom and neither to Kozlowski on the video itself nor to the Tyco shareholders watching the video.] (PR Newswire, "Fox News, Pentagon, Kozlowski and Michael Jackson on List of 10 Worst 2003 PR Gaffes; Ninth Annual PR Blunders List Unveiled," 12/16/2003.)

(3) sadism *n.*: **algolagnia**. See *masochism*

sadistic (as in cruel) *adj.*: **fell** (*n.*: **fellness**). See *cruel*

sadly (to relate) *adv.*: **miserabile dictu**. See *unhappily*

sadness *n.*: **dolor** (*adj.*: **dolorous**) ❖ [NBC president Bob] Wright sounds as if he'd be positively relieved if Letterman would pack up [and leave] just so long as he doesn't have to see an unhappy Dave roaming the halls anymore! But this would be a serious mistake for NBC, because despite Dave's **dolor**, there's still no talk show funnier or more exciting than *Late Night*. (Ken Tucker, "Blues in the Night—David Letterman's Contempt for His Lot in Life After Being Passed Over for the *Tonight Show* Seems to Grow with Every *Late Night*," *Entertainment Weekly*, 7/17/1992, p. 42.)

(2) sadness (as in depression) *n.*: **cafard** [French]. See *depression*

(3) sadness (as in inability to experience pleasure or happiness) *n.*: **anhedonia**. See *unhappiness*

(4) sadness (as in world-weariness or sentimental pessimism over the world's problems) *adj.*: **Weltschmerz** [German]. See *pessimism*

(5) sadness (as part of depressed state) *n.*: **dysphoria**. See *depression*

(6) sadness (express . . . over) *v.t.*: **bewail**. See *lament*

(7) sadness (to fret or complain, including as a result of . . .) *v.i.*: **repine**. See *complain*

(8) sadness (out of the depths of . . . or despair) *n., adv.*: **de profundis**. See *despair*

safecracker *n.*: **yegg**. ❖ From the *Greensboro Daily News*, Dec. 15–21, 1949—**Yeggs** managed to cut through a safe at Belk Department Store in downtown Greensboro but an alert

policeman walking a beat at 3 a.m. foiled their getaway plans and saved the store $138,000 in U.S. savings bonds. (*Piedmont Triad [NC] News & Record*, "100 Years Ago," 12/15/1999.)

safeguard (against attack or danger) *n.*: **bulwark**. See *protection*

(2) safeguard (intended to . . . against evil) *adj.*: **apotropaic**. See *protect*

(3) safeguard *v.t.*: **forfend**. See *protect*

safe haven *n.*: **querencia**. [Spanish. In Spanish bullfighting, the "querencia" is the area to which the bull returns between charges; where he feels safe and/or emboldened. It can be used more generally to refer to any safe haven.] ❖ By the time you read this, *National Review* will have been uprooted from the wonderful old rabbit warren we have inhabited for all but the first two years of our corporate existence. Its managing editor will have been uprooted from the **querencia** she has inhabited for 23 of those 39 years—an office that a visitor recently described as "that little cranny filled with paper." (Linda Bridges, "These Hallowed Halls," *National Review*, 12/31/1996.)

(2) safe haven (as in small, usu. temporary defensive fortification) *n.*: **redoubt**. See *refuge*

sage (as in wise) *adj.*: **sapient**. See *wise*

sail (along swiftly and easily, used esp. of clouds) *v.i.*: **scud**. See *move*

(2) sail (as in glide, through the air like a glider) *n., v.i.*: **volplane**. See *glide*

saints (literature dealing with lives of . . .) *n.*: **hagiology**. ❖ Reflecting on the day DiMaggio's streak finally ended, [Robert W. Creamer] writes, "I used to wonder why there were so many saints in the Christian **hagiology**. . . . But in our own secular times Western civilization, proud of its pragmatic Enlightenment, has created its own saints" [like DiMaggio]. (Ron Fimrite, Books, *Sports Illustrated*, 7/1/1991, p. 7.)

(2) saints (worship of . . .) *n.*: **hagiolatry**. ❖ The concluding chapter [describes] an unprecedented surge in **hagiolatry** and pilgrimage rites connected to the shrines of venerated "saints." (Susan Einbinder, review of *Sephardi Religious Responses to Modernity*, by Norman A. Stillman, *Journal of the American Oriental Society*, 1/12/1998, p. 109.)

salacious (as in lewd or lustful) *adj.*: **lubricious**. See *lewd*

(2) salacious (as in lustful) *adj.*: **lickerish**. See *lustful*

(3) salacious (as in scandalous or risqué) *adj.*: **scabrous**. See *scandalous*

salaried (employees, as opposed to lower-class wage earners) *n.*: **salariat**. See *employees*

salary *n.*: **emolument**. See *wages*

sale *n.*: **vendition**. ❖ This is, to be sure, less a triumph for trains and train stations than for preservation and commerce. Union Station. . . is a historic building that has been saved not by the revitalization of its original function but by its conversion into yet another stylish emporium for the **vendition** of consumer goods to a populace whose capacity for consumption and display is bottomless. (Jonathan Yardley, "The New Union Station—A Terminal Patient Revived," *Washington Post*, 9/26/1988.)

saliva (dribbling from the mouth) *v.t.*, *n.*: **slaver**. See *drool*

sallow (as in pale, and often sickly) *adj.*: **etiolated**. See *pale*

salty *adj.*: **brackish**. ❖ The Apalachicola, Carrabelle and St. Marks Rivers meet the salty gulf to form a **brackish** paradise for oysters, shrimp and fish between the mainland and the barrier islands of St. George, St. Vincent and Dog Island. (Craig Walker, "Florida's 'Forgotten Coast' Is Unforgettable Experience," *Washington Times*, 8/19/2000.)

(2) salty *adj.*: **briny**. ❖ When pro football's lowly Philadelphia Eagles soared over the Dallas Cowboys in their season opener, several Eagles players credited an unlikely factor: pickle juice. Seems that before the game Eagles trainer Rick M. Burkholder said the **briny** stuff would help balance his players' electrolytes and prevent dehydration. . . . [The Eagles are] still downing the salty stuff. (Eileen Glanton, "Eagleade," *Forbes*, 10/16/2000, p. 62a.)

salutation (relating to a . . . , where the purpose is to establish a mood of sociability rather than to communicate information or ideas, such as "have a nice day") *adj.*: **phatic**. See *pleasantries*

salvation (having the power or intent to bring about . . .) *adj.*: **salvific**. The "only way" that Robert J. Dole can defeat President Clinton is by proposing a major cut in taxes, says flat-tax champion . . . Malcolm S. "Steve" Forbes. "Colin Powell is not going to save him. Mother Teresa is not going to save him," said the magazine publisher who spent more than $36 million to finance a failed run for the presidency built around the purportedly **salvific** power of a single-rate income tax. (Blaine Harden, "Dole's Only Hope, Forbes Says, Is Offering Major Cut in Taxes," *Washington Post*, 6/29/1996.)

same (having the . . . nature, substance, or essence) *adj.*: **consubstantial**. See *identical*

sanctimonious (hypocritically . . .) *adj.*: **pharisaical**. See *self-righteous*

(2) sanctimonious (or hypocritical, pious, and/or insincere speech) *n.*: **cant**. See *pious*

(3) sanctimonious (person, esp. one who hypocritically affects religious piety) *n.*: **Tartuffe** (or **tartuffe**). See *hypocrite*

(4) sanctimonious (persons who are . . . and critical of others) *n.pl.*: **unco guid** (preceded by "the"). See *self-righteous*

(5) sanctimonious *adj.*: **Pecksniffian**. See *self-righteous*

sanction (as in approve, esp. to confirm officially) *v.t.*: **homologate**. See *approve*

(2) sanction (as in giving one's stamp of approval) *n.*: **nihil obstat** [Latin]. See *approval*

(3) sanction (officially) *v.t.*: **approbate**. See *authorize*

sanctioned (as in official, act, declaration, or statement, as in with the authority of one's office) *adv.*, *adj.*: **ex cathedra**. See *official*

sanctuary (as in safe haven) *n.*: **querencia**. See *safe haven*

sanctum *n.*: **adytum**. ❖ [Elizabeth Cady Stanton wrote:] There is a solitude which each and every one of us has always carried with him, . . . the solitude of self. Our inner being which we call ourself, no eye nor touch of man or angel has ever pierced. It is more hidden than the caves of the gnome; the sacred **adytum** of the oracle. . . . Such is individual life. (Alice Leuchtag, "Elizabeth Cady Stanton: Freethinker and Radical Revisionist," *Humanist*, 9/19/1996, p. 29.)

sand (of, relating to, or resembling; sandy) *adj*.: **arenaceous**. ❖ As the tension surrounding the war in Iraq heightens, the United States continues to look for new resolutions for the **arenaceous** Persian Gulf chokehold. (Eric Howerton, "Bats Could Be Secret Weapon," University Wire, 3/27/2003.)

sandal (with woven leather strips) *n*.: **huarache**. ❖ By now [Tom] Clancy thrillers have evolved into something of a summer ritual, each hitting the bookstores just in time to be snatched up and tossed in the beach bag along with the **huarache** sandals and the aloe vera. (Andrew Ferguson, Books & Ideas: "Tom Clancy's Star Wars Story: His Latest Thriller Has That Patent Insider Feel," *Fortune*, 7/18/1988, p. 101.)

sandstorm (esp. in Arabia and Africa) *n*.: **haboob**. ❖ The mission was under strict radio silence. But Col. Guidry said one of his lingering regrets is that he didn't break that silence to relay a message to the helicopter pilots who were flying off the USS *Nimitz* in the Persian Gulf that might have warned them of the **haboob**. . . . One helicopter crew had instrument failures in the swirling sand clouds and aborted the mission. (Michael Hedges, "Disaster Foiled Rescue in Iran; 20 Years Ago, Crash 'Lit up the World,'" *Washington Times*, 4/25/2000.)

sane *adj*.: **compos mentis**. ❖ The pop star who swore at the Duchess of York in front of a global audience on live television was brought up to be a "well-mannered child who never got into trouble," his mother said yesterday. . . . [S]he wondered if he had been plied with too much to drink and "was not really **compos mentis**" when he made his outburst. (Sean

O'Neill, "He's a Nice Lad, Says Swearing Star's Mum: Pop Singer Who Insulted the Duchess of York on Live TV," *Daily Telegraph* [London], 11/14/1998.)

sanitize (a book or a piece of writing in a prudish manner) *v.t.*: **bowdlerize**. See *edit*

sap (as in weaken or deprive of strength) *v.t.*: **enervate**. See *debilitate*

sarcastic (bitingly . . .) *adj*.: **mordant**. ❖ Dole's darts have injected about the only amusement there has been in this presidential campaign—but far from being rewarded, he has been castigated. Dole is called sarcastic, sardonic, **mordant** and, most often, mean. People seem to think his biting wit bares too many teeth, prompting even his handlers to debate whether to "let Dole be Dole." (Neal Gabler, "No Fooling—Dole Is a Funny Guy," *Newsday*, 3/25/1996.)

sashay (about so as to attract attention) *v.i.*: **tit-tup**. See *strut*

Satan *n*.: **Beelzebub**. ❖ But Manson's well-publicized Church of Satan membership has helped fuel rumors of onstage animal and virgin sacrifices . . . though he evidently no more believes in a personal **Beelzebub** than a personal Jesus. (Chris Willman, "Manson Mmmbad: Out from Under Hanson's Feel-Good Rock Crawls the Blasphemous Marilyn Manson, Mom and Dad's Worst Nightmare," *Entertainment Weekly*, 7/25/1997, p. 36.)

satanic *adj*.: **Mephistophelean**. See *devilish*

satiate (to the point of excess, esp. things sweet) *v.t.*: **cloy**. ❖ If the seasonal sweetness is starting to **cloy**, try a tart taste of *Bah! Humbug!*[,] the holiday family show from the Imaginary Theatre Company. The musical spoof by Jack Herrick upholds Dickens' message of generosity and caring, but it's updated with engaging songs, slapstick humor and contemporary references. (Judith Newmark, "*Bah! Humbug!* Spoofs Dickens, Shares Theme," *St. Louis Post-Dispatch*, 12/16/1996.)

satirize (esp. by ridiculing or making fun of someone) *n., v.t.*: **pasquinade**. ❖ Joseph Biden, the Democratic senator from Delaware, lost his credibility during the 1988 presidential race when he was caught plagiarizing a speech. (Both [Gary] Hart and Biden were **pasquinaded** in other jokes: What's the title of Gary Hart's new book? *Six Inches From the Presidency*. Did you hear Joe Biden was writing his autobiography? It's called *Iacocca*.) (Alan Dundes, "What's So Funny?" *Mother Jones*, 1/11/1996, p. 18.)

satisfaction (as in happiness) *n.*: **felicity**. See *happiness*

   (2) satisfaction (delusive or illusory) *n.*: **fool's paradise**. See *illusion*

   (3) satisfaction (from others' misfortunes) *n.*: **schadenfreude** [German]. See *sadism*

   (4) satisfaction (from witnessing others' misfortunes) *n.*: **Roman holiday**. See *sadism*

   (5) satisfaction *n.*: **eudemonia** (or **eudaemonia**). See *happiness*

   (6) satisfaction *n.*: **oblectation**. See *pleasure*

satisfy (as in appease) *v.t.*: **dulcify**. See *appease*

saturate (as in soak) *v.t.*: **imbrue**. See *soak*

saucy (girl) *n., adj.*: **hoyden**. See *tomboy*

sausage *n.*: **banger** [British]. ❖ The latest notch on the commission's Fair Trading Act enforcement belt is a meaty settlement with the Thorndon New World supermarket after its beef sausages were found to have been made from mutton. Commission chairman John Belgrave is promising to sniff out any more bent **bangers**. (*Sunday Star Times* [New Zealand], "Loose Change," 9/3/2000.)

savage (as in untamed) *adj.*: **ferine**. See *untamed*

   (2) savage (as in barbarous) *adj.*: **Hunnish**. See *barbarous*

save (having the power or intent to . . . , as in bring about salvation) *adj.*: **salvific**. See *salvation*

savor (the taste of) *v.t.*: **degust**. ❖ The De Pelikaan tea and coffee room, in Zutphen, is a haven where one can **degust** to one's fill and then amble out with a gift-wrapped package for one's love, or merely for the love of fine tea and coffee. (Jonathan Bell, "A. Garsen Coffee/Tea Retailer Opens De Pelikaan Tea Room," *Tea & Coffee Trade Journal*, 12/1/1990.)

savory *adj.*: **esculent**. See *edible*

   (2) savory *adj.*: **sapid**. See *tasty*

say (as in declare) *v.t.*: **asseverate**. See *declare*

saying (as in phrase or expression) *n.*: **locution**. See *phrase*

   (2) saying (at the start of a literary piece setting forth a theme or message) *n.*: **epigraph**. See *quotation*

   (3) saying (pithy . . .) *n.*: **gnome** (*adj.*: **gnomic**). See *catchphrase*

   (4) saying (witty or clever . . . or line) *n.*: **bon mot**. See *line*

saying *n.*: **apothegm**. ❖ The old **apothegm** reiterated by those who reject stricter gun-control laws takes on a different resonance if it's paraphrased this way: "Guns don't kill children—children kill children." (*Newsweek*, "The Death of Innocence?" 4/3/2000, p. 18.)

sayings (given to stating . . . , esp. in a moralizing way) *adj.*: **sententious**. See *aphoristic*

scam (esp. something that at first seems a wonderful discovery or development, but that turns to be a . . . or a delusion) *n.*: **mare's nest**. See *hoax*

scan (a quick cursory . . .) *n.*: **Cook's tour**. [The "Cook" in this term refers to Thomas Cook, the nineteenth-century English travel agent whose organized tours were the first travel packages in which everything was arranged for the customer. The term is also used to refer to a tour that shows only the highlights of a place or thing. See *tour*. Also, a note on the word "scan" itself: Its formal definition is "to examine something closely and carefully," which is the opposite of how many people use it. In fact, its usage in the sense of "skimming" has become so common over the years that this opposite sense of the word is now considered acceptable as well. The word "perusal" has gone through a similar lexical journey, although its use in the sense of "skimming" is considered somewhat less acceptable.] ❖ The 2006 NBA Finals . . . pits a pair of first-timers, the Dallas Mavericks and Miami Heat, in one of the more intriguing and potentially exciting NBA Finals in years. . . . Not only are the franchises new to this event, so, too, are most of the players. Therefore, here is a **Cook's tour**, if you will, of the two teams who have the NBA's eyes and ears for up to the next two weeks. (Peter May, "Comparisons That Don't Factor into Decision," *Boston Globe*, 6/7/2006.)

(2) scan (quick . . . , as in glance) *n.*: **coup d'oeil** [French]. See *glance*

scandal (as in dishonor to one's reputation) *n.*: **blot (or stain) on one's escutcheon** idiom. See *dishonor*

scandalmonger *n.*: **quidnunc**. See *busybody*

scandalous *adj.*: **flagitious**. ❖ Tories and Liberals vied for the support of the rich, and the more or less discreet sale of honours became the recognized means of securing that support. That happy arrangement came unstuck when Lloyd George sold honours in a particularly **flagitious** way to some exceptionally dubious personages. (Geoffrey Wheatcroft, "Wanted: A Better Way to Fund Our Political Parties," *Independent on Sunday*, 7/25/1999.)

(2) scandalous *adj.*: **scabrous**. ❖ Last week NBC Nightly News gravely confirmed a Drudge Report item that Clinton and Lewinsky once had sex after he attended Easter services. No big deal. More **scabrous** stuff than that bounces regularly from cyberland to Jay Leno without stopping for the niceties of confirmation. (Richard Lacayo, Nation: "The Politics of Yuck," *Time*, 9/14/1998, p. 40.)

scanty (as in meager) *adj.*: **mingy**. See *meager*

(2) scanty *n.*: **exiguous**. See *meager*

scar *n.*: **cicatrix**. ❖ Today Laumann's leg, after seven operations, has a principal scar running from midcalf to ankle, from which small tributaries of **cicatrix** extend. (Michael Farber, "Battle Scarred: Canadian Rower Silken Laumann Has Fought Through Pain—In and Out of Competition," *Sports Illustrated*, 7/21/1996, p. 34.)

(2) scar (as in to make a small or shallow cut in the skin) *v.t.*: **scarify**. See *cut*

scare *v.t.*: **affright**. ❖ They erupt like indignant metal jungle birds, and they whoop all night. They make American cities sound like luna-

tic rain forests, all the wildlife **affrighted**, violated, outraged, shrieking. Like the hungry infant's cry, the car alarm is designed to be unignorable—that is, unendurable. (Lance Morrow, "The Thing That Screams Wolf—What Thief Has Ever Been Deterred by Those Unendurable Car Alarms? They're a Crime in Themselves," *Time*, 6/24/1991, p. 46.)

scared (and cautious and indecisive) *adj.*: **Prufrockian**. See *timid*

(2) scared (as in cowardly) *adj.*: **pusillanimous**. See *cowardly*

(3) scared (as in cowardly) *adj.*: **retromingent**. See *cowardly*

(4) scared *adj.*: **tremulous**. See *fearful*

scatter (as in branch out) *v.i.*: **ramify**. See *branch out*

(2) scatter (tending to . . . or break up) *adj.*: **fissiparous**. See *break up*

scatterbrained (person) *n.*: **featherhead**. See *flighty*

(2) scatterbrained (person) *n.*: **flibbertigibbet**. See *flighty*

scattershot (as in covering a wide range in an indiscriminate way) *adj., n.*: **blunderbuss**. A blunderbuss was a short, wide-mouthed gun used to scatter shot at close range. Today, the word describes a clumsy person or can refer to actions taken or statements made that are broader than necessary to hit their target or accomplish their goal (and may miss the target or goal altogether).] ❖ Unlike chemotherapy and radiation, **blunderbuss** weapons that attack healthy as well as cancerous cells and can cause severe side effects, the new [drugs] are designed to kill cancer cells alone. In principle, they should eliminate malignancies more effectively while being far gentler on the patient. (Nicholas Wade, "Scientists View New Wave of Cancer Drugs," *New York Times*, 5/29/2001.)

scavenge (about or through) *v.t.*: **fossick** [Australian]. See *rummage*

scene (as in commotion) *n.*: **bobbery**. See *commotion*

(2) scene (as in commotion) *n.*: **kerfuffle**. See *commotion*

(3) scene (as in setting or physical environment) *n.*: **mise-en-scène** [French; putting on stage]. See *setting*

scheme (secret . . . or group of plotters) *n.*: **cabal**. See *plot*

schemers (group of . . .) *n.*: **camarilla**. See *advisors*

scheming (and evil or shameless woman) *n.*: **jezebel** (sometimes cap.). See *woman*

   (2) scheming (esp. underhanded) *n.*: **jiggery-pokery**. See *trickery*

schizophrenic (as in two-faced) *adj.*: **Janus-faced**. See *two-faced*

schmaltzy *adj.*: **mawkish**. See *sentimental*

scholar (as in lover of learning) *n.*: **philomath**.

   ❖ Thirty years earlier, [Benjamin] Franklin's fellow **philomath** Nathaniel Ames had written in his widely read New England almanac for 1758: "The curious have observ'd that the progress of humane literature (like the sun) is from the East to the West; thus it has traveled through Asia and Europe, and now is at the eastern shore of America." . . . America's rising sun was then the symbol not only of a new political system but of a new civilization. (Thomas Wendel, "America's Rising Sun; Two Hundred Years Ago," *National Review*, 7/13/1984.)

   (2) scholar (as in person who is very knowledgeable in many areas) *n.*: **polymath**. [This word and "philomath" are fairly close synonyms, and in most instances a person who is one will likely be the other as well. The distinction is that a philomath is one who loves the learning process, while a polymath is one who already is knowledgeable in many areas.] ❖ A self-educated **polymath** endowed with formidable charm and considerable intellect, [Benjamin] Franklin quickly became the leading figure in colonial politics, literature, science, and social reform. (Alan Taylor, "For the Benefit of Mr. Kite," *New Republic*, 3/19/2001.)

scholarly (as in literary, community) *n.*: **republic of letters**. See *literary*

   (2) scholarly (as in pedantic) *adj.*: **donnish**. See *pedantic*

(3) scholarly (of a . . . but pedantic word or term) *adj.*: **inkhorn**. See *pedantic*

(4) scholarly (person, esp. in intellectual or literary circles) *n.*: **mandarin**. See *influential*

(5) scholarly (woman with . . . or literary interests) *n.*: **bluestocking**. See *woman*

(6) scholarly (write or speak in a . . . manner, often used in a derogatory fashion) *v.i.*: **lucubrate**. See *discourse*

(7) scholarly *adj.*: donnish. See *bookish*

scholarship (excess striving for or preoccupation with . . .) *n.*: **epistemophilia**. See *knowledge*

   (2) scholarship (which is actually superficial) *n.*: **sciolism**. See *superficial*

schoolteacher *n.*: **pedagogue**. See *teacher*

scold *v.t.*: **flay**. See *criticize*

   (2) scold *v.t.*: **objurgate**. See *criticize*

scolding (as in criticism) *n.*: **animadversion** (*v.t.*: **animadvert**). See *criticism*

   (2) scolding (in speech) *n.*: **philippic**. See *tirade*

(3) scolding (woman who is domineering and . . .) *n.*: **virago**. See *shrew*

(4) scolding (woman) *n.*: **Xanthippe**. See *shrew*

(5) scolding (woman, as in shrew) *n.*: **harridan**. See *shrew*

(6) scolding (woman, as in shrew) *n.*: **termagant**. See *shrew*

(7) scolding (woman, as in shrew) *n.*: **vixen**. See *shrew*

scorn (treat with . . .) *v.t.*: **contemn**. ❖ Schopenhauer defined the arrogance no great man is without—the one that **contemns** the views of his contemporaries and lets him, undisturbed, create what they censure, and despise what they praise. (John Simon, review of *The Spanish Prisoner*, *National Review*, 5/4/1998, p. 59.)

   (2) scorn (being subject to . . . , esp. public) *n.*: **obloquy**. See *abuse*

(3) scorn (express . . .) *idiom*: **cock a snook**. See *thumb one's nose*

(4) scorn *v.t.* or *n.*: **misprision** (*v.t.*: **misprize**). See *disdain*

scornful (as in haughty or condescending) *adj.*: **toplofty**. See *haughty*

(2) scornful (toward another, often by being insulting or by humiliating) *adj.*: **contumelious**. See *contemptuous*

(3) scornful *adj.*: **opprobrious** (*n.*: **opprobrium**). See *contemptuous*

scorpion *n.*: **arachnid**. ❖ I was doing 70 when Brian, a decorous and soft-spoken man, politely informed Claudia that a black scorpion was crawling up her bare leg. Aaaaaah! I turned hard and braked on dirt. Brian executed the intruder, garnering new respect from the womenfolk. There was no point speculating how the **arachnid** had joined us. (Alan Behr, "Yucatan Peninsula/A Coastal Warming in Mexico," *Newsday*, 10/6/1996.)

scoundrel (or rascal) *n.*: **scapegrace**. ❖ Dissolute and profligate, elegant and hypnotically charming, Silas [Ruthvyn] has squandered vast sums of money, married a barmaid, committed the usual unspeakable crimes, possibly even murder. . . . [His brother Austin], though a **scapegrace** [himself] in his younger days, could be guilty of such devilry, and he longs to restore the family name. (Michael Dirda, "A Classic of Terror—and Unsettling Ambiguity," *Washington Post*, 2/1/2004.)

(2) scoundrel (or unprincipled person) *n.*: **blackguard**. ❖ It should be obvious what the problem is if you are ever to win an election in a democracy when you think the other party is a crowd of buffoons in thrall to a cabal of **blackguards**. To begin with, it means that your campaign discourse must be designed not to persuade voters, but to deceive them. Worse, it precludes your ever examining your opponents' premises, arguments and conclusions in good faith. (Frank Wilson, "Misunderestimating May Cost You," *Philadelphia Inquirer*, 11/14/2004.)

(3) scoundrel (or thief) *n.*: **gonif**, **ganef**, or **goniff** [Yiddish]. See *thief*

(4) scoundrel *n.*: **rapscallion**. See *rascal*

scour (as in examine closely, esp. for purposes of surveillance) *v.t.*: **perlustrate**. See *examine*

scream (like a cat in heat) *v.i.*: **caterwaul**. See *screech*

(2) scream (or yelp, bark, or screech) *v.t.*, *n.*: yawp. See *shriek*

screaming (as in shrill, sound made by bagpipes) *n.*: **skirl**. See *bagpipes*

screech (like a cat in heat) *v.i.*: **caterwaul**. ❖ [Singer James Brown] doesn't bounce back from those splits quite so fast anymore. He still knows, however, how to **caterwaul** as if someone had just dropped an anvil on his bunion and make it sound not only passionate but musical. (Ralph Novak, Picks & Pans, *People*, 11/10/1986, p. 9.)

(2) screech (or yelp, bark, or squawk) *v.t.*, *n.*: **yawp**. See *shriek*

screeching (of a sound or noise that is . . . , grating, harsh, or otherwise unpleasant) *adj.*: **stridulous**. See *grating*

screwed up (situation that is . . . or chaotic or complicated) *n.*: **mare's nest**. See *chaotic*

screw up (esp. a golf shot) *v.t.*, *n.*: **foozle**. See *botch*

scrutinize (closely, esp. for purposes of surveillance) *v.t.*: **perlustrate**. See *examine*

sculpted (into rock) *adj.*: **rupestrian**. See *carved*

sea (across or beyond the . . . ; coming from across or beyond the . . .) *adj.*: **transmarine**. ❖ In his new book, *To Rule the Waves*, [Arthur] Herman turns to another institution that contributed no less vitally to the spread of liberal order: the British navy. John Hawkins, Francis Drake, Walter Raleigh [all] came from Devon [and] none was an altogether amiable specimen. . . . But the daring seamanship and enterprising spirit of the Devon mariners hastened the collapse of Spain's **transmarine** empire and prepared the way for Britain's dominion over the seas. (Michael Know Beran, "His Majesty's Blue Domain," *National Review*, 11/29/2004.)

(2) sea (of or pertaining to the ocean or . . .) *adj.*: **pelagic**. ❖ Aboard the *Shogun*, a 90-foot mother ship, we would sail southward from San Diego to the rich fishing grounds off the Baja Peninsula and, using only fly-tackle, attempt to capture **pelagic** beasts that are usually the quarry of big-game fishermen armed with giant reels and trolling rods: striped marlin, yellowfin tuna and, most elusive of all, wahoo. (Philip Caputo, "California Dreamin'—Baja Style," *Sports Afield*, 11/1/1994, p. 102.)

(3) sea (of or relating to the . . . or ocean) *adj.*: **thalassic**. ❖ In summer, a great **thalassic** yearning washes over Rhode Islanders from Woonsocket to Westerly, drawing them to swim, sail, fish—and eat. Rhode Island may lack the wide-open spaces and purple mountain majesties of bigger states, but its clamshack cuisine probably beats what they're eating this summer in Nebraska and Wyoming. (Carol McCabe, "Clamming Up in Rhode Island," *Washington Post*, 8/13/2006.

sealed (completely . . .) *adj.*: **hermetic**. ❖ Today's [college] recruiting showpieces are instead mammoth training complexes, combination indoor practice facilities and weight rooms situated a few steps from the dorms, allowing football players to exist in a sort of **hermetic** theme park. (Alexander Wolff, "Football Dorms," *Sports Illustrated*, 10/14/1991, p. 52.)

seal of approval *n.*: **nihil obstat** [Latin]. See *approval*

search (about or through, as in rummage) *v.t.*: **fossick** [Australian]. See *rummage*

search out (through careful or skillful examination or investigation) *v.t.*: **expiscate**. See *discover*

seas (supremacy on the . . .) *n.*: **thalassocracy**. See *supremacy*

seashore (of or on a . . .) *n., adj.*: **littoral**. See *shore*

seasickness *n.*: **mal de mer** [French]. ❖ After opining recently in this section's Travel Q&A column that a lower-deck cabin is the best place to avoid seasickness on a cruise, we heard otherwise from lots of readers, many of whom offered their own advice for heading off **mal de mer**. We wondered: What really works? . . . Results: Bigger is better. Any large cruise ship worth its salt has a built-in stabilizer. (Jennifer Huget, "Lab Report: Seasickness," *Washington Post*, 3/9/2003.)

seclusion (social . . .) *n.*: **purdah**. ❖ [Hillary Clinton's] wild, subversive earnestness has been put on the back burner. She has been in **purdah**, taken the veil, donned the [robe] of political invisibility, played second string to her husband, and spent her days like a Victorian heroine on some White House couch. (John O'Sullivan, "She's Baaack!" *National Review*, 11/10/1997, p. 4.)

second (as in, in a . . . , as in very shortly) *n.*: **trice** (as in "in a trice"). See *quickly*

secondary (actor to the protagonist in classical Greek drama) *n.*: **deuteragonist** [now used in the sense of one who plays second fiddle or serves as a foil to another]. ❖ Jennifer Paterson became famous as half of television's most improbable culinary duo [as a star of the British TV show *Two Fat Ladies*]. She cut such an extraordinary figure that it was easy to overlook the fact that she was, for most of her life, a **deuteragonist** rather than a main player. Her wit was considerable but it was reactive rather than initiatory. (Jonathan Meades, "Before She Was Fat," *Times* [London], 9/2/2001.)

(2) secondary (phenomenon that accompanies or results from another) *n.*: **epiphenomenon**. See *phenomenon*

(3) secondary (rank, esp. in the military) *n.*: **subaltern**. See *subordinate*

second-class (as in acting subservient as opposed to leading) *adj.*: **sequacious**. See *subservient*

Second Coming *n.*: **Parousia** [Greek]. ❖ With these thoughts in mind, as we continue our lifelong preparation for the coming of the risen Christ, all who claim the title of Christian must plan ahead for a face-to-face meeting with Jesus Christ. It matters not whether that meeting occurs at the **Parousia** or comes personally as quickly as today with a heart attack or an accident. (*Piedmont Triad [NC] News & Record*, "Christians Must Learn to Follow God's Example," 5/14/2000.)

(2) Second Coming (belief in the . . . of Jesus, spec. that He will return in visible form, set up a theocratic kingdom, usher in the millennium, and reign for 1,000 years) *n.*: **chiliasm**. See *Jesus*

second fiddle *n.*: **deuteragonist**. See *secondary*

secrecy *n.*: **hugger-mugger**. ❖ [Before George W. Bush could name Richard Cheney as his running mate], a bit of **hugger-mugger** had to be carried out. Cheney, a long-time resident of Texas, had to sneak over to Wyoming, where he once carpet-bagged as a congressman, to change his voter registration to dodge Constitutional strictures against two candidates from the same state sharing a ticket. (*St. Petersburg Times* [Russia], "Read It and Veep," 8/1/2000.)

(2) secrecy (as in, in concealment) *adv.*: **doggo** (esp. as in "lying doggo"; slang). See *concealment*

secret (most . . . parts, thoughts, or places) *n.*: **penetralia**. ❖ The Elgin marbles rate among the greatest treasures of art history. [They are on traveling display in a museum in huge cardboard boxes.] The installation is also strange because it confounds the experience of cowering through the **penetralia** of some priceless archaeological site with the experience of a dense warehouse full of packed fridges. (Robert Nelson, "Boxes Have Lost Their Marbles," *Age* [Melbourne], 12/14/1994.)

(2) secret (as in, of, or relating to a court, legislative body, or other group that meets in private, and often makes decisions that are harsh or arbitrary) *adj.*: **star chamber**. See *closeddoor*

(3) secret (codes hidden in various forms of communication) *n.*: **steganography**. See *codes*

secret name *n.*: **cryptonym**. See *code name*

secretary (as in one who takes dictation) *n.*: **amanuensis**. ❖ When it came time to take the bar exam, Bartlett petitioned the New York Board of Law Examiners for special arrangements [due to an alleged reading disability]. She wanted unlimited time for the test, access to food and drink, a private room and the use of an **amanuensis** to record her answers. . . . After her third failure [of the bar exam], she

sued the board. (Ruth Shalit, "Why Johnny Can't Read, Write or Sit Still," *New Republic*, 8/25/1997.)

secretly (as in privately) *adj.*: **in petto** [Italian]. See *privately*

(2) secretly (as in privately) *adv., adj.*: **in camera**. See *privately*

section (as in portion) *n.*: **moiety**. See *portion*

section off (esp. into districts or geographic regions) *v.t.*: **cantonize**. See *divide*

sections (usually, but not necessarily, in reference to literary . . . , as in fragments, or to disjointed quotations) *n.pl.*: **disjecta membra** [Latin]. See *bits and pieces*

sedate (as in desensitize) *v.t.*: **hyposensitize**. See *desensitize*

(2) sedate (as in to dull or deaden) *v.t.*: **narcotize**. See *deaden*

sedative (as in sleep-inducing) *adj.*: **soporific**. See *sleep-inducing*

(2) sedative (as in something that induces forgetfulness of or indifference to pain, suffering, or sorrow) *n.*: **nepenthe**. See *narcotic*

seduce (as in bewitch or enchant) *v.t.*: **ensorcell** (or **ensorcel**). See *enchant*

seducer (man who is a . . . of women) *n.*: **Lothario**. See *playboy*

seduction (as in lure or temptation) *n.*: **Lorelei call**. See *lure*

seductive (and charming woman) *n.*: **Circe**. See *enchantress*

(2) seductive (as in alluring) *adj.*: **illecebrous**. See *alluring*

(3) seductive (as in alluring) *adj.*: **siren**. [See also the nouns *siren call* and *Lorelei call* under *lure*.] See *alluring*

see (as in understand, thoroughly and/or intuitively) *v.t.*: **grok**. See *understand*

(2) see (something that may be difficult to discern) *v.t.*: **descry**. See *perceive*

(3) see (wonderful to . . .) *adv.*: **mirabile visu** [Latin]. See *behold*

seedy (as in unkempt or slovenly) *adj.*: **frowzy**. See *messy*

seeing (everything . . . in one view) *adj.*: **panoptic**. See *visible*

seek out (through careful or skillful examination or investigation) *v.t.*: **expiscate**. See *discover*

seep (as in cause to escape from proper channels, esp. a liquid or something that flows) *v.i.*: **extravasate**. See *exude*

seething *adj.*: **furibund**. See *furious*

see-through (as in sheer or transparent) *adj.*: **diaphanous**. See *transparent*

(2) see-through (as in sheer or transparent) *adj.*: **gossamer**. See *transparent*

segment (as in portion) *n.*: **moiety**. See *portion*

segregate (as in consider separately) *v.t.*: **prescind** (generally as in "prescind from"). See *isolate*

(2) segregate (from others, as in isolate) *v.t.*: **enisle**. See *isolate*

segregated (as in against the world) *adv., adj.*: **contra mundum** [Latin]. See *against the world*

(2) segregated (as in things that cannot be mixed) *adj.*: **immiscible**. See *incompatible*

seize (for oneself without permission) *v.t.*: **expropriate**. ❖ As Iraq lays claim to Kuwait, so might Syria, Turkey, and Iran decide it's time to **expropriate** Iraqi territory they believe falls more naturally within their borders. (Lee Smith, "War Special Report: What Comes Next?" *Fortune*, 2/11/1991, p. 36.)

(2) seize (as in usurp) *v.t.*: **accroach**. See *usurp*

(3) seize (for oneself without right) *v.t.*: **arrogate**. See *claim*

(4) seize (money unfairly and in excessive amounts) *v.t.*: **mulct**. See *extract*

(5) seize (property to compel payment of debts) *v.t.*: **distrain**. See *confiscate*

seizing (adapted for . . . , esp. a tail) *adj.*: **prehensile**. See *grasping*

seizure (forcible . . . of another's property) *n.*: **rapine**. See *looting*

select (as in choice or excellent) *adj.*: **eximious**. See *excellent*

selection (as in excerpt, esp. from the Bible) *n.*: **pericope**. See *excerpt*

self-assurance (and poise) *n.*: **aplomb**. See *confidence*

(2) self-assurance (excess . . .) *adj.*: **hubris**. See *arrogance*

self-confidence (and poise) *n.*: **aplomb**. See *confidence*

(2) self-confidence (excess . . .) *adj.*: **hubris**. See *arrogance*

self-control (as in marked by simplicity, frugality, self-restraint, and/or . . .) *adj.*: **Lacedaemonian**. See *spartan*

(2) self-control (as in moderation) *n.*: **sophrosyne**. See *moderation*

(3) self-control (as in self-restraint) *n.*: **continence**. See *self-restraint*

self-controlled *adj.*: **phlegmatic**. See *even-tempered*

self-delusion (living in a world of . . . , with a glorified or romanticized conception of oneself, as a result of boredom in one's life) *n.*: **Bovarism**. [This word derives from personality traits of the principal character in the novel *Madame Bovary*, by Gustave Flaubert]. ❖ If she concentrates solely on fantasies and the things she can't have, it's because neurosis has cut her off from reality. More than a melancholic form of affectivity, **Bovarism** is a malady of perception. (Bertrand Poirot-Delpech, "Flaubert's Fool," *Manchester Guardian Weekly*, 8/30/1998.)

self-denial (as in person who practices extreme . . . , esp. for spiritual improvement) *n., adj.*: **ascetic**. See *austerity*

self-discipline (as in marked by simplicity, frugality, self-restraint, and/or . . .) *adj.*: **Lacedaemonian**. See *spartan*

(2) self-discipline (person who practices extreme . . . , esp. for spiritual improvement) *n., adj.*: **ascetic**. See *austerity*

(3) self-discipline (as in self-restraint) *n.*: **continence**. See *self-restraint*

self-esteem *n.*: **amour-propre** [French]. ❖ [Actor Michael] Douglas, with *Fatal Attraction* and *Basic Instinct* behind him, knows all about playing male victimization without total loss of **amour-propre**. (Richard Schickel, The Arts & Media/Cinema: "Sexual Harassment Is a Good Subject for Legal Briefs," *Time* International, 2/6/1995, p. 58.)

self-generated *adj.*: **autogenous**. ❖ With the support of the Korea Employers' Federation, the advocates maintain that a leased labor law should be legislated. They claim that leased work has been created by the **autogenous** needs of the labor market—demand and supply. (Kim Young-Ock, "The Unstable Transition of Female Employment and Related Policy Tasks," Contemporary Women's Issues Database, 1/1/1996, p. 107.)

self-gratification (as in masturbation) *n.*: **auto-erotism**. See *masturbation*

(2) self-gratification (as in masturbation) *n.*: **onanism**. See *masturbation*

selfhood (as in self-identity) *n.*: **ipseity**. See *self-identity*

self-identity *n.*: **ipseity**. ❖ American military exports to World War II Britain included . . . the worst attitudes and fatal repercussions of racism. Britain reeled at such prejudice. John Bull, the personification of their **ipseity**, knew precious little of Uncle Sam, our father figure, let alone Jim Crow, his seedy Southern cousin. All that slave stuff in America, it was thought, surely ended with the Civil War. (Paul Dean, "Fighting Racism with a Segregated Army," *Los Angeles Times*, 3/13/1988.)

self-important (as in pompous) *adj.*: **flatulent**. See *pompous*

(2) self-important (person or official) *n.*: **high muck-a-muck** (or **high-muck-a-muck**). See *bigwig*

(3) self-important (person or official) *n.*: **panjandrum**. See *bigwig*

(4) self-important *adj.*: **hoity-toity**. See *pompous*

self-indulgence (esp. from eating or drinking too much) *n.*: **crapulence**. See *indulgence*

self-indulgent (person, spec. someone excessively devoted to luxury or sensual pleasures) *n.*: **voluptuary**. See *hedonist* and *sensualist*

(2) self-indulgent *adj.*: **apolaustic**. See *hedonistic*

self-inflicted (wound) *n.*: **podiacide**. See *shooting oneself in the foot*

self-interest (making an argument appealing to one's monetary . . .) *n.*: **argumentum ad crumenam** [Latin]. See *argument*

selfish (person) *n.*: **selfist**. ❖ [Under the heading of "values clarification,"] math, phonics, spelling, and grammar became anathema, as did . . . anything "judgmental" toward the "alternate lifestyles" that emerged from closets in the Sixties. The results were predictable: diminished academic achievement, moral anarchy, and the viruslike spread of a **selfist** subculture characterized by the repressed maturity and cultural illiteracy that is so apparent that even the state is now alarmed. (Paul Papendick, "It's Time to Restore Values to Education," *Bergen County [NJ] Record*, 3/4/1992).

self-opinion (overly high . . . , esp. of a little man) *n.*: **cockalorum**. See *boastful*

(2) self-opinion (overly high . . . , spec. the delusion that one possesses superior intelligence) *n.*: **sophomania**. See *delusion*

self-proclaimed *adj.*: **soi-disant** [French]. See *self-styled*

self-produced *adj.*: **autogenous**. See *self-generated*

self-regard (unduly high . . . , esp. of a little man) *n.*: **cockalorum**. See *boastful*

(2) self-regard (overly high . . . , spec. the delusion that one possesses superior intelligence) *n.*: **sophomania**. See *delusion*

self-reliant (country or region) *n.*: **autarky**. See *self-sufficient*

self-respect *n.*: **amour-propre** [French]. See *self-esteem*

self-restraint *n.*: **continence**. ❖ [Sir Joshua Reynolds's 1788 painting *The Continence of Scipio*, commissioned by Prince Grigory Potemkin,] depicts the Roman general Scipio Africanus nobly turning a captured Carthaginian maiden back to her boyfriend. The painting was apparently a tribute to Potemkin's honor and restraint as a military leader, although reportedly **continence** was not one of his virtues. (Grace Glueck, "Catherine the Great Shopper, Buying British," *New York Times*, 11/29/1996.)

(2) self-restraint (as in moderation) *n.*: **sophrosyne**. See *moderation*

(3) self-restraint (as in person who practices extreme . . . , esp. for spiritual improvement) *n.*, *adj.*: **ascetic**. See *austerity*

self-righteous (hypocritically . . .) *adj.*: **Pecksniffian** [after Seth Pecksniff, a character in the Charles Dickens novel *Martin Chuzzlewit*]. ❖ *George* magazine (founded and edited by JFK Jr.) [showed] a picture of Kennedy apparently nude, "artfully seated [showing] only limbs, chest, and face as he ponders a dangling apple," in the words of the AP. . . . Moreover, in the same issue of his magazine, Mr. Kennedy was delivering a **Pecksniffian** lecture to assorted cousins for licentious behavior. (William F. Buckley Jr., "The Honored Guest," *National Review*, 6/14/1999.)

(2) self-righteous (hypocritically . . .) *adj.*: **pharisaical** [as in characteristic of the Pharisees, an ancient Jewish sect]. ❖ What a dreadful thing, that a mother was so poor that she was inclined to abort one of her children. Couldn't she be helped? The pro-abortion people [muttered] that it was an outrageous breach of medical confidentiality that the story should come out at all: a somewhat **Pharisaical** comment in the light of skillful media manipulation from the same sources when the case suited them. (Mary Kenny, "Death before Birth," *National Review*, 9/30/1996.)

(3) self-righteous (persons who are . . .) *n.pl.*: **unco guid** (preceded by "the"). [This Scottish term comes from a 1786 poem by Robert Burns, "Address to the Unco Guid, or the Rigidly Righteous." It is not required that such persons be hypocritical, but it is required that they continually point out the faults of others.] ❖ Scotland's smokers have respected the ban on smoking in public places, with no more than the odd grumble at this restriction to their freedom. But they have not given in to the bullying and moral pressure exerted by the **unco guid**. They have not, as expected, stubbed out their cigarettes. Over the counter sales of cigarettes have risen by 5 per cent since the ban was imposed. This act of defiance . . . makes you proud to be a Scot. (Allan Massie, "Why

Gordon Won't Rock the Holyrood Boat," *Daily Mail* [London], 10/18/2006.)

(4) self-righteous (person, esp. one who hypocritically affects religious piety) *n.*: **Tartuffe** (or **tartuffe**). See *hypocrite*

(5) self-righteous (speech) *n.*: **cant**. See *pious*

(6) self-righteous (of one who is . . .) *adj.*: **bien-pensant**. See *right-thinking*

self-styled *adj.*: **soi-disant** [French]. ❖ It is such a bloody bore when the weather is so hot and one's **soi-disant** boyfriend refuses to go anywhere nice with you. (Helen Fielding, *Bridget Jones's Diary*, Viking [1998], p. 124.)

self-sufficient (country or region) *n.*: **autarky**. ❖ But in an interdependent world well into the Third Industrial Revolution, as the latest explosive advances in technology and communications are sometimes known, **autarky** and isolation are no longer an option. Just ask the Albanians. (Strobe Talbott, World: "America Abroad: And Now for the Sequels," *Time*, 9/9/1991, p. 44.)

self-taught (person) *n.*: **autodidact** (*adj.*: **autodidactic**). ❖ The only way to master anything is **autodidactically**. Lessons are just for the companionship. (Erik Tarloff, *The Man Who Wrote the Book*, Crown [2000], p. 104.)

sell (museum items in order to purchase more) *v.t.*: **deaccession**. ❖ In 1990, to pay for the acquisition of a 300-piece collection of minimalist and conceptual art owned by Count Giuseppe Panza di Biumo, Krens **deaccessioned** three works from [the Guggenheim] museum's permanent collection. (*Washington Post*, "Object Lesson on Museums' Future," 11/2/2001.)

seller (esp. of quack medicines) *n.*: **mountebank**. See *huckster*

selling (act of . . .) *n.*: **vendition**. See *sale*

sellout (relating to a . . . of one's soul to the devil) *adj.*: **Mephistophelean** [after the devil in the Faust legend to whom Faust sold his soul]. ❖ The unwritten clause [in the contract pursuant to which boxer Sonny Liston obtained a manager], the **Mephistophelean** clause, the only clause that mattered, stipulated silently that Sonny now belonged, body and soul to [the Mob]. (Nick Tosches, *The Devil and Sonny Liston*, Little Brown [2000], p. 108.)

semblance (as in representation) *n.*: **simulacrum**. See *representation*

semi-conscious (pertaining to . . . state just before waking) *adj.*: **hypnopompic**. ❧ In my customarily prolonged **hypnopompic** condition on Saturday morning, I became aware that there was a government "initiative" about passports. (Bryan Appleyard, "My Life as a Sock Puppet," *New Statesman*, 2/26/2007.).

semiserious (as in half serious, half joking) *adj.*: **jocoserious**. [This word is not universally recognized in print dictionaries, it can be commonly found in online dictionaries, it is a useful word, and it has the imprimatur of Williams College English professor Robert Bell, who wrote *Jocoserious Joyce: The Fate of Folly in "Ulysses."*] ❧ Life, in [the author's] **jocoserious** estimate, is a flatulent farce: "The truth was awful; that's why you had religion, romantic novels, football," opines one character, while another, sensing his exclusion from the mainstream, recognises "that there was no one else who had his tastes: that he was a part of the apart." (Henry Hitchings, review of *Don't Read This Book If You're Stupid*, by Tibor Fischer, *Independent* [London], 1/2/2000.)

send-off (as in parting words) *n.*: **envoi** [French]. See *parting words*

(2) send-off (act of giving a . . .) *n.*: **valediction**. See *farewell*

senility (that comes with old age) *n.*: **caducity**. See *old age*

seniors (of or relating to . . . , esp. women) *adj.*: **blue-rinse**. See *elderly*

sense (that something is going to occur) *n.*: **presentiment**. See *premonition*

sense of humor (having a . . . , as in ability or tendency to laugh) *n.*: **risibility**. See *laugh*

(2) sense of humor (person who has no . . .) *n.*: **agelast**. See *humorless*

sensible (as in logical) *adj.*: **ratiocinative**. See *logical*

(2) sensible (as in right-thinking) *adj.*: **bien-pensant**. See *right-thinking*

sensualist (as in one whose life is given over to sensual pleasures) *n.*: **voluptuary** [see also *hedonist*]. ❧ Someone who rejoices in sensory experience; a sensualist is someone concerned with gratifying his sexual appetites of all time—not Cleopatra, Marilyn Monroe, Proust, or any of the other obvious **voluptuaries**— was a handicapped woman with several senses gone. Blind, deaf, mute, Helen Keller's remaining senses were so finely attuned that when she put her hands on the radio to enjoy music, she could tell the difference between the cornets and the strings. (Diane Ackerman, "There Is No Way in Which to Understand the World without First Detecting It; Through the Radar-Net of Our Senses," *Fort Lauderdale Sun-Sentinel*, 7/7/2000.)

sensuous (and luxurious) *adj.*: **sybaritic**. See *luxurious*

sentence (which is left unfinished because the speaker is unwilling or unable to continue or because the rest of the message is implicit) *n.*: **aposiopesis**. See *statement*

sentencing (of convicted persons, spec. burning of heretics at the stake) *n.*: **auto-da-fé**. See *execution*

sentimental (in an excessive or contrived way) *adj.*: **bathetic**. ❧ Right now, aside from **bathetic** song tributes and the mastications of the self-loathing news media, no one knows what to do about Diana's death; the public, for its part, is mesmerized by its operatic grief. (Bruce Handy, "After Princess Diana: I Can't Laugh without You: With Comedy and Mourning, Timing Is Everything, *Time*, 9/22/1997, p. 34.)

(2) sentimental (overly . . .) *adj.*: **mawkish**. ❧ Where great passion leaves off and **mawkishness** begins, I'm not sure. But our tendency to scoff at the possibility of the former and to label genuine and profound feelings as maudlin makes it difficult to enter the realm of gentleness required to understand the story of Francesca Johnson and Robert Kincaid. (Robert

James Waller, *The Bridges of Madison County*, Warner Books [1992], p. xii.)

(3) sentimental (of or relating to something that is pretty in a superficially . . . way) *adj.*: **chocolate-box**. See *pretty*

(4) sentimental (affectedly or excessively . . . , quaint or dainty) *adj.*: **twee**. See *quaint*

sentimentality (which is excessive or contrived) *n.*: **bathos**. ❖ A weepie, in movie-speak, is a film that relies on a strong dose of sentimentality for its forward momentum. . . . But what of a weepie that doesn't work? . . . [*Autumn in New York*] manages to pull out all the mawkish stops without prompting in its viewers so much as a half-hearted sniffle. [The movie is] equal parts perversity and **bathos**. (Adina Hoffman, "An Affair to Forget," *Jerusalem Post*, 1/12/2001.)

separable *adj.*: **dissociable**. ❖ Said recognised that Israel's exemption from the normal criteria by which nations are measured owed everything to the Holocaust. But while recognising its unique significance, he did not see why its legacy of trauma and horror should be exploited to deprive the Palestinians, a people who were "absolutely **dissociable** from what has been an entirely European complicity," of their rights. (*Irish Times*, "Bold Advocate of Palestinian Cause," 9/27/2003.)

separate (into component parts) *v.i.*: **disaggregate**. ❖ Torre believes that unless educational programs which are designed for Hispanics are redesigned with Puerto Ricans specifically in mind, the needs of Puerto Ricans students will be ignored every time. . . . "We [Puerto Ricans have] been made 'Hispanics.' We need to **disaggregate** the data by subgroup. Otherwise the needs of the subgroups will not be met," she says. (*Black Issues in Higher Education*, "Reaching Out, but in Which Direction? The Future Focus of Academic Outreach Programs," 2/20/1997.)

(2) separate (into thin layers) *v.i.*: **delaminate**. ❖ With many [paint] strippers, the softened paint finish begins to swell. This swelling produces tension forces that cause the paint layers to **delaminate** from one another and the wood or metal you are refinishing. (Tim Carter, "Paint Strippers Require You to Read Label, Be Patient," *Minneapolis Star Tribune*, 5/22/1997.)

(3) separate (esp. from one's accustomed environment) *v.t.*: **deracinate**. See *uproot*

(4) separate (esp. into districts or geographic regions) *v.t.*: **cantonize**. See *divide*

(5) separate (from others, as in isolate) *v.t.*: **enisle**. See *isolate*

(6) separate (out, as in consider separately) *v.t.*: **prescind** (generally as in "prescind from"). See *isolate*

(7) separate (state or quality of being . . . , as in different, from others) *n.*: **alterity**. See *different*

(8) separate (tending to . . . or disintegrate) *adj.*: **fissiparous**. See *break up*

(9) separate (as in differentiate) *v.t.*, *v.i.*: **secern**. See *differentiate*

separated (from outside influences) *adj.*: **hermetic**. See *sealed*

(2) separated *adj.*: **cloven**. See *split*

separateness (as in that quality which makes one thing different from any other) *n.*: **haecceity** (or **haeccity**). See *individuality*

separating (act of . . . into parts) *n.*: **fission**. See *splitting*

(2) separating *adj.*: **diacritical**. See *distinguishing*

separation *n.*: **diremption**. ❖ Sin is a breach in one's relationship to others, to the creation and to God [, and evil] makes the re-establishment of the relationship and healing appear impossible. The bond is forever broken. That is why evil is so chilling. Its victory results in complete **diremption**, the loss of all hope of relationship, atonement, or redemption. (Andrew Kimbrell, "Confronting Evil," *Tikkun*, 11/1/2001.)

(2) separation (often due to division, within a group or union) *n.*: **scission**. See *split*

(3) separation (relating to or attempting to create . . . , esp. within the Christian church) *adj.*: **schismatic**. See *disunity*

sequence *n.*: **consecution**. ❖ Subdivide each topic into studies; each study into lessons; each lesson into specific facts and formulae. Let the child proceed step by step to master each one of these separate parts, and at last he will have covered the entire ground. . . . Thus emphasis is put upon the logical subdivisions and **consecutions** of subject matter. (Judy W. Kugelmass, "Educating Children with Learning Disabilities in Foxfire Classrooms," *Journal of Learning Disabilities*, 11/1/1995, p. 545.)

(2) sequence (as in chain or link) *n.*: **catenation** (*v.t.*: **catenate**). See *chain*

serene *adj.*: **equable**. ❖ But, as the seventh youngest of the nine children born to Jim and Jocelyn Rafter in the bleak copper [Australian] mining town of Mount Isa, [U.S. Open champion Patrick Rafter] was, as he says, "kept level" in the matter of humility, though he acknowledges a temper lurks beneath that **equable** exterior. (Ronald Atkin, interview with Patrick Rafter, *Independent on Sunday*, 8/29/1999.)

(2) serene (and carefree time) *adj.*: **prelapsarian**. See *innocent*

(3) serene (as in a place that is . . . , rustic, and simple) *adj.*: **Arcadian**. See *pastoral*

serenity (as in peace of mind) *n.*: **heartsease**. See *peace of mind*

serial (as in book published in installments) *n.*: **fascicle**. See *book*

series (as in chain or link) *n.*: **catenation** (*v.t.*: **catenate**). See *chain*

serious (as in critical, stage or period) *n.*, *adj.*: **climacteric**. See *critical*

(2) serious (partly . . . and partly joking) *adj.*: **jocoserious**. See *semiserious*

sermonizing (relating to or in the nature of . . . , esp. on a practical, rather than theological, matter) *adj.*: **homiletic**. See *preaching*

servant (as in aide or assistant) *n.*: **factotum**. See *assistant*

(2) servant (as in willing tool of another) *n.*: **âme damnée** [French]. See *lackey*

servile (person) *n.*: **lickspittle**. See *sycophant*

(2) servile (to act in a . . . manner) *v.i.*: **genuflect**. See *kneel*

(3) servile (to be . . . toward) *v.i.*: **truckle**. See *kowtow*

(4) servile (to behave toward in a . . . manner) *v.t.*: **bootlick**. See *kowtow*

(5) servile *adj.*: **sequacious**. See *subservient*

servitude (as in forced work for little or no pay) *n.*: **corvée**. ❖ For what makes a woman is a specific social relation to a man, a relation that we have previously called servitude, a relation which implies personal and physical obligation as well as economic obligation ("forced residence," domestic **corvée**, conjugal duties, unlimited production of children, etc.), a relation which lesbians escape by refusing to become or to stay heterosexual. (Jacob Hale, "Are Lesbians Women?" *Hypatia*, 3/1/1996, p. 94.)

(2) servitude (to free from . . .) *v.t.*: **manumit**. See *emancipate*

(3) servitude *n.*: **thralldom**. See *bondage*

set (close together, side by side, or in proper order) *v.t.*: **collocate**. See *place*

set apart (from others, as in isolate) *v.t.*: **enisle**. See *isolate*

set aside (as in consider separately) *v.t.*: **prescind** (generally as in "prescind from"). See *isolate*

setting (or physical environment) *n.*: **mise-en-scène** [French: putting on stage. It is not always hyphenated]. ❖ [T]he blighted streets and conveniently vacant buildings way east of Bunker Hill are enjoying a newfound stardom. Directors, production designers and location managers turn to them, drawn by all the built-in glamour and elaborate, decaying detail, for a readymade, post-apocalyptic **mise en scène**. The rundown area bordering skid row is, on nearly any weekday . . . crowded with movie trailers. (Mary Melton, Movies: "We'll Fake Manhattan," *Los Angeles Times*, 8/30/1998.)

settlement (temporary . . . between opposing parties pending final deal) *n.*: **modus vivendi** [Latin]. See *truce*

seven (group of . . . , or a week) *n.*: **hebdomad** (*adj.*: **hebdomadal**). See *weekly*

severe (as in . . . remarks) *adj.*: **astringent**. See *harsh*

severing (often from or within a group or union) *n*.: **scission**. See *split*

sewer *n*.: **cloaca**. ❖ [The Thames River] was "dirty" in a most literal sense, too, since for many years all the sewers of London ran directly into its water, creating a vast **cloaca** of stench and disease. (Peter Ackroyd, "In Praise of London's 'Old Father,'" *Newsweek* International, 11/22/1999, p. 76.)

sex (absence of or decline in desire for . . .) *n*.: **anaphrodisia**. ❖ *Donahue* 10 a.m. on Channel 2—**Anaphrodisia**: Women who hate to have sex. (Jennifer Erickson, "Today's TV Tips Prime Time," *Atlanta Journal-Constitution*, 11/16/1992.)

(2) sex *idiom*: **slap and tickle**. [This chiefly British term usually refers to sexual activity short of intercourse, such as cuddling or kissing, but sometimes refers to intercourse itself. Cole Porter famously used the term in his song "Most Gentlemen Don't Like Love": "As Madam Sappho in some sonnet said / 'A slap and a tickle / Is all that the fickle / Male / Ever has in his head.'"] ❖ We fear for Callum Best's taste. The dishy son of [soccer star] George Best has found himself a rather unfortunate new friend—Jordan. . . . After rejecting most of London's finest ladies he has turned to big-boobed Jordan for a spot of fun. But instead of a bit of **slap and tickle**, the pair enjoy shopping together. It'll be games of chess next. (Jessica Callan, "3a.m.: Booby Prize," *Mirror* [London], 10/5/2001.)

(3) sex (boy who has . . . with a man) *n*.: **catamite**. ❖ [O]f another uncle [the author writes]: "He was addicted to vice and debauchery. He drank wine continually. He kept a lot of **catamites**, and in his realm wherever there was a comely, beardless youth, he did everything he could to turn him into a **catamite**." (Amitav Ghosh, review of *The Baburnama*, by Zahiruddin Mohammad Babur, translated by Wheeler M. Thackson, *New Republic*, 1/6/1997.)

(4) sex (excessively interested in) *adj*.: **hypersexual**. ❖ REM sleep seems to play a central role in regulating sex drive. Animal studies point the way: Cats that are deprived of REM sleep show dramatic increases in drive-oriented behaviors. They become more aggressive, develop a greater appetite, and become **hypersexual**. (Michael Segell, "The Secrets of Sleep," *Esquire*, 10/1/1994, p. 123.)

(5) sex (or marriage involving persons of different races) *n*.: **miscegenation**. ❖ Gerald Morgan Jr., secretary of the Monticello Association of the Descendants of Thomas Jefferson—which currently consists only of white descendants—says it would be a "moral impossibility" for Jefferson to have impregnated slaves, given his vehement opposition to **miscegenation**. (Barbra Murray, "Clearing the Heirs," *U.S. News & World Report*, 12/22/1997, p. 54.)

(6) sex (as in intercourse, spec. insertion of penis into vagina) *n*.: **intromission** (*v.t.*: **intromit**). See *penetration*

(7) sex (as in the act of . . .) *n*.: **venery**. See *intercourse*

(8) sex (excessive desire for . . . by a man) *n*.: **satyriasis**. See *horniness*

(9) sex (man who has . . . with a boy) *n*.: **pederast**. See *sodomizer*

(10) sex (one having characteristics or reproductive organs of each . . .) *n*.: **hermaphrodite.** See *bisexual*

(11) sex (outside of marriage) *n*.: **hetaerism**. See *affair*

(12) sex (nonpenetrative . . . between two women) *n*.: **tribadism**. ❖ [T]he romantic comedy *Rescuing Desire* comes out against penetration, although more subtly. Middle-aged, baby dyke Toni is counseled by her more experienced lesbian friend that she doesn't need her recently purchased dildo and other toys for lesbian sex. Sex scenes clearly signify **tribadism** . . . and oral sex, but penetration seems left out of the performance. (Mary Conway, "Inhabiting the Phallus," Contemporary Women's Issues Database, 5/1/1996.)

(13) sex *n*.: **houghmagandy** (Scottish). See *intercourse*

sex talk (or swearing to relieve tension) *n.*: **lalo-chezia**. See *swearing*

sexual (relating to or exhibiting . . . behavior in many forms) *adj.*: **pansexual**. ❖ In his persona, meanwhile, [the singer Prince] presented himself as a sort of **pansexual** sprite. Tiny, mascara wearing, lubricious, he gave erotically charged performances and bestowed on his records titles like Lovesexy. (David E. Thigpen, The Arts & Media/Music: "Born Again—Years After Prince Suppressed It, His Fabled Black Album Appears," *Time*, 12/12/1994, p. 94.)

(2) sexual (excessive . . . desire) *n.*: **erotomania**. ❖ It was quickly revealed that [actor Bob Crane] had a passion for promiscuous sex that was only matched by his passion for documenting that passion. . . . Crane was also a pioneer of the now booming phenomenon of do-it-yourself video porn. . . . [T]he hours of tapes and stacks of photographs shot by Crane . . . amounted to a virtual museum of first-person **erotomania**. (Geoff Pevere, "Addicted to the Wrong Kind of Love," *Toronto Star*, 9/8/2002.)

(3) sexual (of or relating to illicit . . . love) *adj.*: **paphian** (or **Paphian**). ❖ [W]henever [Casanova] is laid low with venereal disease—a not infrequent occurrence in these volumes—he typically reviles the unlucky woman he believes to have infected him: numerous are the outbursts in these memoirs against the "whores," "wretches," and "she-monsters" who have passed on to him the **Paphian** disorder. (Terry Castle, "Boogie Nights," *New Republic*, 11/3/1997.)

(4) sexual (as in . . . lovemaking) *adj.*: **amatory** See *lovemaking*

(5) sexual (attraction to animals) *n.*: **zoophilia**. See *bestiality*

(6) sexual (attraction to old people) *n.*: **gerontophilia**. See *lust*

(7) sexual (boy who has . . . relations with a man) *n.*: **catamite**. See *sex*

(8) sexual (desire to look at . . . scenes or images) *n.*: **scopophilia**. See *voyeurism*

(9) sexual (excessive . . . craving by a man) *n.*: **satyriasis**. See *horniness*

(10) sexual (excitement from rubbing against something or someone) *n.*: **frottage**. See *rubbing*

(11) sexual (having a . . . desire) *adj.*: **concupiscent** (*n.*: **concupiscence**). See *lustful*

(12) sexual (intercourse) *n.*: **venery**. See *intercourse*

(13) sexual (preference for unusual . . . practices) *n.*: **paraphilia**. See *deviant*

(14) sexual (study of . . . material) *n.*: **erotology**. See *erotic*

sexual privilege *n.*: **droit de seigneur**. See *entitlement*

sexy *adj.*: **toothsome**. ❖ Sexiest leading lady: . . . The hottest Welsh import since Richard Burton, Catherine Zeta-Jones turns on not only her intended, Michael Douglas, but 28% of those surveyed. Hot on her heels: **toothsome** Julia Roberts (27%). (*InStyle*, "What's Sexy Now!" 9/1/2000, p. 564.)

(2) sexy (as in flirtatious glance) *n.*: **oeillade** [French]. See *glance*

shabby (as in unkempt or slovenly) *adj.*: **frowzy**. See *messy*

(2) shabby *adj.*: **tatterdemalion**. See *ragged*

shade (giving . . .) *adj.*: **umbrageous**. ❖ Masking his steps on the crunchy snow by timing them with the elk's audible footfalls, the hunter moved through the lodgepole pines. Dawn resolved itself into a thin, **umbrageous** light. (Ted Kerasote, "The New Hunter," *Sports Afield*, 11/1/1998, p. 78.)

(2) shade (providing . . .) *adj.*: **umbriferous**. ❖ For most, however, the charm of Surrey hides in its villages, many approached by lanes beneath an enveloping canopy of trees, for in spite of losing nearly 2 million trees in the 1987 hurricane this is an **umbriferous** county. (David Hoppit, "There's More to Surrey Than Suburbs," *Financial Times* [London], 6/27/1992, p. 8.)

(3) shade (having only one . . . of color) *adj.*: **monochromatic**. See *color*

(4) shade *n.*: **tincture**. See *hue*

shaded (by trees or bushes, or set in the woods) *adj.*: **bosky**. See *trees*

shadow *n.*: **penumbra**. ❖ It's been a good grass year in this part of Wyoming half a state away from the Presidential **penumbra** cast by the vacationing Clintons—a late spring, plenty of water, intermittent thunderstorms, just enough rain to put some extra hurry into haying. (Verlyn Klinkenborg, "Where Good Bridges Make Good Neighbors," *New York Times*, 8/28/1995.)

shadow-boxing *n.*: **sciamachy**. ❖ [T]he Champ is in full-time training now, jumping rope, sparring with Floyd, doing his **sciamachy**. (Jeffery Ewener, "Yo! Ontario's 'Rocky' Steps into the Ring," *Toronto Star*, 4/11/1994.)

shadows (interplay of . . . and light, often in a pictorial representation) *n.*: **chiaroscuro**. See *light*

shady (as in giving shade) *adj.*: **umbrageous**. See *shade*

(2) shady (morality or taste) *adj.*: **louche**. See *questionable*

shake (rapidly or spasmodically) *v.i.*: **judder**. ❖ The car was serviced at 12,000 miles in Caithness in March 1994 before I moved to Lincolnshire. Then, noticing severe wheel **judder**, I took the car to a Skegness dealer, who greased the suspension and told me to bring the car back if it got worse. (*Daily Telegraph* [London], unsigned letter to Honest John, motoring columnist, 9/12/1998.)

Shakespeare (worship of . . .) *n.*: **bardolatry**. ❖ [In Germany], in the 18th century, Shakespeare enthralled scholars, actors and directors in such numbers that Goethe was moved to ruminate on the rampant **bardolatry** in an essay titled "Shakespeare ad Infinitum." (Barry Hillenbrand, The Arts & Media/Theater: "Can This Be Shakespeare?" *Time* International, 12/5/1994, p. 52.)

shaking *adj.*: **tremulous**. See *quivering*

shallow (as in superficial knowledge of a subject) *n.*: **sciolism**. See *superficial*

sham *n.*: **postiche**. ❖ The celebration of Black History Month invariably heightens my cynicism, a political **postiche** on an otherwise racially indifferent calendar, save for Reverend King's sadly over-commercialized, mid-

January birthday remembrance. (Rotan E. Lee, "Contract Law Makes Case for Reparations," *Philadelphia Tribune*, 2/15/2005.)

(2) sham (as in something that is impressive-looking on the outside but which hides or covers up undesirable conditions or facts) *n.*: **Potemkin village**. See *facade*

shame (being subject to . . . , esp. public) *n.*: **obloquy**. See *abuse*

(2) shame (to one's reputation) *n.*: **blot (or stain) on one's escutcheon** *idiom*. See *dishonor*

shameful *adj.*: **opprobrious** (*n.*: **opprobrium**). See *contemptuous*

shameless (and conceited person) *n.*: **jackanapes**. See *conceited*

(2) shameless (and scheming woman) *n.*: **jezebel** (sometimes cap.). See *woman*

(3) shameless (and unprincipled person) *n.*: **reprobate**. See *unprincipled*

shamelessness *n.*: **impudicity**. See *brashness*

shantytown (esp. on the outskirts of a city) *n.*: **bidonville**. ["Bidon" is French for "container for liquids," and this word refers to a town built of oil drums, tin cans, or other similar containers. Often—though not necessarily—it refers to shantytowns in France or North Africa.] ❖ You pass the La Saline slum [in Haiti], the lesser known but no less horrific cousin of Cité Soleil. It is a hive of commotion, strapped together with plastic tarps, sheet metal and sticks. No one knows the actual populations of these **bidonvilles**, which, despite the daily toll of disease and hunger and violence, continue to swell with displaced peasants from the country. (Bill Duryea, "The Unbuilt Nation," *St. Petersburg [FL] Times*, 5/25/2003.)

(2) shantytown (esp. in Brazil) *n.*: **favela**. See *slum*

shape (as in physique) *n.*: **somatotype**. See *physique*

(2) shape (distinctive . . . or outline, often of a face) *adj.*: **lineament** (often **lineaments**). See *contour*

shaped (capable of being . . . , such as with plastic, clay, or earth) *adj.*: **fictile**. See *molded*

shapely (as in busty) *adj.*: **bathycolpian**. See *busty*

(2) shapely (as in busty) *adj.*: **hypermammiferous**. See *busty*

(3) shapely (rear end) *adj.*: **callipygian**. See *rear end*

share (as in portion) *n.*: **moiety**. See *portion*

sharp (agreeably . . . in taste or flavor) *adj.*: **piquant**. See *zesty*

(2) sharp (as in . . . remarks) *adj.*: **astringent**. See *harsh*

(3) sharp (as in biting or tart) *adj.*: **acidulous**. See *tart*

(4) sharp (as in having a penetrating quality) *adj.*: **gimlet** (esp. as in "gimlet eye"). See *penetrating*

(5) sharp (as in incisive or perceptive) *adj.*: **trenchant**. See *incisive*

(6) sharp (to taste or smell) *adj.*: **acrid**. See *pungent*

sharpness (as in incisiveness) *adj.*: **acuity**. See *keenness*

shave (one's head) *v.t.*, *n.*: **tonsure**. ❖ The pre-Christian Greeks shaved the heads of their slaves, and the tradition survived for as long as slavery did, even into 19th-century America. Imitating slaves, the first Christian monks adopted the monastic **tonsure** as a sign of submission to God. (Colby Cosh, "The Shape of Things to Come," Alberta Report/Western Report, 10/14/1996, p. 26.)

sheath (for a dagger, sword, or knife) *n.*: **scabbard**. ❖ Edmund Burke, lamenting the death of chivalry, once thundered that a thousand swords should have leaped from their **scabbards** to prevent Queen Marie Antoinette from being dragged to the guillotine by a mob of French revolutionaries. (Norman Podhoretz, "'Sexgate,' the Sisterhood, and Mr. Bumble," Commentary, 6/1/1998, p. 23.)

shed (a skin or covering) *v.t.*, *v.i.*: **exuviate**. ❖ It's the Zhang Yimou factor that remains both her agony and ecstasy: hard as she tries to **exuviate** his influence, her contemporaries insist she's defined by it. (Stephen Short, "She Makes Magic: With Her Mesmerizing Per-

formances, Zhang Ziyi Is Casting a Spell on Audiences Beyond Her Native China," *Time International*, 12/11/2000.)

(2) shed (with one slope or pitch) *n.*: **lean-to**. ❖ Anchor a tarp over a log or a partially overturned canoe or boat. For more room, lash a cross-pole between two trees to make a **lean-to** out of the tarp. (Anthony Acerrano, "How to Stay Alive!" *Sports Afield*, 7/1/1995, p. 68.)

(3) shed *v.i.*: **abscise**. ❖ What is true decline? It often begins only with patches of leaves being smaller than normal and perhaps discolored. These same leaves may drop, or **abscise**, prematurely. (John Ball, "Going, Going, Gone: Diagnosing Tree Decline," *Grounds Maintenance*, 9/1/1999.)

sheep (of, relating to, or characteristic of) *adj.*: **ovine**. ❖ Hello, Dolly [a cloned sheep], brave new **ovine**; art thou a wolf in sheep's cloning? (*Time*, unsigned letter to the editor, 3/31/1997, p. 10.)

sheepish (as in shy, and/or sullen, and/or socially withdrawn or inexperienced) *adj.*: **farouche** [French]. See *shy*

sheer *adj.*: **diaphanous**. See *transparent*

(2) sheer *adj.*: **gossamer**. See *transparent*

shell (of a turtle, like a protective covering) *n.*: **carapace**. ❖ All marriages begin in myth. The myth is the **carapace** under which the real marriage takes shape; the cracking of the **carapace**, like the breakup of the ice on a spring-swollen river, is a deafening thing. (Lynn Darling, "For Better and Worse," *Esquire*, 5/1/1996, p. 58.)

shell game (as in swindle) *n.*, *v.t.*: **thimblerig**. See *swindle*

shelter (as in surround, often protectively) *v.t.*: **embosom**. See *surround*

(2) shelter (place of . . . , as in small, usu. temporary defensive fortification) *n.*: **redoubt**. See *refuge*

(3) shelter (as in safe haven) *n.*: **querencia**. See *safe haven*

shelve (as in discontinue, esp. a session of Parliament) *v.t.*: **prorogue**. See *discontinue*

shield (usually in the form of buffer states,

against nations considered potentially aggressive or ideologically dangerous) *n.*: **cordon sanitaire** [French]. See *buffer*

shift (in a sentence from one construction to a second, grammatically inconsistent construction) *n.*: **anacoluthon**. [This can be intentional, such as when used for rhetorical effect, and unintentional, such as when the speaker changes ideas or focus in midsentence.] ❖ [In a competition asking for limericks based on words beginning with the letters "ai" to "ar," reader Chris Doyle submitted the following:] A sentence begins on a track; / But suddenly changes its tack; / Let's put a sleuth on; / This **anacoluthon**; / And—whoa, get a load of that rack!" (Chris Doyle, letter to the editor, *Washington Post*, 9/19/2004.)

(2) shift (a . . . regarding one's beliefs, causes, or policies) *n.*: **tergiversation** (*v.i.*: **tergiversate**). See *change of mind*

(3) shift (esp. regarding one's beliefs, causes, or policies) *n.*: **bouleversement** [French]. See *change of mind*

(4) shift (sudden . . . of events, often in a literary work) *n.*: **peripeteia**. See *turnaround*

shifting (about) *adj.*: **ambulant** (*v.i.*: **ambulate**, *adj.*: **ambulatory**). See *moving*

shiftless (person) *n.*: **wastrel**. See *slacker*

shifty (as in crafty) *adj.*: **jesuitical** (sometimes cap.). See *crafty*

(2) shifty (as in deceitful conduct) *n.*: **skullduggery**. See *deceitfulness*

shimmering (lightly over a surface) *adj.*: **lambent**. ❖ An inconstant breeze stirred through the valley, and sometimes the wild grass seemed to roll like ocean waves across the slopes, softly aglimmer with **lambent** lunar light. (Dean Koontz, *Intensity*, Bantam [2000], p. 17.)

(2) shimmering *adj.*: **coruscant**. See *glittering*

(3) shimmering *adj.*: **scintillescent**. See *sparkling*

shining (esp. with gold or tinsel) *adj.*: **clinquant**. See *glittering*

(2) shining (softly . . .) *adj.*: **lambent**. See *shimmering*

(3) shining *adj.*: **effulgent**. See *bright*

(4) shining *adj.*: **fulgurant**. See *bright*

(5) shining *adj.*: **lucent**. See *glowing*

(6) shining *adj.*: **refulgent**. See *bright*

(7) shining *adj.*: **scintillescent**. See *sparkling*

(8) shining (like a diamond) *adj.*: **diamantine**. See *diamonds*

shirk (work by pretending to be sick or incapacitated) *v.i.*: **malinger**. ❖ Players are regarded [by team owners] as overpaid louts who greedily want more than they deserve. . . . When a player is injured, he is suspected of **malingering** if he doesn't return to action immediately—unless the bone is sticking through the meat. (Ron Mix, "So Little Gain for the Pain; Striking NFL Players Deserve Much, Much More," *Sports Illustrated*, 10/19/1987, p. 54.)

shirker *n.*, *v.i.*: **goldbrick**. ❖ [V]oters rarely have the option of firing [elected officials] until the end of their term. So you can lollygag for a few years—if that's your preference. . . . Which brings us to Jefferson County Treasurer Mark Paschall, who managed to drag himself into the office on only 132 days last year, according to county records. A **goldbrick**? Quite possibly. But there's nothing to be done about it until 2006. (*Denver Rocky Mountain News*, "On Point," 1/15/2004.)

(2) shirker *n.*: **embusque** [French]. See *slacker*

shit (eating) *adj.*: **scatophagous**. See *excrement*

(2) shit (esp. that of sea birds) *n.*: **guano**. See *bird dung*

(3) shit (feeding on) *n.*: **coprophagous**. See *excrement*

(4) shit (interest in . . . , often sexual) *n.*: **coprophilia**. See *excrement*

(5) shit (obsession with) *n.*: **coprology**. See *excrement*

(6) shit (of or relating to) *adj.*: **stercoraceous**. See *excrement*

(7) shit (study of or obsession with) *n.*: **scatology**. See *excrement*

(8) shit *n.*: **egesta**. See *excrement*

shivering (fit of . . . with cold alternating with fever) *n.*: **ague**. See *chills*

shoemaker *n.*: **cordwainer**. ❖ Until the capitalist era, that is, for thousands and thousands of years up to only two centuries ago, the history of work was, with certain specialized exceptions, the history of craftsmanship. . . . The potter made clay vessels; the cobbler or **cordwainer**, footwear; the weaver, cloth; the tailor, clothing; and so on. (Harry Braverman, "The Making of the U.S. Working Class," *Monthly Review*, 11/1/1994, p. 14.)

shooting oneself in the foot *n.*: **podiacide**. ❖ [This word is not yet dictionary-recognized, but it is a great word that is increasing in popularity. Combining root forms for "foot" and "killing," it was coined by U.N. ambassador Michael Bolton in reference to a speech by Venezuelan president Hugo Chávez. Venezuela was being nominated to the U.N. Security Council but lost the nomination as a result of Chávez's speech. Bolton said: "President Chávez's unconscionable speech to the General Assembly . . . was taken by many of the members of the General Assembly to be indicative of how they'd behave on the council. And it was—it was an act of **podiacide**." Today, the word is increasing in circulation to refer to any self-inflicted wound, as in the following example, which derives from the criticism Joe Biden received for calling Barack Obama "articulate."] ❖ Joe Biden learned the hard way that pointing out Obama's oratory skills is a good way to commit political **podiacide**. It's certain that he is still limping from that comment. Compared to Bush, yes, Obama is quite articulate—but then so is Larry the Cable Guy. Biden must have meant something else, but when the gun went off and the bullet pierced his foot, there was no time for damage control. (D. E. Carson, "Yes, but What Does He Mean, Change," www.broowaha.com/article.php?id=3150, 2/22/2008.)

shopping (compulsion for . . .) *n.*: **oniomania**. ❖ About 90 percent of compulsive shoppers are women. . . . Most are so overcome by feelings of guilt about their spending that only another trip to the shops can make them feel better. . . . Women may have a higher incidence of **oniomania** because of the way they respond to lower-than-normal levels of seratonin. (James Langton, "Cure Being Tested for Shop-Till-You-Drop Syndrome," *Washington Times*, 6/12/2000.)

shore (of or on a . . .) *n.*, *adj.*: **littoral**. ❖ His descriptions of poverty-stricken shore life accord most faithfully with contemporary accounts. The world of the seaweed collectors had become, by 1836, something of a stock-in-trade of **littoral** writing. (James Hamilton-Paterson, review of *Signals of Distress*, by Jim Crace, *New Republic*, 5/6/1996, p. 38.)

short (and squat) *adj.*: **fubsy**. See *squat*

(2) short (speech or writing being very . . . , as in terse) *adj.*: **elliptical**. See *terse*

shortchange (as in overly restricting or limiting, as to amount or share) *v.t.*: **scant**. See *stint*

(2) shortchange (as in to deal with or treat inadequately or neglectfully) *v.t.*: **scant**. See *slight*

shortcoming (tragic . . . , esp. in a literary character) *n.*: **hamartia**. See *flaw*

shortened (something . . .) *n.*: **bobtail**. See *abridged*

shorthand *n.*: **tachygraphy**. ❖ [Samuel] Pepys's Cambridge years were formative. While there he learnt Shelton's **Tachygraphy**, a form of shorthand invaluable for lecture notes but which later came in handy for encrypting his fruitier diary entries. (*Daily Telegraph* [London], "Peterborough: New Peep at Pepys," 2/23/1999.)

(2) shorthand (as in code words, spec. words conveying an innocent meaning to an outsider but with a concealed meaning to an informed person, often to avoid censorship or punishment) *n.*: **Aesopian language**. See *code words*

(3) shorthand (where a part is used to stand for the whole or vice versa) *n.*: **synecdoche**. See *figure of speech*

shortly (very . . . , as in, in an instant) *n.*: **trice** (as in "in a trice"). See *quickly*

(2) shortly *adv.*: **anon**. See *momentarily*

shout (as in screech, like a cat in heat) *v.i.*: **caterwaul**. See *screech*

show (as in send a signal) *v.t.*, *v.i.*: **semaphore**. See *signal*

(2) show (violent . . . in which shame, degradation, or harm is inflicted on a person, often for the enjoyment of onlookers) *n.*: **Roman holiday**. See *spectacle*

showcase (glass . . .) *n.*: **vitrine**. ❖ The dining room, paneled in dark oak with leaded-glass windows, is the focal point for her collection of Chinese Export porcelain. She and Wick designed a glass **vitrine** along one wall to showcase the pieces. (Kirsten Rohrs, "A Music-Loving Couple Orchestrates the Holiday," *Colonial Homes*, 1/1/1997, p. 44.)

shower (as in downpour) *n.*: **cataract**. See *downpour*

show-off (talk or person) *n.*: **cockalorum**. See *boastful*

(2) show-off *n.*: **Gascon** (act of being a . . .) *n.*: **Gasconade**. See *braggart*

show off (relating to speech that is designed to . . .) *adj.*: **epideictic**. See *impress*

showy (but cheap or tasteless, or such an object) *adj.*, *n.*: **gimcrack**. ❖ On Tuesday the Absolutely Fabulous star Joanna Lumley will open a giant multiplex cinema at the Great North Leisure Park, just outside Finchley, north London. . . . To those who loathe the stench of fried food, hate the tinny beat of endless muzak, and deplore the **gimcrack** architecture topped with a grinning Daffy Duck, it is Absolutely Horrid. (Catherine Pepinster, "In England's Green and Multiplexed Land," *Independent on Sunday*, 7/7/1996.)

(2) showy *adj.*: **orchidaceous**. [This adjective is sometimes used to refer to the beauty of a thing, but more frequently it is used to refer to its showy or ostentatious qualities, as in the example given here.] ❖ [At Taillevent restaurant in Paris,] everything remains simple, understated, correct, Timeless. . . . And space, space, space. There's no clutter; no outlandish designer flatware or china; no **orchidaceous**,

wordy wine lists or menus with the requisite undercooked tuna, fantasy salads and crème brûlée. (James, Villas, "Why Taillevent Thrives," *Town & Country*, 3/1/1998.)

(3) showy (but cheap, or such an object) *adj.*, *n.*: **brummagem**. ❖ Robert Altman is American film's chief artisan of costume jewelry. At first glance, the design seems cunning, the gold and the jewels seem rich. Before long, we can see that the design is a mere contraption, the ingredients are gilt and glass. It doesn't take long in Altman's latest, *Kansas City* (Fine Line), for the **brummagem** to show. (Stanley Kauffmann, review of *Kansas City*, *New Republic*, 9/9/1996, p. 37.)

(4) showy (ornamentation that is . . . or superfluous or frilly) *n.*: **furbelow**. See *ornamentation*

(5) showy (esp. regarding speaking or writing style) *adj.*: **magniloquent**. See *pompous*

(6) showy (esp. regarding speaking or writing style) *adj.*: **orotund**. See *pompous*

(7) showy (in a gaudy way) *adj.*: **meretricious**. See *gaudy*

(8) showy *adj.*: **baroque**. See *ornate*

(9) showy *adj.*: **florid**. See *ornate*

(10) showy (as in pompous, speech or writing) *adj.*: **fustian**. See *pompous*

shreds (as in bits and pieces) *n.*: **flinders**. See *bits and pieces*

shrew *n.*: **harridan**. ❖ Set Up a Job Jar. Sure, grandma has used this tactic for ages. But why should that disqualify it? The beauty of the job jar is that husbands see the demanded tasks as issuing from an unemotional cylinder of glass rather than a finger-wagging **harridan**. (Elizabeth Rapoport, "8 Ways to Get Your Husband to Help," *Redbook*, 12/1/1995, p. 53.)

(2) shrew *n.*: **termagant**. ❖ [Arianna Huffington] is the author of six books . . . , a friend to the rich and powerful on two continents, the mother of two young daughters, an intellectual advocate of spiritual awakening . . . , a conservative chat-show hostess, and a reputed **termagant** with the servants. Whew! (Walter Shaprio, "The $20 Million Man," profile of California Republican Michael Huggington, *Esquire*, 10/1/1994, p. 60.)

(3) shrew *n.*: **virago**. ❖ Enlarging on themes from his earlier books, Mr. Nagel depicts [John Quincy Adams's mother] Abigail Adams as a driving, ambitious, nagging **virago**, a perfect "calamity" of a parent, especially in contrast to her husband, John Adams. (Catherine Allgor, "John Quincy Adams: Public Success—and Private Pain," *Washington Times*, 10/12/1997.)

(4) shrew *n.*: **vixen**. ❖ [Winnie Mandela has] been called a shrew. A **vixen**. . . . Baleka Kgotsisile of the ANC Women's League . . . admires Winnie's power, energy and dynamism, but says[,] "The problem with Winnie is that if you don't want to play her game by her rules, she walks away; she simply doesn't play. That is not good for building an organization." (Nokwanda Sithole, "Winnie Mandela: Her Story," *Essence*, 4/1/1994, p. 76.)

(5) shrew *n.*: **Xanthippe** [derives from Socrates' wife, who had such a reputation]. ❖ Remember . . . when a young man and woman couldn't be left alone in room without a chaperone? . . . This hag . . . had a sense of moral outrage which moved her to find evil in a caress. Now this modern day **Xanthippe** runs a sexist women's organization which denies the existence of false abuse allegations and expects millions of American fathers to accept supervised visitation with their own children. (Francis King, "Taliban Movement Gains Strength in the United States," *Fathering*, 9/28/2001.)

shrewd (artfully . . . or cunning) *adj.*: **pawky**. [This chiefly British word often is used with reference to a person's sense of humor, but not always, as in the following example.] ❖ [I called up the Crib Corporation, which writes term papers for students.] ME: Uh, are the professors familiar with your service? I mean, do they ever check papers out? CRIB: Nope. Nobody ever bothers about that. . . . Don't worry, we keep records of the colleges we send

each paper to. The **pawky**, self-congratulating nerve of that yo-yo. I wanted to take a fungo bat and leave him for street pizza somewhere. (D. Keith Mano, "The Cheating Industry," *National Review*, 6/5/1987.)

(2) shrewd *adj.*: **perspicacious**. See *astute*

shriek (or bark, squawk, or screech) *v.t.*, *n.*: **yawp**. ❖ "Woman Uses Glass Eye to Spy on Philandering Husband"; "Help Me Find My Spaceman Lover"; "Nine-Year-Old Boy Is World's Youngest Hit Man"—the headlines of supermarket tabloids supply the titles of Robert Olen Butler's captivating new collection of stories, "Tabloid Dreams." . . . Tabloid headlines capture the **yawp** of the carnival barker: Step right up and see the wonder of the ages. (*Seattle Post-Intelligencer*, "Tabloid Headlines Frame Writer's Search for Truth Among Fantasies," 11/23/1996.)

shrieking (as in shrill, sound made by bagpipes) *n.*: **skirl**. See *bagpipes*

shrill (of a sound or noise that is . . . , grating, harsh, or otherwise unpleasant) *adj.*: **stridulous**. See *grating*

(2) shrill (sound made by bagpipes) *n.*: **skirl**. See *bagpipes*

shrink (back out of fear or desire to shy away from) *v.i.*: **resile**. See *recoil*

(2) shrink (back out of fear or shying away from) *v.i.*: **blench**. See *flinch*

(3) shrink (back, as in recoil, due to fear or intimidation) *v.t.*: **quail**. See *recoil*

shrinkage (as in reduction in size of a swollen object; e.g., loss of erection) *n.*: **detumescence**. ❖ The interesting thing about these lines on impotence is that they were written by a man who died in his 34th year. . . . Still, as we all know today, involuntary **detumescence** can strike at any moment, even when the victim is young and wishes only to demonstrate his love for a woman. (Henry Porter, "If You Want a Good Time, Pay for It," *Independent on Sunday*, 7/12/1998.)

shrivel *v.i.*: **wizen**. ❖ Unfortunately, pumpkins and squashes start to rot after a few months, while most other gourds slowly dry out and turn a pale straw color. Some gourds keep their full, rounded or warty shape, while others **wizen** a little. (*Denver Rocky Mountain News*, "The Fertile Mind," 10/19/1997.)

shrubs (mass of . . .) *n.*: **boscage**. See *bushes*

shudder (from moment of intense excitement) *n.*: **frisson** [French]. ❖ The thing about exploring a guy's back while he's lying face-down is that he's at your mercy—and that's a major turn-on for both of you. Plus, there's so much possibility for serious **frissons** along the length of that gorgeous and muscular terrain. "My guy loves it when I slowly travel up his back with my tongue to his neck," says one woman. "It makes him quiver all over." (Pamela Lister, "5,000 Men Reveal: Their Other Hot Spots," *Redbook*, 12/1/2000, p. 120.)

(2) shudder (as in flinch) *v.i.*: **blench**. See *flinch*

(3) shudder (rapidly or spasmodically) *v.i.*: **judder**. See *shake*

shun (as in treat with contempt) *v.t.*: **contemn**. See *scorn*

shunned (or ostracized) *v.t.*: **sent to Coventry** [British]. See *ostracized*

shutter (window . . . with adjustable horizontal slats) *n.*: **jalousie**. See *window blind*

shy (and/or sullen and/or socially withdrawn or inexperienced) *adj.*: **farouche**. [French. One who is described as "farouche" may have one, two, or all of the above traits, and the example given here suggests all three. It is from an essay by the novelist Elizabeth Bowen about herself. See also *untamed*.] ❖ Perhaps one emotional reason why one may write is the need to work off, out of the system, the sense of being solitary and **farouche**. Solitary and **farouche** people don't have relationships: they are quite unrelatable. If you and I were capable of being altogether house-trained and made jolly, we should be nicer people but not writers. (Chris Hopkins [quoting the Elizabeth Bowen essay referenced above], "Elizabeth Bowen," *Review of Contemporary Fiction*, 6/22/2001.)

(2) shy (and cautious and indecisive) *adj.*: **Prufrockian**. See *timid*

(3) shy (and unassertive person) *n.*: **milquetoast**. See *unassertive*

(4) shy (as in timid and unassertive person) *n.*: **nebbish** [Yiddish]. See *timid*

(5) shy (esp. from lack of self-confidence) *adj.*: **diffident**. See *timid*

(6) shy away *v.i.*: **resile**. See *recoil*

sickening (as in overly sentimental) *adj.*: **mawkish**. See *sentimental*

sickly (and weak person, esp. one morbidly concerned with his own health) *n., adj.*: **valetudinarian**. ❖ At 71, after two heart attacks, he has adopted a distinctly **valetudinarian** demeanor. (Brooke Allen, review of *Starting Out in the Evening*, by Brian Morton, *New Leader*, 12/29/1997, p. 25.)

(2) sickly (as in pale) *adj.*: **etiolated**. See *pale*

(3) sickly (elderly person) *n.*: **Struldbrug**. See *decrepit*

sickness (caused by a physician) *adj.*: **iatrogenic**. See *disease*

(2) sickness (-causing, as in disease-causing) *adj.*: **morbific**. See *disease*

(3) sickness (esp. from eating or drinking too much) *n.*: **crapulence**. See *indulgence*

(4) sickness (fear of) *n.*: **nosophobia**. See *disease*

(5) sickness (of a . . . or disease that has no known cause) *adj.*: **idiopathic** (*n.*: **idiopathy**). See *illness*

(6) sickness (of or relating to a . . . developed by a patient while in a hospital) *adj.*: **nosocomial**. See *hospital*

(7) sickness (pretend to have a . . . or other incapacity to avoid work) *v.i.*: **malinger**. See *shirk*

(8) sickness (early symptom of . . . , esp. migraines, herpes, or depression) *n.*: **prodrome**. See *symptom*

sickout (esp. by policemen) *n.*: **blue flu**. ❖ When a "**blue flu**" epidemic empties the Seattle police department, Lt. Lou Boldt and the few members still working are stretched to their limits, not unlike the nerves of a reader paging through this engrossing new novel.

(Laurie Trimble, "Engrossing Cops-and-Robbers Tale Starts with a Round of 'Blue Flu,'" *Dallas Morning News*, 7/8/2000.)

side dish *n.pl.*: **entremets**. ❖ According to the food historian Giles MacDonagh, he ingested "a hundred Ostend oysters, 12 Pré-Salé mutton cutlets, a duckling with turnips, a brace of roast partridges, a sole Normand, without counting hors d'oeuvres, **entremets**, fruits, etc." (Bee Wilson, "La Gastronomie Humaine," *New Statesman*, 7/19/1999.)

sidestep (as in avert or ward off) *v.t.*: **forfend**. See *avert*

sideways *adv.*: **crabwise**. [This word, often seen in the phrase "moving crabwise," can be used both literally, as in the example here, and figuratively. See *indirectly*.].❖ [The Marine pointed to] the row of chairs along the glass front wall. This was not in Victor's plans. As he walked to the chairs, he would have to face the window. And the watchers. Still wearing his glasses and beret, Victor started moving **crabwise**, while constantly looking at something very interesting on the blank interior wall. He knew he had to keep his head turned away from the surveillance camera. (R. Jellinek, "Freedom Run," *Courier-Mail* [Brisbane, Australia], 12/18/1993.)

siege (of or relating to being under . . .) *adj.*: **obsidional**. See *besieged*

sighing (as in panting) *adj.*: **suspirious** (*v.t.*: **suspire**). See *panting*

sight (having poor . . . , as in nearly blind) *adj.*: **purblind**. See *blind*

(2) sight (loss of) *n.*: **amaurosis**. See *blindness*

sightseers (person who guides . . .) *n.*: **cicerone**. See *tour guide*

sign (early . . . of disease) *n.*: **prodrome**. See *symptom*

(2) sign (or symbol that gives information nonverbally) *n.*: **glyph** See *symbol*

(3) sign (showing an idea without words; e.g., "$," or Chinese or Japanese symbols) *n.*: **ideogram**. See *symbol*

signal (audio . . . that sounds a warning or alert)

n.: **klaxon**. [Klaxon is a trademark for an electromechanical horn or alerting device, which emits a rather blaring noise. The word is generally used (lower case) to refer to an audio alert or a warning of things to come.] ❖ [Walt Disney's] hacking cough was dreaded not only among his employees, who regarded it as a kind of **klaxon** of Walt's impending arrival, but among his own family. (Neal Gabler, *Walt Disney*, Knopf [2006], p. 626.)

(2) signal *v.t., v.i.*: **semaphore** (spec. a visual signal such as flags or mechanical arms, but often used in the broader sense of taking any action to send a signal). ❖ [Warner Bros. cast of cartoon characters included] Porky Pig [as] the harassed middle-management type [and] Elmer Fudd [as] the chronic, choleric dupe. Bugs Bunny . . . became the cartoon Cagney— urban, crafty, pugnacious—and then the blasé underhare who wins every battle without ever mussing his aplomb; one raised eyebrow was enough to **semaphore** his superiority to the carnage around him. (Richard Corliss, "Chuck Reducks: Chuck Jones Just Made Cartoons, but They Were Far More Than Kid Stuff," *Time*, 3/4/2002.)

significance (of equal . . .) *n.*: **equiponderance**. See *importance*

significant (of an event or period that is . . .) *adj.*: **epochal**. See *momentous*

(2) significant (person in a field or organization) *n.*: **wallah**. See *notable*

(3) significant (things) *n.pl.*: **notabilia**. See *noteworthy*

signify (as in portend) *v.t.*: **betoken**. See *portend*

signs (spec. the study and analysis of . . . and symbols as part of communication, as for example in language, gesture, clothing, and behavior) *n.pl.*: **semiotics**. See *communication*

silence *n.*: **harpocracy** (*adj.*: **harpocratic**). [Harpocrates is the Greek god of silence. Recall also that Harpo Marx was the silent one in the Marx brothers films.] ❖ [W]hat we do not know is [Martin] Heidegger's blend of motives for [being a member of the Nazi Party]. Cowardice? Opportunism? Stubbornness? Principle? And if principle, which? Heidegger's **harpocracy** has guaranteed that no one knows how to weight the elements that Heidegger saw . . . in Nazism. (Eric Rothstein, "Heidegger's Silence," *Clío*, 1/1/1998.)

silent *v.i., adj., adv.*: **mumchance** [British]. ❖ There's a group of people, some would say severely misguided, who huddle together for warmth in my name, calling themselves Togs (Terry's Old Geezers). They are the grist to my mill, the only reason I don't sit **mumchance** in front of a microphone every morning. Their letters, their warmth, their wit, make it worthwhile rising in the gloom of an early winter's morning. (Terry Wogan, Wogans World, *Sunday Telegraph*, 2/4/2007.)

silky (as in velvety) *adj.*: **velutinous**. See *velvety*

silliness (as in nonsense) *n.*: **codswallop** [British]. See *nonsense*

silly (as in absurd or preposterous) *adj.*: **fatuous**. See *foolish*

    (2) silly (as in flighty or scatterbrained person) *n.*: **flibbertigibbet**. See *flighty*

    (3) silly (as in laughable) *adj.*: **gelastic**. See *laughable*

    (4) silly (as in laughable) *adj.*: **risible**. See *laughable*

silver (resembling) *adj.*: **argentine**. ❖ [A] moment ago, we are almost certain, we saw the brief silver flash of a tailing permit. . . . The fish makes an initial run of about 150 yards in the direction she came from, and her companion sticks right with her, two fleeing spirits in their **argentine** brilliance. (Dan Gerber, "Permit: The Most Difficult Fish in the World," *Sports Afield*, 9/1/1994, p. 92.)

similar (as in related) *adj.*: **cognate**. See *related*

similarity (of sounds) *n.*: **assonance**. ❖ In fact, internal rhyme and **assonance** have long been a trademark of one-hit wonders. A look back suggests that Chumbawamba has just one hit left in them. Scritti Politti 1 [top 10 hit]; Kajagoogoo: 1; Bananarama: 0; Oingo Boingo: 5; Milli Vanilli: 3; Blues Magoos: 1. (Joel Stein, People, *Time*, 12/08/1997, p. 111.)

    (2) similarity (as in resemblance) *n.*: **simulacrum**. See *representation*

simple (and carefree time) *adj.*: **prelapsarian**. See *innocent*

    (2) simple (as in clear, in thought or expression) *adj.*: **luculent.** See *clear*

    (3) simple (as in clear, in thought or expression) *adj.*: **pellucid.** See *clear*

    (4) simple (as in guileless) *n.*: **artless**. See *guileless*

    (5) simple (as in understandable) *adj.*: **limpid**. See *understandable*

    (6) simple (as in understandable) *adj.*: **perspicuous**. See *understandable*

    (7) simple *adj.*: **abecedarian**. See *basic*

simpleton *n.*: **jobbernowl** [British]. See *idiot*

    (2) simpleton *n.*: **mooncalf**. See *fool*

simplicity (false or insincere showing of . . . , as in naivete) *adj.*: **faux-naïf** [French]. See *naive*

    (2) simplicity (in speech or writing) *n.*: **pabulum** (or **pablum**). See *triteness*

simultaneous (existence in two places) *n.*: **bilocation**. ❖ One [nineteenth-century magician] is renowned for an impossible trick where he seems to be in two places at once; the other is spurred to create a more stunning **bilocation** act using the new technology of electricity. (Gene Lyons, Books: The Week, *Entertainment Weekly*, 11/1/1996, p. 64.)

simultaneously (as in all at once) *adv.*: **holus-bolus**. [This word is used in two related but distinct ways, although the usages are sometimes interchangeable. One is "all at once" or "simultaneously," which is the sense given here. The other is "in the entirety" or "completely," the example for which is under "entirety."] ❖ [Under] Canada's recent constitutional referendum [which was rejected] some federal powers would have been decentralized, federal and provincial premiers strengthened, Quebec designated a "distinct society" and aboriginal peoples' "inherent right to self-government" vaguely acknowledged, among other realignments. Stupidly, the referendum forced citizens to assess all these changes **holus-bolus**, Yes or No. (Carl Wilson, "No, Canada," *Nation*, 12/14/1992.)

sin (study of . . .) *n.*: **hamartiology**. ❖ The question is why do we need to repent? We must first understand **hamartiology**, the doctrine of sin and what sin is. I would define sin as any thought or act or state of being that does not conform to the absolute holiness of God, which incurs guilt before God. (Bucas Sterling, III, "Perfection Rests on Principles," *Washington Times*, 8/22/2005.)

(2) sin (confession of . . .) *n.*: **peccavi**. See *confession*

(3) sin (small or trifling . . .) *n.*: **peccadillo**. See *infraction*

(4) sin (as in wrongdoing, by its own nature or natural law rather than because prohibited by statute) *n.*: **malum in se** [Latin]. See *wrongdoing*

(5) sin (because it is prohibited by statute rather than because the conduct is wrong by its own nature or natural law) *n.*: **malum prohibitum**. See *crime*

sinful *adj.*: **peccant**. ❖ [Otis] did less well by his son, Delmore, whom he hasn't seen since Delmore was eight. . . . [But Otis has a] current, lovingly savvy woman (there must be redemption even for a formerly **peccant** father). (John Simon, review of *Lone Star*, *National Review*, 7/29/1996, p. 54.)

(2) sinful (as in wicked) *adj.*: **flagitious**. See *wicked*

(3) sinful *adj.*: **iniquitous**. See *wicked*

(4) sinful *adj.*: **malefic**. See *evil*

(5) sinful *adj.*: **malevolent**. See *evil*

singer (female . . . who speaks, rather than sings, the lyrics) *n.*: **diseuse** [French] (male singer: **diseur**). ❖ [S]ingers like Frank Sinatra . . . learned the value of honoring a lyric [from Mabel Mercer]. To an extent, that was because, in the last decades of her colorful life, she was less chanteuse than **diseuse**. She, of course, knew the melodies of the songs she chose to interpret, but only followed them when so inclined. Rather, she regarded songs as monologues to be acted with passion and insouciance. (David Finkle, "Oh Happy Day! CDs from Mabel to Michael," *Back Stage*, 7/19/2002.)

singing (responsive . . . or chanting) *n.*: **antiphony**. See *chanting*

(2) singing (and speaking combined together) *n.*: **sprechgesang** [German]. See *speaking*

single (state of being . . . , or nonrecognition or nonregulation of marriage) *n.*: **agamy**. See *unmarried*

(2) single (woman, whether divorced, widowed, or never married) *n.*: **feme sole**. See *woman*

singular (as in occurring one time only) *adj.*: one-off [British]. See *one-time*

(2) singular (as in specific to one person or thing) *adj.*: **idiographic**. See *unique*

(3) singular (as in unique) *adj.*: **sui generis** [Latin]. See *unique*

(4) singular (person or thing) *n.*: **rara avis** [Latin]. See *rarity*

sinister *adj.*: **baleful**. ❖ The successful mapping of the entire human genetic code is such a stupendous feat—and so full of potential for good—that it seems almost gratuitous to start worrying about downsides. Yet I do worry—and not primarily about the **baleful** uses to which the new information could possibly be put: invasions of privacy, ranking of human beings by insurance risk, that sort of thing. (William Raspberry, "Genetic Side Effects," *Washington Post*, 6/30/2000.)

(2) sinister *adj.*: **iniquitous**. See *wicked*

(3) sinister *adj.*: **malefic**. See *evil*

(4) sinister *adj.*: **malevolent**. See *evil*

sink (cause to . . . into mud) *v.t.*: **bemire**. See *mud*

(2) sink (to the bottom of the ocean) *v.i.*: **go to Davy Jones's locker**. See *ocean*

sinking (as in worsening) *adj.*: **ingravescent**. See *worsening*

sinless *adj.*: **impeccant**. See *faultless*

sissy *n.*: **pantywaist**. ❖ In any event, that Bradley attack—and another on Gore for arriving late to the Democrats' anti-tobacco efforts—was clumsy. Bradley is no **pantywaist** in debates; he's trying to be combative. But the "sharp elbows" he promised supporters last year are not finding Gore's rib cage. (Jonathan

Alter, "Bumps along the High Road," *Newsweek*, 1/24/2000, p. 52.)

(2) sissy (as in coward) *n.*: **poltroon**. See *coward*

sister (of or relating to a . . . , or sisterly) *adj.*: **sororal**. ❖ They are not sisters, nor are they named Banger. But Suzette and Vinnie share a **sororal** connection that stretches back decades, to an era when "sex, drugs and rock 'n' roll" summarized an enviable lifestyle. (Bob Ross, "Hawn, Sarandon Put Comic Bang in *Sisters*," *Tampa Tribune*, 9/20/2002.)

site (as in condition of being located in a particular place) *n.*: **ubiety**. See *place*

sit still (ability to . . .) *n.*: **sitzfleisch**. See *endure*

situation (which is difficult or complex) *n.*: **nodus**. See *complication*

skeletal (as in emaciated, esp. as to children as a result of malnutrition) *adj.*: **marasmic**. See *emaciated*

skeleton key (spec. something such as a . . . that allows one to gain access or pass at will) *n.*: **passe-partout** [French]. See *passkey*

skeptic (as in one with no faith or religion) *n.*, *adj.*: **nullifidian**. See *nonbeliever*

skeptical *adj.*: **zetetic**. ❖ The ostensible aim of Mr. Randi's hoax [i.e., convincing researchers that two boys had paranormal powers] was to make psychic researchers rely more widely on the advice of magicians. . . . [However,] the editor of **Zetetic** *Scholar*, a journal devoted to the skeptical analysis of paranormal claims, [stated:] "In no way will his project teach psychic researchers a lesson and make them more likely to trust to magicians' advice." (William Broad, "Magician's Effort to Debunk Scientists Raises Ethical Issues," *New York Times*, 2/15/1983.)

sketch (out in an incomplete way) *v.t.*: **adumbrate**. See *outline*

skill (area of . . .) *n.*: **métier** [French]. See *forte*

(2) skill (person's area of) *n.*: **bailiwick**. See *expertise*

skilled (at handling all matters) *adj.*: **omnicompetent**. See *competent*

skillful *adj.*: **habile**. ❖ The first [choice for the West] was to tolerate Slobodan Milosevic's police and military campaign. . . . The other choice was a NATO military intervention. . . . Thanks to [the dilemma that both choices seemed to lead to disaster], and to the **habile** cunning, combined with ruthlessness, which has made Milosevic the man he is, the West has lost influence over Yugoslav events. (William Pfaff, "NATO Should Halt the Yugoslav Offensive in Kosovo," *Chicago Tribune*, 9/8/1998.)

(2) skillful (or adept) *adj.* **au fait**. [French; lit. to the fact. This term also means familiar with or informed about. See *familiar*.] ❖ I get the impression from our rather-stilted conversation that patience and warmth aren't virtues [British comedian Rhona Cameron is] that familiar with. On the other hand, she's utterly **au fait** with humour, quick-wittedness and the kind of acerbic but well-placed asides which make her one of Britain's top comics. (Hannah Jones, "Rumble Outside the Jungle," *Western Mail* [Cardiff, Wales], 7/18/2003.)

(3) skillful (as in resourceful, person) *n.*: **debrouillard** (or **débrouillard**) [French]. See *resourceful*

skillfulness (or subtlety, esp. in political or business dealings) *n.*: **Italian hands** [often used in the phrase "fine Italian hands."]. See *subtlety*

skim (a quick cursory . . .) *n.*: **Cook's tour**. See *scan*

skimp (as in overly restrict or . . . , as to amount or share) *v.t.*: **scant**. See *stint*

skimpy (as in meager) *adj.*: **mingy**. See *meager*

(2) skimpy *n.*: **exiguous**. See *meager*

skin (of, relating to, or affecting) *adj.*, *n.*: **cutaneous**. ❖ The American Academy of Dermatology urges that [tattoo] artists be trained, regulated and licensed in precautions having to do with "sanitation, sterilization, **cutaneous** anatomy." (Amy Dickinson, "Why Not Tattoo? Kids Love 'Em, but Parents Can Point Out That They're One Form of Foolery That Won't Go Away," *Time*, 11/22/1999, p. 113.)

(2) skin (tingling or prickling sensation with respect to) *n.*: **paresthesia**. See *prickling*

skinflint *n*.: **lickpenny**. See *miser*

skinny (esp. in a pale or corpselike way) *adj*.: **cadaverous**. See *corpselike*

skirmish *n*.: **velitation**. ❖ You could draw straws to figure out which one broke the [NHL Florida] Panthers' back concerning general manager Mike Keenan. Pick one: The Panthers' failure to make more than a ripple in free agency this summer [or] Keenan's various clashes, some serious, some just **velitations**, with Panthers' upper management and coach Jacques Martin. (David J. Neal, "Keenan Yielded Mixed Results in Role with Panthers," *Miami Herald*, 9/3/2006.)

(2) skirmish (as in brawl, esp. public) *n*.: **affray**. See *brawl*

skull (study of shape of) *n*.: **phrenology**. ❖ Modern **phrenology** was developed in the late 1700s by Austrian physician Franz Joseph Gall, who felt that the form of the head represents the form of the brain, and thus reflects the development of brain organs. (Jim Bernstein, "Vital Signs/Oddity/Head Cases," *Newsday*, 9/26/1999.)

sky (as in heavens) *n*.: **welkin**. See *heavens*

(2) sky (of or relating to the . . . or heavens) *adj*.: **empyreal**. See *celestial*

sky-blue *adj*.: **cerulean**. See *blue*

slacker *n*.: **wastrel**. ❖ Hard as he partied, [NBA player Walt "Clyde" Frazier] always worked harder. Not so [son] Walt. Clyde gave Walt a jump rope to quicken his feet. It went unused. He gave him exercises to improve his lateral movement. Nada. . . . But don't get the idea that Walt was a **wastrel**. "I always stressed his being a good kid and a good student," says Clyde. From an early age, Walt was both. (Jack Friedman, "Jocks: Belatedly Learning That Father Knows Best, Walt Frazier III Tries to Be a Clyde Off the Old Block," *People*, 2/27/1989, p. 73.)

(2) slacker *n*.: **embusque** [French]. ❖ All along I had been convinced that the United States ought to aid in the struggle against Germany. With that conviction, it was plainly up to me to do more than drive an ambulance. The more I saw the splendour of the fight the French were fighting, the more I felt like an **embusque**—what the British call a "shirker." So I made up my mind to go into aviation. (James R. McConnell, "True Stories of the Great War: II—Story of the Personnel of the Escadrille, *History of the World*, 1/1/1992.)

(3) slacker (as in one who avoids work or assigned duties) *n*., *v.i*.: **goldbrick**. See *goldbrick*

(4) slacker (as in person who stays in bed out of laziness) *n*.: **slugabed**. See *lazy*

slander (so as to humiliate or disgrace) *v.t*.: **traduce**. See *malign*

(2) slander *n*.: **calumniate** *(v.t*.: **calumny**). See *malign*

(3) slander *v.t*.: **asperse**. See *defame*

(4) slander (as in the destroying of one's reputation) *n*.: **famicide**. See *defamation*

slant (as in downward slope) *n*.: **declivity** (*adj*.: **declivitous**). See *decline*

(2) slant (as in upward slope) *n*.: **acclivity** (*adj*.: **acclivitous**). See *incline*

(3) slant (esp. extending down from a fortification) *n*.: **glacis**. See *decline*

slate *n.pl*.: **papabili** [Italian]. See *candidates*

slaughter (large-scale . . . or sacrifice) *n*.: **hecatomb**. ❖ It is unlikely that even the Serbian "irregulars" in Kosovo have exceeded what they accomplished in that Bosnian "safe haven" in July 1995: the organized killing and interment of perhaps 10,000 male captives. That **hecatomb** was carved out . . . as NATO troops stood by and exchanged pleasantries with the overworked executioners. (Christopher Hitchens, "Minority Report: Srebrenica Revisited," *Nation*, 4/19/1999, p. 8.)

(2) slaughter (mass . . . of unresisting persons) *n*.: **battue** [French]. See *killing*

slaughterhouse *n*.: **abattoir**. ❖ Now it is impossible to find meat of any kind, except chicken, in Delhi. A high court ruled that the city's main Idgah **abattoir** was killing too many animals. More than 12,500 sheep, goats and buffaloes a day were slaughtered there under infernal conditions. (Tim McGirk, "Out of India: Hindu Right-Wing Takes Tough Line in Beef about Meat," *Independent* [London], 4/30/1994.)

slave (female . . . in a harem or concubine) *n.*: **odalisque**. See *concubine*

(2) slave (willing tool or . . . of another) *n.*: **âme damnée** [French]. See *lackey*

(3) slave *v.i.*: **moil**. See *toil*

slave driver (as in strict disciplinarian) *n.*: **martinet**. See *disciplinarian*

(2) slave driver (brutal . . .) *n.*: **Simon Legree**. See *taskmaster*

slave labor (as in forced work for little or no pay) *n.*: **corvée**. See *servitude*

slavery (to free from . . .) *v.t.*: **manumit**. See *emancipate*

(2) slavery *n.*: **thralldom**. See *bondage*

slaves (group of . . . or prisoners chained together) *n.*: **coffle**. See *prisoners*

slavish (person who is . . . , as in hardworking) *n.*: **Stakhanovite**. See *workaholic*

slay (by strangling or cutting the throat) *v.t.*: **garrote**. See *strangle*

(2) slay (by strangling or cutting the throat) *v.t.*: **jugulate**. See *strangle*

slaying (of a king) *n.*: **regicide**. See *killing*

(2) slaying (of one's brother or sister) *n.*: **fratricide**. See *murder*

(3) slaying (of one's father) *n.*: **patricide**. See *killing*

(4) slaying (of one's mother) *n.*: **matricide**. See *killing*

(5) slaying (of one's parent or close relative) *n.*: **parricide**. See *killing*

(6) slaying (of wife by her husband) *adj.*: **uxoricide**. See *killing*

sleek (as in elegant and fashionable) *adj.*: **soigné** [French]. See *elegant*

sleep (sudden attacks of deep . . .) *n.*: **narcolepsy**. ❖ Symptoms of **narcolepsy** include excessive daytime sleepiness (even dropping off to sleep at any time, whether it be watching TV or driving a car). (Kathleen A. Rickard, M.D, "Solving the Mysteries of Sleep," *USA Today Magazine*, 7/1/1997.)

sleep-inducing *adj.*: **soporific**. ❖ She [has] been lobbying to have U.S. high schools start later. Some begin classes as early as 7:10 a.m. . . . Schoolmates Arthur Law and William Hui, both 15, go to bed around midnight and are up by 7. They often fall asleep in class, lulled, they say, by the **soporific** effect of social studies or French. (Jennifer Hunter, "Are You Getting Enough: Accidents, Mistakes, Forgetfulness, Impaired Judgment—Canadians Pay a Steep Price for Their Restless Nights," *Maclean's*, 4/17/2000, p. 42.)

sleepiness *n.*: **somnolence**. ❖ **Somnolence** seemed to be an altogether appropriate state for my return to Congo-Brazzaville. . . . [N]othing much ever seemed to happen here. Indeed, bored foreigners often joked about the place, calling it Rip Van Winkle's village, because of its reputation for immutable sleepiness. (Howard French, A *Continent for the Taking*, Knopf [2004], p. 69.)

(2) sleepiness (relating to period of . . . just before falling asleep) *adj.*: **hypnagogic**. See *drowsiness*

(3) sleepiness (as in condition of stupor or unconsciousness resulting from narcotic drugs) *n.*: **narcosis**. See *stupor*

sleepless (night) *n.*: **white night**. ❖ And his coachhouse parties, **white nights** in which no one had trouble staying awake, were legendary. (*Maclean's*, "Wild Nights in Movieland: How Toronto's Film Festival Came of Age While Grappling with the Egos and Appetites of Hollywood Stars," 8/28/2000, p. 30.)

sleepy (as in sluggish or lethargic) *adj.*: **torpid**. See *lethargic*

sleight of hand *n.*: **prestidigitation**. ❖ He tells us that until he saw [Bill] Bradley play [basketball], he'd lost interest in the game because it had, by the sixties, "attracted exhibitionists who seemed to be more intent on amazing a crowd with aimless **prestidigitation** than with advancing their team by giving a sound performance." (Ron Rosenbaum, "The Revolt of the Basketball Liberals," *Esquire*, 6/1/1995, p. 102.)

(2) sleight of hand *n.*: **legerdemain**. See *trickery*

slender (and/or graceful) *adj.*: **gracile**. [Many dictionaries define this word as "slender" and "graceful" simultaneously, while others define it as either one or the other.] ❖ The oldest human remains from Australia, about 45,000 years in age, have quite thin or **gracile** bones, whereas fossils from 20,000 years ago are robust. The new findings suggest that the difference must stem from some internal process like adaptation to climatic change, and not to interbreeding with the archaic species Homo erectus, as some have suggested. (Nicholas Wade, "From DNA Analysis, Clues to a Single Australian Migration," *New York Times*, 5/8/2007.)

(2) slender (body type) *adj.*: **ectomorphic**. See *lean*

(3) slender (and graceful woman) *n.*: **sylph**. See *woman*

slick (as in slippery) *adj.*: **lubricious**. See *slippery*

slide (a . . . down an incline such as a snowy mountain) *n.*: **glissade**. ❖ He perches on the edge of the desk, and a small **glissade** of dislodged documents slides smoothly away into the wastepaper basket. (Michael Frayn, *Headlong*, Metropolitan Books [1999], p. 87.)

(2) slide (downward . . .) *n.*: **declension**. See *decline*

slight (as in to deal with or treat inadequately or neglectfully) *v.t.*: **scant**. [The use of "scant" as an adjective is of course common, but its use as a verb is less so, and its definitions as a verb are distinct from those as an adjective. See also *stint*.] ❖ Walt [Disney] asked [his wife, Lillian,] what she thought of the name Mickey. "I said it sounded better than Mortimer and that's how Mickey was born. . . . [However, in the mid-1930s Walt recalled,] "After trying various names out on my friends, I decided to call him Mickey Mouse," thus **scanting** Lillian's contribution. (Neal Gabler, *Walt Disney*, Knopf [2007], p. 114.)

(2) slight (as in slender and/or graceful) *adj.*: **gracile**. See *slender*

slim (body type) *adj.*: **ectomorphic**. See *lean*

slimy (as in greasy, oily, or unctuous) *adj.*: **pinguid**. See *oily*

slip (of the tongue) *n.*: **parapraxis**. See *blunder*

slip of the pen *n.*: **lapsus calami** [Latin]. ❖ How many of you, I wonder, spotted my **lapsus calami** of yesterday? . . . Let me quote you the offending passage: "Of the many towns and cities on the rivers Elbe and Oder affected by the catastrophic floods of summer 2002, Prague was perhaps the most severely hit." Oops! As every schoolchild knows, Prague lies neither on the Oder nor the Elbe, but on the River Vltava. (Brendan McWilliams, "Kepler a Big Part of Prague's History," *Irish Times*, 6/4/2004.)

slip of the tongue *n.*: **lapsus linguae** [Latin]. ❖ President Bush was smart to choose Spain as his gateway to Europe last week. The Spaniards appreciated the gesture. . . . True, Bush mispronounced the name of Spain's Prime Minister José Maria Aznar, but not even that **lapsus linguae** could sour the mood in the first meeting between the two conservatives. (*Los Angeles Times*, "Bush's Gateway to Europe," 6/22/2001.)

slippage (downward . . .) *n.*: **declension**. See *decline*

slippery (lit. soapy) *adj.*: **saponaceous**. ❖ Perhaps the most revealing incident is the chapter on the kidnapping of Roger Tamraz. Tamraz, a **saponaceous** Lebanese businessman with US citizenship, became known to the American public in September 1997, when he testified before the Senate Finance Committee on a contribution of $300,000 he had dropped into the Democratic Party coffers. (Walid Harb, Books & the Arts: " 'Snake Eat Snake,' " *Nation*, 07/19/1999, p. 25.)

(2) slippery *adj.*: **lubricious**. ❖ Because of their **lubricious** nature, silicones have been added to both aerosol and pump hair spray formulas to reduce friction (and therefore clogging) during spraying. (M. D. Berthiaume, "Silicones in Hair Fixatives & Finishing Products: A Brief Review," *Drug & Cosmetic Industry*, 5/1/1995, p. 60.)

slit *n.*: **aperture**. ❖ I'm told the women of Yemen are particularly beautiful but it's impossible to tell since they are all—at least those over the age of 14—swathed head to toe in swishing black drapery, with the full hijab hiding the face as well as the hair and neck. A few women allow for a narrow **aperture** to reveal their enchanting kohl-painted eyes. (*Toronto Star*, "Bare Arms Draw Daggers, Sweet Words Greet Visitor," 7/28/2000.)

slobber *v.i., n.*: **slaver**. See *drool*

slogan (pithy . . .) *n.*: **gnome** (*adj.*: **gnomic**). See *catchphrase*

   (2) slogan *n.*: **shibboleth**. See *catchword*

slope (downward . . . , esp. extending down from a fortification) *n.*: **glacis**. See *decline*

   (2) slope (downward) *n.*: **declivity** (*adj.*: **declivitous**). See *decline*

   (3) slope (steep . . . , as in cliff) *n.*: **escarpment**. See *cliff*

   (4) slope (upward) *n.*: **acclivity** (*adj.*: **acclivitous**). See *incline*

slothful (person, who stays in bed out of laziness) *n.*: **slugabed**. See *lazy*

   (2) slothful *adj.*: **fainéant** [French]. See *lazy*

slothfulness (sometimes in matters spiritual, and sometimes leading to depression) *n.*: **acedia**. See *apathy*

slovenly (person) *n.*: **grobian**. See *boor*

   (2) slovenly *adj.*: **frowzy**. See *messy*

slow (tempo) *adv.*: **andante**. ❖ The message was clear: under new management, the Catskill Mountains could go far. But . . . Mac Robbins, a fast man with a one-liner, was playing it **andante** today: "It's a sad, sad time. What can you say? It's the passing of what used to be." (Stefan Kanfer, American Scene: "In New York: Simon Says Condo," *Time*, 10/27/1986.)

   (2) slow (abnormally . . . heart rate) *n.*: **bradycardia**. See *heartbeat*

   (3) slow (as in moving like a slug) *adj.*: **limacine**. See *slug*

   (4) slow (in understanding or perception) *adj.*: **purblind**. See *obtuse*

slowing (engaging in . . . tactics, esp. as a means to wear out an opponent or avoid confrontation) *adj.*: **Fabian**. See *dilatory*

slow-witted (esp. used of a person, as in . . . and confused) *adj.*: **addlepated**. See *confused*

   (2) slow-witted *adj.*: **gormless** [British]. See *unintelligent*

slug (of, relating to, resembling, or moving like) *adj.*: **limacine**. ❖ The California State Board of Accountancy . . . has not distinguished itself . . . as a force disciplining dishonest or incompetent accounting practice. It has been effectively moribund in both capacities, remaining in a **limacine** stupor as the profession it regulates has failed to sound the warning call in the face of the largest series of accounting frauds in American financial history: the savings and loan debacle. (Julianne D'Angelo, "There's No Accounting How Far the Board of Accountancy Will Go," *National Public Accountant*, 12/1/1999.)

sluggish *adj.*: **logy**. ❖ The doctors prescribed powerful tranquilizers, Haldol and Clonopin, which helped control the seizures but made him **logy** and incapable of performing at a major league level. (Richard Demak, "Fighting the Enemy Within: Jim Eisenreich's Promising Major League Career Was Derailed by a Mysterious Ailment, but Now He's Working His Way Back," *Sports Illustrated*, 6/22/1987, p. 40.)

   (2) sluggish *adj.*: **bovine**. ❖ [Boxer Ray] Mercer spent two days in detention before being arraigned before Supreme Court Justice George Roberts yesterday [for trying to fix a fight]. His face had the gentle and almost **bovine** look familiar in old heavyweights who will to the wars no more. (Murray Kempton, "They'll Back You Only if It's Worth It," *Newsday*, 6/30/1993.)

   (3) sluggish (as in appearing lifeless) *adj.*: **exanimate**. See *lifeless*

   (4) sluggish (as in relating to, resembling, or moving like a slug) *adj.*: **limacine**. See *slug*

   (5) sluggish (as in weakened) *adj.*: **etiolated**. See *weakened*

   (6) sluggish *adj.*: **torpid**. See *lethargic*

sluggishness (as in lethargy) *n.*: **hebetude**. See *lethargy*

   (2) sluggishness (sometimes in matters spiritual, and sometimes leading to depression) *n.*: **acedia**. See *apathy*

(3) sluggishness *n.*: **torpor**. See *lethargy*

(4) sluggishness (as in condition of stupor or unconsciousness resulting from narcotic drugs) *n.*: **narcosis**. See *stupor*

slum (esp. in Brazil) *n.*: **favela**. ❖ Forget Carnival and the girl from Ipanema. The hot new attractions for visitors to Rio de Janeiro are the **favelas**—those infamous, scruffy, often felonious shantytowns that cling to Rio's sheer peaks. (*Newsweek*, "Slumming Is Hot in Rio," 4/17/2000, p. 74.)

(2) slum (as in shantytown) *n.*: **bidonville**. See *shantytown*

slum-ridden *adj.*: **Dickensian**. See *ghettolike*

slur (ethnic . . .) *n.*: **ethnophaulism**. ❖ Her suggestion that the name "Chief" given an Indian serviceman "indiscriminately . . . by his white buddies" signifies respect and does not constitute an **ethnophaulism**, ignores the historical use of this term, the qualities and functions of ethnic slurs, and indicates an insensitivity to the Native experience. (Alison Bernstein, "American Indians and World War II: Toward a New Era in Indian Affairs," *American Indian Quarterly*, 6/22/1993.)

(2) slur (as in insult, delivered while leaving the scene) *n.*: **Parthian shot**. See *parting shot*

slut *n.*: **roundheel**. ❖ K—: "That she's expected to be both sexually liberated and autonomous and assertive, and yet at the same time she's still conscious of the old respectable-girl-versus-slut dichotomy, and knows that some girls still let themselves be used sexually out of a basic lack of self-respect, and she still recoils at the idea of ever being seen as this kind of pathetic **roundheel** sort of woman." (David Foster Wallace, "Brief Interviews with Hideous Men," short story, *Harper's*, 10/1/1998.)

sly (artfully . . . or cunning) *adj.*: **pawky**. See *shrewd*

(2) sly (as in crafty) *adj.*: **jesuitical** (sometimes cap.). See *crafty*

(3) sly (characterized by . . . and cunning conduct, esp. in regard to the pursuit and maintenance of political or other power) *adj.*: **Machiavellian**. See *deceitful*

small (very . . .) *adj.*: **bantam**. See *tiny*

(2) small (very . . .) *adj.*: **Lilliputian**. See *tiny*

(3) small (very . . .) *adj.*: **minikin**. See *tiny*

small-breasted (condition of being overly . . .) *n.*: **micromastia**. See *breasts*

small-minded (state of being . . .) *n.*: **parvanimity**. ❖ But the most worrying trend is that Turkey is in the throes of a tug-of-war between the so-called "deep state" of nationalists whose exceeding **parvanimity** leads them to fight tooth and nail those reforms [toward enforcing rights and civil liberties] versus those who are moving Turkey forward in decidedly guarded steps. (Dr. Harry Hagopian, "A Test Case for the European Union?" www.newropeans-magazine.org/content/view/3148/90/, 12/27/2005.)

small talk (idle . . .) *n.*: **palaver**. ❖ How much sharing of personal information at work should you do? How much is too much? And on the other side, how do you handle personal questions flung your way at the office? . . . Of course, we're just talking about everyday random **palaver** here. We're not talking about serious illness or major personal catastrophes. (Amy Joyce, "Too Personal for Professionals? Office Chitchat Can Be Harmless, but Sometimes It Crosses That Blurry Line," *Washington Post*, 4/7/2002.)

(2) small talk *n.*: **bavardage**. See *chitchat*

smart aleck *n.*: **wisenheimer**. ❖ Once upon a time, the big thrill for young **wisenheimers** who perched on Santa's lap was to pull off the old guy's fake beard. But these days, according to a new study, 95% of mall Santas are "Natural Santas"—that is, they have their own beard. (Daniel Eisenberg, Notebook, *Time*, 12/22/1997, p. 11.)

(2) smart aleck (and conceited person) *n.*: **jackanapes**. See *conceited*

smell (of or relating to sense of . . .) *adj.*: **olfactory**. ❖ While we must rely on only three quarters of a square inch of **olfactory** equipment—as opposed to ten square inches on a dog and twenty-four square feet on a shark, which can smell a drop of blood from miles away—the human nose can still be turned into a powerful antenna. (Cal Fussman, "Fee-fi-fo-fum, I Smell . . . Orange Peel, Leather, and My Daughter's Diaper," *Esquire*, 9/1/1998, p. 168.)

(2) smell (loss of sense of . . .) *n*.: **anosmia**. ❖ Why is it difficult to smell a fragrance on yourself? "Because you develop **anosmia**," says Antonia Bellanca, a top perfumer. "Your sense of smell becomes saturated, and your brain turns off to the fragrance." (Lois Joy Johnson, "Scents and Sensibility," *Ladies' Home Journal*, 5/1/1996, p. 148.)

(3) smell (bad . . . from body sweat) *n*.: **bromidrosis**. See *sweat*

(4) smell (bad . . . from waste or decayed matter) *n*.: **effluvium**. See *odor*

(5) smell (foul) *n*.: **fetor**. See *stench*

(6) smell (which is fragrant) *n*.: **ambrosia** (*adj*.: **ambrosial**) See *flavor*

smelling (like, or reminiscent of) *adj*.: **redolent**. See *reminiscent*

smelly *adj*.: **fetid**. ❖ Ask any economist to name the top 100 appreciating assets, and it is highly unlikely that old sneakers would make anyone's list. Yet the value of those decrepit shoes in the back of your closet—yes, even the ones that reek worse than **fetid** feta—may well have increased by a multiple akin to Amazon. com's stock. (L. Jon Wertheim, "The Smell of Money—There's a Hot Resale Market for Fetid Old Sneakers," *Sports Illustrated*, 11/16/1998, p. R1.)

(2) smelly *adj*.: **graveolent**. ❖ Garibaldi left his island retreat in the Mediterranean and took up a new cause. . . : diverting the **graveolent**, disease-ridden River Tiber away from Rome by building over it a Parisian-style boulevard, which he dreamt would become a wonder of the modern world. (*Economist*, "So Close, and Yet So Far; The Eternal City," 7/9/2005.)

(3) smelly *adj*.: **mephitic** (*n*.: **mephitis**). ❖ An organization called the Human Ecology Action League has declared: "Perfume is going to be the tobacco smoke of tomorrow."

To those who want to make America scent-free, perfume vapor, like nicotine smoke, is a **mephitic** poison in the nose, like the smell of a reeky skunk. (Richard Klein, "Get a Whiff of This: Breaking the Smell Barrier," *New Republic*, 2/6/1995, p. 18.)

(4) smelly *adj*.: **noisome**. ❖ Odor caused by gum or mouth disease or that originates in the gastrointestinal system is impervious to brushing, rinsing and chewing, says [one dentist]. For common bad breath, mints are also a bad idea, says Kliossis. "You're feeding the bacteria with sugar—it's actually making the problem worse." He says regular brushing and flossing ought to take care of most **noisome** aromas. (Bo Emerson, "The Dragon Slayers: Our Minty Obssession with the Monster in Our Mouths," *Atlanta Journal-Constitution*, 11/8/2001.)

(5) smelly (atmosphere of crowded or poorly ventilated area) *n*.: **fug**. See *musty*

smile (in a silly, self-conscious, or affected manner, or say something in such a fashion) *v.i.*, *n*.: **simper**. See *smirk*

smiling (as in cheerful) *adj*.: **riant**. See *cheerful*

smirk (in a silly, self-conscious, or affected manner, or say something in such a fashion) *v.i.*, *n*.: **simper**. ❖ One heinous transgression is making another woman feel like half a woman because she didn't deliver her child "naturally." . . . One day, during our mothers' group, [a woman] announced in a **simpering** voice that she had been able to put her daughter on her chest two seconds after birth (as opposed to those of us who'd had cesareans and had to wait several minutes). (Ellen Welty, "My Friend, My Rival," *Redbook*, 5/1/1995, p. 116.)

smoky (and sooty) *adj*.: **fuliginous**. See *sooty*

smooch *v.t.*: **osculate**. See *kiss*

smooth (sound) *adj*.: **euphonious** (*n*.: **euphony**). See *melodious*

(2) smooth (sounding) *adj*.: **dulcet**. See *melodious*

(3) smooth (voice or sound) *adj*.: **mellifluous**. See *melodious*

(4) smooth (voice or sound) *adj*.: **mellisonant**. See *melodious*

smothering (phenomenon of a . . . mother who is overprotective and controlling of her sons, thus hindering their maturation and emotional development) *n*.: **momism**. See *mother*

smudged (or impure) *adj., v.t.*: **maculate**. See *impure*

smutty *adj*.: **fescennine**. See *obscene*

snail (as in relating to, resembling, or moving like a slug) *adj*.: **limacine**. See *slug*

snake (of, relating to, or resembling) *adj*.: **colubrine**. ❖ What do you get when you book one of the biggest house DJs on the planet into one of Cambridge's smallest clubs? We're guessing a serious party. . . . Doors open at 8; we advise getting to Central Square early. By the time the music starts throbbing at 9, there will undoubtedly be a **colubrine** line slithering down Mass. Ave. (Christopher Muther, Go! Wednesday, *Boston Globe*, 3/6/2002.)

snakes (of, resembling, or relating to) *adj*.: **ophidian**. ❖ The implication is clearly that the land should belong to those who work it: "Grampa killed Indians, Pa killed snakes for the land," writes Steinbeck, assuming the collective voice of Tom Joad and his generation. . . . Steinbeck saw no irony in the farmers' staking their claim to the land on their having cleared it of its previous human and **ophidian** inhabitants via genocide. (Eva Resnikova, *"Grapes of Wrath," National Review*, 6/11/1990.)

snared (capable of being . . .) *adj*.: **illaqueable**. See *ensnared*

snarl (as in confused or disarrayed mass) *n*.: **welter**. See *jumble*

(2) snarl (as in entangle) *v.t.*: **embrangle**. See *entangle*

sneaking (as in lying in wait for prey, often used of insects) *adj*.: **lochetic**. See *ambushing*

sneaky (as in crafty) *adj*.: **jesuitical** (sometimes cap.). See *crafty*

(2) sneaky (characterized by . . . and cunning conduct, esp. in regard to the pursuit and maintenance of political or other power) *adj*.: **Machiavellian**. See *deceitful*

(3) sneaky (as in deceitful conduct) *n*.: **skullduggery**. See *deceitfulness*

(4) sneaky (scheming or trickery) *n*.: **jiggerypokery**. See *trickery*

sneeze (or the act of sneezing) *n*.: **sternutation**. ❖ [A]nybody who lives with hay fever or has a predilection for robust **sternutation** knows that a gusty "achoo!" can often produce worse consequences than a few dirty looks at the salad bar. (Bob Molinaro, "Cubs Find Out Sneezing Is Ill Wind That Blows No Good," *Virginian-Pilot*, 5/24/2004.)

snitch (on) *v.i.*: **peach**. See *tattle*

(2) snitch (or accuser) *n*.: **delator**. See *accuser*

snivel (in a whiny or whimpering way) *v.i.*: **pule**. See *whimper*

(2) snivel (weakly) *v.i.*: **mewl**. See *whimper*

snob (esp. someone who seeks to associate with or flatter persons of rank or high social status) *n*.: **tufthunter**. See *hanger-on*

snobbish (as in haughty or condescending) *adj*.: **toplofty**. See *haughty*

snoop (as in eavesdrop) *v.t.*: **earwig**. See *eavesdrop*

(2) snoop (one who would . . . into other's affairs) *n*.: **quidnunc**. See *busybody*

snoring (characterized by loud . . . sounds) *adj*.: **stertorous**. ❖ [B]ut when, three days later, Elvis' condition dramatically worsened and his breathing became noticeably **stertorous**, the worried physician had no choice but to admit him to the hospital. (Peter Guralnick, *Careless Love: The Unmaking of Elvis Presley*, Little Brown [1999], p. 515.)

snowy *adj*.: **niveous**. ❖ Apart from Shakespeare, no other writer is more visible than Mark Twain. No other creature, excluding T. rex, has been returned to life more frequently than the man with the **niveous** hair, roustabout mustache and ivory-and-cream suit. (George Myers Jr., "Twain's Mark Most American of Writers; Still Has Country's Number," *Columbus [OH] Dispatch*, 2/9/1997.)

snub (as in to deal with or treat inadequately or neglectfully) *v.t.*: **scant**. See *slight*

(2) snub (as in treat with contempt) *v.t.*: **contemn**. See *scorn*

snubbing (as in disdain) *n*.: **misprision** (*v.t.*: **misprize**). See *disdain*

soak (flax to separate fibers) *v.t.*: **ret**. See *moisten*

(2) soak *v.t.*: **imbrue**. ❖ That very night Black Partridge, a friendly chief, delivered to Heald a medal which had been given him by the Americans, saying he could not restrain his young men who were resolved to **imbrue** their hands in the blood of the white people, and he would no longer wear that token of friendship. (Benson J. Lossing, *Our Country*, Volume 5, chapter 93, *U.S. History*, 9/1/1990.)

soak up (as in incorporate, the ideas or attitudes of others, esp. parents, into one's own personality) *v.t.*: **introject**. See *incorporate*

soapy *adj*.: **saponaceous**. ❖ I learned that day that lather and taste buds do not mix, for Mother washed my mouth out with Ivory Soap. . . . Yes, she was right to teach me that some words were wrong to utter, but I wish that that **saponaceous** experience had somehow taught me to consider why I would later want to use certain words rather than simply not to use them. (Thomas Nunnally, "Word Up, Word Down," *National Forum*, 4/1/1995, p. 36.)

soar (as in glide, through the air like a glider) *n*., *v.i.*: **volplane**. See *glide*

soaring (esp. too high for safety) *adj*.: **Icarian**. ❖ Gyrating exchange rates—led by the dollar's **Icarian** rise and fall—are the worst offenders of global economic order these days. (Sylvia Nasar, "What Governments Should Be Doing," *Fortune*, 3/14/1988.)

sob (as in wail) *v.i.*: **ululate**. See *wail*

(2) sob (in a whiny or whimpering way) *v.i.*: **pule**. See *whimper*

(3) sob (in lament for the dead) *v.i.*: **keen**. See *wail*

sobbing (of or relating to) *adj*.: **lachrymal**. See *tears*

(2) sobbing *adj*.: **lachrymose**. See *tearful*

so-called (by oneself) *adj*.: **soi-disant** [French]. See *self-styled*

sociable (and pleasant) *adj*.: **sympathique** [French]. See *genial*

social (and festive) *adj*.: **Anacreontic**. See *convivial*

social climber (esp. having attained a position without effort or merit) *n*.: **arriviste**. See *upstart*

(2) social climber *n*.: **parvenu**. See *upstart*

social-climbing (by marrying someone of a higher social class, used esp. of women) *n*.: **hypergamy**. See *marriage*

social structures (breakdown or collapse of . . .) *n*.: **anomie**. See *breakdown*

society (which is based on either strong interpersonal relationships and common values among its members [**gemeinschaft**—see *community*] or impersonal such relationships [**gesellschaft**—see *association*, which includes an example that uses both terms]) [German].

(2) society (as in community, united by close personal bonds) *n*.: **gemeinschaft** [German]. See *community*

(3) society (fashionable . . .) *n*.: **beau monde** [French]. See *high society*

(4) society (fashionable . . .) *n*.: **bon ton** [French]. See *high society*

sodomizer (as in man who performs sodomy on or has sex with a boy) *n*.: **pederast**. ❖ Pederasts in particular have lots of help in finding a good time in Asia, Africa or Latin America. . . . One of the most notorious guides to world sex spas for homosexuals seeking boys is called the Spartacus International Gay Guide. (Michael S. Serrill, "Defiling the Children—In the Basest Effect of the Burgeoning Sex Trade, the Search for Newer Thrills Has Chained Increasing Numbers of Girls and Boys to Prostitution," *Time*, 6/21/1993, p. 52.)

soft (as in quiet) *adj*., *adv*., *n*.: **pianissimo**. See *quiet*

(2) soft (as in velvety) *adj*. **velutinous**. See *velvety*

soil *v.t.*: **besmirch**. See *tarnish*

(2) soil (with mud) *v.t.*: **bemire**. See *mud*

(3) soil *v.t.*: **begrime**. See *dirty*

soiled (or impure) *adj*., *v.t.*: **maculate**. See *impure*

soldier (British . . .) *n*.: **Tommy Atkins** [based

on Thomas Atkins, a fictitious name used in sample blank military forms for the British army]. ❖ It's a sad legacy from the days when Brittania ruled the world with its legions of working-class soldiers doing the dirty work from Canada to Egypt, from India to China. Today the descendants of **Tommy Atkins** find themselves on the dole, with the manufacturing jobs gone off to the colonies Britain once ruled. Their only release, it seems, is to follow their soccer teams, get blind drunk and wreak havoc. (Jack Todd, "Englush Soccer's Shame," *Gazette* [Montreal], 6/18/2004.)

(2) soldier (or, relating to, or suggesting) *adj.*: **martial**. See *warlike*

solicitude (treat another with excessive . . .) *n.*, *v.t.*: **wet-nurse**. See *coddle*

solid (having a . . . and muscular body build) *adj.*: **mesomorphic**. See *muscular*

solitary (person, as in recluse, esp. for religious reasons) *n.*: **eremite**. See *recluse*

(2) solitary (as in socially withdrawn or inexperienced and/or shy and/or sullen) *adj.*: **farouche** [French]. See *shy*

solitude (social . . .) *n.*: **purdah**. See *seclusion*

solution (to a problem, or objective, as in the thing that is being looked for) *n.*: **quaesitum**. See *objective*

somber (as in suggestive of a funeral) *adj.*: **sepulchral**. See *funereal*

(2) somber (or grumpy mood) *n.pl.*: **mulligrubs**. See *grumpiness*

sometimes *adv.*: **betimes**. ❖ I can't say we had any affection for [our teacher], but we respected him and never gave him any guff. We read Caesar; then we read Cicero; then we read Virgil, and **betimes** we made side trips either in class or in Latin club to look at other writers, even to a couple of Milton's Latin poems. (John Gould, "On the Verge, a Boost from Virgil," *Christian Science Monitor*, 2/18/2000.)

son (of or relating to a daughter or . . .) *adj.*: **filial**. See *offspring*

song (of a gondolier) *n.*: **barcarole**. ❖ 2:49 P.M.: The gondolier is in full-throated **barcarole** when, suddenly, he clutches his chest,

grimacing horribly, and lurches backward into the canal, taking his oar with him. I assume a massive coronary. (Mark Leyner, "Gondola!" *Esquire*, 4/1/1997, p. 54.)

(2) song (or poem in celebration of a pending marriage) *n.*: **prothalamion**. ❖ Perhaps the greatest English marriage verse remains the **prothalamion** that Edmund Spenser wrote for the double wedding of the Earl of Worcester's daughters in 1596. Each verse ends with the line "Sweet Thames! run softly till I end my song" as the two brides sail into London and past the Temple, "where now the studious lawyers have their bowers." (Boyd Tonkin, "Motion Makes Media Wait for His Royal Wedding Verse," *Independent* [London], 6/18/1999.)

(3) song (or poem in honor of a bride or bridegroom) *n.*: **epithalamium**. See *toast*

(4) song (or poem of mourning) *n.*: **threnody**. See *requiem*

sonorous *adj.*: **orotund**. ❖ The P.A. system carried her "Star Spangled Banner" over infield dirt, outfield grass and bleacher brick. Annie's operatic soprano drowned everything in its path, rolling in a flood of **orotund** vowels. (Franz Lidz, Focus: "Belting It Out of the Park: Anthem Annie Aims to Sing in Every Baseball Stadium in the Major Leagues," *Sports Illustrated*, 9/18/1995, p. R1.)

soon (very . . . , as in, in an instant) *n.*: **trice** (as in "in a trice"). See *quickly*

(2) soon *adv.*: **anon**. See *momentarily*

soot (abnormal fear of . . . and dirt) *n.*: **mysophobia**. See *fear*

soothe (as in placate) *v.t.*: **propitiate**. See *placate*

soothing (lotion or balm) *n.*: **demulcent**. ❖ Comfrey is often called knit-bone and healing herb. . . . Glycerin is used [as an ingredient in comfrey] because it is a **demulcent** and is so healing. (Joseph Van Seters, "Comfrey: The Forgotten Herb," *Mother Earth News*, 12/1/1994, p. 18.)

(2) soothing (of pain, distress, or tension) *adj.*: **anodyne**. ❖ In his ideal America, marijuana would be **anodyne**, better than medicine. More like one of those cheerful balms that help take a rough corner or two off life—like a latte grande with skim, or a Disney theme park. (Hanna Rosin, "California Gears Up for a Long, Strange Trip," *New Republic*, 2/17/1997.)

(3) soothing (used often of a medicinal treatment) *adj.*: **balsamic**. ❖ Torn between Valium and Prozac, she reached instead for her new Stress-Begone Potpourri. According to the label, its lovely flowers and colorful leaves had been perfumed with a mystical combination of floral and **balsamic** notes that the ancient Aztecs had turned to when they needed soothing and comforting after a particularly stressful day of human sacrifices and tortures. (Peter Dichter, "I Smell a Lawsuit," *Drug & Cosmetic Industry*, 6/1/1998, p. 71.)

(4) soothing (to the ear) *adj.*: **dulcet**. See *melodious*

(5) soothing (agent) *n.*: **anodyne**. See *pain reliever*

(6) soothing (as in reducing stress or anxiety, often used with respect to medications) *adj.*: **anxiolytic** (*n.*: a product that has this effect). See *relaxing*

soothsayer (by using lightning or animal innards) *n.*: **haruspex**. See *fortune-teller*

sooty *adj.*: **fuliginous**. ❖ London, by reason of the excessive [cold air hindering] the ascent of the smoke, was . . . filled with the **fuliginous** steam. (*Earth Explorer*, "When Nature Roars," 2/1/1995.)

sophisticated (as in elegant) *adj.*: **Chesterfieldian**. See *elegant*

(2) sophisticated (as in refined or elegant) *adj.*: **raffiné** (or **raffine**) [French]. See *refined*

(3) sophisticated (as in trendy and wealthy young people) *n.*: **jeunesse dorée** [French]. See *fashionable*

(4) sophisticated (as in well-bred, esp. those aspiring or pretending to be well-bred) *adj.*: **lace-curtain**. See *well-bred*

sophistry *n.*: **casuistry**. See *fallacious*

sorcery *n.*: **necromancy**. See *black magic*

sorrow (as in depression) *n.*: **cafard** [French]. See *depression*

(2) sorrow (express . . . over) *v.t.*: **bewail**. See *lament*

(3) sorrow *n.*: **dolor** (*adj.*: **dolorous**). See *sadness*

(4) sorrow (out of the depths of . . . or despair) *n., adv.*: **de profundis**. See *despair*

sorrowful (often regarding something gone) *adj.*: **elegiac**. ❖ [Richard] Danielpour addressed the audience from the stage to explain the genesis of his trio, *A Child's Reliquary*, which he composed last year to mark the death of a colleague's 18-month-old son. "I know of nothing more tragic or heartbreaking than the death of a child," he said, and yet the music inspired by the occasion was much more than just **elegiac**. (Jeremy Eichler, "A Glimpse at the Piano Trio Times Three," *Newsday*, 5/8/2000.)

(2) sorrowful (sounds) *adj.*: **plangent**. See *mournful*

(3) sorrowful *adj.*: **tristful**. See *sad*

(4) sorrowful (or pitiful) *adj.*: **ruthful**. See *pitiful*

sorry (to relate) *adv.*: **miserabile dictu**. See *unhappily*

(2) sorry (as in pitiful) *adj.*: **ruthful**. See *pitiful*

sort (into separate parts) *v.i.*: **disaggregate**. See *separate*

(2) sort (as in classify) *v.t.*: **taxonomize**. See *classify*

sorts (of all . . .) *adj.*: **omnifarious**. See *varied*

soul *n.*: **anima**. ❖ Dear Dr. Fox: I was having a debate with a friend about whether animals have souls. I said yes, and she said "prove it." What's your answer, Doc? [Answer:] . . . The spirit, or animating principle, can be objectively observed but cannot be weighed or measured. Cut off an animal's head and see what happens. Same for humans. You're left with a body and the **anima** has gone. (Michael Fox, DVM, "Do Animals Have Souls? Tell the Doc," *St. Louis Post-Dispatch*, 6/8/1997.)

(2) soul (or vital spirit) *n.*: **pneuma** [Greek]. ❖ Eva Mendes, who is publicizing the new release *The Spirit* (oh yes, even the **pneuma**

needs a publicist in this age) gave a most creative response when asked by *USAToday.com* what she'd steal if she knew she'd never get caught. "Kate Winslet's roles," Eva said. "She is the most amazing actress in the world." (Tirdad Derakhshani, Sideshow, *Philadelphia Inquirer*, 12/31/2008.)

(3) soul (loss of the . . . , as in damnation) *n.*: **perdition**. See *damnation*

sound (which repeats, such as a drumbeat, machine-gun fire, or hoofs of a galloping horse) *n.*: **rataplan**. ❖ Gore accused Dukakis of being "absurdly timid" in criticizing [Jesse] Jackson, declared that "we're not choosing a preacher, we're choosing a president," and finally, after garnering what he thought was the coveted endorsement of Ed Koch, stood by as the irascible mayor delivered a **rataplan** of one-liners about [Jackson]. (Ellen Nakashima, "13 Ways of Looking at Al Gore and Race," *Washington Post*, 4/23/2000.)

(2) sound *n.*: **sonority**. ❖ And perhaps I'm simply a poor bet for her or anybody, since I so like the [ringing bells] of early romance, yet lack the urge to do more than ignore it when that sweet **sonority** threatens to develop into something else. (Richard Ford, *Independence Day*, Knopf [1995], p. 10.)

(3) sound (which is unpleasant or discordant) *n.*: **dissonance**. ❖ [After the jockey fell into unconsciousness and slid off the horse during the race,] there was the awful **dissonance** of the lone horse galloping riderless. (Laura Hillenbrand, *Seabiscuit*, Random House [2001], p. 330.)

(4) sound (fear of) *n.*: **phonophobia**. See *fear*

(5) sound (financially . . . , esp. with respect to a plan, deal, or investment that can be trusted completely because it is supposedly safe and sure to succeed) *adj.*: **copper-bottomed** [British]. See *sure-fire*

(6) sound (of . . . mind) *adj.*: **compos mentis**. See *sane*

(7) sound (which is full and rich) *adj.*: **orotund**. See *sonorous*

(8) sound (which is pleasant) *adj.*: **euphonious** (*n.*: **euphony**). See *melodious*

(9) sound (words having the same . . . , but different meaning) *adj.*: **homophonic**. See *pronunciation*

sounds (which are pleasing to the ear) *adj.*: **dulcet**. See *melodious*

sour (or tending to become . . .) *adj.*: **acescent**. ❖ "I know you two are young and sophisticated and gritty and shocking and cool and aware," said Uncle Robert, surprising even himself with the **acescent** nature of his discourse. . . . "You see life as shock and sensation. You are very, very wrong. Life is all about tedium, and routine, and grim survival, and getting from one day to the next, and hoping to get a little pleasure out of a lot of pain. . . ." (Miles Kingston, "That's the Trouble with Easter: It's All Death and Sex," *Independent* [London], 3/30/2007.)

(2) sour (as in tangy or tart) *adj.*: **acidulous**. See *tart*

source (principal . . .) *n.*: **wellhead**. ❖ In Portland, where your sex life is considered your business unless it affects the air quality, the response was not warm. To a number of locals, the sole consolation was that Lewinsky and Bleiler—unlike Packwood and Harding—were not really local products, but came from the **wellhead** of all dubious outbursts, Southern California. (David Sarasohn, "L'Affaire Lewinsky Rocks the Weirdness Capital," *Newsday*, 2/8/1998.)

(2) source (as in root) *n.*: **taproot**. See *root*

source and origin *n.*: **fons et origo** [Latin]. ❖ Philadelphia has the awesome Philly Cheese Steak, an unapologetic symphony of protein, carbohydrate and fat that no visitor can leave without sampling. The epicentre of the cheese steak, the **fons et origo** of the indigestible delicacy, is in an Italian-American neighbourhood in South Philadelphia. There you'll find Pat's King of Steaks, where Pat Olivieri had a eureka moment in 1930. Why not combine cheese, beef, onions and Italian bread? (Ludovic Hunter-Tilney, "Prandial Pleasure—

Philadelphia Story," *Financial Times* [London], 7/31/2004.)

sourpuss (as in person who never laughs) *n.*: **agelast**. See *humorless*

south (of, pertaining to, or coming from the . . . , esp. lower Southern Hemisphere) *adj.*: **austral**. ❖ No aircraft landing has ever been attempted at the South Pole during the **austral** winter due to the severe cold, high winds and total darkness, experts say. (Associated Press, as printed in *Newsday*, "Medical Airdrop over South Pole a Success," 7/14/1999.)

space (adequate . . . for living) *n.*: **lebensraum** [German]. See *breathing space*

(2) space (as in gap) *n.*: **lacuna**. See *gap*

(3) space (between teeth) *n.*: **diastema**. See *gap*

(4) space (esp. between the end of a sovereign's reign and the ascension of a successor) *n.*: **interregnum**. See *interval*

(5) space (esp. small . . . between things or events) *n.*: **interstice**. See *gap*

spacious *adj.*: **capacious**. ❖ The new building was tall and **capacious**, and although today it is filled to bursting with more than a million books, back in 1857 it had only a few thousand volumes and plenty of extra space to spare. (Simon Winchester, *The Professor and the Madman*, HarperCollins [1998], p. 77.)

spacy (person, as in an impractical, contemplative person with no clear occupation or income) *n.*: **luftmensch** [lit. man of air; German, Yiddish]. See *dreamer*

Spanish (-speaking neighborhood) *n.*: **barrio**. ❖ In the **barrios** of Los Angeles, an Argentine can watch the latest movies from his homeland at any of a dozen theaters, while a Guatemalan can find a soccer league composed entirely of players from the country he left. (George J. Church, "A Melding of Cultures: Latins, the Largest New Group, Are Making Their Presence Felt," *Time*, 7/8/1985, p. 36.)

sparing (as in not indulgent) *adj.*: **abstemious**. See *restrained*

sparkle *v.i.*: **coruscate**. ❖ In the best of this writing [by Ralph McInerny]—including *The*

Priest (1973), *Connolly's Life* (1983), *Leave of Absence* (1986), and the novels featuring his detective protagonist Father Rodger Dowling—are found gems of **coruscating** insight. (*Christianity Today*, "Football, Neo-Thomism and the Silver Age of Catholic Higher Education," 9/10/96.)

sparkling *adj.*: **scintillescent**. ❖ When Juan Ponce de Leon lookèd toward the coast from his ship on Easter Sunday 1513, he saw **scintillescent** beaches and a land as flat as a welcome mat. No trouble naming the place on the day of Florida, or Feast of Flowers. He pronounced it Floreeda, just as they do 480 years later in Spanish-speaking environs of the world's most famous beach—now in the world's most famous state. (A.E.P. Wall. "Lost? If So, Floridians Have Only Ourselves to Blame," *Orlando Sentinel*, 10/6/1993.)

(2) sparkling (esp. with gold or tinsel) *adj.*: **clinquant**. See *glittering*

(3) sparkling *adj.*: **coruscant**. See *glittering*

(4) sparkling (like a diamond) *adj.*: **diamantine**. See *diamonds*

spartan (as in marked by simplicity, frugality, self-discipline, and/or self-restraint) *adj.*: **Lacedaemonian** [derives from Lacedaemon, the ancient Greek city of Sparta] . ❖ [In] *Manhood at Harvard* [author] Kim Townsend [states that at] the end of the 19th century Harvard University fostered . . . many of the ideals . . . that were to dominate American culture in the first half of the 20th century. . . . A real man rose to challenges, didn't whimper, complain or turn tail but rather embodied an almost **Lacedaemonian** self-discipline and a truly Christian generosity. (*Washington Post*, Hardcovers in Brief, 11/3/1996.)

spasms (as in convulsions, during or after pregnancy) *n.*: **eclampsia**. See *convulsions*

spastic *adj.*: **clonic**. ❖ "The two most common forms are **clonic** repetitions like cartoon character Porky Pig with his 'Th-th-th-that's all, folks!'" says Dr. Bernard Landes, an audiologist and speech pathologist in Long Beach, Calif. (Carole Rust, "Stuttering Is Common in

Toddlers and Usually Curable," *Dallas Morning News*, 6/2/1998.)

speak (esp. in a long-winded or pompous manner) *v.i.*: **bloviate**. ❖ Guess times aren't what they used to be for Harvard Law School. Apparently, the venerable institution feels its professors—aside from a famous handful—aren't being quoted enough in the press. So the news office is sending out word to the media . . . that Harvard Law has many experts available to **bloviate** at the drop of a [hat]. (Al Kamen, "Inquiring Minds and Monica," *Washington Post*, 4/3/2001.)

(2) speak (at length) *v.i.*: **perorate** (*n*.: **peroration**). See *monologue*

(3) speak (inability to . . . due to brain injury) *n*.: **aphasia**. See *uncomprehending*

(4) speak (inability to . . . due to hoarseness): **dysphonia**. See *hoarseness*

(5) speak (or write at length on a subject) *v.i.*: **expatiate**. See *expound*

(6) speak (or write in a scholarly manner, often used in a derogatory fashion) *v.i.*: **lucubrate**. See *discourse*

(7) speak (pompously, loudly, or theatrically) *v.i.*: **declaim**. See *proclaim*

(8) speak (quickly and excitedly) *v.t.*: **burble** See *gush*

(9) speak (to . . . to an absent person or thing) *v.t.*: **apostrophize**. See *address*

speaker (or writer who is dull and boring) *n*.: **dryasdust**. See *boring*

speaking (and singing combined together) *n*.: **sprechgesang** (sometimes cap.). [German for speech-song. The most well-known example of this technique, where the performer's vocals are halfway between speaking and singing, is Rex Harrison's performance as Henry Higgins in *My Fair Lady*; hence this example.] ❖ In a few minutes [before the Broadway premiere of *My Fair Lady* in 1956], the curtain would rise, and Rex Harrison would ask, in the rhetorical **Sprechgesang** he had made his own, "Why can't the English teach their children how to speak?" (Richard Stirling, *Julie Andrews,* St. Martin's Press (2008), p. 81.)

(2) speaking (fear of . . . aloud) *n*.: **phonophobia**. See *fear*

(3) speaking (having a good feel for what is linguistically appropriate when . . .) *n*.: **sprachgefühl** [German]. See *language*

spear *n*.: **assegai**. ❖ If he had lived in the time of the legendary King Shaka, Sifiso Nkabinde would have been a 19th century Zulu warrior, destined to live and die by the **assegai**. (Peter Hawthorne, Africa: "Bloodlines of the Zulu: The Assassination of a Latter-day Tribal Warlord Reignites One of South Africa's Bitterest Conflicts," *Time* International, 2/8/1999, p. 35.)

specialty (area of . . .) *n*.: **métier** [French]. See *forte*

specific (as in particularized) *adj.* **pointillistic**. See *particularized*

(2) specific (to one person or thing) *adj.*: **idiographic**. See *unique*

(3) specific (word that is more . . . than another given word) *n*.: **hyponym**. See *word*

specifically *adv.*: **ex professo** [Latin]. See *expressly*

specious (as in relating to reasoning that sounds plausible but is false or insincere) *adj.*: **meretricious**. ❖ It wouldn't be entirely fair to blame [John] McCain for the bilious mess his party has become. The most vehement of the Republican faithful live in an alternate universe, fermented by decades of Rush Limbaugh's brilliantly **meretricious** baloney and Sean Hannity's low-rent bullying. (Joe Klein, "McCain Summoned Old-Fashioned Antigovernment Outrage in the Final Debate," *Time*, 10/27/2008.)

(2) specious (engaging in argument that may be . . .) *adj., n.*: **eristic**. ❖ The law, roundly stated, tells us that you may not kill another person except in self-defense. The Menendez brothers had no such excuse, but they were got off by a lawyer who mesmerized the jury into rogue theories of psychological compulsions. Such arguments go to **eristic** legal lengths. (William F. Buckley Jr., "The Susan Smith Case," *National Review*, 8/28/1995, p. 54.)

(3) specious (reasoning) *n.*: **syllogism** (*adj.*: **syllogistic**). [A syllogism involves deductive reasoning consisting of a major premise (for example, all human beings are mortal), a minor premise (for example, I am a human being) and a conclusion (I am mortal). Thus a syllogistic argument is not necessarily specious. However, when the conclusion does not follow from the major and minor premise, whether intentionally or not, the reasoning, though still a syllogism, is specious.] ❖ Your May 12 front-page article on consumers moving away from mini-vans and toward sport utility vehicles shows the **syllogistic** reasoning that goes into buying, say, a Toyota Land Cruiser: People who buy these vehicles are rugged; I bought one; therefore, I am rugged. (Thomas Olafson, letter to the editor, *New York Times*, 5/14/1997.)

(4) specious (argument, usually, but not necessarily, related to philosophy) *n.*: **philosophism**. See *argument*

(5) specious (reasoning intended to . . . rationalize or mislead) *n.*: **casuistry**. See *fallacious*

(6) specious (and/or illogical argument) *n.*: **choplogic**. See *fallacy*

(7) specious (argument wherein one proves or disproves a point that is not at issue) *n.*: **ignoratio elenchi** [Latin]. See *irrelevancy*

speckled (with a darker color) *adj.*: **brindled**. See *spotted*

spectacle (violent . . . in which shame, degradation, or harm is inflicted on a person, often for the enjoyment of onlookers) *n.*: **Roman holiday** [derives from gladiatorial combats of the ancient Roman circus staged for the entertainment of the audience]. ❖ The last time a convict was executed in broad daylight [in 1936], 20,000 people showed up. . . . Most of us probably don't want to see someone put to death, but a lot of people do. . . . [Reporters] wrote that souvenir hunters rushed the body, and that the sheriff created a "**Roman holiday**." (Kim Ode, "Should We See the Execution [of Timothy McVeigh]? It Might Teach Us a Lesson," *Minneapolis Star Tribune*, 4/28/2001.)

(2) spectacle (or ceremony that is pretentious) *n.*: **mummery**. See *ceremony*

specter *n.*: **wraith**. See *apparition*

speculation (sometimes in stocks) *n.*: **agiotage**. ❖ The secretary of the Dagestani Security Council said on Monday that there will be no total mobilization in Dagestan. . . . According to [the secretary], the **agiotage** around the statement of the Dagestani Security Council issued on Sunday is explained by technical mistakes. (ITAR-TASS, "No Total Mobilization in Dagestan—Security Council," 9/6/1999.)

speech (pattern that is unique to each person) *n.*: **idiolect**. ❖ And you've finally abandoned that flawed notion of Standard English as a superior dialect. Now it's time for a naked look in your linguistic mirror. Take a closer look. See the unique way you put words together? That's your **idiolect**: your personal dialect. That's your language; no one else has it. (Chris Redgate, "The Red Pencil," *Washington Post*, 5/17/2001.)

(2) speech (formal . . .) *n.*: **allocution**. ❖ During an **allocution** that left him hoarse, Mr. Craig attacked from every angle the truth and constitutionality of Article I, charging perjury [by President Clinton] before the grand jury. (Frank J. Murray, "President's Defense Team Attacks Seriousness of Charges," *Washington Times*, 1/21/1999.)

(3) speech (of or relating to . . . that is ornate, flowery, forceful, and/or eloquent) *adj.*: **Ciceronian**. [Marcus Tullius Cicero (106–43 B.C.) was a Roman statesman, politican, orator, and philosopher. References to speaking in his style can mean one or more of the foregoing, depending on the context.] ❖ Oxford University mooted the idea of establishing a business school six years ago, prompting 500 black-gowned dons to storm into the 17th-century Sheldonian Theatre in protest. Harvard's business school dates from 1908. Cambridge succumbed in 1990. But outraged Oxonians unleashed volleys of **Ciceronian** oratory, arguing that the groves of academe should be out of bounds to commerce. (Tara Pepper, "Oxford's Business Blues," *Newsweek*, 9/2/2002.)

(4) speech (as in common language between people of different languages) *n.*: **lingua franca**. See *language*

(5) speech (common . . . of the people) *n.*: **vulgate**. See *vernacular*

(6) speech (free . . .) *n.*: **parrhesia**. See *free speech*

(7) speech (having a good feel for what is linguistically appropriate in . . .) *n.*: **sprachgefühl** [German]. See *language*

(8) speech (inability to comprehend . . . or written words due to brain injury) *n.*: **aphasia**. See *uncomprehending*

(9) speech (lengthy) *n.*: **peroration**. See *monologue*

(10) speech (or writing that is affected and high-flown) *adj.*: **euphuistic.** See *affected*

(11) speech (or writing that is cryptic or obscure, esp. deliberately) *adj.*: **elliptical**. See *cryptic*

(12) speech (or writing that is pompous or bombastic) *n.*: **grandiloquence**. See *pomposity*

(13) speech (or writing that is trite or simplistic) *n.*: **pablum**. See *triteness*

(14) speech (regional . . . or dialect) *n.*: **patois**. See *dialect*

(15) speech (relating to . . . where the purpose is to establish a mood of sociability rather than to communicate information or ideas, such as "have a nice day") *adj.*: **phatic**. See *pleasantries*

(16) speech (relating to . . . that is designed to impress or for dramatic effect) *adj.*: **epideictic**. See *impress*

(17) speech (unintelligible . . . , esp. heard in certain Christian congregations) *n.*: **glossolalia**. See *unintelligible*

(18) speech (very enthusiastic or excited . . . or writing) *n.*: **dithyramb**. See *enthusiastic*

(19) speech (which is full and rich) *adj.*: **orotund**. See *sonorous*

(20) speech (which is hypocritical, sanctimonious, pious, and/or insincere) *n.*: **cant**. See *pious*

(21) speech (which is wordy or repetitious) *n.*: **logorrhea**. See *verbosity*

speech defect (spec. a defective articulation of the letters "l" or "r") *n.*: **lallation**. [This word also means unintelligible baby talk.] ❖ **Lallation** it's called, the difficulty Asians have in pronouncing "L" and "R" in English. For years it prompted adolescent jokes about "flied lice" and "I went to U.C.R.A." The wisecracks have waned as Japan has given America lessons in quality and industry. No one is heard to mock the Honda Acula or the Sony Warkman. (*New York Times*, "Cowboys and Japanese," 3/8/1988.)

speechless (lit. loss of voice due to disease, injury, or psychological causes) *n.*: **aphonia**. See *laryngitis*

speed *n.*: **alacrity**. ❖ [The Porsche 911 Turbo] also goes around corners. Which is just as well, for it can bridge the gap between them with such **alacrity** that a less than faithful chassis would be a serious oversight. (Dave Moore, "Big Boys' Toy Story—Fast But Silent Porsche 911 Turbo," *Press* [Canterbury, New Zealand], 12/6/2000.)

(2) speed *n.*: **celerity**. ❖ Only a coach, or an old offensive lineman, would find a center captivating. The rest of us, hypnotized over the years by television, usually follow the same old path; our eyes go where the football goes. But if you have a chance to watch the Steelers through your lenses instead of a TV camera's, watch [Dermontti] Dawson. You will marvel at the **celerity** and dexterity displayed by this 6-2, 290-pound lineman. (Dennis Dillon, "The Best, Hands Down," *Sporting News*, 9/2/1996.)

(3) speed (at top . . .) *adv.*: **tantivy**. See *top speed*

speedy (as in hasty) *adj.*: **festinate**. See *hasty*

(2) speedy *adj.*: **velocious**. See *fast*

(3) speedy *adv.*: **tantivy**. See *top speed*

spellbind (as in bewitch or enchant) *v.t.*: **ensorcell** (or **ensorcel**). See *enchant*

spelling (art or study of correct . . .) *n.*: **orthography**. ❖ Our educational practices are now so bizarre that they would defy the pen of a Jonathan Swift to satirize them. [Where] I work, for example, the teachers have received instructions that they are not to impart the traditional disciplines of spelling and grammar. Pettifogging attention to details of syntax and **orthography** is said to inhibit children's creativity and powers of self-expression. (Theodore Dalrymple, "Oxford's Lofty Image to the Contrary, Brits Revel in a Cult of Stupidity," *Minneapolis Star Tribune*, 1/30/1995.)

(2) spelling (bad . . .) *n.*: **cacography**. ❖ Poor spellers and bad typists can get somewhere, thanks to a new friend on the Internet. [The operators of typo.net] have taken advantage of **cacography** in a novel way. . . . They [have] registered more than 90 of the most probable misspellings of popular Web addresses . . . for processing by typo.net. (Thomas Holcomb, "Nerds Inc. Turns Typos Into On-Line Advertising," *New York Times*, 6/2/1997.)

(3) spelling (expert) *n.*: **orthographer**. ❖ After 10 tense rounds, Jody-Anne Maxwell, 12, of Kingston, Jamaica, correctly spelled chiaroscurist (an artist who emphasizes light and dark), outspelling 248 finalists in the Scripps Howard National Spelling Bee last week. The young **orthographer**—the first from outside the continental U.S.—won $10,000, a trophy, and other prizes. (*U.S. News & World Report*, "Phil Hartman; Alice Walton; Lyle and Erik Menendez; Jody-Anne Maxwell," 6/8/1998.)

spent (as in weakened) *adj.*: **etiolated**. See *weakened*

sphere (as in area of activity or interest) *n.*: **purlieu**. See *domain*

(2) sphere *n.*: **ambit**. See *realm*

spicy (agreeably . . . in taste or flavor) *adj.*: **piquant**. See *zesty*

spider *n.*: **arachnid**. ❖ Spiders often send shivers down our spines, turn dreams into nightmares and clutter our ceilings with discarded webs. They are also beautiful creatures, these **arachnids**, with their soft curves, graceful movements and long, sleek legs, says artist Jack Plummer. (Kathy A. Goolsby, "Artist's Creepy Spiders Capture Art Gallery Spotlight," *Arlington Morning News*, 1/9/2000.)

spiders (fear of . . .) *n.*: **arachnophobia**. ❖ According to a recent survey, **arachnophobia** is the UK's second most common phobia (after public speaking). In other words, more people are scared of spiders than are scared of death itself. (*Daily Telegraph* [London], "Health and Well-being: Spiders Are Not Out to Get You," 2/18/2000.)

spin (a log by rotating with the feet) *v.t.*: **birl**. See *logrolling*

spine (curvature of the . . .) *n.*: **lordosis**. ❖ Recently retired Cowboy defensive tackle Randy White was another swaybacked athlete. For linemen like White, a few extra pounds and pronounced **lordosis** mean more leverage and strength. Besides, who wants to tell White he's paunchy? Heck, I would even be afraid to tell him he has pronounced **lordosis**. (Jack McCallum, "Gut Feelings: Hey Guys, Don't Look Down—Something May Be Gaining on You," *Sports Illustrated*, 7/30/1990, p. 56.)

spineless (or a person who is . . .) *adj.*, *n.*: **namby-pamby**. ❖ But whether hawk or dove, many strategists still seem to favor only one of the two paths [to picking stocks]. Can that really be the answer? Choose one road for 2001 and stick to it? No way, I say. I don't want to sound **namby-pamby**, but I think you have to own stocks from both the old world and new. (Andy Serwer, "Investor's Guide 2001: Street Life—The Split-Screen Market This Year Has Thrown Many Investors for a Loop," *Fortune*, 12/18/2000, p. 226.)

(2) spineless (as in cowardly) *adj.*: **pusillanimous**. See *cowardly*

(3) spineless (as in cowardly) *adj.*: **retromingent**. See *cowardly*

(4) spineless (condition of being . . . , as in weak-willed) *n.*: **akrasia** [Greek]. See *weak-willed*

spinning (as in whirling) *adj.*: **vortical**. See *whirling*

(2) spinning (or spiraling motion, often an ocean current) *n.*: **gyre**. See *spiraling*

spinning off (act of . . . into parts) *n.*: **fission**. See *splitting*

spiny (as in prickly) *adj*.: **echinate**. See *prickly*

spiral *adj*.: **helical**. ❖ The spiral staircase leading to Tim Tully's office and laboratory at Cold Spring Harbor Laboratories in New York represents the **helical** structure of DNA. (Judy Silber, "Scientist Probes Beyond 'Genes Are Everything' Thesis," *Christian Science Monitor*, 8/27/1998.)

spiraling (motion, often an ocean current) *n*.: **gyre**. ❖ Widening **gyre**. The escalating expenses and tuition costs of the 1980s have led to a dangerous financial spiral in higher education. State and federal aid together rose 50 percent, less than half the rate of increase in college costs. (Betsy Wagner, "The High Cost of Learning," *U.S. News & World Report*, 6/21/1993.)

spirit (as in vigor, energy, and enthusiasm) *n*.: **élan** [French]. ❖ If Ueberroth is an impresario embodying the renewed American spirit, that **élan** has taken up residence most notably among the generation of Americans called yuppies, the young urban professionals (aged roughly from the mid-20s to the late 30s) who are supplying much of the bright entrepreneurial energy driving the American economy. (Lance Morrow, "Man of the Year: Feeling Proud Again, Olympic Organizer Peter Ueberroth Puts on an Extraordinary Spectacle, Showing What America's Entrepreneurial Spirit Can Do," *Time*, 1/7/1985, p. 20.)

(2) spirit (of an era) *n*.: **zeitgeist**. ❖ Every decade is remembered for some expression of its **zeitgeist**. By their actions and their deeds, overindulgent Americans have unwittingly branded the last decade of the old millennium The Narcissistic '90s. (*Washington Times*, "Culture, et Cetera," 11/30/1999.)

(3) spirit (distinctive . . . of a place) *n*.: **genius loci** [Latin]. ❖ For more than 30 years Sir Nicholas threw his energy and, when available, his money into renovation of his home, which he once described as "the centre of my existence." As the purchaser will soon discover, he is still the castle's **genius loci**, with almost every corner of the house and grounds reflect-

ing his exuberantly complex personality. (Tom Kidd, Property: "A Tower That Mary Queen of Scots Was Pleased to Sleep in—Fordell Castle, in Fife," *Daily Telegraph* [London], 8/14/1999.)

(4) spirit (evil . . . who has sex with sleeping women) *n*.: **incubus**. See *demon*

(5) spirit (evil female . . . who has sex with sleeping men) *n*.: **succubus**. See *demon*

(6) spirit (vital . . . or soul) *n*.: **pneuma** [Greek]. See *soul*

(7) spirit (as in aura or impalpable emanation) *n*.: **effluvium**. See *aura*

spirited *adj*.: **mettlesome**. ❖ The $1 billion for housing gives purpose, and the soul is flourishing, a lively urban soul that fulfills the two love letters to New York spelled out uniquely in brass letters on the plaza fence. [One] from Walt Whitman: "City of the sea! . . . Proud and passionate city—**mettlesome**, mad, extravagant city!" (Bonnie Angelo, Living: "Where the Skyline Meets the Shore—After a Massive Recycling Effort, a Lively Neighborhood Blooms in the Shadow of Wall Street," *Time*, 10/23/1989, p. 82.)

(2) spirited (as in exuberant) *adj*.: **yeasty**. See *exuberant*

(3) spirited (as in jolly) *adj*.: **Falstaffian**. See *jovial*

(4) spirited (girl) *n*., *adj*.: **hoyden**. See *tomboy*

spiritual (pertaining to knowledge of . . . or intellectual things) *adj*.: **gnostic**. ❖ Unhappily, the Markhams, out of ignorance and pigheadedness, have failed to intuit the one **gnostic** truth of real estate (a truth impossible to reveal without seeming dishonest and cynical): that people never find or buy the house they say they want. (Richard Ford, *Independence Day*, Knopf [1995], p. 24.)

spit (dribbling from the mouth) *v.t.*, *n*.: **slaver**. See *drool*

spiteful (one who is . . .) *n*.: **tricoteuse**. See *knitter*. [See the note at "knitter" for why this word can be synonymous with spiteful.]

spitting (while speaking) *adj*.: **sialoquent**. ❖ I once knew a fellow named Fritz; / Who spoke with conspicuous spritz; / Whatever he'd say; / Came out with a spray; / His **sialoquent** spurts gave me fits! (Chloe S. Yarmouth, quoted in *There's a Word for It!* by Charles Harrington Elster, Pocket Books [2005], p. 197.)

spittoon *n*.: **cuspidor**. [This word is noteworthy primarily because James Joyce declared it his favorite in the English language.] ❖ [At] the hot sauce tasting event in Pasadena . . . nobody rolled sauce around in their mouths, sucked air over it, stared ruminatively and then spat it into a discreet **cuspidor**. They just swallowed and gasped. (Charles Perry, "Hot-Sauce Tasters: Time to Get Out Your Hankies," *Chicago Sun-Times*, 12/8/1994.)

splash (light . . .) *n*.: **plash**. ❖ They burble, they babble, they **plash**. . . . No matter how you describe the calm-down sound of water trickling over polished stones into a serene pool, Zen-inspired tabletop relaxation fountains—now available just about everywhere—are making a big splash this holiday shopping season. (Don Oldenburg, Focus: "A Cash Niagara from Desktop Waterfalls," *Washington Post*, 12/21/1999.)

splendid (as in of the highest quality) *n*.: **first water** (usu. as in "of the first water"). See *quality*

(2) splendid *adj*.: **frabjous** (often as in "Oh frabjous day!"). See *wonderful*

(3) splendid *adj*.: **galumptious**. See *excellent*

(4) splendid *adj*.: **palmary**. See *excellent*

(5) splendid *adj*.: **skookum**. See *excellent*

splintering (relating to or attempting to create a . . . , or a breach of union, esp. within the Christian church) *adj*.: **schmismatic**. See *disunity*

splinters *n*.: **flinders**. See *bits and pieces*

split (often from or within a group or union) *n*.: **scission**. ❖ The Scottish Nationalist Party and the Northern (formerly Lombard) League both pretend that their **scission** from Great Britain or the Italian Republic will pose no problems and may even pass unnoticed within a united Europe. (G. M. Tamas, "A Legacy of Empire," *Wilson Quarterly*, 1/1/1994, p. 77.)

(2) split *adj*.: **cloven**. ❖ A fast-growing population in a region **cloven** by the borders of New Mexico, Texas and Mexico could be facing a crisis not far down the road—where to find enough water to supply the demands of more people and expanding industry. (*Dallas Morning News*, "Water Crisis Threatens Rio Grande Cities," 7/12/1999.)

(3) split (open) *v.t.*, *v.i.*, *n*.: **fissure**. See *crack*

(4) split (esp. into districts or geographic regions) *v.t.*: **cantonize**. See *divide*

(5) split (into thin layers) *v.i.*: **delaminate**. See *separate*

split apart (tending to break into, . . . or disintegrate) *adj*.: **fissiparous**. See *break up*

splitting (act of . . . into parts) *n*.: **fission**. ❖ After an uncharacteristically long wait of nine months, Michael Dingman, 58, is spinning off yet another part of his Henley Group, a conglomerate given to amoeba-like **fission**: This makes the fourth time it has divided itself since it was created three years ago. (Alan Deutschman, People: "Spin Control," *Fortune*, 11/6/1989, p. 195.)

(2) splitting (into two parts, esp. by tearing apart or violent separation) *n*.: **diremption**. See *separation*

spoil (as in treat with excessive concern) *n*., *v.t.*: **wet-nurse**. See *coddle*

(2) spoil (or indulge another person in an overprotective way) *v.t.*: **mollycoddle**. See *overprotect*

(3) spoil *v.i.*: **cosset**. See *pamper*

spoilsport (or anyone who is prudish or hostile with respect to minor vices or forms of popular entertainment) *n*.: **wowser** [Australian slang]. See *killjoy*

spoken (not capable of being . . .) *adj*.: **ineffable**. See *indescribable*

(2) spoken *adj*.: **nuncupative**. See *oral*

spokesman *n*.: **prolocutor**. ❖ To appreciate McCurry's talents [as President Clinton's spokesman], transport yourself back and picture [President Nixon's spokesman] Ronald Ziegler dealing with Watergate. Bland, insipid, wind-him-up-and-listen-to-him-recite. He never gave a substantive answer to a question in six years. . . . George Bush's **prolocutor** Marlin Fitzwater was also able, but too stiff. (Joseph Spear, "Mike McCurry: Simply, the Best," *San Jose [CA] Mercury News*, 7/31/1998.) **(2) spokesman** (or leader esp. for a political cause) *n.*: **fugleman**. See *leader*

spokesperson (spec. a character in a book, play, or movie who appears to act as a mouthpiece for the opinions of the author) *n.*: **raisonneur** [French]. See *mouthpiece*

sponge (off of) *v.t.*: **cadge**. See *mooch*

sponger (as in one who mooches) *n.*: **schnorrer** [Yiddish; slang]. See *moocher*

spontaneous (as in unrehearsed) *adj.*: **autoschediastic**. See *unrehearsed*

spooky *adj.*: **eldritch**. See *eerie*

spot (something which may be difficult to discern) *v.t.*: **descry**. See *perceive*

spotlight (being in the . . .) *n.*: **réclame** [French]. See *publicity*

spotted (esp. in black and white) *adj.*: **piebald**. ❖ Sarah Jane Hurley [is] a drunken derelict known as Cow Lady because of her black-and-white spotted coat. . . . When a fellow street person wearing the trademark **piebald** coat is murdered, Cow Lady realizes . . . that once they realize they've killed the wrong woman, she will be next. (Gail Cooke, "Intricate Intrigue Hits Home," *Dallas Morning News*, 7/26/1998.) **(2) spotted** (with a darker color) *adj.*: **brindled**. ❖ On a summer's day now, mint-green pastures are dotted with the tall, **brindled** cows, their white coats sporting distinctive brown markings. Their black-patched eyes resemble natural sunglasses. (*St. Louis Post-Dispatch*, "Friend or Foe? Cows Were Both in '44," 9/5/1994.) **(3) spotted** *adj.*: **dappled**. ❖ Gateway computers, manufactured at North Sioux City, are packed in boxes printed to look like the black-and-white **dappled** hide of a cow because the company was founded by the son of a Sioux City cattle buyer. (George F. Will, "Meanwhile, in South Dakota," *Washington Post*, 5/13/1999.) **(4) spotted** (as if by drops) *adj.*: **guttate**. See *drops*

spouse (or associate or partner) *n.*: **yokefellow**. See *partner*
(2) spouse (who is unfaithful) *n.*: **bedswerver**. See *unfaithful*
(3) spouse *n.*: **helpmeet**. See *helpmate*

spray (esp. with holy water) *v.t.*: **asperse**. See *sprinkle*

spread (false charges or rumors) *v.t.*: **asperse**. See *defame*
(2) spread (news or a rumor about) *v.t.*: **bruit**. See *rumor*
(3) spread (over a surface in a scattered way) *v.t.*: **bestrew**. See *cover*

spread out (as in branch out) *v.i.*: **ramify**. See *branch out*

sprightly (and magical) *adj.*: **elfin**. ❖ For reasons as difficult to identify as the gradations of excellence that turn silver to gold, sports fans quadrennially [i.e., in every Olympic Games] bestow their affection on an **elfin** gymnast. (Jill Smolowe, Olympic Special Section: "Sprite Fight: Which of the Extraordinary Tumbling Pixies Will Become the Seoul Sweetheart?" *Time*, 9/19/1988, p. 54.) **(2) sprightly** (as in nimble) *adj.*: **lightsome**. See *nimble*

spring (back, as in recoil) *v.i.*: **resile**. See *recoil*

sprinkle (esp. with holy water) *v.t.*: **asperse**. ❖ Even Sixtus V, who insisted on having his obelisks **aspersed** with holy water to cast out their devils, admired the brilliance of the Egyptians who had been able to carve such great stones. (Anthony Grafton, "The Obelisks' Tale," *New Republic*, 11/24/1997.)

spruce up *v.t.*: **titivate**. ❖ Of all the charges that technophobes level against the computer, one that is undeniably true is that it is ugly. . . . Computer firms have attempted to **titivate** their technology by encasing it in svelte, matte-black plastic. (*Economist*, "Monitor, Monitor on the Wall," 11/8/1997.)

spry (as in nimble) *adj.*: **lightsome**. See *nimble*

spunky (girl) *n., adj.*: **hoyden**. See *tomboy*

spur (as in stimulus) *n.*: **fillip**. See *stimulus*

spurious (and/or illogical argument) *n.*: **choplogic**. See *fallacy*

(2) spurious (reasoning) *n.*: **syllogism**. See *specious*

spy (on, as in eavesdrop) *v.t.*: **earwig**. See *eavesdrop*

squander (something away) *v.t.*: **fribble**. ❖ But it isn't so much this ill-conceived and high-handed notion of billing me for product not delivered [Internet access services] that fuels my ire, but the fact that without my permission you will have a full month's use of mine and thousands of others' millions of dollars to fritter and **fribble** and squander. A pox on your house, sir! (Unsigned letter to the editor, *Denver Rocky Mountain News*, 5/30/1999.)

squat (and fat) *adj.*: **fubsy**. ❖ Well, it was another night of *The Simpsons* for Bill and Hillary. In separate dens, no doubt. The rest of us got Monica [Lewinsky], the **fubsy** Lolita. . . . I'm not saying that the [Barbara] Walters interview didn't teach me a lot. I now know that being a fat girl in Beverly Hills is hell on earth. Barbara certainly didn't miss the point, bringing up Monica's weight problem half a dozen times. (Michael Harris, "Temptress Monica Revealed," *Ottawa Sun*, 3/4/1999.)

(2) squat (condition of having a . . . physique) *n.*: **embonpoint**. See *plump*

(3) squat (having a short . . . physique) *adj.*: **pyknic**. See *stocky*

squawk (or yelp, bark, or screech) *v.t.*, *n.*: **yawp**. See *shriek*

squeal (on, as in tattle) *v.i.*: **peach**. See *tattle*

squealer (or accuser) *n.*: **delator**. See *accuser*

squeeze out (or cause to escape from proper channels, esp. a liquid or something that flows) *v.t.*: **extravasate**. See *exude*

stab *v.t.*: **lancinate**. See *pierce*

stability *n.*: **ballast**. ❖ For months, the Smiths have sought in vain to find a four-bedroom house in the North Babylon school district, where all the children are established. With the free-floating uncertainty in their lives, the Smiths want school to be the **ballast** for the kids. (Paul Vitello, "No Home and No Answers," *Newsday*, 6/19/1997.)

stable (as in incapable of being overthrown, driven out, or subdued by force) *adj.*: **inexpugnable**. See *impregnable*

stage setting (or physical environment) *n.*: **mise-en-scène** [French; putting on stage]. See *setting*

stagnant (place or situation) *n.*: **backwater**. ❖ But as Gore tries to tar Bush by portraying Texas as some kind of third-world **backwater**, he'd be wise to recall 1992, the last time a governor ran for president. Because if there's one state that does worse than Texas in the rankings game, it's Arkansas [where Bill Clinton is from]. (Scott S. Greenberger, Election 2000: "Gore's New Strategy: Attack Texas as Backward," *Atlanta Journal-Constitution*, 4/16/2000.)

(2) stagnant (as in not moving or temporarily inactive) *adj.*: **quiescent**. See *inactive*

stain (with blood) *v.t.*: **ensanguine**. ❖ The Reformation, which was to divide and **ensanguine** Europe, and divides western Christendom even now, was irretrievably on its way. (*Economist*, "Reform and Rome—Luther on the Stand: 1521," 12/31/1999.)

(2) stain (as in dishonor to one's reputation) *n.*: **blot (or stain) on one's escutcheon** *idiom*. See *dishonor*

(3) stain *v.t.*: **begrime**. See *dirty*

(4) stain *v.t.*: **besmirch**. See *tarnish*

stained (or impure) *adj.*, *v.t.*: **maculate**. See *impure*

staining (of or relating to . . . , as in dyeing) *adj.*: **tinctorial**. See *dyeing*

stale (as in musty) *adj.*: **fusty**. See *musty*

(2) stale (atmosphere of crowded or poorly ventilated area) *n.*: **fug**. See *musty*

stalking (as in lying in wait for prey, often used of insects) *adj.*: **lochetic**. See *ambushing*

stalling (engaging in . . . tactics, esp. as a means to wear out an opponent or avoid confrontation) *adj.*: **Fabian**. See *dilatory*

stammering (words such as "um," "uh," "you know," etc.) *n.*: **embolalia (or embololalia)**. ❖ My recent column on filler words, such as *you know, well, uh,* and *basically,* has provoked numerous responses [as to the best word for that]. . . . **Embololalia (or embolalia)** seem to fit, but I suspect that most of us, in trying to say, uh, **embololalia**, would find ourselves resorting to it. (Jack Smith, "**Embololalia** or **Embolalia**: It's . . . Er . . . Static to Our Ears," *Los Angeles Times*, 8/19/1991.)

stamp of approval *n.*: **nihil obstat** [Latin]. See *approval*

standard (as in original model or example) *n.*: **archetype**. See *model*

standing (of or relating to . . . upright) *n.*: **ortho-static**. ❖ For example, body fluid changes during space flight can cause astronauts to suffer from dizziness and lightheadedness when they return to Earth—a condition called **orthostatic** intolerance. Most space travelers cannot stand quietly for 10 minutes just after landing without feeling faint. (Earl Lane, "Space Aches/Scientists Are Just Beginning to Study the Biological Effects on Astronauts," *Newsday*, 10/13/1998.)

star (shooting . . .) *n.*: **bolide**. See *fireball*

starchy *adj.*: **farinaceous**. ❖ But it's the pastas that should turn any conversation away from films, philosophy and the unexplained. Actually, you could revel in pastas here. With two or three diners, all friends of the **farinaceous**, you might end up sampling nine of them—certainly an adventure in small portions. (Peter M. Gianotti, Dining Out, *Newsday*, 5/9/1993.)

stars (cluster of . . . smaller than a constellation) *n.*: **asterism**. ❖ The Winter Circle comprises six named stars. . . . The six stars are in an oval-shaped **asterism** easily spotted because all the stars in the large pattern are similar in brightness to the naked eye—except Sirius. But that is the best star to spot to find the rest. (Michael Alicea, "Everyday Phrases Reveal Ignorance of Astronomy," *Palm Beach Post*, 4/23/2000.)

(2) stars (of or relating to . . . or constellations) *adj.*: **sidereal**. ❖ It's war! In the year 2063, Earth's space colonists are suddenly under attack from a brutal race of extraterrestrial marauders. . . . As if they weren't trouble enough for our **sidereal** settlers, there are also packs of robots knocking around the planets who are identical to humans except for their

spooky X-pupil eyes. (David Hiltbrand, Picks & Pans: Tube, *People*, 11/6/1995, p. 15.)

(3) stars (of, relating to, or resembling) *adj.*: **astral**. ❖ Religious millennialists have yet to be heard from in great numbers, but before the end of this year there will be all kinds of predictions and movements and staged events. Astronomers, too, may get conjunctivitis trying to find new millennium stars, and astrologers may get conjunctionitis trying to give us the meaning of **astral** relations for the new era. (James S. Chesnut, "New Millennium? Bah, Humbug," *Tampa Tribune*, 9/18/1999.)

start (again, as in renewal or restoration of something after decay, lapse of time, or dilapidation) *n.*: **instauration**. See *restoration*

(2) start (existing from the . . . , as in innate) *adj.*: **connate**. See *innate*

(3) start (from the) *adv.*: **ab initio** [Latin]. See *beginning*

(4) start (from the) *adv.*: **ab ovo** [Latin]. See *beginning*

(5) start (often to a speech or writing) *n.*: **exordium**. See *introduction*

start and finish *n.*: **alpha and omega**. See *beginning and end*

starter (as in beginner) *n.*: **abecedarian**. See *beginner*

starting (as in coming into being) *adj.*: **nascent**. See *emerging*

starting point (as in assumption or set of assumptions) *n.*: **donnée** [French]. See *assumption*

startling (as in sudden, or unexpected) *adj.*: **subitaneous**. See *sudden*

starvation (of child leading to progressive wasting away) *n.*: **marasmus**. See *malnourishment*

starving (and thus emaciated, esp. as to children as a result of malnutrition) *adj.*: **marasmic**. See *emaciated*

(2) starving (as in hungry) *adj.*: **esurient**. See *hungry*

state (as in announce) *v.t.*: **annunciate**. See *announce*

(2) state (as in condition) *n.*: **fettle**. See *condition*

(3) state (as in declare, publicly, solemnly, or formally) *v.t.*: **nuncupate**. See *declare*

(4) state *v.t.*: **asseverate**. See *declare*

stately (as befitting a baron) *adj.*: **baronial**. ❖ [Cardinal John] O'Connor has often publicly questioned his own abilities and accomplishments. For years, he has said how uncomfortable it felt to him, a painter's son from a south Philadelphia rowhouse, to live in the **baronial** 1880 archbishop's mansion behind St. Patrick's. (Rick Hampson, "Courage Carries 'American Pope,'" *USA Today*, 1/17/2000.)

(2) stately (of a . . . woman, often voluptuous) *adj.*: **Junoesque**. See *voluptuous*

statement (which is left unfinished because the speaker is unwilling or unable to continue or because the rest of the message is implicit) *n.*: **aposiopesis**. ❖ **Aposiopesis** [is] a favorite device of Hollywood gangsters. Every time you start a statement and leave the second part unexpressed, you are committing aposiopesis. "Well, I oughta . . ." "Why, you little . . ." (Goldie Morgentaler, "Whatever You Say, There Is Probably a Term for It," *Gazette* [Montreal], 1/21/1995.

(2) statement (in which one references an issue by saying that one will not discuss it; e.g., "I'm not even going to get into the character issue.") *n.*: **apophasis**. See *figure of speech*

(3) statement (made without proof or support) *n.*: **ipse dixit** [Latin]. See *allegation*

(4) statement (or expression or phrase that is elegant, concise, witty, and/or well put) *n.*: **atticism**. See *expression*

(5) statement (which is official, as in with the authority of one's office) *adv., adj.*: **ex cathedra**. See *official*

state of mind (normal . . .) *n.*: **euthymia**. See *mood*

stationary (as in not moving or temporarily inactive) *adj.*: **quiescent**. See *inactive*

status (as in condition) *n.*: **fettle**. See *condition*

status quo (favoring the . . . as in hatred or fear of anything new or different) *n.*: **misoneism** (person holding this view: **misoneist**). See *conservatism*

(2) status quo (person who favors the . . . , spec. a person who is opposed to advancements in technology) *n.*: **Luddite**. See *traditionalist*

(3) status quo (spec. a person who is opposed to individual or political reform or enlightenment) *n.*: **obscurant** (doctrine of such opposition: **obscurantism**). See *traditionalist*

stay put (ability to . . .) *n.*: **sitzfleisch**. See *endure*

steadfast (as in one who clings to an opinion or belief even after being shown that it is wrong) *n.*: **mumpsimus**. See *stubborn*

(2) steadfast (in holding to a belief or opinion) *adj.*: **pertinacious**. See *stubborn*

steadiness *n.*: **ballast**. See *stability*

steady (in rhythm or tempo) *adj.*: **metronomic**. ❖ [T]he next day you delight in the way the light splashes on the snow, or the **metronomic** plop of an icicle melting in the noon glare. Mood swings are built into the Minnesota temperament. (James Lileks, "Want the Tar Pit to Go? Don't Hold Your Breath," *Minneapolis Star Tribune*, 11/7/1997.)

(2) steady (as in unvarying) *adj.*: **equable**. See *unvarying*

steal (as in embezzle) *v.t., v.i.*: **peculate**. ❖ [The Mazda] Miata gets passersby smiling and talking. . . . Other conspicuous cars are costly and imposing and draw hate waves, as they are intended to. Decent householders glare, knowing you couldn't own the thing unless you were a drug dealer or a **peculating** [bureaucrat]. (John Skow, Living: "Miatific Bliss in Five Gears, This Is Definitely Not Your Father's Hupmobile," *Time*, 10/2/1989, p. 91.)

(2) steal (as in embezzle) *v.i.*: **defalcate**. See *embezzle*

steep *adj.*: **declivitous** (*n.*: **declivity**). See *decline*

steer (as in channel) *v.t.*: **canalize**. See *channel*

stench *n.*: **fetor**. ❖ All sorts of processes can create a stink. A major sewage lift station at Cadiz and the river may contribute to the problem downtown. A rendering plant occasionally insults the olfactory nerves of Cadillac Heights residents. But the central plant is the likely culprit for the **fetor** wafting along the river on summer nights. (*Dallas Morning News*, "Stinky Problem: Whatever the Odor Is, Dallas Needs to Eliminate It," 2/23/1999.)

(2) stench (having a . . .) *adj.*: **mephitic** (*n.*: **mephitis**). See *smelly*

(3) stench *adj.*: **noisome**. See *smelly*

stenography (as in writing in shorthand) *n.*: **tachygraphy**. See *shorthand*

step down (from an office or position) *v.t.*: **demit** (as in demit office). See *resign*

stepmother (of or relating to) *adj.*: **novercal**. ❖ Her **novercal** guardian observed [that the girl appeared to have been molested]. The kid also seemed unusually downcast and found it extremely difficult to look her stepmother up in the eye. (Kwame Okoampa-Ahoofe, "Pedophile or Pedo-Contra?" *New York Beacon*, 8/20/2003.)

sterile *adj.*: **acarpous**. ❖ But, according to the doomsayers, if a satellite doesn't clobber you into the next millennium, there's always the danger its plutonium payload will turn your neighbourhood area into an **acarpous** wasteland. (Adrian Bradley, "Space Junk Roulette," *Australian*, 11/19/1996.)

stern (and unyielding) *adj.*: **flinty**. ❖ For all his passionate concern about injustice across the board, [Supreme Court Justice William] Brennan was not a **flinty** moralist in person. . . . Genuinely curious about the interests of people he talked to, he was the most naturally friendly person I have ever known. (Nat Hentoff, "Brennan Believed Constitution Lived," *Denver Rocky Mountain News*, 8/4/1997.)

(2) stern (as in . . . remarks) *adj.*: **astringent**. See *harsh*

steward (as in butler) *n.*: **major-domo**. See *butler*

stick (instrument such as a . . . for punishing children) *n.*: **ferule**. See *paddle*

(2) stick (tightly and tenaciously to another person or thing—one who does so) *n.*: **limpet**. See *clinger*

(3) stick (tightly and tenaciously to another person or thing—one who does so) *n.*: **remora**. See *clinger*

stickler (person who is a . . . in observing established rules or customs, esp. with regard to religious observances) *n.*: **precisian**. ❖ The distinction between ["can" and "may"] has been much discussed. Generally, *can* expresses physical or mental ability <he can lift 500 pounds>; *may* expresses permission or authorization <the guests may now enter>. . . . Although only an insufferable **precisian** would insist on observing the distinction in speech or informal writing (especially in questions such as "Can I wait until August?"), it's often advisable to distinguish between these words. (Bryan A. Garner, "Can," *Oxford Dictionary of American Usage and Style* [2000], p. 128.)

(2) stickler (rigid . . . for rules and procedures) *n.*: **martinet**. See *disciplinarian*

sticky *adj.*: **glutinous**. ❖ I remembered the **glutinous** stashes of spearmint gum that the boys at the school run by my parents used to leave under dining room tables, chapel hassocks and behind bedsteads. (Quentin Letts, Features: "By Gum, I'll Blow You Away—Discarded Chewing Gum Is the Plague of the Modern City," *Daily Telegraph* [London], 10/22/1997.)

(2) sticky *adj.*: **mucilaginous**. ❖ Some folks may assert, tentatively, that [marshmallow] is made from a marsh plant called the mallow or maybe the marsh mallow. Indeed, it used to be based on the **mucilaginous** sap from the root of the marsh mallow, but that was very long ago, and people who offer that explanation are only guessing. (Al Sicherman, "Making Marshmallows; Easy, Fast and Fat-Free," *Minneapolis Star Tribune*, 12/22/1996.)

(3) sticky *adj.*: **viscid**. ❖ Honey bees are on the buzz. Why? You guessed it. Flowers are blooming. It's time for the bees to get out there, find the nectar, wing it back to the hive and convert it into sweet, **viscid** honey. (Walter Nicholls, "Bees Do It," *Washington Post*, 4/7/1999.)

(4) sticky (situation or problem) *n.*: **nodus**. See *complication*

stiff (as in hardened) *adj.*: **sclerotic**. See *hardened*

stiffen *v.t.*: **anneal**. See *strengthen*

stiffness (in relations between people) *n*.: **froideur** [French]. See *chilliness*

stigma (as in dishonor to one's reputation) *n*.: **blot (or stain) on one's escutcheon** *idiom*. See *dishonor*

still (as in nevertheless) *adv*.: **withal**. See *nevertheless*

(2) still (as in not moving or temporarily inactive) *adj*.: **quiescent**. See *inactive*

stilted (as in contrived) *adj*.: **voulu** [French]. See *contrived*

stimulate (as in enliven) *v.t.*: **vivify**. See *enliven*

stimulating *adj*.: **piquant**. ❖ Examine the following strategies for stimulating babies to learn. . . . Sometimes during the day, turn on the tape player and play any music that is **piquant** and engaging. (*Atlanta Inquirer*, "Parenting for Education: 'Babes in Arms' Learning," 8/29/1998.)

(2) stimulating (as in restorative, esp. with respect to effect of certain drugs or medications) *adj*.: **analeptic**. See *restorative*

stimulation (source of . . . , as in inspiration) *n*.: **Pierian spring**. See *inspiration*

stimulus (as in boost, spur or prod) *n*.: **fillip**. ❖ [T]he West has an interest in making Ukraine less dependent on Russian energy. . . . But financing these reactors is a curious way to help Ukraine. The purpose seems as much to give a **fillip** to the West's sagging nuclear industry as to avert another potential environmental disaster. (*Economist*, "Nuclear Blackmail," 3/1/1997.)

(2) stimulus (as in creative inspiration) *n*.: **afflatus**. See *inspiration*

stinging (skin condition characterized by . . . or itching; hives) *n*.: **urticaria**. See *itching*

stingy *adj*.: **cheeseparing**. ❖ Writing his books indeed seemed almost to become John's compensation for not selling books. . . . **Cheeseparing** advances, marketplace invisibility, scant prospect of reaching more than a handful of readers—more than enough reasons for a writer not to get up in the morning, or to peel off into magazine work or teaching. Not John. He was up and at the keyboard before sunrise every day . . . (Bruce McCall, "On Writers and Writing; The Most Successful Writer," *New York Times*, 9/29/2002.)

(2) stingy *adj*.: **costive**. ❖ Yet at the same time there was something **costive** about [artist Jasper] Johns, in sharp contrast to the effusive generosity of Robert Rauschenberg's vision. He didn't want to give anything away. (Robert Hughes, "Behind the Sacred Aura: Jasper Johns Gives Nothing Away, but His Cool, Lovely Mastery of Indirection Finally Becomes Claustrophobic," *Time*, 11/11/1996, p. 76.)

(3) stingy *adj*.: **mingy**. [This is likely a blended word—also known as a portmanteau word—which combines "mean" and "stingy." However, in actual usage, it is generally used as a synonym for "stingy" or for the less pejorative "meager."] ❖ When I wrote skeptically four years ago about the spread of computerized checkout clerks, I said that it was nothing more than a cost-saving conspiracy by **mingy** merchants who'd devised a way to get the customers to do work they should be paying a clerk to do. That part remains true. Machines work more cheaply than people. And the merchant is getting you, the customer, to do a task that once was part of the service he was being paid to provide. (Dave Addis, "Sometimes, Face-to-Screen Is Better Than Face-to-Face," *Virginian-Pilot*, 11/19/2003.)

(4) stingy *adj*.: **niggardly**. ❖ Postponed or **niggardly** 401(k) contributions are still the easiest routes to a destitute retirement. (Richard S. Teitelbaum, Retirement Guide/Special Issue: "How Your 401(k) Can Make You Rich: You're the Boss of Your Retirement Plan, and the Stakes Are Enormous," *Fortune*, 7/24/1995, p. 74.)

(5) stingy *adj*.: **penurious**. ❖ Then there are the whispers that Cincinnati, the most **penurious** franchise in the league, hired [coach] Dave Shula in part because he came cheaply. (Michael Kinsley, "Jaw to Jaw," *Sporting News*, 10/3/1994.)

stink (as in bad odor from waste or decayed matter) *n*.: **effluvium**. See *odor*

(2) stink (from body sweat) *n.*: **bromidrosis**. See *sweat*

(3) stink *n.*: **fetor**. See *stench*

stinking *adj.*: **graveolent**. See *smelly*

stinky *adj.*: **fetid**. See *smelly*

(2) stinky *adj.*: **mephitic** (*n.*: **mephitis**). See *smelly*

(3) stinky *adj.*: **noisome**. See *smelly*

stint (as in overly restricting or limiting, as to amount or share) *v.t.*: **scant**. [The use of "scant" as an adjective is of course common, but its use as a verb is less so, and its definitions as a verb are distinct from those as an adjective. See also *slight*.] ❖ Did Harvard applaud [President Lawrence] Summers for this attempt to make [Professor Cornel] West meet his professorial obligations? Not on your life. . . . The opportunity was rejected. Summers's backpedaling leaves West free to keep on **scanting** his scholarly responsibilities while dipping his toe into politics and popular culture, whining all the while about being "disrespected" by Summers. (Jonathan Yardley, "Harvard's Gates of Power," *Washington Post*, 1/14/2002.)

stipulating (for the sake of argument) *adv.*: **concesso non dato** [Italian; sometimes **dato non concesso**]. ❖ Even supposing, **concesso non dato**, that my legal agreement [to republish my text without my permission] were not necessary, how can one justify that Mr. Wolin "forgot," for months and months, to ask me, at least out of courtesy, for my authorization to include a long text of mine in his book? Did he think I was dead? (Jacques Derrida, letter to the editor, *New York Review of Books*, 2/25/1993.)

stir (as in commotion) *n.*: **bobbery**. See *commotion*

(2) stir (as in commotion) *n.*: **kerfuffle**. See *commotion*

(3) stir (as in commotion) *n.*: **maelstrom**. See *commotion*

(4) stir (as in commotion) *n.*: **pother**. See *commotion*

(5) stir (as in fuss, over a trifling matter) *n.*: **foofaraw**. See *fuss*

stock certificates (hobby of collecting old . . .) *n.*: **scripophily**. ❖ Turns out those tanking tech stocks sometimes are worth the paper they're printed on. On websites like eBay and **Scripophily**.com, there's a lively market for original stock certificates—collectibles that can fetch more than the stock's share value. [Example:] eToys—Share value $0 (defunct)—Sold for $58. (*Time* International [Spanish Edition], Notebook, 7/30/2001.)

stocky (having a short . . . physique) *adj.*: **pyknic**. ❖ There are three basic types of body builds [, one of which is] endomorphic, characterized by predominance of structure developed from endodermal layers of embryo, that is, internal organs. And also characterized by a large abdomen, general roundness, hence of the **pyknic** (wonder if the spelling is a coincidence) type. (Pearl Swiggum, "Falling Wallpaper Creates Major Family Catastrophe," *Wisconsin State Journal*, 3/6/1995.)

(2) stocky (condition of having a . . . physique) *n.*: **embonpoint**. See *plump*

stockyard (as in slaughterhouse) *n.*: **abattoir**. See *slaughterhouse*

stoic (as in unemotional or even-tempered) *adj.*: **phlegmatic**. See *even-tempered*

(2) stoic (as in unfeeling, person, as in one who is interested only in cold, hard facts, with little concern for emotion or human needs) *n.*: **Gradgrind**. See *unfeeling*

stomach (of, relating to, or associated with) *n.*: **gastric**. ❖ "My first advice would be moderation in the size of the meal and the amount of alcohol consumed," said Dr. J. Patrick Waring, a specialist in digestive disorders at Emory University School of Medicine in Atlanta. That's because a big meal sets you up for **gastric** distress. (M.A.J. McKenna, "Festive Feasts Can Make Us Bloated Beasts," *Palm Beach Post*, 12/6/1999.)

(2) stomach (surgical excision into . . . usually for feeding) *n.*: **gastrotomy**. ❖ Three of the six children in the Bellevue class have been fed through **gastrotomy** tubes, or "G-tubes," in their stomachs because they reject oral feed-ings. (Mike Lindblom, "Therapy Intended to Help Youngsters Overcome Fear of Food," *Dallas Morning News*, 2/20/2000.)

(3) stomach (or mouth or jaws of a carnivorous animal) *n.*: **maw**. See *mouth*

stomachache *n.pl.* but sing. or pl. in construction: **collywobbles**. See *bellyache*

stomp (as in move heavily or clumsily) *v.i.*: **galumph**. See *tromp*

stonewalling (engaging in . . . tactics, esp. as a means to wear out an opponent or avoid confrontation) *adj.*: **Fabian**. See *dilatory*

stoning (death by . . .) *n.*: **lapidation**. ❖ Why do self-appointed Muslim leaders find it so hard to condemn the practice of stoning women for adultery? . . . Muslim Council of Britain leader, Dr. Muhammad Abdul Bari gave a feeble answer at the weekend when asked whether **lapidation** is ever justified: "It depends what sort of stoning and what circumstances." (Joan Smith, "Patriarchs with Hearts of Stone," *Independent* [London], 11/15/2007.)

stony (as in unfeeling, person, as in one who is interested only in cold, hard facts, with little concern for emotion or human needs) *n.*: **Gradgrind**. See *unfeeling*

stool pigeon (or accuser) *n.*: **delator**. See *accuser*

stop (up) *v.t.*: **occlude**. See *block*

(2) stop (as in put an end to) *v.t.*: **quietus** (as in "put the quietus to"). See *termination*

storage place (esp. for hiding valuables or goods) *n.*: **cache**. See *hiding place*

storm (as in commotion) *n.*: **maelstrom**. See *commotion*

stormy *adj.*: **procellous**. It was a Stygian [i.e., dark] and **procellous** night. (E. F. Porter, "Thesaurus: 5th Edition of Roget's Masterwork Appears," *St. Louis Post-Dispatch*, 8/8/1992.)

story (as in fable) *n.*: **apologue**. See *fable*

(2) story (which is false, often deliberately) *n.*: **canard**. See *hoax*

storytelling (of or relating to great . . .) *adj.*: **Scheherazadean** [This word derives from *One Thousand and One Nights*, in which the Persian king Shahryar, stung by his wife's infidelity, has her executed and marries a succession of virgins. He believes that all women are unfaithful, and every morning sends his latest wife to be beheaded. Scheherazade volunteers to spend a night with him, and starts telling a wonderful story, unfinished before she falls asleep. The king keeps Scheherazade alive as he eagerly anticipates its conclusion and then subsequent stories, and she eventually becomes his queen.] ❖ [Kim Stanley Robinson's] *The Years of Rice and Salt* is for the most part a magnificent and endlessly fascinating book. Setting himself the **Scheherazadean** labor of holding his readers through a chain of tales, a series of endings and beginnings in which we must let go of one story and then quickly be caught up again in the next, he pulls it off with a trapeze artist's grace. (Laura Miller, review of *The Years of Rice and Salt*, by Kim Stanley Robinson, *Salon.com*, 3/6/2002.)

stout (having a . . . physique) *n.*: **embonpoint**. See *plump*

(2) stout (having a short . . . physique) *adj.*: **pyknic**. See *stocky*

straight (of or relating to standing . . .) *n.*: **orthostatic**. See *standing*

straight-haired *adj.*: **lissotrichous**. See *hair*

strain (positive form of . . . , as in stress, brought on, for example, by a job promotion or a new baby) *n.*: **eustress**. See *stress*

strained (use or misuse of words or phrase, sometimes deliberate) *n.*: **catachresis**. See *misuse*

straitlaced (and intolerant conventionality) *n.*: **Grundyism**. See *puritanical*

(2) straitlaced (as in prim or prudish) *adj.*: **missish**. See *prim*

(3) straitlaced (person or anyone who is puritanical, prudish, or hostile with respect to minor vices or forms of popular entertainment) *n.*: **wowser** [Australian slang]. See *killjoy*

strange (as in eccentric) *adj.*: **pixilated**. See *eccentric*

(2) strange (as in eerie) *adj.*: **eldritch**. See *eerie*

(3) strange (as in otherworldly) *adj.*: **fey**. See *otherworldly*

(4) strange (as in unconventional) *adj.*: **outré** [French]. See *unconventional*

(5) strange *adj.*: **selcouth**. See *unusual*

stranger *n.*: **inconnu** [French]. ❖ [Five years ago, Penguin Publishers] rejected a manuscript about a boy wizard [Harry Potter] by a penniless, unknown Edinburgh-based author [J. K. Rowling]. Penguin had no intention of being wrong-footed again, so [they paid] Eoin Colfer . . . a little-known author, £500,000 [for his children's book]. Colfer isn't quite the impoverished **inconnu** that Rowling was but his story has a similar charm. (Anne Johnstone, "Mixed-up World with a New Spin on the Art of Fantasy," *Herald* [Glasgow], 5/12/2001.)

(2) stranger (as in foreigner, from another country or place) *n.*: **outlander**. See *foreigner*

(3) stranger (as in outcast) *n.*: **Ishmael**. See *outcast*

strangle *v.t.*: **garrote**. ❖ 7:00 A.M. I would like to unfold Brian's precious pocket square and **garrote** him with it. I have seen Golf Central four times, and must endure four more replays over the next two hours. I am Bill Murray in *Groundhog Day*. I am Charlie on the MTA. (Austin Murphy, Golf Plus: "Get Me Outta Here—Watching the Golf Channel for 48 Straight Hours Was Nearly the Undoing of the Author," *Sports Illustrated*, 7/10/1995, p. G8.)

(2) strangle *v.t.*: **jugulate**. ❖ As Douglas Hurd, who refused to sign the letter, could see full well, this is not an attempt to change Tory policy on the single European currency. It is an attempt to **jugulate** William Hague; or at least to begin the tightening of the ligature about his youthful neck. (Boris Johnson, Politics: "Savaged by a Dead Sheep," *Daily Telegraph* [London], 1/7/1998.)

strapping (having a . . . body build) *adj.*: **mesomorphic**. See *muscular*

stray (from the subject) *v.i.*: **divagate**. See *digress*

streaked (with a darker color) *adj.*: **brindled**. See *spotted*

stream (small) *n.*: **rivulet**. ❖ Neuwiller's lan-

guage lab lies off Mill Creek, a marshy **rivulet** near his home on Maryland's Eastern Shore. "You've got to listen to a lot of geese to speak goose," he says. "I've listened to them my whole life." (Franz Lidz, Outdoors, *Sports Illustrated*, 2/21/1994, p. 86.)

(2) stream (of, relating to, or inhabiting) *adj.*: **fluvial**. See *river*

(3) stream (of or relating to moving water such as a . . .) *adj.*: **lotic**. See *water*

(4) stream (of or occurring in a . . . or lake) *adj.*: **limnetic**. See *water*

streaming (smoothly or copiously) *adj.*: **profluent**. See *flowing*

street show *n.*: **raree show**. ❖ Some things need not be belabored: like, for instance, that the [baseball] players and owners, in an orgy of selfishness right out of Neronian Rome, irretrievably polluted a century-old national myth—the myth that this game, of all games, was not just another **raree show**, but was based on a contract of common passion for the game itself between the players and the spectators. (Frank McConnell, "Baseball," *Commonweal*, 11/18/1994, p. 31.)

strength (as in power or might) *n.*: **puissance**. See *power*

(2) strength (deprive of . . .) *v.t.*: **geld**. See *weaken*

(3) strength (loss of . . . or muscle tone due to extreme emotional stimulus) *n.*: **cataplexy**. See *muscle tone*

strengthen *v.t.*: **anneal**. ❖ Yet these smaller manufacturers and service companies are a vital and vulnerable part of U.S. competitiveness. . . . If these companies are not **annealed** by the fire of global competition, they will burn in it. Says Earl Landesman, an A. T. Kearney consultant: "Those just sitting in the U.S. will be blindsided." (Thomas A. Stewart, "The New American Century—Where We Stand," *Fortune*, 6/10/1991, p. 12.)

strengthener (as in something that invigorates) *adj.*, *n.*: **roborant**. See *invigorating*

strenuous (as in laborious) *adj.*: **operose**. See *laborious*

(2) strenuous (task, esp. of cleaning up or remedying bad situations) *n.*: **Augean task**. See *Herculean*

stress (positive form of . . . brought on, for example, by a job promotion or a new baby) *n.*: **eustress**. ❖ **Eustress** is a priming of the system so that you can be on top of your game. It is a state characterized by "alertness, quick decision-making and the ability to react in an appropriate manner." **Eustress** makes one feel energetic and confident (if a little nervous). While distress responds to a challenge with, "Oh, no!" **eustress** says, "Bring it on." (Elwin Green, "Using Stress to Enrich Your Job and Life," *Chicago Sun-Times*, 9/3/2007.)

(2) stress (period of . . . , sometimes, but not necessarily, economic) *n.*: **locust years**. See *hardship*

stretching (and yawning) *n.*: **pandiculation**. See *yawning*

strict *adj.*: **monastic**. ❖ Although [the head of the Thai Power of Virtue Party] doesn't set **monastic** standards for party members—many businessmen are on the ticket and his handpicked replacement for governor is a flashy millionaire architect—he runs the party with a military style that may deter potential allies. (Jay Branegan, "He Wears a Simple Mor-hom, or Farmer's Shirt, and Sandals," *Time International*, 3/23/1992, p. 42.)

strictness (esp. with respect to moral or ethical principles) *n.*: **rigorism**. See *rigidity*

(2) strictness (of one's religious practices) *n.*: **orthopraxy**. See *orthodoxy*

strife (as in heated disagreement or friction between groups) *n.*: **ruction**. See *dissension*

(2) strife (of or relating to . . . within a group or country) *adj.*: **internecine**. See *dissension*

(3) strife (or conflict among the gods) *n.*: **theomachy**. See *gods*

strike (on basis of alleged sickness, esp. by policemen) *n.*: **blue flu**. See *sickout*

(2) strike (repeatedly, often used figuratively) *v.t.*: **buffet**. See *hit*

striking (as in dazzling, in effect) *adj.*: **foudroyant** [French]. See *dazzling*

(2) striking (spec. the act of one object . . . a stationary object, usually applied to ships) *n.*: **allision**. See *collision*

strip tease (artist) *n.*: **ecdysiast**. ❖ By day a computer consultant at a Wall Street bank, Miller morphs at night into an offbeat writer who adds zip to what he considers the staid form of obituary writing. . . . Minneapolis-born stripper Lili St. Cyr, who died early this year, was "one of the finest **ecdysiasts** ever," he raved, then recounted her famed bathtub routine. (Liz Leyden, "On the Web, Special Parting Words; Good-bye! Rewrites Obituaries to Give Fuller Account of the Dead," *Washington Post*, 11/27/1999.)

striving (mental process marked by . . . to do something) *n.*: **conation**. See *determination*

(2) striving (the . . . to achieve a particular goal or desire) *n.*: **nisus**. See *goal*

stroke (as in caress or fondle) *v.i.*: **canoodle** (often "canoodle with"). See *caress*

stroking (gentle . . . used in massage) *n.*: **effleurage**. ❖ Helping executives and office workers unwind on the spot, Ms. Valentino, who is from Lindenhurst, carries her custom-designed 10-pound [massage] chair in an over-sized guitar case from bankers' offices to law firms. At rates that amount to about a dollar a minute, she soothes with **effleurage** and pinches and rolls the skin and muscles on necks until she gets the kinks out. (Marcelle Fischler, "Having a Bad Day? She Rubs It Away," *New York Times*, 5/10/1998.)

stroll (a slow, leisurely . . .) *n.*: **paseo**. ❖ The brochures, of course, portray glossy twenty somethings, but those thronging the cafes and terraces are mostly over 60, or else families with young children. Snatches of conversation are in Dutch, German, Portuguese and English, interspersed with Spanish. You can spot the northern Europeans because they walk faster than the leisurely art of the **paseo** strictly requires. (Elizabeth Nash, Beaches, *Independent* [London], 7/12/1997.)

(2) stroll (about, esp. as in roam or wander) *v.t.*, *v.i.*: **perambulate**. See *roam*

(3) stroll (about, esp. as in roam or wander) *v.t., v.i.*: **peregrinate**. See *roam*

stroller (as in one who strolls through city streets idly or aimlessly) *n.*: **flâneur** [French]; (strolling *n.*: **flânerie**). See *wanderer*

strong (and courageous woman) *n.*: **virago**. See *woman*

(2) strong (as in sharp or bitter to taste or smell) *adj.*: **acrid**. See *pungent*

struggle (engaged in a . . .) *adj.*: **agonistes**. [Greek. This is a postpositive adjective (pronounced ag-uh-NIS-teez), meaning that it follows the word being modified, as in the case of "food aplenty" and "bargains galore." It typically refers to a person engaged in a struggle, as in the example that follows, or an embattled place or thing, It derives from John Milton's 1671 poem "Samson Agonistes," which draws on the Old Testament story of Samson in which he is captured by the Philistines and has his hair cut off and his eyes cut out.] ❖ [In regard to the impeachment hearings,] Democrats still have every opportunity to decide whether they will contribute to a wise and timely solution to the Clinton **agonistes**, or whether they will obstruct, obfuscate and trivialize the proceedings. (*Washington Times*, "Democrats and Impeachment," 9/9/1998.)

(2) struggle (for an idea or principle) *n.*: **jihad**. See *crusade*

(3) struggle (in the soul between good vs. evil) *n.*: **psychomachia**. See *good vs. evil*

(4) struggle (of or relating to . . . within a group or country) *adj.*: **internecine**. See *dissension*

(5) struggle (people who . . . , as in fight, as if to the death) *n.*: **Kilkenny cats** (esp. as in "fight like Kilkenny cats"). See *fight*

strut (about so as to attract attention) *v.i.*: **tittup**. ❖ It's 9 pm . . . and a party at the Rebecca Hossack Gallery is spilling on to the pavement. . . . Terry Major-Ball in a sensible overcoat blinks sleepily at the vision of the cocktail babes **tittupping** by on high heels: Amy and Bella (16), the hostess's absurdly tall daughters, two hormonal volcanoes with angel's wings

attached to their backs. (John Walsh, "Rebecca, Queen of the Desert," *Independent* [London], 3/28/1998.)

strutting (behavior) *n.*: **fanfaronade**. See *bravado*

(2) strutting (person in a vain manner) *n.*: **popinjay**. See *vain*

stubborn (as in resistant to control or authority) *adj.*: **refractory**. ❖ Intractable debt, stubborn state needs, whimsical and **refractory** legislators, a staggering economy, all stirred in a mix of double binds on the issue of taxation, surely will try even [the] considerable talents and energy [of California governor Arnold Schwarzenegger]. (Herbert Gold, "He Came, He Saw, He Compromised: The Further Adventures of Arnold S., Alpha Male," *Sacramento Bee*, 12/28/2003.)

(2) stubborn (in holding to a belief or opinion) *adj.*: **pertinaceous**. ❖ Traditionalists clutch for old stereotypes. Men are initiatory, rational, aggressive, ambitious. Women are receptive, passive, nurturing, intuitive. . . . [These stereotypes] appear to represent a deep-seated fear of losing the assurance of differences—a **pertinacious** insistence that, without hard-line definitions, we shall all soon become androgynous clones. (Kathryn Hume, "Why Can't a Woman/Man Be More Like a Man/Woman?" *Minneapolis Star Tribune*, 3/17/1995.)

(3) stubborn (person, as in one who clings to an opinion or belief even after being shown that it is wrong) *n.*: **mumpsimus**. [This unusual but non-archaic word was invented by a fifteenth-century English priest, who, when corrected for reading the nonsense phrase "quod in ore mumpsimus" (instead of saying "quod in ore sumpsimus," or "which we have taken into the mouth") in the mass, replied, "I will not change my old mumpsimus for your new sumpsimus"]. ❖ [Thoroughbred trainer Laura de Seroux] has been training her horses at San Luis Rey Downs and taking them by van to [other tracks] just before they race [which has been a successful approach for her. She said:] "[There are] people who say you can't win training at [one track] and shipping [to another], who say you have to be at the track where you race. They're being **mumpsimus**." [This is not a completely correct use of the word, since technically "mumpsimus" is a noun referring either to the person clinging to the erroneous belief or to the belief itself. It is not an adjective. However, though many articles discuss what a wonderful word it is, there are nevertheless not many examples of it (other than those that discuss the word merely by defining it), so beggars can't be choosers.] (Hank Wesch, "Word Is, De Seroux Has Come Up with Winning Vocabulary," *San Diego Union-Tribune*, 8/10/2002.)

(4) stubborn *adj.*: **pervicacious**. ❖ [Becoming] an "ingredient brand" . . . require[s] that "emotional associations" of the brand are developed in the consumer's mind. Most manufacturing-led businesses . . . understand the functional processes of protecting a patent or reducing the cost of a component but when it comes to developing and sustaining a consumer brand, they have a somewhat **pervicacious** view that engineering logic will win. (Kevin Thompson, "Strix Has Set Itself a Big Challenge," *Financial Times* [London], 10/19/2004.)

(5) stubborn (as in narrow-minded) *adj.*: **hidebound**. See *narrow-minded*

(6) stubborn (as in obstinate) *adj.*: **contumacious**. See *obstinate*

(7) stubborn (as in resisting constraint or compulsion) *adj.*: **renitent**. See *resistant*

(8) stubborn (in a contrary or disobedient way) *adj.*: **froward**. See *contrary*

(9) stubborn (old man) *n.*: **alter kocker** [Yiddish]. See *old man*

(10) stubborn (person or thing that clings to something tenaciously, whether literally or figuratively) *n.*: **limpet**. See *clinger*

(11) stubborn (to make or become . . .) *v.t.*, *adj.*: **indurate**. See *harden*

stubbornness (spec. refusing to consider a change in one's beliefs, opinions, or policies, esp. in politics) *n.*: **standpatism**. ❖ [T]he world's enclaves of great prosperity—the United States, Europe and Japan—are mainly content with what they have. . . . But the conservatism becomes self-defeating when it prevents countries from moving against undeniable problems. In the U.S., Congress and the White House can't ax unneeded programs. . . . People feel entitled; someone might suffer. Japan and Europe are even more tightly tied to **standpatism**. (Robert Samuelson, "Fat and Prosperous," *Newsweek*, 5/22/2002.)

stubby (having a . . . physique) *n.*: **embonpoint**. See *plump*

(2) stubby (having a short . . . physique) *adj.*: **pyknic**. See *stocky*

student (of a subject at a beginning level) *n.*: **catechumen**. See *beginner*

studious (as in pedantic) *adj.*: **donnish**. See *pedantic*

(2) studious (as in scholarly or bookish) *adj.*: **donnish**. See *bookish*

study (as in analyze closely) *v.t.*: **anatomize**. See *analyze*

(2) study (as in analyze, that which has already occurred; i.e., to project into the past) *v.t.*: **retroject**. See *analyze*

(3) study (as in examine closely, esp. for purposes of surveillance) *v.t.*: **perlustrate**. See *examine*

(4) study (as in formal analysis or discussion of a subject) *n.*: **disquisition**. See *discourse*

(5) study (of matters outside oneself, i.e., the outside world) *n.*: **extrospection** (*adj.*: **extrospective**). See *observation*

stuff (as in junk or paraphernalia) *n.*: **trumpery**. See *junk*

stuffy (and intolerant conventionality) *n.*: **Grundyism**. See *puritanical*

(2) stuffy (as in musty) *adj.*: **fusty**. See *musty*

(3) stuffy (as in pedantic) *adj.*: **donnish**. See *pedantic*

(4) stuffy (atmosphere of a crowded or poorly ventilated area) *n.*: **fug**. See *musty*

stunning (in effect) *adj.*: **foudroyant** [French]. See *dazzling*

stunt (as in prank) *n.*: **dido**. See *prank*

stupid (person) *n.*: **dullard**. ❖ I disagree with a Dec. 17 editorial stating that "the acute shortage of flu vaccine . . . could not have been predicted." The [media has] been serving up the possibility of a "really bad flu season" for months to a public already alarmed by anthrax, smallpox, monkeypox and severe acute respiratory syndrome. Only a **dullard** would be surprised by the increase in demand. (Jeffrey Sartin, letter to the editor, *Washington Post*, 12/26/2003.)

(2) stupid (person) *n.*: **dummkopf** [German]. ❖ [Merging the National and American Leagues] is the worst idea in the history of baseball. . . . [T]he National and American leagues are priceless brand names built up over a hundred years. Even the biggest corporate **dummkopf** knows that brand names with as much recognition as McDonald's and as much history as Coca-Cola are irreplaceable. (Charles Krauthammer, "A Batty Idea from Barons of Baseball," *Denver Rocky Mountain News*, 8/4/1997.)

(3) stupid (equally . . .) *adj.*: **unasinous**. ❖ For months now, this semi-insane gink seething with envy and hatred has been waging a vicious vendetta in this forum. Hiding behind computer screens and other people's names, this . . . troll and his **unasinous** counterpart in Melbourne or Sydney have been [spewing on] each other across cyberspace. (www.topix .com/forum/world/mauritius/TK8JQF03NPR 58V4NO/p3, 9/10/2008.)

(4) stupid (as in foolish) *adj.*: **barmy** [British]. See *foolish*

(5) stupid (as in slow to understand or perceive) *adj.*: **purblind**. See *obtuse*

(6) stupid (class of people regarded as . . . or unenlightened) *n.*: **booboisie**. See *unsophisticated*

(7) stupid (esp. used of a person, as in . . . and confused) *adj.*: **addlepated**. See *confused*

(8) stupid (lit. brainless) *adj.*: **excerebrose**. See *brainless*

(9) stupid (or dull or ignorant or obtuse or uncultured) *adj.*: **Boeotian**. See *dull*

(10) stupid (or foolish, in a smug or complacent manner) *adj.*: **fatuous**. See *foolish*

(11) stupid (person or loser or idiot or anyone generally not worthy of respect) *n.*: **schmendrick** or **shmendrik** [Yiddish]. See *fool*

(12) stupid (person) *n.*: **jobbernowl** [British]. See *idiot*

(13) stupid (person) *n.*: **mooncalf**. See *fool*

(14) stupid (person, as in one mentally deficient from birth) *n.*: **ament**. See *moron*

(15) stupid *adj.*: **gormless** [British]. See *unintelligent*

(16) stupid (as in foolish) *adj.*: **balmy**. See *foolish*

stupidity *n.*: **bêtise** [French]. ❖ [T]he Republicans have only themselves to blame for the **bêtise** of indicting Mr. Clinton on Monica Lewinsky charges. The counts were bound to be mischaracterised as "lying about sex," and bound to serve as a perverse vindication for the President. If that is all his persecutors could find, we keep hearing, there cannot be much else. (Anbrose Evans-Pritchard, Comment: "Republicans Let Clinton Off the Hook," *Daily Telegraph* [London], 2/10/1999.)

(2) stupidity (as in nonsense) *n.*: **folderol** (or **falderal**). See *nonsense*

(3) stupidity (as in nonsense) *n.*: **trumpery**. See *nonsense*

stupor (condition of . . . or unconsciousness resulting from narcotic drugs) *n.*: **narcosis**. [This word is often used figuratively, as in the following example (which is when it can be synonymous with lethargy, sluggishness, and the like), as well as literally.] ❖ Entertainment is, by definition, diversion; diversion becomes addiction; scandal provides intellectual and moral **narcosis**. Everyone knows how the stupor is attained and that, after this fix, there will be another, then another. If not Bill and Hillary, then the Bobbitts and the Simpsons. (Philip Gold, "Candy Is Dandy but Scandal Is Grander," *Insight on the News*, 8/29/2004.)

sturdy (having a . . . and muscular body build) *adj.*: **mesomorphic**. See *muscular*

style (out of . . .) *adj.*: **démodé** [French]. See *outmoded*

(2) style (the latest . . . or fad) *n.*: **dernier cri** [French]. See *trend*

stylish (and wealthy young people) *n.*: **jeunesse dorée** [French]. See *fashionable*

(2) stylish (as in elegant and fashionable) *adj.*: **soigné** [French]. See *elegant*

(3) stylish (as in elegant) *adj.*: **Chesterfieldian**. See *elegant*

(4) stylish *adj.*: **nobby** [British]. See *elegant*

(5) stylish *adj.*: **raffiné** (or **raffine**) [French]. See *refined*

suave (as in elegant) *adj.*: **Chesterfieldian**. See *elegant*

(2) suave (as in refined or elegant) *adj.*: **raffiné** (or **raffine**) [French]. See *refined*

subject (as in problem, which is difficult for a beginner or one who is inexperienced) *n.*: **pons asinorum** [Latin]. See *problem*

subjective (as in taking place entirely within the mind) *adj.*: **immanent**. ❖ The following remarks . . . consider a definite condition in which history appears to be concentrated into a single focal point, like those traditionally found in the utopian images of the thinkers. . . . The historical task is to disclose this **immanent** state of perfection and make it absolute, to make it visible and dominant in the present. (Michael Andre Bernstein, "Walter Benjamin's Long, Limited View: One-Way Street," *New Republic*, 12/8/1997.)

subjugated (as in subjected to external controls and impositions; i.e., the opposite of autonomous) *adj.*: **heteronomous** (*n.*: heteronomy). ❖ Piaget cited more commonplace examples of autonomy and heteronomy. He interviewed children between the ages of 6 and 14 and asked them, for example, why it is bad to tell lies. Young **heteronomous** children replied, "Because you get punished when you tell lies." Piaget asked, "Would it be okay to tell lies if you were not punished for them?" The young children answered yes. Their judgment of matters of right and wrong was obviously governed by others. (Ann Dominick, "The Six National Goals; a Road to Disappointment," *Phi Delta Kappan*, 5/1/1994.)

subjugation *n.*: **thralldom**. See *bondage*

sublime (as in of or related to the sky or heavens) *adj.*: See *celestial*

submerge (as in soak) *v.t.*: **imbrue**. See *soak*

submission (as in marked by insistence on rigid conformity to a belief, system, or course of action without regard to individual differences) *adj.*: **procrustean** (*n.*: **Procrustean bed**). See *conformity*

submissive (overly . . . or devoted to one's wife) *adj.*: **uxorious**. See *devoted*

(2) submissive (to be . . . toward) *v.i.*: **truckle**. See *kowtow*

(3) submissive *adj.*: **sequacious**. See *subservient*

(4) submissive *adj.*: **biddable**. See *obedient*

subordinate (esp. in the military) *n.*: **subaltern**. ❖ The longing for authority and **subaltern** mentality was widespread in those who found appeal in the early Nazi movement. (Ian Kershaw, *Hitler*, Norton [1998], p. 295.)

(2) subordinate (apt to act . . . as opposed to leading) *adj.*: **sequacious**. See *subservient*

(3) subordinate (bureaucrat) *n.*: **satrap**. See *bureaucrat*

(4) subordinate (loyal . . . , esp. of a political leader) *n.*: **apparatchik**. See *underling*

subservient (being . . . as opposed to leading) *adj.*: **sequacious**. ❖ [In 1945, Janet Kalven] called for "an education that will give young women a vision of the family as the vital cell of the social organism, and that will inspire them with the great ambitions of being queens in the home." By which she did not mean a **sequacious** to the Man of the House, picking up his dirty underwear and serving him Budweisers during commercials, but rather a partner in the management of a "small, diversified family firm." (Bill Kauffman, "The Way of Love: Dorothy Day and the American Right," *Whole Earth*, 6/22/2000.)

(2) subservient (person) *n.*: **lickspittle**. See *sycophant*

(3) subservient (to be . . . toward) *v.i.*: **truckle**. See *kowtow*

substance (of two things having an identical . . .) *adj.*: **consubstantial**. See *identical*

(2) substance (the . . . of a matter, as in the bottom line, the main point, the essence, etc.) *n.*: **tachlis** (esp. as in "talk tachlis") [Yiddish]. See *essence*

substitute *n.*: **succedaneum** (suk-si-DAY-nee-uhm). ❖ A Favre **succedaneum**. Turns out, "Faux Favre" has upstaged the real thing. When they couldn't book the real Brett Favre, the ad agency . . . had to improvise. In a 30-second television spot promoting Green Bay, a family shows friends slides from their trip to Green Bay. In each frame, the family appears in different tourist spots—zoo, railroad museum— with a cardboard cutout of their good buddy Favre. (*Wisconsin State Journal*, "Baby Orangutan Thriving," 6/3/2001.)

(2) substitute (esp. of a doctor or clergyman) *n.*: **locum tenens**. See *temporary*

substitution (as in using one word or phrase in substitution for something with which it is usually associated, such as using "city hall" to refer to city government) *n.*: **metonymy**. See *figure of speech*

subtlety (esp. in political or business dealings) *n.*: **Italian hands** [often used in the phrase "fine Italian hands"]. ❖ Mr Amato is noted for his political subtlety in a country in which the advocates of the historic compromise between the Christian Democrats and the Communists once spoke in terms of "converging parallels." He has, therefore, the finest of fine **Italian hands** and will need to use all his talents to see through whatever electoral legislation is necessary following next month's referendum. (*Irish Times*, "Amato Takes Office," 4/27/2000.)

(2) subtlety (raised within the context of a philosophical or theological debate; also used in reference to such a debate itself) *n.*: **quodlibet**. [This word can be used in a complimentary fashion, to praise the subtlety of the argument, or in a pejorative fashion, to suggest that the argument is overly subtle and thus in the nature of a technicality. The example used here shows the latter sense of the word, although, to be sure, the author is being facetious at this point in his article. See also the use of this word under *debate*.] ❖ Common confusion about the words *its* and *it's* and of the apostrophe in general are signs of the declining respect for grammar and reading. . . . It's? Its? How complicated can this be? How difficult is it to teach a sixth grader how to punctuate correctly? [But] why worry about such **quodlibets**? When was the last time anyone even noticed? (Charles S. Larson, "Its Academic, or Is It? Soon, No One Will Care about Correct Grammar, and the Apostrophe Will Disappear into Infinity," *Newsweek*, 11/6/1995.)

suburb *n.*: **banlieu**. [often pl., like the word "suburb" itself, as in banlieues or banlieux. This French word usually refers to the suburban areas outside the major cities in France itself, especially Paris, but is used to refer to suburban areas elsewhere as well.] ❖ [A] Robert Graham sculpture—a woman's mirror-bright torso donated to ornament a bleak traffic circle—has stirred hostility not in some bourgeois "**banlieu**," but in the freewheeling Los Angeles community of Venice, Graham's adopted hometown. Since art patron Roy Doumani offered it up, it's been the talk of Venice. (Patt Morrison, "Public Art, Public Outrage: A Delicate Balance," *Madison [WI] Capital Times*, 8/20/2005.)

subversive (as in traitors or group that is working within a country to support an enemy and which may engage in espionage, sabotage, or other subversive activities) *n.*: **fifth column**. See *traitors*

succeed (often at another's expense) *v.i.*: **batten**. See *thrive*

success (notable or conspicuous . . .) *n.*: **éclat**. ❖ The roll call of artists and writers who have suffered attacks from those less fortunate is long and distinguished. . . . [Playwright Neil] Simon should content himself with the great **éclat** he enjoys and stop worrying about what some newspaper twit writes about him. (Jonathan Yardley, review of *The Play Goes On*, by Neil Simon, *Washington Post*, 10/10/1999.)

(2) success (with the critics but not the public) *n.*: **succès d'estime** [French]. ❖ Reclusive playwright Sam Shepard has pulled a startling switch.... Often teased as the "Masked Man of the American Theater," Shepard is suddenly a wide-screen, posterized movie star playing legendary jet jockey Chuck Yeager in the American epic *The Right Stuff*. Sure, Shepard's done other films (*Days of Heaven*, *Resurrection*, *Raggedy Man*), but they fall into the **succès d'estime** category, seen by too few to endanger his cult status. (*People*, "He Has It All as a Laureate of Stage and Screen: So Now What's He Want? Anonymity," 1/2/1984.)

(3) success (celebrating . . . , as in victory) *adj.*: **epinician**. See *victory*

succinct (saying) *n.*: **gnome** (*adj.*: **gnomic**). See *catchphrase*

succulent *adj.*: **toothsome**. See *tasty*

sucker (as in one easily duped) *n.*: **gudgeon**. ❖ *Novocaine* [follows the] tradition of suckers and saps corrupted by the come-ons of a leggy dame. . . . Susan Ivy [is a dental] patient who doesn't blink twice when she asks Dr. [Frank] Sangster . . . : "Have you ever done it in the chair?" . . . When, after his illicit office clinch with the saucy Susan, a whole cache of prescription painkillers has gone missing, Frank realizes he's been played for a monkey, a patsy, a gull, a **gudgeon**. (Steven Rea, review of *Novocaine*, Knight Ridder/Tribune News Service, 11/14/2001.)

(2) sucker (as in gullible person) *n.*: **gobemouche** [French]. See *gullible*

(3) sucker (as in to deceive or cheat, or the person being cheated or deceived) *n.*: **gull**. See *deceive*

sudden (as in impetuous) *adj.*: **gadarene**. See *impetuous*

(2) sudden (or unexpected) *adj.*: **subitaneous**. ❖ Bartimo was so disappointed [that an article he edited about Micron Technology had to be reviewed by Micron executives before publication] that he quit the $55,000-a-year job after only a month. [The newspaper's attorney said] Bartimo used the Micron story as an "excuse" to quit and that the *Statesman's* only strategy was "limited to making sure the door did not strike his posterior during his **subitaneous** egress." (Howard Kurtz, "Jack Germond: One Part Whiskey, No Part Salad," *Washington Post*, 1/17/2000.)

sufferance (in the face of adversity) *n.*: **longanimity**. See *patience*

suffering (experience of intense . . .) *n.*: **Calvary** [based on hill near Jerusalem where Jesus was crucified]. ❖ In recent weeks the flamboyant [soccer goalie Fabien] Barthez . . . has committed a series of spectacularly awful errors. . . . [I]f goalkeeping is a treacherous business in which even Popes have to jettison the dogma of infallibility . . . few muddied custodians have known the **Calvary** recently being experienced by the once exuberant Barthez. His descent has been nothing less than vertiginous. (James Lawton, "The Goalkeeper's Fear of . . . Losing It," *Independent* [London], 11/27/2001.)

(2) suffering (as in place, condition, or society filled with . . . ; spec., opposite of utopia) *n.*: **dystopia**. See *hell*

(3) suffering (occasion or place of great . . .) *n.*: **Gethsemane**. See *hell*

(4) suffering (occasion or place of great . . .) *n.*: **Golgotha**. See *hell*

(5) suffering (place or occasion of great . . .) *n.*: **Gehenna**. See *hell*

sugar-coat (as in make pleasant or less harsh) *v.t.*: **edulcorate**. See *sweeten*

suggesting (as in urging someone to take a course of action) *adj.*: **hortatory**. See *urging*

suggestion (as in small amount) *n.*: **soupçon** [French]. See *trace*

(2) suggestion (relating to the giving of a . . . , as in advice) *adj.*: **paraenetic** (*n.*: **paraenesis**). See *advice*

(3) suggestion (as in word to the wise) *phr.*: **verbum sap** [Latin]. See *word to the wise*

suggestive (of, or smelling like, used with "of") *adj.*: **redolent**. See *reminiscent*

(2) suggestive (rather than a literal representation, esp. with respect to objects of worship) *adj.*: **aniconic**. See *symbolic*

suicide (commit . . . by setting oneself on fire) *v.t.*: **immolate**. ❖ When Thic Quang Duc **immolated** himself on a Saigon street in 1963, it was news around the world and helped set the stage for the U.S.-backed assassination of Diem. (William McGurn, "Good Morning, Vietnam: On the Long Road to Freedom and Prosperity, Vietnam Is Taking the First Halting Steps," *National Review*, 5/15/1995, p. 51.)

(2) suicide *n.*: **felo-de-se** (*pl.* **felones-de-se**). [Latin; lit. felon of himself. Technically, for this term to apply, the perpetrator must be adult and mentally competent. The term can refer to the person or to the act.] ❖ [By 1985, there were] 220,000 suicides occurring each year [from people administering pesticides to themselves]. Realizing that something had to be done, the United Nations Food and Agriculture Organization produced a set of guidelines for industrial pesticide companies, in the hopes of checking this pandemic *felo-de-se*. (Jason Lott, "Suicide Ready to Drink," *Daily Pennsylvanian*, 2/7/2005.)

(3) suicide *n.*: **seppuku**. [This word refers specifically to a ritual suicide by disembowelment formerly practiced by Japanese samurai. However, it is often used as a synonym for suicide generally (whether literal or figurative), as in the following example.] ❖ The Democratic Party commits **seppuku** in the heartland by coming across as indifferent to people's doubts about abortions or even as pro-abortion. A *New York Times* poll in January found that 61 percent of Americans favor tighter restrictions on abortion, or even a ban, while only 36 percent agree with the Democratic Party position backing current abortion law. (Nicholas D. Kristof, "Who Gets It? Hillary," *New York Times*, 3/16/2005.)

suitable (as in appropriate) *adj.*: **felicitous**. See *appropriate*

(2) suitable *adj.*: **comme il faut** [French]. See *proper*

(3) suitable *n.*: **apposite**. See *relevant*

suitcase (large . . . , opening into two compartments) *n.*: **portmanteau**. ❖ So a week later the official sent up a leather **portmanteau** by rail: It held a frock coat and three waistcoats. (Simon Winchester, *The Professor and the Madman*, HarperCollins [1998], p. 121.)

suitor *n.*: **swain**. [This word is also sometimes defined as boyfriend or male admirer, neither of which is necessarily the same as a suitor, as illustrated by the example.] ❖ Dear Diane: At first, my boyfriend treated me like a queen, giving me everything I wanted. But over the past four months, he has changed. . . . Now he never kisses me like he used to. [Signed] Watching TV, Again. Dear Watching TV: . . . Things are out of balance, and you seem to be waiting for your boyfriend to change back to the attentive **swain** he was when you first started dating. You may have a long wait! (Diane Crowley, "Her Lover's Turned Cool and It Has Her Steamed," *Chicago Sun-Times*, 12/11/1990.)

suits (as in persistent instigation of lawsuits, esp. groundless ones) *n.*: **barratry**. See *lawsuits*

sulk *v.t.*: **mump** [British]. ❖ Question: My 14-year-old daughter says she is not coming on holiday to Spain with us, even though it is all booked. She wants to go camping with her friends instead. . . . [W]hat do we do? Answer: Carry her on to the plane. . .. She's got to learn the financial facts of life. Of course, she's going to **mump** and moan, but parents have to crack the whip sometimes and this is one of them. (Joan Burnie, Just Joan, *Daily Record* [Scotland], 7/10/2000.)

(2) sulk (as in pout) *n.*: **moue** [French]. See *pout*

sulkiness *n.pl.*: **mulligrubs**. See *grumpiness*

sullen *adj.*: **saturnine**. ❖ Even a casual inspection of Benjamin's occasional writings over these years reveals the seeds of self-destruction. Not only do many of his chosen topics . . . reflect a temperament drawn toward disaster. Several others, such as "Left-Wing Melancholy," echo his **saturnine** disposition, a gnawing sense that life itself—certainly his own—was a disaster waiting to happen. (Haim Chertok, "Benjamin: A Powerhouse Failure," *Jerusalem Post*, 10/1/1999.)

(2) sullen (and/or shy and/or socially withdrawn or inexperienced) *adj.*: **farouche** [French]. See *shy*

(3) sullen (mood) *n.pl.*: **mulligrubs**. See *grumpiness*

sullied (or impure) *adj., v.t.*: **maculate**. See *impure*

sully *v.t.*: **besmirch**. See *tarnish*

summarize *v.t.*: **précis** [French]. ❖ The theatre, which has a strict policy on not admitting latecomers until a suitable break, is to start giving the aforementioned latecomers a synopsis in the foyer of what they have missed. . . . Of course, it would have taken a confident female member of staff to **précis** the first 20 minutes of Nicole Kidman in *The Blue Room*. (David Lister, Arts Diary, *Independent* [London], 2/6/1999.)

(2) summarize (the flavor or essence of something, as if by boiling down) *v.t.*: **decoct**. See *boil down*

summary (thorough . . . of existing knowledge on a subject) *phr.*: **état present** [French]. ❖ [T]o write a thorough **état present** of [Samuel] Beckett criticism could easily require a book-length study. In 2003 alone, no fewer than 75 books that discuss Beckett as a main or secondary topic have been published. (Jeanne-Sarah de Larquier, "Beckett's Molloy," *French Forum*, 9/22/2004.)

(2) summary (spec. a memorandum containing . . . or outline of an agreement or diplomatic negotiations) *n.*: **aide-mémoire** [French]. See *memorandum*

summer (of, like, or relating to) *adj.*: **aestival** (or **estival**). ❖ Four-fifteen of a turquoise afternoon. Cloudless, becalmed, **estival**. Wind bearing east off the ocean, eight knots and ebbing trays of iced tea floating through the Turf Club at Del Mar, two knots and tinkling. Sea gulls circling the infield lake, their flaps and landing gear down, hovering. (William Nack, "Four-fifteen on a Turquoise Afternoon: Cloudless, Becalmed," *Sports Illustrated*, 7/15/1991, p. 68.)

(2) summer (spend the . . . in a state of relative inactivity) *v.i.*: **aestivate**. See *laze*

summit (as in highest point that can be attained or the ultimate degree, as of a condition or quality) *n.*: **ne plus ultra**. See *ultimate*

(2) summit (the . . . , as in the pinnacle) *n.*: **Parnassus**. See *pinnacle*

(3) summit *n.*: **apogee**. See *height*

sun (having the . . . as the center) *adj.*: **heliocentric**. ❖ [Copernicus's] startling conclusion: the so-called retrograde motion could be best explained by a **heliocentric** universe. "Finally," he wrote in the math-filled argument published shortly before his death, "we shall place the sun himself at the center of the universe." (Johanna McGeary, Person of the Century, *Time*, 12/31/1999, p. 162.)

(2) sun (near or relating to) *adj.*: **heliacal**. [This adjective is especially used in reference to the first visible rising of a celestial object in the morning sky after conjunction with the Sun; or the last visible setting of a celestial object in the evening sky before conjunction.] ❖ In Rome, two millenia past, the hot weather was known as "dog days" which ran through Aug. 11. It was named for the **heliacal** rising of the Dog Star. Now, the Dog Star doesn't rise with the Sun until late in August. But the name persists. (Ray Murphy, "Billowing Clouds," *Boston Globe*, 6/28/1990.)

sunbathe *v.t.*: **apricate**. ❖ Have you ever **apricated** in the nude? Fifteen percent of Americans have done so, researchers say. (L. M. Boyd, "The Grab Bag," *San Francisco Chronicle*, 1/2/1994.)

sundown (of, relating to or occurring in . . . or evening) *adj.*: **vespertine**. See *evening*

(2) sundown *n.*: **gloaming**. See *twilight*

sunrise (of or relating to . . .) *adj.*: **matutinal**. See *morning*

superb (as in first-class) *adj.*: **pukka**. See *first-class*

(2) superb (as in of the highest quality) *n.*:

first water (usu. as in "of the first water"). See *quality*

(3) superb *adj.*: **mirific**. See *wonderful*

(4) superb *adj.*: **palmary**. See *excellent*

(5) superb *adj.*: **skookum**. See *excellent*

superficial (knowledge of a subject with a pretense of learnedness) *n.*: **sciolism**. ❧ [T]alk-show hosts [sit] on their almighty thrones [with their] fingers on the cut-off buttons ready to spring into action at the slightest hint of statements that could expose the hosts' shallowness. . . . I feel that if host stations were, by law, forced to allow time for rebuttals by individuals or groups . . . unfairly attacked through this medium, most hosts would rapidly seek work elsewhere, unable to face certain exposure of their **sciolism** and hypocrisy. (Jean Paquette, letter to the editor, *Gazette* [Montreal, Quebec], 10/11/1996.)

(2) superficial (describe in a . . . or incomplete way) *v.t.*: **adumbrate**. See *outline*

(3) superficial (as in outward appearance, as opposed to the substance that lies beneath) *n.*, *n.pl.*: **superficies**. See *appearance*

superficialiality (speech or writing) *n.*: **pablum** (or **pabulum**). See *triteness*

superfluous *adj.*: **excrescent**. ❧ Byatt seems rather fond of **excrescent** commentary, and **excrescent** material in general, packing vast amounts of it into the book. The theorising about language, art, mathematics and the DNA of snails never fully justifies its inclusion. It is often done through the mouths of peripheral characters who are introduced purely for that purpose. (Hugo Barnacle, Books: "Has AS Byatt Lost the Plot?" *Independent* [London], 5/4/1996.)

(2) superfluous *adj.*: **supererogatory**. [This word has both a positive and a negative sense. In the positive sense, it means exceeding the call of duty or what is required. See *exceeding*. In the negative sense (which is more common), it means superfluous or unnecessary. The following is an example of the negative sense.] ❧ For our purposes, the [Southern California] earthquake of 1971 was **super-**erogatory, unnecessary, gilding the lily, as Hollywood has always been wont to do. The real earthquake, the cultural revolution that upended the film industry, began a decade earlier. (Peter Biskind, *Easy Riders, Raging Bulls*, Simon & Schuster [1998], p. 14.)

(3) superfluous (word or phrase) *n.*: **pleonasm**. See *redundancy*

(4) superfluous (words) *n.*: **macrology**. See *verbosity*

(5) superfluous (ornamentation that is . . . or showy or frilly) *n.*: **furbelow**. See *ornamentation*

superhuman (person who is . . . , as in hardworking) *n.*: **Stakhanovite**. See *workaholic*

superior (. . . view of one's own ethnic group) *n.*: **ethnocentric**. ❧ Japanese writer Shintaro Ishihara doesn't apologize for what some critics call xenophobia. "I am a nationalist," he said. "I like sumo and I like kabuki, but I don't necessarily have **ethnocentric** ideas that everything Japanese is better." (Tim Larimer, Asia: "Maverick, Patriot . . . Governor!" *Time* International, 4/26/1999, p. 23.)

(2) superior (in rank, class, status, or value) *adj.*: **superordinate**. ❧ "There is no reason to seal any information which has no bearing on the potential harm to the child. The fact that the defendant might want to protect her own privacy does not prevail over the social value of **superordinate** importance of openness and transparency," Judge Kiteley wrote in a comprehensive ruling released last September. (Shannon Kari, "Documents Sealed in Thomson Custody Case: Court Ruling Aimed at Safeguarding Privacy of Media Mogul's Grandchild," *Ottawa Citizen*, 2/14/2003)

(3) superior (as in condescending) *adj.*, *adv.*: **de haut en bas** [French]. See *condescending*

(4) superior (as in first-class) *adj.*: **pukka**. See *first-class*

(5) superior (as in haughty or condescending) *adj.*: **toplofty**. See *haughty*

(6) superior (as in haughty) *adj.*: **fastuous**. See *haughty*

(7) superior (as in pompous or haughty) *adj.*: **hoity-toity**. See *pompous*

superiority *n.*: **meliority**. ❖ At first glance, he was nobody special, with no special talent[, but he had] a penis the size of a horse's. Yet it was this prodigious endowment that set John Holmes apart. . . . He saw, dangling freakishly between his legs, the key to a future of unimaginable wealth and opportunity. Sometimes a physical **meliority** could do that. Think of basketball star Kareem Abdul-Jabbar, a full head taller than his rivals on the court. (Shane Danielsen, "Rise and Fall of a Porn Star," *Weekend Australian*, 2/7/1998.)

supernatural *adj.*: **numinous**. ❖ [T]he very best children's books, however fantastical, always seem to have such characters, in the sense that we find them in naturalistic novels, vivid, individual, and, however grotesque, with some element of reality at their base. . . . But in North Wind . . . MacDonald did create a goddess of authentic **numinous** power, beneficent and destructive, sinking ships and drowning those aboard. (Richard Jenkyns, "Phallus in Wonderland," *New Republic*, 10/26/1998.)

(2) supernatural *adj.*: **preternatural** ❖ Countless odes have been sung to [basketball player Michael] Jordan's uncanny, unearthly, **preternatural** ability to defy gravity. (Richard Stengel, "Yo, Michael! You're the Best! Jordan Rises—and Rises—to the Occasion, Removing the Last Shadow of Imperfection from His Peerless Career," *Time*, 6/24/1991, p. 47.)

supervise (students taking an examination) *v.i.*: **invigilate**. See *proctor*

supervisor (brutal . . . , as in taskmaster) *n.*: **Simon Legree**. See *taskmaster*

supplemental (as in originating from the outside; extrinsic) *adj.*: **adscititious**. See *extrinsic*

supplication (spec. a prayer mentioning things held to be sacred) *n.*: **obsecration**. See *entreaty*

supplies (or baggage or equipment or any object that hinders progress or movement) *n.pl.*: **impedimenta**. See *baggage*

supply (to the point of excess, esp. things sweet) *v.t.*: **cloy**. See *satiate*

support (on which something is built) *n.*: **warp and woof**. See *foundation*

(2) support (persons hired to yell . . . at a performance) *n.*: **claque**. See *applaud*

supporter (loyal or subservient . . . or military person, esp. who supports or protects a political leader) *n.*: **Janissary** [after an elite force of celibate Christians who protected the Ottoman throne from the fifteenth century onward]. ❖ [Romanian dictator] Nicolae Ceausescu and his wife Elena are dead [having been executed after an uprising]—victims of a people too frightened of him and the wall of modern **Janissaries** he constructed around himself to wait for a public trial and measured judgment of his crimes against them. (Hannah Pakula, "Under the Eye of 'the Big C,'" *Washington Post*, 12/27/1989.)

(2) supporter (strong . . . of a cause, religion, or activity) *n.*: **votary**. ❖ As the labor secretary-designate, Mrs. Chavez was the most provocative Bush nominee, and the most inspired. Big Labor feared she might challenge the privileges unions now enjoy—such as immunity from election laws and Supreme Court edicts. She also could have transformed the department into an advocate of the New Economy, not just a **votary** of the old. (Tony Snow, "Resourcefulness under Fire," *Washington Times*, 1/14/2001.)

(3) supporter (of a cause) *n.*: **paladin**. See *proponent*

(4) supporter (generous . . . , esp. of the arts) *n.*: **Maecenas**. See *benefactor*

(5) supporter *adj.*: **acolyte**. See *follower*

supposed (as in invented or substituted with fraudulent intent) *adj.*: **supposititious**. ❖ Not only were [the Russians] submitted to a long and horrifying experience based on a false historical theory; they were also robbed of knowledge of the historical facts. . . . First, a **supposititious** "class" scheme was imposed on every public fact: so that, for example, a wholly invented class of [wealthy farmers] was created and real people were assigned to it, and then repressed by the million. (Robert Conquest, "History, Humanity, and Truth," *National Review*, 6/7/1993.)

(2) supposed *adj.*: **putative**. ❖ In one of [Roz Chast's] most famous cartoons, the careless foibles of motherhood are turned into the stuff of legend through a **putative** ad for "Bad Mom Cards (Collect the Entire Set!)." The pictured examples: ". . . Gloria B.—Promised to take daughter to the mall after school—and then didn't." (Fred Kaplan, "Drawing from Life/ Roz Chast Has Been Drawing Cartoons for the *New Yorker* for 19 Years," *Boston Globe*, 5/21/1995.)

suppress (as in put an end to) *v.t.*: **quietus** (as in "put the quietus to"). See *termination*

supremacy (naval . . .) *n.*: **thalassocracy**. ❖ The real force of the Etruscans, however, was on the seas. . . . As early as the 5th century B.C. the Etruscans were exploring the southern coast of what would become the Italian peninsula. This **thalassocracy**, or dominion of the seas, gave the Etruscans tremendous potential for trade as well as piracy. (Greg Burke, "Masters of Power and Pleasure—A Display of Etruscan Arts and Crafts Reveals a Civilization That Seemed to Enjoy a Good Fight as Much as a Good Party," *Time* International, 2/12/2001, p. 54.)

(2) supremacy (of one political state over others) *n.*: **hegemony**. See *dominance*

(3) supremacy (as in domination, of a nation or group over another) *n.*: **suzerainty**. See *domination*

(4) supremacy (as in superiority or state of being better) *n.*: **meliority**. See *superiority*

sure (as in unavoidable) *adj.*: **ineluctable**. See *unavoidable*

sure thing (esp. with respect to a plan, deal, or investment that can be trusted completely because it is supposedly safe and sure to succeed) *adj.*: **copper-bottomed** [British]. ❖ People laugh when I say there are sometimes bets available which give a **copper-bottomed** guarantee of profit—but that's because I usually say it when I've sucked a helium balloon and my voice sounds all

squeaky. (Derek McGovern, Sports Betting, *Mirror* [London], 8/9/2003.)

surface (appearance, as opposed to the substance that lies beneath) *n.*, *n.pl.*: **superficies**. See *appearance*

surliness *n.pl.*: **mulligrubs**. See *grumpiness*

surly *adj.*: **atrabilious**. ❖ Maneka's cause was the environment, and she set herself up as a temperamental Green Queen. . . . Her most recent public utterances have been richly **atrabilious**. Newspapers reported her anger on returning from an overseas trip to find that her official bungalow had been forcibly occupied by a newly elected member of Parliament. (*New Republic*, "Gandhi Crest," 9/2/91.)

(2) surly *adj.*: **bilious**. ❖ The old arrogance typified by the **bilious** head of the House Resources Committee, Alaskan Don Young—who once vowed revenge on "the wafflestomping, intellectual bunch of idiots" known as environmentalists—lost some of its strut, but none of its purposefulness. (B. J. Bergman, "Environmental Impact," *Sierra*, 9/19/1998, p. 50.)

(3) surly (person) *n.*: **crosspatch**. See *grouch*

(4) surly (and/or shy and/or socially withdrawn or inexperienced) *adj.*: **farouche** [French]. See *shy*

(5) surly *adj.*: **liverish**. See *irritable*

(6) surly *adj.*: **querulous**. See *peevish*

(7) surly *adj.*: **shirty**. See *irritable*

surname *n.*: **cognomen**. ❖ I've got a new favorite site. It's called How Stuff Works and is found easily at www.howstuffworks.com. . . . Its material is written by Marshall Brain (yes, that seems to be his apt **cognomen**) and features superlatively lucid explanations of the mechanics of the world around us for those of us who don't have a clue. (Jay Bailey, "Sign of the Times," *Jerusalem Post*, 2/12/1999.)

surpass (the limits, resources, or capabilities of) *v.t.*: **beggar**. ❖ It somewhat **beggars** belief that the museum turned his job application down. (Simon Winchester, *The Professor and the Madman*, HarperCollins [1998], p. 37.)

surpassing (as in going above and beyond the call of duty or what is required) *adj.*: **supererogatory**. See *exceeding*

surplus *n.*: **nimiety**. See *excess*

surprise (as in sudden turnaround of events, often in a literary work) *n.*: **peripeteia**. See *turnaround*

surrender (an office or position) *v.t.*: **demit** (as in "demit office"). See *resign*

(2) surrender (as in give back, often a territory) *v.t.*: **retrocede**. See *give back*

(3) surrender (esp. responsibility or duty) *v.t.*: **abnegate**. See *renounce*

surround (often protectively) *v.t.*: **embosom**. ❖ The community [of Aspen, Colorado,] sits along the Roaring Fork River, high in the central Colorado Rockies. Peaks **embosom** the town. (*Newsday*, "Aspen at 50," 1/12/1997.)

(2) surround *v.t.*: **girdle**. ❖ I dressed and left my motel, then turned off the commercial strip along Highway 192, past the white polymerized vinyl picket fence that **girdles** the town [of Celebration, Florida], and the water tower that is no water tower at all, just a stagy billboard. (Alexander Wolff, *Big Game, Small World*, Warner Books [2002], p. 69.)

surrounding *adj.*: **ambient**. ❖ That oxygen-deprived state is called hypoxia, and that's basically the state you're in whenever you're above 24-, 25,000 feet on Everest, with or without supplemental oxygen. . . . You're wearing supplemental oxygen, but it's mixed with **ambient** air. (Marty Moss-Coane, "Everest," *Fresh Air*, NPR, 11/11/1997.)

(2) surrounding *adj.*: **circumambient**. ❖ But it is Joan Plowright who walks away with top honors [in *Tea with Mussolini*] in a performance that blends warmth and pawkiness, sparkle and gravitas, heart and backbone. So perfect a being could hardly exist, but the actress makes her grittily alive without allowing the occasionally **circumambient** sentimentality to creep into her work. (John Simon, "Notting Hill," *National Review*, 6/28/1999.)

(3) surrounding *adj.*: **circumjacent**. ❖ Currently in China only 3 million bank cards among the total of over 400 million possess the function of credit card. There is a big gap in credit card businesses between domestic banks and those of **circumjacent** countries. (AsiaInfo Services, "CMB President Talks Bank Internationalization," 12/9/2002.)

surroundings (as in place one frequents) *n.*: **purlieu(s)**. See *hangout*

survey (of a subject) *n.*: **conspectus**. ❖ *America in Black and White* [is a] comprehensive survey of the issues of race in America. . . . Out of the hundreds of cogent observations in their historical **conspectus**, let me begin with this one: black anger and white surrender have become a staple of contemporary racial discourse. (Kenneth S. Lynn, review of *America in Black and White*, by Stephan Thernstrom and Abigail Thernstrom, *American Spectator*, 10/1/1997.)

(2) survey (quick . . . , as in glance) *n.*: **coup d'oeil** [French]. See *glance*

suspect (morality or taste) *adj.*: **louche**. See *questionable*

suspend (as in discontinue, esp. a session of Parliament) *v.t.*: **prorogue**. See *discontinue*

suspenders (for trousers) *n.pl.*: **galluses**. ❖ Bavarians cling as tightly to their traditional dress—Lederhosen (leather pants), knee socks, brightly embroidered **galluses**, hats sporting a white eagle's feather—as Texans do to string ties, cowboy boots, and Stetsons. (*German Life*, "Bavarian Farm Vacations," 5/31/1997.)

suspense (in a state of . . .) *idiom*: **on tenterhooks**. ❖ Russia is **on tenterhooks** waiting to see if its parliament today will confirm President Boris Yeltsin's appointment of Viktor Chernomyrdin as prime minister. (*Washington Times*, "Russians Turn to Barter to Keep Wheels Turning," 9/7/1998.)

sustenance (as in nourishment) *n.*: **alimentation**. See *nourishment*

(2) sustenance (esp. insipid, like baby food) *n.*: **pabulum** (also **pablum**). See *insipid*

swaggering (behavior) *n.*: **fanfaronade**. See *bravado*

(2) swaggering (person) *n.*: **Gascon** (act

of being a . . . person *n.*: **Gasconade**). See *braggart*

swallow (greedily) *v.t.*: **englut**. ❖ [T]he current fashion among non-profit companies [is] accepting "enhancement money" to [name] their theaters after corporate sponsors such as American Airlines. [This is] the theatrical version of the hostile takeover. "**Englut** and devour"—the name that Mel Brooks once invented for a Hollywood studio—is becoming the motto of the American stage. (*New Republic*, "Robert Brustein on Theater," 9/18/2000.)

(2) swallow (as in guzzle) *v.t., v.i.*: **ingurgitate**. See *guzzle*

swallowing (act or process of) *n.*: **deglutition**. ❖ Justice, or more pointedly the judge, in this case should have been more compassionate. "There is a point beyond which even justice becomes unjust," Sophocles said. "Justice untempered by feeling is too bitter and husky a morsel for human **deglutition**," wrote Charlotte Brontë. (*Filipino Express*, "Observer: Death of an Abused Wife," 10/18/1998.)

swamp *n.*: **fen**. ❖ The process of reworking natural topography to suit the needs of an urbanizing and industrializing society was refined by 1900. . . . Draining the **fens** in England is one classic example, and the infilling of Boston's Back Bay and the waterfront expansion of New York are well-known urban instances in this country. (Craig E. Colten, "Industrial Topography, Groundwater, and the Contours of Environmental Knowledge," *Geographical Review*, 4/1/1998, p. 199.)

swamps (of or relating to still water, such as . . .) *adj.*: **lentic**. See *water*

swampy *adj.*: **paludal**. ❖ Bud DeWitt's Swamp Omelet doesn't take its name from any **paludal** odor, texture, or appearance. The name refers only to its place of birth: a duck-hunting camp, where it's served to hunters when they return from swampy blinds with cold feet and ravening hunger. (*Sunset*, "His Cowboy Beans Are Assertive, Not Aggressive," 5/1/1984.)

(2) swampy *adj.*: **quaggy**. See *marshy*

swanky *adj.*: **nobby** [British]. See *elegant*

(2) swanky *adj.*: **soigné** [French]. See *elegant*

swarm *v.i.*: **pullulate**. See *teem*

swastika *n.*: **Hakenkreuz** [German; lit. hooked cross]. ❖ Himmler, the chicken-farmer who considered himself the reincarnation of Heinrich I, loved pagan symbols such as the **Hakenkreuz** on the Nazi flag and the Wolfsangel of the Waffen-SS Division "Das Reich" (whose achievements include locking the 642 villagers of Oradour in their church and burning them to death). (Alex Berlyne, "Nasty Rune," *Jerusalem Post*, 5/5/1995.)

swearing (or dirty talk to relieve tension) *n.*: **lalochezia**. ❖ As of late I've realized that I suffer from **lalochezia**. Maybe suffer isn't quite the right word, since I rather enjoy spewing expletives when I have some steam to blow off. . . . I think at least twice a week I go into an under-the-breath tirade where every other word pretty much guarantees my ticket to hell. (www.projectfutility.net/my-disability.htm, 8/22/2003.)

(2) swearing (excessive . . . , esp. involuntarily when mentally ill) *n.*: **coprolalia**. See *cursing*

sweat (an agent that causes . . . , or having the power to cause . . .) *n., adj.*: **diaphoretic**. ❖ Borage tea is another possibility. Apparently it's excellent for soothing sore throats. . . . [T]he word "borage" is a Latinised version of the Arabic abu arak, which means "father of sweat"—a term due no doubt to its use as a **diaphoretic**. (Grant Simon, "The Beauty of Borage," *Evening Post* [Wellington, New Zealand], 12/5/1996.)

(2) sweat (foul-smelling . . .) *n.*: **bromidrosis**. ❖ Q: "I can't take off my shoes because my feet smell horrible. What can I do?" Sara, 18, Salt Lake City, UT. A: "You may have **bromidrosis**, a disorder you can get if your feet sweat a lot. What happens is, bacteria live off your sweat and cause an odor." (Kristen Kemp, "Your Most Intimate Body Questions—Answered!" *CosmoGirl!* 9/1/2003.)

(3) sweat (inducing . . .) *adj.*: **sudatory**. ❖ The mud is applied to part or all of the body (except the chest) at a temperature of between

104 and 118 degrees. . . . "Good perspiration reaction; very good for a first-time patient," she remarked. . . . After 18 minutes I showered off the mud. . . . Then it was time to go up to my room for the "**sudatory** reaction," an hour's rest given over to still more perspiration. (The mud pack can raise the body temperature several degrees.) (Frederika Randall, "Mud, Glorious Mud in Hills Near Padua," *New York Times*, 4/5/1992.)

(4) sweat (inducing) *adj.*: **sudorific**. ❖ [At the Earth Sanctuary Day Spa you] step into a midnight blue bath filled with warm water. . . . The heat soon induces you into a **sudorific** stupor and you can either drift off to sleep or try to read the thoughtfully provided book on the benefits of water therapy. Once sufficiently sweaty, you're asked to dry off. (Samuel Ee, "Revenge of the Little White Ball," *Business Times* [Singapore], 4/26/2002.)

(5) sweat (in a . . . , as in distress) *n.*: **swivet** (as in "in a swivet") *informal*. See *distress*

(6) sweat (cause . . . by subjecting person or thing to intense heat) *v.t.*: **parboil**. See *heat*

sweeping *adj.*: **pandemic**. See *widespread*

sweet (sounding) *adj.*: **mellifluous**. See *melodious*

(2) sweet (sounding) *adj.*: **mellisonant**. See *melodious*

sweeten (as in make pleasant or less harsh) *v.t.*: **edulcorate**. ❖ [I]ndependently produced movies permit film-makers to tackle themes that the major studios, pressured by the need to attain the widest possible audience, would either **edulcorate** beyond all recognition or reject outright. No major, patently, would ever have financed *Trust* or *Sex, Lies and Videotape* or *Drugstore Cowboy* or *Reservoir Dogs* or *Metropolitan*. (Gilbert Adair, "War of Independents," *Sunday Times* [London], 11/26/1995.)

sweetheart (female) *n.*: **inamorata**. See *girlfriend*

(2) sweetheart (male . . .) *n.*: **inamorato**. See *boyfriend*

(3) sweetheart (my . . .) *n.*: **mavoureen** [Irish]. See *darling*

(4) sweetheart *n.*: **acushla** [Irish]. See *darling*

sweet talk *n.*: **palaver**. ❖ Such success didn't always appear to be in the cards, although at 14 [singer Barry] White had already developed a reputation for smooth **palaver** and made money counseling adults in his Los Angeles neighborhood about their relationships. (Steve Jones, "Barry White's Love Has 'Stayin' Power,'" *USA Today*, 9/3/1999.)

(2) sweet talk (as in compliment, which is empty, meaningless, or insincere) *n.*: **flummery**. See *compliment*

(3) sweet talk (by flattery) *n.*: **blandishment** (*v.t.*: **blandish**). See *flattery*

swelling (or inflammation of skin due to exposure to cold) *n.*: **chilblains**. See *inflammation*

(2) swelling (reduction of a . . . to normal size; e.g., loss of erection) *n.*: **detumescence**. See *shrinkage*

sweltering (as in of or relating to dog days of summer) *adj.*: **canicular**. See *dog days*

swerve (from a course or intended path) *v.t.*: **yaw**. See *veer*

swiftness *n.*: **celerity**. See *speed*

swimming (of or relating to . . .) *adj.*: **natatorial**. ❖ Some golfers might throw up their hands in surrender after a slice or a shanked five-iron, but how many pack up their clubs and become world-class in a fallback sport? Swimmer Ed Moses has done that with only two years of full-time training. So meteoric has his rise through the **natatorial** ranks been that he seems to have answered the commandment of his sign-waving mother, Sissy. (Brian Cazeneuve, "Leaving the Links to Pick up a Stroke—With Three World Cup Wins, Former Golfer Ed Moses Proved Water's No Hazard," *Sports Illustrated*, 11/29/1999, p. R20.)

(2) swimming (pool, esp. indoor) *n.*: **natatorium**. See *pool*

swindle *n.*, *v.t.*: **thimblerig**. [This word refers specifically to a rigged shell game, but "swindle" better conveys the sense that the word can be used as a noun or a verb.] ❖ [H. Ross Perot] is an enterpriser who has built his fortune in intimate collaboration with the grand old firm of Skull and Duggery. . . . Government has become a conspiratorial partnership of the governors and the greedy; and there cannot exist a **thimblerig** that a President Perot wouldn't recognize on sight because he has in his time rigged no end of thimbles himself. (Murray Kempton, "A Den of Sinners Looks to Its Master," *Newsday*, 6/12/1992.)

(2) swindle *v.t.*: **bunco**. ❖ Samuel Adams . . . belonged to the tradition of the American West, "full of liars and braggarts." He saw profit in recognition by the federal government, and in 1867 **buncoed** a tiny mining town into providing [supplies for his trip]. His boats quickly came apart on the boulders, but that didn't deter Adams from claiming he had accomplished the trip, and lobbying Congress for money. (James Conaway, "Fakers of the Frontier; Great Exploration Hoaxes," *Washington Post*, 12/17/1982.)

(3) swindle (as in cheat) *v.t.*: **euchre**. See *cheat*

(4) swindle (as in deceive) *v.t.*: **hornswoggle**. See *deceive*

(5) swindle *v.t.*: **mulct**. See *defraud*

(6) swindle *v.t.*, *v.i.*: **cozen**. See *defraud*

(7) swindle (as in deceive) *v.t.*: **gull**. See *deceive*

swine (of or relating to) *adj.*: **porcine**. See *pigs*

swing (with arms like a monkey) *v.i.*: **brachiate**. ❖ *The Good Seed* [by Mark Leyner] describes a sperm bank on the 71st floor of the Empire State Building: "You can pick a donor with Mensa membership going back to the *Mayflower* and a breakfront filled with gymnastics trophies, and end up giving birth to a slavering **brachiating** moron." (Elaine Gale, "Successful Offbeat Writer/Mark Leyner's Popularity Fueled by a Unique Style," *Minneapolis Star Tribune*, 4/17/1995.)

swirling (or spiraling motion, often an ocean current) *n.*: **gyre**. See *spiraling*

swollen (used often of body parts such as a penis) *adj.*: **tumescent**. ❖ For if . . . the jury is left to decide on the oral evidence alone [in Paula Jones's lawsuit against President Clinton], then her lawyers may well be able to argue, "OK. So our client has enjoyed numerous sexual liaisons—which means she is all the more qualified to recognise an abnormally **tumescent** penis when she sees one." (John Carlin, "No Moles, No Growths," *Independent on Sunday*, 11/16/1997.)

(2) swollen *adj.*: **dropsical**. [This word is the adjectival form of dropsy, which means swollen with an excessive amount of fluid, like edema. It is used more generally to refer to anything (whether or not a person) exhibiting swollen, bloated, or inflated characteristics.] ❖ [French president] Chirac instituted tough welfare reforms in order to cut the budget deficit [but] even more spending cuts [were] needed. [So the government instituted] a collection of cuts, caps, freezes, charges and taxes. . . . It is certainly good to see Jacques Chirac start to tackle France's health and welfare system. The task of reforming a **dropsical** welfare state is not a pleasant one, as plenty of governments elsewhere will attest. (*Economist*, "Third Time Plucky; Jacques Chirac's Government Has Made Some Bold Welfare Reforms, but a Lot Remains to Be Done," 11/18/1995.)

(3) swollen *adj.*: **tumid**. ❖ There are some troubled taters in East Texas. Stunted by drought when young, the sweet potatoes ballooned into misshapen giants when heavy rains fell later in July. Now they are more **tumid** than tuber. They are as big as footballs. (*Dallas Morning News*, "Too-Big Tubers: A Sad Fate Awaits Gigantic Sweet Potatoes," 10/31/1996.)

(4) swollen (reduction of a . . . object to normal size; e.g., loss of erection) *n.*: **detumescence**. See *shrinkage*

sycophant *n.*: **lickspittle**. ❖ Perhaps [Secretary of Energy Bill] Richardson himself deserves some of the blame for his predicament. Too eager to please, he constantly agrees to run fool's errands for his boss [President Clinton]. Acynic might even call him a **lickspittle**. (Franklin Foer, "Bill Richardson, Masochist," *New Republic*, 7/3/2000.)

(2) sycophant (as in willing tool or servant of another) *n.*: **âme damnée** [French]. See *lackey*

(3) sycophant (esp. someone who seeks to associate with or flatter persons of rank or high social status) *n.*: **tuft-hunter**. See *hanger-on*

sycophantic (esp. praise or flattery) *adj.*: **fulsome**. ❖ [T]he most salient single technique of all the conventions . . . is the use of the crippled, the sick and the lately deceased for political effect. . . . At the Reform Party convention, **fulsome** tributes were paid to Ross Perot by a Vietnamese soldier who had aided American prisoners of war (whose agonies were described). (Jonathan Schell, "Convention Tears Are Cheap," *Newsday*, 9/1/1996.)

(2) sycophantic *adj.*: **gnathonic**. ❖ Ideally, the new San Francisco fire chief would be selected from a qualified pool of experienced and competent aspirants with acknowledged backgrounds in firefighting and administration. Unfortunately, the next chief will probably be a poster boy (or girl) for diversity or a **gnathonic** . . . backer of Mayor Brown. (Edward J. Fitzpatrick, letter to the editor, *Chicago Tribune*, 5/27/1990.)

(3) sycophantic (to behave toward in a . . . manner) *v.t.*: **bootlick**. See *kowtow*

sycophants *n.*: **claque**. See *admirers*

syllables (having more than three . . .) *adj.*: **polysyllabic**. ❖ *Firing Line*, the eminently civil talk show . . . was ending its run after more than 33 years on the air. And William F. Buckley Jr., the spiritual force of America's conservatives and the professor with the famously **polysyllabic** vocabulary, was cementing his record as the longest active host of a TV show. (Paul D. Colford, "A Conversation Comes to an End/On TV's *Firing Line*, Host William F. Buckley Jr. and Guests Would Talk—at Length. It's the Sort of Talk That's Been Overtaken by the Sound Bite," *Newsday*, 12/21/1999.)

symbol (or sign that gives information nonverbally) *n.*: **glyph**. ❖ One of the **glyphs** that has been imposed on the American consciousness since illiteracy and immigration made

such retrogression necessary is . . . a band running diagonally across a circle, a synonym for the word "no." If combined with a drawing of a cigarette it means "no smoking." If combined with a big letter P, it means "no parking." (Bob Wiemer, "NAFTA'S Glyphs Are Sinister Lunacies," *Newsday*, 8/26/1996.)

(2) symbol (representing an idea without words; e.g., "$," or Chinese or Japanese symbols) *n.*: **ideogram**. ❖ Why have the Japanese latched onto faxing more than electronic mail? It all boils down to this: In Japan, where writing the language requires oodles of **ideograms** and two systems of syllables in hundreds of different combinations, it is easier to hand-write messages than to find the right combination of computer keys. (Karen de Witt, "Floods of Free-Flowing Fax a Daily Fact of Life in Japan," *Minneapolis Star Tribune*, 11/24/1995.)

(3) symbol (an inspiring . . . , esp. a flag or banner) *n.*: **oriflamme**. See *banner*

(4) symbol (as in figure of speech, where a part is used to stand for the whole, or vice versa) *n.*: **synecdoche**. See *figure of speech*

symbolic (rather than literal representation, esp. with respect to objects of worship) *adj.*: **aniconic**. ❖ Antiquarian authors of the second century . . . described an age before art in which primitive peoples worshiped unformed, **aniconic** images such as rocks and planks. To their way of thinking, this simple age preceded a subsequent "age of art," a period in which worship was transformed by the introduction of images created with aesthetic sense and skill. (Sarah Guberti Bassett, "Excellent Offerings: The Lausos Collection in Constantinople," *Art Bulletin*, 3/1/2000.)

symbols (spec. the study and analysis of . . . and signs as part of communication, as for example in language, gesture, clothing, and behavior) *n.*: **semiotics**. See *communication*

sympathetic (as in compassionate or pitiful) *adj.*: **ruthful**. See *compassionate* and *pitiful*

sympathizer (false . . . , as in one who discourages another by offering remarks that supposedly have the opposite intent) *n.*: **Job's comforter**. See *comforter*

sympathizers (as in traitors or group of . . . working within a country to support an enemy and who may engage in espionage, sabotage, or other subversive activities) *n.*: **fifth column**. See *traitors*

symptom (early . . . of disease, esp. migraines, herpes or depression) *n.*: **prodrome**. ❖ The **prodrome** is a familiar concept in the area of migraines, where people may develop problems concentrating, or extreme sensitivity to light or sound, days before an actual headache. (Karen Patterson, "Early Warning System; Research Shows Quick Action Can Head off Psychosis, Impairment," *Dallas Morning News*, 8/11/2003.)

synonyms (study of subtle distinctions or nuances between words that are . . . or otherwise similar) *n.*: **synonymy**. ❖ *The Artful Nuance*, by Rod Evan, is **synonymy** delivered with a hair-splitter's delight: "A *naked* person is totally bare, wearing nothing; a *nude* person has become nude by removing clothes." . . . A *homonym* is a word like another in sound and spelling but different in meaning. . . . A *homophone* is a word pronounced the same but different in meaning from another, regardless of whether the spelling the same: *Heir* and *air* are homophones. (William Safire, "Making Glad the Heart of Adulthood," *New York Times*, 12/21/2008.)

synopsis *n.*: **conspectus**. See *survey*

(2) synopsis *n.*: **précis** [French]. See *summary*

tacky (as in sticky) *adj.*: **mucilaginous**. See *sticky*

(2) tacky (or kitschy religious or devotional ornament) *n.*: **bondieuserie** [French]. See *ornament*

tactile *adj.*: **haptic**. See *touch*

tactless (person who makes . . . comments that seem to be offering sympathy but instead make the person feel worse, either intentionally or unintentionally) *n.*: **Job's comforter**.

(2) tactless (comments) *n.*: **dontopedalogy**. See *foot-in-mouth*

tail (toward or located near) *adj.*: **caudal**. ❖ The lower tip of the walleye's **caudal** fin is white-tipped, while the sauger's isn't. (Jerry Davis, "Walleye Wonderland—Anglers on Thin Ice, but Chase Coveted Fish Anyway," *Wisconsin State Journal*, 1/21/1996.)

tailing (as in lying in wait for prey, often used of insects) *adj.*: **lochetic**. See *ambushing*

tainted (morally . . .) *v.t.*: **cankered**. See *corrupted*

take (a person or group from one place to another forcibly, whether literally or figuratively) *v.t.*: **frog-march**. See *march*

(2) take (for oneself without permission) *v.t.*: **expropriate**. See *seize*

(3) take (for oneself without right) *v.t.*: **arrogate**. See *claim*

(4) take (property to compel payment of debts) *v.t.*: **distrain**. See *confiscate*

take back (as in renounce or disavow) *v.t.*: **abjure**. See *renounce*

take in (as in ingest) *v.t.*: **incept**. See *ingest*

take it or leave it (as in choice of taking what is offered or nothing; i.e., no real option at all) *n.*: **Hobson's choice**. See *choice*

take on (as in incorporate, the ideas or attitudes of others, esp. parents, into one's own personality) *v.t.*: **introject**. See *incorporate*

takeover (sudden attempt at government . . .) *n.*: **putsch**. See *coup*

take over (as in usurp) *v.t.*: **accroach**. See *usurp*

take place *v.t.*: **betide**. See *happen*

(2) take place (as in result) *v.i.*: **eventuate**. See *result*

taking (forcible . . . of another's property) *n.*: **rapine**. See *looting*

tale (as in fable) *n.*: **apologue**. See *fable*

(2) tale (as in lie) *n.*: **fabulation** (one who does so: **fabulist**). See *lie*

talent (area of . . .) *n.*: **métier** [French]. See *forte*

talk (about, esp. at length) *v.i.*, *n.*: **descant**. ❖ [Handwriting expert Elias Samas] can **descant** for an hour on the secrets a single letter may conceal. "Take the letter 'T,'" he says. "I can give you 30 interpretations on the way people write that letter." (Drew Fetherston, "City & Co./He's Got Analysis Down to a T/Handwriting Expert Sees Past Alphabet's Letters," *Newsday*, 11/26/2000.)

(2) talk (as in discussion) *n.*: **interlocution**. See *discussion*

(3) talk (as in discussion, esp. about art or literature) *n.*: **conversazione** [Italian]. See *conversation*

(4) talk (at length) *v.i.*: **perorate** *(n.*: **peroration**). See *monologue*

(5) talk (between three people) *n.*: **trialogue**. See *conversation*

(6) talk (between two people or groups in which neither side hears or understands or pays attention to the other) *n.*: **dialogue de sourds** [French]. See *dialogue*

(7) talk (casual . . . , as in chitchat) *n.*: **persiflage**. See *chitchat*

(8) talk (casually) *n.*: **chinwag** [slang]. See *chat*

(9) talk (casually) *v.i.*: **confabulate**. See *chat*

(10) talk (formal . . .) *n.*: **allocution**. See *speech*

(11) talk (in a foolish or inept way, or . . . nonsense) *v.i.*, *n.*: **piffle**. See *nonsense*

(12) talk (inability to . . . due to brain injury) *n.*: **aphasia**. See *uncomprehending*

(13) talk (inability to . . . due to hoarseness) *n.*: **dysphonia**. See *hoarseness*

(14) talk (informal . . . , as in chat or discussion) *n.*: **causerie**. See *chat*

(15) talk (light or playful back and forth . . .) *n.*: **badinage**. See *banter*

(16) talk (on a topic, esp. in a long-winded or pompous manner) *v.i.*: **bloviate**. See *speak*

(17) talk (one skilled at dinner . . .) *n.*: **deipnosophist**. See *conversation*

(18) talk (or write at length on a subject) *v.i.*: **expatiate**. See *expound*

(19) talk (pompously, loudly, or theatrically) *v.i.*: **declaim**. See *proclaim*

(20) talk (quickly and excitedly) *v.t.*: **burble** See *gush*

(21) talk (small . . . , as in chitchat) *n.*: **bavardage**. See *chitchat*

(22) talk (to . . . to an absent person or thing) *v.t.*: **apostrophize**. See *address*

talkative (as in characterized by a ready and easy flow of words) *adj.*: **voluble**. ❖ You have to be very specific about what you ask women. If, for example, you missed a Redskins game, and you know a woman who saw it, never, ever ask, "What happened?" Unless you have nowhere to go until Thursday. . . . Left to their own devices, girls go through life **volubly** answering essay questions. (Tony Kornheiser, *Pumping Irony*, Times Books [1995], p. 248.)

(2) talkative (as in verbose) *adj.*: **inaniloquent**. See *verbose*

(3) talkative (condition of being overly . . .) *n.*: **logorrhea**. See *verbosity*

(4) talkative (mania for being overly . . .) *n.*: **cacoëthes loquendi** [Latin]. See *talking*

(5) talkative (very . . . person) *n.*: **magpie**

talkativeness (spec. obsessive repetition of meaningless words and phrases) *n.*: **verbigeration**. See *repetition*

talker (incessant . . . , as in chatterbox) *n.*: **magpie**

talking (mania for . . . too much) *n.*: **cacoëthes loquendi** [Latin]. ❖ [T]here sprang up a waggish tradition [among Samuel Taylor Coleridge's biographers] . . . of mocking the style of his prolixity, but none of preserving its contents. . . . [H]is biographers have had to settle for indicating the fact of his **cacoëthes loquendi**. What we get is the impression of a man who, in the excellent poolhall phrase, too rarely stopped talking and started chalking. (Ben Downing, "A Jelly Minus Its Mould," review of *Coleridge:*

Darker Reflections, 1804–1834, by Richard Holmes, *New Criterion*, 6/1/1999.)

(2) talking (and singing combined together) *n.*: **sprechgesang** [German]. See *speaking*

talks (esp. at the start of negotiations) *n.*: **pourparler** [French]. See *discussion*

tameness (as in gentleness) *n.*: **mansuetude**. See *gentleness*

tan *v.t.*: **apricate**. See *sunbathe*

tangent (as in digression) *n.*: **excursus**. See *digression*

(2) tangent (as in passing comment) *n.*: **obiter dictum** [Latin]. See *passing comment*

tangible *adj.*: **tactile**. ❖ But like all Olympics, this will be a place where the world's greatest athletes vie for a shot at immortality. For Koons and every other person playing a role, Nagano [Japan] will forever be the place where their dreams, once broad and abstract, take on the **tactile** dimensions of an overstuffed bag, a racing bib, an Olympic uniform, or a gold medal. (Sam Walker, "Testing Olympic Dreams on Ice and Snow . . . Among the Palm Trees," *Christian Science Monitor*, 2/6/1998.)

tangle (as in confused or disarrayed mass) *n.*: **welter**. See *jumble*

(2) tangle (as in entangle) *v.t.*: **embrangle**. See *entangle*

tangled (capable of being . . . , as in ensnared) *adj.*: **illaqueable**. See *ensnared*

tangy (agreeably . . . in taste or flavor) *adj.*: **piquant**. See *zesty*

(2) tangy (as in tart) *adj.*: **acidulous**. See *tart*

tantalizing *adj.*: **sirenic**. [See also the nouns *siren call* and *Lorelei call* under *lure*.] See *alluring*

tantrum (marked by a sudden or violent . . .) *adj.*: **vesuvian** (esp. as in . . . temper). See *temper*

(2) tantrum *n.*: **boutade** [French]. See *temper tantrum*

tapering (or coming to a point) *adj.*: **acuminate**. See *pointed*

target (as in the thing that is being looked for; also the answer to a problem) *n.*: **quaesitum**. See *objective*

tarnish *v.t.*: **besmirch**. ❖ "Never in all of this

four years of activity have I ever said anything to **besmirch** anyone's reputation. I think we owe one another as a part of basic human dignity treating one another with dignity and with respect and basic civility. That's the way I was trained in the law." (*Atlanta Journal-Constitution,* "The Paula Jones Decision: Excerpts," 4/3/1998.)

tarnished (or impure) *adj., v.t.:* **maculate**. See *impure*

tart *adj.:* **acidulous**. ❖ People seem to think [Senator Robert Dole's] biting wit bares too many teeth, prompting even his handlers to debate whether to "let Dole be Dole." Dole's **acidulous** wit underscores how humorless the Bush and Bill Clinton years have been compared with past administrations. (Neal Gabler, "No Fooling—Dole Is a Funny Guy," *Newsday,* 3/25/1996.)

(2) tart (agreeably . . . in taste or flavor) *adj.:* **piquant**. See *zesty*

(3) tart (as in . . . remarks) *adj.:* **astringent**. See *harsh*

(4) tart (or tending to become . . . , as in sour) *adj.:* **acescent**. See *sour*

taskmaster (brutal . . .) *n.:* **Simon Legree** [after the cruel slave dealer in Harriet Beecher Stowe's 1852 novel *Uncle Tom's Cabin*]. ❖ Nearly half of the 3rd Infantry's 20,000 still in Iraq have been deployed at least six months, some more than a year. Yesterday, they were told that their departure from Iraq would be delayed a second time. . . . [D]oes it make sense, spending what we do to recruit volunteers—and then leave them with an ill-defined mission under conditions that only a **Simon Legree** could think reasonable? (Lionel Van Deerlin, "Our Fighting Forces in a Sour Mood," *San Diego Union-Tribune,* 7/16/2003.)

taste (as in personal preference) *n.:* **de gustibus**. [Latin, often used as part of the expression "de gustibus non est disputandum," as in "there is no disputing about taste." This phrase is sometimes used pejoratively, as in questioning the taste of others, and sometimes not, as in merely pointing out that everyone has his own opinion.] ❖ Two of the most traditional approaches [determining what goes on TV are paternalism, which] derives its authority from the conviction that culture is all about providing the public with what it needs rather than what it wants, [and populism, which] defers meekly to the relativistic assumption that **de gustibus non est disputandum**; it does not so much judge quality as merely rubberstamp the ratings. (Graham McCann, "How to Define the Indefinable: Television," *Financial Times* [London], 3/26/2003.)

(2) taste (of or relating to sense of . . .) *adj.:* **gustatory**. ❖ Among the **gustatory** delights of Cajun country: An alligator sausage and seafood gumbo. (Anne Rochell Konigsmark, "Cajun Spice Marking Three Centuries of French Flavor in Louisiana, a Year's Worth of Festivals Has the Good Times Really Rolling on the Bayou," *Atlanta Journal-Constitution,* 5/30/1999.)

(3) taste (savor the . . . of) *v.t.:* **degust**. See *savor*

tasteless (and cheap or showy, or such an object) *adj., n.:* **gimcrack**. See *showy*

(2) tasteless (or inappropriate comments) *n.:* **dontopedalogy**. See *foot-in-mouth*

tasting (act or faculty of . . .) *n.:* **gustation**. ❖ Describing the enormous respect she has gained for **gustation**, Allende tells of a lecture in which a Jewish guru gave his students a rosy grape and instructed them to spend no less than 20 minutes eating it. (Jessica Lee, "*Aphrodite* Serves Orgy of Epicurean Delights," *USA Today,* 4/2/1998.)

tasty *adj.:* **sapid**. ❖ In previous reviews, I've raved about the elegant and earthy lobster-and-truffle sausage, the **sapid** sea bass with coarse salt poached in lobster oil, and the indescribably complex and delectable ballottine of lamb stuffed with ground veal, sweet-breads and truffles. (James Villas, "Why Taillevent Thrives," *Town & Country,* 3/1/1998, p. 134.)

(2) tasty *adj.:* **toothsome**. ❖ A highly buffed, $1-million stainless steel kitchen opens onto one side of the dining room so diners can watch while a dozen pleated white toques bob and weave. There, chef Philippe Feret and his team assemble their **toothsome** French classics. (Jane Freiman, Dining Out, *Newsday*, 11/11/1994.)

(3) tasty (said esp. of food or drink that is so good that one wants more) *adj.*: **moreish** [chiefly British]. See *addictive*

(4) tasty *adj.*: **esculent**. See *edible*

tattered *adj.*: **tatterdemalion**. See *ragged*

tatters (as in bits and pieces) *n.*: **flinders**. See *bits and pieces*

tattle (on) *v.i.*: **peach**. ❖ A few days ago a rumor spread like fire through a straw rick that "Deep Throat," [the] world's most famous news source, was [Alexander Haig]. What made this story far-fetched was not that Haig had been a big shot in the Nixon White House in Watergate days, so wouldn't have **peached** on his boss. . . . [Rather, it was implausible] on literacy grounds [since,] he is utterly incapable of making anything perfectly clear once he starts to talk. (Russell Baker, Tiresome News Dept., *New York Times*, 10/7/1989.)

tattler (or accuser) *n.*: **delator**. See *accuser*

taunt (as in insult, which is clever or polite) *n.*: **asteism**. See *insult*

tawdry *adj.*: **meretricious**. See *vulgar*

teach *v.t.*: **catechize**. ❖ A tireless army of social workers, nurses, and home visitors targeted poor families in the tenements of New York and Chicago, **catechizing** them in scrubbing, sweeping, dusting, and disinfecting. (Roy Porter, "The Enemy Within," *New Republic*, 4/20/1998.)

teacher *n.*: **pedagogue**. ❖ "Truthfully, if someone gave Andre [Agassi] a million dollars to go to Wimbledon, he'd still want to go home," said his coach, tennis **pedagogue** Nick Bollettieri, after Agassi's 4–6, 6–2, 7–5, 5–7, 6–0, sorry-tank's-empty loss to [Mats] Wilander [in the 1988 French Open]. (Alexander Wolff, "Mats Mania It Wasn't," *Sports Illustrated*, 6/13/1988, p. 26.)

(2) teacher (of Christianity) *n.*: **catechist**. See *Christianity*

teaching (as in tenet) *n.*: **shibboleth**. See *principle*

(2) teaching (of adults) *n.*: **andragogy**. See *adult education*

teammate (as in close partner or associate , often but not always, one in marriage) *n.*: **yokefellow**. See *partner*

tear (apart) *v.t.*: **rive** (past tense: **riven**). ❖ Her 12-year marriage and her husband's subsequent illness [AIDS] cast Pearson, a poet and Mormon, into a complex drama in which she was not only **riven** with self-doubts but forced to reconcile her deep feelings for her husband and a religion that regards a homosexual life-style as an ex-communicable offense. (Kristin McMurran, "Sequel: Carol Lynn Pearson Pens a Moving Memoir on Her Gay Husband's Death from AIDS," *People*, 2/2/1987, p. 91.)

tearful *adj.*: **lachrymose**. ❖ This is not to belittle [Senator Robert] Dole's genuine emotion as he battled to hold back the tears on Wednesday. No one in public life is so stoical and yet so **lachrymose**. Dole's eyes mist each time he returns to his hometown of Russell, Kansas. (Walter Shapiro, " 'Citizen Bob' Chooses: All or Nothing," *USA Today*, 5/17/1996.)

(2) tearful *adj.*: **larmoyant** [French]. ❖ There's something else that moves Baselitz deeply—his own early paintings. "Yes, it is true," he tells me, laughing with a hint of tears of joy. "I am very sentimental and **larmoyant** about my own early work. It is like . . . crying for no reason. That is the situation in which I find myself." (Michael Glover, "The Grotesque World of Georg Baselitz," *Belfast Telegraph*, 9/8/2007.)

tearing (adapted for . . . apart flesh) *adj.*: **carnassial** (*n.*: a tooth so adapted). See *tooth*

tears (of or relating to) *adj.*: **lachrymal**. ❖ **Lachrymal** Gender Gap—At the Ramsey Clinic's Dry Eye and Tear Research Center in St. Paul, Minn., William H. Frey II [found that] boys and girls up to age 12 cry with the same frequency, but afterward, girls cry more. After age 18, women cry almost four times as frequently as men. (Mary Ann Hogan, "Just Cry, Cry, Cry," *Newsday*, 3/12/1994.)

tease (as in joke) *v.i.*, *n.*: **jape**. See *joke*

(2) tease (esp. through the use of satire) *v.t.*: **pasquinade**. See *satirize*

teasing (good-natured . . .) *n.*: **raillery**.❖ Some people still joke about British food, but for the last 20 years their **raillery** has been way off the mark. The British have been luxuriating in a food revolution that has stocked their supermarkets with a cornucopia of good things and brought them an array of splendid (if expensive) restaurants. All this has been partly powered by immigrants, many from Asia, who brought new foods with them. (Claire Hopley, "From Marzipan to Pork Pies, Sampling Britain's Cornucopia," *Washington Times*, 1/18/2004.)

(2) teasing (playfully) *n.*, *v.t.*, *v.i.*: **chaff**. ❖ To call someone hideously ugly was capable of being defamatory; whether it was so or not must depend on the circumstances of the case. . . . Lord Justice Millett, dissenting, said **chaff** and banter were not defamatory, and even serious imputations were not actionable if no one would take them seriously. (Paul Magrath, Law Report: "'Hideously Ugly' Tag Could Be Defamatory," *Independent* [London], 10/4/1996.)

technicality (as in a subtle point raised within the context of a philosophical or theological debate; also refers to such a debate itself) *n.*: **quodlibet**. See *subtlety*

tedious (passage or section in a book, speech, or work of performing art) *n.*: **longueur**. ❖ [T]he Federation commemoration stumbles on and on with no end in sight. Speech followed dreary speech. . . . Birth of democracy . . . historic event . . . national spirit . . . great debt . . . supreme sacrifice . . . heavy responsibility . . . unique values . . . challenges that lie ahead, dah-dedah; you could feel the frontal lobes turning to porridge as the **longueurs** yawned to infinity. (*Sydney Morning Herald*, "Vaudeville, Boredville, the Bums Were Numb," 5/12/2001.)

(2) tedious (writer or speaker) *n.*: **dryasdust**. See *boring*

(3) tedious (as in bland, though wanting to appear grandiose or having pretensions of grandeur) *adj.*: **blandiose**. See *bland*

(4) tedious (as in uninteresting or dull) *adj.*: **jejune**. See *uninteresting*

tedium (of life) *n.*: **tedium vitae** [Latin]. ❖ In the case of a mentally sound person who wishes to die—such as one suffering from persistent pain or just pervaded by **tedium vitae**—government not only ignores his will but endeavors actively to block its implementation. Yet when it came to Terri Schiavo, who found herself as defenseless as any human being can possibly be, government not only failed to protect her but actively participated in taking her life. (Mauro Lucentini, letter to the editor, *Commentary*, 10/1/2005.)

teem *v.i.*: **pullulate**. ❖ And far from rising above anxiety, classical Greek art **pullulated** with horrors: snakes, monsters, decapitated Gorgons, all designed to ward off the terrors of the spirit world. (Robert Hughes, Art: "The Masterpiece Road Show—An Exhibit of Ancient Greek Sculpture Is Used to Advance a Specious Political Argument," *Time*, 1/11/1993, p. 48.)

teeming (with) *adj.*: **aswarm**. ❖ As tea, silk and porcelain lured Marco Polo, word of outsized human treasure drew me to China. I'd heard that the country's basketball courts were **aswarm** with big men. (Alexander Wolff, Olympics 2000/Basketball: "The Great Wall—China Has Three Towering NBA Prospects in Its Frontcourt—and 100 More 7-footers in Reserve, If You Believe the Rumors, *Sports Illustrated*, 9/11/2000, p. 148.)

teenager (male . . . , esp. in the late teens) *n.*: **ephebe** (*adj.*: **ephebic**). See *boy*

teeth (arrangement of . . .) *n.*: **dentition**. ❖ [Bad fake teeth] fit seamlessly into our obsessions with grossout comedy, kitsch and "hillbilly" humor. From Mike Myers's snaggled but sexy **dentition** in the *Austin Powers* films to Jim Carrey's antics in the current *Me, Myself & Irene* and 1994's *Dumb & Dumber*, fake buckteeth are just another landmark on our endless landscape of crass culture. (Ian Shapira, "Less Taste, More Fillings; The Roots of the Fake Bad Teeth Fad," *Washington Post*, 7/4/2000.)

(2) teeth (having many . . .) *adj.*: **multidentate**. ❖ [In the movie *The Faculty*], a group of student eccentrics—pretty attractive eccentrics, but that's what they tell us—is the last line of defense between total world domination by hideous **multidentate** slithering beasts. (John Anderson, "And You Thought Algebra Was Tough," *Newsday*, 12/28/199.)

(3) teeth (adapted for tearing flesh) *n.*, *adj.*: **carnassial**. See *tooth*

(4) teeth (clenching or grinding of . . . , during sleep) *n.*: **bruxism**. See *grinding*

(5) teeth (decay of . . .) *n.*: **caries** (*adj.*: **carious**). See *decay*

(6) teeth (gap or space between . . .) *n.*: **diastema**. See *gap*

(7) teeth (having no . . .) *adj.*: **edentulous**. See *toothless*

tell (as in confide, one's thoughts or feelings) *v.t.*, *v.i.*: **unbosom**. See *confide*

(2) tell (on, as in tattle) *v.i.*: **peach**. See *tattle*

tell apart *v.t.*, *v.i.*: **secern**. See *differentiate*

temerity *n.*: **hardihood**. See *gall*

temper (having a violent or unpredictable . . .) *adj.*: **vesuvian** (esp. as in . . . temper). ❖ [Philadelphia A's pitcher Lefty] Grove had a **vesuvian** temper that was quite as famous as his fastball, and he left behind him a trail of wrecked water coolers and ruined lockers. There were many days when players, particularly skittish rookies, dared not speak to him as he observed the world from the long shadows of his bony scowl. (William Nack, "Lost in History: From 1929 to 1931, the Philadelphia A's Were the Best Team in Baseball," *Sports Illustrated*, 8/19/1996, p. 74.)

(2) temper (as in harden or strengthen) *v.t.*: **anneal**. See *strengthen*

(3) temper (bad or ill . . .) *n.*: **bile**. See *bitterness*

(4) temper (bad or ill . . .) *n.*: **choler** (*adj.*: **choleric**). See *anger*

temperate (as in not indulgent) *adj.*: **abstemious**. See *restrained*

temperature (abnormally high body . . .) *n.*: **hyperthermia**. ❖ In the last week, 11 deaths have been attributed to the wave of blast-furnace heat. . . . The Dallas County medical examiner's office has ruled 16 deaths since June 1 as related at least in part to **hyperthermia**. (Jason Sickles, "Dallas County Declares Emergency as Deaths from Heat Climb to 16," *Arlington Morning News*, 7/15/1998.)

(2) temperature (abnormally low body . . .) *n.*: **hypothermia**. ❖ With the holidays over, the big chill has settled in, along with the special gifts that only eight more weeks of winter can bring—frostbite and **hypothermia**. (Kathy Wollard, "Test Yourself," *Newsday*, 1/26/1999.)

temperence *n.*: **sophrosyne**. See *moderation*

temper tantrum *n.*: **boutade** [French]. ❖ Many a rising scholar has sipped [Michael Fleury's] champagne in the baroque disorder of his study, learnt from his wisdom and been alarmed by his outrageous **boutades**. With his towering stature and air of authority, Fleury seemed destined to rule, and his gift for invective . . . sustained him in many a controversy. (*Times* [London], "Michael Fleury," 4/15/2002.)

temporary (esp. a doctor or clergyman) *n.*: **locum tenens**. ❖ Some hospitals use temporary physicians on a regular basis. "A lot of people in the urban areas are looking at **locum tenens** as a . . . practice management tool," Mr. Robb said. (Carla D'Nan, "Temporary Doctors Ease Texas' Staffing Shortages in Hospitals," *Dallas Morning News*, 2/27/2000.)

(2) temporary (esp. with respect to political office holders) *adj.*, *adv.*: **ad interim**. ❖ [President Andrew Johnson] decided to rid himself of [Secretary of War] Stanton once and for all, this time in defiance of the Tenure of Office Act. In February 1868 he announced the appointment of Lorenzo Thomas as secretary **ad interim**, whereupon the House passed a resolution of impeachment. (*Reader's Compan-*

ion to American History, "Andrew Johnson," 1/1/1991.)

(3) temporary (as in fleeting) *adj.*: **fugacious**. See *fleeting*

(4) temporary (as in lasting only briefly) *adj.*: **evanescent**. See *transient*

tempt (someone to do something by coaxing or flattery) *v.t.*: **inveigle**. See *lure*

temptation (of another by flattery) *n.*: **blandishment** (*v.t.*: **blandish**). See *flattery*

(2) temptation *n.*: **Lorelei call**. See *lure*

(3) temptation *n.*: **siren call**. See *lure*

tempting (as in alluring) *adj.*: **illecebrous**. See *alluring*

(2) tempting (said esp. of food or drink that is so good that one wants more) *adj.*: **moreish** [chiefly British]. See *addictive*

(3) tempting *adj.*: **sirenic**. [See also the nouns *siren call* and *Lorelei call* under *lure*.] See *alluring*

tenacious (in effort or application) *adj.*: **sedulous**. See *diligent*

(2) tenacious (in holding to a belief or opinion) *adj.*: **pertinacious**. See *stubborn*

tendency (as in personal preference) *n.*: **de gustibus** [Latin]. See *taste*

tender (as in compassionate) *adj.*: **ruthful**. See *compassionate*

tenet *n.*: **shibboleth**. See *principle*

tension (a state of nervous . . . often with irritability) *n.*: **fantod** [usu. "fantods," and often as in "gives one the fantods"]. ❖ Faced with [having to take a geography test, I] would be hyperventilating. I get nervous just figuring out that Jefferson is in Jackson County but Louisville is the county seat of Jefferson County in my own home state. If the word "test" gives you the **fantods**, contemplate a test that is simple to take, doesn't reflect on your intelligence and has no wrong answers. Consider performing a soil test on your landscape. (Walter Reeves, "Soil Tests Have All the Right Answers," *Atlanta Journal-Constitution,* 1/23/2003.)

(2) tension (as in nervousness) *n.pl.* but sing. or pl. in construction: **collywobbles**. See *bellyache*

(3) tension (positive form of . . . brought on, for example, by a job promotion or a new baby) *n.*: **eustress**. See *stress*

tenuous *adj.*: **gossamer**. ❖ In the nether world of prosecutorial logic, a federal investigation of the Monica Lewinsky matter was justified by the **gossamer** connection between the president's alleged efforts to cover up his complicity in the Whitewater bank fraud—a charge that has never been made, much less proven—and his easier-to-prove efforts to conceal his sex life from Paula Jones's lawyers. (Harvey A. Silverglate, "Starr Teachers," *Reason,* 5/1/1999.)

term (of a . . . or name consisting of one word) *adj.*: **monomial**. See *name*

(2) term (of a . . . or word that is pedantic) *adj.*: **inkhorn**. See *pedantic*

(3) term (or name consisting of one word) *n.*: **mononym**. See *name*

(4) term (relating to or explaining a name or a . . .) *adj.*: **onomastic**. See *name*

terminate (as in dismiss, from a position of command or authority—often military—and especially for disciplinary reasons) *v.t.*: **cashier**. See *dismiss*

termination *n.*: **quietus**. [This word, which comes indirectly from Latin—he is (at rest)—has a number of different meanings, all of which have in common the termination or cessation of something. They include: (1) anything that serves to suppress, check, abolish, or eliminate; (2) a release from life (death); or (3) a discharge, as of a duty or debt. The word can be used as a noun, as in the first two examples given here—it is used first in the first sense above and then in the second, with regard to death. Just as frequently, if not more often, it is used as part of the verb phrase "put the quietus to," which is the third example given.] ❖ All the investigations of Reagan-Bush, malfeasance and defalcation, from Iran/contra to B.C.C.I., were given the **quietus** once Clinton came to office. (Christopher Hitchens, Minority Report, *Nation,* 9/25/1995.) ❖ Even in life, Johnny Cash dressed for death, favoring the funereal colors of a perpetual mourner.

Hence his nickname, the Man in Black. Death also lurked in the country great's catalogue; that was especially true during his final decade. . . . But no album in Cash's catalogue explores **quietus** quite like his latest CD, the posthumously released and positively extraordinary *American V: A Hundred Highways*. (J. Freedom du Lac, "Johnny Cash's Failing Voice Sang a Strong Farewell," *Washington Post*, 7/5/2006.) ❖ Once you do make it to the entrees, you'll be equally intrigued. A deceptively simple turkey breast is stuffed with Fontina cheese . . . and served with a La Famiglia di Robert Mondavi Sangiovese that should **put the quietus to** that only white-wine-with-poultry nonsense. (Eve Zibart, "Fare Minded; A Toast to Grapeseed," *Washington Post*, 5/19/2000.)

(2) termination (as in ending) *n.*: **desinence**. See *ending*

terrible (person) *n.*: **caitiff**. See *despicable*

terrific *adj.*: **frabjous** (often as in "Oh frabjous day!"). See *wonderful*

(2) terrific *adj.*: **galluptious** [slang]. See *wonderful*

(3) terrific *adj.*: **mirific**. See *wonderful*

(4) terrific (generally used in the sense of select, choice, or distinguished) *adj.*: **eximious**. See *excellent*

(5) terrific (as in excellent) *adj.*: **galumptious** [slang]. See *excellent*

(6) terrific (as in excellent) *adj.*: **palmary**. See *excellent*

(7) terrific (as in excellent) *adj.*: **skookum**. See *excellent*

(8) terrific (as in first-class) *adj.*: **pukka**. See *first-class*

(9) terrific (as in of the highest quality) *n.*: **first water** (usu. as in "of the first water"). See *quality*

terrify *v.t.*: **affright**. See *scare*

terror (deliberate use of . . . and fear as a military tactic used by the Germans to break the will of the enemy) *n.*: **Schrecklichkeit** [German]. ❖ In 1775, Major John Pitcairn . . . recommended that British forces should sack and burn New England towns until the colonists

gave up. This policy was supported by other British leaders . . . who had experience of war in central Europe, where **Schrecklichkeit** was widely used. (David Fisher, *Washington's Crossing*, Oxford University Press [2004], p. 75.)

terror (as in panic) *n.*: **Torschlusspanik** [German]. See *panic*

terse (speech or writing that is . . .) *adj.*: **elliptical**. ❖ Amy Hempel . . . is a leading exponent of minimalist fiction. . . . The idea is to avoid conventional narrative development and dramatic climaxes and achieve your effect in an **elliptical** way—a few terse, oblique details, images, lines of dialogue, yielding a sudden illumination or at least a tangible mood. (*Entertainment Weekly*, review of *At the Gates of the Animal Kingdom*, by Amy Hempel, 3/9/1990, p. 27.)

test (as in problem, which is difficult for a beginner or one who is inexperienced) *n.*: **pons asinorum** [Latin]. See *problem*

testicle (having only one . . .) *adj.*: **monorchid**. ❖ Worse, [Adolf Hitler] had been born **monorchid**, an unfortunate anatomical deficiency. . . . The fact was confirmed by an autopsy performed on the *Führer's* corpse by Red Army pathologists. (*Daily Telegraph* [London], obituary of Robert Waite, 10/28/1999.)

(2) testicle (surgical removal of a . . . , or both) *n.*: **orchiectomy**. ❖ Though it has been used in the US as elsewhere—on 397 prisoners in San Diego in the early Fifties, for example—the Supreme Court in 1985 ruled that **orchiectomy** was a cruel and unusual punishment. No one has yet been sentenced to chemical castration under the new laws, but when they are, civil liberties groups are geared up to challenge them as an invasion of bodily privacy. (Tim Cornwell, "Castration by Knife May Be the Kindest Cut After All," *Independent on Sunday*, 7/20/1997.)

test out *v.t.*: **assay**. See *experiment*

testy (as in grumpy, mood) *n.pl.*: **mulligrubs**. See *grumpiness*

(2) testy *adj.*: **querulous**. See *peevish*

(3) testy *adj.*: **splenetic**. See *irritable*

(4) testy *adj.*: **tetchy**. See *grouchy*

(5) testy *adj.*: **waspish**. See *irritable*

text (earliest version of a . . . or musical score) *n.*: **urtext** [German]. See *original*

textbook (as in handbook or manual) *n.*: **enchiridion**. See *handbook*

(2) textbook (as in primer) *n.*: **hornbook**. See *primer*

theater (of or relating to the art of the . . . or drama, esp. the writing of plays) *adj.*: **dramaturgic**. ❖ **Dramaturgic** precision isn't always necessary. In fact, sometimes a sprawling theatrical mess fascinates with eerie mystery, audacious characters and striking imagery. *Messalina*, which opened Friday at Red Eye in Minneapolis, is such an animal— a wobbly play in search of a dynamic telling. (Graydon Royce, "In a Muddled *Messalina*, 2 Performances Stand Out," *Minneapolis Star Tribune*, 10/8/2006.)

(2) theater (total . . .) *n.*: **Gesamtkunstwerk** [German]. See *work of art*

theatrical (overly . . . behavior) *n., adj.*: **operatics**. See *melodramatic*

themselves (between or among . . .) *adj., adv.*: **inter se** [Latin]. ❖ Consequently, the [Australian] Federal Government took the case to the High Court. One of its duties is to hear **inter se** disputes between the Commonwealth [of Australia] and the states. (Daryl Best, "Australia's Greentime History," *History Today*, 10/1/1997, p. 9.)

theories (spec. doctrines to be believed; articles of faith) *n.pl.* **credenda**. See *beliefs*

theory (which is complicated and often illogical) *n.*: **choplogic**. See *fallacy*

thesaurus (spec. a list, or the study, of the subtle distinctions or nuances between words that are synonyms or otherwise similar) *n.*: **synonymy**. [A synonymy is not precisely a thesaurus because most thesauruses (besides this one) simply list synonyms for a given base word without explaining how those synonyms may differ in nuance from each other, as does a synonymy.] See *synonyms*

(2) thesaurus *n.*: **synonymicon**. [The first book that was close to a dictionary was published in 1604 and entitled *A Table Alphabeticall, conteyning and teaching the true writing and understanding of hard usuall English words. . . .*] ❖ The book was by today's standards more a **synonymicon** than a true dictionary—it offered very brief (often one-word) glosses rather than true definitions. (Simon Winchester, *The Meaning of Everything*, Oxford [2003], p. 22.)

thesis (as in formal analysis or discussion of a subject) *n.*: **disquisition**. See *discourse*

thicken *v.t., v.i.*: **inspissate**. ❖ The rangers, one of several patrols combing the frontier to monitor Indian activity, "observed an **inspissate[d]** Juice, like Molasses, distilling from the Tree. They found it sweet and by this Process of Nature learn'd to improve it into Sugar." (*Washington Post*, "1000 Years of Loudoun; 'Crossroads of the Indian World,'" 12/5/1999.)

thicket (of trees or shrubs) *n.*: **copse**. ❖ The summit itself (794 feet above Lake Superior) is cloaked with thick **copses** of sugar maple and birch, but a short hike east or west will lead you to rocky outcroppings with unobstructed views. (Jim Gorman, "Jawdroppers: 21 Wilderness Vistas So Big, So Beautiful That They Inspire Profound Sentiments Like, 'Wow!'" *Backpacker*, 4/1/1997, p. 56.)

(2) thicket *n.*: **boscage**. See *bushes*

thick-skinned *adj.*: **pachydermatous**. ❖ If [former Governor] Edwin Edwards had stormed out of the room every time his integrity was questioned, we'd never have gotten anything done. [Present Governor] Foster, though he looks **pachydermatous** enough, is evidently not yet used to the slings and arrows of outrageous—or outraged—senators. (James Gill, "The Governor's Temper Tantrum," *New Orleans Times-Picayune*, 6/12/1996.)

thief (caught red-handed) *n.*: **backberend**. ❖ I shout to the warden-in-chief, / That I've spotted a **backberend** thief. / On the forested track, / With a buck on his back: / "There's the venison! Now—where's the beef?" (Tim Alborn,

The Omnificent English Dictionary in Limerick Form [oedilf.com], 10/11/2005.)

(2) thief (spec. an adult who instructs children how to steal) *n.*: **Fagin** [based on a character in the Charles Dickens novel *Oliver Twist* who teaches children to be pickpockets]. ❖ Young armed robbers would walk into a jewelry store. . . . One would hammer a glass display. . . . Another would scoop up the spoils. . . . But a single clue, a handgun carelessly left behind in a car, turned out to be the thread that led investigators to a modern-day **Fagin** who recruited teens in Flatbush to rob jewelry stores in Baltimore and then found Baltimore teens to pull heists in Brooklyn. (Michele Salcedo, "'Fagin' Gang Busted/Robbery Ring Faces Prison Sentences," *Newsday*, 7/14/1997.)

(2) thief *n.*: **gonif** or **ganef** or **goniff** [Yiddish]. ❖ "They're robbing me blind!" she cried. She harangued anyone who would listen with tales accusing her elderly brother of stealing $20,000 and a six-carat diamond that her late husband, the diamond broker, had given her. "He's a **gonif**!" she would spit. (Amy Dickinson, "The Case of the Stolen Stradivarius; The Diva Was on Her Deathbed, the Dastardly Deed Was Done, but Who Done It?" *Washington Post*, 5/9/1999.)

thievery *n.*: **brigandage** thief (*n.*: **brigand**). See *robbery*

thin (and/or graceful) *adj.*: **gracile**. See *slender*

(2) thin (body type) *adj.*: **ectomorphic**. See *lean*

(3) thin (esp. in a pale or corpselike way) *adj.*: **cadaverous**. See *corpselike*

thing-in-itself (the reality of something as it appears, as opposed to how it is perceived by the senses) *n.*: **noumenon**. [This concept was developed by Immanuel Kant in his 1781 essay "Critique of Pure Reason." It is the opposite of "phenomenon," which is something that is known or derived through the senses as opposed to through the mind. Kant's philosophies are sometimes used as a rebuttal to atheism, as in the example here.] ❖ [T]he reality we apprehend is not reality in itself. It

is merely our experience or "take" on it. Kant's startling claim is that we have no basis for assuming that a material perception of reality ever resembles reality itself. . . . Some atheists have understood Kant to be denying the existence of external reality or of arguing that all of reality is "in the mind." [Rather,] he insists that the **noumenon** obviously exists because it is what gives rise to phenomena. (Dinesh D'Souza, "What Atheists Kant Refute," *Christian Science Monitor*, 10/17/2007.)

things (as in junk or paraphernalia) *n.*: **trumpery**. See *junk*

(2) things (everyday . . . , esp. those that show the lifestyle of a people) *n.pl.*: **realia**. See *objects*

think (about something, often used as a directive, as in "Consider this:") *v.t.*: **perpend**. See *consider*

(2) think (about, as in analyze closely) *v.t.*: **anatomize**. See *analyze*

(3) think (logically) *v.i.*: **ratiocinate**. See *analyze*

(4) think *v.t.*: **cerebrate**. ❖ Yet [TV star Tim] Allen is more inclined to **cerebrate** about success than to celebrate it—his antic imagination and rapid-fire mouth are offset by a warily analytical mind. (*Entertainment Weekly*, "The Entertainers—Tim Allen—A No. 1 Show, a No. 1 Book, Now That's Horsepower," 12/30/1994, p. 20.)

(5) think *v.t.*: **cogitate**. ❖ For a month or so, volunteers spent fourteen hours each day in darkness. As other animals do, the subjects would sleep awhile, wake up out of a dream, think about the dream or **cogitate** casually about some other topic for a couple of hours, then fall back to sleep. (Michael Segell, "The Secrets of Sleep," *Esquire*, 10/1/1994, p. 123.)

thinker (as in one who pretends to be a philosopher) *n.*: **philosophaster**. See *philosophy*

thinking *n.*: **mentation**. ❖ Dear Dr. Donohue: My mother and two of her sisters have senile dementia. What is it? How does it start? A: Dementia is a diminished state of **mentation** —trouble remembering, reasoning, learning, etc. "Senile" refers to aging, a term considered passé in this connection today. Old age has little to do with dementia. (Dr. Paul Donohue, "Steroids Aren't Tops in Fighting Arthritis," *St. Louis Post-Dispatch*, 9/6/1993.)

(2) thinking (staring at one's belly-button as an aid to . . . , as in meditation) *n.:* **omphaloskepsis**. See *meditation*

think up (by full and careful consideration, an idea, plan, theory, or explanation) *v.t.:* **excogitate**. See *devise*

third (choice, as in middle ground) *n.:* **tertium quid** [Latin for "third thing"]. See *middle ground*

third-person (person who refers to himself or herself in the . . .) *n.:* **illeist**. ❖ I've read that some famous sports figures become **illeists** during press conferences: "He (meaning the speaker) has to work more on his free throws." I have but one thing to say about that, "Redgate finds that sort of thing somewhat irritating." (Chris Redgate, "The Red Pencil," *Washington Post*, 3/15/2000.)

thorny (as in prickly) *adj.:* **echinate**. See *prickly*

thorough (as in total or complete, usually used with "nonsense") *adj.:* **arrant**. See *total*

thought (about which one is obsessed) *n.:* **idée fixe** [French]. See *obsession*

(2) thought (as in concept or idea that can be expressed in one word) *n.:* **holophrasis** (*adj.:* **holophrastic**). See *idea*

(3) thought (spoken . . . that is left unfinished because the speaker is unwilling or unable to continue or because the rest of the message is implicit) *n.:* **aposiopesis**. See *statement*

(4) thought (about matters outside oneself, i.e., the outside world) *n.:* **extrospection** (*adj.:* **extrospective**). See *observation*

(5) thought (staring at one's belly-button as an aid to . . . , as in meditation) *n.:* **omphaloskepsis**. See *meditation*

thoughtless (person who makes . . . comments that seem to be offering sympathy but instead make the person feel worse, either intentionally or unintentionally) *n.:* **Job's comforter**. See *comforter*

thoughts (spec. doctrines to be believed; articles of faith) *n.pl.* **credenda**. See *beliefs*

thousand (a . . . years) *n.:* **chiliad**. See *millennium*

thrash (generally used figuratively) *v.t.:* **larrup**. See *whip*

threadbare *adj.:* **tatterdemalion**. See *ragged*

threat (as in suggesting the use of force to settle an issue or argument) *n.:* **argumentum ad baculum** [Latin for "to the stick" or "to the rod"]. ❖ In *The Godfather*, when the mafioso . . . "make[s] him an offer he can't refuse" he is using an **argument[um] ad baculum**, or rod, in rod's modern slang sense of pistol. (Philip Howard, "Rhetoric and All That Rot," *Times* [London], 4/12/1991.)

(2) threat (empty or harmless . . .) *n.:* **brutum fulmen** [Latin]. ❖ What is in the heels of the Court is not the wisdom of the act of the incumbent President in proposing amendments to the Constitution, but his constitutional authority to perform such act [which is an issue this Court may decide. Should it be found that he cannot amend the Constitution, his promise to do so] would merely be a **brutum fulmen**. (Justice Reynato S. Puno, "Dissenting Opinion in the Case of *Lambino v. Commission on Elections*," *Manila Bulletin*, 10/27/2006.)

(3) threat (spec. acting as if or threatening that a future event, usually unwanted, has already occurred by reference to an event that precedes it; for example, "if you look at my diary, you're dead") *n.:* **prolepsis**. See *prediction*

threaten (someone with divine punishment) *v.i.:* **comminate**. ❖ As a useful corrective [to all the positive publicity surrounding the millennium], this column will, from now until the McMillennium, be chronicling the . . . plethora of . . . wrong turnings of the past thousand years. . . . And what shall we have a go at? What horrors shall we denounce and **comminate**? Well . . . could be almost anything. There's an [embarrassment of riches], to be frank. (Michael Bywater, "Fed Up Already with All the Millennium Gush? Read On . . . ," *Observer Review* [London], 1/31/1999.)

threatening (or menacing) *adj.*: **minatory**. See *menacing*

threesome *n.*: **troilism** person engaged (*n.*, *adj.*: **troilist**). [This word is usually defined with reference to a ménage à trois (see *ménage à trois*). However, it is also sometimes used in a nonsexual sense, as in the example given.] ❖ Valentine's Day is the busiest, most booked-up night of the year for restaurants, so you would think that restaurateurs would be happy. Of course they are not. (They are never happy). They complain bitterly, claiming that only tables for two can be sold. . . . Restaurateurs would be pleased if the ridiculously old-fashioned notion of a romantic twosome could be extended to **troilism**, at least, and preferably double-dating . . . (*Evening Standard* [London], "Two's Company, Three's Better," 2/13/2001.)

thrill (as in moment of intense excitement) *n.*: **frisson** [French]. See *shudder*

thrive (often at another's expense) *v.i.*: **batten**. ❖ The bureaucracy has effectively run Japan for the past four decades, and it **battens** on its power—not to mention the plum private-sector jobs that go to many senior government officials when they retire. A recent study by Tokyo Shoko Research, for example, discovered that nearly 1 in 5 construction-company board members is a former bureaucrat. (Edward W. Desmond, Japan: "Hosokawa's Way— Abandoning Traditional Politics, the Prime Minister Muscles Through a Political Reform That Points the Way Toward Even More Profound Change," *Time*, 11/29/1993, p. 20.)

throng (of people) *n.*: **ruck**. See *multitude*

throughout *adv.*: **passim**. [Latin. This word, well known to attorneys and literary scholars, is used to cite a word, phrase, or concept that may be found throughout a work of another. It can also be used to refer to a trait or idea that occurs on an ongoing basis with respect to persons, places, or things. There are two different examples of the word presented here, which show both of these uses.] ❖ Now that America is worrying about the dollar's decline, the administration's new treasury secretary, John Snow, is under attack. . . . In framing his pronouncements on exchange rates, his best bet would be to establish a reputation for profundity by saying nothing, or by making whatever he does say unintelligible (Alan Greenspan, **passim**). (*Economist*, "The Diminishing Dollar," 5/24/2003.) ❖ [In the opera *Hansel and Gretel*,] the only sequences of words I could hear were those sung by the two males, Father and Witch. The children were inaudible **passim** . . . (Michael Tanner, "Old Hat," *Spectator*, 3/20/2004.)

throw (something or someone out of a window) *v.t.*: **defenestrate** (*n.*: **defenestration**). ❖ The first problem for the prosecution, however, came when Kid Twist, while under police guard at the Half Moon Hotel in Coney Island, sailed out his window and down five stories to his death. To this day, Kid Twist's **defenestration** remains a mystery, if only to the New York City Police Department. (David Remnick, *King of the World*, Random House [1998], p. 60.)

throwing up (act of . . .) *n.*: **emesis**. See *vomiting*

(2) throwing up (an agent that causes . . .) *n.*: **emetic**. See *vomiting*

throw up (making an effort to . . . , by retching) *v.i.*: **keck**. See *vomit*

thrust (oneself or one's ideas forward in an unwelcome way) *v.t.*: **obtrude**. See *impose*

thrust out *v.t.*: **extrude**. See *push out*

thumb one's nose *idiom*: **cock a snook** [or **cock a snoot**; slang—primarily British]. ❖ Almost wherever he turned in the U.S., Prime Minister Shamir has been quizzed on Israel's relations with South Africa. . . . Since Israel is so heavily dependent upon the U.S. and, therefore, on public opinion [there], it cannot simply **cock a snook**, like others do, at its American critics. So, Mr. Shamir dutifully . . . voiced assurances that Israel was gradually scaling down its South African connection. (*Jerusalem Post*, "The Whipping Boy," 11/19/1989.)

thunderbolt *n.*: **coup de foudre**. [French.

Though literally meaning "thunderbolt," this is almost always used in the sense of "love at first sight."] See *love at first sight*

ticks (study of . . . and mites) *n.*: **acarology** (person who does so: **acarologist**). ❖ Although most people squirm at the thought of ticks and mites, dozens of students and researchers have gathered on the Ohio State University campus to learn more about these bloodsucking creatures. The **Acarology** Laboratory's 50th annual Summer Program provides a three-week schedule filled with informational workshops providing the latest facts and discoveries about ticks and mites. (Leslie Stimel, "Ticks, Mites Top Ohio State U. Program Menu," University Wire, 6/29/2000.)

tidy *adj.*: **in Bristol fashion**. [This British term is often (but not always) applied to boats and is often used as part of the phrase "shipshape and Bristol fashion." It is believed that the term derives from the fact that ships moored at Bristol Harbour were beached at low tide and could tip over, so they had to be sturdy and the goods in their holds securely stowed.] ❖ Unlike four years ago, when [Lowell] Weicker as [Connecticut] Governor-elect was presented a proposed budget with a $1.6 billion revenue shortfall on top of a $562 million deficit for the current year, Mr. Rowland received a two-year budget that was in balance and within the state's legal spending limit. "In short, we hand over a ship of state that has the hatches battened down and is **in Bristol fashion**," Mr. Weicker said. (George Judson, "Weicker Gives Budget Plan but Rowland Sees Problem," *New York Times*, 11/16/1994.)

tie (as in bond) *n.*: **vinculum**. See *bond*

   (2) tie (as in chain or link) *n.*: **catenation** (*v.t.*: **catenate**). See *chain*

   (3) tie (together) *v.t.*: **colligate**. See *unite*

tight-fisted (as in stingy) *adj.*: **cheeseparing**. See *stingy*

   (2) tight-fisted (as in stingy) *adj.*: **mingy**. See *stingy*

tightrope walker *n.*: **funambulist**. ❖ As Richard learned, walking the museum's tightrope

gives you a better appreciation of what real **funambulists** . . . do at higher heights on thinner wires! (Fern Shen, "The Greatest Science on Earth," *Washington Post*, 10/13/2005.)

   (2) tightrope walker (or one who balances things) *n.*: **equilibrist**. See *balancer*

tightwad *n.*: **lickpenny**. See *miser*

tilt (as in downward slope) *n.*: **declivity** (*adj.*: **declivitous**). See *decline*

   (2) tilt (as in upward slope) *n.*: **acclivity** (*adj.*: **acclivitous**). See *incline*

   (3) tilt (esp. extending down from a fortification) *n.*: **glacis**. See *decline*

time (measurement of) *n.*: **chronometry**. ❖ It is no longer enough, in these complex times, for a college hoopster to have a thorough knowledge of his team's motion offense and a firm grasp of the principles of man-to-man defense. He must also master the **chronometry** of as many as six time zones in order to know when to call his girlfriend. (Austin Murphy, College Basketball: "Basket Case—Our Travel-Weary Correspondent Flew to the Ends of the Earth—Well, O.K., to Hawaii and Alaska—to Find Out That the Best Teams in the Early Going Were Local Rivals," *Sports Illustrated*, 12/8/1997, p. 74.)

   (2) time (science of measuring . . . or making timepieces) *n.*: **horology**. ❖ In the early 19th century, the [American] clockmakers practically invented mass production, using interchangeable parts even before the Springfield Artillery Co. did so. By the early 1840s, American producers were able to export $2 clocks to Britain and undercut English manufacturers by $8 and more. Naturally, the English makers, long the leaders in **horology**, accused the Americans of dumping. (Rita Koselka, "Made in the U.S.A.," *Forbes*, 6/15/1987.)

   (3) time (esp. short . . . between things or events) *n.*: **interstice**. See *gap*

   (4) time (of or over the same . . . period) *adj.*: **coetaneous**. See *contemporaneous*

   (5) time (of the same . . . period) *adj.*: **coeval**. See *contemporaneous* and *contemporary*

time being (for the . . .) *n.*: **nonce** (used as "for the nonce"). ❖ The shacks were shoddy and the university was certain to raze them, but for the **nonce** they were boarded up. (Lars Eighner, *Travels with Lizbeth*, St. Martin's Press [1993], p. 191.)

timeless *adj.*: **atemporal**. ❖ [Hermès menswear designer Veronique] Nichanian says she tries to design in an "**atemporal**" style. "There is an evolution, a gradual change. But you can always put my clothes together, even if you buy them two or three seasons apart." (Alix Sharkey, Fashion: "She Has Designs on Men," *Independent* [London], 11/25/1998.)

timid (and cautious and indecisive) *adj.*: **Prufrockian**. [This adjective derives from T. S. Eliot's 1915 poem *The Love Song of J. Alfred Prufrock*. Prufrock is an aging man who regrets the hesitancy and cautiousness with which he has lived his life. The example given relates to Larry McMurtry's novel *Anything for Billy* and refers to the narrator.] ❖ Striking the **Prufrockian** pose, [Ben Sippy] worries about his decaying body, the romances he passed up as a youth, the timidities of his life. (David Brooks; Books, *Wall Street Journal*, 10/6/1988.)

(2) timid (esp. from lack of self-confidence) *adj.*: **diffident**. ❖ Weaker women are really strong women in disguise: They need nurturing in order to bring out their self-confidence, but the good stuff is within, waiting to be tapped. (The very same applies to shy, **diffident** men.) (Susan Deitz, "Single File/Not Just Feminists Want Some Respect," *Newsday*, 10/4/1998.)

(3) timid (person) *n.*: **nebbish** [Yiddish]. ❖ The eternal second banana [George Bush], the man thought too timid to sculpt his own political persona . . . the bland campaigner who ended one debate by apologizing for his lack of eloquence—this consensus choice as political **nebbish** suddenly transformed himself into the prim reaper who could not be denied. (Laurence I. Barrett., Nation: "Bush by a Shutout; After His Southern Sweep, the Vice President Builds Really 'Big Mo,'" *Time*, 3/21/1988, p. 14.)

(4) timid (and/or sullen and/or socially withdrawn or inexperienced) *adj.*: **farouche** [French]. See *shy*

(5) timid (and unassertive person) *n.*: **milquetoast**. See *unassertive*

(6) timid (as in cowardly) *adj.*: **pusillanimous**. See *cowardly*

(7) timid (as in cowardly) *adj.*: **retromingent**. See *cowardly*

(8) timid (as in spineless or indecisive, or such a person) *adj., n.*: **namby-pamby**. See *spineless*

tinge (as in trace or small amount of) *n.*: **tincture**. See *trace*

tingle (from moment of intense excitement) *n.*: **frisson** [French]. See *shudder*

tingling (or prickling of skin sensation) *n.*: **paresthesia**. See *prickling*

(2) tingling (or prickling or itching sensation that insects are crawling on you) *n.*: **formication**. See *prickling*

tint *n.*: **tincture**. See *hue*

tiny *adj., n.*: **Lilliputian** [based on the Lilliputians, a people in *Gulliver's Travels*, by Jonathan Swift]. ❖ Pister is just one of thousands of scientists and engineers around the world who have immersed themselves in the **Lilliputian** world of micromachines, convinced not only that small is beautiful but that it is also the wave of the technological future. One Japanese firm has assembled tiny parts into a working automobile the size of a grain of rice. (Leon Jaroff, Global Agenda: "Tiny Technology: A New Lilliputian World of Micromachines: Scientists Are Creating Wasp-Size Helicopters and Building Mechanical Systems on Slivers of Silicon," *Time* International, 12/2/1996, p. 58.)

(2) tiny *adj.*: **bantam**. ❖ Furnish your rooms with what Seidman and Cohen call "psychic comforts." These are the small, often affordable touches that inspire you to relax: warm towels, fresh flowers, a CD player in the bath. Replace **bantam** throw pillows with oversized, down-stuffed pillows that practically telegraph their invitation from across the room. (Dylan Landis, "Live in Style and Comfort," *Minneapolis Star Tribune*, 9/19/1996.)

(3) tiny *adj.*: **minikin** [This word is generally

described in dictionaries as rare or obsolete. However, it still appears with sufficient frequency in modern usage to render it appropriate for inclusion herein.] ❖ We're going to go out on a limb—or perhaps a vine—and guess that when you buy a pumpkin, it's usually for decorative, not culinary, purposes. Pumpkins are one of nature's lovelier creations, in their shades of orange ranging from sherbet to burnt umber, and in sizes from **minikin** to gargantuan. (Jane Dornbusch, "So Many Pumpkins, So Little Time—Carve a New Niche for Versatile Squash," *Boston Herald*, 10/29/2000.)

tip (as in extra or unexpected gift or benefit, sometimes as thanks for a purchase) *n.*: **lagniappe**. See *gift*

   (2) tip (as in gratuity) *n.*: **pourboire** [French]. See *gratuity*

   (3) tip (in Near Eastern countries, esp. to expedite service) *n.*: **baksheesh**. See *gratuity*

tiptoe (as in ballet step on point of toe) *n.*: **pas de bouree** [French]. ❖ I have learned not to ignore this warning from [my dog] Lizbeth, whether I perceive the tiny [fire] ants or not, but to remove ourselves at Lizbeth's first **pas de bouree**. (Lars Eighner, *Travels with Lizbeth*, St. Martin's Press [1993], p. 123.)

tip-top (as in excellent) *adj.*: **palmary**. See *excellent*

   (2) tip-top (as in first-class) *adj.*: **pukka**. See *first-class*

   (3) tip-top *adj.*: **galumptious**. See *excellent*

tirade *n.*: **philippic**. ❖ Cleaves . . . launched into a biting tirade directed at his teammates. . . . Cleaves's **philippic** wasn't exactly borrowed from the win-one-for-the-Gipper school of oratory; another player summarized the crux of his message as, "Y'all motherf——s better get your s—— together!" But it got his point across just the same. (Seth Davis, NCAA's Midwest Regionals: "Following the Leader: The Spartans Paid Heed to a Lively Locker-Room Lecture from Mateen Cleaves and Secured a Return Trip to the Final Four," *Sports Illustrated*, 4/12/2000, p. 62.)

   (2) tirade *n.*: **jeremiad**. See *complaint*

tired (as in weakened) *adj.*: **etiolated**. See *weakened*

   (2) tired (chronically . . .) *adj.*: **neurasthenic**. See *fatigued*

tiring (as in laborious) *adj.*: **operose**. See *laborious*

title (substitution of a . . . , as in epithet, for a person's proper name) *n.*: **antonomasia**. See *epithet*

tizzy (in a . . . , as in distress) *n.*: **swivet** (as in "in a swivet") *informal*. See *distress*

toady (as in willing tool or servant of another) *n.*: **âme damnée** [French]. See *lackey*

   (2) toady (esp. someone who seeks to associate with or flatter persons of rank or high social status) *n.*: **tuft-hunter**. See *hanger-on*

   (3) toady *n.*: **lickspittle**. See *sycophant*

   (4) toady *n.*: **running dog**. See *lackey*

   (5) toady *v.i.*: **truckle**. See *kowtow*

toadying (as in sycophantic) *adj.*: **gnathonic**. See *sycophantic*

toast (in the form of a song or poem in honor of a bride or bridegroom) *n.*: **epithalamium**. ❖ I shout [over] the phone at her. "Guess what—I'm getting married!" The shocked silence that greets this news goes on forever—at least until my money runs out. "Congratulations, hen," a man says as I come out of the phone box. "I hope you'll be very happy," and I must make do with his whiskey-laced **epithalamium**. (Kate Atkinson, *Behind the Scenes at the Museum*, St. Martin's Press [1998], p. 312.)

toddler *n.*: **moppet**. See *child*

to-do (as in commotion) *n.*: **bobbery**. See *commotion*

   (2) to-do (as in commotion) *n.*: **kerfuffle**. See *commotion*

   (3) to-do (over a trifling matter) *n.*: **foofaraw**. See *fuss*

toe (big . . .) *n.*: **hallux**. See *big toe*

toes (having more than normal number of . . . or fingers) *adj.*: **polydactyl**. ❖ Often, states have different criteria for diagnosing birth defects. Missouri does not consider **polydactyl** infants, those born with more than five fingers or toes, as having a birth defect, for example. Other states do. (David J. Mitchell, "Tracking Birth Defects Is Goal of Bond's: Bill Proposal Calls for Spending $70 Million Over the Next Two Years," *St. Louis Post-Dispatch*, 3/17/1998.)

together (as in simultaneously or all at once) *adv.*: **holus-bolus**. See *simultaneously*

toil *v.i.*: **moil**. ❖ "Deepak Chopra will go down as one of the greatest medical salesmen in history," says Dr. John Renner, a critic who has been following his career. Why **moil** for years in therapy with an overpriced shrink if you can simply transcend the maze of the self? Why accept the narrow, negative definition of reality imposed by parents and society and "realistic" friends if you can have a much more expansive version? (Chip Brown, "Deepak Chopra Has [Sniff] a Cold," *Esquire*, 10/1/1995, p. 118.)

(2) toil (forced . . . for little or no pay) *n.*: **corvée**. See *servitude*

toilet (communal) *n.*: **cloaca**. See *latrine*

tolerance (in the face of adversity or suffering) *n.*: **longaminity**. See *patience*

tolerant (of other views and opinions) *adj.*: **latitudinarian**. See *open-minded*

tomboy (as in girl who is high-spirited or boisterous) *n.*: **hoyden**. ❖ Espied by the legionnaires as a potential recruit, she is asked to help out at a catechism class for a gaggle of foulmouthed, streetwise little **hoydens**, whose recitation of the Hail Mary sounds "taunting and lewd, like a jeering chant from an angry crowd at a football game." (John Elson, Books: "Dirt from the Old Sod," *Time*, 8/30/1993, p. 64.)

(2) tomboy (as in girl with playful or impish appeal) *n.*: **gamine** [French]. See *girl*

tongue (of or relating to) *adj.*: **lingual**. ❖ Even if you've already pierced your tongue, you can still come to your senses. The body has an amazing ability to heal itself. . . . But if you absolutely must persist in **lingual** lunacy, at the very least keep your tongue jewelry clean, don't wear it at night or while you're eating, and, whatever you do, don't bite down! (Christine Gorman, Your Health: "A Risky Fashion— Piercing Your Tongue Leaves You Vulnerable

to Cracked Teeth, Infection and Other Bodily Danger," *Time*, 8/31/1998, p. 77.)

(2) tongue (of, resembling, or relating to) *adj.*: **glossal**. ❖ [How do] chameleons capture creatures nearly one-sixth their size—the equivalent of a human bagging a large turkey—using only their **glossal** appendages[?] Granted, the lizards' slingshot tongues are comparatively longer than humans' tongues, but that still doesn't account for chameleons' prodigious snaring abilities. (*National Wildlife*, "Slip of the Tongue," 4/1/2001.)

(3) tongue *n.*: **lingua** [Latin]. ❖ Contrary to popular belief, Latin is not a dead language. In fact, it's alive and well and riding the bestseller lists in the form of Latin for All Occasions, a **lingua**-in-bucca [tongue-in-cheek] book by Henry Beard on how to spice up your conversation with Latin phrases. (Steve Wulf, Scorecard: "Contrary to Popular Belief, Latin Is Not a Dead Language," *Sports Illustrated*, 1/14/1991, p. 9.)

tongues (gift of . . .) *n.*: **glossolalia**. See *unintelligible*

too (as in moreover) *adv.*: **withal**. See *moreover*

tool (willing . . . or servant of another) *n.*: **âme damnée** [French]. See *lackey*

too much *n.*: **nimiety**. See *excess*

tooth (adapted for tearing flesh) *n., adj.*: **carnassial**. ❖ This opening program goes back to the demise of the dinosaurs to discover the roots of the carnivores, and to reveal a vital key to their success: the development of the **carnassial** tooth. (*Dallas Morning News*, "Science Fare," 4/22/1996.)

tooth decay (or bone decay) *n.*: **caries**. See *decay*

toothless *adj.*: **edentulous**. ❖ Dentists gave Fifty-Year Awards to fluoridating water systems including: seven West Virginia and 5 Kentucky water districts. Yet, 42% of mostly fluoridated West Virginians and Kentuckians are **edentulous**, the country's worst toothless rates. (PR Newswire, "Dentists Award the Cavity-Prone and Toothless," 5/25/2004.)

top (as in "the . . . of") *n.*: **apogee**. See *height*

(2) top (as in highest point that can be attained or the ultimate degree, as of a condition or quality) *n*.: **ne plus ultra**. See *ultimate*

(3) top (the . . . , as in the pinnacle) *n*.: **Parnassus**. See *pinnacle*

top speed (at . . .) *adv*.: **tantivy**. ❖ This column's first annual Psychic Award goes to [Scott] Sklamba, who admitted before he entered the contest [as to what to name the NBA franchise that was supposedly moving from Minnesota to New Orleans, but did not, as predicted by Sklamba] that he was ready "to place the right side of my brain into warp, **tantivy** overdrive" for the effort [as to what to name the team]. (Angus Lind, "The Columnist Who Cried Wolf," *New Orleans Times-Picayune*, 6/22/1994.)

topic (as in problem, which is difficult for a beginner or one who is inexperienced) *n*.: **pons asinorum** [Latin]. See *problem*

top-notch *adj*.: **palmary**. See *excellent*

(2) top-notch *adj*.: **skookum**. See *excellent*

torch (lighted) *n*.: **flambeau**. ❖ Though [American Steve] Timons wasn't able to close [Russian Jaroslav] Antonov down, he kept him from setting the Soviets on fire [in the 1988 men's Olympic volleyball tournament]. Meanwhile, the Americans were an emotional **flambeau**. (Bruce Anderson, Volleyball: "West Bests East: The U.S. Men Spiked Their Rivals and Drinking Buddies, the Soviets, for the Gold," *Sports Illustrated*, 10/10/1988, p. 104.)

torment (as in instance or place of great suffering) *n*.: **Gehenna**. See *hell*

(2) torment (as in instance or place of great suffering) *n*.: **Gethsemane**. See *hell*

(3) torment (as in instance or place of great suffering) *n*.: **Golgotha**. See *hell*

(4) torment (as in place, condition or society filled with . . . ; spec., opposite of utopia) *n*.: **dystopia**. See *hell*

tormented (as if by a witch or by unfounded fears) *adj*.: **hagridden**. ❖ [W]e can solve the AIDS scourge only [by] burying the overmastering but quite hollow colour [i.e., race] arrogance that has **hagridden** Europe for so many

centuries, causing totally unnecessary misery not only to people of other colours but also to Europeans themselves. (Philip Ochieng, "'Foreign Girls' and AIDS—Stigma from the West," Africa News Service, 12/6/1998.)

torn (apart) *v.t.* **riven** (present tense: **rive**). See *tear*

tornado (as in whirlwind) *n*.: **tourbillion**. See *whirlwind*

torpor (sometimes in matters spiritual, and sometimes leading to depression) *n*.: **acedia**. See *apathy*

tortoise (of or relating to a . . . or turtle) *adj*.: **chelonian**. ❖ Timmy the Tortoise has put up with some indignities in his time. But heaven knows how the Duke of Devonshire's cabbage-chewing **chelonian** lodger will deal with Powderham Castle's summer guests. For Alice Cooper, the outlandish American singer, is to play a concert there in July, along with a raft of his fellow "monsters of rock." (Simon Davis, "Peterborough: Timmy Eyes Up the Monsters of Rock," *Daily Telegraph* [London], 3/20/1999.)

(2) tortoise (of or relating to a . . . or turtle) *adj*.: **testudinate**. See *turtle*

tortuous *adj*.: **anfractuous** (*n*.: **anfractuosity**). ❖ Everything [at Kennebunkport, Maine,] looked just as the nation remembers it: that familiar house, with its gray shingled siding and mullioned windows and stone chimney; the surf pounding the **anfractuous** New England coastline; the fresh-clipped lawn, where daily briefings once charted the early escalation of the Persian Gulf War. (David Von Drehle, "Campaign Diary; Father, Son Talk of Their Relationship; For Candidate Bush, a Pause on Dad's 75th Birthday, *Washington Post*, 6/14/1999.)

(2) tortuous *adj*.: **vermiculate**. ❖ Again and again, as Duncan Grant's **vermiculate** private life unwinds, his biographer makes him somehow preposterous. All sex is preposterous, perhaps, and it's difficult to write about, especially when it remains, as homosexuality was for most of Duncan Grant's life, illegal and so wreathed with euphemism and an increasingly dated "naughtiness." (Candia McWilliam, Books: "The Bells! The Bells!" *Independent* [London], 6/8/1997.)

(3) tortuous (as in twisted) *adj.*: **tortile**. See *twisted*

torture (final or severest . . . , esp. by a judge or accuser) *n.*: **question extraordinaire**. [French. This term derives from the judicial system in France prior to the French Revolution. In order to extract confessions, suspects could be subject to *question ordinaire* (ordinary questioning), the ordinary form of torture, or the *question extraordinaire* (extraordinary questioning), with increased brutality.] ❖ [In Montreal, in 1734, Angélique was accused of arson.] She would be forced to . . . confess to her crime and apologize humbly for it. Then her hands would be chopped off, [and] she would be hanged until unconscious. . . . [Later] the sentence [was] mitigated. Angélique's hands would be spared but she would not escape la **question extraordinaire**. . . . Amidst unspeakable agony, her lower leg bones were slowly shattered. (Desmond Morton, "An Incendiary Tale," *Literary Review of Canada*, 4/1/2006.)

(2) torture (by beating the soles of the feet with a stick) *n.*, *v.t.* **bastinado**. See *beating*

toss (something or someone out of a window) *v.t.*: **defenestrate** (*n.*: **defenestration**). See *throw*

total (usually used with "nonsense") *adj.*: **arrant**. ❖ Some people think there are too many bowl games (three more have applied for certification this year), and I believe this to be **arrant** nonsense. Too many bowl games in America? In the land of the free and the home of the roadside reptile farm? You might as well say we have too many beauty queens. (Charles P. Pierce, "The Naked Guy Wore Clothes and the Beauty Queen Left Early," *Esquire*, 12/1/1998, p. 50.)

(2) total (esp. as in . . . power) *adj.*: **plenary**. See *complete*

totality (viewed in the ... of the circumstances)

adv.: **sub specie aeternitatis** [Latin]. See *big picture*

totally (as in, in the entirety) *adv.*: **holus-bolus**. See *entirety*

touch (esp. for medical reasons) *v.t.*: **palpate** (*n.*: **palpation**). ❖ Lift the breast and lay it flat in the palm of your hand. Sandwich the breast by placing the other palm down over it. **Palpate** carefully with the top hand all the way along and across the breast, feeling for any thickening or lumps. (Lisa Jones Townsel, "Good Defense: A Monthly Breast Self-Exam," *St. Louis Post-Dispatch*, 10/31/1998, p. 39.) ❖ My mother's struggle [with breast cancer], which lasted 21 years, has become part of my medical history, carefully chronicled in manila folders at the doctor's office. It has meant especially diligent **palpations** from my gynecologist. (Joanne Kaufman, "Will I Inherit My Mother's Disease?" *Redbook*, 2/1/1997, p. 49.)

(2) touch (of or relating to sense of . . .) *adj.*: **haptic**. ❖ There is something extremely tactile about [Jackson Pollock's] art; he's an artist, like Vincent van Gogh, who had to feel the forms, whose responses to the world were more **haptic** than visual. (John Zeaman, "The Shape of Things to Come," *Bergen County [NJ] Record*, 10/25/1997.)

(3) touch (loving to . . .) *adj.*: **thigmophilic**. ❖ Yeah, there's a lot of scurrying, and [the rats] run along the walls, and this is an amazing thing to me. The phrase that pest control people use is **thigmophilic**. It means "touch loving." They love to touch. They love to be against the wall. (Robert Sullivan, "Robert Sullivan Discusses the Rats of New York," NPR, Morning Edition, 4/8/2004.)

(4) touch (as in small amount) *n.*: **soupçon** [French]. See *trace*

(5) touch (as in trace or small amount of) *n.*: **tincture**. See *trace*

(6) touch (of, relating to, or perceptible to sense of) *adj.*: **tactile**. See *tangible*

touched (appearing . . . as if under a spell) *adj.*: **fey**. See *crazy*

(2) touched (as in slightly insane, often used humorously) *adj.*: **tetched**. See *crazy*

touchy (as in peevish or grouchy) *adj.*: **tetchy**. See *grouchy*

tough (as in thick-skinned) *adj.*: **pachydermatous**. See *thick-skinned*

toughen *v.t.*: **anneal**. See *strengthen*

toupee (or hairpiece) *n.*: **postiche**. See *hairpiece*

tour (quick . . . that shows only the highlights of a place or thing in a cursory manner) *n.*: **Cook's tour**. [The "Cook" in this term refers to Thomas Cook, the nineteenth-century English travel agent whose organized tours were the first travel packages where everything was arranged for the customer. The term is also used to refer more generally to any kind of quick scan. See *scan*.] ❖ Time and again in *The Know-It-All*, his witty, serendipitous **Cook's tour** of human knowledge, A. J. Jacobs wonders what impelled him to read the *Encyclopedia Britannica*, all 32 volumes and 33,000 pages of it, from cover to cover to cover. [He] offers various psychological and even Freudian explanations, but he never mentions the most likely reason—he had a book contract. (Harper Barnes, "You Know What? Britannica Reader Didn't Get It All Right, *St. Louis Post-Dispatch*, 9/29/2004.)

tour guide *n.*: **cicerone**. ❖ At the end of this 500-page account readers are left with the grateful feeling that they have been led through the labyrinth of Russian names, events and cataclysms by a charming and witty guide, not an odious, mercenary **cicerone**. (Tatyana Tolstaya, review of *Lenin's Tomb: The Last Days of the Soviet Empire*, by David Remnick, *New Republic*, 4/11/1994, p. 29.)

tower (over, as in dominate) *v.t.*: **bestride**. See *dominate*

to wit (as in namely) *adv.*: **scilicet**. See *namely*

(2) to wit (as in namely) *adv.*: **videlicet**. See *namely*

trace (as in small amount) *n.*: **soupçon** [French]. ❖ [E]ven as they take their first steps against porno chic, the French aren't likely to stop selling and celebrating sex. But a **soupçon** of moral outrage may do France, and the world, some good. (Stephen Baker, Commentary: "Why 'Porno Chic' Is Riling the French," *Business Week*, 7/30/2001.)

(2) trace (as in small amount) *n.*: **tincture**. ❖ Gradually, the Democratic party withdrew from the [Kennedy] family, leaving them members only of the Kennedy party. John Jr. escaped all this. He maintained at least a **tincture** of the promise that Ted and the others had leeched out of the Legacy. (Peter Collier, "A Kennedy Apart," *National Review*, 8/9/1999.)

track (closely to a line, rule, or principle) *v.i.*: **hew**. See *conform*

tracking (as in lying in wait for prey, often used of insects) *adj.*: **lochetic**. See *ambushing*

trade (as in profession) *n.*: **métier** [French]. See *profession*

tradition (excessive reverence for . . . or forebears) *adj.*: **filiopietistic**. See *old-fashioned*

traditionalism (as in hatred or fear of anything new or different) *n.*: **misoneism** (person holding this view: **misoneist**). See *conservatism*

traditionalist (spec. a person who is opposed to advancements in technology) *n.*: **Luddite**. [The word is based on a group of British workers who destroyed laborsaving textile machinery between 1811 and 1816 for fear that the machinery would reduce employment. It is generally, but not always, used disparagingly.] ❖ [Al Gore's] role as an enemy of medical progress should come as no surprise. When biotech **Luddite** Jeremy Rifkin wrote *Algeny*—a diatribe against gene-based drug development in which he implied that the human life span should revert to that enjoyed before the Bronze Age so that mankind could be closer to nature—it was Al Gore who wrote the glowing blurb that Rifkin has given us "an insightful critique of the changing way in which mankind views nature." (Robert Goldberg, "The Luddite: [Al Gore] Invented the Internet?" *National Review*, 8/14/2000.)

(2) traditionalist (spec. a person who is opposed to individual or political reform or enlightenment) *n.*: **obscurant** (doctrine of such opposition: **obscurantism**). ❖ The shah was "our guy," an absolute ruler who was secularizing the country and freeing his people from the shackles of religious superstition and **obscurantism**. It never occurred to our foreign policy thinkers and experts that the people of Iran wanted their **obscurantism** and old-fashioned religion. (Andrew Greeley, "U.S. Keeps Making Mistakes in Mideast," *Chicago Sun-Times*, 2/23/2007.)

tragedy (as in episode having the quality of a nightmare) *n.*: **Walpurgis Night**. See *nightmare*

trail (slowly) *v.i.*: **draggle**. See *follow*

train *v.t.*: **catechize**. See *teach*

trained (to show a conditioned response) *adj.*: **Pavlovian**. See *conditioned*

traitor (esp. who aids an invading enemy) *n.*: **quisling**. ❖ The German-speaking countries aren't alone with this shame. When French President Jacques Chirac was mayor of Paris, his son-in-law lived in a building seized from Jews by French **quislings** during World War II. (Walter Russell Mead, "Long After War, Nazi Taint Lives On in Europe," *Minneapolis Star Tribune*, 11/10/1996.)

(2) traitor (esp. who betrays under guise of friendship) *n.*: **Judas**. See *betrayer*

traitorous (as in unfaithful or disloyal) *adj.*: **perfidious**. See *unfaithful*

traitors (or group of sympathizers working within a country to support an enemy and who may engage in espionage, sabotage, or other subversive activities) *n.*: **fifth column** [derives from the name given to sympathizers of the four rebel columns who advanced on Madrid during the 1936 Spanish civil war]. ❖ One thing about Osama [bin Laden] and his flacks, they know how to manipulate our media. Drop a tape on them and they stand up and salute. He has a built-in propaganda machine working for him. All I can say is that it's a good thing they didn't have American TV at the time of Hitler. TV news, especially cable, seems to be Osama's mindless **fifth column**. (Marvin Kitman, "Enough with Osama Cable," *Newsday*, 2/23/2003.)

tramp (as in move heavily or clumsily) *v.i.*: **galumph**. See *tromp*

(2) tramp *n.*: **clochard** [French]. See *vagrant*

trance (unintelligible speech given as if in a . . . , esp. heard in certain Christian congregations) *n.*: **glossolalia**. See *unintelligible*

tranquil (and carefree time) *adj.*: **prelapsarian**. See *innocent*

(2) tranquil (as in a place that is . . . , rustic and simple) *adj.*: **Arcadian**. See *pastoral*

(3) tranquil *adj.*: **equable**. See *serene*

tranquillity *n.*: **quietude**. ❖ [T]he American people are simply not in a revolutionary mood. And why should they be? This is an era of profound political and social **quietude**. (Charles Krauthammer, Conservatives: "Quit Whining and Enjoy Winning," *Newsday*, 10/7/1997.)

(2) tranquillity (as in peace of mind) *n.*: **heartsease**. See *peace of mind*

(3) tranquillity *n.*: **ataraxy** (or **ataraxia**). See *calmness*

tranquilizer (as in something that induces forgetfulness or oblivion of pain, suffering, or sorrow) *n.*: **nepenthe**. See *narcotic*

tranquilizing (as in reducing stress or anxiety, often used with respect to medications) *adj.*: **anxiolytic** (*n.*: a product that has this effect). See *relaxing*

(2) tranquilizing (as in sleep-inducing) *adj.*: **soporific**. See *sleep-inducing*

transcend (as in surpass the limits, resources, or capabilities of) *v.t.*: **beggar**. See *surpass*

transcending (as in going above and beyond the call of duty or what is required) *adj.*: **supererogatory**. See *exceeding*

transfer (to oneself without permission) *v.t.*: **expropriate**. See *seize*

transform (esp. in a strange, grotesque, or humorous way) *v.t.*: **transmogrify**. ❖ In 1962 Bette [Davis] costarred with Joan Crawford in Hollywood's camp classic, *Whatever Happened to Baby Jane?* Playing a child star **transmogrified** by time into a demented crone, she pulled off one of Hollywood's grandest grotesques. Yet inside this horror comic sight gag, Bette finds a touching and tragic character. (Brad

Darrach, "Grande Dame," *People*, 10/23/1989, p. 82.)

transformation (complete . . .) *n.*: **permutation**. ❖ As countless observers have pointed out, Madonna has held our fascination these many years by both periodically reinventing herself, and by going out of her way to shock us a little more with every **permutation**. So far, the formula has worked like a charm. (Bill Ervolino, "Oh, No! More About Madonna, *Bergen County [NJ] Record*, 10/18/1992.)

(2) transformation (spec. a fundamental . . . of mind or character, esp. a spiritual conversion) *n.*: **metanoia** [Greek for "repentance"]. See *conversion*

transgression (because it is prohibited by statute rather than because the conduct is wrong by its own nature or natural law) *n.*: **malum prohibitum**. See *crime*

(2) transgression (by its own nature or natural law rather than because prohibited by statute) *n.*: **malum in se** [Latin]. See *wrongdoing*

transient *adj.*: **evanescent**. ❖ Each political season begins with a prayerful belief that this time the public and the press will get it right—that we will select a president based on substance and stature rather than attack ads, **evanescent** polls and a cockeyed primary calendar. (*USA Today*, "Candidates Dodging the Issues Convention," 1/5/1996.)

(2) transient *adj.*: **fugacious**. See *fleeting*

transition (spec. a fundamental transformation of mind or character, esp. a spiritual conversion) *n.*: **metanoia**. See *conversion*

transitional (or intermediate state, phase, or condition) *adj.*: **liminal**. [This word is the adjectival form of "limen," which is Latin for "threshold."] ❖ *Jolted* is funny and smart and fast paced. And it's written with real love for that fascinating **liminal** creature called the young teenager, for whom the sky is always just about to fall. (Tim Wynne-Jones, "Electrifying," *Globe and Mail* [Toronto], 9/13/2008.)

translating (as in interpretative, often of a document or text, such as scripture) *n.*: **hermeneutic**. See *interpretation*

translation (which is literal) *n.*: **metaphrase** (also, *v.t.*: to translate literally). ❖ *The Aeneid* seems to be something major translators turn to only when they have run out of Homer or Dante and still need something meaty to get their chops into. . . . Dryden's translation of *The Aeneid* (1697) remains an unmatched achievement. . . . Dryden's beginning has the advantage of a word-for-word **metaphrase** of the Virgil—"Arma virumque cano"—and in the same rhythm too. (A. E. Stallings, "The Historical Present," *American Scholar*, 1/1/2007.)

translator (and guide for travelers, esp. where Arabic, Turkish, or Persian is spoken) *n.*: **dragoman**. See *guide*

translucent *adj.*: **diaphanous**. See *transparent*

(2) translucent *adj.*: **gossamer**. See *transparent*

transmit (as in send a signal) *v.t.*, *v.i.*: **semaphore**. See *signal*

transparent (esp. as in easily understood or seen through, like motives) *adj.*: **transpicuous**. ❖ At first, I wasn't real surprised when [Britney Spears] started hanging out with Paris [Hilton]. I mean, if you were depressed and trapped by a family and everything, wouldn't you want to break out? . . . But then Brit-Brit started, you know, flashing her bits. And the pole-dancing lessons. She can be so **transpicuous**. Clearly—I mean, clearly—she's trying to send me a message. She wants to [date me again]. (Jonathan Last, "When Truth Is Transpicuous," *Philadelphia Inquirer*, 12/13/2006.)

(2) transparent *adj.*: **diaphanous**. ❖ Webster's defines "glamor," which is fashion's favorite buzzword for spring, as "bewitching charm." But most women would have to be under a pretty potent incantation before donning some of the almost wanton creations that slunk off runways for the upcoming season: teetering high heels, slit-to-there skirts, glove-fitting suits and **diaphanous** blouses leaving nothing to the imagination. (Denise Flaim, "Spring Fashion—Glamor Gets Real," *Newsday*, 3/9/1995.)

(3) transparent *adj.*: **gossamer**. ❖ During the Mogul empire, the muslin woven in Dacca was so **gossamer** that it was said to be lighter than a cobweb. Legend has it that the 17th century Emperor Aurangzeb rebuked his daughter for being naked when she was actually wearing seven layers of sheer muslin. (Marguerite Johnson, "Fashion, Like So Much in India, Goes Back to Ancient Times," *Time* International, 5/17/1993, p. 44.)

(4) transparent (like glass) *adj.*: **hyaline**. See *glassy*

trapped (capable of being . . .) *adj.*: **illaqueable**. See *ensnared*

trapping (as in lying in wait for prey, often used of insects) *adj.*: **lochetic**. See *ambushing*

trappings *n.*: **habiliment(s)**. ❖ What we would now consider our multicultural diversity was in fact greater at that time than it is today . . . but it was not much in evidence as a phenomenon. Everyone, it seems, had decided to mute differences under the **habiliments** of a common culture. (Nathan Glazer, "Social and Political Stability," *Commentary*, 11/1/1995, p. 62.)

(2) trappings (as in finery) *n.*: **caparison**. See *finery*

(3) trappings (showy . . . , as in finery) *n.*: **frippery**. See *finery*

trash (accumulation of . . . , esp. prehistoric) *n.*: **midden**. ❖ In some cases the **midden** gives clues to the diets of prehistoric people. Along the shores of the Hudson River at Croton Point, New York, archaeologists found a **midden** of oyster shells several meters deep and four hectares (10 acres) in area. Generations of Indians must have gathered oysters for food and thrown away the shells. (*Earth Explorer*, "Trashy Treasures," 2/1/1995.)

(2) trash *n.*: **dross**. ❖ Why wait around for authors to turn themselves into celebrities when it's possible to sign up people who are already famous or semi-so? Whether such folk could actually write novels mattered hardly at all. Turning unmitigated **dross** into **dross** that will sell is how editors and, sotto voce, ghost-writers earn their keep. (Paul Gray, "Damsel in Distress—Random House Scorned Joan Collins' Manuscripts and the Dispute Wound Up in Court. So Whither the Celebrity Novel?" *Time*, 2/19/1996, p. 75.)

(3) trash *n.*: **offal**. ❖ A mountain of garbage is to become one of the most romantic vistas on Long Island. Long known as "Merrick Mountain," the Hempstead Town trash heap is about to begin a two-year, $15-million transformation into Overlook Park at Merrick. Perched atop some 3 million tons of **offal**, visitors will be able to see the Robert Moses Causeway to the east and the Manhattan skyline to the west. (Issac Guzman, "In Hempstead, Mound of Muck Fertilizes a Park—'Merrick Mountain' Will Become a Spot for Nature and Exercise Enthusiasts," *Newsday*, 5/11/1997.)

(4) trash (as in garbage) *n.*: **spilth**. See *garbage*

(5) trash (as in printed material that is trivial) *n.*: **bumf** [British]. See *junk*

(6) trash (study of a culture by examining its . . .) *n.*: **garbology**. See *garbage*

(7) trash *n.*: **detritus**. See *debris*

travail (period of . . . , sometimes, but not necessarily, economic) *n.*: **locust years**. See *hardship*

travel (compulsion to . . . or wander) *n.*: **dromomania**. ❖ [Edwina Ashley, for a time the richest woman in England] developed a textbook case of **dromomania**, becoming so addicted to compulsive travel that once she forgot her children, leaving them in Hungary with their governess. (Florence King, "Mountbatten's Wild, Beloved Edwina," *Washington Times*, 10/7/1991.)

(2) travel (able to . . . freely in a given environment; used of species) *adj.*: **vagile**. See *move*

(3) travel (about, esp. on foot and esp. as in roam or wander) *v.t.*, *v.i.*: **perambulate**. See *roam*

(4) travel (about, esp. on foot and esp. as in roam or wander) *v.t.*, *v.i.*: **peregrinate**. See *roam*

(5) travel (to a sacred place or shrine, esp. to Mecca) *n.*: **hadj**. See *pilgrimage*

traveler *n.*: **viator**. ❖ It is a question of caveat **viator**. If you travel to countries which have Draconian penalties [e.g., Saudi Arabia] and commit a crime, you cannot expect to be heard and punished according to Western European norms. (*Daily Telegraph* [London], "Leading Article: The Saudi Lash," 9/24/1997.)

traverse (a body of water, esp, in a shallow part) *v.t.*: **ford**. See *cross*

tray *n.*: **salver**. ❖ By Jeeves, the butler is back. Like a note on a silver **salver**, the decision by Rupert Murdoch's former valet to tell all in the latest edition of *Punch* has drawn attention to the return of that ultimate status symbol, the gentleman's gentleman. (Cole Moreton, Focus: "What the Butler Saw . . . and Told," *Independent on Sunday*, 7/5/1998.)

treacherous (as in perilous) *adj.*: **parlous**. See *perilous*

(2) treacherous (as in unfaithful or disloyal) *adj.*: **perfidious**. See *unfaithful*

(3) treacherous (or despicable) *adj.*: **reptilian**. See *despicable*

treasonist (esp. who aids an invading enemy) *n.*: **quisling**. See *traitor*

treasonists (as in traitors or group of . . . working within a country to support an enemy and who may engage in espionage, sabotage, or other subversive activities) *n.*: **fifth column**. See *traitors*

treasures (of a household) *n.pl.*: **lares and penates**. ❖ On April 23, an auctioneer at New York's Sotheby's will start the bidding on furniture, jewelry and odds and ends belonging to one of this century's most famous women [Jacqueline Onassis]. She was also one of its most private, a circumstance seemingly at odds with her family's putting up her **lares and penates** for public consumption. (*Minneapolis Star Tribune*, "Even at the Auction of Her Effects, Jackie O Will Remain Elusive," 3/28/1996.)

treat (as in delicacy or delight) *n.*: **bonne bouche** [French]. See *delicacy*

treatise (as in formal analysis or discussion of a subject) *n.*: **disquisition**. See *discourse*

treatment (supposed . . . , which is untested or unproved) *n.*: **nostrum**. See *remedy*

treaty (as in pact) *n.*: **amicabilis concordia**. See *pact*

trees (having many . . . , or set in the woods) *adj.*: **bosky**. ❖ Elbert and Anne Chapman are Greens. They are spiritual siblings of those militant environmentalists who are giving European governments fits. Greens dress in rough-hewn woolens and sneakers and breathe the more liberating air of the '60s. They rail against industrial pollution and ache to dwell in **bosky** bucolia. (Holly Wheelwright, Retirement Planning: "Your Cost of Living: Adding It Up," *Money*, 11/8/1989, p. 14.)

(2) trees (relating to, resembling, or living in) *adj.*: **arboreal**. ❖ The tree-saving tendency is part of the wider picture of Nimby [not in my back yard] environmentalism, the distinctive badge of those with time and money to waste. This **arboreal** sentimentality won't die out with the older generation, for even the young are bursting with [tree] lunacy. "Save the rainforests" is the modern version of the Children's Crusade. (Jane Jakeman, "A Nation Obsessed by Large Lumps of Wood," *Independent* [London], 12/30/1994.)

(3) trees (having many . . .) *adj.*: **arboreous**. See *wooded*

(4) trees (mass of . . . or bushes) *n.*: **boscage**. See *bushes*

tree-shaped *adj.*: **dendriform**. ❖ "Tree" columns have a history: It is often said that the Doric column was inspired by a tree in ancient Greece. In our time, one thinks of the "forest" of steel in the great railway sheds, or of Frank Lloyd Wright's "**dendriform**" columns at the Johnson Wax Building in Wisconsin (though they look more like flowers than trees). (Benjamin Forgey, "One Fine Heavy-Metal Act; The New Nissan Pavilion, a Concert of Steel and Nature," *Washington Post*, 6/3/1995.)

tree trunk *n.*: **bole**. ❖ Climbing that old fig-tree, though, had been our tactical master-stroke. The buffalo circled the sturdy trunk endlessly and with increasing irascibility, occasionally standing on its hind legs, with forefeet propped against the **bole**, in vain attempts to haul us down out of there. (Donald Macintosh, Travel: "Book Award: Up a Fig-Tree without a Gun," *Daily Telegraph* [London], 7/17/1999.)

trek (difficult or painful . . .) *n.*: **via dolorosa**. See *ordeal*

(2) trek (to a sacred place or shrine, esp. to Mecca) *n.*: **hadj**. See *pilgrimage*

tremble (rapidly or spasmodically) *v.i.*: **judder**. See *shake*

trembling *adj.*: **tremulous**. See *quivering*

trend (the latest . . .) *n.*: **dernier cri** [French]. ❖ [I have] a reflexive need to test-drive the newest exercise contraption in the faint hope that it will do what the Stairmaster, treadmill and Nordic Track before it could not: lure me to the gym with any semblance of consistency. So it was hardly a volitional act that led me to experience the cardiovascular **dernier cri**, a spinning class, at my Manhattan gym. (L. Jon Wertheim, "Eyes Shut, Ears Open, Mind Puzzled Spinning May Be the Latest Craze, but One Skeptical Practitioner Finds It Flaky," *Sports Illustrated*, 7/13/1998, p. R10.)

trends (one who adopts current . . .) *n.*: **weathercock**. See *fickle*

trendsetter (as in arbiter, on matters of taste, fashion, style, protocol, etc.) *n.*: **arbiter elegantiae** [Latin]. See *arbiter*

trendy (and wealthy young people) *n.*: **jeunesse dorée** [French]. See *fashionable*

(2) trendy (not . . .) *adj.*: **démodé** [French]. See *outmoded*

tribulation (period of . . . , sometimes, but not necessarily, economic) *n.*: **locust years**. See *hardship*

tribute (formal expression of . . .) *n.*: **encomium** (one who delivers praise or . . . *n.*: **encomiast**). ❖ In a memorial service filled with military pageantry, tearful reminiscences and glowing **encomiums**, Goldwater, who was 89 when he died Friday of natural causes, was hailed as a man of honesty and principle to a fault and a

politician who did more than any other to set the Republican Party on its current conservative course. (*Minneapolis Star Tribune*, "Goldwater Honored as Man of Principle and Blunt Honesty/Politicians Join Citizens in Saying Goodbye," 6/4/1998.)

(2) tribute *n.*: **panegyric** (one who gives tribute *n.*: **panegyrist**). ❖ Though time, history, and cinema have somewhat passed it by, Sergei Eisenstein's *Alexander Nevsky* is still a great Russian bear of a film, a ritualistic **panegyric** to the beauty of warriors in battle, and to the concept of homeland above all. (*Magill's Survey of Cinema*, "*Alexander Nevsky*," 6/15/1995.)

(3) tribute (as in give a prize to) *v.t.*: **premiate**. See *award*

(4) tribute (or to bestow . . . upon) *n.*, *v.t.*: **garland**. See *accolade*

(5) tribute (paying . . . , lit. kissing of the hand) *n.*: **baisemain** [French]. See *kissing*

trick (as in cheat) *v.t.*: **euchre**. See *cheat*

(2) trick (as in deceive or defraud) *v.t.*, *v.i.*: **cozen**. See *defraud*

(3) trick (as in deceive) *v.t.*: **humbug**. See *deceive*

(4) trick (as in prank) *n.*: **dido**. See *prank*

(5) trick (as in swindle) *v.t.*: **bunco**. See *swindle*

(6) trick (or force someone into doing something, esp. by fraud or coercion) *v.t.*: **shanghai** (person who does so *n.*: **shanghaier**). See *coerce*

(7) trick (as in deceive) *v.t.*: **gull**. See *deceive*

trickery (sometimes in a deceitful way) *n.*: **legerdemain**. ❖ Indeed, the footnotes can be the most important part of an annual report. They provide details of the accounting practices the company used in preparing the report. You can pick up hints from footnotes that the company took unusual measures to enhance its profits. A change in accounting procedures can sometimes signal bookkeeping **legerdemain**. (Robin Micheli, "Investing Basics: A Few Key Items in an Annual Report Can Tell You a Lot," *Money*, 3/1/1988, p. 181.)

(2) trickery *n.:* **jiggery-pokery**. ❖ Conveniently enough, the revisions have made it more likely that the economy will fulfill the pledge made by Keizo Obuchi, the prime minister, of 0.6% growth for this fiscal year. . . . But not everyone is happy with all the statistical **jiggery-pokery**. In a recent report, the IMF noted dryly that Japan's statistical methods were "not well understood outside of the Economic Planning Agency." (*Economist*, "Japanese Statistics: The Mystery of Numbers," 12/11/1999.)

(3) trickery (as in sleight of hand) *n.:* **prestidigitation**. See *sleight of hand*

trickle (as in light splash) *n.:* **plash**. See *splash*

tricky (as in crafty) *adj.:* **jesuitical** (sometimes cap.). See *crafty*

(2) tricky (characterized by . . . and cunning conduct, esp. in regard to the pursuit and maintenance of political or other power) *adj.:* **Machiavellian**. See *deceitful*

(3) tricky (as in deceitful conduct) *n.:* **skullduggery**. See *deceitfulness*

(4) tricky (situation or problem) *n.:* **nodus**. See *complication*

trifle (as in idle or waste time) *v.i.:* **footle** (usu. as in "footle around"). See *dawdle*

trifling (thing or matter) *n.:* **bagatelle**. ❖ Needless to say, [Jeffrey] Katzenberg has everything to prove in the partnership [Dreamworks SKG]; he even mortgaged his house to raise the $33m down payment on his share of the company, a mere **bagatelle** for the immensely more wealthy [Steven] Spielberg and [David] Geffen. (Roger Clarke, Film: "The Great White Shark of Tinseltown," *Independent* [London], 12/10/1998.)

(2) trifling (a fuss over a . . . matter) *n.:* **foofaraw**. See *fuss*

(3) trifling (as in vain or worthless) *adj.:* **nugatory**. See *worthless* and *unimportant*

(4) trifling *adj.:* **footling** [chiefly British]. See *unimportant*

(5) trifling *adj.:* **nugacious**. See *trivial*

(6) trifling *adj.:* **picayune**. See *trivial*

(7) trifling *adj.:* **piffling**. See *trivial*

trinket *n.:* **bibelot**. ❖ We are living in a time of such wealth that people can fritter their money away on useless but scrumptious desirables like . . . little silver boxes designed 100 years ago for the safe conveyance, in one's pocket or purse, of a few wooden matches. These **bibelots** were made at the turn of the last century, a period of similar wealth and ostentatious consumption. (Carol R. Richards, "Again, Spending for the Sake of Spending," *Newsday*, 2/4/2000.)

(2) trinket *n.:* **bijou**. ❖ "Oh, it's beautiful," she says quietly, turning the Neanderthal [fox tooth] pendant in her fingers, peering at it over her glasses. "It's beautiful and it's moving. A 35,000-year-old **bijou**—isn't that moving?" (Robert Kunzig, "Learning to Love Neanderthals," *Discover*, 8/1/1999.)

(3) trinket *n.:* **gewgaw**. ❖ Just turn on the TV. Pick up a catalog. Walk into almost any department store, and there it is—along with mounds of other gimmicky gadgets and garish **gewgaws** that . . . the world can live without. (James A. Russell, "What the World Needs Now . . . Is Not Another Gimmicky Gadget or Worthless Doohickey," *St. Louis Post-Dispatch*, 9/9/1995.)

(4) trinket (as in gadget) *n.:* **whigmaleerie**. See *gadget*

trip (to a sacred place or shrine, esp. to Mecca) *n.:* **hadj**. See *pilgrimage*

trite (as in excessive or contrived sentimentality) *adj.:* **bathetic**. See *sentimental*

(2) trite (one who utters . . . remarks, as in platitudes) *n.:* **platitudinarian**. See *platitudes*

(3) trite (remark or statement) *n.:* **platitude**. See *cliché*

triteness (speech or writing) *n.:* **pablum** [also **pabulum**]. ❖ But on Israel and the Middle East, the audience wanted mush [from the candidates]. And that's exactly what it got: **pablum** that offered a gloss of reassurance while revealing almost nothing of what these candidates really think about the spectacular changes—and the enormous dangers—in the region. (James D. Besser, "Candidates Dishing

Out Cheap Slogans," *Baltimore Jewish Times*, 10/21/1994.)

(2) triteness (as in excessive or contrived sentimentality) *n*.: **bathos**. See *sentimentality*

triumph (celebrating . . .) *adj*.: **epinician**. See *victory*

(2) triumph (in which one comes from behind to win at the last moment) *n*.: **Garrison finish**. See *victory*

(3) triumph (with the critics but not the public) *n*.: **succès d'estime** [French]. See *success*

trivial *adj*.: **nugacious**. ❖ Should an appointed bureaucracy award tax funds to anyone it chooses to write, photograph, paint or otherwise depict [pornography?] . . . The market is there. . . . But it shouldn't be the public's money. What's needed is a wall of separation between crud and state. Let **nugacious** trash be provided not by government but by free enterprise, as it is on television. (A.E.P. Wall, "Separation of Crud and State? No Tax Money for Trash," *Orlando Sentinel*, 11/15/1990.)

(2) trivial *adj*.: **picayune**. ❖ Some referees, however, took F.I.F.A.'s instructions much too seriously. Their cautionary yellow cards were flashed with abandon, often for infractions as **picayune** as failing to throw a ball into play quickly enough or neglecting to form a proper defensive wall for a free kick. (Barry Hillenbrand, USA 94: "The Defining Moment of the 1994 World Cup Came Early," *Time* International, 7/18/1994, p. 36.)

(3) trivial *adj*.: **piffling**. ❖ This depressing development [high unemployment in some former Communist countries] is overshadowed by a much more peculiar one. A few countries have managed to keep unemployment rates remarkably low. The Czech Republic, for one, has a rate of only 3.4%. In Russia a mere 2.4% of the workforce is officially registered unemployed; in Ukraine it is a **piffling** 0.4%. What can explain this? (*Economist*, "A Puzzling Job," 2/18/1995, p. 70.)

(4) trivial (a fuss over a . . . matter) *n*.: **foofaraw**. See *fuss*

(5) trivial (as in fault, offense, or sin that is forgivable) *adj*.: **venial**. See *forgivable*

(6) trivial (or worthless matter) *n*.: **dross**. See *worthless*

(7) trivial *adj*.: **footling** [chiefly British]. See *unimportant*

(8) trivial *adj*.: **nugatory**. See *unimportant*

tromp (as in move heavily or clumsily) *v.i.*: **galumph**. ❖ So they reinvented Godzilla. Instead of barrel legs that **galumph** through the Ginza, Godzilla now has runner's calves to bolt down Broadway. (Howard Chua-Eoan, The Arts/Cinema: "Godzilla Redux—The Monster That Has Made a Meal of Tokyo for Decades Is Back, This Time with an Appetite for New York City," *Time* International, 7/6/1998, p. 26.)

trouble *n*.: **tsuris** [Yiddish]. ❖ Against any human [chess] player, [Garry Kasparov] would have moved aggressively and gone for the win. But he wasn't playing against a human. "I still have a chance of making a blunder. . . . So with all those facts, it was reduced to a simple decision [agree to a draw]. To lose is a disaster." [The computer] suffered none of this **tsuris**. "I'm calculating publicity factors, scientific factors, psychological factors, while the machine is just taking account of the chess factors," moans Kasparov. (Steven Levy, "Machine vs. Man: Checkmate," *Newsweek*, 7/21/2003.)

(2) trouble (as in bother or inconvenience) *v.t.*: **discommode**. See *inconvenience*

(3) trouble (as in bother or inconvenience) *v.t.*: **incommode**. See *inconvenience*

troublemaker *n*.: **scapegrace**. See *scoundrel*

(2) troublemaker *n*.: **stormy petrel**. See *inciter*

troublemaking (behavior, as in mischief) *n*.: **doggery** [i.e., doglike behavior]. See *mischief*

truce (temporary . . . between opposing parties pending final deal) *n*.: **modus vivendi** [Latin]. ❖ The Christmas recess signaled a make-or-break time for the [settlement] effort [in Northern Ireland]. . . . If the republicans and unionists did not find some grounds for pursuing a **modus vivendi** by this May, conciliators feared, the talks might seem futile to everyone, giving way to summer confrontations and street violence. (James Walsh, Europe: "Out of the Labyrinth—At Last, Northern Ireland Gets a Peace Plan with Light at the End of the Tunnel," *Time* International, 1/26/1998, p. 28.)

true (appearing to be . . . or accurate) *adj.*: **verisimilar**. See *realistic*

(2) true (as in genuine) *adj.*: **echt** [German]. See *genuine*

(3) true (as in reflecting reality) *adj.*: **veridical**. See *realistic*

(4) true (necessarily . . . , as in incontrovertible) *adj.*: **apodictic**. See *incontrovertible*

truncated (something . . .) *n.*: **bobtail**. See *abridged*

trunk (of a tree) *n.*: **bole**. See *tree trunk*

trust (as in reliance on . . . alone rather than reason, esp. in philosophical or religious matters) *n.*: **fideism**. See *faith*

trusting (as in credulous) *adj.*: **ultrafidian** [Latin]. See *credulous*

truth (historical . . .) *n.*: **historicity**. See *authenticity*

(2) truth (relating to a story in which . . . and fiction are mixed together) *adj.*: **Pirandellian**. See *reality*

(3) truth (the reality of something as it appears, as opposed to how it is perceived by the senses) *n.*: **noumenon**. See *thing-in-itself*

truthful *adj.*: **veridical** [see also this word under "realistic," in the sense of "reflecting reality"]. ❖ The concept of a sudden, uncharacteristic adherence to the truth is not new either, Jim Carrey having recently played a lawyer magically condemned to a **veridical** 24 hours in *Liar, Liar*. (James Gill, "Beatty Movie Right on the Money," *New Orleans Times-Picayune*, 5/27/1998.)

try (the . . . to achieve a particular goal or desire) *n.*: **nisus**. See *goal*

try out *v.t.*: **assay**. See *experiment*

tug (used to . . .) *adj.*: **tractive**. See *pull*

tumble (esp. from a position of strength) *n.*: **dégringolade** [French]. See *downfall*

tumult (as in chaos) *n.*: **tohubuhu**. See *chaos*

(2) tumult (as in hubbub) *n.*: **charivari**. See *hubbub*

(3) tumult *n.*: **maelstrom**. See *commotion*

(4) tumult *n.*: **pother**. See *commotion*

turbulent (situation) *n.*: **maelstrom**. See *commotion*

(2) turbulent (situation) *n.*: **pother**. See *commotion*

turkey (of or relating to the domestic fowl, including . . .) *adj.*: **gallinaceous**. See *fowl*

turmoil (as in chaos) *n.*: **tohubuhu**. See *chaos*

(2) turmoil (movement toward or degree of . . . in a system or society) *n.*: **entropy**. See *disorder*

(3) turmoil (of or relating to . . . within a group or country) *adj.*: **internecine**. See *dissension*

(4) turmoil *n.*: **maelstrom**. See *commotion*

(5) turmoil *n.*: **pother**. See *commotion*

turn (away from a course or intended path) *v.t.*: **yaw**. See *veer*

turnaround (sudden . . . of events, often in a literary work) *n.*: **peripeteia**. ❖ Although scalped in Atlanta, this year's Cleveland Indians, in case you hadn't noticed, posted the best record in baseball. Given their five excruciating decades as patsies of the American league, even for someone who has never sat down in Cleveland to change flights, their **peripeteia** was exhilarating. (Haim Chertok, "Rooting for the Home Team Brings out the Confessions of a Revolving Fan," *Jerusalem Post*, 11/17/1995.)

(2) turnaround (a . . . regarding one's beliefs, causes, or policies) *n.*: **tergiversation** (*v.i.*: **tergiversate**). See *change of mind*

(3) turnaround (as in reversal of policy or position) *n.*: **volte-face** [French]. See *about-face*

(4) turnaround (regarding one's beliefs, causes, or policies) *n.*: **bouleversement** [French]. See *change of mind*

turncoat (esp. who aids an invading enemy) *n.*: **quisling**. See *traitor*

(2) turncoat (esp. who betrays under guise of friendship) *n.*: **Judas**. See *betrayer*

turncoats (as in traitors or group of . . . working within a country to support an enemy and who may engage in espionage, sabotage, or other subversive activities) *n*.: **fifth column**. See *traitors*

turned up (esp. a nose) *adj*.: **retroussé** [French]. See *nose*

turning (and twisting) *adj*.: **flexuous**. See *waving*
(2) turning (as in whirling) *adj*.: **vortical**. See *whirling*
(3) turning (outward from the center in all directions, as if from a dome) *adj*.: **quaquaversal**. See *dipping*

turn inside out *v.t*.: **evaginate**. See *inside out*

turn over (as in give back, often a territory) *v.t*.: **retrocede**. See *give back*

turns (full of . . . , as in tortuous) *adj*.: **anfractuous** (*n*.: **anfractuosity**). See *tortuous*

turtle (of or relating to a . . . or tortoise) *adj*.: **testudinate**. ❖ [Maryland Terrapin (terrapin being a type of turtle) coach Gary] Williams went to work mending fences [after sanctions were imposed on the basketball program]. And he devised a recruiting strategy that centered on high school underclassmen, who would come in after the worst of the sanctions expired. Fortunately for him, he found a few good ones with **testudinate** instincts. (Jack McCallum, "Back from the Depths—Maryland Is an ACC Power Once Again, Ending a Decline That Began with Len Bias's Death," *Sports Illustrated*, 2/20/1995, p. 20.)
(2) turtle (of or relating to a . . . or tortoise) *adj*.: **chelonian**. See *tortoise*
(3) turtle (shell, like a protective covering) *n*.: **carapace**. See *shell*

tutor *n*.: **pedagogue**. See *teacher*

twelve (group of . . .) *n*.: **dodcatet**. ❖ It can reasonably be said that *A Dance to the Music of Time*, Anthony Powell's monumental 12-part novel about English manners, society, politics and power, still begs for an American counterpart. . . . The title of the first volume in Powell's **dodecatet**, *A Question of Upbringing*, came to him while driving with a friend. (Graydon Carter, "Lucky George," *New York Times Book Review*, 11/14/2008.)

twilight (of or relating to) *adj*.: **crepuscular**.

❖ My current hate list is made up of three types of people[, among them] dog-owners who permit their animals to "foul the public footpath" (actually, "permit" is a very poor word for those **crepuscular** pooch-lovers who take their animals out at twilight or dawn with the express purpose of fouling the footpath). (David Aaronovitch, "Off with His Head, and Other Sweet Revenges," *Independent* [London], 5/29/1997.)
(2) twilight *n*.: **gloaming**. ❖ The Duel at Dusk, Part II, featuring the Orioles and the Cleveland Indians, will start at 4:15 ET, just as the sun starts to slip behind the third-base grandstand at Camden Yards. . . . The effects of that diminishing light and whether batters will be able to see pitches in the **gloaming** dominated conversations Tuesday afternoon. (Mel Antonen, "Orioles, Indians Fear Shadows Today—Players Agree Pitchers Gain Most in Twilight Starts," *USA Today*, 10/15/1997.)
(3) twilight (of or relating to) *adj*.: **vespertine**. See *evening*

twin (ghostly . . . of a living person) *n*.: **doppelgänger**. ❖ Before I left, my sister gave me a card. It shows a hiker, stooped beneath his backpack at a bend in the trail. He wears a startled expression as he encounters a briefcase-toting **doppelgänger** of himself in a business suit. The caption: "Stanley was deeply disappointed when, high in the Himalayas, he found his true self." (Mike Klesius, "Everyman's Everest; Any Hearty Hiker Can Climb the Killer Mountain's Smaller Neighbor—Without Disappearing into Thin Air," *Washington Post*, 6/27/1999.)

twinkling (as in emitting flashes of light) *adj*.: **coruscant**. See *glittering*
(2) twinkling (as in, in a . . .) *n*.: **trice** (as in "in a trice"). See *quickly*
(3) twinkling (esp. with gold or tinsel) *adj*.: **clinquant**. See *glittering*
(4) twinkling (lightly over a surface) *adj*.: **lambent**. See *shimmering*
(5) twinkling *adj*.: **scintillescent**. See *sparkling*

twisted *adj*.: **tortile**. ❖ Fred Phelps [is] the

virulently anti-gay leader of Westboro Baptist Church. [Its members carry signs that] say such despicable things as "God Hates Fags." The question I want to raise about all of this is why religion sometimes gets so abused in this way . . . . Phelps certainly is not alone in his **tortile** and malignant theology nor in the revolting way he chooses to behave in support of its know-nothingism. (Bill Tammeus, "Wholesome versus Destructive Religion," Knight-Ridder Tribune News Service, 9/4/2001.)

(2) twisted (as in tortuous) *adj.*: **anfractuous** (*n.*: **anfractuosity**). See *tortuous*

twister (as in whirlwind) *n.*: **tourbillion**. See *whirlwind*

twisting (and turning) *adj.*: **flexuous**. See *waving*

(2) twisting (as in tortuous) *adj.*: **vermiculate**. See *tortuous*

twitter (like a bird) *v.i.*: **chitter**. See *chirp*

two-faced (as in hypocritical) *adj.*: **Janus-faced**. [This word is based on Janus, the god of gates or doorways, depicted with two faces looking in opposite directions. Sometimes it has a nonpejorative meaning, in the sense of merely having two contrasting aspects or sides (as shown in the first example), and sometimes it has a pejorative meaning, such as hypocritical (as shown in the second example)]. ❖ There's something about the sport itself that makes it suited to Georgia. The state's identity has long been **Janus-faced**, part good ol' boy with a gun rack on his truck, part genteel Man in Full, just back from the quail hunt. Football's mix of testosterone-driven violence and elegance and dash accommodates both sensibilities. (L. Jon Wertheim, "Dawg Days: All Is Right Again in Georgia, Where the Beloved Bulldogs Have Reclaimed Their Gridiron Legacy," *Sports Illustrated*, 12/23/2002.) ❖ [President Bush's] message to the world has been . . . free trade is an unalloyed good that leads to the enrichment of all involved. . . . Unfortunately, Bush has weakened his hand by agreeing to exempt large segments of the U.S. economy from the less fortunate short-term outcomes of free trade [through tariffs on foreign countries and subsidies]. If a foreign nation pursued the **Janus-faced** trade policies coming out of his administration, George W. Bush would yell foul. (Avrum D. Lank, "Bush Is Two-faced on Free Trade," *Milwaukee Journal Sentinel*, 5/31/2002.)

two-sided *adj.*: **Janus-faced**. See *two-faced*

twosome (arranged in or forming a . . .) *adj.*: **jugate**. See *pair*

(2) twosome (two individuals or units regarded as a . . .) *n.*: **dyad**. See *pair*

(3) twosome *n.*: **duumvirate**. See *duo*

tying (act of . . . or binding up or together) *n.*: **ligature**. ❖ Auto-erotic asphyxiation—also known as "scarfing"—aims to increase sensation at orgasm. One psychologist said yesterday that sex involving **ligature** is "said to be among the most powerful orgasmic experiences a man can have." It is also extremely dangerous and doctors warned that anyone indulging in it should seek sexual counseling immediately. (Celia Hall, "Fatal Hazards of a Dangerous Sexual Practice," *Independent* [London], 2/9/1994.)

type (original . . . or example) *n.*: **archetype**. See *model*

types (of all . . .) *adj.*: **omnifarious**. See *varied*

typical (as in usual or customary) *adj.*: **wonted**. See *customary*

tyrannical (ruthlessly and violently . . .) *adj.*: **jackbooted**. See *oppressive*

tyrant (potential . . . , as in dictator) *n.*: **man on horseback**. See *dictator*

UFOs (study of . . .) *n.*: **UFOlogy**. ❖ [The book] *Communion* seems to signal a dramatic new era in **UFOlogy**. This time around an increasing number of everyday folk are claiming not merely to have spotted saucer-shaped spacecraft, but to have had disagreeable encounters with creepy travelers from another Time, Space, or Universe. (Michelle Green, "Making Communion with Another World—America's Fascination with UFOs Booms Again as Three New Books Suggest That Humanoids Are Here," *People*, 5/11/1987, p. 34.)

ugly (repulsive or terrifying woman) *n.*: **gorgon**. ❖ [T]he most memorable film noir villainesses were formidable and unmistakably alluring. You search in vain for some of the same charisma in the new killer women of the movies. Instead they are unfeeling, unimaginative, unattractive **gorgons**, and [you wonder what] disturbing cultural malaise . . . is producing this virulent wave of revulsion toward women who want to take charge. (Stephen Farber, Movies—Commentary: "That's No Lady—That's Our Nightmare," *Los Angeles Times*, 3/18/2001.)

(2) ugly (old woman) *n.*: **beldam**. See *hag*

(3) ugly (woman who is old) *n.*: **crone**. See *hag*

ultimate (degree, as of a condition or quality, or the highest point that can be attained) *n.*: **ne plus ultra**. [This term means (go) no more beyond (this point).] ❖ If to hustle is human and to con divine, the art of the extended con must have reached the **ne plus ultra** of its divinity in the U.S. in the 1920s and '30s, when oily operators like Oscar Hartzell and John R. Brinkley were pulling down staggering fortunes by filling people's hearts with hope and their heads with hooey. (Douglas Cruickshank, "The Art of the Scam," *Salon.com*, 5/6/2002.)

(2) ultimate (as in decisive remark, blow, or factor) *n.*: **sockdolager**. See *decisive*

(3) ultimate (as in most distant, or remote, destination or goal) *n.*: **ultima Thule**. See *distant*

(4) ultimate (to the . . .) *adv.*: **à l'outrance** [French]. See *utmost*

ultraconservative (in beliefs and often stuffy, pompous, and /or elderly) *adj.*, *n.*: **Colonel Blimp**. See *conservative*

umbrella *n.*: **bumbershoot**. ❖ Some of the heaviest rain downtown fell during lunch hour. Umbrella-armed pedestrians scurrying for food turned sidewalks into **bumbershoot** battlegrounds. (Jingle Davis, "Georgia Welcomes Needed Rain," *Atlanta Journal-Constitution*, 7/28/1998.)

unable (as in powerless) *adj.*: **impuissant**. See *powerless*

unalterable (as in offering no possibility of return) *adj.*: **irremeable**. See *irreversible*

unambiguous *adj.*: **univocal**. ❖ David Klinghoffer seeks to defend Mel Gibson's film about the death of Jesus, *The Passion*, on the basis of corroborative statements found in the Talmud and medieval writings. However, those sources are neither **univocal** nor reliable. [The] ancient rabbinic writings . . . were recorded decades after the fact and represent political, theological and polemic tendencies, not historiography. (Rabbi Dan Shevitz, letter to the editor, *Los Angeles Times*, 1/5/2004.)

(2) unambiguous (as in clear, in thought or expression) *adj.*: **luculent**. See *clear*

unamusing (as in person who tries to be funny but is not) *n.*: **witling**. See *humorless*

unanimity (of the human race throughout history on an issue) *n.*: **consensus genitum** [Latin]. See *consensus*

unanimously *adj.*, *adv.*: **nem con** [Latin; short for *nemine contradicente*]. See *unopposed*

unanticipated (event that may be an act of God) *n.*: **force majeure**. ❖ But if there's a fire, flood, strike, or other mishap classed as an act of God (**force majeure**), the builder can further extend occupancy [of the buyer at the builder's development] without limit and without having to pay compensation or provide accommodation [to the buyer]. (*Toronto Star*, "Builders Allowed Some Delays," 7/3/1999.)

(2) unanticipated (or sudden) *adj.*: **subitaneous**. See *sudden*

unapologetic (as in unrepentant) *adj.*: **impenitent**. See *unrepentant*

unarmed (as in vulnerable, person or thing): *n.*: **clay pigeon**. See *vulnerable*

unashamed *adj.*: **impenitent**. See *unrepentant*

unasked *adj.*: **unbidden**. See *uninvited*

unassertive (and timid person) *n.*: **milquetoast**. ❖ [Warren Buffet]: "Mergers will be motivated by very good considerations. There truly are synergies in a great many mergers. But whether there are synergies or not, they are going to keep happening. You don't get to be the CEO of a big company by being a **milquetoast**. You are not devoid of animal spirits." (Brent Schlender, "The Bill & Warren Show—What Do You Get When You Put a Billionaire Buddy Act in Front of 350 Students? $84 Billion of Inspiration," *Fortune*, 7/20/1998, p. 48.)

(2) unassertive (person) *n.*: **nebbish** [Yiddish]. See *timid*

unattractive (woman who is old) *n.*: **crone**. See *hag*

unavailing (as in vain or worthless) *adj.*: **nugatory**.

(2) unavailing (efforts that are laborious but . . .) *adj.*: **Sisyphean**. See *futile*

(3) unavailing *adj.*: **bootless**. See *futile*

(4) unavailing *adj.*: **otiose**. See *useless*

unavoidable *adj.*: **ineluctable**. ❖ [T]he much maligned welfare system seems particularly ripe for experimental reform—and not just because it is universally detested. In fact, the case for experimental reform stems from two **ineluctable** truths. The first is that no one knows for sure how to slash the welfare rolls, short of simply cutting off benefits. The second is that the problem of dependency has now reached epidemic proportions. (David Whitman, "Welfare: An Agenda for Change," *U.S. News & World Report*, 10/5/1992.)

unavoidably (as in whether willingly or desired or not) *adv.*: **nolens volens** [Latin]. ❖ Within a few years the Great War had blown away the entire [Austro-Hungarian] empire and, **nolens volens**, laid the foundations for Nazism. When Vienna became part of Nazi Germany in 1938, [Jewish Austrian photographer Dr. Emil] Mayer and his wife committed suicide. He was 68. (Meir Ronnen, "Early Cameraman Was Nazi Victim," *Jerusalem Post*, 7/25/2003.)

unaware (as in ignorant) *adj.*: **nescient** (*n.*: **nescience**). See *ignorant*

unbalanced (slightly mentally . . . , often used humorously) *adj.*: **tetched**. See *crazy*

unbefitting (as in undignified) *adj.*: **infra dig**. See *undignified*

unbeliever (as in one with no faith or religion) *n., adj.*: **nullifidian**. See *nonbeliever*

unbending (as in hardened) *adj.*: **sclerotic**. See *hardened*

unbiased (as in neutral) *adj.*: **adiaphorous**. See *neutral*

(2) unbiased (uncompromisingly . . . , as in just) *n.*: **Rhadamanthine**. See *just*

unblemished (as in faultless or sinless) *adj.*: **impeccant**. See *faultless*

unbounded (in exhibiting emotion or celebration) *adj.*: **saturnalian**. See *uninhibited*

unbreakable *adj.*: **infrangible**. ❖ Concrete, that most common and **infrangible** of surfaces, is accessible to everyone. Yet it is virtually virgin terrain for professional sports. The founders of [Roller Hockey International] have recognized this and are taking full advantage of it. (Kelli Anderson, Roller Hockey: "That Professional Sports Had Entered Uncharted Territory Was Clear," *Sports Illustrated*, 8/16/1993, p. 50.)

(2) unbreakable *adj.*: **irrefrangible**. ❖ Things I learned en route to looking up other things: That "fascism" as a political term was adopted by Mussolini from one of Aesop's fables showing that while sticks could be easily broken one by one, they were irrefrangible if tied together in a bundle. (Sydney J. Harris, "Police Departments Rocked by Lawsuit Mania," *Chicago Tribune*, 10/1/1986.)

uncanny (as in eerie) *adj.*: **eldritch**. See *eerie*

uncaring (as in cruel) *adj.*: **fell** (*n.*: **fellness**). See *cruel*

(2) uncaring (as in thick-skinned) *adj.*: **pachydermatous**. See *thick-skinned*

(3) uncaring (person, as in one who is interested only in cold, hard facts, with little concern for emotion or human needs) *n.*: **Gradgrind**. See *unfeeling*

uncertain (in terms of the effect that one action or activity will have on another) *adj.*: **Heisenbergian**. [In 1932, the German physicist Werner Heisenberg won a Nobel Prize for his uncertainty principle, which roughly provides that increasing the accuracy of measurement of one observable quantity increases the uncertainty with which other quantities may be known. For example, if one determines the temperature of a glass of water by putting a thermometer in it, the warmth or coolness of the thermometer will alter the temperature of the water. The word is more generally used to describe a situation in which one action or activity may effect another, but in uncertain or unknowable ways. The following example is taken from an article that discusses the fact that some colleges admit a higher percentage of male applicants than female applicants because they have so many more qualified female applicants.] ❖ In the end, targeting applications to schools with historically better admit rates for either gender is a **Heisenbergian** exercise, where the previous year's data will influence the next year's applicant pool in unknown ways. (Alex Kingsbury, "Admittedly Unequal," *U.S. News & World Report*, 6/25/2007.)

(2) uncertain (and cautious and indecisive) *adj.*: **Prufrockian**. See *timid*

(3) uncertain (as in equivocal, word, phrase, or expression) *n.*: **equivoque**. See *equivocal*

(4) uncertain (as in having multiple interpretations or signifying different things) *adj.*: **multivocal**. See *ambiguous*

(5) uncertain (as in indecisive) *adj.*, *v.i.*, *n.*: **shilly-shally**. See *vacillate*

(6) uncertain (as in unpredictable outcome) *adj.*: **aleatory**. See *unpredictable*

(7) uncertain (or undecided person, esp.

regarding political issues) *n.*: **mugwump**. See *undecided*

uncertainty (as in chronic inability to make decisions) *n.*: **abulia** (also spelled **aboulia**). See *indecisiveness*

(2) uncertainty (as in the dilemma of being given a choice between two equally appealing alternatives and thus being able to choose neither one) *n.*: **Buridan's ass**. See *paralysis*

(3) uncertainty (esp. as in beyond . . .) *n.*: **peradventure**. See *doubt*

(4) uncertainty (expression of . . . as to one's opinion on an issue, esp. arising from awareness of an opposing viewpoint) *n.*: **aporia**. See *doubt*

(5) uncertainty *n.*: **dubiety**. See *doubtfulness*

unchanging (as in everlasting) *adj.*: **sempiternal**. See *everlasting*

(2) unchanging (as in stagnant or backward place or situation) *n.*: **backwater**. See *stagnant*

(3) unchanging (in rhythm or tempo) *adj.*: **metronomic**. See *steady*

(4) unchanging *adj.*: **equable**. See *unvarying*

uncivilized (person, as in Neanderthal) *n.*: **troglodyte**. See *Neanderthal*

(2) uncivilized *adj.*: **gothic**. See *barbaric*

unclean (as in unkempt or slovenly) *adj.*: **frowzy**. See *messy*

uncleanliness (abnormal fear of . . .) *n.*: **mysophobia**. See *fear*

unclear (as in a failure to perceive something clearly or accurately or not being based on clear observation or analysis as a result of being cross-eyed, literally or figuratively) *adj.*: **strabismic**. See *cross-eyed*

(2) unclear (as in cryptic or obscure speech or writing, esp. deliberately) *adj.*: **elliptical**. See *cryptic*

(3) unclear (as in equivocal, word, phrase, or expression) *n.*: **equivoque**. See *equivocal*

(4) unclear (as in subject to two different interpretations) *adj.*: **amphibolous**. See *ambiguous*

(5) unclear (in terms of the effect that one

action or activity will have on another) *adj.*: **Heisenbergian**. See *uncertain*

(6) unclear (or cryptic or ambiguous) *adj.*: **sibylline** (or **sybilline**; often cap.). See *cryptic*

(7) unclear (use of . . . words) *n.*: **parisology**. See *ambiguous*

(8) unclear *adj.*: **Delphic**. See *ambiguous*

uncoded (language) *adj.*: **en clair** [French]. ❖ There being no documents regulating concealed command and control, clear-text assignment of combat missions occurred from time to time. On July 3, 1941, for example, this **en clair** radio telegram was sent: "All Air Force combined units at the Western Front shall immediately destroy by all forces in echeloned air groups tanks and crossings in the area Bobruisk, Pavlov, Tagorsky . . ." (V. I. Medvedev, "Progress in Front Aviation Communications During the Great Patriotic War," *Military Thought*, 4/1/2005.)

uncomfortable (as in bothersome) *adj.*: **pestiferous**. See *bothersome*

(2) uncomfortable (by not affording enough space) *adj.*: **incommodious**. See *cramped*

uncommitted (or undecided person, esp. regarding political issues) *n.*: **mugwump**. See *undecided*

uncommon (as in unconventional) *adj.*: **outré** [French]. See *unconventional*

(2) uncommon (very . . . person or thing) *n.*: **rara avis** [Latin]. See *rarity*

(3) uncommon *adj.*: **selcouth**. See *unusual*

(4) uncommon *adj.*: **recherché** [French]. See *rare*

uncomplicated (as in elementary or basic) *adj.*: **abecedarian**. See *basic*

uncomplimentary (or expressing disapproval) *adj.*: **dyslogistic**. ❖ The Office of the Chief of Public Affairs has reviewed the most recent screenplay for the feature motion picture *Forrest Gump*. In its current form, the Department of the Army cannot recommend approval of this project [in part because] . . . the improbable behavior of uniformed personnel and the portrayal of active and ex-service members is

dyslogistic. The "mooning" of a president by a uniformed soldier is not acceptable cinematic license. (Mitchell Markovitz, letter to the editor, *Harper's*, 11/1/2001.)

(2) uncomplimentary (as in faultfinding) *adj.*: **captious**. See *faultfinding*

(3) uncomplimentary (person) *n.*: **smellfungus**. See *faultfinder*

uncomprehending (spoken or written words due to brain injury) *n.*: **aphasia**. ❖ Aphasia is not caused by paralysis but by damage to the parts of the brain that turn our thoughts into words we can say and write, and turn the words we hear and read into thoughts we understand. Talking, listening, reading and writing are all more or less equally impaired in **aphasia**. (Richard C. Katz, "Helping Aphasia Victims Communicate," *Arizona Republic*, 7/15/1999.)

uncompromising (position, esp. with respect to moral or ethical principles or practices) *n.*: **rigorism**. See *rigidity*

unconcern (esp. on matters of politics or religion) *n.*: **Laodiceanism**. See *indifference*

unconciousness (as in condition of stupor or . . . resulting from narcotic drugs) *n.*: **narcosis**. See *stupor*

unconditional (as in complete or unlimited, esp as in . . . power) *adj.*: **plenary**. See *complete*

unconnected (of or relating to events that occur close in time but are . . . to each other) *adj.*: **acausal**. [This word stems from a 1952 article by Swiss psychologist Carl Gustav Jung on synchronicity, which he described as two or more events that are causally unrelated (i.e., they are "acausal") but which are parallel or which occur together in a meaningful manner; in Jung's words, there is "meaningful coincidence."] ❖ In an **acausal** world, where cause and effect are not connected through time, artists are joyous because "unpredictability is the life of their paintings, their music, their novels." Everyone here lives in the moment, and since the present has little effect on the future, few people pause to think about the consequences of their actions. (Michiko Kakutani, review of

Einstein's Dreams, by Alan Lightman, *New York Times*, 1/5/2003.)

unconquerable (as in incapable of being overthrown, driven out or subdued by force) *adj.*: **inexpugnable**. See *impregnable*

unconscious *n.*: **insensate**. ❖ She wasn't capable of running over him while he lay **insensate**. (Dean Koontz, *Intensity*, Knopf [1995], p. 295.)

uncontradicted (as in unopposed) *adj., adv.*: **nem con** [Latin; short for *nemine contradicente*]. See *unopposed*

uncontrollable (and undisciplined person) *n.*: **bashi-bazouk** [Turkish]. See *undisciplined*

(2) uncontrollable (as in resistant to control or authority) *adj.*: **refractory**. See *stubborn*

(3) uncontrollable (as in unruly) *adj.*: **indocile**. See *unruly*

(4) uncontrollable (event that may be an act of God) *n.*: **force majeure**. See *unanticipated*

uncontrolled (as in impetuous) *adj.*: **gadarene**. See *impetuous*

unconventional (holding . . . opinions or having an . . . perspective) *adj.*: **heterodox** (*n.*: **heterodoxy**). ❖ His growing . . . **heterodoxy** could, with hindsight, be seen as the first overt signs of a growing alienation from convention and society that would later evolve into a radical sense of separateness and disconnection. (Sylvia Nasar, *A Beautiful Mind*, Simon & Schuster [1998], p. 143.)

(2) unconventional *adj.*: **outré** [French]. ❖ It's exciting to discover in a new guide, published since the Marriage Act relaxed the rules last year, more than 500 attractively **outré** places to get married. Depending on your personality traits, the Reptile House at London Zoo may strike you as the ideal place to tie the knot. Or perhaps the Bass Museum of Brewing? (*Independent* [London], "The Weasel, an Exquisite New Torture to Inflict on Friends and Relatives," 2/24/1996.)

(3) unconventional (thinker, esp. on matters of morals and religion) *n.*: **libertine**. See *freethinker*

uncoordinated (as in clumsy) *adj.*: **lumpish**. See *clumsy*

uncouth (person) *n.*: **grobian**. See *boor*

(2) uncouth (person) *n.*: **yahoo**. See *boor*

uncover (through careful or skillful examination or investigation) *v.t.* **expiscate**. See *discover*

(2) uncover *v.t.*: **disinter**. See *disclose*

unctuous *adj.*: **oleaginous**. ❖ I can say awful things to a president or member of Congress, but for some reason, I tremble before **oleaginous** [car] salesmen. You know the type: They spend half of their time scampering off to confer with unseen managers, only to return with sheaves of paper purporting to show the "true factory invoice." And once we have completed the ugly deal, they stalk us by mailing out desk calendars at Christmas. (Tony Snow, "Minivan Shopping Is Poor Cure for Washington Blahs," *Dallas Morning News*, 6/30/1996.)

(2) unctuous (as in greasy or oily) *adj.*: **pinguid**. See *oily*

(3) unctuous *adj.*: **fulsome**. See *insincere*

uncultivated (person) *n.*: **grobian**. See *boor*

uncultured *adj.*: **philistine**. ❖ The intellectual left [in England] hated Thatcherism because it seemed so **philistine**. Yet the Thatcherite indifference to culture, the separation of the cultural classes from power, had the paradoxical effect of allowing a certain eccentric freedom. It was, after all, under Thatcher . . . that the Saatchi Collection, the most ambitious private museum of cutting-edge art in the world, got built and prospered. (Adam Gopnik, "Cool Britannia—Tony Blair's Regime Is Transforming the Way Britain Thinks About Itself," *Sunday Telegraph* [London], 7/13/1997.)

(2) uncultured (class of people regarded as . . .) *n.*: **booboisie**. See *unsophisticated*

(3) uncultured (or dull or stupid or ignorant or stupid) *adj.*: **Boeotian**. See *dull*

undebatable *adj.*: **irrefragable**. See *unquestionable*

undecided (or neutral person, esp. regarding political issues) *n.*: **mugwump**. ❖ The **mugwump** vote. Historically, undecided voters have tended to break against the incumbent, and Democrats believe this year will prove no different. A new Pew poll showed that [John]

Kerry has made more gains among swing voters this past month than Bush, and surveys show undecided voters are unhappy with the direction of the country. (Liz Marlantes, "Candidates Vie to Be 'Safe' Choice," *Christian Science Monitor*, 10/28/2004.)

(2) undecided (as in chronic inability to make decisions) *n.*: **abulia** (or **aboulia**). See *indecisiveness*

undeniable *adj.*: **irrefragable**. See *unquestionable*

under (lying . . .) *adj.*: **subjacent**. See *below*

underage (period when one is . . .) *n.*: **nonage**. See *youth*

underbrush *n.*: **boscage**. See *bushes*

underclass (of society) *n.*: **lumpenproletariat**.
❖ Americans, male and female, who listen to talk radio (two-thirds of whom say they find it a significant source of information and ideas) are affluent and well-educated. These Americans may not be the "overclass" that so many gabble about these days, but they're not exactly the **lumpenproletariat**. (Frank Gaffney Jr., "Talking a Stereotype to Death," *Washington Times*, 10/9/1995.)

under cover (as in, in concealment) *adv.*: **doggo** (esp. as in "lying doggo"; slang). See *concealment*

underdog (champion of the . . .) *n.*: **infracaninophile**. ❖ I'll admit that I didn't even pretend to be an **infracaninophile** when little Florida A & M's basketball team was pitted against Duke in the opening round of the NCAA tournament last season. Pulling for an underdog, you see, doesn't have to be taken to the ludicrous stage. (D. L. Stanley, "Infracaninophiles Have Their Reasons," *Atlanta Inquirer*, 1/6/2001.)

underestimate (as in undervalue) *v.t.*: **mizprize**. See *undervalue*

underground (publishing system or publication of government-banned literature, or the literature produced by such a system) *n.*: **samizdat** [originally referred to secret publication of government-banned literature in the Soviet Union]. ❖ In 1969 Daniel Ellsberg . . . smuggled from his office safe a top-secret government study detailing American involvement in Vietnam. [He] duplicated the so-called Pentagon Papers, a page at a time on a first-generation Xerox machine. Ellsberg leaked the **samizdat** to antiwar leaders and reporters, including the *New York Times*'s Neil Sheehan. (David Greenberg, "The Insider," *Washington Post*, 7/22/2001.)

underhanded (as in unscrupulous) *adj.*: **jackleg**. See *unscrupulous*

(2) underhanded (characterized by . . . and cunning conduct, esp. in regard to the pursuit and maintenance of political or other power) *adj.*: **Machiavellian**. See *deceitful*

(3) underhanded (conduct) *n.*: **skullduggery**. See *deceitfulness*

(4) underhanded (scheming or trickery) *n.*: **jiggery-pokery**. See *trickery*

underling (loyal . . . , esp. of a political leader) *n.*: **apparatchik**. ❖ To date, [Russian President Vladimir] Putin has carried out the policies of other men, the perfect faceless **apparatchik**. (Bill Powell, "Russia's Mystery Man," *Newsweek International*, 1/17/2000, p. 30.)

undermine (as in deprive of strength) *v.t.*: **geld**. See *weaken*

undernourishment (condition of . . . of a child) *n.*: **marasmus**. See *malnourishment*

underpinning (on which something is built) *n.*: **warp and woof**. See *foundation*

underprivileged (people, as in lowest class of society) *n.*: **lumpenproletariat**. See *underclass*

underrate *v.t.*: **mizprize**. See *undervalue*

understand (thoroughly and/or intuitively) *v.t.*: **grok**. [This word was coined by Robert Heinlein in his 1961 science fiction novel *Stranger in a Strange Land*.] ❖ Katy Borner of Indiana University is an expert in information visualization, or displaying large amounts of data in ways that allow us to unlock the hidden meaning. While the Web provides a rising flood of information, our brains can't digest it all and our tools, like search engines, are too primitive to **grok** patterns, trends, and communities within a social network. (Maura Welch, "Building a Macroscope," *Boston Globe*, 5/1/2006.)

(2) understand (based on past experience) *v.t.*: **apperceive**. See *comprehend*

(3) understand (difficult to . . .) *adj.*: **recondite**. See *complicated*

(4) understand (inability to . . . spoken or written words due to brain injury) *n.*: **aphasia**. See *uncomprehending*

understandable *adj.*: **limpid**. ❖ Unlike other recent biographers of Darwin . . . Miss Browne does not dwell on the complex social, political and psychological background of his scientific work. . . . Instead the reader is given an exceptionally **limpid** and focused description of how Darwin gradually pieced together his theory from his geological, biological and anthropological observations. (*Economist*, review of *Charles Darwin: Voyaging—A Biography*, Volume I, by Janet Browne; *Darwin's Dangerous Idea: Evolution and the Meanings of Life*, by Daniel C. Dennett; and *Why We Get Sick: The New Science of Darwinian Medicine*, by Randolph M. Nesse and George C. Williams, 7/29/1995, p. 65.)

(2) understandable (as in clearly understood) *adj.*: **perspicuous**. ❖ One [of the Principles of Mathematics] was the "theory of descriptions" which purported to solve a problem that Plato had wrestled with, namely how one can think and speak of non-existent things. The theory showed how various tricky propositions could be translated into something more **perspicuous** and less puzzling; it soon came to be seen as a model of how to philosophise. (*Economist*, "The Philosophers That Sophie Skipped," 12/7/1996, p. 79.)

(3) understandable (as in clear, in thought or expression) *adj.*: **luculent**. See *clear*

(4) understandable (in thought or expression) *adj.*: **pellucid**. See *clear*

(5) understandable (to the general public) *adj.*: **exoteric**. See *accessible*

understanding (as in pact) *n.*: **amicabilis concordia**. See *pact*

(2) understanding (as in compassionate) *adj.*: **ruthful**. See *compassionate*

(3) understanding (spec. a recognition of one's errors, and a return to a sane, sound, or correct position and the . . . gained from the experience) *n.*: **resipiscence**. See *reformation*

(4) understanding (as in perception or awareness) *n.*: **ken**. See *perception*

(5) understanding (moment of . . . , often the point in the plot at which the protagonist recognizes his or her or some other character's true identity or discovers the true nature of his or her own situation) *n.*: **anagnorisis**. See *recognition*

(6) understanding (of other views and opinions) *adj.*: **latitudinarian**. See *open-minded*

(7) understanding (sudden . . .) *n.*: **epiphany**. See *realization*

understatement (as in "He's not bad.") *n.*: **litotes**. ❖ In another column, I expounded the art of **litotes**, by which we damn with faint praise or praise with faint damns. The usual example is, "She's not a bad soprano," which is subtly different from saying that the lady is a good soprano. (James Kilpatrick, "When Counseling Erring Writers, You Better Have Right Stuff," *Denver Rocky Mountain News*, 12/28/1997.)

(2) understatement *n.*: **meiosis**. ❖ Of the two common types of irony, understatement or **meiosis** ("This assignment required more than a minute") generally is better received than overstatement or hyperbole ("This assignment took forever"). (Stephen Wilbers, "Humor Can Be a Powerful Communications Tool," *Minneapolis Star Tribune*, 6/27/1997.)

understood (easily . . . or seen through, likes motives) *adj.*: **transpicuous**. See *transparent*

undervalue *v.t.*: **mizprize**. [This verb also means to hold in disdain, and in this example, the word could be used in both senses. See also *disdain*.] ❖ I have been a fan of [the TV show] *Friends* in the past, and many is the argument I have had with sophisticated folk who seek to dispraise it, **misprize** it and set it at naught. On these occasions, the theme of my argument is that we should not presume to patronise

Friends when the professionalism and sheer classiness of its writing and ensemble performance simply kick British ass. (Peter Bradshaw, "Friends We Can Do Without," *Evening Standard* [London], 1/8/1999.)

underworld (relating to gods and spirits of the . . .) *adj.*: **chthonic.** ❖ In the phrase "in heaven and on earth and under the earth," Philippians would recognize the areas in which the cosmic and **chthonic** powers were thought to rule. (Edgar Krentz, "Work Out Your Own Salvation," *Christian Century*, 9/11/1996.)

undignified *adj.*: **infra dig.** ❖ Increasingly MBAs must search in the hidden job market (Hello, Uncle Herbert?), a disturbingly **infra dig** undertaking for folks who just paid $70,000 for what they thought was the heights. (Alan Deutschman, Careers: "The Trouble with MBAs," *Fortune*, 7/29/1991, p. 67.)

undiplomatic (person who makes . . . comments that seem to be offering sympathy but instead make the person feel worse, either intentionally or unintentionally) *n.*: **Job's comforter.** See *comforter*

(2) undiplomatic (comment that seems to be offering sympathy but instead makes the person feel worse, either intentionally or unintentionally) *n.*: **Job's comforter.** See *comforter*

(3) undiplomatic (or tasteless comments) *n.*: **dontopedalogy.** See *foot-in-mouth*

undisciplined (and uncontrollable person) *n.*: **bashi-bazouk** [Turkish; derives from the irregular, undisciplined, mounted mercenary soldiers of the Ottoman army]. ❖ I admit it: I cut through. To get . . . to my daughter's school, I drive through residential streets in Homeland. . . . This commuter traffic does not please residents of Homeland, to whom apparently, we motorists on our way to school and work are a crowd of **bashi-bazouks** galloping over the hill to plunder their houses and slaughter their cattle. (John McIntyre, "Cruising Through Homeland," *Baltimore Sun*, 1/18/1999.)

unearthly (as in eerie) *adj.*: **eldritch.** See *eerie*

unease (positive form of . . . , as in stress, brought on, for example, by a job promotion or a new baby) *n.*: **eustress.** See *stress*

uneasiness (as in a state of tense and nervous . . . often with irritability) *n.* **fantod.** See *tension*

(2) uneasiness (in a state of . . .) *idiom*: **on tenterhooks.** See *suspense*

(3) uneasiness *n.*: **inquietude.** See *anxiety*

uneasy (to make . . . , as in disconcert) *v.t.*: **discomfit.** See *disconcert*

uneducated (as in ignorant) *adj.*: **nescient** (*n.*: **nescience**). See *ignorant*

(2) uneducated (as in unenlightened) *adj.*: **benighted.** See *unenlightened*

(3) uneducated (class of people regarded as . . . , as in unsophisticated) *n.*: **booboisie.** See *unsophisticated*

unemotional (or even-tempered) *adj.*: **phlegmatic.** See *even-tempered*

(2) unemotional (person, as in one who is interested only in cold, hard facts, with little concern for emotion or human needs) *n.*: **Gradgrind.** See *unfeeling*

unending (as in everlasting) *adj.*: **sempiternal.** See *everlasting*

unendingly *adv.*: **in aeternum** [Latin]. See *forever*

unenlightened *adj.*: **benighted.** ❖ We hear an awful lot about teenagers these days. According to the tabloids, they are lazy, feckless and ignorant. According to just about everyone, including the Office of National Statistics, they are having too much sex. According to some experts, we have only ourselves to blame. If teenagers are **benighted**, it's because we have left them in the dark. (Maureen Freely, "They Never Tell Us the Things We Really Want to Know," *Independent* [London], 11/1/1999.)

(2) unenlightened (as in ignorant) *adj.*: **nescient** (*n.*: **nescience**). See *ignorant*

(3) unenlightened (class of people regarded as . . .) *n.*: **booboisie.** See *unsophisticated*

(4) unenlightened *adj.*: **philistine.** See *uncultured*

unequalled (person or thing) *n.*: **nonesuch.** See *paragon*

unequivocal *adj.*: **univocal.** See *unambiguous*

unethical (as in unscrupulous) *adj.*: **jackleg**. See *unscrupulous*

(2) unethical (characterized by . . . and cunning conduct, esp. in regard to the pursuit and maintenance of political or other power) *adj.*: **Machiavellian**. See *deceitful*

(3) unethical (conduct) *n.*: **skullduggery**. See *deceitfulness*

(4) unethical (person, spec. one who accepts bribes) *n.*: **boodler**. See *corrupt*

uneven (as in irregularly notched toothed or indented) *adj.*: **erose**. ❖ Dear Al: I want to install wooden paneling in our den, which has a stone fireplace. How can I best hide the gaps where the **erose** edges of the fireplace and the straight edges of the paneling meet? [Answer] Don't hide the gaps. Do away with them by cutting the paneling to conform with the uneven stone surface. (Al Carrell, Super Handyman, *St. Louis Post-Dispatch*, 7/7/1995.)

unexpected (event that may be an act of God) *n.*: **force majeure**. See *unanticipated*

(2) unexpected (or sudden) *adj.*: **subitaneous**. See *sudden*

unexplained (as in involving factors not to be comprehended based on reason alone) *adj.*: **suprarational**. See *incomprehensible*

unexplorable (in depth, meaning, or significance) *adj.*: **unplumbable**. ❖ Fascinating organization, the U.S. Postal Service. Hard to fathom, though. To take just one question of **unplumbable** depth, how do you suppose the fellows decide which artists will get to do those "love" stamps? (Daniel Seligman, "Love in the Post Office, and Other Matters," *Fortune*, 8/19/1985, p. 219.)

unfair (in matters of discrimination between groups) *adj.*: **invidious**. See *discriminatory*

unfaithful (spouse) *n.*: **bedswerver**. ❖ When a **bedswerver**'s hungry for spice, / It's unlikely she'll heed the advice / When her conscience yells, "Don't!" / And I'm guessing she won't / Give a thought to adultery's price. (Mike Scholtes, *The Omnificent English Dictionary in Limerick Form* [oedilf.com], 4/6/2006.)

(2) unfaithful (to a belief, duty, or cause) *adj.*: **recreant**. ❖ All right, here is the cardinal [John O'Connor] who troubles our comfort with his insistence that a sin is a sin and must be reproved with severity as it is to be absolved with mercy. . . . Of course he abrades; he would be **recreant** to duty if he didn't. (Murray Kempton, "The Politics of Profanity," *Newsday*, 10/23/1994.)

(3) unfaithful *adj.*: **perfidious**. ❖ Tory wives . . . are never more themselves than when standing by a faithless husband who has just betrayed them to the flashbulbs of the newshounds and the sniggers of the world. . . . [T]hey descend in an unbroken line, brave smiles hiding the heartache. That at least is the tabloid reading: wife's trusting innocence shattered at one leap by **perfidious** male. (Rosalind Miles, "A Necessary Backdrop in the Roadshow of His Life," *Independent* [London], 1/7/1994.)

(4) unfaithful (man married to an . . . wife) *n.*: **cuckold** (*v.t.*: to make a . . . of). See *adulterous*

unfashionable *adj.*: **démodé** [French]. See *outmoded*

unfathomable (through investigation or scrutiny) *adj.*: **inscrutable**. See *mysterious*

unfeeling (person, as in one who is interested only in cold, hard facts, with little concern for emotion or human needs) *n.*: **Gradgrind**. [This word is based on Thomas Gradgrind, from *Hard Times*, by Charles Dickens. Gradgrind had such a personality and valued practicality and materialism above all else.] ❖ In [her book on Julius Caesar,] McCullough is very much a **Gradgrind** when it comes to facts: They are all that is needful, presented, it must be said, without color or animation to detract from their merit. Even descriptions of battles— which are cursory for a work devoted to the life of one of the world's greatest generals—have all the movement and drive of origami instructions. . . . McCullough's [writing is] leaden [in the] way it sits on the page. (Katherine A. Powers, review of *The October Horse*, by Colleen McCullough, *Washington Post*, 12/15/2002.)

(2) unfeeling (as in cruel) *adj.*: **fell** (*n.*: **fellness**). See *cruel*

(3) unfeeling (as in inanimate) *adj.*: **insensate**. See *inanimate*

(4) unfeeling (as in medication causing inability to feel pain) *n.*: **analgesia**. See *numbness*

(5) unfeeling (as in thick-skinned) *adj.*: **pachydermatous**. See *thick-skinned*

unfit (mentally) *adj.*: **non compos mentis** [Latin]. See *insane*

unfitting (as in things that do not mix together) *adj.*: **immiscible**. See *incompatible*

(2) unfitting *adj.*: **malapropos**. See *inappropriate*

unflappability *n.*: **ataraxy** (or **ataraxia**). See *calmness*

unflappable (as in unemotional or even-tempered) *adj.*: **phlegmatic**. See *even-tempered*

(2) unflappable *adj.*: **equable**. See *serene*

unflattering (or expressing disapproval) *adj.*: **dyslogistic**. See *uncomplimentary*

unfocused (as in actions taken or statements made that are broader than necessary to hit their target or accomplish their goal) *adj.*, *n.*: **blunderbuss**. See *scattershot*

unforgivable (as in unpardonable) *adj.*: **irremissible**. See *unpardonable*

unforseen (event that may be an act of God) *n.*: **force majeure**. See *unanticipated*

(2) unforseen (occurrence, leading to an awkward or embarrassing situation) *n.*: **contretemps**. See *mishap*

(3) unforseen (or sudden) *adj.*: **subitaneous**. See *sudden*

unfortunate *adj.*: **infelicitous**. ❖ Ideally, an *SI* swimsuit shoot should take six weeks or so, with each model brought to the location for about a week. Campbell has found through experience that two models sharing one photographer can be an **infelicitous** triangle. Often one of the women feels she's playing second fiddle. (Frank Deford, "Lights, Camera, Action! Our Master at Combining Models with Swimsuits and Scenery," *Sports Illustrated*, 2/7/1989, p. 51.)

(2) unfortunate (occurrence, leading to an awkward or embarrassing situation) *n.*: **contretemps**. See *mishap*

(3) unfortunate (perpetually . . . person) *n.*: **schlimazel** [Yiddish]. See *unlucky*

(4) unfortunate *n.*, *adj.*: **hoodoo**. See *bad luck*

unfortunately (to relate) *adv.*: **miserabile dictu**. See *unhappily*

unfriendliness (as in chilly relations between people) *n.*: **froideur** [French]. See *chilliness*

unfulfilled (or frustrated in realizing one's goals) *adj.*: **manque** (as in "artist . . . "). See *frustrated*

unfunny (as in person who tries to be funny but is not) *n.*: **witling**. See *humorless*

ungainly *adj.*: **lumpish**. See *clumsy*

ungraceful *adj.*: **lumpish**. See *clumsy*

ungrammatical (spec. an error in speaking or writing because of trying too hard to be grammatically correct) *n.*: **hypercorrection**. See *error*

unhappily (to relate) *adv.*: **miserabile dictu** [Latin]. ❖ My old friend took it very well, I thought, when he read that a Moog synthesizer had been placed in a museum. . . . Wasn't it only last week that the most famous of synthesizers was at the cutting edge of modern art? . . . And now, **miserabile dictu**, the first commercially produced model has gone to its reward, acquired by the Stearns Collection of Musical Instruments at the University of Michigan. (Donal Henahan, "And in This Gallery, We See the Ancient Moog," *New York Times*, 2/5/1989.)

unhappiness (as in inability to experience pleasure or happiness) *n.*: **anhedonia** (*adj.*: **anhedonic**). ❖ The numbers are not good. Clurman says 63 per cent of us wish we could be doing something else with our lives. . . . A good friend theorizes that she and I repeatedly mentally return to the republic of **anhedonia** because our families are from Saskatchewan. We don't do fun well. So we went shopping. (Jennifer Wells, "No Fun at Mall These Days," *Toronto Star*, 1/31/2003.)

(2) unhappiness (as in instance or place of . . .) *n.*: **Gehenna**. See *hell*

(3) unhappiness (as in instance or place of . . .) *n.*: **Gethsemane**. See *hell*

(4) unhappiness (as in instance or place of . . .) *n.*: **Golgotha**. See *hell*

(5) unhappiness (as in place, condition, or society filled with . . . ; spec., opposite of utopia) *n.*: **dystopia**. See *hell*

(6) unhappiness (as in world-weariness or sentimental pessimism over the world's problems) *adj.*: **Weltschmerz** [German]. See *pessimism*

(7) unhappiness (experience of intense . . . , as in suffering) *n.*: **Calvary**. See *suffering*

(8) unhappiness (general feeling of . . . as form of depression) *n.*: **dysphoria**. See *depression*

(9) unhappiness (to fret or complain, including as a result of . . .) *v.i.*: **repine**. See *complain*

(10) unhappiness *n.*: **megrims** (pl. of megrim) [also means migraine headache]. See *headache*

unhappy (as in dejected) *adj.*: **chapfallen**. See *dejected*

(2) unhappy (as in dismal and gloomy) *adj.*: **acherontic**. See *gloomy*

(3) unhappy (as in miserable or wretched, esp. as to poverty) *adj.*: **abject**. See *wretched*

(4) unhappy (as in unfortunate) *adj.*: **infelicitous**. See *unfortunate*

(5) unhappy (chronically . . .) *adj., n.*: **dysthymic**. See *depressed*

(6) unhappy (or grumpy mood) *n.pl.*: **mulligrubs**. See *grumpiness*

unhealthy (atmosphere or influence) *n.*: **miasma**. See *noxious*

(2) unhealthy (or unwholesome) *adj.*: **insalubrious**. See *unwholesome*

unhinged (slightly mentally . . . , often used humorously) *adj.*: **tetched**. See *crazy*

uniform (as in unvarying) *adj.*: **equable**. See *unvarying*

unimaginative (as in uninspired) *adj.*: **invita Minerva** [Latin]. See *uninspired*

unimportant (or insignificant) *adj.*: **nugatory**. ❖ Immigration is not needed economically; its contribution to the prosperity of native-born Americans is **nugatory**; and along with bilingualism, multiculturalism, and the cultural balkanization promoted by quotas, it helps to undermine the sense of a common American identity. (John O'Sullivan, "Going West?" *National Review*, 12/11/1995, p. 58.)

(2) unimportant *adj.*: **footling** [chiefly British]. ❖ The objection that commentators of the right make about Michael Moore is, generally, that his arguments are facile. . . . But the tearing up of the Constitution and Bill of Rights is happening [under President Bush] with surprising speed and reach. . . . Moore lists the erosion of liberty with enough precision to make objections to his flippancy seem **footling**. (Nicholas Lezard, review of *Dude, Where's My Country?* by Michael Moore, *Guardian* [London], 6/12/2004.)

(3) unimportant (as in trivial) *adj.*: **piffling**. See *trivial*

(4) unimportant (as in useless) *adj.*: **inutile**. See *useless*

(5) unimportant (or worthless matter) *n.*: **dross**. See *worthless*

(6) unimportant (something which is . . . , as in useless) *n.*: **vermiform appendix**. See *useless*

(7) unimportant (thing or matter) *n.*: **bagatelle**. See *trifling*

(8) unimportant *adj.*: **nugacious**. See *trivial*

(9) unimportant *adj.*: **picayune**. See *trivial*

uninformed (as in ignorant) *adj.*: **nescient** (*n.*: **nescience**). See *ignorant*

(2) uninformed (as in unenlightened) *adj.*: **benighted**. See *unenlightened*

(3) uninformed (class of people regarded as . . . or unenlightened) *n.*: **booboisie**. See *unsophisticated*

uninhibited (in exhibiting emotion or celebration) *adj.*: **saturnalian**. ❖ The young New Yorker [Zia Jaffrey, author of *The Invisibles: A Tale of the Eunuchs of India*,] perceived that the

Hijra, lower in caste even than the Untouchable dung-cleaners, somehow cut to the heart of the paradox of India. They were clownish and **saturnalian** in spirit: "I thought of them almost like Shakespearian fools, being given permission to comment on society and speak their mind in the way that no one else could." (Roger Clarke, "Caste Aside," *Independent* [London], 7/29/1997.)

uninspired *adj.*: **invita Minerva**. [Latin; lit. Minerva unwilling. Minerva is the Roman goddess of wisdom and patroness of the arts. If she deserts you, your work will be uninspired. The background to the example that follows is that John Harris, the *Washington Post* national political editor, had written that Daniel Froomkin's *Washington Post* blog, White House Briefing, could be wrongly construed as coming from a neutral reporter rather than from a liberal columnist, which Mr. Harris considered Mr. Froomkin to be. The responsive posts on the *Washington Post* Web site took strong exception to Mr. Harris's position.] ❖ Dear Mr. Harris: [Regarding] your elaborate, though rather "**invita Minerva**," position paper . . . let me be the first to tell you that your opening statement ["Since my comments about Dan Froomkin . . . have attracted some attention, I'd like to briefly respond."] is indicative of how little you . . . have thought before setting out to attack Froomkin's column. (Pleno Jure, blog .washingtonpost.com/washpostblog/2005/12/ froomkin_on_white_house_briefing.html, 12/13/2005.)

unintelligent *adj.*: **gormless** [British]. ❖ [I]n the Royal Pioneer Corps in the Fifties, I was frequently involved in preparing paperwork for courts martial. . . . They all had three things in common. The prosecuting officer was an intelligent, ambitious captain (he became a brigadier). The defense was conducted by a rather **gormless** National Service second lieutenant. I don't recall anyone being found not guilty. (John Aulton, letter to the editor, *Independent* [London], 3/1/1997.)

(2) unintelligent (esp. used of a person, as in . . . and confused) *adj.*: **addlepated**. See *confused*

unintelligible (speech, esp. heard in certain Christian congregations) *n.*: **glossolalia**. ❖ **Glossolalia** happens when people are so filled with the Holy Spirit, with a kind of rapture, that they speak in words and sounds that are not recognizable. It conveys the ecstasy of God's spirit within them. (Martha Sawyer Allen, "Footsteps of Paul/Hunting for the Holy Spirit," *Minneapolis Star Tribune*, 9/18/1999.)

uninterested *adj.*: **pococurante**. See *apathetic*

uninteresting *adj.*: **jejune**. ❖ "There's a magnetic field here," explains [actor Peter] O'Toole. "I'm attracted to these larger-than-life roles, and they to me." Offscreen, Peter was living a life that made some of his characters look almost **jejune**. Drinking and carousing, he became a mythic figure at home and abroad. (Andrea Chambers, Stage: "Though He Is Plagued by a Custody Fight over His Son, Peter O'Toole Is a Triumph in *Pygmalion*," *People*, 6/29/1987, p. 96.)

(2) uninteresting (as in bland, though wanting to appear grandiose or having pretensions of grandeur) *adj.*: **blandiose**. See *bland*

uninvited *adj.*: **unbidden**. ❖ When my children were very little, they were afraid of the dark. I appointed myself their Guardian Angel, always ready to protect them from the **unbidden** monsters of their dreams. (Peggy Dolgin, "500 Words or Less—Fearful Angel," *Newsday*, 6/28/1993.)

unique (as in one of a kind) *adj.*: **sui generis** [Latin]. ❖ The Holocaust was a **sui generis** event that has a historically specific explanation. (Daniel Goldhagen, *Hitler's Willing Executioners*, Knopf [1996], p. 419.)

(2) unique (as in specific to one person or thing) *adj.*: **idiographic**. ❖ Luckily for you, I am a student of **idiographic** psychology, which is the science of attempting to understand the unique aspects of a particular individual and happily I think I have diagnosed your problem. You are a "personality" when it's plain that you need to be a "celebrity." (Shay

Healy, "Ah, Mr Cowen! Yes, I've Been Expecting You. New image, Is It? Follow Me," *Daily Mail* [London], 8/29/2009.

(3) unique (as in occurring one time only) *adj.*: **one-off** [British]. See *one-time*

(4) unique (or rare person or thing) *n.*: **rara avis** [Latin]. See *rarity*

uniqueness (as in that quality that makes one thing different from any other) *n.*: **haecceity** (or **haeccity**). See *individuality*

unit (as a . . .) *adv.*: **en bloc** [French]. See *whole*

unite *v.t.*: **colligate**. ❖ [The] reconstruction [of the values of Nigerian society] becomes mandatory as a result of the heterogeneous ethnic-cultural composition of the Nigerian nation. It also amounts to attempts to discover the binding thread that can **colligate** and guarantee a successful coexistence within this larger political unit. (Onyemaechi Udumukwu, "Ideology and the Dialectics of Action: [Chinua] Achebe and [Festus] Iyayi, *Research in African Literatures*, 9/1/1996, p. 34.)

(2) unite (as in blend) *v.t.*, *v.i.*: **inosculate**. See *blend*

(3) unite (as in bring together) *v.t.*: **conflate**. See *combine*

(4) unite (as with glue) *v.t.*: **agglutinate**. See *adhere*

(5) unite (in a series or chain) *v.t.*, *adj.*: **concatenate** (*n.*: **concatenation**). See *connect*

united (by a close relationship) *adj.*: **affined**. See *connected*

(2) united (closely . . .) *adj.*: **coadunate**. See *joined*

(3) united (of things that cannot be . . .) *adj.*: **immiscible**. See *incompatible*

uniting (or reconciling of opposing viewpoints or beliefs) *adj.*: **syncretic** (or **syncretistic**). See *reconciling*

unity (concerned with establishing . . . among churches or religions) *adj.*: **ecumenical**. See *churches*

universal (in scope or applicability) *adj.*: **ecumenical**. ❖ [N]orthern Ireland's Betty Williams, co-winner of the 1976 Nobel Peace Prize, told graduating seniors at Quinnipiac College in Hamden, Conn., "Men have made enough mess of the world, and it's about time they moved over." At Texas A&M, Democratic Senator Lloyd Bentsen was more **ecumenical** in his exhortation: "You are our best hope for the future," he said. "Don't blow it." (*Time*, Education: "New Prospects, Old Values," 6/17/1985, p. 68.)

(2) universal (as in widespread) *adj.*: **pandemic**. See *widespread*

universally (viewed . . .) *adv.*: **sub specie aeternitatis** [Latin]. See *big picture*

universality (as in breadth of inclusiveness) *n.*: **catholicity** [*adj.*: **catholic**]. ❖ Maidanek was genuinely a mixed-race [concentration] camp, and its victims included large numbers of Europeans, Russians, and Poles as well as ethnic Jews. That **catholicity** made it easier to describe in the press. (Catherine Merridale, *Ivan's Army*, Metropolitan Books [2006], p. 295.)

universe (study of evolution of) *n.*: **cosmogony**. ❖ The mind resists reducing **cosmogony** to cartoons. On the other hand, what could be more in the spirit of Coyote and Road Runner than the Big Bang [theory of evolution]? (Lance Morrow, Viewpoint: "Mars as Divine Cartoon," *Time*, 8/19/1996, p. 65.)

unkempt *adj.*: **blowsy** (or **blowzy**). See *disheveled*

(2) unkempt *adj.*: **frowzy**. See *messy*

unkind (as in wicked) *adj.*: **flagitious**. See *wicked*

unknowable (in depth, meaning, or significance) *adj.*: **unplumbable**. See *unexplorable*

(2) unknowable (in terms of the effect that one action or activity will have on another) *adj.*: **Heisenbergian**. See *uncertain*

unknown (person) *n.*: **inconnu** [French]. See *stranger*

unlikelihood (statement of . . . , expressed in the form of an exaggerated comparison with a more obvious impossibility; for example: "the sky will fall before I get married.") *n.*: **adynaton**. ❖ Ten days ago, I was asking Boris Johnson if he was going to be the next editor of the

Daily Telegraph and he said: "I think the possibility is so remote, it's more likely that I would be blinded by a champagne cork, decapitated by a Frisbee or locked in a disused fridge. What [is that] called in ancient poetry, where you list a series of things, the adunata? . . . Anyway, it's highly unlikely." [As the author later discovered, the word that Mr. Johnson had in mind was "**adynaton**" rather than "adunata."] (Lynn Barber, "Charmed, I'm Sure," *Observer* [London], 10/5/2003.)

unlimited (esp as in . . . power) *adj.*: **plenary**. See *complete*

unlucky (perpetually . . . person) *n.*: **schlimazel** [Yiddish. The counterpart to this word is "schlemiel," a habitual bumbler. Thus, the schlemiel will spill his soup and it will land on the schlimazel]. ❖ Anderson plays the genial **schlimazel**. . . . [H]e spends a great deal of time taking people to the airport, a chore one has to be tricked into. . . . When traveling himself, he inevitably gets a plane on which all the overhead compartments are full, even if he's the first passenger to board. And then the flight attendant handing out the peanuts mysteriously passes him by. (John J. O'Connor, "A Comic Who Finds Humor in the Everyday," *New York Times*, 9/14/1998.)

    (2) unlucky *n., adj.*: **hoodoo**. See *bad luck*

unmanageable (as in uncontrollable and undisciplined person) *n.*: **bashi-bazouk** [Turkish]. See *undisciplined*

    (2) unmanageable (as in unruly) *adj.*: **indocile**. See *unruly*

    (3) unmanageable (as in resistant to control or authority) *adj.*: **refractory**. See *stubborn*

unmanly (person) *n.*: **pantywaist**. See *sissy*

    (2) unmanly *adj.*: **epicene**. See *effeminate*

unmarried (state of being . . . , or nonrecognition or nonregulation of marriage) *n.* **agamy**. ❖ [T]he low birth-rate [in Europe] is not a function of **agamy** but of low fertility of married couples. (Kingsley Davis, "Kingsley Davis on Reproductive Institutions and the Pressure for Population," *Population and Development Review*, 9/1/1997.)

    (2) unmarried (woman, whether divorced, widowed, or never married) *n.*: **feme sole**. See *woman*

unmatched (person or thing) *n.*: **nonesuch**. See *paragon*

unmelodious *adj.*: **scrannel**. See *cacophonous*

unmitigated (usually used with "nonsense") *adj.*: **arrant**. See *total*

unmoved (as in, in the original position) *adj., adv.*: **in situ** [Latin]. ❖ [O]pening arguments cannot be delivered until tomorrow, precisely because much prosecution evidence is still **in situ** as exhibit material over at the Muhammad trial. It will need to be hauled back and forth, submitted into evidence here but required for jury deliberation in Virginia Beach. (Rosie DiManno, "Doodling Sniper Suspect Keeps Pace with Artists," *Toronto Star*, 11/12/2003.)

unnamed (as in anonymous) *adj.*: **innominate**. See *anonymous*

unnatural (as in artificial) *adj.*: **factitious**. See *artificial*

    (2) unnatural (as in contrived) *adj.*: **voulu** [French]. See *contrived*

unnecessary (as in superfluous) *adj.*: **excrescent**. See *superfluous*

    (2) unnecessary (as in superfluous) *adj.*: **supererogatory**. See *superfluous*

    (3) unnecessary (word or phrase) *n.*: **pleonasm**. See *redundancy*

    (4) unnecessary (words) *n.*: **macrology**. See *verbosity*

unopposed *adj., adv.*: **nem con** [Latin; short for *nemine contradicente*]. ❖ At the end of February, [Hong Kong's] highly unpopular chief executive, Tung Chee-hwa, was handed another five-year term. This was not because he had done a great job, but because China's leaders wanted him to stay in office. An electoral college packed with Hong Kong business leaders and politicians fearful of opposing China's wishes therefore re-elected him **nem con**. (*Economist*, "Rivals More than Ever—Hong Kong and Shanghai," 3/30/2002.)

unoriginal (as in uninspired) *adj.*: **invita Minerva** [Latin]. See *uninspired*

unorthodox (holding . . . opinions or having an . . . perspective) *adj.*: **heterodox** (*n.*: **heterodoxy**). See *unconventional*

unorthodox *adj.*: **outré** [French]. See *unconventional*

unpalatable *adj.*: **brackish**. ❖ Coffee grinders are fanatical? Not if you hate bad coffee. For years, I was convinced I didn't like coffee. Finally it dawned on me: I liked coffee-flavored things. Maybe I'd been drinking bad coffee. I began a near-maniacal program to produce coffee that wasn't sour and **brackish**. In the process, I acquired a coffee grinder, and I haven't been without one since. (Ann Lemons, "It's a Grind," *St. Louis Post-Dispatch*, 4/26/1997.)

unpardonable *adj.*: **irremissible**. ❖ The Christian code known as the Apostolic Decrees formulated three **irremissible** sins: idolatry, adultery, and [homicide]. (Sarah Currie, "The Killer Within: Christianity and the Invention of Murder in the Roman World," *Journal of Feminist Cultural Studies*, 7/31/1996, p. 153.)

unpolished (or poorly put together, esp. with respect to a piece of writing or a speech) *adj.*: **incondite**. See *crude*

unpredictable (or uncertain outcome) *adj.*: **aleatory**. ❖ [Quoting Thomas Dewey:] Man finds himself living in an **aleatory** world; his existence involves, to put it baldly, a gamble. The world is a scene of risk; it is uncertain, unstable, uncannily unstable. Its dangers are irregular, inconstant, not to be counted upon as to their times and seasons. (Stephen Holmes, review of *John Dewey and the High Tide of American Liberalism*, by Alan Ryan, *New Republic*, 3/11/1996, p. 40.)

(2) unpredictable (in terms of the effect that one action or activity will have on another) *adj.*: **Heisenbergian**. See *uncertain*

unprincipled (person) *n.*: **reprobate**. ❖ When Bill Clinton first ran for president, nobody doubted his devotion to issues or penchant for plunging into the vagaries of public policy. Nor did the public question his political skill. We merely wondered whether he was a **reprobate**. (Now we know.) (Tony Snow,

"In Leisurely Pursuit," *Washington Times*, 11/14/1999.)

(2) unprincipled (behavior) *n.*: **knavery**. See *corruption*

(3) unprincipled (characterized by . . . and cunning methods, esp. in regard to the pursuit and maintenance of political or other power) *adj.*: **Machiavellian**. See *deceitful*

(4) unprincipled (conduct) *n.*: **skullduggery**. See *deceitfulness*

(5) unprincipled (government by the most . . . people) *n.*: **kakistocracy**. See *government*

(6) unprincipled (person) *n.*: **blackguard**. See *scoundrel*

unprogressive (person, spec. a person who is opposed to advancements in technology) *n.*: **Luddite**. See *traditionalist*

(2) unprogressive (spec. a person who is opposed to individual or political reform or enlightenment) *n.*: **obscurant** (doctrine of such opposition: **obscurantism**). See *traditionalist*

unprotected (as in vulnerable, person or thing): *n.*: **clay pigeon**. See *vulnerable*

unqualified (as in complete or unlimited, esp. as in . . . power) *adj.*: **plenary**. See *complete*

(2) unqualified (government by the most . . . people) *n.*: **kakistocracy**. See *government*

unquestionable *adj.*: **irrefragable**. ❖ [T]he California Civil Rights Initiative [Proposition 209] . . . was the model of justice and simplicity: the state cannot discriminate, either for or against individuals or groups, in employment, education, or contracting. But Judge Henderson believes that this prohibition against discrimination is itself discriminatory! By his **irrefragable** logic, the Fourteenth Amendment's command that "No State shall . . . deny to any person . . . equal protection of the laws" is unconstitutional! (Edward J. Erler, "Popped 209," *National Review*, 2/10/1997, p. W1.)

unquestioning (and loyal assistant) *n.*: **myrmidon**. See *assistant*

unreal (as in artificial) *adj.*: **factitious**. See *artificial*

(2) unreal (as in delusional) *adj.*: **fatuous**. See *delusional*

unrealistic *adj.*: **chimerical**. Even if tobacco's opponents could achieve the **chimerical** goal of eliminating smoking by minors, they would not be satisfied. (Jacob Sullum, "Let's Make a Deal," *Reason*, 10/1/1997, p. 26.)

(2) unrealistic (as in idealistic but likely impractical or . . .) *adj.*: **quixotic**. See *idealistic*

(3) unrealistic (conduct, as in idealistic without regard to practicality) *n.*: **knight-errantry**. See *idealistic*

(4) unrealistic (spec. the tendency to see things as more beautiful than they really are) *n.*: **kalopsia**. See *rose-colored glasses*

unreasonable (as in fallacious or illogical argument) *n.*: **paralogism** (*adj.*: **paralogical**). See *fallacy*

unrefined (as in indifferent or antagonistic to artistic or cultural values) *adj.*: **philistine**. See *uncultured*

(2) unrefined (or poorly put together, esp. with respect to a piece of writing or a speech) *adj.*: **incondite**. See *crude*

(3) unrefined (person) *n.*: **grobian**. See *boor*

(4) unrefined (person) *n.*: **yahoo**. See *boor*

unrehearsed *adj.*: **autoschediastic**. ❖ Her performance last night was fantastic. / By turns she was sweet and sarcastic. / She emoted and quipped, / And without any script! / It was utterly **autoschediastic**. (Sheila B., *The Omnificent English Dictionary in Limerick Form* [oedilf.com], 8/1/2005.)

unrelated (of or relating to events that occur close in time but are . . . to each other) *adj.*: **acausal**. See *unconnected*

unremorseful *adj.*: **impenitent**. See *unrepentant*

unrepentant *adj.*: **impenitent** ❖ Judge William Kelsay on Monday sentenced former Judge William Danser . . . to 90 days' house arrest and 400 hours of community service for cutting special, lenient deals for friends and pro athletes. . . . [Danser has not] apologized for his behavior. . . . And he said, in ridiculing the **impenitent** defendants, "Maybe I was foolish to come to court and think I might hear some kind of public apology." (Dan Reed, "Ex-

Judge Avoids Jail in Ticket Scheme," *San Jose Mercury News*, 7/27/2004.)

unreserved (and reckless person) *n.*: **rantipole**. See *wild*

(2) unreserved (in exhibiting emotion or celebration) *adj.*: **saturnalian**. See *uninhibited*

unrest *n.*: **maelstrom**. See *commotion*

(2) unrest *n.*: **pother**. See *commotion*

unrestrained (as in impetuous) *adj.*: **gadarene**. See *impetuous*

(2) unrestrained (in exhibiting emotion or celebration) *adj.*: **saturnalian**. See *uninhibited*

(3) unrestrained (morally or sexually) *adj.*, *n.*: **libertine**. See *promiscuous*

unrivaled (person or thing) *n.*: **nonesuch**. See *paragon*

unruly *adj.*: **indocile**. ❖ The Guadalupe River rowdies are rearing their ugly heads of dysfunction. For years, this marauding group of **indociles** has swarmed down on the Guadalupe River on Labor Day, leaving a path of destruction along the river similar to that of the Exxon *Valdez*. How difficult can it be to ban alcohol from these individuals? How much is the ecology of the river worth in dollars? (Steve Ochoa, "Sound Off," *San Antonio Express-News*, 9/3/2000.)

(2) unruly (as in resistant to control or authority) *adj.*: **refractory**. See *stubborn*

(3) unruly (as in uncontrollable and undisciplined, person) *n.*: **bashi-bazouk** [Turkish]. See *undisciplined*

unsafe (as in perilous) *adj.*: **parlous**. See *perilous*

unscrupulous *adj.*: **jackleg**. ❖ Be wary, he said, of offers . . . to invest in short-term investments or promissory notes with enticingly high interest rates dangled as a profitable return. Be especially wary, he added, when the pitch includes such phrases as "it really does work" and "fully guaranteed." And **jackleg** investment outfits often have high-sounding words like "global" and "trust" in their titles, he noted. (Larry Wilkerson, "In the Season of Giving, Some Folks Get Taken," *Atlanta Journal-Constitution*, 12/7/2000.)

(2) unscrupulous (behavior) *n*.: **knavery**. See *corruption*

(3) unscrupulous (characterized by . . . and cunning methods, esp. in regard to the pursuit and maintenance of political or other power) *adj*.: **Machiavellian**. See *deceitful*

(4) unscrupulous (conduct) *n*.: **skullduggery**. See *deceitfulness*

(5) unscrupulous (politician) *n*.: **highbinder**. See *corrupt*

unseat *v.t.* **unhorse**. ❖ [Lynn Martin] puts onions on her lunchtime hot dogs. Onions and dill pickles and tomatoes and celery salt. [She] has been scarfing down such hot dogs from the same vendor on Chicago's northwest side, in the neighborhood where she grew up and from which she is mounting a campaign to **unhorse** Democratic Sen. Paul Simon, who is 61. The hot dogs, loaded in the Chicago manner, pack a political message: I am from Chicago and my opponent is from Dixie. (George F. Will, "Paul Simon's Problem," *Washington Post*, 1/18/1990.)

unseemly (as in indecent) *adj*.: **ostrobogulous**. See *indecent*

(2) unseemly (as in undignified) *adj*.: **infra dig**. See *undignified*

unseen (nearly . . .) *adj*.: **liminal**. See *invisible*

unsociable (as in socially withdrawn or inexperienced and/or shy and/or sullen) *adj*.: **farouche** [French]. See *shy*

unsophisticated (class of people regarded as . . .) *n*.: **booboisie**. ❖ [T]he myth of a heartland filled with **booboisie**—dear to intellectuals and the consultants who claim to control the populace—is etched in stone in this land. The daring thought that citizens are enlightened and knowledgeable, due to profound changes in the economy and in the new multiplicity of information sources, is too daring. (Douglas Davis, "Puritanical Pols Ignore Polls, Other Big 'P': Privacy," *Arizona Republic*, 12/27/1998.)

(2) unsophisticated (false or insincere showing of . . . or naive behavior) *adj*.: **faux-naïf** [French]. See *naive*

(3) unsophisticated *n*.: **artless**. See *crude*

unsound (argument in which a false conclusion is drawn from two premises, neither of which conveys information about all members of the designated class) *n*.: **undistributed middle**. See *fallacy*

(2) unsound (argument, spec. where one argues that because event B followed event A, then event A must have caused event B) *n*.: **post hoc, ergo propter hoc** [Latin for "after this, therefore, because of this"]. See *fallacy*

(3) unsound (as in fallacious or illogical argument) *n*.: **paralogism** (*adj*.: **paralogical**). See *fallacy*

(4) unsound (mentally) *adj*.: **non compos mentis** [Latin]. See *insane*

unspeakable (as in indescribable) *adj*.: **ineffable**. See *indescribable*

unspontaneous (as in contrived) *adj*.: **voulu** [French]. See *contrived*

unstable (as in changeable) *adj*.: **labile**. See *changeable*

unsteady (as in changeable) *adj*.: **labile**. See *changeable*

unsuccessful *adj*.: **abortive**. ❖ [Saddam Hussein's] first venture into subversive politics came in 1956 when, as a new member of the Baath Party, he participated in an **abortive** coup against King Faisal II. (Jill Smolowe, Iraq: "Sword of the Arabs—Brutal Perhaps, but Only as Crazy as a Desert Fox, Saddam Hussein Mounts a Crude Push for Middle East Supremacy and Worries the World," *Time*, 6/11/1990, p. 32.)

unsuitable (as in things that do not mix together) *adj*.: **immiscible**. See *incompatible*

(2) unsuitable *adj*.: **malapropos**. See *inappropriate*

unsupported (as in fallacious or illogical argument) *n*.: **paralogism** (*adj*.: **paralogical**). See *fallacy*

unsure (and cautious and indecisive) *adj*.: **Prufrockian**. See *timid*

(2) unsure (as in indecisive) *adj*., *v.i.*, *n*.: **shilly-shally**. See *vacillate*

(3) unsure (as to one's opinion on an issue,

esp. arising from awareness of an opposing viewpoint) *n.*: **aporia**. See *doubt*

(4) unsure (in terms of the effect that one action or activity will have on another) *adj.*: **Heisenbergian**. See *uncertain*

(5) unsure (or undecided person, esp. regarding political issues) *n.*: **mugwump**. See *undecided*

(6) unsure (as in chronic inability to make decisions) *n.*: **abulia** (or **aboulia**). See *indecisiveness*

untamed *adj.*: **farouche** [French]. ❖ True, in the concerto's finale she discarded the tempo set by her conductor, Emmanuel Krivine, and decided on a more congenial, faster one for herself. But on her new recording of the Chopin concertos with Charles Dutoit—released on EMI last month—she is obedient, less **farouche**. (Dermot Clinch, "Molto Agitato," *New Statesman*, 4/2/1999.)

(2) untamed *adj.*: **feral**. ❖ On part of that land they had built a private zoo, to which they charged admission. . . . I said it sounded like a good place to start. It would be good to take a look at the animals in confinement before we went thrashing around in the bush after **feral** ones. (Bil Gilbert, "Nasty Little Devil," *Sports Illustrated*, 11/21/1994, p. 72.)

unthinking (repetition of ideas that have been drilled into the speaker or that reflect the opinions of the powers that be) *v.t., v.i., n.*: **duckspeak**. See *recite*

untidy *adj.*: **frowzy**. See *messy*

untimely (as in a statement, thought, knowledge, or action that comes to mind or occurs after the fact when it is too late to act on it, such as locking the barn door after the cows have left) *n.*: **afterwit**. See *belated*

untroubled (and carefree time) *adj.*: **prelapsarian**. See *innocent*

(2) untroubled *adj.*: **dégagé** [French]. See *easygoing*

(3) untroubled (or carefree behavior) *n.*: **rhathymia**. See *carefree*

untruthful (abnormal propensity for being . . . , esp. by embellishing) *n.*: **mythomania**. See *embellishment*

(2) untruthful *adj.*: **mendacious**. See *dishonest*

unusable *adj.*: **inutile**. See *useless*

unusual *adj.*: **selcouth**. [This word is probably archaic, but there are some recent usages.] ❖ State Labor Relations Board hearing examiner Timothy Tietze ruled that the Northwest Area School Board did not commit an unfair labor practice when it voted to give the public 10 days to review any tentative teacher contract before the board votes on it. . . . Tietze says the resolution to have a 10-day public review arose from "a set of **selcouth** circumstances." (Mark Guydish, "NW Area Union's Complaint Dismissed," *Wilkes-Barre [PA] Times-Leader*, 3/2/2007.)

(2) unusual (as in departing from the standard or norm) *adj.*: **heteroclite**. See *abnormal*

(3) unusual (as in eccentric) *adj.*: **pixilated**. See *eccentric*

(4) unusual (as in supernatural) *adj.*: **preternatural**. See *supernatural*

(5) unusual (as in unconventional) *adj.*: **outré** [French]. See *unconventional*

(6) unusual (holding . . . opinions or having an . . . perspective) *adj.*: **heterodox** (*n.*: **heterodoxy**). See *unconventional*

(7) unusual (very . . . person or thing) *n.*: **rara avis** [Latin]. See *rarity*

(8) unusual *adj.*: **recherché** [French]. See *rare*

unvarying *adj.*: **equable**. ❖ Its gardens, rich in fuchsias and roses, flourish in the damp, **equable** climate. (Michel Arnaud, "A Great Little Dane," description of Falsled Kro, rural inn near Millinge, Denmark, *Town & Country*, 10/1/1995, p. 118.)

(2) unvarying (in rhythm or tempo) *adj.*: **metronomic**. See *steady*

unwavering (as in one who clings to an opinion or belief even after being shown that it is wrong) *n.*: **mumpsimus**. See *stubborn*

(2) unwavering (as in stubborn) *adj.*: **pervicacious**. See *stubborn*

(3) unwavering (in holding to a belief or opinion) *adj.*: **pertinacious**. See *stubborn*

unwelcome *adj.*: **persona non grata** [Latin]. ❖ In his newspaper interview, Mr. Wolf revealed that he wanted to immigrate to Israel in 1991, apparently when he was declared **persona non grata** by the Russians, who were under pressure by the German government to send him back. (John O. Koehler, "Israel Welcomes Terrorists' Best Friend," *Washington Times*, 7/28/1996.)

(2) unwelcome (as in not asked or invited) *adj.*: **unbidden**. See *uninvited*

unwholesome *adj.*: **insalubrious**. ❖ Next to the garment district—in an even more **insalubrious** part of [Los Angeles], heavily populated with drunks—is Toy-town, home to more than 100 businesses, most of them owned by Chinese immigrants. (*Economist*, "How to Remake a City," 5/31/1997.)

(2) unwholesome (or harmful) *adj.*: **noisome**. See *harmful*

unwillingness *n.*: **nolition**. ❖ We may speculate that after [the many disturbances in European life during the last few decades (the war in Algeria, terrorism, etc.)], these countries may be suffering from a kind of fatigue . . . or the weakening of the will, including the will to exist. . . . On the other hand, this may only appear to be the case. These countries may only appear to lack the will or volition to continue existing whereas, in reality, there is no such **nolition**. (Victor Perez-Diaz, "The Role of Civil Nations in the Making of Europe," *Social Research*, 12/22/2000.)

unyielding (and stern) *adj.*: **flinty**. See *stern*

(2) unyielding (as in hardened) *adj.*: **sclerotic**. See *hardened*

(3) unyielding (as in one who clings to an opinion or belief even after being shown that it is wrong) *n.*: **mumpsimus**. See *stubborn*

(4) unyielding (as in stubborn) *adj.*: **pervicacious**. See *stubborn*

(5) unyielding (in holding to a belief or opinion) *adj.*: **pertinacious**. See *stubborn*

(6) unyielding (position, esp. with respect to moral or ethical principles or practices) *n.*: **rigorism**. See *rigidity*

upbeat (as in one habitually expecting an upturn in one's fortunes, sometimes without justification) *adj.*: **Micawberish** (*n.*: **Micawber**). See *optimistic*

(2) upbeat (esp. blindly or naively) *adj.*: **Panglossian**. See *optimistic*

(3) upbeat (excessively or unrealistically . . . person) *n.*: **Pollyanna**. See *optimistic*

upbraid (as in criticize) *v.t.*: **flay**. See *criticize*

(2) upbraid *v.t.*: **objurgate**. See *criticize*

upbraiding (being subject to verbal . . . , esp. public) *n.*: **obloquy**. See *abuse*

updating (of an organization to meet contemporary conditions, esp. as proposed by Pope John XXIII with respect to the Catholic church after Vatican II) *n.*: **aggiornamento** [Italian]. ❖ [After] World War II, Lavrenty Beria . . . counterposed a "reformist" program to the policy of retrenchment. . . . He put forward a decidedly liberal program, proposing to loosen some of the strictures of central planning and to allow a measure of "decentralization." In foreign policy, he proposed an **aggiornamento**—no direct confrontation with the West, the neutralization of Germany—in a way a forerunner of the detente of the 1970s. (Laurent Murawiec, "Putin's Precursors," National Interest, 6/22/2000.)

(2) updating (esp. a scholarly critical . . . , as in revision) *n.*: **recension**. See *revision*

upheaval (as in chaos) *n.*: **tohubuhu**. See *chaos*

(2) upheaval *n.*: **maelstrom**. See *commotion*

(3) upheaval *n.*: **pother**. See *commotion*

upper class (as in fashionable society) *n.*: **beau monde** [French]. See *high society*

(2) upper class (as in fashionable society) *n.*: **bon ton** [French]. See *high society*

(3) upper class (esp. those aspiring or pretending to be . . .) *adj.*: **lace-curtain**. See *wellbred*

(4) upper class (study of or focus on the . . . , esp. in artistic works) *n.*: **plutography**. See *wealth*

uppercase (letter) *n.*: **majuscule**. ❖ A had its bomb, B its movie, C its section and D its day. Now E is having its era. . . . You must have seen its amazing breakthrough performance in e-mail. Soon there were E-Stamps, E-trade, e-Toys.com, e-etc. Now, E's got capital status; as we like to say, E is "E-biquitous!" . . . What versions does E come in? You can get E in a manly, three-pronged **majuscule** or a dainty, curly [lower case] that almost looks like a smiley face! (Jesse Green, "E-nough Already," *Washington Post*, 11/21/1999.)

upright (of or relating to standing . . .) *n.*: **orthostatic**. See *standing*

uprightness (as in virtue or integrity) *n.*: **probity**. See *integrity*

uprising (against existing social or artistic conventions) *n.*: **titanism** (often cap.). See *revolt*

   (2) uprising (or riot) *n.*: **émeute** [French]. See *riot*

   (3) uprising (peasant's . . .) *n.*: **jacquerie**. See *revolt*

   (4) uprising *n.*: **émeute** [French]. See *rebellion*

uproar (as in commotion) *n.*: **bobbery**. See *commotion*

   (2) uproar (as in commotion) *n.*: **kerfuffle**. See *commotion*

   (3) uproar *n.*: **maelstrom**. See *commotion*

   (4) uproar *n.*: **pother**. See *commotion*

uproot (esp. from one's accustomed environment) *v.t.*: **deracinate**. ❖ The "re-potting hypothesis" blames American mobility: Frequent re-potting of plants damages roots, and frequent changes of residence—blame economic dynamism, the automobile, suburbanization, the lure of the Sun Belt—produce a **deracinated** population. (George Will, "Democracy Is Healthy If Bowling Leagues Are," *Newsday*, 1/5/1995.)

uprooted (of . . . people having lost class status) *adj.*: **lumpen**. See *displaced*

upset (as in angry) *adj.*: **wroth**. See *angry*

   (2) upset (as in defeat by . . .) *v.t.*: **unhorse**. See *defeat*

   (3) upset (as in indignant) *n.*: **dudgeon** (often expressed as "in high dudgeon"). See *indignant*

   (4) upset (extremely) *adj.*: **apoplectic**. See *angry*

upstart (esp. social or economic) *n.*: **parvenu**. ❖ Mocked for his pompous speaking style and his pompadour hair style, his overweening ambition and his underwhelming intellect, he seems to be a stereotype of the social climbing **parvenu** who somehow manages to keep insinuating himself into a better class of society, but can't stop his embarrassed hosts from laughing behind his back. (Mark A. Heller, "David Levy: Not Such a Buffoon," *Jerusalem Post*, 12/4/1998.)

   (2) upstart (social or economic, esp. having attained a position without effort or merit) *n.*: **arriviste**. ❖ The real reason [Arianna Huffington] has been so angrily attacked [for writing a biography of Pablo Picasso], she argues, is that the art establishment perceives her as a dilettante and **arriviste**. "It's not a question of having an art degree," she says, "but whether or not you have been certified by the clique." (Dan Chu, Pages: "An Unflattering Portrait of Picasso Leaves Art Critics in a Hanging Frame of Mind," *People*, 7/25/1988, p. 50.)

upstream (of fish that swim . . .) *adj.*: **anadromous**. See *fish*

up-to-date (being . . . with or informed about something) *adj.*: **au fait** [French]. See *familiar*

upward (slope) *n.*: **acclivity** (*adj.*: **acclivitous**). See *incline*

urban (densely populated . . . area) *n.*: **megalopolis**. See *crowded*

   (2) urban (region) *n.*: **conurbation**. See *metropolis*

urbane (and intelligent person) *n.*: **bel esprit**. See *cultivated*

   (2) urbane (as in elegant) *adj.*: **Chesterfieldian**. See *elegant*

   (3) urbane (as in refined or elegant) *adj.*: **raffiné** (or **raffine**) [French]. See *refined*

   (4) urbane (as in well-bred, esp. those aspiring or pretending to be well-bred) *adj.*: **lace-curtain**. See *well-bred*

urge (as in irresistible compulsion) *n.*: **cacoëthes**. See *compulsion*

   (2) urge (mental process marked by . . . to do something) *n.*: **conation**. See *determination*

(3) urge *v.t.*: **adjure**. See *plead*

urgent *adj.*: **clamant**. ❖ [The headline is a play on words, as the article refers to a decline in clam population in Babylon, Long Island.] (Joie Tyrrell, In Babylon: "A **Clamant** Try to Boost Numbers," *Newsday*, 11/7/ 1999.)

(2) urgent *adj.*: **necessitous**. ❖ A black Fairfax County police officer whose white supervisor asked him to shine the supervisor's shoes was justified in resigning from the police department because working conditions were "just too oppressive," a state examiner has ruled. [The examiner] wrote that Jackson, who said he feared for his safety after complaining that his supervisor's remark was racist, had "compelling and **necessitous**" reasons for resigning. (Patricia Davis, "Treatment Drove Black Officer Out of Fairfax Force, Ruling Says," *Washington Post*, 10/28/1992.)

urging (someone to take a course of action) *adj.*: **hortatory**. ❖ [Writer Meg Greenfield] loved argument and continued a tradition under which [*Washington*] *Post* editorials avoided **hortatory** calls to action in favor of making points by marshaling facts. (J. Y. Smith, obituary of Meg Greenfield, *Washington Post*, 5/14/1999.)

(2) urging (or inciting or inspiring to action) *adj.*: **proceleusmatic**. See *exhorting*

urinate *v.i.*: **micturate**. ❖ Also, in 1996 Stephen Herek's film [*101 Dalmations*] can dare show something old Walt [Disney] could never have allowed: a **micturating** puppy. The benefits of such frankness are debatable. Should your kiddies shriek with laughter at the sight of wee-wee, you might want to consider abandoning them. (Kevin Jackson, "101 Dalmatians, One Real Bitch," *Independent on Sunday*, 12/15/1996.)

urinating (backwards) *adj., n.*: **retromingent**. [This word refers to urinating backwards (when used as an adjective, which is the example given here) or animals that do so (when used as a noun). However, while the connection to the actual definition is vague, it has also taken on a slang definition of "cowardly,"

in addition to being used as a kind of general, all-purpose insulting way to describe a person, such as "idiotic" or "moronic." See *cowardly*.] ❖ I noticed two large gray stones and as we neared them, they turned into two rhinos. It is not like TV. The space and the feeling of vulnerability become amplified. Realizing a rhino can outrun a man does not help. Moreover they can pierce a car with their horn and flip it over. Even more insulting you cannot sneak up behind them as they are powerfully **retromingent**. (Allen Pittman, "Physical Training Traditions," www.apittman.com/africa2.shtml [2005].)

urine (uncontrolled or involuntary discharge of) *n.*: **enuresis**. See *bed-wetting*

usage (new . . . , phrase or word) *n.*: **neologism**. See *word*

use (right of . . . of property, especially land, belonging to another) *n.*: **usufruct**. ❖ By late 1946, [Albert] Einstein was pushing to seeking to sell the remaining house and give control of the money to a legal guardian for [his son]. But [his ex-wife] had the **usufruct** of the house . . . and she was terrified of surrendering any control. (Walter Isaacson, *Einstein*, Simon & Schuster [2007], p. 516.)

useful *adj.*: **utile**. ❖ Of all of the pickups on the road, the 2003 Chevy Avalanche is certainly one of the most **utile**. That is, not only [are] there such things as the midgate that allows the vehicle to change from two rows of seats in the cab to a single row and additional cargo space, when it comes to cargo, there are two lockable storage compartments in the cargo box. (*Automotive Design & Production*, "Dimensionally Like a Rock," 4/1/2003.)

useless (something that is . . .) *n.*: **vermiform appendix**. [This term derives the body part of that name, which is generally considered unnecessary.] ❖ Many [voters] have strong expectations of Gore. President Clinton regularly introduces Gore as the most active vice president in American history, and few challenge the idea. Contrasted with the image of the vice president as the **vermiform appen-**

dix of American government, Gore has been a close presidential adviser with his own responsibilities in streamlining government, dealing with Russia and environmental themes. (*Sunday Oregonian*, "Democrats Should Pick Gore," 2/27/2000.)

(2) useless *adj.*: **inutile**. ❖ Bush has also considered ending a nascent program under which the United States would pay Russia to render plutonium **inutile** for weapons use by burning it at atomic power plants. (Gregg Easterbrook, "The Real Danger Is Nuclear," *New Republic*, 11/5/2001.)

(3) useless *adj.*: **otiose**. ❖ [The] blind infatuation [of the mass media and penal experts] with taxpayer-funded **otiose** rehabilitation programs and crusading against the alleged "root" causes of crime, i.e., poverty, unemployment, malparenting . . . , deters their acknowledging the obvious and fuels unconstructive whining against tough but condign punishments. (Bruce Fein, "Treating Criminals with the Contempt They Deserve," *Washington Times*, 1/8/1996.)

(4) useless (as in superfluous) *adj.*: **excrescent**. See *superfluous*

(5) useless (as in superfluous) *adj.*: **supererogatory**. See *superfluous*

(6) useless (as in vain or worthless) *adj.*: **nugatory**. See *worthless*

(7) useless (efforts that are laborious but . . .) *adj.*: **Sisyphean**. See *futile*

(8) useless (as in futile activity) *n.*: **mug's game** [British informal]. See *futile*

(9) useless (mission or project) *n.*: **fool's errand**. See *hopeless*

(10) useless (or futile) *adj.*: **bootless**. See *futile*

(11) useless (relating to the view that all human striving and aspiration is . . . , or people who hold such a view) *adj.*, *n.*: **futilitarian**. See *futile*

usual *adj.*: **wonted**. See *customary*

usurp *v.t.*: **accroach**. ❖ It was an article in the charge of treason, or, as it was then styled, of **accroaching** royal power, against Mortimer, that he intermeddled in the king's household without the assent of this council. (Henry Hallam, "History of Europe During The Middle Ages: Part XXV," *History of the World*, 1/1/1992.)

utmost (to the . . .) *adv.*: **à l'outrance** [French]. ❖ Yet the foreign policy events of the White House of Mr. Clinton that will be remembered are more in terms of military power than of durable peacemaking: the twin interventions in Bosnia and Kosovo, the series of small engagements against Iraq, the missile strikes on Sudan and Afghanistan. None of these was the kind of [war] **à l'outrance** threatened and in some cases waged by his predecessors. (Andrew Marshall, "A President in Search of His Legacy," *Independent* [London], 7/10/2000.)

(2) utmost (as in the ultimate degree, as of a condition or quality, or the highest point that can be attained) *n.*: **ne plus ultra**. See *ultimate*

utopia (as in place of extreme luxury and ease where physical comforts and pleasures are always at hand) *n.*: **Cockaigne**. See *paradise*

(2) utopia (in which everyone rules equally) *n.*: **pantisocracy**. See *government*

(3) utopia (spec. a place of fabulous wealth or opportunity) *n.*: **El Dorado**. See *paradise*

(4) utopia *n.*: **Xanadu**. See *paradise*

utopian (spec., having the characteristics of a mythical romantic place) *adj.*: **Ruritanian**. See *paradise*

utter (as in total or complete, usually used with "nonsense") *adj.*: **arrant**. See *total*

vacillate (as in being indecisive) *adj., v.i., n.*: **shilly-shally**. ❖ [In the Truman administration, as contrasted with the Clinton administration,] there was no **shilly-shallying** over the role of First Lady. (David Ellis, Up Front: "Wild About Harry—The Late President's Daughter and His Biographer Separate Bush and Clinton from the Tried and Truman," *People*, 9/21/1992, p. 52.)

vacillating (as in fickle, person whose opinion is always changing as the wind blows, like a weathervane) *n.*: **girouette** [French]. See *weathervane*

vacillation (as in chronic inability to make decisions) *n.*: **abulia** (or **aboulia**). See *indecisiveness*

vagabond *n.*: **clochard** [French]. See *vagrant*

vagina (of or relating to) *adj.*: **yonic**. ❖ [The exhibition by] sculptor Cathy de Monchaux [includes] a collection of sexually explicit photographs of women. . . . Natalie Angier writes: "As symbols go, the phallus is a yawn." . . . But the vagina, now there's a Rorschach with legs. You can make of it practically anything you want, need or dread. . . . This, Cathy de Monchaux knows. Which is not to say that the artist's work is all about the **yonic**. (Michael O'Sullivan, "De Monchaux's Female Form and Function," *Washington Post*, 8/11/2000.)

(2) vagina (insertion of penis into . . .) *n.*: **intromission** (*v.t.*: **intromit**). See *penetration*

vagrant *n.*: **clochard** [French]. ❖ And then there are the disquieting, all too visible symptoms of what's become known as the economic malaise—metro cars animated by unemployed young men hawking newspapers, passed-out **clochards** sleeping in doorways, train stations crawling with brutish, suspicious cops. (Judith Sullivan, Letter from Paris: "Resisting Change, One Ballot at a Time," *Newsday*, 6/1/1997.)

vague (as in cryptic speech or writing, esp. deliberately) *adj.*: **elliptical**. See *cryptic*

(2) vague (or cryptic or ambiguous) *adj.*: **sibylline** (or **sybilline**; often cap.). See *cryptic*

(3) vague *adj.*: **Delphic**. See *ambiguous*

vain (person) *n.*: **fop**. ❖ If makeup represents the worst possible cosmetic combo (fake and detectable), muscles represent the best (obvious and real). [W]riter Sam Fussell . . . in a 1991 book about his bodybuilding career . . . describes the advent of a new male subspecies: the muscle **fop**. (Alan Farnham, "Male Vanity: You're So Vain I Bet You Think This Story's About You," *Fortune*, 9/9/1996, p. 66.)

(2) vain (person) *n.*: **popinjay**. ❖ The variance between [a vain man's] perception of himself and the public's is simply too wide. Thus one's irritation when senior golfer Jim Colbert cocks his finger and struts like a **popinjay** after sinking a putt vanishes when you see that under his floppy white hat lies the world's lousiest rug. (Tad Friend, "You Look Great," *Esquire*, 3/1/1997, p. 71.)

(3) vain (and conceited person) *n.*: **coxcomb**. See *conceited*

(4) vain (as in unsuccessful) *adj.*: **abortive**. See *unsuccessful*

(5) vain (as in useless or futile) *adj.*: **bootless**. See *futile*

(6) vain (as in useless or ineffective) *adj.*: **otiose**. See *useless*

(7) vain (as in without substance or worth) *adj.*: **nugatory**. See *worthless*

(8) vain (efforts which are laborious but in . . .) *adj.*: **Sisyphean**. See *futile*

(9) vain (like a peacock) *adj.*: **pavonine**. See *peacock*

(10) vain (mission or project) *n.*: **fool's errand**. See *hopeless*

(11) vain (relating to the view that all human striving and aspiration is in . . . , or people who hold such a view) *adj., n.*: **futilitarian**. See *futile*

valedictory (as in parting words) *n.*: **envoi** [French]. See *parting words*

valid (as in legitimate; acceptable) *adj.*: **cromulent**. See *legitimate*

value (under a new standard, esp. one that differs from conventional norms) *v.t.*: **transvaluate**. See *evaluate*

valueless (as in useless) *adj.*: **inutile**. See *useless*

(2) valueless (deeming something as . . .) *n.*: **floccinaucinihilipilification**. See *worthless*

(3) valueless (something that is . . .) *n.*: **vermiform appendix**. See *useless*

(4) valueless (thing or matter) *n.*: **bagatelle**. See *trifling*

(5) valueless *adj.*: **nugatory**. See *worthless*

values (study of . . .) *n.*: **axiology**. ❖ It should not be perpetually accepted that what is intangible is automatically immeasurable. For example, to quantify good and bad behaviour[,] a system of values audit needs to be introduced. Values auditing is not a new idea. Years ago, the science of values or axiology was developed. It is claimed that **axiology** makes possible the objective measurement of value as accurately as a thermometer measures temperature. (Dr. Abu Bakar Abdul Majeed, "Probing Good and Evil Thoughts," *New Straits Times* [Malaysia], 11/18/2000.)

(2) values (of a person, people, or culture) *n.*: **ethos**. See *character*

vanish *v.t.*: **evanesce**. See *disappear*

vanishing (as in lasting only briefly) *adj.*: **evanescent**. See *transient*

vanity (full of . . . and boastful) *adj.*: **vainglorious**. See *boastful*

variable (as in changeable) *adj.*: **labile**. See *changeable*

(2) variable (as in fickle, person whose opinion is always changing as the wind blows, like a weathervane) *n.*: **girouette** [French]. See *weathervane*

varied (as in of all varieties) *adj.*: **omnifarious**. ❖ Ms. Ono says both the music and art of her late husband [John Lennon] were profoundly influenced by his **omnifarious** interests, including metaphysics and UFOs. (Thomas Rop, "When She's 64 . . . Yoko Ono—Will We Still Need Her? Will We Still Heed Her?" *Dallas Morning News*, 1/13/1997.)

(2) varied (composed of . . . items) *adj.*: **farraginous**. See *mixed*

(3) varied (often used of a performer or artist) *adj.*: **protean**. See *versatile*

(4) varied *adj.*: **multifarious**. See *versatile*

variety (as in dissimilarity) *n.*: **heterogeneity** (*adj.*: **heterogeneous**). See *dissimilar*

(2) variety (as in diversity) *n.*: **variegation** (*v.t.*: **variegate**). See *diversity*

(3) variety (as in region populated by people from a . . . of countries or backgrounds) *n.*: **cosmopolis**. See *diversity*

(4) variety (having great . . .) *adj.*: **multifarious**. See *versatile*

veer (from a course or intended path) *v.t.*: **yaw**. ❖ At last week's U.S. Open a television camera . . . captured—and no doubt added to—the anxiety of the world's best golfers as they teed off on the most traumatic opening hole in tournament golf. [P]anic visited the eyes of third-round leader Ernie Els, who watched his tee shot . . . **yaw** left toward terra incognita. (John Garrity, *Golf Plus*, *Sports Illustrated*, 6/27/1994, p. 44.)

vegetables (mixture of . . . and/or fruits) *n.*: **macédoine** [French]. See *mixture*

veil (or disguise) *n.*, *v.t.*: **vizard**. See *disguise*

veiled (as in dark, misty, and gloomy) *adj.*: **caliginous**. See *dark*

velvety *adj.*: **velutinous**. ❖ With the exception of his soundtrack to *When Harry Met Sally . . .* , when he rejuvenated standards with his elegant clinking and **velutinous** vocals, [Harry] Connick's albums have been somewhat unsatisfying. (Michael Corcoran, "Peppers Red-Hot, but Lack 'Magik,'" *Chicago Sun-Times*, 10/6/1991.)

venerate (often in a servile manner) *v.i.*: **genuflect**. See *kneel*

veneration (not necessarily sincere or unforced) *n.*: **obeisance**. See *homage*

(2) veneration (of dead people) *n.*: **necrolatry**. See *worship*

vengeful (one who is . . .) *n.*: **tricoteuse**. See *knitter*. [See the note at "knitter" for why this word can be synonymous with vengeful.]

venture (which is fruitless or hopeless) *n.*: **fool's errand**

veracious (as in reflecting reality) *adj.*: **veridical**. See *realistic*

verbal *adj.*, *adv.*: **viva voce** [Latin]. ❖ Yesterday I got one from an editor . . . who wanted permission to quote something I said to him in a phone conversation last summer. I asked him not to, explaining that **viva voce** quotes are dangerous; they might be picked up and requoted wrong, either by accident or design, and there would be no published version under my byline to prove what I really said. (Florence King, The Misanthrope's Corner, *National Review*, 12/31/1996, p. 60.)

(2) verbal *adj.*: **nuncupative**. See *oral*

verbatim (as in the very words used by a writer or speaker) *phr.*: **ipsissima verba** [Latin]. See *words*

(2) verbatim (translation) *n.*: **metaphrase**. See *translation*

verbose *adj.*: **inaniloquent**. [Note that the word is "inaniloquent," not "ineloquent" or "inaneloquent"; its roots are "inanis" (inane) and "loqui" (speak).] ❖ One of the greatest fears of a writer is that s/he would be considered **inaniloquent** rather than eloquent. (William R. Long, "Inamorata/Inamorato," www.drbilllong.com/Prefixes/Inamorata.html, 8/10/2005.)

(2) verbose (as in rambling) *adj.*: **discursive**. See *rambling*

(3) verbose (as in characterized by a ready and easy flow of words) *adj.*: **voluble**. See *talkative*

(4) verbose (mania for being . . .) *n.*: **cacoëthes loquendi** [Latin]. See *talking*

verbosity *n.*: **circumlocution**. ❖ When Ferdinand Magellan circumnavigated the globe in the early 16th century, he proved the world was round, thus providing a valuable service to humankind. But when we use **circumlocution** in writing—when we use an excessive number of words to arrive at our destination—we do a great disservice to our readers: We waste their time. (Stephen Wilbers, "Get to the Point, So You Don't Waste Readers' Time," *Minneapolis Star Tribune*, 9/4/1998.)

(2) verbosity *n.*: **logorrhea**. ❖ Frankly, I would have enjoyed a few moments of silence instead of the **logorrhea**, talkiness and banal-

ities offered by anchors for two hours [during the O. J. Simpson chase]. (Liz Smith, "That O. J. Coverage," *Newsday*, 6/21/1994.)

(3) verbosity *n.*: **macrology**. [This word can be used in a "macro" sense, as in any speech or piece of writing that is unnecessarily long and contains superfluousness, or in a "micro" sense of redundancy of words, for which a synonym would be "pleonasm" (see *redundancy*)]. ❖ The term "focusing on core businesses" is often just chief executive **macrology**, something that sounds good in the annual report. (Tim Knapton, "Sharper Focus Has AWA Looking Like a Winner," *Australian Financial Review*, 2/7/1998.)

(4) verbosity *n.*: **periphrasis** (*adj.*: **periphrastc**). ❖ As you will have discerned from my strikingly unadorned, almost Amish-style prose, I'm an earthy, New Age kind of a guy. Honest. Not for me the style-obsessed grandiloquent **periphrasis** of other, more arch columnists. (David Benedict, Theatre: Reviews, *Independent* [London], 8/30/1997.)

(5) verbosity (spec. obsessive repetition of meaningless words and phrases) *n.*: **verbigeration**. See *repetition*

(6) verbosity (through use of unnecessary words or phrases) *n.*: **pleonasm**. See *redundancy*

vernacular (as in speech used by members of the underworld or a particular group) *n.*: **argot**. ❖ Until last week, most stock-market investors were confident that the U.S. economy was not headed for a recession anytime soon. A slowdown, when it came, was expected to be gradual—a soft landing, in the economic **argot**. (*Time*, "The Economy—Headed for a Hard Landing? 7/10/1989, p. 47.)

(2) vernacular (as in speech used by members of the underworld or a particular group) *n.*: **cant**. ❖ **Cant** is often associated with gangs who wish to keep their activities secret. As Cardozo-Freeman (1984) explains, "Secret languages are a thriving folk tradition constantly used, particularly in segregation and the hole." (Peter M. Wittenberg, "Language and

Communication in Prison," *Federal Probation*, 12/1/1996, p. 45.)

(3) vernacular *n.*: **vulgate**. ❖ Stretching a cultural point, Eszterhas is a kind of modern-day American Dante, telling us again the true story we have just lived through—the Clinton impeachment—using the coarse and vulgar way people really talk these days (the real "**vulgate**," so to speak). (Liz Smith, "Red-Hot Rhapsody," *Newsday*, 7/18/2000.)

(4) vernacular (as in vocabulary) *n.*: **lexicon**. See *vocabulary*

(5) vernacular (regional . . .) *n.*: **patois**. See *dialect*

versatile (often used of a performer or artist) *adj.*: **protean**. ❖ So now at last one sees the work whole—more than 240 paintings, drawings, prints, sculptures and ceramics, the outpouring of a **protean** talent [Paul Gauguin] who influenced the course of modern painting more than anyone except Cézanne. (Robert Hughes, Art: "Seeing Gauguin Whole—At Last a Masterly Exhibition Corrects Myths and Moonshine About the Pioneering Painter," *Time*, 5/9/1988, p. 76.)

(2) versatile *adj.*: **multifarious**. ❖ Nevertheless, [*The Black Album* by Prince] is a rich and complex record by one of pop's most talented, **multifarious** performers. (David E. Thigpen, The Arts & Media/Rock Music, *Time International*, 1/9/1995, p. 47.)

vestibule (spec. the passageway in a stadium that connects the outer concourse to the interior of the stadium itself) *n.*: **vomitory**. See *corridor*

vestige (as in trace or small amount of) *n.*: **tincture**. See *trace*

vex *v.t.*: **chivvy**. See *pester*

vial *n.*: **ampoule**. ❖ Ayalon police are investigating two incidents at Holon's Wolfson Hospital, in which doctors noticed that the **ampoules** of ephedrine they were about to inject into their patients seemed "strange." (Raine Marcus, "Police Probe Ampoule Case," *Jerusalem Post*, 6/25/1995.)

vibrate (rapidly or spasmodically) *v.i.*: **judder**. See *shake*

vice (place of . . . , as in corruption) *n.*: **Augean stable**. See *corruption*

vicinity (physical . . .) *n.*: **vicinage**. ❖ We demand a jury trial and overwhelming proof of guilt in criminal cases to prevent government oppression, persecution or harassment. The twin rights of the defendant operate by requiring each element of a crime to be found by a cross-section of his peers in the **vicinage**. (Bruce Fein, "Freestyle Law When Sentences Are Imposed," *Washington Times*, 12/25/2001.)

(2) vicinity *n.*: **purlieu**. ❖ Neither does Richler ask an equally obvious question about the missing element in his Arab-Jewish equation: in which cafes in Damascus have Syrian novelists argued for the legitimacy and moral necessity of Israel? In what **purlieu** of Montreal is there a Canadian-Arab writer making the case for the Jews? (Edward Alexander, review of *This Year in Jerusalem*, by Mordecai Richler, *Commentary*, 1/1/1995, p. 82.)

victory (celebrating . . .) *adj.*: **epinician**. [The title of the article gives the context of this passage.] ❖ The victories won, the **epinician** attitudes abandoned, the heroes departed, in the Village and the Town that are the realities of Wimbledon, normal life is reasserted. (Brian Sewell, "Wimbledon Is Hell: As the Tennis-Loving Crowds Descend on London's Most Famous Suburb, Our Columnist and Irate SW19 Resident Is in the Midst of the Worst Fortnight of His Year," *Evening Standard* [London], 6/28/2004.)

(2) victory (in which one comes from behind to win at the last moment) *n.*: **Garrison finish**. [This term derives from Edward "Snapper" Garrison, an American jockey whose practice was to hold a horse back for most of a race and then come on with a driving sprint in the stretch. The example here is not technically correct, since a Garrison finish requires one to be victorious; it is not merely a last-second surge followed by defeat. Nevertheless, it gives a sense of the term.] ❖ Mike Dukakis went from 17 points ahead [of George H. W. Bush] in July to 17 points behind in October—a loss in confidence by one-third of the electorate—before closing with a **Garrison finish**. (David Nyhan, "One Voter in 20 Made the Difference for the Republican Ticket," *Boston Globe*, 11/10/1988.)

(3) victory (obtained only at great cost to the victor) *n.*: **Cadmean victory**. See *Pyrrhic victory*

view (as in tenet) *n.*: **shibboleth**. See *principle*

(2) view (of the world) *n.*: **weltanschauung** [German]. See *worldview*

(3) view (preconceived . . . on an issue) *n.*: **parti pris** [French]. See *preconception*

(4) view (seeing everything in one . . .) *adj.*: **panoptic**. See *visible*

(5) view (which is odd, stubborn, or whimsical) *n.*: **crotchet**. See *notion*

viewpoint (centered on male . . .) *adj.*: **androcentric**. See *male*

(2) viewpoint (which is controversial, or a person who holds one) *n.*: **polemic**. See *controversy*

views (spec. doctrines to be believed; articles of faith) *n.pl.*: **credenda**. See *beliefs*

vigilant (as in on the lookout) *idiom*: **on the qui vive**. See *lookout*

(2) vigilant (person) *n.*: **Argus**. See *watchful*

vigor (as in energy coupled with a will to succeed) *n.*: **spizzerinctum**. See *energy*

(2) vigor (lack of . . . from having no energy or nourishment) *n.*: **inanition**. See *exhaustion*

(3) vigor (lacking . . .) *adj.*: **bovine**. See *sluggish*

(4) vigor (lacking . . .) *adj.*: **logy**. See *sluggish*

(5) vigor *n.*: **brio**. See *energy*

(6) vigor *n.*: **élan** [French]. See *spirit*

vilification (being subject to . . . , esp. public) *n.*: **obloquy**. See *abuse*

villain (as in scoundrel or unprincipled person) *n.*: **blackguard**. See *scoundrel*

villainous (as in wicked) *adj.*: **flagitious**. See *wicked*

(2) villainous *adj.*: **malefic**. See *evil*

(3) villainous *adj.*: **malevolent**. See *evil*

vindication (finding . . . through testimony of others) *n.*: **compurgation**. See *acquittal*

vindictive (one who is . . .) *n.*: **tricoteuse**. See *knitter*. [See the note at "knitter" for why this word can be synonymous with vindictive.]

vinegar *n.*: **acetum**. ❖ The other simple pleasure Casanova extols repeatedly is salad. He would add anchovies and hard-boiled eggs to the green leaves and then dress them with olive oil (from Lucca, if possible) and herb-flavoured vinegar (he favoured a brand called **acetum** quattuor latronum—"four thieves vinegar"). (Matthew Sturgis, Food and Drink: "Darling, I Eat Your Hair—Casanova's Voracious Appetite Was Not Confined to the Bedroom," *Daily Telegraph* [London], 5/30/1998.)

vintage (wine of superior quality) *n.*: **supernaculum**. See *wine*

violence (initiate . . .) *v.i.*: **aggress**. See *fight*

violent (in the manner of an oppressive and despotic organization) *adj.*: **jackbooted**. See *oppressive*

(2) violent (spectacle in which shame, degradation, or harm is inflicted on a person, often for the enjoyment of onlookers) *n.*: **Roman holiday**. See *spectacle*

VIP (in a field or organization) *n.*: **wallah**. See *notable*

(2) VIP (or self-important person or official) *n.*: **high muck-a-muck** (or **high-muck-a-muck**). See *bigwig*

(3) VIP (or self-important person or official) *n.*: **panjandrum**. See *bigwig*

(4) VIP *n.*: **padishah**. See *emperor*

(5) VIP *n.*: **nabob**. See *bigwig*

(6) VIP *n.*: **satrap**. See *bigwig*

virginal *adj.*: **vestal**. See *chaste*

virgin birth *n.*: **parthenogenesis**. [This word is used in the biblical sense and, even more frequently, when referring to the animal world.] ❖ [Was Jesus born of the Virgin Mary?] [W]e know that the word translated as "virgin," namely *almah*, means only "a young woman." In any case, **parthenogenesis** is not possible for human mammals, and even if this law were relaxed in just one case, it would not prove that the resulting infant had any divine power. (Christopher Hitchens, *God Is Not Great*, Twelve Books/Hachette [2007], p. 115.)

Virgin Mary (worship of . . .) *n*.: **mariolatry**. ❖ An authoritarian who believed that world Catholicism should be rigidly controlled from the Vatican, [Pope Pius XII] was in the tradition of the despotic popes, whose ranks include Pius IX, Pius X and the present incumbent [John Paul II]. All these authoritarians vigorously promoted **mariolatry** in all its forms; the Virgin Mary has always been used as an anti-liberal or anti-communist icon. (Frank McLynn, Books: "A Pontiff Stripped of His Lies," *Independent on Sunday*, 9/26/1999.)

virile (relating to or concerned with being . . .) *adj*.: **priapic**. See *manly*

virtue (lit. humanity; often used in the sense of decency) *n*.: **menschlichkeit** [German, Yiddish]. See *decency*

(2) **virtue** (personal . . . , as in honor) *n*.: **izzat** [Hindi]. See *honor*

(3) **virtue** *n*.: **probity**. See *integrity*

visible (everything . . . in one view) *adj*.: **panoptic**. ❖ Now [Jerome, Arizona,] is a sun-dappled conglomeration of large wooden homes with sunporches, steep stone stairways, charming restaurants, and **panoptic** views of Sycamore Canyon and the Mogollon Rim. (Brad Gooch, "Red Rocks West," *Harper's Bazaar*, 10/1/1995, p. 159.)

vision (having poor . . . , as in nearly blind) *adj*.: **purblind**. See *blind*

(2) **vision** (loss of . . .) *n*.: **amaurosis**. See *blindness*

visionary *n*.: **fantast**. ❖ Stars, Dream Factory a **Fantast** Plot? . . . [D]raw near and listen closely as officials in both Nassau and Suffolk hype their vision of Long Island's newest industry. The movie industry is big business, and officials in Nassau and Suffolk Counties want to capture Hollywood's eye with proposals for an outside-the-filmway studio. (Jessica Kowal, Eye on Long Island: "The Industry Scene," *Newsday*, 1/22/1995.)

(2) **visionary** *adj*.: **fey**. See *clairvoyant*

visitor (as in foreigner, from another country or place) *n*.: **outlander**. See *foreigner*

visualize (as in to conceive of or form an image

of) *v.t.*: **ideate**. ❖ Because I like reporting better than **ideating** I try as often as I can to let the reporting generate the idea. People frequently ask, "Where do you get your ideas from?" There's no simple answer. (Sydney H. Schanberg, "The Best Ideas Come from Your Bones," *Newsday*, 8/20/1993.)

vitality (as in energy coupled with a will to succeed) *n*.: **spizzerinctum**. See *energy*

(2) **vitality** (lack of . . . from having no energy or nourishment) *n*.: **inanition**. See *exhaustion*

(3) **vitality** (lacking . . .) *adj*.: **bovine**. See *sluggish*

(4) **vitality** (lacking . . .) *adj*.: **logy**. See *sluggish*

(5) **vitality** *n*.: **brio**. See *energy*

vocabulary *n*.: **lexicon**. ❖ The Godfather did more than hit it big. It became a part of the American **lexicon**, the source of catch-phrases still in use more than a quarter of a century later—for example, "I made him an offer he couldn't refuse." (Harry Levins, "Puzo Hour Equals 35 Minutes," *St. Louis Post-Dispatch*, 7/28/1996.)

(2) **vocabulary** *n*.: **word-hoard**. ❖ Some writers [when giving speeches] conserve their **word-hoard** like squirrels preparing for winter, but [Martin] Amis gives as good value in person as he does on the page. (Allison Pearson, "Martin Amis: Allison Pearson Strips Away the Hype and Finds a Clever, Funny Human," *Daily Telegraph* [London], 10/4/1997.)

(3) **vocabulary** (of or relating to) *adj*.: **lexical**. See *words*

(4) **vocabulary** (specialized . . . or speech used by a particular group) *n*.: **argot**. See *vernacular*

(5) **vocabulary** (used by members of the underworld or a particular group) *n*.: **cant**. See *vernacular*

vociferous (and boisterous) *adj*.: **strepitous**. See *loud*

vogue (not in . . .) *adj*.: **démodé** [French]. See *outmoded*

voice (loss of . . . due to disease, injury, or psychological causes) *n*.: **aphonia**. See *laryngitis*

(2) voice (which is full and rich) *adj.*: **orotund**. See *sonorous*

voices (fear of or aversion to . . .) *n.*: **phonophobia**. See *fear*

volatile (potentially . . . place or situation) *n.*: **tinderbox**. See *explosive*

volcanic (eruption) *adj.*: **pelean** (sometimes cap.). ❖ **Pelean** volcanoes are named for Mt. Pelee, which exploded in Martinique in 1902 and killed 36,000 people. Instead of spitting fiery lava, which flows at less than a mile a day, **Pelean** volcanoes explode in deadly avalanches of superheated gas, steam and rocks—called pyroclastic flows, literally "fiery rocks"—that roar down the slopes at speeds up to 100 m.p.h. (Bob Drogin, "Mt. Pinatubo: Scientists' Countdown to Eruption," *Los Angeles Times*, 6/27/1991.)

volcano (landslide from . . .) *n.*: **lahar**. ❖ Huge **lahar** building on Mt Ruapehu . . . A HUGE mudslide that threatens to wipe out bridges, roads and power pylons is building on Mt Ruapehu. (Jon Morgan, "Huge Lahar Building on Mt. Ruapehu," *Dominion* [Wellington, New Zealand], 4/12/2001.)

volcanos (study of) *n.*: **volcanology**. ❖ For University of Oregon geology professor Kathy Cashman, Mount St. Helens picked a horrible time to get lively. The southwestern Washington volcano is the reason Cashman chose **volcanology** as a career, and she studied the 1980–86 eruptions there long after others lost interest. But she has missed the recent spell of activity while on sabbatical in Italy. (Scott Maben, "Scientist Returns to Familiar Volcano," *Eugene [OR] Register-Guard*, 10/10/2004.)

volition (mental process marked by . . . to do something) *n.*: **conation**. See *determination*

voluntary (as in optional) *adj.*: **facultative**. See *optional*

voluptuous (woman, often with stately or regal bearing) *adj.*: **Junoesque** [after ancient Roman goddess Juno, wife of Jupiter]. ❖ After rejections from countless modeling agencies, [Anna Nicole Smith was selected to be in *Playboy* magazine]. Her **Junoesque** appeal led straight to a three-year contract with Guess? "I always wanted to get back to be smaller than I was," she says. "But I just couldn't. Now I feel very good about it, and I wouldn't change my figure for anything." (*People*, "Anna Nicole Smith Is Livin' Large and Loving It," 9/20/1993, p. 76.)

(2) voluptuous (as in busty) *adj.*: **bathycolpian**. See *busty*

(3) voluptuous (young woman) *n.*: **houri** [French]. See *woman*

(4) voluptuous (as in busty) *adj.*: **hypermammiferous**. See *busty*

vomit (make an effort to . . . , by retching) *v.i.*: **keck**. ❖ [T]hrowing up has been a relief for moviemakers since before *The Exorcist*. . . . And while the blueberry pie barf-athon in 1986's *Stand by Me* is memorable, it is the rotund Mr. Creosote . . . in Monty Python's 1983 comedy epic *The Meaning of Life* who remains the **kecking** king. [Note that "keck" refers to making the effort to vomit as opposed to vomiting itself, but although this example is not technically accurate, the concept is clear.] (*Entertainment Weekly*, "Hurls, Hurls, Hurls!" 7/31/1998.)

vomiting (act of . . .) *n.*: **emesis**. ❖ Michigan: Of patients who received marijuana, 71.1 percent reported results ranging from no **emesis** at all to moderate nausea and increased appetite. About 90 percent chose to continue using marijuana as an anti-nausea therapy. (Barbara Yost, "The Straight Dope/Don't Expect Your Physician to Say 'Smoke Two Joints, and Call Me in the Morning,'" *Arizona Republic*, 1/7/1999.)

(2) vomiting (an agent which causes . . .) *n.*: **emetic**. ❖ Of course, there are people who can and do stick to diets religiously (quite literally, in some cases), but the rest of us will do anything to try to cheat the system. . . . Then, if I had a pound for every laxative, **emetic**, diuretic, anorectic or amphetamine swallowed in the cause of weight loss, I shouldn't need to be writing this article. (Rose Shepherd, "Slim Chance," *Independent* [London], 1/11/1997.)

voodoo *n.*: **necromancy**. See *black magic*

voracious *adj.*: **edacious**. ❖ [W]e were privy to

a bloodbath between two women (the daughters of Muhammad Ali and Joe Frazier) the run-up to which benefitted from a healthy dose of media hype.... [My friend] thinks it's admirable that Laila Ali and Jacqui Frazier-Lyde went after each other, took loads of punches, earned six figures in prize money apiece and were greeted by an **edacious** and fawning media. (Bonnie Erbe, "Progress for Women Will Not Be Found in the Ring or a Shoe Box," *Ventura County Star*, 6/20/2001.)

(2) voracious (as in hungry) *adj.*: **esurient**. See *hungry*

vote (direct . . . where electorate exercises right of self-determination) *n.*: **plebiscite**. See *election*

voyage (difficult or painful . . .) *n.*: **via dolorosa**. See *ordeal*

voyeurism (as in desire to look at erotic scenes or images) *n.*: **scopophilia**. ❖ "In studies of **scopophilia** made in Denmark in the 1970's, twice as many men as women reported experiencing excitement from the visual pleasure of watching heterosexually pornographic materials, 22% of the men as opposed to the 11% of the women." (*Literature Film Quarterly*, "Shakespeare, Zeffirelli and the Homosexual Gays," 10/1/92.)

vulgar *adj.*: **meretricious**. ❖ "We didn't copyright the X [movie rating]," Valenti says. "So it was pilfered by pornographers. It became so soiled and tainted that the X became synonymous with the most tawdry and **meretricious** kind of work." (Marshall Fine, "My, How the Movies Have Changed: 25 Years after *Midnight Cowboy*," Gannett News Service, 2/24/1994.)

(2) vulgar (and abusive woman) *n.*: **fishwife**. See *woman*

(3) vulgar (compulsive . . . behavior) *n.*: **copropraxia**. See *obscene*

(4) vulgar *adj.*: **fescennine**. See *obscene*

vulnerable (person or thing): *n.*: **clay pigeon**. ❖ [I]t was the same season that [Indianapolis Colts defensive end Dwight] Freeney finally grew tired of soccer, or at least grew frustrated from facing the incessant barrage of shots while acting as the uniformed **clay pigeon** in the Bloomfield goal. When he finally did make his way to the football field, the attraction wasn't just the game, but the fact that his brother Hugh was the starting quarterback. (Kevin Dupont, "Holding Up His End," *Boston Herald*, 1/16/2005.)

(2) vulnerable (as in a journey or passage, with dangers on both sides) *idiom*: **between Scylla and Charybdis**. See *precarious*

waffle (as in avoid a straight answer) *v.t.*: **tergiversate**. See *evade*

wages *n.*: **emolument**. ❖ [Baseball's umpires] . . . backed themselves into a corner [by resigning en masse], and baseball is letting them have exactly what they deserve [by accepting the resignations]. It obviously has taken them completely by surprise, but they have just learned that they are not irreplaceable and that their **emoluments** are not entitlements. (Jonathan Yardley, "Victimization Strikes Out," *Washington Post*, 8/2/1999.)

waiflike *adj.*: **gamine** [French]. ❖ Everywhere else it may be the year of the woman. But in fashion, this is the year of the waif. Models like Claudia Schiffer, Christy Turlington, Naomi Campbell and Linda Evangelista—the glamour amazons with their hyper hair, teeth and curves—are being edged out by a budding crop of **gamines**—wan, wistful, doe-eyed and as thin as adolescent boys. (Tracy Achor Hayes, "The Waif of the Future," *St. Louis Post-Dispatch*, 7/29/1993.)

wail (in lament for the dead) *v.i.*: **keen**. ❖ When word spread through the convent, recalls one nun, "Everybody rushed to [the Mother Teresa's] room. They were all around her, wailing and hugging the Mother's body." The sisters' **keening** was heard by the communists, whose party headquarters are next door, and they tipped off journalists that Teresa had died. (Tim McGirk, *Religion: "'Our Mother Is Gone!'"* In a Lavish Ceremony That Mother Teresa Would Have Scorned, Calcutta and the Rest of the World Bid a Touching Farewell to an Angel of Mercy," *Time* International, 9/22/1997, p. 54.)

(2) wail *v.i.*: **ululate**. ❖ "They guided and helped Mossad elements in the assassination of my husband," [Fathia Shkaki] told reporters at Damascus Airport soon after her late husband's body arrived on a special Tunisian aircraft. She **ululated** as the coffin, wrapped in a Palestinian flag, was taken off the plane. (Jon Immanuel, "Shkaki to Be Buried Today," *Jerusalem Post*, 11/1/1995.)

(3) wail (like a cat in heat) *v.i.*: **caterwaul**. See *screech*

wailing (in Irish folklore, female spirit who predicts death by . . .) *n.*: **banshee**. ❖ He came over, did Sean McDonald, in 1976. He came here with his parents and his brother, John, from Dublin, where only once did the **banshee** wail into the night to announce the death of a cop. (Jimmy Breslin, "He Came from Ireland to Hear a Banshee in Bronx," *Newsday*, 3/17/1994.)

waiting (as in anticipatory) *adj.*: **prevenient**. See *anticipatory*

walk (around something, esp. as part of a ritual) *v.t.*: **circumambulate**. ❖ On a snowy morning, prayer beads in his hand, the king of Lo is **circumambulating** his walled city, Lo Monthang. (Claudia Glenn Dowling, "Isolated in the Himalayas for Centuries, the Fabled Kingdom of Lo Finally Opens Its Gates to the Modern World: The Last Days of Shangri-La," *Life*, 2/1/1993, p. 78.)

(2) walk (a slow, leisurely . . .) *n.*: **paseo**. See *stroll*

(3) walk (affectedly to attract attention) *v.i.*: **tittup**. See *strut*

(4) walk (esp. as in roam or wander) *v.t., v.i.*: **perambulate**. See *roam*

(5) walk (esp. as in roam or wander) *v.t., v.i.*: **peregrinate**. See *roam*

walker (as in one who strolls through city streets idly or aimlessly) *n.*: **flâneur** [French]; (wandering *n.*: **flânerie**). See *wanderer*

walking (faster and faster involuntarily) *n.*: **festination**. ❖ In **festination**, the person takes short steps, barely clearing the ground. As walking continues, the steps become progressively rapid, almost to the point of a loping gait. **Festination** is one sign of Parkinson's disease. (Dr. Paul Donohue, "Festination: Warning Sign of Parkinson's Disease," *St. Louis Post-Dispatch*, 12/15/1995.)

(2) walking (of . . . with soles of feet entirely on the ground, as humans and bears do) *adj.*: **plantigrade**. ❖ I'm just about to stick my head out [of the tent] to take a peek when Mar-ian blows her nose loudly. The next sound we hear is that of stampeding **plantigrade** feet. Charlie follows the tracks in the dew, and reports that the cubs fled for hundreds of yards out of sight. "Bears don't like to be surprised," Maureen explains. (Paul Rauber, "Running with Bears," *Sierra*, 3/1/1999.)

(3) walking *idiom*: **shank's mare** (or **shank's pony**). [This term is Scottish and dates from the eighteenth century, when "shank" was another word for "shin." Beyond that, however, the derivation of the term is obscure, though usage is not uncommon today.] ❖ Arthur Cotton Moore is the latest to refer to the "closing" of Pennsylvania Avenue in front of the White House That most famous American street is not closed; only motorized vehicles are excluded. If Mr. Moore and others who share his feelings would get out of their vehicles and try **shank's mare** for transportation, they would find an environment that is pleasant, urban and fully consistent with its historic setting. (Robert Morris, "The Avenue Is Open," *Washington Post*, 2/10/1996.)

(4) walking (about) *adj.*: **ambulant** (*v.i.*: **ambulate**, *adj.*: **ambulatory**). See *moving*

walkout (on basis of alleged sickness, esp. by policemen) *n.*: **blue flu**. See *sickout*

wall (as in a low, temporary, quickly built fortification) *n.*: **breastwork**. See *fortification*

wan (and often sickly) *adj.*: **etiolated**. See *pale*

(2) wan (as from absence of sunlight) *adj.*: **etiolated**. See *pale*

(3) wan (as in pale or corpselike) *adj.*: **cadaverous**. See *corpselike*

wander (about, esp. on foot) *v.t.*, *v.i.*: **perambulate**. See *roam*

(2) wander (about, esp. on foot) *v.t.*, *v.i.*: **peregrinate**. See *roam*

(3) wander (aimlessly) *v.i.*: **maunder**. See *roam*

(4) wander (compulsion to . . . or travel) *n.*: **dromomania**. See *travel*

(5) wander (from the subject) *v.i.*: **divagate**. See *digress*

wanderer (as in one who strolls through city streets idly or aimlessly) *n.*: **flâneur** [French] (idling *n.*: **flânerie**). ❖ All that is missing from a footloose, fanciful exhibit in Bonn of nearly 1,000 shoes is Cinderella's glass slipper and a donation from the Imelda Marcos collection. . . . "My ideal viewer," [said the show's creator], "is a **flâneur**, a Charles Baudelaire sauntering down a boulevard, enjoying its glamour." (Emily Mitchell, Sightings: Dance/United States, *Time* International, 1/3/1994, p. 55.)

wandering (as in digressive) *adj.*: **excursive**. See *digressive*

want (as in need or require) *v.t.*: **desiderate**. ❖ Keynes was quite dismissive of governments and government-controlled central banks from this point of view. He argued that "it is natural, after what we have experienced, that prudent people should **desiderate** a standard of value which is independent of finance ministers and state banks." (Philip Arestis, "The Independence of Central Banks: A Nonconventional Perspective," *Journal of Economic Issues*, 3/1/1995, p. 161.)

(2) want (as in strong craving) *n.*: **avidity**. See *craving*

(3) want (slight or faint . . .) *n.*: **velleity**. See *hope*

(4) want (strong . . . , as in craving) *n.*: **appetence**. See *craving*

wanting (esp. something one once had but has no more) *n.*: **desiderium**. See *longing*

(2) wanting (strongly) *adj.*: **appetent** (*n.*: **appetence**). See *desirous*

(3) wanting *adj.*: **athirst**. See *eager*

wanton (as in lewd or lustful) *adj.*: **lickerish**. See *lustful*

(2) wanton (as in lewd or lustful) *adj.*: **lubricious**. See *lewd*

war (engaged in a . . . , as in struggle) *adj.*: **agonistes**. See *struggle*

(2) war (or relating to or suggesting) *adj.*: **martial**. See *warlike*

ward off *v.t.*: **forfend**. See *avert*

warfare (marked by a lack of aggression or progress) *n.*: **sitzkrieg**. ❖ One of the draft resolutions Congress considered but did not pass last week called on President Bush to postpone military action against Iraq and give sanctions time to work. . . . [However,] Saudi Arabia, Egypt and Syria are nervous about keeping so many U.S. troops in the region indefinitely. The entire coalition could come unglued if the **sitzkrieg** continues much longer. (Bruce W. Nelan, The Gulf: "Can Sanctions Still Do the Job? Given Time, the Embargo Would Cripple Iraq, But That Does Not Mean Saddam Would Pull Out of Kuwait," *Time*, 1/21/1991, p. 40.)

warlike *adj.*: **martial**. ❖ There is a ridiculously **martial** air to all this [turkey hunting]. Guns slung, head nets smashed around our necks, camo boat cushions banging into the backs of our knees, we walk singlefile back up along the treeline, away from the forested hill. (Guy Martin, "Operation Turkey," *Sports Afield*, 12/1/1995, p. 143.)

(2) warlike (as in belief that political power is best achieved through use of force) *n.*: **machtpolitik** [German]. See *politics*

(3) warlike *adj.*: **bellicose**. See *belligerent*

warm (and cozy) *adj.*: **gemütlich** [German]. See *cozy*

(2) warm (as in genial and pleasant) *adj.*: **sympathique** [French]. See *genial*

(3) warm (as in of or relating to dog days of summer) *adj.*: **canicular**. See *dog days*

warmed-over (food or old material) *n.*, *adj.*: **rechauffé** [French]. ❖ John Barton's entertainment by, and about, the kings, queens and notables of England has always had a considerable charm in its 40-year history. But this current tour, presented by Duncan C. Weldon and Paul Elliott (men who do much to ensure quality theatre is kept alive in this country), has a kind of **rechauffé** feel to it, as though it has been warmed up from the production scene last year in Stratford. (Richard Edmonds, Culture—Review: "Sinden Is a Storyteller Supreme," *Birmingham Post*, 9/10/2003.)

warmth (as in cordiality) *n.*: **empressement** [French]. See *cordiality*

warning (serving as a . . . or alarm) *adj.*: **apos-emetic**. [This term is used especially with regard to certain animals whose coloration warns would-be predators of their poisonous properties, as in the phrase "aposematic coloring."] ❖ Being poisonous doesn't help them survive if they've already become a meal, so they advertise their toxicity. It doesn't take hungry animals with color vision long to learn the color code for "nasty." . . . The commonest creatures with **aposematic** coloring are bees, wasps and yellow jackets, and "there are fleets of flies and beetles that look like yellow jackets," Poulson said. (K. O. Dawes, "Toxic Animals Come with Warning Labels," *Chicago Sun-Times*, 11/8/1992).

(2) warning *n.*: **alarum**. ❖ Here we go again. No sooner had the Senate, despite the nearly universal predictions to the contrary, passed the campaign finance reform bill than the **alarums** and dirges about its fate recommenced. Tom DeLay would fight it in the House! (Elizabeth Drew, "McCain's Baby; Opposing Campaign Reform Won't Be Easy This Time Around," *Washington Post*, 5/8/2001.)

(3) warning (as in alarm bell) *n.*: **tocsin**. See *alarm*

(4) warning (as in suggesting the use of force to settle an issue or argument) *n.*: **argumentum ad baculum** [Latin]. See *threat*

(5) warning (as in threat, which is empty or harmless) *n.*: **brutum fulmen** [Latin]

(6) warning (audio . . .) *n.*: **klaxon**. See *signal*

(7) warning (as in word to the wise) *phr.*: **verbum sap** [Latin]. See *word to the wise*

warped (as in twisted) *adj.*: **tortile**. See *twisted*

warranted (esp. in reference to a punishment) *adj.*: **condign**. See *deserved*

wart *n.*: **verruca**. ❖ The son has a whopping great **verruca**, which is so far resisting everything me and the pharmacist on the corner are throwing at it. So, when the colleague presents me with a [concoction], I take it home and present it to the son, who whips off his sock and in his eagerness to get rid of the **verruca**, manages to pour most of the liquid onto the bedroom carpet. (*Daily Post*, "Inside Out," 12/17/2002.)

warts (of, relating to, or resembling) *adj.*: **verrucous**. ❖ Sometimes the condition [crusted scabies] causes scaly, **verrucous**-like plaques that cover large areas anywhere on the body. (Chet Scerra, "Scabies: Tips for Diagnosing and Cautions about Treatment," *Modern Medicine*, 3/1/1996, p. 27.)

wary (as in watchful, person) *n.*: **Argus**. See *watchful*

wash (as in cleanse) *v.t., v.i.*: **depurate**. See *cleanse*

washing (like detergent) *v.t.*: **detersive**. See *cleansing*

(2) washing (of the body) *n.*: **ablution**. See *cleansing*

wasps (of, relating to, or resembling) *adj.*: **vespine**. ❖ August is a truly dreadful month for those who write daily for a living. I have too often written laudatorily of the only citizen whose season it is, the common wasp, to be comfortable doing it yet again. What could I do to ease the unbearable burden of writing through the full month of August, and also spare the world yet another column of winsomely **vespine** musings? (Kevin Myers, An Irishman's Diary, *Irish Times*, 9/6/2000.)

waste (parts, esp. from an animal) *n.*: **offal**. ❖ This is a preliminary list of European products that the United States is threatening with 100% tariffs in a dispute with the European Union over hormone-treated beef. . . . Edible **offal** of bovine animals, swine, sheep, goats, horses, etc., fresh, chilled or frozen. (*USA Today*, "Preliminary 100% Tariff Targets," 3/23/1999.) See *trash*

(2) waste (as in printed material that is trivial) *n.*: **bumf** [British]. See *junk*

(3) waste (away) *n., v.i.*: **atrophy**. See *wither*

(4) waste (from the body) *n.*: **egesta**. See *excrement*

(5) waste (matter) *n.*: **dross**. See *trash*

(6) waste (or squander something) *v.t.*: **fribble**. See *squander*

waste time (as in hesitate to act due to indecision) *v.i.*: **dither**. See *procrastinate*

(2) waste time (as in procrastinate or hesitate to act) *v.i.*: **shilly-shally**. See *procrastinate*

wasting (of the body resulting from chronic disease) *n.*: **cachexia**. ❖ Despite its legacy of tragic birth defects in newborn infants 30 years ago, thalidomide is showing encouraging signs of being a potent weapon against a variety of ailments, including . . . the AIDS-associated wasting disorder, **cachexia**. (Robert Cooke, "Thalidomide: A Nasty Drug Changes Its Spots: Once Linked with Tragic Birth Defects, It Now May Help Fight Other Serious Health Problems," *Newsday*, 6/14/1994.)

(2) wasting (of child's body due to malnourishment) *n.*: **marasmus**. See *malnourishment*

wasting away (progressive . . .) *adj.*: **tabescent**. ❖ While others were indulging in preemptive fumbles behind the Ruddington Methodist Chapel, . . . I was inhabiting a sensual desert, refreshed only by the occasional trip up Mickleborough Hill where, beneath the roots of a **tabescent** sycamore tree, I had buried . . . a copy of *Parade* magazine with an interesting artistic feature on Cyd Charisse's legs. (Michael Bywater, "Believe It or Not: I Was a Teenage Toy Boy Too," *Independent on Sunday*, 8/10/1997.)

(2) wasting away (esp. as to children as a result of malnutrition) *adj.*: **marasmic**. See *emaciated*

watch (as in on the . . .) *n.*: **on the qui vive** idiom. See *lookout*

(2) watch (esp. for changes in trends) *n.*: **weather eye** (esp. as in "keep a weather eye"). See *lookout*

(3) watch (over students taking an examination) *v.i.*: **invigilate**. See *proctor*

watchdog *n.*: **Cerberus** [derives from the three-headed dog assigned to guard the entrance to Hades in Greek mythology]. ❖ *American Playhouse*, the public television dramatic series . . . provides PBS with 12 programs a year, which makes it the nation's most prolific independent film outlet, not to mention a sort of cultural watchdog in the hellish world of commercial film making—**Cerberus** at the gates of Hollywood. (Bruce Weber, Television: "Big Movies on Little Budgets," *New York Times*, 05/17/1992.)

watches (science of making . . . or clocks) *n.*: **horology**. See *time*

watchful (person) *n.*: **Argus**. [Derives from the giant in Greek mythology who had 100 eyes and was made guardian of the land of Io. It is sometimes used as an adjective, as in "Argus-eyed."] ❖ [Actor Gregg Thomas] is often described as a physical actor. Off stage, he strides with a bounding gait. He watches people with **Argus** eyes, keenly observant, vigilant. (Elizabeth Cronin, "Leading Man—This Seattle Actor Has Paid His Dues to Get Starring, Challenging Roles," *Seattle Times*, 9/16/1990.)

water (containing . . . , esp. crystallized) *adj.*: **hydrous**. ❖ [T]hermodynamic data suggest that ice in contact with anhydrous minerals like those in Apollo and Luna soil samples will eventually react, forming **hydrous** minerals in which the constituents of water are chemically bound into the mineral crystals. (A. B. Binder, "No Ice on the Moon?" *Science*, 7/23/1999.)

(2) water (of or relating to moving . . . , such as rivers, streams, and springs) *adj.*: **lotic**. Dams alter the physical, chemical, and biological attributes of rivers by blocking the movement of fishes, converting **lotic** habitats to lentic [still-water] habitats, altering the flow regime, and increasing siltation upstream from and scouring downstream from the dam. (Jeremy Tiemann, "Effects of Lowhead Dams on Freshwater Mussels in the Neosho River, Kansas," *Transactions of the Kansas Academy of Science*, 10/1/2002.)

(3) water (of or relating to still . . . , such as lakes, ponds, dams, and swamps) *adj.*: **lentic**. ❖ The great barred frog was also found across a large range of stream sizes as well as at **lentic** water bodies such as dams. (Wendy Pyper, "The Great Frog Survey," *Ecos*, 1/1/2003.)

(4) water (of or relating to underground . . .) *n.*: **phreatic**. ❖ The first scare occurred on Tuesday, July 18th, when what the volcanologists term a "**phreatic** eruption"—a steam

explosion caused by the interaction between molten rock material or very hot solid rock and groundwater—set off fears that a major eruption was imminent. (George John, "In the Shadow of a Volcano," *Caribbean Today*, 7/31/1996.)

(5) water (of or occurring in . . . such as lakes or ponds) *adj.*: **limnetic**. ❖ In all, [The Nature Conservatory] has about a thousand preserves scattered throughout the country. The smallest, half an acre, is on Scotia Lake Island, near Schenectady, N.Y., and has a good but tiny bit of undisturbed **limnetic** woodland. (Bil Gilbert, "The Nature Conservancy Game," *Sports Illustrated*, 10/20/1986, p. 86.)

(6) water (of, like, or relating to) *adj.*: **aqueous**. ❖ The largest reservoir in northeastern Colorado at 6.5 miles long, it offers retirees—and unretirees, for that matter—a number of **aqueous** activities, such as boating and swimming. (James B. Meadow, "End of the Rainbow for Many, the Golden Years Lie in Fort Collins," *Denver Rocky Mountain News*, 6/7/1999.)

(7) water (pure . . .) *n.*: **aqua pura**. ❖ As the global population expands, putting pressure on the limited supply of clean freshwater, more armed conflict over who gets access to **aqua pura** seems inevitable. (Michael S. Serrill, Water: "Wells Running Dry, Rampant Waste and Pollution of Our Most Vital Resource Create a Crisis That Could Lead to Future Armed Conflicts," *Time* International, 11/1/1997, p. 16.)

(8) water (of or relating to, as in the sea or ocean) *adj.*: **thalassic**. See *sea*

(9) water (consisting of . . . and land) *adj.*: **terraqueous**. See *land*

(10) water (fear or dread of . . .) *n.*: **hydrophobia**. See *fear*

(11) water (of or relating to hot . . .) *adj.*: **hydrothermal**. See *hot water*

water bank (of or relating to a . . .) *adj.*: **riparian**. ❖ Most states also enforced **riparian** law, which provides that all who have property abutting a waterway or body of water have the right to normal use of the water, but may not reduce its use and enjoyment by others and downstream users. (Roger Meiners, "Get the Government Out of Environmental Control," *USA Today Magazine*, 5/1/1996.)

watercolor *n.*: **aquarelle** [French]. ❖ It was Dali's **aquarelle** Sun King, which he painted half a century ago as an expression of his admiration for Louis XIV, that inspired the fragrance of the same name. (Greer Fay Cashman, "The Sweet Smell of Summer," *Jerusalem Post*, 8/28/1997.)

watered-down *adj.*: **anodyne**. See *bland*

waterfall (very large or high . . .) *n.*: **cataract**. ❖ The roar of the plunging cascade and the fine spray that rises 500 m above Victoria Falls are aptly captured in the great **cataract's** local tribal name, mosioatunya—the smoke that thunders. (Peter Hawthorne, Environment: "Too Many Trips to the Falls—The Battle Is On to Save Africa's Great Scenic Wonder from the Ravages of a Tourist Boom," *Time* International, 7/1/1996, p. 40.)

watery (eyes or runny nose) *adj.*: **rheumy**. ❖ He always had a flamboyantly coloured silk handkerchief tucked into one sleeve so he could make regular dabs at his **rheumy** eyes. (Val McDermid, *A Place of Execution,* St. Martin's Press [2000], p. 221.)

(2) watery (as in full of puddles) *adj.*: **plashy**. See *puddles*

wavelength (on the same . . .) *adj.*: **simpatico**. See *compatible*

waver (as in indecisive) *adj., v.i., n.*: **shilly-shally**. See *vacillate*

wavering (as in chronic inability to make decisions) *n.*: **abulia** (or **aboulia**). See *indecisiveness*

waves (resembling . . . in appearance or motion) *adj.*: **undulant**. ❖ Undoubtedly, doctors and dentists who have aquariums in their offices have instinctively sensed what recent research has shown: Concentrating on the **undulant** motion of fish and seaweed is relaxing and anxiety-reducing for patients. (Catherine Houck, "The 9 Best Ways to Destress," *Good Housekeeping*, 9/1/1995, p. 82.)

waving (as in bending or winding) *adj.*: **flexuous**. ❖ [In *Tales of Beatnik Glory*, Ed Sanders] chronicl[es] an anxious generation that sought strategic interment, an embunkered generation that found consolation and community within the magic space of a private urban zone, willing (indeed needing) to live not within the **flexuous** tensions of engagement but rather within the energizing logic of retreat and separation. His is a Beat generation not on the road but in the shelter. (Joseph Dewey, "Helter Shelter: Strategic Interment in *Tales of Beatnik Glory*," *Review of Contemporary Fiction*, 3/22/1999.)

way of speaking *n.*: **façon de parler** [French]. ❖ For Mr. Searle, the idea of the brain as computer remains . . . just a metaphor that can mistakenly be taken literally. [For example]: "The gastrointestinal tract is a highly intelligent organ. . . . [Although this is not of course literally true], the idea that the gut shows intelligent behavior is only a harmless **façon de parler** that is not likely to lead anyone into serious error. (Anthony Gottlieb, "The Lesson of the Drunk and the Streetlight," *New York Times*, 10/11/1992.)

weak (from loss or lack of body strength) *adj.*: **asthenic** (*n.*: **asthenia**). ❖ While it could be argued that [the Nissan Pathfinder is] understressed and thus promises longevity as well as requiring only 87-octane fuel, it looks rather **asthenic** compared to even such a six-cylinder as Jeep (195 hp/225 foot-pounds) or Blazer (190 hp/250 foot-pounds) offers. (Alan Vonderhaar, "When I Received the Nissan Pathfinder," Gannett News Service, 2/2/1999.)

(2) weak (and sickly person, esp. one morbidly concerned with his own health) *n., adj.*: **valetudinarian**. See *sickly*

(3) weak (as in ineffective) *adj.*: **feckless**. See *ineffective*

(4) weak (as in pale, and often sickly) *adj.*: **etiolated**. See *pale*

(5) weak (as in powerless) *adj.*: **impuissant**. See *powerless*

(6) weak (as in spineless or indecisive, or such a person) *adj., n.*: **namby-pamby**. See *spineless*

weaken (as in deprive of strength) *v.t.*: **geld**. ❖ [T]he great American middle class wants [federal programs left intact, including] its Social Security, its Medicare, its long-term care, its tax credits, [etc.] . . . Any unreconstructed conservative who threatens to take them away . . . does so at his peril. That is why conservatives have changed the subject. They have given up on the campaign to **geld** the federal government. (Jack Beatty, "How the GOP Went Wrong," *Washington Post*, 9/11/1994.)

(2) weaken (as in deprive of strength) *v.t.*: **enervate**. See *debilitate*

(3) weaken (in value, amount or degree) *v.t.*: **attenuate**. See *lessen*

weakened *adj.*: **etiolated** [The primary sense of this word is the weakened effect on a plant caused by depriving it of exposure to sunlight (which also accounts for this word meaning "pale"). However, it is also more generally used to refer to anything weakened or enfeebled.] ❖ [In 1996, the] gender war turned its attention from female victimhood to male identity crises, and by most accounts the male sperm-count dropped to little more than **etiolated** dribble. Estrogen fall-out was blamed, but it may well have been exacerbated by The Girlie Show. (Oliver Bennett, 1996: "The Year That Went Pop," *Independent* [London], 12/29/1996.)

(2) weakened (chronically . . . , as in fatigued) *adj.*: **neurasthenic**. See *fatigued*

weakening (esp. of moral principles or civil order) *n.*: **labefaction**. ❖ As a black minister in Washington, I know that it is iconoclastic for me to blame the general **labefaction** [of] the present D.C. administration [i.e., Marion Barry] for making a black and white coalition impossible. Washington is divided by race [and] it has become politically advantageous to maintain that division. (Kirk D. Monroe, letter to the editor, *Washington Post*, 5/21/1989.)

weak-minded (condition of being . . .) *n.*: **akrasia** [Greek]. See *weak-willed*

(2) weak-minded (state of being . . . , as in indecisiveness) *n.*: **abulia**. See *indecisiveness*

weak-willed (condition of being . . .) *n.*: **akrasia** (also **acrasia**) *adj.*: **akratic**. [This Greek word refers to a situation in which a person knows the best course of action to take yet is unable to take it because of a lack of willpower or self-control. It has been contrasted with the word "licentious" in the *Oxford Dictionary of Philosophy* as follows: "In contrast with the person suffering from akrasia, who feels the conflict yet succumbs to temptation, the licentious person is supposed to feel no conflict at all between low desire and the promptings of a better self or a higher reason. . . . It is thus more fun being licentious than being akratic."]. ❖ In fact, some attitudes that might be attributed to my purchase [of ice cream], e.g., I must desire to gain weight if I am opting for the hot fudge sundae, might be false (a competing desire won the mental battle or **akrasia** stepped in). Indeed, one cannot even infer that I am indifferent to gaining weight—perhaps I have made a deal with myself to skip dinner in exchange for this treat. (Kimberly Ferzan, "Opaque Recklessness," *Journal of Criminal Law and Criminology*, 3/22/2001.)

wealth (devotion to the pursuit of . . .) *n.*: **mammonism**. ❖ The survey revealed that **mammonism**, or the principle of the almighty dollar, is strong in Korea with 46 percent of those polled agreeing that money can buy happiness. (*Korea Times*, "44 Pct of Koreans Feel More Dejected After IMF," 2/21/1999.)

(2) wealth (source of great . . .) *n.*: **Golconda** [based on city in India where diamond mines were once located]. ❖ Harvard provides the Democrats with brainy talent. Hollywood delivers the glamour. But for money, there's no place like New York City's Upper East Side, especially ZIP code 10021, a **Golconda** of campaign cash for Democratic candidates. (W. John Moore, "Lobbying & Law: Mr. Gore's and Mr. Bradley's Neighborhood," *National Journal*, 8/14/1999.)

(3) wealth (study of or focus on . . . , esp. in artistic works) *n.*: **plutography**. ❖ **Plutography** is to money what pornography is to sex, explains the 56-year-old pioneer of the New Journalism [author Tom Wolfe], emphasizing that "today it is impossible to be too ostentatious." (R. Z. Sheppard, review of *The Bonfire of the Vanities*, by Tom Wolfe, *Time*, 11/9/1987, p. 101.)

(4) wealth (worship of or devotion to . . .) *n.*: **plutolatry**. ❖ When it comes time to choose a career, the majority of Harvard folk are unable to pose the crucial question to themselves: What can I do with my life that is existentially meaningful? . . . Hordes of people dedicate their lives to the ravenous chasing of money—a spiritually bankrupt **plutolatry**—as if money were anything other than a *means* to some end. (Jonathan Jacoby, *Anti-Social Behavior*, 11/4/1999.)

(5) wealth *n.*: **pelf**. ❖ The carrot isn't always monetary. In advertising, show business, and journalism, people work themselves to the nub for glitz and glory more than for **pelf**. (Ford S. Worthy, Executive Life: "You're Probably Working Too Hard," *Fortune*, 4/27/1987, p. 133.)

(6) wealth (of or relating to the gaining of . . .) *adj.*: **chrematistic**. See *monetary*

wealthy (and/or prominent person) *n.*: **nabob**. See *bigwig*

(2) wealthy (government by the . . .) *n.*: **plutocracy**. See *government*

(3) wealthy (government by the . . . , i.e., in proportion to wealth or property ownership) *n.*: **timocracy**. See *government*

wear (away by friction or scraping) *v.t.*: **abrade**. See *chafe*

weariness (as in tedium, of life) *n.*: **tedium vitae** [Latin]. See *tedium*

(2) weariness (from lack of energy or nourishment) *n.*: **inanition**. See *exhaustion*

wearing apparel *n.*: **raiment**. See *clothing*

wearying (as in laborious) *adj.*: **operose**. See *laborious*

weathervane *n.*: **girouette**. [French. This word is often used in a derogatory fashion to refer to someone whose opinion is always changing as the wind blows, as in the following example.] ❖ ADQ Leader Mario Dumont has weath-

ered Premier Jean Charest's name-calling in recent weeks, and says he doesn't take it to heart. . . . The Liberal premier has repeatedly called Dumont a **girouette**, saying he changes his opinions like a weather vane shifts with the wind. (CBC.ca, "Pig, Liar, Buffoon, Yes-man . . . Weather Vane?" 10/17/2007.)

wedding (of or relating to a . . .) *adj.*: **hymeneal**. ❖ The tasteful [Donald] Trump–[Marla] Maples nuptial ceremony took place last night. The low-key **hymeneal** rites were attended by all of Donald's and Marla's closest friends, with the exception of Mike Tyson, the pugilist, who was detained. (Sydney H. Schanberg, "Donald and Marla—This Is a Love Story?" *Newsday*, 12/21/1993.)

week *n.*: **hebdomad** (weekly) *adj.*: **hebdomadal**. ❖ Sadly, the vast majority of humanity, and even a large majority of Jews, do not have the time or the strength to remind themselves that they have a soul, a spirit. Shabbat could be a **hebdomadal** reminder of that, for if we observe it properly, we do not merely feed our bellies with those Shabbat delicacies, but we also feed that soul, that spirit. (Moshe Kohn, "How Judaism Trains Us to Achieve Spirituality," *Jerusalem Post*, 10/13/1995.)

weep (in lament for the dead) *v.i.*: **keen**. See *wail*

weeping (given to . . .) *adj.*: **larmoyant**. See *tearful*

(2) weeping (of or relating to) *adj.*: **lachrymal**. See *tears*

weepy *adj.*: **lachrymose**. See *tearful*

weight (or heaviness, esp. of a person) *n.*: **avoirdupois**. [This word is sometimes used in a neutral sense simply to refer to the weight a person carries, and sometimes is used to refer to a person being overweight.] ❖ In the ensuing two years Gibson blew up to more than 400 pounds as he ate an overabundance of fast foods, and he caught the eye of recruiters from Indiana, Purdue and Wisconsin, who detected the soul of an athlete beneath all the **avoirdupois**. (Tim Crothers, "Gibson Pruned His Weight to 371 and Blossomed into a Bulldozer of a Blocker Who Probably Will Be the First Lineman Taken in the NFL Draft," *Sports Illustrated*, 2/22/1999, p. 56.)

(2) weight (loss resulting from chronic disease) *n.*: **cachexia**. See *wasting*

weird (as in eccentric) *adj.*: **pixilated**. See *eccentric*

(2) weird (as in eerie) *adj.*: **eldritch**. See *eerie*

(3) weird (as in perplexing) *adj.*: **quisquous**. See *perplexing*

(4) weird (as in departing from the standard or norm) *adj.*: **heteroclite**. See *abnormal*

welfare (general . . . of the community) *n.*: **weal**. See *well-being*

(2) welfare (general . . . , as in well-being) *n.*: **commonweal**. See *well-being*

well-being (general . . .) *n.*: **commonweal**. ❖ It is a four-alarm national embarrassment that here, on the doormat of the 21st century, we're still debating whether and how to teach evolution to schoolchildren. No other developed country finds Darwin a menace to the **commonweal**. None of the major organized religions opposes the theory of evolution. (Curt Suplee, "Facts of Faith," *Washington Post*, 4/11/1999.)

(2) well-being *n.*: **weal**. [This word can be used in the sense of prosperity and happiness (often as in "weal or woe" or "weal and woe"), or in the sense of the general well-being of the community. The first example demonstrates the former sense and the second example demonstrates the latter.] ❖ Because we recognize that the **weal and woe** of others is as real as our own, we also recognize that factors bearing on their well-being should enter into our own practical accounting, albeit not with the same weighting that one's own good (and that of one's loved ones) carries. (Loren Lomasky, review of *Generosity: Virtue in Civil Society*, by Tibor Machin, *Reason*, 5/1/1998, p. 58.) ❖ Clinton campaigned for the presidency stressing themes that lie at the center of the new politics [columnist E. J.] Dionne favors—the intelligent use of government to

improve the public **weal**. (Ronald Radosh, review of *They Only Look Dead: Why Progressives Will Dominate the Next Political Era*, by E. J. Dionne, *Commentary*, 6/1/1996, p. 62.)

(3) well-being *n.*: **eudemonia** (or **eudaemonia**). See *happiness*

well-bred (esp. those aspiring or pretending to be . . .) *adj.*: **lace-curtain**. ❖ Every year, Vrdolyak, then the 10th Ward alderman and de facto mayor of Chicago, would open his home to politicians, tough guys with funny nicknames such as "Ox" and "Crazy Joe," and neighborhood people. It was the kind of party where bagmen would drink with iron workers and bankers. There were no **lace-curtain** pretensions at these parties. They were for drinking and eating and politics . . . (John Kass, "Vrdolyak Always a Good Judge of Power," *Chicago Tribune*, 5/11/2007.)

well-endowed (as in busty) *adj.*: **bathycolpian**. See *busty*

(2) well-endowed (as in busty) *adj.*: **hypermammiferous**. See *busty*

well-groomed *adj.*: **soigné** [French]. See *elegant*

well-informed (being . . . with or familiar with something) *adj.*: **au fait** [French]. See *familiar*

well-read (as in literary, community) *n.*: **republic of letters**. See *literary*

well-versed (being . . . with or familiar with something) *adj.*: **au fait** [French]. See *familiar*

welt (on the skin) *n.*: **weal**. ❖ Along with room attendants who burst in at inopportune moments, bed bugs are just one more essential component of these establishments and waking to find itchy red **weals** all over our bottoms is part and parcel of the experience. (Jeremy Atiyah, "Stop Trashing Bedbugs!" *Independent on Sunday*, 9/14/1997.)

werewolf (ability to assume characteristics of or delusion where one thinks one is a . . .) *n.*: **lycanthropy**. ❖ Once upon a time, in the gloriously disreputable days of *I Was a Teenage Werewolf* (1957) and *Werewolves on Wheels* (1971) and *I Married a Werewolf* (a/k/a *Werewolf in a Girl's Dormitory*, 1961) and *Face of* *the Screaming Werewolf* (1959), **lycanthropy** was strictly midnight fodder for the unwashed hordes of gore fans. (Kevin Jackson, Film: "The Werewolf as Social-Climber," *Independent*, 8/25/1994.)

(2) werewolf *n.:* **loup-garou** [French]. ❖ Looking for a model for a mythical, wolf-like **loup-garou**, he used a photograph of Tiffany, his black-and-white spaniel-terrier mix, who had died five years earlier. To convey the spirit of the ghostly **loup-garou**, Rodrigue painted Tiffany blue. (Michael J. Neill, Arts: "Howling Success: How Much Is That Doggy? If It's Blue, $150,000," *People*, 12/7/1992, p. 131.)

(3) werewolf *n.:* **lycanthrope**. ❖ By the time Michael Landon began attacking classmates in *I Was a Teenage Werewolf* (1957), the cinematic **lycanthrope** seemed on the verge of extinction. (*Entertainment Weekly*, "Werewolves? Everywhere! *Wolf* Joins a Pack of Monster Movies Gone Astray," 1/13/1995, p. 68.)

wet (as in like liquid or tending to become liquid) *adj.:* **liquescent**. See *liquid*

(2) wet (from rain) *adj.:* **pluvial** or **pluvious**. See *rain*

whim *n.:* **boutade** [French]. ❖ [On his new album,] Tori Kudo and his associates make skewed, strange and gentle music. At times the 41 tracks (many are mere **boutades**) recall [The Velvet Underground]. [H]alfway through, you're won over by his whimsy. (Luke Bainbridge, "The Next 15," *Observer*, 11/16/2003.)

(2) whim (as in notion that is odd, stubborn, or whimsical) *n.:* **crotchet**. See *notion*

whimper (or whine) *v.i.:* **pule**. ❖ The [President Clinton] impeachment fight had been over for weeks, the outcome clear as day: Senate Democrats would block conviction; House managers would whine and **pule** about how they were prevented from presenting a proper prosecution. (Michelle Cottle, "On The Hill: Played Out," *New Republic*, 3/1/1999.)

(2) whimper *v.i.:* **mewl**. ❖ Women are never so macho as when beauty is at stake. Show us a large cockroach and we're **mewling** sissies,

but bring out a pan of hot wax that's going right onto our flesh, and suddenly we're as tough and impassive as Arnold Schwarzenegger in *The Terminator*. (Lynn Snowden, "Beauty Hurts," *Harper's Bazaar*, 7/1/1995, p. 124.)

whine *v.i.:* **girn** [Scottish]. ❖ (Alan Cochrane, Comment: "We'll Have Only Ourselves to Blame but, Says Alan Cochrane, That Won't Stop His Fellow Scots '**Girning**' About the English," *Daily Telegraph*, 5/6/1999.)

whine *v.i.:* **pule**. See *whimper*

(2) whine (weakly) *v.i.:* **mewl**. See *whimper*

whining (as in complaining) *adj.:* **querulous**. See *peevish*

whip (generally used figuratively) *v.t.:* **larrup**. ❖ Andy Benes, who was **larruped**, 10-7, by the Giants in St. Louis, will take a 7-7 mark against them into Friday's series opener. (Sports Network, "St. Louis Cardinals Team Notes," 6/7/1996.)

(2) whip *n.,* (to flog with a . . .) *v.t.:* **knout**. [This was a whip used in imperial Russia.] ❖ George [H. W.] Bush took a terrible fall over the budget agreement. But so . . . did the Democratic leaders. Usually he does not equate himself with them. He allows his chief of staff, John H. Sununu, to treat members the way a 19th century Russian landowner treated the serfs. The premise is that the lout understands only the **knout**. (Mary McGrory, "Trouble on the Home Front," *Washington Post*, 10/11/1990.)

(3) whip *v.t.:* **flagellate**. See *criticize*

whipping (the soles of the feet with a stick as a form of punishment or torture) *n., v.t.:* **bastinado**. See *beating*

whirling *adj.:* **vortical**. ❖ [James] Dyson . . . set out to create a vacuum that doesn't lose suction. He says it took 5,127 prototypes to develop his concept of a spinning air stream that uses centrifugal force to extract dirt and debris. . . . He found that his **vortical** design removed even fine dust particles from the air, so almost none escaped to clog the motor fan or pollute the house. (Laura Fisher Kaiser, "Papa's Got a Brand-New Bagless," *Washington Post*, 2/20/2003.)

(2) whirling (or spiraling motion, often an ocean current) *n.*: **gyre**. See *spiraling*

whirlwind *n.*: **tourbillion**. ❖ Lemmer clips the larger windsock to the halyard, runs it up the flagpole a bit, then fastens the smaller sock on. He pulls the windsocks up the pole and ties the halyard to a cleat. The wind fills the socks and they become **tourbillions** of color; they are tornadoes devouring a crayon factory and turned on their sides. (Crocker Stevenson, "Kite Shop Offers Summer Answers That Are Blowing in the Wind," *Milwaukee Journal Sentinel*, 7/22/2004.)

whispered (said in . . . tones, not to be overheard) *adv., adj.*: **sotto voce**. ❖ On the subject of swings, the world's top golfers can be as gossipy as seventh-graders at a slumber party. So it is said, **sotto voce**, that Leonard doesn't hit the ball that well. (Ivan Maisel, Golf Plus/U.S. Open Preview, *Sports Illustrated*, 6/15/1998, p. G38.)

whispering (or rustling sound) *n.*: **susurrous**. ❖ [When my book, *Town without Rivers*, opens, Reka has] just gotten out of prison for killing her lover and has gone back to the town where she grew up. . . . She was accustomed to . . . porch sitters falling silent as she appeared, their **susurrous** gossip rising faintly like wind through pine needles as she passed into what they considered out of earshot. (Interview: Michael Parker Reads a Portion of His Novel *Towns Without Rivers*, NPR, *All Things Considered*, 7/19/2001.)

whistle *v.i.*: **siffle**. ❖ Since I noticed [that "lower classes" don't whistle a tune anymore], I've checked the places where it used to happen, and it isn't happening. You can hang about under a ladder with a chap up it painting a window [or] peer under a car where another chap is lying on his back on one of those trolley things . . . and you won't catch a note, not so much as a canary's bleep, not a single **siffle**. (Hannah Pool, "Jackdaw," *Guardian* [London], 7/25/1997.)

whistling (as in to make a soft rustling sound) *v.i.*: **sough**. See *rustling*

white (of an egg) *n.*: **albumen**. ❖ Medieval Europeans raiding gull colonies marveled at how some eggs contained nutritious yolk and **albumen** while others, apparently identical, held a baby bird, and still others were rotten. (Laura Erickson, "No Yoke: Egg Came Before Chicken," *Minneapolis Star Tribune*, 4/17/1995, p. 15.)

(2) white (as in pale, as from absence of sunlight) *adj.*: **etiolated**. See *pale*

(3) white (becoming . . .) *adj.*: **albescent**. See *whitish*

(4) white (covered with . . . or gray hair as if with age) *adj.*: **hoary**. See *gray*

white-hot *adj.*: **candescent**. ❖ Straight ahead and side-to-side, the **candescent** glow [of the street light] offers a measure of safety. (Jim Bencivenga, "Fencing Heaven," *Christian Science Monitor*, 8/2/2001.)

whitish (or turning white) *adj.*: **canascent**. ❖ The calendar said it was spring, but the weather said different. Boston was being battered by a nasty nor'easter, and 10 miles north in Lynnfield, the snow swirled out of a **canescent** sky. (Robert Parker, "Robert Parker Brings a Soft Touch to the Hard-Boiled School of Mystery Writing," *People*, 5/7/1984, p. 58.)

(2) whitish *adj.*: **albescent**. ❖ As for [Michael] Jackson, do you think he has a clue just how strange he looks? With his cruelly abridged nose, **albescent** skin, glassy eyes and startled expression—and an outfit that included those metallic shin guards—he looked like he had stepped out of a Peter Max cartoon. (David Hiltbrand, Picks & Pans: Tube, *People*, 7/3/1995, p. 15.)

whole (as a . . .) *adv.*: **en bloc** [French]. ❖ But 15 years later, as many had predicted, a majority of French Quebecers voted to split, their will thwarted by nonfrancophones, including Jews who voted **en bloc** to keep Quebec Canadian. (Ron Csillag, "Jews Consider Bidding Quebec 'Adieu,'" *Jerusalem Post*, 11/30/1995.)

wholly (as in, in the entirety) *adv.*: **holus-bolus**. See *entirety*

whore *n.*: **bawd**. See *prostitute*

(2) whore *n.*: **demimondaine**. See *prostitute*

(3) whore *n.*: **fancy woman**. See *prostitute*

(4) whore *n.*: **trollop**. See *prostitute*

whorehouse *n.*: **bagnio**. See *brothel*

whores (as a group) *n.*: **demimonde**. See *prostitutes*

who's who (as in a series of short biographical sketches) *n.*: **prosopography**. See *biography*

wicked *adj.*: **facinorous**. ❖ U.S. District Judge Garland Burrell said allowing the federal government to return to [confessed Unabomber Theodore Kaczynski] his rambling personal journal, in which he put down his innermost thoughts while living in a rural Montana cabin, would effectively "preserve for posterity some evidence of the evils wrought by his **facinorous** Unabomber actions." (Michael Taylor, "Unabomber Journal Stays Secret," *San Francisco Chronicle*, 3/10/2004.)

(2) wicked *adj.*: **flagitious**. ❖ [In Dr. Seuss's "How the Grinch Stole Christmas"] the Grinch [is] a nefarious, **flagitious**, sly, nasty, troublesome, bad-tempered, intolerant and foul-smelling character who, for reasons never fully explained, lives in a cave above the town. (Robin Greer, "Carrey Christmas," *News Letter* [Belfast, Ireland], 12/1/2000.)

(3) wicked *adj.*: **iniquitous**. ❖ To begin with, Sir Jeremy suggests . . . that mine is a simpleminded version of history [i.e., the cold war], in which a perfectly virtuous West triumphs over a thoroughly **iniquitous** East. (*Commentary*, "CNN's *Cold War*," 7/1/1999.)

(4) wicked (as in devilish) *adj.*: **Mephistophelean**. See *devilish*

(5) wicked (person) *n.*: **caitiff**. See *despicable*

(6) wicked *adj.*: **malefic**. See *evil*

(7) wicked *adj.*: **malevolent**. See *evil*

wide (and flat, like a spatula) *adj.*: **spatulate**. See *flat*

widen (in scope) *v.t.*: **aggrandize**. See *expand*

wideness (as in diversity) *n.*: **variegation** (*v.t.*: **variegate**). See *diversity*

wide-ranging (state of being . . . , as in breadth of inclusiveness) *n.*: **catholicity** [*adj.*: **catholic**]. See *universality*

widespread *adj.*: **pandemic**. ❖ But with renewed emphasis on a more family-oriented service and the embarrassing legacy of scandals such as Tailhook, the Pentagon appears to be cracking down on adultery and related offenses. But it is not just allegations of **pandemic** sexual misconduct, such as those at the Aberdeen Proving Ground, attracting prosecutors' attention. (Tamara Jones, "One Lieutenant's Adultery," *Newsday*, 5/13/1997.)

(2) widespread *adj.*: **regnant**. ❖ Consequently the debate seems to have been polarized and stalled by the crosscurrents of white backlash, black rage, and liberal despair. African American scholar Derrick Bell conveys some of the **regnant** frustration: "We have made progress in everything, yet nothing has changed." (Dinesh D'Souza, "Myth of the Racist Cabbie," *National Review*, 10/9/1995, p. 36.)

(3) widespread (in scope or applicability) *adj.*: **ecumenical**. See *universal*

widow *n.*: **relict**. ❖ Other countries in South Asia are also exponents of widows' and daughters' politics. Bangladesh, for example, is [ruled by Khaleda Zia] the **relict** of President Zia Rahman, assassinated [in 1981]. (*Economist*, "Only Widows and Orphans?" 5/8/1999.)

widowhood *n.*: **viduity**. ❖ It's a matter for conjecture how far [Queen Elizabeth II] can discharge her role as mother to the nation, aged 74, while "Mummy" [the Queen Mother]—or, as her daughter used to style her, "the Problem"—continues to grind out her interminable **viduity**. (Glen Newey, "You're No Better Than a Stuffed Badger, Ma'am; Long Live the Republic—Even Her Daughter Calls Her 'The Problem,'" *New Statesman*, 8/7/2000.)

wife (having one . . . at a time) *n.*: **monogyny**. ❖ In retrospect, I have to say that **monogyny** isn't all that bad. Sure it lacks variety and the thrill of getting caught and telling lies, but it has its subtle compensations. Deception and betrayal aren't everything, after all. (Dick Dougherty, "A Lot of Married Men Like Me Are Consumed by Regret," Gannett News Service, 8/11/1999.)

(2) wife (of, relating to, or having characteristics of) *adj.*: **uxorial**. ❖ Only a few months ago, I had been a struggling reporter, a nice girl from Nebraska who could outsit them on a barstool. Now, I was going to become a society wife, the **uxorial** ornament of a legend, tyrant, and infamous playboy. It was unbelievable, even to me. (Lynn Woodward, "Be Careful What You Wish For . . . It Might Come True," *Cosmopolitan*, 5/1/1994, p. 274.)

(3) wife (murder of . . . by her husband) *adj.*: **uxoricide**. See *killing*

(4) wife (or husband who is unfaithful) *n.*: **bedswerver**. See *unfaithful*

(5) wife (overly devoted to or submissive to one's . . .) *adj.*: **uxorious**. See *devoted*

(6) wife (who is overly devoted to her husband) *adj.*: **maritorious**. See *devoted*

(7) wife (esp. when referring to a traditional . . . who may, for example, stay at home and raise the children) *n.*: **helpmeet**. See *helpmate*

(8) wife (having more than one . . . at a time) *n.*: **polygyny**. See *polygamy*

wig (esp. worn by men in 17th and 18th centuries) *n.*: **peruke**. ❖ The old moguls hated movies where people wore powdered wigs and wrote with feathers. So this film's first images should set the old bosses spinning in their mausoleums. A gentleman's **peruke** is affixed, a lady's bosom powdered. (Richard Corliss, Cinema: "Lust Is a Thing with Feathers," *Time*, 1/16/1989, p. 64.)

(2) wig (or hairpiece) *n.*: **postiche**. See *hairpiece*

wild (and reckless person) *n.*: **rantipole**. ❖ [The play] could be an extension of Bragg's fascination with self-destructive stars, inspired by his first-rate biography of Richard Burton. [The lead in the play] goes for a Burton, giving us not just the **rantipole** boozer and the insecure star but also implying an educated distaste for the whole business of masquerade. (Michael Billington, "Tragic Hero Who Goes for a Burton," *Guardian* [London], 7/10/1992.)

(2) wild (as in frenzied) *adj.*: **corybantic**. See *frenzied*

(3) wild (as in uncontrollable and undisciplined person) *n.*: **bashi-bazouk** [Turkish]. See *undisciplined*

(4) wild (as in untamed) *adj.*: **ferine**. See *untamed*

(5) wild (sexually) *adj., n.*: **libertine**. See *promiscuous*

(6) wild *adj.*: **farouche** [French]. See *untamed*

wildness (emotional . . . , as in frenzy, esp. as caused by something unattainable) *n.*: **nympholepsy**. [This word often, though not always, refers to an erotic frenzy.] See *frenzy*

will (mental process marked by having . . . to do something) *n.*: **conation**. See *determination*

willful (as in premeditated) *adj.*: **prepense** (usually used as part of the phrase "malice prepense"). See *premeditated*

(2) willful (as in stubborn) *adj.*: **pervicacious**. See *stubborn*

willpower (lack of . . .) *n.*: **abulia** (or **aboulia**). [Another related definition of this word is a chronic inability to make decisions. See *indecisiveness*.] ❖ Thus when he comes to praise those who recognize poverty as owing as much to circumstances as to **abulia**, his discussion immediately widens to include spiritual truth and the reception of The Word. (Henry Golemba, "'Distant Dinners' in Crane's *Maggie*: Representing 'The Other Half,'" *Essays in Literature*, 9/22/1994, p. 235.)

willy-nilly (as in whether willingly or desired or not) *adv.*: **nolens volens** [Latin]. See *unavoidably*

wily (as in crafty) *adj.*: **jesuitical** (sometimes cap.). See *crafty*

(2) wily (characterized by . . . and cunning conduct, esp. in regard to the pursuit and maintenance of political or other power) *adj.*: **Machiavellian**. See *deceitful*

(3) wily (as in deceitful conduct) *n.*: **skullduggery**. See *deceitfulness*

wimp (as in coward) *n.*: **poltroon**. See *coward*

(2) wimp *n.*: **pantywaist**. See *sissy*

wimpy (being . . . , as in weak-willed) *n.*: **akrasia** [Greek]. See *weak-willed*

win (in which one comes from behind to win at the last moment) *n.*: **Garrison finish**. See *victory*

wince *v.i.*: **blench**. See *flinch*

wind (in and out) *v.i.*: **sinuate**. ❖ They crossed the far stone wall that marked the top of the Seep Square and, cutting left again, began to **sinuate** their way up through the thorn apples. (Robert F. Jones, "Are You Lonesome Tonight?" *Sports Afield*, 10/1/1994, p. 90.)

(2) wind (of, relating to, caused by or carried by) *adj.*: **eolian** (or **aeolian**). ❖ Two formerly peaceful streets in this town of 453 bear the savage mark of a tornado. Houses splintered. Trees stripped. Cars in storefronts. Baby carriages impaled on posts. It's all the work of set decorators bent on reproducing an **eolian** nightmare. (Marco R. Della Cava, "*Apollo 13* Star Plunges Right into *Twister*," *USA Today*, 7/7/1995.)

(3) wind (gentle . . .) *n.*: **zephyr**. See *breeze*

(4) wind (sudden violent gust of . . .) *n.*: **williwaw**. See *gust*

wind currents (pertaining to rising . . .) *adj.*: **anabatic**. ❖ Winds, such as katabatic (downslope) and **anabatic** (upslope) breezes, are generated thermotopographically. Land and sea breezes result from thermal circulation systems, which are generated by contrasting thermal responses of land and water. (Paul John Beggs, "An Integrated Environmental Asthma Model," *Archives of Environmental Health*, 3/13/1995, p. 87.)

windfall (as in lucky find) *n.*: **trouvaille** [French]. See *find*

winding (as in bending or waving) *adj.*: **flexuous**. See *waving*

(2) winding (full of . . . turns, as in tortuous) *adj.*: **anfractuous** (*n.*: **anfractuosity**). See *tortuous*

(3) winding (as in tortuous) *adj.*: **vermiculate**. See *tortuous*

window (bay . . .) *n.*: **oriel**. ❖ The newer Renaissance section [of the Rothenburg town hall], built in 1572, replaced the portion destroyed in the fire. It's decorated with intricate friezes, an **oriel** extending the building's full height, and a large stone portico opening onto the square. (*Frommer's Europe*, "Germany: 3, The Romantic Road," 1/1/1998.)

(2) window (throw something or someone out of a . . .) *v.t.*: **defenestrate** (*n.*: **defenestration**). See *throw*

window blind (with adjustable horizontal slats) *n.*: **jalousie**. ❖ Begun lived in a cell measuring about 10 ft. long and 5 ft. wide. It contained two narrow wooden cots and an open toilet. At one end was a small window that let in narrow strips of light. "It had metal **jalousies** to keep out the sun and block the view to the prison yard," Begun said. (James O. Jackson, "Soviet Union—A Day in the Depths of the Gulag," *Time*, 3/9/1987, p. 52.)

windows (having . . .) *adj.*: **fenestrated** (*n.*: **fenestration**). ❖ Tucked beneath the soaring roof, the Siffs' bedroom is spacious and full of light, but its sloping walls make it cozy as a bear's den. A quartet of windows frames a panorama of pines and snowy hills. "It's as if you're in a great tree house!" he declares. Luckily, the other end, though less **fenestrated**, is elegant too. (Kenneth Miller, "The Way We Live: Dream House '95," *Life*, 5/1/1996, p. 102.) ❖ "If this is some cheap bill-collecting dodge, I'll throw the sonofabitch out the window." "There is no **fenestration** in this building," said Wismer Strook, "only glass walls." (Tom Wolfe, *A Man in Full*, Farrar, Straus and Giroux [1998], p. 550.)

(2) windows (one that cuts and fits glass for) *n.*: **glazier**. ❖ Remember that glass pane on the terrace door that cracked last year when your toddler whacked it with his toy hammer? The one you've been meaning to take to the **glazier**? The one you doctored with masking tape? . . . Well, replacing a windowpane is not the work of wizards. (Tal Katz, "Installing New Glass in a Window Need Not be a Complete Pane," *Jerusalem Post*, 2/23/1995.)

wine (body, color, and taste of) *n.*: **vinosity**. ❖ Most important, add a little grape-juice concentrate. I know it is expensive, I agree it is a cheat, but nothing else gives the wine that round **vinosity** that distinguishes wine from Appellation Controlee Rat's Urine. (Michael Buerk, Wine: "Why Chateau Buerk Is the Stuff for Me," *Daily Telegraph*, 6/6/1998.)

(2) wine (lover or connoisseur) *n.*: **oenophile**. ❖ This favorite of discriminating Manhattanites is well stocked, so you'll be too. As for gifts, that fussy **oenophile** on your list won't balk at an imperial bottle of 1978 Chateau Lafite-Rothschild ($1,450). (Joshua B. Adams, "T&C's New York Holidays," *Town & Country*, 12/1/1994, p. 125.)

(3) wine (of superior quality, which is so good that it is drunk to the last drop) *n.*: **supernaculum**. [This word is Latin for "upon the nail," referring to the custom of leaving only enough in the glass to make a bead on the fingernail.] ❖ There are now more than 400 commercial vineyards in England and Wales, plus countless hobby enterprises, and most of them got through a difficult spring with buds intact. One might even produce the **supernaculum** of 1991. (David Hoppit, Property: "Bibulous Bargain-Hunting," *Financial Times* [London], 10/12/1991.)

(4) wine (of, relating to, or made with) *n.*: **vinous**. ❖ Terrible, terrible news! Rich yuppies are lapping up all the great wines. No price is too steep for a Wall Streeter when his palate craves **vinous** delight. A restaurant wine bill can run to thousands of dollars when these conspicuous consumers are in the bibulous vein. (Russell Baker, "When a Bottle Costs $1,975, What's Inside Isn't the Point," *Minneapolis Star Tribune*, 2/23/1998.)

(5) wine (person who drinks a lot of . . .) *n.*: **winebibber**. ❖ Robert Finigan's *Private Guide to Wines* newsletter likes Opus One very much. He suspects, however, that people are buying it to show it off—not drink it—because drinking a $50 wine would be a conspicuous presumption. If you're more **winebibber** than collector, Finigan advises waiting until Opus One is discounted, as he thinks it inevitably will be before too long. (*Money*, "Magnum Opus," 5/1/1984.)

(6) wine (study of) *n.*: **enology**. ❖ Richard Vine (that's right, Vine—and his Ph.D. is in agricultural economics) is one of America's foremost authorities on agriculture's most glamorous product. He has written an authoritative textbook on wine, and teaches **enology** at Purdue University in West Lafayette, IN. (Joseph Scott, "A Good [Cheap] Bottle of Wine," *Good Housekeeping*, 8/1/1996, p. 39.)

(7) wine (having the color of red . . .) *adj.*: **vinaceous**. See *red wine*

wings (insects that have shed their . . . or of or about such insects) *n.*, *adj.*: **dealate**. ❖ **Dealates**: Only 1 percent of the tens of thousands of [termites] survive the process of leaving the colony, landing and looking for a mate. Those that survive will pair off, beat their wings from their bodies, and begin a highly structured mating ritual. (*New Orleans Times-Picayune*, "Fortress of Destruction," 6/29/1998.)

(2) wings (without . . .) *adj.*: **apterous**. ❖ To test this notion, they compared genes in flies and crustaceans, which are insects' closest relatives with gills. . . . They discovered that two previously discovered insect wing genes, called pdm and **apterous**, were hidden in the DNA of the flightless crustaceans. (*ScienceNOW*, "The Origin of Insect Flight," 2/12/1997.)

wink *v.i.*: **nictitate**. See *blink*

winking (spasmodic . . . of one or both eyes) *n.*: **blepharospasm**. See *blinking*

winner (with the critics but not the public) *n.*: **succès d'estime** [French]. See *success*

winning (celebrating . . .) *adj.*: **epinician**. See *victory*

winter (of, related to, or occurring in) *adj.*: **brumal**. ❖ Two days before I was due to arrive at Branford [for a January duck hunt], a **brumal** wind howled down from Canada, the shore areas of the Sound froze over, and we spent our day feeding stale bread to ragged bands of disconsolate mallards standing on the ice in the cove near his house. (Nelson Bryant, Outdoors: "Ducks Elusive in Trip to Sound," *New York Times*, 1/14/1985.)

(2) winter (of, relating to, or occurring in) *adj*.: **hibernal**. ❖ [W]e made up an entire 156-person field out of threesomes. In each, the golfers have a common bond. Can you guess what it is? . . . David Frost, Andy North, Don January. . . . [Answer:] **Hibernal**. (Michael Bamberger, Golf Plus/U.S. Open Preview, *Sports Illustrated*, 6/14/1999, p. G12.)

(3) winter (of, relating to, or occurring in) *adj*.: **hiemal**. ❖ Attending a Jimmy Buffett concert is like participating in a spring break frat bash for baby boomers. Defying balmy but decidedly **hiemal** temperatures, graying fans of the beach-bum balladeer arrived for his sold-out Madison Square Garden gig in full Parrot Head regalia. (Letta Tayler, "A Baby-Boomer Break/Buffett Gives High-Flying Parrot Heads What They Want," *Newsday*, 2/21/1998.)

wipe out (as in abolish) *v.t*.: **extirpate**. See *abolish*

(2) wipe out (as in put an end to) *v.t*.: **quietus** (as in "put the quietus to"). See *termination*

wisdom (superficial . . . on a subject) *n*.: **sciolism**. See *superficial*

(2) wisdom (universal . . .) *n*.: **pansophy** (*adj*.: **pansophic**). See *knowledge*

(3) wisdom (spec. a recognition of one's errors, and a return to a sane, sound, or correct position and the . . . gained from the experience) *n*.: **resipiscence**. See *reformation*

wise *adj*.: **sapient**. ❖ [S]urprisingly, there has hitherto been no systematic account of [C. S. Lewis's conversion to Christianity]. David C. Downing seeks to fill this [gap.] Coming from a **sapient** Lewis scholar, Downing's narrative is precise and rounded; it also contains many intelligent insights into Lewis's work. . . . [I]t is still of considerable worth to Lewis critics and of use to all scholars of modern Christian thought. (Adam Schwartz, review of *The Most Reluctant Convert: C. S. Lewis's Journey to Faith*, by David C. Downing, *Christianity and Literature*, 9/22/2002.)

wise guy (and conceited person) *n*.: **jackanapes**. See *conceited*

(2) wise guy (as in buffoon, who is some-times boastful) *n*.: **Scaramouch**. See *buffoon*

(3) wise guy (as in smart aleck) *n*.: **wisenheimer**. See *smart aleck*

wish (as in strong craving) *n*.: **avidity**. See *craving*

(2) wish (for) *v.t*.: **desiderate**. See *want*

(3) wish (slight or faint . . .) *n*.: **velleity**. See *hope*

(4) wish (which is delusive or not realistically obtainable) *n*.: **will-o'-the-wisp**. See *pipe dream*

wishing (for something, esp. for something one once had but has no more) *n*.: **desiderium**. See *longing*

(2) wishing (strongly . . . for) *adj*.: **appetent** (*n*.: **appetence**). See *desirous*

wishy-washy (as in chronic inability to make decisions) *n*.: **abulia** (or **aboulia**). See *indecisiveness*

(2) wishy-washy *adj*., *n*.: **namby-pamby**. See *spineless*

wistful *adj*.: **tristful**. See *sad*

wit *n*.: **jocosity**. See *humor*

witch (as in shrew) *n*.: **harridan**. See *shrew*

(2) witch (as in shrew) *n*.: **termagant**. See *shrew*

(3) witch (as in shrew) *n*.: **virago**. See *shrew*

(4) witch (as in shrew) *n*.: **vixen**. See *shrew*

(5) witch (as in shrew) *n*.: **Xanthippe**. See *shrew*

(6) witch (as in ugly old woman) *n*.: **beldam**. See *hag*

witchcraft *n*.: **necromancy**. See *black magic*

witches (assembly of . . .) *n*.: **coven**. ❖ Now the witches are forced to confront a question their predecessors faced since the dawn of Christianity: Should they retreat back into secret **covens**, or try their luck in the open market of America's scattered spirituality? (Hanna Rosin, "An Army Controversy: Should the Witches Be Welcome? Flap over Wiccans Tests Military's Religious Tolerance," *Washington Post*, 6/8/1999.)

witchlike (old woman) *n*.: **crone**. See *hag*

with all respect (to) *prep*.: **pace** [Latin]. See *respectfully*

withdraw (as in recoil) *v.i.*: **resile**. See *recoil*

(2) withdraw (from office or membership) *v.i.*: **demit** (as in demit office). See *resign*

withdrawal (desperate . . . , as in retreat) *n.*: **Dunkirk**. See *retreat*

(2) withdrawal (social . . .) *n.*: **purdah**. See *seclusion*

withdrawn (socially . . . or inexperienced and/or shy and/or sullen) *adj.*: **farouche** [French]. See *shy*

wither (away) *n., v.i.*: **atrophy**. ❖ The greatest threat to our nation's future is not economic, but moral. "Middle class morality" is under siege—all around we see the results of the **atrophying** of personal responsibility and the breakdown of the family. Leaders like Clinton can only make things worse. (Katherine Kersten, "Why Feminist Crusaders Are Silent on Clinton," *Minneapolis Star Tribune*, 2/11/1998.)

(2) wither *v.i.*: **wizen**. See *shrivel*

withered (old woman) *n.*: **crone**. See *hag*

without (anythig better) *adv.*: **faute de mieux** [French]. See *lacking*

(2) without (from . . .) *adv.*: **ab extra** [Latin]. See *externally*

witness (based on eyewitness observation) *adj.*: **autoptic**. See *eyewitness*

witty (sayings) *n.pl.*: **facetiae**. ❖ The story about Ann Richards of Texas quotes the two sound bites that made her famous. She changed the names, but the **facetiae** were familiar. The one about Bush being born with a silver foot in his mouth she lifted from Lily Tomlin. The one about Ginger Rogers doing whatever Fred Astaire did but backwards and in heels was lifted from a lecture by Linda Ellerbee, who says she overheard it on a bus. (P. M. Zall, letter to the editor, *Los Angeles Times*, 10/22/1989.)

(2) witty *adj.*: **waggish**. ❖ In one of his **waggish** moments, Henry Kissinger once commented, "There cannot be a crisis next week. My schedule is already full." (James Walsh, "Confronting Chaos," *Time*, 10/18/1993, p. 20.)

(3) witty (person who tries to be . . . but is not) *n.*: **witling**. See *humorless*

(4) witty (line) *n.*: **bon mot** [French]. See *quip*

(5) witty (line) *n.*: **epigram**. See *quip*

wizardry *n.*: **necromancy**. See *magic*

wobbly (as in quivering) *adj.*: **tremulous**. See *quivering*

wolf (characteristic of or resembling) *adj.*: **lupine**. ❖ Few actors are as entertaining as [Jack] Nicholson when he cuts loose (i.e., *Batman* and *The Shining*), but such an approach would nosedive [the movie] *Wolf*. He plays it perfectly, even under Rick Baker's mounds of makeup. He's always had a **lupine** edge to his work, anyway. (Mark Burger, "Nicholson Steals the Show in *Wolf*," *Jewish Journal*, 6/23/1994.)

(2) wolf (ability to assume characteristics of or delusion where one thinks he is a . . .) *n.*: **lycanthropy**. See *werewolf*

woman. See also *women*

woman (beautiful and alluring . . .) *n.*: **houri** [French]. ❖ Ask any shortstop what it's like trying to turn a double play when the base runner barreling toward him is a suicide bomber who believes that his martyrdom will ensure a place for his family in paradise and unlimited access to hundreds of virginal **houris**. It's intense, baby! (Mark Leyner, "The Most Dangerous Games," *Esquire*, 10/1/1997, p. 64.)

(2) woman (French working-class young . . .) *n.*: **grisette** [French]. ❖ Some [women who eventually became prostitutes] were upperclass girls, down on their luck, who chose to service rich men rather than serve as governesses to their children. . . . Many more were born into a life of poverty, earning paltry livings as **grisettes**, or seamstresses, before emerging like glittering butterflies from the grey muslin dresses that gave them their name. (Lucy Moore, "How to Get Ahead in Bed," *Sunday Times* [London], 2/24/2002.)

(3) woman (who is scheming and evil) *n.*: **jezebel** (sometimes cap.). ❖ "Bobby, I think I can handle a good-looking girl reporter." Seen it happen again and again. They come in, bat their pretty eyes at you, cross their legs a few times, and before you know, it's "I shouldn't really be telling you this" and "Would you like to see our confidential files?" Beware of **Jezebels** with tape recorders." (Christopher Buckley, *Thank You for Smoking*, Random House [1994], p. 71.)

(4) woman (frenzied or raging . . .) *n*.: **maenad**. ❖ While men everywhere winced [when Lorena Bobbitt cut off her husband's penis], a lot of women were gleefully triumphant. . . . Now the submissive pinup was suddenly revealed as a screaming **maenad**. "Lorena Bobbitt's a total heroine," says punk singer Maffeo. (Tad Friend, "Yes," *Esquire*, 2/1/1994, p. 48.)

(5) woman (who is coarse and abusive) *n*.: **fishwife**. ❖ The market puts on a good show: huge quantities of fish and a rich running dialogue between the dealers, which tends to go along the lines of: "*@$$! my brother you @/*X!" "Oh yeah? Well, I'll *&%XO you, you ?!OX*$!" It doesn't take long to work out where the phrase "swears like a **fishwife**" comes from. (Tim Dowling, "Welcome to Fishville," *Sunday Telegraph* [London], 4/19/1998.)

(6) woman (having the form or appearance of) *adj*.: **gynecomorphous**. ❖ How the love of a man has directed the course of their lives is the unifying theme [in three novellas by Mary Gordon], and it does not seem beside the point to view the book[,] as a whole, as a probe into the limits of feminism. What Gordon seems to be saying . . . is that women are defined by their bodies, by their femaleness, their **gynecomorphous** selves. (Colleen Kelly Warren, "Illuminating Inner Thoughts," *St. Louis Post-Dispatch*, 10/10/1993.)

(7) woman (who is slender and graceful) *n*.: **sylph**. ❖ The first song [I dance to at the strip club] is "Brick House," an homage to women who butter their potatoes. This is not a song for a **sylph**. A diminutive dancer I know played it one night and was humiliated when a man in the audience shouted out, "But you're flat!" (Lily Burana, *Strip City*, Talk Miramax Books [2001], p. 174.)

(8) woman (who is strong and courageous) *n*.:

virago. ❖ Feminists don't like strong women because too many **viragos** would put them out of business. To prosper they need a steady supply of women who exemplify the other V-word, "victim." (Florence King, The Misanthrope's Corner, *National Review*, 3/10/1997, p. 64.)

(9) woman (who is unconventionally attractive) *n*.: **jolie laide** (or **jolie-laide**). [French, for "pretty-ugly." This term refers to a woman who is attractive in an unconventional or unusual way, or more literally, pretty and ugly at the same time. (The masculine form would be "joli laid." See *handsome*.) It can also be applied to inanimate objects, and can be used as an adjective. See *pretty* for an example. A similar term is "belle laide," which means "beautifully-ugly" and which can also be used as a noun or as an adjective; an example is provided under *beautiful*.] ❖ [Opera singer Maria Callas,] a **jolie laide** with hard, bony features and a startlingly long nose, . . . contrived through sheer force of will to persuade audiences that she was a great beauty with an even greater voice. (Terry Teachout, "The Voice," *New York Times*, 8/26/2001.)

(10) woman (single . . . , whether divorced, widowed, or never married) *n*.: **feme sole**. ❖ Flavia Luisinha De Souza (in her 50s—"Don't print my age. I want to keep them guessing!"): "I made up my mind at 16 that I didn't want to get married," said this petite woman who runs a music studio. . . . She didn't quite say "So there!" but it was there alright! So you can guess that she has no qualms about being [a] **feme sole**. (*New Straits Times*, "Single, and It Feels So Right!" 4/15/2002.)

(11) woman (of or relating to a . . .) *adj*.: **gynecoid**. ❖ Researchers refer to the pear-shaped body as **gynecoid** in part because mostly women develop this type: Extra weight in the rear, thighs and hips. When a woman talks about her "saddlebags" she is talking about a pear shape. (Bob Condor, "Scientists Weigh in with New Ideas on Fatness," *Seattle Post-Intelligencer*, 10/29/2007.)

(12) woman (regarded as ugly, repulsive, or terrifying) *n.*: **gorgon**. ❖ [T]he most memorable film noir villainesses were formidable and unmistakably alluring. You search in vain for some of the same charisma in the new killer women of the movies. Instead they are unfeeling, unimaginative, unattractive **gorgons**, and [you wonder what] disturbing cultural malaise . . . is producing this virulent wave of revulsion toward women who want to take charge. (Stephen Farber, Movies: "That's No Lady—That's Our Nightmare, *Los Angeles Times*, 3/18/2001.)

(13) woman (who hates men) *n.*: **misandrist**. ❖ Feminist ideologues have recently falsely accused men of being wildly abusive to woman on Super Bowl Sunday. They have held men responsible for 150,000 anorexia deaths each year. . . . My book [*Who Stole Feminsim?*] documents a widespread ongoing campaign of mean-spirited, socially divisive, **misandrist** Ms/information. (Christina Hoff Sommers, Letters from the People, *St. Louis Post-Dispatch*, 8/29/1994.)

(14) woman (with scholarly or literary interests) *n.*: **bluestocking**. ❖ At 59, slender with close-cut hair, [Pauline] Maier appears more outdoorsy than professorial, a self-described "Radcliffe **bluestocking**" who quickly belies that description with an infectious laugh. (Michael Kenney, "A New Look at Exceptional Document/Author: Plain Folk Shaped Declaration of Independence," *Minneapolis Star Tribune*, 7/9/1997.)

(15) woman (attractive young . . . who is flighty and flamboyant) *n.*: **frippet** [British; informal]. ❖ All in all, my take on the breakfast [boat] trip is: do it with your wife. If it's your wife, you know you're with someone you get along with. . . . [B]eing taken to a lovely hotel and out on the river for breakfast is really something your wife . . . deserves more than some snake-hipped little **frippet** who'd be off at the drop of a wallet, don't you think? (Michael Bywater, "One Man in a Boat—But Who Should He Take?" *Independent* [London], 5/14/2000.)

(16) woman (intriguing . . .) *n.*: **intrigante**. ❖ [Frenchwoman Olympia Mancini (1638–1708) was, by nature, an **intrigante**. Shortly after her marriage, she became involved in various intrigues at Court. There were rumours that prior to her marriage, she was briefly the mistress of Louis XIV. While not exactly beautiful, Olympia was described as possessing great charm and indisputable fascination. (en.wikipedia.org/wiki/Olympia_Mancini, "Olympia Mancini.")

(17) woman (regarded as vicious and scolding) *n.*: **harridan**. See *shrew*

(18) woman (relating to a . . . right after childbirth) *adj.*: **puerperal**. See *postpartum*

(19) woman (right after childbirth) *n.*: **puerperium**. See *postpartum*

(20) woman (shrewish . . .) *n.*: **vixen**. See *shrew*

(21) woman (old and ugly) *n.*: **crone**. See *hag*

(22) woman (state of being a . . .) *n.*: **muliebrity**. See *femininity*

(23) woman (who is a shrew) *n.*: **termagant**. See *shrew*

(24) woman (who is a shrew) *n.*: **Xanthippe**. See *shrew*

(25) woman (who is charming and seductive) *n.*: **Circe**. See *enchantress*

(26) woman (who is head of a household) *n.*: **materfamilias** [Latin]. See *head of household*

(27) woman (who is married) *n.*: **feme covert**. See *married*

(28) woman (who is old and ugly) *n.*: **beldam**. See *hag*

(29) woman (condition of a . . . having masculine tendencies) *n.*: **viraginity** (*adj.*: **viraginous**). See *masculine*

(30) woman (girl or young . . . who is impish or playful) *n.*: **gamine** [French]. See *girl*

(31) woman (hired to do cleaning work) *n.*: **charwoman**. See *maid*

(32) woman (of a . . . who is stately and regal, esp. tending toward voluptuous) *adj.*: **Junoesque**. See *voluptuous*

(33) woman (of or like an old . . .) *adj.*: **anile**. See *old woman*

(34) woman (of or relating to a . . . who has never given birth) *adj.:* **nulliparous**. See *childless*

(35) woman (who is pregnant for the first time or has had only one child) *n.:* **primipara**. See *pregnant*

(36) woman (with whom one is in love or has an intimate relationship) *n.:* **inamorata**. See *girlfriend*

(37) woman (young . . . who is high-spirited or boisterous) *n.:* **hoyden**. See *tomboy*

womanhood *n.:* **muliebrity**. See *femininity*

womanizer (as in lecherous man or playboy) *n.:* **roué** [French]. See *playboy*

(2) womanizer (as in man who seduces women) *n.:* **Lothario**. See *playboy*

(3) womanizer *n.:* **rakehell**. See *libertine*

women. See also *woman*

women (as a group) *n.:* **distaff** (often as in "distaff side"). ❖ Womantrek is for women only. Husbands, boyfriends, brothers and sons need not apply. Bordas, 41, hastens to explain that Womantrek is not an exercise in antimale discrimination. Rather, its aim is to create a **distaff** equivalent of male bonding. (Dan Chu, "When Bonnie Bordas Leads a Wilderness Tour, There's No Male Call at All," *People*, 5/8/1989, p. 135.)

(2) women (fear of) *n.:* **gynophobia**. ❖ [W]hat [the movie] *Going All the Way* is really about . . . is the same old male-bonding misogyny. Male-bonding **gynophobia** may be a little more exact. Sonny and Gunner don't hate women so much as live in mortal fear of them. That's why Sonny and Gunner are always running off to the bar together, or out to the old football field. That's where these would-be ladies' men are happiest—alone, together. (Stephen Whitty, "*All The Way* Not as Deep as It Pretends," *New Orleans Times-Picayune*, 12/12/1997.)

(3) women (fond of . . .) *adj.:* **philogynous**. (*n.:* **philogyny**) ❖ [To promote her book *Misogynies*, feminist writer Joan] Smith gave a reading at the radical Silver Moon bookshop. . . . Accompanying her, as representative of the New Man supreme, was husband Francis Wheen, (who is hailed in *Misogynies* as "living proof of the possibility of a **philogynous** future"). (*Sunday Times* [London], Diary, 5/6/1990.) ❖ [I]ndustry and commerce will be looking for an extra 1.5 million employees over the next five years but . . . fewer than a million new employees will come forward; 83 per cent of these will be women. Not out of **philogyny** then, but out of desperation, employers are rushing to make working practices less prejudicial to those who would like at least the choice of whether to have children. (Elizabeth Heron, "Graduate Careers: Wanted: Women with Skills; Workplace Conditions Are Changing as Employers Gear Up to Meet a Different Job Market," *Independent* [London], 2/15/1990.)

(4) women (kept by wealthy lovers or protectors) *n.:* **demimonde**. ❖ Gigi's family is part of the **demimonde**, the class of women in 19th century France who were supported by well-to-do lovers or protectors. (Gerry Kowarsky, "With Help of Act Inc, Humor in *Gigi* Withstands Test of Time," *St. Louis Post-Dispatch*, 7/22/1999.)

(5) women (person who hates . . .) *n.:* **misogynist**. See *hatred*

(6) women (government by or political or social dominance by) *n.:* **gynocracy**. See *government*

(7) women (government or society or group ruled by) *n.:* **gynarchy**. See *government*

wonderful (to relate) *adv.:* **mirabile dictu** [Latin]. ❖ Some food is transformed by a recipe. A hot dog, for example, is nothing like meat. Nor are potato chips like a spud. But other recipes amplify the essential qualities of an ingredient; crabcakes, for example. . . . In our crabcake search, we found a lot of variation and, **mirable dictu**, no bad crabcakes. Some, notably those at Legal Seafood, were good, meaty and satisfying. (*Boston Globe*, "Crabcakes," 7/30/1992.)

(2) wonderful *adj.:* **frabjous**. [This derives from the line "O frabjous day! Calloh! Callay!" in Lewis Carroll's *Through the Looking-*

Glass (1872). The speaker is expressing his pleasure upon discovering that the Jabberwock has been killed: "he chortled in his joy"— "chortled" itself being a more well-known Carroll coinage stemming from the same source.] ❖ Oh, **Frabjous** Day! A real American man would rather miss Thanksgiving day dinner than Super Bowl Sunday, the true national campfire. . . . For those lucky enough to actually be there . . . it is the heartiest party of the year, the macho New Year's Eve, especially now that this endless TV day has been reaffirmed by billion-dollar network contracts. (Robert Lipsyte, "Backtalk; On Such a Macho Day, Reality Is a Blur," *New York Times*, 1/25/1998.)

(3) wonderful *adj.*: **galluptious** [slang]. ❖ He painted his own little bestiary of self-styled animals and other friends with as much glee and gimlet-eyed subtlety as he used to play a rhinocerous on stage. His creatures are genetic mixtures that are sometimes as ludicrous as a cross between a Chihuahua and a peccary. But they are blessed with such personalities and presence that they have their own **galluptious** but unimpeachable reality. (David Shirey, "Art Paintings by Zero Mostel Make the Viewer Chuckle and Think," *New York Times*, 7/27/1980.)

(4) wonderful *adj.*: **mirific**. [This word also means working wonders or miraculous, though it is not used as such in this example.] ❖ [She] was largely indifferent to food. . . . She smoked a good deal, and I suspect she looked forward to the end of a meal more than to the start of one, whether the fare was Rose's **mirific** stews and soups and breads, or Peter's scrambled eggs, or a veal paprikasch . . . or a quick sandwich in a local pub. (Bruce Kellner, "Miss Young, My Darling: A Memoir," *Review of Contemporary Fiction*, 6/22/2000.)

(5) wonderful *adj.*: **galumptious**. See *excellent*

(6) wonderful (as in of the highest quality) *n.*: **first water** (usu. as in "of the first water"). See *quality*

(7) wonderful (to behold) *adv.*: **mirabile visu** [Latin]. See *behold*

(8) wonderful *adj.*: **palmary**. See *excellent*

(9) wonderful *adj.*: **skookum**. See *excellent*

wood (of, relating to, or having the texture or appearance of) *adj.*: **ligneous**. ❖ The tree-saving tendency is part of the wider picture of Nimby [not in my back yard] environmentalism, the distinctive badge of those with time and money to waste. This arboreal sentimentality won't die out with the older generation, for even the young are bursting with **ligneous** lunacy. "Save the rainforests" is the modern version of the Children's Crusade. (Jane Jakeman, "A Nation Obsessed by Large Lumps of Wood," *Independent* [London], 12/30/1994.)

wooded *adj.*: **arboreous**. ❖ However, Monona is a Tree City, it owes its uniqueness to its **arboreous** nature, and one wonders if a regulation curtailing wholesale removal of greens would not be in order. (J. T. Carstensen, "Downing of Monona Trees Cries for Regulations," *Wisconsin State Journal*, 8/28/1995.)

(2) wooded *adj.*: **sylvan**. ❖ For more than 30 years, Ed and Eva Gumbert's 230-acre farm on the Etowah River in north Cherokee County has been their **sylvan** haven. It was . . . a world of soaring hawks, majestic hardwood trees and unspoiled blue-ridged vistas. (Julie B. Hairston, "Asphalt Rumble—Proposed Northern Arc Has Proved a Dividing Highway, from Northside vs. Southside to Neighbor vs. Neighbor," *Atlanta Journal-Constitution*, 2/4/2002.)

woods (of or relating to . . . , or having many trees) *adj.*: **bosky**. See *trees*

(2) woods (of or relating to) *adj.*: **sylvan**. See *wooded*

woody *adj.*: **ligneous**. See *wood*

wool (or hair or fur that covers the body of a mammal) *n.*: **pelage**. See *hair*

woolly (having a . . . appearance) *adj.*: **flocculent**. See *fluffy*

word. See also *words*

word (invented just for a particular occasion) *n.*: **nonce word**. ❖ Lexicographers must beware the dreaded one-time-only "**nonce**" **word**, such as "Disneyitis" or "Borkability" (which means, by the way, the potential for a candidate to be damaged by a media campaign). Coined to live in one article, **nonce words** die like mayflies. (Liesl Schillinger, NYC: "What's the Word? The New Three-Volume Random House Slang Dictionary Is Right Up One Lexicographer's Alley," *Newsday*, 5/2/1994.)

(2) word (just the right . . . or phrase) *n*.: **mot juste** [French]. ❖ He is in such a rush to say so many things that he cannot always be bothered to find the **mot juste**: if *guys* is his trademark noun, *helluva* is Iacocca's favorite modifier. (Kurt Andersen, "A Spunky Tycoon Turned Superstar: Straight-Talking Lee Iacocca Becomes America's Hottest New Folk Hero," *Time*, 4/1/1985, p. 30.)

(3) word (long . . . , or one given to the use of) *n*., *adj*.: **sesquipedalian**. ❖ The longest word in the works of Shakespeare (*Love's Labour's Lost*) is honorificabilitudinitatibus, truly **sesquipedalian** but rarely used. (Laurence McNamee, "Dous-ies," *Dallas Morning News*, 4/27/1997.)

(4) word (even longer . . . , or one given to the use of) *n*., *adj*.: **hippopotomonstrosesquipedalian**. ❖ Infamous quiz show contestant Herbert Stempel's "out of the park" definition of "floccinaucinihilipilification"—"the longest word in the English language"—landed in foul territory when he claimed "that's from Shakespeare" ("The Man with All the Answers," Style, Sept. 27). The word was first used in 1741, more than a century after Shakespeare's death. . . . Perhaps your editors should be more careful when dealing with such **hippopotomonstrosesquipedalian** . . . matters. (Edward J. Seiler, "Free for All," *Washington Post*, 10/1/1994.)

(5) word (misuse of . . . , by confusing a similar one) *n*.: **malapropism**. ❖ When Dent was fired [by New York Yankee owner George Steinbrenner], Peterson, in a neat **malapropism**, said, "George has been languishing long and hard over this decision." (Tim Kurkjian, "The Boss Strikes Again—George Steinbrenner's Yanks Sank, So He Fired the Manager, Of Course," *Sports Illustrated*, 6/18/1990, p. 48.)

(6) word (new . . . , phrase, or expression) *n*.: **neologism**. ❖ Back during Watergate, the President's men were always having to announce that he had "misspoke himself," an odd **neologism** that made it sound as though Nixon had just wet his pants. Just once it would be nice to hear a White House press secretary say, "The President made a faux pas." (Christopher Buckley, "Hoof in Mouth," *Forbes FYI*, 5/4/1998, p. 31.)

(7) word (or form that has only one recorded use) *n*.: **hapax legomenon** [Greek]. ❖ Blimah is a biblical **hapax legomenon**, appearing in Job 26:7, within a paean to God's might as creator: "He it is who stretches out Zaphon over chaos; Who suspended earth over blimah." (Azzan Yadin, "A Web of Chaos: Bialik and Nietzsche on Language, Truth, and the Death of God," *Prooftexts: A Journal of Jewish Literary History*, 3/22/2001.)

(8) word (or phrase that is brand-new and created in the hope that others will use it and make it recognized) *n*.: **protologism**. [This word is not yet recognized in print dictionaries, but it is useful and is found increasingly in online dictionaries. It differs from the word "neologism," which is a newly coined word, in that neologisms are words that have already been in public usage by authors other than their inventors. Thus, a protologism is even newer than a neologism, and as soon as it finds its way onto Web sites and into newspapers, journals, and books, it will become a neologism.] ❖ As I had never seen [the phrase "totus porcus" as used by Patrick Buchanan] before, I looked it up at ask.com. Nothing. OK, so then I googled the phrase. Only 80 hits. The same search on Yahoo! gave 106 hits. Wikipedia returned zero hits. The number of hits is too low for the phrase to be a neologism, but the usage by Patrick Buchanan surely makes it a **protologism** on the rise. (C. Scott Willy, *cs-willy.com/ overlooked*, 5/8/2007.) [Buchanan had stated:

"But we had best discover why it was our forefathers, who created this country, rejected, *totus porcus*, the nonsense we spout today about egalitarianism." The author of this piece submitted that "totus porcus" means "the whole hog."]

(9) word (or phrase that used to stand alone but then requires a modifier due to changes in technology or other new developments) *n.*: **retronym**. [Among numerous examples are acoustic guitar, manual typewriter, natural childbirth, terrestrial radio, regular coffee, day baseball, conventional weapons, natural turf, cloth diaper, and two-parent family.] *USA Today: The Television Show* . . . is of course an offshoot of the six-year-old national newspaper (which Gannett employees now refer to by the **retronym** "USA-Today-the-newspaper"), which in turn was designed to be something like a newspaper for television viewers. (Marjorie Williams, "Now, Here's the Good News . . . *USA Today*'s TV Spinoff, Focusing on 'the Journalism of Hope,'" *Washington Post*, 9/12/1988.)

(10) word (that is more specific than another given word) *n.*: **hyponym**. [For example, spaniel and puppy are hyponyms in relation to dog. The more general word is called the hypernym.] ❖ [T]he Thesaurus features more than 60 new "panels" devoted to **hyponyms**, ranging from terms used in accounting to famous waterfalls. . . . Types of forest and woodland, for example, include: chaparral, garrigue, igapo, maquis, montane, selva and taiga. (Mark Sanderson, The Literary Life, *Sunday Telegraph* [London], 6/13/2004.)

(11) word (which derives from the name of a real or fictitious person) *n.*: **eponym** (*adj.*: **eponymous**). ❖ The point to sadomasochistic sex, one assumes, is knowing when to stop. . . . The [movie *Quills*] uses the life of the Marquis de Sade (1740–1814), the French aristocrat turned literary pornographer (whose very name became the **eponym** for the painful sex practices he wrote about), to examine the rights of an artist versus the rights of society. (Leah Rozen, Screen/Picks & Pans, *People*, 12/4/2000.)

(12) word (definition of a . . . or phrase in a dictionary or elsewhere) *n.*: **definiens**. See *definition*

(13) word (distortion or destruction of sense of . . .) *n.*: **verbicide**. See *distortion*

(14) word (of a . . . that is pedantic) *adj.*: **inkhorn**. See *pedantic*

(15) word (of or relating to a . . . that is more generic than another given word) *adj.*: **superordinate**. See *generic*

(16) word (or phrase that is being defined in a dictionary or elsewhere) *n.*: **definiendum**. See *definition*

word-for-word (translation) *n.*: **metaphrase**. See *translation*

wordiness (spec. obsessive repetition of meaningless words and phrases) *n.*: **verbigeration**. See *repetition*

(2) wordiness (through use of unnecessary words or phrases) *n.*: **pleonasm**. See *redundancy*

(3) wordiness *n.*: **circumlocution**. See *verbosity*

(4) wordiness *n.*: **logorrhea**. See *verbosity*

(5) wordiness *n.*: **macrology**. See *verbosity*

(6) wordiness *n.*: **periphrasis**. See *verbosity*

word list *n.*: **onomasticon**. ❖ Bodies are sometimes lost or stolen. He returned them. . . . Not only was his profession unrecognized, there was not even a word for what he did. Words such as "brigand," or "pirate," or perhaps "body hunter" give some vague notion of it. Even the . . . **onomasticon** was of no help to her. While she was able to find all sorts of names for mythological and religious figures who aided and abetted the human world, there was no name to be found for what he did. So she would call him "the body retriever," an invention of her own. (Manya Steinkoler, "The Body Retriever," *Literature and Psychology*, 3/22/2002.)

(2) word list *n.*: **lexicon**. See *dictionary*

word of mouth (by . . .) *adj.*, *adv.*: **viva voce** [Latin]. See *verbal*

word play *n.*: **paronomasia**. ❖ Rosten's humor depends on comic dialect, the solecism, the pun, the malapropism . . . [and] **paronoma-**

sia. (Don Nilsen, "Humorous Contemporary Jewish-American Authors: An Overview of the Criticism," *Melus*, 12/1/1996, p. 71.)

(2) word play (as in pun) *n*.: **paronomasia**. See *pun*

words. See also *word*

words (aversion to or fear of) *n*.: **logophobia**. ❖ Does using a large vocabulary make you "elitist"? . . . The author of *A Little Stranger*, castigated in many review pages, wonders if her attackers suffer from **logophobia**. (Candia McWilliam, In My View, *Times* [London], 1/29/1989.)

(2) words (dispute about or battle of . . .) *n*.: **logomachy**. ❖ A **logomachy** about "discrimination" and "equal opportunity" is unlikely to solve a subtle distributive problem encountered in intercollegiate athletics, but colleges can foster harmony if they are allowed to adopt local policies of distributive justice. (Louis M. Guenin, "A Choice of Extent," *National Forum*, 3/22/1997, p. 22.)

(3) words (excessive use of or obsession with) *n*.: **verbomania**. ❖ [Today's] lawyers fall victim to the belief that all human experience can be verbalized. . . . [But] if one looks back in the history of the law, it appears that the use of demonstrative evidence was much more widespread . . . in 19th century courtrooms than it is today. Perhaps this historical curiosity tends to confirm my hypothesis concerning the source of [today's] lawyers' **verbomania**. (Mark Foster, "Demonstrative Evidence Often Speaks Louder Than Words," *Legal Times*, 7/1982, p. A2.)

(4) words (love of) *n*.: **logophilia**. ❖ Where most rock music is fueled by booze, drugs and a cranky dissatisfaction, the John Huss Moderate Combo's tunes are propelled by pure **logophilia**. Clever, playful and indefatigable, Huss' wordplay dominates his songs with unexpected rhymes and kaleidoscopic imagery. (Rick Reger, Music, Concert Line, *Chicago Tribune*, 1/24/1997.)

(5) words (obsession with . . .) *n*.: **logomania**. ❖ Thumbing through [Dr. Johnson's]

dictionary . . . can create many a pleasurable afternoon for the irrepressible **logomaniac**. (Tracy Lee Simmons, "Johnson's Canon; On the Trail of the Great Lexicographer," *Weekly Standard* [London], 5/29/2006.)

(6) words (of or relating to) *adj*.: **lexical**. ❖ One good authority suggests that "an educated speaker of English can understand, and potentially use, at least 50,000 words." . . . But *Chambers Dictionary*, the official Scrabble dictionary in Britain, has some 300,000 words, and the *Oxford English Dictionary* has 500,000. . . . What are we to make of such **lexical** waste, such idle riches? (Thomas Sutcliffe, "Glossary/Scrabbling for Linguistic Domination," *Independent* [London], 11/24/1994.)

(7) words (of or relating to) *adj*.: **wordish**. [This word is usually listed in dictionaries (if at all) as "obscure," but the author of the passage below, the former principal editor of *The New Oxford American Dictionary* (Second Edition), opines that it is a legitimate word.] ❖ Funner. Impactful. Blowiest. Territorialism. Multifunctionality. Dialoguey. Dancey. Thrifting. Chillaxing. . . . Someone, somewhere, is using [these words] with a disclaimer like "I know it's not a real word . . ." . . . But if all these words look **wordish**, sound **wordish**, and act **wordish**, why are they all hedged about with the namby-pamby "I know it's not a real word" disclaimers? (Erin McKean, "I Know It's Not a Word, but . . . , *Boston Globe*, 8/3/2008.)

(8) words (pronounced alike, but meaning is different) *n*.: **homophone**. ❖ You warned about body piercing and noted precautions to be taken against infections in those who "can't resist a naval ring." Isn't a naval ring something worn only by Annapolis graduates? Guess you meant navel. Ah, for a spell checker that warns about **homophones**! (Unsigned letter to the editor*, Time*, 7/12/1999, p. 8.)

(9) words (study of) *n*.: **logology**. ❖ The essence of **logology** is discovering word patterns, as in palindromes, e.g., deified; tautonyms, e.g., murmur; words dependent on alphabetic order, e.g., almost; and isograms, long words in which no letter appears more than once, e.g., ambidextrously. (Howard Richler, "A Logologist Could Probably Turn Water into Wine," *Montreal Gazette*, 3/28/1998.)

(10) words (condition of forgetting . . . or the right one) *n.*: **lethologica**. ❖ Words. I've always loved them. That's why it bothers me that lately I've been plagued with **lethologica**. . . . So now, when I can't remember a word, I have an out. I just apologize and explain that I am suffering from a condition known as . . . "Let's see, it's right on the tip of my tongue. It begins with an 'L,' no, no, an 'A,' or is it a 'T'?" (Barbara Rolek, "This Meat Loaf a Celebration for Taste Buds," *Northwest Indiana Post-Tribune*, 9/18/2002.)

(11) words (the very . . . used by a writer or speaker) *phr.*: **ipsissima verba** [Latin.] ❖ [T]he English translation of Valerian Albanov's *In the Land of White Death* is a valuable addition to expeditionary lore. Albanov (1881–1919) [was on] a scouting expedition in search of new hunting grounds for big game—polar bears, seals and walruses. Much of the book's touted value comes from the fact that it relates Albanov's own account of his own ordeal, his **ipsissima verba**. (Caroline Alexander, "The Second-Worst Journey in the World," *New York Times*, 12/10/2000.)

(12) words (excessive use of . . .) *n.*: **circumlocution**. See *verbosity*

(13) words (excessive use of . . .) *n.*: **logorrhea**. See *verbosity*

(14) words (excessive use of . . .) *n.*: **periphrasis**. See *verbosity*

(15) words (given to the use of long . . .) *adj.*: **sesquipedalian**. See *word*

(16) words (having a good feel for what is linguistically appropriate in using spoken or written . . .) *n.*: **sprachgefühl** [German]. See *language*

(17) words (having more than three syllables) *adj.*: **polysyllabic**. See *syllables*

(18) words (inability to recall meaning of . . . or using them incorrectly) *n.*: **paramnesia**. See *amnesia*

(19) words (inability to understand spoken or written . . . due to brain injury) *n.*: **aphasia**. See *uncomprehending*

(20) words (misuse or strained use of . . . or phrases, sometimes deliberate) *n.*: **catachresis**. See *misuse*

(21) words (one who studies . . . and language) *n.*: **philologist**. See *linguist*

(22) words (or speech used by members of the underworld or a particular group) *n.*: **argot**. See *vernacular*

(23) words (or speech used by members of the underworld or a particular group) *n.*: **cant**. See *vernacular*

(24) words (which are meaningless or deceptive) *n.*: **flummery**. See *meaningless*

word to the wise *phr.*: **verbum sap** [Latin]. ❖ Norris Hoyt, in discussing the possible U.S. casualty count in a war against Iraq, wrote [that the Germans lost 280,000 in Stalingrad and did not take the city, though only 400,000 people lived there, as contrasted with 6 million in Baghdad. However, there is little] to suggest that the 400,000 loyal subjects of Stalingrad . . . contributed significantly to the German losses. Mr. Hoyt's **verbum sap** sounds more like a red herring. (Alfred E. Alby, letter to the editor, *Washington Post*, 10/2/2002.)

wordy (as in rambling) *adj.*: **discursive**. See *rambling*

(2) wordy (as in verbose) *adj.*: **inaniloquent**. See *verbose*

(3) wordy (mania for being overly . . . , in speech) *n.*: **cacoëthes loquendi** [Latin]. See *talking*

work (doing . . . only when the boss is watching) *n.*: **eyeservice**. [Although this word may not appear in any dictionaries, its does appear in the King James Version of the Bible. Colossians 3:22: "Servants, obey in all things your masters according to the flesh; not with eyeservice, as menpleasers; but in singleness of heart, fearing God." Thus, while obviously not a common word, it is nevertheless presumably mentioned and discussed in English-speaking churches all over the world every Sunday (as evidenced in part by the example) and, in that sense, is not archaic. Plus, it's a useful word.] ❖ Do you work hard or hardly work? My pastor posed this question recently during a sermon. He asked members of the congregation if they engaged in "**eyeservice**." . . . In other words, do you work hard only when the boss has his or her eyes on you? (Michelle Singletary, "Working Wonders," *Washington Post*, 1/9/2003.)

(2) work (as in toil) *v.i.*: **moil**. See *toil*

(3) work (avoider) *n.*: **embusque** [French]. See *slacker*

(4) work (forced . . . for little or no pay) *n.*: **corvee**. See *servitude*

workaholic *n.*: **Stakhanovite**. [This word derives from Alexei Stakhanov, a Russian miner who devised a system to award recognition and special privileges to Soviet workers for output beyond production norms. Although a noun, the word is frequently used in the adjectival sense of "hardworking" or "obsessive."] ❖ The first thing you must understand about [baby-boomers] is how hard they work. Among them a 60-hour week is standard, with many—especially the younger ones, the singles, and the entrepreneurs—reporting 70, 80, even 90 hours on the job each week. Experts confirm the boomers' reports of **Stakhanovite** schedules. (Walter Kiechel III, "The Workaholic Generation," *Fortune*, 4/10/1989.)

worker (Mexican . . . allowed to work in United States) *n.*: **bracero**. See *laborer*

(2) worker (who works solely for a fee, esp. one hired to perform tasks that are dangerous, offensive, or menial) *n.*: **hireling**. See *mercenary*

workers (who are salaried, as opposed to lower-class wage earners) *n.*: **salariat**. See *employees*

work of art (total . . .) *n.*: **Gesamtkunstwerk**. [German. This is a concept of German composer Richard Wagner, referring to an ideal combination of performing arts, including music, drama, decor, etc., resulting in total theater, as in opera. It is intended to be a complimentary term, though it is not used as such in the following example.] ❖ Like Hitler before him, Saddam Hussein is, after his fashion, an artist and an aesthete. Since his accession to the purple in 1979, he has led his people in a choreographed **Gesamtkunstwerk** of light and sound, folkloric costumes and overblown mythology, in which each Iraqi, no matter how humble, has played a part. (James Gardner, "One with Nineveh and Tyre," *National Review*, 5/13/1991.)

workshop (spec. a final effort made by architectural students to complete a solution to a problem within an allotted time, but sometimes used to refer to any kind of . . . or brainstorming session) *n.*: **charette** (or **charrette**). ❖ A six-day design workshop starting tonight will bring together neighborhood residents, business owners and public agencies to brainstorm about the future of the area from Uptown to Lyndale Av. S. and Lake St. Called the West Lake Design **Charette**, the workshop will tackle a range of issues, from parking proposals to a Metro Transit bus layover station. (Linda Mack, "Uptown Workshop Will Seek Solutions for a Neighborhood Swamped with Cars," *Minneapolis Star Tribune*, 4/16/1998.)

worldview *n.*: **weltanschauung** [German]. ❖ [Marlon is an excellent African American Scrabble player who is having bad luck on his tile draws.] I point out that the problem may not be Marlon's letters but Marlon's **weltanschauung**. "Surely he doesn't think The Man is fixing his tiles," Matt says. He doesn't have to think it's racial, I say. (Stefan Fatsis, *Word Freak*, Houghton Mifflin [2001], p. 279.)

worms (of, relating to, resembling or caused by) *adj.*: **vermicular**. ❖ Another artist who mixes media audaciously and goes for complex conceptual effects is Mona Hatoum. . . . She is also greatly concerned, in various ways, with the **vermicular**, writhing shapes of intestines and the metamorphosis of domestic items into something strange and nasty. (Martin Gayford, The Arts: "As Majestically Italian as Olive Oil and Garlic Art," *Sunday Telegraph* [London], 8/30/1998.)

worm-shaped (or resembling a worm) *adj.*: **vermiform**. ❖ Even more eccentric is Eric Roy's *Worm on Quartz*, a fantasy in which a smoky quartz suggests an abstract sea cucumber with an inlaid and colorful **vermiform** shape on its back. (Donald Miller, "Cases of Wonder: Jewel Beauty, Museum Treasures at Carnegie," *Pittsburgh Post-Gazette*, 3/20/1999.)

worn-out (and broken-down) *adj.*: **raddled**. ❖ Thus you get . . . what seems likely to be the most tasteless scene of the year in which Ethan gets to give a **raddled** old hooker (played by 50's sex bomb Mamie Van Doren, who really must need the money to endure such degrading treatment) a bed bath and a grope. (*Birmingham Post*, "Culture: It's Slack by Name and Slack by Nature," 5/10/2002.)

(2) worn-out (chronically . . . , as in fatigued) *adj.*: **neurasthenic**. See *fatigued*

(3) worn-out (as in decrepit) *adj.*: **spavined**. See *decrepit*

worried (as if by a witch or by unfounded fears) *adj.*: **hagridden**. See *tormented*

worries (as in nervousness) *n.pl.* but sing. or pl. in construction: **collywobbles**. See *bellyache*

worry *v.t., v.i., n.*: **cark**. ❖ I don't remember all our dogs, because they were many and they constantly faced danger and were more expendable than dogs nurtured in the lap of luxury without **cark** or care. (John Gould, "The Life and Times of Farm Dogs," *Christian Science Monitor*, 4/17/1998.)

(2) worry (as in a state of nervous tension, often with irritability) *n.*: **fantod**. See *tension*

(3) worry (as in anxiety) *n.*: **inquietude**. See *anxiety*

(4) worry (as in trouble) *n.*: **tsuris** [Yiddish]. See *trouble*

(5) worry (or complain) *v.i.*: **repine**. See *complain*

(6) worry (positive form of . . . brought on, for example, by a job promotion or a new baby) *n.*: **eustress**. See *stress*

(7) worry (state of . . .) *n.*: **swivet** (as in "in a swivet") informal. See *distress*

worrywart (as in pessimist who continually warns of a disastrous future) *n.*: **Jeremiah**. See *pessimist*

worsening *adj.*: **ingravescent**. ❖ To Americans who worry that their country is going the way of ancient Rome, only faster, two of the most alarming trends are the **ingravescent** influence of money in politics and the exponential growth of gambling. As was inevitable, these have merged. . . . [T]he gambling industry poured nearly $4 million in "soft money" into the Democratic and Republican parties last year. (Martin Dyckman, "Gambling Interests Invest in Politics," *St. Petersburg [FL] Times*, 7/8/1997.)

worship (of dead people) *n.*: **necrolatry**. ❖ While many of the most devout of the Elvis People are concurrently devout Christians—and there are those who think that referring to Elvis as "The King" is blasphemous—there is a strain of Elvis worship that veers close to **necrolatry**. (Philip Martin, "In the Land of Elvis, Death Meant Never Being Obsolete," *Arkansas Democrat-Gazette*, 8/19/2001.)

(2) worship (not necessarily sincere or unforced) *n.*: **obeisance**. See *homage*

(3) worship (of women) *n.*: **philogyny**. See *women*

(4) worship (often in a servile manner) *v.i.*: **genuflect**. See *kneel*

worshipful (biography) *n.*: **hagiography** (*adj.*: **hagiographic**). See *biography*

worst *adj.*: **pessimal**. ❖ Local governments should have complete discretion to use allocated federal reconstruction dollars for maintenance. . . . In that way, local governments could choose optimal strategies for the use of all tax dollars available to them, rather than the "**pessimal**" one they now employ. (Lucius J. Riccio, "An Ounce of Prevention," *Newsday*, 8/4/1992.)

worthless (deeming something as . . .) *n.*: **floccinaucinihilipilification** ❖ [North Carolina Senator Jesse Helms:] "I note your distress at my **floccinaucinihilipilification** of the Comprehensive Test Ban Treaty." (*Perspectives, Newsweek*, 8/9/1999.)

(2) worthless (matter) *n.*: **dross**. ❖ [The Clinton impeachment trial] was supposed to be a monumental event, a sombre and historical process that either demonstrated America at its best or America at its worst. But most assuredly, it was not expected to tumble immediately into the **dross** of daytime television drudgery, as insignificant and non-compelling as the endlessly scrolling TV listings. (*Toronto Star*, "Bill in Reruns but Hillary Eyes New Show," 1/18/1999.)

(3) worthless *adj.*: **nugatory**. ❖ Judge Bork raises yet another argument, which is that the President has the power to pardon anyone accused or convicted of "offenses against the United States" and thus could render any conviction **nugatory** by pardoning himself. (Daniel E. Troy, "The Indictment Option," *National Review*, 4/6/1998, p. 26.)

(4) worthless (as in made without regard to quality) *adj.*: **catchpenny**. See *inferior*

(5) worthless (as in useless) *adj.*: **inutile**. See *useless*

(6) worthless (something that is . . .) *n.*: **vermiform appendix**. See *useless*

wrapping (act of . . . , tying, or binding up or together) *n.*: **ligature**. See *tying*

wreath (for the head) *n.*: **chaplet**. See *garland*

wretched (esp. as to poverty) *adj.*: **abject**. ❖ Women now make up more than half of the estimated 50 million Chinese living in **abject** poverty, it was reported yesterday amid calls for greater government intervention. (*Washington Times*, "More Than Half of Nation's 50 Million Poor Are Women," 4/9/1999.)

(2) wretched (as in despicable, person) *n.*: **caitiff**. See *despicable*

wrinkle *n., v.t.*: **rimple**. ❖ [In the Bush-Gore 2000 election fight,] Bob Dole recommended that both campaigns agree to take a second look at invalidated ballots from military personnel. Noting that a hand recount in South Florida is carefully scrutinizing ballots for "a dimple, a pimple or **rimple**," Dole argued, "If you're going to do that, you ought to look at the intent of the military absentee ballots."

(Kathy Kiely, "Bush Fights Rejection of Military Ballots—Officials Mark 1,420 Overseas Votes Invalid," *USA Today*, 11/20/2000.)

wrinkled (very . . .) *adj.*: **rugose**. ❖ A couple of years ago, right before an endometrial biopsy, [the nurse] and the female gynecologist stared suddenly at my [vagina]. Was it shrunken and dry like an old woman's supposedly is? Was it too colorful—more purple than pink? [Was] its inside unusually **rugose**, both characteristics said to be indicative of a woman who enjoys sex and has had a lot of it? (Joanna Frueh, "Vaginal Aesthetics," *Hypatia*, 9/22/2003.)

write (inability to . . .) *n.*: **disgraphia**. ❖ Some [children] have auditory processing problems; some are dyslexic and don't see words the way other children do; some have **disgraphia**, a writing disorder; and some have attention deficit disorder. (Ellen Sweets, "Lap-Time Lessons: Parents Can Give Children the Gift of an Early Love of Reading," *Dallas Morning News*, 6/2/1998.)

(2) write (irresistible compulsion to . . .) *n.*: **cacoëthes scribendi** [Latin]. ❖ The diametrically opposite disorder is writer's itch. "Scribble, scribble, scribble, Mr. Gibbon," George III (or, some say, his brother, the Duke of Gloucester) famously buttonholed the historian of the Decline and Fall of the Roman Empire. Linked to the libido sciendi, this **cacoëthes scribendi** had already reached epidemic proportions by the Renaissance. (Roy Porter, "Reading Is Bad for Your Health," *History Today*, 3/1/1998, p. 11.)

(3) write (or speak at length on a subject) *v.i.*: **expatiate**. See *expound*

(4) write (or speak in a scholarly manner, often used in a derogatory fashion) *v.i.*: **lucubrate**. See *discourse*

(5) write *v.t.*: **indite**. See *compose*

writer (of fiction, esp. who writes in quantity) *n.*: **fictioneer**. See *novelist*

(2) writer (or speaker who is dull and boring) *n.*: **dryasdust**. See *boring*

(3) writer (professional . . .) *n.*: **wordmonger**. See *author*

writer's cramp *n.*: **graphospasm**. ❖ Q. Regarding your article "Crashes are no accident, says reader": So, what do we call an "accident" if it is not an accident? I was a Naval OSHA inspector for several years, inspecting 21 ships for safety hazards. The Navy calls them "mishaps." . . . A. Gee, [I] love language. That is why [I] took up writing despite the risk of a mishap and possible **graphospasm**. (Bob Weber, "It's the Key to 3-Minute Warning," *Chicago Tribune*, 2/23/2003.)

writing (of . . . that is clear and elegant) *adj.*: **Addisonian** [after English essayist Joseph Addison (1672–1719)]. ❖ And then you met him. You did if you were a working journalist in New York or covered a national political campaign. [Murray Kempton] enjoyed being in a group of reporters; he liked to try out ideas for columns, dropping fully formed **Addisonian** sentences into conversation to see which ones got a nod or a laugh. The winners turned up in the next day's paper. (David Von Drehle, "A Journalist's Singular Voice," *Washington Post*, 5/6/1997.)

(2) writing (or speech characterized by the affected choice of obscure words) *n.*: **lexiphanicism** (*adj.*: **lexiphanic**). ❖ Can a book be both funny and tiresome? It is not the logorrhoea [wordiness] of the narrator, Harry Driscoll, that bothers me, nor his **lexiphanic** prose . . . (I love reading with a dictionary to hand). (Debra Adelaide, In Short, *Sydney Morning Herald*, 3/29/2003.)

(3) writing (of . . . that is concise, precise, or refined; lit. "as if engraved in a precious stone") *adj.*: **lapidary**. ❖ [Kennedy Fraser] trusts her keen eye, her subject matter and good writing to tell her stories. . . . Fraser has produced a book of exquisite set pieces—compelling stories told in seamless narrative, in **lapidary** prose. (Maureen Dezell, review of *Ornament and Silence: Essays on Women's Lives*, by Kennedy Fraser, *Boston Globe*, 1/30/1997.)

(4) writing (poor . . . , esp. characterized by the affected choice of archaic words) *n.*: **tushery**. ❖ This novel, set in the last days of Rome in the Eastern Empire, . . . tells the story of [a woman] who discovers that she is a born doctor . . . , but soon realises that there is no room for her in a society where medicine is the province of men. As a piece of historical romance it is saved from **tushery** by down-to-earth writing and a quite remarkable amount of information about early medicine which proves fascinating in itself. (Robery Nye, review of *The Beacon at Alexandria*, by Gillian Bradshaw, *Guardian* [London], 2/6/1987.)

(5) writing (such as poetry or certain works of fiction, valued for their aesthetic qualities rather than to provide information or instruction) *n.pl.* but *sing.* in construction: **belles-lettres** [French]. See *literature*

(6) writing (study of . . . , as in handwriting, esp. to study character) *n.*: **graphology**. See *handwriting*

(7) writing (of, by, or pertaining to . . . by an author) *adj.*: **auctorial**. See *author*

(8) writing (table) *n.*: **escritoire**. See *desk*

(9) writing (enthusiastic or excited . . . or speech) *n.*: **dithyramb**. See *enthusiastic*

(10) writing (having a good feel for what is linguistically appropriate when . . .) *n.*: **sprachgefühl** [German]. See *language*

(11) writing (in shorthand) *n.*: **tachygraphy**. See *shorthand*

(12) writing (inability to understand . . . due to a brain injury) *n.*: **aphasia**. See *uncomprehending*

(13) writing (or speech that is as in affected and high-flown) *adj.*: **euphuistic.** See *affected*

(14) writing (or speech that is cryptic or obscure, esp. deliberately) *adj.*: **elliptical**. See *cryptic*

(15) writing (or speech that is pompous or bombastic) *n.*: **grandiloquence**. See *pomposity*

(16) writing (or speech that is trite or simplistic) *n.*: **pablum** (also **pabulum**). See *triteness*

writings (collection of . . . by an author) *n.*: **chrestomathy**. See *anthology*

(2) writings (or artistic works created in the author's or artist's youth) *n.*: **juvenilia**. See *compositions*

written material (inability to read or understand) *n.*: **alexia**. ❖ Researchers conducting studies on **alexia** found that damage to certain areas of the left hemisphere resulted in the inability to read and write; individuals could not recognize words and their respective meanings at an automatic level. (Karen J. Rooney, "Dyslexia Revisited: History, Educational Philosophy, and Clinical Assessment Applications," *Intervention in School & Clinic*, 9/1/1995, p. 6.)

wrong (engaging in argument that may be . . . , as in specious) *adj., n.*: **eristic**. See *specious*

(2) wrong (reasoning that is intended to mislead or rationalize) *n.*: **casuistry**. See *fallacious*

wrongdoer *n.*: **malefactor**. ❖ In the crowded western part of New Delhi sits a vast but packed prison surrounded by high yellow walls. Built in 1958 for a few thousand thieves, murderers and other **malefactors**, Tihar Jail is now home to more than 11,500 prisoners. (Meenakshi Ganguly, Asia: "A Place to Call Home—New Delhi's Tihar Jail Has Gone from Being an Unruly Hellhole to a Global Model for Prison Reform," *Time* International, 12/11/2000, p. 32.)

(2) wrongdoer *n.*: **miscreant**. ❖ Although the U.S. claims the legal right to try anyone for the murder of an American citizen abroad, prosecutors first have to get their hands on the suspect, and that has proved a major stumbling block even in cases where **miscreants** are firmly identified. (Johanna McGeary, World: "Sifting for Answers—As the Dead Are Buried, the Gritty Work of Finding the Terrorists Proceeds Slowly in Africa," *Time*, 8/24/1998, p. 48.)

wrongdoing (in public office) *n.*: **malversation**. ❖ A third charge is that [President Clinton's first-term national security adviser Anthony] Lake is guilty of **malversation**, the evidence being a token $5,000 fine he was assessed by the Justice Department for failing to sell several stock holdings promptly. (Jacob Heilbrunn, "Dr. Maybe Heads for the CIA," *New Republic*, 3/24/1997.)

(2) wrongdoing (in public office) *n.*: **misprision**. ❖ Last week [on a talk show, Washington, D.C. mayor Marion Barry was] disingenuous, as he danced around responsibility for any of the city's problems. When the talk shifted to the number of court-appointed receivers who have taken over city agencies and functions, once again Mr. Barry failed to acknowledge the **misprision**. (Jonetta Ross Barras, "Say You're Sorry, Mayor Barry," *Washington Post*, 2/28/1997.)

(3) wrongdoing (or evil by its own nature or natural law rather than because prohibited by statute) *n.*: **malum in se**. [Latin. The counterpart to this term, *malum prohibitum*, refers to an offense prohibited by statute but not inherently wrong or evil. See *crime*.] ❖ [Marijuana smokers] haven't really done anything wrong. Smoking marijuana affects no one else, infringes upon no one's rights and is not **malum in se**. Nonetheless, these people will now forever be classified into a category that places them among the murderers, rapists and kidnappers of society. Those criminals deserve the label "ex-convict." Contrarily, someone who lights a blunt in the privacy of his own room doesn't. (Edward Fu, "Should Drugs Be Legalized," University Wire, 3/8/2006)

(4) wrongdoing (confession of . . .) *n.*: **peccavi**. See *confession*

x-rays (not transparent to . . .) *adj.*: **radiopaque**.
❖ If you've always wondered how to trans-
late plethysmograph (an electronic device to
monitor the amount of blood in the body),
head degausser (a demagnetizer on the head
of an electronic speaker) and **radiopaque**
(insulation against x-rays) into Hebrew, you
now have a new source of information. (Judy
Siegel-Itzkovich, "Seeds of Hope Beneath
Charred Remains," *Jerusalem Post*, 11/1/1998.)

X

yawning (and stretching) *n*.: **pandiculation**. ❖ His constantly changing answering-machine message has featured recitations on the pre-sleep state of "**pandiculation**" and sportscast-style accounts of the recent Short-Kasparov chess match. (Peter Goodman, "Piano Forte: The Pianist from Central Casting He's Not; But Awadagin Pratt Goes His Own Way, and It's Paying Off," *Newsday*, 1/9/1994.)

year (awful . . .) *n*.: **annus horribilis** [Latin]. ❖ The Queen famously called 1992—a year of separations, divorce and scandal—her **annus horribilis**. The emotional low point may have come on Nov. 20, her 45th wedding anniversary, when Windsor Castle caught fire. (James Collins, "Restoring the Windsors [And Windsor Castle, Too]," *Time*, 12/1/1997, p. 60.)

(2) year (great . . .) *n*.: **annus terrificus** [Latin]. ❖ [The good things that happened in 1992] may not be a solid trend, only a faint glimmering, a tiding. Even so, if the tiding is genuine, then it would be justified, with a suitable bow to the Queen [who called 1992 an "annus horribilis"], to rename 1992: **annus terrificus**! (*Time*, The Best of 1992: "Standouts, From Pained Royals to Royal Pains to the Aristocrats of Talent," 1/4/1993, p. 53.)

(3) year (of wonders) *n*.: **annus mirabilis** [Latin]. ❖ The year 1492 was Spain's **annus mirabilis**, a year of marvels. A Spanish Pope was elected that year, a Borja from Catalonia. (He was called Borgia in Italy, where the Two Sicilies already had Spanish rulers.) King Ferdinand and Queen Isabella, who had just united their kingdoms, drove the Moors from the Spanish peninsula by a military victory at Granada. (Garry Wills, History: "1492 vs. 1892 vs. 1992: At Three Imperial Moments, Three Columbuses Reveal Something about Their Different Eras," *Time*, 10/7/1991, p. 61.)

yearn (for) *v.t.*: **desiderate**. See *want*

yearning (esp. for something one once had but has no more) *n*.: **desiderium**. See *longing*

(2) yearning (strongly . . .) *adj*.: **appetent** (*n*.: **appetence**). See *desirous*

(3) yearning *n*.: **appetence**. See *craving*

(4) yearning *n*.: **avidity**. See *craving*

yell (as in screech) *v.i.*: **caterwaul**. See *screech*

(2) yell (or yelp, bark, or screech) *v.t., n.*: **yawp**. See *shriek*

yellow (strong . . .) *adj*.: **gamboge**. ❖ His belly is no longer swollen [having just received a new liver]. His skin is pink, not **gamboge** yellow. He can eat. He can live. (Michael Bywater, "Giving the Greatest Gift of All," *Independent on Sunday*, 6/15/1997.)

yelp (or yelp, bark, or screech) *v.t., n.*: **yawp**. See *shriek*

yen (condition involving . . . to eat nonfood items) *n*.: **pica**. See *craving*

(2) yen (having a strong . . .) *adj*.: **appetent** (*n*.: **appetence**). See *desirous*

yes man *n*.: **lickspittle**. See *sycophant*

yesterday (of or relating to) *adj*.: **hesternal**. ❖ I'll say this: every day I learn something new; such sudden purity; all those **hesternal** woes severed; liberated from the grief of the body, its ridiculous needs. (Sharon McCartney, "Marie Antoinette's Last Thoughts," *Queen's Quarterly*, 9/22/2006.)

yet *adv*.: **withal**. See *nevertheless*

young (admiration for or fascination with . . . people) *n*.: **juvenophilia**. ❖ Do we need another waist-deep wallow in the 1960s, ensconcing us cheek by jowl with Frank Rizzo and Eldridge Cleaver, Sam Yorty and Mark Rudd, Lester Maddox and Herbert Marcuse and other long-forgotten bit players in a period drama? Do we need to be reminded of that era's gaseous **juvenophilia**, like *Time* magazine's celebration of Americans 25 or younger as 1967's "Man of the Year"[?] (George Will, review of *Nixonland*, by Rick Perlstein, *New York Times Book Review*, 5/11/2008.)

(2) young *adj*.: **neanic**. ❖ [In 1964,] the world was being made aware of something called the Free Speech Movement. [A graduate student at UC–Berkeley, Jack Weinberg, stated]: "We don't trust anybody over 30." Despite being beyond the deadline set by this whimsical imperative of **neanic** gerontology. . . . I managed to write a couple of pieces about

Y

the FSM. (Gene Marine, "Geezers of the FSM," *San Francisco Examiner*, 9/25/1994.)

(3) young (being or becoming . . .) *adj.*: **juvenescent** (*n.*: **juvenescence**). ❖ By the time he was 24, Pete Townshend, the guitar-spinning auteur of the seminal 1960s rock group the Who, had secured a permanent place in the annals of pop culture. His song "My Generation," with its **juvenescent** proclamation, "Hope I die before I get old," had become the anthem of the Woodstock era. (Janice Simpson, "Pete, We Can Hear You," *Time*, 7/12/1993.)

(4) young (government by the . . .) *n.*: **neocracy**. See *government*

(5) young (hatred of . . . people) *n.*: **misopedia**. See *hatred*

youngster (male . . . who is awkward and clumsy) *n.*: **hobbledehoy**. See *clumsy*

(2) youngster *n.*: **moppet**. See *child*

youth (period of one's . . .) *n.*: **nonage**. [This word specifically refers to the period of time during which one is a minor and is also sometimes used to refer to a period of one's immaturity.] ❖ [I]t is a boo-boo to write that something is "very unique" or "rather unique." A proposal is either unique or it isn't. . . . In its pure form, the adjective simply does not take modifiers of comparison, intensification or degree. In my **nonage** as a writer who writes about usage, I speculated 20 years ago that English has "at least a score" of absolute adjectives. (James J. Kilpatrick, " 'Rather Unique' Is Somewhat Impossible," *Chicago Sun-Times*, 3/7/2004.)

(2) youth (male . . . who is awkward and clumsy) *n.*: **hobbledehoy**. See *clumsy*

youthful (being or becoming . . .) *adj.*: **juvenescent** (*n.*: **juvenescence**). See *young*

(2) youthful *adj.*: **neanic**. See *young*

zeal (as in full of energy) *n.*: **brio**. See *energy*

    (2) zeal (undue . . . for one subject or idea) *n.*: **monomania**

    (3) zeal (excessive or unbridled . . . , as in enthusiasm) *n.* **schwarmerei** [German]. See *enthusiasm*

zealot *n.*: **energumen**. See *fanatic*

zealous *adj.*: **perfervid**. See *impassioned*

zenith (as in highest point that can be attained or the ultimate degree, as of a condition or quality) *n.*: **ne plus ultra**. See *ultimate*

zesty (agreeably . . . in taste or flavor) *adj.*: **piquant**. ❖ In ancient times, Arab traders spread tales that precious Eastern spices grew in lakes guarded by winged animals. Later, explorers risked death searching for a seagoing spice route. . . . Indian "fusion"—the cross-fertilization of traditional Western cuisine with the aromatic and **piquant** flavors of the East—has arrived. (Linda Kulman, "Hotter Than Ginger Spice," *U.S. News & World Report*, 3/22/1999.)

zigzagging *adj.*: **flexuous**. See *waving*

Z